MEDICAL LAW

Bradford Hospitals **NHS**
NHS Trust

Medical Library

Bradford Royal infirmary

Bradford, BD9 6RJ

Tel 01274 364130   Fax 01274 364704

Fines are chargeable on this book if you keep it beyond the
agreed date.
10p per day / 50p per week
You may renew the book by calling into the Library, in writing.
by phone – 36 4130 - or by email -
medical.library2@bradfordhospitals.nhs.uk

MEDICAL LAW

TEXT, CASES, AND MATERIALS

EMILY JACKSON

OXFORD

UNIVERSITY PRESS

OXFORD

UNIVERSITY PRESS

Great Clarendon Street, Oxford OX2 6DP

Oxford University Press is a department of the University of Oxford.
It furthers the University's objective of excellence in research, scholarship,
and education by publishing worldwide in

Oxford New York

Auckland Cape Town Dar es Salaam Hong Kong Karachi
Kuala Lumpur Madrid Melbourne Mexico City Nairobi
New Delhi Shanghai Taipei Toronto

With offices in

Argentina Austria Brazil Chile Czech Republic France Greece
Guatemala Hungary Italy Japan Poland Portugal Singapore
South Korea Switzerland Thailand Turkey Ukraine Vietnam

Oxford is a registered trade mark of Oxford University Press
in the UK and in certain other countries

Published in the United States
by Oxford University Press Inc., New York

British Library Cataloguing in Publication Data

Data available

Library of Congress Cataloging in Publication Data

Data available

Typeset by RefineCatch Limited, Bungay, Suffolk
Printed in Great Britain by
Antony Rowe Ltd, Chippenham, Wiltshire

ISBN 0–19–926127–X   978–0–19–926127–7

1 3 5 7 9 10 8 6 4 2

To Emma and Sophie Jackson

PREFACE

My intention in writing this book has been to provide students of medical or health care law and ethics with both a textbook and a source of relevant materials. The text should be sufficiently accessible to be useful to undergraduate students with no prior knowledge of either law or medicine, but also in-depth enough to be interesting to postgraduate students already familiar with the field. Obviously, for reasons of space, it is impossible for one book to exactly match every possible medical law curriculum, and there will inevitably be areas that some readers may wish I had covered in more depth. With such issues—for example the retained organs scandal—I have flagged up other relevant sources where more detailed analysis may be found.

Many of the subjects covered in this book are contentious and newsworthy. This makes them exciting both to teach and to study, but also means that there are likely to be many interesting new developments during the life of this book. Wherever possible, I have tried to flag-up likely future directions.

People often have strongly held views on medical law and ethics, and in this book I have included extracts which embody a number of diverse perspectives. My aim has been to explain and describe current medical law, and provide balanced analysis of the issues, not to offer my personal views. There are places where my opinions may become evident, but this should not prevent readers from forming their own judgements.

While writing this book I have acquired many debts of gratitude. To begin with, I would like to thank Jane Kavanagh at OUP, who first suggested that I should consider writing a medical law textbook, and Sarah Hyland, who has been a helpful and supportive editor.

I have learned a great deal from the students who have studied medical law with me, both at LSE and Queen Mary, and I would like to thank three in particular, who worked as my research assistants at various points during the writing of this book. Aimee Daruwala and Nicola McGuigan sifted through and photocopied a growing mountain of material, and Stuart Andrews heroically read the whole draft manuscript prior to publication. His comments and suggestions were invaluable.

My colleagues at LSE, Queen Mary, the HFEA, and elsewhere, have been encouraging and inspiring, and I would particularly like to thank Marie Fox, Ellie Lee, John Harris, Simon Jenkins, Suzi Leather, Sheila McLean, Mavis Maclean, Katherine O'Donovan, Mike Redmayne, Helen Reece, Nik Rose, Sally Sheldon, and Juliet Tizzard.

I could not have written this book without the support of my closest friends, whose confidence in my ability to complete this project kept me going when it seemed like an overwhelmingly daunting task, and whose unfailingly excellent company helped to take my mind off the whole thing at critical moments. I am especially grateful to Jonathan Brenton, Hugh Collins, Alison Cox, Nicola Lacey, Rebecca Mead, Ciarán O'Meara, Duncan Paterson, Henry Phillips, Robert Phillips, Paul Raffield, Monica Thurnauer, and Matthew Weait.

Finally, I would like to thank my father, Douglas Jackson, and my sister-in-law, Sue Jackson, for being incredibly supportive over the past three years. When I started writing this book, I benefited enormously from conversations with my late brother, Rupert Jackson, about the reality of life as a consultant in an overstretched NHS accident and emergency department and intensive care unit. This book is dedicated to his daughters, Emma and Sophie, with all my love.

Emily Jackson

October 2005

ACKNOWLEDGEMENTS

Grateful acknowledgement is made to all the authors and publishers of copyright material which appears in this book, and in particular to the following for permission to reprint material from the sources indicated:

Albany Law Review for extracts from Eileen L McDonagh, 'My Body, My Consent: Securing the Constitutional Right to Abortion Funding', (1999) 62 *Albany Law Review* 1057.

American Psychological Association for extracts from Dan W Brock, 'Misconceived Sources of Opposition to Physician-Assisted Suicide', (2000) 6 *Psychology, Public Policy, and Law*; and Margot White and Daniel Callahan, 'Oregon's First Year: The Medicalization of Control', (2000) 6 *Psychology, Public Policy, and Law*.

American Society of Law, Medicine and Ethics for extracts from Frances Miller, 'Denial of Health Care and Informed Consent in English and American Law Extracts', (1992) 18 *American Journal of Law and Medicine*.

Blackwell Publishers for extracts from Helen Draper & Tom Sorrell, 'Patients' Responsibilities', (2002) 16 *Bioethics*; Helga Kuhse 'Clinical ethics and nursing: "yes" to caring, but "no" to a female ethics of care', (1995) 9 *Bioethics*; Darren Shickle, 'Public Preferences for Health Care: Prioritisation in the United Kingdom', (1997) 11 *Bioethics*; Paul McNeill, 'Paying People to Participate in Research: Why Not?', (1997) 11 *Bioethics*; Florencia Luna, 'Vulnerable Populations and Morally Tainted Experiments', (1997) 11 *Bioethics*; Paquita de Zulueta, 'Randomised Placebo-Controlled Trials and HIV-Infected Pregnant Women in Developing Countries: Ethical Imperialism or Unethical Exploitation', (2001) 15 *Bioethics*; Massimo Reichlin, 'The Argument from Potential: A Reappraisal', (1997) 11 *Bioethics*; Julian Savulescu, 'The Embryonic Stem Cell Lottery and the Cannibalization of Human Beings', (2002) 16 *Bioethics*; David Resnik, 'Regulating the Market in Human Eggs', (2001) 15 *Bioethics*; Robert Lee & Derek Morgan, 'Sterilisation and Mental Handicap: Sapping the Strength of the State', (1998) 14 *Journal of Law and Society*; Peter Conrad and Deborah Potter, 'Human growth hormone and the temptations of biomedical enhancement', (2004) 26 *Sociology of Health and Illness*; Judith Jarvis Thomson, 'A Defence of Abortion', (1971) 1 *Philosophy and Public Affairs*; Henry S Richardson, 'Specifying norms as a way to resolve concrete ethical problems', (1990) 19 *Philosophy and Public Affairs*; Loren E Lomasky, 'Medical Progress and National Health Care', (1980) 10 *Philosophy and Public Affairs*; Norman Daniels, 'Health-Care Needs and Distributive Justice', (1981) 10 *Philosophy and Public Affairs*; Christopher Tollefsen, 'Embryos, Individuals, and Persons: An Argument Against Embryo Creation and Research', (2001) 18 *Journal of Applied Philosophy*; Susan M Wolf, Jeffrey P Kahn, John E Wagner, 'Using Preimplantation Genetic Diagnosis to Create a Stem Cell Donor: Issues, Guidelines and Limits', (2003) 31 *Journal of Law, Medicine and Ethics*; Roger Brownsword, 'Stem Cells, Superman, and the Report of the Select committee', (2002) 65 *Modern Law*

Review; John Griffiths, 'Assisted Suicide in the Netherlands: The Chabot Case', (1995) 58 *Modern Law Review*; Paula Case, 'Secondary Iatrogenic Harm: Claims for Psychiatric Damage Following a Death Caused by Medical Error', (2004) 67 *Modern Law Review*; Nigel Lowe & Satvinder Juss, 'Medical Treatment–Pragmatism and the Search for Principle', (1993) 56 *Modern Law Review*; Dermot Feenan, 'Common Law Access to Medical Records', (1996) 59 *Modern Law Review*; Genevra Richardson, 'Autonomy, Guardianship and Mental Disorder: One Problem, Two Solutions', (2002) 65 *Modern Law Review*; Harvey Teff, 'Regulation under the Medicines Act 1968: A continuing prescription for health', (1984) 47 *Modern Law Review*; Christopher Hodges, 'Development Risks: Unanswered Questions', (1998) 61 *Modern Law Review*; Laura Hoyano, 'Misconceptions about Wrongful Conception', (2002) 65 *Modern Law Review*; Margaret Brazier, 'Patient autonomy and consent to treatment: the role of the law?', (1987) 7 *Legal Studies*; and Katherine O'Donovan and Roy Gilbar, 'The Loved Ones: Families, Intimates and Patient Autonomy', (2003) 23 *Legal Studies*.

Extracts from the *British Medical Journal* and the *Journal of Medical Ethics* are reproduced with the permission of the BMJ Publishing Group.

Cambridge University Press for extracts from Edmund D Pellegrino, 'Intersections of Western biomedical ethics and world culture: problematic and possibility', (1992) 3 *Cambridge Quarterly of Healthcare Ethics*; Bernard Williams, *Making Sense of Humanity and Other Philosophical Papers* (1995); Stephen Munzer, *A Theory of Property* (1990); John Harris, 'The Age-Indifference Principle and Equality', (2005) 14 *Cambridge Quarterly of Healthcare Ethics*; Martin Smith & Heidi Foster, 'Morally Managing Medical Mistakes', (2000) 9 *Cambridge Quarterly of Healthcare Ethics*; Allen E Buchanan & Dan W Brock, *Deciding for Others: The Ethics of Surrogate Decision Making* (1989); Onora O'Neill, *Autonomy and Trust in Bioethics* (2002); Peter Singer & Karen Dawson, 'IVF technology and the argument from potential'; and Helga Kuhse and Peter Singer, 'Individuals, humans and persons: The issue of moral status', in P Singer et al. (eds), *Embryo Experimentation* (1990); John Harris, 'Stem Cells, Sex, and Procreation', (2003) 12 *Cambridge Quarterly of Healthcare*; and John Keown, *Euthanasia, Ethics and Public Policy: An Argument against Legalisation* (2002). Reproduced by permission of Cambridge University Press.

Cavendish Publishing for extracts from Biggs, H, 'I Don't Want to be a Burden! A Feminist Reflects on Women's Experiences of Death and Dying', pp. 279–95 and Fox, M, 'Research Bodies: Feminist Perspectives on Clinical Research', pp. 115–34 in Sheldon, S and Thomson, M (eds), *Feminist Perspectives on Health Care Law* (1998) London: Cavendish Publishing.

Connecticut Law Review for extracts from Jessica Berg, 'Grave Secrets: Legal and Ethical Analysis of Postmortem Confidentiality', (2001) 34 *Connecticut Law Review*.

Crown copyright material is reproduced under Class Licence Number C01P0000148 with the permission of OPSI and the Queen's Printer for Scotland.

Extracts from *Wisconsin Law Review* are reproduced with the permission of the Daily Reporter Publishing Company.

Extracts from *Journal of Health Politics, Policy and Law* are reproduced with the permission of Duke University Press.

Elsevier for extracts from I Kennedy, RA Sells, AS Daar, RD Guttmann, R Hoffenberg, M Lock, J Radcliffe-Richards, N Tilney and for the International Forum for Transplant Ethics, 'The case for "presumed consent" in organ donation', reprinted from *The Lancet*, vol. 351, pp. 147–52, © 1998; J Radcliffe-Richards, AS Daar, RD Guttmann, R Hoffenberg, I Kennedy, M Lock, RA Sells, N Tilney, 'The case for allowing kidney sales. International Forum for Transplant Ethics', reprinted from *The Lancet*, vol. 351, pp. 1950–2, © 1998; and Peter Singer, 'Xenotransplantation and Speciesism', reprinted from *Transplantation Proceedings*, vol. 24, pp. 728–32, © 1992; Charles Foster, 'It should be, therefore it is', reprinted from *New Law Journal*, vol. 154, © 2004; with permission from Elsevier.

The General Medical Council for extracts from *Confidentiality: Protecting and Providing Information* (GMC, 2004) http://www.gmc-uk.org/guidance/library/confidentiality.asp; *Serious Communicable Diseases Guidance to Doctors*, (London, GMC, 1997) http://www.gmc-uk.org/guidance/library/serious_communicable_diseases.asp; *Research: The Role and Responsibilities of Doctors*, (GMC, 2002) available at http://www.gmc-uk.org/; and *Withholding and Withdrawing Life-prolonging Treatments: Good Practice in Decision-making*, (London GMC, August 2002).

Georgetown University Press for extracts from Bonnie Steinbock, 'The Concept of Coercion and Long-Term Contraceptives', in Moskowitz, Ellen and Jennings, Bruce, *Coerced Contraception? Moral and Policy Challenges of Long-Acting Birth Control* (Washington D.C.: Georgetown UP, 1996).

Hart Publishing for Eric Matthews, 'Mental and Physical Illness–An Unsustainable Separation?', in N Eastman and J Peay (eds) *Law Without Enforcement: Integrating Mental Health and Justice* (1999); and Rhona Schulz, 'Surrogacy in Israel: An Analysis of the Law in Practice' in R Cook, SD Sclater with F Kaganas (eds), *Surrogate Motherhood: International Perspectives* (2003).

The Harvard Law Review Association for extracts from Frederick Schauer, 'Slippery Slopes', (1985) 99 *Harvard Law Review*, © 1985 by the Harvard Law Review Association; Margaret Jane Radin, 'Market-Inalienability', (1987) 100 *Harvard Law Review* © 1987 by the Harvard Law Review Association.

Extracts from the *Hastings Law Journal* are reproduced with the permission of Hastings School of Law.

Human Fertilisation and Embryology Authority for extracts from *Sex Selection: options for regulation*, © Human Fertilisation and Embryology Authority 2003.

Indiana University Press for extracts from AL Caplan, *Am I my Brother's Keeper? The Ethical Frontiers of Biomedicine* (1997); and Christine Overall, 'Frozen Embryos and "Fathers' Rights": Parenthood and Decision-Making in the Cryopreservation of Embryos', in Callahan, Joan (ed.) *Reproduction, Ethics and the Law: Feminist Responses* (Bloomington and Indianapolis: Indiana UP, 1995).

Extracts from *The Law Reports, The Weekly Law Reports, English Reports* and *Family Law Reports* are reproduced with the permission of the Incorporated Council of Law Reporting for England and Wales.

Extracts from John Marshall, 'Experiment on Human Embryos: Sentience as the cut-off point?', in GR Dunstan and MJ Seller (eds), *The Status of the Human Embryo: Perspectives from Moral Tradition* (1998); and Bill New & Julian Le Grand, *Rationing in the NHS: Principles and Pragmatism* (1996) are reproduced with the permission of the King's Fund, www.kingsfund.org.uk.

Extracts from the *All England Reports* and *The Times Law Reports* are reproduced with the permission of LexisNexis.

The *London Review of Books* and Lord Chief Justice Stephen Sedley for extracts from Stephen Sedley, 'Short Cuts', (2005) 27 *London Review of Books*.

Extracts from *Nature Reviews Genetics* are reproduced with the permission of Macmillan Publishers.

Extracts from the *New England Journal of Medicine* are reproduced with the permission of Massachusetts Medical Society.

McGraw-Hill Publishers for extracts from Amy Gutmann, 'For and Against Equal Access to Health Care', *Milbank Memorial Fund Quarterly/Health and Society* (1981) 59, and in *Classic Works in Medical Ethics*, Gregory Pence (ed.) (Boston: McGraw-Hill, 1998).

Medical Research Council for extracts from *Personal Information in Medical Research*, © 2000 Medical Research Council.

Nuffield Trust for extracts from Richard Sykes, *New Medicines, The Practice of Medicine, and Public Policy* (London, Nuffield Trust, 2000).

Extracts from *The Journal of Mental Health Law* are reproduced with the permission of Northumbria Law Press (Law School, Northumbria University).

Oxford University Press for extracts from John A Robertson, 'Extending preimplantation genetic diagnosis: the ethical debate: Ethical issues in new uses of preimplantation genetic diagnosis', (2003) 18 *Human Reproduction*, © European Society of Human Reproduction and Embryology, reproduced by permission of Oxford University Press/*Human Reproduction*; Hilary Putnam, 'Cloning People'; John Harris, 'Clones, Genes and Human Rights'; Ian Wilmut, 'Dolly: The Age of Biological Control'; and Jonathan Glover, 'Eugenics and Human Rights', in J Burley (ed.), *The Genetic Revolution and Human Rights* (OUP, 1999); Michael Jones, 'Breach of Duty'; and Andrew Grubb, 'Consent to Treatment: The Competent Patient', in A Grubb with J Laing (eds), *Principles of Medical Law* 2nd edition (OUP, 2004); Ian Kennedy, *Treat Me Right*, (OUP, 1988); and Ian Kennedy, 'The Fiduciary Relationship and its Application to Doctors' in P Birks (ed.), *Wrongs and Remedies in the Twenty-first Century* (Oxford: Clarendon Press, 1986). Reproduced by permission of Oxford University Press.

Extracts from *Medical Law Review, Current Legal Problems, Journal of Law, Policy and the Family, International and Comparative Law Quarterly, Human Reproduction* and the *Oxford Journal of Legal Studies* are reproduced with the permission of Oxford University Press and the authors.

Penguin Books for extracts from Jonathan Glover, *Causing Death and Saving Lives* (1977).

Random House, Inc. for extracts from Ronald Dworkin, *Life's Dominion: An Argument about Abortion and Euthanasia.*

Royal College of Psychiatrists for extracts from *Evidence submitted to the Joint Committee on the Draft Mental Health Bill* (RCP, 2004).

South Carolina Law Review for extracts from Jane Stapleton, 'Bugs in Anglo-American Products Liability', (2002) 53 *South Carolina Law Review.*

Extracts from *Feminist Legal Studies, Ethical Theory and Moral Practice, Medicine, Health Care and Philosophy* and the *European Journal of Health Law* are reproduced with the permission of Springer.

Extracts from *St Louis University Law Journal* are reproduced with the permission of St Louis University School of Law.

Extracts from *Stanford Law and Policy Review* and *Stanford Law Review* are reproduced with the permission of Stanford School of Law.

Extracts from *Journal of Medicine and Philosophy, Journal of Social Welfare and Family Law* and *American Journal of Bioethics* are reproduced with the permission of the Taylor & Francis Group.

Extracts from *Texas International Law Journal* and *Texas Law Review* are reproduced with the permission of University of Texas School of Law.

Thomson Publishing Services for extracts from Robin Oppenheim, 'The "Mosaic" of Tort Law: The Duty of Care Question', (2003) *Journal of Personal Injury Law;* '(on the application of Smeaton) v Secretary of State for Health', (2002) *Criminal Law Review* 664; Richard HS Tur, *Legislative Technique and Human Rights: The Sad Case of Assisted Suicide* (2003) Sweet & Maxwell; Charles Pugh and Marcus Pilgerstorfer, *The Development Risk Defence: Knowledge, Discoverability and Creative Leaps* (2004) Sweet and Maxwell.

Extracts from *Law Quarterly Review, Journal of Personal Injury Law, Criminal Law Review* and *Modern Law Review* are reproduced with the permission of Thomson Publishing Services.

University of California Press for extracts from Marlene Gerber Fried, 'Abortion in the United States–Legal but Inaccessible', in R Solinger (ed.), *Abortion Wars: A Half Century of Struggle 1950–2000* (Berkeley, University of California Press, 1998).

Extracts from Allen Buchanan, 'Ethical Responsibilities of Patients and Clinical Geneticists', (1998) 1 *Journal of Health Care, Law and Policy*. Reproduced with the permission of the University of Maryland School of Law.

University of Pennsylvania Press for extracts from Alexander Morgan Capron, 'Informed Consent in Catastrophic Disease Research and Treatment', (1974) 123 *University of Pennsylvania Law Review*.

Extracts from Lori Andrews, 'Beyond Doctrinal Boundaries: A Legal Framework for Surrogate Motherhood', (1995) 81 *Virginia Law Review*, reproduced with the permission of the Virginia Law Review Association.

Extracts from Lori B Andrews, 'A Conceptual Framework for Genetic Policy: Comparing the Medical, Public Health and Fundamental Rights Models', (2001) 79 *Washington University Journal of Law and Policy*; and Rebecca Dresser, 'Patient Advocates in Research: New Possibilities, New Problems', (2003) 11 *Washington University Journal of Law and Policy*; reproduced with the permission of Washington University School of Law.

Extracts from Katherine T Bartlett, 'Re-expressing Parenthood' (1998) 98 *Yale Law Journal*; and Marjorie Maguire Schulz, 'From Informed Consent to Patient Choice: A New Protected Interest', (1985) 95 *Yale Law Journal*; reproduced with the permission of the Yale Law Journal Company, Inc.

Extracts from Deborah Lupton, 'The Body, Medicine and Society' reproduced by permission of Oxford University Press Australia from *Second Opinion: An Introduction to Health Sociology*, 3rd edition 2005, Germov (ed.) Oxford University Press, www.oup.com.au.

Extracts from Mary Ann Warren, 'On the Moral and Legal Status of Abortion' (1973) 1 *The Monist* 43–61.

Extracts from Ruth Faden, Tom L Beauchamp, with Nancy M P King, *A History and Theory of Informed Consent* (OUP, 1986), reproduced by permission of Oxford University Press.

Extracts from Margaret Pabst Battin, *The Least Worst Death: Essays in Bioethics on the End of Life* (OUP, 1994), reproduced by permission of Oxford University Press.

Every effort has been made to clear the necessary permissions. If notified, the publisher will undertake to rectify any errors or omissions at the earliest opportunity.

CONTENTS

TABLE OF CASES

TABLE OF STATUTES

Page references in **bold** indicate that the text is reproduced in full.

TABLE OF STATUTORY INSTRUMENTS

Page references in **bold** indicate that the text is reproduced in full.

TABLE OF TREATIES, CONVENTIONS AND EUROPEAN LEGISLATION

1

AN INTRODUCTION TO BIOETHICS

1. CENTRAL ISSUES

1. Conventional medical ethics focused on the doctor–patient encounter. Bioethics' remit is much broader, taking in the dilemmas raised by new technologies.

2. Religious perspectives on bioethics tend to be less individualistic than secular approaches. Few now believe that modern medicine is 'usurping God's will', rather medical progress is, within limits, supported by most religious bioethicists.

3. There is an important difference between consequentialist and deontological reasoning. Consequentialists judge an action by its consequences, whereas deontological reasoning is less pragmatic, and starts from the premise that respecting a person's rights and autonomy is important for its own sake.

4. The 'principlist' approach lays out four key principles: autonomy, beneficence, non-maleficence and justice, which can be brought to bear on medical dilemmas. In contrast, casuistry involves reasoning by analogy from other similar cases. Virtue ethics is concerned with working out what a 'virtuous' person would do. And a feminist ethics of care rejects the dominant emphasis upon patient autonomy, and values relationships more highly.

5. Arguments from 'human dignity' or respect for the 'sanctity of human life' have particular resonance in the medical context, but their meaning, and the extent to which they are religiously inspired, is opaque.

6. Slippery slope claims are often essentially empirical claims, and effective regulation might be the best way to accommodate them.

2. INTRODUCTION

The purpose of this chapter is to provide an introduction to bioethical reasoning. The words 'ethics' and 'morality' derive from the Greek (*ethos*) and Latin (*mores*), meaning 'customs'. In their ordinary usage, the words have slightly different connotations. 'Morality' often implies a restrictive, and perhaps religiously inspired, code of conduct. 'Ethics' tends to refer to the systematic analysis of what it might mean to lead a decent life. Medical ethics is a branch of applied ethics, and it is principally concerned with how we should go about resolving particularly difficult questions that arise from the practice of medicine.

As we shall see throughout this book, it is impossible to study medical law without also confronting complex ethical dilemmas. For example:

- When is it acceptable for doctors to withhold lifesaving treatment from a profoundly handicapped baby?

- Should parents be allowed to choose their children's sex?
- What, if anything, would be wrong with paying someone to 'donate' one of their kidneys?
- Should an anorexic teenager be force-fed?
- Should scientists be allowed to carry out experiments on human embryos?
- What limits, if any, should be placed upon women's access to abortion?
- Should voluntary euthanasia be legalized?

It would be difficult to work out the appropriate *legal* response to such questions without also considering their ethical dimension. While this is principally a book about medical law, it would be artificial to draw a sharp distinction between medical law and medical ethics. Rather throughout this book we will be considering how law should respond to the ethical dilemmas thrown up by the practice of medicine.

This opening chapter attempts to summarize various ways in which we might go about resolving, or at least discussing, these ethical problems. We begin by looking at what we might mean by 'medical ethics', and the newer term 'bioethics'. Next we consider seven different types of ethical reasoning. When justifying a preference for a particular outcome in the field of medical law and ethics, it is common for people to ground their argument in reasons such as the need to respect 'human dignity' or the 'sanctity of human life', or to appeal to the dangers of the 'slippery slope', and we consider what these various claims involve. We conclude by looking at changing attitudes towards the human body within medical law and ethics.

3. BIOETHICS

While medical ethics has a very long history, bioethics is a relatively new discipline. Conventionally, medical ethics has been concerned with the ethics of good medical practice, that is with what it means to be a good doctor. Ethical rules or codes of conduct were guidelines that the medical profession imposed upon itself in order to ensure that doctors' behaviour towards both their colleagues and their patients met appropriate standards of moral decency. Unsurprisingly, therefore, the vantage point was always that of the doctor himself: how should the doctor obtain consent; when can a doctor breach his duty of confidentiality; and so on. Medical practice was strongly paternalistic: doctors were under a duty to act in their patients' best interests, but it was doctors (as opposed to the patients themselves) who decided what those interests were. In the next extract Susan Sherwin argues that conventional medical ethics also tended to marginalize both the patient's perspective and the broader social causes of ill health.

Susan Sherwin[1]

Until very recently, conscientious physicians were actually trained to act paternalistically toward their patients, to treat patients according to the physician's own judgement about what would be

---

[1] 'A Relational Approach to Autonomy in Healthcare' in Susan Sherwin (ed), *The Politics of Women's Health: Exploring Agency and Autonomy* (Temple UP Philadelphia 1998) 19–47, 21.

best for their patients, with little regard for each patient's own perspectives or preferences. The problem with this arrangement, however, is that health care may involve such intimate and central aspects of a patient's life—including, for example, matters such as health, illness, reproduction, death, dying, bodily integrity, nutrition, lifestyle, self-image, disability, sexuality, and psychological well-being—that it is difficult for anyone other than the patient to make choices that will be compatible with that patient's personal value system . . . Whenever possible, then, these types of choices should be made by the person whose life is central to the treatment considered. The principle of respect for patient autonomy is aimed at clarifying and protecting patients' ultimate right to make up their own minds about the specific health services they receive.

A striking feature of most . . . discussions about patient autonomy is their exclusive focus on individual patients; this pattern mirrors medicine's consistent tendency to approach illness as primarily a problem of particular patients . . . Within the medical tradition, suffering is located and addressed in the individuals who experience it rather than in the social arrangements that may be responsible for causing the problem. Instead of exploring the cultural context that tolerates and even supports practices such as war, pollution, sexual violence, and systemic unemployment—practices that contribute to much of the illness that occupies modern medicine—physicians generally respond to the symptoms troubling particular patients in isolation from the context that produces these conditions.

In contrast, Heather Draper and Tom Sorrell argue that medical ethics has tended to ignore patients' *obligations*, and has usually focused exclusively on the duties of doctors.

Heather Draper and Tom Sorrell[2]

Medical ethics is one-sided. It dwells on the ethical obligations of doctors to the exclusion of those of patients . . .

In comparison to what it asks of doctors, mainstream medical ethics makes very few demands of patients, and these usually begin and end with consent. Traditionally medical ethics has asserted that, as autonomous agents, competent patients must be allowed to decide for themselves the course of their medical treatment, and even whether to be treated at all. . . . Little or nothing is said about what kinds of decisions patients *ought* to make. Nor is much said about their responsibilities for making good rather than bad decisions. Indeed . . . mainstream medical ethics implies that a competent patient's decision is good simply by virtue of having been made by the patient. At times it seems as though patients never make, or cannot make, bad decisions . . .

In welfare states, discussion about the use of limited resources extends naturally to a consideration of whether citizens have some sort of moral obligation, other things being equal, to limit their demands on these resources. If the answer is 'Yes', then there may be a civic obligation to follow preventive health measures recommended by one's doctor. If one is advised to stop smoking or over-eating, and one disregards that advice, so that one's condition deteriorates to the point that expensive treatment is required to keep one alive, one may be doing something doubly wrong—breaking obligations to oneself and breaking civic obligations not to use public resources unnecessarily . . .

In short, there are duties not to use health services casually. . . . Someone who indulges their hypochondria by frequent visits to the GP, or who summons an ambulance after getting sunburn; someone who knowingly presents himself at an emergency room with nothing more than severe indigestion; or who calls out a doctor because he needs a prescription that could be filled in office

---

[2] 'Patients' Responsibilities in Medical Ethics' (2002) 16 Bioethics 335–51, 335, 337–8, 343–5.

hours next day; all of these patients do something morally wrong, wrong primarily because they have taken away time and resources better spent on more urgent cases . . .

[P]atients who are generally able to consent or refuse consent to medical treatment or to follow medical advice are presumed by mainstream medical ethics to be autonomous. If genuinely autonomous, they must be expected to take responsibility for the decisions that they make—including responsibility for any resulting ill health.

Bioethics' remit is generally assumed to be much wider than that of traditional medical ethics. It emerged as a distinctive discipline in the 1960s in response to a number of different factors. First, rapid technological progress was posing some complex dilemmas, particularly at the beginning and end of life. Effective contraception, safe abortion and artificial respirators all raised new and difficult questions which went beyond ethical conduct within the doctor–patient encounter. For example, once it became possible to (a) perform organ transplants, and (b) keep a patient's heart beating after death, it was necessary to ask whether these 'brain-dead' patients could be a legitimate source of organs for transplantation.

Secondly, medical paternalism was beginning to be challenged, and the principle of patient autonomy was instead ascendant. Patients no longer automatically deferred to doctors' superior medical expertise but were increasingly willing to insist upon their 'rights' and to challenge unsatisfactory treatment through litigation.

In the next extract, Helga Kuhse and Peter Singer discuss the origins and remit of bioethics.

Helga Kuhse and Peter Singer[3]

Since the 1960s, ethical problems in health care and the biomedical sciences have gripped the public consciousness in unprecedented ways. In part, this is the result of new and sometimes revolutionary developments in the biomedical sciences and in clinical medicine . . . These technological breakthroughs, however, have not been the only factor in the increasing interest in ethical problems in this area. Another factor has been a growing concern about the power exercised by doctors and scientists, which shows itself in concern to assert 'patients' rights' and the rights of the community as a whole to be involved in decisions that affect them. This has meant greater public awareness of the value-laden nature of medical decision making, and a critical questioning of the basis on which such decisions are made . . .

It was in the climate of such new ethical issues and choices that the field of inquiry now known as 'bioethics' was born. The word was not originally used in this sense. Van Rensselaer Potter originally proposed the term for a 'science of survival' in the ecological sense—that is, an interdisciplinary study aimed at ensuring the preservation of the biosphere. This terminology never became widely established, however, and instead 'bioethics' came to refer to the growing interest in the ethical issues arising from health care and the biomedical sciences . . .

Although the term itself is new, and the prominence of bioethics owes much to recent developments in the biomedical sciences, bioethics can also be seen as a modern version of a much older field of thought, namely medical ethics . . . Traditionally, medical ethics has focused primarily on the doctor–patient relationship and on the virtues possessed by the good doctor. It has also been very much concerned with relations between colleagues within the profession . . . Bioethics, on the other hand, is a more overtly critical and reflective enterprise. Not limited to questioning the

---

[3] 'What is bioethics? A historical introduction' 3–11 in Helga Kuhse and Peter Singer (eds), *A Companion to Bioethics* (Blackwell Oxford 1998) 3–4.

ethical dimensions of doctor–patient and doctor–doctor relationships, it goes well beyond the scope of traditional medical ethics in several ways. First, its goal is not the development of, or adherence to, a code or set of precepts, but a better understanding of the issues. Second, it is prepared to ask deep philosophical questions about the nature of ethics, the value of life, what it is to be a person, the significance of being human. Third, it embraces issues of public policy and the direction and control of science.

4. HOW SHOULD WE MAKE DIFFICULT ETHICAL DECISIONS?

Many people have 'gut feelings' or intuitive reactions to ethical dilemmas: it is very common for people to say of a controversial medical practice, such as reproductive cloning or animal-to-human organ transplantation: 'I just think it's wrong.' If everyone shared the same 'gut feelings', it would be relatively easy to translate this shared popular consensus into regulation. But in a heterogeneous society, disagreement is of course inevitable. And in the absence of consensus, we need to find some mechanism for resolving ethical dilemmas that goes beyond an appeal to our 'gut instincts'. As we will see in the following sections, bioethicists are principally concerned with trying to work out what this mechanism should be.

(a) RELIGIOUS BIOETHICS

There has always been an interesting relationship between religion and the practice of medicine. In the past, the belief that illness has a spiritual origin was commonplace. As a result, people sought cures through prayer and appeals to divine mercy, rather than from the medical profession. While the comprehensive rejection of medical expertise on religious grounds is now rare, there are still many people whose religious beliefs ground their anxiety about modern medicine's unprecedented power to create and to destroy life. Within a secular and culturally diverse society, however, religion tends to be regarded as a matter of private faith. As a result, while religious leaders' pronouncements on bioethics may be of central importance to the adherents of particular religions, their role in public discourse, and in shaping public policy is less clear.

In the next extract Daniel Callahan suggests that because all religions have a long and rich history of grappling with questions that are of central importance to medical law and ethics—such as the meaning of life or death—religious perspectives might be a particularly useful resource for the comparatively new discipline of secular bioethics.

Daniel Callahan[4]
The most striking change over the past two decades or so has been the secularisation of bioethics. The field has moved from one dominated by religious and medical traditions to one now increasingly shaped by philosophical and legal concepts. The consequence has been a mode of public

---

[4] 'Religion and the Secularization of Bioethics' (1990) 20 Hastings Center Report 2–4.

discourse that emphasizes secular themes: universal rights, individual self-direction, procedural justice and a systematic denial of either a common good or a transcendent individual good.

Religious convictions are thought 'personal' in two senses: they bespeak a particular cultural and ethnic background, and they reveal someone's inner life . . . The net result of this narrowing of philosophy and the disappearance or denaturing of religion in public discourse is a triple threat. It leaves us, first of all, too heavily dependent upon the law as the working source of morality. The language of the courts and legislatures becomes our only shared means of discourse. That leaves a great number fearful of the law (as seems the case with many physicians) or dependent upon the law to determine the rightness of actions, which it can rarely do since it tells us better what is forbidden or acceptable, than what is commendable or right.

It leaves us, secondly, bereft of the accumulated wisdom and knowledge that are the fruit of long-established religious traditions. I do not have to be a Jew to find it profitable and illuminating to see how the great rabbinical teachers have tried to understand moral problems over the centuries. Nor will Jews find it utterly useless to explore what the popes, or the leading Protestant divines, have had to say about ethics. . . .

It leaves us, thirdly, forced to pretend that we are not creatures both of particular moral communities and the sprawling inchoate general community that we celebrate as an expression of our pluralism. Yet that pluralism becomes a form of oppression if, in its very name, we are told to shut up in public about our private lives and beliefs and talk a form of what Jeffrey Stout has called moral Esperanto. The rules of that language are that it deny the concreteness and irregularities of real communities, that it eschew vision and speculation about goals and meaning, and that it enshrine the discourse of wary strangers (especially that of rights) as the preferred mode of daily relations.

Although there are obviously differences between religions, a number of similarities within religious approaches to bioethics might be identified. First, religious bioethics tend to emphasize the intrinsic rightness or wrongness of a particular course of action, and be less swayed by pragmatic or consequentialist arguments. In relation to euthanasia, for example, a religious perspective would concentrate upon the legitimacy or otherwise of bringing about another person's death, rather than the practical difficulties in policing doctors' behaviour.

Secondly, religions tend to share two principal moral concerns: (a) love for one's neighbour (almost every religion, for example, contains some version of the Golden Rule: that you should treat your neighbour as you would expect to be treated yourself); and (b) a sense of awe and respect for 'God's creation', and most especially for human life.

In the next extract, Hazel Markwell and Barry Brown describe how Roman Catholics' fundamental belief in the sanctity of life informs their response to a wide variety of bioethical questions.

Hazel Markwell and Barry Brown[5]

There is a long tradition of bioethical reasoning within the Roman Catholic faith, a tradition that extends from Augustine's writings on suicide in the early Middle Ages to recent papal teachings on euthanasia and reproductive technologies. Roman Catholic bioethics . . . comprises a complex set

---

[5] 'Bioethics for Clinicians: Catholic Bioethics' (2001) 165 Canadian Medical Association Journal 189–92, 189.

of positions that have their origins in scripture, the writings of the Doctors of the Church, papal encyclicals, and reflections by contemporary Catholic theologians and philosophers . . .

Fundamental to Catholic bioethics is a belief in the sanctity of life: the value of a human life, as a creation of God and a gift in trust, is beyond human evaluation and authority. God maintains dominion over it. In this view, we are stewards, not owners, of our own bodies and are accountable to God for the life that has been given to us.

Applied to medicine, then, religious perspectives tend to be less individualistic than secular bioethics, and to start from the premise that life is a gift which is not ours to destroy. This leads them to place less emphasis upon patient autonomy than secular approaches.

Thirdly, every religion has been confronted by the question of how far man should be allowed to 'interfere' with the natural order. Their answers have varied dramatically—from the idea that modern medicine is usurping divine power and frustrating God's will, to the more progressive (and much more common) view that man's quest for knowledge, and hence medical progress, is itself part of God's creation. In the next extract, Paul Badham explains this shift in the context of Christianity.

Paul Badham[6]

[M]edical ethics provides the largest number of instances where Christians today almost unanimously accept as good practices which their predecessors in the faith regarded as evil. For many centuries Christians forbade the giving of medicine, deeming it equivalent to the practice of sorcery. The practice of surgery, the study of anatomy and the dissection of corpses for medical research were all at one time firmly forbidden. Later the practices of inoculation and vaccination faced fierce theological opposition. Indeed in 1829 Pope Leo XII declared that whoever decided to be vaccinated was no longer a child of God; smallpox was a judgement of God, vaccination was a challenge to heaven. For similar reasons the initial use of quinine against malaria was denounced by many Christians. The introduction of anaesthesia and, above all, the use of chloroform in childbirth were seen as directly challenging the biblical judgement that, because of their inheritance of the guilt of Eve's original sin, all women must face the penalty that 'in pain you shall bring forth children'. Consequently the use of chloroform in childbirth was vigorously attacked from public pulpits throughout Britain and the United States . . .

The root objection to all the medical practices mentioned above was the belief that the duty of human beings was to submit in patience to what God had willed. All innovations in medical practice were initially seen as implying a lack of faith and trust in God's good purposes. Doctors were accused of 'playing God', of being unwilling to accept that God knows what is right for a particular person, of prying into sacred mysteries and areas of God's own prerogative. Yet gradually all mainstream Christian churches have modified their teaching, and the formerly criticized activity of the doctor has itself come to be seen as itself a channel of God's love and the vehicle of his providence. Consequently although the practice of medicine faced opposition in earlier centuries, a very close relationship now exists between doctors and clergy . . . Christians today are happy to think of doctors as fulfilling the will of God in restoring to heath persons struck down by curable illness.

It would be a mistake to imply that there is a single Jewish tradition, nevertheless,

6 'Theological examination of the case for euthanasia' in Paul Badham and Paul Ballard, *Facing Death: An Interdisciplinary Approach* (Cardiff University of Wales Press Cardiff 1996) 101–16, 103.

Jewish perspectives on bioethics tend to share the conviction that our bodies belong to God, and that we are therefore under a duty to care for them. This leads both to an emphasis on preventative medicine, and, as Shimon Glick explains in the next extract, to the belief that the treatment of illness is obligatory, on the part of both physicians and their patients.

Shimon Glick[7]

Consonant with the high priority given to life, the Jewish tradition, unlike Anglo-Saxon law, *requires* the physician to respond to any patient's call for help. . . . But just as the physician is obligated to render care, so too, the seeking of care by the patient is mandatory. The reason for this obligation is that, in our Jewish tradition, man does not possess title to his life or his body. Man is but the steward of the divine possession which he has been privileged to receive. The terms of that stewardship are not of man's choice, but are determined by G/d's commands. We forbid suicide and require man to take all reasonable steps to preserve life and health. When beneficence conflicts with autonomy, the former is given precedence by Judaism, a view clearly in conflict with the modern Western consensus. While such a violation of autonomy for the patient's good is not enforceable in our modern pluralistic societies, it has full sanction in the Jewish tradition, and Jewish courts may enforce medical treatment when unequivocally indicated.

In the deliberations as to permissibility of a given act, its being 'natural' or 'unnatural' plays little role. In our tradition, the world is regarded as a deliberately unfinished product placed in the trust of man—himself a finite and imperfect being. Man is expected, indeed commanded . . . to engage in completing . . . the work of the Creator . . .

Man is neither to worship Nature as do the pagans, nor is he to be intimidated by it. He is commanded to control Nature and to exploit it constructively. Healing the ill . . . is therefore not only theologically acceptable, but is mandated. This eagerness to modify Nature, together with the great value placed on human life, contributed to the exalted place occupied by the healing profession in Jewish tradition.

Mainstream Muslim theologians agree that technological intervention in nature, so long as its purpose is to improve human welfare, does not contravene the prohibition against changing God's creation. Indeed, it has been argued that scientific research is protected by the *Shari'a*, and that medicine is a religious duty in every community. Preventative medicine—through the *Shari'a*'s rulings on hygiene and self-restraint— is encouraged. The Islamic Code of Medical Ethics, for example, states that:

The natural prophylaxis against some diseases rests in the revival of such religious values as chastity, purity, self-restraint, and refraining from advertently or inadvertently inflicting harm on self or others. To preach these values is preventative medicine and therefore lies within the jurisdiction and obligation of the medical profession.[8]

Fourthly, religious bioethics are generally more strongly normative than secular bio-ethics. Whereas secular bioethics might accept that there is no *right* answer to a particularly controversial ethical question, and might instead concentrate upon devising an acceptable procedure through which a compromise position might be reached,

[7] 'A View from Sinai: a Jewish Perspective on Biomedical Ethics' in E Pellegrino, P Mazzarella, and P Corsi (eds), *Transcultural Dimensions* (University Publishing Group Frederick, MD 1992) 73–82, 76–7.

[8] Issued by the International Organisation of Islamic Medicine (later called the Islamic Organisation of Medical Sciences) in 1981.

religious bioethics would be more likely to reach a definite, normative conclusion. Fifthly, religious perspectives on ethical dilemmas tend to consist in the interpretation of past authority, and are always to some extent constrained by the written or oral teachings or texts of the particular tradition.

(b) SECULAR BIOETHICS

While it would be a mistake to gloss over the internal disagreements that are common *within* the various religious traditions, the existence of a source of authority, or multiple sources, provides an obvious starting point for ethical reasoning on a particular issue, and the rich web of interpretative precedent should—in theory at least—lead religious scholars towards the *right* answer. In contrast, secular bioethics has no obvious starting point, and is much less certain about whether a right answer exists.

Within secular bioethics, are there nevertheless some shared and universally accepted values? In the next extract, Edmund Pellegrino argues that respect for human dignity is a secular principle that transcends cultural difference.

Edmund D Pellegrino[9]

In more cultures than ever before, there is recognition of the moral rights of patients to participate in decisions that affect them, to protection of confidentiality, to humane treatment, and to access to healthcare. There is a long way to go before unanimity is achieved, but it is clear that older models of physician-dominated relationships are under scrutiny everywhere....

Growing recognition of the moral rights of patients, their special vulnerability as sick persons, and their dependency on the physician's knowledge constitute the empirical foundations of a morally defensible ethic of medicine. Those cultural systems that violate such norms cannot be given equal moral standing with systems that respect these norms, not because the cultural systems that support human and patients' rights are *per se* superior but because the protection of human rights is grounded in something more fundamental than culture—the deference owed to all human beings *qua* human beings. This is a norm by which every culture may be judged.

To be sure, the present idea of respect for the self-determination of patients originated in contemporary bioethics, which in its present form is a product of Western ... conceptions of ethics. However, we must not forget that it has been only two decades since even Western medical ethics abandoned the stance of medical authoritarianism. It did so because it recognized that the duty of respect for the moral right of patient autonomy is grounded in the rights and moral claims all human beings have on one another. Patient self-determination happens to have been first emphasized by 'Western' medical ethics, but it should be universally recognized because of its metacultural justification, not its propagation by Western medicine. The dignity of the human person is not something that can be continually asserted or denied. It transcends culture because it resides inalienably in what it is to be a human being ...

The ethical system of any culture is morally defensible because it is grounded in truths that transcend that culture; it is not morally defensible simply because it is the product of a particular culture ... The fact of cultural difference does not necessitate absolute cultural relativism. Rather it energizes the search for those ethical elements that transcend particular cultures.

If secular bioethics is not looking for the right answer to a difficult ethical dilemma,

---

[9] 'Intersections of Western Biomedical ethics and world culture: problematic and possibility' (1992) 3 Cambridge Quarterly of Healthcare Ethics 191–6, 193–5.

what is it doing? One possibility might be that reasoned argument and deliberation is a rational way to resolve difficult questions, where a number of conflicting views exist. In the next extract, Tim Dare argues that the requirement to give reasons, or to justify one's moral views is an especially important feature of ethical reasoning.

Tim Dare[10]

If a position of mine is to count as an ethical position I must produce reasons for it. This is not to say that I must articulate a complex moral theory or even state a moral principle that I am following for my position to count as moral. But in practice there are certain sorts of reasons or responses which will not do. Because a mere prejudice, for instance, is precisely a belief that is not supported by reasons, I cannot offer mere prejudices in support of my position. Similarly, mere emotional reactions will not count as reasons . . . This is not to say that ethical positions should be unemotional or dispassionate. On the contrary, we should care about our moral views. But emotional reactions should be prompted by or grounded in moral judgments and not vice versa. And if my position is based upon propositions of fact which are not only false but so implausible that they fail even the minimal standards of evidence I impose upon others I will likely be offering not reasons but instead showing that I can think of no genuine reasons for my position at all . . .

Perhaps most importantly, the role of reasons imposes a constraint of consistency. Consistency requires that if there are exactly the same reasons in support of one course of action as there are in support of another, then those actions will be equally right or equally wrong—they will be equally well supported or undercut by reasons.

In the next extract, Dan Brock further suggests that, to be persuasive, the reasons we give for our moral judgments must be ones that others can accept.

Dan W Brock[11]

[M]oral judgments are unlike some judgments of taste and moral disagreements are unlike some disagreements over matters of taste, because moral judgments must be backed by reasons. If you like vanilla ice cream and I like chocolate, we can just accept this as a difference in taste—there is no correct preference about flavours of ice cream, and if asked why I prefer chocolate, I may be able to repeat only that it tastes better to me. Unlike matters of taste, moral judgments, for example, about whether voluntary euthanasia is wrong, must be backed with reasons . . . [T]he very process of having and offering reasons for our moral judgments is the principal feature distinguishing morality from mere expressions of simple taste or preference.

Because the principal role of moral judgments is to guide action . . . moral judgments are subject to a special worry. The worry is that they may be no more than a hodgepodge of thinly veiled rationalizations and biases reflecting our own self-interest, prejudices, and arbitrary preferences. General moral principles or theories can help allay this worry by explaining these judgments: they are shown to fit, and to be derivable and made from, a coherent, unified moral conception. We come to see that our particular moral judgments have a coherent identifiably moral source, heretofore likely only implicit, and are not merely a cover for our prejudices and self-interest.

[A]ny conclusions that a particular moral disagreement is in principle irresolvable should come only at the end of a full, but failed, attempt to resolve the disagreement.

---

[10] 'Applied Ethics, Challenges to' in Ruth Chadwick (ed), *Encyclopaedia of Applied Ethics* 1(1) (Academic Press San Diego 1997) 183–90, 183–5.
[11] 'Public Moral Discourse' in LW Sumner and Joseph Boyle (eds), *Philosophical Perspectives on Bioethics* (University of Toronto Press Toronto 1996) 271–96, 283–4, 289, 292, 294.

In a liberal democracy, public policy that requires everyone to act in specific ways should not be based on sectarian views reasonably rejected by substantial segments of the population. This is a goal that cannot always be realized for all policy, certainly in practice, but I believe in theory as well; still, it is an important goal nonetheless. It implies, for example, that public policy should not be based on specific religious beliefs that many do not share. Not only public policies themselves, but the reasons that are offered in their support in policy debate should not be reasons that others can reasonably reject as a basis for public policy in a pluralistic society.

(1) MORAL THEORIES

The question of how we should work out what would be the right or wrong thing to do has formed the basis of moral philosophy for thousands of years. There is insufficient space here to fully describe the extensive and rich philosophical literature from which medical ethics has borrowed. But it is worth noting that two traditions in particular have often pulled in different directions when applied to medical dilemmas. Teleological (from the Greek *telos*: consequences) theories judge the rightness or wrongness of an action in terms of its likely *consequences*. So to argue that legalizing euthanasia might damage the doctor–patient relationship would be an example of consequentialist or teleological reasoning. Utilitarianism—or the idea that we should act so as to maximize the amount of pleasure or happiness within society—is the most well-known teleological theory. Deontological (from the Greek *deontos*: duty) theories, in contrast, insist that the intrinsic rightness or wrongness of an action does not depend upon its consequences, but rather upon whether it is consistent with certain *basic moral principles*. An example might be basing an argument for the legalization of euthanasia upon the principle that we should respect the autonomous decisions of competent adults. The writings of the philosopher Immanuel Kant (1724–1804) are often used as an example of deontological moral theory. Let us consider each in turn.

(a) Utilitarianism

Utilitarianism emerged as a secular alternative to Christian ethics in the late eighteenth and early nineteenth centuries through the work of Jeremy Bentham (1748–1832), and later John Stuart Mill (1806–73), whose father was one of Bentham's pupils. According to utilitarianism, morality lies not in religious obedience, but in the maximization of human welfare. Because the pleasure and wellbeing of each human being matters equally, utilitarianism is an essentially egalitarian theory.

A utilitarian is interested only in the *consequences* of an action, not whether it is intrinsically either right or wrong. An example might be the question of whether we should keep our promises. A utilitarian would have to say that there can be both good and bad consequences from keeping a promise. Where the good consequences outweigh the bad consequences, it will be right to keep the promise, but when the reverse is true, the promise should be broken. The problem with this is that it ignores the fact that simply having made a promise to another person offers a compelling reason to keep it.

A variation on utilitarianism, called 'rule utilitarianism', provides a partial solution to some of the defects of utilitarian moral reasoning. A rule utilitarian would ask not which *action* will maximize welfare, but rather which *general rules* will, on the whole, lead to the best consequences. When deciding whether doctors should respect patient confidentiality, for example, a strict utilitarian would answer: 'it depends'. Sometimes it might be good to keep patients' records secret, but at other times it might not. This case-by-case approach would require doctors to predict the consequences of both revealing and not revealing information about each of their patients. This would clearly be an unmanageable task, which would itself have negative consequences because the provision of health care services would grind to a halt. So a rule utilitarian might say that it is, *on the whole*, better to impose a duty on doctors to respect their patients' confidentiality since this rule will tend to maximize wellbeing.

Another problem with utilitarianism is its *quantitative* approach to welfare. If killing one healthy person would enable us to transfer her organs into five patients who would otherwise die, surely the utilitarian would be forced to conclude that this would be the right thing to do. Again, rule utilitarianism might offer a way to avoid this unpalatable conclusion: applying the principle that doctors should 'above all do no harm' will, in general, tend to have better consequences than allowing doctors to kill their patients in order to save more lives.

Of course, as Kevin Wildes explains, utilitarianism depends upon the existence of a mechanism through which different outcomes can be ranked, otherwise it would be impossible to tell whether consequence A is preferable to consequence B.

Kevin Wildes[12]

The appeal to the consequences of one's decisions brings no more success [in resolving moral controversies], because it faces the problem of how to assess and evaluate different consequences. For example, some believe that living somewhat longer as a result of chemotherapy is a better consequence, even with the side-effects, than dying. Yet for others, living a life unimpaired by treatment is a more important outcome than extending the length of life. To make a judgment among consequences one needs an agreed-upon method by which to rank the outcomes. Therefore a consequentialist must build in some presuppositions about the assessment and ranking of values, both to evaluate possible outcomes of ethical choices and to know which outcomes are more desirable and should be given priority. . . . Consequentialist accounts therefore, are no better than those of intuitionists for purposes of demonstrating which set of outcomes is preferable because such a judgment requires an authoritative means of ranking benefits and harms. We are left in a position in which there is no way to judge between methods of valuing consequences except by appeal to our own moral sense.

(b) Kantianism

The aspect of Kant's philosophy that we are particularly interested in here is his 'categorical imperative'. Kant himself gives four formulations of the Categorical Imperative, two of which are worth singling out here:

(a) Act only on that maxim whereby you can at the same time will that it should become a universal law.

(b) So act as to treat humanity, whether in your own person or in that of any other, never solely as a means but always also as an end.

---

[12] 'Particularism in Bioethics: Balancing Secular and Religious Concerns' (1994) 53 Maryland Law Review 1220, 1228.

The first imperative requires us to act *consistently* and *justly*. The latter (which is more commonly cited by medical ethicists) demands that we do not ever treat another person—or allow ourselves to be treated—purely in order to satisfy another's purposes.

Both are in some sense negative tests for actions, that is they tell us what we must *not* do: one must not act inconsistently, and one must not use another person solely for one's own ends. They do not consist in positive prescriptions for action: not all acts that conform to the categorical imperative are ones that we ought to perform. Furthermore, as John Rawls has pointed out, it would be 'a serious misconception to think of the Categorical Imperative procedure as an algorithm intended to yield, more or less mechanically, a correct judgement'.[13] Rather, he suggests that the point of the categorical imperative may simply be to inculcate 'a form of moral reflection that could reasonably be used to check the purity of our motives'.[14] Similarly, in the next extract, Onora O'Neill argues that Kant was interested in 'principled autonomy', or the giving of reasons which others might understand.

Onora O'Neill[15]

The evidence that Kant's account of autonomy is not a conception of individual autonomy is easily assembled. He never speaks of an *autonomous self* or *autonomous persons* or *autonomous individuals*, but rather of the *autonomy of reason*, or the *autonomy of ethics*, or the *autonomy of principles* and of the *autonomy of willing* . . . For Kant autonomy is *not a form of self-expression*, it is a matter of acting on certain sorts of principles . . . Nor are those who act with principled autonomy committed to any distinctive form of individualism; principled autonomy is expressed in action whose principle *could be adopted by all others*.

To make either thinking or proposals for action followable by others we must impose structure on them: we must make our underlying principles of communication and proposals for action that are law-like or principled; if we do not, we do not offer reasons for thinking or for acting . . .

Autonomy in thinking is no more—but also no less—than the attempt to conduct thinking (speaking, writing) on principles on which all others whom we address could also conduct their thinking (speaking, writing). Autonomy in action is also no more—but also no less—that the attempt to act on principles on which all others could act . . .

So 'self-legislation' is not a mysterious phrase for describing merely arbitrary ways in which a free individual might or might not act. It is the basic characteristic of ways of thinking or willing that are conducted with sufficient discipline to be followable or accessible to others. Such ways of thinking and acting must be lawlike rather than lawless, and will thereby be in principle intelligible to others, and open to their criticism, rebuttal or reasoned argument.

In contrast, Barbara Secker is concerned that Kantian autonomy, with its emphasis upon independence and rationality, asks too much of patients.

Barbara Secker[16]

[G]iven the nature of patienthood, the Kantian concept of autonomy demands too much of patients. This idealistic concept is of little practical relevance in health contexts where patients, on

---

[13] John Rawls, *Lectures on the History of Moral Philosophy* (Barbara Herman (ed)) (Harvard UP Cambridge, MA 2000) 166.

[14] Ibid, 148.

[15] *Autonomy and Trust in Bioethics* (CUP Cambridge 2002) 83–5, 91, 93.

[16] 'The Appearance of Kant's deontology in contemporary Kantianism: concepts of patient autonomy in bioethics' (1999) 24 Journal of Medicine and Philosophy 43–66, 50–1.

the whole, bear little resemblance to the Kantian free, independent, exclusively rational individual . . .

Moreover, the highly rationalistic, individualistic Kantian account appears to assume that all that patients need to qualify as autonomous, in addition to the requisite intrinsic capacities . . . is negative freedom. However, patients frequently are in vulnerable positions, are unable to act on their decisions, and require that positive measures be taken on their behalf. . . .

If we appeal to the Kantian view (based on an ideal of the self as independent and exclusively rational), very few, if any, patients will be regarded as autonomous. Actual patients are likely to be dependent or interdependent, and their decision-making capacity is not always based (exclusively) on reason.

My second concern is that Kantian autonomy appears to place a premium on independence. The corresponding normative assumptions about the nature of human capacities and interaction may contribute to the devaluing of those patients who may be dependent and vulnerable . . . [I]f autonomy is morally valuable, and if autonomy is associated with independence, then dependence is regarded as morally inadequate and, consequently, those who are dependent are devalued . . . The nature of patienthood, however, is partially characterized by dependency of one kind or another . . .

My third criticism of the Kantian concept is that it may promote paternalism better than it promotes patient autonomy. Because the Kantian concept is not well suited for application to patients and yet still is one of the dominant accounts, I am concerned that patients may be measured against its rigorous standards, that the majority will not 'measure up' and that some health care professionals and institutions may attempt to justify wholesale paternalism.

(2) PRINCIPLISM AND ITS CRITICS

While applying moral philosophy to medical dilemmas can undoubtedly enrich our reasoning process, it will seldom provide clear prescriptions for doctors faced with difficult moral dilemmas. So, for example, a doctor might be told that: 'A utilitarian would do X, and a Kantian would do Y' which might be interesting, but is not terribly helpful.

A more practical way to decide medical questions was set out in Tom Beauchamp and James Childress's groundbreaking book *Principles of Biomedical Ethics*, now in its fifth edition. Beauchamp and Childress distilled four basic principles—autonomy, non-maleficence, beneficence, and justice—and argued that these could be used to guide medical decision-making.

(a) The word *autonomy*—from the Greek *autos* (self) and *nomos* (rule)—initially referred to the self-rule of independent cities. It has since been extended to mean individual self-governance, and encompasses a cluster of interests such as liberty, privacy and freedom of choice. In relation to medicine, respect for autonomy tends to mean giving competent adults the right to make their own decisions about their medical treatment.

(b) *Non-maleficence*, or the duty to 'above all do no harm' (*primum non nocere*) has its origins in the Hippocratic oath. So, for example, it could be argued that removing a kidney from a living donor potentially breaches the doctors duty to 'do no harm', since it involves major surgery which could have no health benefit for the living organ donor.

(c) *Beneficence*, or the duty to 'do good' has clear parallels with religious ethics' emphasis upon compassion and helping others. Whenever a patient wants to make a decision which her doctor believes to be contrary to her best interests, the principles of autonomy and beneficence (and perhaps also non-maleficence) will come into conflict, and we will need to decide which should have priority.

(d) *Justice* is often interpreted to mean that we should treat like cases alike. But of course this depends upon being able to tell when cases are either 'like' or 'unlike'. When allocating lungs for transplant, do we act justly by making non-smokers a lower priority than smokers (i.e. are these 'unlike' cases?), or should the only relevant criteria be clinical need, in which case the smoker and the non-smoker are 'like' cases? In relation to health care, it is seldom possible to give every patient immediate access to the best medical treatment, so justice instead demands that we ration scarce resources fairly and transparently.

These principles are more 'user-friendly' than Kantian moral philosophy or Utilitarianism, but they nevertheless borrow from both deontological and teleological reasoning. So respect for patient autonomy might be described as a deontological principle because it is valuable regardless of the consequences of the patient's decision. On the other hand, beneficence may be a teleological principle because we can only act beneficently if we have some conception of whether the action will increase the patient's welfare.

Commonly, more than one principle will be relevant, and they will often pull in different directions. Indeed, almost every contentious medical question could be framed as a conflict between two or more of these basic principles. It might even be argued that the reason why awkward cases are agonizing is precisely because they are cases in which principles that many of us would accept are in conflict with each other. Consider euthanasia, for example. The principle of autonomy might suggest that we should respect a competent patient's wish to die. Against this, the principle of non-maleficence might lead us to conclude that doctors should never actively cause a patient's death.

So while the principlist approach might enable us to describe a moral dilemma as a conflict between competing principles, it will rarely dictate any particular outcome. Rather, as Tom L Beauchamp and James F Childress admit in the next extract, when principles conflict there is no escaping the need to decide which factor is more important in the particular circumstances. One solution might be to rank the principles, but any hierarchy requires justification which cannot be provided by the principles themselves. If, for example, we want to say that autonomy should take priority over beneficence, either in general, or in a particular case, then we need to explain why.

Tom L Beauchamp and James F Childress[17]
A set of principles in a moral account should function as an analytical framework that expresses the general values underlying rules in the common morality. These principles can then function as

[17] TL Beauchamp and JF Childress, *Principles of Biomedical Ethics* (5th edn OUP Oxford 2001) 12, 15–16, 18–19.

guidelines for professional ethics . . . [W]e defend four clusters of moral principles that serve this function. The four clusters are (1) *respect for autonomy* (a norm of respecting the decision-making capacities of autonomous persons), (2) *nonmaleficence* (a norm of avoiding the causation of harm), (3) *beneficence* (a group of norms for providing benefits and balancing benefits against risks and costs), and (4) *justice* (a group of norms for distributing benefits, risks, and costs fairly).

Nonmaleficence and beneficence have played a central historical role in medical ethics, whereas respect for autonomy and justice were neglected in traditional medical ethics. . . .

Our four clusters of principles do not constitute a general moral theory. They provide only a framework for identifying and reflecting on moral problems. The framework is spare, because prima facie principles do not contain sufficient content to address the nuances of many moral circumstances. We therefore need to examine how to specify and balance these abstract principles. . . .

Specification is a process of reducing the indeterminateness of abstract norms and providing them with action guiding content. For example, without further specification, 'do no harm' is an all-too-bare starting point for thinking through problems, such as assisted suicide and euthanasia. It will not adequately guide action when norms conflict. . . .

Principles, rules and rights require balancing no less than specification. We need both methods because each addresses a dimension of moral principles and rules range and scope, in the case of specification, and weight or strength, in the case of balancing. Specification entails a substantive refinement of the range of scope of norms, whereas balancing consists of deliberation and judgment about the relative weights or strength of norms. Balancing is especially important for reaching judgments in individual cases, and specification is especially useful for policy development. . . .

As a response to criticisms that the model of balancing is too intuitive and open-ended—lacking in a commitment to firm principles—we can list a few conditions that reduce the amount of intuition involved. The following conditions must be met to justify infringing one prima facie norm in order to adhere to another.

1. Better reasons can be offered to act on the overriding norm than on the infringed norm. . . .

2. The moral objective justifying the infringement must have a realistic prospect of achievement.

3. The infringement is necessary in that no morally preferable alternative can be substituted.

4. The infringement selected must be the least possible infringement, commensurate with achieving the primary goal of the action.

5. The agent must seek to minimize any negative effects of the infringement.

6. The agent must act impartially in regard to all affected parties.

Beauchamp and Childress's approach has a number of critics. In the next extract, K Danner Clouse and Bernard Gert argue that, rather than clarifying difficult questions, principlism may be unsystematic and misleading.

K Danner Clouse and Bernard Gert[18]

We believe that the 'principles of biomedical ethics' approach is mistaken and misleading. Principlism is mistaken about the nature of morality and is misleading as to the foundations of ethics . . .

Our bottom line, starkly put, is that 'principle', as conceived by the proponents of Principlism, is a

[18] 'A Critique of Principlism' (1990) 15 Journal of Medicine and Philosophy 219–36, 220, 222–3, 229, 232–3.

misnomer and that 'principles' so conceived cannot function as they are in fact claimed to be functioning by those who purport to employ them. At best, 'principles' operate primarily as checklists naming issues worth remembering when considering a biomedical moral issue. At worst 'principles' obscure and confuse moral reasoning by their failure to be guidelines and by their eclectic and unsystematic use of moral theory . . .

If the principle is not a clear, direct imperative at all, but simply a collection of suggestions and observations, occasionally conflicting, then he will not know what is really guiding his action nor what facts to regard as relevant nor how to justify his action. The language of principlism suggests that he has applied a principle which is morally well-established and hence prima facie correct. But a closer look at the situation shows that in fact he has looked at and weighed many diverse moral considerations, which are superficially interrelated and herded under a chapter heading named for the 'principle' in question . . . This actually amounts simply to thinking about the case from diverse and conflicting points of view . . .

Taking what is properly the moral ideal of helping others (and hence not morally required), and lumping it under a 'principle' of beneficence along with genuine duties (which are required), eg, the duty of health care professionals to help their patients, leads to confusion and misunderstanding. The confusion basically results from treating beneficence as if it were morally required just as noninterference with the freedom of others is morally required.

The appeal of principlism is that it makes use of those features of each ethical theory that seems to have the most support. Thus, in proposing the principle of beneficence, it acknowledges that Mill was right in being concerned with consequences . . . In proposing the principle of autonomy, it acknowledges that Kant was right in emphasising the importance of the individual person . . . But there is no attempt to see how these different concerns can be blended together as integrated parts of a single adequate theory, rather than disparate concerns derived from several competing theories.

(3) CASUISTRY

Dissatisfaction with the principlist approach to bioethics has led to a resurgence of interest in casuistry. Casuistry involves case-based reasoning, where instead of starting with broad, abstract principles (a top-down approach), we instead begin with our response to concrete cases and reason by analogy (a bottom-up approach). This is, as John Arras points out, undoubtedly similar to the judiciary's incremental development of the common law.

John D Arras[19]
Developed in the early Middle-Ages as a method of bringing abstract and universal ethico-religious precepts to bear on particular moral situations, casuistry has had a checkered history. In the hands of expert practitioners during its salad days in the sixteenth and seventeenth centuries, casuistry generated a rich and morally sensitive literature devoted to numerous real-life ethical problems, such as truth-telling, usury, and the limits of revenge. By the late seventeenth century, however, casuistical reasoning had degenerated into a notoriously sordid form of logic-chopping in the service of personal expediency. To this day, the very term 'casuistry' conjures up pejorative images of disingenuous argument and moral laxity.

In spite of casuistry's tarnished reputation, some philosophers have claimed that casuistry, shorn of its unfortunate excesses, has much to teach us about the resolution of moral problems in

[19] 'Getting Down to Cases: The revival of casuistry in bioethics' (1991) 16 Journal of Medicine and Philosophy 29–51, 29–30, 34–6.

medicine. Indeed through the work of Albert Jonsen and Stephen Toulmin this 'new Casuistry' has emerged as a definite alternative to the hegemony of the so-called 'applied ethics' method of moral analysis that has dominated most bioethical scholarship and teaching since the early 1970s.

Contrary to deductivist ethical theories, wherein principles are said to preexist the actual cases to which they apply, the new casuistry contends that ethical principles are 'discovered' in the cases themselves, just as common law legal principles are developed in and through judicial decisions on particular legal cases ... Rather than stemming originally from some ethical theory, such as Utilitarianism, these principles are said to emerge gradually from reflection upon our responses to particular cases ...

In the applied ethics model, principles not only 'come before' our practices in the sense of being antecedently derived from theory before being applied to cases; they also have priority over practices in the sense that their function is to justify (or criticize) practices ... It is just the reverse for the new casuists, who sometimes imply that ethical principles are nothing more than mere *summaries* of meanings already embedded in our actual practices. Rather than serving as a justification for certain practices, principles within the new casuistry often merely seem to *report* in summary fashion what we have already decided ...

In contrast to the deductivist method, whose principles glide unsullied over the facts, the principles of the new casuistry are always subject to further revision and articulation in light of new cases.

In the next extract, Albert Jonsen argues that no moral dilemma is entirely novel, and that it therefore makes sense to look at how analogous dilemmas have been resolved in the past.

Albert R Jonsen[20]

No ethical problem is completely unprecedented. Regardless how novel, it bears some resemblance to problems that are more familiar. The more familiar ones will often be ones for which resolutions have been offered and sometimes accepted. Thus, one compares the new case with the more familiar one. That comparison almost always involves seeking for the similarities and differences in circumstance. Occasionally, in the more novel cases, one will recognize that the topics under which the moral discussion proceeds are inadequate because the practice or institution has manifestly or subtly changed. In this view, ethical reasoning is primarily reasoning by analogy, seeking to identify cases similar to the one under scrutiny and to discern whether the changed circumstances justify a different judgement in the new case than they did in the former.

In essence, casuistry's starting point is the idea that moral certainty derives from our shared intuitive response to so-called paradigm cases. There are a number of problems with this. First, even if we do believe that our intuitions will sometimes embody universally valid moral judgements—an example might be condemnation of Nazi doctors' abuse of research subjects during the Second World War—these are the exception rather than the norm. Moreover, it is not clear that our intuitive response to 'easy' cases actually helps us very much when we are faced with much tougher moral choices. For example, let us imagine that we all agree that it would be unethical to kill disabled children. How would that assist us when we are faced with the much more finely balanced question of whether it could ever be ethical to withdraw life-sustaining medical treatment from a very severely handicapped neonate?

[20] 'Casuistry: An Alternative or Complement to Principles' (1995) 5 Kennedy Institute of Ethics Journal 237–51, 245.

Secondly, case based reasoning will only yield a definite answer if there is some consensus upon what counts as a relevant similarity. Is abortion relevantly similar to murder (the killing of an innocent human being), or is it relevantly similar to contraception (allowing women to control their reproductive capacity)? Without underlying agreement on certain fundamental moral questions, casuistry provides us with little concrete guidance.

Thirdly, the analogy with the common law is imperfect. The common law contains a system of *binding* precedent, and identifies individuals (that is, judges) whose interpretation of previous cases is *authoritative*. In the field of bioethics, not only is there no common morality to guide decision-making, but also there are no clearly identifiable moral 'experts' to adjudicate on competing interpretations of previous authority.

Fourthly, it is not clear how we can be guided by decisions in previous cases unless those decisions are distilled into some sort of general principle. We could, for example, say that depriving someone of their liberty would normally be wrong, but we might also be able to think of exceptional circumstances in which detention might be justified, perhaps because someone suffers from such a serious mental illness that she would otherwise pose a serious risk of harm to herself, or others. So we distill from this reasoning process the *general principle* that compulsory detention will be legitimate only where there is a serious risk of harm.

(4) THE RELATIONSHIP BETWEEN PRINCIPLISM AND CASUISTRY

Rather than treating principlism and casuistry as diametrically opposed approaches to bioethical dilemmas, it might be more helpful to see them as complementary. In the next extract, Henry Richardson advocates an amalgamation of principlism and casuistry which he calls *specification*. Essentially this means that we rely upon *case-based reasoning* in order to illuminate what our *general principles* actually mean.

Henry S Richardson[21]
[T]he norms to which we are commonly committed are not plausibly viewed as formally absolute . . . Rather, they are typically qualified, at least implicitly, by variants of 'generally' or 'for the most part'. This sort of looseness is a common feature of our norms as we find them, whether they be prohibitions, positive duties or ends . . . The kind of looseness our norms allow is often thought of as making implicit room for exceptions . . .

While the model of specification begins with norms that allow for latitude, it also ends with them . . . The central assertion of the model of specification is that specifying our norms is the most important aspect of resolving concrete ethical problems, so that once our norms are adequately specified for a given context, it will be sufficiently obvious what ought to be done. . . .

Are there rational constraints on specification? Unless there were it would be hard to see how specification could be anything but a special employment of intuition. I will propose a coherence standard for the rationality of specification . . . A (successful) theory importantly makes intelligible logical connections among the norms to which one is committed that do not merely demonstrate that they are logically compatible with each other, but also explain some of them in terms of others . . .

I have argued that the model of specification is not only distinct from the pure models of

[21] 'Specifying norms as a way to resolve concrete ethical problems' (1990) 19 Philosophy and Public Affairs 279–310, 293–4, 300, 308.

application and balancing and their hybrids, but also superior to each of them . . . It benefits from a considerable degree of casuistical flexibility without sacrificing a potentially intimate tie to guiding theories; and it is able to proceed from norms looser and hence more acceptable than the completely universal ones required by the deductivist . . . By showing, without relying upon universal norms, how a theory might remain stable in the face of conflicts, the model of specification also undercuts the argument for ethical skepticism that departs from the fact that norms will conflict.

The decisive advantage of the model of specification lies in its attitude to conflicts of norms. Whereas the pure model of application is bedeviled by conflicts and the pure model of intuitive balancing sails through them untouched, the model of specification learns from the conflicts it faces, exploiting their friction to push off toward a more concrete and definite understanding of the relevant norms.

(5) VIRTUE ETHICS

Recent interest in virtue ethics, which derives from Ancient Greek philosophy, emerged as a reaction to a number of perceived disadvantages with the theories discussed in the previous sections. Virtue ethicists have, for example, drawn attention to the minimal ethical content of most moral theories. Both Kantianism and utilitarianism lead us to evaluate acts according to whether they are permissible, rather than whether they would be the *best* or the *right* thing to do. In contrast, a virtue ethicist would maintain that people should always try to do the right thing for the right reason.

One important feature of virtue ethics is its rejection of the idea that patient autonomy is an absolute or overriding virtue. This means that the fact that an individual wants to do something is not in itself a reason for thinking that it would be the right thing to do. For example, in relation to euthanasia, Philippa Foot has argued that simply wanting to die is not enough to make death a good thing for a person.[22] Rather causing a person's death could only be the right thing to do if her life lacks certain basic human goods, such as friendship and support.

Similarly, in Chapter 10, we encounter Rosalind Hursthouse's argument that the morality of a woman's decision to have an abortion depends upon the character she manifests in electing to terminate a new human life.[23] According to Hursthouse, parenthood is intrinsically good and so a woman who fails to appreciate this, and wants an abortion because, for example, pregnancy would interfere with her holiday plans, has not reflected with due seriousness, and has therefore not made a virtuous decision. In contrast, a woman who knows that she would be unable to provide a child with the basic minimum human goods has acted virtuously in trying to prevent that child's miserable existence.

Virtue ethics therefore depends upon being able to work out what a virtuous person would do in any situation. But even if we could amass a list of objectively good virtues (honesty, compassion, kindness, justice, etc), it is clear that these will sometimes point in different directions. In the NHS, doctors often have to select which of the patients on their waiting list should have priority for the available beds. Should non-urgent patients who have already waited for six months be given priority, or

---

[22] 'Euthanasia' (1977) 6 Philosophy and Public Affairs 85–112.
[23] 'Virtue Theory and Abortion' (1991) 20 Philosophy and Public Affairs 223–46.

should the bed always go to the patient with the most immediately pressing need? The virtues of fairness and compassion may be relevant here, but they do not tell us how to allocate a vacant bed.

Or let us imagine that a doctor who is advising a couple on the chance that their second child would have the same inherited condition as their first discovers, as a result of genetic tests, that the husband could not be father of the first child. Does she act virtuously by being honest with the husband? Or would a virtuous person reveal this information only to the wife, or not at all?

It has also been pointed out that virtuous people will sometimes act wrongly despite having good intentions. Robert Veatch, for example, says that he is 'concerned about well-intentioned, bungling do-gooders'.[24] A doctor who withholds a diagnosis of terminal cancer from her patient may be acting out of compassion, but it still might be the wrong thing to do.

(6) FEMINISM AND THE ETHICS OF CARE

There are a number of reasons for feminists' dissatisfaction with conventional medical ethics. First, medical ethics used to be principally concerned with the doctor–patient encounter, and the medical profession was, until comparatively recently, heavily male-dominated. Women, on the other hand, are disproportionately represented among patients. Their reproductive capacity; their role as principal carers for both children and the elderly; and their greater life expectancy combine to make women more frequent users of medical services than men. Women are also more likely to be employed in the health services as *carers*, either as nurses (whose role, until fairly recently, was confined to carrying out doctors' orders) or as auxiliary staff. So when medical ethicists focus upon the dilemmas facing *doctors*, they are ignoring the equally important moral dilemmas that might be encountered by patients, or by nurses and other health care workers.

Secondly, drawing on the influential and controversial work of psychologist Carol Gilligan, feminist theorists have argued that abstract moral reasoning in general, and an emphasis on individualistic principles such as autonomy in particular, are both distinctively male. Women's existence, they maintain, is characterized by connections with others, especially through pregnancy and childrearing, and that this makes them value relationships more highly than individual autonomy. Gilligan describes that,

The psychology of women that has consistently been described as distinctive in its greater orientation toward relationships and interdependence implies a more contextual mode of judgment and a different moral understanding. Given the differences in women's conceptions of self and morality, women bring to the life cycle a different point of view and order human experience in terms of different priorities.[25]

On this analysis, whereas a male doctor might regard patients as collections of symptoms to be diagnosed and treated, a female doctor would be more likely to empathize with her patients, and to nurture their holistic wellbeing.

---

[24] R Veatch 'The danger of virtue' (1988) 13 Journal of Medicine and Philosophy 13.
[25] C Gilligan, *In a Different Voice* (Harvard UP Cambridge, MA 1982) 22.

A third and related point is that the dominant principle of medical ethics, namely patient autonomy, presupposes an independent, largely self-sufficient individual who is able to weigh information in order to reach a rational decision about his medical treatment. Yet of course, few patients meet this sort of exacting standard. Illness commonly creates dependency and vulnerability. And in any event, a model of moral reasoning which privileges the rational, self-directed individual relies on a partial and inaccurate understanding of what it is to be human. All of us were completely dependent on others at the beginning of our lives, and most of us will be unable to function independently before we die.

Taken together, these three criticisms of conventional bioethics have led to feminist interest in an ethic of care, which—in short—takes for granted the inevitability of dependency and requires us to treat others with sympathy and compassion. So in relation to euthanasia, for example, an ethic of care might require us to empathize with the plight of terminally ill patients. This does not, however, actually tell us very much about the legitimacy or otherwise of euthanasia. Depending on one's perspective, an ethic of care could be used to argue in favour of legalized euthanasia, so that distressed patients do not have to endure frightening or painful deaths, or alternatively, it might lead to the opposite conclusion, if we are principally concerned about the possibility of vulnerable patients feeling pressurized into requesting euthanasia. If an unconscious patient in urgent need of a blood transfusion is carrying a card stating that she is a Jehovah's Witness who wishes to refuse the use of blood products, does an ethic of care demand that doctors respect her wishes and allow her to die, or should they treat her without consent and save her life?

In short, 'care' is an inherently vague concept, which could be used to justify almost any plausible moral argument. In addition to its essential ambiguity, there is also a danger of reinforcing the stereotype that self-sacrifice and care come naturally to women, and by implication, that values such as justice do not. Regarding the bond of motherhood as the principal source of women's moral judgement is also unsatisfactory because it is simply impossible to care for everyone in the way that one cares for one's own child. An ethic of care might be an appealing ideal, but it cannot tell us how we should act when it is impossible to provide optimum care to everybody. Rationing scarce medical resources must be informed by principles of justice, rather than care.

In the following extract, Helga Kuhse criticizes the idea that an ethic of care can replace ethical principles and reasoned argument.

Helga Kuhse[26]

Is ethics gendered? Do women and men approach ethics differently? The answer of many thinkers has been 'yes'. Rousseau thought that abstract truths and general principles are 'beyond a woman's grasp . . .; woman observes, man reasons'. Schopenhauer bluntly proclaimed: 'the fundamental fault of the female character is that it has *no sense of justice*'. This 'weakness in their reasoning faculty', Schopenhauer continued, 'also explains why women show more sympathy for the unfortunate than men' . . . Freud believed that 'for women the level of what is ethically normal is different from what it is in men.' Women, he wrote, 'show less sense of justice than men'. On

---

[26] 'Clinical ethics and nursing: "yes" to caring, but "no" to a female ethics of care' (1995) 9 Bioethics 207–19, 207–11, 214–16.

these views, then, men and women not only approach ethics differently, but insofar as women were thought to lack a head for abstract principles, and a sense of justice, their ethical approach was also regarded as somewhat defective and inferior to that of men . . .

There is [a] school of thought that holds that traditional male thinkers, while wrong on much else, were right . . . that women and men do approach ethics differently. This school of thought rejects the idea that women are *incapable* of abstract, principled thinking; rather, and much more fundamentally, it claims that principled ethical thinking is not the only valid (or best) approach to ethics. There is, according to this view, an alternative 'female' approach to ethics which is based not on abstract 'male' ethical principles or wide generalisations, but on 'care', that is, on receptivity and responsiveness to the needs of others . . .

[T]he assumption is that caring, in its sensitive attention to the particularities of the situation can give the right answer. But this is not so. Sensitivity and particularity alone can not guide action . . . Without principles of some sort—and it is of course an open question what these principles should be—there can be no ethical discourse, no justification—only particularities and unguided feelings; neither will have any persuasive powers for others, nor should they have persuasive power for us . . .

If women . . . excessively devalue reasoned argument, if they dismiss ethical principles and norms and hold that notions of impartiality and universalizability have no place in a female ethics of care, then they will be left without the theoretical tools necessary to condemn some actions or practices, and to defend others. Bereft of a universal ethical language, women will be unable to participate in ethical discourse . . .

(c) COMMON JUSTIFICATORY STRATEGIES

(1) HUMAN DIGNITY; THE SANCTITY OF HUMAN LIFE AND PLAYING GOD

A common response to novel or controversial medical techniques—such as euthanasia, surrogacy, cloning and abortion—is to argue that they interfere with human dignity; or that they are at odds with the sanctity of human life; or that they would involve human beings 'playing God'. International agreements on biomedicine have also emphasized the importance of respect for human dignity: the preamble to the Council of Europe Convention on Human Rights and Biomedicine requires signatories 'to take such measures as are necessary to safeguard human dignity and the fundamental rights and freedoms of the individual with regard to the application of biology and medicine'.

But what do these phrases actually mean? In the next extract, Ruth Chadwick attempts to pin down what might be meant by the expression 'playing God'.

Ruth F Chadwick[27]
[I]t seems clear that the use of the term 'playing God' normally indicates moral disapproval on the part of the speaker, but it is not obvious what is supposed to be bad about taking the decision. Let us consider alternative ways of looking at the question.

(a) God's prerogative
From a religious point of view the objection may be that it is for God to give life and for God to

[27] 'Playing God' (1989) 3 Cogito 186–93, 188.

take it away. Such a view notoriously has the difficulty however that is seems to imply the rejection of medicine altogether . . .

(b) Letting nature take its course

Here the playing-God objection is interpreted as a claim that human beings are interfering with the course of nature, and that this is wrong. As such it can be, and has been, fairly easily answered . . . John Stuart Mill points out that it is impossible for humans to let nature take its course because every human action has an impact, however slight, upon nature.

(c) Equality

A third possibility . . . is that the objection expresses an intuition about equality . . . The suggestion may be that human beings have lives that are of equal value and that it is therefore wrong for one set of people to judge that the lives of others are of less value. . . .

(d) Omniscience

A further claim about equality may be involved here. The suggestion would be that one thing that human beings have in common is that their knowledge is limited. Those who take decisions about the quality of the lives of others are aspiring to the kind of omniscience that is simply not available to them . . .

Because of the fact that actions describable as playing God are seen as going beyond human limits, they are frequently actions that human beings have not been in a position to take before. They may be in possession of a new type of technology, for example, and the question is raised as to whether it should be used. In such cases assessing the consequences is not a simple matter, especially where changes are envisaged that will affect future generations . . .

The playing-God objection may be useful, then, in that it reminds us that certain things have unpredictable and possibly disastrous consequences. But it seems doubtful that it can provide a conclusive argument against a certain course of action.

In a secular society, what might it mean to say that human life is sacred? In the next extract, Ronald Dworkin suggests that there is a universal, and not necessarily religious, sense of awe at the 'miracle' of human creation.

Ronald Dworkin[28]

Something is sacred or inviolable when its deliberate destruction would dishonour what ought to be honoured. . . . The idea that each individual human life is inviolable is . . . rooted, like our concern for the survival of our species as a whole, in two combined and intersecting bases of the sacred: natural *and* human creation. Any human creature, including the most immature embryo, is a triumph of divine or evolutionary creation, which produces a complex, reasoning being from, as it were, nothing, and also of what we often call the 'miracle' of human reproduction, which makes each new human being both different from and yet a continuation of the human beings who created it. . . .

The life of a single human organism commands respect and protection, then, no matter in what form or shape, because of the complex creative investment it represents and because of our wonder at the divine or evolutionary processes that produce new lives from old ones, at the processes of nation and community and language through which a human being will come to absorb and continue hundreds of generations of cultures and forms of life and value, and, finally, when mental life has begun and flourishes, at the process of internal personal creation and judgement by which a person will make and remake himself, a mysterious, inescapable process in

---

[28] *Life's Dominion: An Argument about Abortion and Euthanasia* (HarperCollins London 1993) 83–4.

which we each participate, and which is therefore the most powerful and inevitable source of empathy and communion we have with every other creature who faces the same frightening challenge. The horror we feel in the wilful destruction of a human life reflects our shared inarticulate sense of the intrinsic importance of each of these dimensions of investment.

On the other hand, Peter Singer argues that the 'sanctity of human life', which he condemns as speciesist, derives from a specifically Christian moral tradition.

Peter Singer[29]

People often say that life is sacred. They almost never mean what they say. They do not mean, as their words seem to imply, that *all* life is sacred. If they did, killing a pig or even pulling up a cabbage would be as contrary to their doctrine as infanticide. So when in the context of medical ethics people talk of the sanctity of life, it is the sanctity of *human* life that they really mean . . .

[W]hat is the position when we compare severely and irreparably retarded human infants with nonhuman animals like pigs and dogs, monkeys and apes? I think we are forced to conclude that in at least some cases the human infant does not possess any characteristics or capacities that are not also possessed, to an equal or higher degree, by many nonhuman animals. This is true of such capacities as the capacity to feel pain, to act intentionally, to solve problems, and to communicate with and relate to other beings; and it is also true of such characteristics as self-awareness, a sense of one's own existence over time, concern for other beings, and curiosity. In all these respects adult members of the species I have mentioned equal or surpass many retarded infant members of our own species . . .

So when we decide to treat one being—the severely and irreparably retarded infant—in one way, and the other being—the pig or monkey—in another way, there seems to be no difference between the two that we can appeal to in defense of our discrimination . . . The doctrine of the sanctity of human life, as it is commonly understood, has at its core a discrimination on the basis of species and nothing else . . .

The doctrine of the sanctity of all human life, and the seriousness with which the killing of any member of our species is regarded, mark off the Christian ethical and cultural tradition from almost all others . . . [T]he Christian tradition is distinctive for the sharpness of the line it draws between all beings that are members of our species and all other beings. . . .

There can be no doubt that the change in European attitudes to abortion and infanticide is a product of the coming of Christianity . . . [T]he change occurred not because of some general broadening of people's moral concern that was part of a more enlightened moral outlook, but because of the Christian doctrine that all born of human parents have immortal souls and are destined for an eternity of bliss or for everlasting torment . . . To kill a human being was an act of fearful significance, since it consigned him or her to an eternal fate . . . The unborn fetus, from the moment it acquired its soul, was destined to rise again on the day of judgment and face its Judge. If its responsibility for the sin of Adam had not been removed by baptism, it was doomed to hell for ever.

[T]he intuitions which lie behind [the doctrine of the sanctity of human life] are not insights of self-evident moral truths, but the historically conditioned product of doctrines about immortality, original sin and damnation which hardly anyone now accepts; doctrines so obnoxious, in fact, that if anyone did accept them, we should be inclined to discount any other moral views he held. Although advocates of the doctrine of the sanctity of human life now frequently try to give their position some secular justification, there can be no possible justification for making the boundary

---

[29] *Unsanctifying Human Life: Essays on Ethics* (H Kuhse (ed)) (Blackwell Oxford 2002) 217, 219–22, 228.

of sanctity run parallel with the boundary of our own species, unless we invoke some belief about immortal souls.

Human dignity is an especially vague and ambiguous concept. In particular, its scope is potentially wider than respect for persons or human rights. We might, for example, be required to treat an embryo or a corpse, neither of which is a person or rights' holder, with *dignity*. We might not have to behave as though an embryo or a corpse was a human person, but neither are we entitled to use and dispose of them as if they were *things*.

In the next extract, Deryck Beyleveld and Roger Brownsword argue that the concept of human dignity has undergone a significant shift in meaning in recent years. Respect for human dignity used to mean promoting autonomous choice, which they describe as 'human dignity as empowerment'. According to Joseph Raz, for example,

Respecting human dignity entails treating humans as persons capable of planning and plotting their future. Thus, respecting people's dignity includes respecting their autonomy, their right to control their future. . . . An insult offends a person's dignity if it consists of or implies a denial that he is an autonomous person or that he deserves to be treated as one.[30]

In recent years, however, Beyleveld and Brownsword suggest that human dignity is instead being invoked in order to *restrict* individual's choices, which they refer to as 'human dignity as constraint'. This is commonly done by arguing that a controversial medical practice is 'against human nature'.

Deryck Beyleveld and Roger Brownsword[31]

What we have called 'human dignity as empowerment' equates human dignity with the capacity to make unforced choices, and, from here, constructs a regime of human rights centred on the promotion of individual autonomy . . . With human dignity as empowerment, life is not free of tragic choices; but it is for each person to make his or her own informed choice, tragic or otherwise. . . . In this version of what we have called 'human dignity as constraint', we find 'free' action distinctively limited by reference to the duty not to compromise one's own dignity . . .

Many persons feel that a number of scientific interventions are 'unnatural', and cite this as the reason why it is wrong to employ them. This reaction may be linked to the idea that such interventions are contrary to dignity by the following reasoning. Dignity is the property by virtue of which human beings have moral rights or moral standing. All human beings have dignity simply by virtue of being human. Dignity is thus an essential part of human nature. Therefore, to act contrary to human nature is to act contrary to human dignity, and it might, then, be alleged that, for example, assisted reproduction itself is against nature; or 70-year-old women bearing children is against nature; or lesbianism is against nature; or men bearing children is against nature. . . .

An attempt to explicate respect for human dignity in terms of human nature is not without its problems even if couched within a framework that links having dignity to being human (in a biological sense) . . . Suppose that it is held that it is unnatural for a lesbian woman to bear a child, or for a man to bear a child. What is meant by saying that it is unnatural? Clearly, it cannot be meant that it goes against the laws of nature. If something is contrary to the laws of nature then it cannot (physically) happen. And, if it is not possible for it to happen then there is no need to prescribe that it ought not to happen or to take steps to prevent it from happening.

---

[30] J Raz, *The Authority of Law* (OUP Oxford 1979) 221.
[31] *Human Dignity in Bioethics and Biolaw* (OUP Oxford 2001) 64–5, 229–30.

Perhaps, then, what is meant is that it cannot happen without human intervention. However, there are so many things that cannot happen without human intervention that this threatens to imply that human action itself is contrary to human nature. Certainly, anyone who adopts such a view must, it seems, hold that all medical intervention without which a person would die is contrary to human nature.

(2) THE SLIPPERY SLOPE

Another common objection to controversial medical practices is that they might represent the first step on a slippery slope. This a consequentialist argument in that it does not appeal to the intrinsic wrongness of a particular technique; rather as Frederick Schauer explains, the fear is that allowing something that may seem fairly innocuous in itself might have unforeseeable, uncontrollable or dangerous consequences.

Frederick Schauer[32]

Sometimes the warning is of 'a foot in the door,' and the British often refer to 'the thin edge of the wedge.' Most commonly we are told to beware of the 'slippery slope'. Yet regardless of the term employed, the phenomenon referred to is the same. The single argumentative claim supported by each of these metaphors, as well as by many others, is that a particular act, seemingly innocuous when taken in isolation, may yet lead to a future host of similar but increasingly pernicious events. But why should this be? What induces people to believe that in some cases neither doctrinal limits nor judicial intervention can prevent the slide down the slippery slope? . . .

As a start we can say that a slippery slope argument necessarily contains the implicit concession that the proposed resolution of the instant case is not itself troublesome. By focusing on the consequences for future cases, we implicitly concede that this instance is itself innocuous, or perhaps even desirable. If we felt otherwise, then we would not employ the slippery slope argument, but would rather claim much more simply that this case, in itself, is impermissible. By implicitly conceding that the instant case is, by itself, unobjectionable, the slippery slope argument directs our attention and our fears to the danger case in the future. It is not permitting the instant case that worries us, but rather the possibility that permitting the instant case will lead to the danger case. . . .

A slippery slope claim implicitly or explicitly urges that the instant case distorts or skews the normal risk functions so that the descent from this decision to the danger case may be more slippery than the normal passage from one case to the next. Thus, what can distinguish a slippery slope claim from other warnings about the future is the identification of factors increasing the likelihood not only of slippage, but of slippage in the particular direction that takes us from the instant case to the danger case. The task confronting one who makes a slippery slope argument is thus to identify possible sources of this skewed risk factor . . .

Thus the persuasive slippery slope argument must draw upon those largely empirical circumstances that might skew the otherwise equally likely danger cases systematically in one direction rather than another. For without empirical evidence of such systematic skewing, the slippery slope argument has nothing on which to stand.

In the next extract, Bernard Williams contrasts two different types of slippery slope claim: the 'horrible result' argument and the 'arbitrary result' argument. He also

[32] 'Slippery Slopes' (1985) 99 Harvard Law Review 361, 361–2, 368–9, 376, 382.

explains that slippery slope arguments do not necessarily justify banning a practice, rather a different response might be regulation which draws a line between acceptable and unacceptable practices. We return to this point in Chapter 16 (p. 956) when we consider the legalization of euthanasia.

Bernard Williams[33]

In many ethical connections, including those in which the discussion concerns what the law should be, there is a well-known argument against allowing some practice, that it leads to a slippery slope. The argument is often applied to matters of medical practice. If X is allowed, the argument goes, then there will be a *natural progression* to Y; and since the argument is intended as an objection to X, Y is presumably agreed to be objectionable, while X is not (though of course it may be objectionable to the proponent of the argument—the slippery slope may be only one of his objections to it) . . .

First it is worth distinguishing two types of slippery slope argument. The first type—the *horrible result* argument—objects, roughly speaking, to what is at the bottom of the slope. The second type objects to the fact that it is a slope: this may be called the *arbitrary result* argument. . . .

All of the arguments that I shall be considering use the idea that there is no point at which one can non-arbitrarily get off the slope once one has got onto it—that is what makes the slope slippery. Arguments that belong to the first type that I have distinguished involve, in addition, the further idea that there is a clearly objectionable practice to which the slope leads. The second type of argument, by contrast, relies merely on the point that after one has got on to the slope, subsequent discriminations will be arbitrary . . .

The first requirement is that it should be probable in actual social fact that such a process will occur. This requires that there should be some motive for people to move from one step to the next. Suppose it is plausible that there will be a slide, and that there will be, at each stage, pressure to take the next step. What follows from that? The slippery slope argument concludes that one should not start, and that the first case should not be allowed, on the ground that after the first step there is nowhere to stop . . .

But there is an obvious alternative. Granted that we are now considering cases in which a definite rule of practice is needed, we have the alternative of drawing a sharp line between cases that are allowed and cases that are not . . . Is drawing a line in this way reasonable? Can it be effective? The answer to both these questions seems to me evidently to be 'Yes, Sometimes' . . .

[T]he slippery slope argument should be properly understood as in good part an empirical, consequentialist argument . . . Seen in this light, it seems to me that the slippery-slope style of argument can carry weight, and is to be taken seriously; but that, equally, it need not necessarily carry the day, in the sense of proving that the first step should never be taken. We may, instead, take the path of drawing a line, and that is a perfectly reasonable reaction, in the right circumstances, to the challenge that is indeed posed by the slippery slope considerations.

5. THE BODY

In recent years, there has been a great deal of academic interest in 'the body'. For our purposes, two particular themes are worth highlighting. First, in the past medical knowledge about the body was believed to be scientific, and hence neutral and

---

[33] *Making Sense of Humanity and Other Philosophical Papers* (CUP Cambridge 1995) 213–14, 220–1.

objective. In recent years, however, sociologists have argued that medicine *controls* our bodies, first, by defining illness and abnormality, and, secondly, by instilling us with a sense of responsibility for the state of our bodies. Secondly, our relationship with our bodies is difficult to classify according to conventional legal norms. Let us explore both these themes in turn.

(a) THE SOCIAL CONSTRUCTION OF THE BODY

Medicine undoubtedly has the power to decide what counts as an illness. In the nineteenth century, for example, masturbation was believed to be a dangerous illness which produced a cluster of symptoms, including vertigo, loss of hearing and memory, and headaches, and which had some very serious long-term consequences, such as heart disease, insanity, blindness, and even death. While this now seems like a comical example of Victorian ignorance and prudery, today other natural processes, such as the menopause, are increasingly treated as 'medical conditions', in need of professional intervention and control.

In the next extract Deborah Lupton fleshes out the claim that medical knowledge about the body is not neutral, but instead embodies a set of cultural and political assumptions.

Deborah Lupton[34]

Social theorists who are interested in the body and medicine deny that medical knowledge, or indeed any other type of knowledge, can be regarded as neutral, scientific or politically disinterested. Rather, like the body or any other phenomenon, medicine is socially constructed, is mediated through social understandings, and has political effects. For instance, while we may think that the version of the human body presented in a medical textbook is 'scientific truth' and therefore politically neutral, closer examination reveals conventions of representation that support wider sociocultural and political assumptions and objectives. The body in such textbooks is nearly always that of a young white male, suggesting that this type of body is the 'real' or 'normal' human body, against which other bodies (those of women, people of non-white ethnicity, or the elderly) are considered 'abnormal' . . .

A discussion of embodiment in relation to medicine need not focus only on the bodies of patients, but also on those who care for them. The work of medical practitioners, nurses and other health care professionals requires an ability to objectify patients' bodies to a certain extent, for to allow one's emotions to intrude too far into the patients' bodies can prove disabling. Just as the ritualised procedures in the operating theatre serve to protect patients' feelings, they also protect the surgeons from feelings of shame, disgust, or guilt that may arise from cutting into the patients' bodies and thereby causing them injury. If patients were not rendered anonymous, turned into bodies rather than maintained as people, it would be more difficult to operate upon them . . .

Throughout the history of scientific medicine, medical and public health knowledges have been employed to distinguish and differentiate between 'normal', 'healthy' bodies and those that are regarded as 'abnormal', 'diseased' or 'deviant'. The male European body has been represented as the archetypical normal, healthy body . . . By way of contrast, the female body, the bodies of the working classes or the poor, non-white bodies, and homosexual bodies have been singled out as

---

[34] 'The Body, Medicine and Society' in John Germow (ed), *Second Opinion: An Introduction to Health Sociology* (OUP Oxford 1998) 121–35, 122, 128, 130–2.

diseased, passive, contaminating, dirty and lacking self-control. There is a symbiotic relationship, therefore, between identifying the bodies of particular social groups (such as women, non-Whites, the working class, or homosexuals) as being uncontrolled, dirty, and as a result, more susceptible to illness, disease and early death, and the reproduction of the notion that such groups are inferior to the dominant social group (that is, well-off, white, heterosexual men). . . .

Since the eighteenth century, Africa has been portrayed as the breeding ground of disease—a place of dark, dank pestilence, where white travellers should be ever-vigilant. . . . The 'Orient' has also been regarded as an exotic place where health risks lurk. In contemporary public health discourses, this tendency remains. Certain countries—such as Thailand, for example—are represented as 'danger sites' for Western men because of the possibility that they might contract AIDS from having sex with local sex workers. There is little concern about the possibility that the male clients themselves may infect the sex workers. . . .

Compared with the male body, the female body has been represented as sickly, weak, and susceptible to illness. Women are typically described in the legal, medical and early social scientific literature as possessing problematic and unruly bodies, with their sexual and reproductive capacities requiring constant surveillance and regulation. Particularly in the nineteenth and twentieth centuries, medical assumptions about women—for example, that they were prone to uncontrolled emotional outbursts, which in turn were produced by the uterus, or that their natural place was in the home rather than participating in the public sphere—have contributed to the control of women and their confinement to the domestic sphere.

In the next extract, Bill Hughes argues that the ill and dependent body is increasingly seen as a reflection of the patient's weakness or failure. In part, this is because preventative medicine emphasizes the individual's responsibility for her own health, and may downplay some of the wider social causes of ill health, such as poverty.

Bill Hughes[35]

As health maintenance—as opposed to curative—strategies emerge as the priority in contemporary patterns of health care, then responsibility for health shifts from the professional to the lay person . . . There can be no doubt that this apparent democratisation of the relationship between professional and patient suited western governments intent on reducing public expenditure and squeezing the welfare state. The ideas of self care and health maintenance as the responsibility of the lay person rather than the professional became, in the 1980s, important ideological tools in the privatisation of healthcare activities. In the contemporary, secular, deregulated world, a good deal of the policing of human behaviour—which is traditionally invested in the powers of religion and law—is carried out in the name of health . . . Medical knowledge, often in the form of behavioural prescriptions, challenges the population to be healthy, to adopt healthy behaviours and to choose healthy places to live and work.

Disease—in at least some of its manifestations—can now be regarded as a failure of health maintenance, a sign of an improper relationship to one's body and to what one does with it.

(b) DO WE OWN OUR BODIES?

In contemporary bioethics, the question of whether we have rights in our bodies akin to ownership emerges in debates about surrogacy and payment for organ donation.

[35] 'Medicalized Bodies' in Philip Hancock, Bill Hughes, Elizabeth Jagger, Kevin Paterson, Rachel Russell, Emmanuelle Tulle-Winton, and Melissa Tyler (eds), *The Body, Culture and Society: An Introduction* (Open UP Milton Keynes 2000) 12–28, 17–19, 23.

Certainly, some of the rights that we have over our bodies look very like property rights: a right to use them, to exclude others, and to be compensated for negligently inflicted damage are all rights that also commonly exist in relation to things that we own. On the other hand, it is less clear whether we possess another right that we would normally associate with ownership, namely the right to transfer for value.

In the next extract Stephen Munzer argues that while it would not make sense to say that we have full ownership of our bodies, we do possess some more limited property rights in them.

Stephen Munzer[36]

[S]ome hold that the body should be thought of as property and emphasize that each person owns or has title to himself or herself. Others maintain that the body ought not to be thought of as property at all, and indeed that it demeans human beings to think of them or their bodies as property. In contrast, the position advocated here is that, insofar as one takes an overall view, people do not own, but have some limited property rights in, their bodies. . . .

It is unhelpful to say that no body rights are property rights. It is also unhelpful to say that all body rights are property rights . . . Since both extreme views should be rejected, one must provide a criterion for classifying some, but not all, body rights as property rights. The most useful criterion is transferability . . .

[O]ne can divide all body rights into personal rights and property rights. Personal rights are body rights that protect interests or choices other than the choice to transfer. Property rights are body rights that protect the choice to transfer . . . One can subdivide property rights in the body into weak and strong varieties. A weak property right involves only a choice to transfer gratuitously. A strong property right involves a choice to transfer for value.

[T]ransferability is a highly important feature of property as usually understood. And transferability is even more important in the special case of body rights because of their close connection with autonomy . . .

[I]t is a mistake to characterize body rights, jointly or individually, as self-ownership. Taken jointly, the body rights of each person amount not to ownership but only to a weaker package of limited property rights. Considered individually, the body rights of each person are not all in the same boat. Most body rights are personal rather than property rights; examples are rights not to be murdered, not to be searched without a warrant or just cause . . . and to exclude others from sexual or other physical contact. Some body rights are property rights—whether weak, such as the right to donate an organ upon death, or strong, such as the right to sell semen; but these weak and strong property rights are neither so numerous nor so central as to establish that persons 'own' themselves.

6. CONCLUSION

In the remainder of this book, we will see that, in recent years, there has been a shift from a paternalistic model of medical decision-making, based upon the idea that 'doctor knows best', towards an autonomy model, which assumes that a competent adult patient should have an almost absolute right to refuse medical treatment. It would, however, be a mistake to regard patient autonomy as the overriding value in *all*

---

[36] *A Theory of Property* (CUP Cambridge 1990) 37–8, 43, 45, 47, 48–9, 56.

medical decision-making. The right to autonomy is a *negative* right to prevent unwanted intervention, and patients do not have the right to demand access to medical treatment when resources are unavailable; or when treatment would be against their doctors' clinical judgement; or when parliament has decided that the treatment in question is ethically unacceptable, examples currently include human reproductive cloning and female circumcision.

The problem for the law is that there will be very few cases when there is agreement over the legitimacy of controversial medical practices. There will never be any consensus over whether euthanasia should be legalized, for example, or whether it is legitimate to experiment on embryos. In this chapter, we have focused mainly upon how we might go about *discussing* these questions. We could, for example, look at the *consequences* of regulating in one way or another. So, in relation to euthanasia, we could ask whether legalization would, on balance, make life better or worse for sick and vulnerable patients. We could also think about what *principles* might be at stake, and how the tension between autonomy and non-maleficence should be resolved. It might be important to think about what arguments grounded in human dignity or respect for the *sanctity of human life* mean in this context, and whether there is a *slippery slope* that either could, or could not, be contained through regulation. None of these considerations can tell us what to do, however, and undoubtedly most of us will also bring our own values and experiences to bear on these questions. In relation to euthanasia, for example, someone with strong religious convictions will be influenced by their faith, and someone who has seen a relative die a protracted and painful death may find that that experience shapes their judgement. Our 'gut instincts' will inevitably often provide the starting point for our reasoning process, but it is important to remember that, on their own, there is no reason why anyone else should find them persuasive.

7. FURTHER READING

BEAUCHAMP, TOM L and CHILDRESS, JAMES F, *Principles of Biomedical Ethics* (5th edn OUP Oxford 2001).

BEYLEVELD, DERYCK and BROWNSWORD, ROGER, *Human Dignity in Bioethics and Biolaw* (OUP Oxford 2001).

HARRIS, JOHN (ed), *Bioethics* (OUP Oxford 2001).

KUHSE, HELGA, 'Clinical ethics and nursing: "yes" to caring, but "no" to a female ethics of care' (1995) 9 Bioethics.

KUHSE, HELGA and SINGER, PETER (eds), *A Companion to Bioethics* (Blackwell Oxford 1998).

MORGAN, DEREK, *Issues in Medical Law and Ethics* (Cavendish London 2001) chs 1 and 2.

O'NEILL, ONORA, *Autonomy and Trust in Bioethics* (CUP Cambridge 2002).

2

RESOURCE ALLOCATION

1. CENTRAL ISSUES

1. There are a number of different possible rationing strategies; such as equal access to treatment; rationing according to clinical need; maximizing health gains, through the QALY approach; discriminating on the grounds of age; taking individual responsibility for ill-health into account; rationing according to ability to pay; singling out certain types of excluded treatment; rationing by diluting the standard of care, and finally, random allocation of treatment.

2. It is also important to decide *who* should be charged with making rationing decisions. Both doctors and politicians would rather avoid making these tough choices, and

decision-making is now increasingly delegated to the National Institute of Clinical Excellence (NICE).

3. Patients may want to challenge rationing decisions, and this is principally done via judicial review. Historically the judiciary has been reluctant to interfere with decisions about the allocation of scarce resources. There have been some important recent exceptions, but it is not yet clear whether they represent a decisive trend towards more pro-active judicial scrutiny.

4. Patients might also want to seek treatment abroad, and within the EU, their right to do so may be protected by law.

2. INTRODUCTION

In this chapter we examine the complex and politically contentious question of resource allocation, or rationing. Our principal emphasis will be on the rationing of National Health Service (NHS) expenditure, rather than other scarce goods, such as organs (which we consider separately in Chapter 12). At the outset, it is interesting to note a subtle shift in the meaning of the word 'rationing' over the course of the twentieth century. Rationing used to mean that people should be entitled to a fixed quota of resources: an obvious example would be the rationing of food and other household goods during and immediately after the Second World War. This was conspicuously egalitarian: deprivation was to be shared equally across society as part of a collective commitment to the national good. Now, however, rationing is generally assumed to refer to the discretionary allocation of resources. The burden of deprivation instead appears to be distributed unevenly across society, leading to concerns about the arbitrariness of rationing decisions. Rationing by discretion is also, of course, much more difficult to monitor and challenge than a system based upon fixed entitlements.

Since the NHS first started treating patients in 1948, demand for healthcare services has far outstripped the NHS's capacity to supply them. In the first section of this chapter, we consider some of the reasons why NHS resources are overstretched, but we also examine the arguments of those who believe that rationing should be unnecessary. For example, some people would argue that the UK could afford to divert sufficient funds to the NHS to eliminate the need for services to be rationed. After all, there appears to be no shortage of money in certain other sectors of the economy, such as sport or the entertainment industry. Alternatively, it is claimed that reducing inefficiency and waste by ensuring that treatments are only provided when they meet some threshold level of effectiveness would again largely remove the need to make 'tragic choices' about the allocation of scarce NHS funds. But while increasing public spending on the NHS and eliminating inappropriate use of resources are clearly worthwhile goals, for the foreseeable future it is unlikely that the NHS will be able to provide immediate access to optimum care for every citizen in the UK.

If some sort of rationing is inevitable, it is important to distinguish between the various different levels at which resource allocation decisions may be taken. At the macro level, political choices must be made about how much public money should be spent on the NHS in the light of the other competing demands upon the nation's resources. Within the health budget, priorities must be set in order to determine how much money should be spent on different types of healthcare: what proportion of the NHS budget should be spent on primary care (that is, the patient's first point of contact with the health service, usually provided by general practitioners) compared with hospitals, for example? Within limits set by central government, such as specific targets for the treatment of particular diseases, health authorities have to distribute resources between different branches of medicine. What proportion should be spent on mental health services, for example, or on obstetric care? At the micro level, it might be necessary to choose between individual patients, perhaps in order to work out which one should be given the only available bed in an intensive care unit.

In an ideal world, these invidious choices would be unnecessary, but if such decisions are inevitable, it is important to ensure that they are taken fairly. In the second section we consider how we might distinguish between fair and unfair ways to allocate scarce resources, at both the macro and the micro levels. While it is clear that certain patient characteristics, such as race, should be irrelevant, huge disagreement exists over whether it might be reasonable to take into account other factors, such as an individual's age, or her responsibility for her own ill health.

In addition to working out the criteria which should inform a fair system of resource allocation, it is also important to decide who should be responsible for making these decisions. Ought responsibility to rest with central government, or with local health authorities? Is it important to take public opinion into account, and if so, how might this best be done? Should choices about how to meet people's health needs, within the resources available, be delegated to individual clinicians? In the UK, the National Institute for Clinical Excellence[1] (NICE) was set up in 1999 in order to judge the clinical and cost-effectiveness of treatments and make

---

[1] Since 2005 the National Institute for Health and Clinical Excellence.

recommendations about their provision within the NHS, and we also assess NICE's impact.

Finally, we look at the ways in which choices about the allocation of resources might be challenged, principally of course by disgruntled patients who believe that they have been unfairly denied access to appropriate treatment. As a public body, the NHS's choices may be subject to judicial review. In practice, however, patients have only succeeded in proving that the NHS has acted irrationally, unreasonably or unlawfully in a tiny minority of cases. Because the Secretary of State for Health is under a statutory duty to provide certain health services, such as aftercare for the mentally ill, a patient who has been denied treatment on grounds of cost might also be able to bring an action for breach of statutory duty. Again, such actions are seldom successful. Finally, might the Human Rights Act 1998 offer some protection to patients who have been refused treatment? Could the right to life under Article 2 impose a duty on the NHS to make life-prolonging treatment available to anyone whose life would otherwise be in danger? Given the long history of the courts' reluctance to interfere with choices about the allocation of NHS resources, and their apparent recognition that funds—even for life-saving treatment—are inevitably limited, it seems unlikely that the Human Rights Act will offer patients an effective new mechanism for challenging rationing decisions.

3. THE SCARCITY OF RESOURCES

After the end of the Second World War, a labour government was elected under Clement Attlee which promised to massively expand welfare provision, and in particular to introduce a national health service. Before the NHS was set up in 1948 (under the National Health Service Act 1946), it had been thought that providing the whole population with free and comprehensive health care, in addition to the other social services which were to be made available through the welfare state, might improve the nation's health, and thus lead to a diminishing demand for health care services. David Hunter explains that:

the NHS was founded on a fallacy: that there was a finite amount of ill-health in the population which, once removed, would result in the maintenance of health and the provision of health care becoming cheaper as the need for it dropped off. What has happened is that success in health care has resulted in people living longer potentially to be ill more often and therefore consume more resources.[2]

From the outset, it became obvious that the costs of providing care were going to exceed the available resources. Prescription charges were introduced in 1951, leading to the resignation of Aneurin Bevan, the chief architect of the NHS and its first Secretary of State for Health.

Over the last six decades, successive governments have increased spending on the NHS at above the rate of inflation, and the proportion of the UK's gross national

---

[2] David J Hunter, *Desperately Seeking Solutions: Rationing Health Care* (Longman London 1997) 20.

product (GNP) spent on health has risen from 5 per cent in the 1980s to 7 per cent in 2000. Yet the NHS continues to be chronically underfunded, and its inadequacies are a continual source of popular dissatisfaction, media interest, and political strife. Why is this? A combination of factors probably contribute to the persistence of a financial crisis in the NHS despite increased government spending, and to the widespread perception that the NHS cannot cope with the demands placed upon it.

First, the NHS may be a victim of its own success. Life expectancy has increased dramatically since the 1940s. Our need for medical care is concentrated in our last years of life, and so extending the period of old age massively increases demand for health services. And it is the very elderly sector of the population which is set to increase most rapidly in the future. By 2031 the proportion of the UK's population which will be over 85 is predicted to grow from 1.9 per cent of the population to 3.5 per cent.[3]

Secondly, technological and scientific progress has led to the availability of more sophisticated (and expensive) treatments for a wide variety of conditions. The continual development of new treatment options inevitably places increasing demands upon the NHS budget. Third, patients' expectations have risen dramatically since the 1940s. Most of the UK's population have been able to take the NHS's existence for granted throughout their lives, and have tended to take for granted that free and comprehensive health care should be available as of right. Patients are increasingly well informed about the availability of different treatments, and more assertive about their 'rights'. Armed with information gathered from the internet, patients may demand access to expensive new treatments, rather than believing that 'doctor knows best'. There is also a tendency to draw a simple causal link between more sophisticated health care and improved health, and thereby overemphasize what the NHS can and should achieve.

Fourthly, when a service is provided free of charge, there are fewer constraints on demand than is the case when people have to pay for it. With no financial disincentives to seeking medical care, people visit their general practitioner (GP) for ailments that are indubitably likely to clear up by themselves without any intervention or treatment. Demand—particularly for primary care services—is therefore especially elastic.

Fifthly, the proportion of the NHS budget spent on secondary care in hospitals has decreased while more money has been diverted to primary care and preventative medicine. Although few would dispute the virtue of keeping as many patients as possible out of hospital, failures in hospital care—such as long waiting times for life-saving operations, or patients being kept on trolleys because of bed shortages—are often particularly stark and newsworthy, adding to the public's perception of the NHS as a failing service. Sixthly, more than half of all NHS resources is spent on salaries,[4] and while still not generous, these have increased above the rate of inflation in recent years. Reductions in the hours worked by junior doctors have also increased pressure

[3] Christopher Newdick, *Who Should we Treat? Rights, Rationing and Resources in the NHS* (2nd edn OUP Oxford 2005) 8.
[4] Ibid, 3.

on the NHS budget. Seventhly, as we shall see in the next chapter, clinical negligence claims represent a significant drain on NHS funds, thereby reducing the amount of money available to improve patient care.

Finally, the problem of healthcare funding appears to be universal. The central problem, as Mark Hall explains, is that providing the whole population with optimum access to medical care would probably absorb all of a country's resources:

When we are ill, we desperately want our doctors to do everything within their power to heal us, regardless of the costs involved. Medical technology has advanced so far, however, that literal adherence to this credo for everyone would consume the entire gross domestic product.[5]

In fact, one study estimated that providing all the healthcare that could be beneficial to each French citizen would cost five and a half times France's gross national product.[6] But although we want money to be no object when we are patients, as taxpayers or purchasers of health insurance we are rather more cost conscious.

A variety of factors are therefore responsible for the NHS's persistent financial difficulties, but it would be a mistake to regard each of these reasons for pressure on the NHS budget as 'problems'. On the contrary, improved life expectancy, better treatments, and higher salaries for nurses are all to be welcomed. If the additional demands placed on the NHS are always likely to outstrip the available resources, we have to think about the best ways to minimize any negative impact upon patient care. Many believe that rationing has become inevitable, and as Alan Maynard explains in the next extract, that the important task now facing the NHS is to ensure that resources are rationed as fairly and as openly as possible.

Alan Maynard[7]

There are two certainties in life: death and scarcity. A long, good-quality life free of pain, disability and distress from birth to death is the exception rather than the rule. Most people confront morbidity over the life-cycle and demand cures and care which are expensive and often of unproven benefit. Principles and practices (mostly only implicit) determine who is left in pain and discomfort, who is treated and who is left to die. The policy issue is therefore not whether, but how, to ration access to health and social care. Society and its political representatives are, however, reluctant to confront this reality . . . A health service in 'political denial' stunts the development of socially agreed rationing principles, that are openly discussed and accountably applied, and creates a market of special pleading on both the demand—(for example patient advocacy groups) and supply side (for example, the pharmaceutical industry). These are organisations with overlapping goals which result in a single demand: spend more!

Before we consider what a fair rationing system might look like, we should acknowledge the arguments of those who argue that this acceptance of the inevitability of rationing is either unnecessary or premature.

First, there are those who would dispute the premise that anyone other than the individual patient/consumer should be responsible for paying for health care services.

---

[5] Mark A Hall, 'Rationing Health Care at the Bedside' (1994) 69 New York University Law Review 693, 694.

[6] Cited in Richard D Lamm, 'Rationing of Health Care: Inevitable and Desirable' (1992) 140 University of Pennsylvania Law Review 1511, 1512.

[7] 'Ethics and health care "underfunding" ' (2001) 27 Journal of Medical Ethics 223–7, 223, 225–6.

Robert Nozick, for example, has argued against any sort of 'patterned' distribution of resources.[8] According to Nozick, provided everyone has acquired their own resources justly, the way in which they choose to spend their wealth is none of the state's business. Taxation is, in Nozick's view, akin to forced labour, and hence illegitimate. If some people choose to spend their own money on health care or medical insurance, and others do not, the distribution of health care that results will be just. An interesting twist on Nozick's theory of distributive justice might be possible, however, if we draw an analogy between ill health and the one legitimate task of what he describes as the 'night-watchman state', namely protecting citizens against aggression. Disease and disability similarly threaten the individual's security, and interfere with her ability to pursue her own goals. If a government has a duty, even in Nozick's minimal state, to ensure that its citizens can freely engage in civil society without being subject to violence and aggression, might it also be possible to argue that public resources could legitimately be devoted to enabling citizens to pursue their own ends free from disease and infirmity?

Secondly, Donald Light argues that it is illegitimate to even contemplate rationing before attempts have been made to eliminate waste and inefficiency within the NHS.[9] Evidence-based medicine, which is intended to help to reduce expenditure upon ineffective or inefficient treatments, is perceived to be a more appropriate solution to the NHS's funding crisis than rationing.

Donald W Light[10]

[T]o say that 'rationing is inevitable and therefore we should focus on how to ration reasonably' is like the medical profession deciding that 'death is inevitable and therefore we should focus on how to die reasonably.' Death is inevitable, but the conclusion denies the whole purpose of medicine. Likewise, our purpose should be to postpone and minimise rationing as much as possible . . .

When the argument that 'rationing is inevitable' is applied not to situations with effectively absolute shortages like liver transplants, but to the healthcare system as a whole, it assumes that there can never be enough money, or surgeons or drugs or child psychiatrists, to satisfy all the needs that people have. . . .

The claim that health needs are bottomless is an empirical question, not an assertion or article of faith. What makes it a myth and an indefensible form of paternalism is that no one making this claim goes out and tests it. Yet the depth of the pit can be determined by taking people in a well funded healthcare system who face no barriers of time, distance, money, or delays and measuring their rates of surgery, or drug use, or visits to the doctor. If the advocates of the bottomless pit are correct, average citizens in such a system would see the doctor every day, take multiple drugs, and have an operation a week . . . In fact, Dutch people or Germans see the doctor and have operations at somewhat higher rates than do the British, but the rates are far from infinite.

What this means is that rationing by any reasonable definition is avoidable, and the British can have a healthcare system without widespread denial of care, waiting lists, run down facilities, and underservice . . .

If the government and the healthcare professions seriously want to minimise the rationing of care to sick patients, they need to address the sorts of waste that have been identified by the

---

[8] *Anarchy, State and Utopia* (Blackwell Oxford 1974).
[9] Donald W Light, 'The real ethics of rationing' (1997) 315 British Medical Journal 112–15.
[10] 'The real ethics of rationing' (1997) 315 British Medical Journal 112–15.

Anti-rationing Group—including overtesting, inappropriate prescribing, the organisation of follow up for new outpatients, and the provision of care by doctors that can be done by nurses. The Anti-rationing Group has concluded that if these sources are eliminated, the waiting lists 'would disappear within a year, never to return.' . . .

Critical to reducing such waste and the need for rationing is the strong implementation of evidence based medicine. So long as good outcomes are not measured and resources directed towards them, everything will be a 'cost' without a benefit and wasteful practices will have equal weight with effective practices.

But while it is undoubtedly true that the NHS could operate more efficiently, it is unlikely that this could wholly eliminate the need to ration services. The NHS spends more than half of its budget on wages, and so huge gains in efficiency would only be possible if staff costs could be significantly reduced. For obvious reasons, it would be undesirable to expect health care professionals to work longer hours for smaller salaries.

Thirdly, it has been suggested that demand for NHS services could be managed more efficiently. This might be done by attempting to persuade the public not to make inappropriate or unnecessary use of health care services. Public education strategies have already been used to inform people that they should not expect their GP to visit them at home during the night unless their condition is extremely serious. Poster campaigns have stressed that ambulances are not there to provide a taxi service for people who would prefer not to make their own way to hospital. Another way to manage demand is to find new ways to meet people's need for advice about their health. Helplines (such as NHS Direct) and information available on the internet[11] allow people to find out whether their symptoms indicate a need for medical intervention without them having to visit their GP. Making the public aware that pharmacists can offer free advice is also intended to help reduce demand for primary care services.

Fourthly, it is sometimes argued that the UK could afford to spend far more of its GNP on health care, and that a massive increase in resources would remove the need for rationing. Devoting more public money to the NHS would mean either that less would be available to other public services, such as education or policing, or that tax rates would have to rise significantly. Both are of course possible. But we should remember that while health is undoubtedly very important, it is clearly not the only thing that matters to us, as is evident from our lifestyles: few of us could claim that we always put our health first when deciding how to occupy our time, or what to eat and drink.

It is certainly true that the UK spends a smaller proportion of its GNP on health than most other European nations, and approximately half as much as the US. Yet comparisons between different countries' expenditure on health services are notoriously difficult and potentially misleading. For example, in the US, health care providers have an incentive to carry out as many tests as possible on an individual patient in order to recoup the maximum amount of money from the insurer. Unnecessary X-rays and other redundant diagnostic tests push up the US's expenditure on health without improving patient care. In some European countries, such as France and

[11]   <http://www.nhsdirect.nhs.uk>.

Germany, a mixed health economy exists whereby compulsory social insurance is topped up by co-payments or charges levied on patients, for which there is now a growing market in private insurance. So although both France and Germany spend more of their GNP on health than the UK, this does not mean that more public money is being lavished on healthcare, but rather that individuals are choosing to divert more of their personal resources to the purchase of top-up insurance. So while it might be true that the government could spend more on health, it is not necessarily obvious that this would completely eliminate the shortage of resources.

In 2000 the World Health Organization[12] attempted to rank national health systems' performance according to the extent to which they achieved three goals:

(1) good health

(2) responsiveness to the population's expectations

(3) fairness of financial contribution.

The results were interesting, not least because—as is evident from the extract reproduced below—there appears to be no correlation between the amount spent on healthcare per capita and a country's rank. Nor does the percentage of care provided privately appear to make any difference. France came first; the UK 18th; and the US was 37th (out of 191 countries).

WHO rank	Country	Expenditure per capita ($)	% private
1	France	2,077	23.6
2	Italy	1,783	32.0
7	Spain	1,218	23.2
10	Japan	1,822	21.7
11	Norway	2,425	17.2
18	United Kingdom	1,461	16.2
20	Switzerland	2,794	26.6
25	Germany	2,424	25.4
32	Australia	2,043	30.7
37	United States	4,178	55.3

4. DIFFERENT RATIONING STRATEGIES

The reality of rationed health care is that patients are deprived of beneficial treatment. If treatment is withheld from a patient because it is not likely to do any good, then this would be a straightforward case of clinical judgment rather than rationing. Depriving individuals of care that might help them is radically at odds with the rule of rescue, that is 'the strong human proclivity to provide aid to identified victims of illness or

---

[12] World Health Report 2000 *Health Systems: Improving Performance* (WHO 2000).

accident'.[13] To say that society does not value patient X sufficiently to spend the £10,000 that it would cost to prevent her death seems unbearably callous. We prefer to maintain the illusion that life is priceless, although as John McKie et al. point out, the reality of rationed healthcare is precisely that there are limits upon what we are prepared to spend on a patient's medical treatment.

John McKie, Jeff Richardson, Peter Singer, Helga Kuhse[14]

Can we place a monetary value on a human life? Many people reject the very idea of doing so. How could we possibly arrive at any figure that would represent the value of a human life? . . . What would we think of a society that, after spending a certain amount in attempting to save the lives of miners trapped after an underground mishap, said that it had reached the limit of the value of the miners' lives, and left them to die rather than spend more on rescuing them?

Yet we do live in a society that allows people to die when it costs too much to save them. It happens all the time, in areas like road safety, workplace safety, overseas aid and in health care . . .

[A] financial limit on our efforts to save human life is present in every national health care budget. We may know that providing better screening to detect the early stages of some forms of cancer would save a specific number of lives, and yet often we do not do it because the cost is too high . . .

Are we then in the position of the society that allows entombed miners to die because the costs of rescuing them are too high? One difference is that, in the case of the miners, we know who the victims are. We can more easily identify with them, and they will presumably have families and friends who will be distraught at their peril and desperate for their rescue . . . In the case of cancer screening programmes, we do not know when we make the decision who will be affected by our decision not to fund the programme, and we may never be able to find out . . .

The difference is psychologically significant. To abandon identifiable people to certain death when they could be saved appears to be a more heartless decision, and to symbolize a lack of concern for human life to a far greater degree, than a failure to reduce the road toll. On reflection, however, it is hard to place much moral weight on this psychological difference. Those killed in car crashes on dangerous intersections, and those who die from preventable cancers, will themselves be people who are no less real than the trapped miners, and their families will grieve no less for their deaths.

Because depriving people of beneficial health care services requires us to sacrifice identifiable individuals' lives or welfare, any rationing system is, as Loren E Lomasky explains, always going to be difficult to justify.

Loren E Lomasky[15]

If resources are indispensable to a group of persons at peril but too limited to accommodate all, to save one life is to sacrifice another. Our moral principles are severely strained by circumstances that require the balancing of one innocent life against another. Such choices, however, promise to intrude on us increasingly.

Two classic examples of triage are the dangerously overloaded lifeboat and the harried medic patching up the wounded on a battlefield. Whatever is done, some salvageable lives will be forfeited.

[13] DC Hadorn, 'The problem of discrimination in health care priority setting' (1992) 268 Journal of the American Medical Association 1454–8, 1454.

[14] The Allocation of Health Care Resources: An Ethical Evaluation of the 'QALY' Approach (Dartmouth Aldershot 1998) 1–3.

[15] 'Medical Progress and National Health Care' (1980) 10 Philosophy and Public Affairs 65–88, 80, 82.

The dreadfulness of these choices though is somewhat softened by the urgency of a crisis: action must be immediate and there is little luxury for reflective deliberation. If called upon to justify his actions, an agent could plead that he was reacting instinctively to the needs of the moment.

Contemporary medical technology is responsible for triage situations of a rather different character. A mechanism is devised that is effective against some previously untreatable condition. Unfortunately, only a small percentage of those afflicted can receive treatment. Who shall be allowed to live? Here decision-makers are dealing with a series of events predictable well in advance. Not enmeshed in a precipitously developing crisis, they are privileged to assume the role of detached administrator. There is, however, a price to be paid for this relative ease: whatever standards are developed and employed are subject to close scrutiny. Those disfavored in the selection process are perfectly entitled to ask why. Persuasive answers will not be easily forthcoming . . .

[W]e possess neither reliable intuitive nor theoretical grounds for making a choice of life against life. Because each human life is owed maximum respect, differential treatment based on precarious judgments of social worth is odious. But to consign individuals to life or death because of the results of a lottery allows impersonal forces to adjudicate in the most deeply personal of crises . . .

Triage is never unproblematic, but on what basis could a creature of the state adopt any principle of selection? Whoever is excluded can justifiably complain that he is thereby being disadvantaged by the very institution whose special duty is to extend equal protection to all persons.

Hidden and implicit mechanisms for allocating scarce resources—such as subsuming cost considerations within clinical discretion—allow politicians, NHS administrators and doctors to avoid explicitly admitting that they are denying some patients treatment which might improve their wellbeing on the grounds of cost. It is also convenient for decision-makers if rationing criteria have the appearance of neutrality and objectivity.

In this section, we examine different criteria which could plausibly be used to ration healthcare services. While we might agree that resources should be allocated fairly, this just begs the question: what do we mean by fair? Do we treat people fairly when we treat them equally? Or should priority always be given to those in the greatest need? Alternatively should we ensure that resources are allocated where they will do most good, using some sort of cost-effectiveness calculation? We could choose to take an individual's responsibility for their own ill health into account; or their social value; or we could opt for a straightforward free market in healthcare in which those who were prepared to spend the most would have access to the best treatment. Finally, we could abandon the search for defensible rationing criteria and instead distribute healthcare resources by some process of random selection.

It is important to remember that a perfectly fair and universally acceptable rationing system is an unrealistic goal. Rather we may instead be looking for ways to allocate scarce resources which attempt to mediate fairly between competing claims on NHS resources. In practice, most people would probably advocate some sort of mixed rationing system, in which a number of different factors are taken into account when allocating resources. For example, an approach based upon the cost-effectiveness of treatment may have to be supplemented by additional criteria, such as urgency of clinical need.

Before we assess potentially fair rationing criteria, it is worth pointing out that some very obviously unfair grounds for distinguishing between patients might never-theless have an effect upon the ways in which resources are allocated in the NHS. First, while it would clearly be unethical for doctors to take a patient's personal appeal into account when deciding whether to offer them treatment, in practice health care pro-fessionals are human beings capable of feeling enormous sympathy for one patient and exasperation with another. Of course, these emotions should not be allowed to colour their clinical judgement, but it would be impossible to guarantee that doctors will never be prompted to do more for a patient out of personal sympathy. Secondly, some patients are simply more demanding and assertive than others, and this will undoubtedly affect their access to NHS resources. A patient who demands a second opinion, or who repeatedly telephones a consultant's secretary may receive care that other patients might not have the confidence or the knowledge to seek out. John Butler interviewed health care professionals about their attitudes to rationing, and as we see in the following extract, concern was expressed about patients' uneven ability to exert pressure upon health care resources.

John Butler[16]

The health visitor was clear about the injustice that could result from rationing by inaccessibiliy, in which the astute and the persistent were rewarded at the expense of those who lacked the know-how to seek out what they wanted. Those who are put off, she said, will not be the better-educated middle-class families, they will be the poorer families who are under-educated and inarticulate . . .

The surgeon, too, expressed his moral concern at the potential for social bias in the innate responsiveness of the service to the pressure exerted upon it by patients. Those who 'push and shove a bit' will often get the best treatment, but they will not be a cross-section of all those waiting to be seen. He recognized it as wrong (albeit, perhaps, unavoidable) that a class bias will ensue through which cases may not always be seen in the order of their clinical urgency. It was the replacement of need by pressure as the determinant of access to secondary care that he saw as wrong.

(a) EQUALITY

Equal distribution of health care resources does not, of course, mean that the NHS's total budget should be divided equally between all UK citizens. Rather, as Amy Gut-mann explains, equality of access instead means that everyone with an equivalent health need should have equivalent access to appropriate care. Patients who are alike in relevant ways should be treated alike, and patients who are unlike each other should be treated in appropriately unlike fashion. But of course this just begs the question: what factors justify treating patients similarly and what factors justify differentiating between them? Is an alcoholic who needs a liver transplant 'like' a non-drinker with a history of liver disease who has a similarly urgent need for a transplant, or does the patient's alcoholism turn them into 'unlike' cases?

---

[16] *The Ethics of Health Care Rationing: Principles and Practices* (Cassell London 1999) 230.

Amy Gutmann[17]

A principle of equal access to health care demands that every person who shares the same type and degree of health need must be given an equally effective chance of receiving appropriate treatment of equal quality so long as that treatment is available to anyone. Stated in this way, the equal access principle does not establish whether a society must provide any particular medical treatment or health care benefit to its needy members . . . The principle requires that if anyone within a society has an opportunity to receive a service or good that satisfies a health need, then everyone who shares the same type and degree of health need must be given an equally effective chance of receiving that service or good.

Since this is a principle of equal access, it does not guarantee equal results . . . Discriminations in health care are permitted if they are based upon type or degree of health need, willingness of informed adults to be treated, and choices of lifestyle among the population. The equal access principle constrains the distribution of opportunities to receive health care to an egalitarian standard, but it does not determine the total level of health care available or the effects of that care (provided the care is of equal quality) upon the health of the population. Of course, even if equality in health care were defined according to an 'equal health' principle, one would still have to admit that a just health care system could not come close to producing an equally healthy population, given the unequal distribution of illness among people and our present medical knowledge . . .

Equal access also places limits upon the market freedoms of some individuals, especially, but not exclusively, the richest members of society. The principle does not permit the purchase of health care to which other similarly needy people do not have effective access . . . Thus, the rigorous implementation of equal access to health care would prevent rich people from spending their extra income for preferred medical services, if those services were not equally accessible to the poor.

It is also worth noting that equal distribution of health services does not necessarily imply that everyone should have access to the same high standard of care. Rather greater equality could be achieved by levelling down so that everyone's medical treatment was equally inadequate.

In practice then, on its own equality does not tell us very much about how to allocate scarce NHS resources. Instead, it supplements other rationing criteria, such as need or cost-effectiveness, by ensuring that these are employed consistently between patients in order to avoid the arbitrary and unfair distribution of resources. It also, as Ian Kennedy suggests, might lead us to give particular priority to the needs of the most disadvantaged and vulnerable members of society.

Ian Kennedy[18]

The notion of justice which I find most convincing is that which tells us that we ought to seek a society in which each person is accepted as of equal moral worth and has equal opportunity to enjoy an equal share of the total sum of society's goods. A particular feature of such a view of what is just is that any attempt to translate it into practice must begin by favouring the weakest and the least advantaged, since these are the people least likely to have the opportunity to enjoy an equal share of what we have, and are thus most in need of help . . .

[17] 'For and Against Equal Access to Health Care' Milbank Memorial Fund Quarterly/Health and Society 59(4) (1981) in *Classic Works in Medical Ethics*, Gregory Pence (ed) (McGraw Hill Boston 1998) 367–81, 368–70.

[18] *Treat Me Right: Essays in Medical Law and Ethics* (Clarendon Press Oxford 1998) 291.

So, if we are concerned with what constitutes a just allocation of resources, my prescription, at the very least, would call for policies aimed at ensuring, as far as possible, that everyone had an equal opportunity to enjoy an equal share of the total net welfare of society.

One ingredient of the net benefits that a society enjoys is health. It follows that a just society must set its policies and write its laws to ensure that everyone, beginning with the least advantaged and most vulnerable, has an equal opportunity to enjoy an equal share of the total net resources allocated to health.

(b) NEEDS

At first sight, distributing NHS resources according to need might appear attractively fair and simple. Needs, after all, have much greater moral force than wants or desires. But the concept of 'need' is remarkably elastic and culturally variable. New technologies will constantly expand our category of medical 'needs'. As Richard Lamm has argued,

[m]edical 'need' is an infinitely expandable concept. We need what is available, and in a creative and inventive society such as our own, there is no end to what we can do to treat aging bodies.[19]

Moreover, need could only operate as a rationing criteria if we were able to construct some sort of hierarchy of needs, so that we could tell whether one patient's need was greater or less than of other candidates for treatment. We would, for example, have to decide whether life-preserving needs are always more important that life-enhancing needs. It could be argued that someone whose life is in danger clearly 'needs' treatment more than someone who will survive without treatment, and that life-saving treatment should always be our first priority. But this would disregard other relevant criteria, such as a person's capacity to benefit from treatment. The life of a patient who is in an irreversible coma can be preserved—at great cost—for many years using artificial ventilation, nutrition, and hydration. It is not clear that this sort of expenditure should necessarily take priority over treatment, such as palliative care, which is capable of alleviating a terminally ill patient's pain and discomfort, but which will not save her life. Similarly, prolonging someone's life for a very short period of time is not necessarily a better use of NHS resources than treatment which might enable another patient to have many years of active and painfree life.

In the next extract, Norman Daniels argues that health needs can be ranked according to the extent to which 'normal species functioning' is impaired. So, for example, someone with a broken hip has their normal opportunity range restricted more than someone with a disfiguring scar, for example, and hence according to Daniels's scheme, hip replacement operations should take priority over cosmetic surgery.

Norman Daniels[20]
A theory of health-care needs should serve two central purposes. First, it should illuminate the sense in which we—at least many of us—think health care is 'special,' that it should be treated

---

[19] Richard D Lamm, 'Rationing of Health Care: Inevitable and Desirable' (1992) 140 University of Pennsylvania Law Review 1511, 1512.
[20] 'Health-Care Needs and Distributive Justice' (1981) 10 Philosophy and Public Affairs 146–79, 146–7, 154, 159, 177.

differently from other social goods. Specifically, even in societies in which people tolerate (and glorify) significant and pervasive inequalities in the distribution of most social goods, many feel there are special reasons of justice for distributing health care more equally . . .

Second, such a theory should provide a basis for distinguishing the more from the less important among the many kinds of things health care does for us. It should tell us which health-care services are 'more special' than others. Thus, a broad category of health-services functions to improve quality of life, not to extend or save it. Some of these services restore or compensate for diminished capacities and functions; others improve life quality in other ways. We do draw distinctions about the urgency and importance of such services. Our theory of health-care needs should provide a basis for a reasonable set of such distinctions. If we can assume some scarcity of healthcare resources, and if we cannot (or should not) rely just on market mechanisms to allocate these resources, then we need such a theory to guide macro-allocation decisions about priorities among health-care needs . . .

What emerges here is the suggestion that we use impairment of the normal opportunity range as a fairly crude measure of the relative importance of health-care needs at the macro level. In general, it will be more important to prevent, cure, or compensate for those disease conditions which involve a greater curtailment of normal opportunity range. . . .

[W]e can characterize health-care needs as things we need to maintain, restore, or compensate for the loss of, normal species-functioning. Since serious impairments of normal functioning diminish our capacities and abilities, they impair individual opportunity range relative to the range normal for our society . . .

My account of health-care needs and their connection to fair equality of opportunity has a number of implications for resource-allocation issues. I have already noted that we get an important distinction between the use of health-care services to meet health-care needs and their use to meet other wants and preferences. The tie of health-care needs to opportunity makes the former use special and important in a way not true of the latter. Moreover, we get a crude criterion— impact on normal opportunity range—for distinguishing the importance of different health-care needs.

There are, however, several problems with Daniels's attempt to prioritize different health needs by the extent to which they interfere with normal species functioning. First, 'normal species functioning' may sound like an objective criterion, but it is in fact quite difficult to pin down. How much infirmity is 'normal' in old age, for example? It is 'normal' for human bodies to fail progressively in old age, yet we would not want to give a low priority to treatment of very elderly patients on the grounds that their infirmity is 'normal'. Secondly, Daniels admits that normal species functioning will be culturally variable. For example, in the UK in 1900, normal species functioning meant a life expectancy of about forty-five years, now it is over 80. More worryingly, normal species functioning depends in part upon the availability of decent health services, leading to a degree of circularity in using 'normal functioning' as a criterion for the distribution of health care. In sub-Saharan Africa, some countries' health systems' inability to respond adequately to the AIDS pandemic is reducing average life expectancy each year. Does this mean that the responsibility of health services in these countries correspondingly dwindles as 'normal species functioning' is diminished? Allan Buchanan, for example, has argued that:

A principle which requires only that resources be allocated so as to assure that everyone attains the normal opportunity range would be inadequate in situations in which the normal opportunity range was unacceptably narrow due to a failure to allocate sufficient resources for health care.[21]

Thirdly, a great many medical treatments attempt to restore 'normal species functioning', and so in conditions of scarcity, the assumption must be that it would be possible to rank particular illnesses and disabilities according to the extent to which they interfere with normal functioning. Treatments for the most debilitating conditions would then take priority over more minor interferences with normal functioning. In practice, however, it would be extremely difficult to construct an objective, population-wide hierarchy because the extent to which someone is debilitated by a particular condition may depend upon their circumstances. For some people, such as surgeons or pilots, losing the sight in one eye will have disastrous consequences, for others its impact upon their quality of life may be comparatively slight.

Finally, there would have to be exceptions to Daniels's classification in order to accommodate valuable medical treatments which do not attempt to 'restore normal species functioning'. Contraception and abortion, for example, are intended to disrupt normal biological processes. Yet in the UK contraception is considered such a cost-effective public good that it is exempt from prescription charges. Pregnancy and childbirth are normal processes, and obstetric care does not restore normal species functioning, yet it seems clear that maternity services are an appropriate use of public money. Palliative care cannot restore normal functioning, but there is no doubt that it should be a high priority in any humane health care system.

It is also worth noting that while many health needs can be met by providing patients with medical treatment, sometimes the best solution to a person's ill-health will lie outside the capabilities of the NHS. A person who is depressed may 'need' a job in order to restore their self esteem. Children suffering from asthma may 'need' to move out of a damp inner city house. It is important to remember that the NHS is always going to be incapable of delivering perfect health to the population, since so much ill-health is caused by factors other than lack of optimum health care.

(c) MAXIMIZING HEALTH GAINS

While it seems uncontroversial that scarce NHS resources should be spent where they are likely to do most good, rationing strategies which attempt to maximize health gains are explicitly utilitarian, and therefore suffer from some of the defects of utilitarianism that we considered in Chapter 1 (see pp. 11–12). Calculating the aggregate health gain across society necessarily involves an interpersonal comparison of harms and benefits. But of course the fact that patient A is more likely to benefit from treatment than patient B is of little interest to patient B when she is denied access to the only treatment which is likely to offer her any chance (albeit a smaller one than patient A) of living a normal healthy life. Deciding to spend a particular sum of money on treatment which is likely to save ten people's lives, in preference to

---

[21] 'The Right to a Decent Minimum of Health Care' (1984) 13 Philosophy and Public Affairs 55–78, 64.

treatment likely to save one person's life may at first sight appear rational and sensible. But if you put yourself in the shoes of the one person whose life is to be sacrificed in order that ten others may live, this decision may look rather different.

(1) ASSESSING COST-EFFECTIVENESS: THE QALY

Quality Adjusted Life Years, known as QALYs, are an attempt to quantify the costs and health gains which can be expected from different treatments, in order to compare their relative cost-effectiveness.[22] The point of QALYs is that they do not only measure the amount of extra life that a particular treatment might generate, but also its quality; the assumption being that we should divert resources to treatments which are likely to offer people the longest periods of healthy and active life. Alan Williams, a QALY enthusiast, explains them as follows:

The essence of a QALY is that it takes a year of healthy life expectancy to be worth 1, but regards a year of unhealthy life expectancy as worth less than 1. Its precise value is lower the worse the quality of life of the unhealthy person (which is what the 'quality adjusted' bit is all about). If being dead is worth zero, it is, in principle, possible for a QALY to be negative, i.e. for the quality of someone's life to be judged worse than being dead.

The general idea is that a beneficial health care activity is one that generates a positive amount of QALYs, and that an efficient health care activity is one where the cost per QALY is as low as it can be. A high priority health care activity is one where the cost-per-QALY is low, and a low priority activity is one where cost-per-QALY is high.[23]

There are therefore various stages to a QALY assessment. First, a quality of life scale must be worked out ranging from 0 (death) to 1.0 (full health). Next, we multiply the patient's life expectancy and quality of life score, both before and after treatment. The difference will be the QALY score. Let us imagine that, without treatment, patient A has 2 years of life left, and her quality of life is judged to be 0.5. Before treatment, her life contains 1 QALY. If treatment X would give her 6 years with a quality of life of 1.0, post-treatment, her life contains 6 QALYs. The QALY value of treatment X is therefore 5. The next stage is to calculate the cost per QALY. So let's imagine that treatment X costs £1000. Since it provides 5 QALYs, the cost per QALY is £200. If an alternative treatment Y costs £10,000 and has a QALY value of 10, its cost per QALY is £1000. Treatment X is therefore more cost effective than treatment Y.

If QALY scores are worked out for a number of different treatments, it should be possible to draw up league tables of treatments in order to work out which offer the best value for money. In the following extract from one such table, we can see that GP advice to stop smoking has a low cost per QALY, while heart transplantation is much more expensive, and neurosurgery on patients with malignant brain tumours appears to be extremely cost-ineffective.

[22] The QALY scale was first developed in the work of Rosser et al. in the 1970s. See further R Rosser and VC Watts 'The measurement of hospital output' (1972) 1 International Journal of Epidemiology 361–8; R Rosser and P Kind 'A scale of values of states of illness: is there a social consensus' (1978) 7 International Journal of Epidemiology 347–58.
[23] 'The Value of QALYs' (1985) 94 Health and Social Service Journal.

Alan M Maynard[24]

QALY of competing therapies: some tentative estimates	Cost/QALY £
Cholesterol testing and diet therapy (adults aged 40–69)	220
GP advice to stop smoking	270
Pacemaker insertion	1100
Hip replacement	1800
Kidney transplant	4710
Breast cancer screening	5780
Heart transplantation	7840
Hospital haemodialysis	21 970
Neurosurgical intervention for malignant brain tumour	107 780

QALYs are an attempt to objectively compare the cost-effectiveness of different treatments in order, as Alan Williams explains, that scarce NHS resources 'do as much good as possible'.

Alan Williams[25]

Common sense tells us that in the face of scarcity we should use our limited resources in such a way that they do as much good as possible. In health care, 'doing good' means improving people's life expectancy and the quality of their lives. Since people value both of these fundamental attributes of life, we need a measure of outcome which incorporates both, and which reflects the fact that most people are willing to sacrifice some quality of life in order to gain some additional life expectancy, and vice versa. This is precisely the role of the QALY. . . . Thus the QALY is to be contrasted with measures such as 'survival rates', commonly used as the sole success criteria in clinical trials, which implicitly assume that only life expectancy is of any concern to people. The essence of the QALY concept is that effects on life expectancy and effects on quality of life are brought together in a single measure, and the bulk of the empirical work involved in making the concept operational is concerned with eliciting the values that people attach to different health states, and the extent to which they regard them as better or worse than being dead . . .

In the presence of scarcity, resources devoted to the health of one person will be denied some other person who might have benefited from them. Clinicians are quite used to this phenomenon with respect to the allocation of their own time, and of any other resources that they control as practice managers. They are trained to discriminate between those who will benefit greatly from treatment and those who won't, and by this means 'clinical priorities' are established, which are based on some broad assessment of risks, benefits and costs. The role of costs here is crucial because they represent sacrifices made by other potential patients who did not get treated. Thus the economists' argument that medical practice should concentrate on those treatments that are known to be cost-effective is designed to ensure that the benefits gained by the treatments that are actually provided should be greater than the benefits sacrificed by those who were denied treatment. That is what 'doing as much good as possible with our limited resources' means.

But while QALYs lend a degree of objectivity to the ranking of medical treatments, they cannot tell us how much money should be allocated to healthcare, nor which

[24] 'Developing the health care market' (1991) 101 The Economic Journal 1277–86.
[25] 'Economics, QALYs and Medical Ethics: A health economist's perspective' in Souzy Dracopoulou (ed), Ethics and Values in Health Care Management (Routledge London 1998) 29–37, 29–31.

treatments should be funded. Kidney transplants may cost more per QALY than cholesterol testing in the above 'league table', but that does not mean that kidney transplants should not be performed within the NHS. Rather QALYs simply provide policymakers with a technical and supposedly objective hierarchy of treatments in order to help them assess and compare cost-effectiveness. As we see later in this chapter, a cost/utility scale was used to rank treatments in Oregon, but it initially led to some profoundly counter-intuitive results: cosmetic breast surgery ranked above treatment for open thigh fractures, for example. So although the QALY scale might offer relevant information to decisionmakers, it is not a substitute for decisionmaking, and there will still be difficult choices to make.

It is also important to note that a number of commentators have challenged the usefulness and fairness of the QALY approach to resource allocation. First, according to the logic of QALYs, transferring resources from technologies which have a high cost per QALY to those with a low cost per QALY will mean that the country's overall health gain will rise without any additional expenditure. The implication is that the purpose of a health service is to generate the maximum number of quality adjusted life years at the lowest cost. QALYs assume that society is neutral as to how these health benefits are distributed across society, and is concerned only with ensuring the maximization of health gains. It makes no difference—for example—whether the years of healthy life go to people who are already in good health or to those whose health is poor. Thus, QALYs have a tendency to ignore the fairness of distribution in favour of an approach concerned only with the total aggregate size of health improvement. In practice, most of us would prefer the NHS to fund high cost interventions for patients with life threatening illnesses, such as cancer and heart disease, rather than offering treatments which might be more cost-effective to those with more trivial complaints, such as hayfever or acne. Our concern is not simply to maximize the aggregate health gain in society at the lowest cost, but rather to ensure that the NHS responds appropriately to those in the greatest need.

Secondly, the emphasis upon maximizing health gains is explicitly utilitarian. By measuring the units of lifetime, rather than treating individuals as separate and intrinsically valuable, QALYs require us to sacrifice some individuals' lives in order to maximize the total health gains to society. If it costs £5,000 to extend five people's lives for a year, and £1,000 to extend one person's life for ten years, QALYs would suggest that the latter is the best use of resources. But as John Harris, one of QALYs most vigorous critics, explains, the five people whose lives are shortened as a result of this calculation might not agree:

What matters is that the person is not prepared to agree that his interest in continued life is of less value than that of anyone else, nor that that interest necessarily varies with the quality of his life nor with his life expectancy. In short, if a person wants continued existence, then, in my view, his interest in continued existence is entitled to be treated as on a par with that of anyone else. All people who want to go on living have an interest in continued existence, the value of which can only be determined by themselves.[26]

[26] J Harris, 'Double jeopardy and the veil of ignorance—a reply' (1995) 21 Journal of Medical Ethics 151–7, 151.

Thirdly, it has been suggested that using QALYs to ration treatment will tend to exacerbate existing discrimination against the elderly and the disabled, whose QALY scores are likely to be fairly low because of their reduced life-expectancy and/or their lower pre-existing quality of life. People who are unlucky enough to suffer from conditions which are very expensive to treat—and this is usually people with very serious illnesses—will also be discriminated against, because the cost per QALY of treating them is always likely to be high. This is, in Harris's words, 'a sort of double jeopardy', whereby people who have already been unlucky enough to be disabled will be further disadvantaged when competing for scarce life-saving treatment.[27] Discriminating against people on the grounds of their quality of life or life expectancy is, according to Harris, 'as unwarranted as it would be to discriminate on the grounds of race or gender'.

This argument has been contested by Peter Singer, John McKie, Helga Kuhse, and Jeff Richardson.[28] They argue that John Harris has overlooked a crucial feature of QALYs, namely that what is measured is the change in a person's health brought about by a particular intervention. The example they give is rather complicated, but can be summarized as follows. Karen is a paraplegic suffering from persistent pain, whose quality of life on the QALY scale is said to be 0.5. Her life-expectancy is 40 years, and so before treatment her life contains 20 QALYs. Let us imagine that a treatment costing $10,000 could eliminate her pain, but would leave her in a wheelchair, and that this would raise her quality of life to 0.75 on the QALY scale. If her life-expectancy continues to be 40 years, she now has 30 QALYs left. In contrast, Lisa has a minor limp, and her quality of life is judged to be 0.95. She too has a life expectancy of 40 years, and without treatment her life contains 38 QALYs. Treatment costing $10,000 dollars would remove her limp and leave her with a quality of life score of 1: her life would now contain 40 QALYs. Spending $10,000 on Lisa yields 2 QALYs, while the same amount of money offers Karen 10 QALYs. In order to maximize QALYs, these resources should be diverted to the paraplegic whose post-treatment quality of life may be lower than Lisa's, but whose QALY gain per dollar spent is higher.

Although it is clearly possible to construct examples in which people with pre-existing disabilities stand to gain more per QALY than those in nearly full health, it is inevitable that trying to maximize the number of life years gained within the NHS will generally skew resources away from services for those whose lives are likely to be short, namely the elderly or patients with incurable terminal illnesses, towards the treatment of younger people, and in particular of children. Palliative care does not offer the prospect of generating any more 'life years', but making a dying person's last days or weeks more comfortable is unquestionably an appropriate use of NHS resources. According to John Harris, again:

The ageism of QALY is inescapable, for any calculation of the life-years generated for a particular patient by a particular therapy must be based on the life expectancy of that patient after treatment. The older the patient is when treated, the fewer the life-years that can be achieved by the therapy . . . [I]t will usually be more QALY efficient to concentrate on areas of medicine which will

[27] id., 'QALYfying the value of life' (1987) 13 Journal of Medical Ethics 117–23, 120.
[28] 'Double jeopardy and the use of QALYs in health care allocation' (1995) 21 Journal of Medical Ethics 144–50.

inevitably generate more QALYs, neonatal care or paediatrics, for example. And equally, to channel resources away from (or deny them altogether to) areas such as geriatric medicine or terminal care.[29]

Fourthly, the QALY approach is inconsistent with the principle that people with equal health needs should have equal access to appropriate medical treatment. Rather, maximizing QALYs means that people with equal need for treatment will not be treated equally, rather as Penelope Mullen and Peter Spurgeon explain, their access to treatment will depend upon the costs of treating them:

Thus systematic discrimination could result against, say, those from ethnic minority groups who require interpreters, those living in poorer housing who might require inpatient stays rather than day surgery and those living in remote sparsely populated locations, etc. To take a hypothetical example, suppose there were a condition, suffered by both men and women, for which treatment gave equal health gain for both sexes but, for some biological reason, treatment for a woman costs far more than treatment for a man. Would it be acceptable to follow the logic of QALY maximisation and give treatment of men higher priority than treatment of women?[30]

Fifthly, when a new treatment is introduced, it may be extremely expensive, but its costs may decrease as the technology becomes cheaper, or as the expense of initial additional staff training is eliminated. The QALY scale might then discourage innovation in favour of established and currently cheaper treatments, even where there might be cost-savings from adopting the new treatment over the longer term.

Sixthly, QALYs assume that it is possible to devise an objective and accurate mechanism for measuring the anticipated length and quality of a person's life. In fact, the medical profession's predictions of future life expectancy are notoriously unreliable, and speculating about the future quality of a person's life will obviously also be inherently uncertain. Treatment outcomes depend upon a wide variety of factors, such as the doctor's skill and the quality of aftercare services, and since the QALY calculation is simply too crude to capture all of the relevant variables, its results will be imprecise and indeterminate.

It could even be argued that it is in fact impossible to reduce such a complex concept as quality of life to a single numerical value between 0 and 1. Advocates of QALYs often appear to assume that devising a quality of life scale would be comparatively straightforward, and rarely explain who would be charged with making these assessments. Would it be people suffering from the particular illness or disability; the medical profession; or members of the public? It could be argued that only people who live with a condition are in any position to judge its effect on their quality of life. But of course it is not easy for such people to make the sort of comparative assessments needed in order to formulate a quality of life scale. Doctors and members of the public may be able to speculate about the relative inconvenience or distress caused by a range of disabilities, especially if they have experience of caring for people with disabling conditions, but they inevitably do so from a position of relative ignorance.

---

[29] John Harris, 'More and Better Justice' in JM Bell and Susan Mendus (eds), *Philosophy and Medical Welfare* (CUP Cambridge 1988) 75–96, 80.

[30] Penelope Mullen and Peter Spurgeon, *Priority Setting and the Public* (Radcliffe Medical Press Abingdon 2000) 42.

Moreover, not only is it very difficult for anyone to judge whether depression might be worse than losing sensation in one's right arm, but also quality of life judgements are necessarily subjective and hence do not lend themselves to the sort of objective quantification which the QALY scales appear to be based upon. The QALY weightings are inevitably arbitrary: how can we tell whether living ten years with a quality of life score of 0.9 is equivalent to living for nine years in perfect health? And they are incapable of taking the individual patient's own preferences and needs into account. For some people, immobility may not greatly interfere with their ability to gain enjoyment from life; for others it will be devastating. Since decisions based upon QALYs might have life and death consequences, it is especially important to remember that QALY scores are grounded in conjecture and guesswork.

Using QALYs at the macro level may, as John Harris suggests, be slightly less objectionable because we would just be deciding that treatment X, in general, leads to better patient outcomes at lower cost than treatment Y. It is at the micro level, when choices have to be made between individual patients that taking QALYs into account would be especially invidious.

John Harris[31]

There are two ways in which QALYs might be used. One is unexceptionable and useful, and fully in line with the assumptions which give QALYs their plausibility. The other is none of these.

QALYs might be used to determine which of rival therapies to give to a particular patient or which procedure to use to treat a particular condition. Clearly the one generating the most QALYs will be the better bet, both for the patient and for a society with scarce resources. However, QALYs might also be used to determine not what treatment to give these patients, but which group of patients to treat, or which conditions to give priority in the allocation of health care resources. It is clear that it is this latter use which Williams has in mind, for he specifically cites as one of the rewards of the development of QALYs, their use in 'priority setting in the health care system in general' . . . It is this use which is I believe positively dangerous and morally indefensible. Why? . . .

It is crucial to realise that the whole plausibility of QALYs depends upon our accepting that they simply involve the generalisation of the 'truth' that 'given the choice a person would prefer a shorter healthier life to a longer period of survival in a state of severe discomfort . . . But whereas it follows from the fact that given the choice a person would prefer a shorter healthier life to a longer one of severe discomfort, that the best treatment for that person is the one yielding the most QALYs, it does not follow that treatments yielding more QALYs are preferable to treatments yielding fewer QALYs where different people are to receive the treatments. That is to say, while it follows from the fact (if it is a fact) that I and everyone else would prefer to have, say, one year of healthy life rather than three years of severe discomfort, that we value healthy existence more than uncomfortable existence for ourselves, it does not follow that where the choice is between three years of discomfort for me or immediate death on the one hand, and one year of health for you or immediate death on the other, that I am somehow committed to the judgement that you ought to be saved rather than me.

[31] 'QALYfying the value of life' (1987) 13 Journal of Medical Ethics 117–23, 118.

(2) A WIDE OR NARROW INTERPRETATION OF COST-EFFECTIVENESS?

When health economists engage in cost-effectiveness analysis of medical treatments, their focus tends to be quite narrowly confined. It would, however, be possible to broaden the scope of these sorts of calculations in a number of ways. First, health is improved not only by direct medical intervention. In fact, healthcare is probably one of the least important factors behind the dramatic improvements in public health that occurred during the twentieth century. Better nutrition, sanitation and workplace safety, and a reduction in poverty levels almost certainly contributed more to the nation's health than medical treatment. It has been estimated that health services affect about 10 per cent of the principal indices for measuring health (such as infant mortality, absences through sickness, and life expectancy), while 90 per cent are determined by factors beyond the control of the NHS, such as environment, nutrition and lifestyle.[32] Could it therefore be argued that the cost-effectiveness of new medical technologies should be judged not only against other medical treatments as in the QALY league tables, but also against other social measures which might in fact lead to greater improvements in health at lower cost? In particular, reducing child poverty levels would be likely to have a dramatic—and quite possibly highly cost-effective— impact upon health, and yet raising welfare payments to poor families does not have the same popular appeal as heroic medical interventions to cure the sick.

In order to engage in a cost–benefit calculation, it is also of course necessary to work out what counts as a benefit. Are we concerned only with the health benefit to the particular individual, or might it be legitimate to take into account other benefits that might accrue from her successful treatment? For example, enabling members of the workforce to return to paid employment has clear social benefits that, if included in the calculation, might lead us to give priority to the treatment of adults of working age, or to those in full-time employment, or even to sub-sections of society who do especially valuable work. Should we take into account whether a patient has depend- ent children who will also benefit from her recovery? In deciding what priority sub- stance abuse treatment programmes should receive, is it relevant that successfully treating drug addiction will not only improve the individual addict's life, but also that of her family and the community in which she lives?

Jonathan Glover argues that it will sometimes be legitimate to take into account any benefit which might accrue to third parties, such as dependent children, when deciding which patient to treat.

Jonathan Glover[33]

If there are two people whose lives are in question and we have to choose to save only one, the number of people dependent on them should be regarded as very important. If other things are equal, but one has no family and the other is the mother of several young children, the case against deciding between them randomly is a strong one . . . Refusal to depart from random choice when knowledge about their dependants is available is to place no value on avoiding the additional misery caused to the children if the mother is not the one saved . . .

---

[32] David J Hunter, *Desperately Seeking Solutions: Rationing Health Care* (Longman London 1997) 18.

[33] *Causing Death and Saving Lives* (Penguin London 1977) 222–3.

If we give some weight to the interests of dependants, should we take into account more generalized side-effects, such as the relative importance of the contributions to society made by different people? There are good grounds for rejecting this as a general policy. It is a truism that we have no agreed standard by which to measure people's relative contribution to society. How does a mother compare with a doctor or a research scientist or a coal-miner? Any list of jobs ranked in order of social value seems, at least at present, to be arbitrary and debatable. It also seems to introduce the offensive division of people into grades . . .

But, while rejecting discrimination based on supposed social worth as a general policy, it would be wrong to rule out the possibility of exceptions in extreme cases. It seems doctrinaire to say that, if Winston Churchill in 1940 had been in the lifeboat situation, it would have been wrong to give him priority.

On the one hand, invoking non-health benefits for third parties as a way of choosing between individual candidates for treatment seems unfair because it violates the principle that people with equal health needs should be given an equal chance to receive appropriate treatment. In the next extract, John Harris argues that discriminating against childless or single people in the distribution of health care resources fails to treat them as individuals whose lives are intrinsically, as opposed to instrumentally, valuable, and offends the basic egalitarian principle that all lives have equal moral worth.

John Harris[34]

[T]here do seem to me to be weighty objections to a preference for those with dependants . . . [T]he feeling that it is somehow more important to rescue those with dependants, when elevated to the level of policy, amounts to a systematic preference of those with families over those without . . . At first glance and particularly to those without dependant children, this looks very much like a covert grading of people into the 'haves' and the 'have-nots'—those who have dependants and those who don't. It might even be seen as a clandestine introduction of some reinforcement of a moral preference for the nuclear family and as an attack both on the childless, and on those with less family-oriented ideas about child-rearing. . . .

Dependence . . . is not simply dependence on parents, and grief and misery are not confined to family relationships. But even if they were, it is unclear that they would constitute adequate reasons for preferring to save one person rather than another. We should not forget that while the bereaved deserve sympathy, by far the greatest loss is to the deceased, and the misfortune of her friends and relations pales into insignificance besides the tragedy to the individual who must die. It seems as obviously offensive systematically to inflict this loss on the childless, and perhaps the friendless, as it would be to grade people in any other way. It seems less than convincing to argue that concentration of attention on 'the interests of dependants' rather than on the merits of individuals, rescues such a policy from the opprobrium of an arbitrary division of society into grades of people, with priority always and automatically accorded to those with families.

Finally, if systematic family preference became overt public policy, it might begin to seem that a relatively cheap form of insurance against a low-priority rating in the rescue stakes would be the acquisition of a family.

It could further be argued that it would in practice be impossible to calculate the non-health benefits of treating a particular individual with any accuracy or certainty.

---

[34] *The Value of Life* (Routledge London 1985) 104–6.

It is difficult enough for doctors to make predictions about their patients' future life expectancy, expecting them to accurately predict their likely contribution to society would be absurd. Even a fairly simple example of an indirect benefit, such as whether a patient has young children, has the capacity to operate unfairly. Not all parents actually support and love their children. Patient Z may be an estranged father who has not had any contact with his children since they were born; should he nevertheless take priority over Patient Y, who is childless but devotes all of her spare time to voluntary work with deprived youngsters? If we instead only want to reward people whose contribution to their children's lives is real and tangible, we would have to engage in a most unpalatable assessment of an individual's moral value.

There is also, as Dan Brock argues, no obvious stopping point once we start to take into account the indirect non-health benefits of treating particular individuals, and an inevitable potential for bias, prejudice and stereotypes would creep into these sorts of assessments.[35] Offering priority to people in high-skilled employment may benefit the country as a whole, but it would be indirectly discriminatory because the people most likely to receive treatment would be white, middle-class men.

On the other hand, where particular types of care, such as substance abuse treatment programmes, are likely to have enormously beneficial effects upon the wellbeing of others, it seems less obviously unjust to use this as an additional reason for diverting funds to this type of treatment. After all, the purpose of the NHS is not only to relieve individual suffering, but also to promote the welfare of the community as a whole. Taking these broader purposes into account when setting health care priorities does not involve claiming that certain people's lives are more valuable than others. As a result, Dan Brock argues below that taking into account indirect non health benefits can be legitimate at a macro level, where the decisions do not involve discriminating against particular individuals on account of their relative usefulness, but rather choosing what proportion of public money should be allocated to the health service in question.

Dan Brock[36]

The closer one is to selecting individual patients competing for scarce health care resources, the more ethically problematic prioritizing their claims on the basis of indirect non health benefits appears to be. I think this may be for three reasons. First, the choice then is more directly between individual persons on the basis of their instrumental non health value to others, not just of the different instrumental value of treating different health needs. Second, we are then directly distributing health resources to individual patients, not just money for different health needs, and so the idea that the resource should be used for the specific purpose it is meant to serve applies more directly. Third, the social roles of those doing the prioritizing or allocating are typically different . . . A common objection to physicians doing 'bedside rationing' is that their commitments are and should be to the individual patients whom they are treating, not to broader social concerns . . . The importance of patients' trust in their physicians' commitment to their medical needs above all else provides a special reason why physicians should not prioritize their efforts by the indirect non health benefits of treating different patients.

---

[35] Dan Brock, 'Separate Spheres and Indirect Benefits' (2003) 1 Cost Effectiveness and Resource Allocation 4. Available online at <http://www.resource-allocation.com/content/1/1/4>.
[36] Ibid, 1/4.

As a rough generalization and all other things being equal, the higher level a macro health care resource allocation or prioritization decision, the more defensible it is to give weight to the indirect non health benefits and costs of alternative resource uses in health care. The closer to micro level choices by health professionals between the needs of their individual patients, the stronger the case that these indirect non health benefits and costs should be ignored on grounds of fairness. However, the policy alternatives are not only to give indirect non health benefits the same weight as direct health benefits, or to give them no weight at all; they can be given some but lesser weight than direct health benefits and costs, though there is no apparent principled answer to how much weight these effects should receive in different contexts. Since the fairness objection to counting these effects in health care resource prioritization is strong, but, so far as I can see, not fully decisive, and because its force is different for different decision making levels and contexts, particular societies might exercise significant discretion through fair, democratic decision procedures about what weight to give them.

While agreeing that social-utilitarian considerations should normally be disregarded, Beauchamp and Childress argue that in exceptional circumstances it may be legitimate to take an individual's social worth into account when rationing treatment.

Tom Beauchamp and James Childress[37]

[J]udgements of comparative social worth are inescapable and acceptable in some situations. For example, in an earthquake when some injured survivors are medical personnel who suffer only minor injuries, they justifiably receive priority of treatment if they are needed to help others. Similarly, in an outbreak of infectious disease, it is justifiable to inoculate physicians and nurses first to enable them to care for others. Under such conditions, a person may receive priority for treatment on grounds of social utility if and only if his or her contribution is indispensable to attaining a major social goal. As in analogous lifeboat cases, we should limit judgements of comparative social value to the specific qualities and skills that are essential to the community's immediate protection without assessing the general social worth of persons. If we limit exceptions based on social utility to emergencies involving necessity, they do not threaten the ordinary moral universe or imply the general acceptability of social-utilitarian calculations in distributing health care.

(d) AGE

The question of whether it is acceptable to take into account a patient's age when rationing treatment has been hotly contested. There are plausible arguments on both sides of this debate. First, it is sometimes argued that treating the elderly will cost more than treating younger people because they may take longer to recover. Treatment is thus less cost-effective. Secondly, there is a greater chance that an older person will suffer from other illnesses or disorders, thus further reducing the likelihood of a successful outcome. Thirdly, because older people will usually have a shorter life-expectancy, the benefits in terms of life years gained from treatment will be less. Fourthly, the older person is more likely to have had what is often described as a 'fair innings', and hence scarce resources should be diverted to younger patients in order to ensure that as many people as possible have the chance to live a normal life-span. According to the fair innings argument, as John Harris explains, the elderly have

[37] *Principles of Biomedical Ethics* (5th edn OUP Oxford 2001) 271.

already had an opportunity to pursue their life plans, and to live a worthwhile and fulfilling life:

What the fair innings argument needs to do is capture and express in a workable form the truth that while it is always a misfortune to die when one wants to go on living, it is not a tragedy to die in old age; but it is on the other hand, both a tragedy and a misfortune to be cut off prematurely.[38]

It is important to distinguish two versions of the 'fair innings' argument. One would simply advocate always favouring younger patients. So a 10-year-old child should be preferred to a 20-year-old; and someone in their thirties should receive priority over someone in their forties. The second would only use age as a reason for distinguishing between patients once an older person has in fact had their 'fair innings', however we might define it. If we set the threshold for a 'fair innings' at 70, for example, there would be no good reason for prioritizing teenagers over those in their twenties since neither has yet had a 'fair innings'.

On the other hand, it could first be argued that assumptions about older people's frailty are generalizations, and fail to take into account the fact that many elderly individuals are extremely fit, whereas some young people are very unhealthy and may stand to gain little from treatment. While age may be one variable that affects a person's prognosis, it is by no means the only or even the most important one, and to use sweeping generalizations about a large and diverse section of the population in order to ration services is arbitrary and unjust. The severity of a person's condition is, in fact, a much more accurate predictor of a person's chance of recovery than their age. And yet we would be reluctant to exclude extremely ill people as a group from health care services. Rather, it is fairer to make an individual assessment about a patient's ability to benefit from medical intervention.

Secondly, concerns about the efficacy of treatment in older people may not be grounded in concrete evidence of ineffectiveness, but rather might arise from their underrepresentation in clinical research trials (considered in Chapter 8, p. 508). By reducing clinicians' confidence in the effectiveness of treatment for older people, ageism in research might therefore have a trickle down effect upon their access to medical treatment. Third, enabling older people to live independently for as long as possible will in fact lead to cost savings in other parts of the health and social services budget by reducing their dependence upon social care services.

Finally, in the next extract John Harris further suggests that age-discrimination in the distribution of healthcare resources amounts to 'the systematic disvaluing of the old', which he argues would have undesirable social consequences.

John Harris[39]

Those who believe in discriminating in favour of the young or against the old must believe that insofar as murder is an injustice it is less of an injustice to murder the old than the young; it is clear that in robbing people of life you take less from them the less life expectancy they have.

A society that accords lower priority in the allocation of resources for healthcare to the old or those with reduced life expectancy is saying, in effect, that their lives are less worth saving, in

---

[38] John Harris, *The Value of Life* (Routledge London 1985) 93.
[39] 'The Age-Indifference Principle and Equality' (2005) 14 Cambridge Quarterly of Healthcare Ethics 93–9.

short, are less valuable. If the right or good done in saving or preserving a life is the less, then so is the wrong done in taking it, which would make, for example, the crime of murder inevitably less serious when the victims are old or terminally ill . . .

The systematic disvaluing of the old or those with life-threatening illness might have a corrosive effect on social morality and community relations more generally. It might, for example, lead to an increasing tolerance of the idea that any and all resources, or even care, devoted to the old or those with life-threatening disease was a waste of time, money, and emotion. Even if this were the right view to take, the sort of society that implemented such views at the level of policy might be increasingly one in which others would feel threatened and uneasy. Moreover, once the old, however defined, had been ruled out of account, the middle-aged would become the old. They would after all have greater elapsed time 'in the bank' and shorter life expectancy ahead than the rest of society and the cycle of argument and discrimination would have a tendency to extend indefinitely, a tendency moreover that would be difficult to restrain.

(e) INDIVIDUAL RESPONSIBILITY FOR ILL-HEALTH

Many diseases and disabilities are caused or exacerbated by a patient's own behaviour. Should this be relevant when allocating scarce resources? If an individual is responsible for creating her own need for healthcare services, should she also bear the cost of her treatment, or perhaps be a lower priority for the expenditure of public money? On the one hand, it might be argued that making access to treatment depend upon whether someone has contributed to their own ill-health could provide a powerful incentive towards greater personal responsibility. But on the other, if the prospect of increased ill-health and/or premature death does not dissuade someone from engaging in unhealthy activities, it is hardly likely that being a low priority for NHS care would do so.

Nevertheless, regardless of its impact upon behaviour, some commentators, such as Robert Blank, have suggested that it is fair and just to take individual responsibility into account when rationing scarce resources.

Robert Blank[40]

At present, an unreasonably high proportion of early deaths result from heart disease and cancer, both tied to some extent to lifestyle . . . Behavioral factors contribute to much of our burden of illness . . .

Reinforcing this trend toward reevaluating the extent of morbidity and mortality that are directly tied to individual behavior is the current concern over the costs of health care . . . Because the need for the most expensive medical interventions such as long-term intensive care and organ transplantation is frequently a product of unhealthy individual action, it is likely that individual behavior that contributes to the need for these massive expenditures will be scrutinized more and more closely.

Moreover, because few persons today pay fully for their own medical care . . . people who try to take care of themselves are helping underwrite the costs incurred by those who fail to do so. Understandably, there is an increasingly vocal demand to shift the monetary burden to those individuals who knowingly take the health risks . . . Considerable initiative for these actions comes from distaste at having to pay for someone else's bad habits.

[40] *Rationing Medicine* (Columbia UP New York 1988) 199–200.

In practice, however, it would be impossible to devise a fair system for accurately attributing responsibility for ill health. First, the obvious examples of smokers, alcoholics and drug abusers may not attract much public sympathy, but these are not the only types of behaviour which may have an adverse effect upon an individual's health. Should we also penalize drivers or cyclists who are injured in road traffic accidents; skin cancer sufferers who sunbathed too much in their youth; athletes with sporting injuries; individuals who subject themselves to too much stress at work; people who eat a lot of junk food? The list of people who may have contributed to their own need for health care services is potentially endless. Secondly, it is also highly questionable whether all unhealthy behaviours are in fact the result of deliberate choice: voluntariness is often a matter of degree. If an individual's parents were both alcoholics and her life has been exceptionally harsh, is she less responsible for her alcohol-related liver damage than someone who just enjoys getting drunk?

Thirdly, smoking, drug use and poor diet tend to correlate with socioeconomic status, hence penalizing smokers or drug users will in practice mean that priority for healthcare services is given to the richest and healthiest sections of society. Fourthly, it is seldom possible to isolate a single causal factor for most diseases. The fact that an individual likes fried food and beer may have contributed to their need for a heart bypass operation, but there are many other possible causes. Commonly genetic predisposition, environmental factors, social conditions and a person's lifestyle will interact with each other to produce a person's susceptibility to a particular disease. Fifthly, accurately identifying voluntary risk-takers would necessarily involve substantial violations of privacy. Finally, as Beauchamp and Childress have pointed out, in practice voluntary risk takers will often cost the NHS *less* over the course of their lifetimes than self-disciplined, fit and abstemious individuals:

Some risk-taking involves less rather than more medical care, because it results in earlier and quicker deaths than might occur if individuals lived longer and developed chronic debilitating conditions . . . 'low-risk' non-smoking men with low blood pressure consistently generate far higher health care costs per year of life than 'high-risk' men who smoke and have high blood pressure.[41]

(f) RELEVANCE OF PUBLIC OPINION

What role should public opinion play in setting priorities within the NHS? On the one hand, the NHS is funded through taxation, and used by almost everyone in the country, and so as both taxpayers and healthcare consumers, perhaps the public should have some say over the distribution of NHS resources. Involving the public in setting healthcare priorities might help to ensure that services are appropriate and meet the population's needs and preferences. Moreover, since depriving individual citizens of beneficial medical treatment on the grounds that it costs too much is so controversial and potentially divisive, public consent to, or agreement with the goals and principles of resource allocation might be advisable. On the other hand, there are

---

[41] Tom L Beauchamp and James F Childress, *Principles of Biomedical Ethics* (5th edn OUP Oxford 2001) 248.

serious difficulties in working out what the public does in fact think about the distri-bution of NHS resources. As Darren Shickle explains, there is some evidence that when asked, the public tends to give highest priority to treatment for children and for life threatening illnesses, and will be less sympathetic towards treatment of the elderly or those who are thought to be responsible for their own ill-health.

Darren Shickle[42]

Despite the limited scope of the public surveys conducted so far, a number of themes have emerged:

- A willingness to pay for experimental, 'high-tech' life-saving treatments rather than more cost-effective treatments which will improve quality of life, which are more likely to maximise utility from the scarce resources available;

- Preference for treating the young rather than the old;

- Preference for treating patients with dependants (e.g. spouse, children) rather than those who have none;

- A willingness to discriminate against those patients who were partially responsible for their illness due to a choice of 'unhealthy' lifestyle (e.g. smoking cigarettes, drinking excess alcohol) . . .

The Cardiff Health Survey asked respondents to choose between two patients who were identical in every respect apart from their age. When asked to choose between a 5-year old and a 70-year old person, 94% of 721 respondents gave priority to the child. The overwhelming majority said that it was a very or quite easy decision to make. Only 1% gave priority to the 70 year old . . . The respondents were also asked to choose between two identical patients aged 35 and 60 years respectively. Again, there was a preference for the younger patient (80%), although over half said the decision was quite or very difficult. 13% of respondents were unable to give a preference . . .

The Cardiff Health Survey also asked respondents to make choices between otherwise identical patients who differed only by marital status. About three quarters of respondents were willing to give a higher priority to the married patient. This preference was only partly related to an assump-tion that the married person would have children. There was a view that marriage carried with it responsibilities which being single did not . . .

As part of the Cardiff Health Survey respondents were also asked to make choices between individuals who could be 'blamed' to some extent for their illness. 74% of respondents were willing to give preference to a non-smoker over a smoker . . . Respondents were also willing to use alcohol intake and diet as a priority discriminator for otherwise identical patients. 80% of respondents said that they would choose a patient with low alcohol intake rather than a heavy drinker.

In the next extract, Bill New and Julian Le Grand point out that respondents to one-off public opinion surveys will seldom be well informed about the competing demands upon the NHS budgets, and will not generally have had time to reflect upon what are indubitably exceptionally complex decisions.

---

[42] 'Public Preferences for Health Care: Prioritisation in the United Kingdom' (1997) 11 Bioethics 277–90, 281, 284–6, 288.

Bill New and Julian Le Grand[43]

[D]irectly involving the public in the decision-making process carries significant dangers . . . There must be a concern that in any [public] meeting the advice gained from the public will emanate from only one section of the population, usually the most affluent, vocal and articulate.

But even if perfectly representative samples of the public can be consulted, the legitimacy of their having a direct influence on resource allocation and rationing will still be deeply problematic. The outcome of such exercises will reflect majority opinion and, although it is hard to be sure what that opinion would be, it is likely that the interests of very old, infirm, mentally ill or disabled people will be neglected in favour of the concerns of the majority. High-technology rescue or repair medicine, for example, can easily be conceived as immediately relevant to us all. Furthermore, it is simply naïve to suppose that the lay public have the requisite knowledge to make many decisions which are of a complex, technical nature.

The traditional method for addressing such issues is representative democracy, whereby officials are appointed or elected to be responsible for taking and implementing decisions on behalf of the whole community. Encouraging direct decision-making by community groups would, it might be argued, constitute a fundamental break with this tradition, and would have the unfortunate consequence of allowing public officials to absolve themselves of the consequences of their actions, claiming that they simply 'did what the public wanted'.

Political decision-making—and that is what rationing decisions are—must be open to challenge, scrutiny and debate, and those who make the decisions must bear the responsibility for and deal with the consequences of those decisions. If not, poor decision-making can result. Why, for example, should members of the public make considered judgements when they do not face the prospect of being challenged on them, nor of answering for any unfavourable consequences? Accountability would, under these circumstances, be weakened. Political decisions will always be a compromise, arbitrating between different groups in society, made by people who represent the whole community and not just one set of interests. The general 'public' are not accountable in this sense. Thus, while the public must constitute one part of a system of representative democracy— that of scrutineers, consultants and ultimate arbiters of who should represent them—they should be involved to a greater degree with caution.

There is also the problem that the public's attitude towards healthcare rationing will depend upon whether they are making choices as taxpayers or as patients. As taxpayers, most people do not want massive increases in income tax. As patients, however, we want the best medical care available. These two desires are simply contradictory. When we are desperately ill, we do not want to be told that the NHS has better things to spend its money on than saving our life. But as taxpayers, we accept the inevitability of such judgments. This is not just a problem of incompatible personal preferences, but reflects a wider conflict between the rule of rescue and cost-effectiveness analysis. In general, we have much more sympathy for identifiable individuals whose needs are now great than we do for unknown people whose lives may be in danger in the future. This is sometimes called the statistical lives paradox,[44] and was evident in the public's response to the Child B case, discussed below at p. 84. Denying treatment to one identifiable and very ill child will often attract greater

---

[43] *Rationing in the NHS: Principles and Pragmatism* (King's Fund London 1996).

[44] A Weale, 'Statistical lives and the principle of maximum benefit' (1979) 5 Journal of Medical Ethics 185–95, 186.

condemnation than deciding not to invest in services which would be likely to save hundreds of—as yet unidentifiable—children's lives in the future.

(g) ABILITY TO PAY

A free market in healthcare would replace rationing with market forces. Consumers would be free to purchase health care, either at the point of use or via insurance schemes, and services would be supplied to meet this demand. Treatment which nobody wished to purchase would simply not be available. Some people have suggested that a free market system might have certain advantages, such as deterring inappropriate use of healthcare services. However, there are many reasons why a free market in medical treatment is an unattractive proposition.

Most importantly, there would always be people who were unable to afford treatment and insurance, and who would therefore die easily preventable deaths and be forced to live in extreme pain and discomfort if society was not prepared to cover the costs of essential care. Our consumption of healthcare resources is concentrated in our last years of life, when we will often be least able to pay for the healthcare that we need. Even allowing for the pooling of risk via insurance, there is an inverse correlation between socioeconomic status and good health. Insurance premiums are set according to risk rather than wealth, so in a free market the cost of insurance would generally be highest for those with the least resources. A society which had such little concern for the lives of its poorest and sickest members would be a depressingly bleak place to live.

Secondly, although charges might deter some people from approaching the doctor for trivial or minor conditions, evidence appears to indicate that charges tend to lower demand for all types of care. People often do not know in advance if their symptoms are trivial or significant, and discouraging them from seeking medical advice will in practice reduce the likelihood of early diagnosis, which in turn will reduce the clinical and cost effectiveness of their treatment.

Thirdly, in general patients do not choose medical treatment, in the same way as they might choose to purchase other goods and services. A free market is supposed to work because consumers are able to exercise choice over their spending: they will not buy goods or services which they do not want, and are able to select providers which best meet their needs. Patients are unlike purchasers of other consumer goods, however. Nobody wants medical treatment for its own sake, instead healthcare is generally needed because people are ill and would prefer not to be. Efficient markets also depend in part upon informed and discerning consumers. But there is a fundamental information imbalance in the doctor/patient relationship, and patients are unable to exercise much control (other than the straightforward right of refusal) over which treatments they receive.

Fourthly, because few people could afford to pay for acute medical treatment as they needed it, and no one would want to face the additional stress of borrowing money when they were seriously ill, a free market in healthcare would tend to operate through insurance schemes. And there are a number of specific problems that arise from using private insurance to cover the costs of healthcare:

First, some health risks will usually be considered uninsurable. Many insurance policies exclude certain conditions, such as self-inflicted injuries, drug abuse, HIV/AIDS, or major epidemics. Very elderly people, or those with serious pre-existing conditions may find it very difficult or even impossible to purchase health insurance. There would therefore always have to be a state-funded safety net to cover the treatment of risks which private companies choose to exclude from their insurance policies. Thus, the problem of rationing publicly funded care remains.

Secondly, when risks are pooled through insurance, low-risk patients will often be charged premiums that appear to be higher than their anticipated benefits, and they may therefore decide that purchasing insurance is not worthwhile. As a result, high-risk individuals' premiums will be even higher, and may prove to be unaffordable, thus increasing the proportion of the population which is uninsured and dependent, again, on the publicly funded safety-net.

Thirdly, because insurance insulates the patient from the real costs of care, it encourages people to make more use of medical services than they would under a straightforward free market. Fourthly, insurance schemes will also tend to give health care providers an incentive to overtreat, and thus waste resources for no additional health gain.

Finally, the administration costs of multiple private insurers are much higher than those of state-run systems. The US spends much more than any other developed country on health, yet 45 million Americans have no insurance, and Americans are not any healthier than residents of European countries which spend half as much on their national health services. In fact, as we saw from the table reproduced above at p. 40, healthcare in the US ranked 37th in the WHO 'league table'.

Rationing according to the patient's ability to pay might appear to be fundamentally incompatible with the NHS's core principle that healthcare should be free at the point of delivery. But in fact, the original National Health Service Act 1946 contained provisions which allowed patients to pay extra for what was known as an 'amenity bed'. These 'section 4' patients would receive the same clinical care as ordinary NHS patients, but their accommodation would be more comfortable and private than the normal open wards. And this idea that patients should be able to receive care within the NHS, with supplementary charges for additional services or treatments that are more expensive than the basic NHS standard of care, is gaining ground among some health economists. For example, allowing NHS hospitals to offer pregnant women the option of paying for an elective caesarean, while receiving NHS antenatal care, relieves the pressure on NHS resources and expands patient choice, both of which seem like laudable goals. But of course it is only richer patients who would be able to afford better services and additional choices, which appears to be at odds with the basic principle that health care services should be distributed according to need, rather than ability to pay.

Certain healthcare services, such as infertility treatment, are routinely provided in the private sector. Very few people now receive free dental or optical care. Long term residential care generally has to be paid for by the patients themselves. In addition, an increasing proportion of the services which are routinely provided by the NHS can also be purchased privately, and private patients will usually be treated more quickly than those who have to wait for publicly funded care. Approximately 11 per cent of the UK population is now covered by private medical insurance, and the number of people paying directly for elective surgery continues to rise each year. This is clearly rationing according to ability to pay rather than need, and it has become a normal feature of health care provision in the UK.

A mixture of public and private provision of health care services does then exist in the UK, but a reluctance to admit that one of the founding principles of the NHS has been compromised means that the relationship between the public and the private sector lacks clarity and transparency. The British Medical Association has advocated greater honesty about the inability of the NHS to provide free and comprehensive healthcare. It argues that the NHS should continue to be publicly funded, and to provide care which is free at the point of use, but that it is unrealistic to expect such a service to be fully comprehensive:

The concept of the NHS as a comprehensive service may have outlived its usefulness. It will be increasingly common to see treatments which are judged to be of limited clinical effectiveness, not cost-effective or an inappropriate use of public funds, excluded from this system. The role of the private sector in meeting demands for these and other treatments will inevitably grow in import-ance, particularly in the self-pay sector as patients seek specific treatments which are explicitly excluded from the NHS. This growth should be encouraged and facilitated, although tax or other fiscal incentives would be an inequitable and inefficient means of doing so.[45]

It is also important to remember that a parallel private insurance sector is not a simple 'add-on' to the NHS. Instead, the two interact with each other. The NHS subsidizes the private sector through allowing its employees to carry out private treatment within NHS hospitals, and by permitting NHS consultants to maintain private prac-tices. In order to meet Government targets, it is also increasingly common for NHS trusts to purchase private sector care for their patients. It has been estimated that between 50–60,000 NHS-funded operations are carried out in the private sector each year.[46]

In recent years, there has been increasing government interest in public/private partnerships which are intended both to supplement the resources available for public services and also to modernize their management. One example is the Private Finance Initiative (PFI), through which the state pays private companies to build and maintain hospitals, and more recently to provide some clinical services. For patients, treatment continues to be free at the point of use. Whether or not PFIs in fact represent value for money is a matter of some controversy. There are, for example, those who argue that the PFI hospital building programme offers short-term savings for the Treasury, and thus may serve politicians' ends, but that these arrangements are not necessarily in the longer term interests of the NHS.

Purchasing clinical services from the private sector is even more controversial. When the public sector invites tenders from private companies, it is usually under a

---

[45] *British Medical Association Healthcare Funding Review* (BMA London 2001) available at <http://www.bma.org.uk/>.
[46] Christopher Newdick, *Who Should we Treat? Rights, Rationing and Resources in the NHS* (2nd edn OUP Oxford 2005) 233.

duty to select the cheapest bid. Since most of the NHS's resources are spent on wages, private sector clinical services would generally only be able to improve efficiency if they lower employment costs, for example by reducing staffing levels, or altering the skill-mix among employees. Ancillary and catering services have long been contracted out to the private sector, where the lowest bids will generally come from companies which pay their staff very little. Poor working conditions and morale among ancillary workers inevitably affects the standard of service provided to patients.

(h) DEFINING A PACKAGE OF CARE

This type of rationing involves setting limits upon the treatments which will be funded by the state. A core package of essential services would be provided free of charge, but other services would only be available privately. Rationing policies which exclude particular treatments clearly lend themselves to openness and transparency. It is comparatively easy to understand an NHS trust's decision to decide which procedures it is not prepared to fund. Public expectations of the health service could then be based upon clearly defined limits. The NHS would continue to provide universal access to a basic healthcare package, but would no longer claim to offer every citizen every possible type of medical treatment.

In some other countries, most notably in New Zealand, Holland, and the US state of Oregon, there have been explicit attempts to devise packages of healthcare services. These have not proved to be overwhelmingly successful. In New Zealand, the Core Services Committee could not find any treatment or area of service within the current range of provision which could be completely excluded. So, 'in something of an anti-climax, the Committee recommended that "core" be defined as being what was already being provided prior to the reforms'.[47]

The Dutch established the Dunning Committee to define a core healthcare package, and its report proposed four criteria to be taken into account when deciding whether treatments should be included: (1) necessity, (2) effectiveness, (3) efficiency and (4) whether it would be inappropriate for individuals to be responsible for paying for the treatment. These four filters were intended to screen out treatments, and the Committee had advocated public funding for every procedure which fulfilled all four criteria. Because too many treatments satisfied this initial filter, waiting lists then had to be used to set priorities.

In 1988, in response to a budgetary shortfall, Oregon's state legislature suspended Medicaid funding for all organ transplants.[48] Following the high profile case of Coby Howard, a 7-year-old boy who had been denied a bone marrow transplant, resource allocation became a central political issue. The purpose of the 1989 Oregon health plan was to ensure that all citizens with an income at or below the federally defined poverty level received publicly funded medical treatment. Previously Medicaid services had only been available to citizens with incomes of 58 per cent or less than this

---

[47] M Cooper, 'Core services and the New Zealand Health Reforms' in R Maxwell (ed), *Rationing Health Care* (Churchill Livingstone London 1995) 799–807, 805.

[48] LM Fleck, 'Just caring: Oregon, health care rationing, and informed democratic deliberation' (1994) 19 Journal of Medicine and Philopsophy 367–88, 375.

official poverty line. In order to increase the number of citizens covered by Medicaid, Oregon decided instead to restrict the services which would be available as part of the basic healthcare package. Different condition/treatment pairs (such as appendicitis/appendectomy) would be ranked in order of priority by an appointed commission which took into account both community views and the cost–benefit ratio of different treatments. Once the commission had drawn up a league table of different treatments, the state would decide, in the light of the total it wanted to spend, where the line should be drawn in this prioritized list. Treatments above the line would be funded by Medicaid for all poor citizens, treatments below would be excluded.[49] At first, the rankings produced some rather bizarre results. Cosmetic breast surgery, for example, ranked higher than treatment for open thigh fractures; and tooth capping higher than appendectomy. The list was subsequently revised, giving highest priority to treatment for pneumonia and TB. Initially, Oregon chose to fund the top 565 (out of 696) condition/treatment pairs.

In Oregon, an attempt was made to involve the public in the setting of healthcare priorities.[50] First, a telephone survey of 1001 citizens was carried out, although the results were later disregarded following concerns about bias. In particular, it was thought that the public's evaluation of different health states was incapable of reflecting the perspective of people living with disabilities. Secondly, a total of forty-seven public meetings were held in local town halls. The average attendance at these was twenty-two, most of whom were health care professionals rather than the Medicaid patients whose medical treatment was to be rationed.[51] The Oregon health plan did succeed in increasing the number of citizens eligible for Medicaid by 100,000, thus reducing the proportion of the population which is uninsured, although it should be noted that this was only partly achieved by restricting access to certain treatments. Instead, Oregon's state legislature imposed a new tobacco tax in order to fund this increased coverage.

Some health authorities in the UK have specified that they will not fund certain procedures such as tattoo removal, sterilization reversal, or gender reassignment surgery. The reason for identifying these low priority interventions and excluding them from NHS coverage is not that such treatments are ineffective, nor that they are a significant drain on NHS resources. Rather the purpose of such restrictions is to reflect the judgement that certain procedures are not appropriately provided within a publicly funded health service. Tattoo removal or sterilization reversal in fact cost very little compared with, for example, the maintenance of an intensive care unit. A refusal to fund such marginal procedures may help to clarify what it is reasonable to expect from the NHS, but it will not solve its funding crisis.

Moreover, blanket exclusions will themselves often be both unfair and unlawful (see below pp. 87–9). Tattoo removal may seem trivial, but what if a person was tattooed while he was a prisoner of war? Any exclusions must be able to accommodate

---

[49] Newdick, *Who Should we Treat? Rights, Rationing and Resources in the NHS* (2nd edn OUP Oxford 2005) 33.

[50] LM Fleck, 'Just caring: Oregon, health care rationing, and informed democratic deliberation' (1994) 19 *Journal of Medicine and Philosophy* 367–88, 375.

[51] Newdick, *Who Should we Treat? Rights, Rationing and Resources in the NHS*, 37.

exceptional cases, and this individualized assessment of need will itself cost money. Policies which exclude relatively trivial medical procedures are never likely to yield the sort of cost savings that would be necessary to obviate the need for further rationing techniques.

In practice, this sort of explicit, highly visible prioritization of services is much less significant than the much less obvious types of rationing which, as we see in the following section, permeate the entire NHS, namely rationing by diluting the standard of care.

(i) RATIONING BY DILUTION

Rationing by dilution involves offering less care than is ideal; perhaps by carrying out fewer diagnostic tests, or by spending less time with patients. It has, for example, been estimated that extending the average GP consultation time to ten minutes would require a 30 per cent increase in the number of GPs, with obvious cost implications.[52] Health services in the UK continue to be available to everyone, but no one gets optimum treatment. Giving all patients access to slightly substandard care appears to be more politically expedient than openly denying coverage to certain patients. When choosing between different drugs or other medical devices, doctors might not select the most effective and expensive option, and instead offer treatment which satisfies their legal duty of care but is not the best available. Hospitals do not always spend enough money on services such as cleaning and catering, so that patients are provided with poor food and a less than ideal environment. Run-down NHS buildings may not be renovated or rebuilt. Rationing by delay means that patients have to wait to be treated, perhaps by waiting for an appointment with their GP, or by being put on a waiting list for hospital treatment. Delays in treating patients may reduce demand because some patients will get better while waiting to see a doctor, and others may die. Rationing by termination involves patients being discharged from hospital earlier than might be desirable. According to Donald Light:

The NHS already rations on a massive scale. The NHS rations by delay to get on waiting lists, and then on the waiting lists themselves, and then with the further wait after an appointment has been made. It rations by undersupply of staff, doctors, machines, facilities, etc; by undercapitalisation of run down facilities; by dilution of tests done and services received; by discharge earlier than desirable; and by outright denial to even the chance to wait or be undertreated.[53]

In short, the UK's universal health service is sustained by spreading its resources extremely thinly.

(j) LOTTERIES

As we saw earlier, rationing inevitably means that some patients will be deprived of potentially beneficial medical treatment. Because it is so hard to defend denying an identifiable individual appropriate healthcare on the grounds of cost, would it be

52 British Medical Association, Briefing note of the National Plan for the NHS, 18 July 2000.
53 Donald W Light, 'The real ethics of rationing' (1997) 315 British Medical Journal 112–15.

preferable to opt for some sort of random selection process, such as a lottery, which would allow decisionmakers to avoid choosing between equally deserving potential recipients? Avoiding what Jonathan Glover refers to as 'the unpleasantness of making non-random choices between people's lives'[54] is then the principal merit of distribution by lottery:

Even deciding by lot must be fairly unpleasant, but it must be much more distressing to decide by making judgements about the value of the lives of different people.[55]

In addition to being less stressful for doctors, and perhaps for patients too,[56] random selection would probably be an efficient and comparatively cheap way to distribute resources, and thus might have financial advantages for the NHS as a whole. In one sense, a lottery would also be egalitarian, since everyone has an equal chance of benefiting from the randomly allocated treatment. But on the other hand, a lottery would not be capable of targeting resources where they are most needed, or where they are likely to do most good. Relatively fit and healthy individuals would have as much chance of getting treatment as patients whose lives are in danger.

Lotteries are sometimes used when we cannot come up with rational and defensible reasons for choosing between people. Citizens are randomly allocated to jury service, for example. And in times of war, conscription to military service has been done on a random basis. Because most people believe that there *are* rational and defensible reasons for distinguishing between different patients, random selection has few supporters. But if none of the criteria we have considered in the previous sections in fact offer a fair way of setting priorities within the NHS, the overt egalitarianism of random distribution might have some merit.

5. RESOURCE ALLOCATION IN THE NHS

(a) GOVERNMENT POLICY

There continues to be strong public support for the idea of a healthcare system which is free at the point of use, and which provides everyone with access to the same standard of health care. Other former state-run enterprises, such as nationalized industries and the transport system, are now largely run on free-market principles, but the public appears to be stubbornly resistant to the idea of a free market in health care. Hence, the feared political implications of abandoning a commitment to a fully funded and comprehensive NHS have led successive governments to maintain the fiction that the NHS is currently providing such a service, when in fact the reality is rather different. Some treatments are, as we saw earlier, specifically excluded from NHS coverage. But of much more practical significance is the routine dilution of the standard of care patients receive.

---

[54] *Causing Death and Saving Lives* (Penguin London 1977) 219.
[55] Ibid.
[56] Tom L Beauchamp and James F Childress, *Principles of Biomedical Ethics* (5th edn OUP Oxford 2001) 268.

Although the Treasury decides how much money the NHS should receive from public funds each year, the government does not generally become involved in resource allocation decisions within the NHS. Rather it has largely delegated this task to NHS trusts, and to NICE, both of which are discussed below. The principal ways in which government policies do influence spending priorities in the NHS is through the setting of targets, such as waiting time initiatives, and through National Service Frameworks (NSFs), such as the NHS Cancer Plan, which are designed to set national standards for the treatment of particular conditions. In order to meet these targets, health authorities must divert resources to the chosen area, inevitably leaving less money for other types of healthcare.

On a few rare occasions, resource allocation decisions have been taken directly by the Secretary of State for Health. One notable example was his attempt to specify how sildenafil (Viagra) should be rationed within the NHS. Initially a Department of Health circular was issued stating that 'doctors should not prescribe sildenafil. Health authorities are also advised not to support the provision of sildenafil at NHS expense . . . other than in exceptional circumstances.' The circular was successfully challenged by Pfizer, the manufacturer of Viagra. Collins J held that by stating 'in bald terms that Viagra should not be prescribed', the circular purported to override GPs' clinical judgement, which would place them in breach of their terms of service. Subsequently the Secretary of State issued Regulations which specified that NHS prescriptions could only be issued to certain categories of patients, such as those suffering from specified medical conditions. These restrictions were confirmed by the Secretary of State when he reviewed his policy a year later. The reason he gave was that unrestricted prescribing of sildenafil would cost the NHS £125 million per year. In contrast, restricted prescribing was costing £25 million. Pfizer again sought judicial review of this policy, arguing that it did not comply with Article 7.3 of the Council Directive (EEC 89/105), known as the Transparency Directive, which states that:

Any decision to exclude an individual medicinal product from the coverage of the national health insurance system shall contain a statement of reasons based on objective and verifiable criteria.

The Court of Appeal rejected Pfizer's claim.[57] Simon Brown LJ argued that the Secretary of State's decision that unrestricted access to Viagra was unaffordable was essentially a political judgment:

[T]he decision to restrict the use of Viagra was not based on its clinical or cost-effectiveness but rather on the Secretary of State's assessing the need it addressed as having a lower priority than other calls on NHS funds, such assessment involving an essentially political judgment.

And Buxton LJ explained that the requirements of the Transparency Directive were easily satisfied:

For the criteria to be 'verifiable', all that is necessary is that they should be published and available, in particular to would-be importers, to satisfy themselves that they do not contain disguised restrictions on intra-Community trade. And the measures are 'objective' . . . if they are based on a legitimate aim, that of improving the economics of the state health system.

[57] R (on the application of Pfizer Ltd) v Secretary of State for Health [2002] EWCA Civ 1566, (2002) 70 BMLR 219.

The criterion adopted by the Secretary of State in this case fully meets those requirements. And that is all that the directive requires, that the criteria used by the member state should meet its (fairly modest) objectives. What the directive plainly does not require, and what would be wholly inappropriate in view of its objectives, is that each decision applying the criteria should be subject to the detailed scrutiny and exposition of the merits and economics of particular medicinal products that the applicants seek to achieve in this case.

In the next extract, Keith Syrett suggests that the decision in *Pfizer* follows the pattern of judicial self-restraint which is also evident in the judicial review cases which we consider below, at pp. 82–91.

Keith Syrett[58]

Pfizer, albeit *obiter*, also offers firm evidence of a continued unwillingness on the part of the judiciary to fashion the principles of domestic public law into a mechanism for overseeing the transparency of such decision-making. Simon Brown LJ accepted the argument, which the Secretary of State had outlined in his letter, that the decision as to whether Viagra should be provided on the NHS was 'an essentially political judgment, that is not within the province of a reviewing court'.

It is apparent from this case that neither European nor domestic legal principles are likely to offer any significant assistance to those who wish to see greater transparency in decision-making on the allocation of health care resources. Taken overall, therefore, *Pfizer* follows a pattern of 'judicial self-restraint' in this field . . .

Similarly, in *Pfizer*, the Court's categorisation of the decision as 'political' and therefore as effectively insulated from judicial scrutiny performed much the same function as the 'ritual invocation of *Wednesbury* principles' in the earlier cases . . . The Secretary of State was placed under only the most minimal of obligations of transparency: all that was demanded by the court was that he provide some information to establish that the decision was 'political' in that it was based upon his assessment that Viagra had a lower priority than other calls upon NHS funding. He was not required to offer any form of account of how these priorities had been determined in effect, it was enough for him merely to 'toll the bell of tight resources'. . . . The failure to demand a more comprehensive justification is perhaps all the more regrettable since there had been indications in the intervening cases of *Fisher* and *A, D and G* that the courts were becoming more prepared to impose an explanatory obligation upon bodies making decisions on the allocation of limited health care resources.

(b) NHS POLICY

The internal market in healthcare was created by the then Conservative government in 1991 (through the NHS and Community Care Act 1990) to introduce greater efficiency and financial accountability into the NHS, and to enhance consumer/patient choice. By separating the roles of purchasers (at that time, health authorities and GP fundholders) and providers (NHS Trusts) of healthcare, the intention was that both purchasers and providers would pay closer attention to whether services represented good value for money. Whereas previously, any rationing in the NHS was hidden and operated mainly through clinical discretion, in 1991 the Government

---

[58] 'Impotence or Importance? Judicial Review in an Era of Explicit NHS Rationing' (2004) 67 Modern Law Review 289–304.

explicitly delegated the task of rationing—that is, setting priorities and evaluating the cost-effectiveness of treatment options—to health authorities and GP fundholders. Although as we see below, the Labour government elected in 1997 has made significant changes to the organization of the NHS, decisions about which treatments to 'purchase' continue to be taken at local level, principally by primary care trusts.

Until recently resources were distributed to health authorities in the UK according to a weighted capitation formula, which takes into account population size, adjusted for age, relative need, and unavoidable local cost differences. The National Health Service Reform and Health Care Professions Act 2002 introduced a number of changes to the way in which NHS resources are allocated. In particular, it introduced a degree of 'performance related' funding. It amended the National Health Service Act 1977, section 97C of which now provides that:

Where the Secretary of State has made an initial determination of the amount to be allotted for any year [to a Strategic Health authority or] to a Health authority under subsection (3) above, he may increase the initial amount by a further sum if it appears to him that over a period notified to the Authority—

(a) they satisfied any objectives notified to them as objectives to be met in performing their functions, or

(b) they performed well against any criteria notified to them as criteria relevant to the satisfactory performance of their functions.

A 'star-rating' system for hospitals has been introduced, giving hospital trusts which achieve the maximum three stars additional funds and greater autonomy. The key indicators which govern this performance related funding are the number of patients waiting more than eighteen months for in-patient treatment; the number of patients waiting more than twenty-six weeks for outpatient treatment; the number of patients waiting on trolleys for more than twelve hours; whether cancer patients have to wait more than two weeks for a hospital appointment; the standard of cleanliness and financial probity. The Audit Commission has criticized the star-rating system as a rather crude and at times inaccurate measure of a hospital's performance:

Some trusts which, because they were given three stars, may be eligible to apply for freedoms as NHS Foundation trusts, were judged by auditors to be performing poorly and as having management shortcomings.[59]

Since 2004 hospitals have also been eligible to apply for Foundation Trust status, which will offer even greater financial and decision-making freedom. In contrast, hospital trusts which receive zero stars must immediately develop recovery plans and unless performance improves, their management may be put out to tender, either to other NHS Trusts or to the private sector. And in the next extract, ACL Davies is sceptical about two claims made for Foundation Hospitals, namely that they will be both responsive to local needs and autonomous.

---

[59] *Achieving the NHS Plan: Assessment of current performance, likely future progress and capacity to improve* (Audit Commission, 2003) para 42.

ACL Davies[60]

[I]n a national service, autonomy may bring the benefits of responsiveness to local needs, and innovation. But not everyone accepts that these are genuine benefits. Since the NHS is funded through national taxation, patients expect to receive the same service regardless of where they live. If an area with a predominantly elderly population decides to cut funding for fertility treatment in order to pay for better services for stroke victims, this can be portrayed either favourably, as responsiveness to local needs, or unfavourably, as a 'postcode lottery', which access to treatment depends on where a patient lives.

[T]here is an important debate about the correct balance between accountability and autonomy in the NHS. While some may resent yet another set of reforms which promises autonomy but fails to deliver it, others may be relieved to discover that the balance has been struck in favour of accountability for Foundation Trusts. But what is most worrying is the way in which a gap has opened up between the reality of accountability and the rhetoric of autonomy surrounding Foundation Trusts. It is claimed that Foundation Trusts will be free to do as they please subject only to the light-touch licensing regime operated by the independent regulator. But, as this article has shown, this claim is questionable. The danger is that the rhetoric of autonomy will make the relationship between the Department of Health and Foundation Trusts wholly untransparent. The Department of Health may be able to deny all responsibility for the activities of Foundation Trusts, when in practice it has a substantial degree of control over what they do. Parliament and the public—not the Secretary of State—stand to lose influence over Foundation Trusts.

In 2002, approximately thirty strategic health authorities were created to replace around one hundred health authorities.[61] These are responsible for agreeing performance targets with the Department of Health, and for issuing guidance to the NHS trusts in their area. They are also supposed to take steps to involve patients and the wider public in developing services, and for ensuring compliance with guidance from the Healthcare Commission and other regulatory bodies. The 2002 reforms also introduced primary care trusts (PCTs), and there are now about three hundred of them, which are responsible for purchasing medical treatment for local communities from NHS Trusts, and for making arrangements for the provision of GP services. Their role is to assess local health needs, and to ensure that they meet national targets, while keeping strictly within their financial allocations. Although the Department of Health has described these changes as 'shifting the balance of power' towards local decision-making,[62] at the same time it has set up so many regulatory and supervisory bodies to set standards and monitor compliance, that local decision making is heavily constrained by centralized policy strategies.

In any event, it is not necessarily clear that local decision-making within the NHS is the best way to promote patient care. It can, for example, enable the government to delegate blame for inadequate services. Moreover, with 300 PCTs setting different health priorities, the continued existence of the 'postcode lottery', whereby a patient's access to treatment may depend principally upon where she lives, is not surprising. In addition, it may not be cost efficient to provide facilities for the treatment of

---

[60] 'Foundation Hospitals: A New Approach to Accountability and Autonomy in the Public Services' (2004) Public Law 808–28, 812–13, 828.

[61] Section 8 of the National Health Service Reform and Health Care Professions Act 2002 amended the National Health Service Act 1977 s. 8.

[62] *Shifting the Balance of Power: The Next Steps* (Department of Health, 2002).

comparatively rare diseases at local level. While PCTs are meant to set up consortia in larger regions to address this problem, there is obviously a danger that some patients with unusual medical conditions might not have straightforward access to specialist healthcare services.

(c) CLINICAL DISCRETION

For a number of reasons, the medical profession may be ill equipped to make rationing decisions. First, the doctor's primary ethical duty is do the best for her patient, rather than make broad policy decisions about competing priorities. Medical ethics has been dominated by individualistic values, such as beneficence and autonomy; in contrast, economic analysis tends to be broadly utilitarian. There is perhaps an irreconcilable conflict between the goal of diverting health care resources where they will do most good, and acting in the best interests of a particular patient. Having conducted empirical research into the attitudes of physicians to rationing, van Delden et al. found that:

Physicians tend to primarily look to the government for making allocation decisions. In their view, their primary concern should be the interests of their patients. They accept that their decisions influence the distribution of means and are willing to take this into account, but choosing between patients is not their job.[63]

Secondly, the medical profession's training equips them to make individual treatment decisions, rather than to manage budgets effectively. Thirdly, doctors are at the sharp end of rationing decisions, unlike politicians or health authority managers. It is undoubtedly exceptionally difficult for a doctor to have to tell her patient that there is more that could be done, but that there are not sufficient funds to do it.

Fourthly, doctors fear that knowingly withholding potentially beneficial treatment from a patient will leave them open to litigation. As we saw in Chapter 3, the standard of care in negligence is objective, and insufficient resources do not necessarily offer a defence.

But however admirable the professional ideal of complete devotion to each patient's best interests might be, doctors cannot avoid making rationing decisions because choosing to allocate money to one patient inevitably means that there is less money to spend on other people. If the NHS has finite resources, all clinical decisions are effectively choices about resource allocation. And it is increasingly recognized that where funds are limited, the ethical ideal that doctors must always give each of their patients the best available treatment—regardless of its cost—is simply unsustainable. Let us imagine a patient with muscle pain. Drug X will relieve her pain for ten hours; drug Y will give her five hours of pain relief. If clinical effectiveness is the sole consideration, drug X is the best option for this patient. But let us imagine that a single dose of drug X costs £10, while drug Y costs 10p. Each hour of pain relief using drug X costs £1, while drug Y gives an hour of pain relief for 2p. Clearly drug Y is a

[63] JJM van Delden, AM Vrakking, A van der Heide, and PJ van der Maas, 'Medical decision making in scarcity situations' (2004) 30 Journal of Medical Ethics, 207–11.

much more cost-effective treatment, and a doctor who continued to prescribe Drug X without good reason would be wasting NHS resources.

In practice, doctors do recognize that they have obligations to others which will sometimes override their duty towards an individual patient. Ranaan Gillon gives the example of a GP who is listening to a patient's account of his personal anguish when a fifty-five year old man with chest pain collapses in the waiting room. Of course, he says, the doctor would choose to subordinate the interests of the patient in his consulting room in favour of the person outside.[64]

Indeed, the judiciary has acknowledged that it is legitimate for clinicians to take the resources available for other patients into account when making treatment decisions. For example, in *R v North Derbyshire Health Authority, ex parte Fisher*,[65] Dyson J held that:

When deciding whether to prescribe treatment to a patient, a clinician has to have regard to many factors, including the resources available for that treatment and the needs of and likely benefit to that patient, as compared with other patients who are likely to be suitable for that treatment during the financial year.

And in *Arthur J S Hall & Co (A Firm) v Simons*,[66] Lord Hoffmann drew an analogy between lawyers' and doctors' duties to third parties:

The doctor, for example, owes a duty to the individual patient. But he also owes a duty to his other patients which may prevent him from giving one patient the treatment or resources he would ideally prefer.

It should also be remembered that there are a number of other situations in which doctors routinely take the interests of third parties and society as a whole into account when making decisions. In Chapter 6, we see that patient confidentiality can be breached in certain circumstances in order to prevent harm to third parties. And in Chapter 8 we will see that the primary goal of a doctor who is carrying out a randomized controlled trial is to generate valuable knowledge, rather than to promote her patients' wellbeing. Similarly, in a live organ donor transplant, the surgeon's intention is also clearly to benefit the recipient rather than the donor.

In the UK, doctors have seldom explicitly acknowledged that they are rationing medical treatment, and instead cost–benefit considerations have been absorbed within their clinical discretion, making it very difficult for patients to tell whether their doctor has taken the costs of treatment into account when recommending a particular course of action. For example, if a patient is suffering symptoms which are very likely to be caused by a minor illness, but there is a remote chance that something much more serious is wrong with them, doctors will often adopt a 'wait and see' approach, even though there is a very small chance the patient might benefit from undergoing expensive investigative procedures immediately. Few doctors would regard this as an example of rationing, but instead would argue that they were exercising their clinical judgement.

---

[64] Raanan Gillon, 'Ethics, Economics and General Practice', in Gavin Mooney and Alistair McGuire (eds), *Medical Ethics and Economics in Health Care* (OUP Oxford 1988) 114–34, 116.

[65] (1997) 38 BMLR 76 (QBD).

[66] [2002] 1 AC 615, 690.

It is also common for interventions to be targeted at 'high risk' groups. Flu vaccines are available free of charge to the over 75s. Unless there is a family history of breast cancer, regular mammograms are provided only to women over the age of 50. Yet it is undoubtedly true that younger people might benefit from being vaccinated against flu, and that regular breast cancer screening for women in their 40s could save lives. The principal, albeit not overtly articulated, justification for restricting patients' access to these sorts of services is cost. As Ranaan Gillon has explained:

If one were to take thoroughly to heart the idea that as curative doctors we should never allow concern for cost to others to deflect us from doing whatever we could to benefit our patients, then diagnostic services would be overwhelmed as we tested for rare but possible problems.[67]

As we saw earlier, rationing by dilution, in which patients are offered affordable and adequate, but not necessarily absolutely optimum care, has become a routine feature of clinical practice within the NHS. It is barely perceptible as rationing, and is therefore much less open to scrutiny than some of the more explicit rationing mechanisms that we considered earlier.

In the next extract, Keith Syrett explains that until the creation of the internal market in healthcare in 1991, few patients were even aware that medical treatment was rationed.

Keith Syrett[68]

[F]or many years, rationing in the NHS was not a matter of significant political or public debate. This was in part because lower expectations in the early years of the Service led to acceptance that deficiencies in provision were simply a fact of life. More significantly, most rationing took place under cover of clinical judgment: that is, it was *implicit*, in that 'the reasoning involved [was] not clearly stated to anyone except . . . the person making the decision'. Medical professionals effectively 'converted' political decisions on resource allocation into clinical decisions about treatment by 'internalising' resource limits and providing justification for denial on medical grounds by portraying the decision as optimal or routine in the specific circumstances. Suspicion that such decisions were in reality dictated by resource considerations tended to be minimal because of the existence of high levels of trust between doctors and patients, premised upon the belief that physicians possessed both expertise and access to all medical resources necessary for effective care and that they would act as dedicated patient advocates in attempting to secure these. In this manner, clinical judgment 'render[ed] the process of rationing as it were politically invisible, by fragmenting it across space and time into individualised and private transactions between doctors and patients. The result was that the NHS was able to maintain the fiction of meeting everyone's needs'.

(d) NICE

The National Institute for Health and Clinical Excellence (previously the National Institute for Clinical Excellence), or NICE, is a special health authority which was set up by statutory instrument in 1999 in part to make resource allocation decisions in

---

[67] Raanan Gillon, 'Ethics, Economics and General Practice', in Gavin Mooney and Alistair McGuire (eds), *Medical Ethics and Economics in Health Care* (OUP Oxford 1988) 114–34, 128.

[68] 'Impotence or Importance? Judicial Review in an Era of Explicit NHS Rationing' (2004) 67 Modern Law Review 289–304.

the NHS more explicit and transparent, and to address the problem of the 'postcode lottery'. Its official purpose is to provide patients, health care professionals and the public 'with authoritative, robust and reliable guidance on current best practice',[69] and to appraise the clinical and cost-effectiveness of both new and existing medical treatments and technologies. In this chapter, we are principally concerned with NICE's appraisals of new and existing treatments and its guidance about their provision within the NHS. Approximately forty appraisals are carried out each year by NICE's independent advisory committees which are made up of doctors, statisticians, health economists, and patient advocates. Appraisals can recommend: (1) the treatment's unrestricted use in the NHS; (2) its restricted use confined to certain categories of patients; (3) its use to be confined to clinical trials; or (4) that it should not be used in the NHS.

As we saw earlier, some commentators have suggested that reducing NHS expenditure upon ineffective or inefficient treatments would largely eliminate the need to ration services. In essence, NICE adopts a middle ground: it promotes evidence-based medicine, but does not regard it as a complete solution to the problem of scarce resources in the NHS. Even treatments which have been proved to be clinically effective may not reach some threshold level of cost-effectiveness, and NICE would then recommend that they are not offered within the NHS at all, or that their availability should be restricted to certain categories of patients. So, for example, NICE recommended that the obesity drug orlistat (brand name Xenical) should only be prescribed to patients who have already lost some weight through making changes to their diet and lifestyle.

NICE's decision-making process is undoubtedly open and transparent: all of NICE's appraisals are available on its website, and before decisions are finalized, there is an opportunity for 'stakeholders'—such as patient groups and the medical profession—to comment upon its draft conclusions. There is also a right of appeal for interested groups who will be directly affected by NICE guidance. In the next extract Keith Syrett explains that one consequence of NICE's commitment to transparency is undoubtedly that its decisions will be more open to challenge by interested parties.

Keith Syrett[70]

[I]t is clear that NICE has a . . . role in making 'tough choices' on the allocation of resources. Indeed, notwithstanding assertions to the contrary, the establishment of NICE—especially its technology appraisal function—appears to mark 'the beginning of explicit, national rationing' in the NHS.

This is significant because it has been powerfully argued that explicit resource allocation decisions are inherently more unstable than decisions which can be presented as based upon clinical necessity, even if these are also in reality dictated by resource considerations. The greater visibility of the process thus increases the potential for conflict. This may already be seen in the responses to certain Institute decisions. Refusal to authorise the use of an intervention has been opposed by patients and their representatives. On the other hand, approval has been contested by professionals seeking to preserve their clinical and managerial discretion with the consequence

[69] NICE, *A Guide to Our Work* (NICE, 1999) <http://www.nice.org.uk/>.
[70] 'Nice Work? Rationing, Review and the "Legitimacy Problem" in the new NHS' (2002) 10 Medical Law Review 1, 3–5.

that geographical variations in access to treatment have tended to persist. Elsewhere, patients requiring other services have lost out as resources are diverted to fund 'NICE-approved' interventions. The controversy generated has been manifested in media campaigns, Parliamentary debate and threats of legal action.

NICE has been the subject of two reviews since it was set up. First by the House of Commons Health Select Committee in 2002,[71] which recommended that there should be a further external review, which was then carried out by The World Health Organization Regional Office for Europe in 2003.[72] Despite being impressed by NICE's openness and transparency, and broadly supportive of its aims, both reports indicated that there was room for improvement.

A number of criticisms have been made of NICE in its first years of operation. First, NICE is charged with making two rather different types of judgement: first, it must assess technical, scientific evidence of a treatment's efficacy, and secondly, it must make a value judgement about whether it is appropriate for the NHS to fund the treatment. The only people qualified to make the first sort of assessment are experts who are capable of evaluating complex scientific data. And this aspect of NICE's role in appraising the clinical efficacy of new treatments arguably duplicates certain tasks which are already performed by the Medicines and Healthcare products Regulatory Agency (see Chapter 9 for more on the MHRA's role).

The second sort of judgement which NICE must make does not necessarily require technical expertise, and perhaps should instead reflect community values about the nature and purposes of the NHS. As a result of NICE's ambiguous dual role, the question of its appropriate membership is rather complicated. Members of the public are not qualified to make judgements about whether a particular treatment works, but might be able to contribute to discussions over whether it represents good enough value for money. In response to concern over the public's underrepresentation in its decisions, NICE has set up a citizens' council which will meet twice a year to consider 'generic' issues, rather than to contribute to decisions about individual treatments. It is, however, worth noting Keith Syrett's scepticism about the council's somewhat limited powers.

Keith Syrett[73]

However, the [citizen's] council suffers from significant limitations. It operates merely in an advisory capacity, and the institute is not bound to act on its recommendations. It has no power to instigate investigations, topics being referred to it by the institute or as a result of ministerial suggestion. It is intended merely to consider questions of a general nature and will only in exceptional circumstances address those matters which arise in the course of a technology appraisal. Perhaps most significantly, it is intended that the council shall only meet twice a year, for some six days in total. For these reasons, it has been criticized as a token gesture.

Secondly, the status of NICE guidance is unclear. It is, in fact, not legally binding on clinicians and health authorities, and yet it has tended to be treated as such by health

[71] Second Report, 2002

[72] Suzanne Hill et al., *Technology Appraisal Programme of the National Institute for Clinical Excellence: A Review by WHO* (WHO Europe 2003).

[73] 'A Technocratic Fix to the "Legitimacy Problem"? The Blair Government and Health Care Rationing in the United Kingdom' (2003) 28 Journal of Health Politics, Policy and Law 715.

authorities, doctors, and the media. This is perhaps unsurprising given that the Government has explicitly said that it expects NICE guidelines to be implemented throughout the NHS. Moreover, Directions issued in January 2002, instruct health authorities that any treatments which have been approved by NICE should normally be available to patients within three months.[74] Of course the critical word here is 'normally'. Would it, for example, be acceptable to decide not to fund a NICE approved treatment on the grounds that resources were scarce? The answer seems to be 'no'. In its response to the House of Commons Select Committee on Health's report, the government explained what was meant by 'normally':

The word 'normally' was included on the advice of Counsel to cover unusual circumstances outside the control of PCTs such as disruption to the supply of a medicine. The context in which the Direction was issued makes clear that scarce resources is not a good reason for failure to implement NICE guidance ... Health authorities and PCTs are expected to manage their budgets so that patients can be guaranteed that if a treatment recommended by NICE is appropriate for them, they will receive it.[75]

If a patient is denied treatment which has been recommended by NICE, it may assist them when seeking judicial review of a decision to refuse access to treatment. NICE guidance does not, however, give patients a right to treatment which is endorsed by NICE. Although there may be a duty on NHS institutions to fund NICE recommended treatments, there is no duty on doctors to use them, rather the question of what treatment is appropriate for a particular patient remains a question of clinical discretion, although obviously doctors would be expected to have regard to authoritative guidance on a treatment's clinical effectiveness.

Thirdly, despite the quasi-mandatory status of NICE recommendations, extra money is seldom put aside to fund their implementation, and so health authorities must strive to find the resources to pay for NICE-approved technologies and treatments from elsewhere in their budgets. This has had two consequences. First, different health authorities will choose to make savings in different ways, resulting in a new 'postcode lottery', as the cuts in coverage necessary to implement NICE's recommendations are made unevenly throughout the country. Secondly, despite its quasi-mandatory status, implementation of NICE recommendations is, as the Chairman of NICE suggests in the following extract, variable.

Michael Rawlins[76]

The extent to which NICE guidance has been implemented is unclear and the evidence (so far largely unpublished) is contradictory. There are, unquestionably, examples of local uptake of NICE guidance, and national data suggest that for some topics, clinical practice has substantially changed. Nevertheless, work commissioned by NICE and others suggests that uptake of the Institute's appraisal guidance is variable. The effect of our guidelines and interventional procedures advice on clinical practice is still too early to tell.

Fourthly, NICE's 'topic selection' process is not random, but rather is intended to

---

[74] *Directions to Health Authorities, Primary Care Trusts and NHS Trusts in England* (DH, 11 Dec 2001).

[75] *Government response to the Health Committee's 2nd report of session 2001–02 on National Institute for Clinical Excellence* (Cm 5611, 2002) 9.

[76] 'Five NICE years' (2005) 365 The Lancet 904–8.

ensure that NICE issues guidance on particularly controversial or expensive treatments or technologies in a rolling programme of appraisals. The Secretary of State decides which treatments should be subject to appraisal by NICE, on the advice of the Advisory Committee on Topic Selection, which contains representatives from the Department of Health, NHS Trusts, patient groups and the pharmaceutical industry. It would, of course, be impossible to subject every available medical procedure to the sort of rigorous assessment carried out by NICE. On average, each appraisal takes sixty-two weeks from the start of the process to the close of a possible appeal and the issuing of the final guidance. It is, of course, clearly sensible for NICE to ensure that it appraises new or expensive treatments first, but when coupled with the duty to fund NICE recommendations, the result may be that patients who suffer from certain conditions do not benefit from this prioritized funding. As the House of Commons Select Committee on Health points out, this may mean that the standard of care a patient can expect to receive will depend upon whether or not she has a 'politically correct' disease.

House of Commons Select Committee on Health[77]

77. The Government's recent directive announcing that implementation of NICE's recommendations on technology appraisals will be mandatory within three months of their issue can be seen as a positive step towards ensuring that NICE's guidance is acted on in the right way. Although the implementation of NICE's recommendations will not be 'mandatory' in the sense that NICE recommendations will override individual clinical judgement, health authorities and PCTs will have to ensure that the funding is available and the infrastructure in place to enable clinicians to act on NICE's recommendations. However, clinicians and commissioners of care are concerned that without specific 'extra' funding this will lead to inequities in the funding and provision of treatments and services which are not subject to NICE appraisal. The NHS Alliance argued that, because of mandatory funding, 'In the pursuit of national equity, there is a real danger of producing an even more sinister form of rationing than postcode prescribing—based on whether or not a patient has a "politically correct" disease'.

Fifthly, giving 'interested parties'—such as patient groups and the pharmaceutical industry—a right to make representations and a right of appeal has led to the criticism that NICE might be too easily swayed by powerful lobbying organizations. For example, the first NICE appraisal was of the flu drug zanamivir (brand name Relenza). NICE found that it would reduce episodes of flu from 6 days, on average, to 5, and reduce the risk of complications by 6 per cent, at a total cost to the NHS of £10 million. NICE initially recommended that it should not be available within the NHS, but its manufacturer, Glaxo Wellcome (now GlaxoSmithKline), launched an appeal. NICE reconsidered and its revised recommendation was that Relenza should be available to certain high-risk patient groups. In the next extract, Keith Syrett explains how by revealing NICE's susceptibility to lobbying by interested parties, this sort of decision may pose a threat to its legitimacy.

Keith Syrett[78]

The underlying suspicion of the motivation behind the decision which was evident among certain

---

[77] *2nd Report of Session 2001–02 on National Institute for Clinical Excellence*, para 68.
[78] 'A Technocratic Fix to the "Legitimacy Problem"? The Blair Government and Health Care Rationing in the United Kingdom' (2003) 28 Journal of Health Politics, Policy and Law 715.

elements of the medical profession in this case is also illustrative of the key obstacle hampering NICE's attainment of legitimacy among members of the public. This is the fact that priority-setting is 'inescapably a political process' in which debate and discussion between different interests and the articulation of conflicting values as to the goals of health care are inevitable. The campaigns mounted by Glaxo-Wellcome on zanamivir and by the Multiple Sclerosis Society on beta-interferon and glatiramer acetate demonstrate how 'evidence becomes an instrument of politics rather than a substitute for it', as lobby interests seek to infiltrate and manipulate the decision-making process in their favour. The visibility and centrality of NICE as a decision-making body, as compared with implicit, fragmented decisions undertaken by clinicians renders it especially susceptible to contestation by what have been labeled 'vocal, middle-class elites'.

There is then the danger that certain diseases and treatments will receive preferential treatment over other conditions which may be just as deserving, but which lack skilled and powerful advocates. The World Health Organization review found that approximately 38 per cent of NICE's final appraisals had been appealed. And it is certainly worth noting that NICE appears to be reluctant to recommend that any treatments or technologies should not be provided at all within the NHS. Of its first fifty appraisals, NICE recommended that sixteen should be available for routine use; thirty for selective use; and four for use only in research settings. None were wholly excluded from NHS coverage. Given the government's insistence that NICE guidance should be followed, it may in practice increase the pressure on NHS resources. NICE itself has estimated that its recommendations may cost the NHS an additional £575 million, and Richard Cookson et al. argue that NICE may have become the pharmaceutical industry's 'golden goose'.

Richard Cookson, David McDaid, and Alan Maynard[79]

NICE has concluded that all of the new pharmaceuticals it has appraised are cost effective and has refused to rank them in any form of hierarchy—not even a grading of 'high,' 'medium,' or 'low' cost effectiveness, let alone a full scale league table. As a consequence, health authorities are slavishly funding marginally cost effective drugs approved by NICE and diverting funding away from more cost effective existing services that lack politically powerful advocates (for example, hip replacements and cataract surgery). NICE has effectively become an advocacy mechanism by which lobbies of specialists and their supporters in the pharmaceutical industry extract more public money from the NHS. Instead of challenging the pharmaceutical industry to show value for money, NICE has become their 'golden goose.'

There are also concerns about equity. NICE places heavy emphasis on reducing 'postcode prescribing' of interventions. With fixed budgets, however, NICE guidance that is adopted will be funded by cutting (or by diluting, delaying, deterring, or deflecting) other services. Local decisions about such cuts will vary. As a consequence, geographical variations in quality of care may actually increase for those less fortunate services bereft of attention from NICE. Worse, the focus on postcode prescribing may divert attention from other goals relating to equity. For example, individual patients from the professional classes may prove particularly adept at insisting that NICE guidance is followed in their particular cases. This might exacerbate inequalities in access to high quality health care.

To remedy these problems, NICE needs to become a national healthcare rationing agency . . .

---

[79] 'Wrong SIGN, NICE mess: is national guidance distorting allocation of resources?' (2001) 323 British Medical Journal 743–5.

NICE needs to start saying 'no' to costly and relatively cost ineffective new drugs and devices. Rationing of new technologies is essential for political as well as economic reasons. Without politically acceptable ways of doing this, technology will continue to fuel the widening gap between public expectations and public willingness to pay for the NHS. The wider this gap grows the greater the risk that wealthier patients will turn to the private sector for their core health services, leading ultimately to the NHS becoming a rump service used only by the poor and the unhealthy.

Sixthly, despite its commitment to open and transparent decisionmaking, in practice NICE routinely withholds the evidence upon which its appraisals are based because pharmaceutical companies have specified that the relevant information was supplied in confidence. In its review of NICE's first years of operation, the House of Commons select committee on health recommended that all evidence submitted to NICE should be available for public scrutiny.

Seventhly, although NICE is specifically charged with appraising a treatment or technology's cost-effectiveness, it is not absolutely clear what criteria they are using for judging whether a treatment represents adequate value for money. This problem was highlighted in the World Health Organization review:

One particular criterion about which there is confusion is the use of a threshold or benchmark for value for money. On the one hand, it appears that there may be a threshold (£30,000/QALY) being used informally when considering technologies and this figure was mentioned by almost everyone the Review team consulted. On the other hand, there have been statements by NICE that the Committee is not using a threshold, and some of the Committee members publicly take exception to the idea that a threshold is an appropriate approach to decision-making.[80]

6. CHALLENGING RATIONING DECISIONS

(a) JUDICIAL REVIEW

Because rationing decisions will often involve denying patients potentially beneficial treatment on the grounds that the resources could be better spent elsewhere, it is vitally important that the decision-making process is fair and reasonable. Decision-making should be unbiased and consistent; decision-makers must ensure that all relevant considerations are taken into account, and should be prepared to give reasons for their decisions. Patients should have a right to be heard, and to challenge decisions.

Judicial review is available to scrutinize the legality but not the merits of decisions taken by public authorities. A patient who believes that a health authority has deprived them of appropriate treatment can apply for judicial review, but only on the grounds that the decision was taken unlawfully, that is that the healthy authority acted outside of its statutory powers; or irrationally, that is the decision is so unreasonable that no reasonable health authority could have come to the same decision (known as *Wednesbury*[81] unreasonableness). An action could also be brought for judicial review on the grounds that it infringed an applicant's rights under the Human Rights Act.

---

[80] Suzanne Hill et al., *Technology Appraisal Programme of the National Institute for Clinical Excellence: A Review by WHO* (WHO Europe 2003) 31.
[81] *Wednesbury Corporation v Minister of Housing and Local Government* [1966] 2 QB 275.

In practice, the courts have proved extremely reluctant to criticize funding decisions. In *R v Central Birmingham Health Authority, ex parte Walker*,[82] a non-urgent operation required by a premature baby was postponed on a number of occasions due to a shortage of nurses. The baby's mother applied for judicial review of the decision to postpone, but the Court of Appeal refused her application. Having pointed out that 'resources are, and perhaps always will be, finite', Sir John Donaldson MR found that:

It is not for this court, or indeed any court, to substitute its own judgment for the judgment of those who are responsible for the allocation of resources. This court could only intervene where it was satisfied that there was a prima facie case, not only of failing to allocate resources in the way in which others would think that resources should be allocated, but of a failure to allocate resources to an extent which was Wednesbury unreasonable, if one likes to use the lawyers' jargon, or, in simpler words, which involves a breach of a public law duty.

A year later, in *R v Central Birmingham Health Authority, ex parte Collier*,[83] the Court of Appeal was faced with a similar issue. This time, the little boy had had a number of unsuccessful heart operations, and was in desperate need of open heart surgery. Despite being at the top of the waiting list, the operation was postponed several times because of a shortage of both beds and nurses in the intensive care unit. The boy's father applied for judicial review, but the Court of Appeal found that his son's situation was 'not different in any relevant respect from that which obtained in the Walker case', and rejected his application:

Sir Stephen Brown[84]

There is no complaint of bad faith by the health authority. It is not suggested that they are in any way dragging their feet . . . [T]here is no suggestion here that the hospital authority has behaved in a way which is deserving of condemnation or criticism. What is suggested is that somehow more resources should be made available to enable the hospital authorities to ensure that the treatment is immediately given.

Of course this is a hearing before a court. This is not the forum in which a court can properly express opinions upon the way in which national resources are allocated or distributed. They may be very good reasons why the resources in this case do not allow all the beds in the hospital to be used at this particular time . . .

From the legal point of view, in the absence of any evidence which could begin to show that there was a failure to allocate resources in this instance in circumstances which would make it unreasonable in the Wednesbury sense to make those resources available, there can be no arguable case. I am bound to say that, whilst I have for my part every sympathy with the position of Mr Collier and his family and can understand their pressing anxiety in the case of their little boy, it does seem to me unfortunate that this procedure has been adopted. It is wholly misconceived in my view. The courts of this country cannot arrange the lists in the hospital, and, if it is not evidence that they are not being arranged properly due to some unreasonableness in the Wednesbury sense on the part of the authority, the courts cannot, and should not, be asked to intervene.

The decision in *Collier* has been sharply criticized by Christopher Newdick, who argues that it is:

---

[82] (1987) 3 BMLR 32. [83] Unreported, 6 Jan 1988.
[84] *R v Central Birmingham Health Authority, ex parte Collier*, unreported, 6 Jan 1988.

[o]ne of the most unsatisfactory cases ever to have emanated from the Court of Appeal in England . . . The case is unsettling because neither the applicant nor the court appeared to know how, or why, facilities could not be made available for this undeniably urgent operation. On any Hippocratic assessment of the case, its merits could hardly have been greater: the case was urgent, surgery was life-saving and well-understood, and the prospects of success were good. How could any reasonable system of priorities sensibly have abandoned such a deserving case?[85]

More recently Christopher Newdick has suggested that '*Collier* should now be regarded as wrongly decided for failing to assess the reasons for the decision to refuse treatment.'[86]

The judicial review case which attracted most media attention was undoubtedly the 'Child B' case, or *R v Cambridge Health Authority, ex parte B*.[87] Jaymee Bowen, whose name was initially concealed in order to protect her from the knowledge of the seriousness of her illness, was first diagnosed with acute lymphoblastic leukaemia when she was 5 years old. She recovered, but at the age of 10 developed acute myeloid leukaemia. Consultants at Addenbrookes Hospital in Cambridge, and at the Royal Marsden Hospital in London agreed that the only possible treatment (intensive chemotherapy and a second bone marrow transplant) would be very unlikely to succeed and was not in her best interests. Her father sought opinions from other doctors in the UK and in the US. Treatment in the US would have been prohibitively expensive, but he did find one doctor at the Hammersmith Hospital in London who was prepared to treat his daughter privately, and he sought an extracontractual referral from Cambridge and Huntingdon health authority to pay for the £75,000 treatment. His request was refused, and he applied for judicial review of this decision. At first instance, Laws J called upon the health authority to justify its decision by explaining the priorities which had led it to refuse to fund Child B's treatment:

where the question is whether the life of a ten year old child might be saved, by more than a slim chance, the responsible authority must in my judgment do more than toll the bell of tight resources. They must explain the priorities that have led them to decline to fund the treatment.[88]

Later the same day, the Court of Appeal overturned his judgment on the grounds that the health authority had acted rationally and fairly, and that court intervention in such a case would be misguided.

R v Cambridge Health Authority, ex parte B[89]

B, a girl born in 1984, was diagnosed in 1990 as suffering from non-Hodgkin's lymphoma and common acute lymphoblastic leukaemia and treated successfully at that time with chemotherapy. In December 1993 she developed acute myeloid leukaemia and received a second course of chemotherapy, total body irradiation and a bone marrow transplant. When she suffered a relapse of that condition in January 1995 the doctors who had previously treated her considered that a third course of chemotherapy and a second bone marrow transplant would not be in her best

---

[85] Christopher Newdick, 'Public Health Ethics and Clinical Freedom' (1998) 14 Journal of Contemporary Health Law and Policy (1998) 335, 354.
[86] 'The Organisation of Health Care' 3–82, in A Grubb with J Laing (eds), *Principles of Medical Law* (2nd edn OUP Oxford 2004) 44.
[87] [1995] 1 WLR 898.   [88] (1995) 25 BMLR 16, 17.   [89] [1995] 1 WLR 898.

interests. Her father applied to the health authority on her behalf for the funding of such treatment at hospital in London, where treatment would be administered as a two-stage process; further chemotherapy, with an estimated chance of success at between 10 and 20 per cent and at a cost of £15,000, would, if successful, be followed by a second bone marrow transplant, with the same estimated chance of success and at a cost of £60,000. The health authority refused. At first instance Laws J directed the health authority to reconsider its decision. The Court of Appeal overruled his decision, and reinstated the health authority's original decision.

Sir Thomas Bingham MR

I have no doubt that in a perfect world any treatment which a patient, or a patient's family, sought would be provided if doctors were willing to give it, no matter how much it cost, particularly when a life was potentially at stake. It would however, in my view, be shutting one's eyes to the real world if the court were to proceed on the basis that we do live in such a world. It is common knowledge that health authorities of all kinds are constantly pressed to make ends meet. They cannot pay their nurses as much as they would like; they cannot provide all the treatments they would like; they cannot purchase all the extremely expensive medical equipment they would like; they cannot carry out all the research they would like; they cannot build all the hospitals and specialist units they would like. Difficult and agonising judgments have to be made as to how a limited budget is best allocated to the maximum advantage of the maximum number of patients. That is not a judgment which the court can make. In my judgment, it is not something that a health authority such as this authority can be fairly criticised for not advancing before the court.

The case attracted intense and lurid media interest—*The Sun*'s headline was 'Condemned by Bank Balance' and the *Daily Mail*'s was 'Sentenced to Death'. Media attitudes towards the case did differ however, with some commentators condemning the health authority for effectively depriving a little girl of her only chance of survival, and others arguing that such tough choices were now inevitable within the NHS. It was, however, generally agreed that the Child B case was an example of rationing. Interestingly though, the then Chief Executive of Cambridge and Huntingdon health authority has challenged this assumption, contending that the decision had been made solely on the basis of Jaymee Bowen's best interests. There had, he argued, been no decision to withdraw funding for the treatment which her doctors had recommended, rather the consensus of expert opinion among the doctors who had been treating Jaymee Bowen was that the treatment requested by her father would be ineffective and inappropriate:

Our decision was not motivated by a shortage of money and in reality had little ever to do with the current debate about healthcare rationing.[90]

Following the intense publicity, an anonymous private benefactor came forward to pay for Jaymee Bowen's treatment. The consultant who had agreed to treat Jaymee privately decided against a second bone marrow transplant, and instead gave her an experimental treatment known as a donor lymphocyte infusion. Jaymee survived for a few more months and died in May 1996.

---

[90] Stephen Thornton, 'The Child B case—reflections of a chief' (1997) 314 British Medical Journal 1838.

One of the reasons why the courts have proved extremely reluctant to overturn a health authority's decision not to fund a particular patient's treatment is that they are not in a position to know about the other—possibly more compelling—claims upon its resources. If funds are diverted to patient A, there may not be enough to pay for the treatment of patients B, C, or D, none of whom has been represented before the court.

In *Re J (A Minor)*,[91] J had suffered serious head injuries when he was one month old. He was profoundly mentally and physically handicapped, and the doctors treating him agreed that mechanical ventilation or other life-saving measures should not be employed if he should suffer a life-threatening event. J's mother, however, wanted such measures to be taken. Although the decision to withhold treatment was not made for financial reasons, Lord Donaldson nevertheless took into account the possible existence of other patients who might benefit more from treatment:

I would stress the absolute undesirability of the court making an order which may have the effect of compelling a doctor or health authority to make available scarce resources (both human and material) to a particular child, without knowing whether or not there are other patients to whom those resources might more advantageously be devoted.

More recently, there have been a few cases in which the courts have found that health authorities have acted unlawfully when deciding not to fund particular treatments. In *R v North Derbyshire Health Authority, ex parte Fisher*,[92] Dyson J criticized a Health authority's decision not to fund Beta-Interferon except in conjunction with clinical trials. Since no trials were scheduled to take place, this amounted to a blanket ban, which was inconsistent with a Department of Health circular which had asked health authorities:

to develop and implement local arrangements to manage the entry of such drugs into the NHS . . .; and in particular, to initiate and continue prescribing of Beta-Interferon through hospitals.

Although the circular had only issued guidance and not directions, the health authority was under a duty to take it into consideration. According to Dyson J:

The respondents had to have regard to that national policy. They were not obliged to follow the policy, but if they decided to depart from it, they had to give clear reasons for so doing, and those reasons would have been susceptible to a Wednesbury challenge . . . Moreover, if the respondents failed properly to understand the circular, then their policy would be as defective as if no regard had been paid to the policy at all.

The health authority was held to have acted unreasonably by ignoring the Department of Health circular, and their policy on Beta Interferon therefore had to be reconsidered, taking proper account of NHS national policy.

The case of *R v North West Lancashire Health Authority, ex parte A and Others*[93] is, at first sight, an exceptional case in which patients were successful in establishing that a health authority had acted unlawfully in depriving them of treatment on the grounds of costs. In 1995, the health authority had adopted a restrictive referral policy for transsexuals seeking gender reassignment surgery at the country's only specialist Gender Identity Clinic at the Charing Cross Hospital in London. Three applicants

---

[91] [1992] 4 All ER 614.   [92] (1997) 38 BMLR 76 (QBD).   [93] [2000] 1 WLR 977.

who had had their requests for extra-contractual referrals turned down applied for judicial review. Auld LJ agreed that health authorities were entitled to make lists of treatments which were and were not a priority, and he agreed that it would 'make sense' to give gender reassignment surgery a lower priority than treatment for cancer, heart disease, or kidney failure. But he found that the policy did not make adequate provision for an individual's exceptional circumstances to be taken into account, and that the policy should be reformulated in order to (a) properly acknowledge that transsexualism is an illness, and (b) make effective provision for exceptions in individual cases.

In practice, of course, it is possible that the health authority could still refuse to fund these applicants' gender reassignment surgery, but satisfy the Court of Appeal that it was not operating a blanket ban by offering *reasons* for the decisions to refuse funding in each individual's case. Could it then be argued that the practical consequence of the decision in *NW Lancashire* is not to ensure that disgruntled patients receive treatment, but to instead offer them a personalized justification for a refusal to treat them? In Derek Morgan's words:

The right to health care becomes in fact a right to transparency about the tragic choices that are being negotiated.[94]

But while the judgment in *NW Lancashire* could simply result in a largely cosmetic exercise, the duty to articulate reasons does at least force health authorities to examine the fairness and consistency of their decisions.

R v North West Lancashire Health Authority, ex parte A and Others[95]

The applicants suffered from gender identity dysphoria. Two of them had been diagnosed to have a clinical need for gender reassignment surgery. The third was awaiting assessment of suitability for surgery. The health authority in 1995 had allocated a low priority to such surgery, which it considered achieved little or no clinical gain, and had decided that it would not pay for gender reassignment surgery or specialist counselling outside its own district. The only specialist clinic for dealing with gender identity dysphoria was at a London hospital. The policy was revised in 1998 to place gender reassignment surgery in a category of procedures which had not been tested by carefully conducted scientific research and where it was unclear whether the procedures were effective, ineffective or harmful. The policy stipulated that such procedures should be commissioned with caution and subject to a formal evaluation to ensure cost-effective use of resources. It authorized the director of public health and health policy to consider exceptions on the basis of overriding clinical need, but stipulated that 'such exceptions will be rare, unpredictable and will usually be based on circumstances that could not have been predicted at the time when the policy was adopted.' The authority refused requests by the applicants to be referred to the clinic in London. On their applications for judicial review, Hidden J quashed the authority's decisions and its policy, and ordered that the cases of the applicants be considered afresh. The Court of Appeal upheld his decision.

Auld LJ

[I]t is an unhappy but unavoidable feature of state funded health care that regional health authorities have to establish certain priorities in funding different treatments from their finite

[94] *Issues in Medical Law and Ethics* (Cavendish London 2001) 58.
[95] [2000] 1 WLR 977.

resources. It is natural that each authority, in establishing its own priorities, will give greater priority to life-threatening and other grave illnesses than to others obviously less demanding of medical intervention. The precise allocation and weighting of priorities is clearly a matter of judgment for each authority, keeping well in mind its statutory obligations to meet the reasonable requirements of all those within its area for which it is responsible. It makes sense to have a policy for the purpose—indeed, it might well be irrational not to have one—and it makes sense too that, in settling on such a policy, an authority would normally place treatment of transsexualism lower in its scale of priorities than, say, cancer or heart disease or kidney failure. Authorities might reasonably differ as to precisely where in the scale transsexualism should be placed and as to the criteria for determining the appropriateness and need for treatment of it in individual cases. It is proper for an authority to adopt a general policy for the exercise of such an administrative discretion, to allow for exceptions from it in 'exceptional circumstances' and to leave those circumstances undefined. In my view, a policy to place transsexualism low in an order of priorities of illnesses for treatment and to deny it treatment save in exceptional circumstances such as overriding clinical need is not in principle irrational, provided that the policy genuinely recognises the possibility of there being an overriding clinical need and requires each request for treatment to be considered on its individual merits . . .

Accordingly, given the authority's acknowledgement that transsexualism is an illness, its policy, in my view, is flawed in two important respects. First, it does not in truth treat transsexualism as an illness, but as an attitude or state of mind which does not warrant medical treatment. Second, the ostensible provision that it makes for exceptions in individual cases and its manner of considering them amount effectively to the operation of a 'blanket policy' against funding treatment for the condition because it does not believe in such treatment. . . .

The authority should reformulate its policy to give proper weight to its acknowledgement that transsexualism is an illness, apply that weighting when setting its level of priority for treatment and make effective provision for exceptions in individual cases from any general policy restricting the funding of treatment for it.

Buxton LJ

A number of propositions are clearly established, mainly by the decision of this court in R v. Cambridge Health Authority, ex parte B. They are: (1) A health authority can legitimately, indeed must, make choices between the various claims on its budget when, as will usually be the case, it does not have sufficient funds to meet all of those claims. (2) In making those decisions the authority can legitimately take into account a wide range of considerations, including the proven success or otherwise of the proposed treatment; the seriousness of the condition that the treatment is intended to relieve; and the cost of that treatment. (3) The court cannot substitute its decision for that of the authority, either in respect of the medical judgments that the authority makes, or in respect of its view of priorities . . .

It follows from the foregoing propositions that a health authority can in the course of performing these functions determine that it will provide no treatment at all for a particular condition, even if the condition is medically recognised as an illness requiring intervention that is categorised as medical and curative, rather than merely cosmetic or a matter of convenience or lifestyle.

In all of this, the court's only role is to require that such decisions are taken in accordance with equally well known principles of public law. Those principles include a requirement that the decisions are rationally based upon a proper consideration of the facts. The more important the interest of the citizen that the decision affects, the greater will be the degree of consideration that is required of the decision-maker. A decision that, as is the evidence in this case, seriously affects the citizen's health will require substantial consideration, and be subject to careful scrutiny by the court as to its rationality . . .

I am not satisfied that the decisions of the health authority in this case met these criteria. . . .

When the matter is remitted there will still, of course, be many factors that the health authority can properly take into account that may well point towards the original decision being maintained. Those include the cost of the procedures, underlined by expert evidence that once a patient has started on the course of counselling and review that course must necessarily be carried through to surgery in those cases where that is advised; the comparatively small number of patients needing gender reassignment treatment; and the costs and demands of other procedures.

R v North and East Devon Health Authority, ex parte Coughlan[96] is an even more exceptional case. Miss Coughlan had been seriously injured in a road traffic accident in 1971. She was tetraplegic and required constant care. In 1993, she and seven other seriously disabled patients were moved to Mardon House, a purpose built unit, which they were assured would be their 'home for life'. In 1996, the health authority recommended that Mardon House should be closed, although it accepted that it had a continuing commitment to finance the care received by the residents to whom this promise had been made. Miss Coughlan applied for judicial review. The Court of Appeal found that the patients had a legitimate expectation not only to be treated fairly and impartially by the health authority, but also to the substantive benefit of a home for life in Mardon House. Frustrating that expectation would be so unfair that it would amount to an abuse of power. Lord Woolf even suggested that a failure to honour the substantive promise made to the applicant was 'equivalent to a breach of contract in private law'. Indeed the Court of Appeal appeared to employ the principle of estoppel in order to protect Miss Coughlan's reasonable reliance upon the health authority's representations.

R v North and East Devon Health Authority, ex parte Coughlan[97]

The applicant, who was severely injured in a road accident in 1971, was tetraplegic, doubly incontinent, partially paralysed in the respiratory tract and suffered from recurrent headaches. In 1993 she and seven comparably disabled patients were moved with their agreement from a hospital which the health authority wished to close to Mardon House, a National Health Service facility for the long-term disabled, which the health authority assured them would be their home for life. In 1998, following public consultation, the health authority decided to close Mardon House. On an application for judicial review of the closure decision, Hidden J quashed the decision to close Mardon House. The Court of Appeal upheld his decision.

Lord Woolf MR

[I]t is necessary to begin by examining the court's role where what is in issue is a promise as to how it would behave in the future made by a public body when exercising a statutory function . . .

What is still the subject of some controversy is the court's role when a member of the public, as a result of a promise or other conduct, has a legitimate expectation that he will be treated in one way and the public body wishes to treat him or her in a different way. Here the starting point has to be to ask what in the circumstances the member of the public could legitimately expect.

There are at least three possible outcomes. (a) The court may decide that the public authority is only required to bear in mind its previous policy or other representation, giving it the weight it

---

[96] [2001] QB 213.   [97] [2001] QB 213.

thinks right, but no more, before deciding whether to change course. Here the court is confined to reviewing the decision on Wednesbury grounds . . . (b) On the other hand the court may decide that the promise or practice induces a legitimate expectation of, for example, being consulted before a particular decision is taken. Here it is uncontentious that the court itself will require the opportunity for consultation to be given unless there is an overriding reason to resile from it . . . (c) Where the court considers that a lawful promise or practice has induced a legitimate expectation of a benefit which is substantive, not simply procedural, authority now establishes that here too the court will in a proper case decide whether to frustrate the expectation is so unfair that to take a new and different course will amount to an abuse of power. Here, once the legitimacy of the expectation is established, the court will have the task of weighing the requirements of fairness against any overriding interest relied upon for the change of policy . . .

There has never been any question that the propriety of a breach by a public authority of a legitimate expectation of the second category, of a procedural benefit—typically a promise of being heard or consulted—is a matter for full review by the court. The court has, in other words, to examine the relevant circumstances and to decide for itself whether what happened was fair . . . But in relation to a legitimate expectation of a substantive benefit (such as a promise of a home for life) doubt has been cast upon whether the same standard of review applies. Instead it is suggested that the proper standard is the so-called Wednesbury standard which is applied to the generality of executive decisions. This touches the intrinsic quality of the decision, as opposed to the means by which it has been reached, only where the decision is irrational or . . . immoral . . .

It is, however, clear from the health authority's evidence and submissions that it did not consider that it had a legal responsibility or commitment to provide a home, as distinct from care or funding of care, for the applicant and her fellow residents. It considered that . . . the provision of care services to the current residents had become 'excessively expensive,' having regard to the needs of the majority of disabled people in the authority's area . . .

But the cheaper option favoured by the health authority misses the essential point of the promise which had been given. The fact is that the health authority has not offered to the applicant an equivalent facility to replace what was promised to her. The health authority's undertaking to fund her care for the remainder of her life is substantially different in nature and effect from the earlier promise that care for her would be provided at Mardon House. That place would be her home for as long as she chose to live there.

We have no hesitation in concluding that the decision to move Miss Coughlan against her will and in breach of the health authority's own promise was in the circumstances unfair. It was unfair because it frustrated her legitimate expectation of having a home for life in Mardon House. There was no overriding public interest which justified it.

It is however important to remember that one of the reasons for treating public law differently from private law is that public authorities have a duty to balance competing claims upon their resources. The health authority's evidence to the Court of Appeal stated that Mardon House had become:

a prohibitively expensive white elephant. The unit was not financially viable. Its continued operation was dependent upon the Authority supporting it at an excessively high cost. This did not represent value for money and left fewer resources available for other services.[98]

While it of course honourable to keep one's promises, maintaining Mardon House

---

[98] [2001] QB 213.

might jeopardize the health authority's ability to offer services to other patients, whose interests were not represented in this case. Could it be argued that in *Coughlan* the Court of Appeal were in fact judging the merits, as opposed to the legality of the authority's decision?

On the other hand, Paul Craig and Soren Schonberg suggest that the Court of Appeal in *Coughlan* rightly separated two different exercises of power by the Health authority: the promise to Miss Coughlan and the policy decision to close Mardon House. They agree that the policy change was not unreasonable in the *Wednesbury* sense, but that the breach of promise amounted to an abuse of power.

Paul Craig and Soren Schonberg[99]

[T]here were two lawful exercises of power in this type of case: the promise and the policy change. It was this consideration which led the Court of Appeal to distinguish between two standards of judicial review of discretion. There was, on the one hand, bare or intrinsic irrationality, which allowed the court to intervene to quash a decision which defied comprehension . . . Such cases were rare. Irrationality also embraced decisions made on the basis of flawed logic. . . . It was acknowledged that the present decision might well pass a rationality test cast in these terms.

There was, on the other hand, the possibility of intervention on the ground of abuse of power. A power which had been abused had not been lawfully exercised. . . .

The court in Coughlan was, therefore, correct in rejecting a test of bare or intrinsic rationality as the standard for review in [this] category of case. To countenance judicial intervention only where the contested decision either defied comprehension, or was based on flawed logic, under-values the nature of the applicant's interest, and would provide scant protection for the individual. The decision to close Mardon House would, as recognised in Coughlan, 'not easily be challenged as irrational', in either of these senses. In cases of this kind a bare rationality test would, as noted earlier, constitute the public authority judge in its own cause. The recognition that bare or intrinsic rationality was ill-suited to this type of case required the court to fashion some other standard of review.

The court in Coughlan chose to base review on abuse of power. To resile from a prior assurance could be unfair and hence an abuse of power. The court would view a legitimate expectation within the statutory context in which it had arisen, thereby preserving 'the important principle that the executive's policy-making powers should not be trammelled'. Policy, and the reasons for changing it, were for the public authority, and would not ordinarily be open to judicial review. The court's task was limited to asking whether the application of the policy to an individual who had been led to expect something different was a just exercise of power.

Are *NW Lancashire* and *Coughlan* simply exceptional decisions, or do they represent a trend towards increased willingness, on the part of the judiciary, to challenge funding decisions? According to Christopher Newdick, the latter is true, and in the next section we consider whether the Human Rights Act has also played a part in encouraging the courts to play a more active role in scrutinizing the fairness of rationing in the NHS.[100]

---

[99] 'Substantive Legitimate Expectations after *Coughlan*' (2000) Public Law, 684–701, 690–1, 698.
[100] Christopher Newdick, *Who Should we Treat? Rights, Rationing and Resources in the NHS* (2nd edn OUP Oxford 2005).

(b) THE HUMAN RIGHTS ACT 1998

Could a disgruntled patient who is denied access to medical treatment invoke the Human Rights Act 1998 in order to challenge the decision? If a patient is denied treatment which might save her life, for example, would it be possible to argue that her right to life, protected under Article 2, has been violated? Certainly Article 2 does not only oblige public bodies to refrain from deliberately taking its citizens' lives, but can also require them to take adequate measures to protect life. And it is possible to imagine circumstances in which a failure to provide any life-saving treatment at all to a critically ill patient might infringe Article 2. But it is extremely unlikely that patients could routinely invoke Article 2 in order to force health authorities to fund treatment which has been refused on the grounds of cost or clinical judgement.

The European Court of Human Rights has generally been slow to interfere with resource allocation decisions within public services. In the context of providing policing services, for example, the European Court of Human Rights found that the right to life should not be interpreted in a way which imposed a disproportionate burden on public authorities:

As to the alleged failure of the authorities to protect the rights to life of Ali and Ahmet Osman . . . bearing in mind the difficulties involved in policing modern societies, the unpredictability of human conduct and the operational choices which must be made in terms of priorities and resources, such an obligation must be interpreted in a way which does not impose an impossible or disproportionate burden on the authorities. Accordingly, not every claimed risk to life can entail for the authorities a Convention requirement to take operational measures to prevent that risk from materialising.[101]

In *Scialacqua v Italy*,[102] the European Commission dismissed an applicant's claim that the Italian public health service was obliged by Article 2 to pay for medicines which he claimed had improved his condition. If faced with such a case in the UK, the judiciary would be likely to follow the approach evident in the judicial review cases described earlier. Provided that a decision not to fund treatment had been taken fairly and rationally, it is improbable that it would be overturned by the courts.

Alternatively might a refusal to fund treatment be challenged under Article 8, the right to respect for one's private and family life, or if sufficiently serious, could a denial of medical treatment ever amount to 'inhuman or degrading treatment' under Article 3, and might a disgruntled patient be able to claim that they were discriminated against in the exercise of their Convention rights under Article 14? All three claims were made by the applicants in questions in *NW Lancashire Health Authority v A, D and G*,[103] discussed in the previous section, and were briskly dismissed by the Court of Appeal. Auld LJ found that 'in any event, Art 8 imposes no positive obligations to provide treatment', and went on to say,

It is plain, in my view, that article 3 was not designed for circumstances of this sort of case where the challenge is as to a health authority's allocation of finite funds between competing demands. As Hidden J observed, in rejecting similar submissions below:

---

[101] *Osman v UK* (Case 87/1997/871/1083) [1999] 1 FLR 193.
[102] (1998) 26 EHRR CD164.   [103] [2000] 1 WLR 977.

'The Convention does not give the applicants rights to free healthcare in general or to gender reassignment surgery in particular. Even if the applicants had such a right it would be qualified by the respondent's right to determine healthcare priorities in the light of its limited resources'.

Auld LJ also described resort to Article 14 as 'misconceived':

That is not a matter of sexual or any other discrimination against which the law provides protection; it is a matter of different priorities for different illnesses, a matter of medical judgment.

Buxton LJ was similarly dismissive. Article 3, he said, did not apply to resource allocation decisions:

Article 3 of the ECHR addresses positive conduct by public officials of a high degree of seriousness and opprobrium. It has never been applied to merely policy decisions on the allocation of resources, such as the present case is concerned with.

And on Articles 8 and 14, Buxton LJ held that:

it is plain that in this case there has occurred no interference with either the applicants' private life or with their sexuality . . . Such an interference could hardly be founded on a refusal to fund medical treatment.

It is impossible to see how the applicants have been the victims of discrimination on grounds of sex. True it is that they seek a particular treatment related to their sexuality; but that has been refused not because of that sexuality, but on grounds of allocation of resources. If it were an act of discrimination simply to refuse treatment that was related to sexuality, the health authority would be obliged to provide such treatment in every case, whatever the other calls on its resources.

At first instance in *R (on the application of Watts) v Bedford Primary Care Trust*,[104] discussed further in the following section, Munby J again rejected the claim that having to wait a year for a hip replacement operation, with all the pain and suffering to be endured in the meantime, might be in breach of Article 3:

Article 3 is not engaged unless the 'ill-treatment' in question attains a minimum level of severity and involves actual bodily injury or intense physical or mental suffering. However that is not this case. Making every allowance for the constant pain and suffering that the claimant was having to endure—and I do not seek in any way to minimise it—the simple fact in my judgment is that nothing she had to endure was so severe or so humiliating as to engage article 3.[105]

But while it would be difficult for a claimant to establish that any denial of medical treatment infringed their rights under the Human Rights Act 1998, it is certainly not impossible. In *Price v United Kingdom*[106] the prison authorities could not cope with the special needs of a four-limb-deficient thalidomide victim with numerous health problems including defective kidneys. The Court found that there had been a breach of Article 3:

There is no evidence in this case of any positive intention to humiliate or debase the applicant. However, the Court considers that to detain a severely disabled person in conditions where she is dangerously cold, risks developing sores because her bed is too hard or unreachable, and is unable

---

104 [2003] EWHC 2228 (Admin).   105 [2003] EWHC 2228 (Admin).
106 (2001) 34 EHRR 1285.

to go to the toilet or keep clean without the greatest of difficulty, constitutes degrading treatment contrary to article 3.[107]

And in the next extract, David O'Sullivan argues that it might be possible for Article 14 and Article 2 to be invoked where a patient is denied life-saving treatment on the grounds of age or disability.

David O'Sullivan[108]

Acknowledging that the right to life is engaged in decisions regarding the funding of treatment would bring into play the non-discrimination provision in article 14 of the Convention. Article 14 places on authorities the obligation to secure the Convention rights without discrimination on any ground. There is an illustrative (rather than exhaustive) list of prohibited grounds such as sex, race and religion which includes 'social origin . . . property, birth or other status'. A refusal of potentially life-saving treatment which was based in part on the supposedly marginal nature of somebody's life in terms of their employment may constitute discrimination on grounds of social origin or other status and breach article 14 in conjunction with article 2 (the right to life). It may also be argued that a refusal of such treatment because of the advanced age of the patient would breach article 14 taken together with article 2. In the event of such an argument, the court would have to consider whether such a distinction constitutes unlawful discrimination or legitimate differentiation with some reasonable and objective justification.

Importantly, the Human Rights Act 1998 has led to a greater emphasis upon the proportionality of decisions to restrict access to medical treatment. Interferences with convention rights must be justified according to whether they serve a legitimate aim, are necessary in a democratic society, and proportionate to the aim being pursued. In the next extract, Christopher Newdick suggests that the Human Rights Act would have made a difference to the court's decision in 1988 in *ex p Collier*, discussed above at p. 83.

Christopher Newdick[109]

Let us now reflect on the case of *Collier v Birmingham Health Authority*, in which a boy of four was not given life-saving heart surgery, despite being top of his consultant's list of patients. No satisfactory explanation was offered for the failure, but the court refused to intervene in the matter. Both the domestic law of judicial review and the Human Rights Act 1998 would now take a close interest in the case, to ensure that the circumstances of the case were lawful, perhaps under the right to life provisions of article 2, or respect for private and family life under article 8. . . . Thus, aided by the Human Rights Act 1998, the courts have rightly become willing to subject decisions of this nature to more intense scrutiny to ensure that discretion has been exercised in a reasonable and proportionate manner. This approach reflects a more general movement in the balance of power between individuals and public authorities.

(c) SEEKING TREATMENT ABROAD

Could a patient who has been denied treatment in the UK, or who wants to avoid UK waiting lists seek reimbursement for treatment abroad? Article 49 of the EC Treaty

---

[107] [2003] EWHC 2228 (Admin).

[108] 'The Allocation of Scarce Resources and the Right to Life under the European Convention on Human Rights' (1998) Public Law 389–95, 394–5.

[109] Christopher Newdick, *Who Should we Treat? Rights, Rationing and Resources in the NHS* (2nd edn OUP Oxford 2005) 127–8.

prohibits restrictions on the freedom to provide services which are 'normally provided for remuneration' within the EU. Unquestionably this covers private medical treatment, and the ECJ has also held that remuneration exists in some types of publicly funded treatment.[110] But while Article 49 may enable patients to seek treatment abroad, it confers no right to be reimbursed for such treatment. As amended Article 22 of Council Regulation No 1408/71, which coordinates national social security systems, allows Member States to decide whether to authorize reimbursement for treatment abroad, but states that authorization:

may not be refused where the treatment in question is among the benefits provided for by the legislation of the Member State on whose territory the person concerned resides and where he cannot be given such treatment within the time normally necessary for obtaining the treatment in question in the Member State of residence, taking account of his current state of health and the probable course of the disease.

This means that patients cannot claim financial support for treatment abroad where the treatment in question is unavailable within the NHS. Whether or not the provision can be used to avoid NHS waiting lists depends, of course, upon how 'the time normally necessary for obtaining the treatment in question' is to be interpreted. It seems clear that patients cannot expect the NHS to pay for treatment abroad just because they cannot be treated immediately in the UK. Instead, it is only where the waiting time in the UK amounts to 'undue delay' that it will be possible to invoke Article 22 to demand access to services in another country.

The European Court of Justice has taken the view that there will be circumstances in which a nation is entitled to restrict its citizens' access to treatment abroad, but, as Gareth Davies explains, only if this would impede the national healthcare system's capacity to function effectively. The likelihood of this sort of harm has to be established on a case by case basis.

Gareth Davies[111]

In Müller-Fauré[112] the Court of Justice has made clear that restricting patients to receiving medical services from their domestic health systems is often contrary to EC Treaty rules on the free movement of services, particularly where the treatment is not in-patient. The patient should generally be able to go abroad for treatment at the expense of their national health authority. This has structural and financial repercussions for health care systems in several Member States, including the United Kingdom, whose systems are premised upon captive patients. It also has broader implications for welfare harmonisation and provision in the European Union. Exceptions are possible, where the implications for the national health system would be very serious, but Müller-Fauré indicates that the Court will not allow national courts or authorities to rely on these too freely. . . .

The Member States' central fear is that patients going abroad, usually to avoid waiting lists, will result in higher costs. Not only will the national authorities lose their control over the rate of treatment, and hence spending, but they will also be left with possibly half-empty institutions.

---

[110] Case C-158/96 Kohll v Union de Caisses de Maladie [1998] ECR I-1931.

[111] 'Health and Efficiency: Community Law and National Health Systems in the Light of Müller-Fauré' (2004) 67 Modern Law Review 94–107.

[112] Case C-385/99 Müller-Fauré v Onderlinge Waarborgmaatschappij OZ Zorgverzekeringen and van Riet v Onderlinge Waarborgmaatschappij ZAO Zorgverzekeringen, judgment of 13 May 2003.

These cannot simply be closed down, because maintaining the national medical infrastructure is a matter of strategic and public health importance. Therefore the state will be forced to operate an inefficient system, adding an extra burden to its budget.

Since economic reasons do not justify restrictions on free movement, this fear is usually presented in a slightly convoluted form. The Member States claim that the extra cost burden, and loss of control, is such that their chosen system in fact becomes unviable. It is not the money itself that worries us, they say, but the breakdown of our national health scheme. This the Court has accepted as a legitimate reason for restrictions. However, there are no trump cards in Community law, and it is a question for each case whether the risk really is great enough to justify the loss of patient, and provider, freedom.

The question of whether or not European law entitles a patient on an NHS waiting list to be reimbursed for treatment in another Member State arose for the first time in the UK in *R (on the application of Watts) v Bedford Primary Care Trust and Another*.[113] Yvonne Watts sought a hip replacement operation in France in order to avoid the NHS waiting time of approximately one year. Her local NHS Trust refused to fund the operation, and she challenged this decision, arguing that it was contrary to her free movement rights under EU law. The critical question was whether the waiting list meant that the patient would be subject to 'undue delay'. The Court of Appeal asked for further clarification from the European Court of Justice on a number of questions, among them:

Is the United Kingdom National Health Service entitled to refuse to authorise a patient's treatment in another Member State if it reasonably judges that to do so in the particular and similar cases would dislocate its system of administering priorities through waiting lists?

R (on the application of Watts) v Bedford Primary Care Trust and Another[114]
The claimant, who was 72 years old, needed hip replacement surgery. She was on an NHS waiting list where the waiting times was approximately one year. Mrs Watts sought reimbursement for treatment in France, on the grounds that she had enforceable rights under European Community law (specifically under Art 49 of the EC Treaty and Art 22 of Council Regulation No 1408/71) to be treated in another Member State if the NHS is unable to provide appropriate treatment within the timescale indicated by the patient's medical condition and medical needs.

May LJ
We consider that the court should proceed on an assumption that, if the NHS were required to pay the cost of some of its patients having treatment abroad at a time earlier than they would receive it in the United Kingdom, this would require additional resources.

The budget allocated, as a matter of governmental policy, to the NHS is not currently large enough to enable all who wish to have treatment, regardless of its urgency, to receive it promptly. The NHS could, as a matter of policy, have mitigated this situation by restricting the types of treatment provided. We imagine that some present or future Member States do not have health services which provide the range of treatments provided by the NHS. Instead, the NHS applies its finite resources by according priorities to different treatments and by having regard to the urgency of individual cases. This results at present in some quite lengthy waiting lists for less urgent treatment . . .

We are not clear that the Court of Justice intended to require that those who wished to jump

---

113 [2004] EWCA CIV 166 [2004] All ER (D) 349 (Feb).   114 Ibid.

the queue by having medical treatment in another Member State are able, if necessary, by so doing to dictate an increase in what may be an already strained national health service budget; or to force the postponement of more urgent treatment needed by others.

At the time of writing it is not known what the ECJ's response to the Court of Appeal's questions will be, but in the next extract Christopher Newdick suggests that if a right to treatment abroad to avoid overlong waiting lists is recognized, this may benefit stronger patients at the expense of those who are unable to travel in order to 'jump' UK waiting lists.

Christopher Newdick[115]

The case of Watts v Secretary of State for Health (2004) creates the possibility that primary care trusts may be obliged to pay for the hospital care that patients receive in the EU. The European Court of Justice (ECJ) has said that patients from Germany and Holland may do so if (1) the health care in question is covered by the health insurance system operating in the patient's own Member State, (2) the treatment is 'normal in the professional circles concerned', in that it is 'sufficiently tried and tested by international medical science', and (3) the same or equally effective treatment cannot be obtained at home 'without undue delay.'

The Court of Appeal referred the case to the ECJ in order for specific questions to be answered. Once answers have been provided, the matter will be re-heard by the Court of Appeal and it will apply the solutions suggested. The questions referred by the Court go to the heart of the NHS: Is the UK court obliged to ignore the fact that this approach may require increased NHS funding? May the NHS refuse to authorise treatment abroad in the interests of equal and fair waiting lists? Can some jump the NHS waiting lists? And by what criteria should 'undue delay' be judged, according to individual need, or institutional standards?

To introduce a European right to travel will do much to benefit the strong and articulate. But it ignores those who cannot travel, or inarticulate patients who do not press for their rights.

A system which skews health care rights in this way has little to recommend it.

(d) NEGLIGENCE

Could an NHS trust's decision to offer care that is less than ideal on grounds of cost represent a breach of their primary duty of care to patients? As we see in the next chapter, health authorities, and now NHS trusts do owe a duty to provide an acceptable standard of care. Because the standard of care in negligence is assessed objectively, lack of resources is, in theory at least, irrelevant. In *Bull v Devon Area Health Authority*,[116] a case we consider again in the next chapter, Exeter City Hospital operated on two sites, and its resources were evidently severely stretched: Slade LJ suggested that 'in cases where multiple births were involved, the system in operation at the hospital in 1970 was obviously operating on a knife-edge'. During the delivery of Mrs Bull's twins, unsuccessful attempts were made to summon a registrar, and a consultant finally arrived to deliver the second twin over an hour later, during which time he had been deprived of oxygen and as a result was left profoundly mentally and

---

[115] 'Rights to Treatment in the EU? UK Clinical Ethics Network' <http://www.ethics-network.org.uk/comment/newdick.htm> (last visited 24 Apr 2005).

[116] (1989) 22 BMLR 79 (CA).

physically disabled. The Court of Appeal was clear that limited resources was not necessarily a defence to an allegation of negligence; Mustill LJ, for example, said that:

it is not necessarily an answer to allegations of unsafety that there were insufficient resources to enable the administrators to do everything which they would like to do.

Nevertheless, the Court of Appeal accepted that less than ideal care will sometimes be inevitable. Here a delay of 15 to 20 minutes in summoning a registrar or consultant would have been acceptable, but the delay of 68 minutes amounted to negligence. Dillon LJ accepted that it would not be reasonable to expect the same standard of care and treatment at Exeter City Hospital as it would from a 'centre of excellence'. The Hospital was not under a duty to have a system in place which would eliminate the possibility of any delay. Rather the duty was to provide 'a staff *reasonably sufficient* for the foreseeable requirements of the patient' (my emphasis).

(e) BREACH OF STATUTORY DUTY

If a patient could argue that a health authority was under a statutory duty to provide them with particular treatment, an action for breach of statutory duty may appear to offer a more positive avenue for redress. A statutory duty is not the same as a discretionary power, which means that a lack of resources cannot provide an excuse for failing to fulfil the duty imposed by statute. In the context of educational provision, the House of Lords has suggested that:

The courts should be slow to downgrade such [statutory] duties into what are, in effect, mere discretions over which the court would have little real control.[117]

Clearly the National Health Service Act creates a duty on the part of the Secretary of State:

National Health Service Act 1977
1 Secretary of State's duty as to health service

(1) It is the Secretary of State's duty to continue the promotion in England and Wales of a comprehensive health service designed to secure improvement—

(a) in the physical and mental health of the people of those countries, and

(b) in the prevention, diagnosis and treatment of illness,

and for that purpose to provide or secure the effective provision of services in accordance with this Act.

(2) The services so provided shall be free of charge except in so far as the making and recovery of charges is expressly provided for by or under any enactment, whenever passed . . .

s. 3(1) It is the Secretary of State's duty to provide throughout England and Wales, to such extent as he considers necessary to meet all reasonable requirements—

(a) hospital accommodation;

---

[117] *R v East Sussex CC ex p. Tandy* [1988] AC 714, per Lord Browne-Wilkinson at 749.

(b) other accommodation for the purpose of any service provided under this Act;

(c) medical, dental, nursing and ambulance services;

(d) such other facilities for the care of expectant and nursing mothers and young children as he considers are appropriate as part of the health service;

(e) such facilities for the prevention of illness, the care of persons suffering from illness and the after-care of persons who have suffered from illness as he considers are appropriate as part of the health service;

(f) such other services as are required for the diagnosis and treatment of illness.

Notice, however, that the Secretary of State's statutory duty under the Health Service Act is not to *provide* comprehensive access to all types of medical treatment, but rather to *promote* a comprehensive health service. In *Coughlan*,[118] Lord Woolf admitted that the duty to promote a comprehensive NHS was very far from a duty to *ensure* that the service was comprehensive:

When exercising his judgment [the Secretary of State] has to bear in mind the comprehensive service which he is under a duty to promote as set out in section 1 [of the National Health Service Act 1977]. However, as long as he pays due regard to that duty, the fact that the service will not be comprehensive does not mean that he is necessarily contravening either section 1 or section 3. The truth is that, while he has the duty to continue to promote a comprehensive free health service and he must never, in making a decision under section 3, disregard that duty, a comprehensive health service may never, for human, financial and other resource reasons, be achievable. Recent history has demonstrated that the pace of developments as to what is possible by way of medical treatment, coupled with the ever increasing expectations of the public, mean that the resources of the NHS are and are likely to continue, at least in the foreseeable future, to be insufficient to meet demand.

It is generally accepted that there will always be types of medical care which the NHS simply cannot afford to offer free of charge. Working adult patients have to pay prescription charges; patients must contribute to the costs of dental and optical care; counsellors and psychotherapists often charge for their services; cosmetic surgery is seldom available on the NHS. The Secretary of State's duty is therefore to ensure that the NHS provides an *adequate* service, whatever that might mean. Because, as Rudolf Klein has explained, 'the frontiers of adequacy have never been defined',[119] and adequacy remains a rather 'fuzzy and elastic notion',[120] it would be very difficult to *prove* that the Secretary of State was ever actually in breach of the duty to 'continue the promotion' of a comprehensive NHS.

The duties imposed upon the Secretary of State by the 1977 Act are clearly very general in nature, and involve the exercise of his discretion. Furthermore, the Secretary of State is entitled to delegate his duties under the Act to strategic health authorities, special health authorities and primary care trusts (PCTs) and NHS Trusts. But even if it was possible to prove that there had in fact been a breach of the duty to

---

[118] [2001] QB 213.
[119] Rudolf Klein 'Defining a Package of NHS Healthcare services: the case against' in Bill New (ed), *Rationing: Talk and Action in Health Care* (BMJ London 1997) 85–94, 85.
[120] Ibid, 85–94, 86.

promote a comprehensive health service, or to provide hospital accommodation or medical services, a patient would only be able to claim a remedy in tort if the court judged that parliament had intended that individuals should have a *private law* remedy for any breach of the duties in sections 1 and 3 of the Act. Under the 1977 Act there is no penalty or remedy prescribed for breach of the duties imposed upon the Secretary of State. And in the context of other social services, the House of Lords has confirmed that the purpose of legislation is to benefit society as a whole, rather than to offer remedies to individual citizens.[121]

A few cases, such as *Hincks* extracted below, have considered and rejected the possibility of an action for breach of the statutory duty in sections 1 and 3 of the National Health Service Act.

R v Secretary of State for Social Services, ex parte Hincks[122]

In 1971 plans were approved by the Secretary of State for additional orthopaedic services at a hospital but they could not be carried out as the money made available was less than the lowest tender. In 1978 the scheme was put off for ten years. The applicants, who had been on the waiting list for orthopaedic surgery for several years, sought a declaration that the Secretary of State was in breach of his duty under the National Health Service Act 1977 to 'provide throughout England and Wales to such extent as he considers necessary to meet all reasonable requirements (a) hospital accommodation . . . (c) medical services'.

Lord Denning MR

[A]s the discussion proceeded, it seemed to me inevitable that this provision had to be implied into s 3, 'to such extent as he considers necessary to meet all reasonable requirements such as can be provided within the resources available'. That seems to me to be a very necessary implication to put on that section, in accordance with the general legislative purpose. It cannot be supposed that the Secretary of State has to provide all the latest equipment. As Oliver LJ said in the course of argument, it cannot be supposed that the Secretary of State has to provide all the kidney machines which are asked for, or for all the new developments such as heart transplants in every case where people would benefit from them . . . It cannot be that the Secretary of State has a duty to provide everything that is asked for in the changed circumstances which have come about. That includes the numerous pills that people take nowadays: it cannot be said that he has to provide all these free for everybody.

I would like to read a few words from the judgment of Wien J, who gave a very comprehensive and good judgment in this matter. He said:

'The question remains: has there been a breach of duty? Counsel for the [Secretary of State] submits that section 3 does not impose an absolute duty. I agree. He further submits it does, by virtue of the discretion given, include an evaluation of financial resources or the lack of them is at the root of the whole problem in this case. If funds were unlimited, then of course regions and areas could go ahead and provide all sorts of services. But funds are not unlimited. The funds are voted by Parliament, and the health service has to do the best it can with the total allocation of financial resources.'

I agree with that approach of the judge in this case. . . . The Secretary of State says that he is doing the best he can with the financial resources available to him: and I do not think that he can be faulted in the matter.

---

[121] See, for example, the comments of Lord Browne-Wilkinson in *X v Bedfordshire CC* [1995] 3 All ER 353.
[122] (1980) 1 BMLR 93 (CA).

Bridge LJ

As the evidence shows and as we all know as a matter of common knowledge, the health service currently falls far short of what everyone would regard as the optimum desirable standard. That is very largely a situation which is brought about by lack of resources, lack of suitable equipment, lack of suitably qualified personnel, and above all lack of adequate finance.

I feel extremely sorry for the particular applicants in this case who have to wait a long time, not being emergency cases, for necessary surgery. They share that misfortune with thousands up and down the country. I only hope that they have not been encouraged to think that these proceedings offered any real prospects that this court could enhance the standards of the National Health Service, because any such encouragement would be based upon manifest illusion.

Similarly in *Re HIV Haemophiliac Litigation*,[123] Rougier J had held that it was plain that Parliament did not intend there to be a cause of action for any member of the public affected by breach of the duties in the National Health Service Act, and this was upheld by the Court of Appeal. Ralph Gibson LJ said:

For my part, I share the judge's view of the apparent nature of the duties imposed by the 1977 Act. They do not clearly demonstrate the intention of Parliament to impose a duty which is to be enforced by individual civil action.

In contrast, a rather more specific obligation is imposed on health authorities by section 117 of the Mental Health Act 1983:

Mental Health Act 1983

s.117(2) it shall be the duty of the district health authority . . . to provide . . . after-care services for any person to whom this section applies until such time as the district health authority . . . are satisfied that the person concerned is no longer in need of such services.

This is not a vague duty to *promote* aftercare, instead it is clear that there is a duty to *provide* appropriate services for patients who have been discharged from mental hospitals. Nevertheless, the courts have been reluctant to find health authorities liable to individual patients for failing to make appropriate provision. In *Clunis v Camden and Islington HA*,[124] a case we consider again in the next chapter, a patient, Christopher Clunis, had suffered from a severe mental disorder for several years. He had been discharged, but was plainly not being properly cared for in the community. Clunis had been waving screwdrivers and talking about devils, but was not taken to a place of safety, and a few hours later he killed Jonathan Zito in a London tube station. Following his conviction for manslaughter, Clunis brought an action against the health authority for failure to ensure he was assessed and treated, which would have resulted in hospital admission and prevented Zito's killing. The underlying purpose of his claim was to enable Jayne Zito, the murdered man's widow, to sue him for damages. The Court of Appeal rejected Clunis's claim on the grounds that it arose out of his commission of a criminal offence, and it would therefore be contrary to public policy to allow him to succeed. This would have been sufficient grounds for dismissing Clunis's application, but the Court of Appeal also rejected his claim that the health

---

123 (1990) 41 BMLR 171.   124 [1998] QB 978.

authority could be liable for their breach of their statutory duty under section 117(2) of the Mental Health Act 1983. Beldam LJ argued that:

the primary method of enforcement of the obligations under section 117 is by complaint to the Secretary of State. No doubt, too, a decision by the district health authority or the local social services authority under the section is liable to judicial review at the instance of a patient . . . [But] the wording of the section is not apposite to create a private law cause of action for failure to carry out the duties under the statute.

Clunis had further maintained that the health authority owed him a common law duty of care to provide aftercare services, but this was again rejected by the Court of Appeal. The Court held that a common law duty could not be superimposed upon a statutory duty in order to circumvent the statutory framework.

7. CONCLUSION

One thing is certain: there will never be sufficient funds devoted to the NHS to eliminate the need to make tough choices about the allocation of scarce resources. While opposition politicians may claim that reducing waste would enable them to achieve the holy grail of improving public services *and* cutting taxes, the evidence suggests that it will always be impossible to provide immediate access to optimum health care, free at the point of use, to every citizen. The important question is therefore not *whether* to ration treatment within the NHS, but *how* to do this in the fairest possible way. Priorities must be set at the macro level between different sorts of healthcare services, and at the micro level it may be necessary to choose which patient should be given a scarce resource, such as a bed in an intensive care unit. It is also important to work out who should be charged with making these difficult decisions: doctors, politicians, the general public, or a body such as NICE.

Fairness also demands that people who are affected by a funding decision should be able to challenge it, and hold the decision-maker to account. Does judicial review adequately fulfil this function? As we have seen, there has been a tradition of judicial deference to health authorities' funding decisions, much like the judicial deference to clinical judgement embodied in the *Bolam* test (considered in Chapter 3). In recent years, there appears to be evidence of a shift towards more proactive judicial scrutiny of funding choices within the NHS, but the judiciary exercises no control over the overarching Treasury decision about how much public money should be allocated to the NHS, which will ultimately dictate the extent to which trusts must ration their services.

In the UK we are, as all politicians know, very attached to the principle of universal access to free healthcare. But is this feasible? Certainly few of us are willing to pay much higher rates of income tax, and so rationing by dilution within the NHS has become inevitable. But is it also worth thinking about whether it would be preferable to confront more directly the possibility of a mixed healthcare system, in which patients sometimes have to contribute directly to the costs of their care? In relation to some treatments, such as dentistry, optometry and fertility treatment, such a system already exists. Extending this mixed health economy to acute care is, for anyone brought up in the UK, profoundly counter-intuitive, but in the coming years, we may have to acknowledge that the utopian post-war dream of a completely comprehensive and entirely free NHS is no longer possible, and that the best we can hope for is transparency and fairness in the allocation of scarce resources.

8. FURTHER READING

CRAIG, PAUL and SCHONBERG, SOREN, 'Substantive Legitimate Expectations after *Coughlan*' (2000) Public Law 684–701.

DAVIES, GARETH, 'Health and Efficiency: Community Law and National Health Systems in the Light of Müller-Fauré' (2004) 67 Modern Law Review 94–107.

HARRIS, JOHN, 'Double jeopardy and the use of QALYs in health care allocation' (1995) 21 Journal of Medical Ethics 144–50.

HARRIS, JOHN, 'The Age-Indifference Principle and Equality' (2005) 14 Cambridge Quarterly of Healthcare Ethics 93–9.

LIGHT, DONALD W, 'The real ethics of rationing' (1997) 315 British Medical Journal 112–15.

MAYNARD, ALAN, 'Ethics and health care "underfunding" ' (2001) 27 Journal of Medical Ethics 223–7.

NEW, BILL and GRAND, JULIAN LE, *Rationing in the NHS: Principles and Pragmatism* (King's Fund London 1996).

NEWDICK, CHRISTOPHER, *Who Should we Treat? Rights, Rationing and Resources in the NHS* 2nd edn (OUP Oxford 2005).

SYRETT, KEITH, 'Nice Work? Rationing, Review and the "Legitimacy Problem" in the new NHS' (2002) 10 Medical Law Review 1.

SYRETT, KEITH, 'Impotence or Importance? Judicial Review in an Era of Explicit NHS Rationing' (2004) 67 Modern Law Review 289–304.

3

MEDICAL MALPRACTICE

1. CENTRAL ISSUES

1. Actions for breach of contract are possible if a patient has paid for her medical treatment. In practice, however, contracts will generally contain an implied term that the doctor will exercise reasonable care and skill, and this is indistinguishable from the duty to take reasonable care in the tort of negligence.

2. Usually establishing that a doctor owes her patient a duty of care will be straightforward. More complex issues arise if a third party wishes to sue a doctor, perhaps because the doctor failed to prevent a patient from causing harm to others.

3. The standard of care to be expected of doctors has been dominated by the *Bolam* test, as modified by *Bolitho:* the doctor will not be guilty of negligence if she has acted in accord-

ance with a practice accepted as proper by a responsible body of medical opinion, provided that that opinion is capable of withstanding logical analysis.

4. Next the claimant must prove that the doctor's breach of duty caused her injuries. This is often particularly difficult in medical negligence cases because, by definition, the patient is usually *already* ill, and so there are immediately at least two possible causes of her poor health.

5. There is a great deal wrong with the clinical negligence system: it is costly and inefficient, and claimants are seldom successful. More importantly still, it fosters a 'blame culture', which makes learning from mistakes less likely.

2. INTRODUCTION

In this chapter, we consider the law's response to medical treatment which has gone wrong. Conventionally, it has been assumed that people who have been injured as a result of inadequate medical treatment will want to seek financial compensation. In reality, evidence appears to suggest that an explanation, an apology, and reassurance that the incident will not be repeated are much more important to patients than monetary redress. In one study of people affected by medical injuries, 60 per cent wanted an apology, explanation or inquiry into the cause of the incident, only 11 per cent thought that financial compensation was the most appropriate remedy.[1]

Despite failing to offer patients their preferred remedies, the volume of clinical negligence cases has increased dramatically over the last thirty years. Where treatment is provided privately, there will be a contract between the health care provider and the

---

[1] *Making Amends: A consultation paper setting out proposals for reforming the approach to clinical negligence in the NHS* (DH 2003) 75.

patient, and so an action for breach of contract may be possible. There is no contract between NHS patients and their doctors, and so in the public sector, disgruntled patients will have to sue in tort. In practice, however, there is little difference between these two actions. In both cases, the courts will ask whether the doctor has breached her duty of care, and whether that breach caused the claimant's loss.

We begin this chapter by looking briefly at the possibility of an action for breach of contract, before exploring the different stages involved in a clinical negligence claim. Tort and contract are not the only possible responses to inadequate medical treatment, and mention is also made of the NHS complaints system; the possibility of disciplinary action by the General Medical Council (GMC); and the circumstances in which a doctor might be prosecuted for gross negligence.

In recent years, there has been increasing criticism of the way in which medical mishaps are dealt with. The clinical negligence system costs the NHS a great deal of money but arguably works to hamper rather than promote improved patient care. By fostering a 'blame culture' it offers a disincentive to health care workers to own up to adverse events and near-misses, making learning from mistakes less likely. It also fails to provide patients with the apologies and explanations which are so important to them. In the last sections of this chapter, we look at these criticisms in detail, and we evaluate the proposed reforms of the clinical negligence system.

In this chapter, we will focus upon *doctor's* mistakes, rather than those of other healthcare workers. This is partly because doctors are principally responsible for patient care, and are therefore also responsible for their negligent choices and actions, and partly because historically the bulk of litigation has been against the medical profession, and so there is comparatively little case law addressing nurses' duties of care.

It should also be noted that two 'special cases' in the tort of negligence are dealt with elsewhere in this book. The question of liability for failing to provide sufficient information to patients, and the possibility of liability for occurrences before birth, are covered in Chapters 5 and 11 respectively. Of course the basic principles of negligence which are the subject of this chapter are equally applicable in these cases, but because each raises a number of distinctive questions, they warrant separate discussion.

3. BREACH OF CONTRACT

If health care is provided in the private sector, the patient will have a contract with her doctor and/or with the clinic or hospital where she receives treatment. The nature of these contracts varies. For example, a patient may make an agreement directly with a doctor, who will then arrange for the patient's admission, or alternatively the patient's agreement may be made with the hospital, which then employs a doctor to provide the necessary services. The terms of contracts for private health care will also differ. Some contracts contain terms naming a specific individual as the treating doctor. Breach of this sort of contractual term could give rise to an action for breach of contract.

Contracts for private health care will also contain terms which are implied by statute. An example might be the supply of medical devices, which must—under sections 4 and 9 of the Supply of Goods and Services Act 1982—be of satisfactory quality and fit for their purpose. Statutory limits on the use of exclusion clauses also apply. Under section 2(1) of the Unfair Contract Terms Act 1977, it is not possible to exclude or restrict liability for death or personal injury caused by negligence.

It is possible, if unlikely, that a contract could contain an express term guaranteeing the outcome of the procedure. Few doctors would ever choose to give such a warranty, however, and it has become clear that the courts will be very slow to imply such a term into a contract for healthcare services. The point was considered by the Court of Appeal in *Eyre v Measday*:

Eyre v Measday[2]

Mrs Eyre (the plaintiff) underwent a private sterilization operation carried out by the defendant gynaecologist, who had stated that the operation 'must be regarded as a permanent procedure'. A year later, Mrs Eyre became pregnant and gave birth to a child. She brought an action against the defendant for damages for breach of contract. The judge dismissed her claim and she appealed unsuccessfully to the Court of Appeal.

Slade LJ

I think there is no doubt that the plaintiff would have been entitled reasonably to assume that the defendant was warranting that the operation would be performed with reasonable care and skill. . . . The contract did, in my opinion, include an implied warranty of that nature. However, that inference on its own does not enable the plaintiff to succeed in the present case. She has to go further. She has to suggest, and it is suggested on her behalf, that the defendant, by necessary implication, committed himself to an unqualified guarantee as to the success of the particular operation proposed, in achieving its purpose of sterilising her, even though he were to exercise all due care and skill in performing it. The suggestion is that the guarantee went beyond due care and skill and extended to an unqualified warranty that the plaintiff would be absolutely sterile. . . .

But, in my opinion, in the absence of any express warranty, the court should be slow to imply against a medical man an unqualified warranty as to the results of an intended operation, for the very simple reason that, objectively speaking, it is most unlikely that a responsible medical man would intend to give a warranty of this nature. Of course, objectively speaking, it is likely that he would give a guarantee that he would do what he had undertaken to do with reasonable care and skill but it is quite another matter to say that he has committed himself to the extent suggested in the present case. . . .

I am afraid that, in my view, if they had wanted a guarantee of the nature which they now assert, they should have specifically asked for it.

This was followed a year later by the Court of Appeal in *Thake v Maurice*,[3] another sterilization case, in which Neill LJ stated,

I do not consider that a reasonable person would have expected a responsible medical man to be intending to give a guarantee. Medicine, though a highly skilled profession, is not, and is not generally regarded as being, an exact science. The reasonable man would have expected the defendant to exercise all the proper skill and care of a surgeon in that speciality he would not in my view have expected the defendant to give a guarantee of 100% success.

---

[2] [1986] 1 All ER 488.   [3] [1986] QB 644.

The Court of Appeal in *Thake* did accept that there might be some circumstances in which a guarantee of success might reasonably be inferred: Nourse LJ gave the example of an operation to amputate a limb. A patient who goes into hospital to have their right leg amputated could reasonably expect that the operation will in fact remove their right leg. But such cases are likely to be extremely rare, and much more commonly, a reasonable person could not expect a doctor to guarantee a successful outcome.

Note that in both *Eyre v Measday* and *Thake v Maurice* the Court of Appeal considered that the contract did contain an implied term guaranteeing that the doctor would exercise reasonable care and skill. In practice, this is indistinguishable from the duty to take reasonable care in the tort of negligence, owed by all doctors to their patients. Because the vast majority of malpractice claims are brought in negligence, rather than for breach of contract, it is within our discussion of clinical negligence actions that we flesh out what might be meant by 'reasonable care and skill'. It should, however, be noted that the courts would be guided by similar considerations when considering cases for breach of a contract's implied term warranting that the doctor will exercise reasonable care.

As private health care becomes more common, and as patients increasingly see themselves as consumers exercising choice, rather than as grateful recipients of the NHS's beneficence, might contract have a more central role to play in framing the doctor–patient relationship? In the next extract, Harvey Teff critically evaluates some of the arguments for greater emphasis upon contractual ordering in the medical context.

Harvey Teff[4]

In certain respects, the relationship between doctor and patient does have more affinity with contract than with tort . . . To begin with, it is a *relationship*. Medical encounters differ from stock situations in tort in that the parties are seldom total strangers to one another prior to the event precipitating litigation. There is, in principle, scope for negotiation about the terms of the arrangements which they make; the doctor is paid for having undertaken to provide professional services to the patient . . .

[A]s the public service ethic of the NHS progressively gives way to a more commercial one, health care is more readily perceived as a commodity and its provision as a matter of private ordering. The more this altered perception takes root, the stronger might appear to be the case for a contractual framework, with terms designed by the parties, in place of externally imposed criteria, largely shaped by the medical profession via the *Bolam* . . . approach. If the doctor–patient relationship is truly envisaged as consensual and especially if patient autonomy is to be taken seriously, what could be more natural, mutually acceptable, and effective than for the parties to frame the terms of engagement to suit individual circumstances? . . .

Under a conception of medicine as trade, all patients would be entitled to negotiate for a higher standard of treatment than that required under tort law—as is already in principle possible with private medicine—or indeed to opt for a lower one, through a waiver of tort rights and the dismantling of statutory protections . . .

The courts have so far held the line on familiar public policy grounds. Maintenance of high

[4] *Reasonable Care: Legal Perspectives on the Doctor–Patient Relationship* (Oxford Clarendon Press 1994) 164–5, 167, 169.

standards in health care is seen as an overriding need, not to be jeopardized by allowing providers to exercise their bargaining power to the detriment of relatively vulnerable and inadequately informed patients. Such a change of regime could, it is argued, easily lead to a widespread diminution of standards, contrary to the interests of patients and difficult to reconcile with the ethical obligations of doctors . . .

Freedom of contract is of little avail if the doctor nearly always has a better understanding of the medical indications and knows more about the nature and quality of proposed treatment and available options. . . .

If the absence of an arm's length relationship should make us question private contractual ordering even for fully competent adult patients, it would . . . seem wholly misconceived for the innumerable treatment decisions that have to be made for the very young, the geriatric and the mentally disturbed.

4. NEGLIGENCE

In order to succeed in an action in negligence, the claimant must establish

(a) that she is owed a duty of care by the defendant (this will usually be the doctor who is treating the patient, and her employer will be vicariously liable for her negligence)

(b) that the defendant breached that duty by failing to exercise reasonable care

(c) that the breach of duty caused the claimant's injuries, and that those injuries are not too remote.

Finally, there are a number of defences which may be available to the defendant.

Let us examine each of these stages in turn.

(a) THE EXISTENCE OF A DUTY OF CARE

The existence of a duty of care within the doctor–patient (or nurse–patient) relationship can generally be taken for granted. It is a well-established duty situation, and it is unimaginable that a doctor, or other health care worker, who had made a mistake during medical treatment would attempt to argue that she did not owe her patient a duty of care. The duty will be to exercise reasonable care and skill in diagnosis, advice and treatment. Provided that the doctor committed the tort in the course of her employment—which will invariably be the case in clinical negligence cases—her employer (the NHS trust) will be vicariously liable for her negligence. In three situations, however, the question of the existence of a duty of care becomes slightly more complicated.

(1) WHEN DOES THE DOCTOR–PATIENT RELATIONSHIP COME INTO BEING?

Usually of course the existence of a doctor–patient relationship will be obvious. But there might be times when the question of whether a particular individual was in fact the doctor's patient at the relevant time is not straightforward. Because a doctor is under no obligation to treat a 'stranger', it is important to know when the transition from 'stranger' to 'patient' takes place. The common law position is that a duty of care is imposed upon the doctor once she has *assumed responsibility* for the patient's care.

For GPs, it might be said that an individual becomes their patient under the NHS (Choice of Medical Practitioner) Regulations 1998 as soon as she is registered on their list,[5] however the duty of care will generally arise only when the doctor knows of the patient's need for medical services. For some patients, such as those over the age of 75, who must be offered an annual consultation, the doctor's duty of care might extend to seeking out the patient, but normally it is only when the patient requests the doctor's assistance that the duty of care comes into being.

In hospitals, a doctor–patient relationship exists once the doctor has undertaken to provide medical services to the patient. In a casualty department, the duty may arise as soon as the patient presents herself for treatment, before she is actually seen by a doctor. This issue arose in *Barnett v Chelsea and Kensington Hospital Management Committee*:

Barnett v Chelsea and Kensington Hospital Management Committee[6]

After drinking tea later discovered to have contained arsenic, three nightwatchmen had started vomiting and attended the casualty department of the defendant's hospital. The nurse telephoned the casualty officer, Dr Banerjee, who told her to tell them to go home and call their own doctors. He did not see the men, who died hours later from arsenic poisoning. Despite not having seen the men, Nield J held that Dr Banerjee had undertaken to exercise reasonable care and did owe them a duty of care, which he had breached by failing to examine them himself. A widow of one of the men sued in negligence. Nield J found that there was a duty of care. (Later in this chapter we will see that her action failed on the question of causation.)

Nield J

In my judgment, there was here such a close and direct relationship between the hospital and the watchmen that there was imposed on the hospital a duty of care which they owed to the watchmen. Thus I have no doubt that Nurse Corbett and Dr. Banerjee were under a duty to the deceased to exercise that skill and care which is to be expected of persons in such positions acting reasonably. . . .

Without doubt Dr. Banerjee should have seen and examined the deceased. His failure to do either cannot be described as an excusable error as has been submitted, it was negligence. It is unfortunate that Dr. Banerjee was himself at the time a tired and unwell doctor, but there was no-one else to do that which it was his duty to do. Having examined the deceased I think that the first and provisional diagnosis would have been one of food poisoning.

(2) WHO ELSE MIGHT OWE PRIMARY DUTIES OF CARE TO PATIENTS?

In addition to being vicariously liable for its employees' negligence, might the health authority or NHS trust owe a primary duty of care to patients to ensure that they receive adequate treatment? The Court of Appeal in *Wisher v Essex AHA*,[7] a case we consider in more detail below at pp. 136–7, clearly thought it was possible for a health authority to owe patients a primary, non-delegable duty of care to provide properly skilled medical staff, and an adequately equipped hospital.

[5] SI 1992/635. [6] [1969] 1 QB 428. [7] [1986] 3 All ER 801.

Sir Nicolas Browne-Wilkinson VC

In my judgment, a health authority which so conducts its hospital that it fails to provide doctors of sufficient skill and experience to give the treatment offered at the hospital may be directly liable in negligence to the patient. Although we were told in argument that no case has ever been decided on this ground and that it is not the practice to formulate claims in this way, I can see no reason why, in principle, the health authority should not be so liable if its organisation is at fault . . .

Claims against a health authority that it has itself been directly negligent, as opposed to vicariously liable for the negligence of its doctors, will, of course, raise awkward questions. To what extent should the authority be held liable if (eg in the use of junior housemen) it is only adopting a practice hallowed by tradition? Should the authority be liable if it demonstrates that, due to the financial stringency under which it operates, it cannot afford to fill the posts with those possessing the necessary experience? But, in my judgment, the law should not be distorted by making findings of personal fault against individual doctors who are, in truth, not at fault in order to avoid such questions. To do so would be to cloud the real issues which arise.

Glidewell LJ

I agree with Sir Nicolas Browne-Wilkinson V-C that there seems to be no reason in principle why, in a suitable case different on its facts from this, a hospital management committee should not be held directly liable in negligence for failing to provide sufficient qualified and competent medical staff.

One problem with this primary duty is that, as we saw in the previous chapter, NHS trusts inevitably operate with scarce resources: there is probably always more that could be done to improve the standard of healthcare services. While courts may be prepared to impose some minimum standard of care, they are generally reluctant to interfere with policy decisions about the allocation of limited resources. In *Bull v Devon AHA* we can see the Court of Appeal attempting to draw a distinction between the hospital's duty to provide minimally adequate treatment, for which it could be liable in negligence, and its freedom to choose how to organize its services within the limited funds available to it.

Bull v Devon AHA[8]

Mrs Bull brought an action against Devon Health Authority on behalf of her severely handicapped son, one of twins, who had been injured as a result of a delay in the registrar's arrival during childbirth. The system for urgently summoning an obstetrician had broken down, and there was a delay of about an hour before the registrar arrived. The health authority argued that such a delay was unavoidable because the hospital operated on two sites so there would inevitably be times when doctors were needed on both. The Court of Appeal rejected this, and held that the system had failed to provide an acceptable level of care.

Dillon LJ

We have had a certain amount of discussion in the course of the argument as to whether the law should impose, or a patient should have the right to expect, the same standard of care and treatment from a local district hospital such as the defendant's hospital in the present case as from a 'centre of excellence'—a major teaching hospital in London or Oxbridge or a large modern hospital in a large city. Obviously, there are highly specialised medical services which a district hospital does not have the equipment to provide and does not hold itself out as ready to provide.

---

[8] [1993] 4 Med LR 117 (CA).

But this case is not about highly specialised services like that. The Exeter City Hospital provides a maternity service for expectant mothers, and any hospital which provides such a service ought to be able to cope with the not particularly out of the way case of a healthy young mother in somewhat premature labour with twins. . . .

In my judgment, the plaintiff has succeeded in proving, by the ordinary civil standards of proof, that the failure to provide for Mrs Bull the prompt attendance she needed was attributable to the negligence of the defendants in implementing an unreliable and essentially unsatisfactory system for calling the registrar.

So while Mrs Bull was not entitled to expect that an obstetrician would be available immediately, waiting for an hour fell below the minimum standard of care that the hospital were under a duty to provide. If, say, the registrar had been bleeped and arrived within 15 minutes, Mrs Bull's action would probably have failed.

In principle then, there will be a non-delegable duty on health authorities to provide adequate treatment, but usually it will be more straightforward to find the health authority liable through its vicarious liability for an employee's negligence, where difficult distinctions between operational and policy decisions do not arise.

The primary duty to provide adequate treatment might be more significant, however, where, as is increasingly common, a patient's treatment has been contracted out to a private hospital. In such cases, the NHS trust will continue to be liable for a failure to arrange adequate care, even though it is not the doctors' employer. Of course the NHS trust will normally have made an arrangement with the private hospital to indemnify them against any liability, but the patient herself will be able to sue the NHS trust.

It is not just health authorities who might owe primary duties of care to patients. In *Re HIV Haemophiliac Litigation*[9] haemophiliac patients who had suffered damage after transfusion with HIV-contaminated blood products brought an action against, among others, the Secretary of State for Health for negligence in purchasing blood from America; for failing to heat-treat blood; and for failing to warn patients of the risks of contamination. The defendant argued first that there was not a relationship of sufficient proximity between these claimants and the Secretary of State because they were not individually identifiable; and secondly, that it would not be just and reasonable to impose a duty of care, because the allocation of resources by the Secretary of State was not justiciable in an action in negligence. Because the Secretary of State has considerable discretion in exercising his duties, judicial review would normally be more appropriate than an action in negligence. Nevertheless, the Court of Appeal said that the case could proceed to trial because there was at least an arguable case. Bingham LJ held that:

where, as here, foreseeability by a defendant of severe personal injury to a person such as the plaintiff is shown, and the existence of a proximate relationship between plaintiff and defendant is accepted, the plaintiff is well on his way to establishing the existence of a duty of care. He may still fail to do so if it is held that imposition of such a duty on the defendant would not in all the circumstances be just and reasonable, but it is by no means clear to me at this preliminary stage that the department's submissions on that aspect must prevail.

[9] [1990] NLJR 1349 962.

The case was then settled by the Government, and so did not proceed to a full hearing. Usually, it will be very difficult to argue that the Secretary of State for Health owed individual patients a duty of care. Establishing the requisite proximity will often be impossible, as we can see from the following case.

Danns v Department of Health[10]

Mrs Danns had become pregnant seven years after Mr Danns had undergone an apparently successful vasectomy in 1983. A study published in the *British Medical Journal* in 1984 had indicated that there was a risk of spontaneous reversal many years after a vasectomy, and there-after it became normal practice to warn patients of this risk. The Danns brought an action against the Department of Health for failure to take steps to disseminate this information to the 1.5 million people estimated to be relying upon pre-1984 vasectomies as their only method of birth control. The Court of Appeal found that the Department of Health did not owe Mr and Mrs Danns a duty of care.

Roch LJ

[T]he Department did not owe the plaintiff a duty at common law to take reasonable care, for the reason that there did not exist as between the plaintiffs and the defendants that degree of the proximity which the law requires. The plaintiffs were not the defendants' neighbours. . . . I agree with the Judge when . . . he said:

> Yet further, I would also hold that requirements of fairness, justice and reasonableness do not require the Department to give to the public at large the warnings contended for by the plaintiffs in this action.

(3) COULD HEALTHCARE WORKERS EVER OWE NON-PATIENTS A DUTY OF CARE?

Usually of course the only person likely to be injured or to suffer loss if a doctor or other healthcare worker makes a mistake is the patient herself, and, as we have seen, the existence of a duty of care between doctor and patient will usually be unproblem-atic. But could a third party ever be owed a duty of care by a healthcare professional? In the next sections, we highlight four different scenarios in which this question might arise:

- Wrongful conception
- Psychiatric injury
- Failure to prevent the patient from causing harm
- Medical examinations

(a) 'Wrongful conception'

Where a sterilization operation has been carried out negligently, or a patient has been given negligent advice about its success, it is, as we see in Chapter 11, possible to recover damages in tort for the pain and discomfort associated with pregnancy and childbirth. These are, of course, suffered only by women. Where a man's sterilization has failed, the 'damage' is therefore suffered not by the patient himself, but by a third

---

[10] [1998] PIQR P226.

party. She will generally only be able to recover damages if she was within the doctor's contemplation at the time of the operation, because she was the patient's wife or partner. In *McFarlane v Tayside Health Board*,[11] a case we consider in detail in Chapter 11, the patient was married, and not only was his wife's reliance upon the assurances that sterility had been achieved foreseeable, but also she was in a sufficiently proximate relationship with her husband's doctors. In contrast, in *Goodwill v BPAS*,[12] the court decided that a doctor carrying out a vasectomy does not owe a duty to his patient's *future* sexual partners.

Goodwill v BPAS[13]

The patient had had a vasectomy organized by the defendants. He had been told that the operation had been successful, and that he no longer needed to use contraception. Three years later he met the claimant and had sex with her, having told her about his vasectomy. She had also consulted her doctor who assured her there was little chance of her becoming pregnant. Unfortunately the sterilization operation had not in fact succeeded and Ms Goodwill became pregnant, and subsequently gave birth to a daughter. She brought an action against the defendants claiming damages for loss of income; the expenses of pregnancy and childbirth; and the cost of raising her daughter.

Peter Gibson LJ

The defendants were not in a sufficient or any special relationship with the plaintiff such as gives rise to a duty of care. I cannot see that it can properly be said of the defendants that they voluntarily assumed responsibility to the plaintiff when giving advice to Mr MacKinlay. At that time they had no knowledge of her, she was not an existing sexual partner of Mr MacKinlay but was merely, like any other woman in the world, a potential future sexual partner of his, that is to say a member of an indeterminately large class of females who might have sexual relations with Mr MacKinlay during his lifetime.

(b) Psychiatric injury

A different sort of case in which a non-patient might suffer injury is where a patient's relative suffers psychiatric injury, such as post traumatic stress disorder (PTSD), as a result of witnessing her negligent medical treatment. In such cases, the third party is plainly a secondary victim, and so the limiting principles developed in cases such as *Alcock v Chief Constable of South Yorkshire*[14] and *White v Chief Constable of South Yorkshire*[15] apply. In short, the claimant must have a close relationship with the victim; she must be close in time and space to the incident; she must witness it, or its immediate aftermath, with her unaided senses; and she must suffer a recognizable psychiatric illness as a result.[16]

In *Sion v Hampstead Health Authority*,[17] a father had stayed in hospital with his son who had been injured in a motor-cycle accident. His son lapsed into a coma and died fourteen days later. The father alleged that the hospital treating him had been negligent, and claimed damages for his own psychiatric illness. His claim was dismissed

---

[11] [2000] 2 AC 59.   [12] [1996] 2 All ER 161.   [13] [1996] 2 All ER 161.
[14] [1992] 1 AC 310.   [15] [1999] 2 AC 455.
[16] Both *Alcock* and *White* arose out the Hillsborough stadium disaster in 1989, and involved claims brought by friends or relatives (*Alcock*) and policemen (*White*).
[17] *The Times* 10 June 1994.

by the Court of Appeal on the grounds that, as Staughton LJ explained, there had been

no sudden appreciation by sight or sound of a horrifying event. On the contrary, the report describes a process continuing for some time, from first arrival at the hospital to the appreciation of medical negligence after the inquest. In particular, the son's death when it occurred was not surprising but expected.

Similarly in *Taylor v Somerset Health Authority*, Auld J found that there had not been a sufficiently traumatic 'event' to bring the deceased's wife's visit to the mortuary within the 'immediate aftermath' of his death:

Taylor v Somerset Health Authority[18]
Mrs Taylor's husband had had a heart attack and died at work. His death was the result of the health authority's admitted negligence in failing to diagnose his serious heart disease. She attended the hospital mortuary within an hour of the death to view his body in order to satisfy her disbelief that he was in fact dead. Mrs Taylor sought damages for the psychiatric illness she claimed that she had suffered as a result.

Auld J
The immediate aftermath extension is one which has been introduced as an exception to the general principle established in accident cases that a plaintiff can only recover damages for psychiatric injury when the accident and the primary injury or death caused by it occurred within his sight or hearing. There are two notions implicit in this exception cautiously introduced and cautiously continued by the House of Lords. They are of:

(1) an external, traumatic, event caused by the defendant's breach of duty which immediately causes some person injury or death; and

(2) a perception by the plaintiff of the event as it happens, normally by his presence at the scene, or exposure to the scene and/or to the primary victim so shortly afterwards that the shock of the event as well as of its consequence is brought home to him.

There was no such event here other than the final consequence of Mr Taylor's progressively deteriorating heart condition. . . . In my judgment, his death at work and the subsequent transference of his body to the hospital where Mrs Taylor was informed of what had happened and where she saw the body do not constitute such an event. . . .

Here, the main purpose of Mrs Taylor's visit to the mortuary was to confirm or otherwise the information that she had received from the doctor that her husband was dead. Apart from the obvious shock to her of the sight of his dead body, it bore no marks or signs to her of the sort that would have conjured up for her the circumstances of his fatal attack. . . . In my view, the fact that Mrs Taylor's main purpose in viewing her husband's body in the mortuary was to settle her disbelief as to his reported death is not capable of being part of any possible immediate aftermath in the circumstances of this case.

In contrast, in *Tredget and Tredget v Bexley HA*,[19] a mother and father succeeded in an action for psychiatric injury suffered as a result of their baby's traumatic delivery and his death within forty-eight hours. Judge White explained:

Although lasting for over 48 hours from the onset of labour to the death, this effectively was one

---

[18] (1993) 16 BMLR 63.   [19] [1994] 5 Med LR 178.

event. Of course, it was not in the nature of an immediate catastrophe which lasts only a few seconds—panic in a stadium or a motor accident—but one just as traumatic for those immediately involved as participants as each of the parents were.

The law should be, and in my judgment is, 'fluid enough' not simply to recognise one type of traumatic event and to shut its eyes to another.

More recently, in *North Glamorgan NHS Trust v Walters*, a mother who witnessed her baby's distressing final 36 hours was said to have suffered the requisite 'shock'.

North Glamorgan NHS Trust v Walters[20]

The claimant, Ms Walters, was with her baby in hospital when he suffered a fit: he was covered in blood and his body was stiff. She was assured that it was very unlikely that he had suffered any serious damage. In fact he had irreparable brain damage, and died thirty-six hours later, after life-support was withdrawn. The hospital admitted that the child's death was the result of negligence. The claimant successfully sued for damages for her pathological grief reaction, and the defendant's appeal to the Court of Appeal was dismissed.

Ward LJ

In my judgment on the facts of this case there was an inexorable progression from the moment when the fit occurred as a result of the failure of the hospital properly to diagnose and then to treat the baby, the fit causing the brain damage which shortly thereafter made termination of this child's life inevitable and the dreadful climax when the child died in her arms. It is a seamless tale with an obvious beginning and an equally obvious end. It was played out over a period of 36 hours, which for her both at the time and as subsequently recollected was undoubtedly one drawn-out experience. . . .

This is not a case of the gradual dawning of realisation that her child's life had been put in danger by the defendant's negligence. A consequence of that negligence was that the child was seized with convulsion. She was there witnessing the effect of that damage to her child. The necessary proximity in space and time is satisfied. The assault on her nervous system had begun and she reeled under successive blows as each was delivered. It comes as no surprise to me that when her new baby was ill she should suffer the flashbacks of 36 horrendous hours which wreaked havoc upon her mind.

And in one of the most strikingly 'claimant friendly' judgments in recent years, *Frogatt v Chesterfield and North Derbyshire Royal Hospital NHS Trust*,[21] Forbes J allowed a patient's husband and son to recover damages for the psychiatric conditions they had developed after discovering that she had had an unnecessary mastectomy following negligent misdiagnosis of breast cancer: the shocking 'events' were (in the case of the husband) seeing his wife naked, and (in the case of the son) overhearing a telephone conversation:

Forbes J

In Mr Froggatt's case, his sudden appreciation of the trauma that had been suffered by Mrs Froggatt as the result of the Defendant's negligence occurred when he saw her undressed for the first time after the mastectomy. He was quite unprepared for what he saw and he was profoundly and lastingly shocked by it. As a result, his sleep became fitful, he became generally agitated and he suffered an adjustment disorder that lasted for about one and a half years. . . .

---

[20] [2002] EWCA Civ 1792, [2003] PIQR 232.   [21] [2002] All ER (D) 218.

In Dane's case, the sudden appreciation came as a result of overhearing his mother's telephone conversation and his immediate belief, based on the negligent advice that had been given to his mother and that she felt obliged to repeat to him, that she had cancer and was likely to die. He was completely unprepared for such a shock and, as a result, he suffered a moderate Post Traumatic Stress Disorder.

In the next extract, Paula Case discusses some of the special problems facing relatives seeking to claim for psychiatric illnesses triggered by their relatives' negligent medical treatment.

Paula Case[22]

Although relatives affected by an iatrogenic death in the family may (or may not) suffer any one of a number of psychiatric disorders, there are particular difficulties for claimants where the major triggering factor of the illness is regarded as the experience of bereavement, as opposed to witnessing a horrific external event which causes bereavement. The relative is unlikely to witness at first hand the 'sudden shocking event' currently required by English law as, unlike the typical accident environment, the hospital is a highly controlled space where the family's view of tragedy is often occluded by the intervention of hospital personnel . . .

Having demonstrated a recognised psychiatric illness, the relative of the MAV [medical accident victim], as a secondary victim, must then prove that the psychiatric harm was a foreseeable result of the negligence . . . In the cases under discussion the defendant will likely be an NHS trust or clinician, and so presumably will be possessed of greater knowledge of the cause and effect of psychiatric symptoms than the 'educated layman'. This fact, combined with the visibility of the patient's family in the hospital environment, make it tempting to assume that the foreseeability of psychiatric harm following the unnecessary death in hospital of a relative could readily be established.

The claimant will generally not witness the moment of their relative's demise and may rely on viewing the deceased's body after death as the 'shocking event' which caused the harm. Where the relative is absent during the events which caused the death of the deceased, an attempt to rely on identification of the body after death as the 'shocking event' is likely to fail . . . In *Alcock*, their Lordships agreed that secondary victims must demonstrate that their injury be caused by a 'sudden appreciation by sight or sound of a horrifying event which violently agitates the mind'.

The sudden shocking event requirement presents particular problems in hospital cases, because it might be argued by defendants that the 'suddenness' of the shocking event is negated by the reasons that brought the MAV to hospital. In other words, the probability of deterioration is known merely by the fact that the MAV was in hospital . . .

Implicit in the sudden shocking event condition is the requirement of a single event triggering the harm, as opposed to the cumulative onslaught of traumatic circumstances. The rejection of claims on the basis that the harm was caused by the cumulative effect of events and the gradual realisation of the defendant's wrong, has also been a particular problem in cases pertaining to alleged medical negligence.

Psychiatric injury might also be caused to non-patients by the communication of traumatic information. It would be difficult to fit this within the *Alcock* criteria, on the grounds that the claimant is supposed to have witnessed the shocking event with her unaided senses, as opposed to just being told about it. However, if information is

[22] 'Secondary Iatrogenic Harm: Claims for Psychiatric Damage Following a Death Caused by Medical Error' (2004) 67 Modern Law Review 561–87, 562, 570–1, 573–4.

communicated negligently, might it be possible for a relative to claim that she is a primary victim, and hence that the distinction between physical and psychiatric injury is less important?

At first sight, this might seem improbable, given that it has generally been assumed that primary victims must have been *physically* endangered by the defendant's negligence. In *Page v Smith*,[23] for example, Lord Lloyd said that to be a primary victim, the claimant had to be 'within the range of foreseeable physical injury'. A different approach was, however, adopted in *Farrell v Avon HA*.[24] When the claimant arrived at the hospital following the birth of his son, he was wrongly informed that his baby had died, and was given a dead baby to hold for 20 minutes. He was then told that there had been a mistake, and his son was in fact alive and well. Bursell J held that the claimant was a primary victim because he was directly involved in the traumatic incident, and he was therefore able to recover for his PTSD.

In contrast, in *Powell v Boldaz*[25] the claimants said that they had suffered psychiatric injury as a result of false information being provided to them after their son's negligent treatment and subsequent death. The Court of Appeal dismissed their claim on the grounds that their son's doctors could not owe his parents a duty of care because they had not been called upon to treat them as patients.

Stuart Smith LJ

I propose to consider, first, whether a sufficient relationship of proximity existed. It must be appreciated that although the plaintiffs were patients of the defendants in the sense that they were on their register, the only patient who was seeking medical advice and treatment was Robert. It was to him that the defendants owed a duty of care. The discharge of that duty in the case of a young child will often involve giving advice and instruction to the parents so that they can administer the appropriate medication, observe relevant symptoms and seek further medical assistance if need be. In giving such advice, the doctor obviously owes a duty to be careful. But the duty is owed to the child, not to the parents. . . .

After the death, the defendants may owe the plaintiffs a duty of care; but this depends upon whether they are called upon, or undertake, to treat them as patients. . . .

I do not think that a doctor who has been treating a patient who has died, who tells relatives what has happened, thereby undertakes the doctor–patient relationship towards the relatives. It is a situation that calls for sensitivity, tact and discretion. But the mere fact that the communicator is a doctor, does not, without more, mean that he undertakes the doctor–patient relationship. . . .

If the relatives concerned happen to be on the doctor's register as patients, the position, in my judgment, is no different.

With respect, the authority of *Powell* is open to question since, as we have seen in *Farrell* and *Frogatt*, it would not appear to be true that a doctor can owe a duty of care to individuals *only* if she has been called upon, or has undertaken to treat them. Here the question was whether the defendants owed a duty not to harm the claimants, and so the question of whether they were also under a duty to *treat* the claimants was not, strictly speaking, relevant.

---

[23] [1996] AC 155.   [24] [2001] Lloyd's Rep Med 458.   [25] [1998] Lloyd's Rep Med 116 CA.

(c) Failure to prevent the patient causing harm

There are a number of ways in which patients who are not offered proper advice or treatment might pose a risk to others. First, if a doctor knows that her patient is unfit to drive, she would almost certainly be under a duty to advise her of the dangers of driving. Should the doctor fail to advise such a patient not to drive, a third party might be injured as a result. Secondly, patients with infectious or contagious diseases clearly pose a risk to third parties, and hence a doctor's negligent failure to diagnose her patient's condition, or to offer her appropriate advice or treatment might put others at risk. Thirdly, if a doctor does not section an obviously dangerous psychiatric patient (see further Chapter 7), it is foreseeable that a third party might be attacked. In all these situations, could a doctor owe these foreseeably injured non-patients a duty of care?

It is important to remember that in such cases the doctor has not directly *caused* the third party's injury, rather she would be being sued for an omission, or a failure to prevent harm from occurring. As a result, the three stage test from *Caparo v Dickman*[26] applies: (1) the claimant's injury must be foreseeable; (2) there must be a proximate relationship between the claimant and the doctor; and (3) the imposition of a duty must be fair, just and reasonable in all the circumstances. While it might be relatively straightforward to establish foreseeability, proving that there is a sufficient relationship of proximity and that imposing a duty of care would be fair, just and reasonable will often be much more problematic.

The question of a duty to protect a member of the public against a dangerous psychiatric patient arose in *Palmer v Tees Health Authority*.[27]

Palmer v Tees Health Authority[28]

In 1994 a man called Armstrong, with a long history of psychiatric problems, abducted, sexually assaulted and murdered Rosie Palmer, who was four years old. The claimant (Rosie's mother) claimed that the defendants failed to diagnose that there was a real, substantial and foreseeable risk of Armstrong committing serious sexual offences against children, and as a result they failed to provide him with adequate treatment. She argued that the defendants should therefore be liable for Rosie's death, and for her own post-traumatic stress disorder and pathological grief reaction. It was not disputed that the injuries to Rosie and her mother were arguably foreseeable; but the judge held that there was no sufficient proximity and that it was not fair, just and reasonable to impose a duty of care upon the defendants. Her appeal was dismissed.

Stuart-Smith LJ

An additional reason why in my judgment in this case it is at least necessary for the victim to be identifiable (though as I have indicated it may not be sufficient) to establish proximity, is that it seems to me that the most effective way of providing protection would be to give warning to the victim, his or her parents or social services so that some protective measure can be made. . . .

It may be a somewhat novel approach to the question of proximity, but it seems to me to be a relevant consideration to ask what the defendant could have done to avoid the danger, if the suggested precautions ie committal under s.3 of the Mental Health Act or treatment are likely to be of doubtful effectiveness, and the most effective precaution cannot be taken because the

---

[26] [1990] 2 AC 605.   [27] [1999] Lloyd's Rep Med 351 CA.   [28] Ibid.

defendant does not know who to warn. This consideration suggests to me that the Court would be unwise to hold that there is sufficient proximity.

For these reasons I would uphold the judge's conclusion that there is no proximity between the defendants and Rosie. The claim in respect of her injury and death must fail and so must the claimant's brought on her own behalf.

No cases involving non-patients suing health authorities for their failure to prevent a patient from causing injuries through dangerous driving or infectious disease have arisen in the UK, but it seems likely that the courts would find that injuring other road users or infecting close contacts were foreseeable consequences of the failure to provide reasonable care to the patient. Where injuries are caused by dangerous driving, as in *Palmer* it is very unlikely that there would be a sufficient relationship of proximity between the doctor and the third party. In the case of infectious or contagious disease, unless both the claimant's existence and her risk of infection were known to the doctor, it would again be difficult to argue that there was a sufficiently proximate relationship. Even if the claimant was identifiable in advance as someone likely to be infected by the patient, perhaps because the doctor knew about their sexual relationship, other considerations, such as the duty to protect patient confidentiality (considered in Chapter 6), might mean that it would not be fair, just or reasonable to impose a duty to protect the third party from infection.

It should, however, be noted that in *Osman v UK*,[29] the European Court of Rights held that state authorities could be under a duty to take positive action to protect a third party whose life is in danger where they knew or ought to have known of the existence of a real and immediate risk to the person's life. *Osman* involved a case against the police, and so its implications in the health context are unclear, especially since the police are not bound by the same duty of confidentiality as doctors.

(d) Medical examinations

Finally, could a doctor who has been employed to carry out a medical examination owe a duty of care to the person who is examined? Until recently, doctors were only under the minimal duty not to actually injure the individual during the examination. In *X (Minors) v Bedfordshire County Council*[30] the House of Lords held that a psychiatrist who was employed by the local authority to interview a child as part of a child protection inquiry did not owe the child a duty of care, other than the duty not to damage her during the examination.

A similar approach was evident in *Kapfunde v Abbey National Plc.*[31] Mrs Kapfunde had had her application for a permanent post turned down following Dr Daniel's assessment of the company's standard medical questionnaire, which revealed that she had sickle cell anaemia. She brought an action in negligence against Abbey National and Dr Daniel, claiming damages for the economic loss which she suffered as a result of not getting the job. The Court of Appeal held that there was no duty of care. Kennedy LJ explained that:

Dr Daniels was instructed by Abbey National to advise on the appellant's suitability for

---

[29] (Case 87/1997/871/1083) [1999] 1 FLR 193.   [30] [1995] 2 AC 633 HL.
[31] [1999] ICR 1, (1999) 45 BMLR 176.

employment. She was obliged to acquaint herself with Abbey National's criteria for employment and to consider the questionnaire which the appellant had completed with proper professional skill and care in order to give proper advice to Abbey National. But these duties were owed to Abbey National and not to the appellant. There was no pre-existing relationship between Dr Daniels and the appellant from which a duty of care to the appellant could be derived. The only relationship between them was that between the giver of advice and the subject of the advice; and that is not enough.

More recently, it seems that someone who is employed by a third party to examine an individual could, in certain circumstances, owe that individual a duty of care. In *Phelps v Hillingdon LBC*,[32] for example, the House of Lords held that an educational psychologist employed by a local authority could owe the children whom they examine a duty of care. Lord Slynn held that:

it is long and well-established, now elementary, that persons exercising a particular skill or profession may owe a duty of care in the performance to people who it can be foreseen will be injured if due skill and care are not exercised, and if injury or damage can be shown to have been caused by the lack of care. Such duty does not depend on the existence of any contractual relationship between the person causing and the person suffering the damage. A doctor, an accountant and an engineer are plainly such a person. . . .

The fact that the educational psychologist owes a duty to the authority to exercise skill and care in the performance of his contract of employment does not mean that no duty of care can be or is owed to the child.

And in *D v East Berkshire Community Health NHS Trust*,[33] the Court of Appeal had held that a doctor examining a child where there is a suspicion that the child has been abused undoubtedly owes the child a duty of care. Lord Phillips MR held that:

In so far as the position of a child is concerned, we have reached the firm conclusion that the decision in Bedfordshire cannot survive the 1998 [Human Rights] Act. Where child abuse is suspected the interests of the child are paramount: Given the obligation of the local authority to respect a child's convention rights, the recognition of a duty of care to the child on the part of those involved should not have a significantly adverse effect on the manner in which they perform their duties.

The case then went to the House of Lords on the question of whether the doctor in such circumstances might *also* owe a duty of care to the parents. The House of Lords decided that this would create an unacceptable conflict of interest, and so any duty of care must be owed to the child alone.

JD v East Berkshire Community Health NHS Trust[34]

Allegations of child abuse, which subsequently proved to be unfounded, had been made against parents. The parents claimed damages from the NHS trusts for psychiatric harm alleged to have been caused by the false accusations and their consequences.

Lord Rodger

In considering whether it would be fair, just and reasonable to impose such a duty, a court has to have regard, however, to all the circumstances and, in particular, to the doctors' admitted duty to

---

[32] [2000] 4 All ER 504.   [33] [2003] EWCA Civ 1151, [2004] 2 WLR 58.
[34] [2005] UKHL 23 (Transcript on Lexis).

the children. The duty to the children is simply to exercise reasonable care and skill in diagnosing and treating any condition from which they may be suffering. In carrying out that duty the doctors have regard only to the interests of the children. Suppose, however, that they were also under a duty to the parents not to cause them psychiatric harm by concluding that they might have abused their child. Then, in deciding how to proceed, the doctors would always have to take account of the risk that they might harm the parents in this way. There would be not one but two sets of interests to be considered. Acting on, or persisting in, a suspicion of abuse might well be reasonable when only the child's interests were engaged, but unreasonable if the interests of the parents had also to be taken into account. Of its very nature, therefore, this kind of duty of care to the parents would cut across the duty of care to the children. . . .

[I]f contrary to my view, a duty of care were to be imposed in favour of the parents in these cases, I could see no proper basis for then failing to extend it to other members of the family, to friends of the family, to teachers and to child-minders—in short, to anyone who might come under suspicion of having abused the child. The potentially wide range of this supposed additional duty could only add to the risk that it would compromise the key duty of care to the children.

As a result of these latter decisions, Andrew Grubb has suggested that the general proposition advanced in *X v Bedfordshire* that a doctor engaged by a third party owes only the limited duty not to injure the claimant during an examination 'cannot stand with subsequent pronouncements in *Phelps* and should no longer be considered sound law'.[35]

(b) BREACH

(1) WHAT IS THE STANDARD OF CARE?

Having established (usually very straightforwardly) that she was owed a duty of care, the next stage for a claimant in a negligence action is to prove that the doctor breached her duty of care. In the law of tort generally, when deciding whether some precaution should have been taken against a foreseeable risk, the courts will weigh a number of factors, including (i) the magnitude of the risk; (ii) the gravity of the consequences should the risk materialize; (iii) the difficulty and cost of taking the precaution in question; (iv) the utility of the defendant's conduct, etc. Hence, if the likelihood of the harm materializing is low, and the potential consequences trivial, it may be reasonable not to take precautions against it. On the other hand, if the risk is high; or if its consequences are likely to be grave; or if it could be very easily eliminated, then a reasonable person might take steps to prevent the risk materializing. The standard of care must be assessed in terms of the individual patient, so if the doctor knows that her patient is unusually susceptible to a particular risk, then a reasonable doctor would take that into account.

The standard of care will be assessed at the time when the alleged negligence occurred; so if the claimant was injured during childbirth twenty years ago but only now brings an action for her injuries, the obstetrician will be judged by the standards of reasonable and responsible obstetric care twenty years previously. In *Roe v Minister*

---

[35] 'Duties in Contract and Tort' in A Grubb With J Laing (eds), *Principles of Medical Law* (2nd edn OUP Oxford 2004) 313–68, 366.

of Health,[36] heard in 1954, the defendants had administered contaminated anaesthetic to the claimant in 1947, but at that time the risk of contamination was unknown. The Court of Appeal found that there had been no negligence, Denning LJ famously saying 'We must not look at the 1947 accident with 1954 spectacles.' In 1951, a leading textbook had warned against the practice which led to the accident in *Roe*, and Denning LJ therefore went on to say:

If the hospitals were to continue the practice after this warning, they could not complain if they were found guilty of negligence. But the warning had not been given at the time of this accident. Indeed, it was the extraordinary accident to these two men which first disclosed the danger. Nowadays it would be negligence not to realise the danger, but it was not then.

Of course, the standard of care which can be expected of doctors is not that of the reasonable man or woman on the street, rather it is the standard of the reasonable medical practitioner. In a negligence action, this means it will be necessary to establish that the doctor did not act as a reasonable doctor, skilled in the particular speciality, would have done. A GP must act as a reasonable GP; a neurosurgeon as a reasonable neurosurgeon, and so on. If a GP were to attempt a specialist procedure, such as anaesthesia, she would be judged by the standard of a reasonable anaesthetist. If the GP is unable to meet this standard, then she will be negligent for undertaking treatment beyond her competence.

The central problem in judging the standard of care is that reasonable doctors within the same area of expertise may disagree about how best to treat an individual patient. If differences of medical opinion are inevitable, how can the court decide which view should be preferred? As many law students will recall, the answer to this question has been dominated by what has become known as the *Bolam* test.

Bolam v Friern Hospital Management Committee[37]

Mr Bolam, who was suffering from mental illness, was advised by a consultant at the defendants' hospital to undergo electroconvulsive therapy (ECT). He was not warned of the very small risk of fracture. He was not given relaxant drugs, nor was he physically restrained. Mr Bolam sustained a fractured hip during treatment. At the time, medical opinion on the desirability of warning patients of the risk of fracture, and the use of relaxant drugs and physical restraint varied. He sued the defendants for negligence, but lost. (In 1957, negligence actions were decided by juries.)

McNair J (in his direction to the jury)

But where you get a situation which involves the use of some special skill or competence, then the test whether there has been negligence or not is not the test of the man on the top of a Clapham omnibus, because he has not got this special skill. The test is the standard of the ordinary skilled man exercising and professing to have that special skill. A man need not possess the highest skill at the risk of being found negligent. It is well established law that it is sufficient if he exercises the ordinary skill of an ordinary competent man exercising that particular art. . . .

A doctor is not guilty of negligence if he has acted in accordance with a practice accepted as proper by a responsible body of medical men skilled in that particular art . . . Putting it the other way round, a doctor is not negligent, if he is acting in accordance with such a practice, merely because there is a body of opinion that takes a contrary view. At the same time, that does not mean

---

[36] [1954] 2 QB 66.   [37] [1957] WLR 582.

that a medical man can obstinately and pig-headedly carry on with some old technique if it has been proved to be contrary to what is really substantially the whole of informed medical opinion. Otherwise you might get men today saying: 'I don't believe in anaesthetics. I don't believe in antiseptics. I am going to continue to do my surgery in the way it was done in the eighteenth century'. That clearly would be wrong.

Although *Bolam v Friern Hospital Management Committee*[38] was itself only a first instance decision, and one of the last medical negligence cases to come before a jury, McNair J's formula was subsequently approved by the House of Lords in *Whitehouse v Jordan*[39] and *Maynard v West Midlands*, extracted below.

The *Bolam* test treats medical negligence differently from other negligence actions. When deciding whether an employer or a driver, for example, has been negligent, the standard of care is set by the *court* using the device of the reasonable man. When the defendant is a doctor, however, the standard of care has tended to be set by *other doctors*, via the *Bolam* test. This judicial deference to medical opinion is partly due to the complexity of medical evidence, but might also be explained by a sense of professional solidarity, and by the high regard in which the medical profession has conventionally been held. Note, for example, Mustill LJ's comments from the Court of Appeal's judgment in *Wilsher v Essex AHA*,[40] discussed more fully later.

Mustill LJ

Here we have a medical unit which would never have existed but for the energy and public spirit of Dr. Hardy. If the unit had not been there, the plaintiff would probably have died. The doctors and nurses worked all kinds of hours to look after the baby. They safely brought it through the perilous shoals of its early life. For all that we know, they far surpassed on numerous occasions the standard of reasonable care. Yet it is said that for one lapse they (and not just their employers) are to be held liable in damages. Nobody could criticise the mother for doing her best to secure her son's financial future. But has not the law taken a wrong turning if an action of this kind is to succeed?

If the courts are reluctant to question the evidence of a 'responsible' medical practitioner, does this mean that a doctor can avoid liability for negligence if she finds one respectable expert witness who will say that they would have acted in the same way? This would appear to have been the conclusion from *Maynard v West Midlands RHA*.[41]

Maynard v West Midlands RHA[42]

The claimant's symptoms suggested that she was suffering either from tuberculosis (TB) or from Hodgkin's disease. In fact she had TB, but her doctors recommended that she should undergo a test for Hodgkin's disease which posed a risk of damaging her vocal chords. This risk materialized. She presented expert evidence that the likelihood of her symptoms being Hodgkin's disease and not TB was so small that it did not justify assuming this risk. The trial judge was persuaded by the claimant's evidence and found that the defendant had exposed her to an unreasonable risk. On appeal, the Court of Appeal reversed the judge's decision, holding that there had been no negligence. Her appeal to the House of Lords was dismissed.

---

[38] [1957] WLR 582.   [39] [1981] 1 WLR 246.   [40] [1987] 1 QB 730.
[41] [1985] 1 All ER 635.   [42] Ibid.

Lord Scarman

A case which is based on an allegation that a fully considered decision of two consultants in the field of their special skill was negligent clearly presents certain difficulties of proof. It is not enough to show that there is a body of competent professional opinion which considers that theirs was a wrong decision, if there also exists a body of professional opinion, equally competent, which supports the decision as reasonable in the circumstances. It is not enough to show that subsequent events show that the operation need never have been performed, if at the time the decision to operate was taken it was reasonable in the sense that a responsible body of medical opinion would have accepted it as proper. . . .

Differences of opinion and practice exist, and will always exist, in the medical as in other professions. There is seldom any one answer exclusive of all others to problems of professional judgment. A court may prefer one body of opinion to the other, but that is no basis for a conclusion of negligence. . . .

I have to say that a judge's 'preference' for one body of distinguished professional opinion to another also professionally distinguished is not sufficient to establish negligence in a practitioner whose actions have received the seal of approval of those whose opinions, truthfully expressed, honestly held, were not preferred. . . . For in the realm of diagnosis and treatment negligence is not established by preferring one respectable body of professional opinion to another.

In *Maynard*, notice that Lord Scarman suggests that the courts should defer to the opinions of expert witnesses if they are 'truthfully expressed, honestly held', which implies that the court will only scrutinize the *credibility* of witnesses, rather than the content of their evidence. In *Hills v Potter*,[43] while rejecting the accusation of excessive deference to the medical profession, Hirst J nonetheless appeared to confine the court's role to judging whether there is, in fact, a 'substantial' body of opinion, and whether it is 'respectable', 'responsible' and 'experienced'. Again, these factors appear to go to the credibility of the witnesses, and not to the reasonableness of their views.

I do not accept the argument . . . that, by adopting the Bolam principle, the court in effect abdicates its power of decision to the doctors. In every case the court must be satisfied that the standard contended for on their behalf accords with that upheld by a substantial body of medical opinion, and that this body of medical opinion is both respectable and responsible, and experienced in this particular field of medicine.

Despite Hirst J's reference to the need for the body of medical opinion to be 'substantial', in other cases it has not mattered if the defendant and her expert witness are in a tiny minority. In *De Freitas v O'Brien*,[44] for example, expert evidence showed that a tiny minority of neurosurgeons would have endorsed the defendant's conduct, but the Court of Appeal nevertheless found that he had not been negligent.

There had, however, been one notable exception to the court's apparent reluctance to review the substance, as opposed to just the credibility, of expert evidence. In *Hucks v Cole*, a case decided in 1960 but not reported until 1994, the Court of Appeal rejected the evidence of the defendant's expert witnesses, and found that the doctor had been negligent despite the claims of other doctors that they would have acted in the same way.

---

[43] [1984] 1 WLR 641.   [44] [1995] 6 Med LR 108.

Hucks v Cole[45]

The claimant was a pregnant woman with a septic finger. Her doctor failed to prescribe penicillin, and the patient suffered puerperal fever as a result. Four expert witnesses testified that they too would not have prescribed penicillin in these circumstances, but the Court of Appeal found that this did not determine the matter and that the doctor had breached his duty of care.

Sachs LJ

When the evidence shows that a lacuna in professional practice exists by which risks of grave danger are knowingly taken, then, however small the risks, the court must anxiously examine that lacuna—particularly if the risks can be easily and inexpensively avoided. If the court finds, on an analysis of the reasons given for not taking those precautions that, in the light of current professional knowledge, there is no proper basis for the lacuna, and that it is definitely not reasonable that those risks should have been taken, its function is to state that fact and where necessary to state that it constitutes negligence. In such a case the practice will no doubt thereafter be altered to the benefit of patients.

On such occasions the fact that other practitioners would have done the same thing as the defendant practitioner is a very weighty matter to be put on the scales on his behalf; but it is not . . . conclusive. The court must be vigilant to see whether the reasons given for putting a patient at risk are valid in the light of any well-known advance in medical knowledge, or whether they stem from a residual adherence to out-of-date ideas—a tendency which in the present case may well have affected the views of at any rate one of the defendant's witnesses, who, at a considerable age, seemed not to have any particular respect for laboratory results . . .

Despite the fact that the risk could have been avoided by adopting a course that was easy, efficient and inexpensive, and which would have entailed only minimal chances of disadvantages to the patient, the evidence of the four defence experts to the effect that they and other responsible members of the medical profession would have taken the same risk in the same circumstances has naturally caused me to hesitate considerably on two points. Firstly, whether the failure of the defendant to turn over to penicillin treatment during the relevant period was unreasonable. On this, however, I was in the end fully satisfied that . . . failure to do this was not merely wrong but clearly unreasonable. The reasons given by the four experts do not to my mind stand up to analysis. . . .

Doctor Cole knowingly took an easily avoidable risk which elementary teaching had instructed him to avoid; and the fact that others say they would have done the same neither ought to nor can in the present case excuse him in an action for negligence however sympathetic one may be to him.

Then in 1997, in *Bolitho v City and Hackney HA*, the House of Lords adopted a more robust version of the *Bolam* test, and the excessively deferential interpretation adopted in cases like *Maynard* and *De Freitas* must now be in doubt.

Bolitho v City and Hackney HA[46]

A two year old boy had suffered severe brain damage after admission to hospital for respiratory problems. He subsequently died. The paediatric registrar had failed to attend him, but even if she had attended, she would not have intubated him. Intubation was the only procedure which could have prevented respiratory failure, but it was not without risks. The expert witnesses for each side expressed diametrically opposed views about whether the failure to intubate was reasonable. The boy's mother's appeal to the House of Lords was dismissed, because on the facts, the House of Lords held that the registrar had not breached her duty of care, but the case is important for Lord

---

[45] [1993] 4 Med LR 393.   [46] [1997] 4 All ER 771.

Browne-Wilkinson's comments on the circumstances in which the court would decide that there had been negligence despite expert evidence agreeing with the defendant's course of action.

Lord Browne-Wilkinson

[I]n my view, the court is not bound to hold that a defendant doctor escapes liability for negligent treatment or diagnosis just because he leads evidence from a number of medical experts who are genuinely of opinion that the defendant's treatment or diagnosis accorded with sound medical practice. In Bolam's case McNair J stated that the defendant had to have acted in accordance with the practice accepted as proper by a 'responsible body of medical men'. Later he referred to 'a standard of practice recognised as proper by a competent reasonable body of opinion'. Again, in the passage which I have cited from Maynard's case, Lord Scarman refers to a 'respectable' body of professional opinion. The use of these adjectives—responsible, reasonable and respectable—all show that the court has to be satisfied that the exponents of the body of opinion relied on can demonstrate that such opinion has a logical basis. In particular, in cases involving, as they so often do, the weighing of risks against benefits, the judge before accepting a body of opinion as being responsible, reasonable or respectable, will need to be satisfied that, in forming their views, the experts have directed their minds to the question of comparative risks and benefits and have reached a defensible conclusion on the matter. . . .

In the vast majority of cases the fact that distinguished experts in the field are of a particular opinion will demonstrate the reasonableness of that opinion. In particular, where there are questions of assessment of the relative risks and benefits of adopting a particular medical practice, a reasonable view necessarily presupposes that the relative risks and benefits have been weighed by the experts in forming their opinions. But if, in a rare case, it can be demonstrated that the professional opinion is not capable of withstanding logical analysis, the judge is entitled to hold that the body of opinion is not reasonable or responsible.

I emphasise that, in my view, it will very seldom be right for a judge to reach the conclusion that views genuinely held by a competent medical expert are unreasonable. The assessment of medical risks and benefits is a matter of clinical judgment which a judge would not normally be able to make without expert evidence. As the quotation from Lord Scarman makes clear, it would be wrong to allow such assessment to deteriorate into seeking to persuade the judge to prefer one of two views both of which are capable of being logically supported. It is only where a judge can be satisfied that the body of expert opinion cannot be logically supported at all that such opinion will not provide the bench mark by reference to which the defendant's conduct falls to be assessed.

I turn to consider whether this is one of those rare cases. Like the Court of Appeal, in my judgment it plainly is not.

Following *Bolitho*, the views of expert witnesses' must not only be honestly and sincerely held, but must also be *defensible*, in the sense that they must be 'capable of withstanding logical analysis?' What does this mean in practice?

The *Bolitho* approach to the *Bolam* test has subsequently been applied in a number of cases. In *Wisniewski v Central Manchester Health Authority*,[47] there was disagreement between the expert witnesses over the reasonableness of the defendant's failure to carry out a procedure which would have detected that the baby's umbilical cord was wrapped around his neck during childbirth. Brooke LJ explained that

Hucks v Cole itself was unquestionably one of the rare cases which Lord Browne-Wilkinson had in

---

[47] [1998] Lloyd's Rep Med 223 CA.

mind. . . . In my judgment the present case falls unquestionably on the other side of the line, and it is quite impossible for a court to hold that the views sincerely held by Mr Macdonald (an eminent consultant and an impressive witness) and Professor Thomas cannot logically be supported at all. . . .

[T]he views expressed by Mr Macdonald and Professor Thomas were views which could be logically supported and held by responsible doctors.

There have, however, been a few 'rare cases' in which the courts have been willing to challenge the logic or defensibility of medical authority. In *Reynolds v North Tyneside Health Authority*,[48] Gross J found that the failure to examine the claimant's mother properly during childbirth, which caused the claimant's asphyxia, and resulting cerebral palsy, was one of those 'rare cases' in which the court should be prepared to disregard expert evidence:

Gross J

[C]ommon practice in the profession in question, while a most useful guide in setting standards, is not conclusive of the question of breach of duty. By way of illustration, a defendant is not to be exonerated because others too are negligent or common professional practice is slack. Accordingly, where the defence to a charge of negligence entails reliance on a body of professional opinion, the court must be satisfied that such opinion has a logical basis and has reached a defensible conclusion on the matter in question. . . .

In the circumstances, it was logical to conduct an immediate VE [vaginal examination] on admission when the membranes had ruptured and the head was 3/5 palpable in the abdomen. That conclusion was supported by evidence of competent practice at the time. There was no or no sufficient evidence of any contrary practice.

If, notwithstanding the above, there was a contrary body of opinion that would not have conducted VEs when the foetal head was 3/5 palpable (without other complications), then this was one of those rare cases where the Court could and should conclude that such body of opinion was unreasonable, irresponsible, illogical and indefensible. . . .

In any event, even if there was any such contrary practice, or body of opinion, then the only reason articulated in its support for not conducting an immediate VE, namely the risk of infection, does not withstand scrutiny. Where the sole reason relied upon in support of a practice is untenable, it follows (at least absent very special circumstances) that the practice itself is not defensible and lacks a logical basis. That is the case here. The suggested contrary practice (or body of opinion) is neither defensible nor logical. Having carefully examined the evidence, this is one of those rare cases where it is appropriate to conclude that there is a lacuna in the practice for which there is no proper basis. Put another way, insofar as any such contrary practice turns on the risk of infection, I would be unable to accept that its proponents had (i) properly directed their minds to the comparative risks and benefits and (ii) reached a defensible conclusion.

And in *Marriott v West Midlands RHA*, the Court of Appeal decided that the evidence given by the expert witness who defended the doctor's conduct could not be logically supported.

Marriott v West Midlands RHA[49]

Mr Marriott had suffered a head injury and had been unconscious for 20–30 minutes. He was taken to hospital but discharged. For the next week he was lethargic, suffered from headaches, and

---

[48] Unreported, 30 May 2002.   [49] [1999] Lloyds Rep Med 23.

had no appetite. His GP, Dr Patel, attended him but said there was nothing wrong. Four days later Mr Marriott's condition deteriorated and he lost consciousness. He had to undergo surgery to remove a haematoma, and was left permanently disabled. One expert witness supported Dr Patel's judgment, while another claimed that it had been negligent not to refer Mr Marriott back to the hospital.

Beldam LJ

The judge then identified the area of disagreement which lay, she said, in the element of discretion which a reasonably prudent doctor would exercise whether or not to advise readmission to hospital.

'Furthermore, whilst a Court must plainly be reluctant to depart from the opinion of an apparently careful and prudent general practitioner, I have concluded that, if there is a body of professional opinion which supports the course of leaving a patient who has some 7 days previously sustained a severe head injury at home in circumstances where he continues to complain of headaches, drowsiness etc, and where there continues to be a risk of the existence of an intracranial lesion which could cause a sudden and disastrous collapse, then such approach is not reasonably prudent. It may well be that, if in the vast majority of cases, the risk is very small. Nevertheless, the consequence, if things go wrong, are disastrous to the patient. In such circumstances, it is my view that the only reasonably prudent course in any case where a general practitioner remains of the view that there is a risk of an intracranial lesion such as to warrant the carrying out of neurological testing and the giving of further head injury instructions, then the only prudent course judged from the point of view of the patient is to re-admit for further testing and observation.'

She thus held that Dr Patel's decision on 11 October not to refer the plaintiff back to hospital was negligent. . . .

It was open to the judge to hold that, in the circumstances as she found them to have been, it could not be a reasonable exercise of a general practitioner's discretion to leave a patient at home and not to refer him back to hospital. Accordingly, I would dismiss the appeal.

In the next extract, Lord Woolf (writing extra-judicially) explores the reasons for this shift away from the *Bolam* test.

Lord Woolf [50]

[U]ntil recently the courts treated the medical profession with excessive deference, but recently the position has changed. It is my judgment that it has changed for the better . . .

What is it that has caused the change? I would identify the following causes.

First, today the courts have a less deferential approach to those in authority. The growth in judicial review has resulted in the judiciary becoming accustomed to setting aside decisions of those engaged on behalf of the Crown in public affairs, from a Minister of the Crown downwards. By comparison the medical profession and the Health Service were small beer.

Secondly, while there has been the huge growth in the scale of litigation, including actions brought against hospital trusts and the medical profession, the proportion of successful medical negligence claims in England is put at only 17 per cent. The courts became increasingly conscious of the difficulties which bona fide claimants had in successfully establishing claims.

Thirdly, there had developed an increasing awareness of patients' rights. The public's

---

[50] 'Are the Courts Excessively Deferential to the Medical Profession?' (2001) 9 Medical Law Review 1–16, 1–5.

expectations of what the profession should achieve have grown . . . The move to a rights-based society has fundamentally changed the behaviour of the courts.

Fourthly, the 'automatic presumption of beneficence' has been dented by a series of well-publicised scandals . . . Almost daily there are reports in the media suggesting that there is something amiss with our health treatment.

Fifthly, our courts were aware that courts at the highest level of other Commonwealth jurisdictions, particularly Canada and Australia, were rejecting the approach of the English courts. They were subjecting the actions of the medical profession to a closer scrutiny than the English courts . . .

Sixthly, medical negligence litigation was revealed as being a disaster area. The Health Service and the insurance industry had to be required to change their approach to handling litigation. They appeared to consider that every case was worth fighting . . . The annual cost of medical negligence litigation is estimated to be at least equivalent to building, running and staffing one new hospital annually. The litigation was particularly bitter and often singularly unproductive . . .

Seventhly, recently a series of cases have come before the courts that raised fundamental questions of medical ethics. . . . The courts, having had to struggle with issues such as these, were prepared to adopt a more proactive approach to resolving conflicts as to more traditional medical issues.

Eighthly, a final influence that will be of increasing importance and probably played a part in the case of some of the factors I have already mention was first the proposal for and subsequently the incorporation into English domestic law of the European Convention of Human Rights.

Harvey Teff argues that the courts' increasing willingness to scrutinize the *content* of expert evidence is especially welcome, given lawyers' tendency to treat expert witnesses as 'hired hands'.

Harvey Teff[51]

Reassertion at the highest level of the court's role in scrutinizing professional practice is welcome, not least because of current concerns about the dynamics of providing expert evidence for the purposes of adversarial litigation. Some law firms' choice of experts is apt to depend too much on perceived presentational skills and acuity in advancing the client's case, and too little on detached expertise. To the extent that solicitors 'shop around' until a sympathetic expert is found, differential resources, of funding and access to expertise, will typically favour institutional defendants such as health authorities or hospital trusts . . .

A very recent survey of 500 expert witnesses revealed that 70% of them said that they had been asked by lawyers to modify their report or opinion in some way and that around one-third had done so. Most of the resulting amendments would have taken the form of innocent clarification and correction of factual errors in reports. However, about a quarter of the respondents' recorded comments are more equivocal, in some instances acknowledging the alteration of opinions . . . Despite the requirement 'that expert evidence presented to the court should be and should be seen to be the independent product of the expert uninfluenced as to form or content by the exigencies of litigation', it remains the case that 'expert witnesses instructed on behalf of parties to litigation often tend . . . to espouse the cause of those instructing them to a greater or lesser extent, on occasion becoming more partisan than the parties' . . .

One prominent medicolegal authority has bluntly declared that '*Bolam* will only work fairly if

---

[51] 'The Standard of Care in Medical Negligence—Moving on from *Bolam*?' (1998) 18 Oxford Journal of Legal Studies 473–84, 481–3.

the use of hired hands as defence medical experts is eliminated. It would then be possible to talk of a responsible body of medical opinion' . . .

Increasingly, the cases contain elaborate treatment of the medical issues, coupled with signs of more independent and critical judicial appraisal of expert evidence on the requisite standard of care. They may not yet display the distaste for the *Bolam* model expressed in the Australian High Court when it decided *Rogers v Whitaker*, but the measured approach now endorsed by the House of Lords in *Bolitho* should reduce the risk of legitimating the lowest common denominator of accepted practice.

The NHS Litigation Authority (whose role we consider below at p. 171) operates a Clinical Negligence Scheme for trusts (CNST) which sets its own approved risk management standards. The CNST operates as a quasi-insurance system for NHS trusts, so there are obvious economic incentives for trusts to ensure compliance with the CNST's risk management standards. The Royal Colleges of Medicine now routinely issue best practice guidance, and the National Institute of Clinical Excellence (whose role we considered in the previous chapter) is responsible for developing its own treatment protocols. Within the NHS increased reliance is being placed upon medical audit, or the systematic review of the quality of care and of diagnostic and treatment processes. Most hospitals now have audit departments which are responsible for monitoring the effectiveness of treatments. In the future, it may become increasingly difficult for doctors to ignore clear evidence of a particular treatment's inefficacy.

This does not necessarily mean that any doctor who deviates from accepted practice will inevitably be found negligent if something goes wrong. If that were the case, then no doctor could ever try a new technique without risking being sued, and medical progress would be hampered. Guidelines are, by definition, not mandatory. Nevertheless, although evidence of a departure from accepted practice is not necessarily determinative, as we can see in the following case, it may help a claimant who is seeking to prove negligence.

Clark v MacLennan[52]

After the birth of her first child, the claimant suffered from stress incontinence. The first defendant, a gynaecologist, performed an operation a month later, although it was normal practice among gynaecologists not to perform such an operation until at least three months after birth, in order to ensure its success and to prevent the risk of haemorrhage. The operation was not successful and after it was performed haemorrhage occurred. Two further operations were necessary, but neither was successful, and the claimant was left permanently disabled.

Peter Pain J

[W]here there is a situation in which a general duty of care arises and there is a failure to take a precaution, and that very damage occurs against which the precaution is designed to be a protection, then the burden lies on the defendant to show that he was not in breach of duty as well as to show that the damage did not result from his breach of duty. I shall therefore apply this approach to the evidence in this case. I first have to ask myself whether the plaintiff has established that it is a general practice among gynaecologists that an anterior colporrhaphy should not ordinarily be performed until at least three months after birth. . . . I am satisfied that this is the general

---

[52] [1983] 1 All ER 416.

practice. . . . Exceptions can be considered, but they require justification. . . . This is the general practice among gynaecologists and any departure from it requires justification.

Having considered all the points raised by the defendants, I hold that the defendants have failed to establish that it was justifiable to perform the operation of anterior colporrhaphy on the plaintiff only four weeks after birth. Consequently, there was a breach of the duty of care owed to the plaintiff.

In the next extract, Margaret Brazier and José Miola argue that these developments, coupled with the decision in *Bolitho*, indicate that the courts may be not only more willing to challenge medical evidence, but also will increasingly be better equipped to do so.

Margaret Brazier and Jose Miola[53]

Most importantly, *Bolitho* has been decided at a time when other developments also point to a revolution in the way medical malpractice is judged. Medicine itself is changing with practitioners increasingly evaluating their own practice and seeking to develop evidence-based medicine. The traditional guardians of clinical standards, the Royal Colleges of Medicine, have over the last decade become more and more proactive, issuing guidelines about good practice with reference to treatments and procedures . . . [T]he National Institute for Clinical Excellence (NICE) has been established to develop guidelines for good practice, not just in the context of new drug treatments, but in a much wider sphere of reviewing all forms of therapies and procedures. . . . The judge confronted by individual experts who disagree about good practice will in certain cases be able to refer to something approaching a 'gold standard'. . . .

[NICE's] central purpose is to rationalise and co-ordinate clinical guidance on effective treatment, in appropriate cases developing something close to protocols on disease management. Presumably such guidance will be written lucidly, in terms intelligible to judges in medical malpractice claims. The judge will have access to material, independent of the particular dispute before him, enabling him to assess the logic of the parties' cases. *Bolitho*, plus more ready access to clinical guidelines, suggests a more proactive role for judges assessing expert evidence. Nor will clinical guidelines necessarily be the only source of judicial guidance on the logic of the evidence presented by the parties. The burgeoning literature on medical developments, often presented in a style comprehensible to lay people, may also be resorted to much more frequently in litigation. *Bolitho* demands that doctors explain their practice. Doctors themselves are developing tools which will enable judges to review those explanations.

In contrast, in the next extract Brian Hurwitz explains that guidelines, by definition, are meant to have general application and might not take the particular patient's circumstances into account.

Brian Hurwitz[54]

Evidence based guidelines are standardised specifications of care that apply to the general condition and not necessarily to the particular clinical situation at hand; they therefore require extrapolation to an individual patient's circumstances. Guidelines are synthesised from many sources of information and may create a false sense of consensus, may mask or underplay controversy, and can rapidly become out of date as a result of new findings. Many guidelines face more or less well grounded degrees of dissent much of the time . . .

[53] 'Bye-Bye Bolam: A Medical Litigation Revolution?' (2000) 8 Medical Law Review 85–114, 104–5.
[54] 'How does evidence based guidance influence determinations of medical negligence?' (2004) 329 British Medical Journal, 1024–28.

Some degree of discretion lies at the heart of clinical judgment, which has to take account of competing influences on decision making such as the patient's choice, healthcare targets, costs, and incentives. But discretion requires to be exercised in accordance with the patient's best interests and within professional bounds. This will often, but not always, entail acting in accord with authoritative guidelines.

Harvey Teff also expresses some reservations about the move towards a 'guideline mentality'.

Harvey Teff[55]

Yet as [clinical guidelines] do become more 'authoritative', the perceived epitome of 'best practice', they could, even without displacing *Bolam*, create pressure to reverse the onus of proof, requiring the doctor to establish that failure to adhere to guidelines was not negligent. Granting such a high level of putative authority to guidelines would, it is submitted, be undesirable. They are not designed *as* legal rules. Depending on their provenance, they may offer a counsel of perfection that is locally unattainable, or be too undemanding, perhaps unduly influenced by considerations of cost-containment. Equally, there are often reasonable grounds for arguing that seemingly controlling guidelines, derived from population studies, are either not meant to, or did not in fact, cover the particular clinical circumstances.

In view of such inevitable limitations, it would be inappropriate for guidelines to become the sole basis of liability, and imprudent to make them a key, or even, *prima facie*, determinant, especially if this would encourage more people to initiate misconceived claims when guidelines had not been followed . . . In any event, clinical discretion is increasingly likely to be constrained, whether by purchaser or trust-driven demands, or through doctors' fears that, in the era of clinical governance, non-conformity will invite legal sanction . . .

There are serious implications for health-care providers if clinical discretion is unduly constrained by the developments outlined above . . . If one begins with the inarticulate premise that guidelines are intrinsically desirable, it is all too easy to assume that they will be appropriately developed, widely applicable and properly applied. Thus beguiled, we are tempted to understate the hold of established working practices, and to minimize the possible chilling effect of a guidelines mentality on medical expertise and innovation. Reluctance to innovate for fear of litigation may become more pronounced because, by definition, it is normally hard to demonstrate that *new* health technologies are evidence-based. . . . More broadly, guidelines are liable to divert the attention of the clinician from what constitutes 'health' for the particular patient . . .

If EBM [evidence based medicine] becomes the 'new deity in clinical medicine', it could herald the dominance of a new kind of medical paternalism—'*the guideline knows best*'.

(2) IS THE STANDARD OF CARE FIXED?

It is normally said that the standard of care in tort law is objective. Many law students will recall the case of *Nettleship v Weston*,[56] in which a learner driver was found to be negligent for failing to meet the standard of care which could be expected of a reasonably experienced driver. Does this mean that the standard of care in medical negligence is fixed and objectively determined, or might it vary according to the

---

[55] 'Clinical Guidelines, Negligence and Medical Practice' in M Freeman and A Lewis, *Current Legal Issues: Law and Medicine* vol 3 (OUP Oxford 2000) 67–80, 77–9.
[56] [1971] 2 QB 691.

circumstances? In the next sections we look at whether it would be reasonable to expect a lower standard of care in four different situations:

- if resources are scarce;
- if the doctor is treating the patient in an emergency;
- if the doctor is inexperienced;
- if the doctor is practising alternative medicine.

(a) Scarce resources

In determining what standard of care would be reasonable, should the court take into account the scarcity of resources? Clearly within the NHS the standard of care could, if there were unlimited funds, often be much higher. For example, optimum maternity care might involve providing each pregnant woman with her own midwife, and ensuring that a consultant obstetrician is present during every birth. Given finite resources, that level of care could only be provided to a small number of women. The NHS is however committed to offering maternity care to every pregnant woman in the UK, and inevitably the standard of care which can realistically be provided to the whole population will fail to meet this unaffordable ideal. Of course, this political reality makes judging the standard of care in negligence especially difficult. If less than perfect care is inevitable, how do courts tell when treatment has failed to meet an acceptable standard?

In *Knight v Home Office*, insufficient resources did not offer a complete defence, but were nonetheless relevant to the standard of care which could be expected in a prison hospital.

Knight v Home Office[57]

A mentally ill prisoner was being held in the hospital wing of Brixton prison. He received treatment that would not have come up to the standards that could be expected in a mental hospital: he had not been offered counselling, and was not put on continuous observation. He hanged himself. On behalf of his estate, it was argued that the Home Office had breached their duty to provide him with appropriate care.

Pill J

It is for the court to consider what standard of care is appropriate to the particular relationship and in the particular situation. It is not a complete defence for a government department any more than it would be for a private individual or organisation to say that no funds are available for additional safety measures.

I cannot accept what was at one time submitted by counsel for the defendants that the plaintiffs' only remedy would be a political one. To take an extreme example, if the evidence was that no funds were available to provide any medical facilities in a large prison there would be a failure to achieve the standard of care appropriate for prisoners.

In making the decision as to the standard to be demanded the court must, however, bear in mind as one factor that resources available for the public service are limited and that the allocation of resources is a matter for Parliament.

I am unable to accept the submission that the law requires the standard of care in a prison

---

[57] [1990] 3 All ER 237.

hospital to be as high as the standard of care for all purposes in a psychiatric hospital outside prison. I am unable to accept that the practices in a prison hospital are to be judged in all respects by the standard appropriate to a psychiatric hospital outside prison. There may be circumstances in which the standard of care in a prison falls below that which would be expected in a psychiatric hospital without the prison authority being negligent. Even in a medical situation outside prison, the standard of care required will vary with the context. The facilities available to deal with an emergency in a general practitioner's surgery cannot be expected to be as ample as those available in the casualty department of a general hospital, for example.

As Pill J makes clear, a prison is undoubtedly under a duty to provide a basic minimum level of medical care to prisoners. In *Brooks v Home Office*,[58] a case involving a remand prisoner with a high risk pregnancy, Garland J said:

I cannot regard Knight as authority for the proposition that the plaintiff should not, while detained in Holloway, be entitled to expect the same level of antenatal care, both for herself and her unborn infants, as if she were at liberty, subject of course to the constraints of having to be escorted and, to some extent, movement being retarded by those requirements.

The prison had failed to make an immediate appointment when a scan revealed that one of the prisoner's twins had not grown as expected. On the facts, there was no liability because a delay of two days in making an appointment would have been reasonable, and would not have prevented the weaker twin's stillbirth.

Similarly, in *Bull v Devon AHA*,[59] discussed earlier, the Court of Appeal held that a certain minimum *and fixed* standard of care should be met regardless of the hospital's financial constraints. It was no excuse to a failure to provide this *minimum* standard of care that the hospital had limited resources. Let us take the common example of delays in being seen in a busy accident and emergency department. It would almost certainly not be negligent to expect people with minor injuries to wait for several hours, but a similar failure to attend to someone who had had a heart attack would fail to meet this basic minimum standard of care, and the fact that the hospital was operating with limited resources would offer no excuse.

In the next extract Christian Witting criticizes the courts' reluctance to permit the standard of care to fluctuate according to the available resources, although he also notes that one disadvantage of a variable standard of care is that patients who are injured through the provision of substandard services might be denied compensation.

Christian Witting[60]

[I]t will be contended that the application of negligence principles is usually predicated upon a number of factual elements including the ability of a decision-maker to decide differently and to act in a way that avoids the infliction of harm. In the NHS context, this means that it is only reasonable to impose liability upon NHS employees where they have the ability to change their practices and thereby ensure that patients are not injured by way of medical mishaps. The ability to do these things is often dependent upon the availability of funds to employ extra staff and obtain extra bed space and equipment. Where this is not possible, the response of the law to under-funding must be to alter the criteria by which determinations of negligence are made. . . .

---

[58] [1999] 2 FLR 33 QBD.   [59] [1993] 4 Med LR 117 (CA).
[60] 'National Health Service Rationing: Implications For The Standard Of Care In Negligence' (2001) 21 Oxford Journal of Legal Studies 443.

Just as the courts in judicial review cases have deferred to the wisdom of hospitals and to their professional employees when determining how scarce resources should be allocated, so they must recognise the impossibility of maintaining ideal standards of care in the face of a government policy which tacitly accepts that a small proportion of NHS treatments will result in mishaps and accidents. The standard of care must be modified in cases of systemic negligence, where this is the consequence of under-funding. To attribute 'fault' to hospitals and front-line medical staff in these cases is to impose liability upon parties who are unlikely to have the ability to avoid the causation of harm to patients. They are causally insignificant parties.

It has been argued that scope exists within current rules on the standard of care to recognise the reality of NHS under-funding. This scope is to be found in the simple requirement that those who act must act reasonably in the circumstances of the particular case. The fact of under-funding, and of the inevitable systemic failures to which this gives rise, are important circumstances that the courts must take into account. . . .

The real difficulty, of course, lies in attempting to justify the denial of compensation to those who are injured as a result of diluted or sub-standard care brought about by under-funding. Justice would seem to demand that there be compensation for these patients. However, if the argument set out in this paper is accepted, there is little which would justify payment of such compensation by health authorities, NHS hospitals or their professional employees.

(b) Emergencies

In an emergency, it might be difficult for doctors to provide the same standard of care as might normally be expected. Following a major disaster, such as a train crash or bomb blast, hospitals may be overwhelmed with casualties. A doctor who is off duty may stop at the roadside to assist the victims of a road traffic accident, when lack of equipment will inevitably compromise the standard of care which she can provide. In such circumstances, would it be reasonable to expect a lower standard of care than normal?

GP contracts specify that, if available, they must offer treatment in an emergency to patients in their practice area who are not on their list, and whose own doctors are unable to give immediate treatment.[61] In general, however, off-duty doctors in the UK are not under a duty to offer assistance if they come upon a medical emergency. Nevertheless, a failure to assist in an emergency might prompt disciplinary action by the General Medical Council, whose guidance on the duties of a doctor states that

In an emergency, wherever it may arise, you must offer anyone at risk the assistance you could reasonably be expected to provide.[62]

Once a doctor has undertaken to offer care to an injured person, she undoubtedly assumes a duty of care. But since what is expected of doctors is 'reasonable care', it is appropriate to take into account the situation in which the doctor is administering treatment. It would, for example, not be reasonable to expect a doctor who has been called out to the site of a train crash to provide the level of care that would be available in a well-equipped intensive care unit. Indeed in *Wilsher v Essex Area Health Authority*[63] Mustill LJ said:

---

[61] The National Health Service (General Medical Services) Regulations 1992 SI 1992/635 Sch 2, para 4(h).
[62] *Good Medical Practice* (GMC London 2001) para 9.   [63] [1987] 1 QB 730.

I accept that full allowance must be made for the fact that certain aspects of treatment may have to be carried out in what one witness . . . called 'battle conditions'. An emergency may overburden resources and, if an individual is forced by circumstances to do too many things at once, the fact that he does one of them incorrectly should not lightly be taken as negligence.

(c) Inexperience

Should a doctor's inexperience affect the standard of care which can reasonably be expected of her? On the one hand, doctors have to learn by experience, and it would seem harsh for junior doctors to be potentially liable in negligence for their inability to reach the standard of care which might be expected from a more experienced doctor. But on the other hand, if the standard of care patients are entitled to expect fluctuated according to the doctor's experience, patients would be well advised to refuse to be treated by anyone who is not highly experienced, and the system through which junior doctors learn 'on the job' would break down. This issue arose in *Wilsher v Essex AHA*,[64] and although the junior doctor was ultimately exonerated because he had taken the reasonable step of asking a registrar for assistance, a majority of the Court of Appeal held that the standard of care should not be lower for inexperienced doctors. (Note that it was only on the issue of causation that appeal was made to the House of Lords, which we consider below at p. 142, and so it is the Court of Appeal judgment which is relevant to the question of whether the junior doctor had breached his duty of care.)

Wilsher v Essex Area Health Authority[65]

Martin Wilsher was born prematurely suffering from various illnesses. While he was in the special care baby unit, a junior and inexperienced doctor mistakenly inserted a catheter into a vein rather than an artery, and then asked the senior registrar to check what he had done. The registrar failed to see the mistake and some hours later, when replacing the catheter, did exactly the same thing himself. In both instances Martin Wilsher was given excess oxygen. He alleged that the excess oxygen in his bloodstream had caused an incurable condition of the retina resulting in near blindness.

Mustill LJ

To my mind, this notion of a duty tailored to the actor, rather than to the act which he elects to perform, has no place in the law of tort. Indeed, the defendants did not contend that it could be justified by any reported authority on the general law of tort. Instead, it was suggested that the medical profession is a special case. Public hospital medicine has always been organised so that young doctors and nurses learn on the job. If the hospitals abstained from using inexperienced people, they could not staff their wards and theatres, and the junior staff could never learn. The longer-term interests of patients as a whole are best served by maintaining the present system, even if this may diminish the legal rights of the individual patient, for, after all, medicine is about curing, not litigation.

I acknowledge the appeal of this argument, and recognise that a young hospital doctor who must get onto the wards in order to qualify without necessarily being able to decide what kind of patient he is going to meet is not in the same position as another professional man who has a real choice whether or not to practice in a particular field. Nevertheless, I cannot accept that there

---

[64] [1987] 1 QB 730.   [65] Ibid.

should be a special rule for doctors in public hospitals . . . To my mind, it would be a false step to subordinate the legitimate expectation of the patient that he will receive from each person concerned with his care a degree of skill appropriate to the task which he undertakes to an understandable wish to minimise the psychological and financial pressures on hard-pressed young doctors.

Glidewell LJ

In my view, the law requires the trainee or learner to be judged by the same standard as his more experienced colleagues. If it did not, inexperience would frequently be urged as a defence to an action for professional negligence.

If this test appears unduly harsh in relation to the inexperienced, I should add that, in my view, the inexperienced doctor called on to exercise a specialist skill will, as part of that skill, seek the advice and help of his superiors when he does or may need it. If he does seek such help, he will often have satisfied the test, even though he may himself have made a mistake. It is for this reason that I agree that Dr Wiles was not negligent. He made a mistake in inserting the catheter into a vein, and a second mistake in not recognising the signs that he had done so on the X-ray. But, having done what he thought right, he asked Dr Kawa, the senior registrar, to check what he had done, and Dr Kawa did so. Dr Kawa failed to recognise the indication on the X-ray that the catheter was in the vein, and some hours later himself inserted a replacement catheter, again in the vein, and again failed to recognise that it was in the vein. Whichever of the suggested tests of negligence should be applied to Dr Wiles, we are all agreed that Dr Kawa was negligent, and that the defendants must therefore be liable for any damage to the plaintiff proved to have been caused by that negligence.

Sir Nicolas Browne-Wilkinson VC (dissenting)

I cannot accept that the standard of care required of an individual doctor holding a post in a hospital is an objective standard to be determined irrespective of his experience or the reason why he is occupying the post in question.

In English law, liability for personal injury requires a finding of personal fault (eg negligence) against someone. In cases of vicarious liability such as this, there must have been personal fault by the employee or agent of the defendant for whom the defendant is held vicariously liable. Therefore, even though no claim is made against the individual doctor, the liability of the defendant health authority is dependent on a finding of personal fault by one or more of the individual doctors. . . .

The houseman has to take up his post in order to gain full professional qualification; anyone who, like Dr Wiles, wishes to obtain specialist skills has to learn those skills by taking a post in a specialist unit. In my judgment, such doctors cannot in fairness be said to be at fault if, at the start of their time, they lack the very skills which they are seeking to acquire. . . .

In my judgment, so long as the English law rests liability on personal fault, a doctor who has properly accepted a post in a hospital in order to gain necessary experience should only be held liable for acts or omissions which a careful doctor with his qualifications and experience would not have done or omitted. It follows that, in my view, the health authority could not be held vicariously liable . . . for the acts of such a learner who has come up to those standards, notwithstanding that the post he held required greater experience than he in fact possessed.

Recall that earlier we saw that Glidewell LJ and Sir Nicolas Browne-Wilkinson VC agreed that a failure to provide adequate supervision of junior medical staff might also represent a breach of the hospital's *primary* non-delegable duty of care to provide a safe system of treatment.

(d) Complementary and alternative medicine

How should the courts determine the standard of care which can reasonably be expected of practitioner of complementary or alternative medicine. Should a Chinese herbalist be judged against the reasonable practitioner of Chinese herbal medicine, or should he be expected to meet the same standard of care as an orthodox clinician? Interestingly there have been virtually no reported cases brought by patients who claim that they have been injured as a result of alternative therapies. This is not necessarily because such treatments have a high level of safety, rather it is also possible that patients who believe that they have been left worse off after resorting to alternative medical treatments are less likely to complain, and in particular may be reluctant to consult a conventional doctor about their symptoms. The issue has arisen only once in the UK, in *Shakoor v Situ.*

Shakoor v Situ[66]

KS, a practitioner of traditional Chinese herbal medicine (CHM), was consulted by a patient about a skin condition for which the only orthodox medical treatment was surgery. After taking nine doses of the herbal remedy, the patient suffered acute liver failure and died. It had been established that, on the balance of probabilities, his death was probably caused by the remedy, which had produced an extremely rare and unpredictable reaction. Papers published in orthodox medical journals had suggested that the ingestion of a similar medicine gave rise to the risk of liver damage and, in one case, had caused death. KS stated that his knowledge of Chinese medical textbooks and periodicals had led him to believe that the remedy was completely safe.

Bernard Livesey QC

Is he to be judged by the standards of the reasonably careful practitioner of CHM or according to the standards applicable to orthodox medical practitioners in this country? There is not any authority on this point in this country or, so far as I am aware after appropriate searches, in other common law jurisdictions. . . .

The Chinese herbalist, for example, does not hold himself out as a practitioner of orthodox medicine. More particularly, the patient has usually had the choice of going to an orthodox practitioner but has rejected him in favour of the alternative practitioner for reasons personal and best known to himself and almost certainly at some personal financial cost . . . The decision of the patient may be enlightened and informed or based on ignorance and superstition. Whatever the basis of his decision, it seems to me that the fact that the patient has chosen to reject the orthodox and prefer the alternative practitioner is something important which must be taken into account. Why should he later be able to complain that the alternative practitioner has not provided him with skill and care in accordance with the standards of those orthodox practitioners whom he has rejected?

On the other hand, it is of course obviously true to say that the alternative practitioner has chosen to practice in this country alongside a system of orthodox medicine and must abide by the laws and standards prevailing in this country . . .

[W]here he prescribes a remedy which is taken by a patient it is not enough to say that the remedy is traditional and believed not to be harmful, he has a duty to ensure that the remedy is not actually or potentially harmful . . . An alternative practitioner who prescribes a remedy must take steps to satisfy himself that there has not been any adverse report in such journals on the remedy which ought to affect the use he makes of it. That is not to say that he must take a range of publications himself. It should be enough if he subscribes to an 'association' which arranges to search the relevant literature and promptly report any material publication to him. The relevant literature will be that which would be taken by an orthodox practitioner practising at the level of speciality at which the alternative practitioner holds himself out. If he does not subscribe to such an association the practitioner will not have discharged his duty to inform himself properly and may act at his peril.

Accordingly, a claimant may succeed in an action against an alternative practitioner for negligently prescribing a remedy either by calling an expert in the speciality in question to assert and prove that the defendant has failed to exercise the skill and care appropriate to that art . . . Alternatively, the claimant may prove that the prevailing standard of skill and care 'in that art' is deficient in this country having regard to risks which were not and should have been taken into account. . . .

In these circumstances, I find that the defendant was not in breach of his duty to the deceased. I am satisfied that he acted in accordance with the standard of care appropriate to TCHM as properly practised in accordance with the standards required in this country. The fact that the deceased died in consequence of the medication, as the doctors have on a balance of probability agreed, is a tragic accident but not the fault of the defendant.

In short, there would seem to be two ways in which a claimant might establish negligence on the part of an alternative medical practitioner. First, she could attempt to prove that the defendant did not meet the standard of care of the reasonable practitioner of that particular 'art'. Secondly, even if the defendant did act as a reasonable alternative practitioner, it would still be open to the claimant to establish that the prevailing standard of care in that 'art' is itself deficient, on the grounds that it fails to take proper account of well-publicized evidence of toxicity.

(3) PROOF OF BREACH

It is for the claimant to prove on the balance of probabilities that the defendant has breached her duty of care. The maxim *res ipsa loquitur* (the thing speaks for itself) allows the courts, in certain circumstances, to draw an inference that the defendant was negligent. There is some dispute over whether it reverses the burden of proof, such that it is for the defendant to prove that she was *not* negligent, or alternatively whether the burden of proof remains with the claimant, but the facts appear to give rise to an inference of negligence, which might be rebutted by evidence that the defendant had not in fact been negligent. The better view is almost certainly that the burden of proof remains with the claimant, but there is of course little difference in practice between asking the defendant to justify actions which have raised an inference of negligence, and reversing the burden of proof.

The maxim will apply where an accident would not normally happen unless someone had been negligent. An example might be if a surgical instrument is left inside the patient's body after surgery. It would be difficult to think of circumstances in which this had occurred, but no one had breached their duty of care towards the patient. Similarly, if a patient went into hospital in order to have her gangrenous right leg amputated, and her healthy left leg was amputated instead, again the inference might reasonably be drawn that the surgeon had been negligent.

Essentially then, *res ipsa loquitur* is just an elaborate way of saying that there will occasionally be circumstances in which a judge would be entitled to find that the defendant had been negligent without evidence from expert witnesses confirming that the defendant's actions fell below the appropriate standard of care. It will apply then only to very simple cases where negligence can readily be inferred by a lay person, from the facts themselves. However, in clinical negligence cases, the claimant will seldom be able to make out her case without expert evidence.

Hobhouse LJ's judgment in *Ratcliffe v Plymouth and Torbay Health Authority* offers a helpful explanation of the limited application *res ipsa loquitur* is likely to have in actions against doctors.

Ratcliffe v Plymouth and Torbay Health Authority[67]

Mr Ratcliffe underwent an operation on his right ankle in one of the defendants' hospitals. He was given a spinal anaesthetic to relieve post-operative pain. The operation itself was a success, but he was left with a serious neurological defect on the right side, causing a total loss of sensation in his leg, severe pain and penile numbness. He contended that this raised an inference that the spinal anaesthetic had been given negligently. His claim was dismissed by Mantell J, and the Court of Appeal dismissed his appeal.

Hobhouse LJ

Res ipsa loquitur is no more than a convenient Latin phrase used to describe the proof of facts which are sufficient to support an inference that a defendant was negligent and therefore to establish a prima facie case against him. . . . The burden of proving the negligence of the defendant remains throughout upon the plaintiff. The burden is on the plaintiff at the start of the trial and, absent an admission by the defendant, is still upon the plaintiff at the conclusion of the trial . . . The plaintiff may or may not have needed to call evidence to establish a prima facie case. The admitted facts may suffice for that purpose . . .

If the facts of the present case had been that the plaintiff had gone into the operating theatre to have an arthrodesis to his right ankle and had come out of the theatre with his right ankle untouched and an arthrodesis to his left ankle, clearly no expert evidence would be required to support an inference of negligence on the part of the defendants. 'In the ordinary course of things', that does not happen if those conducting the operation have used proper care. . . . In practice, save in the most extreme cases of blatant negligence, the plaintiff will have to adduce at least some expert evidence to get his case upon its feet. . . .

Res ipsa loquitur is not a principle of law: it does not relate to, or raise, any presumption. It is merely a guide to help to identify when a prima facie case is being made out. Where expert and factual evidence has been called on both sides at a trial, its usefulness will normally have long since been exhausted.

(c) CAUSATION

Once a claimant has established that the doctor has breached her duty of care, she still has to prove that it was this breach of duty which caused her injuries. In practice, causation poses particular difficulties in medical negligence actions because there will usually be at least two possible causes of the patient's injury: the doctor's actions and

---

[67] [1998] Lloyd's Rep Med 168.

the patient's pre-existing condition. Where there are multiple causes, proving caus-ation on the balance of probabilities is especially problematic. The patient's health may have deteriorated even if the care she received was non-negligent, so often what has been lost is the *chance* of being restored to health. The courts are therefore often forced to speculate about what *might* have happened if the doctor had not in fact breached her duty of care.

(1) THE 'BUT FOR' TEST

The standard test for causation is often referred to as the 'but for' test: but for the defendant's negligence, would the claimant have suffered the injuries in question? In the medical context, this means that the claimant must show that their injury was caused by the doctor's negligence, rather than being a consequence of her pre-existing condition. It is not enough to show both that the doctor breached her duty of care, and that the claimant's health has got worse, rather there must be a causal link between these two events. So, for example, if a doctor makes a mistake in diagnosis, but a correct diagnosis would not have made a difference, the doctor's negligence has not caused the claimant's injury.

A case where the application of the 'but for' test was straightforward was *Barnett v Chelsea and Kensington Hospital Management Committee.*

Barnett v Chelsea and Kensington Hospital Management Committee[68]
See above p. 109 for the facts.

Nield J
It remains to consider whether it is shown that the deceased's death was caused by this negligence or whether, as the defendants have said, the deceased must have died in any event. . . .

There has been put before me a timetable which, I think, is of much importance. The deceased attended at the casualty department at 8.05 or 8.10 a.m. If Dr Banerjee had got up and dressed and come to see the three men and examined them and decided to admit them, the deceased could not have been in bed in a ward before 11 a.m. I accept Dr. Goulding's evidence that an intravenous drip would not have been set up before 12 noon . . . Dr. Lockett, dealing with this, said 'If [the deceased] had not been treated until after 12 noon the chances of survival were not good' . . .

If the principal condition is one of enzyme disturbance—as I am of the view that it was here—then the only method of treatment which is likely to succeed is the use of the specific or antidote which is commonly called B.A.L. Dr. Gouding said this in the course of his evidence:

The only way to deal with this is to use the specific B.A.L. I see no reasonable prospect of the deceased being given B.A.L. before the time at which he died . . .

I regard that evidence as very moderate, and that it might be a true assessment of the situation to say that there was no chance of B.A.L. being administered before the death of the deceased.

For these reasons, I find that the plaintiff has failed to establish, on the grounds of probability, that the defendants' negligence caused the death of the deceased.

It is not always possible to predict with this degree of certainty what would have happened to the claimant if they had been properly treated. More commonly, the

[68] [1969] 1 QB 428.

doctor's negligence *might* or *might not* have made a difference. In such cases the application of the 'but for' test is much more complicated. In particular, as we can see from the House of Lord's judgment in *Wilsher*, in medical cases there will often be multiple possible causes which means that it will be particularly difficult to prove, on the balance of probabilities, which one caused the claimant's injuries.

Wilsher v Essex Area Health Authority[69]

Martin Wilsher was born prematurely suffering from various illnesses. On two occasions, he was given excess oxygen. He was diagnosed with an incurable condition of the retina (RLF) which resulted in near blindness. This could have been caused by excess oxygen, but there were five other possible causes. At the trial the medical evidence was inconclusive whether the excess oxygen had caused or materially contributed to his condition. The trial judge and the Court of Appeal held that the hospital was to be taken as having caused the injury notwithstanding that it was not possible to ascertain the contribution made by the hospital's breach of duty. The health authority successfully appealed to the House of Lords.

Lord Bridge

In the Court of Appeal in the instant case Sir Nicolas Browne-Wilkinson V-C, being in a minority, expressed his view on causation with understandable caution. But I am quite unable to find any fault with the following passage in his dissenting judgment:

'. . . There are a number of different agents which could have caused the RLF. Excess oxygen was one of them. The defendants failed to take reasonable precautions to prevent one of the possible causative agents (eg excess oxygen) from causing RLF. But no one can tell in this case whether excess oxygen did or did not cause or contribute to the RLF suffered by the plaintiff. The plaintiff's RLF may have been caused by some completely different agent or agents, eg hypercarbia, intraventricular haemorrhage, apnoea or patent ductus arteriosus. . . . This baby suffered from each of those conditions at various times in the first two months of his life. There is no satisfactory evidence that excess oxygen is more likely than any of those other four candidates to have caused RLF in this baby. To my mind, the occurrence of RLF following a failure to take a necessary precaution to prevent excess oxygen causing RLF provides no evidence and raises no presumption that it was excess oxygen rather than one or more of the four other possible agents which caused or contributed to RLF in this case. The position, to my mind, is wholly different from that in McGhee, where there was only one candidate (brick dust) which could have caused the dermatitis, and the failure to take a precaution against brick dust causing dermatitis was followed by dermatitis caused by brick dust. In such a case, I can see the common sense, if not the logic, of holding that, in the absence of any other evidence, the failure to take the precaution caused or contributed to the dermatitis. To the extent that certain members of the House of Lords decided the question on inferences from evidence or presumptions, I do not consider that the present case falls within their reasoning. A failure to take preventive measures against one out of five possible causes is no evidence as to which of those five caused the injury.' . . .

[W]hether we like it or not, the law, which only Parliament can change, requires proof of fault causing damage as the basis of liability in tort. We should do society nothing but disservice if we made the forensic process still more unpredictable and hazardous by distorting the law to accommodate the exigencies of what may seem hard cases.

[69] [1988] 1 AC 1074.

Complicated issues are also raised when the doctor's breach of duty deprives the patient of the *chance* of recovery, as we can see from *Hotson v East Berkshire AHA*.

Hotson v East Berkshire AHA[70]

When he was thirteen years old, the claimant injured his hip in a fall. He was taken to a hospital run by the defendant health authority, where the injury was not correctly diagnosed, and was sent home. After five days of severe pain, he was taken back to the hospital where a proper diagnosis was made and he was given emergency treatment. He subsequently developed a severe medical condition leaving him with a major permanent disability. At the trial, the judge found that even if the claimant's injury had been diagnosed and treated immediately, there was still a 75% risk of his disability developing, but that the breach of duty had turned that risk into an inevitability, thus denying the claimant a 25% chance of a good recovery. The judge awarded the claimant 25% of the full value of the damages awardable for the claimant's disability. The Court of Appeal affirmed the judge's decision. The authority successfully appealed to the House of Lords.

Lord Bridge

On the basis of these findings [the judge] held, as a matter of law, that the plaintiff was entitled to damages for the loss of the 25% chance that, if the injury had been promptly diagnosed and treated, it would not have resulted in avascular necrosis of the epiphysis and the plaintiff would have made a very nearly full recovery. . . . He reached the conclusion that the question was one of quantification and thus arrived at his award to the plaintiff of one quarter of the damages appropriate to compensate him for the consequences of the avascular necrosis.

It is here, with respect, that I part company with the judge. The plaintiff's claim was for damages for physical injury and consequential loss alleged to have been caused by the authority's breach of their duty of care. In some cases, perhaps particularly medical negligence cases, causation may be so shrouded in mystery that the court can only measure statistical chances. But that was not so here. On the evidence there was a clear conflict as to what had caused the avascular necrosis. The authority's evidence was that the sole cause was the original traumatic injury to the hip. The plaintiff's evidence . . . was that the delay in treatment was a material contributory cause. This was a conflict, like any other about some relevant past event, which the judge could not avoid resolving on a balance of probabilities. Unless the plaintiff proved on a balance of probabilities that the delayed treatment was at least a material contributory cause of the avascular necrosis he failed on the issue of causation and no question of quantification could arise. . . .

The upshot is that the appeal must be allowed on the narrow ground that the plaintiff failed to establish a cause of action in respect of the avascular necrosis and its consequences.

Lord Ackner

To my mind, the first issue which the judge had to determine was an issue of causation: did the breach of duty cause the damage alleged? If it did not, as the judge so held, then no question of quantifying damage arises. The debate on the loss of a chance cannot arise where there has been a positive finding that before the duty arose the damage complained of had already been sustained or had become inevitable. . . .

I have sought to stress that this case was a relatively simple case concerned with the proof of causation, on which the plaintiff failed, because he was unable to prove, on the balance of probabilities, that his deformed hip was caused by the authority's breach of duty in delaying over a period of five days a proper diagnosis and treatment. Where causation is in issue, the judge decides that issue on the balance of the probabilities. . . .

---

[70] [1987] 1 AC 750.

Once liability is established, on the balance of probabilities, the loss which the plaintiff has sustained is payable in full. It is not discounted by reducing his claim by the extent to which he has failed to prove his case with 100% certainty.

According to *Hotson*, the courts must just be satisfied that it is *more likely than not* that the claimant's injuries would have been avoided if the doctor had not been negligent. If there is a 55 per cent chance that the patient would have made a complete recovery if she had received non-negligent treatment, she can recover in full. Whereas if there is a 45 per cent chance of recovery, her claim fails because she has not proved on the balance of probabilities that her injuries were caused by the defendant's negligence. The problem with framing the issue in this way is that the courts are engaged in an inevitably hypothetical inquiry about what *might have happened* if the doctor had not acted as she did, and this sort of speculation is not well suited to precise quantification in percentage terms.

In the following case, the question for the judge was whether a heavy drinker would have stopped drinking if he had been told he had end-stage liver disease. On the evidence of his wife, the judge found that he would have done. For obvious reasons, it is impossible to judge the truth or falsity of this finding.

Hutchinson v Epsom and St Helier NHS Trust[71]

The claimant's husband was obese and a heavy drinker. He had attended hospital where blood tests were taken and he was asked about his alcohol consumption. Despite abnormal blood test results, liver function tests were not carried out and his liver disease was not detected. If it had been, he would have been advised to stop drinking and lose weight. He died the following year. The question for the court was whether the failure to advise him to stop drinking caused his death.

John Royce QC

Would the deceased have given up drink had he been properly warned? This is not an easy question to decide. It is clear on the evidence, as I have found, that he was a considerable drinker. He was very fond of his wine in particular . . . What would he have been told? The evidence is that he would have been told, 'If you don't stop drinking you will be dead in twelve months or perhaps two years'. That is a stark warning. Mrs Hutchinson gave evidence on this issue. She said, 'I believe he would have given up had he been told this.' . . . Having listened to Mrs Hutchinson in the witness box and seen her during this trial, it is clear to me that there is considerable force in what she says. Undoubtedly he would have had the motivation. In my judgment, she is probably right. Had he been given that stark warning when he should have been, he would, on the balance of probabilities, have stopped drinking. . . .

For the reasons set out earlier in this judgment, it follows that the claimant has proved that negligence in this case was at least a material contribution to the damage that was suffered, that damage was the cause of the deceased's death, and in consequence this claim must succeed in full.

In a non-medical case, *Fairchild v Glenhaven Funeral Services*,[72] the House of Lords has recently allowed a claim to succeed despite the claimants' inability to prove which of several employers, all of whom had exposed them to asbestos, had caused their mesothelioma (a rare form of lung cancer caused by exposure to asbestos). This more 'claimant-friendly' decision is, however, unlikely to have much impact upon the

---

[71] [2002] EWHC 2363.   [72] [2002] UKHL 22, [2003] 1 AC 32.

difficulties in proving causation in medical negligence cases because the House of Lords expressly approved the more restrictive approach to causation in *Wilsher*. Lord Bingham, for example, said:

It is plain, in my respectful opinion, that the House was right to allow the defendants' appeal in *Wilsher* for the reasons which the Vice-Chancellor had given and which the House approved. It is one thing to treat an increase of risk as equivalent to the making of a material contribution where a single noxious agent is involved, but quite another where any one of a number of noxious agents may equally probably have caused the damage.

And Lord Hoffmann further suggested that:

the political and economic arguments involved in the massive increase in the liability of the National Health Service . . . are far more complicated than the reasons . . . for imposing liability upon an employer who has failed to take simple precautions.

And in *Gregg v Scott*,[73] a case in which a GP's failure either to correctly diagnose a lymphoma (a type of cancer), or to refer the patient to a specialist, reduced his chance of survival from 42 per cent to 25 per cent, a majority of the House of Lords confirmed that *Fairchild* did not affect the requirement that the claimant must prove causation on the balance of probabilities:

Lord Hoffmann

In effect, the Appellant submits that the exceptional rule in Fairchild should be generalised and damages awarded in all cases in which the defendant may have caused an injury and has increased the likelihood of the injury being suffered. . . .

It should first be noted that adopting such a rule would involve abandoning a good deal of authority. The rule which the House is asked to adopt is the very rule which it rejected in Wilsher's case. Yet Wilsher's case was expressly approved by the House in Fairchild. Hotson too would have to be overruled. Furthermore, the House would be dismantling all the qualifications and restrictions with which it so recently hedged the Fairchild exception. There seem to me to be no new arguments or change of circumstances which could justify such a radical departure from precedent . . .

[A] wholesale adoption of possible rather than probable causation as the criterion of liability would be so radical a change in our law as to amount to a legislative act. It would have enormous consequences for insurance companies and the National Health Service. In company with my noble and learned friends Lord Phillips of Worth Matravers and Baroness Hale of Richmond, I think that any such change should be left to Parliament.

Lord Phillips

It is always likely to be much easier to resolve issues of causation on balance of probabilities than to identify in terms of percentage the effect that clinical negligence had on the chances of a favourable outcome. This reality is a policy factor that weighs against the introduction into this area of a right to compensation for the loss of a chance. A robust test which produces rough justice may be preferable to a test that on occasion will be difficult, if not impossible, to apply with confidence in practice . . .

In Fairchild v Glenhaven Funeral Services Ltd this House made a change in the law of negligence in the interests of justice . . . In this case Lord Nicholls of Birkenhead proposes a different

---

[73] [2005] UKHL 2 (transcript on Lexis).

approach in the case of a doctor whose negligence has decreased the chance that a patient will be cured of a disease. Under that proposal the doctor will be liable to the extent that his negligence has reduced the chance of a cure. My Lords, it seems to me that there is a danger, if special tests of causation are developed piecemeal to deal with perceived injustices in particular factual situations, that the coherence of our common law will be destroyed.

Under our law as it is at present, and subject to the exception in Fairchild, a claimant will only succeed if, on balance of probability the negligence is the cause of the injury. If there is a possibility, but not a probability, that the negligence caused the injury, the claimant will recover nothing in respect of the breach of duty. . . .

The complications of this case have persuaded me that it is not a suitable vehicle for introducing into the law of clinical negligence the right to recover damages for the loss of a chance of a cure. Awarding damages for the reduction of the prospect of a cure, when the long term result of treatment is still uncertain, is not a satisfactory exercise. Where medical treatment has resulted in an adverse outcome and negligence has increased the chance of that outcome, there may be a case for permitting a recovery of damages that is proportionate to the increase in the chance of the adverse outcome. That is not a case that has been made out on the present appeal.

It is worth noting the final paragraph in this extract from Lord Phillips' judgment. By the time the case reached the House of Lords, Mr Gregg's chance of survival now looked rather better than 25 per cent, and in such circumstances, Lord Phillips thought that he should not be able to recover for the loss of a chance of a cure. On a different set of facts, Lord Phillips implies that he would not, in principle, be hostile to such claims. Given this, and the powerful speeches from the two dissenting judges, Lord Hope and Lord Nicholls (see below), it seems likely that the courts will soon revisit the question of whether the conventional approach to causation set out in *Hotson* and *Wilsher*, works unfairly where the patient has lost a less than 50–50 chance of recovery.

Lord Nicholls (dissenting)

A patient is suffering from cancer. His prospects are uncertain. He has a 45% chance of recovery. Unfortunately his doctor negligently misdiagnoses his condition as benign. So the necessary treatment is delayed for months. As a result the patient's prospects of recovery become nil or almost nil. Has the patient a claim for damages against the doctor? No, the House was told. The patient could recover damages if his initial prospects of recovery had been more than 50%. But because they were less than 50% he can recover nothing.

This surely cannot be the state of the law today. It would be irrational and indefensible. The loss of a 45% prospect of recovery is just as much a real loss for a patient as the loss of a 55% prospect of recovery. In both cases the doctor was in breach of his duty to his patient. In both cases the patient was worse off. He lost something of importance and value. But, it is said, in one case the patient has a remedy, in the other he does not.

This would make no sort of sense. It would mean that in the 45% case the doctor's duty would be hollow. The duty would be empty of content. For the reasons which follow I reject this suggested distinction. The common law does not compel courts to proceed in such an unreal fashion. I would hold that a patient has a right to a remedy as much where his prospects of recovery were less than 50–50 as where they exceeded 50–50. . . .

It cannot be right to adopt a procedure having the effect that, in law, a patient's prospects of recovery are treated as non-existent whenever they exist but fall short of 50%. If the law were to proceed in this way it would deserve to be likened to the proverbial ass . . .

The way ahead must surely be to recognise that where a patient is suffering from illness or injury and his prospects of recovery are attended with a significant degree of medical uncertainty, and he suffers a significant diminution of his prospects of recovery by reason of medical negligence whether of diagnosis or treatment, that diminution constitutes actionable damage. This is so whether the patient's prospects immediately before the negligence exceeded or fell short of 50% . . .

The present state of the law is crude to an extent bordering on arbitrariness. It means that a patient with a 60% chance of recovery reduced to a 40% prospect by medical negligence can obtain compensation. But he can obtain nothing if his prospects were reduced from 40% to nil. This is rough justice indeed. By way of contrast, the approach set out above meets the perceived need for an appropriate remedy in both these situations and does no more than reflect fairly and rationally the loss suffered by a patient in these situations.

(2) REMOTENESS

There is another hurdle to overcome once a claimant has succeeded in proving factual causation: it is also necessary to establish that the type of damage is not too remote. According to the *Wagon Mound*[74] test for remoteness, the type of damage must be foreseeable, although its extent, and the manner in which it occurred, need not be. Normally in clinical negligence cases the *type* of damage will be some sort of physical injury, which is obviously a foreseeable consequence of negligent medical care. As a result, there are few medical cases where remoteness has been an issue.

One exception is *R v Croydon Health Authority*.[75] The claimant had undergone a pre-employment chest X-ray, and the radiographer failed to alert her to an abnormality (primary pulmonary hypertension or PPH), which would be exacerbated by pregnancy. She argued that if she had known that she had PPH, she would not have become pregnant. The Court of Appeal dismissed her claim for the costs arising from the birth of her child on the grounds that they were too remote. Kennedy LJ held that:

The damage was, as is sometimes said, too remote. The chain of events had too many links. . . . We understand that the radiologist never actually saw the plaintiff, and he probably knew very little about her except her age. He would no doubt have accepted that, in so far as he failed to observe an abnormality which could have affected her fitness for work as an employee of the health authority in the immediate future, that was something for which he should be held accountable, but her domestic circumstances were not his affair.

In *Page v Smith*[76] the House of Lords held that provided physical injury was foreseeable, the defendant might also be liable if the claimant suffers psychiatric injury as a result of her negligence. Hence, if it is foreseeable that a doctor's negligence will physically injure her patient, then the doctor will also be liable if the patient in fact suffers psychiatric injury, even if no physical injury in fact results. According to Lord Lloyd:

it was enough to ask whether the defendant should have reasonably foreseen that the plaintiff might suffer physical injury as a result of the defendant's negligence, so as to bring him within the range of the defendant's duty of care. It was unnecessary to ask, as a separate question, whether

---

[74] [1961] AC 388.   [75] (1997) 40 BMLR 40.   [76] [1996] AC 155.

the defendant should reasonably have foreseen injury by shock; and it is irrelevant that the plaintiff did not, in fact, suffer any external physical injury.

In *The Creutzfeldt-Jakob Disease Litigation; Group B Plaintiffs v Medical Research Council*[77] the claimants were children, handicapped by dwarfism, who had taken part in a clinical experimental trial with a type of human growth hormone (Hartree HGH). It later became clear that this was capable of infecting them with Creutzfeldt-Jacob Disease (CJD). All of the children became aware that they were at risk of developing CJD. On a trial of the preliminary issues, Morland J held that it was possible to recover damages for the psychiatric injury that had been caused by this knowledge.

Morland J

I am satisfied that when the defendants breached their duty of care to them by being responsible for injecting them with potentially lethal Hartree HGH they should have reasonably foreseen that, if deaths occurred from CJD caused by HGH contaminated with the CJD agent, some of the recipients of that HGH, including some of normal phlegm and ordinary fortitude, might well suffer psychiatric injury on becoming aware of the risk to them. . . . The defendants as tortfeasors committed a wrong upon the Group B plaintiffs by imperilling their lives from a terrible fatal disease. It was reasonably foreseeable that, if the worst fears were realised and deaths from CJD occurred, Hartree HGH recipients, both those of normal fortitude and those more vulnerable, might suffer psychiatric injury. I cannot see in the facts and circumstances of this litigation why public policy, including social and economic policy considerations, should exclude them from compensation.

A further dimension to remoteness is the question of whether an intervening act or decision has broken the chain of causation. If a psychiatric patient who was known to be a suicide risk succeeds in committing suicide as a result of a negligent failure to keep her under appropriate surveillance, has the chain of causation been broken by the patient's own action in deliberately taking her own life? In *Kirkham v Chief Constable of Greater Manchester*,[78] the court rejected the claim that the deceased's suicide had been a *novus actus* on the grounds that it was the very act which the defendants had been under a duty to prevent. And in *Reeves v Commissioner of Police of the Metropolis*,[79] another case in which a prisoner committed suicide, Lord Jauncey dismissed the argument that his decision to take his own life constituted a *novus actus*.

The deceased's suicide was the precise event to which the duty was directed and as an actus it was accordingly neither novus nor interveniens.

Instead, as we see below, the House of Lords used the defence of contributory negligence to reduce the damages payable to his estate.

Where there was no prior indication that a patient was at risk of committing suicide, her actions would be much more likely to break the chain of causation. In *Hyde v Tameside AHA*,[80] the claimant was being treated in a general hospital for a physical disability. He became depressed and jumped out of a window, leaving him permanently disabled. The Court of Appeal held that the hospital staff were not under a duty to prevent him from attempting to commit suicide.

[77] [2000] Lloyd's Rep Med 161.   [78] [1990] 2 QB 283.   [79] [2000] 1 AC 360.
[80] *The Times* 15 Apr 1981.

(d) DEFENCES

Various defences to an action in negligence are possible. A partial defence would exist if the patient had been contributorily negligent, perhaps because she discharged herself from hospital against medical advice. Under section 1 of the Law Reform (Contributory Negligence) Act 1945, damages can be reduced in proportion to the extent of the claimant's responsibility for her injuries. So might a patient's failure to follow medical instructions, or to accurately describe her symptoms, amount to contributory negligence? Most instances of non-compliance or inaccuracy are unlikely to affect a patient's award, because many, if not most, patients fail to comply exactly with their doctor's instructions, and it is often difficult for patients to precisely articulate their symptoms. But a patient who completely ignores her doctor's advice might be found to bear some responsibility if her condition deteriorates.

Another situation in which the question of the patient's contributory negligence might arise is if a patient succeeds in harming herself when the doctors treating her were under a duty to prevent such behaviour. If she could be said to be responsible for her own actions, a reduction in damages on the grounds of contributory negligence might be possible. This was the preferred solution in *Reeves v Commissioner of Police of the Metropolis*,[81] where Lord Hoffmann explained:

a 100 per cent apportionment of responsibility to Mr. Lynch gives no weight at all to the policy of the law in imposing a duty of care upon the police. . . . The apportionment must recognise that a purpose of the duty accepted by the commissioner in this case is to demonstrate publicly that the police do have a responsibility for taking reasonable care to prevent prisoners from committing suicide. On the other hand, respect must be paid to the finding of fact that Mr. Lynch was 'of sound mind.' . . . In these circumstances, I think that the right answer is . . . to apportion responsibility equally.

Where the patient has been wholly responsible for her injuries, this may simply lead to a finding that the doctor had not been negligent at all. For example, in *Venner v North East Essex Health Authority and Another*[82] a woman who was about to undergo a sterilization operation was advised to come off the contraceptive pill, but to take other contraceptive precautions prior to the operation. Before the operation she was asked whether there was any chance that she could be pregnant, to which she answered 'no', despite the fact that she and her husband had engaged in unprotected sexual intercourse. She was in fact pregnant when the operation took place, and subsequently gave birth to a healthy child. Tucker J found that there had been no negligence, and the patient herself—a mature woman who understood the likelihood of conception—was responsible for her pregnancy.

Tucker J

I am satisfied that the normal routine as described by these witnesses was adhered to in the case of the plaintiff. I find that she was advised to use an alternative method of contraception or to abstain. She was a mature woman with more than average experience of gynaecological problems. She was fully aware of the almost inevitable consequences in her case of indulging in unprotected intercourse. I am quite sure she understood what she was being told. . . .

[81] [2000] 1 AC 360.   [82] *The Times* 21 Feb 1987.

Where, as here, a mature and sensible woman is asked a question to which only she knows the answer, then she bears a real responsibility to give an accurate and truthful answer. It is not incumbent upon a medical man in the position of the second defendant to pry further into the intimate details of her life. . . . Only two people knew that unprotected intercourse had taken place, the plaintiff and her husband. She knew of the probable consequences of such intercourse. She ought to have told the second defendant that it had taken place, but she did not . . . Why did the plaintiff indulge in unprotected sexual intercourse at all? The plaintiff says it was because she was not advised against it . . . In my judgment if a woman conducts herself in that way contrary to advice and then gives an answer which is less than frank it can scarcely be said that the operating gynaecologist is responsible for the continuing pregnancy.

The defence of *volenti non fit injuria* is extremely unlikely to affect clinical negligence claims. It is difficult to imagine a case in which the patient was said to have voluntarily assumed the risk of being injured by the doctor's negligence.

In contrast, there have been cases where the defence of illegality or *ex turpi causa non oritur actio* has been raised. In *Clunis v Camden and Islington Health Authority*,[83] a case we considered in the previous chapter, involving a mental patient who killed a tube passenger, the Court of Appeal applied the maxim of *ex turpi causa non oritur actio* to reject his claim against the health authority for their failure to ensure he was properly assessed and treated:

Beldam LJ

In our view, the plaintiff's claim does arise out of and depend upon proof of his commission of a criminal offence. . . . In the present case the plaintiff has been convicted of a serious criminal offence. In such a case, public policy would in our judgment preclude the court from entertaining the plaintiff's claim unless it could be said that he did not know the nature and quality of his act, or that what he was doing was wrong. The offence of murder was reduced to one of manslaughter by reason of the plaintiff's mental disorder but his mental state did not justify a verdict of not guilty by reason of insanity. Consequently, though his responsibility for killing Mr Zito is diminished, he must be taken to have known what he was doing and that it was wrong. . . .

The court ought not to allow itself to be made an instrument to enforce obligations alleged to arise out of the plaintiff's own criminal act and we would therefore allow the appeal on this ground.

(e) LIMITATION PERIODS

If the patient's loss is financial, there is a six year limitation period.[84] Most personal injury cases must be brought within three years either of the date when the injury occurred, or the date when the patient realized, or should have realized, that she might be able to sue.[85] If the patient dies as a result of her injuries, her relatives have three years from the date of death, or from the date when they realize, or should have realized, that an action could be brought.[86] Section 14 of the Limitation Act sets out when the three year period starts to run:

---

[83] [1988] QB 978 CA.   [84] Limitation Act 1980 ss 2 and 5.   [85] Ibid, ss 11(4) and 14(1).
[86] Ibid, ss 11(5) and 14(1).

Limitation Act 1980 section 14

(1) . . . references to a person's date of knowledge are references to the date on which he first had knowledge of the following facts—

    (a) that the injury in question was significant; and

    (b) that the injury was attributable in whole or in part to the act or omission which is alleged to constitute negligence . . .; and

    (c) the identity of the defendant; and

    (d) if it is alleged that the act or omission was that of a person other than the defendant, the identity of that person and the additional facts supporting the bringing of an action against the defendant. . . .

(2) For the purposes of this section an injury is significant if the person whose date of knowledge is in question would reasonably have considered it sufficiently serious to justify his instituting proceedings for damages . . .

(3) For the purposes of this section a person's knowledge includes knowledge which he might reasonably have been expected to acquire—

    (a) from facts observable or ascertainable by him; or

    (b) from facts ascertainable by him with the help of medical or other appropriate expert advice which it is reasonable for him to seek;

but a person shall not be fixed under this subsection with knowledge of a fact ascertainable only with the help of expert advice so long as he has taken all reasonable steps to obtain (and, where appropriate, to act on) that advice.

One of the problems section 14 presents in medical cases is that it may be particularly difficult for an individual to determine whether their injury was 'attributable in whole or in part to the act or omission which is alleged to constitute negligence'. Medical treatment is not always successful, and so an individual whose condition deteriorates may have just been unlucky. As we can see from the following case, it is not necessary for the claimant to *know* that their injuries are due to negligence, rather time starts to run when they could be said to have constructive knowledge of the *possibility* of litigation.

Forbes v Wandsworth Health Authority[87]

In October 1982 Mr Forbes had an operation on his left leg. The operation was not a success, nor was a second operation carried out the next day. Mr Forbes' leg had to be amputated. In June 1991 he consulted a solicitor. Advice from a vascular surgeon obtained in October 1992 suggested that the amputation could have been avoided if the second operation had been carried out sooner. In December 1992 Mr Forbes issued proceedings against the defendant health authority, and the judge said that his action was not time-barred because he had no reason to suspect or think that the removal of his leg was due to the act or omission of the defendant. The health authority appealed but before the case was heard by the Court of Appeal, Mr Forbes died. By a majority the Court of Appeal allowed the health authority's appeal.

---

[87] [1997] QB 402 CA.

Stuart-Smith LJ

It seems to me that where, as here, the plaintiff expected or at least hoped that the operation would be successful and it manifestly was not, with the result that he sustained a major injury, a reasonable man of moderate intelligence, such as the deceased, if he thought about the matter, would say that the lack of success was 'either just one of those things, a risk of the operation or something may have gone wrong and there may have been a want of care; I do not know which, but if I am ever to make a claim, I must find out'.

In my judgment, any other construction would make the 1980 Act unworkable since a plaintiff could delay indefinitely before seeking expert advice and say, as the deceased did in this case, I had no occasion to seek it earlier. He would therefore be able, as of right, to bring the action, no matter how many years had elapsed. This is contrary to the whole purpose of the 1980 Act which is to prevent defendants being vexed by stale claims which it is no longer possible to contest. . . .

I have come to the conclusion, therefore, that in the circumstances of this case the deceased did have constructive knowledge.

For children or incompetent adults, the limitation period does not begin to run until they become competent.[88] In such cases, it is obviously possible to sue many years after the alleged negligent act, when evidence as to the precise circumstances which led to the claimant's injuries may no longer be reliable.

In addition, section 33 of the Limitation Act 1980 gives the court a discretion to extend the limitation period where it would be equitable to do so. In making this judgment, the court has to balance the degree to which the statutory limitation period prejudices the claimant, with the degree to which an extension of that period will prejudice the defendant. The court will have regard to a number of factors, such as the reasons for the delay, and the conduct of both parties. Contrast *Smith v Leicestershire Health Authority*, where the court said that it would have been persuaded to exercise its discretion under section 33, and *Forbes v Wandsworth Health Authority*, where it declined to do so.

Smith v Leicestershire Health Authority[89]

When she was a child, Mrs Smith, who was now aged fifty-four, had her condition misdiagnosed, resulting in her having an operation which caused tetraplegia. The possibility of an action in negligence only became apparent twenty-five years later. In deciding whether it should exercise its discretion under section 33, the Court of Appeal found that to do so would be of tremendous importance to the claimant, while not unduly prejudicing the defendants

Roch LJ

The degree to which the provisions of s. 11 of the 1980 Act would prejudice the plaintiff far outweighs the prejudice to the defendants that a direction under s. 33 of the Act would create. The plaintiff has a terrible disability for which it has now been established that the defendants are tortiously liable. The extent to which the defendants themselves may be worse off because the claim was not brought prior to 1 April 1990 pales in comparison with the loss to the plaintiff if a court were not to exercise its discretion in her favour. . . .

In this case, all the expert witnesses were agreed that the radiologist at the defendants hospitals had fallen below proper standards for a radiologist in the 1950s, and the judge unhesitatingly accepted that evidence. Causation does not change with the passage of time. . . .

---

[88] Limitation Act 1980 s 28.   [89] [1998] Lloyd's Rep Med 77.

This is not even a case where the defendants could complain that had the proceedings been brought in the 1960s or 1970s the plaintiff would have been unable to establish the causal connection, whereas advances in medical science between the 1970s and the 1990s had enabled her to do so. Causation was established by the acceptance of the defendants expert evidence. For these reasons we would had it been necessary have exercised our discretion under s. 33 in the plaintiffs favour.

Forbes v Wandsworth Health Authority[90]
For facts, see above.

Stuart Smith LJ
[I]t is necessary to consider the effect of s 33 of the 1980 Act. . . . This gives rise to the question whether in the circumstances this court must now exercise its discretion afresh. . . . But for one feature, this might prove to be a difficult and important question. That feature is the death of Mr Forbes between the trial of the preliminary point and the appeal. That is a new situation which to my mind undoubtedly affects the exercise of discretion under s 33, if for no other reason than that the potential damages recoverable for the benefit of the estate of the deceased are significantly less than they would have been if the deceased were still alive. No damages for pain, suffering and loss of amenity can be recovered for any period after the death, and the claim for future cost of care, aids and appliances . . . will not be recoverable. . . .

There is a further problem caused by excessive delay in medical negligence cases. The court is concerned with acceptable standards of medical practice in 1982. With the best will in the world it is not always easy, where medical science and practice has progressed over the years, for experts to put themselves back into the standard of the day, now 14 years ago. Although in theory this may be a difficulty that affects both sides, in practice it often presents more difficulty for the defence since recent advances which affect current opinion have to be ignored. . . .

There is a further aspect which is relevant to consideration of the exercise of discretion under s 33. That is the strength of the plaintiff's case. . . . Taking a broad view of the plaintiff's chances of success on the material available, I have to say that I can only regard them as modest. For all these reasons, I have come to the conclusion that the court should not exercise discretion in favour of the plaintiff.

In the next extract, Richard Lewis explains the justification for limitation periods:

Richard Lewis[91]
There is general agreement over the aims of the law of limitation. First, it provides finality so that sooner or later an incident or transgression which might have led to a claim can be safely treated as closed by all concerned. Secondly, it gives defendants a degree of protection from stale claims which they can no longer properly contest. And thirdly it provides an incentive to plaintiffs to commence proceedings without delay. This is closely related to the need to protect defendants from old claims but goes further in that it also recognises that the trial of disputes on complete or unreliable evidence is prejudicial to the public interest in the proper administration of justice. These objectives must of course be balanced against the interests of plaintiffs and the law now attaches very great weight to the need to give injured persons a fair chance to commence proceedings; hence the date of knowledge provisions and the section 33 discretion.

---

[90] [1997] QB 402 CA.
[91] 'The Limitation Period in Medical Negligence Claims' (1998) 6 Medical Law Review 62–98, 64.

5. THE NHS COMPLAINTS SYSTEM

Patients who are dissatisfied with their medical treatment will not necessarily either choose, or be eligible to pursue an action in negligence. Such patients may nevertheless want to complain about the care they received. The NHS complaints system has recently undergone a complete overhaul. In 2003, the Department of Health published *NHS complaints reform—making things right*, its proposals for reform of the NHS complaints process. The Health and Social Care (Community Health and Standards) Act 2003 put these reforms into place. The intention was (1) to make the system more flexible so that there are a range of ways in which people can express concerns about the services they have received; (2) to improve local resolution; (3) to shift responsibility for independent review to the Healthcare Commission; and (4) to ensure that information about complaints and their causes are used to raise the standard of patient care.

Every NHS trust and Primary Care trust now has its own Patient Advice and Liaison Service (PALS) with staff available to listen to patients' concerns, and to offer information and support. These support staff will liaise with other staff and managers to help resolve problems before a formal complaint is made. Local resolution is the next stage, and it is usually successful—only 2 per cent of complaints progress beyond the local resolution stage. The Department of Health has produced a *Good Practice Toolkit* for local resolution, to ensure that it works consistently across the NHS. An Independent Complaints Advocacy Service (ICAS) has also been set up to ensure that complainants have access to support in articulating their concerns and in navigating the complaints system.

If local resolution fails, the Commission for Healthcare Audit and Inspection, known as the Healthcare Commission, is responsible for managing the independent review stage of the complaints process. A complaint must be made to the Healthcare Commission within two months of receiving a formal written response from the NHS trust or GP's practice. The Healthcare Commission will review individual cases in order to assess whether further action is required, and if so, what. It will usually seek an explanation and an acknowledgement of what went wrong, and if warranted, an apology. It can also recommend that the healthcare provider makes changes so that lessons are learned, and the same thing does not happen again. There is no power to award compensation. The Healthcare Commission also promotes the systematic use of feedback from complaints through its inspection processes.

If a case is particularly complex, or remains unresolved after review by the Healthcare Commission, recourse may be had to the Ombudsman.[92] The Health Service Ombudsman looks into complaints made by or on behalf of people who have suffered because of unsatisfactory treatment or service within the NHS. The complaint has to be made within a year from when the patient became aware of the events which are the subject of the complaint, and the patient must show that she has suffered some hardship or injustice. It is not usually possible to obtain damages, although in some

---

[92] <http://www.ombudsman.org.uk>.

rare circumstances, where the person involved can prove that they have suffered financial loss, the ombudsman can order some financial payment. This happens in fewer than ten cases each year.[93]

The Ombudsman does not investigate cases where the complainant could bring an action for negligence, unless it would not be reasonable to expect her to pursue a legal remedy. However, in some circumstances the Ombudsman will take on complaints about negligent treatment, provided that the complainant undertakes not to start legal proceedings.

The Health Service Ombudsman received 4,703 new complaints during 2003/4. Most of these were deemed to be premature because they had failed to exhaust local resolution. In 2003/4, 342 grievances were investigated, of which 244 (71 per cent) were upheld. The three subjects on which the most grievances were received were clinical treatment (49 per cent), complaint handling (19 per cent) and written and oral communication (8 per cent).[94]

6. THE GENERAL MEDICAL COUNCIL

In serious cases, a disgruntled patient might also report a doctor to the General Medical Council (GMC), and if found to be guilty of serious professional misconduct, the doctor can be struck off or suspended from the medical register, or conditions may be imposed upon her practice, such as a requirement that she refrains from carrying out a particular procedure. In the past, appeals from GMC decisions were to the Privy Council, but the National Health Service Reform and Healthcare Professions Act 2002 provides that appeals must now be made to the High Court. The 2002 Act also set up the Council for the Regulation of Healthcare Professionals, which regulates professional bodies like the GMC and the Nursing and Midwifery Council. It is intended to ensure consistency, and can refer disciplinary decisions directly to the High Court if it judges them to have been too lenient.

While doctors' mistakes will seldom amount to 'serious professional misconduct', serious cases of negligence can result in disciplinary action. In *McCandless v GMC*,[95] the appellant had been struck off the medical register, and appealed to the Privy Council, arguing that 'serious professional misconduct' implied that the conduct had to have been morally blameworthy. The appellant admitted that he had been negligent, but said that an honest mistake could not amount to serious professional misconduct. The Privy Council rejected his appeal. Lord Hoffmann said that:

the possible penalties available to the committee, which used to be confined to the ultimate sanction of erasure, have been extended to include suspension and the imposition of conditions upon practise. This suggests that the offence was intended to include serious cases of negligence . . . [T]he public has higher expectations of doctors and members of other self-governing professions. Their governing bodies are under a corresponding duty to protect the public against the genially incompetent as well as the deliberate wrongdoers.

[93] Health Service Ombudsman for England Annual Report 2003–04 <http://www.ombudsman.org.uk/>.
[94] Ibid.
[95] [1996] 1WLR 167.

The Medical (Professional Performance) Act 1995 introduced a new procedure for suspending a doctor from the register, or making registration conditional upon retraining or avoiding a particular procedure, where she is guilty of 'seriously deficient performance'. Seriously deficient performance is defined as 'a departure from good professional practice, whether or not it is covered by specific GMC guidance, sufficiently serious to call into question a doctor's registration'. Obviously this definition is somewhat question-begging, nevertheless it is clearly not necessary to prove that patients have been harmed by the doctor's 'seriously deficient performance'.

It is not only patients who might want to report the conduct of an incompetent doctor. Other healthcare workers will often be better placed than patients to spot unusually poor results, or inadequate care. The GMC's guide to good medical practice states that doctors must report a colleague whom they suspect to be unfit to practice,[96] and a similar duty is placed on nurses by the Nursing and Midwifery Council.

In practice, however, it is often difficult for doctors and nurses to raise concerns about a colleague's poor performance. Stephen Bolsin, the 'whistleblower' who reported his doubts about the practice of paediatric cardiac surgery at the Bristol Royal Infirmary was ostracized by the medical establishment, and eventually emigrated to Australia. Since 1999, the Public Interest Disclosure Act 1998 has given protection against dismissal and victimization to employees who have disclosed information in the public interest. And a Health Service Circular now requires each NHS trust and Health Authority to investigate staff concerns, and to guarantee that staff who raise concerns responsibly and reasonably will be protected against victimization.[97] It remains to be seen whether this will remove some of the cultural and institutional barriers to open reporting. Certainly, Julia Burrows' empirical research found that comparatively few nurses would report concerns about risky GPs:

Julia Burrows[98]

Only 61 per cent of nurses said they would report a concern about 'risky' GP performance, 6 per cent said they would not, while 33 per cent were unsure. Only 37 per cent knew whom to report it to . . . The nurses were given options to choose regarding the reasons they might not report concerns. The two most likely reasons to stop them reporting anything was a feeling it might not make a difference anyway . . . and a lack of trust in the authority or manager to take appropriate action . . . Nearly one third of the nurses questioned said that during their career they had had concerns about GPs' performance to the extent they felt patients were at risk, yet over half of these did not report them. Of the 47 per cent who did report the concern, no action was taken in more than half of cases. . . . In my study, of the seven nurses who had raised their concern about specific GP performance, six of these (86 per cent) felt that the response they received was not adequate to protect patients. . . . It is suggested that the situation where more than a third of nurses are unsure whether or not they would report a GP even when they feel patients could be at risk, has worrying implications for patient safety. Even among those who feel they would report a concern, there was little clarity about the correct procedures for doing this.

---

[96] *Good Medical Practice* (GMC London 2001) paras 26–7.   [97] HSC 1999/198.
[98] 'Telling Tales and Saving Lives: Whistleblowing—the Role of Professional Colleagues in Protecting Patients from Dangerous Doctors' (2001) 9 Medical Law Review 110–29, 121–3, 125.

The GMC also now has a role in the ongoing scrutiny of doctors' standard of care. Historically, doctors were admitted to the medical register on qualification, and no further checks were made unless the doctor's performance gave rise to serious concern. From April 2005, in order to practise medicine in the UK, doctors must hold a licence to practise. To retain this licence, doctors will have to 'revalidate' every five years, by demonstrating that they remain up to date and fit to practise. The purpose of revalidation is to shift the emphasis away from simply checking a doctor's initial qualifications towards regular assessment of the doctor's ability to provide appropriate care. Doctors must now *prove* that their own practice over the previous five years has been in line with the principles set out in the GMC's guide to the duties of a doctor, *Good Medical Practice*. This means routinely collecting and keeping data and information drawn from their day-to-day medical practice. The GMC also demands evidence of participation in an internal appraisal scheme.

7. THE CRIMINAL LAW

In extreme cases, might a doctor's misconduct lead to criminal liability? If death is caused by gross negligence, a conviction for manslaughter is possible, making it important to be able to tell when negligence is 'gross'. The question came before the Court of Appeal in *R v Prentice*.

R v Prentice; R v Sullman[99]
Two young doctors failed to check the labels before injecting cytotoxic drugs into the patient's spine. The patient died. They were charged with manslaughter, and convicted. Their appeals were successful on the grounds that the jury had not been properly directed as to the proper test of involuntary manslaughter by breach of a professional duty of care.

Lord Taylor CJ
The ingredients of involuntary manslaughter by breach of duty which need to be proved are:

   (1) The existence of the duty.

   (2) A breach of the duty causing death.

   (3) Gross negligence which the jury consider justifies a criminal conviction. . . .

[W]e consider proof of any of the following states of mind in the defendant may properly lead a jury to make a finding of gross negligence:

   (a) Indifference to an obvious risk of injury to health.

   (b) Actual foresight of the risk coupled with the determination nevertheless to run it.

   (c) An appreciation of the risk coupled with an intention to avoid it but also coupled with such a high degree of negligence in the attempted avoidance as the jury consider justifies conviction.

   (d) Inattention or failure to advert to a serious risk which goes beyond 'mere inadvertence' in respect of an obvious and important matter which the defendant's duty demanded he should address. . . .

[99] [1994] QB 302.

The question for the jury should have been whether, in the case of each doctor they were sure that the failure to ascertain the correct mode of administering the drug and to ensure that only that mode was adopted was grossly negligent to the point of criminality, having regard to all the excuses and mitigating circumstances in the case.

Of those, there were many. Doctor Prentice was required to give the treatment without the consultant who prescribed it giving any instruction or thought as to who should do so. This, despite the fact that Doctor Prentice was inexperienced, reluctant to give the treatment and wholly unaware . . . of the likely fatal consequences of giving the drug he did by lumbar puncture. . . .

Had the directions to the jury left it open to them to take these matters into account on the specific issue of gross negligence which we hold was the right issue, they may well, in our judgment, have concluded that the prosecution had failed to establish that essential ingredient. Accordingly, in our view, the appeals of these two appellants must be allowed and their convictions quashed.

A year later the House of Lords in *R v Adomako* eschewed such a specific direction to the jury. Instead, they endorsed a rather circular definition: negligence is 'gross' when it is so bad that it should be criminal.

R v Adomako[100]

The defendant was the anaesthetist during an eye operation. He failed to notice that the tube from the ventilator had become disconnected. The patient suffered a cardiac arrest, and subsequently died. The defendant was charged with manslaughter. At his trial it was conceded on behalf of the defendant that he had been negligent. The judge directed the jury that the test to be applied was whether the defendant had been guilty of gross negligence. The defendant was convicted. His appeal to the Court of Appeal was dismissed, and he appealed to the House of Lords.

Lord Mackay

[I]n my opinion the ordinary principles of the law of negligence apply to ascertain whether or not the defendant has been in breach of a duty of care towards the victim who has died. If such breach of duty is established the next question is whether that breach of duty caused the death of the victim. If so, the jury must go on to consider whether that breach of duty should be characterised as gross negligence and therefore as a crime. This will depend on the seriousness of the breach of duty committed by the defendant in all the circumstances in which the defendant was placed when it occurred. The jury will have to consider whether the extent to which the defendant's conduct departed from the proper standard of care incumbent upon him, involving as it must have done a risk of death to the patient, was such that it should be judged criminal.

It is true that to a certain extent this involves an element of circularity, but in this branch of the law I do not believe that is fatal to its being correct as a test of how far conduct must depart from accepted standards to be characterised as criminal. This is necessarily a question of degree and an attempt to specify that degree more closely is I think likely to achieve only a spurious precision. The essence of the matter, which is supremely a jury question, is whether, having regard to the risk of death involved, the conduct of the defendant was so bad in all the circumstances as to amount in their judgment to a criminal act or omission. . . .

I entirely agree with the view that the circumstances to which a charge of involuntary man-slaughter may apply are so various that it is unwise to attempt to categorise or detail specimen directions.

[100] [1995] 1 AC 1.

This circular definition was subsequently applied by the Court of Appeal in *R v Becker*,[101] where Tuckey LJ explained that the

judge told the jury four times that they had to find the negligence criminal. Further definition of gross was not required as Adomako makes clear. . . . [T]he jury had to face the crucial issue which, as the judge said, was for them and not for the doctors to decide. That is to say, whether the mistake which the appellant made was so bad that they could characterise it as a crime.

In recent years, there has been an increase in the number of prosecutions against doctors for manslaughter. RE Ferner found that seventeen doctors were charged with manslaughter in the 1990s, compared with two in each of the preceding two decades.[102] This, he suggests, is unlikely to point to an eightfold increase in gross negligence. Rather, more plausible explanations are an increased tendency to involve the police, and greater willingness on the part of the Crown Prosecution Service to prosecute doctors, perhaps because it perceives that juries have become more likely to convict.[103] Ferner goes on to suggest that the criminal law will usually be an inappropriate response to medical errors:

Convicting doctors of manslaughter may satisfy a desire for retribution, but deters careful consideration of the ways of preventing tragedies from recurring.[104]

And in the next extract, Jon Holbrook argues that an increased willingness to prosecute doctors who have simply made mistakes points to a shift in our attitude towards accidents.

Jon Holbrook[105]

This increase in prosecutions for medical manslaughter reflects society's changed attitude towards the notion of gross negligence. In 1925 the Court of Appeal stressed the importance of the negligence having to be gross when it said the accused's negligence must go beyond a mere matter of compensation between subjects and show such disregard for the life and safety of others as to amount to a crime against the state and conduct deserving of punishment. In a 19th century case the court had noted that 'if there was only the kind of forgetfulness which is common to everybody, or if there was a slight want of skill . . . it would be wrong to proceed against a man criminally in respect of such injury.' The court then gave as an example of gross negligence the surgeon who operated while drunk. In other words, previous generations were concerned to ensure that doctors were not prosecuted for the sort of mistake that a reasonably competent doctor could make due to an error of judgment or by mischance or misadventure.

But social attitudes to accidents have changed. [There is] a social intolerance towards 'accidents' as being events that have an innocent origin. This changed approach must have had an effect on the medical authorities, police, Crown Prosecution Service, lawyers, judges, and jurors who are involved in medical accidents that result in death. The test of gross negligence has been an element of gross negligence manslaughter for well over a 100 years, but its application to the surgery and hospital ward has changed in recent years. Our modern day intolerance of accidents as innocent events has tended to turn medical mistakes resulting in death into tragedies calling for criminal investigation.

---

[101] Unreported 19 June 2000.
[102] Medication errors that have led to manslaughter charges (2000) 321 British Medical Journal 1212–16.
[103] Ibid.   [104] Ibid.
[105] The criminalization of fatal medical mistakes (2003) 327 British Medical Journal 1118–19.

8. PROBLEMS WITH CLINICAL NEGLIGENCE

There is widespread dissatisfaction with the clinical negligence system. A National Audit Office report, *Handling Clinical Negligence Claims in England*, found that in 1999/2000 clinical negligence cases lasted, on average, five-and-a-half years.[106] Protracted legal proceedings mean that the legal costs of a case are often greater than any damages the claimant receives. Annual NHS expenditure on clinical negligence has risen from £1 million in 1974/5 to £446 million in 2001/2.[107] The legal and administrative costs exceed the damages awarded in most claims under £50,000. Indeed for smaller claims—those where claimant receives between £10,000 and £25,000—the legal and administrative costs exceed the size of the award in 76 per cent of cases.[108] As a result of extended limitation periods for latent injuries, and for cases involving children and mentally incapacitated adults, there is also a significant backlog of claims, which the National Audit Office estimates will cost the NHS £5.25 billion.[109]

The value of claims has also risen dramatically in recent years. In the mid-1970s the average award in a clinical negligence claim was £1454, by 2002 it was £259,038.[110] The highest damages are paid for birth-related brain damage: despite representing only 5 per cent of all clinical negligence actions, 60 per cent of annual expenditure on litigation is spent on these cases.[111] On average, the damages in a successful cerebral palsy claim are £670,000, but payments in some cases are much higher—as much as £5.5 million in one case.[112]

Regardless of how deserving individual claimants' cases might be, it must be acknowledged that diverting NHS funds to the payment of damages inevitably reduces the amount of money available for patient care. As Alan Merry and Alexander McCall Smith explain:

If damages become payable, then that means that there is a correspondingly reduced amount available for the maintenance of wards and equipment, the purchase of drugs or the provision of treatment. A medium-sized award, therefore, may be crudely translated into ten fewer hip replacements.[113]

This concern was also expressed by Sir Nicolas Browne-Wilkinson V-C in *Wilsher v Essex AHA*:[114]

In the modern world with its technological refinements, is it sensible to persist in making compensation for those who suffer from shortcomings in technologically advanced treatment depend on proof of fault, a process which the present case illustrates can consume years in time and huge sums of money in costs? Given limited resources, what balance is to be struck in the allocation of such resources between compensating those whose treatment is not wholly successful and the provision of required treatment for the world at large?

---

[106] National Audit Office, *Handling Clinical Negligence Claims in England* (NAO 2001).
[107] *Making Amends: A consultation paper setting out proposals for reforming the approach to clinical negligence in the NHS* (DH 2003) 60.
[108] Ibid, 70.   [109] Ibid, 72.   [110] Ibid, 65.   [111] Ibid, 47.   [112] Ibid, 50.
[113] *Errors, Medicine and the Law* (CUP Cambridge 2001) 212.
[114] [1987] 1 QB 730.

In the following extract, John Harris suggests that victims of medical negligence should compete for scarce NHS funds according to the same rationing criteria that exist throughout the NHS, rather than, as happens now, being given absolute priority.

John Harris[115]

In most healthcare systems the need to prioritise patients for care and to ration the resources available is now well recognised. . . . However, one group of claimants for healthcare resources have been guaranteed top priority for receipt of funds available for health care—victims of medical accidents. This fact has been scarcely noted and its justice seldom questioned. . . .

If people who need treatment to save their life can be told that scarcity of resources does not allow them to be treated, why, equally, should not people who need legal redress and compensation (out of the same limited pot of money) be told that the resources necessary to fund the professional help and compensation that they need are either exhausted or committed to those with a greater need?

How can compensation automatically and necessarily be a higher moral or political priority than treatment? . . . If public resources available for patient care are to be cash limited and patients forced to compete for priority within those limits, why should not the same be true of access to litigation and compensation? Why, in short, are some victims of medical accidents given priority over the victims of all other types of accidents, injuries, and illnesses?

If these questions are pertinent the need for compensation for medical accidents should perhaps be regarded as an illness that is expensive to treat and affects comparatively few people. . . . I think it plausible to insist that the health related needs of victims of medical accidents or negligence compete on at least an equal footing with other such needs rather than having automatic and absolute priority. . . .

The courts doubtless see themselves as addressing the justice of the claims of the plaintiff before them. But in so doing they take decisions which have the direct effect of denying or postponing the, arguably, equally or more urgent and just cases of other claimants to fair access to the public resources available for health care. The important question, I believe, is whether it is just for awards of damages to be enforced when the effect of so doing may be to deny more important or urgent claims on the same budget.

As we have seen, proving breach of duty *and* causation are formidable obstacles, and most of those patients who do seek compensation will receive nothing. And of course not all patients who have suffered injury as a result of their medical treatment will choose to sue the NHS trust where they were treated. Some patients may not realize that they are eligible to bring an action in negligence. Others, as Linda Mulcahy explains in the following extract, may simply decide that the difficulties of pursuing a legal claim outweigh the small chance of receiving compensation.

Linda Mulcahy[116]

Studies of the link between medical negligence claims and medical mishaps have also found that claiming is an atypical response to medical mishap. Danzon's seminal study of the relationship between adverse events and medical negligence claims found that only 1 in 25 negligent injuries resulted in compensation through the malpractice system.

[115] 'The injustice of compensation for victims of medical accidents' (1997) 314 British Medical Journal 1821.
[116] L Mulcahy, *Disputing Doctors: The socio-legal dynamics of complaints about medical care* (Open UP Maidenhead 2003) 64–6.

It is also clear from empirical studies that many people do not express their grievance in a formal setting because they do not know how to, fear retribution and defensive responses or because they do not believe that it would make a difference to their lives or the lives of others . . . It has also been argued that a key reason why people do not complain about doctors is that they feel doubly vulnerable. If they are long-term sick or likely to need future care, they may feel that the risk of upsetting the doctor and jeopardizing their future care is too great . . .

Evidence suggests that lack of knowledge about how and where to complain may still be a problem for some groups . . . But there are many other reasons why dissatisfaction and grievances do not evolve into complaints or claims, which have nothing to do with the hostility of the legal system. Patients may also *choose* not to make a complaint or clinical negligence claim . . . for some, avoiding disputes is a positive and rational choice. Asked why they had not voiced their dissatisfaction, this subset said they had other priorities, wished to put negative experiences behind them or avoid confrontation.

It is also worth noting that claimants are less likely to succeed in clinical negligence actions than they are in other sorts of cases: only 24 per cent of clinical negligence cases funded by the Legal Services Commission are successful.[117] Hence for the majority of claimants, stressful and expensive litigation will end in disappointment. Research appears to indicate that even where claimants are awarded damages, many remain dissatisfied because they have not been given an explanation, an apology, or reassurance that the same thing will not happen again.[118]

Nevertheless, despite high levels of dissatisfaction, patients have been increasingly willing to sue when their medical treatment goes wrong. In the late 1970s, there were about 700 claims each year against doctors, dentists and pharmacists; by 2002/3, the NHS Litigation Authority was receiving 6,797 claims per year.[119] Increasing resort to the courts has raised fears that the UK is moving towards a US-style 'compensation culture', in which the fear of litigation means that doctors increasingly practice 'defensive medicine', that is they choose treatment which is legally safest, rather than in the best interests of their patients. For example, it has been argued that excessively high caesarean delivery rates in the US are an example of defensive medicine in action: obstetricians in the US are, on average, sued three times in their careers,[120] and, as a result, insurance premiums in these high-risk specialities are becoming unaffordable.

As Michael Jones points out in the next extract, the claim that fear of being sued might prompt doctors to practice defensive medicine is difficult to evaluate, because there will be times when the more cautious approach which may result from the prospect of litigation if something goes wrong will in fact lead to better patient care. For example, a dentist who refuses to administer a general anaesthetic because she is concerned about the prospect of being sued is almost certainly also acting in the best interests of her patients.

[117] National Audit Office, *Handling Clinical Negligence Claims in England* (NAO 2001) 5.
[118] L Mulcahy, *Disputing Doctors: The socio-legal dynamics of complaints about medical care* (Open UP Maidenhead 2003) 96.
[119] *Making Amends: A consultation paper setting out proposals for reforming the approach to clinical negligence in the NHS* (DH 2003) 58.
[120] Ibid, 27.

Michael Jones[121]

The increase in medical malpractice litigation over the last 15 or 20 years has been accompanied by claims that, in response to the threat of litigation, doctors now practise defensively. This involves undertaking procedures which are not medically justified but are designed to protect the doctor from a claim for negligence. The most commonly cited examples are unnecessary diagnostic tests, such as X-rays, and unnecessary caesarean deliveries. However, applying the *Bolam* test, a reasonable doctor would not undertake an *unnecessary* procedure and so a doctor could not avoid a finding of negligence by performing one. In fact, to the extent that the procedure carries some inherent risk, a practitioner acting in this way may increase his chances of being sued. Moreover, there is little clear understanding within the medical profession of what the term 'defensive medicine' means. 'Defensive' may mean simply treating patients conservatively or even 'more carefully', and this begs the question whether that treatment option is medically justified in the patient's interests. Nonetheless, the courts have apparently acknowledged the existence of the phenomenon of defensive medicine, despite the fact that there is virtually no empirical, as opposed to anecdotal evidence of such practices in this country.

Another criticism made of the clinical negligence system is the practice of including the cost of private care in the award, even though the claimant may, in fact, receive her treatment within the NHS. This inevitably increases the size of awards, and there is the danger that patients may be overcompensated if they choose to be treated in the NHS, despite having received damages which were intended to pay for private care.

Successful claimants have usually received any damages in a lump sum, which causes further problems. Lump sum awards are based upon predictions about the claimant's future needs and life expectancy, and since these amount to little more than informed guesswork, over or under compensation is inevitable. Indeed, even if the patient dies unexpectedly shortly after an award is made, her relatives are entitled to keep the damages which were intended to provide for her care throughout her lifetime.

One solution would be to move towards periodical payments. These would require ongoing contact between the claimant and the NHS trust, and so might incur higher administration costs. Nevertheless they might have a number of advantages:

- they would reassure the claimant that her funds are not going to run out if she lives longer than expected;
- they would avoid the need for lawyers to argue over the claimant's likely life expectancy, which, for obvious reasons, can be distressing for the claimant and her family;
- they would more accurately meet the claimant's needs;
- cases could be settled more quickly because there would be no need to assess the claimant's full future care needs;
- the NHS would be able to budget to meet periodical payments more effectively.

In 2003, section 2 of the Damages Act 1996 was amended to provide that a court may order that damages take the form of periodical payments, either wholly or in part.

[121] 'Breach of Duty' in A Grubb with J Laing (eds), *Principles of Medical Law* (2nd edn OUP Oxford 2004) 369–441, 402–3.

Finally, it is also worth remembering that most people who have to live with serious illness and disability will not receive any damages at all. Only those who can establish that another's negligence caused their ill-health will receive generous financial assistance with the costs of their care. The needs of brain damaged babies, for example, are identical regardless of whether their disabilities were caused by negligent obstetric care or a congenital condition. Is it fair that some brain damaged infants receive millions of pounds to pay for private treatment for the rest of their lives, while other babies with identical practical needs receive nothing? A social security system, or welfare state, which allocates resources according to need might then be fairer than the tort of negligence.

It is not just the expense, inconvenience and unfairness of negligence claims which has come under attack. Even more importantly, as we see in the next section, it is increasingly recognized that the clinical negligence system works to obstruct efforts to ensure that mistakes are not repeated.

(a) A NEW APPROACH: LEARNING FROM MISTAKES

If adverse events result from human error, the tort system is not necessarily an effective way to ensure such errors are not repeated. Conventionally, negligence is supposed to raise standards of behaviour through the deterrent effect of the prospect of having to pay damages should things go wrong. Doctors, however, will very seldom pay damages themselves. Instead these will be met by their employers, or in the case of GPs and some private doctors, by the Medical Defence Unions. Of course doctors may fear being sued for the damage a finding of negligence could do to their reputation, but paradoxically the most egregious examples of negligence will tend to be settled quickly and quietly by the NHS trust, and will attract little publicity. Furthermore, as Alan Merry and Alexander McCall Smith point out:

A point which is often misunderstood is that human error, being by definition unintentional, is not easily deterred.[122]

For example, most doctors will have prescribed or administered the wrong drug, or the wrong dose of a drug, to a patient at some point in their career. Usually these mistakes are harmless, and often go unnoticed. But if the patient dies or is injured as a result, the doctor (or in practice, her employer) may be sued in negligence. Alan Merry and Alexander McCall Smith argue in the next extract that this is an example of 'outcome bias': culpability depends on the consequences of an action, rather than upon its blameworthiness. A system of deterrence built upon such haphazard foundations is unlikely to work. Instead a more effective way to prevent human error is to anticipate likely mistakes, such as drug administration errors, and design systems which are intended to minimize the risk materializing.

Alan Merry and Alexander McCall Smith[123]

Most drug errors are harmless, and as such pass unpunished and almost without comment . . .

---

[122] *Errors, Medicine and the Law* (CUP Cambridge 2001) 2.
[123] Ibid, 46–7, 51.

However, harm does occur occasionally. When it does, the severity of the consequences may be quite out of proportion to the magnitude of the error, and is usually related to chance more than to the degree of negligence involved . . . It is not our position that these errors should be accepted—indeed, much greater effort is warranted to reduce their occurrence. However, given the frequency of drug errors overall, the conclusion does seem inescapable that the factor which plays the greatest role in the allocation of blame for these errors is their outcome. It is the result that is being judged, not the action. In other words *outcome bias* is compounding the effect of *moral luck*. . . .

The fact that deterrence is relatively ineffective in this regard does not imply that nothing can be done about the problem of error . . . Not only is it too limited to focus on the operator, but in reality the operator is the part of the system most difficult to make error-free, because, of course, operators are humans.

Merry and McCall Smith have also argued that the negative impact litigation has upon individual doctors is also unlikely to improve the standard of patient care:

Alan Merry and Alexander McCall Smith[124]

Working under a threat of litigation creates a climate of fear, which cannot be conducive to the best use of human resources within the medical system. Moreover, the impact on a doctor, once a complaint has been made, is likely to be deleterious to his or her subsequent discharge of professional duties. The adverse effect of excessive stress on performance is well known, and a person experiencing the trauma of litigation is therefore likely to be a greater safety risk than one who is not under such personal pressure.

Recent evidence suggests that medical mishaps are common: it has been estimated that 10% of hospital inpatient admissions result in an adverse event, and that these cost the NHS up to £2 billion a year in additional bed days.[125] Many adverse events have serious consequences: a recent study found that a third of adverse events led to moderate or great disability, or death.[126] Each year, nearly 10,000 serious adverse reactions to drugs are reported, and around 1150 people who have been in recent contact with mental health service commit suicide. Research suggests that as many as 70 per cent of adverse incidents are preventable.[127] The National Audit Office has estimated that, at any one time, 9 per cent of patients have an infection, such as MRSA (methicillin-resistant Staphylococcus aureus), which has been acquired during their stay in hospital. The effects vary from extended length of stay, to permanent disability and, in at least 5000 patients each year, death. These hospital acquired infections are estimated to cost the NHS nearly £1 billion each year, and at least 15 per cent of them are preventable.[128]

In the next extract Paul Barach and Stephen D Small draw attention to a difference between the NHS and other high-risk activities, where human error is anticipated, and learning from mistakes is the norm.

---

[124] Ibid, 217.

[125] Department of Health Expert Group, *An Organisation with a Memory* (DH 2000) viii.

[126] Charles Vincent et al., 'Adverse events in British hospitals: preliminary retrospective record review' (2001) 322 British Medical Journal 517–19.

[127] Department of Health Expert Group, *An Organisation with a Memory* (DH 2000) 26.

[128] *Improving patient care by reducing the risk of hospital acquired infection: a progress report* (NAO London 2004) 1.

Paul Barach and Stephen D Small[129]

Non-punitive, protected, voluntary incident reporting systems in high risk non-medical domains have grown to produce large amounts of essential process information unobtainable by other means. Non-medical incident reporting systems have evolved over the past three decades to emphasise near misses, in addition to adverse events, to encourage confidentiality over anonymity, and to move beyond traditional linear thinking about human error, to analyses of multiple causation at the level of systems.

For healthcare reporting systems there must be incentives to promote voluntary reporting— completely, confidentially, and objectively. Reporting should be the right, easy, and safe policy for healthcare professionals. To maximise the usefulness of incident reporting systems there will be a need to balance accountability, system transparency, and protections for reporters. . . .

The top priority must be to design systems geared to preventing, detecting, and minimising effects of undesirable combinations of design, performance, and circumstance. Experience with non-medical incident reporting systems in aviation, nuclear power technology, and petrochemical processing, offer lessons applicable to the design of safety reporting systems in health care.

Open reporting of adverse incidents and 'near-misses' would ensure that medical staff are able to learn from them. But the adversarial negligence system provides very strong disincentives to admitting mistakes. An open reporting system depends upon moving away from a 'blame culture', which inevitably deters medical staff from being open about their mistakes. It might also be promoted by making reporting mandatory, confidential and anonymized.

In *An Organisation with A Memory*, the Department of Health's Expert Group contrasted a person-centred approach to mistakes, such as that embodied by the clinical negligence system, where the emphasis is upon discovering who was at fault, and a systems approach, which assumes that humans are fallible and that errors are inevitable. The problem with the person-centred approach is that by trying to apportion individual blame, systemic reasons for adverse events may be missed, and effective learning hampered.

Department of Health Expert Group[130]

- When things go wrong whether in health care or in another environment, the response has often been an attempt to identify an individual or individuals who must carry the blame. The focus of incident analysis has tended to be on the events immediately surrounding an adverse event, and in particular on the human acts or omissions immediately preceding the event itself . . .

- Human error may sometimes be the factor that immediately precipitates a serious failure, but there are usually deeper, systemic factors at work which if addressed would have prevented the error or acted as a safety-net to mitigate its consequences . . .

- There is evidence that 'safety cultures', where open reporting and balanced analysis are encouraged in principle and by example, can have a positive and quantifiable impact on the performance of organisations. 'Blame cultures' on the other hand can encourage people to cover up errors for fear of retribution and act against the identification of the true causes of

---

[129] 'Reporting and preventing medical mishaps: lessons from non-medical near miss reporting systems' (2000) 320 British Medical Journal 759–63.

[130] *An Organisation with a Memory* (DH 2000) viii–ix, 21 available at <http://www.dh.gov.uk>.

failure because they focus heavily on individual actions and largely ignore the role of under-lying systems. The culture of the NHS still errs too much toward the latter.

- Reporting systems are vital in providing a core of sound representative information on which to base analysis and recommendations. Experience in other sectors demonstrates the value of systematic approaches to recording and reporting adverse events and the merits of quarrying information on 'near misses' as well as events which actually result in harm. The NHS does not compare well with best practice in either of these areas. . . .

- When an adverse event occurs, the important issue is not who made the error but how and why did the defences fail and what factors helped to create the conditions in which the errors occurred . . .

- Human error is commonly blamed for failures because it is often the most readily identifiable factor operating in the period just prior to an adverse event. Yet two important facts about human error are often overlooked. First, the best people can make the worst mistakes. Second, far from being random, errors fall into recurrent patterns. The same set of circum-stances can provoke similar mistakes, regardless of the people involved. Any attempt at risk management that focuses primarily upon the supposed mental processes underlying error (forgetfulness, inattention, carelessness, negligence, and the like) and does not seek out and remove these situational 'error traps' is sure to fail. . . .

- The possibility of developing design solutions to specific hazards is under-explored in health care. In other sectors significant efforts are being made to design equipment and products in a way which helps to minimise potential hazards, yet despite one or two examples of good practice which demonstrate its applicability to health care this approach has not yet been applied extensively or systematically in the NHS.

A further recommendation from the Expert Group relates to the importance of reporting not only adverse events themselves, but also near misses. If data is only collected from incidents which in fact result in serious harm, this risks 'skewing learning towards a very small cross-section of accidents'.[131] In the aviation industry, for example, pilots are under a duty to report near misses since these are likely to yield useful information which might help to ensure that similar mistakes, which might cause serious accidents, are not made in the future. If only crashes were analysed, there would be much less opportunity to learn from mistakes.

This reasoning was developed in the Final Report of the Bristol Royal Infirmary Inquiry, which began as a public inquiry into the abnormally high death rate for paediatric cardiac surgery at Bristol Royal Infirmary, but which ultimately acted as a review of the NHS's response to adverse events. The Bristol Inquiry's robust conclusion was that clinical negligence litigation should be abolished.

Bristol Royal Infirmary Inquiry[132]
Chapter 26

28 Clinical negligence litigation does not represent a systematic approach to accountability, far less to the proper analysis of error. Rather, it is an entirely haphazard process. Further-more, any system of accountability, to be effective, requires that there be openness about

---

[131] Department of Health Expert Group, *An Organisation with a Memory* (DH 2000) 39.
[132] *Learning from Bristol: the report of the public inquiry into children's heart surgery at the Bristol Royal Infirmary 1984–1995* Cm 5207 (2001) <http://www.bristol-inquiry.org.uk/>.

who is accountable and for what. There is no such parallel in the system of clinical negligence litigation. Few cases ever actually see the light of day in court. Indeed in many of the more obvious cases of error, where it is clear to the trust, the NHS Litigation Authority, or a defence society, that a hospital or a particular professional was at fault, the claim is settled and no public airing of the issues ever takes place. What might be learned from such cases cannot thus be shared across the NHS. Other hospitals and healthcare professionals, indeed even those in the same institution, may not learn of, and thus from, the case. Paradoxically, those cases which are not settled, and thus become publicly known, tend to be those in which it is less certain that a hospital or a particular professional was at fault. Thus, at its extreme, we have the bizarre situation under the current system of clinical negligence litigation, in which the worst excesses rarely come into view, while the more borderline cases attract the attention of the press and public. This is a far cry from any system for holding the NHS to account for its conduct and its errors. . . .

30 By institutionalising blame it breeds defensiveness. The instinct is to cover up and deny. Errors cannot be treasured if, by acknowledging them, the healthcare professional or hospital may be sued. . . .

33 It is our view, therefore, that the culture and the practice of clinical negligence litigation work against the interests of patients' safety. The system is positively counter-productive, in that it provides a clear incentive not to report, or to cover up, an error or incident. And, once covered up, no one can learn from it and the next patient is exposed to the same or a similar risk.

35 Ultimately, we take the view that it will not be possible to achieve an environment of full, open reporting within the NHS when, outside it, there exists a litigation system the incentives of which press in the opposite direction. We believe that the way forward lies in the abolition of clinical negligence litigation, taking clinical error out of the courts and the tort system. It should be replaced by effective systems for identifying, analysing, learning from and preventing errors along with all other sentinel events. There must also be a new approach to compensating those patients harmed through such events.

36 Within the NHS itself, a policy of reporting sentinel events which is both open and non-punitive should be pursued. (By a non-punitive policy we mean a policy which expressly indicates that the NHS prizes information and it will not punish those who report errors, including their own, except in circumstances of criminal behaviour.)

The crucial point is that instead of expecting that medical staff will never make mistakes, it is more realistic to assume the inevitability of human error, and to try to build protections into the system to try to minimize their adverse effects. To take a mundane example, the designers of word processing packages take it for granted that users are likely to close documents without remembering to save their work. As a result, prompting mechanisms are built into computer software to remind users that they might want to save documents before exiting them, and back-up documents are generated automatically.

In relation to medical practice, a systems approach might involve practices such as ensuring that different drugs do not have confusingly similar packaging, or that drugs with similar names are not stored together, thus reducing the risk of confusing them. The Chief Pharmaceutical Officer's Report *Building a Safer NHS for Patients: Improv-*

ing Medication Safety[133] lays out a number of strategies for reducing medication errors, such as automatic double checking by a second person in defined high risk situations; discussing medication with patients and carers at the time of administration; and readily distinguishable wristbands for patients with known allergies.[134]

In relation to assisted conception, particular interest in avoiding adverse incidents was generated after the *Leeds* case, considered in Chapter 14 p. 837, in which a woman's eggs were fertilized with the wrong man's sperm. Human fallibility means that the risk of this sort of mistake cannot be eliminated, but it can be reduced. As a result, there are now witnessing requirements to ensure that at least two people confirm the patients' identity. Rather than just relying upon the patient's name as an identifier, additional information such as their date of birth and hospital number must also be recorded, in order to reduce the likelihood of error when different patients have similar names.

Openness about mistakes is not only important in order to identify 'error traps'— such as misleadingly similar drugs' packaging—and put in place systems to ensure that the risk of human error is minimized. It is also important from the point of view of patients who have been the victims of medical mishaps. As we have seen, patients are often much more interested in obtaining an explanation and an apology than financial compensation. Indeed litigation is more likely where patients believe that there has been a cover-up or that a mistake has gone unacknowledged. Vincent et al.'s study of the motivations of litigants found that the decision to take legal action was determined not only by the original injury, but also by insensitive handling and poor communication afterwards. Patients who had decided to sue were seeking greater honesty; an acknowledgement of the severity of the trauma they had suffered; and assurances that lessons had been learnt from their experiences:

Communication assumes a special importance when things have gone wrong. Patients often blame doctors not so much for the original mistakes, as for a lack of openness or willingness to explain.[135]

It is also important to remember that responsibility is not synonymous with blame. As Berlinger and Wu point out, doctors who admit their mistakes and work to ensure that they and others learn from them are undoubtedly taking responsibility for their conduct.

N Berlinger and A W Wu[136]

Responsibility should not be confused with blame, although that is too often the sense in which it is used in discussions of medical error and in particular of medical malpractice. Rather, the individual who takes responsibility within a systems approach will be committed to 'prospective responsibility': discussing and analysing mistakes, improving practices, and fulfilling his or her role obligations, including the duty to disclose . . .

Simply 'telling the truth', and even apologising, are unlikely in themselves to fulfil a patient's

---

[133] DH 2004.

[134] *Building a Safer NHS for Patients: Improving Medication Safety* (DH 2004) 9.

[135] C Vincent et al., 'Why do people sue doctors? A study of patients and relatives taking legal action' (1994) 343 The Lancet 1609–13, 1613.

[136] 'Subtracting insult from injury: addressing cultural expectations in the disclosure of medical error' (2005) 31 Journal of Medical Ethics 106–8.

expectations. Demonstrating to the injured patient and the family that their experience has been treated seriously, and that measures have been taken to prevent a recurrence, constitute the next step of the process. Other actions that physicians and hospitals can take include: providing fair compensation for injuries, with the burden of compensation shared among responsible parties; offering patients and families access to counselling services; and inviting them to contribute to the hospital's quality improvement process by sharing their experience.

In the next extract, Martin Smith and Heidi Foster argue that the disclosure of medical mistakes is justified by a variety of different types of ethical reasoning (which we considered in Chapter 1).

Martin Smith and Heidi Foster[137]

After a mistake has occurred, are honesty and apology the best policies? What values, virtues, and consequences support or discourage the disclosure of medical mistakes? . . .

Pertaining to rights-based reasoning, honest and candid communication followed by apology are a sign and a support of patients' rights to respectful treatment and care, and to self-determination. Patients . . . have a right to medical information about themselves . . . If an error or mistake occurs during the healthcare delivery process, the general right to medical information about oneself includes a right to this additional information that affects one's care. A patients' rights-based approach, focused on the dual and intertwined rights of respect and autonomy, supports a generalized practice of open discussion and truthful disclosure of medical mistakes.

From the perspective of professional duties and responsibilities, a primary ethical duty is to respect the dignity of patients by promoting their best interests . . . In most cases a patient's best interests are promoted through disclosure and an offer of relevant information, including mistakes made by the professionals in the provision of that patient's care.

A consideration of professional virtues or character traits also supports the general principle of disclosing mistakes with forthrightness . . . The virtue of truthfulness is ultimately essential for an effective professional–patient relationship because relationships cannot endure failures of truthfulness for long . . .

Finally, in ethically evaluating disclosure of mistakes from a consequentialist perspective, consideration needs to be given to the harms and benefits to all 'parties' who stand to be harmed or benefited by disclosure and apology . . . On the harm side of the ledger, disclosure is not always a benign activity. Patients can be emotionally fragile or in the middle of life-threatening situations; a disclosure of a mistake at that moment, similar to the giving of 'bad news' in such situations, could be detrimental to patient welfare and best interests. If mistakes are disclosed, patients or families might worry unnecessarily about other aspects of their care, and such worry might cause stress, discourage patients from seeking necessary care, and lead them to reject beneficial interventions in the future . . . Also in the current climate of healthcare, professionals could have their reputations, careers, livelihoods, referrals, staff privileges, and future employment opportunities jeopardized if they disclose a serious mistake.

On the benefit side of disclosure, patients . . . who have greater clarity and understanding of the medical situation may make better healthcare decisions . . . Honest disclosure can provide them with explanations and understanding . . ., give consolation that lessons have been learned, promote acceptance and closure about what transpired, and eliminate lawsuits filed to find out what really happened . . . Similarly, just as damage to professional reputations could occur by disclosure, so too could damage to professional reputations occur by non-disclosure. A perceived 'cover-up'

[137] 'Morally Managing Medical Mistakes' (2000) 9 Cambridge Quarterly of Healthcare Ethics 38–53, 45–7.

could lead a patient or family member to conclude that the professional is disloyal or untrustworthy . . .

Finally, consideration should also be given to the benefits to the healthcare system in general if disclosure and apology become a professional standard . . . Although the terms are paradoxical, mistakes can be viewed as 'gems' and 'treasures' because much can be learned from them for the betterment of future patients . . .

The above ethical considerations bring us to this conclusion: as a guiding principle, professionals should begin with a premise that all mistakes should be disclosed and accompanied by an apology, unless strong reasons exist to do otherwise.

(b) REFORM

Before the introduction of the NHS Redress Bill, there had been a number of attempts to improve the functioning of the clinical negligence system. The NHS Litigation Authority (NHSLA) was set up in 1995, and it has encouraged the earlier admission of liability, and the provision of explanations and apologies. This led to some reductions in the time taken to settle claims: new cases now take, on average, 1.19 years to settle, and older claims under four years, a reduction of eighteen months since the National Audit Office's analysis of claims in 1999/2000.[138] The NHSLA has used a specialized panel of solicitors, and has also promoted wider use of mediation.

Mediation, along with other types of alternative dispute resolution (ADR), is increasingly advocated as a way to avoid some of the defects of litigation. Typically in mediation a neutral third party will attempt to facilitate negotiation between the parties. It is non-adversarial, and the aim is to arrive at a consensual solution. Unlike judges, mediators do not have the power to impose settlements. In 1995, the NHS launched a medical negligence mediation pilot scheme. It attracted few cases—only twelve during three years—but a financial settlement was reached in all but one case, with average awards of £34,000.[139] Perhaps more importantly, other remedies were also made available to claimants, such as public apologies; explanations of decisions; offers to visit the department in order to see the improvements that had been put in place; new treatment plans; and information about the burial place of a miscarried fetus.[140]

The reforms to the civil justice system, prompted by Lord Woolf's report *Access to Justice*, have also gone some way towards streamlining clinical negligence claims, which Lord Woolf identified as the area where civil justice was 'failing most conspicuously'.[141] In 1998 the *Pre-Action Protocol for the Resolution of Clinical Disputes* was issued. Its purpose is to encourage openness, and to reduce the need to resort to adversarial litigation. Parties are now given incentives to settle actions quickly, and to make use of mediation. Patients initially send letters of claim, which identify the alleged negligence, and the injuries and losses suffered as a result. The NHS trust (or

[138] *Making Amends: A consultation paper setting out proposals for reforming the approach to clinical negligence in the NHS* (DH 2003) 92.
[139] L Mulcahy et al., *Mediating Medical Negligence Claims: An Option for the Future?* (HMSO London 1999) xiv.
[140] Ibid.
[141] Lord Woolf, *Access to Justice: Final Report to the Lord Chancellor on the Civil Justice System* (HMSO London 1996) 15.2.

other defendant) must respond within three months, either admitting the claim, or denying it with specific answers to the allegations made by the patient.

Where a trial does go to court, pre-trial agreements to determine what the court will be asked to decide are now encouraged, and the Court has a more pro-active role in case management. The new Civil Procedure Rules[142] emphasize that expert witnesses' primary duty is to assist the court to discover the truth, and not to offer partisan evidence to support one party's point of view, and in straightforward cases, the judge can appoint a single expert. Where more experts are used, they may be invited to submit a joint report.

The Clinical Negligence Scheme for trusts (CNST), administered by the NHSLA, was set up in 1995 in order to help NHS trusts to fund negligence litigation by pooling funds, so that one high value case does not threaten an NHS trust's capacity to carry out its other responsibilities. As a condition for discounted premiums, it requires the development of clinical incident reporting systems to ensure compliance with its risk management standards.

Set up in 2001, the National Patient Safety Agency (NPSA) runs a mandatory reporting system for logging all failures, mistakes, errors and near-misses across the health service. It is intended to introduce a streamlined approach to dealing with errors and mistakes, and ensure that lessons are learnt and spread throughout the health service. In 2004 the NPSA launched the national reporting and learning system (NRLS). This mainly extracts information from existing local risk management systems, but NHS employees are also able to report directly to the system through an online form. Information is anonymized, and the staff and patients involved in any incident are not identifiable.

In 2001 the National Clinical Assessment Authority, now the National Clinical Assessment Service (NCAS), was set up to support the NHS in dealing with doctors and dentists whose performance gives cause for concern. It provides advice about the local handling of cases, and can carry out clinical performance assessments, and make recommendations about how to address any problems which have been identified. The NCAS will undertake assessments where the concern is not so grave that patients are seriously at risk: such cases should still be handled by the GMC.

As we saw in Chapter 2, the Department of Health already produces NHS performance data, through which NHS trusts receive a 'star rating', of between zero and three stars, which is used to judge the degree of independence the trust is allowed in making management decisions.[143] In its response to the Bristol Inquiry, the Department of Health said that it intends to produce ratings of individual consultants, although the wisdom of this development has been challenged by Christopher Newdick:

Christopher Newdick[144]

[A]s we have seen, the government intends to publish consultant-specific data from which patients will be able to see how individual doctors perform relative to their peers. This provides a basis on

---

[142] 1998/3132, pursuant to the Civil Procedure Act 1997.

[143] Department of Health, *NHS performance ratings: acute trusts, specialist trusts, ambulance trusts, mental health trusts 2001/02* (DoH London 2002).

[144] 'NHS Governance after *Bristol*: Holding On, or Letting Go?' (2002) 10 Medical Law Review 111–31, 119–20.

which to make better-informed decisions and an upward pressure on clinical standards. Doctors and NHS trusts hospital employers will be keen that their performance in the league table is attractive to patients, their medical advisors and to the new NHS regulators. Under pressure of *performance management*, however, will doctors become reluctant to undertake difficult cases for fear of damaging their clinical performance statistics? Unless the process of audit is sufficiently sensitive to record the levels of difficulty presented by individual cases, bare statistics could suggest that the most experienced surgeons who undertake the most difficult cases and, therefore, achieve the least good results in terms of successful outcomes, are the least competent. Clearly, this would be entirely misleading. More generally, 'difficult' cases might be refused care for fear of damaging the position of surgeon, or the hospital, in the table.

The concern is illuminated by research conducted by the National Bureau of Economic Research into cardiac surgery in New York and Pennsylvania . . . The Bureau made three key findings. First, performance data led to substantial patient selection by hospitals and, in particular, a decline in the severity of the illness of patients receiving coronary artery bypass graft . . . Secondly, the system led to more serious cases being assigned to hospitals with greater expertise and tended to reduce the heterogeneity of patients admitted to individual hospitals for surgery. On the other hand, this effect did not lead to any increase in substantial health benefits. Thirdly, the system discouraged the admission of very sick patients: 'more severely ill patients experienced dramatically worsened health outcomes'.

As we saw earlier, the NHS complaints system has also been reformed recently. Unfortunately, however, the complaints and the claims systems still largely operate independently, with patients having to choose whether to lodge a complaint or to pursue a claim. It would perhaps make more sense to have a single-track system, providing all patients with an explanation, apology and assurance that steps have been taken to avoid repetition.

In its review of clinical negligence, the government acknowledged that there had been significant recent improvements in the system, but it argued that fundamental reform remained necessary. It was not persuaded to move towards a no-fault compensation scheme, however. Although such schemes also exist in Denmark, Sweden and Finland, and to a limited extent in France, the most well known example is in New Zealand where a no-fault scheme has been in place since 1972, and it is described below by the Chief Medical Officer in *Making Amends*:

Making Amends[145]

Compensation is payable for 'personal injury by accident'. Personal injury caused by medical mishap or medical error is included within the definition of personal injury. A medical mishap is defined as when the patient was provided with the correct treatment, properly given, but the patient had a complication which was both rare and severe. A medical mishap is rare if it would not occur in more than 1% of cases in which the treatment is given. It is not rare if the patient knows the risks before treatment started. A medical mishap is severe if the patient was in hospital for at least 14 days or was significantly disabled for at least 14 days or the patient died.

A medical error is defined as 'the failure of a registered health professional to observe a standard of care and skill reasonably expected in the circumstances', (similar to the Bolam

---

[145] *Making Amends: A consultation paper setting out proposals for reforming the approach to clinical negligence in the NHS* (DH 2003) 99.

test . . .). Causation must be demonstrated. The claim must be made within 12 months of the injury . . .

Payments are made for medical treatment, loss of earnings (80% of pre-injury earnings up to a certain limit), transport and accommodation costs and death benefits . . .

The cost of claims is met by a combination of general taxation, premiums charged to medical practitioners and levies on employers . . .

A key feature of the New Zealand scheme is that claimants are prevented from seeking common law damages.

In 2004 the New Zealand government relaxed the limiting criteria, and victims may now receive compensation even if the mishap was not rare and there was no fault involved.

Although removing the need to prove fault would undoubtedly simplify and speed up the process of compensation, the problem of establishing causation remains, and as we have seen, in medical cases this is a significant obstacle. It also means that arbitrary lines will continue to be drawn between patients who are eligible for compensation because they can prove that their injuries were caused by a medical mishap, and those who cannot. As we have seen, the needs of a brain damaged baby are the same, regardless of whether its injuries were caused by asphyxia at birth or a congenital disability. A no-fault compensation scheme would continue to distinguish between patients on grounds other than need.

No-fault schemes may be cheaper to administer, but they are also likely to attract higher numbers of claims, and may therefore end up costing more than the clinical negligence system. In New Zealand for example, the proportion of the population making claims each year is more than double that in England,[146] and the Chief Medical Officer estimated that a no-fault scheme would be unaffordable for the NHS:

Estimates suggest that even with a 25% reduction in the current level of compensation the cost of a true no-fault compensation scheme would vary between £1.6 billion per year (if 19% of eligible claimants claimed) to almost £4 billion (if 28% of eligible claimants claimed). This compares with £400 million spent on clinical negligence in 2001.[147]

A no fault scheme would also fail to address patients' desire for apologies and explanations, and would not necessarily promote learning from mistakes. Nevertheless, it is the preferred solution of the British Medical Association:

British Medical Association[148]

- The BMA has long supported the introduction of a no fault compensation scheme for medical injuries and believes that such a system should have maximum financial limits . . .

- The present tort-based procedures destroy the proper relationship between patient and doctor, introducing a confrontational element, totally foreign to the mutual trust which should exist. The procedures encourage concealment and lack of frankness on the part of the doctor, just when it is most undesirable. . . .

- A no fault compensation system would offer a choice to the individual. Instead of those few

---

[146] *Making Amends*, 106.   [147] Ibid, 112.
[148] *Funding—no fault compensation for medical injuries* (2003) <http://www.bma.org.uk>.

individuals able to establish that the care they had received was negligent being awarded very large sums in compensation, patients suffering unforeseen injury during their medical care would be compensated reasonably for the damage they have endured and, where appropriate, dependants compensated for financial loss.

- It is the sincere hope of the profession that, whatever other benefits might result from a no fault scheme, the absence of the threat of litigation would ensure much greater frankness in explaining the nature and cause of any mishap to the patient concerned, encouraging accountability by the doctor to his/her patient who is, after all, the person most entitled to require it. . . .

- The current adversarial system contributes to the blame culture which prevents health professionals being open about mistakes and learning from them.

Having rejected both the status quo and a move towards a no-fault compensation system, in *Making Amends*[149] the Chief Medical Officer laid out the Government's preferred solution, the NHS Redress Scheme:

Making Amends[150]
An NHS Redress Scheme should be introduced to provide investigations when things go wrong; remedial treatment and care when needed; explanations and apologies; and financial compensation in certain circumstances.

Harm to a patient may come to light as the result of an adverse event, a complaint, or a claim from a solicitor. In all cases, the response should be:

- An investigation of the incident which is alleged to have caused harm and of the harm that has resulted;
- Provision of an explanation to the patient and of the action proposed to prevent repetition;
- The development and delivery of a package of care providing remedial treatment, therapy and arrangements for continuing care where needed;

The proposed NHS Redress Scheme would provide a mechanism for organising this response and in suitable cases considering whether payment for pain and suffering, for out of pocket expenses and for care or treatment which the NHS could not provide should be made. The requirement would be to reach a decision on the case within six months from the initial approach from the patient . . .

- Patients would be eligible for payment for serious shortcomings in NHS care if the harm could have been avoided and if the adverse outcome was not the result of the natural progression of the illness. Payment would be made:

  - by a local NHS trust for reimbursement of the cost of the care leading to harm (or similar amount)

  - by a national body for amounts up to £30,000 . . .

- A package of care would be provided in cash or kind according to the severity of the impairment, judged according to the ability to perform the daily tasks of living, and would comprise:

---

[149] *Making Amends: A consultation paper setting out proposals for reforming the approach to clinical negligence in the NHS* (DH 2003) 16.
[150] Ibid, 119, 16–18.

- a managed care package

- a monthly payment for the costs of care (at home or in a residential setting) which cannot be provided through a care package (in the most severe cases this could be up to £100,000 per annum)

- one-off lump sum payments for home adaptations and equipment at intervals throughout the child's life (in the most severe cases, this could be up to £50,000)

- an initial payment in compensation for pain, suffering and loss of amenity capped at £50,000. . . .

• The new NHS Redress Scheme would not take away a person's right to sue through the Courts but:

- . . . there would be a presumption that they had first applied to the NHS Redress Scheme

- those accepting packages of care and compensation under the NHS Redress Scheme would be required to waive their right to go to court on the same case.

• For cases that do not fall within the criteria of the scheme:

- there would be an expectation that mediation would be used as a first step and pre-action protocols would require mediation to be attempted in specified types of cases. Acceptance of a mediation package would be binding

- there would be strong encouragement of the use of periodical payments in larger value cases, including 'out of court' settlements

- the costs of future care would no longer reflect the cost of private treatment

- specialist training would be provided to judges handling clinical negligence cases . . .

• Statutory provisions would be introduced to encourage openness in the reporting of adverse events. This would encompass:

- a duty of candour requiring clinicians and health service managers to inform patients about actions which have resulted in harm

- exemption from disciplinary action for those reporting adverse events or medical errors (except where there is a criminal offence or where it would not be safe for the professional to continue to treat patients)

- legal privilege would be provided for reports and information identifying adverse events except where the information was not recorded in the medical record.

The introduction of an NHS Redress Bill was announced in the Queen's Speech in 2005, and is likely to become an Act in 2005/6. At the time of writing the Bill has not been published and so the extent to which it will embody the proposals in *Making Amends* is as yet unclear, although the Government has specified that the proposed NHS Redress Scheme for severely neurologically impaired babies, proposed in Making Amends, will not now go ahead.

According to *Making Amends* then, the critical ingredients of a claim will be that

(a) there has been a serious shortcoming in NHS care, and

(b) that the harm could have been avoided, and

(c) that the adverse outcome was not the result of the natural progression of the illness.

It will of course be necessary to establish what counts as a 'serious shortcoming' in care. And it will also be necessary to prove causation, which as we have seen is a considerable obstacle to a successful claim.

One important new dimension of NHS Redress will be the obligation not just to offer financial compensation but to instead ensure that the claimant is provided with a package of care to meet their needs, and to emphasize the importance of rehabilitation. Mediation would also be encouraged as a first step. In the next extract, Brian Capstick explains that there is a risk that the proposed scheme will encourage more claims, without necessarily reducing the clinical negligence burden.

Brian Capstick[151]

The redress scheme proposes that hospitals investigate all adverse events, not only in response to a complaint or claim by the patient. . . . Although prompt investigation of adverse events that lead to serious injury is a sound risk management measure, investigating the larger number of adverse events that cause only minor harm will greatly increase the workload.

When an investigation shows that something has gone wrong, clinicians will have to disclose this to the patient or family. This will be part of a new statutory duty of candour . . . Although candour may disarm some potential claimants, others may construe the admission as an invitation to pursue a claim.

The next step for people who decide to pursue a smaller claim would be for the hospital to develop and deliver a package of remedial care. However, since care is in theory already provided to people who need it, it is not clear what this provision would add unless it permits queue jumping or treatment that would not normally be available under the NHS. . . .

Patients will be eligible for payment for 'serious shortcomings' in NHS care if the harm could have been avoided and if the adverse outcome was not the result of the natural progression of the illness. It is not clear whether 'serious shortcomings in NHS care' will be a softer test than the existing test of negligence but, if it is softer, the success rate for claimants could rise. . . .

By removing the risk that the loser may ultimately have to pay the winner's legal costs, the proposed scheme removes any deterrent to borderline or frivolous claims. Coupled with the duty of candour and the publicity that would no doubt attend a national scheme, this could boost the compensation culture that, up to now, it has been public policy to prevent. . . .

[T]he scheme's promise of possible compensation for no outlay by the claimant and at no risk is likely to encourage more claimants rather than reduce them. People who discover that they have a good claim in negligence when they apply to the scheme are likely to switch to a negligence based claim to get the higher levels of compensation available from the courts. The result may be that the number of claims may rise and the scheme will only add a new class of beneficiary . . .

As it stands, *Making Amends* proposes to make it easier to pursue small claims . . ., without necessarily reducing the number of claims processed through the conventional legal system and perhaps encouraging even more of them.

---

[151] 'The future of clinical negligence litigation?' (2004) 328 British Medical Journal 457–9.

9. CONCLUSION

It is commonly said that tort law serves two purposes: compensation and deterrence. In the context of medical negligence, we have seen, first, that it does not offer an efficient compensation scheme for patients who suffer injury or damage as a result of negligent treatment, and, second, that it does not effectively deter poor practices or encourage good ones. Worse still, not only is tort law costly and inefficient, it may actually contribute towards the repetition of mistakes by fostering a 'blame culture' and inhibiting open reporting of errors, which is, of course, the best way to ensure that they are not repeated. The government's announcement that it intends to reform the clinical negligence system is therefore to be welcomed, but at the time of writing, it is impossible to predict whether its proposed replacement, the NHS redress scheme, will be a success.

Will lower administration costs and lower awards be off-set by increases in the number of claims? Will the new scheme remove the obstacles to open reporting, or will the need to establish that there has been a 'serious shortcoming' in NHS care mean that it will still be necessary to *blame* an individual doctor, or other health care provider? If so, it is unlikely to fulfil the Bristol Inquiry's recommendation that we should 'treasure' mistakes, in order to learn effectively from them. And, of course, the NHS redress scheme will continue to distinguish between people whose illnesses or disabilities can be attributed to 'serious shortcomings' in NHS care, and those who have become unwell or disabled as a result of natural processes. In 1970, with the first publication of *Accidents, Compensation and the Law*, Patrick Atiyah drew attention to the unfairness of drawing a distinction between individuals with identical needs in this way, and his remarks undoubtedly remain pertinent today.

Patrick Atiyah[152]

Injuries and accidents may be divided into two categories according to whether or not they are caused by the actions (or inaction) of some human person. In the tort system this distinction marks the line between liability and no-liability because compensation for injury or illness will be recoverable in a tort action only if one of its immediate or proximate causes was the conduct of some human person other than the plaintiff . . .

The distinction between human and natural causes can produce some striking results. Why, for example, should a child born disabled as a result of negligence on the part of the doctor who delivered the child be entitled to substantial compensation from the tort system, while the child born with similar congenital disabilities receives no common law damages? . . . It has been suggested that the view that brain-damaged babies deserve more generous compensation than the congenitally disabled is rooted in the desire for accountability, not compensation. More generally, it might be argued that compensating victims of human causes at a higher level than victims of natural causes is a way of giving effect to notions of personal responsibility: a person should be required to pay compensation for injuries if, but only if, that person was in some sense responsible for the disabilities. But there are many ways of holding people accountable for their actions other than making them pay compensation; and even if we accept that compensation for injuries caused

---

[152] Peter Cane, *Atiyah's Accidents, Compensation and the Law* (5th edn Butterworths London 1993) 331–2.

by humans ought to be paid for by those who cause them, it does not follow that those injured and disabled by human causes should be treated more generously than those injured and disabled by natural causes.

Nevertheless, if compensation for disabilities was paid by individuals, the argument based on personal responsibility might have some force. However, we have seen that most tort compensation is not paid by individuals, but by insurers . . . and in this light it is less clear why tort-type benefits should only be available to those injured by human action. On the whole, those disabled people who can recover tort damages . . . are much better provided for than those disabled people who must rely on social security benefits alone. Can this be justified in the light of the fact that the tort system and the social security system are, in effect, both financed by the public at large?

10. FURTHER READING

Bristol Royal Infirmary Inquiry, *Learning from Bristol: the report of the public inquiry into children's heart surgery at the Bristol Royal Infirmary 1984–1995* <http://www.bristol-inquiry.org.uk/>.

CASE, PAULA, 'Secondary Iatrogenic Harm: Claims for Psychiatric Damage Following a Death Caused by Medical Error' (2004) 67 Modern Law Review 561–87.

Department of Health Expert Group, *An Organisation with a Memory* (DH 2000) available at <http://www.dh.gov.uk>.

HARRIS, JOHN, 'The injustice of compensation for victims of medical accidents' (1997) 314 British Medical Journal 1821.

Making Amends: A consultation paper setting out proposals for reforming the approach to clinical negligence in the NHS (DH 2003) available at <http://www.dh.gov.uk>.

MERRY, ALAN, and McCALL SMITH, ALEXANDER, *Errors, Medicine and the Law* (CUP Cambridge 2001).

NEWDICK, CHRISTOPHER, 'NHS Governance after *Bristol*: Holding On, or Letting Go?' (2002) 10 Medical Law Review 111–13.

SMITH, MARTIN, and FOSTER, HEIDI, 'Morally Managing Medical Mistakes' (2000) 9 Cambridge Quarterly of Healthcare Ethics 38–53.

TEFF, HARVEY, *Reasonable Care: Legal Perspectives on the Doctor–Patient Relationship* (Clarendon Press Oxford 1994).

TEFF, HARVEY, 'The Standard of Care in Medical Negligence—Moving on from *Bolam*?' (1998) 18 Oxford Journal of Legal Studies 473–84.

WITTING, CHRISTIAN, 'National Health Service Rationing: Implications For The Standard Of Care In Negligence' (2001) 21 Oxford Journal of Legal Studies 443.

WOOLF, LORD, 'Are the Courts Excessively Deferential to the Medical Profession?' (2001) 9 Medical Law Review 1–16.

4
CONSENT I: CAPACITY AND VOLUNTARINESS

1. CENTRAL ISSUES

1. A patient must consent to medical treatment, otherwise it might be both an assault and a battery.

2. The principle of patient autonomy means that every competent adult patient has the *right* to refuse medical treatment, even if her reasons are bizarre, irrational or non-existent, and even if her refusal will result in her death.

3. This right extends to advance refusals of treatment, provided first, that the patient was competent when she made the decision, and second, that the refusal precisely covers her present situation.

4. Patients who lack capacity can be treated without consent, and slightly different rules apply depending on the reason for the patient's incompetence.

5. In an emergency, doctors are entitled to do what is necessary to save the patient's life or prevent serious injury.

6. Incompetent adults can be treated in their best interests, and this has a wider meaning that just their best *clinical* interests. When the Mental Capacity Act 2005 comes into force, the treatment of incompetent adults will be governed by statute rather than the common law.

7. Parents normally give consent to their children's medical treatment, unless there is a dispute or the treatment is especially controversial.

8. Mature minors can also acquire the right to consent to treatment, but not, apparently, the right to refuse life-saving treatment.

9. The patient's consent must have been given voluntarily, that is it must not have been vitiated by undue influence or coercion. In practice, both are uncommon, although not unprecedented, in relation to medical treatment.

2. INTRODUCTION

One of the first principles of medical law is that a competent adult patient must give her consent to medical treatment. As Cardozo J famously said in the US case, *Schloendorff v New York Hospital*:[1]

Every human being of adult years and sound mind has a right to determine what shall be done with his own body; and a surgeon who performs an operation without his patient's consent, commits an assault.

---

[1] 105 NE 92 (1914).

Touching a person without her consent, however benevolently, is prima facie unlawful. For consent to be valid, first the patient must have the capacity to consent; secondly, her consent must be given voluntarily; and thirdly she must understand the nature of the treatment to which she has consented. We deal with the first two criteria in this chapter. The following chapter is devoted to the question of how much information might be required before a patient's consent is adequately 'informed'.

We begin by noting that consent has a legal, a moral, and a clinical function. Legally, consent is necessary in order to convert what would otherwise be an unlawful touching or assault into a lawful practice. It serves then to protect medical practitioners from both prosecution and civil liability. Morally, consent is required in order to respect the patient's right to self-determination. And clinically, a patient's consent will make it easier to treat her, and her cooperation may contribute towards the treatment's success.

Having established the necessity of obtaining the patient's consent to medical treatment, we go on to consider what happens when a patient *cannot* give consent. Different rules apply depending upon the reasons for the patient's lack of capacity, and we separately consider (a) emergencies, (b) incompetent adults, and (c) children. Finally, we turn to the requirement that the patient's consent must have been given voluntarily, and we consider three factors that might undermine the patient's ability to freely consent to medical treatment: coercion, undue influence, and mistake.

3. THE CONSENT REQUIREMENT

(a) CRIMINAL LAW

It is widely believed that it is the patient's consent to medical treatment which prevents it from being both a civil wrong and a criminal assault. According to Lord Donaldson MR in *Re R (Wardship) (A Minor: Consent to Treatment)*:[2]

It is trite law that in general a doctor is not entitled to treat a patient without the consent of someone who is authorised to give that consent. If he does so, he will be liable in damages for trespass to the person and may be guilty of a criminal assault.

A hard-line libertarian would regard the patient's consent as not only a *necessary* but also a *sufficient* justification for medical treatment. Hence if a patient consents to have her healthy limbs amputated, or to undergo female circumcision, then a libertarian would contend that her consent transforms what would otherwise be an assault into a lawful practice. In contrast, a more paternalistic approach would specify further criteria, such as the qualifications of the person carrying out the procedure and the intention to benefit the patient, which would have to be satisfied in order to prevent an operation from amounting to an assault.

Certainly the English criminal law does not adopt a hard-line libertarian approach. At common law, consent will not normally offer a defence to the infliction of actual or grievous bodily harm. In the *Attorney General's Reference (No 6 of 1980)*,[3] the Court of

---

[2] [1992] Fam 11.   [3] [1981] QB 715.

Appeal had to address the question of whether, if two people fought (other than in the course of sport) it could be a defence to a charge of assault that the victim consented to fight:

Lord Lane CJ

[S]tarting with the proposition that ordinarily an act consented to will not constitute an assault, the question is: at what point does the public interest require the court to hold otherwise? . . .

The answer to this question, in our judgment, is that it is not in the public interest that people should try to cause, or should cause, each other actual bodily harm for no good reason. Minor struggles are another matter. So, in our judgment, it is immaterial whether the act occurs in private or in public; it is an assault if actual bodily harm is intended and/or caused.

Two questions arise from this. First, does medical treatment involve actual bodily harm, and secondly, what might count as a 'good reason'? On the first point, while some activities, such as examining a patient, will not cause any 'bodily harm', for others the answer is clearly 'yes'. Surgery, for example, involves cutting the body in a way which could undoubtedly be described as 'grievous bodily harm'. On the question of whether doctors have a 'good reason' for causing actual or grievous bodily harm, note that the Court of Appeal refers to the accepted legality of, among other things, 'reasonable surgical interference . . . as needed in the public interest'.

Lord Lane CJ

Nothing which we have said is intended to cast doubt upon the accepted legality of properly conducted games and sports, lawful chastisement or correction, reasonable surgical interference, dangerous exhibitions, etc. These apparent exceptions can be justified as involving the exercise of a legal right, in the case of chastisement or correction, or as needed in the public interest, in the other cases.

In *R v Brown*,[4] a case in which the House of Lords decided that occasioning actual bodily harm during consensual sado-masochistic practices was an offence, the Lords agreed that 'proper' medical treatment does not constitute a criminal offence, but as Lord Mustill explains, this exception cannot derive solely from the patient's consent.

Lord Mustill

Many of the acts done by surgeons would be very serious crimes if done by anyone else, and yet the surgeons incur no liability. Actual consent, or the substitute for consent deemed by the law to exist where an emergency creates a need for action, is an essential element in this immunity; but it cannot be a direct explanation for it, since much of the bodily invasion involved in surgery lies well above any point at which consent could even arguably be regarded as furnishing a defence. Why is this so? The answer must in my opinion be that proper medical treatment, for which actual or deemed consent is a prerequisite, is in a category of its own.

Lord Mustill had made similar remarks a year earlier in *Airedale NHS Trust v Bland*:[5]

Lord Mustill

[T]here is a point higher up the scale than common assault at which consent in general ceases to form a defence to a criminal charge. . . . If one person cuts off the hand of another it is no answer to say that the amputee consented to what was done.

---

[4] [1994] 1 AC 212.   [5] [1993] AC 789.

How is it that, consistently with the proposition just stated, a doctor can with immunity perform on a consenting patient an act which would be a very serious crime if done by someone else? The answer must be that bodily invasions in the course of proper medical treatment stand completely outside the criminal law. The reason why the consent of the patient is so important is not that it furnishes a defence in itself, but because it is usually essential to the propriety of medical treatment.

So at common law, it seems to be well established that, for public interest reasons, 'reasonable' or 'proper' medical treatment stands completely outside the criminal law. Of course, the use of words such as 'reasonable' and 'proper' means that not every surgical operation will be legal. Amputating a patient's healthy limbs in order to increase their income from begging, for example, would undoubtedly constitute an offence.

More complicated is the question of whether amputating a healthy limb when its presence appears to cause the patient considerable distress could ever be legitimate. In 2000 a great deal of media attention was generated when it was revealed that a surgeon in Scotland had performed elective single-leg amputations on two physically healthy individuals with psychiatric disorders. Both individuals were suffering from a rare sort of body dysmorphic disorder in which the patient wishes to be an amputee.[6] The surgeon involved said that 'at follow up, both patients remain delighted with their new state'.[7] On the one hand, operating in order to transform a non-disabled individual into a disabled one self-evidently causes grievous bodily harm, and seems manifestly 'unreasonable'. Yet, on the other hand, we now accept as 'reasonable' both gender reassignment surgery and cosmetic surgery, and in both cases, the purpose is similarly to alter the patient's physical body so that it better fits her preferred body image.

Under section 18 of the Offences Against the Person Act 1861, it is an offence 'unlawfully and maliciously . . . to cause any grievous bodily harm with intent'. It is undoubtedly true that surgery will generally cause grievous bodily harm. Since maliciously simply means 'subjectively recklessly', that is, with awareness or foresight of the risk of harm, the critical word here is 'unlawfully', which implies that intentionally causing grievous bodily harm might sometimes be done *lawfully*. Again 'reasonable' medical treatment, carried out with the patient's consent seems an obvious example. Just as at common law, however, it is possible that certain sorts of medical treatment might be regarded as offences under section 18, regardless of whether the patient consented. Female circumcision is specifically proscribed by the Female Genital Mutilation Act 2003, but it is also possible that it might also be an offence both at common law, and by virtue of the Offences Against the Person Act. It undoubtedly causes grievous bodily harm, and would not fit within the 'reasonable surgical interference' exception.

---

[6] Sarah Ramsay 'Controversy over UK surgeon who amputated healthy limbs' (2000) 355 The Lancet 476.
[7] Ibid.

(b) CIVIL LAW

Consent will prevent a doctor from being liable for the tort of battery. Provided that the patient consented to treatment, there could be no possibility of an action to recover damages in tort for unlawful touching. If a patient wishes to claim that their consent was not 'real', perhaps because they were not told what they were consenting to, or because they were coerced into agreeing to the treatment, then an action for battery might be possible. In practice, such actions are extremely rare. As we see in the next chapter, very few patients are ever able to persuade a court that their apparent consent was defective due to a lack of information, and later in this chapter, we see that coercion and undue influence are also very unlikely to vitiate a patient's consent.

(c) THE FORM CONSENT SHOULD TAKE

There is no common law requirement that consent to medical treatment must be in writing. There are a few procedures, such as fertility treatment, where a statutory requirement to obtain written consent exists,[8] but this is exceptional. In most routine medical treatment the patient's consent can be inferred from her conduct. If I put out my arm to have a blood sample taken, the doctor or nurse can legitimately assume that I am consenting to having a needle stuck into my vein. In most patient encounters with health care professionals, formal consent procedures are non-existent. Rather, by seeking treatment and complying with instructions, the patient indicates her willingness to be treated. It might also be argued that the patient's conduct creates an estoppel, such that it would be inequitable to allow her to subsequently claim that she had not in fact consented to the treatment in question.

Where the treatment involves surgery, it is good medical practice, albeit not a legal requirement, to obtain the patient's consent in writing, usually by the patient signing a standard consent form. It is, however, important to remember that the consent form does not amount to a contract between the doctor and her patient. Rather the patient's consent must be ongoing throughout her treatment, and she is free to withdraw her consent at any time. Signing a consent form does not affect the patient's right to refuse to undergo the operation.

(d) THE PRINCIPLE OF AUTONOMY

The principle that a competent adult must not be treated without her consent is clearly directed towards protecting both her autonomy and her bodily integrity. As we can see from the following judicial statements, every competent adult patient has the *right* to refuse medical treatment, even if her reasons are bizarre, irrational or non-existent, and even if her refusal will result in her death.

The case of *Airedale NHS Trust v Bland*[9] (which we consider in detail in Chapter 16) contains strong confirmation of the priority that must be given to the principle of patient self-determination:

---

[8] Human Fertilization and Embryology Act 1990, Schedule 3(1).   [9] [1993] AC 789.

Lord Mustill

If the patient is capable of making a decision on whether to permit treatment, . . . his choice must be obeyed even if on any objective view it is contrary to his best interests.

Lord Goff

[T]he principle of self-determination requires that respect must be given to the wishes of the patient, so that if an adult patient of sound mind refuses, however unreasonably, to consent to treatment or care by which his life would or might be prolonged, the doctors responsible for his care must give effect to his wishes, even though they do not consider it to be in his best interests to do.

In *Re T*,[10] all three judges in the Court of Appeal again articulated a robust commitment to patient autonomy:

Lord Donaldson MR

An adult patient who, like Miss T, suffers from no mental incapacity has an absolute right to choose whether to consent to medical treatment, to refuse it or to choose one rather than another of the treatments being offered. . . . This right of choice is not limited to decisions which others might regard as sensible. It exists notwithstanding that the reasons for making the choice are rational, irrational, unknown or even non-existent.

Butler-Sloss LJ

A man or woman of full age and sound understanding may choose to reject medical advice and medical or surgical treatment either partially or in its entirety. A decision to refuse medical treatment by a patient capable of making the decision does not have to be sensible, rational or well-considered.

Staughton LJ

An adult whose mental capacity is unimpaired has the right to decide for herself whether she will or will not receive medical or surgical treatment, even in circumstances where she is likely or even certain to die in the absence of treatment. Thus far the law is clear.

Of course, it is also now necessary to consider whether the patient's right to make her own medical decisions might be protected by the Human Rights Act 1998. A number of convention rights might be relevant here, such as Article 2 (the right to life); Article 3 (the right not to be subjected to inhuman or degrading treatment); Article 5 (the right to liberty); Article 8 (respect for private and family life); and Article 9 (respect for religious views).

Respect for patient autonomy is also undoubtedly considered to be good medical practice. The British Medical Association, for example, advises doctors that:

It is well established in law and ethics that competent adults have the right to refuse any medical treatment, even if that refusal results in their death.[11]

It seems then to be settled law that competent adult patients have the right to make *irrational* and *life-threatening* decisions to refuse medical treatment. In the next extract, Julian Savulescu and Richard W Momeyer defend the patient's right to make

---

[10] [1993] Fam 95.
[11] British Medical Association, *Withholding and withdrawing life-prolonging medical treatment: guidance for decision making* (2nd edn 2001), para 9.1.

irrational decisions, but they nevertheless suggest that efforts should be made to promote rational, critical deliberation.

Julian Savulescu and Richard W Momeyer[12]

Our contention is that being autonomous requires that a person hold rational beliefs. We distinguish between rational choice and rational belief. Being autonomous may not require that one's choices and actions are rational. But it does require that one's beliefs which ground those choices are rational . . .

We do not respect autonomy when we encourage people to act on irrational beliefs. Rather, such beliefs limit a person's autonomy . . . Since holding true beliefs is necessary to be autonomous, we do not respect autonomy when we allow patients to act on irrational beliefs. Should physicians override choices based on irrational beliefs? Should life-saving blood transfusions be given to Jehovah's Witnesses against their wishes? . . .

We believe there are reasons against taking this radical departure from the notion of informed consent . . .

The first reason is consequentialist: if we allow doctors to override choices based on some species of irrationality, then other Jehovah's Witnesses will be distressed at the thought their decisions will be overriden. The general misery and distrust of medicine that would result would reduce the value of such a policy . . .

Secondly, though a practice of allowing people to act out of wilful ignorance or irrationality may not promote their autonomy in the short term, respect for autonomy is not the only ground for non-interference in another person's life. It is surely enough that it is his life, and that he ought to be allowed to do what there is no good reason to do, if he chooses. . . .

Thirdly, *requiring* that choice be grounded on rational beliefs before it is respected is fraught with dangers. Those who claim to know Truth with certainty are at least as dangerous as those who claim to know Right and Good with certainty . . .

In the end, deferral to irrationality, to partial autonomy, to imperfect consent and to unexplored values and metaphysical beliefs in patients may be necessary, even morally required. But before reaching this point, a physician committed to the highest standard of care will exercise her talents as an educator to promote greater rationality in patients. Not to make the effort to promote rational, critical deliberation is to risk a very contemporary form of patient abandonment: abandonment to human irrationality . . .

If an ethic of respect for persons in contemporary medicine rules out—except in the most extreme cases—coercion as a response to patient irrationality, it also makes more imperative a 'critical educator' response to patient irrationality.

Other commentators, such as Shimon Glick, have argued that when a patient is taking a life and death decision, there are times when a degree of paternalism would be justifiable.

Shimon Glick[13]

I would like to suggest . . . that it is high time that the pendulum which has swung from overbearing, autocratic and insensitive paternalism to an often cruel and dangerous autonomy, be allowed to swing back to a more moderate and sensible balance between autonomy and beneficence . . .

---

[12] 'Should informed consent be based upon rational beliefs?' (1997) 23 Journal of Medical Ethics 282–8, 282, 287–8.
[13] 'The morality of coercion' (2000) 26 Journal of Medical Ethics 393–5.

[O]ftentimes individuals under acute stress may make hasty tragic decisions which they subsequently, under more careful consideration, regret . . .

I would hope that even the most devoted advocates of autonomy might accept the premise that a patient who is frightened and stressed, may not be fully autonomous; his/her refusal should therefore be assigned less weight.

It is tragic to accept such a patient's refusal automatically at face value, even if a team of psychiatrists and lawyers judge that person legally competent . . .

In addition, autonomy is of no value to a dead person. By permitting a patient to die avoidably, when it is virtually certain that were he saved against his present protest he would be grateful, one is granting that person his short term 'autonomous' wish while depriving him of his long term autonomy . . .

I am not advocating a return to insensitive, arrogant paternalism, which places little or no value on individual patients' opinions and values, and arrogates to the physician the absolute right to select therapy, under the guise of always knowing what is best for the patient. But when a thoughtful ethics committee listens carefully to a patient's viewpoint, and is convinced that the patient's welfare demands a particular treatment, and that the patient, too, will subsequently be grateful for such intervention, I believe it to be ethically appropriate to overrule the patient's objections.

In Chapter 1, we looked at the principle of patient autonomy (see further p. 22), and saw that some commentators have suggested that it is an excessively individualistic value. Giving the competent adult patient an absolute right to reject life-saving medical treatment ignores the impact that this might have upon other people, such as her dependants. Here there may be a tension between a patient's *legal* right to determine what is done to her body, and her *moral* obligations to others. Let us imagine that X shares an extremely rare blood group with her sister, Y, who is in urgent need of a blood transfusion. Legally X cannot be compelled to donate blood to Y, even though this is a procedure which will cause X minimal pain and discomfort and is virtually risk-free, but which might save Y's life. We might, however, criticize X for failing to meet her *moral* duty of easy rescue, that is, the 'presumption that refusing to save another person's life when doing so is virtually costless to the person in a position to act, is seriously wrong'.[14]

(e) PREGNANT WOMEN'S AUTONOMY?

In *Re T*,[15] Lord Donaldson mooted one possible exception to the right to refuse treatment:

The only possible qualification is a case in which the choice may lead to the death of a viable foetus. That is not this case and, if and when it arises, the courts will be faced with a novel problem of considerable legal and ethical complexity.

Later the same year, just such a case arose. In *Re S (Adult: Refusal of Treatment)*,[16] Mrs S wanted to refuse a caesarean section on religious grounds (she was described as a

---

[14] JL Nelson, *Hippocrates' Maze: Ethical Explorations of the Medical Labyrinth* (Rowman and Littlefield New York 2003) 119.
[15] [1993] Fam 95.   [16] [1992] 4 All ER 671.

'born-again Christian'). Her competence was not in doubt. An emergency application was made, and after an *ex parte* hearing lasting less than two hours, Sir Stephen Brown granted a declaration that the operation would be lawful. He suggested that there was 'some American authority' which suggested that the US courts would be likely to grant a declaration in circumstances such as these. On this point, with respect, Sir Stephen Brown was mistaken. In the only case he mentions, *Re AC*,[17] the decision had in fact been that the caesarean which had been carried out on Angela Carder against her wishes had been unlawful, and should not have been performed.

In addition to being an unlawful infringement of the competent adult patient's right to refuse unwanted medical treatment, forcing women to have caesarean sections against their will is ultimately likely to result in poorer outcomes for fetuses, since women who object to surgical delivery might be deterred from seeking any medical attention during pregnancy and labour.

Re S is almost certainly now of historical interest only. In two subsequent cases, the Court of Appeal has confirmed that pregnancy does not diminish the competent adult patient's right to refuse unwanted medical intervention. In *Re MB (An Adult: Medical Treatment)*,[18] although in the event MB was judged temporarily incompetent on the grounds of her needle phobia, Butler-Sloss LJ referred to *Re S* as 'a decision the correctness of which we must now call in doubt'. Instead she was emphatic that:

A competent woman who has the capacity to decide may, for religious reasons, other reasons, for rational or irrational reasons or for no reason at all, choose not to have medical intervention, even though the consequence may be the death or serious handicap of the child she bears, or her own death.

A year later, in *St George's NHS Trust v S*[19] the emergency caesarean section which had been performed upon S against her wishes was held to be a trespass. Judge LJ strongly defended the pregnant woman's right to refuse treatment which could save her fetus's life, even if her decision might appear to be 'morally repugnant'.

Judge LJ

In our judgment while pregnancy increases the personal responsibilities of a woman it does not diminish her entitlement to decide whether or not to undergo medical treatment. Although human, and protected by the law in a number of different ways . . ., an unborn child is not a separate person from its mother. Its need for medical assistance does not prevail over her rights. She is entitled not to be forced to submit to an invasion of her body against her will, whether her own life or that of her unborn child depends on it. Her right is not reduced or diminished merely because her decision to exercise it may appear morally repugnant.

As Rebecca Bailey-Harris points out in the next extract, the Court of Appeal's judgment in *St George's NHS Trust v S* represents an especially robust assertion of the principle of patient autonomy.

Rebecca Bailey-Harris[20]

The entire judgment (delivered by Judge L.J. on behalf of the court) is permeated by the theme of patient autonomy and the obligation of a free society to guard that autonomy from erosion. This

---

[17] [1990] 573 A 2d 1235.   [18] [1997] 2 FLR 426.   [19] [1999] Fam 26.
[20] 'Pregnancy, Autonomy and Refusal of Medical Treatment' (1998) 114 Law Quarterly Review 550–5.

reasoning led to a robust reassertion of the common law right of a competent adult to refuse treatment ... Here the court held that S was competent throughout; bizarre, eccentric and irrational thinking does not per se indicate incompetence.

(f) ADVANCE DIRECTIVES

In order to protect patient autonomy, it is not just contemporaneous refusals of medical treatment which must be respected. We consider advance refusals (sometimes known as advance directives or living wills) in more detail in Chapter 16 p. 934 when we look at end of life decision making. An advance refusal will be binding on the medical practitioners involved in the patient's care if, first, the patient was competent when she executed the advance refusal; and, secondly, it fits her current predicament; and, thirdly, the patient had not subsequently changed her mind. An obvious example might be a card, carried by a Jehovah's Witness, which specifies that in no circumstances would they consent to receive a blood transfusion.

In practice, however, it is very unusual for patients to draw up advance directives which are precise enough to be legally binding. It is almost impossible to foresee every medical eventuality when making an advance directive, and any lack of fit between the advance refusal and the patient's present circumstances will lead to doubt about its validity, and medical staff will therefore feel justified in ignoring it. Because the patient is now incompetent, it may also be difficult to establish that she was actually competent when she made her decision. There is also always a risk that the patient may have changed her mind since making the advance directive.

More complicated still is the argument that it is *never* possible for an advance directive to have been sufficiently well informed because, by definition, the competent adult does not know what it is like to be incompetent. If I decide that I would not want my life prolonged if I were to become severely demented, I am making that judgment with no knowledge of what it feels like to be severely demented. It might seem a horrifying prospect to me now, but it is possible that once I become demented, I will, in fact, appear to be cheerful and to gain pleasure from my existence. In Chapter 16 at p. 938, we explore the disagreement over whether respect for autonomy means that an incompetent adult should be bound by her previous choices, since these reflect her 'real' preferences, or whether she is effectively now a different person, whose previous values no longer exist, and whose present interests should take priority.

In any event, it seems clear that where there is any doubt over the validity of an advance refusal of life-saving treatment, the English courts will resolve that doubt 'in favour of the preservation of life'.[21] In *HE v A Hospital NHS Trust*,[22] the question of the validity of an advance directive arose. The patient, whose condition was now life-threatening, had executed an advance directive refusing blood products when she was a Jehovah's Witness. She had since abandoned her religion in order to marry her Muslim fiancé. In addition, she had not mentioned the advance directive to the medical staff involved in her care, and she had told relatives that she did not want to

---

[21] *Re T (Adult: Refusal of Treatment)* [1993] Fam 95, per Lord Donaldson.
[22] [2003] EWHC 1017 (Fam), [2003] 2 FLR 408.

die. Munby J held that the advance directive 'cannot have survived her deliberate, implemented, decision to abandon that faith and to revert to being a Muslim'.

Munby J

[A]lthough the burden of proof on the issue of capacity is on those who seek to dispute it, the burden of proof is otherwise on those who seek to establish the existence and continuing validity and applicability of an advance directive. So if there is doubt that doubt falls to be resolved in favour of the preservation of life ... Where, as here, life is at stake, the evidence must be scrutinised with especial care. The continuing validity and applicability of the advance directive must be clearly established by convincing and inherently reliable evidence . . .

Whether there truly is some real reason to doubt, whether the doubt is a real doubt or only some speculative or fanciful doubt, will inevitably depend on the circumstances. Holding the balance involves awesome responsibility. Too ready a submission to speculative or merely fanciful doubts will rob advance directives of their utility and may condemn those who in truth do not want to be treated to what they would see as indignity or worse. (I am acutely conscious of, and trust I am properly sensitive to, the profound sense of violation that Jehovah's Witnesses feel if forced to submit to blood transfusions against their will.) Too sceptical a reaction to well-founded suggestions that circumstances have changed may turn an advance directive into a death warrant for a patient who in truth wants to be treated.

At the end of the day, and however unhelpful for hard-pressed doctors this seeming platitude may be, it must all depend on the facts. All I would add is that the longer the time which has elapsed since an advance directive was made, and the greater the apparent changes in the patient's circumstances since then, the more doubt there is likely to be as to its continuing validity and applicability. There will be cases in which, as I have said, there will need to be especially close, rigorous and anxious scrutiny.

It is noteworthy that Munby J implies that the burden of proof of capacity is reversed when the patient has issued an advance directive, and that such patients no longer benefit from the presumption of competence which applies when patients make contemporaneous decisions. Of course, it is easy to understand why the courts might be cautious when it is difficult to tell whether a patient really intended to refuse life-saving treatment in the circumstances in which she now finds herself. Nevertheless, it is clear that this presumption against following the patient's previously expressed wishes, unless there is 'convincing and inherently reliable evidence' of its validity, may mean that there are times when patients are given treatment which they tried, when competent, to refuse.

To be binding, an advance refusal must precisely specify the treatment which is being refused. Yet few patients make these sorts of detailed requests. It is much more common for people to express a general desire not to be kept alive if they become a 'vegetable', for example. As we can see from the following case, even repeated and clear assertions that a patient would not want to be kept alive once she was no longer able to recognize her own children were held to be insufficiently precise to qualify as a binding advance directive.

W Healthcare NHS Trust v H[23]

KH suffered acutely from multiple sclerosis. Although she remained conscious, she was disorien-

---

[23] [2004] EWCA Civ 1324.

tated and no longer recognized her closest family members. She was fed by a PEG (percutaneous gastrostomy) tube, could not swallow, was doubly incontinent, and required twenty-four hour care. When the PEG tube became dislodged, the question whether it should be reinserted arose. There was evidence from her friends and family members that she had said repeatedly that if the time came when she could no longer recognize her daughters, she did not want to be kept alive.

Brooke LJ

The next question when what is being proposed amounts to a trespass is whether there is a clear exposition of the patient's wishes before she became incapable, which is capable in law of amounting to a direction as to how she wishes to be treated when no longer capable of taking decisions for herself. The logic behind this is that the important principle of personal autonomy means that each one of us, certainly when we become an adult, are capable of saying no to any infringement of our bodily integrity. The insertion of a PEG tube would certainly be an infringement of KH's bodily integrity. If we say this clearly at a time when we are capable of expressing our wishes, then that clear declaration is binding on those who would have the responsibility for our care when we are no longer competent. But the declaration has to be clear and it has to be referable to the particular circumstances. . . .

I am of the clear view that the judge was correct in finding that there was not an advance directive which was sufficiently clear to amount to a direction that she preferred to be deprived of food and drink for a period of time which would lead to her death in all circumstances. There is no evidence that she was aware of the nature of this choice, or the unpleasantness or otherwise of death by starvation, and it would be departing from established principles of English law if one was to hold that there was an advance directive which was established and relevant in the circumstances in the present case, despite the very strong expression of her wishes which came through in the evidence.

While in practice it may be difficult to establish that an advance directive is valid, it is certainly not impossible. In *Re AK (Adult Patient) (Medical Treatment: Consent)*[24] (extracted in Chapter 16), a 19-year-old man suffering from motor neurone disease requested that the doctors should remove him from the artificial ventilator two weeks after he finally lost all ability to communicate. Hughes J held that:

In the present case the expressions of AK's decision are recent and are made not on any hypothetical basis but in the fullest possible knowledge of impending reality. I am satisfied that they genuinely represent his considered wishes and should be treated as such . . .

Given that his express wishes are clear, the conclusion follows from what I have said that once the conditions which he has stipulated arise it will be unlawful to continue invasive ventilation.

4. INCAPACITY

As we have seen, if a patient is judged to be competent, their consent or refusal of medical treatment is decisive. In contrast, if a patient is incompetent, they may be treated without their consent. Clearly it is therefore vitally important to be able to tell when a patient either is or is not competent.

---

[24] [2001] 1 FLR 129.

(a) DEFINING INCAPACITY

How might we assess decision-making capacity? Two approaches can be distinguished: one based upon *status* and the other upon *function*.

- According to the status approach, certain categories of patients are presumed to be incompetent because of their status, regardless of their real decision-making ability. A fifteen year old child, for example, might be presumed to be incompetent because of her age, even though in fact her powers of reasoning outstrip those of many adults.

- The functional approach instead focuses on the individual's actual capabilities. A child would not automatically be disqualified from taking decisions about her medical treatment, rather her competence would depend upon whether she is in fact able to make the particular decision.

Although the status approach benefits from ease of application—it is much more straightforward to discover a child's age than it is to individually assess her decision-making capacity—it is, as Ian Kennedy points out, the functional approach which better promotes the principle of patient self-determination;

Ian Kennedy[25]

The fundamental flaw in the status approach is that it takes no account of the individuality of each person. Respect for autonomy, however, involves respect for each person's individuality. It demands, therefore, that any criterion intended to determine when someone is incapable of being autonomous should, equally, be respectful of that person's individuality. Merely placing him in a class is far too gross a test of incapacity. It denies respect to the individual as an individual, and must therefore be rejected . . .

It should be clear from what has been said so far that the only valid criterion of capacity is the ability of the particular individual to comprehend the nature and consequences of the proposed procedure. This is a test which is specific to each individual and thus maximizes respect for each person's autonomy. It makes maturity the crucial determinant, the maturity that consists in having a stable set of values and outlook on life and the ability to weigh the proposed procedure in the light of these so as to arrive at a considered decision.

It seems clear, from cases such as *Re C*[26] and *Gillick*[27] (see below pp. 196 and 233), that the English courts adopt a combination of the status and the functional approaches to capacity: all adults are presumed to be competent, and all children under the age of 16 are presumed to be incompetent, by virtue of their minority. But although these twin presumptions are status based, they are simply starting points, and the *actual* decision-making capacity of mentally impaired adults or older children should be assessed using the functional approach, where it is the individual's capabilities, and not their membership of a particular social group, which matters. As we see later, in practice, the courts have tended to invoke an unqualified 'status' approach to capacity when children wish to take life-threatening decisions.

This amalgamation of functional and status based tests for capacity retains some of

---

[25] *Treat Me Right* (OUP Oxford 1988) 57–8.   [26] [1994] 1 All ER 819 [1994] 1 WLR 290.
[27] [1984] QB 581.

the disadvantages of a pure status based approach. All the evidence appears to suggest that while the decision-making capacity of young children clearly differs from that of adults, by the time children reach the age of about 14, many are able to reason as effectively as people who are 18 years old. Nevertheless, English law will require the 14-year-old to prove that she has the requisite capacity, while the 18-year-old will be presumed competent, and the burden of proof would instead lie with those who seek to establish that she is in fact incompetent.

Although plainly a more effective way to protect patient autonomy, the functional approach does, however, beg the question of exactly how we tell whether an individual is capable of making her own medical decisions. Clearly, the test should focus upon the patient's decision-making *process*, rather than the *content* of her decision. A test for capacity which assessed the *reasonableness* of a patient's choice is synonymous with benevolent paternalism, and inconsistent with the principle of patient autonomy, which, if it is to mean anything, must protect the patient's right to make decisions that others believe to be misguided. Instead, a patient should be considered competent if she meets a *minimum threshold level of decision-making ability*, and once she has satisfied this test, the *wisdom* of any particular decision she might take should be immaterial. According to the British Medical Association:

The fact that an individual has made a decision which appears to others to be irrational or unjustified should not be taken as evidence that the individual lacks the mental capacity to make that decision.[28]

It is also important to remember that, in reality, capacity is a question of degree. Although patients at either end of the spectrum might be readily identified as either competent or incompetent, towards the middle it will be difficult to determine where the line should lie. As Michael Gunn explains:

Capacity/incapacity are not concepts with clear a priori boundaries. They appear on a continuum which ranges from full capacity at one end to full incapacity at the other end. There are, therefore, degrees of capacity. The challenge is to choose the right level to set as the gateway to decision-making and respect for persons and autonomy.[29]

Normally it is assumed that adult patients have the capacity to consent to treatment. Decision-making capacity only tends to become an issue in two situations. First, if the patient belongs to a group whose members often or normally lack capacity, health care professionals may be alerted to the possibility that she will not be able to give a valid consent to treatment. This will be true of children, unconscious patients, and people suffering from certain mental disorders.

Secondly, if the patient's doctors believe that her decision is seriously misguided or irrational, they are more likely to question her decision-making capacity. The irrationality of a patient's choice does not justify a finding of incompetence, however. On the contrary, as we have seen, if competent, a patient's decision must be respected regardless of how foolish or irrational it may seem. But it is probably inevitable that

---

[28] British Medical Association, *Withholding and withdrawing life-prolonging medical treatment: guidance for decision making* (2nd edn 2001) paras 9.1–9.3.
[29] M. Gunn, 'The Meaning of Incapacity' (1994) 2 Medical Law Review 8.

doctors will be more likely to question a patient's capacity when she refuses to consent to a proposed treatment, than when she agrees with the doctor's recommendation.

Of course, if the medical profession is unlikely to challenge a patient's decision-making capacity when she has *consented* to the proposed treatment, the pool of patients who are currently labelled incompetent will be smaller than it would be if *all* patients' decision-making capacity was individually scrutinized and assessed. In the study discussed in the next extract, Raymont et al. assessed the decision-making capacity of acutely ill medical inpatients, and found that almost half of them lacked capacity, but since none of them had refused treatment, the treating doctors had not questioned their decision-making capacity.

Vanessa Raymont, William Bingley, Alec Buchanan, Anthony S David, Peter Hayward, Simon Wessely, and Matthew Hotopf[30]

Our study suggests that in routine clinical practice, doctors most usually fail to identify that patients with significant cognitive impairment do not have capacity. If we accept that a high proportion of acutely ill medical inpatients do not have mental capacity to make decisions about current treatment, our findings have implications for clinical practice, legislation, and the doctor–patient relationship. The current position is to assume capacity unless there is strong evidence to the contrary. We suspect that a substantial proportion of patients with decisional difficulties place their trust in doctors, and passively acquiesce with treatment plans. Thus, incapacity is frequently overlooked. . . .

[T]he high proportion of medical patients who are treated without being able to give valid consent is striking, with very few checks being in place . . . A substantial proportion of inpatients in any general medical ward do not have capacity to make informed treatment decisions, a situation that is rarely recognised by doctors . . . However, to accept the passive acquiescence of such patients as evidence of true consent would be dangerous when important and irreversible decisions need to be made. Before making such decisions, the clinician should have considered the possibility that the patient is unable to give valid consent.

In this chapter, we divide incompetent patients into three groups: those who are temporarily incapacitated in an emergency; mentally incompetent adults; and children. It is, however, important to remember, as Carl Elliott makes clear in the following extract, that there will be enormous differences between incompetent patients. For example, a premature baby and a mature 17-year-old are both children, but their mental abilities and their health needs could hardly be more different.

Carl Elliott[31]

[T]he very fact that all incompetent and marginally competent patients are often lumped together in the same category says something about the way the field has evolved . . . [I]dentifying it as the most morally relevant feature about a patient downplays the fact that incompetent and marginally competent patients comprise a vastly diverse range of human beings who present very different ethical problems. From an ethical point of view, an anencephalic [a baby born without an upper brain], a 65 year old woman with Alzheimer's disease, a violent man with schizophrenia and a 6 year old with incurable lymphoma are probably divided by more than they share. Not only do

---

[30] 'Prevalence of mental incapacity in medical inpatients and associated risk factors: cross-sectional study' (2004) 364 The Lancet 1421–7.
[31] 'Patients doubtfully capable or incapable of consent' in H Kuhse and P Singer (eds), *A Companion to Bioethics* (Blackwell Oxford 1998) 452–62, 452.

different incompetent patients present different ethical problems, they occupy radically different places in our moral and emotional lives. We generally think of children, for example, in ways very different from the ways we think of incompetent adults. While our attitudes to incompetent adults are often centred on respect for the patient's previous values and the narrative of her past life, our moral attitudes towards children are commonly located within notions of dependence, protection, growth and the child's relationship to her parents.

(b) EMERGENCIES

A patient suffering from short-term incapacity, perhaps because she is unconscious or heavily sedated, might need urgent medical treatment but be unable to give consent. When a patient is attended at the scene of an accident, or when someone is first brought into an accident and emergency department, for example, they may be unconscious, and therefore incapable of consenting to their own medical treatment. It would clearly be absurd if a patient's inability to consent prevented her from receiving emergency medical treatment. Treatment in these circumstances is justified by invoking the doctrine of necessity. In *Re F*,[32] a case we consider in detail below, Lord Goff explained the doctrine of necessity as follows:

Lord Goff

[T]he basic requirements, applicable in these cases of necessity, that, to fall within the principle, not only (1) must there be a necessity to act when it is not practicable to communicate with the assisted person, but also (2) the action taken must be such as a reasonable person would in all the circumstances take, acting in the best interests of the assisted person . . .

Where, for example, a surgeon performs an operation without his consent on a patient temporarily rendered unconscious in an accident, he should do no more than is reasonably required, in the best interests of the patient, before he recovers consciousness. I can see no practical difficulty arising from this requirement, which derives from the fact that the patient is expected before long to regain consciousness and can then be consulted about longer term measures.

A different type of emergency might emerge when a patient is unconscious during surgery, and the surgeon notices that there is something seriously wrong with the patient which had not been anticipated when she gave consent. In these circumstances, the principle of necessity justifies medical intervention provided that it would be unreasonable, and not just inconvenient, to wait until the patient regains consciousness and capacity, and is able to make her own decision about the treatment in question.

The Department of Health's standard consent form *Patient agreement to investigation or treatment* contains a clause which states:

I understand that any procedure in addition to those described on this form will only be carried out if it is necessary to save my life or to prevent serious harm to my health.[33]

This does not amount to express consent to any additional procedure, since as we will see in the following chapter, consent will only be valid if the patient has been

---

[32] [1990] 2 AC 1 HL.   [33] <http://www.dh.gov.uk/assetRoot/04/01/90/34/04019034.pdf>.

informed 'in broad terms' about the nature of the procedure.[34] It is unlikely that the courts would find that this sort of clause justified more intrusive treatment than would be justified in any event at common law, by virtue of the doctrine of necessity. Rather the better interpretation of this sort of clause is that it alerts the patient in advance to the possible application of the principle of necessity, should the doctors discover a condition which, if not treated immediately, might cause death or serious injury.

It is the principle of necessity which justifies doctors trying to save the lives of people who have attempted to commit suicide. In such circumstances, it will rarely be possible to be certain either that the patient definitely intended to end her life, or that she was competent when she attempted to commit suicide. Attempts to save the person's life would therefore be lawful by virtue of the common law justification of necessity.

(c) INCOMPETENT ADULTS

Until the Mental Capacity Act 2005 comes into force, probably in 2007, it is the common law which applies to the medical treatment of mentally incapacitated adults. Since much of the Act simply codifies and clarifies the existing common law principles, with a few notable additions, it is important to have a good understanding of both the new legislation *and* the position at common law.

(1) AT COMMON LAW

(a) Presumption of capacity and the *Re C* test

In order to protect patients' autonomy, there is first, a presumption of capacity, and, secondly, this can be rebutted only if, on the functional approach, this patient is unable to make her own decisions. The presumption of capacity is especially important when the patient in question suffers from some sort of mental disorder. It means that however mentally ill a patient might be, and however foolish the decision she wishes to take, she still (in theory, at least) benefits from the presumption that she is able to take decisions about her own medical treatment, and it would be for her doctors to prove otherwise.

The leading English case on capacity, and an excellent illustration of the fact that mental illness and mental incapacity are not synonymous with each other, is *Re C*.

Re C[35]

C was a patient at Broadmoor hospital. He was sixty-eight years old and suffered from chronic paranoid schizophrenia. He had grandiose delusions that he had had an international career in medicine, during which he had never lost a patient. He developed gangrene and his consultant was of the view that, unless his leg was amputated, he had an 85% chance of death. C said that he would rather die with two feet than live with one. Although the danger of death was averted without amputation this time, there was a risk that his condition would deteriorate, and he would

---

[34] *Chatterton v Gerson* [1981] QB 432.   [35] [1994] 1 All ER 819, [1994] 1 WLR 290.

need amputation in the future. C's solicitor sought, and was granted, a declaration that no amputation should take place without C's written consent.

Thorpe J

I consider helpful Dr E's analysis of the decision-making process into three stages:

- first, comprehending and retaining treatment information,
- secondly, believing it and,
- thirdly, weighing it in the balance to arrive at choice.

Applying that test to my findings on the evidence, I am completely satisfied that the presumption that Mr C has the right of self-determination has not been displaced. Although his general capacity is impaired by schizophrenia, it has not been established that he does not sufficiently understand the nature, purpose and effects of the treatment he refuses. Indeed, I am satisfied that he has understood and retained the relevant treatment information, that in his own way he believes it, and that in the same fashion he has arrived at a clear choice.

Notice that C was clearly seriously mentally ill, and suffering from delusions, and that the decision he wished to take might have had very serious adverse consequences, but he was still judged capable of coming to a decision about whether or not to have his leg amputated.

A number of cases have since confirmed that people who are mentally ill may nevertheless be competent to make life and death decisions. For example, in *Re JT (Adult: Refusal of Medical Treatment)*[36] a woman who suffered from learning difficulties and severe behavioural disturbance was nevertheless judged to have capacity under the *Re C* test, and her refusal to consent to dialysis treatment was respected. And in *Secretary of State for the Home Department v Robb*,[37] Thorpe J held that a prisoner on hunger strike who suffered from a personality disorder was competent, and that it would therefore have been unlawful to force-feed him.

The test Thorpe J applied has come to be known as the *Re C* test. It has subsequently been confirmed by the Court of Appeal in *Re MB*,[38] and it undoubtedly formed the basis of the statutory test for incapacity in the Mental Capacity Act 2005 (see below p. 218). In short, Thorpe J proposed a three stage test for establishing a patient's capacity:

(1) Can the patient comprehend and retain the relevant information?

(2) Is he able to believe it?

(3) Is he able to weigh the information, balancing risks and benefits, in order to arrive at a choice?

In *Re MB* Butler-Sloss LJ initially appeared to qualify the *Re C* test by missing out the second stage:

A person lacks capacity if some impairment or disturbance of mental functioning renders the person unable to make a decision whether to consent to or to refuse treatment. That inability to make a decision will occur when:

---

[36] [1998] 1 FLR 48.   [37] [1995] 1 FLR 412.   [38] *Re MB* [1997] 1 FCR 274.

(a) the patient is unable to comprehend and retain the information which is material to the decision, especially as to the likely consequences of having or not having the treatment in question.

(b) the patient is unable to use the information and weigh it in the balance as part of the process of arriving at the decision.

However at a number of points the Court of Appeal directly approved the *Re C* test without qualification, and the better interpretation is almost certainly that the Court of Appeal meant to confirm that Thorpe J's three stage test applies to the determination of capacity.

Despite receiving broad approval from the judiciary and parliament alike, the *Re C* test does contain a few ambiguities. First, the principle that the patient can understand treatment information is clearly important, since decisions based upon inadequate understanding might not reflect the patient's real preferences. But how well a patient is able to understand information may depend more upon how the information is presented and communicated, than upon her mental capabilities. Research has indicated that it is possible to improve an individual's ability to satisfy a capacity assessment, by using simple language or presenting information with the help of pictures rather than words.[39] This suggests that evidence that a patient lacks decision-making capacity should not automatically lead to their classification as incompetent, but rather should first prompt attempts to enhance their ability to make decisions, using more appropriate information-giving techniques. Only when it becomes clear that the person cannot understand simplified information should it be acceptable to treat her without consent.

Secondly, it is often assumed that a patient will only be judged incompetent if they have some *mental* disorder which prevents them from making a decision. Yet the pain, fatigue and disorientation caused by chronic *physical* illness, not to mention the influence of medication, can also disrupt the patient's ability to weigh information in the balance to arrive at a choice. A patient who is in unbearable pain, for example, may not be capable of weighing the side-effects of painkilling drugs against her immediate and overwhelming need for pain relief. Recall that Raymont et al.'s study found that almost 50 per cent of acutely ill medical inpatients lacked capacity but, as Raymont et al. pointed out, this sort of incapacity—unlike that resulting from mental disorder—commonly goes unnoticed.[40]

Thirdly, what if the patient is capable of making a decision, but is unable to communicate it? In almost all cases, it will be possible to enable patients to communicate their wishes, but in some extreme situations—such as when the patient is suffering from what is known as 'locked in' syndrome—despite the patient's competence, it will be impossible to find out what decision she wishes to make. In such circumstances, the competent patient will have to be treated as if she were incompetent, and treatment without consent would be lawful.

Fourthly, the *Re C* test's approach to irrational decision-making is somewhat

---

[39] MJ Gunn et al. 'Decision-Making Capacity' (1999) 7 Medical Law Review 269–306, 283.

[40] 'Prevalence of mental incapacity in medical inpatients and associated risk factors: cross-sectional study' (2004) 364 The Lancet 1421–7.

ambiguous. On the one hand, it seems clear that provided a patient satisfies the *Re C* test, it does not matter whether the decision she wants to take is irrational, or based upon her own peculiar values or beliefs. As Lord Donaldson MR explained in *Re T*:[41]

the patient's right of choice exists whether the reasons for making that choice are rational, irrational, unknown or even non-existent.

On the other hand it is sometimes difficult to draw the line between a person's bizarre and irrational wishes, which must nevertheless be respected, and evidence of a person's inability to come to a reasoned decision about their treatment, as demanded by the third stage of the *Re C* test. For example, it has been stated on a number of occasions that the competent adult patient is entitled to refuse treatment 'for no reason at all'.[42] Yet making a decision for no reason at all would appear to indicate that the patient has not weighed information in the balance to arrive at a choice, and hence would appear to fail the third limb of the *Re C* test for capacity.

In reality, when a patient wishes to refuse potentially life-saving treatment, the courts will generally tend to inquire into her reasons for wanting treatment to discontinue. In *Re B (Adult: Refusal of Medical Treatment)*, a case which we consider in detail in Chapter 16, Dame Elizabeth Butler-Sloss's finding that Ms B was competent certainly appeared to have been influenced by the consistency and rationality of her *reasons* for wishing ventilation to be discontinued.

In *Re MB*,[43] Butler-Sloss LJ suggested that although irrationality is not the same as incompetence, it might sometimes amount to *evidence* of incompetence:

Although it might be thought that irrationality sits uneasily with competence to decide, panic, indecisiveness and irrationality in themselves do not as such amount to incompetence, but they may be symptoms or evidence of incompetence.

Similarly, in *Re T*, Lord Donaldson suggested that a bizarre or unusual decision might sometimes offer supporting evidence if there are other grounds for questioning the patient's competence:

That his choice is contrary to what is to be expected of the vast majority of adults is only relevant if there are other reasons for doubting his capacity to decide. The nature of his choice or the terms in which it is expressed may then tip the balance.

In *NHS Trust v T (Adult Patient: Refusal of Medical Treatment)*,[44] Ms T had attempted to execute an advance directive refusing the blood transfusions she needed regularly because of her tendency to self-harm through blood-letting. In her advance directive, she explained her reasons for refusing blood transfusions as follows:

I believe my blood is evil, carrying evil around my body. Although the blood given in transfusions is perfectly healthy/clean once given to me it mixes with my own and also becomes evil. Contaminated by my own. Therefore the volume of evil blood in my body will have increased and likewise the danger of my committing acts of evil.

Charles J stressed that making a bizarre or irrational decision was not sufficient for a

[41] [1993] Fam 95.
[42] *Re MB* [1997] 1 FCR 274 per Butler-Sloss LJ.
[43] *Re MB* [1997] 1 FCR 274.
[44] [2004] EWHC 1279 (Fam), [2005] 1 All ER 387.

finding of incapacity, but nevertheless found that her belief that blood was evil amounted to a disorder of the mind:

Charles J

If there are difficulties in deciding whether the patient has sufficient mental capacity, particularly if the refusal may have grave consequences for the patient, it is most important that those considering the issue should not confuse the question of mental capacity with the nature of the decision made by the patient, however grave the consequences. The view of the patient may reflect a difference in values rather than an absence of competence and the assessment of capacity should be approached with this firmly in mind. The doctors must not allow their emotional reaction to or strong disagreement with the decision of the patient to cloud their judgment in answering the primary question whether the patient has the mental capacity to make the decision. . . .

Ms T's references to her blood being evil equate to the example given that 'the blood is poisoned because it is red'. From that it seems to me that this assertion and belief of Ms T is a misconception of reality which can more readily be accepted to be, and on the present evidence should be accepted to be, a disorder of the mind and further or alternatively symptoms or evidence of incompetence.

Cases involving anorexic patients are a particularly good example of the rather blurred line between the protection of the competent patient's right to take irrational *decisions*, and the questioning of capacity on the grounds of the patient's irrational *decision-making*. In a number of cases, the courts have found that anorexics are incompetent, and have authorized force-feeding without their consent.[45] This is because the disease creates an inability to understand, believe, and weigh treatment information in order to arrive at a choice, and thus anorexic patients will commonly fail the *Re C* test. The courts thus appear to believe that a sharp distinction can be drawn between C's (irrational) delusions of grandeur—which did not cast doubt upon his competence—and an anorexic's (irrational) belief that she is fat, which demonstrates her inability to weigh information in order to arrive at a choice.

Heather Draper has also pointed out an interesting distinction between chronic undereating usually caused by psychological problems, where a finding of incapacity and the authorization of force-feeding is relatively straightforward, and chronic *over-eating*, which might similarly be prompted by psychological problems such as low self-esteem, and which will sometimes be similarly life-threatening, but where compulsory treatment would be extremely unlikely.[46] Of course one explanation is that anorexia is classified as a mental illness in the International Classification of Diseases (ICD-10), whereas extreme gluttony is not, although it should be noted that this classification is not universally accepted, and that, in any event, mental illness is not synonymous with incapacity.[47] Draper has also contrasted an anorexic's refusal of food with a woman's rejection of radical mastectomy:

Let us take a step back from the emotionally charged issue of anorexia and consider a parallel

---

[45] *Re W* [1993] Fam 64 CA; *South West Hertfordshire Health Authority v B* [1994] 2 FCR 1051.

[46] 'Anorexia nervosa and respecting a refusal of life-prolonging therapy: a limited justification' (2000) 14 Bioethics 120–33, 131.

[47] Ibid, 130; Rebecca Dresser, 'Feeding the Hunger Artists: Legal Issues in Treating Anorexia Nervosa' [1984] Wisconsin Law Review 297, 328–9.

case—that of a woman who knows that with a radical mastectomy and chemotherapy she has a good chance of recovering from breast cancer but who refuses to have the operation because, in her opinion, living with only one breast or no breasts at all will be intolerable. She is *also* making a decision based on her perception of her body image and we might think that this is an irrational perception. Nevertheless, operating without her consent is unthinkable.[48]

It is important to remember that a patient might be competent to make some decisions but not others. In *Re MB*[49] the patient suffered from a needle phobia which meant she could not consent to the injection of an anaesthetic prior to the performance of a caesarean section, to which she *had* consented. Her needle phobia had rendered her temporarily incompetent to make the decision to refuse the injection, although the court appeared to indicate that she *was* capable of giving consent to the caesarean section itself.

In *Re MB*, the Court of Appeal also approved Lord Donaldson's statement from *Re T*, that:

What matters is that the doctors should consider whether at that time he had a capacity which was commensurate with the gravity of the decision which he purported to make. The more serious the decision, the greater the capacity required.

Butler-Sloss LJ confirming that:

The graver the consequences of the decision, the commensurately greater the level of competence is required to take the decision.

With respect, in some ways this is rather odd. As Tom Buller explains in the next extract, if the test for capacity is directed towards evaluating someone's decision-making *ability*, that should be independent of the outcome of any decision that they might take.

Tom Buller[50]

[U]ntil one can point to a direct relationship between the risk of a decision and its difficulty, it appears arbitrary to demand that the riskier the decision, the higher the standard of competence required. There may be other good reasons for protecting patients from risky decisions, but this concern is the proper domain of paternalism, not competence . . .

Perhaps the underlying problem [with a risk-relative standard of competence] is that risk is being asked to do work for which it is not suited. The risks or consequences of an action or decision function in the same way that other informational elements do, namely for providing the agent with reasons for choosing one option rather than the other. If we grant risk this informational role and, in addition, the level-setting role, then we undermine the notion of decision-making in general. . . .

The goal of protecting the well-being of questionably competent patients is a laudable one, and there may be good paternalistic reasons for demanding a higher standard of competence for a patient to choose to reject life-sustaining treatment than to accept it; however these are reasons, legitimate or otherwise, for overriding a patient's decision, rather than reasons for determining whether the patient is competent or not.

[48] 'Treating anorexics without consent: some reservations' (1998) 24 Journal of Medical Ethics 5–7, 6.
[49] *Re MB* [1997] 1 FCR 274.
[50] 'Competence and risk-relativity' (2001) 15 Bioethics 93–109, 107–9.

In contrast, in the next extract Allen E Buchanan and Dan W Brock defend a risk-relative standard of competence.

Allen E Buchanan and Dan W Brock[51]

There is an important implication of this view that the standard of competence ought to vary in part with the expected harms or benefits to the patient of acting in according with the patient's choice—namely, that just because a patient is competent to consent to a treatment, it does *not* follow that the patient is competent to refuse it. For example, consent to a low-risk life-saving procedure by an otherwise healthy individual should require only a minimal level of competence, but refusal of that same procedure by such an individual should require the highest level of competence . . .

According to the decision-relative concept of competence, the greater the potential harm to the individual of accepting his or her choice, the higher the standard of competence. From this it follows that a finding of incompetence is more likely in precisely those circumstances in which the case for paternalism is strongest—cases in which great harm can be easily avoided by taking the decision out of the individual's hands. The variable standard leaves patients with some right to make bad choices, but does not make that right unlimited without regard for the patient's well-being. Thus the concept of competence favored here allows paternalism in situations in which the case for paternalism seems strongest, while at the same time preserving the law's fundamental tenet that in health care people may be treated paternalistically only when they are incompetent to make their own decisions . . .

[T]here are not two distinct questions of whether the patient is competent and then whether, even if competent, paternalistic setting aside of the patient's choice about treatment is justified. Instead, there is the one question of whether the patient's exercise of decision-making capacities on this occasion has been sufficiently defective and has yielded a decision sufficiently contrary to the patient's good to warrant setting aside the patient's choice by deeming him or her incompetent.

To introduce the qualification that greater capacity is needed when the outcome might be serious or irreversible leaves considerable scope for paternalism: it would make the test for capacity harder to satisfy if a patient wants to make a decision which her doctors believe to be seriously wrong. It also appears to reverse the burden of proof of competence: the presumption of capacity means that it should *always* be for the doctors to establish that a patient lacks capacity, the adult patient should never have to prove that she is competent to make the decision in question.

On the other hand, capacity is almost certainly *task*-specific: that is, many people are competent to make some decisions, but not others. Someone might be able to understand what is involved in having a broken arm set in plaster, but not to weigh up the risks and benefits of more complex treatment, such as chemotherapy. But it would be a mistake to confuse the *complexity* or *difficulty* of a decision, with the *gravity of its outcome*. As Tom Beauchamp and James Childress point out, some decisions with very serious consequences might be relatively easy to understand, while other less risky choices could be extremely complex. Hence, the standard of competence should vary according to the reasoning *capacity* which is necessary to understand the decision

---

[51] *Deciding for Others: The Ethics of Surrogate Decision Making* (CUP Cambridge 1989) 62–3.

itself, and not according to the *risks* which might flow from making the decision in one way or another.[52]

Tom Beauchamp and James Childress[53]

A single core meaning of the word *competence* applies in all contexts. That meaning is 'the ability to perform a task.' By contrast to this core meaning, the *criteria* of particular competencies vary from context to context because the criteria are relative to specific tasks . . . The competence to decide is therefore relative to the particular decision to be made. A person should rarely be judged incompetent with respect to every sphere of life . . . Competence is therefore best understood as specific rather than global: It depends not only on a person's abilities but also on how that person's abilities match the particular decision-making task he or she confronts.

Competence may vary over time and be intermittent. Many persons are incompetent to do something at one point in time but competent to perform the same task at another point in time . . . It is correct to say that the threshold level of competence to decide will rise as the complexity or difficulty of a task increases (deciding about spinal fusion, say, as contrasted with deciding whether to take a minor tranquilizer). However, the level of competence to decide does not rise as the risk of an outcome increases. No basis exists for believing that risky decisions require more ability at decision-making than less risky decisions. To the contrary, a solid basis exists for believing that many non-risky decisions require more ability at decision-making than many risky decisions. For persons whose competence is in question, it also seems disrespectful of their autonomy to say, in effect, 'You are competent to decide what to do with your children, what to do with your financial affairs, and whether to be in this hospital, but you are not competent to refuse to be intubated or catheterized because of the increased risk.'

We can avoid these problems by recognizing that the level of *evidence* for determining competence should vary according to risk, while competence itself varies only along a scale of difficulty in decision-making.

(b) The best interests test

Once it has been established that a patient lacks capacity, how should she be treated? As we can see in the following sections, at common law, the courts have fashioned a 'best interests' test out of the doctrine of necessity.

A *Necessity*

If medical treatment is lawful only if the doctor has first obtained an effective consent, where does this leave incompetent adults who cannot give a valid consent to treatment? Since at common law, no one else has the power to consent to an adult's medical treatment, there would seem to be an obvious gap here. In *Re F*, a case involving the proposed sterilization of a mentally incompetent adult woman, the House of Lords considered that the impossibility of obtaining effective consent could not possibly mean that incompetent adults should be deprived of medical treatment. Instead, based upon the same principle of necessity which justifies treating the temporarily unconscious patient in an emergency, the Law Lords agreed that doctors could treat incompetent adult patients in their best interests.

---

[52] See further, Ian Wilks, 'The debate over risk-related standards of competence' (1997) 11 Bioethics 413–26.

[53] *Principles of Biomedical Ethics* (5th edn OUP Oxford 2001) 70, 76.

In Re F (Mental Patient: Sterilisation)[54]

F, a thirty-six year-old mentally handicapped woman, was a voluntary inpatient in a mental hospital. She had formed a sexual relationship with a male patient. The hospital staff considered that she would be unable to cope with the effects of pregnancy and giving birth, and that, since all other forms of contraception were unsuitable and it was considered undesirable to further curtail F's limited freedom of movement in order to prevent sexual activity, it would be in her best interests to be sterilized. F's mother, who also wished her to be sterilized, issued an originating summons seeking a declaration from the court that such an operation would not be unlawful.

Lord Brandon

There are, however, cases where adult patients cannot give or refuse their consent to an operation or other treatment. One case is where, as a result of an accident or otherwise, an adult patient is unconscious and an operation or other treatment cannot be safely delayed until he or she recovers consciousness. Another case is where a patient, though adult, cannot by reason of mental disability understand the nature or purpose of an operation or other treatment. The common law would be seriously defective if it failed to provide a solution to the problem created by such inability to consent. In my opinion, however, the common law does not so fail. In my opinion, the solution to the problem which the common law provides is that a doctor can lawfully operate on, or give other treatment to, adult patients who are incapable, for one reason or another, of consenting to his doing so, provided that the operation or other treatment concerned is in the best interests of such patients. The operation or other treatment will be in their best interests if, but only if, it is carried out in order either to save their lives, or to ensure improvement or prevent deterioration in their physical or mental health.

Lord Goff

The general rule is that consent is necessary to render such treatment lawful. If such treatment administered without consent is not to be unlawful, it has to be justified on some other principle.

Upon what principle can medical treatment be justified when given without consent? We are searching for a principle upon which, in limited circumstances, recognition may be given to a need, in the interests of the patient, that treatment should be given to him in circumstances where he is (temporarily or permanently) disabled from consenting to it. It is this criterion of a need which points to the principle of necessity as providing justification . . .

But where the state of affairs is permanent or semi-permanent, as may be so in the case of a mentally disordered person, there is no point in waiting to obtain the patient's consent. The need to care for him is obvious; and the doctor must then act in the best interests of his patient, just as if he had received his patient's consent so to do. Were this not so, much useful treatment and care could, in theory at least, be denied to the unfortunate.

In the judgments in *Re F*, there appears to be some slippage between the word 'necessity', with its implication that doctors should treat only when treatment is in fact *necessary*, and 'best interests', which implies that non-essential treatment can be given, provided that it would promote the patient's wellbeing. This was explained by Lord Bridge on the grounds that if the principle of necessity only justified life-saving treatment, incompetent patients might be deprived of beneficial medical care:

It seems to me to be axiomatic that treatment which is necessary to preserve the life, health or well being of the patient may lawfully be given without consent. But if a rigid criterion of necessity

[54] [1990] 2 AC 1 HL.

were to be applied to determine what is and what is not lawful in the treatment of the unconscious and the incompetent, many of those unfortunate enough to be deprived of the capacity to make or communicate rational decisions by accident, illness or unsoundness of mind might be deprived of treatment which it would be entirely beneficial for them to receive.

The best interests test is often contrasted with the substituted judgment test, commonly employed by courts in the US. The substituted judgment test involves the court attempting to discover what decision *this* individual would be likely to make if she were competent. It is less overtly paternalistic than the best interests test, since it attempts to extend the principle of self-determination to patients who are in fact incapable of making their own decisions.

The substituted judgment test is not without difficulties, however. In the next extract, Carl Elliott points out the inherent difficulty of trying to imagine what it would be like to be someone else.

Carl Elliott[55]

Imaginatively sharing another person's particular, subjective point of view, however, requires imagining a logical impossibility. It asks the question: what would it be like for me, if I were someone else? And while I may be able more or less to approximate another person's experience by imagining what it would be like for me to undergo that experience, this becomes more and more difficult with patients whose experience is vastly different from mine. The most problematic cases arise when we must imagine what life is like for a person whose mental life appears radically different from our own, as a result of mental retardation, mental disability or mental illness. This kind of imaginative leap requires us to imagine what it would be like not to have the mental abilities that we have, including those by virtue of which we are able to imagine—a difficult leap indeed, and not without its dangers . . . There are at least two serious dangers here. One danger comes with trying to imagine the experience of the permanently unconscious, such as anencephalic babies or permanently vegetative persons. This is the danger of imagining, in Nagel's words, that 'there is something that it is like' to be permanently unconscious . . .

The other serious danger is that of underestimating the quality of a mentally impaired or disabled person's life. The fact that I would not want to live such a life, or the fact that I would not regard my life as worthwhile if I were to lose my mental faculties, says little about the quality of that person's life.

In practice, unless the patient was formerly competent and had clearly expressed her views on how she should be treated if she were to become incompetent (in which case this might be an example of an advance directive rather than substituted judgment), the substituted judgment test might just be a more patient-centred way to describe the best interests test. In the absence of very clear evidence, such as unusual religious beliefs, it is extremely unlikely that a court would apply the substituted judgment test and decide that an incompetent adult would have chosen to make a decision which her doctors believe to be contrary to her best interests. Moreover, the best interests test in practice requires doctors to ask not what would be in the best interests of a hypothetical reasonable patient, but rather what would be in the best interests of *this particular* patient, with her own values and preferences. Hence, as Lord Donaldson

---

[55] 'Patients doubtfully capable or incapable of consent' in H Kuhse and P Singer (eds), *A Companion to Bioethics* (Blackwell Oxford 1998) 452–62, 458.

suggested in *Re T*, it seems clear that the incompetent patient's wishes are plainly relevant to the doctor's assessment of her best interests:

Consultation with the next of kin has a further advantage in that it may reveal information as to the personal circumstances of the patient and as to the choice which the patient might have made, if he or she had been in a position to make it. Neither the personal circumstances of the patient nor a speculative answer to the question 'What would the patient have chosen?' can bind the practitioner in his choice of whether or not to treat or how to treat or justify him in acting contrary to a clearly established anticipatory refusal to accept treatment but they are factors to be taken into account by him in forming a clinical judgment as to what is in the best interests of the patient.

The Department of Health's *Form for adults who are unable to consent to investigation or treatment* states that:

'Best interests' go far wider than 'best medical interests', and include factors such as the patient's wishes and beliefs when competent, their current wishes, their general well-being and their spiritual and religious welfare.

Hoffmann LJ, in the Court of Appeal judgment in *Bland* certainly believed that there might be little difference in practice between the substituted judgment and best interests tests:

The patient's best interests would normally also include having respect paid to what seems most likely to have been his own views on the subject. To this extent I think that what the American courts have called 'substituted judgment' may be subsumed within the English concept of best interests.

As we see later, the best interests test in the Mental Capacity Act 2005 explicitly incorporates reference to the previously competent patient's preferences.

B How relevant is Bolam?

If doctors are entitled to treat incompetent patients in their best interests, it is obviously important to offer doctors some guidance about what 'best interests' actually means. In *Re F*[56] the House of Lords suggested that the criterion for determining whether treatment is in the best interests of an incompetent adult should be whether it satisfies the familiar *Bolam* test (described in the previous chapter p. 122). The standard of care demanded by the tort of negligence should, on this view, also govern the decision about what care should be provided to incapacitated adults.

Lord Griffiths

The doctor . . . must give the treatment that he considers to be in the best interests of his patient, and the standard of care required of the doctor will be that laid down in *Bolam v Friern Hospital Management Committee*.

Lord Brandon

In order that the performance of such operations on, and the giving of such other treatment to, such adults should be lawful, they must be in their best interests. If doctors were to be required, in deciding whether an operation or other treatment was in the best interests of adults incompetent

---

[56] [1990] 2 AC 1 HL.

to give consent, to apply some test more stringent than the *Bolam* test, the result would be that such adults would, in some circumstances at least, be deprived of the benefit of medical treatment which adults competent to give consent would enjoy. In my opinion it would be wrong for the law, in its concern to protect such adults, to produce such a result.

Lord Goff

I have said that the doctor has to act in the best interests of the assisted person. In the case of routine treatment of mentally disordered persons, there should be little difficulty in applying this principle. In the case of more serious treatment, I recognise that its application may create problems for the medical profession; however, in making decisions about treatment, the doctor must act in accordance with a responsible and competent body of relevant professional opinion, on the principles set down in *Bolam v Friern Hospital Management Committee*.

The Court of Appeal in *Re F* had taken a different view,[57] and more recent cases have reverted to their opinion that the *Bolam* test cannot decisively establish whether a particular treatment is in the patient's best interests.

In *Re S* and *Re A* (below) the Court of Appeal has persuasively argued that treating a patient in her best interests is not synonymous with treating her non-negligently. The Court of Appeal has pointed out that there are in fact two duties: first, doctors must act in accordance with proper professional standards, that is they must satisfy the *Bolam* test; and, second, they must act in the best interests of the particular patient. The *Bolam* test may approve several different courses of action as being within the reasonable range of clinical judgment, but, logically, the *best* interests test should give only one answer.

In Re S (Adult Patient: Sterilisation)[58]

The patient, a twenty-nine year-old woman with severe learning difficulties, was distressed by her menstrual periods. Her mother applied for a declaration that it would be lawful to perform a sterilisation or hysterectomy. The judge made the declaration, but this was overturned by the Court of Appeal.

Dame Elizabeth Butler-Sloss P

This ground raises a question of law as to the correct approach of the court to the best interests of a patient without the mental capacity to consent to an operation and the relevance of the *Bolam* test to that judicial inquiry . . .

I would suggest that the starting point of any medical decision would be the principles enunciated in the *Bolam* test and that a doctor ought not to make any decision about a patient that does not fall within the broad spectrum of the *Bolam* test. The duty to act in accordance with responsible and competent professional opinion may give the doctor more than one option since there may well be more than one acceptable medical opinion. When the doctor moves on to consider the best interests of the patient he/she has to choose the best option, often from a range of options. As Mr Munby has pointed out, the best interests test ought, logically, to give only one answer.

In these difficult cases where the medical profession seeks a declaration as to lawfulness of the proposed treatment, the judge, not the doctor, has the duty to decide whether such treatment is in the best interests of the patient. The judicial decision ought to provide the best answer not a range of alternative answers. There may, of course, be situations where the answer may not be obvious

---

[57] *The Times* 8 Dec 1988.   [58] [2001] Fam 15.

and alternatives may have to be tried. It is still at any one point the best option of that moment which should be chosen. . . .

As I have set out earlier in this judgment, the principle of best interests as applied by the court extends beyond the considerations set out in the *Bolam* case. The judicial decision will incorporate broader ethical, social, moral and welfare considerations . . .

The question, however, for the judge was not was the proposed treatment within the range of acceptable opinion among competent and responsible practitioners, but was it in the best interests of S? The *Bolam* test was, in my view, irrelevant to the judicial decision, once the judge was satisfied that the range of options was within the range of acceptable opinion among competent and responsible practitioners. If it was not, I would hope a surgeon would not operate, even if a declaration was given by the court.

Thorpe LJ

The *Bolam* test was of course developed in order to enable courts to determine the boundaries of medical responsibility for treatment that has gone wrong, and usually disastrously wrong. So at first blush it would seem an unlikely import in determining the best interests of an adult too disabled to decide for him- or herself. . . .

[I]n determining the welfare of the patient the *Bolam* test is applied only at the outset to ensure that the treatment proposed is recognised as proper by a responsible body of medical opinion skilled in delivering that particular treatment. That may be a necessary check in an exercise where it would be impossible to be over scrupulous. But I find it hard to imagine in practice a disputed trial before a judge of the Division in which a responsible party proposed for an incompetent patient a treatment that did not satisfy the *Bolam* test. In practice the dispute will generally require the court to choose between two or more possible treatments both or all of which comfortably pass the *Bolam* test. . . . In deciding what is best for the disabled patient the judge must have regard to the patient's welfare as the paramount consideration. That embraces issues far wider than the medical. Indeed it would be undesirable and probably impossible to set bounds to what is relevant to a welfare determination. In my opinion the *Bolam* case has no contribution to make to this second and determinative stage of the judicial decision.

And in *Re A*,[59] a case we consider below at p. 211, in which the mother of a mentally disabled man sought the court's approval for carrying out a vasectomy, Dame Elizabeth Butler-Sloss made a similar point.

Dame Elizabeth Butler-Sloss P

Another question which arises from the decision in *Re F* is the relationship of best interests to the 'Bolam test'. Doctors charged with the decisions about the future treatment of patients and whether such treatment would, in the cases of those lacking capacity to make their own decisions, be in their best interests, have to act at all times in accordance with a responsible and competent body of relevant professional opinion. That is the professional standard set for those who make such decisions. The doctor, acting to that required standard, has, in my view, a second duty, that is to say, he must act in the best interests of a mentally incapacitated patient. I do not consider that the two duties have been conflated into one requirement.

With respect, this more recent interpretation of the best interests test seems clearly right. The *Bolam* test was developed in order to determine whether a doctor should be liable in negligence for medical treatment *which had already been given*, and *which had*

---

[59] [2000] 1 FLR 549.

already gone wrong. Ascribing responsibility in medical negligence, and determining *prospectively* what treatment a particular patient should be given are obviously entirely different exercises. It is perhaps right that a doctor should not be held liable for a patient's injury unless negligence can be proved on the balance of probabilities. But where, as in *Re F, Re S,* and *Re A,* there is an application for the sterilization of a mentally incompetent person, the doctor should have to prove that sterilization would be the best possible option, not simply that it is treatment which reaches some minimum level of acceptability.

It could even be argued that applying the *Bolam* test to an assessment of a patient's best interests effectively emasculates the court's protective function. A doctor seeking court approval for proposed treatment in circumstances where *no competent or responsible body of medical opinion would countenance it* is extremely unlikely to get as far as a court hearing. Thorpe LJ recognized this in *Re S*:

I find it hard to imagine in practice a disputed trial before a judge . . . in which a responsible party proposed for an incompetent patient a treatment that did not satisfy the *Bolam* test.

In addition to an overemphasis upon the *Bolam* test, in some of the cases which followed *Re F,* the interpretation of the 'best interests' test was also particularly unfortunate. There was, for example, a tendency to take for granted the fertility of the mentally handicapped women whose proposed sterilizations were declared lawful. The courts did not always make a fertility assessment an essential precondition to sterilization, so it is possible that some infertile women may have had wholly unnecessary invasive surgery. In both *Re W (Mental Patient: Sterilisation),*[60] and *Re HG,*[61] sexual intercourse was unlikely but sterilization was still held to be in the woman's best interests. Even when the chance of sexual contact has been taken into account, a mentally handicapped woman's 'attractiveness' has sometimes been assumed to be synonymous with the likelihood of sexual activity.[62] Regardless of whether it is true that a woman's vulnerability to unwanted sexual attention is increased by her physical attractiveness, sterilization is obviously not the optimum solution for mentally handicapped women who are at risk of sexual assault. As Sheila McLean points out, removing the possibility of assault or abuse is a better preventative strategy than sterilization.

Sheila McLean[63]

Certainly . . . we may wish to protect people from exploitation, but it is equally clear that sterilising them does not achieve this. In fact, removing the risk of pregnancy might make disabled people even more vulnerable to sexual exploitation . . . Sterilisation does not mean that they will not be vulnerable to sexual assault, unsuitable liaisons or sexually transmitted diseases. All it does is to ensure that no conception takes place, reinforcing the earlier suggestion that the actual reasons given for non-consensual sterilisations are not the same as those which are overtly given. . . .

In many of the cases, it is in fact clear that the 'best interests' test will be met where there is a

---

[60] [1993] 1 FLR 381.   [61] [1993] 1 FLR 588.
[62] *Re P (A Minor)(Wardship: Sterilisation)* [1989] 1 FLR 182; *Re LC (Medical Treatment: Sterilisation)* [1997] 2 FLR 258.
[63] *Old Law, New Medicine* (Pandora London 1999) 100.

congruence of clinical recommendation, parental support and judicial inclination. The reported cases have shown . . . that medical willingness to sterilise, especially when coupled with parental approval, has been a critical predictor of the outcome, even if the woman is not in a sexual relationship and her fertility has never been assessed . . .

Perhaps inevitably, the UK courts have also depended heavily, as is their wont, on the *Bolam* test. This test uses acceptable medical practice as a yardstick of whether or not the operation in question was properly carried out. But the test is designed to judge the **competence** of a medical procedure—it is not designed to test its **lawfulness**, and it is therefore entirely inappropriate in such cases . . . And as Brazier points out, 'For the woman, if the *Bolam* test and the *Bolam* test alone establishes the lawfulness of surgery then judicial intervention does little more than protect her from the complete maverick whom none of his colleagues would back in his decision to sterilise her'.

Although note that Ranaan Gillon suggests that sterilization may be preferable to total sexual segregation.

Ranaan Gillon[64]

[I]t is hard to see why it can *never* be in the best interests of a severely mentally handicapped person to be sterilised if it is accepted that it can sometimes be in the best interests of a mentally normal woman to be sterilised . . .

If the question of such women's best interests is pursued it becomes less and less clear that sterilisation is necessarily against their best interests. Given for example the pervasive assumption that pregnancy must if at all possible be avoided, women in such circumstances are likely to be subjected to considerably more repressive control over their contacts with men, and especially mentally handicapped men, in the hospitals, hostels and day centres where severely handicapped people often spend much of their time. Indeed, only total sexual segregation can guarantee the avoidance of pregnancy. On the other hand if the possibility of pregnancy is eliminated by some effective means of contraception the ordinary mixed social intercourse becomes a much easier option.

[S]uppose it is accepted that (a) ordinary social life, including the mixing of the sexes, is desirable for severely mentally handicapped people too, and (b) that in the nature of mixed sex social life it is impossible to eliminate the possibility that sexually developed members of such a group will from time to time have sexual intercourse, . . . and (c) that it is important to ensure that no pregnancy results from any such intercourse, then the desirability of effective contraception follows. However, even if contraception is accepted as desirable it may still be argued that other reversible and less dangerous forms of contraception are preferable to sterilisation which is usually irreversible and involves a surgical operation.

So far as the irreversibility is concerned this only seems to be important if there is some realistic chance that the severely mentally handicapped person will develop sufficiently to become capable of parenting and being allowed to parent a child . . . Where there is some realistic chance of such development then it does indeed seem in the best interests of the woman not to have an irreversible sterilisation. However, in many cases no such realistic chance of maturation to a state compatible with parenthood exists—and then the irreversibility of the operation seems to be irrelevant.

More recently, there is evidence that the courts are requiring conclusive *proof* that sterilization is necessary to protect the incompetent adults' health. In *Re S (Medical*

---

[64] 'On sterilising severely mentally handicapped people' (1987) 13 Journal of Medical Ethics 59–61, 59–60.

Treatment: Adult Sterilisation),[65] for example, there was no evidence that S was having a consensual sexual relationship, rather her mother was concerned that she might be at risk of sexual abuse in the future. The court refused to grant a declaration that sterilization would be lawful on the grounds that there should be an identifiable, rather than a speculative risk of harm which sterilization was intended to prevent. And a Practice Note from the Official Solicitor has confirmed the Court of Appeal's approach:

Practice Note[66]

In any medical case, the claimant must adduce evidence from a responsible medical practitioner not only (1) that performing the particular operation would not be negligent, but also (2) that it is necessary in the best interests of the patient. The court's jurisdiction is to declare the best interests of the patient on the application of a welfare test analogous to that applied in wardship. The judicial decision will incorporate broader ethical, social, moral and welfare considerations. Emotional, psychological and social benefit to the patient will be considered. The court will wish to prepare a balance sheet listing the advantages and disadvantages of the procedure for the patient. If potential advantages and disadvantages are to be relied on then the court will wish to assess in percentage terms the likelihood of them in fact occurring . . .

An operation must address a current real need. It must be shown that the patient is capable of conception and is having or is likely to have full sexual intercourse. Any risk of pregnancy should be identifiable rather than speculative.

C Only medical interests?

It seems clear that the best interests test not only takes into account the patient's immediate clinical needs, but might also accommodate her emotional or psychological interests. In the sterilization cases considered in the previous section, it is clear that the courts have taken into account factors other than the *medical* risks of pregnancy, and been influenced by the *social* benefits of avoiding pregnancy. This question was particularly conspicuous in *Re A*, which involved an application to sterilize a mentally incapable man. Here there could be no clinical benefit to A from his sterilization. Although the Court of Appeal rejected this application, it nevertheless left open the possibility that the decision might be reversed if A's circumstances changed and it became evident that his freedom of movement and association was being restricted in order to avoid the risk that he might engage in unprotected sexual intercourse.

Re A (Medical Treatment: Male Sterilisation)[67]

A, who was twenty-eight years old, had Down Syndrome and was on the borderline between significant and severe impairment of intelligence. He lived with his sixty-three year old mother who provided him with a high degree of care and supervision. However, the mother's health was not good and her concern was that, when A moved into local authority care, he might have a sexual relationship resulting in the birth of a child and he would be unable to understand the consequences, and she disapproved very strongly of a man walking away from responsibility. Accordingly, his mother applied to the High Court for a declaration that a vasectomy operation was in A's best interests and could lawfully be performed on him despite his inability to consent to it. The

---

[65] [1998] 1 FLR 944.

[66] Practice Note (Official Solicitor: Declaratory proceedings: Medical and Welfare Decisions for Adults who Lack Capacity) [2001] 2 FLR 158.

[67] [2000] 1 FLR 549.

judge refused to grant the declaration, and the mother's appeal was rejected by the Court of Appeal.

Dame Elizabeth Butler-Sloss P

An application on behalf of a man for sterilisation is not the equivalent of an application in respect of a woman. It is not a matter of equality of the sexes but a balancing exercise on a case by case basis. There are obvious biological differences and sexual intercourse for a woman carries the risk of pregnancy which patently it does not for a man. Indeed there is no direct consequence for a man of sexual intercourse other than the possibility of sexually transmitted diseases. There may be psychological consequences for him in pregnancy or in the birth of his child. He may be required to take responsibility for the child after birth and may, in certain circumstances attract disapproval and criticism. In the case of a man who is mentally incapacitated, neither the fact of the birth of a child nor disapproval of his conduct is likely to impinge on him to a significant degree other than in exceptional circumstances. His freedom of movement might in certain instances be restricted and consequently his quality of life might be diminished. It is possible that there may be other disadvantages to the person concerned which might lead a court to decide to approve the operation. It may be necessary to evaluate the nature and degree of risk attached to approval of or refusal to approve the operation to sterilise. But the task in each case is to balance all the relevant factors and to decide what are the best interests of the person unable to make his own decision.

    In the present appeal it is necessary to focus upon the best interests of A himself. It is clear from the evidence of his mother that, as long as she cares for him, he will continue to be subjected to the present regime of close supervision. . . . When in due course he goes into local authority care, the degree of freedom might be affected by the fear that he might form a sexual relationship with another resident. It would however, in my view, be likely that the woman concerned would be the object of protection rather than A. If his quality of life were, however, to be diminished, that would be a reason to seek at that time a hearing before a High Court judge to grant a declaration that sterilisation would then be in A's best interests.

Thorpe LJ

In conclusion although I agree that this appeal must be dismissed I would like to emphasise that its failure does not preclude a fresh application in the future on fresh evidence.

Perhaps the best example of a broad interpretation of the best interests test is *Re Y*,[68] where acting as a bone marrow donor to a desperately ill sibling was held to be in the best interests of an incompetent adult. Here there could be no possible *medical* benefit to the patient from undergoing an invasive procedure in order to donate bone marrow to her sister. Rather the donation was authorized on the grounds that it would be of immeasurable benefit to her *mother* (who was already in poor health), as well as to her sister, who might otherwise die. Because both her mother and sister would be profoundly grateful to Y, the operation was said to be for her 'emotional, psychological and social benefit'.

Re Y (Mental Incapacity: Bone Marrow Transplant)[69]

The plaintiff suffered from a bone marrow disorder, and the only realistic prospect of recovery for the plaintiff was a bone marrow transplant operation from a compatible donor. The plaintiff's sister, the defendant, appeared to be a suitable donor. The defendant was severely mentally and physically handicapped and was incapable of giving her consent to bone marrow donation. The

---

[68] [1996] 2 FLR 787, [1997] 2 WLR 556.   [69] Ibid.

plaintiff sought a declaration that it would be lawful to carry out preliminary blood tests and a bone marrow harvesting operation under general anaesthetic, despite the fact that the defendant could not give her consent.

Connell J

The test to be applied was whether it was in the best interests of the defendant for the procedures to take place. The fact that the process would benefit the plaintiff was not relevant, unless, as a result of the defendant helping the plaintiff the best interests of the defendant were served. . . .

If the plaintiff dies, this is bound to have an adverse effect upon her mother who already suffers from significant ill health. One lay witness took the gloomy view that this event would prove fatal to the mother, but in any event her ability to visit the defendant would be handicapped significantly, not only by a likely deterioration in her health, but also by the need which would then arise for her to look after her only grandchild.

In this situation, the defendant would clearly be harmed by the reduction in or loss of contact to her mother. Accordingly, it is to the benefit of the defendant that she should act as donor to her sister, because in this way her positive relationship with her mother is most likely to be prolonged. Further, if the transplant occurs, this is likely to improve the defendant's relationship with her mother who in her heart clearly wishes it to take place and also to improve her relationship with the plaintiff who will be eternally grateful to her.

The disadvantages to the defendant of the harvesting procedure are very small . . .

It is doubtful that this case would act as a useful precedent in cases where the surgery involved is more intrusive than in this case, where the evidence shows that the bone marrow harvested is speedily regenerated and that a healthy individual can donate as much as two pints with no long-term consequences at all. Thus, the bone marrow donated by the defendant will cause her no loss and she will suffer no real long-term risk.

There were three factors which contributed to this decision that a self-evidently non-therapeutic procedure could nevertheless be in the best interests of an incompetent adult. First, the procedure must carry a very low or minimal risk. Bone marrow donation causes some discomfort, and there is always a small risk associated with the use of a general anaesthetic. It is, however, generally considered a low-risk procedure. Note that Connell J explicitly stated that his judgment would not be a useful precedent in cases where the surgery involved is more intrusive, such as solid organ donation.

Secondly, in this case there was no evidence that the incompetent adult objected to the donation. Although not specifically addressed by Connell J, it is difficult to imagine that a court would find that a non-therapeutic medical procedure was in the best interests of a patient who was actively resisting it.

Thirdly, there would have to be some plausible benefit to the incompetent adult herself. In Re Y this was satisfied by the patient's close relationship with her mother, which might be adversely affected by her sister's death. If the incompetent patient was incapable of valuing relationships at all, perhaps because she was in a persistent vegetative state, then it is unlikely that bone marrow donation could be said to be in her best interests. The fact that a particular procedure will provide a very substantial benefit to a third party cannot justify imposing it upon an incompetent adult unless there is evidence that it will also benefit the patient herself. In the sterilization cases, for example, the courts have generally insisted that the operation must benefit the woman herself, and the fact that it might make life easier for the patient's carers should be irrelevant.

(c) Court involvement

At common law, there is no possibility of proxy consent to the medical treatment of an incompetent adult. Despite common perceptions to the contrary, the next of kin has absolutely no formal legal role. And since the Crown lost its prerogative power as *parens patriae* under the Mental Health Act 1959, the courts cannot *consent* to an incompetent adult's treatment. Rather the legal position is that treatment which is in the incompetent patient's best interests is lawful, and treatment which is not in her best interests is unlawful. The courts cannot convert unlawful treatment into lawful treatment, their role is instead confined to *declaring* that a particular procedure would be in the patient's best interests, and hence lawful. The declaration does not change anything, however, and the treatment would have been equally lawful without the court's declaration, so in effect the court is simply *confirming* the treatment's legality.

In most cases, then, court approval is strictly speaking unnecessary, and the purpose of seeking a declaration will be to reassure the doctors, and perhaps the patient's carers too, that the proposed treatment is indeed lawful. It would also be possible to seek a declaration that a decision *not* to treat an incompetent adult would be lawful, as in *Re D (Medical Treatment: Mentally Disabled Patient)*,[70] discussed below, when the patient's unwillingness to cooperate made it impossible to provide dialysis treatment. Again, the principal purpose of the application was to reassure the doctors that their proposed *non-treatment* would be lawful.

For a number of especially controversial medical procedures, the courts have however suggested that they should be involved as a matter of course. First, sterilization operations carried out for contraceptive purposes have been treated differently from cases in which sterility is a side-effect of the treatment of an illness, such as ovarian cancer, when court involvement would not normally be necessary.[71] In *Re F*, there was some disagreement over whether court approval for contraceptive sterilization was mandatory, or merely desirable. The minority view was that of Lord Griffiths, who argued that a sterilization operation should *never* go ahead without leave of a High Court judge.

Lord Griffiths

But I cannot agree that it is satisfactory to leave this grave decision with all its social implications in the hands of those having the care of the patient with only the expectation that they will have the wisdom to obtain a declaration of lawfulness before the operation is performed. In my view the law ought to be that they must obtain the approval of the court before they sterilise a woman incapable of giving consent and that it is unlawful to sterilise without that consent. I believe that it is open to your Lordships to develop a common law rule to this effect.

In contrast, the majority held court involvement was not necessary, but was 'highly desirable as a matter of good practice':

---

[70] [1988] 2 FLR 22.   [71] See, eg, *Re GF (Medical Treatment)* [1992] 1 FLR 293.

Lord Brandon

[T]he lawfulness of a doctor operating on, or giving other treatment to, an adult patient disabled from giving consent, will depend not on any approval or sanction of a court, but on the question whether the operation or other treatment is in the best interests of the patient concerned. That is, from a practical point of view, just as well, for, if every operation to be performed, or other treatment to be given, required the approval or sanction of the court, the whole process of medical care for such patients would grind to a halt.

That is not the end of the matter, however, for there remains a further question to be considered. That question is whether, in the case of an operation for the sterilisation of an adult woman of child-bearing age, who is mentally disabled from giving or refusing her consent to it, although involvement of the court is not strictly necessary as a matter of law, it is nevertheless highly desirable as a matter of good practice. In considering that question, it is necessary to have regard to the special features of such an operation. These features are: first, the operation will in most cases be irreversible; secondly, by reason of the general irreversibility of the operation, the almost certain result of it will be to deprive the woman concerned of what is widely, and as I think rightly, regarded as one of the fundamental rights of a woman, namely, the right to bear children; thirdly, the deprivation of that right gives rise to moral and emotional considerations to which many people attach great importance; fourthly, if the question whether the operation is in the best interests of the woman is left to be decided without the involvement of the court, there may be a greater risk of it being decided wrongly, or at least of it being thought to have been decided wrongly; fifthly, if there is no involvement of the court, there is a risk of the operation being carried out for improper reasons or with improper motives; and, sixthly, involvement of the court in the decision to operate, if that is the decision reached, should serve to protect the doctor or doctors who perform the operation, and any others who may be concerned in it, from subsequent adverse criticisms or claims.

Having regard to all these matters, I am clearly of the opinion that, although in the case of an operation of the kind under discussion involvement of the court is not strictly necessary as a matter of law, it is nevertheless highly desirable as a matter of good practice.

There may be cases of other special operations to which similar considerations would apply. I think it best, however, to leave such other cases to be examined as and when they arise.

The majority's view that court approval was desirable but not necessary is probably to be preferred, since it is difficult to see what legal justification there could be for *requiring* the court to exercise its declaratory jurisdiction. Rather any doctor who did not seek the court's approval for a sterilization operation might have failed to comply with good clinical practice, and be in breach of his duty of care.

Secondly, cases involving the withdrawal of artificial hydration and nutrition from patients in a persistent vegetative state have routinely been brought before the courts. In *Airedale NHS Trust v Bland*,[72] Lord Keith agreed with the Court of Appeal's suggestion that court approval would be necessary until the appropriate 'body of experience and practice had been built up':

Lord Keith

The decision whether or not the continued treatment and care of a PVS patient confers any benefit on him is essentially one for the practitioners in charge of his case. The question is whether

---

[72] [1993] AC 789.

any decision that it does not and that the treatment and care should therefore be discontinued should as a matter of routine be brought before the Family Division for endorsement or the reverse. The view taken by the President of the Family Division and the Court of Appeal was that it should, at least for the time being and until a body of experience and practice has been built up which might obviate the need for application in every case. As Sir Thomas Bingham M.R. said, this would be in the interests of the protection of patients, the protection of doctors, the reassurance of the patients' families and the reassurance of the public. I respectfully agree that these considerations render desirable the practice of application.

Thirdly, recall that in *Re F*, Lord Brandon said that '[t]here may be cases of other special operations to which similar considerations would apply', but he thought it best 'to leave such other cases to be examined as and when they arise'. In *Re Y*, discussed above, Connell J suggested that:

this case fell within a category of cases in which, if on any future occasion there was a need or a wish to perform a bone marrow harvesting procedure on an adult incompetent, it was appropriate for the matter first to be ventilated in court before the procedures took place.

Court approval should therefore routinely be sought where the treatment is particularly controversial and/or non-therapeutic. Other examples might include living organ donation or gender reassignment surgery. As yet there have been no examples of doctors proposing to carry out such procedures on incompetent adults in the UK, but it could be assumed that the courts would recommend prior judicial scrutiny if such cases arise in the future. It seems clear that abortion is not one of these special cases. In *Re SG (Adult Mental Patient: Abortion)*,[73] a case we consider in Chapter 7, Sir Stephen Brown P decided that when doctors decide that an abortion would be in the best interests of a mentally incapacitated woman, a court declaration will usually be unnecessary.

(d) The use of force

It now seems clear that reasonable force can be used in the course of treatment carried out on incompetent adults.

Norfolk and Norwich NHS Trust v W[74] Johnson J
[I]n circumstances such as the present the court does have a power at common law to authorise the use of reasonable force.

Re MB[75] Butler-Sloss LJ
It would however follow, in our view, from the decision that a patient is not competent to refuse treatment, that such treatment may have to be given against her continued objection if it is in her best interests that the treatment be given despite those objections. The extent of force or compulsion which may become necessary can only be judged in each individual case and by the health professionals.

Since the Human Rights Act 1998 came into force, the use of force must now be qualified by Article 3 (which prohibits inhuman and degrading treatment). In the *Herczelgfalvy* case, which we consider again in Chapter 7 p. 426, force and restraint

---

[73] [1991] FLR 329.   [74] [1996] 2 FLR 613.   [75] *Re MB* [1997] 1 FCR 274.

had been used on a mentally ill patient. The ECHR found that this did not breach Article 3 because it was 'a therapeutic necessity'. The Court held that

a measure which is a therapeutic necessity cannot be regarded as inhuman or degrading. The Court must nevertheless satisfy itself that the medical necessity has been convincingly shown to exist.

It follows that where treatment is *not* a therapeutic necessity, the use of force might amount to a violation of Article 3.

Of course, the fact that the courts *can* authorize the use of reasonable force does not mean that they should do so whenever a patient resists treatment. On the contrary, it will seldom be in the best interests of incompetent patients to undergo forced treatment. Where the patient's cooperation is important, the harm that might be done by imposing treatment on an unwilling patient might sometimes outweigh the benefits of treatment, and hence regardless of whether treatment is in her best interests, the doctors might be justified in deciding not to treat the patient against her wishes. This situation arose in *Re D*,[76] where an incompetent adult with end-stage renal failure refused to undergo dialysis. Since he would not keep still, dialysis (which he needed four times a week) could only be provided under general anaesthetic. Given the patient's condition, this would be both impracticable and dangerous. The doctors therefore sought a declaration from the court that it would be lawful not to impose dialysis upon him. Sir Stephen Brown P granted the declaration, finding that it would be in the best interests of the patient, and hence lawful:

not to impose haemodialysis upon him in circumstances in which, in the opinion of the medical practitioners responsible for such treatment, it is not reasonably practicable to do so.

(2) BY STATUTE

The process of reforming the law on incapacity began in 1989, with a Law Commission review. This was followed by four consultation papers, and a final Report, *Mental Incapacity*, in 1995. The Lord Chancellor's Department (now the Department for Constitutional Affairs) then took over the process, issuing a consultation document *Who Decides*, in 1997, followed two years later by proposals for reform *Making Decisions*. Eventually, the Mental Capacity Act was passed in 2005, and it is thought that it will come into force in 2007. Guidance on the implementation and interpretation of the Act will be provided in a Code of Practice, to be issued by the Department for Constitutional Affairs (DCA). At the time of writing, the final Code has not yet been published, but a draft Code was issued in September 2004.

Although it makes a few important changes to the common law, much of the Act simply codifies the existing common law position. Let us examine the key provisions of the Act.

(a) Definition of incapacity

Under section 2(1) of the Mental Capacity Act 2005:

---

[76] (1997) 41 BMLR 81.

a person lacks capacity in relation to a matter if at the material time he is unable to make a decision for himself in relation to the matter because of an impairment of, or a disturbance in the functioning of, the mind or brain.

Section 3(1) lays out what is meant by being 'unable to make a decision':

(1) For the purposes of section 2, a person is unable to make a decision for himself if he is unable—

  (a) to understand the information relevant to the decision,

  (b) to retain that information,

  (c) to use or weigh that information as part of the process of making the decision, or

  (d) to communicate his decision (whether by talking, using sign language or any other means).

There are thus two stages to the assessment of capacity. First, it must be established that the person is suffering from 'an impairment of, or a disturbance in the functioning of, the mind or brain'. This 'diagnostic threshold' means that someone will not fall within the provisions of the Act unless they are suffering from some mental impairment. The draft Code of Practice suggests that a wide variety of conditions will be covered, such as alcohol or drug misuse, delirium, the effects of a head-injury, as well as the more obvious categories of learning difficulties and mental illness.[77]

Secondly, once this diagnostic requirement has been satisfied, it is necessary to work out whether the person is able to make a decision for himself. This second stage is essentially a statutory version of the *Re C* test. Note that section 3(1)(d) also specifies that someone who cannot communicate his decision by any possible means is to be treated in the same way as someone who lacks decision-making capacity. This is, as we have seen, already the case at common law, and both the explanatory notes and the draft Code of Practice suggest that this will apply only to the tiny number of patients, such as those suffering from locked-in syndrome, who cannot communicate *at all*, not even by squeezing an arm or blinking an eyelid.[78]

The test for capacity in the Act is therefore functional and 'decision-specific'. A person cannot be labelled 'incapable' simply because they have a particular medical condition or diagnosis. Rather their decision-making ability must also be individually assessed in the light of the particular decision to be taken. Section 2 also makes it clear that a lack of capacity cannot be established merely by reference to a person's age, appearance, or any condition or aspect of a person's behaviour which might lead others to make unjustified assumptions about their capacity. Under section 1, the common law presumption of capacity is incorporated, as is the principle that making an unwise decision does not demonstrate that a person lacks capacity.

1(2) A person must be assumed to have capacity unless it is established that he lacks capacity.

1(4) A person is not to be treated as unable to make a decision merely because he makes an unwise decision.

---

[77] <http://www.dca.gov.uk/menincap/mcbdraftcode.pdf>.

[78] <http://www.dca.gov.uk/menincap/mcbdraftcode.pdf>; *Mental Capacity Bill: Explanatory Notes* (Dec 2004) <http://www.publications.parliament.uk/pa/ld200405/ldbills/013/en/05013x--.htm#end> para 24.

Section 1(3) further provides that 'a person is not to be treated as unable to make a decision unless all practicable steps to help him to do so have been taken without success'. This is bolstered by section 3(2):

3(2) A person is not to be regarded as unable to understand the information relevant to a decision if he is able to understand an explanation of it given to him in a way that is appropriate to his circumstances (using simple language, visual aids or any other means).

Section 3(3) of the Act specifies that someone who can retain information only for short periods of time should nevertheless be entitled to make their own decisions. Hence people in the early stages of Alzheimer's disease, when only their short term memory is compromised, may still have the capacity to exercise control over their medical treatment.

3(3) The fact that a person is able to retain the information relevant to a decision for a short period only does not prevent him from being regarded as able to make the decision.

Normally it will be doctors who decide whether a person lacks capacity in relation to a medical decision, although their assessments can be challenged by an appeal to the court for a declaration. In order to be protected from a charge of battery or assault, a doctor needs to have a 'reasonable belief' that the person lacks capacity. If a doctor treats without consent someone who is in fact capable, and has no grounds for believing that she lacked capacity, an action in tort or even a criminal prosecution is possible.

(b) How should people who lack capacity be treated?

Again, section 1(5) simply confirms the common law position that:

1(5) An act done, or decision made, under this Act for or on behalf of a person who lacks capacity must be done, or made, in his best interests.

Section 1 also contains the 'least restrictive alternative' principle, according to which:

1(6) Before the act is done, or the decision is made, regard must be had to whether the purpose for which it is needed can be as effectively achieved in a way that is less restrictive of the person's rights and freedom of action.

This means that when deciding between possible courses of action, there should be a presumption in favour of the least intrusive one, and it also means that consideration should be given to whether it is necessary to act at all. So, for example, in relation to sterilization, under section 1(6), permanent sterilization must be an option of last resort.

Section 4 fleshes out what factors must be considered when making a determination of what is in a person's best interests:

4(2) The person making the determination must consider all the relevant circumstances and, in particular, take the following steps

(3) He must consider—

(a) whether it is likely that the person will at some time have capacity in relation to the matter in question, and

(b) if it appears likely that he will, when that is likely to be.

(4) He must, so far as reasonably practicable, permit and encourage the person to participate, or to improve his ability to participate, as fully as possible in any act done for him and any decision affecting him . . .

(6) He must consider, so far as is reasonably ascertainable—

(a) the person's past and present wishes and feelings (and, in particular, any relevant written statement made by him when he had capacity),

(b) the beliefs and values that would be likely to influence his decision if he had capacity, and

(c) the other factors that he would be likely to consider if he were able to do so.

(7) He must take into account, if it is practicable and appropriate to consult them, the views of—

(a) anyone named by the person as someone to be consulted on the matter in question or on matters of that kind,

(b) anyone engaged in caring for the person or interested in his welfare,

(c) any donee of a lasting power of attorney granted by the person, and

(d) any deputy appointed for the person by the court,

as to what would be in the person's best interests and, in particular, as to the matters mentioned in subsection (6).

Under section 4(3), regard must be had to whether and when a person is likely to regain capacity. This means that if the person's incapacity is likely to be temporary, it would not be in their best interests for decisions to be taken which could wait until they regain capacity, and can decide for themselves.

Notice that section 4(6) specifies that it is necessary to take into account the person's past wishes and feelings, and any written statement made by him when he had capacity, as well as his beliefs and values. The Act therefore makes it clear that best interests is not to be judged objectively, on purely clinical grounds, but must take into account the individual patient's own perspective.

To this end, sections 35–7 of the Act also provide for the appointment of an Independent Mental Capacity Advocate (IMCA) to support and represent a person who lacks capacity. An IMCA *must* be appointed when an NHS body is proposing to give 'serious medical treatment' to someone without capacity, and no close family member or friend is available to consult about his wishes or feelings. The IMCA's role is to communicate the person's wishes, feelings, beliefs and values and any other relevant information to the decision maker. The IMCA is also able to challenge any decision made about the incapacitated person's treatment.

(c) The use of restraint

Just like at common law, there are times when it is legitimate to use force or restraint under the 2005 Act. The use of force will not attract liability provided the conditions in section 6(2) and (3) are met:

6(2) The first condition is that D reasonably believes that it is necessary to do the act in order to prevent harm to P.

(3) The second is that the act is a proportionate response to—

(a) the likelihood of P's suffering harm, and

(b) the seriousness of that harm.

The draft Code of Practice makes clear that the onus is on the person doing the restraining to prove that it is both a necessary and proportionate response to a non-trivial risk of harm to P.

(d) Proxy decision making

One of the principal changes the Act makes to the common law is by introducing the possibility of proxy medical decision-making for incapacitated adults. This involves the person (P) nominating one or more people, referred to as 'donees', with lasting power of attorney (LPA) who, under section 9(1)(a) will have the authority to make decisions about, among other things, P's personal welfare, or specified matters concerning his personal welfare, when/if he loses capacity. This power undoubtedly extends to taking medical decisions. A donee is only permitted to take decisions about life-sustaining treatment if P has included a clear statement to this effect in the LPA document.

The power of the donee of LPA is, under section 9(4), subject to the provisions of the Act, and in particular to the principles embodied in section 1, and the best interests requirements in section 4. This means that the donee is not empowered to take decisions which are not in the incapacitated person's best interests. It also means that section 4(3) applies, and the donee must take into account whether P is likely to regain capacity in the near future, and, under section 4(6), that the person's past and present wishes and feelings must be considered. If someone has not nominated a 'donee', their close friends or relatives might be consulted under section 4(7)(e) when assessing their best interests, although their views will not be decisive.

Under section 16, it is also open to the court to appoint a deputy to make decisions on behalf of an incapacitated person, or to make the decision itself, although the draft Code of Practice suggests that the appointment of deputies will be unusual in relation to healthcare decisions. Doctors already have the power to act in a person's best interests, and in the case of a dispute, a decision of the court is preferable to the appointment of a deputy. Nevertheless section 17(d) specifies that the deputy's powers extend to 'giving or refusing consent to the carrying out or continuation of a treatment by a person providing health care for P', with one important exception: deputies are not able to refuse consent to life-sustaining treatment.

(e) Advance directives

Sections 24 and 25 specifically deal with advance directives, referred to in the Act as advance decisions. According to the Explanatory Notes, these provisions 'seek to codify and clarify the current common law rules'.[79] Advance decisions are defined in section 24(1):

---

[79] *Mental Capacity Bill: Explanatory Notes* (Dec 2004) <http://www.publications.parliament.uk/pa/ld200405/ldbills/013/en/05013x--.htm#end> para 82.

'Advance decision' is a decision made by a person ('P'), after he has reached 18 and when he has capacity to do so, that if—

   (a) at a later time and in such circumstances as he may specify, a specified treatment is proposed to be carried out or continued by a person providing health care for him, and

   (b) at that time he lacks capacity to consent to the carrying out or continuation of the treatment

the specified treatment is not to be carried out or continued.

Section 24(1) specifies that advance decisions must have been made when an adult was competent, and must specify which treatment should not be carried out or continued when the person (P) lacks capacity. Hence section 24 only covers advance *refusals* of treatment. An advance *request* for treatment would be relevant under section 4(6)(a), above, when deciding what is in a person's best interests, but could not be decisive.

Under section 24(2), it is enough for the treatment which P wishes to refuse to be described in layman's terms, so a failure to use precise technical language will not defeat an advance directive. For most advance decisions, with the exception of refusals of life-saving treatment, there is no need for them to be in writing, so an oral refusal of non-life-sustaining treatment must be complied with. Under section 24(3), a person can withdraw or alter their advance decision at any time when he has capacity to do so, and under sections 24(4) and (5), withdrawals and alterations do not have to be in writing.

Section 25(1) specifies that, to be effective, an advance decision must be both *valid* and *applicable to the treatment.* If a decision is both valid and applicable to the treatment, then under section 26(1) 'the decision has effect as if he had made it, and had had capacity to make it, at the time when the question arises whether the treatment should be carried out or continued'. Section 25(2) defines when a decision will not be *valid*:

25(2) An advance decision is not valid if P—

   (a) has withdrawn the decision at a time when he had capacity to do so,

   (b) has, under a lasting power of attorney created after the advance decision was made, conferred authority on the donee (or, if more than one, any of them) to give or refuse consent to the treatment to which the advance decision relates, or

   (c) has done anything else clearly inconsistent with the advance decision remaining his fixed decision.

Hence, to be valid, there must be no evidence that the P has either withdrawn the decision or conferred authority in relation to the relevant treatment on a donee via a lasting power of attorney. Under section 25(2)(c) the decision is not valid if the P has acted in a way which is 'clearly inconsistent' with the decision. What does this mean? One obvious example might be if someone has explicitly renounced the religious beliefs upon which their decision was based. But it is, of course, possible to imagine situations where it will be difficult to tell whether a person's subsequent actions are 'clearly inconsistent' with the advance decision. For example, the Act does not specify whether the actions which serve to invalidate the advance directive under section 25(2)(c) must have occurred while the P was still competent, or whether the now incompetent P's conduct could also invalidate their advance decision. On the one hand, the failure to specify when the 'clearly inconsistent' actions should take place would seem to lead to the conclusion that *any* inconsistent conduct will invalidate the decision, regardless of when it takes place. Yet on the other hand, since section 24(3) specifies that P may withdraw or alter an advance decision only 'when he has capacity to do so', it might seem odd that an incompetent person is entitled to invalidate their decision *indirectly* by acting inconsistently with it.

The draft Code of Practice recommends that patients should be advised to regularly review and update their advance decisions because a recently reviewed decision is more likely to be found valid than if considerable time has elapsed since it was made.

Section 25(3)–(6) specify when an advance decision will not be *applicable*:

25(3) An advance decision is not applicable to the treatment in question if at the material time P has capacity to give or refuse consent to it.

(4) An advance decision is not applicable to the treatment in question if—

(a) that treatment is not the treatment specified in the advance decision,

(b) any circumstances specified in the advance decision are absent, or

(c) there are reasonable grounds for believing that circumstances exist which P did not antici-pate at the time of the advance decision and which would have affected his decision had he anticipated them.

An advance decision will therefore lapse if the person who executed it regains capacity. Just as at common law, it is also necessary that the advance decision precisely covers the situation in which the P now finds himself, and that there are no reasonable grounds for believing that there has been a change of circumstances which casts doubt upon whether the advance decision would continue to reflect the P's views. Again, advising patients to regularly update their advance decisions may minimize the chance that the decision will be found inapplicable on the grounds either that the patient's own circumstances have changed, or that the patient was not aware of some new medical development, which might have changed his attitude towards treatment.

It is unclear whether section 25(4)(c) could apply to the scenario we considered earlier, where a now demented individual appears to be contented and does not want to die, despite have issued an otherwise binding advance directive refusing life-sustaining treatment in these circumstances. Is the fact that he appears to be happy despite his dementia a circumstance 'which P did not anticipate at the time of the advance decision and which would have affected his decision'? If interpreted in this way, the scope of section 25(4)(c) is potentially extremely broad since it would almost always be possible to argue that P issued their advance decision in a state of relative ignorance about what it would actually be like to be incapacitated.

Section 25(5) and (6) lay down special rules for advance refusals of life-sustaining treatment. The P must specifically acknowledge that he intends to refuse treatment even if this puts his life at risk; the decision must be in writing and signed by P or a representative in P's presence, and the signature must be witnessed. This is more exacting than the common law, under which there is no requirement for an advance refusal to be in writing, regardless of the gravity of its consequences, although as we have seen, there are a number of reasons why an advance refusal of life-sustaining treatment might be found not to apply to the situation in which the patient finds herself.

Where there is doubt about the validity or applicability of an advance decision, under section 26(4) an application can be made to the court for a declaration. While the court's advice is being sought, under 26(5) nothing in the advance decision should prevent the provision of life-sustaining treatment or steps to prevent a deterioration in the P's condition.

(f) The Court of Protection

Section 45 of the Act will set up a new Court of Protection. The Court will have the same power as the High Court, but the intention is that it will build up specialist expertise in matters involving incapacitated individuals, and will be charged with resolving disputes and uncertainties over, for example, whether a person lacks capacity; whether proposed treatment is in his best interests and whether an advance decision is valid and applicable. The draft Code of Practice also suggests that decisions involving PVS patients or non-therapeutic sterilization should continue to be referred to the court, and that other controversial treatment decisions 'involving ethical dilemmas in untested areas' should similarly not be taken without referring the matter to the Court of Protection.[80] An example might be living organ donation.

The draft Code of Practice suggests that where there is a dispute or uncertainty over medical treatment, the application to the Court of Protection should normally be made by the NHS trust, or other body responsible for the patient's care. Any person who is alleged to lack capacity will also be able to make an application, though more usually he will be made a party to the proceedings, and the Official Solicitor may be appointed to protect his interests.

(d) CHILDREN

Childhood covers the period in a person's life from birth to the age of 18. It is however worth remembering that the law adopts a number of different cut-off points for different activities. A ten year old can, in some circumstances, be held criminally responsible for her actions; when she reaches the age of 16 she can have lawful sexual intercourse, marry and buy cigarettes; but she cannot vote until she is 18. So when is she able to consent to medical treatment? As we will see in the following sections, much will depend upon the nature of the medical treatment in question, as well as the child's decision-making capacity. It is also unclear whether a child's ability to consent thereby deprives her parents of their power to consent to medical treatment, or whether this power continues until the child reaches adulthood.

---

[80] <http://www.dca.gov.uk/menincap/mcbdraftcode.pdf>.

(1) PARENTAL CONSENT

Anyone with parental responsibility for a child undoubtedly has the power to consent to her medical treatment. Provided that both parents have parental responsibility, each would normally be able to give a valid consent to their child's medical treatment without consulting the other. The consent of both parents is only necessary for certain treatments, such as non-therapeutic circumcision. In *Re J (Specific Issue Orders: Child's Religious Upbringing and Circumcision)*[81] Dame Elizabeth Butler-Sloss P said:

There is, in my view, a small group of important decisions made on behalf of a child which, in the absence of agreement of those with parental responsibility, ought not to be carried out or arranged by one parent carer although she has parental responsibility under s 2(7) of the Children Act 1989. Such a decision ought not to be made without the specific approval of the court. Sterilisation is one example. . . . The issue of circumcision has not, to my knowledge, previously been considered by this court, but in my view it comes within that group. The decision to circumcise a child on grounds other than medical necessity is a very important one; the operation is irreversible, and should only be carried out where the parents together approve of it or, in the absence of parental agreement, where a court decides that the operation is in the best interests of the child.

In *Re C (Welfare of Child: Immunisation)*,[82] a case in which the mother and the father disagreed over whether their child should receive the MMR vaccine, Thorpe LJ said that:

In my opinion this appeal demonstrates that hotly contested issues of immunisation are to be added to that 'small group of important decisions'.

Hence, where the parents agree with each other, consent to circumcision and vaccination lies within a zone of parental discretion, and the court will not impose its own view of whether the procedure is in the child's best interests. Where the parents cannot agree, the decision will be made by the court according to *its* view of where the child's best interests lie.

If they are married, both parents automatically have parental responsibility. If they are unmarried, the father can acquire parental responsibility (since 2003) by being registered on the child's birth certificate. Prior to 2003, the father had to apply for a court order, or register a formal parental responsibility agreement with the court. Non-parents may also have parental responsibility (perhaps because the child is living with them and they have a residence order), in which case they too would be able to give a valid consent to medical treatment. And non-parents who have care of the child—such as teachers and child-minders—are entitled to do what is reasonable in all the circumstances to safeguard or promote the child's welfare,[83] which might of course mean consenting to *routine* medical treatment, such as having a wound bandaged.

In an emergency, if there is no-one with parental responsibility who is either able or willing to consent to a child's medical treatment, the doctors would be entitled to treat in the absence of consent in order to avoid serious harm or death. In *Gillick v West*

---

[81] [2000] 1 FLR 571.   [82] [2003] EWCA Civ 1148 [2003] 2 FLR 1095 CA.
[83] Children Act 1989 s 3(5)(b).

Norfolk and Wisbech AHA,[84] a case we consider in detail below at p. 233, Lord Templeman said:

I accept that if there is no time to obtain a decision from the court, a doctor may safely carry out treatment in an emergency if the doctor believes the treatment to be vital to the survival or health of an infant and notwithstanding the opposition of a parent or the impossibility of alerting the parent before the treatment is carried out.

Similarly, Lord Scarman suggested that:

Emergency, parental neglect, abandonment of the child, or inability to find the parent are examples of exceptional situations justifying the doctor proceeding to treat the child without parental knowledge and consent.

Where treatment could reasonably be delayed until the parents can be found or a court order obtained, the doctors should not proceed with treatment.

Parents clearly have the ability to consent to medical treatment, but do they also have the right to *refuse*? Parents have the authority to act for the benefit of their children, so their right to consent or to refuse to consent to treatment is abrogated where they seek to make a decision which might harm the child. Hence, if one or both of the parents withhold consent to treatment which the doctors believe to be in the child's best interests, the doctors can seek approval from another source, namely the courts (see below).

(2) COURT INVOLVEMENT

The court's power to authorize the medical treatment of children derives from wardship, its inherent jurisdiction, or more recently from statute. Wardship differs slightly from the inherent jurisdiction—if a child is made a ward of court, the court must make *all* important decisions about her upbringing until the wardship comes to an end, whereas the inherent jurisdiction can apply to a one-off decision. In practice, however, the two are largely indistinguishable. Both derive from the Crown's prerogative power as *parens patriae*, exercised by judges of the High Court, and both give the courts much more sweeping powers than are possessed either by the parents or by a mature minor.

Usually, if a child's parents refuse to consent to treatment which her doctors believe to be necessary, it is the doctors who will apply to the court using wardship or the inherent jurisdiction. It is also possible that another concerned individual might apply if, for example, both the doctors and the parents were proposing to take a step which appeared not be in the child's best interests. This was the case in *Re D (A Minor) (Wardship: Sterilisation)*.[85] D was an 11-year-old girl who suffered from Sotos syndrome and 'had a dull, normal intelligence'. Her behavioural problems, academic skills, and social competence were all improving. As yet, D had shown no interest in the opposite sex, and in any event, she had no opportunity to engage in sexual intercourse because her mother never left her side, and she was never allowed out alone. Nevertheless, D's parents, her paediatrician and a consultant obstetrician had

---

[84] [1984] QB 581.   [85] [1976] 2 WLR 279.

all agreed that D should be sterilized. It was D's educational psychologist who applied to have D made a ward of court, and the question of whether sterilization was in D's best interests was then considered by the court, which made a declaration that the operation should not go ahead.

Heilbron J

A review of the whole of the evidence leads me to the conclusion that in a case of a child of 11 years of age, where the evidence shows that her mental and physical condition and attainments have already improved, and where her future prospects are as yet unpredictable, where the evidence also shows that she is unable as yet to understand and appreciate the implications of this operation and could not give a valid or informed consent, but the likelihood is that in later years she will be able to make her own choice, where, I believe, the frustration and resentment of realising (as she would one day) what had happened, could be devastating, an operation of this nature is, in my view, contra-indicated.

For these, and for the other reasons to which I have adverted, I have come to the conclusion that this operation is neither medically indicated nor necessary, and that it would not be in D's best interests for it to be performed.

In addition to wardship and the inherent jurisdiction, under the Children Act 1989, the court can issue either a specific issue order, or a prohibited steps order[86] to determine what treatment a child should receive. In *Re C (Welfare of Child: Immunisation)*,[87] the fathers of two children who were living with their mothers sought specific issue orders to enable their children, who had received none of the recommended childhood vaccines, to be immunized. The judge ordered each mother to have her child immunized, and the Court of Appeal upheld his decision.

Regardless of the route taken to bring the question of a child's medical treatment before the courts, the decision will be governed by the welfare principle. Under section 1 of the Children Act, in any question affecting a child's upbringing, her welfare must be the 'paramount consideration'.[88] What does this mean in practice?

Most types of medical treatment will self-evidently be therapeutic, and in the best interests of a sick child. A few procedures, however, raise particular problems for the application of the best interests test. Blood tests for the purposes of establishing paternity will generally be allowed: the test itself causes only slight discomfort, and the child might in fact benefit from knowing the truth about her origins.[89] Bone marrow, blood or organ donation (see further Chapter 12 p. 737) are not in a child's best *clinical* interests, although it might be possible to argue that saving a sibling's life by donating bone marrow, for example, is overwhelmingly in the child's emotional best interests. It is less likely that the courts would authorize the removal of a solid organ from a child donor, and as yet no cases have come before the English courts. Another question which is so far untested in English law is whether purely cosmetic surgery could be justified by the best interests test.[90] In Chapter 8, we consider the special issue of non-therapeutic research on children.

---

[86] Section 8(1).   [87] [2003] EWCA Civ 1148 [2003] 2 FLR 1095 CA.
[88] Children Act 1989 s 1(1).
[89] *Re F (A Minor) (Blood Tests: Parental Rights)* [1993] 3 All ER 596; *Re H (A Minor) (Blood Tests: Parental Rights)* [1996] 4 All ER 28.
[90] See further RB Jones, 'Parental consent to cosmetic facial surgery in Down's syndrome' (2000) 26 Journal of Medical Ethics 101–2.

As we can see from the next case, sterilization carried out in order to avoid pregnancy, rather than because of some medical disorder, has also been treated as a special case, and, as with adults, decisions should be made by the court. The Official Solicitor will represent the child's interests.[91]

In Re B (A Minor)[92]

Jeannette was a seventeen year old girl suffering from 'moderate' mental handicap: she was said to have a 'mental age' of six. Expert evidence was that pregnancy would be a 'disaster', and that no other contraceptives were suitable. The House of Lords authorized her sterilization.

Lord Bridge

It is clear beyond argument that for her pregnancy would be an unmitigated disaster. The only question is how she may best be protected against it. The evidence proves overwhelmingly that the right answer is by a simple operation for occlusion of the fallopian tubes and that, quite apart from the question whether the court would have power to authorise such an operation after her 18th birthday, the operation should now be performed without further delay. I find it difficult to understand how anybody examining the facts humanely, compassionately and objectively could reach any other conclusion.

Lord Templeman

In my opinion sterilisation of a girl under 18 should only be carried out with the leave of a High Court judge. A doctor performing a sterilisation operation with the consent of the parents might still be liable in criminal, civil or professional proceedings. A court exercising the wardship jurisdiction emanating from the Crown is the only authority which is empowered to authorise such a drastic step as sterilisation after a full and informed investigation.

Lord Oliver

It is important at the very outset, therefore, to emphasise as strongly as it is possible to do so, that this appeal has nothing whatever to do with eugenics. It is concerned with one primary consideration and one alone, namely the welfare and best interest of this young woman, an interest which is conditioned by the imperative necessity of ensuring, for her own safety and welfare, that she does not become pregnant.

In the next extract, Robert Lee and Derek Morgan offer a number of criticisms of the House of Lords' judgment in *Re B*.

Robert Lee and Derek Morgan[93]

Having stated that Jeannette had a mental age of five or six, the judgments in *Re B* seem to treat Jeannette as if she were simply a child of that age. Jeannette, like all other handicapped people, would be expected to demonstrate different functional abilities across a whole range of skills. Intelligence testing offers little information as to many of these abilities, and in so far as it leads to labels such as 'mental age of five', it misdescribes the mentally handicapped person in a discriminatory fashion. Jeannette may not read at all, unlike many six-year-olds, but she may consistently out-perform most children of that age in terms of socialisation or self-help. In addition, the criterion of 'mental age' was treated as static . . .

---

[91] Practice note (Official Solicitor: 'Declaratory Proceedings: medical and welfare decisions for adults who lack capacity' 2001) 2 FLR 158.

[92] [1987] 2 WLR 1213 [1988] AC 199.

[93] 'Sterilisation and Mental Handicap: Sapping the Strength of the State' (1988) 14 Journal of Law and Society 229–46, 238–9, 242.

Nor will the concept of mental age shed much light upon Jeanette's biological and emotional state as a seventeen-year-old woman. While it may be difficult to grapple with the concept of a physically mature woman manifesting child-like intelligence in some respects, we must be careful that we do not discount and become repulsed by the notion that this person manifests adult sexual desires . . .

The issues relating to both community care and parental wishes lead to another widely voiced criticism: that such sterilisations are a matter of convenience for those who care for women such as Jeanette rather than in her interests . . .

What emerges on this analysis is a grim picture of life for young handicapped women. For example, an apparently cogent reason for sterilisation was that Jeanette was about to attend an adult training centre. Is the assumption that trainees at these centres have the opportunity to disappear to explore sexual intercourse? Why are these centres so underfunded and understaffed that they cannot adequately protect women vulnerable to sexual abuse? . . .

In spite of all the protestations that Jeanette's sterilisation was not merely for convenience, in a broad sense this is clearly untrue. The necessity for the sterilisation in the eyes of the court arose out of their perception that she was at greater risk of pregnancy in the community.

Of course *Re B* should now be read in the light of the courts' more exacting application of the best interests test in adult sterilization cases such as *Re S*, discussed earlier at p. 207.

Most of the cases in which the courts have had to make decisions about a child's medical treatment have involved parents or the child herself objecting to treatment which the doctors believe to be in her best interests. And the difficult question that arises is whether parents (or the child herself) can ever legitimately take a different view from her doctors about precisely where a child's best interests lie. In general, the answer to this question is 'no': the courts have been willing to override parental refusals, and as we see below, refusals by the child too, whenever a child's life or health might be endangered.

For example, in *Re A (Children) (Conjoined Twins: Separation)*,[94] a case we consider in more detail in Chapter 16, p. 980, the Court of Appeal ordered the separation of conjoined twins in order to save the stronger twin's life, despite the parents' refusal to consent to the operation. In *Re C (A Child)(HIV Test)*[95] the mother, who was infected with the HIV virus, rejected conventional medical thinking on the causes and treatment of HIV, and refused to allow her child to be tested for the HIV virus. At first instance, Wilson J overruled her objections on the grounds that it was overwhelmingly in the child's best interests to be tested, and the Court of Appeal refused permission to appeal:

Butler-Sloss LJ

I have no doubt at all, for my part, that it is right that this child should have the test done . . . In my view, the child is clearly at risk if there is ignorance of the child's medical condition. The degree of intrusion into the child of a medical test is slight . . . It does not matter whether the parents are responsible or irresponsible. It matters whether the welfare of the child demands that such a course should be taken . . . This child has the right to have sensible and responsible people find out whether she is or is not HIV positive . . . What seems to me to be crucial is that someone should

---

[94] [2001] Fam 147 CA.   [95] [2000] Fam 48.

find out so that one knows how she should be looked after . . . Either way this child has her own rights. Those rights seem to me to be met at this stage by her being tested to see what her state of health is for the question of knowledge.

There is one exceptional case which appears to point in a different direction. In *Re T (A Minor) (Wardship: Medical Treatment),*[96] the Court of Appeal refused to authorize a liver transplant against the parents' wishes, despite the likelihood that the child would not live beyond the age of two and half without a transplant. Oddly, the Court of Appeal found that this was a case in which there was 'genuine scope for a difference of view between parent and judge', and that the mother's objection to the transplant surgery should therefore be respected. The parents were both healthcare professionals, who had sensibly framed their objection in terms of the distress and discomfort the surgery might cause their son. The Court of Appeal held that their refusal to give consent to the transplant operation was not based upon 'scruple or dogma', and in such cases, it was in the best interests of the child that important decisions about his upbringing be taken by his parents.

Waite LJ

It can only be said safely that there is a scale, at one end of which lies the clear case where parental opposition to medical intervention is prompted by scruple or dogma of a kind which is patently irreconcilable with principles of child health and welfare widely accepted by the generality of mankind; and that at the other end lie highly problematic cases where there is genuine scope for a difference of view between parent and judge . . . [T]here must be a likelihood (though never of course a certainty) that the greater the scope for genuine debate between one view and another the stronger will be the inclination of the court to be influenced by a reflection that in the last analysis the best interests of every child include an expectation that difficult decisions affecting the length and quality of its life will be taken for it by the parent to whom its care has been entrusted by nature.

The case is, however, probably best regarded as a rather idiosyncratic and anomalous judgment. In *Re C (Welfare of Child: Immunisation),*[97] for example, Thorpe LJ said of *Re T*:

However, the outcome of that appeal, denying a child life-prolonging surgery, is unique in our jurisprudence and is explained by the trial judge's erroneous focus on the reasonableness of the mother's rejection of medical opinion.

The court in *Re T* appeared to be swayed by the fact that the child would need to be cared for by his mother after the operation, and that her ability to provide proper care would somehow be compromised if the operation had been carried out without her agreement. The family were living abroad at the time, and the court also took into account the difficulties returning to England for the operation would pose for the family. Since the prognosis was that the child would be likely to die within the next two years without the operation, these factors were perhaps given undue prominence, and most commentators have suggested that this was not in fact a case where there could reasonably be any disagreement about where the child's best interests lay.

---

[96] [1997] 1 WLR 242.   [97] [2003] EWCA Civ 1148 [2003] 2 FLR 1095 CA.

Furthermore, the Court of Appeal appeared to be asking themselves whether the mother's refusal was prompted by her love and concern for her son, whereas, as Marie Fox and Jean McHale point out in the next extract, the proper question is not whether the parents care for their child, but whether the proposed treatment is in the child's best interests. Where parents are Jehovah's Witnesses, for example, and refuse to consent to their child receiving a blood transfusion, the courts will routinely override their decision, despite the fact that the parents' refusal will usually be prompted by their love for their child, whom they genuinely believe will be seriously adversely affected by receiving blood products.

Marie Fox and Jean McHale[98]

In the first place, we would question whether the downplaying of [Jehovah's Witness] beliefs is legitimate. Furthermore, it is debatable whether the Court of Appeal judges were right to be more receptive to the parents' objections in *Re T*, which were rooted in factors other than religious or ethical conviction, including the location of the parties and the nature of the treatment. Although parents may legitimately object to proposed treatment where it is deemed 'heroic' in nature and parental opposition is rooted in the experimental, invasive and/or prolonged nature of the procedure, it would seem that this is not such a case . . . [I]t was a recognised clinical procedure, and one with a high success rate according to some experts . . .

We are given little evidence to support the Court's opinion that this mother was exceptionally devoted. Furthermore, even assuming that this representation is accurate, two troublesome issues arise. First, if we accept the Court's depiction of her as especially caring, it was surely incumbent upon the judges to examine why she was so reluctant to undertake the care of her son following a procedure which could save his life, particularly in view of her professional expertise in this area. Secondly, there is no exploration of the relationship between caring and reasonableness. It must be doubted whether the decisions of an exceptionally caring parent, even one who is a health professional herself, may automatically be deemed reasonable ones.

Of course, it is possible that the courts might become involved because of a different sort of disagreement between the child's parents and her doctors. In *Re J (A Minor) (Child in Care: Medical Treatment)*, a case we will consider again in Chapter 16 p. 976, the doctors caring for J believed that 'it would not be medically appropriate to intervene with intensive therapeutic measures' such as artificial ventilation, if J were to suffer a life-threatening event. J's mother, however, wanted J to be ventilated if he was no longer able to breathe spontaneously. Lord Donaldson MR was clear that the courts would never force doctors to act contrary to their clinical judgment.

Lord Donaldson MR

The fundamental issue in this appeal is whether the court in the exercise of its inherent power to protect the interests of minors should ever require a medical practitioner or health authority acting by a medical practitioner to adopt a course of treatment which in the bona fide clinical judgment of the practitioner concerned is contra-indicated as not being in the best interests of the patient. I have to say that I cannot at present conceive of any circumstances in which this would be other than an abuse of power as directly or indirectly requiring the practitioner to act contrary to the fundamental duty which he owes to his patient. This, subject to obtaining any necessary consent, is to treat the patient in accordance with his own best clinical judgment.

---

[98] 'In Whose Best Interests?' (1996) 60 Modern Law Review 700–9, 703, 705.

Hence, when the court becomes involved in disputes over a child's medical treatment, it can *authorize* the doctors to take such steps as they believe to be in the child's best interests, and it can *overrule* both a parent's and a child's refusal, but it cannot *compel* doctors to do something which is contrary to their clinical judgment. So while it is true that the court's powers extend beyond that of parents and mature children— only a court, for example, can approve a minor's sterilization—the court's powers under the inherent jurisdiction are not in fact 'theoretically limitless', as Lord Donaldson MR suggested in *Re W*,[99] considered below.

(3) THE USE OF FORCE

Undoubtedly, the inherent jurisdiction gives courts the power to authorize the use of reasonable force and detention, in order to ensure that the child receives the treatment in question, otherwise the court's ability to overrule a minor's refusal of treatment, confirmed in both *Re R* and *Re W* (discussed below), would in practice be meaningless. It is, however, important to remember that, as with adults, force should be used only when treatment is a therapeutic necessity, otherwise it might amount to inhuman and degrading treatment, and be prohibited under Article 3 of the Human Rights Act 1998.

In the next extract, Jane Fortin further suggests that the use of force might not survive a challenge under Article 5 (the right to liberty and security). While the detention of persons of 'unsound mind' can be justified under Article 5(1)(e), Fortin suggests that some of the adolescents whose refusals of life-saving treatment have been overridden, such as the boy in *Re E* discussed below at p. 236, were not of 'unsound mind'. Fortin therefore argues that the use of force could only be justified if Article 2 (the right to life) is given priority.

Jane Fortin[100]

The courts might now find it difficult to justify employing the wardship jurisdiction to force an intelligent 16-year-old to undergo treatment against his will, as the High Court did in *Re E (A Minor) (Wardship: Medical Treatment)*. According to Ward J, the boy in that case was not *Gillick*-competent [see below p. 233] because he was unable to grasp the implications of a range of decisions. In particular, he did not have a full understanding of the implication of refusing treatment and choosing to die. But that, surely, is a very far cry from describing him as of 'unsound mind' within Article 5(1)(e) of the Convention. How then is the court to gain its authority to force such a patient to undergo medical treatment without itself infringing Article 5? In such circumstances, it might survive an Article 5 challenge by turning to Article 2 for a solution, when confronted by a teenager refusing life-saving treatment. It might argue that since a minor's rights under the Convention sometimes inevitably conflict, notably his rights under Articles 2 and 5, it must find an appropriate balance between those rights. Although a minor patient is entitled to freedom from restraint under Article 5, this right may be outweighed by the patient's right to life itself, particularly if he lacks the capacity to comprehend the implications of refusing life-saving treatment. Furthermore, Article 2 imposes a positive obligation on all public authorities, including the courts, to take all reasonable steps to preserve life. A court, when exercising its inherent

---

[99] [1993] Fam 64 CA.
[100] 'Children's rights and the use of physical force' (2001) 13 Child and Family Law Quarterly 243.

jurisdiction, might therefore argue that it cannot ignore its duty to save the life of a desperately ill adolescent.

In *A Metropolitan Borough Council v DB*,[101] a case involving a 17-year-old crack cocaine addict who had just given birth and whose health was seriously at risk, Cazalet J did specifically confine the permissible use of force to situations where the minor's life or health was in grave danger. His order stated that:

such reasonable force may be authorised by the local authority to be used to implement such medical treatment to DB as may be considered necessary by the doctors concerned for her to prevent her death or serious deterioration in her health.

And in *Re C (Detention: Medical Treatment)*,[102] Wall J considered that he had the power under the inherent jurisdiction to authorize the use of force in order to detain and treat a 16-year-old girl with anorexia, although he declined to use it in this case because forced treatment was 'antipathetic to the ethos of the clinic':

Since I regard C's presence in the unit and her adherence to its regime as integral parts of her treatment programme, I equally have no doubt that under the inherent jurisdiction I have power not only to direct that she reside in the clinic but also to authorise the use of reasonable force (if necessary) to detain her in the clinic. I am also satisfied that, were it necessary, I have power to authorise the use of reasonable force to C's person in the administration of the clinic's refeeding treatment programme.

He also held that the welfare principle demanded that any court order should direct or authorize the minimum necessary degree of force or restraint, and specify the minimum necessary period of detention:

Any order the court makes should direct or authorise the minimum degree of force or restraint, and in the case of an order directing or authorising the detention of the child the minimum period of detention, consistent with the welfare principle.

(4) THE COMPETENT MINOR

(a) At common law (*Gillick* competence)

Until 1986, it was not clear whether doctors could ever lawfully treat a minor without her parent's consent. Mrs Victoria Gillick's unsuccessful battle to prevent her daughters from receiving contraceptive advice without her consent established that a doctor could provide contraceptive advice to a minor without consulting her parents. Beyond that central point, interpretations of the House of Lords judgment in the *Gillick* case, and its significance for children's medical treatment more generally, vary dramatically. The problem is that there are some key differences between the two leading judgments of Lord Fraser and Lord Scarman, yet the third member of the 3:2 majority in the House of Lords, Lord Bridge, agreed with both of them.

Gillick v West Norfolk and Wisbech AHA[103]
The Department of Health and Social Security (DHSS) issued a Memorandum of Guidance to health authorities which stated that although it would be unusual to provide contraceptive advice

---

[101] [1997] 1 FLR 767. [102] [1997] 2 FLR 180. [103] [1984] QB 581.

and treatment to children under the age of sixteen without parental consent, in exceptional cases it was for a doctor, exercising his clinical judgment, to decide whether contraceptive advice or treatment should be provided. Mrs Gillick, who was the mother of five girls under the age of 16, wrote to her local health authority seeking an assurance from them that no contraceptive advice or treatment would be given to any of her children while under 16 without her knowledge and consent. The health authority refused, and Mrs Gillick sought a declaration that the notice was unlawful. The Court of Appeal overturned Woolf J's rejection of her claim, and then by a 3:2 majority, the House of Lords allowed the DHSS's Appeal.

Lord Fraser

It seems to me verging on the absurd to suggest that a girl or a boy aged 15 could not effectively consent, for example, to have a medical examination of some trivial injury to his body or even to have a broken arm set. Of course the consent of the parents should normally be asked, but they may not be immediately available. Provided the patient, whether a boy or a girl, is capable of understanding what is proposed, and of expressing his or her own wishes, I see no good reason for holding that he or she lacks the capacity to express them validly and effectively and to authorise the medical man to make the examination or give the treatment which he advises. . . .

It is, in my view, contrary to the ordinary experience of mankind, at least in Western Europe in the present century, to say that a child or a young person remains in fact under the complete control of his parents until he attains the definite age of majority, now 18 in the United Kingdom, and that on attaining that age he suddenly acquires independence. In practice most wise parents relax their control gradually as the child develops and encourage him or her to become increasingly independent. Moreover, the degree of parental control actually exercised over a particular child does in practice vary considerably according to his understanding and intelligence and it would, in my opinion, be unrealistic for the courts not to recognise these facts. . . .

Nobody doubts, certainly I do not doubt, that in the overwhelming majority of cases the best judges of a child's welfare are his or her parents. Nor do I doubt that any important medical treatment of a child under 16 would normally only be carried out with the parents' approval. That is why it would and should be 'most unusual' for a doctor to advise a child without the knowledge and consent of the parents on contraceptive matters. . . . But there may be circumstances in which a doctor is a better judge of the medical advice and treatment which will conduce to a girl's welfare than her parents. It is notorious that children of both sexes are often reluctant to confide in their parents about sexual matters, and the DHSS guidance under consideration shows that to abandon the principle of confidentiality for contraceptive advice to girls under 16 might cause some of them not to seek professional advice at all, with the consequence of exposing them to 'the immediate risks of pregnancy and of sexually-transmitted diseases.' . . .

There may well be other cases where the doctor feels that because the girl is under the influence of her sexual partner or for some other reason there is no realistic prospect of her abstaining from intercourse. If that is right it points strongly to the desirability of the doctor being entitled in some cases, in the girl's best interest, to give her contraceptive advice and treatment if necessary without the consent or even the knowledge of her parents. The only practicable course is to entrust the doctor with a discretion to act in accordance with his view of what is best in the interests of the girl who is his patient. He should, of course, always seek to persuade her to tell her parents that she is seeking contraceptive advice, and the nature of the advice that she receives. At least he should seek to persuade her to agree to the doctor's informing the parents. But there may well be cases, and I think there will be some cases, where the girl refuses either to tell the parents herself or to permit the doctor to do so and in such cases, the doctor will, in my opinion, be justified in proceeding without the parents' consent or even knowledge provided he is satisfied on the following matters: (1) that the girl (although under 16 years of age) will understand his advice; (2) that he cannot persuade her to inform her parents or to allow him to inform the parents that she is seeking contraceptive advice; (3) that she is very likely to begin or to continue having sexual intercourse with or without contraceptive treatment; (4) that unless she receives contraceptive advice or treatment her physical or mental health or both are likely to suffer; (5) that her best interests require him to give her contraceptive advice, treatment or both without the parental consent.

Lord Scarman

The principle of the law, as I shall endeavour to show, is that parental rights are derived from parental duty and exist only so long as they are needed for the protection of the person and property of the child . . .

I would hold that as a matter of law the parental right to determine whether or not their minor child below the age of 16 will have medical treatment terminates if and when the child achieves a sufficient understanding and intelligence to enable him or her to understand fully what is proposed. It will be a question of fact whether a child seeking advice has sufficient understanding of what is involved to give a consent valid in law. Until the child achieves the capacity to consent, the parental right to make the decision continues save only in exceptional circumstances. . . .

When applying these conclusions to contraceptive advice and treatment it has to be borne in mind that there is much that has to be understood by a girl under the age of 16 if she is to have legal capacity to consent to such treatment. It is not enough that she should understand the nature of the advice which is being given: she must also have a sufficient maturity to understand what is involved. There are moral and family questions, especially her relationship with her parents; long-term problems associated with the emotional impact of pregnancy and its termination; and there are the risks to health of sexual intercourse at her age, risks which contraception may diminish but cannot eliminate. It follows that a doctor will have to satisfy himself that she is able to appraise these factors before he can safely proceed upon the basis that she has at law capacity to consent to contraceptive treatment. And it further follows that ordinarily the proper course will be for him, as the guidance lays down, first to seek to persuade the girl to bring her parents into consultation, and if she refuses, not to prescribe contraceptive treatment unless he is satisfied that her circumstances are such that he ought to proceed without parental knowledge and consent.

Lord Fraser stuck rather more closely than Lord Scarman to the particular issue of contraceptive treatment, and he laid out several conditions that should be satisfied before a doctor should offer contraceptive advice to a minor without her parents' knowledge. These conditions are principally directed to ensuring that it is in the minor's best medical interests that she is given contraceptive advice or treatment in the absence of parental consent. In effect, the parents' right to consent to their child's treatment cedes to the doctor's judgment about where the child's best interests lie. This is not especially radical.

In contrast, Lord Scarman's judgment appears to be much more far-reaching in scope. He suggests that when the child achieves sufficient maturity and understanding, her parents' right to consent to her medical treatment *disappears altogether*, and is replaced by the minor's right to make her own decisions.

For three reasons, it could, however, be argued that Lord Scarman's judgment is not quite as radical as it initially appears. First, Lord Fraser's was the first judgment to be delivered, and Lord Scarman began his judgment by agreeing with him, without qualification. Secondly, given that Lord Bridge said 'I fully agree with the reasons expressed by both my noble and learned friends', it would appear that Lord Bridge at least believed that Lords Fraser and Scarman were essentially saying similar things. Thirdly, Lord Scarman suggests that the purpose of establishing that the child has capacity is:

to enable him or her to exercise a *wise* choice in his or her own interests. (my emphasis)

Further, he recognized the social reality:

which is that many girls are fully able to make *sensible* decisions about many matters before they reach the age of 16. (my emphasis)

Permitting a child to make 'wise choices' and 'sensible decisions' is plainly not the same thing as a child acquiring an absolute right to make mistakes once she has reached a sufficient level of maturity.

Lord Scarman also appeared to hold children to a higher standard of decision-making capacity than that which applies to adults. In order to be competent, the child had to 'have a sufficient maturity to understand what is involved', such as the 'moral and family questions' and the 'risks to health' associated with a decision to have sex and to use contraceptives. The requirement that the child should have a grasp of 'moral and family questions' contrasts sharply with the much more minimal *Re C* test, discussed earlier at p. 196, which governs adults' decision-making capacity.

In any event, in the cases which have followed *Gillick*, the courts have been extremely reluctant to give mature minors the *right* to make their own medical decisions, especially when the choices they wish to make are life-threatening. This has happened in two different ways.

First, it has proved relatively easy to establish that children who are very seriously ill are not *Gillick* competent. In part, this is because the courts have suggested that capacity is not a free-standing concept, but rather that it has to be judged in the context of the particular decision that the child wishes to take: the more serious the decision, the greater the capacity needed to make it. So a child might be able to consent to having a leg X-rayed, but might not be capable of refusing a life-saving blood transfusion. In *Re S (A Minor)(Consent to Medical Treatment)*,[104] Johnson J found that a 15-year-old girl suffering from thalassaemia who no longer wanted to undergo monthly blood transfusions was not competent to make this decision:

It does not seem to me that her capacity is commensurate with the gravity of the decision which she has made. It seems to me that an understanding that she will die is not enough. For her decision to carry weight she should have a greater understanding of the manner of the death and pain and the distress.

Indeed, it sometimes seems that the test for capacity when the child wishes to make a life and death decision appears to be set so high that no child could ever be deemed sufficiently competent. In *Re E (A Minor) (Wardship: Medical Treatment)*,[105] a 15-year-old boy, A, who was suffering from leukaemia, wished to refuse a blood

---

[104] [1994] 2 FLR 1065.   [105] [1993] 1 FLR 386.

transfusion because of his Jehovah's Witness beliefs. Ward J found that to be *Gillick* competent it was not enough that A knew he would die, but also that he would have to understand the manner of his death and the extent of his and his family's suffering.

Re E (A Minor) (Wardship: Medical Treatment)[106]

A, a 15-year-old boy who was suffering from leukaemia, urgently needed a blood transfusion to save his life. As devout Jehovah's Witnesses, A and his parents had refused to consent. A had been made a ward of court. The hospital authority sought leave of the court to treat A as they considered necessary, including giving transfusions of blood and blood products.

Ward J

I find that A is a boy of sufficient intelligence to be able to take decisions about his own well-being, but I also find that there is a range of decisions of which some are outside his ability fully to grasp their implications. Impressed though I was by his obvious intelligence, by his calm discussion of the implications, by his assertion even that he would refuse well knowing that he may die as a result, in my judgment A does not have a full understanding of the whole implication of what the refusal of that treatment involves . . .

I am quite satisfied that A does not have any sufficient comprehension of the pain he has yet to suffer, of the fear that he will be undergoing, of the distress not only occasioned by that fear but also—and importantly—the distress he will inevitably suffer as he, a loving son, helplessly watches his parents' and his family's distress. They are a close family, and they are a brave family, but I find that he has no realisation of the full implications which lie before him as to the process of dying. He may have some concept of the fact that he will die, but as to the manner of his death and to the extent of his and his family's suffering I find he has not the ability to turn his mind to it nor the will to do so.

If, therefore, this case depended upon my finding of whether or not A is of sufficient understanding and intelligence and maturity to give full and informed consent, I find that he is not . . .

I am far from satisfied that at the age of 15 his will is fully free. He may assert it, but his volition has been conditioned by the very powerful expressions of faith to which all members of the creed adhere. When making this decision, which is a decision of life or death, I have to take account of the fact that teenagers often express views with vehemence and conviction—all the vehemence and conviction of youth! Those of us who have passed beyond callow youth can all remember the convictions we have loudly proclaimed which now we find somewhat embarrassing. I respect this boy's profession of faith, but I cannot discount at least the possibility that he may in later years suffer some diminution in his convictions . . .

There is compelling and overwhelming force in the submission of the Official Solicitor that this court, exercising its prerogative of protection, should be very slow to allow an infant to martyr himself.

In my judgment, A has by the stand he has taken thus far already been and become a martyr for his faith. One has to admire—indeed one is almost baffled by—the courage of the conviction that he expresses. He is, he says, prepared to die for his faith. That makes him a martyr by itself. But I regret that I find it essential for his well-being to protect him from himself and his parents, and so I override his and his parents' decision.

Of course, it is not clear that most adults are capable of fully grasping what it is like to die, and so it could be argued that children are being held to a test for capacity

---

[106] Ibid.

which is more difficult to satisfy than the comparatively undemanding *Re C* test. The durability of A's beliefs was confirmed when he continued to refuse blood after his eighteenth birthday, and died as a result.

In *Re L (Medical Treatment: Gillick Competency)*,[107] Sir Stephen Brown P found that a 14-year-old girl who wanted to refuse a life-saving blood transfusion on religious grounds was not *Gillick* competent. In part this was because she lacked vital information about the likely nature of her predicted death, which had in fact been deliberately withheld from her. This seems, with respect, to be a misreading of the *Gillick* test for competence, which is supposed to judge whether the child is *capable* of understanding information, not whether she has been given sufficient information to enable her to make an informed choice. Since the patient's doctors will largely control her access to information about her condition and her treatment, it would be regrettable if an absence of information automatically led to a finding of incompetence. As Andrew Grubb explains:

> The fact that L was ignorant of the detail that the court required her to understand was hardly her fault. Of itself, this did not render her incompetent; rather, it left her uninformed. It cannot be right that a doctor may manipulate a patient's capacity to make a decision by failing to provide relevant information.[108]

In *Re S*, *Re L*, and *Re E*, the standard of competence demanded of children who wanted to refuse treatment was extremely high, and perhaps even unattainable. It is interesting to consider whether these cases would have been brought before the courts, and identical findings of incompetence made, if these children had instead wanted to *consent* to the treatments in question. An additional difference between the test for capacity in children and adults is that, unlike adults' decision-making capacity, *Gillick* competence is a status which cannot fluctuate on a day-to-day basis, so that an individual is competent on one day and not on another. In *Re R*,[109] a case we consider in detail below, Lord Donaldson held that:

> [E]ven if [R] was capable on a good day of a sufficient degree of understanding to meet the *Gillick* criteria, her mental disability, to the cure or amelioration of which the proposed treatment was directed, was such that on other days she was not only 'Gillick incompetent,' but actually section-able. No child in that situation can be regarded as 'Gillick competent' . . . 'Gillick competence' is a developmental concept and will not be lost or acquired on a day to day or week to week basis.

However, as we saw in *Re MB*,[110] an adult's capacity to make decisions is capable of fluctuating depending upon the circumstances. A test which accommodates fluctuations in a person's ability to make decisions is plainly more protective of patient autonomy than a test which defines someone as competent only where their decision-making capacity is unwavering. An adult is entitled to make choices about her medical treatment while she is competent, even if it is known that there will be times when she will lack capacity. Yet a child with fluctuating capacity is deemed to be incompetent, even when, on a functional approach, her decision-making capacity is not in doubt.

---

[107] [1998] 2 FLR 810.
[108] Commentary on *Re L (Medical Treatment: Gillick Competency)* (1999) 7 Medical Law Review 58–61, 60.
[109] [1992] Fam 11 CA.   [110] *Re MB* [1997] 1 FCR 274.

Again, it appears that children are being held to a more exacting test of capacity than adults.

Secondly, and much more controversially, the Court of Appeal has drawn a curious distinction between consent to treatment and refusal, which significantly narrows the scope of the *Gillick* judgment. *Gillick*, on this view, endows mature minors with the right to consent, but does not give them the right to refuse. It is Lord Donaldson MR in his judgments in *Re R* and *Re W*,[111] discussed below, who first proposed this distinction between consent and refusal, and as we see later, he has come under sustained academic criticism ever since.

In Re R (A Minor) (Wardship: Consent to Treatment)[112]

R, a fifteen year old girl in the care of the local authority, suffered increasingly serious episodes of mental illness characterized by violent and suicidal behaviour. Following one such episode, she was admitted to an adolescent psychiatric unit where the proposed treatment included the compulsory administration of certain anti-psychotic drugs. R, in a lucid interval, indicated that she would refuse any such treatment. The local authority began wardship proceedings, requesting court approval for the administration of the proposed medication without R's consent.

Lord Donaldson MR

Lord Scarman [in *Gillick*] was discussing the parents' right 'to *determine* whether or not their minor child below the age of 16 will have medical treatment' (my emphasis). . . . A right of determination is wider than a right to consent. The parents can only have a right of determination if either the child has no right to consent, that is, is not a keyholder, or the parents hold a master key which could nullify the child's consent. I do not understand Lord Scarman to be saying that, if a child was 'Gillick competent,' to adopt the convenient phrase used in argument, the parents ceased to have an independent right of consent as contrasted with ceasing to have a right of determination, that is, a veto. In a case in which the 'Gillick competent' child refuses treatment, but the parents consent, that consent enables treatment to be undertaken lawfully, but in no way determines that the child shall be so treated. In a case in which the positions are reversed, it is the child's consent which is the enabling factor and again the parents' refusal of consent is not determinative. If Lord Scarman intended to go further than this and to say that in the case of a 'Gillick competent' child, a parent has no right either to consent or to refuse consent, his remarks were obiter, because the only question in issue was Mrs. Gillick's alleged right of veto. Furthermore I consider that they would have been wrong . . .

The . . . refusal of the 'Gillick competent' child is a very important factor in the doctor's decision whether or not to treat, but does not prevent the necessary consent being obtained from another competent source.

Because of the similarities between the decision in *Re R* and that in *Re W*, where the Family Law Reform Act 1969, discussed in the next section, applied, we examine the implications of Lord Donaldson's distinction between consent and refusal after mention has been made of the statute which applies to children aged 16 and 17.

(b) By statute (The Family Law Reform Act 1969)

Children aged 16 or 17 are in a rather curious position. They may, of course, be *Gillick* competent, but in addition the Family Law Reform Act 1969 provides that their

---

[111] [1993] Fam 64 CA.   [112] [1992] Fam 11 CA.

consent to medical treatment shall be as effective as it would be if they were an adult. This means that the capacity of a 16- or 17-year-old will be judged in the same way as for adults. Provided that a 16- or 17-year-old child is competent, there is no need for a doctor to obtain separate consent from her parents.

Family Law Reform Act 1969 section 8

(1) The consent of a minor who has attained the age of sixteen years to any surgical, medical or dental treatment which, in the absence of consent, would constitute a trespass to his person, shall be as effective as it would be if he were of full age; and where a minor has by virtue of this section given an effective consent to any treatment it shall not be necessary to obtain any consent for it from his parent or guardian.

(2) In this section 'surgical, medical or dental treatment' includes any procedure undertaken for the purposes of diagnosis, and this section applies to any procedure (including, in particular, the administration of an anaesthetic) which is ancillary to any treatment as it applies to that treatment.

(3) Nothing in this section shall be construed as making ineffective any consent which would have been effective if this section had not been enacted.

It is worth noting that section 8 only applies to *diagnosis* and *treatment*. Bone marrow or organ donation, and non-therapeutic research are therefore excluded, and the validity of a 16- or 17-year-old's consent to such procedures would be governed by the common law. It is also important to remember that the section merely creates a *presumption* in favour of capacity, which can be rebutted in the same way as the presumption that an adult is competent, namely by evidence that the child is not able to believe, retain and weigh information in the balance in order to arrive at a choice.

The most controversial question raised by section 8 is, as above, whether it applies only to consent, or whether it also gives 16- and 17-year-old children the same right as adults to *refuse* medical treatment. On the one hand, it might be argued that the right to refuse must complement the right to consent, otherwise this becomes the rather thin 'right' merely to agree with the doctor's recommended treatment. A right to agree, unless accompanied by the parallel right to disagree, could hardly be said to protect patient autonomy.

On the other hand, the section itself refers only to the minor's 'consent' being effective, and states that it displaces the *need* to obtain parental consent. Not only is it silent as to refusal, but also section 8(3) specifically states that although the 16- or 17-year-old has become capable of giving an effective consent, this does not render ineffective any consent, such as that of the parents, which existed before the statute was passed. It might then be argued that this section's principal purpose was simply to protect doctors, by enabling them to act lawfully when a 16- or 17-year-old gives consent, rather than to remove the parental right to consent in favour of older children's right to make autonomous decisions. Certainly this was the preferred interpretation of the Court of Appeal in *Re W*, the only case to have considered section 8 in any detail.

Re W (A Minor) (Medical Treatment: Court's Jurisdiction)[113]

W, a sixteen year old girl, was in the care of the local authority. In 1990, she developed symptoms of anorexia nervosa and was admitted to an adolescent residential unit for treatment. When her condition deteriorated the local authority decided, contrary to W's wishes and the opinion of the consultant attending her, to transfer her to a unit specializing in the treatment of eating disorders. W resisted the application on the ground that section 8 of the Family Law Reform Act 1969 conferred on her the same right as an adult to refuse medical treatment so that the court could not override her decision. At first instance, Thorpe J made the declaration sought, and the Court of Appeal rejected W's appeal.

Lord Donaldson MR

On reflection I regret my use in *In Re R (A Minor) (Wardship: Consent to Treatment)* of the keyholder analogy because keys can lock as well as unlock. I now prefer the analogy of the legal 'flak jacket' which protects the doctor from claims by the litigious whether he acquires it from his patient who may be a minor over the age of 16, or a 'Gillick competent' child under that age or from another person having parental responsibilities which include a right to consent to treatment of the minor. Anyone who gives him a flak jacket (that is, consent) may take it back, but the doctor only needs one and so long as he continues to have one he has the legal right to proceed. . . .

[I]t is a feature of anorexia nervosa that it is capable of destroying the ability to make an informed choice. It creates a compulsion to refuse treatment or only to accept treatment which is likely to be ineffective. This attitude is part and parcel of the disease and the more advanced the illness, the more compelling it may become. Where the wishes of the minor are themselves something which the doctors reasonably consider need to be treated in the minor's own best interests, those wishes clearly have a much reduced significance.

There is ample authority for the proposition that the inherent powers of the court under its parens patriae jurisdiction are theoretically limitless and that they certainly extend beyond the powers of a natural parent. There can therefore be no doubt that it has power to override the refusal of a minor, whether over the age of 16 or under that age but 'Gillick competent.' It does not do so by ordering the doctors to treat which, even if within the court's powers, would be an abuse of them or by ordering the minor to accept treatment, but by authorising the doctors to treat the minor in accordance with their clinical judgment, subject to any restrictions which the court may impose.

Balcombe LJ

It will be readily apparent that the section is silent on the question which arises in the present case, namely whether a minor who has attained the age of 16 years has an absolute right to refuse medical treatment. I am quite unable to see how, on any normal reading of the words of the section, it can be construed to confer such a right. The purpose of the section is clear: it is to enable a 16-year-old to consent to medical treatment which, in the absence of consent by the child or its parents, would constitute a trespass to the person. In other words, for this purpose, and for this purpose only, a minor was to be treated as if it were an adult. That the section did not operate to prevent parental consent remaining effective, as well in the case of a child over 16 as in the case of a child under that age, is apparent from the words of subsection (3).

(c) The child's 'right' to refuse treatment: *Re R* and *Re W*

Lord Donaldson's argument in both *Re R* and *Re W* can be simply stated. Doctors

[113] [1993] Fam 64 CA.

must have an effective consent before they can lawfully offer medical treatment. *Gillick* and the Family Law Reform Act 1969 endow certain older children with the right to give a valid consent to medical treatment, and hence allow doctors to proceed without seeking an additional consent from the child's parents. But the parental right to consent is not thereby extinguished, rather it co-exists both with the child's right to consent, and with the court's even broader right to authorize medical treatment through the inherent jurisdiction. Because doctors need only one effective consent, once a child is *Gillick* competent (or 16 or 17-years-old), there are three possible sources of this consent: the parents, the courts, and the mature minor. Consent from any one of these three sources will suffice to protect the doctor from prosecution or liability in tort. That means the parents' or the court's consent will be effective *even if the mature minor refuses to give her consent*. The mature minor therefore has no right to have her refusal respected.

This distinction has subsequently been confirmed in a number of cases. In *Re L (Medical Treatment: Gillick Competency)*,[114] for example, Sir Stephen Brown P went on to say that he would have authorized the transfusion even if L had been competent because of the gravity of her situation:

It is also my view, without any doubt at all, that it would be the appropriate order to make even if I were not justified in coming to the conclusion that she was not so-called '*Gillick* competent'. This is an extreme case, and her position is grave indeed.

And according to Thorpe J in *Re K, W and H (Minors) (Medical Treatment)*:[115]

The decision of the Court of Appeal in *Re R* made it plain that a child with *Gillick* competence can consent to treatment, but that if he or she declines to do so, consent can be given by someone else who has parental rights or responsibilities. Where more than one person has power to consent, only a refusal of all having that power will create a veto.

What reason could there be for distinguishing between consent and refusal in this way? Caroline Bridge explains that:

Withholding consent, in the face of medical diagnosis and prescribed treatment requires a countering of the professional view, a stance against authority. The consequences of refusal are likely to be potentially dangerous and more significant than simply giving consent.[116]

In *Re W*, Lord Donaldson MR did not qualify the courts' right to overrule the mature minor, but Balcombe and Nolan LJJ did attempt to confine the courts' and parents' power to overrule the mature minor's refusal to cases in which the treatment is necessary to prevent death or severe permanent injury.

Lord Nolan

[T]he present state of the law is that an individual who has reached the age of 18 is free to do with his life what he wishes, but it is the duty of the court to ensure so far as it can that children survive to attain that age. To take it a stage further, if the child's welfare is threatened by a serious and imminent risk that the child will suffer grave and irreversible mental or physical harm, then once

---

[114] [1998] 2 FLR 810.   [115] [1993] 1 FLR 854.
[116] 'Religious Beliefs and Teenage Refusal of Medical Treatment' (1999) 62 Modern Law Review 585–94, 590.

again the court when called upon has a duty to intervene . . . Due weight must be given to the child's wishes, but the court is not bound by them.

Lord Balcombe

It will normally be in the best interests of a child of sufficient age and understanding to make an informed decision that the court should respect its integrity as a human being and not lightly override its decision on such a personal matter as medical treatment, all the more so if that treatment is invasive. In my judgment, therefore, the court exercising the inherent jurisdiction in relation to a 16- or 17-year-old child who is not mentally incompetent will, as a matter of course, ascertain the wishes of the child and will approach its decision with a strong predilection to give effect to the child's wishes. . . . Nevertheless, if the court's powers are to be meaningful, there must come a point at which the court, while not disregarding the child's wishes, can override them in the child's own best interests, objectively considered. Clearly such a point will have come if the child is seeking to refuse treatment in circumstances which will in all probability lead to the death of the child or to severe permanent injury.

The courts' underlying presumption here seems to be that, while respecting a mature teenager's decision-making autonomy is important, it is trumped by the principle that society should not permit children to make decisions which will lead to their deaths. It seems that the English courts are applying an unstated principle that the right to make life-ending decisions is governed by a *status* approach to competence: all individuals under the age of eighteen are prevented from choosing to die. The case of *Re E* offers a particularly compelling illustration of the fact that the courts in fact employ a status test for competency to make life-threatening decisions. The child was, it seems, incompetent the day before his eighteenth birthday but competent a day later when he was entitled to, and subsequently did, refuse a blood transfusion. Caroline Bridge persuasively argues:

that judges should not go through the pretence of applying a functional test of capacity when the outcome of the young person's decision is not one that they, or probably society, would countenance. The law should openly declare that welfare reigns when grave decisions with momentous outcomes are considered and recognise that adolescent autonomy is, inevitably, circumscribed.[117]

In the next extract, Andrew Grubb makes a similar point:

Andrew Grubb[118]

Clearly, the court is striving to act on its 'hunch' that society should not let children make a decision to die. In truth, it comes down to no more than the court (as society's instrument) acknowledging that at some point citizens must be allowed to make their own decisions, even ones which others might perceive as harmful to them. That point is the age of majority, which for us is 18 . . . Once that point is reached, the state does not have a compelling interest to prevent rational citizens from reaching (most) decisions. Until that point, however, the protective duty of society permits intervention. If this is the public policy of this country, it would be far better for the courts . . . simply to say so rather than to obfuscate matters by distorting the legal concept of competence.

---

[117] 'Religious Beliefs and Teenage Refusal of Medical Treatment' (1999) 62 Modern Law Review 585–94, 594.
[118] Commentary on *Re L (Medical Treatment: Gillick Competency)* (1999) 7 Medical Law Review 58–61, 61.

In contrast, Nigel Lowe and Satvinder Juss support the Court of Appeal's unstated principle or 'hunch', and argue that paternalism is justified where the child's decision would cause irreparable harm.

Nigel Lowe and Satvinder Juss[119]

Collectively, these decisions [in *Re W*, *Re R* and *Re E*] establish two grounds upon which a child's refusal can be overriden; namely, (1) the inability to make an informed judgment, in which case the refusal carries no weight; and (2) where the child *is* capable of making an informed view, that preference is balanced against the harm to the child's welfare which will ensue if these wishes are observed.

We would support the decisions on either basis because it seems to us wrong for the court to allow a child to refuse treatment that would do him or her irreparable harm. After all, it is perhaps all too easily forgotten that, in the final analysis, a child is still only a child ... Is a child of 'sufficient understanding and intelligence' if he or she acts irrationally? Is autonomy meaningful if it is irrational? ... Balcombe LJ recognised that if W's refusal not to take solid food was not shortly reversed 'she would be likely to suffer permanent damage to her brain and reproductive organs' and not be able to bear children. Can it humanely be argued, in these circumstances, that the court ought not to have intervened? We agree with Ward J that a court should be slow to let a child martyr himself. To those who question how a child can be held able to give a valid consent yet be unable to exercise a power of veto, we would reply that there is a rational difference to be made between giving consent and withholding it. We must start with the assumption that a doctor will act in the best interests of his patient. Hence, if the doctor believes that a particular treatment is necessary for his patient, it is perfectly rational for the law to facilitate this as easily as possible and hence allow a '*Gillick* competent' child to give a valid consent, and also to protect the child against parents opposed to what is professionally considered to be in his best interests. In contrast, it is surely right for the law to be reluctant to allow a *child* of whatever age to be able to veto treatment designed for his or her benefit, particularly if a refusal would lead to the child's death or permanent damage. In other words, the clear and consistent policy of the law is to protect the child against wrong-headed parents and against itself.

In their support for Donaldson's approach, Lowe and Juss are, however, in the minority. Many commentators, such as Ian Kennedy in the next extract, believe that Lord Donaldson's 'gloss' on the House of Lords' judgment in *Gillick* was illegitimate.[120]

Ian Kennedy[121]

But enter now Lord Donaldson. He had clearly taken against *Gillick* and decided that he was going to provide a gloss to it. The gloss he provided is such that if it were accepted as law, the House of Lords would have been overruled by a lower court—a rare legal phenomenon indeed. Lord Donaldson took it upon himself to interpret *Gillick* in such a way that he arrived at the following conclusions. A child over the age of 16 or one under that age who understands what is proposed has the legal capacity to consent. But that capacity is also retained by a parent. Thus, if a child over 16 or under 16 but legally competent consents to treatment the doctor may go ahead. The parents have no right of veto since it is the consent of any of the parties which enables treatment to be carried out despite the child's refusal. The significance of this view cannot be overstated. A

---

[119] 'Medical Treatment—Pragmatism and the Search for Principle' (1993) 56 Modern Law Review 865–72, 871–2.

[120] See also Gillian Douglas, 'The retreat from *Gillick*' (1992) 55 Modern Law Review 569–76.

[121] 'Consent to Treatment: The Capable Person' in C Dyer (ed), *Doctors, Patients and the Law* (Blackwell Oxford 1992) 44–71, 60–1.

party under the age of 18, even though legally competent, would lose the most critical element of the right to self-determination, the right to refuse.

Make of this what you will. If Lord Donaldson is right, it drives a coach and horses through *Gillick* and, if it were law, would amount to a significant amendment to the law relating to capacity in the case of young people. Neither of the other two judges in the Court of Appeal joined Lord Donaldson on this particular flight, reasoning quite rightly that it was unnecessary for the decision they had to reach. In my respectful view, Lord Donaldson is wrong. His interpretation of *Gillick* is unique, which is an achievement given the buckets of ink spilt in analyzing that case. His failure to accept that the power to refuse is no more than the obverse of the power to consent and that they are simply twin aspects of the single right to self-determination borders on the perverse.

Certainly none of the judgments in *Gillick* distinguished between consent and refusal, and instead their focus was upon the rights of mature minors to have their wishes about their medical treatment respected, which would appear to encompass a right of refusal as well as a right to consent.

The distinction between consent and refusal is also inconsistent with sections 38(6) and 44(7) of the Children Act 1989, which specifically state that if a child has 'sufficient understanding to make an informed decision he may refuse to submit to the examination or assessment'. Oddly then, Lord Donaldson MR's judgments in *Re R* and *Re W* permit the Court, in exercising its inherent jurisdiction, to override the express and unambiguous provisions of a statute. This runs counter with the principle that the prerogative power cannot be used to undermine statutory provisions.[122]

In the next extract, John Harris argues that the right to refuse is the necessary corollary of a right to consent, and without it, the right to consent becomes simply a right to acquiesce in a decision which has already been taken.

John Harris[123]

The idea that a child (or anyone) might competently consent to a treatment but not be competent to refuse it is a palpable nonsense, the reasons for which are revealed by a moment's reflection on what a competent consent involves. To give an informed consent you need to understand the nature of the course of action to which you are consenting, which, in medical contexts, will include its probable and possible consequences and side effects and the nature of any alternative measures which might be taken and the consequences of doing nothing.

So, to understand a proposed treatment well enough to consent to it is to understand the consequences of a refusal. And if the consequences of a refusal are understood well enough to consent to the alternative then the refusal must also be competent.

Doubtless the learned, if illogical judges in Re W had the best of intentions. They wanted to act in the best interests of the child . . . [T]here are things which it is sensible to do but not sensible to refuse to do, and perhaps the judges in Re W had these obviously true contrasts in mind. But there cannot be things that we are competent to do but not competent to refuse to do . . .

[W]hen we listen to children but reserve the right to overrule them, we are not respecting their autonomy, nor are we obtaining their consent. Where we ask for their consent in circumstances in which we would not accept a refusal, we are behaving as good adults should towards incompetent children. We are involving the children in processes which will minimise distress and will enhance

---

[122] *AG v De Keyser's Royal Hotel Ltd* [1920] AC 508; *Richards v Richards* [1984] AC 174.
[123] 'Consent and end of life decisions' (2003) 29 Journal of Medical Ethics 10–15, 12.

the building of their capacity for autonomy. We are not, however, obtaining consent or respecting autonomy. Rather, we are securing acquiescence—quite another thing.

Similarly Sarah Elliston suggests that Lord Donaldson's 'gloss' means that children's medical decisions will be respected only if 'they know what is good for them'.

Sarah Elliston[124]

The establishment of competence of a minor . . . appears to be a meaningless exercise. . . .

The situation we are faced with now is that the most that a competent child can expect is that their consent to medical intervention will be determinative. Therefore it may be seriously doubted whether any real question of autonomous decision making by them arises. Their consent is a mere acceptance or endorsement of a procedure that may be authorised to be carried out anyway. . . .

In cases involving children, the opinion of the child's medical practitioner will almost invariably be the decisive factor and they will be given leave to carry out such medical procedures as they deem necessary. This can be demonstrated by the fact that in every reported case the medical practitioners have been given such leave to proceed despite the refusal of consent by the minor. This is the position regardless of whether the child is deemed competent or not or whether their decision is supported by their parents. . . .

An adult patient is asked to consent precisely because it is anticipated that they may, for whatever reason, refuse. Proceeding without permission is a violation of the respect due to the patient in terms of both their bodily integrity and their freedom of choice. Are competent minors really unworthy of similar respect? . . .

It is suggested that, instead of fixing an age below which competent patients may have their refusal of treatment overriden by others, the sole question should be that of competence and that the standard of competence should be the same as that for adults as set out in the judgment in *Re C*, not a redefinition of competence that assumes the patient is incompetent if they do not accept recommended medical treatment. The role of the law regarding consent to medical treatment should be to protect the decision making of competent persons, not the competent person themselves.

At present, the law in England permits those under 18 to have their medical decisions respected if, but only if, they know what is good for them and accept the treatment that is proposed. Such a situation is both illogical and unjust and may have wider implications for the way in which children are viewed in our society, in that it suggests that children are in some way less entitled to full respect as members of our society by virtue of their status.

It could even be argued that the right to refuse unwanted medical treatment is of more fundamental importance than the right to consent. For example, Jane Fortin draws attention to the practical consequences of ordering a fully grown adolescent to have treatment that she does not want:

Despite the implicit authorisation of the use of physical force, the case-law is surprisingly reticent over the practical details. Indeed, the courts have barely mentioned that the implication of author-ising treatment against the wishes of a fully grown adolescent is that he may have to be held down physically to undergo it.[125]

Indeed Lawrence Gostin has gone so far as to argue that:

---

[124] 'If You Know What's Good for You: Refusal of Consent to Medical Treatment by Children' in S McLean (ed), *Contemporary Issues in Law, Medicine and Ethics* (Ashgate Dartmouth 1996) 29–55, 39, 43, 45–6, 52.
[125] 'Children's rights and the use of physical force' (2001) 13 Child and Family Law Quarterly 243.

Nothing degrades a human being more than to have intrusive treatment thrust upon him despite his full understanding of its nature and purpose and his clear will to say 'no'.[126]

Imagine a 15-year-old girl who is pregnant and does not wish to have an abortion. The logical consequence of Lord Donaldson MR's judgments is that even if the girl is *Gillick* competent, both her parents and the courts would retain the right to consent to the abortion, and the operation could therefore proceed despite her refusal. In *Re W* Lord Donaldson MR and Balcombe LJ were undeterred by this 'hair-raising' possibility, on the grounds that it would be unlikely to happen in practice:

Lord Donaldson MR

Hair-raising possibilities were canvassed of abortions being carried out by doctors in reliance upon the consent of parents and despite the refusal of consent by 16- and 17-year-olds. Whilst this may be possible as a matter of law, I do not see any likelihood taking account of medical ethics, unless the abortion was truly in the best interests of the child.

Balcombe LJ

In the course of the arguments before us it was suggested that a construction of section 8 of the Act of 1969 which denies a 16- or 17-year-old girl an absolute right to refuse medical treatment, but leaves it open to her parents to consent to such treatment, could in theory lead to a case where a pregnant 16-year-old refuses an abortion, but her parents consent to her pregnancy being terminated. So it could in theory, but I cannot conceive of a case where a doctor, faced with the refusal of a mentally competent 16-year-old to having an abortion, would terminate the pregnancy merely upon the consent of the girl's parents. Leaving aside all questions of medical ethics, it seems to me inevitable that in such highly unlikely circumstances the matter would have to come before the court. I find it equally difficult to conceive of a case where the court, faced with this problem and applying the approach I have indicated above, would authorise an abortion against the wishes of a mentally competent 16-year-old. The dilemma is therefore more apparent than real.

It is perhaps regrettable that we should have to rely upon doctors' good sense, rather than the law, to ensure that these 'hair-raising possibilities' do not take place.

Recall that at the beginning of this chapter, we noted that consent is necessary both to provide the doctor with a defence to a charge of assault or to liability in damages for trespass, and to protect the patient's autonomy. In relation to children, as John Eekelaar points out in the next extract, on Lord Donaldson's view, it appears that the former purpose of consent is the more important one: doctors need only one effective consent in order to lawfully treat a child, whereas respect for autonomy would involve offering equal protection to the child's right to refuse treatment.

John Eekelaar[127]

Lord Donaldson said that there were two reasons for requiring that a patient consents to medical treatment. The 'clinical' reason was that it made treatment easier. The 'legal' reason was 'to provide those concerned in the treatment with a defence to a criminal charge of assault or battery or a civil claim for damages for trespass to the person'. This is an astonishingly narrow view of the

---

[126] 'Consent to Treatment: The Incapable Person' in C Dyer (ed), *Doctors, Patients and the Law* (Blackwell Oxford 1992) 72–88, 76.
[127] 'White Coats or Flak Jackets? Children and the Courts Again' (1993) 109 Law Quarterly Review 182–7.

requirement, which . . . is surely rooted in the fundamental civil rights of all citizens that their personal integrity should not be infringed without their consent or lawful justification. Lord Donaldson is not unaware of this, for in a later case involving an adult, he relates it to the right 'to choose whether to consent to medical treatment, to refuse it or to choose one rather than another of the treatments being offered . . . notwithstanding that the reasons for making the choice are rational, irrational, unknown or even non-existent': *Re T (An Adult: Refusal of Medical Treatment)*. . . .

Lord Donaldson seems to be reluctant to accept that the law should protect minors, even if competent, in the same manner. Rather, his primary concern is to fashion the law so as to minimise the risk of legal action against doctors.

5. VOLUNTARINESS

The next necessary ingredient of a valid consent to medical treatment is that it should have been given voluntarily. It will, of course, be rare for patients to be coerced by direct threats into consenting to medical treatment, but more subtle forms of pressure are possible. The important question is whether the external pressure was such as to overbear the patient's will.

To begin with, it is important to note that the experience of illness, and the offer of treatment, will often leave a patient feeling that she has no option but to consent. Particularly when the patient's condition is life-threatening, and there is only one possible way in which death might be avoided, the patient will be under considerable pressure to agree to the proposed treatment. Yet the pressurized context in which healthcare choices often have to be made does not mean that patients are incapable of consenting to medical treatment. As PDG Skegg has explained:

Consent is no less effective when it is unwillingly or reluctantly given; few patients would consent to major surgery if it were not for the force of surrounding circumstances, and the knowledge that health or even life may be in jeopardy if they do not consent.[128]

But where there has been coercion, undue influence or a fundamental mistake as to the nature of the procedure, it may be possible to argue that the patient's consent is not real.

(a) COERCION

Coercion may vitiate consent to treatment. If a patient was coerced into consenting to treatment, then her apparent consent will be invalid, and any medical treatment which was carried out may be both an assault and a battery. Ruth Faden et al. define coercion as follows:

Coercion occurs if one party intentionally and successfully influences another by presenting a credible threat of unwanted and avoidable harm so severe that the person is unable to resist acting to avoid it. The three critical features in this definition . . . are that

---

[128] *Law, Ethics and Medicine: Studies in Medical Law* (Clarendon Press Oxford 1984) 97.

1. the agent of influence must *intend* to influence the other person by presenting a severe threat,

2. there must be a credible *threat,* and

3. the threat must be *irresistible.*[129]

On this definition, coercion will very seldom vitiate a patient's consent to medical treatment. In fact, when people talk about coercion in the context of consent to medical treatment, they are usually referring to *persuasion* or *manipulation* or *exploitation*, rather than coercion.

In the next extract, Sally Sheldon and Stephen Wilkinson are critical of arguments that consent to female genital mutilation is necessarily coerced.

Sally Sheldon and Stephen Wilkinson[130]

Opponents of female genital mutilation have argued that only someone who was coerced, manipulated or highly irrational would agree to undergo female genital mutilation and that, therefore, valid informed consent to it is, in practice, impossible . . . The kind of pressure envisaged may take two forms. It may either be *direct* pressure from friends and family who seek to persuade or force women to undergo female genital mutilation or, alternatively, it may be *indirect* pressure to conform to deep-rooted, internalised social expectations.

If the pressure envisaged in this kind of argument is of the first (direct) kind, however, surely this would justify appropriate safeguards to ensure that consent was valid, rather than a complete ban on all female genital mutilation procedures. A good example of such an alternative legal regime would be the UK regulations which impose specific safeguards to ensure that consent is valid and uncoerced where a living donor is genetically unrelated to the donee. On the other hand, if the concern is with general social pressures to conform, is it sustainable simply to *assume* that *no* woman could *ever* rationally consent to female genital mutilation . . .

In any case, if the claim that consent to these procedures can never be valid holds true, then it may also hold true for many forms of cosmetic surgery where the decision to have such surgery results from overt or covert social pressure to conform to certain physical ideals.

Offering someone a large sum of money to become a research subject, or to agree to become a living organ donor is often said to be coercive. Yet it is hard to see how someone is *coerced* by an attractive offer. We certainly would not want to say that someone who receives a very generous job offer has been *coerced*. As Bonnie Steinbock explains in the next extract, an offer might be exploitative, in that it takes advantage of someone's straitened circumstances, but this is not the same thing as coercion.

Bonnie Steinbock[131]

[I]t is often far from clear whether a given policy or program is coercive because the concept is complex, controversial, and often difficult to apply. For example, should we understand coercion narrowly, as involving only physical threats or force? Or can the offering of benefits and incentives

---

[129] Ruth Faden, Tom Beauchamp with Nancy King, *A History and Theory of Informed Consent* (OUP Oxford 1986) 339.

[130] 'Female genital mutilation and cosmetic surgery: regulating non-therapeutic body modification' (1998) 12 Bioethics 263–85, 271–2.

[131] 'The Concept of Coercion and Long-Term Contraceptives' in Ellen Moskowitz and Bruce Jennings, *Coerced Contraception? Moral and Policy Challenges of Long-Acting Birth Control* (Georgetown UP Washington DC 1996) 53–78, 54–6.

to get people to do things they would otherwise not do be coercive? Intuitions differ as to whether a proposal *expands* or *constricts* a person's options, and so enhances or limits freedom . . .

Despite the problematic nature of many coercion claims, the concept of coercion can be useful in evaluating social policies if the concept is carefully and appropriately used. To label a policy 'coercive' is to make a *prima facie* objection to it. However, it should be remembered that coercion is not always unjustified or improper: for example, the coercive sanctions attached to the law to force individuals to obey it. Moreover, some socially desirable ends can only be achieved through mutually agreed-upon coercive policies, such as taxation and immunization . . .

The mere existence of external pressure or influence does not establish coercion. The influence or pressure must be of a kind and an amount that diminishes free choice. The central question for understanding the concept of coercion, then, is *how much, and what kind of influence or pressure deprives actions and decisions of their autonomous character*. As we will see, the question does not have a simple or straightforward answer. Moreover, pressure or influence that does not qualify as coercive may also be morally objectionable if, for example, it exploits a person's desperate situation . . .

Both offers and threats are proposals that provide an external influence or impetus to action. Yet threats coerce, whereas offers generally do not. How can threats be distinguished from offers? The intuitive answer is that threats limit freedom, whereas offers enhance it; that one acts involuntarily in response to a threat, whereas one voluntarily accepts an offer; that the recipient of an offer is free to decline, whereas the recipient of a threat is not. . . .

Incentives, like threats, are ways of trying to get people to do things. Unlike threats, incentives are typically welcome offers that seem morally unobjectionable. Yet sometimes inducements and incentives are alleged to be coercive . . . Offering a poor person money for a body part exploits him or takes advantage of his poverty, but it is not clear that it forces or coerces him.

Incentives to do things that people ordinarily would not consider doing appear to be in the same category as exploitative offers. Whether they are coercive is unclear. However, even if they are not coercive, they may be morally impermissible.

In the next extract, P Bean argues that coercion and pressure are not synonymous. He suggests that coercion involves taking advantage of a patient's vulnerability, and, as a result, that mental patients may be particularly susceptible.

P Bean[132]

In an obvious sense there can be no consent if coercion is used: X cannot be said to be consenting if agreement is extracted with Y's gun . . . Coercion neutralises consent. The problem with coercion, as it affects mental patients . . ., is that it is never as naked as that but may involve more subtle threats of punishments, loss of privileges, threats of further detention etc. Where psychiatric staff say 'we shall do this or that to you unless you consent to this treatment,' they are involved in coercion. Similarly, when they say 'we shall keep you in hospital unless you consent to this treatment' they are also involved in coercion . . .

Assume that hospital staff said to a patient 'unless you consent to this treatment your condition will deteriorate'. Is coercion being exercised here? It is not, according to the interpretation of coercion given here. For the essential difference from coercion, as illustrated in these examples, is that coercion takes unfair advantage of the patient's vulnerability. The latter does not. It accepts his position, provides him with a choice even though the range of choices are limited (in this case, improvement as against deterioration . . . It is not about avoiding psychological pressure, for no

---

[132] *Mental Disorder and Legal Control* (CUP Cambridge 1986) 138–9.

greater psychological pressure could exist than in the latter example, but avoiding psychological pressure that is unfair ... So where consent is extracted with threats of punishment, loss of privileges and threats of further detention this is coercion for it takes unfair advantage of the patient's vulnerability. There is no coercion when the patient is placed under pressure, however severe, even though that pressure may involve life or death choices. A person is not coerced because he is pressurised; he is coerced when his vulnerability is exploited.

In *Freeman v Home Office (No 2)*,[133] a prisoner serving a life sentence claimed that he had received medical treatment which had been administered against his will. He argued that where the doctor is also a prison officer, a patient's consent could never be truly voluntary. The Court of Appeal rejected this argument: whether or not consent had been given voluntarily was a question of fact, and that although the patient's imprisonment might alert the court to the danger that the patient's apparent consent was not a real consent, the voluntariness of the patient's consent would have to be individually assessed in each case. Stephen Brown LJ said:

I find myself in complete agreement with the trial judge that the sole issue raised at the trial, that is to say whether the plaintiff had consented to the administration of the drugs injected into his body, was essentially one of fact.

He then went on to quote with approval the trial judge's statement that:

The right approach, in my judgment, is to say that where, in a prison setting, a doctor has the power to influence a prisoner's situation and prospects a court must be alive to the risk that what may appear, on the face of it, to be real consent is not in fact so.

(b) UNDUE INFLUENCE

In *Re T*,[134] the court recognized that pressure to consent to, or to refuse medical treatment is unlikely to consist in physical force or duress, and much more likely to take the form of persuasion. Of course, many forms of persuasion are wholly legitimate. Doctors and relatives will often try to persuade patients of the merits of undergoing a procedure which they believe will benefit the patient. In *Re T*, Staughton LJ recognized that:

every decision is made as a result of some influence: a patient's decision to consent to an operation will normally be influenced by the surgeon's advice as to what will happen if the operation does not take place.

Further, as Ruth Faden et al. explain:

Frequently in clinical situations, professionals would be morally blameworthy if they did not attempt to persuade their patients to consent to interventions that are medically necessitated. Reasoned argument in defense of an option is itself information, and as such is no less important in ensuring understanding that disclosure of facts ... Paradigmatically, persuasion succeeds by *improving*, and not by undermining, a person's understanding of his or her situation.[135]

---

[133] [1984] 1 All ER 1036.   [134] [1993] Fam 95 CA.
[135] Ruth Faden, Tom Beauchamp with Nancy King, *A History and Theory of Informed Consent* (OUP Oxford 1986) 347, 351.

Whether or not the persuasion amounts to undue influence would have to be established on the facts of each case. One obviously relevant factor, as pointed out in *Re T*, is the relationship between the persuader and the patient, the implication being that the closer the relationship, the harder it may be for the patient to resist complying with their views.

Re T (Adult: Refusal of Treatment)[136]

T's mother was a Jehovah's Witness, and although T was not a member of the sect herself, she had been brought up in accordance with its tenets. On 4 July 1992 when she was 34 weeks pregnant she was admitted to hospital following a road traffic accident. In the afternoon, when only her mother was with her, she stated that she did not want a blood transfusion, that she had been a Jehovah's Witness and retained some beliefs. Her child was stillborn and her condition deteriorated. She was sedated and placed on a ventilator. On 8 July her father, supported by her boyfriend, applied to the court for a declaration that it would not be unlawful for the hospital to administer a transfusion to her in the absence of her consent. The judge granted the declaration, and the Official Solicitor's appeal was dismissed.

Lord Donaldson MR

A special problem may arise if at the time the decision is made the patient has been subjected to the influence of some third party. This is by no means to say that the patient is not entitled to receive and indeed invite advice and assistance from others in reaching a decision, particularly from members of the family. But the doctors have to consider whether the decision is really that of the patient. It is wholly acceptable that the patient should have been persuaded by others of the merits of such a decision and have decided accordingly. It matters not how strong the persuasion was, so long as it did not overbear the independence of the patient's decision. The real question in each such case is 'Does the patient really mean what he says or is he merely saying it for a quiet life, to satisfy someone else or because the advice and persuasion to which he has been subjected is such that he can no longer think and decide for himself?' In other words 'Is it a decision expressed in form only, not in reality?'

When considering the effect of outside influences, two aspects can be of crucial importance. First, the strength of the will of the patient. One who is very tired, in pain or depressed will be much less able to resist having his will overborne than one who is rested, free from pain and cheerful. Second, the relationship of the 'persuader' to the patient may be of crucial importance. The influence of parents on their children or of one spouse on the other can be, but is by no means necessarily, much stronger than would be the case in other relationships. Persuasion based upon religious belief can also be much more compelling and the fact that arguments based upon religious beliefs are being deployed by someone in a very close relationship with the patient will give them added force and should alert the doctors to the possibility—no more—that the patient's capacity or will to decide has been overborne. In other words the patient may not mean what he says.

It is worth noting that in *Re T*, the decision which the court decided had been undermined by undue influence was a *refusal* of treatment, rather than consent. It might be predicted that if T's mother had in contrast persuaded her to *consent* to a life-saving blood transfusion, it is highly unlikely that the doctors would have sought a court declaration that T's apparent consent had been vitiated by her mother's undue influence.

---

[136] [1993] Fam 95 CA.

(c) MISTAKE

A decision may not genuinely reflect the patient's wishes if it is based upon a mis-understanding about the seriousness of the patient's condition, or about the need for treatment. This was again an issue in *Re T* where the patient had been reassured that a blood transfusion might not be necessary, and that equally effective alternatives existed. Her condition had, however, deteriorated since these assurances had been given, thus casting doubt upon the authenticity of her continuing refusal. If the patient's claim is that their apparent consent was vitiated by a mistake, they will generally be arguing that they were inadequately informed about the nature of the treatment, and in particular about its risks or side-effects. We consider this sort of claim in more detail in the following chapter.

6. CONCLUSION

In this chapter we have principally been concerned with the medical treatment of vulnerable patients, such as children and adults who lack capacity. We have seen that a great deal turns on whether a patient has, or does not have, capacity to make a medical decision. If a patient is competent, then the principle of autonomy dominates, and the patient is entitled to refuse treatment, including life-saving treatment, for irrational reasons or even for no reason at all. If, on the other hand, if the patient lacks capacity, doctors are entitled to act paternalistically and to carry out (almost) any treatment which they believe to be in the patient's best interests. Since the consequences of being classified as 'incompetent' or 'lacking capacity' are that one's wishes can legitimately be ignored, it is vitally important both that a clear definition of incapacity exists, and that it is applied objectively and consistently.

For some patients, such as very young children and permanently comatose adults, it will be self-evident that they lack the capacity to make decisions about their medical treatment. However, while the law demands a binary either/or categorization of a patient as either competent or incompetent, the reality is that decision-making cap-acity exists on a spectrum. Towards either end of this spectrum, decisions about whether a patient has capacity will be so obvious as to barely need stating. Towards the middle, however, the decision may be much more difficult. The patient in *Re C* was entitled to refuse amputation, despite his bizarre delusions, whereas an anorexic patient, who is deluded about her need to lose weight, might be deemed incompe-tent, and force-fed against her wishes. Deciding when a patient's unusual or mis-guided decision-making process amounts to incapacity is clearly a complicated and difficult task, and it is evident that considerations other than the patient's innate reasoning abilities are sometimes taken into account. For children, we have seen that the test for capacity is set so high in relation to potentially life-threatening decisions that it would be extraordinary if any child were able to satisfy it.

Since the capacity/incapacity line is so critical, it is also important to consider *who* should be charged with making this assessment. While independent review by the courts is possible, usually the decision will be taken by the patient's doctors. Two important points follow from this. First, doctors are undoubtedly much less likely to question a patient's decision-making capacity when she has agreed to a proposed treatment. This means that uncooperative patients are more likely to be categorized as incompetent, and treated against their wishes. Secondly, once the doctor has determined that a patient lacks capacity, she is then entitled to treat the patient according to *her* assessment of the patient's best interests. In most cases, then, doctors are responsible for applying both the test for incapacity *and* the best interests test, and therefore exercise considerable control over the treatment of incompetent patients.

Of course, all these choices can be brought before the courts, and in the case of especially controversial treatments such as sterilization, court involvement is routine. But in the ordinary run of things, it is important to acknowledge that it is not judges, but rather doctors, who must interpret and apply both the test for capacity and the best interests test.

At the time of writing it is impossible to tell what difference the Mental Capacity Act 2005 might make. Will the codification of many of the common law rules lead to greater clarity and transparency, for example? Will the possibility of appointing a proxy to take medical decisions prove popular? Will many people choose to execute advance decisions? Finally, it will also be interesting to see whether the introduction of legislation covering the treatment of adults who lack capacity might also have an impact upon the courts' approach to cases involving children.

7. FURTHER READING

BRIDGE, CAROLINE, 'Religious Beliefs and Teenage Refusal of Medical Treatment' (1999) 62 Modern Law Review 585–94.

BULLER, TOM, 'Competence and risk-relativity' (2001) 15 Bioethics 93–109.

DOUGLAS, GILLIAN, 'The retreat from *Gillick*' (1992) 55 Modern Law Review 569–76.

DRAPER, HEATHER, 'Anorexia nervosa and respecting a refusal of life-prolonging therapy: a limited justification' (2000) 14 Bioethics 120–33.

DRAPER, HEATHER, 'Treating anorexics without consent: some reservations' (1998) 24 Journal of Medical Ethics 5–7.

EEKELAAR, JOHN, 'White Coats or Flak Jackets? Children and the Courts Again' (1993) 109 Law Quarterly Review 182–7.

FOX, MARIE and McHALE, JEAN, 'In Whose Best Interests?' (1996) 60 Modern Law Review 700–9.

GUNN, MJ et al., 'Decision-Making Capacity' (1999) 7 Medical Law Review 269–306.

JONES, RB, 'Parental consent to cosmetic facial surgery in Down's syndrome' (2000) 26 Journal of Medical Ethics 101–2.

LOWE, NIGEL and JUSS, SATVINDER, 'Medical Treatment—Pragmatism and the Search for Principle' (1993) 56 Modern Law Review 865–72.

McLEAN, SHEILA, *Old Law, New Medicine* (London Pandora 1999) ch 5.

SHELDON, SALLY and WILKINSON, STEPHEN, 'Female genital mutilation and cosmetic surgery: regulating non-therapeutic body modification' (1998) 12 Bioethics 263–85.

5

CONSENT II: UNDERSTANDING

1. CENTRAL ISSUES

1. It is increasingly recognized that patients' consent to medical treatment has to be informed. The difficult question is working out exactly how much information patients need.

2. If a patient was not informed 'in broad terms' about the nature of the medical treatment she has received, her consent was not real and an action in battery is possible. Such cases are, however, rare.

3. More usually, a patient who claims not to have been adequately informed will bring an action in negligence, claiming that by failing to provide sufficient information, the doctor was in breach of her duty of care.

4. The question of how much information is necessary to avoid liability in negligence has

traditionally be governed by the *Bolam* test, that is a doctor is judged by her conformity with responsible medical opinion. In contrast, the reasonable patient test would ask whether the doctor had provided the information which the reasonable patient would want to know.

5. Causation raises particular difficulties for patients who want to argue that their doctors failed to warn them about an adverse side effect. This is because the patient has to prove that, if she had been told about a particular risk, she would have refused to consent to the treatment. This is a necessarily speculative inquiry, made more difficult by the fact that the patient now has the benefit of hindsight.

6. In practice, professional guidance imposes much more onerous duties of information disclosure upon doctors than tort law.

2. INTRODUCTION

One of the first principles of medical law is that a competent adult patient must give their consent to medical treatment. Touching a person without their consent—however benevolently—is prima facie unlawful. For consent to be valid, first it must be given voluntarily; secondly, the patient must have the capacity to consent; and thirdly the patient must understand the nature of the treatment to which she has consented. We dealt with the first two criteria in the previous chapter. Here we are concerned with the question of how much information must be provided to patients before they consent to medical treatment. This issue is often referred to as 'informed consent': Does a patient's consent to medical treatment have to be 'informed'? And if it does, exactly how much information will fulfil this requirement?

In this chapter we begin by considering the ethical justifications for informing patients about their medical treatment. We then turn to explore the legal framework which is supposed to protect patients' interests in information disclosure. As we shall see, neither battery nor negligence has proved capable of capturing all the interests which are at stake when patients are deprived of information that may be necessary before they can reach an informed decision about whether to consent to a proposed course of treatment. In fact, both suffer from significant defects, leading some commentators to suggest that a wholly different approach might be appropriate. We then consider a few alternatives to using the law of tort, and conclude by looking at the gap between the minimum standards of disclosure demanded by tort law with the much more rigorous guidance on informing patients produced by the medical profession itself.

3. WHY INFORM PATIENTS?

In the past doctors were under no duty at all to provide their patients with information about their prognoses, or the advantages and disadvantages of different therapeutic alternatives. On the contrary, the assumption was that doctors would exercise their customary care and skill in deciding upon the best course of action for their patient. Indeed Hippocrates even enjoined physicians to take positive steps to conceal information from their patients:

Perform [your duties] calmly and adroitly, concealing most things from the patient while you are attending to him . . . turning his attention away from what is being done to him; . . . revealing nothing of the patient's future or present condition.[1]

And the Hippocratic Oath itself assumes that treatment decisions are for the doctor alone:

I swear by Apollo and Aesculapius that I will follow that system of regimen which according to *my* ability and judgment *I* consider for the benefit of my patients.[2] (my emphasis)

Until relatively recently, it would not have occurred to doctors that patients too might have the ability or the judgment to make choices about their medical care. It was thought that informing patients about a poor prognosis, possible side effects, or the availability of alternative treatments would be likely to cause distress or confusion, and hence jeopardize the possibility of recovery. Keeping patients in ignorance, and maintaining patients' trust and hope through the illusion of medical certainty was especially important given that most of the available treatments were in fact largely ineffective, and any reported improvements principally resulted from the placebo effect. Silence and, in certain circumstances, deception were themselves intended to achieve medical benefits by maintaining a patient's belief in the possibility of a cure.

There were times, however, when doctors might judge the provision of information to be in a patient's best interests. When surgical procedures were carried out without anaesthetics, for example, it was important for patients to prepare themselves for the infliction of excruciating pain. In the 1767 case *Slater v Baker and Stapleton*[3] a surgeon

---

[1] Hippocrates, *Decorum* (trans. W Jones) (Harvard UP Cambridge Mass. 1967) 267.
[2] Hippocrates, *Oath of Hippocrates*, in 1 Hippocrates 299–301 (WHS Jones trans., 1962).
[3] 2 Wils KB 359, 95 ER 850 (1767).

had, without the patient's consent, refractured his leg and placed it in an experimental apparatus to stretch and strengthen it during healing. The court found that it was the normal practice of surgeons to seek consent before refracturing a patient's leg, and therefore there had been an improper breach of professional conduct. In addition, the court reasoned:

It is reasonable that a patient should be told what is about to be done to him, that he may take courage and put himself in such a situation as to enable him to undergo the operation.

Patients did not have an autonomy-based *right* to be provided with information, rather doctors might sometimes reasonably decide that informing patients about a proposed course of treatment had certain therapeutic advantages.

During the twentieth century, the idea that doctors might be under a duty to offer patients sufficient information to enable them to exercise some control over their medical care took hold. In part, this was a result of the growing importance of the principle of patient autonomy, which we considered in Chapter 1. In addition, advances in medical knowledge meant that there was frequently more than one possible treatment for a patient's condition. Since few treatments are entirely without side-effects or possible adverse consequences, it is often necessary to choose between various therapeutic options, weighing up their relative advantages and disadvantages. While doctors' special skill qualifies them both to diagnose a patient's condition, and to carry out specialist medical procedures, it does not enable them to determine which treatment best accommodates the patient's own priorities. Following a diagnosis of breast cancer, for example, the choice between chemotherapy and mastectomy may be one that is best made by the patient herself in the light of her doctors' advice about each treatment's side-effects and likely success rates. The Hippocratic principle that the doctor should decide which treatment the patient should receive has thus gradually been replaced by the idea that this decision is in fact for the patient herself, and the doctor has been recast as a source of information and expert advice.

In the next extract Michael Jones explains how the imbalance of knowledge and power in the doctor–patient relationship might be redressed, at least in part, by placing doctors under a duty to provide patients with the information they need in order to make informed choices about their care.

Michael Jones[4]

It is a trite observation that the doctor–patient relationship involves a major imbalance of power, some of which stems from social norms—patients expect to be at a disadvantage, because of their lack of knowledge, their lack of training, and sometimes because we want to believe desperately that the doctor is all knowing and all powerful and therefore will definitely make the correct diagnosis and provide a complete cure. Although some of this disparity is inherent in most professional–client relationships those relationships are not generally conducted when the client is ill (and on occasion when the client is at the disadvantage of being naked, apart from a flimsy robe). Part of the imbalance between doctor and patient is due to the patient's lack of information, and, on one view, it is the function of the law to redress the imbalance by providing patients with the 'right' to be given that information, or perhaps more accurately imposing a duty on doctors to

---

[4] 'Informed Consent and other Fairy Stories' (1999) 7 Medical Law Review 103–34, 129.

provide it. There are some within the medical profession who appear to resent the notion that informed consent is part and parcel of 'patient rights'—a patient with rights is a lawsuit waiting to happen. On the other hand, a patient with no rights is a citizen who is stripped of his or her individuality and autonomy, as well as her clothes, as soon as she walks into the surgery or the hospital. Patients cease to be subjects and become objects—objects of concern on the part of the medical profession at best, or objects upon whom the doctor practices his trade, or learns his trade, or, at worst, conducts medical research.

Applying some of the concepts we explored in Chapter 1, it might be possible to detect both deontological and consequentialist justifications for the twin elements of informed consent: (a) to seek the patient's consent prior to treatment; and (b) to ensure that the patient has sufficient information about the proposed course of treatment. The deontological justification is obviously respect for patient self-determination and bodily autonomy. Respect for persons requires us to allow individuals to make their own decisions about their medical treatment, hence the need to gain the patient's consent. And as we saw in Chapter 1, autonomous decision-making is only possible where an individual is free from constraints, such as a lack of relevant information. The principle of patient self-determination therefore demands that patients have access to the information they need in order to choose whether to consent to medical treatment.

The consequentialist justification would instead emphasize the beneficial consequences that flow from involving patients in medical decision-making. Giving patients some control over the medical care that they receive will tend to lead to better outcomes. Patients might, for example, be more likely to comply with a treatment regime that they have chosen for themselves than with one which has been imposed upon them. It might also be argued that imposing a duty on doctors to communicate effectively with their patients should improve the quality of care available to all patients.

But while there may appear to be sound ethical reasons for giving patients enough information to enable them to make informed decisions about their medical treatment, the concept of 'informed consent' is not without its critics. First, it is worth noting that the expression 'informed consent' may be both ambiguous and misleading. It is, for example, commonly used as a convenient shorthand for two separate legal duties: the duty to obtain the patient's consent before treatment, and the duty to ensure that the patient has been adequately informed about the risks and benefits of their therapeutic options. Nor is it not clear whether the word 'informed' refers to the doctor's behaviour or the patient's state of mind. Is consent 'informed' if information has simply been provided before consent is given, regardless of whether the patient has in fact read, listened to, or understood anything? Or must the consent itself have been 'informed' by the patient's prior consideration of all relevant material factors? The leading judgment of the High Court of Australia in *Rogers v Whitaker*,[5] suggested that 'nothing is to be gained by reiterating . . . the oft-used and somewhat amorphous phrase "informed consent" '. It is, the judges argued, 'apt to mislead as it suggests a test of the validity of a patient's consent'. Moreover its rather confusing implication is

---

[5] (1992) 175 CLR 479.

that consent is either informed or uninformed, when in fact no such sharp boundary exists and instead the important issue is working out *how much* information patients might need in order to be adequately—though not fully—informed. PDG Skegg has suggested that:

It is regrettable, although entirely understandable, that it was not the expression 'sufficiently informed consent' which became so common. This would have alerted users to the fact that there is an issue of how informed it is necessary to be, in the context and for the purpose in question.[6]

Secondly, to say that consent should be 'informed' does not tell us exactly how much information should be provided. On the contrary, as we shall see later, it is almost impossible for doctors to know prospectively how much disclosure will be necessary in order to avoid liability in negligence. Thirdly, and as a result of this uncertainty, there is a danger that doctors may feel compelled to disclose too much information to patients. Presenting patients with lengthy and complex consent forms may inhibit rather than promote genuine communication between doctors and their patients. There is, for example, some evidence that patients' understanding of consent forms is inversely related to their length.

Fourthly, simply providing patients with information does not ensure that they have understood everything that they have been told. Not only are hypothetical predictions about risk inherently difficult to understand, but, as Onora O'Neill points out, illness can also undermine an individual's willingness and capacity to digest complex information.

Onora O'Neill[7]

When we are ill or injured we often find it hard to achieve any demanding version of individual autonomy. . . . A person who is ill or injured is highly vulnerable to others, and highly dependent on their action and competence. Robust conceptions of autonomy may seem a burden and even unachievable for patients; mere choosing may be hard enough. And, in fact, the choices that patients are required to make are typically quite limited. It is not as if doctors offer patients a smorgasbord of possible treatments and interventions, a variegated menu of care and cure. Typically a diagnosis is followed with an indication of prognosis and suggestions for treatment to be undertaken. Patients are typically asked to choose from a smallish menu—often a menu of one item—that others have composed and described in simplified terms. This may suit us well when ill, but it is a far cry from any demanding exercise of individual autonomy. . . .

The traditional construction of doctor–patient relations as relations of trust, as quasi-personal, as guided by professional concern for the patient's best interests makes sense to many patients because (if achievable) it would secure what they most need . . .

However, at a time at which the real relations between doctors and patients are no longer personal relationships, nor even one-to-one relationships, but rather relationships between patients and complex organisations staffed by many professionals, the older personal, trust-based model of doctor–patient relationships seems increasingly obsolete. Contemporary relations between professionals and patients are constrained, formalised and regulated in many ways, and may erode patients' reasons for trusting. The very requirements to record and file medical information, for example, while intended to control information and protect patients, can inhibit

---

[6] PDG Skegg, 'English Medical Law and "Informed Consent": An Antipodean Assessment and Alternative' (1999) 7 Medical Law Review 135–65, 138.

[7] *Autonomy and Trust in Bioethics* (CUP Cambridge 2002) 38–9.

doctors' abilities to communicate freely. Doctors, like many other professionals, find themselves pressed to be accountable rather than to be communicative, to conform to regulations rather than to enter relations of trust. As layers of regulation and control are added with the aim of protecting dependent, ignorant and vulnerable patients, as professionals are disciplined by multiple systems of accountability backed by threats of litigation on grounds of professional negligence in case of failure to meet these requirements, relations between patients and professionals are inevitably reshaped. Much is demanded of informed consent requirements if they are to substitute for forms of trust that are no longer achievable ... and safeguard the interests of patients who find strangers at their bedsides.

Fifthly, Jay Katz suggests that one of the key challenges for doctors is to effectively communicate the absence of certainty within medicine. There will, for example, rarely be only one possible course of treatment, and the medical profession is seldom unanimous about the appropriate response to a patient with a particular set of symptoms. Katz suggests that doctors may find it especially difficult to be candid with their patients about this lack of certainty.

Jay Katz[8]

[T]he spectacular technological advances in the diagnosis and treatment of disease, spawned by medical science, provided patients and doctors with ever-increasing therapeutic options, each having its own particular benefits and risks. Thus, for the first time in medical history it is possible, even medically and morally imperative, to give patients a voice in medical decisionmaking. It is possible because knowledge and ignorance can be better specified; it is medically imperative because a variety of treatments are available, each of which can bestow great benefits or inflict grievous harm; it is morally imperative because patients, depending on the lifestyle they wish to lead during and after treatment, must be given a choice ...

The longer I reflect about doctor–patient decisionmaking, the more convinced I am that in this modern age of medical science, which for the first time permits sharing with patients the uncertainties of diagnosis, treatment, and prognosis, the problem of uncertainty poses the most formidable obstacle to disclosure and consent.... Medical uncertainty constitutes a formidable obstacle to joint decisionmaking for a number of reasons: Sharing uncertainties requires physicians to be more aware of them than they commonly are. They must learn how to communicate them to patients and they must shed their embarrassment over acknowledging the true state of their own and of medicine's art and science. Thus, sharing uncertainties requires a willingness to admit ignorance about benefits and risks; to acknowledge the existence of alternatives, each with its own known and unknown consequences; to eschew one single authoritative recommendation; to consider carefully how to present uncertainty so that patients will not be overwhelmed by the information they will receive; and to explore the crucial question of how much uncertainty physicians themselves can tolerate without compromising their effectiveness as healers. To so conduct oneself is most difficult. For, once doctors, on the basis of their clinical experience and knowledge, conclude which treatment is best, they tend to disregard, if not reject, the view of other colleagues who treat the same condition differently. ...

Moreover, acknowledgement of uncertainty is undermined by the threat that it will undermine doctors' authority and sense of superiority. ... All of this suggests that implementation of the idea of informed consent is, to begin with, not a patient problem but a physician problem.

---

[8] 'Informed Consent: Must it Remain a Fairy Tale?' (1993) 10 Journal of Contemporary Health Law and Policy 69, 76, 81–2.

Sixthly, giving patients detailed information about remote risks, and ensuring that they have understood it, takes time, and therefore costs money. Scarce NHS resources might then be diverted to cumbersome consent procedures, which could be more effectively spent on providing medical treatment. Seventhly, doctors have traditionally been concerned that giving a patient information about all of the possible risks and side-effects associated with a particular procedure might confuse and alarm her, and in particular might prompt her to attach disproportionate importance to a very remote risk and refuse treatment which is overwhelmingly likely to be successful. The medical profession's principal goal has tended to be the treatment of disease and the alleviation of pain and disability, rather than the expansion of patient choice. Where a conflict appears to exist between the disclosure of information and the promotion of patient welfare, doctors have often believed that their duty to act in the best interests of their patients should take priority.

Finally, the practice of obtaining consent is commonly limited to a single encounter before treatment begins when the doctor recommends a particular procedure and offers the patient some information about its risks and benefits, before asking the patient to sign a consent form. Yet this model of decision-making is unsatisfactory for two reasons. First, it sits uneasily with the reality of medical treatment, which will rarely involve one single decision, but rather a series of decisions taken as more information becomes available about the patient's condition, and alternative treatment options become plausible. Consent forms exacerbate this false perception that consent is an event, rather than a process which takes place over time. A doctor's duty to communicate effectively with her patients may be especially important *during* treatment, and should not be confined to some brief bureaucratic ritual when the patient is first admitted to hospital. Secondly, although patients are free to withdraw from treatment at any point, some may falsely believe that signing a consent form binds them to its contents. In other contexts, a person who signs a document will usually have made a binding commitment to fulfil their side of the bargain, and it is therefore unsurprising that many patients do not understand that their right to refuse treatment persists throughout their care.

4. LEGAL PROTECTION FOR PATIENTS' INTERESTS IN INFORMATION DISCLOSURE

In the following section we tackle the central problem of what legal claim is appropriate when consent has *not* been properly informed. Does the lack of adequate information vitiate the patient's consent altogether, in which case the claim would lie in battery? Or is the provision of information part of the doctor's ordinary duty of care, meaning that a failure to offer adequate information might ground an action in negligence? In the UK, the duty to obtain the patient's consent prior to treatment is protected by the tort of battery, while the duty to ensure that the patient has been given enough information (whatever that might mean) is normally treated as an aspect of the doctor's ordinary duty of care.

In short, an action in battery will only be successful if the patient did not in fact consent to the medical treatment that she received, and for a number of reasons the courts have been extremely reluctant to hold that a failure to give the patient information about risks or alternatives wholly invalidates the patient's consent. Most cases involving allegations of insufficient disclosure are therefore brought in negligence. But a successful action in negligence requires damage to have been caused by the doctor's breach of duty. Patients who have been inadequately informed prior to undergoing treatment can only bring an action in negligence if they happen to have suffered injury as a result of the doctor's failure to disclose some relevant piece of information. As we see later, this requirement will prove fatal to almost every potential claim, even if there was patently wholly inadequate disclosure prior to treatment.

(a) BATTERY

Trespass to the person can be both a tort (battery) and a crime (assault). A patient's consent to medical treatment will only absolve the medical practitioner from liability in battery for unlawful touching if the consent is 'real': the patient must know what she is consenting to. If a patient consented to a different procedure from that which is in fact performed, her consent will not be effective, and the doctor might be found liable for unlawful touching. An example cited by Bristow J in *Chatterton v Gerson*[9] was a case from the 1940s in which a boy was admitted to hospital in Salford for a tonsillectomy. Due to an administrative error, he was circumcised instead. According to Bristow J, the appropriate cause of action here would have been trespass to the person.

Trespass to the person can also be a criminal offence. *R v Tabassum*,[10] T—who had no medical qualifications at all—was convicted of indecent assault after he persuaded the three complainants to consent to him showing them how to carry out a breast self-examination. Each complainant said they had only consented because they thought T had medical qualifications or relevant training. The Court of Appeal upheld his conviction on the grounds that:

consent was given because they mistakenly believed that the defendant was medically qualified . . . and that, in consequence, the touching was for a medical purpose. As this was not so, there was no true consent.

In contrast, in *R v Richardson*,[11] a dentist continued to treat her patients after she had been suspended from practising. Her patients were not mistaken as to her identity, because she had treated them before, but as to her qualifications to practice. The Court of Appeal stated that:

either there is consent to actions on the part of a person in the mistaken belief that he or they are other than they truly are, in which case it is assault or, short of this, there is no assault.

Because 'the complainants were fully aware of the identity of the appellant', the Court of Appeal overturned her conviction. The concept of the 'identity of the

---

[9] [1981] QB 432.   [10] [2000] 2 Cr App Rep 328 (CA).   [11] 43 BMLR 21 (CA).

person' should not, the court held, be extended to cover a person's qualifications or attributes.

The advantage of an action in battery is that it is not necessary to establish that any physical harm has been caused by the doctor's inadequate disclosure. As we see below, causation represents an almost insuperable obstacle to most claimants' actions in negligence because of the need to prove that proper disclosure would have prompted the patient to reject the proposed course of treatment. Instead, a successful action in battery will lead to compensation for the dignitary harm of being treated without valid consent. This more accurately protects the patient's interest in self-determination because it is the violation of the patient's right to make an informed choice which is being compensated, rather than the materialization—through nobody's fault—of some small risk. Patients who are inadequately informed about an alternative treatment option will only be able to recover in negligence if the treatment that they received in fact goes wrong and they suffer physical injury as a result. Yet arguably, the patient's right to make an informed choice about which therapeutic option best accommodates their particular priorities has been infringed even if their treatment does not happen to cause them physical injury.

It is also no defence to a charge of battery that the doctor was acting in the best interests of her patient, or that she exercised all reasonable care and skill in carrying out the nonconsensual treatment. Evidence of accepted medical practice is also irrelevant: if the failure to provide information to a patient vitiates an apparent consent, the fact that the defendant can point to other doctors who would have acted in the same way will not absolve her of responsibility. Moreover, there could be no 'therapeutic privilege' (discussed below at p. 284) if the cause of action is battery rather than negligence. If certain information is necessary for consent to be real, the doctor is not absolved from a failure to disclose it because she judges that disclosure might cause the patient severe distress or anxiety. Since the concept of therapeutic privilege is inherently paternalistic, and unless narrowly confined could reintroduce a 'doctor knows best' attitude towards the disclosure of information, its irrelevance to an action in battery further protects patient self-determination. The competent adult patient's right to be free from non-consensual touching is almost absolute, and the tort of battery appears to offer strong and uncompromising protection for a patient's right to make treatment decisions for herself.

Despite appearing to go more precisely to the infringement of patient autonomy involved in depriving patients of material information, judges have confined its use to the rare cases in which the patient was misinformed about the nature of the proposed treatment. Provided that the patient agreed to the procedure which was in fact carried out, their consent will be effective and no action in battery will lie. The leading case is *Chatterton v Gerson*, in which Bristow J held that consent would be real as long as the patient had been informed 'in broad terms' about the nature of the procedure.

Chatterton v Gerson[12]
Miss Chatterton suffered chronic and unendurable pain in a post-operative scar, and was sent for treatment to a pain clinic, where the defendant operated to block the sensory nerve. Although the

---

[12] [1981] QB 432 (QBD).

defendant did not recall what he had said to her, his regular practice was to explain to patients before the operation that it would result in numbness, and that it might involve temporary loss of muscle power. Miss Chatterton's recollection was that he did not warn her of the risks of numbness and muscle weakness. She experienced some numbness and after a repeat operation, she lost the sensation in her right leg. There was no allegation that the performance of the operations had been negligent, but the plaintiff claimed in trespass that her consent to operation was vitiated by lack of explanation of what the procedure was and what were its implications; and in negligence that the defendant had breached his duty of care by failing to give the plaintiff such an explanation of the nature and implications of the proposed operation that she could come to an informed decision on whether she wanted to have it.

Bristow J
Trespass to the person and consent
It is clear law that in any context in which consent of the injured party is a defence to what would otherwise be a crime or a civil wrong, the consent must be real. . . .

In my judgment what the court has to do in each case is to look at all the circumstances and say 'Was there a real consent?' I think justice requires that in order to vitiate the reality of consent there must be a greater failure of communication between doctor and patient than that involved in a breach of duty if the claim is based on negligence. When the claim is based on negligence the plaintiff must prove not only the breach of duty to inform, but that had the duty not been broken she would not have chosen to have the operation. Where the claim is based on trespass to the person, once it is shown that the consent is unreal, then what the plaintiff would have decided if she had been given the information which would have prevented vitiation of the reality of her consent is irrelevant.

In my judgment once the patient is informed in broad terms of the nature of the procedure which is intended, and gives her consent, that consent is real, and the cause of the action on which to base a claim for failure to go into risks and implications is negligence, not trespass. Of course if information is withheld in bad faith, the consent will be vitiated by fraud. Of course if by some accident, as in a case in the 1940's in the Salford Hundred Court where a boy was admitted to hospital for tonsilectomy and due to administrative error was circumcised instead, trespass would be the appropriate cause of action against the doctor, though he was as much the victim of the error as the boy. But in my judgment it would be very much against the interests of justice if actions which are really based on a failure by the doctor to perform his duty adequately to inform were pleaded in trespass.

Negligence
[The doctor] ought to warn of what may happen by misfortune however well the operation is done, if there is a real risk of a misfortune inherent in the procedure, as there was in the surgery to the carotid artery in the Canadian case of *Reibl v. Hughes*. In what he says any good doctor has to take into account the personality of the patient, the likelihood of the misfortune, and what in the way of warning is for the particular patient's welfare.

I am not satisfied that Dr. Gerson fell short of his duty to tell the plaintiff of the implications of this operation, properly carried out. . . . I should add that if I had thought that Dr. Gerson had failed in his duty to inform her of the implications inherent in the second injection, I would not have been satisfied that if properly informed the plaintiff would have chosen not to have it.

In *The Creutzfeldt-Jakob Disease Litigation*,[13] the claimants had been treated with

---

13 [1995] 54 BMLR 1 (QBD).

Human Growth Hormone (HGH), which had been extracted from pituitary glands that had been unlawfully harvested from dead bodies. They argued that their consent had been given on the understanding that the drug had been lawfully prepared, and that this ostensible consent was vitiated by the fact that the pituitaries had been unlawfully harvested. Their claim was dismissed by May J who summarized the law as follows:

There is assault and battery when there is physical violation of a person's body without true consent. There is true consent when a person consents to the nature of the act done. There is no English law doctrine of informed consent and a person may succeed in a claim for failure to inform or warn only if the failure alleged amounts to negligence. To frame such a claim in battery is not only deplorable but insupportable in law.

In part, this judicial hostility to the use of battery in medical cases flows from the assumption that battery involves *deliberately* inflicted injury. A doctor who fails to tell a patient about a small inherent risk posed by a proposed course of treatment does not intend to injure her. And because a battery will also often be an assault, judges have been reluctant to criminalize by association a doctor's well-meaning but misguided decision to withhold information from a patient. In *Appleton v Garrett*, extracted below, the dentist deliberately carried out extensive and wholly unnecessary dental treatment for personal financial gain. And it was almost certainly this element of intentional and fraudulent wrongdoing which persuaded the court to find him liable for battery rather than negligence.

Appleton and Others v Garrett[14]

The defendant, Mr Garrett, was a practising dentist in the National Health Service from 1981 to 1988. In 1989 he was struck off the Dental Register as a result of gross overtreatment of patients. The eight claimants (then referred to as plaintiffs) were former patients. The defendant had admitted negligence, but the court had to decide, *inter alia*, whether there could also be liability for trespass to the person.

Dyson J

It is not in dispute that a surgeon who performs an operation without his patient's consent commits an assault for which he is liable in damages.

The evidence undoubtedly establishes that none of these eight plaintiffs was given any information on which to base a suitably informed consent. None was told why Mr Garrett was of the view that massive restorative treatment was required, often on perfect teeth. Typically, the plaintiff went for a normal routine check-up, and was subjected to the course of treatment without any explanation at all . . . I am quite satisfied that the failure to inform in these eight cases was not mere negligence and that Mr Garrett withheld information deliberately and in bad faith. The scale of the unnecessary treatment was so great that it must have been obvious to him that it was indeed unnecessary. The radiographs that he took before he embarked on the treatment showed in many cases that the teeth in these young plaintiffs were free from caries and were in what has been described as 'virgin condition'.

Much of the treatment on these teeth was considerable in its scope and extent. For example, several surfaces of virgin teeth were cut heavily and received large fillings, quite often supported by pins. Others received root canal treatment and crowns . . .

[14] 34 BMLR 23 (QBD).

I conclude therefore that Mr Garrett deliberately embarked on large-scale treatment of these plaintiffs which he knew was unnecessary and that he deliberately withheld from them the information that the treatment was unnecessary because he knew that they would not have consented had they known the true position. . . . I find, therefore, that none of the plaintiffs consented, at any rate to the treatment of those teeth that required no treatment, and that, at least in relation to those teeth, the tort of trespass to the person has been made out.

In *Wells v Surrey AHA*,[15] a sterilization operation was first suggested to the claimant after she had gone into labour, and the operation was performed at the same time as a caesarean section. The court found that the doctor had been negligent in failing to give the claimant 'proper advice' about the advisability of sterilization. Given the absence of adequate advice, and the circumstances in which her consent was obtained, it is hard to believe that this claimant had genuinely understood the implications of the operation to which she consented. Despite this, the court found that her consent had been real. Gerald Robertson suggests that the only explanation for this somewhat surprising result is 'that the court was struggling to avoid the conclusion that the doctor was guilty of the tort of battery'.[16]

A further problem which flows from the tendency to frame consent as a defence to the tort of battery is that a consent will be seen as 'effective' if it precludes legal liability, regardless of whether it is adequately informed. Other purposes of obtaining patients' consent—such as enabling patients to exercise their right of self-determination or improving the quality of patient care—are marginalized by this narrow interpretation of consent. A consent will be 'effective' in protecting a doctor from liability in battery when it may rest upon a significant misapprehension about the risks and benefits of treatment, and thus be wholly 'ineffective' in facilitating meaningful patient choice.

In the next extract, Ian Kennedy suggests that a broader application of the tort of battery might better protect patients' interests in information disclosure.

Ian Kennedy[17]

As for the law of tort, battery has very considerable potential as the vehicle for setting the legal bounds of the doctor–patient relationship. After all, it is concerned with touching and centres on the presence or absence of consent. On the other hand, it carries connotations of intentional wrongdoing and harm which make it appear unsuitable as the medium for mediating between doctors and patients, where the context is one of caring and benevolence. For this reason, the courts in England have set their face against its general use. It has been confined to cases in which the lack of consent is fundamental, going to the very nature and purpose of the touching, or in which the touching takes place despite a patient's explicit refusal.

This is not the place to criticise this judicial response. All that will be said here is that patients' interests could well be better protected if the tort of battery were held to have a wider application. In particular, questions of what has come to be known as 'informed consent' could well be differently analysed and decided. A patient may have consented on the 'nature and purpose' test, but the information provided by the doctor may be so inadequate, in that it failed to respect the

---

[15] *The Times* 29 July 1978.

[16] 'Informed Consent to Medical Treatment' (1981) 97 Law Quarterly Review 102–26, 123.

[17] 'The Fiduciary Relationship and its Application to Doctors' in P Birks (ed), *Wrongs and Remedies in the Twenty-first Century* (Clarendon Press Oxford 1986) 111–40, 113–14.

patient's right to know, so as to be able to choose, that the consent should be regarded as entirely invalid. Such an extension of the tort of battery would restore the law's protection of the symbolic harm represented by the complaint that the patient's right to know was not respected. It would, in other words, reflect a legal response based upon rights.

But even if judges could be persuaded to carve out an extended role for the tort of battery, there are reasons why battery too might offer inadequate protection for patients' right to make informed medical decisions. Medical treatment can only be a battery if there has been some sort of physical contact between doctor and patient. Hence while an action in battery might be relatively straightforward if the treatment in question is surgery, there are many medical decisions which do not involve touching, and which would therefore be unaffected by a more robust application of the tort of battery. The prescription of drugs, for example, does not involve any physical contact, and so a patient who is inadequately informed about a medicine's side effects could not bring an action in battery. A patient who is not told about the risks of *not* consenting to the only treatment which might save her life has not been touched, and so could have no action in battery. As a result, Marjorie Maguire Shultz has argued that:

Defining the scope of an autonomy interest in terms of physical contact with the body has intuitive appeal and offers a certain simplicity of administration. But ultimately, physical contact is too literal a demarcation for what is a much broader, non-tangible interest in patient choice. Health care choices of vast consequence can be made and implemented without such bodily contact as predictably triggers battery analysis. Most notably, this occurs when a doctor makes a decision not to act.[18]

(b) NEGLIGENCE

As we saw in Chapter 3, there are three stages to an action in negligence. First, the defendant must owe the claimant a duty of care of the scope contended for, secondly, he must breach that duty, and thirdly, the breach must have caused the claimant's damage. Let us examine each stage in turn.

(1) THE DUTY OF CARE

If a patient's consent to a medical procedure has been sufficiently informed to be legally effective, and hence to avoid a charge of battery, the patient's only option is to argue that the doctor's failure to disclose information about their treatment amounted to negligence. It is worth noting, as Andrew Grubb explains in the next extract, that this amounts to a duty to act positively rather than to simply refrain from causing harm, and that such duties are exceptional in English law, and generally require special justification.

Andrew Grubb[19]

[I]t is immediately apparent that if the patient is entitled to be informed, the doctor is under a

---

[18] 'From Informed Consent to Patient Choice: A New Protected Interest' (1985) 95 Yale Law Journal 219, 229–30.
[19] 'Consent to Treatment: The Competent Patient' 131–203 in A Grubb with J Laing (eds), *Principles of Medical Law* (2nd edn OUP Oxford 2004) 179–80.

duty to provide the information. To so assert, however, is to place on the doctor a duty of affirmative action. It is trite law that English law regards such a duty as exceptional. While it is one thing to expect people to refrain from careless behaviour, English law, with its aversion to the 'officious intermeddler', will not ordinarily impose a duty to do something on behalf of another. The first step, therefore, is to examine the legal basis for the doctor's duty to inform a patient, so as to obtain valid consent to treatment.

One well-established ground on which a duty to inform could be based would be to find that, as between the doctor and the patient, there exists a 'special relationship', giving rise to a duty to act. The traditional example is the parent–child and, by extension, the teacher–child relationship. In effect, therefore, the duty is derived from the status of the parties. The common law has not, however, regarded the doctor–patient relationship as falling into the category of special relationships. Its legal origins lay in the law of contract and thus in an assumption that the parties were at arm's length. The notion of vulnerability which underpins the law's recognition of a special relationship, while clearly a central feature of modern medicine, did not colour the earlier development of the law. Thus a duty to inform cannot be derived from the existence of a special relationship.

An alternative ground on which English law could base an affirmative duty to inform can be derived from the law of equity . . . English law, however, has never regarded the doctor–patient relationship as fiduciary. Indeed, when asked to do so, the House of Lords expressly refused . . . Thus, any duty to inform cannot be based on a fiduciary relationship.

So, where does the duty come from? Curiously, when the English courts very belatedly got round to examining whether a doctor is under a duty to inform a patient, the legal-technical difficulties involved in actually finding some juristic basis for a duty of affirmative action were largely ignored. Instead, the general duty of care owed by a doctor to a patient was interpreted as extending not only to acts but also omissions, in this case the failure properly to inform.

Despite some ambiguity about the origin of the duty to inform, it is now widely accepted that one aspect of the duty of care which doctors always owe to their patients is to provide them with information about any proposed treatment. The chief problem has then been to work out when the doctor has breached this duty. How much information is required in order to fulfil the doctor's duty of care? As we see in the following sections, the law has struggled to devise a satisfactory test for assessing the adequacy of a doctor's disclosure.

(2) THE STANDARD OF CARE

(a) English law

It is sometimes forgotten that the *Bolam* case itself involved the doctor's failure to warn the patient about the risks involved in electro-convulsive therapy and to advise him that these could be minimized by the use of restraints or muscle relaxants. In a less famous passage from his direction to the jury, McNair J said:

you have to make up your minds whether it has been proved to your satisfaction that when the defendants adopted the practice they did (namely, the practice of saying very little and waiting for questions from the patient), they were falling below a proper standard of competent professional opinion on this question of whether or not it is right to warn. Members of the jury, though it is a matter entirely for you, you may well think that when dealing with a mentally sick man and having a strong belief that his only hope of cure is E.C.T. treatment, a doctor cannot be criticized if he does not stress the dangers which he believes to be minimal involved in that treatment.[20]

In *Hills v Potter*,[21] a first instance case decided just before the Court of Appeal's judgment in *Sidaway*, Hirst J expressed concern about the practical consequences of importing the doctrine of informed consent from Canada and the US:

I therefore reject the argument of counsel for the plaintiff that I should apply the standard laid down in the Canadian and cited United States cases, and I hold that the proper standard is the medical standard, in accordance with *Bolam*'s case . . .

   This, of course, does not mean that I treat the decisions of the Supreme Court of Canada and the cited United States cases with other than the utmost respect. But in my judgment the principles there laid down could only be incorporated in English law as a result of the decision of an appellate court, which would have to balance the considerations canvassed so cogently in the Canadian and United States judgments against the very formidable problems and potential liabilities which would undoubtedly confront medical men if these principles were applied here. It is common knowledge that the extent of these problems and potential liabilities has caused serious anxiety in the United States, whence the principles laid down in the Canadian decisions are derived.

The most authoritative, though by no means clear statement of the law is the House of Lords' 1985 judgment in *Sidaway v Board of Governors of the Bethlem Royal Hospital and the Maudsley Hospital.*[22] Mrs Sidaway complained that she had not been told about an operation's small risk of damage to her spinal column. She claimed that if she had been warned, she would not have had the operation. This small risk had in fact materialized, and Mrs Sidaway was now seriously disabled. The House of Lords unanimously rejected Mrs Sidaway's claim that the failure to warn her of this risk had been negligent. They were also all agreed that the duty to disclose information is part of the doctor's ordinary duty of care. There were, however, very marked differences in their approaches to determining the relevant standard of care.

Sidaway v Board of Governors of the Bethlem Royal Hospital and the Maudsley Hospital[23]

Mrs Sidaway, who had suffered recurrent pain in her neck, right shoulder and arms, underwent an operation in 1974 which was performed by a senior neuro-surgeon at the first defendant's hospital. The operation, even if performed with proper care and skill, carried an inherent, material risk, which was put at between one and two per cent, of damage to the spinal column and the nerve roots. This risk materialized and Mrs Sidaway was left severely disabled. She claimed damages for negligence against the hospital and the executors of the deceased surgeon. Her claim was dismissed by Skinner J and the Court of Appeal. Mrs Sidaway appealed to the House of Lords. The House of Lords unanimously agreed that the failure to warn Mrs Sidaway of the very small risk was not negligent, but their judgments on how to assess the relevant standard of care differed.

Lord Scarman

The case is plainly of great importance. It raises a question which has never before been considered by your Lordships' House. Has the patient a legal right to know, and is the doctor under a legal duty to disclose, the risks inherent in the treatment which the doctor recommends? If the law

---

[20] [1957] 1 WLR 582, at 591.   [21] [1984] 1 WLR 641.   [22] [1985] AC 871.
[23] [1985] AC 871 (HL).

recognises the right and the obligation, is it a right to full disclosure or has the doctor a discretion as to the nature and extent of his disclosure? . . .

The right of 'self-determination'—the description applied by some to what is no more and no less than the right of a patient to determine for himself whether he will or will not accept the doctor's advice—is vividly illustrated where the treatment recommended is surgery. A doctor who operates without the consent of his patient is, save in cases of emergency or mental disability, guilty of the civil wrong of trespass to the person: he is also guilty of the criminal offence of assault. The existence of the patient's right to make his own decision, which may be seen as a basic human right protected by the common law, is the reason why a doctrine embodying a right of the patient to be informed of the risks of surgical treatment has been developed in some jurisdictions in the U.S.A. and has found favour with the Supreme Court of Canada. Known as the 'doctrine of informed consent,' it amounts to this: where there is a 'real' or a 'material' risk inherent in the proposed operation (however competently and skilfully performed) the question whether and to what extent a patient should be warned before he gives his consent is to be answered not by reference to medical practice but by accepting as a matter of law that, subject to all proper exceptions (of which the court, not the profession, is the judge), a patient has a right to be informed of the risks inherent in the treatment which is proposed. The profession, it is said, should not be judge in its own cause: or, less emotively but more correctly, the courts should not allow medical opinion as to what is best for the patient to override the patient's right to decide for himself whether he will submit to the treatment offered him. . . .

But the circumstance that this House is now called upon to explore new ground is no reason why a rule of informed consent should not be recognised and developed by our courts. The common law is adaptable: it would not otherwise have survived over the centuries of its existence. The concept of negligence itself is a development of the law by the judges over the last hundred years or so. . . .

Unless statute has intervened to restrict the range of judge-made law, the common law enables the judges, when faced with a situation where a right recognised by law is not adequately protected, either to extend existing principles to cover the situation or to apply an existing remedy to redress the injustice . . . If, therefore, the failure to warn a patient of the risks inherent in the operation which is recommended does constitute a failure to respect the patient's right to make his own decision, I can see no reason in principle why, if the risk materialises and injury or damage is caused, the law should not recognise and enforce a right in the patient to compensation by way of damages.

One point is clear, however. If failure to warn of risk is actionable in English law, it must be because it is in the circumstances a breach of the doctor's duty of care: in other words, the doctor must be shown to be negligent. . . .

In a medical negligence case where the issue is as to the advice and information given to the patient as to the treatment proposed, the available options, and the risk, the court is concerned primarily with a patient's right. The doctor's duty arises from his patient's rights. If one considers the scope of the doctor's duty by beginning with the right of the patient to make his own decision whether he will or will not undergo the treatment proposed, the right to be informed of significant risk and the doctor's corresponding duty are easy to understand: for the proper implementation of the right requires that the doctor be under a duty to inform his patient of the material risks inherent in the treatment. And it is plainly right that a doctor may avoid liability for failure to warn of a material risk if he can show that he reasonably believed that communication to the patient of the existence of the risk would be detrimental to the health (including, of course, the mental health) of his patient.

Ideally, the court should ask itself whether in the particular circumstances the risk was such that this particular patient would think it significant if he was told it existed. I would think that, as a matter of ethics, this is the test of the doctor's duty. The law, however, operates not in Utopia but in the world as it is: and such an inquiry would prove in practice to be frustrated by the subjectivity of its aim and purpose. The law can, however, do the next best thing, and require the court to answer the question, what would a reasonably prudent patient think significant if in the situation of this patient. The 'prudent patient' cannot, however, always provide the answer for the obvious reason that he is a norm (like the man on the Clapham omnibus), not a real person: and certainly not the patient himself. Hence there is the need that the doctor should have the opportunity of proving that he reasonably believed that disclosure of the risk would be damaging to his patient or contrary to his best interest. This is what the Americans call the doctor's 'therapeutic privilege.' Its true analysis is that it is a defence available to the doctor which, if he invokes it, he must prove. On both the test and the defence medical evidence will, of course, be of great importance. . . .

My conclusion as to the law is therefore this. To the extent that I have indicated I think that English law must recognise a duty of the doctor to warn his patient of risk inherent in the treatment which he is proposing: and especially so, if the treatment be surgery. The critical limitation is that the duty is confined to material risk. The test of materiality is whether in the circumstances of the particular case the court is satisfied that a reasonable person in the patient's position would be likely to attach significance to the risk. Even if the risk be material, the doctor will not be liable if upon a reasonable assessment of his patient's condition he takes the view that a warning would be detrimental to his patient's health.

Lord Diplock

In English jurisprudence the doctor's relationship with his patient which gives rise to the normal duty of care to exercise his skill and judgment to improve the patient's health in any particular respect in which the patient has sought his aid, has hitherto been treated as single comprehensive duty covering all the ways in which a doctor is called upon to exercise his skill and judgment in the improvement of the physical or mental condition of the patient for which his services either as a general practitioner or specialist have been engaged. This general duty is not subject to dissection into a number of component parts to which different criteria of what satisfy the duty of care apply, such as diagnosis, treatment, advice (including warning of any risks of something going wrong however skilfully the treatment advised is carried out). The *Bolam* case itself embraced failure to advise the patient of the risk involved in the electric shock treatment as one of the allegations of negligence against the surgeon as well as negligence in the actual carrying out of treatment in which that risk did result in injury to the patient. . . .

In matters of diagnosis and the carrying out of treatment the court is not tempted to put itself in the surgeon's shoes; it has to rely upon and evaluate expert evidence, remembering that it is no part of its task of evaluation to give effect to any preference it may have for one responsible body of professional opinion over another, provided it is satisfied by the expert evidence that both qualify as responsible bodies of medical opinion. But when it comes to warning about risks, the kind of training and experience that a judge will have undergone at the Bar makes it natural for him to say (correctly) it is my right to decide whether any particular thing is done to my body, and I want to be fully informed of any risks there may be involved of which I am not already aware from my general knowledge as a highly educated man of experience, so that I may form my own judgment as to whether to refuse the advised treatment or not.

No doubt if the patient in fact manifested this attitude by means of questioning, the doctor would tell him whatever it was the patient wanted to know; but we are concerned here with volunteering unsought information about risks of the proposed treatment failing to achieve the result sought or making the patient's physical or mental condition worse rather than better. The only effect that mention of risks can have on the patient's mind, if it has any at all, can be in the direction of deterring the patient from undergoing the treatment which in the expert opinion of the doctor it is in the patient's interest to undergo. To decide what risks the existence of which a patient should be voluntarily warned and the terms in which such warning, if any, should be given, having regard to the effect that the warning may have, is as much an exercise of professional skill and judgment as any other part of the doctor's comprehensive duty of care to the individual patient, and expert medical evidence on this matter should be treated in just the same way. The *Bolam* test should be applied.

Lord Bridge (with whom Lord Keith agreed)

I should perhaps add at this point, although the issue does not strictly arise in this appeal, that, when questioned specifically by a patient of apparently sound mind about risks involved in a particular treatment proposed, the doctor's duty must, in my opinion be to answer both truthfully and as fully as the questioner requires.

I recognise the logical force of the *Canterbury* doctrine [see below p. 281], proceeding from the premise that the patient's right to make his own decision must at all costs be safeguarded against the kind of medical paternalism which assumes that 'doctor knows best.' But, with all respect, I regard the doctrine as quite impractical in application for three principal reasons. First, it gives insufficient weight to the realities of the doctor/patient relationship. A very wide variety of factors must enter into a doctor's clinical judgment not only as to what treatment is appropriate for a particular patient, but also as to how best to communicate to the patient the significant factors necessary to enable the patient to make an informed decision whether to undergo the treatment. The doctor cannot set out to educate the patient to his own standard of medical knowledge of all the relevant factors involved. He may take the view, certainly with some patients, that the very fact of his volunteering, without being asked, information of some remote risk involved in the treatment proposed, even though he describes it as remote, may lead to that risk assuming an undue significance in the patient's calculations. Secondly, it would seem to me quite unrealistic in any medical negligence action to confine the expert medical evidence to an explanation of the primary medical factors involved and to deny the court the benefit of evidence of medical opinion and practice on the particular issue of disclosure which is under consideration. Thirdly, the objective test which Canterbury propounds seems to me to be so imprecise as to be almost meaningless. If it is to be left to individual judges to decide for themselves what 'a reasonable person in the patient's position' would consider a risk of sufficient significance that he should be told about it, the outcome of litigation in this field is likely to be quite unpredictable.

. . . [A] decision what degree of disclosure of risks is best calculated to assist a particular patient to make a rational choice as to whether or not to undergo a particular treatment must primarily be a matter of clinical judgment. It would follow from this that the issue whether non-disclosure in a particular case should be condemned as a breach of the doctor's duty of care is an issue to be decided primarily on the basis of expert medical evidence, applying the *Bolam* test. But I do not see that this approach involves the necessity 'to hand over to the medical profession the entire question of the scope of the duty of disclosure, including the question whether there has been a breach of that duty.' Of course, if there is a conflict of evidence as to whether a responsible body of medical opinion approves of non-disclosure in a particular case, the judge will have to resolve that conflict. But even in a case where, as here, no expert witness in the relevant medical field condemns the non-disclosure as being in conflict with accepted and responsible medical practice, I am of opinion that the judge might in certain circumstances come to the conclusion that disclosure of a particular risk was so obviously necessary to an informed choice on the part of the patient that no reasonably prudent medical man would fail to make it. The kind of case I have in mind would be an operation involving a substantial risk of grave adverse consequences, as, for example, the ten per cent risk of a stroke from the operation which was the subject of the Canadian case of *Reibl v. Hughes.*

Lord Templeman

There is no doubt that a doctor ought to draw the attention of a patient to a danger which may be special in kind or magnitude or special to the patient. . . .

Whenever the occasion arises for the doctor to tell the patient the results of the doctor's diagnosis, the possible methods of treatment and the advantages and disadvantages of the recommended treatment, the doctor must decide in the light of his training and experience and in the light of his knowledge of the patient what should be said and how it should be said. At the same time the doctor is not entitled to make the final decision with regard to treatment which may have disadvantages or dangers. Where the patient's health and future are at stake, the patient must make the final decision. The patient is free to decide whether or not to submit to treatment recommended by the doctor and therefore the doctor impliedly contracts to provide information which is adequate to enable the patient to reach a balanced judgment, subject always to the doctor's own obligation to say and do nothing which the doctor is satisfied will be harmful to the patient. . . .

At the end of the day, the doctor, bearing in mind the best interests of the patient and bearing in mind the patient's right of information which will enable the patient to make a balanced judgment must decide what information should be given to the patient and in what terms that information should be couched.

Lord Diplock thought that the *Bolam* test applied to all aspects of a doctor's duty of care, and saw no reason to treat advice differently from diagnosis and treatment: the doctor's disclosure should therefore be judged by its conformity with responsible medical practice. At the other extreme, Lord Scarman argued that the doctor's duty of disclosure arose from the patient's 'basic human right' to make her own medical decisions. He was persuaded that the common law should follow the example set in cases from Canada and the US, and adopt a 'prudent patient' test (discussed in more detail below at p. 281): the doctor's duty should be to disclose that which a reasonable, prudent person in this patient's position would want to know, subject only to the 'therapeutic privilege', discussed below at p. 284.

Falling somewhere in between are the judgments of Lord Bridge, with whom Lord Keith agreed, and Lord Templeman. Lord Bridge 'recognized the logical force of the doctrine of informed consent', but for three reasons regarded it as 'quite impractical'. First, he said it gave 'insufficient weight to the doctor–patient relationship', because doctors could not be expected to educate patients to their own level of understanding. But, with respect, this makes little sense: the prudent patient test demands *adequate*, not full disclosure. Very remote or trivial risks would not have to be disclosed, because the prudent patient would not consider them material. Secondly, he argued that it would be unrealistic to 'deny the court evidence of medical opinion and practice on disclosure'. It is not entirely clear what he means by this: the fact that evidence of medical practice exists does not necessarily mean that it should be decisive. If there are sound reasons for judging the reasonableness of a doctor's disclosure by what patients generally want to know, then evidence of this—rather than customary medical practice—should be determinative. Thirdly, he said that judging what the reasonable person in the patient's position would want to know is 'almost meaningless', and would lead to unpredictability in litigation. Again, with respect this criticism seems misplaced since the whole tort of negligence depends upon the judiciary's application, and greater specification of the reasonable man test.

Having rejected the prudent patient test, Lord Bridge went on to fashion a modified *Bolam* test. Disclosure, he argued, was *'primarily* a matter of clinical judgment', but this did not mean that the profession was entirely free to set its own standards of disclosure. Rather in certain circumstances, the judge might conclude that a risk ought to have been disclosed even if there was a body of responsible medical opinion which would not have warned the patient of it. The sort of risk he had in mind was 'an operation involving a substantial risk of grave adverse consequences', and the example he gave was a 10 per cent risk of a stroke. But while we know that Lord Bridge believed that a 1–2 per cent risk of spinal cord damage was not a substantial risk of grave adverse consequences, and a 10 per cent risk of a stroke was such a risk, his judgment begs the question of how to draw the line in between these two points of certainty. Is a 5 per cent risk of a stroke sufficient; or a 2 per cent risk of death? Aside from the grey area problem, Ian Kennedy points out that Lord Bridge's qualification to the *Bolam* test also 'beg[s] the central question: "substantial" and "grave" to whom?'[24] It cannot be to the doctor because otherwise this would simply restate the *Bolam* test which Lord Bridge instead intends to qualify. If it is 'substantial and grave' to *this* patient, then this would introduce a subjective patient-orientated standard, which again would be inconsistent with Lord Bridge's rejection of the less radical objective prudent patient test. Instead, Ian Kennedy suggests that Lord Bridge must mean that the *court* should judge whether a particular risk is substantial and grave.[25] Ironically, in practice this assessment would not be very different from what the courts would have to do if they were to apply the prudent patient test which Lord Bridge had earlier dismissed as unworkable.

Lord Templeman also advocated a modified *Bolam* test. There is, he argued, 'no doubt that a doctor ought to draw the attention of a patient to a danger which may be special in kind or magnitude or special to the patient'. When a risk is 'special', the *Bolam* test is not necessarily decisive, and a judge may decide that nondisclosure was negligent despite evidence of its conformity with responsible medical practice. But of course, this again begs the question of what qualifies as a 'special' risk. It is notable that Lord Templeman expressly includes risks which are special to the patient, even though they are not special in kind or magnitude. This looks very like a test which judges the reasonableness of disclosure from the *patient's* rather than the doctor's perspective.

Four years later, the Court of Appeal in *Gold v Haringey HA*[26] adopted a rather surprising interpretation of the judgments in *Sidaway*. Despite the views of Lords Bridge, Keith, and Templeman that it would be negligent not to warn a patient of a

---

[24] *Treat Me Right* (OUP Oxford 1988) 200–1.   [25] Ibid, 201.   [26] [1988] QB 481.

risk which was either 'substantial and grave' or 'special', the Court of Appeal in *Gold* simply stated that the House of Lords in *Sidaway* had applied the *Bolam* test. The only judgment referred to was that of Lord Diplock, whose straightforward application of *Bolam* did not represent the slightly more nuanced approach of the majority.

Gold v Haringey HA[27]

In 1979, the claimant underwent a sterilization operation at the defendants' hospital. She subsequently became pregnant and gave birth to her fourth child. She brought an action for damages for negligence against the defendants alleging, inter alia, that she had not been warned of the failure rate of female sterilization operations and that if she had been warned her husband would have undergone a vasectomy instead. Medical evidence was that a substantial body of responsible doctors would not have given any such warning in 1979. The judge nevertheless found that the defendants had been negligent, and the defendants' appealed to the Court of Appeal. The Court of Appeal allowed their appeal.

Lloyd LJ

In *Sidaway* the House of Lords applied the [*Bolam*] test to a case in which a doctor, before carrying out an operation, failed to warn his patient of a very small risk of very serious injury. It would have been open to the House of Lords to hold that the *Bolam* test applied to negligent diagnosis and negligent treatment, but not negligent advice. In other words, the House of Lords could have adopted the doctrine of 'informed consent' favoured in the United States of America and Canada. But the House of Lords declined to follow that path.

If there had been any doubt on the question, which I do not think there was, it was removed by the speech of Lord Diplock in the *Sidaway* case . . . It is clear from Lord Diplock's speech in *Sidaway* that a doctor's duty of care in relation to diagnosis, treatment and advice, whether the doctor be a specialist or general practitioner, is not to be dissected into its component parts.

Since the judgment in *Sidaway*, there have been very few cases involving the failure to disclose information, and fewer still in which the courts have decided that a doctor's failure to disclose information was negligent. Two rare examples are first, *McAllister v Lewisham and North Southward HA*,[28] in which a failure to disclose a risk of sensory deficit associated with a particular type of brain surgery, which the defendant's own expert witness put at 100 per cent, was found to be negligent. And second, *Smith v Tunbridge Wells Health Authority*,[29] in which Morland J found that while some surgeons in 1988 might not have warned a 28-year-old man of the risk of impotence associated with an operation to repair a rectal prolapse, 'that omission was neither reasonable nor responsible'. In 1999, Michael Jones reported that he had found thirty cases since 1984 in which 'informed consent' was an issue. It was the sole basis of the claim in nine cases.[30] Eleven claimants successfully established that there had been a breach of duty, but four of these then failed to prove causation. Only seven cases had ultimately been successful.

It is not clear that the paucity of litigation in this area can be explained solely by the English courts' failure to adopt a patient-centred test for disclosure. On the contrary, evidence from other countries suggests that there will be little litigation and very few successful claims regardless of whether doctors are under a duty to comply with the

---

[27] Ibid (CA).   [28] [1994] 5 Med LR 343.   [29] Ibid 334, at 339
[30] Michael Jones, 'Informed Consent and other Fairy Stories' (1999) 7 Medical Law Review 103–34.

prudent patient test for disclosure. In Gerald Robertson's study of informed consent cases in Canada in the ten years following *Reibl v Hughes*,[31] the first Canadian case to recognize a prudent patient standard of disclosure, it was the sole basis of only 11 per cent of medical malpractice claims. The informed consent claim was dismissed in 82 per cent of cases (compared with an average failure rate of 44 per cent in other malpractice actions). Of the claimants who managed to prove that there had been a breach of duty, 56 per cent failed to establish causation. Contrary to the assumption underlying the English courts' rejection of the prudent patient test, in practice it does not appear to have opened the much feared 'floodgates'.

Of course, as we saw in Chapter 3, since *Sidaway*, the House of Lords judgment in *Bolitho v City and Hackney HA*[32] modified the *Bolam* test by emphasizing the need for the medical opinion to be 'responsible' and 'reasonable', so that when a doctor seeks to rely upon the evidence of other doctors who say that they would have acted in the same way, the courts will nevertheless be prepared to make a finding of negligence where the professional opinion in question 'is not capable of withstanding logical analysis'. Although Lord Browne-Wilkinson in *Bolitho* was careful to specify that his judgment applied to questions of diagnosis and treatment, and not to disclosure of risk, is *Bolitho* nevertheless evidence of a trend towards greater judicial willingness to challenge clinical judgment?

In *Pearce v United Bristol Healthcare NHS Trusts*, the Court of Appeal did appear to move a little closer to the 'reasonable patient' test in determining whether a risk of stillbirth associated with waiting for a natural birth should have been disclosed to a pregnant woman whose baby was two weeks overdue.

Pearce v United Bristol Healthcare NHS Trust[33]

Tina Pearce's sixth child was about two weeks overdue when she saw the consultant responsible for her care at the respondent hospital, the United Bristol Healthcare Trust. She was very distressed, and begged to have an induced labour or a caesarean section. The consultant, however, thought it appropriate to let nature take its course, and for her to have a normal birth without any medical intervention. He explained that it would be very risky to induce the birth, and that it would take longer for her to recover if she had a caesarean section. She accepted his advice. The baby died in utero a few days later. The following issues were raised at the trial: (1) Should the consultant have advised Mrs Pearce that there was a small increased risk of stillbirth as a result of the delay in delivery? (2) If the consultant should have so advised, would his advice have altered her decision to have a natural birth? The trial judge dismissed Mrs Pearce's claim, and she appealed to the Court of Appeal. Her appeal was dismissed.

Lord Woolf MR

The views of the majority [in *Sidaway*] most clearly appear from the speech of Lord Bridge of Harwich, with which Lord Keith of Kinkel agreed. However, Lord Diplock also gave a speech, which adopted the same approach as that of Lord Bridge. That approach involved applying the *Bolam* test to the giving, or failure to give, advice. . . . While recognising that Lord Templeman's approach is not precisely that of the majority, it seems to me that that statement of Lord Templeman does reflect the law and does not involve taking a different view from the majority. . . .

In a case where it is being alleged that a plaintiff has been deprived of the opportunity to make

---

[31] 114 DLR (3d) 1.   [32] [1998] AC 232.   [33] (1998) 48 BMLR 118 [CA].

a proper decision as to what course he or she should take in relation to treatment, it seems to me to be the law, as indicated in the cases to which I have just referred, that if there is a significant risk which would affect the judgment of a reasonable patient, then in the normal course it is the responsibility of a doctor to inform the patient of that significant risk, if the information is needed so that the patient can determine for him or herself as to what course he or she should adopt. . . .

Turning to the facts of this case, the next question is, therefore, 'Was there a significant risk? . . . [O]n any basis, the increased risk of the stillbirth of Jacqueline, as a result of additional delay, was very small indeed . . . Even looked at comprehensively it comes to something like 0.1–0.2%. The doctors called on behalf of the defendants did not regard that risk as significant; nor do I . . .

Particularly when one bears in mind Mrs Pearce's distressed condition, one cannot criticise Mr Niven's decision not to inform Mrs Pearce of that very, very small additional risk. . . . This is a case where, in my judgment, it would not be proper for the courts to interfere with the clinical opinion of the expert medical man responsible for treating Mrs Pearce.

As to what would have been the consequence if she had been told of this particularly small risk, it is difficult to envisage . . ., but my conclusion is that, in so far as it was possible for this court to make an assessment of this, the inference is that if Mrs Pearce had been able to understand what she had been told about the increased risk, her decision would still have been to follow, reluctantly, the advice of the doctor who was treating her, namely Mr Niven.

But while Lord Woolf MR's statement that 'a significant risk which would affect the judgment of the reasonable patient' should be disclosed appears to indicate a more robust commitment to the patient's right to information, note that in deciding whether the doctors should have disclosed a 0.1–0.2 per cent risk of stillbirth, Lord Woolf said that '*the doctors* called on behalf of the defendants did not regard that risk as significant, nor do I' (my emphasis). Thus he appeared to rely upon the *doctors'* judgment of whether the risk was 'significant', and not on Tina Pearce's own assessment of whether the risk was sufficiently material that it would have affected her decision to accept medical advice and proceed to a natural birth.

Nevertheless, in *Wyatt v Curtis*,[34] a case in which a woman was not warned about the risk of abnormality as a result of her having contracted chicken pox during pregnancy, Sedley LJ suggested that Lord Woolf's approach in *Pearce* 'refines' Lord Bridge's judgment in *Sidaway* by explaining that whether a risk is 'substantial' or 'grave' should be assessed from the patient's and not the doctor's point of view.

Lord Woolf's formulation refines Lord Bridge's test by recognising that what is substantial and what is grave are questions on which the doctor's and the patient's perception may differ, and in relation to which the doctor must therefore have regard to what may be the patient's perception. To the doctor, a chance in a hundred that the patient's chickenpox may produce an abnormality in the foetus may well be an insubstantial chance, and an abnormality may in any case not be grave. To the patient, a new risk which (as I read the judge's appraisal of the expert evidence) doubles, or at least enhances, the background risk of a potentially catastrophic abnormality may well be both substantial and grave, or at least sufficiently real for her to want to make an informed decision about it.

And in the recent House of Lords judgment in *Chester v Afshar*,[35] a case we discuss in

---

[34] [2003] EWCA Civ 1779 judgment available on Lexis.   [35] [2004] UKHL 41, [2004] 3 WLR 927.

detail below at p. 295, Lord Steyn also quoted with approval Lord Woolf's approach, and went on to say:

A surgeon owes a legal duty to a patient to warn him or her in general terms of possible serious risks involved in the procedure. The only qualification is that there may be wholly exceptional cases where objectively in the best interests of the patient the surgeon may be excused from giving a warning. This is, however, irrelevant in the present case. In modern law medical paternalism no longer rules and a patient has a prima facie right to be informed by a surgeon of a small, but well established, risk of serious injury as a result of surgery.

Again notice that while Lord Steyn states that the duty is to warn the patient about 'serious' risks, it is not clear whether the seriousness of the injury should be judged from the patient's or the doctor's perspective. Nevertheless, Lord Steyn's rejection of 'medical paternalism' may be further evidence of a gradual shift towards the adoption of a reasonable patient test.

A further, but less frequently discussed practical problem lies in establishing what information was, in fact, disclosed to the patient. Patients are unlikely to have made notes during their encounter with the doctor, and many years later, may not be able to accurately recall what they were told. Doctors' notes seldom record every detail of the conversations they have had with patients, and it is often difficult for doctors to remember exactly what passed between them and one individual patient, particularly if their encounter took place some years ago. The courts will therefore often be faced with two contradictory accounts of the discussions that took place prior to treatment. Evidence of a doctor's usual practice will sometimes be relevant, though in many cases, the judge will simply have to decide who is the more credible witness. In *Chatterton v Gerson*,[36] for example, Bristow J believed the doctors' account of the pre-operation discussions:

I have come to the conclusion that on the balance of probability Dr. Gerson did give his usual explanation about the intrathecal phenol solution nerve block and its implications of numbness instead of pain plus a possibility of slight muscle weakness, and that the plaintiff's recollection is wrong; and on the evidence before me I so find.

Whereas in the first instance decision in *Chester v Afshar*, the trial judge had preferred the claimant's account on the grounds that it had the 'ring of truth and [was] most unlikely to be the result of either invention or reconstruction'.[37]

Having examined the way in which English law approaches the question of the standard of care, let us now turn to critically evaluate the three possible options: (a) the reasonable doctor test; (b) the prudent patient test, and (c) the subjective standard, as well as the 'therapeutic privilege' exception.

(b) The reasonable doctor test

The reasonable doctor test suffers from a number of disadvantages. First, and most importantly, it does not protect the patient's right to self-determination. The central problem with employing a professional standard test in order to determine what information patients need in order to make informed choices about their medical

---

[36] [1981] QB 432.   [37] [2002] EWCACiv 724, [2003] QB 356.

treatment is that, unlike diagnosis and treatment, this is not a question which requires clinical expertise. On the contrary, if the patient has the right to decide whether to consent to a proposed treatment, she can only exercise meaningful choice over this decision if she has sufficient information to allow her to weigh the advantages and disadvantages of the treatment in question, in the light of her own values and priorities. Medical progress has expanded the range of available treatment options, and there is also always the possibility of declining treatment altogether. As Harry Lesser explains in the next extract, most treatments will have side-effects, the acceptability of which can be judged only from the patient's own perspective. Cancer of the throat can, for example, be treated by surgery or by radiation. Surgery is more effective, but will deprive the patient of normal speech. Only the patient herself can determine whether the higher chance of prolonging life outweighs the reduction in the quality of her life. Harvey Teff, for example, explains that:

The relative importance which patients attach, for example, to quality as against length of life, and to physical integrity or appearance as against diminution of pain, may reflect personal values, circumstances and priorities of which the surgeon, in particular, is initially unaware and may never become sufficiently apprised.[38]

Harry Lesser[39]

The obvious merit of the older model is that it gives the power of decision to the person with the most relevant knowledge; doctors are not of course infallible, but they are more likely to be right than someone ignorant of medicine. However, matters are in practice by no means so simple. In the first place, there is not always a medically best course of action, for two reasons. One is that medicine has at least three aims—to prolong life, to remove obstacles to a person's physical and mental functioning and to relieve suffering. Very often these three all come together . . . But this is not always so; if, for example, the choice is to relieve pain at the cost of leaving patients feeling 'woozy' and confused, or to help them to be mentally alert at the cost of appreciable physical pain, then there is no 'better' course of action, even medically, except in terms of the individual patient's preference, whichever it may be: it is honourable to choose alertness and the price of physical suffering, but in no way dishonourable to choose the reverse . . .

Even where the aim is clear, and agreed on by doctor and patient—for example to cure a particular disease or malfunctioning—it may not be possible to produce a 'right' or 'correct' ordering of the possible lines of treatment. This is because types of treatment can differ in at least five ways: in the likelihood of success, the degree of success possible, the seriousness of the 'side-effects' (which are also not all of the same type), the seriousness of the harm if things go wrong and the degree of risk that things might go wrong. . . . Once again, doctors' expertise enables them to know the possible consequences of various alternatives and to have some idea of their likelihood; but there is still no right answer to the question which alternative is best, which risks are worth taking and which are not, except in terms of what the patient chooses . . .

Even if one can say—as sometimes one can—that a particular treatment is clearly medically best . . . there may still be valid non-medical reasons for rejecting it: it may, for example, be vitally important for someone to postpone going into hospital to attend to essential family or business matters, even if medically they should go in at once.

[38] Harvey Teff, 'Consent to Medical Procedures: Paternalism, Self-Determination or Therapeutic Alliance' (1985) 101 Law Quarterly Review 432–53.
[39] 'The Patient's Right to Information' in Margaret Brazier and Mary Lobjoit (eds), *Protecting the Vulnerable: Autonomy and Consent in Health Care* (Routledge London 1991) 150–60, 153–4.

Secondly, there may be a tension between English law's robust defence of a patient's right to refuse medical treatment 'for rational reasons, for irrational reasons or for no reasons at all',[40] and its much more paternalistic approach to the provision of information. The patient's right to make her own decision about whether to consent to a particular procedure is rigorously protected by the judiciary, and yet the information which may be necessary in order to take full advantage of this right to self-determination can be withheld with relative impunity.

Thirdly, the reasonable doctor test inevitably emphasizes the question of what the doctor actually said: would other doctors have said similar things to patients in these circumstances? But if the purpose of giving information to patients is to ensure informed decision-making, the question should instead be: does the patient have an adequate *understanding* of the relative advantages and disadvantages of treatment. Individual patients' capacity to understand complex information about risk will vary considerably. English is not every patient's first language. Simply offering each patient a standardized information sheet may absolve a doctor of negligence, but it is by no means an ideal way to promote meaningful patient choice.

Fourthly, the emphasis on consent implies a paternalistic model of medical decision-making in which a doctor offers the patient one possible course of treatment, which she can then accept or decline. But there is rarely only one possible course of action, and so framing the issue in this way already implicitly accepts that the doctor should have the power to determine which treatment is appropriate, with the patient's only option being to agree with the doctor, or reject treatment altogether. Choice, on the other hand, is a much more patient-centred concept which might involve much greater emphasis upon the various alternative courses of action open to the patient.

Fifthly, the reasonable doctor test offers little prospective guidance for doctors faced with the question: 'what am I legally required to disclose to this patient?' The rather cryptic and unhelpful answer to this question must be that a doctor should tell the patient that which no reasonably prudent doctor would fail to disclose, as determined retrospectively by a court. Sixthly, it is, as Ian Kennedy points out in the next extract, arguable whether a common professional standard for the disclosure of information could be said to exist at all. But even if it does, customary practice might itself be wholly inadequate and would be perpetuated by a reasonable doctor standard of disclosure.

Ian Kennedy[41]

In the context of the disclosure of information, the very notion of a professional standard is something of a nonsense. *There simply is no such standard,* if only because the profession has not got together to establish which risks should be disclosed to which patients in which circumstances. That the profession has, by contrast, got together and established which treatment should be attempted for which patients is, if you will, strong evidence of what their sphere of competence is and should be. Furthermore, in the absence of a professional standard, the likelihood exists of doctors affirming that Dr X's conduct was, in the circumstances proper, out of some sense, misguided or otherwise, of professional solidarity. If such a state of affairs were to occur, it would

---

[40] See, eg, *Re MB (An Adult: Medical Treatment)* [1997] 2 FLR 426 and *Re T* [1993] Fam 95.
[41] *Treat Me Right* (OUP Oxford 1988) 189–90.

do nothing for patient confidence and could well foster a sense of bitterness of frustration, out of which might grow further litigation. . . .

Is defensive medicine a real possibility, or another example of hyperbole? Again, it is the latter. To begin with, one doctor's defensive medicine may well be another's idea of good practice. In other words, it may simply be a term to describe that kind of careful medicine which ought to be practised, but which some find irksome. Next, to engage in a dialogue with a patient, in which the doctor explains the nature and implications of treatment, can hardly be called defensive medicine. It can only be described properly as good medicine. The legal test need only be that the doctor does what is reasonable in disclosing risks, just as he is required to do in the case of treatment and diagnosis. If sensitive guidance were available on what may be reasonable—what, for example, a prudent patient in a particular patient's circumstances might wish to know, and what amounted to justifiable exceptions—there need be no more defensive medicine than there is now. It is uncertainty about what is ethically and legally called for which may cause doctors to act defensively.

Finally, the reasonable doctor test largely ignores the role of other health care professionals who are not medical practitioners. Nurses, for example, may have more time to spend discussing treatment options, and might be better at communicating with patients than doctors.

The advantage of a reasonable doctor test for the standard of disclosure is its comparative ease of application. Should a doctor be sued in negligence, expert witnesses can—as in other malpractice actions—offer evidence of whether other doctors would in fact have acted in the same way if faced with a similar patient. In contrast, if the test is instead what this patient would want to know, doctors will be forced to guess what might matter to this patient. It is increasingly rare for doctors—particularly those carrying out specialist treatments such as surgery—to have had any contact at all with the patient prior to their admittance to hospital. Without knowing anything about the patient's values and goals, the doctor has no way of determining which pieces of information matter to her. In order to avoid liability, the doctor may therefore be tempted to give the patient more information than she could possibly digest, thereby reducing rather than enhancing her ability to make an informed choice.

(c) The prudent patient test

In order to address the defects of the reasonable doctor test, what has become known as the 'prudent patient' test has gained favour in some states in the US, and in Canada, Australia, and New Zealand. Probably its most famous formulation is taken from the 1972 US case *Canterbury v Spence*: A risk must be disclosed:

when a reasonable person, in what the physician knows or should know to be the patient's position, would be likely to attach significance to the risk or cluster of risks in deciding whether or not to forgo the proposed therapy.

Similarly, in the leading Australian case, *Rogers v Whitaker*,[42] a risk was defined as material if:

[42] (1992) 175 CLR 479.

In the circumstances of the particular case, a reasonable person in the patient's position, if warned of the risk, would be likely to attach significance to it or if the medical practitioner is, or should reasonably be aware that the particular patient, if warned of the risk, would be likely to attach significance to it.

But the prudent patient test is itself not without disadvantages. How are doctors supposed to know in advance what the abstract hypothetical reasonable patient would want to know? Since the standard of care in a particular case could only be conclusively determined *retrospectively* by the courts, the doctor will have to second guess the court's assessment of what a reasonable patient would consider material. Since there are very few cases in this area, and even fewer readily accessible legal judgments, doctors facing a decision about how much information to provide to a particular patient will gain little practical assistance from consulting the law. Instead, they are likely to seek guidance from *other doctors* as to what patients generally want to know. It is easy to see how in practice this test could become indistinguishable from the reasonable doctor test.

The authors of the next extract suggest, perhaps a little optimistically, that any inherent difficulty in knowing what patients want to know will in practice encourage doctors to spend more time finding out what matters to their patients, thus improving patient care.

Paul S Appelbaum, Charles W Lidz, and Alan Meisel[43]

The patient-oriented standard imposes upon physicians more substantial obligations than does the professional standard . . . Physicians have reasonably ready ways of knowing what the [professional] standard is and of complying with it. Medical education and supervised clinical training, formal continuing education, and informal discourse among colleagues all help to inform physicians as to what it is customary to tell patients about treatment. For the same reasons that the content of the standard is easily accessible to physicians, it is relatively simple to establish in a trial, assuming that other physicians are willing to serve as expert witnesses.

By contrast, the content of the patient-oriented standard is especially difficult for physicians to ascertain. The professional standard is factual and therefore empirically determinable; the patient-oriented standard is hypothetical. It requires physicians to disclose the information that a reasonably prudent person would find material to making a decision. . . .

The very difficulty in knowing and applying the patient-oriented standard turns out to be its virtue (though possibly not from physicians' perspective). To determine what a reasonable patient would find material to making a decision, physicians are compelled to engage in a discussion with each patient. In so doing, they act to implement one of the fundamental goals of the idea of informed consent: to inform patients in decision making about their own care.

Against this, it could be argued that, just like the reasonable doctor test, the prudent patient test cannot adequately protect patient self-determination. Individual patients' interest in information will vary dramatically. People have different priorities, beliefs and family histories, all of which will affect the relative importance they attach to the risks and benefits of medical treatment. While all patients would want to know about risks that are very likely to materialize or which have potentially grave consequences, lesser risks may only be significant to certain patients. Giving all patients

---

[43] *Informed Consent: Legal Theory and Clinical Practice* (OUP Oxford 1987) 45–6.

the information that the abstract reasonable patient requires might be preferable to the *Bolam* standard of disclosure, but it will result in some patients being deprived of facts about a proposed treatment which are in fact of vital importance to them. As we shall see later, this problem may be exacerbated by the application of a quasi-objective 'reasonable patient' test for causation. If the claimant must prove not that she herself would have refused treatment if she had been properly informed, but rather that the reasonable patient would not have consented to the treatment in question, the right to act according to one's own preferences and priorities is not protected at all.

(d) The subjective standard

In the next extract, Alexander Capron argues that only a subjective standard of disclosure can adequately protect patient autonomy, since it acknowledges that people have highly variable informational needs, and imposes a duty upon doctors to tailor their disclosures according to the individual patient's own priorities and concerns.

Alexander Morgan Capron[44]

The importance of a subjective rather than an objective standard of materiality can be seen by comparing how well each standard would serve the functions of informed consent. For example, a physician-investigator's self scrutiny is likely to be increased if he has to ask, 'Is this procedure right for this patient, based on what I actually know about him or her?' and not on what is known about the 'reasonable patient'. The very routine nature of the latter does nothing to promote reexamination on the part of the physician-investigator as he plans how he will explain the proposed intervention to the patient-subject. The requirement that the physician-investigator individualize the informing process is consistent with the obligation to individualize the diagnostic and therapeutic processes. Similarly, the respect for the patient-subject as a full human being is better served by a subjective standard.

In practice, however, a subjective standard would prove almost impossible to enforce. Patients will rarely be able to articulate all of their relevant values, background characteristics and goals during a brief consultation. Within the modern and increasingly impersonal health care system, doctors cannot be expected to know enough about their individual patients' characters and beliefs to accurately predict what factors will be material to their decisionmaking, and it would be unfair to hold doctors liable in negligence for their inability to anticipate all of their patients' idiosyncratic values and priorities. On the contrary, patients must rely on their doctors to make judgments about what factors are likely to be important to them. And of course, in making this assessment, doctors will inevitably rely on evidence both of what other doctors generally do in such circumstances, and of what patients generally appear to want to know.

This is not to say that the subjective standard should be completely dismissed as an impractical moral ideal. Rather, while practical considerations mean that it would be difficult for it to ground the test of liability in negligence, it might nevertheless be important for doctors to at least attempt to discover the individual patient's subjective priorities through appropriate questioning. In the next extract, Ruth Faden et al.

---

[44] 'Informed Consent in Catastrophic Disease Research and Treatment' (1974) 123 University of Pennsylvania Law Review 340, 416–17.

advocate a shift away from standards of disclosure towards a duty to enter into an 'informational exchange' with patients.

Ruth R Faden, Tom L Beauchamp, with Nancy MP King[45]

What should a professional disclose in order to obtain consents based on substantial understanding? At first glance it might appear that any attempt is doomed to failure. On the one hand, because there are no intersubjective criteria for distinguishing material from immaterial information, any stock disclosure . . . is inappropriate. Yet if the subjective standard is adopted, it is often difficult, if not impossible, for a physician or a researcher to guess correctly what would be material to a prospective patient or subject, especially a complete stranger . . .

[T]he solution lies not in reformulations of conventional or proposed legal disclosure standards, but rather in the adoption of a different approach to understanding and informed consent—an approach that focuses more broadly on issues of communication, while dispensing with abstract and disembodied issues about proper *standards* of disclosure . . .

From the perspective of informed consent . . ., disclosure standards requiring a specified quantum of information are not only insufficient, but present an entirely misleading approach to the issues. Such disclosure standards are not adequate to protect autonomous decisionmaking, because the emphasis on disclosure is the wrong emphasis. The central question is not merely, 'What facts should the professional provide?' but 'What should the professional ask and say?' and, as we see shortly, 'How should the professional act?' Traditional questions about adequate disclosures need to be reformulated as questions about effective communication. This entails use of a subjective standard of understanding.

The key to effective communication is to invite active participation by patients or subjects in the context of an informational exchange. . . . Professionals would do well to end their traditional preoccupation with disclosure and instead ask questions, elicit the concerns and interests of the patient or subject, and establish a climate that encourages the patient or subject to ask questions. This is the most promising course to ensure that the patient or subject will receive information that is personally material—that is, the kind of description that will permit the subject or patient, on the basis of his or her personal values, desires, and beliefs, to act with substantial autonomy.

Finally, it could also be argued that there is a tension between the therapeutic privilege, discussed in the following section—which is subjectively assessed—and the standard of care. Why should doctors be entitled to take into account the patient's special sensibilities when deciding *not* to tell them about a particular risk, while their special sensibilities are irrelevant to the decision to disclose information?

(e) Therapeutic privilege

In *Sidaway*, Lord Scarman accepted that the 'prudent patient' test should, if it were adopted by English law, be subject to one exception, namely the doctor's therapeutic privilege, according to which there is no duty to disclose information which might be positively harmful to patients. If a doctor believes that a patient's likely reaction to a particular piece of information would be likely to cause a serious deterioration in her condition, then that information may reasonably be withheld. In the next extract, Len Doyal suggests that there may be circumstances in which selective non-communication will in fact protect the patient's capacity to exercise informed choice later on.

---

[45] *A History and Theory of Informed Consent* (OUP Oxford 1986) 306–7.

Len Doyal[46]

[S]uppose that an oncologist is faced with a 'rational' (that is, non-psychiatrically ill) patient who is so anxious about possible bad news that any attempt at complete truth will probably meet with misunderstanding. In this case, a decision to be selective with information may well be taken in order to respect the right of the patient to make an *informed* choice later on. If one froze such a decision in time then no doubt it would appear to be paternalistic. Yet when the process of informing and understanding is seen as precisely that—a process over time involving complex intellectual and emotional interaction between clinician and patient—then accusations of paternalism may not be correct. Of course, there is still the question of how long to sequence the information and what to do if the anxiety does not abate. In practice, the answers to such questions are sometimes unclear because of the contingencies of patient competence and the difficulties of knowing what it means to respect autonomy when confronted with them. Clinicians must just do the best they can. Provided that informed consent remains their *short-term* goal so that any important choices the patient may wish to make is not precluded, and that they are careful not to be selective in their communication for any other reason than to optimize patients' understanding (for example, the patient's distress *per se* or their own discomfort at the patient's reaction to bad news), then their actions are not paternalistic in any invidious sense of the word.

Because the therapeutic privilege exception allows the doctor's paternalistic concern for her patient's best interests to trump the principle of patient self-determination, as Ruth Faden et al. point out, its precise scope must be tightly circumscribed if it is not to undermine the patient's ability to make informed choices about her medical treatment.

Ruth R Faden, Tom L Beauchamp, with Nancy MP King[47]

If framed broadly, [the therapeutic privilege] can permit physicians to withhold information if disclosure would cause *any* countertherapeutic deterioration, however slight, in the physical, psychological, or emotional condition of the patient. If framed narrowly, it can permit the physician to withhold information if and only if the patient's knowledge of the information would have *serious* health-related consequences—for example, by jeopardizing the success of the treatment or harming the patient psychologically by critically impairing relevant decisionmaking processes.

The *Canterbury* decision represents a narrow account:

The [therapeutic privilege] exception obtains [if] risk-disclosure poses such a threat of detriment to the patient as to become unfeasible or contraindicated from a medical point of view. It is recognized that patients occasionally become so ill or emotionally distraught on disclosure as *to foreclose a rational decision,* or complicate or hinder the treatment, or perhaps even pose psychological damage to the patient.

The narrowest possible formulation is narrower still; it is analogous to the incompetence exception, because it can be validly invoked only if the physician reasonably believes disclosure would render the patient incompetent to consent to or refuse the treatment, that is, would render the decision nonautonomous. To invoke the therapeutic privilege under such circumstances does not conflict with respect for autonomy, as an autonomous decision could not be made in any event. However, broader formulations of the privilege that require only 'medical contraindication' of some sort do operate at the expense of autonomy. These formulations may unjustifiably endanger

---

[46] 'Medical Ethics and Moral Indeterminacy' (1990) 17 Journal of Law and Society 1–16, 9.
[47] *A History and Theory of Informed Consent* (OUP Oxford 1986).

autonomous choice altogether, as when the invocation of the privilege is based on the belief that an autonomous patient, if informed, would refuse an indicated therapy for what the medical community views as incorrect or inappropriate reasons.

In particular, it is important that information is not withheld just because it might prompt the patient to refuse treatment which the doctor believes to be in her best interests. If this came within the therapeutic privilege exception, patients' right to refuse treatment would be substantially diminished by the indirect resurrection of the paternalistic assumption that it is doctors alone who should decide what treatment a patient should undergo. A better and narrower formulation would allow doctors to invoke the therapeutic privilege exception only if the patient would suffer physical or mental harm *other than that which the doctor believes would be caused by her decision to refuse to have the treatment in question*. This is enshrined in the GMC's guidance to doctors:

You should not withhold information necessary for decision making unless you judge that disclosure of some relevant information would cause the patient serious harm. In this context serious harm does not mean the patient would become upset, or decide to refuse treatment.[48]

But while therapeutic privilege does allow beneficence (or the doctor's duty to act in her patient's best interests) to trump respect for patient self-determination in certain exceptional circumstances, it is not in practice synonymous with the reasonable doctor test because the presumption is still in favour of disclosure. In order to invoke the therapeutic privilege exception, the burden of proof would be on the doctor to establish that she had reasonable grounds for believing that non-disclosure was indicated in this particular situation.

(f) When and how should information be provided

It is plainly not sufficient that doctors should simply give patients information about a proposed course of treatment without any attempt to ensure that the patient has understood what they have been told. Information must be comprehensible, and should be communicated in a way that facilitates understanding. It is therefore important for health care professionals to take reasonable steps to present information in a way that patients will be able to understand, and to ensure that the context in which disclosures are made is appropriate. If English is not the patient's first language, access to translated information, or to an interpreter might be necessary.

However comprehensive the disclosure, giving a patient information about the risks associated with surgery immediately before or after an operation might nevertheless be negligent. For example, in *Lybert v Warrington HA*[49] the surgeon discussed the irreversibility of sterilization, and the risks of failing to achieve sterility immediately after the patient had undergone the operation. The court concluded that the surgeon had been negligent because the warning was not sufficiently emphatic and clear, and because the timing and the conditions in which it was given were inappropriate.

---

[48] *Seeking patients' consent: the ethical considerations*, Nov 1998, para 10.
[49] [1996] 7 Med LR 71.

It is also important that the task of informing patients about the risks and benefits associated with the various treatment options is taken seriously, and not, for example, delegated to junior medical staff who may have little experience of communicating with patients, and whose ability to answer patients' questions may be limited. There is also a danger that obtaining patients' consent to medical treatment is perceived by some doctors to be a formal bureaucratic legal requirement, that offers protection against future litigation, but which can be fulfilled by the information contained on a standard consent form.

It is difficult to communicate effectively with patients. Studies indicate that patients are seldom able to recall information that has been disclosed to them about their condition and its treatment. It is common for patients to sign consent forms without reading them. Perfect patient comprehension is an unrealistic goal. But nevertheless, health staff should do as much as is reasonable in the circumstances to promote their patients' understanding of relevant factors.

(g) Is there a duty to answer questions?

Although the judgments in *Sidaway* were concerned with the voluntary disclosure of information, Lords Diplock, Bridge and Templeman all appeared to agree that a doctor should be under a duty to answer their patient's questions. Lord Bridge said that the doctor must answer 'truthfully and as fully as the questioner requires'. Lord Diplock contrasted the educated and inquiring patient (the example he used was a judge) for whom the *Bolam* test did not appear to apply because 'the doctor would tell him whatever it was the patient wanted to know'. And Lord Templeman appeared to place the patient who asks questions in the same category as patients whose treatment carries some special risk, where again the *Bolam* test *simpliciter* does not apply.

With respect, this distinction—between the patient who asks questions, who should receive full and truthful information, and the patient who does not, who should be told only what other doctors think is reasonable—may be objectionable for a number of reasons. First, as Margaret Brazier points out, the educated, middle-class patient, who is not intimidated by a consultant's expertise, will have access to a subjectively defined patient-orientated standard of information disclosure: they should be told whatever they want to know. Whereas frightened, inarticulate patients will be confined to the minimal level of information demanded by the modified *Bolam* test.

Margaret Brazier[50]

The judgment in *Sidaway* setting the 'professional standard' for disclosure is limited to what degree of information the doctor must volunteer. The inquisitive patient has a right to know . . . But this distinction between the questioning and the apparently acquiescent patient is another distinction more apparent than real. No guidance is given in *Sidaway* as to what degree of disclosure is triggered by questioning. The Court of Appeal in *Blyth v Bloomsbury AHA* held that a patient inquiring as to the likely risks and side-effects of the injectable long-acting contraceptive Depo-Provera was not entitled to *all* the information the doctor had on the drug. . . .

---

[50] 'Patient autonomy and consent to treatment: the role of the law?' (1987) v 7(2) Legal Studies pp. 169–93, 184, 186.

The Law Lords held unanimously that the patient who requests further information must be answered truthfully and comprehensively. They contended patients' rights were thereby sufficiently protected as the patient who expressly sought to exercise his autonomy was empowered to do so. The practical problems for doctors of applying this 'want to know' test were considered in the previous section. And it has to be doubted whether in any real sense a test which requires the patient to take the initiative can ever genuinely promote patient autonomy. The articulate middle-class patient, whether receiving private or NHS treatment, may well be in a position to initiate discussion of risks and benefits. The less articulate, the apprehensive, those who feel socially ill at ease with the consultant, or whose doctors are hard-pressed in inner city clinics, will be hesitant to initiate discussions. Not 'bothering' the doctor is a deeply entrenched tradition in many parts of Britain. It implies that the patient doubts the doctor's skill, raises fears of offending those who are going to care for you, and may just seem plain rude. It does not follow though that the tradition of patient silence implies lack of interest or desire to participate in decision-making if that opportunity is offered by the doctor.

Secondly, the three Law Lords do not explain *why* patients who ask questions should be entitled to full and truthful answers. Presumably, the justification for this qualification is that a patient has the right to make an autonomous and meaningful choice in the light of information which is relevant and important *to her*. Yet surely there is no reason why this right should be confined to patients who *happen* to be sufficiently educated and confident to know how to ask the correct questions.

Although these obiter statements in *Sidaway* appear to draw a sharp distinction between the doctor's proper response to a patient's questions and her duty to volunteer information, the Court of Appeal in *Blyth v Bloomsbury HA* did not feel compelled to recognize any difference between the two duties, and instead applied the *Bolam* test to the doctor's duty to respond to a patient's specific questions.

Blyth v Bloomsbury Health Authority[51]

During pregnancy it was discovered that Mrs Blyth did not have immunity against rubella. She was advised that she should be immunized immediately after birth, and at the same time given a contraceptive injection, Depo-Provera, in order to ensure that she did not become pregnant for at least three months. After being injected with the drug she suffered unpleasant side effects. She sued the health authority on the ground that the hospital staff had been negligent giving her insufficient information and advice about the possible side effects of Depo-Provera, and that if she had been informed about the possible side effects more fully she would not have agreed to have the injection. At first instance, Mrs Blyth succeeded. The health authority successfully appealed against the finding of negligence.

Kerr LJ

The question of what a plaintiff should be told in answer to a general enquiry cannot be divorced from the *Bolam* test, any more than when no such enquiry is made. In both cases the answer must depend upon the circumstances, the nature of the enquiry, the nature of the information which is available, its reliability, relevance, the condition of the patient, and so forth. Any medical evidence directed to what would be the proper answer in the light of responsible medical opinion and practice—that is to say, the *Bolam* test—must in my view equally be placed in the balance in cases where the patient makes some enquiry, in order to decide whether the response was negligent or not. . . .

[51] [1993] 4 MED LR 151 (CA).

Indeed I am not convinced that the *Bolam* test is irrelevant even in relation to the question of what answers are properly to be given to specific enquiries, or that Lord Diplock or Lord Bridge intended to hold otherwise. It seems to me that there may always be grey areas, with differences of opinion, as to what are the proper answers to be given to any enquiry, even a specific one, in the particular circumstances of any case. However, on the evidence in the present case this point does not arise, since no specific enquiry was found to have been made.

Accordingly, I conclude that the judge erred in finding negligence in relation to what the plaintiff was not told by Dr Burt, whether he relied on the medical evidence or on the obiter remarks in *Sidaway*, or both.

Neill LJ

I do not understand that in the decision of the House of Lords in *Sidaway*, in the passages to which my Lord has already drawn attention, either Lord Diplock or Lord Bridge were laying down any rule of law to the effect that where questions are asked by a patient, or doubts are expressed, a doctor is under an obligation to put the patient in possession of all the information on the subject which may have been available in the files of a consultant, who may have made a special study of the subject. The amount of information to be given must depend upon the circumstances, and as a general proposition it is governed by what is called the *Bolam* test.

In *Poynter v Hillingdon Health Authority*[52] the trial judge found that the parents of a very ill child had not asked sufficiently precise questions to obviate the application of the *Bolam* test.

Poynter v Hillingdon Health Authority[53]

In December 1987, Matthew Poynter, then aged fifteen months, underwent heart transplant surgery. His parents had religious objections to heart transplantation, and felt that they had been pressurized into giving their consent. Immediately after the anaesthetic was administered, the plaintiff's heart stopped and his brain was deprived of oxygen leading to massive irreversible damage. The judge concluded that the risk of this happening was 'no more than 1% and perhaps less'. As a result, the plaintiff was left profoundly disabled, and in need of constant care. Matthew's parents claimed that those responsible for carrying out the surgery had been negligent in failing to warn them of the risk that he might survive the transplant surgery but suffer permanent brain damage.

Sir Maurice Drake

Mr and Mrs Poynter say they wanted all information about the risks arising from the proposed heart transplant, but they do not say that at any time they specifically asked what were the risks of permanent serious disability to Matthew, nor that they asked any question about the risk of permanent brain damage. . . .

My conclusion is that nothing that these parents asked made it known to any of the defendants' medical team that they were being asked to inform them about the risks of serious permanent brain damage or serious permanent disability. The hospital were of course aware of such a risk but assessed it as being only a very small one. They chose not to mention it to the parents.

I have no difficulty in holding that there was, in 1987, a substantial responsible body of medical opinion which would not have disclosed to a patient, or a child patient's parents, the risks of serious complications which amounted to no more than about 1%. . . .

---

[52] 37 BMLR 192.   [53] Ibid.

Applying the *Bolam* test, these defendants are not to be held negligent. Taking into account the observations made in the *Sidaway* case, my finding is that there is nothing in the questions asked by these parents to make the *Bolam* test inapplicable in this case. Even if, contrary to my findings, these parents had asked directly about the risk of serious permanent brain damage, which I find they did not, it is by no means certain that Dr Radley-Smith, or Professor Yacoub would have been under an unqualified duty to tell them of their assessment of a risk of no more than, and probably less than, 1% ... Had they been required to exercise their professional skill, in balancing the desire of the parents to have full information against the possibility that the result of giving that information would have been to deter the parents from consenting to the operation, which those experts strongly believed to be in the best interests of Matthew, I think it is arguable that they were entitled to withhold that information. But that issue does not arise for my consideration since I find, on the facts of this particular case, that there was no duty, in view of the questions asked, to disclose that risk.

More recently, however, in *Pearce v United Bristol Healthcare NHS Trust*[54] Lord Woolf appeared to return to the formulation preferred by the House of Lords in *Sidaway* when he said that 'if a patient asks a doctor about the risk, then the doctor is required to give an honest answer'.

(3) CAUSATION

For a successful action in negligence, the claimant must not only prove the existence of a duty of care and its breach, but also that damage or loss has been caused by the defendant's breach of duty. This means that a failure to disclose material information will only be actionable in negligence if that failure caused the claimant to suffer some injury or loss. The claimant who has managed to establish that her doctor was in breach of the duty to give her sufficient information—itself by no means an easy task, as we have seen—therefore has three further obstacles to a successful claim in negligence. She must prove

(1) that she has suffered an injury that has made her worse off than she would have been if the procedure had not been performed; *and*

(2) that her injury is the materialization of the undisclosed risk or outcome; *and*

(3) that if she had been informed of this risk or outcome, she (or a reasonable patient) would not have consented to the procedure and the injury would not have occurred.

(a) Causation in practice

Applying the 'but for' test to disclosure cases means that we should ask whether, but for the doctor's failure to disclose this information to this patient, the patient would have suffered their injury. So we need to know whether the injury would still have occurred if the patient had been properly informed. Causation will therefore be established if the claimant can prove that proper disclosure would have caused them to decline the treatment which has resulted in their injury. But of course, this question is almost impossible to answer. Not only is it a speculative inquiry about what the

---

[54] (1998) 48 BMLR 118 [CA].

patient might have done in different circumstances, but also by the time the case gets to court the claimant has the benefit of hindsight. She now *knows* that a particular remote risk *has* materialized. From her perspective, the 1 per cent risk of an adverse outcome has ceased to be a remote hypothetical possibility, and has become a 100 per cent certainty. It is therefore likely that the claimant's assertions of what she would have done had she known about the risk will be coloured by her knowledge that she has had the misfortune of being among the 1 per cent of patients whose treatment results in an adverse outcome.

The 'but for' test would ordinarily require us to ask whether *this patient* would have rejected a treatment proposal if she had been properly informed. If *she* would have had the treatment anyway, the doctor's breach of duty did not cause her loss. On the other hand, if *she* would have refused treatment, and hence avoided the risk which has now materialized, causation is established. Causation is thus normally judged subject-ively—we ask whether this claimant would still have suffered the loss even if the defendant had not been negligent. But non-disclosure cases are exceptional in the sense that establishing factual causation is, strictly speaking, impossible because the court must instead resolve a purely hypothetical problem: what would the claim-ant have done in circumstances which, by definition, never existed. As Ian Kennedy explains, concern about relying too heavily on the patient's own testimony in dis-closure cases has led to the adoption of a hybrid subjective/objective test in which objective considerations carry more weight than they would do normally.

Ian Kennedy[55]

If the test is wholly subjective, the plaintiff may be thought to be at too great an advantage, since it is not difficult, with the advantage of hindsight, to claim that she would never have had the treatment had she known. If the test is wholly objective, the common law's traditional approach to causation, that it be determined as a matter of fact on the basis of the evidence, is undermined. As a consequence, there has appeared (as in politics so, in the law!) a third way. Whether expressed as such or not, the Courts have in their decisions sought to steer a course between the two polar positions, so as to fashion a test which avoids the pitfalls which attend both . . . What we see are grand differences of substance, subjective versus objective, melting into shades of emphasis and nuance, such that any close exegesis makes it hard to identify the difference between them. In essence, putting the conclusion first, the difference lies only in the point of departure for the analysis. It will be suggested here that the true key to understanding the difference between the tests lies in where the burden of argument is placed. One alternative is to begin with the assump-tion that the test turns on what the plaintiff says, but then to demand that the plaintiff demon-strates the reasonableness of this position. The alternative is to begin with the assumption that the test turns on what a reasonable person would have done, but then to temper this to a greater or lesser extent by reference to what the plaintiff says. The labels 'objective' and 'subjective' and their variants 'modified objective' or 'hybrid' can then be understood for the shorthand they are. And more importantly, legal analysis and argument can concentrate on which of the two assumptions is to be preferred and, once adopted, what moderating factors should qualify it . . .

[T]he crucial but often overlooked point [is] that there is something special in the analysis of causation in cases of breach of the duty to obtain informed consent. The court is being asked to resolve a hypothetical problem, what would the plaintiff have done if properly informed. This has

---

[55] 'Commentary on *Arndt v Smith*' (1998) 6 Medical Law Review 126–31, 128.

at least two ramifications . . . It argues for a cautious approach and it suggests that invoking the traditional approach of the common law to causation as being a matter of evidence is less persuasive than it may appear.

A hybrid test was employed in *Smith v Barking, Havering and Brentwood HA*.[56] Hutchison J suggested that an objective test should be used to 'test' the truth of the patient's assertion from the witness box that she would not have consented if she had been told about a particular risk. If a reasonable patient would have agreed to the proposed treatment even if she had been told about the particular risk, then the onus would be on the patient to produce some evidence to back up her claim that she would have declined the treatment:

However, there is a peculiar difficulty involved in this sort of case—not least for the plaintiff herself—in giving, after the adverse outcome is known, reliable answers as to what she would have decided before the operation had she been given proper advice as to the risks inherent in it. Accordingly, it would, in my judgment, be right in the ordinary case to give particular weight to the objective assessment. If everything points to the fact that a reasonable patient, properly informed, would have assented to the operation, the assertion from the witness box, made after the adverse outcome is known, in a wholly artificial situation and in the knowledge that the outcome of the case depends upon the assertion being maintained, does not carry great weight unless there are extraneous or additional factors to substantiate it.[57]

But how might a patient prove the truth of what is by definition a hypothetical assertion? While a patient with unusual religious beliefs might be able to demonstrate that she would have acted differently, it will usually be very difficult for a claimant to produce evidence to support her assertion that she would not have acted in the same way as most other patients if presented with information about the remote risks associated with a recommended procedure. And it is at least arguable that the introduction of a rebuttable presumption that the claimant's evidence as to causation is false is inconsistent with basic principles of justice. Furthermore, adopting an objective test for establishing causation will enable the doctor to rely on evidence that patients in general very seldom refuse to consent to the procedure in question. This sort of solid, empirical evidence contrasts sharply with the claimant's easily discredited post hoc assertion that they would not have consented if they had been properly informed.

A further problem with adopting an objective approach to causation is that it confuses the question of the *credibility* of the claimant's evidence with its objective reasonableness. A patient is under no duty to make decisions which are consistent with those of an ordinarily prudent patient. On the contrary,

A mentally competent patient has an absolute right to refuse to consent to medical treatment for any reason, rational or irrational, or for no reason at all, even where that decision may lead to his or her own death.[58]

As Alexander Capron argues in the next extract, testing a claimant's evidence against what a hypothetical reasonable person in her situation would have done significantly

---

[56] (1988) reported [1994] 5 Med LR 285.   [57] At 289.
[58] *Re MB* 38 BMLR 175, per Butler-Sloss LJ.

undermines the patient's right to make foolish or idiosyncratic choices about her medical care. The credibility of evidence from a patient with peculiar priorities should be assessed in the ordinary way—does the judge believe her account?—rather than against a standard of objective reasonableness.

Alexander Morgan Capron[59]

[The patient owes no one a duty to decide prudently or to require for his decision only the facts that an ordinary person would want. The [prudent patient] rule would bar recovery by a patient whose idiosyncratic decisionmaking takes him outside the realm of the 'reasonably prudent person'. This is equivalent to a defense of contributory negligence, which has no place in an action for failure to obtain informed consent. . . .

[T]he importation of the 'reasonable person' standard for causation is as misplaced here as it was in judging materiality of disclosure. An 'individualized test of causation is indicated because informed consent seeks to assure patients the right to make even irrational decisions'. To deny recovery because . . . a reasonable person would not have cared about a certain factor (although . . . the factor did matter to the particular patient-plaintiff) undermines the fundamental purpose of the informed consent rule, the promotion of individual autonomy. The danger that a physician-defendant will be unfairly prejudiced by the patient-plaintiff's testimony is slight. It can be minimized through cross-examination.

And in the next extract, Tony Honoré suggests, in the context of discussion of a Canadian 'failure to warn' case, that the need for additional evidence to back up the claimants hypothetical assertions of what she would have done if properly warned is misleadingly described as an objective approach to causation, but instead should be seen as a necessary adjunct to evidence which is necessarily speculative.

Tony Honoré[60]

In *Arndt v Smith* a mother sued her physician, who had not warned her that her foetus might be injured as a result of the chickenpox she contracted during her pregnancy. When her daughter was born with a congenital injury attributable to the chickenpox, she claimed the cost of raising the child, alleging that, had she been told of the risk, she would have sought an abortion. . . .

The causal issue in such cases turns on a hypothesis about events that did not happen. Did one non-event—the doctor's failure to warn—cause another non-event—the patient's not deciding to have an abortion? [T]here may be little evidence available apart from that of the patient herself. She, after the event, is almost certain to say that, had she been warned, she would have reached a different decision. Otherwise she would not have sued. But her evidence, however honest, is speculative. We cannot know for certain what we would have done in circumstances with which we were never faced. . . .

Assertions about hypothetical conduct therefore need buttressing by more solid evidence about the plaintiff's temperament and beliefs (how keen was she to have a child? was she pro- or anti-abortion?), how great the risks really were and what medical advice would have been given in the light of them. Evidence of this sort may be termed objective, since it does not turn on the plaintiff's say-so. But to adduce it goes, surely, to the discharge of the evidential burden that lies on the plaintiff on the causal issue, not to showing that the issue itself is the objective one: 'would a reasonable patient in her position have decided to opt for an abortion?' . . .

[59] 'Informed Consent in Catastrophic Disease Research and Treatment' 123 University of Pennsylvania Law Review (1974) 340, 410, 420.

[60] 'Causation and Disclosure of Medical Risks' (1998) 114 Law Quarterly Review 52–5, 52–3, 55.

To show after the event that she would have refused or demanded certain treatment a patient must show that she would at the time have had a reason for doing so. It is not enough to say retrospectively that she would have done so, but neither is she bound to demonstrate that an objectively 'reasonable' patient would have done so. Patients of full age and capacity have a right of self-determination in medical matters.

Some cases in the UK have appeared to adopt a more straightforwardly subjective test for causation, tempered only by the judge's assessment as to the witness's credibility as opposed to its substantive reasonableness. In *Gowton v Wolverhampton HA*[61] the trial judge was convinced that the plaintiffs would have continued to rely on the contraceptive pill if they had known about the risk that a vasectomy would spontaneously reverse itself. And in *O'Keefe v Harvey-Kemble*,[62] Neill LJ found that:

there were weighty arguments for the defendant . . . as to why the defendant's version of events should have been preferred; alternatively, that the plaintiff would have been likely to proceed with the operation whatever warnings she received from the defendant. However, in the event, the recorder preferred the recollection of the plaintiff and accepted her evidence as to whether she would have proceeded if she had been fully and properly advised of the attendant risks. Those were essentially findings of fact based on the recorder's assessment of the witnesses, of a kind with which this court will only interfere in rare cases. This is not such a case, in my view.

A further complexity exists where the patient can establish that she would not have consented to have this particular treatment at this time if she had been properly informed, but cannot prove that she would never have undergone the procedure at some point in the future. Here the question of causation becomes especially complicated. Applying the 'but for' test, it could be argued that the patient can prove that the doctor's inadequate disclosure caused her injury because she would not have undergone the operation when she did, and therefore the risk would not have materialized on this occasion. But on the other hand, she might have undergone the same operation—and been exposed to an identical risk of an adverse outcome—at a later date. The issue first came before the English courts in *Chester v Afshar*,[63] and by a 3:2 majority the House of Lords applied the reasoning adopted in an earlier Australian case, *Chappel v Hart*,[64] and found that it was not necessary for a patient to prove that she would have refused the operation for the rest of her life if she had been properly advised. Instead, the fact that 'but for' the defendant's negligence, she might nevertheless have been exposed to the identical risk at a later date would only be relevant when quantifying her loss. Normally, of course, the chance that the slight risk would in fact materialize if she had the operation on another occasion will be very small and so any reduction in damages would be likely to be nominal. The only exception to this is if the claimant is especially susceptible to the particular risk, and so the chance of it materializing in the future will be correspondingly higher, and the reduction in damages would therefore be greater.

Underlying the judgments of the majority of the House of Lords was some reluctance to penalize Miss Chester for her candour in admitting that she could not be

61 [1994] 5 Med LR 432.   62 45 BMLR 74 (CA).
63 [2004] UKHL 41, [2004] 3 WLR 927.   64 (1998) 72 AJLR 1344.

certain that she would not have undergone the operation at some point in the future, even if properly warned. To require her to assert that she would never have undergone the operation would, according to Lord Hope, discriminate against patients who have found the decision as to whether or not to go ahead with treatment difficult.

Chester v Afshar[65]

The defendant Mr Afshar, a neurosurgeon, advised the claimant Miss Chester, who had been suffering from back pain, to undergo an elective surgical procedure on her spine. According to Miss Chester, he did not explain that even if conducted without negligence, this operation carried a small risk (between 0.9–2%) that the claimant would develop cauda equina syndrome. Despite expressing her desire to avoid surgery, the claimant reluctantly agreed and the procedure was carried out three days later. She subsequently developed cauda equina syndrome and brought an action against the defendant in negligence. The judge found that the defendant had negligently failed to warn the claimant of the risk of developing the syndrome; that had she been aware of the risk she would have sought advice on alternatives to surgery and the operation would not have taken place when it did, if at all; but that the defendant had not been negligent in his conduct of the procedure. He held that since the operation would not have taken place when it did, there was a sufficient causal link between the defendant's failure to warn and the damage sustained by the claimant and that link was not broken by the possibility that the claimant might have consented to surgery in the future. The defendant appealed.

Lord Steyn

The starting point is that every individual of adult years and sound mind has a right to decide what may or may not be done with his or her body. Individuals have a right to make important medical decisions affecting their lives for themselves: they have the right to make decisions which doctors regard as ill advised. Surgery performed without the informed consent of the patient is unlawful. The court is the final arbiter of what constitutes informed consent. Usually, informed consent will presuppose a general warning by the surgeon of a significant risk of the surgery . . .

Secondly, not all rights are equally important. But a patient's right to an appropriate warning from a surgeon when faced with surgery ought normatively to be regarded as an important right which must be given effective protection whenever possible.

Thirdly, in the context of attributing legal responsibility, it is necessary to identify precisely the protected legal interests at stake. A rule requiring a doctor to abstain from performing an operation without the informed consent of a patient serves two purposes. It tends to avoid the occurrence of the particular physical injury the risk of which a patient is not prepared to accept. It also ensures that due respect is given to the autonomy and dignity of each patient. . . .

Fourthly, it is a distinctive feature of the present case that but for the surgeon's negligent failure to warn the claimant of the small risk of serious injury the actual injury would not have occurred when it did and the chance of it occurring on a subsequent occasion was very small. It could therefore be said that the breach of the surgeon resulted in the very injury about which the claimant was entitled to be warned . . .

I have come to the conclusion that, as a result of the surgeon's failure to warn the patient, she cannot be said to have given informed consent to the surgery in the full legal sense. Her right of autonomy and dignity can and ought to be vindicated by a narrow and modest departure from traditional causation principles.

---

[65] [2004] UKHL 41, [2004] 3 WLR 927.

Lord Hope

In this case there is no dispute that Mr Afshar owed a duty to Miss Chester to inform her of the risks that were inherent in the proposed surgery, including the risk of paralysis. The duty was owed to her so that she could make her own decision as to whether or not she should undergo the particular course of surgery which he was proposing to carry out. That was the scope of the duty, the existence of which gave effect to her right to be informed before she consented to it. It was unaffected in its scope by the response which Miss Chester would have given had she been told of these risks.

There were three possibilities. She might have agreed to go ahead with the operation despite the risks. Or she might have decided then and there not to have the operation then or at any time in the future. Or she might have decided not to have the operation then but to think the matter over and take further advice, leaving the possibility of having the operation open for the time being. The choice between these alternatives was for her to take, and for her alone. The function of the law is to protect the patient's right to choose. If it is to fulfil that function it must ensure that the duty to inform is respected by the doctor. It will fail to do this if an appropriate remedy cannot be given if the duty is breached and the very risk that the patient should have been told about occurs and she suffers injury. . . .

I would accept that a solution to this problem which is in Miss Chester's favour cannot be based on conventional causation principles. The 'but for' test is easily satisfied, as the trial judge held that she would not have had the operation on 21 November 1994 if the warning had been given. But the risk of which she should have been warned was not created by the failure to warn. It was already there, as an inevitable risk of the operative procedure itself however skilfully and carefully it was carried out. The risk was not increased, nor were the chances of avoiding it lessened, by what Mr Afshar failed to say about it. . . .

Nor does it seem to me that an appeal to common sense alone will provide a satisfactory answer to the problem. . . .

I would prefer to approach the issue which has arisen here as raising an issue of legal policy which a judge must decide. It is whether, in the unusual circumstances of this case, justice requires the normal approach to causation to be modified.

I start with the proposition that the law which imposed the duty to warn on the doctor has at its heart the right of the patient to make an informed choice as to whether, and if so when and by whom, to be operated on. Patients may have, and are entitled to have, different views about these matters. All sorts of factors may be at work here—the patient's hopes and fears and personal circumstances, the nature of the condition that has to be treated and, above all, the patient's own views about whether the risk is worth running for the benefits that may come if the operation is carried out. For some the choice may be easy—simply to agree to or to decline the operation. But for many the choice will be a difficult one, requiring time to think, to take advice and to weigh up the alternatives. The duty is owed as much to the patient who, if warned, would find the decision difficult as to the patient who would find it simple and could give a clear answer to the doctor one way or the other immediately.

To leave the patient who would find the decision difficult without a remedy, as the normal approach to causation would indicate, would render the duty useless in the cases where it may be needed most. This would discriminate against those who cannot honestly say that they would have declined the operation once and for all if they had been warned. I would find that result unacceptable. The function of the law is to enable rights to be vindicated and to provide remedies when duties have been breached. Unless this is done the duty is a hollow one, stripped of all practical force and devoid of all content. It will have lost its ability to protect the patient and thus to fulfil the only purpose which brought it into existence. On policy grounds therefore I would hold that the test of causation is satisfied in this case. The injury was intimately involved with the duty to warn. The duty was owed by the doctor who performed the surgery that Miss Chester consented to. It was the product of the very risk that she should have been warned about when she gave her consent. So I would hold that it can be regarded as having been caused, in the legal sense, by the breach of that duty.

Lord Walker

The surgeon's duty to advise his patient (and in particular, to warn of unavoidable risks of surgery) is a very important part of his professional duty. In *Sidaway*, Lord Scarman described the patient's right to make his own decision as a basic human right. Lord Scarman was delivering a dissenting speech, but the whole House recognised this right; . . . and during the 20 years which have elapsed since *Sidaway* the importance of personal autonomy has been more and more widely recognised . . .

In making a decision which may have a profound effect on her health and well-being a patient is entitled to information and advice about possible alternative or variant treatments. . . . [T]here are real difficulties (especially, perhaps, for a conscientious claimant aware of the fallibility of hindsight) in a claimant asserting that (if warned of the risks) she would never in any circumstances have submitted to surgery. There would be a danger . . . of an honest claimant finding herself without a remedy in circumstances where the surgeon has failed in his professional duty, and the claimant has suffered injury directly within the scope and focus of that duty. I agree with Lord Steyn and Lord Hope that such a claimant ought not to be without a remedy, even if it involves some extension of existing principle . . . Otherwise the surgeon's important duty would in many cases be drained of its content.

In contrast, in their robust dissenting judgments, Lords Bingham and Hoffmann followed the dissenting judgment of McHugh J in *Chappel v Hart*,[66] arguing that Miss Chester had in fact failed the 'but for' test, since the timing of the operation did not affect the risk of injury.

Lord Bingham (dissenting)

[I]n the ordinary run of cases, satisfying the 'but for' test is a necessary if not a sufficient condition of establishing causation. Here, in my opinion, it is not satisfied. Miss Chester has not established that but for the failure to warn she would not have undergone surgery. She has shown that but for the failure to warn she would not have consented to surgery on Monday 21 November 1994. But the timing of the operation is irrelevant to the injury she suffered, for which she claims to be compensated. That injury would have been as liable to occur whenever the surgery was performed and whoever performed it.

Thus the question arises whether Miss Chester should be entitled to recover even though she cannot show that the negligence proved against Mr Afshar was, in any ordinary sense, a cause of her loss. . . .

A claimant is entitled to be compensated for the damage which the negligence of another has caused to him or her. A defendant is bound to compensate the claimant for the damage which his or her negligence has caused the claimant. But the corollaries are also true: a claimant is not entitled to be compensated, and a defendant is not bound to compensate the claimant, for damage not caused by the negligence complained of. The patient's right to be appropriately warned is an important right, which few doctors in the current legal and social climate would consciously or

66 (1998) 72 AJLR 1344.

deliberately violate. I do not for my part think that the law should seek to reinforce that right by providing for the payment of potentially very large damages by a defendant whose violation of that right is not shown to have worsened the physical condition of the claimant.

For these reasons, and also those given by my noble and learned friend Lord Hoffmann, I would allow this appeal.

Lord Hoffmann (dissenting)

The burden is on a claimant to prove that the defendant's breach of duty caused him damage. Where the breach of duty is a failure to warn of a risk, he must prove that he would have taken the opportunity to avoid or reduce that risk. In the context of the present case, that means proving that she would not have had the operation. . . .

The claimant argued that as a matter of law it was sufficient that she would not have had the operation at that time or by that surgeon, even though the evidence was that the risk could have been precisely the same if she had it at another time or by another surgeon. A similar argument has been advanced before this House.

In my opinion this argument is about as logical as saying that if one had been told, on entering a casino, that the odds on no 7 coming up at roulette were only 1 in 37, one would have gone away and come back next week or gone to a different casino. The question is whether one would have taken the opportunity to avoid or reduce the risk, not whether one would have changed the scenario in some irrelevant detail. The judge found as a fact that the risk would have been precisely the same whether it was done then or later or by that competent surgeon or by another.

It follows that the claimant failed to prove that the defendant's breach of duty caused her loss. On ordinary principles of tort law, the defendant is not liable. The remaining question is whether a special rule should be created by which doctors who fail to warn patients of risks should be made insurers against those risks.

The argument for such a rule is that it vindicates the patient's right to choose for herself. Even though the failure to warn did not cause the patient any damage, it was an affront to her personality and leaves her feeling aggrieved.

I can see that there might be a case for a modest solatium in such cases. But the risks which may eventuate will vary greatly in severity and I think there would be great difficulty in fixing a suitable figure. In any case, the cost of litigation over such cases would make the law of torts an unsuitable vehicle for distributing the modest compensation which might be payable.

Below, Andrew Grubb argues that the majority in *Chester* made the right decision.

Andrew Grubb[67]

It is difficult to argue with [the majority's] reasoning. It would undermine the rule and be unjust for a doctor to require a patient to show that she would never have a particular procedure in the future. It is also counterintuitive to think that because the patient may run the risk in the future—by agreeing to and having the procedure—the negligence is not connected to her injury. At worst, she will be exposed to a small risk of injury which is unlikely *then* to eventuate. She had in a real and immediate sense suffered injury that she would not otherwise have suffered. That should be sufficient to establish a causal link.

Against this, Charles Foster agrees with the dissenting judges, and argues that the majority judgments effectively abolish the need for claimants to prove causation.

---

[67] 'Consent to Treatment: The Competent Patient' 131–203 in A Grubb with J Laing (eds), *Principles of Medical Law* (2nd edn OUP Oxford 2004) 200.

Charles Foster[68]

[The majority] accepted that, according to conventional principles of causation, the claimant had to fail. But there was a clear wrong here: the defendant failed to discharge his duty to the claimant. And where there was a wrong, there had to be a remedy. We have all been used to thinking of breach and causation as analytically distinct. That, they said, was wrong. When considering the question of causation, one could not forget why the law imposed on a doctor a duty to abstain from performing an operation. . . .

Why, then, was there a duty to warn? There were two reasons, according to Lord Steyn. First, because the warning tended to avoid the occurrence of injuries, the risk of which the claimant was not prepared to accept. And second, because it ensured 'that due respect is given to the autonomy and dignity of each patient'. The first reason was clearly irrelevant on the facts of this case. The second proved decisive. . . .

This is Alice in Wonderland stuff. Causation is not established but, since it should be, it will be deemed to be. Where a duty exists for some reason that can be described in terms of human rights (and what duty cannot be?) a breach will entitle the claimant to damages on policy grounds, even if causation cannot be proved. The House of Lords has stretched the rules of causation before— notably in *Fairchild v Glenhaven Funeral Services*. But *Chester* goes much further: it abolishes the requirement for causation in any meaningful sense. . . .

The reasoning was, basically: a human right has been breached. That is a bad thing because human rights are important. Therefore, although causation is not really established, we will say that it is. The claimant is therefore entitled, presumably, to damages identical to those that she would have received had she been able to prove that a proper warning would have led her to decline the operation. Surely a more logical thing to do would be to award her the fairly notional damages that she would have got under the European Convention on Human Rights for the article 8 breach she had suffered. Indeed, Lord Hoffmann conceded that 'there might be a case for a modest solatium'.

Causation in consent cases of the *Chester* type has always been difficult to prove. Now it will be easy. Claimants' witness statements will in future, no doubt, say: 'If I had been properly warned, I would have gone off and pondered.' That will be difficult to gainsay . . .

We have always thought of causation as a logical, almost mathematical business. To intrude policy into causation is like saying that two plus two does not equal four because, for policy reasons, it should not. After *Chester*, nothing seems unthinkable.

In the next extract, Jane Stapleton points out the exceptional nature of the duty imposed on the doctor in *Chester* to indemnify the patient against coincidental consequences.

Jane Stapleton[69]

In negligence, many courts are wary about holding D liable for a coincidental consequence of D's tort even if it was foreseeable. . . . Other courts seem willing to extend negligence liability to these consequences. . . . [I]mportant examples are *Chester v Afshar* and *Chappel v Hart*. In both these cases D's breach in failing to warn a patient of the risk of an adverse surgical outcome was part of the history of that adverse consequence to C because, had the warning been given, the evidence was that C would not have had the operation at the time and place he did, and therefore the same freakish consequence would probably not have occurred. The adverse consequence was

---

[68] 'It should be, therefore it is' (2004) 154 New Law Journal 7151.
[69] 'Cause in Fact and the Scope of Liability for Consequences' (2003) 119 Law Quarterly Review 388–425, 419–20.

foreseeable but entirely coincidental. These cases therefore raised the issue of when, if ever, and why coincidental consequences should be judged within the appropriate scope of liability for the tort of negligence.

The map I have sketched of this area of law allows us to see clearly the exceptional nature of the decision, by both courts, that the foreseeable but coincidental consequence of the breach of a fault-based rule was within the appropriate scope of liability. These courts might have formulated an exceptional 'scope' rule which stated, for example, that the vulnerability of a medical patient's autonomy was so extreme that, on policy grounds, this justified exposing to liability for coincidental consequences health care personnel who were in breach of their duty to warn.

Kumaralingam Amirthalingam further argues that the decision in *Chester* reflects an increasing tendency to view causation as a matter of moral accountability rather than factual cause.

Kumaralingam Amirthalingam[70]

Causation is increasingly a proxy for moral accountability. While it was always meant to be a normative inquiry designed to fix liability on a responsible person, courts have been, for the most part, conscious of maintaining a causal link between breach and injury, whether through the traditional 'but for' test or the 'common sense' approach. Recently, causation has transcended its role in attributing causal responsibility and has been used instead to fix liability on a party who, in the court's eyes, ought to have been held accountable even if there were no evidence that that party actually caused the injury. The current mantra is that causation must be seen in the context of the purpose of the law and should not be separated from questions of liability. Effectively, this means that courts may find a defendant causally responsible if at the end of the day, despite the absence of actual evidence of a causal link, it is fair, just and reasonable that the defendant, rather than the plaintiff, should bear the loss. This confuses causation with the broader question of liability, more properly addressed at the duty or remoteness stage.

(b) The problem of causation

For a number of reasons, the requirement that the claimant prove that the inadequate disclosure caused their injury is one of the most unfortunate features of an action in negligence for failure to disclose relevant information. First, the principal purpose of the requirement that doctors should give their patients adequate information is to protect the patient from making uninformed choices about their medical care, *not to prevent physical injury*. If the purpose of giving patients information is to facilitate informed decisionmaking, then any failure to tell a patient about a material factor will have interfered with her ability to make an autonomous choice, regardless of whether she happens to have *also* suffered physical injury as a result. Yet this free-standing interest in the capacity to make an informed choice is not protected by the tort of negligence.

Secondly, as Gerald Robertson points out in the next extract, a successful claim in negligence for failure to disclose a material risk is in practice synonymous with strict liability for medical mishaps. Negligence is incapable of recognizing a patient's inherent interest in material information, and so informed consent instead becomes a route for patients to seek financial compensation for unfortunate but blameless medical outcomes. Doctors who exercised all due care and skill in the performance of an

---

[70] 'Medical Non-Disclosure, Causation and Autonomy' (2002) 118 Law Quarterly Review 540–4, 542.

operation will be found liable for the consequences of an accident which they could have done nothing to prevent just because their pre-operation disclosures were inadequate. Perhaps it would be more appropriate for doctors to be liable for the interference with the patient's ability to reach an informed choice—and we would of course have to think about how to quantify this sort of dignitary injury—but not for the unfortunate but blameless medical mishap.

Gerald Robertson[71]

[A] closer examination of the evolution and development of the doctrine of informed consent in the United States indicates that the promotion of the individual's right to self-determination may not be the true function of the doctrine. Instead it can be argued that its function has been to expand the liability of the medical profession in order to award compensation to a greater number of victims of 'medical accidents' . . .

It is beyond doubt that one effect of the recognition of the doctrine of informed consent is to expand the liability of the medical profession. The explanation for this is quite simple. Courts, particularly in this country, constantly stress the truism that things can go wrong in the course of medical treatment without that treatment having necessarily been performed negligently . . . This means that a large number of patients who suffer injury in the course of medical treatment will, under a fault-based system of compensation such as our own, go without compensation because they are the victims, not of negligent performance of the treatment, but rather of the risks incident thereto. One way in which to remedy this situation, within the present fault-based framework, is to expand liability by making the doctor answerable in damages for failing to warn the patient of these risks prior to undergoing treatment. In this way a greater number of medical accident victims receive compensation, by means of extending the liability of the medical profession beyond the bounds of actual negligent performance of treatment. . . .

However, it can be argued that such expansion of liability was not merely the effect, but rather the purpose, of the development of the doctrine of informed consent in the United States. As [Alan Meisel] indicates:

> The requirement of informed consent to medical treatment has, for at least the past two decades, been used as the cloth from which courts have begun to fashion a no-fault system for compensating persons who have suffered bad results from medical treatment.

Peter Cane also points out this central ambiguity in the purpose of a claim in negligence for inadequate disclosure of risk:

whatever the ideological basis of the duty to warn (or, in other words, the interest which it protects), its importance in practice lies in providing a basis for imposing liability for physical injury not caused by negligence.[72]

It is, however, important to remember that the patient will only be able to recover damages if the injury she sustained was caused by the undisclosed risk. Imagine, for example, that the doctor negligently fails to warn the patient of risk X, and that she can prove that if she had been warned about risk X, she would not have refused to have the treatment in question. In the event, risk X does not materialize, but the patient suffers another unrelated injury as a result of risk Y. In these circumstances,

---

[71] 'Informed Consent to Medical Treatment' (1981) 97 Law Quarterly Review 102–26, 109–10.
[72] 'A Warning about Causation' (1999) 115 Law Quarterly Review 21–7, 23.

'but for' the defendant's negligence, the patient would not have suffered any injury. Can she recover for injury Y? Almost certainly not. This is, in effect, a remoteness question. The injury she in fact suffered was not a foreseeable one, and so it seems likely that on policy grounds it would not be recoverable. In *Chester v Afshar*, Lord Walker distinguished coincidental injuries—such as an unforeseeable accident of anaesthesia or the operating theatre being struck by lightning—from the facts in *Chester*. He argued that Miss Chester's injury did not fall into the same category of coincidental injuries because:

Bare 'but for' causation is powerfully reinforced by the fact that the misfortune which befell the claimant was the very misfortune which was the focus of the surgeon's duty to warn.

So in practice, recovery in non-disclosure cases involves strict liability but only for the particular risk which the doctor negligently failed to mention to the patient.

Thirdly, because the claimant must prove that the inadequate disclosure caused an injury, cases only tend to come before the courts where the patient has not been informed about the risk of an adverse outcome which has then materialized. Adequate information is not, however, confined to disclosure of risks. In order to exercise meaningful choice, it is important that patients are told about alternatives to the proposed treatment. For example, if a patient with breast cancer is not informed about alternatives to radical mastectomy, she has undoubtedly been deprived of the ability to exercise meaningful choice over her treatment. It would however be difficult for her to prove that she has been *harmed* by an operation which successfully removed a tumour. In addition to information about other treatment options, patients might also want to know if their doctor will benefit financially from their decision to opt for a particular course of treatment. Patients may also regard information about who will carry out the procedure, how much experience they have, and their success rates as important. But because, as Marjorie Maguire Shultz explains, a failure to give these other types of information to patients will seldom result in physical injury, equally important aspects of informed choice are marginalized by the law.

Marjorie Maguire Shultz[73]
In many tort actions, factual cause is relatively clear. . . . Invasions of autonomy, however, involve an especially complex and probabilistic analysis. There are multiple issues: Did the doctor's nondisclosure materially invade the patient's interest in choice? What would the patient have chosen had her choice been protected? What would have happened, medically, had the alternate choice been made? Such complexities are unmanageable within the yes/no framework of factual cause; compressed into a single question, they become oversimplified.

Under such a simplified analysis, if individual criteria were used, the very existence of any injury would seem to turn solely on the rather shaky reed of the plaintiff's hindsight testimony. It is not surprising that courts faced with such a compacted ultimate issue moved to adopt objective standards of reasonableness to address the question. If, on the other hand, choice were an independently protected interest, the factual cause issue would be narrower and simpler—whether the patient's right to choose had been encroached upon as a result of a doctor's failure to disclose. . . .

[73] 'From Informed Consent to Patient Choice: A New Protected Interest' (1985) 95 Yale Law Journal 219, 251–2.

[P]reemption of patients' authority by doctors may also give rise to injuries that are real but intangible, or to physical outcomes that are arguably not 'injurious' except from the individual's vantage point. These outcomes may be excluded from negligence doctrine's definitions of harm. Thus, a patient not told about a method of sterilization that is more reversible than the one performed may have difficulty convincing a court that nonreversibility is a cognizable physical injury. A patient who alleges that, properly informed, she would have chosen a lumpectomy rather than a radical mastectomy might find it hard, under existing negligence rules, to characterize the successful operation that removed her breast and eradicated her cancer as having 'injured' her. Similarly, the patient with a desire to go home or to a hospice to die, who is instead maintained alive by hospital machinery, might have difficulty establishing 'injury' under definitions of an interest in physical well-being rather than choice.

In the following extract, Frances Miller discusses a particular type of information which might be increasingly important for patients, but which is again marginalized within a negligence model. As we saw in Chapter 2, rationing of scarce medical resources has become inevitable, and it will not always be possible to provide every patient with the best available treatment. If treatment is withheld on the grounds of cost, are patients entitled to be told this information?

Frances Miller[74]

If physicians withhold the information that potentially beneficial treatment is being denied their patients for economic reasons, they not only usurp the possibility of patient choice or self-help on the matter, but they assume a staggering moral burden. The traditional justification for silence under such circumstances is that it would be cruel and inhumane to tell patients that therapy might help them, but that they have no access to it. One can construct a powerful argument, however, that silence under such circumstances often is not only equally cruel and inhumane, but also morally unacceptable.

Physicians truly are 'playing God' in such circumstances, but they may not have all the facts. Some patients may have their own resources for obtaining medical care about which their doctors are unaware. Others may choose to invest their energies in trying to change rationing policies that affect them detrimentally, rather than passively accepting denial of care as their lot. In any event, many patients may have personal, business or professional priorities and commitments that would change in the light of full, truthful information about their medical conditions and treatment options. To deny patients such information is to compromise the exercise of personal autonomy, the raison d'etre of the informed consent doctrine. . . .

So far, the general public in neither [the US nor the UK] has understood the true extent of existing rationing very well, and patients have often been spared the explicit knowledge that treatment is being withheld from them for reasons having more to do with economics than with their medical best interests. That ignorance is rapidly dissipating in both countries, however. As patients become more aware that they may be the targets of rationing, anger and frustration derived from their helplessness are likely to be focused on the nearest target—the physician-gatekeeper as de facto enemy, because she withholds critical information. But if physicians impart information about beneficial but economically unavailable care as part of their traditional obligation to act in their patients' best interests, the character of physicians changes in those patients' eyes from enemy to ally. Doctors and patients can then work together to improve the way health care resources are allocated.

[74] 'Denial of Health Care and Informed Consent in English and American law' (1992) 18 American Journal of Law and Medicine 37, 70–1.

While it might be difficult to prove that not disclosing the existence of an appropriate treatment which the NHS has decided not to fund *caused* a person's injury or loss, patients might feel particularly aggrieved if their doctor did not let them know that treatment which would be available privately might have a greater chance of success. The BMA's advice to doctors is to tailor disclosure of this sort of information to the individual patient's circumstances.

British Medical Association[75]

The candour which is now generally accepted practice in relation to medical information, however, does not appear automatically to extend to other categories of information which have a direct bearing on patient choice. A particular area of uncertainty which has been highlighted in the media and in correspondence to the BMA concerns the range of options that patients should be told about when there is little or no likelihood of some of those options being funded. Anecdotal evidence bears out the view that doctors frequently base their judgments about discussion of possible options on their assessment of the patient's potential ability to purchase those treatments privately. Some doctors feel acutely embarrassed about having to tell patients that some treatments are only available in the private sector and some think it is wrong to do so if the cost is evidently beyond the patient's means.

The BMA has supported the right of doctors to tell patients about the existence of options which the clinician believes to be potentially beneficial for the patient but has recognised that providing such information can create additional stresses and dilemmas for vulnerable patients so that the manner and timing of the information should be carefully considered and may need to be supported by professional counselling. Some doctors who feel strongly about the benefits of the drug are forthright in expressing their views to patients. Others who would like to prescribe products like Taxol clearly feel they cannot mention it on the grounds that, if not publicly funded, the information creates anxiety or distress or raises unachievable hopes. Knowing that a possible, even if unproven, product exists that may briefly extend the patient's lifespan is likely to make some families feel pressured to incur debts to buy it.

Advice from the BMA's Medical Ethics Committee

Doctors should take their cue from patients as to the amount of information to impart about treatment options. Patients should have as much information as possible about why certain treatments were not available on the NHS (or through their insurer).

Fourthly, actually proving that the inadequate disclosure *caused* the claimant's injury is fraught with difficulty and, as we saw in the previous section, in practice represents a significant obstacle to the chances of bringing a successful action in negligence. Inadequate disclosure of risks will seldom result in any physical injury at all, and hence will usually be immune from potential liability in negligence. But even in cases where a risk has materialized, it is so inherently unlikely that a patient will succeed in proving that inadequate disclosure caused their injury—especially if the risk was a small one—that doctors will hardly ever be held to account for a failure to tell their patients about the risks associated with treatment.

Fifthly, 'cause' appears to have acquired a rather special meaning in failure to warn cases. As Peter Cane has explained, the doctors in these cases rarely 'caused' the injury in question 'in the central sense of the word "cause" as it is used outside the law',

---

[75] *Duty of Candour? Truth Telling and Rationing of Resources* (July 1997).

because 'failure to warn of a risk does not "cause" the materialization of the risk'. Rather the injury has usually been caused by an unfortunate and inherently unlikely combination of circumstances, and the doctor simply *created the situation* in which this extraordinary sequence of events could occur. The question of whether a doctor should be liable for a failure to disclose a risk is more accurately stated as whether she should be liable for creating the situation in which an accidental injury might or (more likely) might not occur.

(c) MOVING AWAY FROM BATTERY AND NEGLIGENCE

The central problem, then, with the current legal mechanisms for protecting a patient's right to information about their treatment is that both battery and negligence have proved to be inadequate. Battery is inadequate because it will only be relevant where the treatment involves unlawful touching, and in any event the courts have tightly circumscribed its application to non-disclosure cases. Negligence requires proof that the lack of information caused physical harm, which of course will seldom be the case when a patient is not given enough information. What alternatives might there be?

In the next extract Joanna Manning describes the system which exists in New Zealand. If a patient wishes to obtain compensation for a doctor's failure to warn her of a particular risk, under the no-fault compensation scheme it will still be necessary to establish a causal link between the failure to warn and physical injury. However, in addition a Code of Rights offers additional protection to patients' interests in information disclosure since it is a breach of the Code not to disclose information which the reasonable patient would consider material. While the Code does not provide financial compensation to patients who have been inadequately informed, doctors are placed under a robust duty to give patients sufficient information to enable them to make informed choices, and given that we have already established that the deterrent effect of negligence in relation to information disclosure is likely to be minimal, the New Zealand system may in practice have more impact upon doctors' behaviour.

Joanna Manning[76]

Since 1996 New Zealand has had a Code of Health and Disability Services Consumers' Rights with the force of law. The Code places heavy emphasis on information disclosure and informed consent . . . The Code committed itself from the outset to the patient-centred standard of disclosure from *Rogers v. Whittaker*. The *Bolam* test was rejected: evidence of professional practice is relevant but not conclusive. . . .

Since 1974 in New Zealand the function of compensation for injury has sensibly been separated from issues of professional accountability . . . A negligent failure to obtain an informed consent where the relevant risk eventuates and results in personal injury is covered by the compensation scheme . . . Thus, there is no need for the Code of Rights to serve the compensatory role . . . The Code of Rights is designed to meet the other, remaining functions served by the civil action, such as vindication, professional accountability, prevention and deterrence . . .

---

[76] 'Informed Consent To Medical Treatment: The Common Law And New Zealand's Code Of Patients' Rights' (2004) 12 Medical Law Review 181.

One of the advantages of the Code is its recognition that a consumer is likely to want a wider range of information than about risks in making decisions about treatment. Right 6, in referring to 'the information that a reasonable consumer, in that consumer's circumstances, would expect to receive', recognises that the information patients might need is not confined to information about risks, but extends to other types of information that may be needed to enable them to make an informed decision about their care . . .

In New Zealand, separating compensation for injury from issues of professional accountability has made possible one of the advantages of the Code for complainants—breach of the Code does not depend upon proof of injury, nor of a causal link between any injury suffered and a breach of a Code Right. The Code does not distinguish between battery and negligence. The prohibition on providing services without informed consent in Right 7(1) applies to all services, not just those involving bodily contact, as required for the tort of battery. It is not necessary to show that the patient suffered harm as a result of a failure to be sufficiently informed. So, it is strictly irrelevant to whether there has been a breach of Right 6 that the Commissioner finds it probable that, even if the health provider had explained the risks of the procedure, the patient would have gone ahead with it in any event. The patient is entitled to appropriate information irrespective of whether it would have been a determinative factor in the decision to proceed. Thus, breaches of Rights 6 and 7(1) of the Code can result where the consumer's right to be sufficiently informed or give an informed consent has not been observed, even though no injury has resulted, where the injury suffered is not physical, or where injury suffered is unrelated to the risk that should have been disclosed. This properly reflects the paramount interest that the duty of disclosure and the concept of informed consent is designed to secure—the individual's autonomy and right to decide in an informed manner, not just the interest in bodily safety.

5. A FIDUCIARY RELATIONSHIP?

If the doctor–patient relationship could be said to be fiduciary in nature, we might have an alternative basis for imposing an obligation on them to disclose material information. And indeed, since equitable duties of disclosure are usually a response to the law's recognition that a relationship involves one party being unusually vulnerable to the other's ability to exercise some discretion or power over her interests, they might seem a promising basis for a more patient-orientated approach to informed consent. The case law, however, is not encouraging. In *Sidaway* in the Court of Appeal,[77] Dunn LJ said that the fiduciary relationship:

has been confined to cases involving the disposition of property, and has never been applied to the nature of the duty which lies upon a doctor in the performance of his professional treatment of his patient. In any event, I do not find it helpful in considering the duty of the doctor to his patient to draw analogies, which are in any case ill-founded, from other branches of the law which have developed in different circumstances and for different reasons.[78]

and Lord Scarman, the only Law Lord to consider the possibility of a fiduciary relationship between doctor and patient, was similarly dismissive:

Counsel for the appellant referred to *Nocton v. Lord Ashburton* in an attempt to persuade your

---

[77] [1984] QB 491.   [78] [1984] QB 491, at 515.

Lordships that the relationship between doctor and patient is of a fiduciary character entitling a patient to equitable relief in the event of a breach of fiduciary duty by the doctor. The attempt fails: there is no comparison to be made between the relationship of doctor and patient with that of solicitor and client, trustee and cestui qui trust or the other relationships treated in equity as of a fiduciary character.[79]

Is Lord Scarman's summary dismissal of the possibility of a fiduciary relationship between doctor and patient justified?

It is uncontroversial the doctor–patient relationship is one of trust and confidence, and, in other contexts, the courts have recognized that it might be fiduciary in character. A presumption of the invalidity of gifts and bequests from patient to doctor, for example, was established in the nineteenth century.[80] And there are obligations which doctors owe to their patients—most obviously, the duty of confidentiality—which are plainly equitable in nature, and which arise because equity has acknowledged the special dependency which exists within the doctor–patient relationship. Conceding that fiduciary relationships normally arise only when property interests are at stake, Margaret Brazier has nevertheless argued that:

in a sense the patient does entrust his most precious property, his body and health to the doctor. Is equity too rigid . . . to expand to fill the inflexibility of tort within the common law?[81]

In some other countries, the courts have suggested that while some aspects of the doctor–patient relationship might involve fiduciary obligations, these should be confined to situations in which neither contract nor tort already provides an adequate remedy. For example, Sopinka J in the Canadian Supreme Court case of *Norberg v Wynrib*[82] suggested that '[f]iduciary duties should not be superimposed on these common law duties simply to improve the nature and extent of the remedy'. In short, if the issue is the doctor's malpractice, equitable remedies would be inappropriate. The doctor's breach of her duty to use appropriate care and skill is not a breach of her fiduciary duty. But while the courts have become accustomed to regarding the duty to provide adequate pre-treatment disclosure as part of the doctor's ordinary duty of care, negligence's requirement that actionable damage should have been caused by the failure to give adequate information has, as we saw in the previous section, rendered the chance of a poorly advised patient succeeding in a negligence action virtually nonexistent. Indeed this point was made persuasively by MacLachlin J in her judgment in *Norberg v Wynrib* when she rejected her colleagues' 'closed commercial view of fiduciary obligations',[83] and suggested that:

Recognising the fiduciary nature of the doctor–patient relationship provides the law with an analytical model by which physicians can be held to the highest standard of dealing with their patients which the trust accorded to them requires . . . . The fact that society encourages us to trust our doctors, to believe that they will be persons worthy of our trust, cannot be ignored as a factor inducing a heightened degree of vulnerability.[84]

Moreover, other self-evidently fiduciary relationships, such as that between agent and

---

[79] [1985] AC 871 at 884. [80] *Rhodes v Bate* (1866) 1 Ch App 252.
[81] 'Patient autonomy and consent to treatment: the role of the law?' (1987) 7 Legal Studies 169–93, 191.
[82] (1992) 138 NR 81 at 176. [83] At 143. [84] At 128 and 137.

principal, are also contractual in nature, so it is not necessarily true that fiduciary obligations can arise only when actions in contract and tort are unavailable.

There are some cases from other countries which have appeared to categorize the doctor's duty of disclosure as a fiduciary obligation. In *Miller v Kennedy*, the State of Washington's Court of Appeals held that:

The duty of the doctor to inform the patient is a fiduciary duty. The patient is entitled to rely upon the physician to tell him what he needs to know about the condition of his body. The patient has the right to chart his own destiny, and the doctor must supply the patient with the material facts the patient will need in order to intelligently chart that destiny with dignity.[85]

But while an equitable basis for the duty of disclosure might initially appear attractive, as Ian Kennedy argues in the following section, there are good reasons to be sceptical about the extent to which recognizing a fiduciary relationship would in fact improve patients' access to adequate information. Since the fiduciary's principal obligation is to act in her 'client's' best interests, a paternalistic approach to information disclosure might be defensible within a fiduciary model. Ian Kennedy goes so far as to describe the 'best interests' test, which would underpin the fiduciary relationship, as 'the anti-principle, the means whereby courts have handed power to doctors by allowing them to determine what should be done',[86] and as a result is sceptical about the progressive potential of fiduciary obligations. He also warns of the dangers of adopting an approach which defines the doctor–patient relationship in terms of the patient's vulnerability and dependence.

Ian Kennedy[87]

The brave new world of the fiduciary relationship looks increasingly, and depressingly, like the bad old days of 'best interests'. As . . . a criterion for setting the proper bounds of the doctor–patient relationship, 'best interests' leaves a lot to be desired! Yet here it is again, wearing new clothes. So far from a legal framework which rejects paternalism for something better, the doctor as fiduciary reduces down to the very same paternalism. . . .

The danger present in adopting the fiduciary relationship approach is that . . . [t]he law reverts to a status approach, fixing the patient in a dependent role and inviting claims of vulnerability. The patient who consents can always argue later that he was too vulnerable or was exploited. He may not succeed but the doctor–patient relationship is once again destabilised by the nature of the legal framework within which it is caused to function . . .

A second criticism flows from what has just been said. The whole tenor of the doctor as fiduciary approach is to perpetuate the notion of the patient as victim. This may seem an odd criticism when throughout this paper I have been trumpeting the power imbalance between doctor and patient. Surely, it can be said, all that the fiduciary relationship approach does is to recognise this imbalance and seek to take account of it. Well, my criticism stands. What the adoption of a fiduciary approach does, in fact, is to entrench the power imbalance, to make it part of the law. This is the last thing which the law should be doing. What we should be looking for is a framework which recognises the difference in power and tries to do something about it; tries in short to redress it.

[85] 522 P.2d 852 at 860.
[86] 'The Fiduciary Relationship and its Application to Doctors' in P Birks (ed), *Wrongs and Remedies in the Twenty-first Century* (Clarendon Press Oxford 1986) 111–40, 138.
[87] Ibid, 139–40

A third and final criticism is that the main contribution of the fiduciary relationship to the doctor–patient relationship is to load onto doctors an ill-defined but wide range of obligations, which they ignore at their peril. This cannot be fair. . . .

In conclusion, therefore, my submission is that the fiduciary relationship as applied to doctors and patients is a false dawn. It does not provide nor should be seen as laying the foundations for a more appropriate legal framework governing them. It is confused jurisprudentially, it infantilises patients, it leaves doctors unsure. Most important it extends the *carte blanche* of 'best interests' when the 'best interests' approach is arguably one of medical law's most glaring weaknesses.

6. GOOD MEDICAL PRACTICE

In the rules governing disclosure of information to patients, we have an excellent example of the gap between tort law and the principles of good medical practice which we considered in Chapter 2. As we have seen in this chapter, tort law imposes fairly minimal requirements on doctors, whereas the codes of practice and guidelines promulgated by the British Medical Association,[88] the General Medical Council, the Royal Colleges, and the Department of Health[89] tend to be much more detailed and expansive. As we can see in the next extract, the profession's own guidance on obtaining patients' consent imposes considerably more onerous duties on the medical profession than the reasonable doctor standard in tort law. While failure to follow the GMC's guidance does not automatically lead to disciplinary action, a significant departure might lead the GMC to issue a warning to the doctor in question.

General Medical Council[90]

Providing sufficient information

4. Patients have a right to information about their condition and the treatment options available to them. The amount of information you give each patient will vary, according to factors such as the nature of the condition, the complexity of the treatment, the risks associated with the treatment or procedure, and the patient's own wishes. For example, patients may need more information to make an informed decision about a procedure which carries a high risk of failure or adverse side effects; or about an investigation for a condition which, if present, could have serious implications for the patient's employment, social or personal life

5. The information which patients want or ought to know, before deciding whether to consent to treatment or an investigation, may include:

- details of the diagnosis, and prognosis, and the likely prognosis if the condition is left untreated;

- uncertainties about the diagnosis including options for further investigation prior to treatment;

- options for treatment or management of the condition, including the option not to treat;

---

[88] British Medical Association, *Consent Tool Kit, Second edition* — Feb 2003 available at <http://www.bma.org.uk/>.

[89] *Reference Guide to Consent for Examination or Treatment* (DH 2001 available at <http://www.dh.gov.uk>).

[90] *Seeking patients' consent: the ethical considerations*, Nov 1998 available at <http://www.gmc-uk.org/standards/consent.htm>.

- the purpose of a proposed investigation or treatment; details of the procedures or therapies involved, including subsidiary treatment such as methods of pain relief; how the patient should prepare for the procedure; and details of what the patient might experience during or after the procedure including common and serious side effects;

- for each option, explanations of the likely benefits and the probabilities of success; and discussion of any serious or frequently occurring risks, and of any lifestyle changes which may be caused by, or necessitated by, the treatment;

- advice about whether a proposed treatment is experimental;

- how and when the patient's condition and any side effects will be monitored or re-assessed;

- the name of the doctor who will have overall responsibility for the treatment and, where appropriate, names of the senior members of his or her team;

- whether doctors in training will be involved, and the extent to which students may be involved in an investigation or treatment;

- a reminder that patients can change their minds about a decision at any time;

- a reminder that patients have a right to seek a second opinion;

- where applicable, details of costs or charges which the patient may have to meet.

6. When providing information you must do your best to find out about patients' individual needs and priorities. For example, patients' beliefs, culture, occupation or other factors may have a bearing on the information they need in order to reach a decision. You should not make assumptions about patients' views, but discuss these matters with them, and ask them whether they have any concerns about the treatment or the risks it may involve. You should provide patients with appropriate information, which should include an explanation of any risks to which they may attach particular significance. Ask patients whether they have understood the information and whether they would like more before making a decision. . . .

Responding to questions
9. You must respond honestly to any questions the patient raises and, as far as possible, answer as fully as the patient wishes. In some cases, a patient may ask about other treatments that are unproven or ineffective. Some patients may want to know whether any of the risks or benefits of treatment are affected by the choice of institution or doctor providing the care. You must answer such questions as fully, accurately and objectively as possible.

Withholding information
10. You should not withhold information necessary for decision making unless you judge that disclosure of some relevant information would cause the patient serious harm. In this context serious harm does not mean the patient would become upset, or decide to refuse treatment.

Presenting information to patients
13. Obtaining informed consent cannot be an isolated event. It involves a continuing dialogue between you and your patients which keeps them abreast of changes in their condition and the treatment or investigation you propose. Whenever possible, you should discuss treatment options at a time when the patient is best able to understand and retain the information. To be sure that your patient understands, you should give clear explanations and give the patient time to ask questions. In particular, you should:

- use up-to-date written material, visual and other aids to explain complex aspects of the investigation, diagnosis or treatment where appropriate and/or practicable;

- make arrangements, wherever possible, to meet particular language and communication needs, for example through translations, independent interpreters, signers, or the patient's representative;

- where appropriate, discuss with patients the possibility of bringing a relative or friend, or making a tape recording of the consultation;

- explain the probabilities of success, or the risk of failure of, or harm associated with options for treatment, using accurate data;

- ensure that information which patients may find distressing is given to them in a considerate way. Provide patients with information about counselling services and patient support groups, where appropriate;

- allow patients sufficient time to reflect, before and after making a decision, especially where the information is complex or the severity of the risks is great. Where patients have difficulty understanding information, or there is a lot of information to absorb, it may be appropriate to provide it in manageable amounts, with appropriate written or other back-up material, over a period of time, or to repeat it;

- involve nursing or other members of the health care team in discussions with the patient, where appropriate. They may have valuable knowledge of the patient's background or particular concerns, for example in identifying what risks the patient should be told about;

- ensure that, where treatment is not to start until some time after consent has been obtained, the patient is given a clear route for reviewing their decision with the person providing the treatment.

Who obtains consent

14. If you are the doctor providing treatment or undertaking an investigation, it is your responsibility to discuss it with the patient and obtain consent, as you will have a comprehensive understanding of the procedure or treatment, how it is carried out, and the risks attached to it. Where this is not practicable, you may delegate these tasks provided you ensure that the person to whom you delegate:

- is suitably trained and qualified;

- has sufficient knowledge of the proposed investigation or treatment, and understands the risks involved;

- acts in accordance with the guidance in this booklet.

You will remain responsible for ensuring that, before you start any treatment, the patient has been given sufficient time and information to make an informed decision, and has given consent to the procedure or investigation.

Since tort law offers virtually no prospective guidance to doctors concerned about how much information to provide, in practice it is to these detailed guidelines that doctors will turn. Hence, the medical profession and the executive have created a doctrine of informed consent which applies de facto to medical treatment in the UK. The judiciary's reluctance to impose a standard of care on doctors which is consistent with the much more widely read and understood standards of good medical practice starts to look increasingly bizarre.

7. CONCLUSION

In this chapter, we have seen that there are significant problems with using tort law to protect patients' interests in informative disclosure, and that instead the profession's own good practice guidelines impose much more robust responsibilities upon doctors. In the final extract, I ask whether this matters.

Emily Jackson[91]

The chief problem with tort law's response to information disclosure is that it points to a significant gap in the law's protection of patient autonomy. It may be true that competent adult patients have an almost absolute right to refuse unwanted treatment. But we have to remember that their ability to take advantage of this right may depend critically upon having sufficient understanding of the relative merits and disadvantages of the available treatments. Yet as we have seen, whether or not patients will get this information still generally lies within the doctor's discretion.

My focus has been the largely impotent role tort law plays in the protection of patients' interests in information disclosure. But does this matter? It might be argued that because, in practice, the guidance doctors receive from the Royal Colleges, the Department of Health, the BMA and the GMC stresses the importance of giving patients sufficient information, the fact that this is not backed up by remedies in tort law is of comparatively little importance . . .

Doctors wanting to know what they should disclose to patients will usually consult professional guidance, rather than the law reports, and so, in practice, the inadequacies of tort law may have little practical impact upon the provision of information to patients. Nevertheless, while most doctors do attempt to find out what each individual patient wants to know, and try to provide this information in an accessible and straightforward way, this is certainly not because of the 'deterrent' effect of tort law. On the contrary, it is *despite* the complete absence of any effective deterrent to inadequate disclosure in the law of tort. Law students are usually told that tort law serves two principal functions: compensation and deterrence. In relation to information disclosure, it serves neither. As a result, I think there is an increasing need to think seriously about abandoning the pretence that tort law offers any protection at all to patients' interests in access to information about their medical treatment.

8. FURTHER READING

Brazier, Margaret, 'Patient autonomy and consent to treatment: the role of the law?' Legal Studies (1987) vol 7(2) 169–93.

Honore, Tony, 'Causation and Disclosure of Medical Risks' (1998) 114 Law Quarterly Review 52–5.

Jackson, Emily, 'Informed Consent to Medical Treatment and the Impotence of Tort' in SAM McLean (ed), *First Do No Harm* (Ashgate Aldershot 2006).

Jones, Michael, 'Informed Consent and other Fairy Stories' (1999) 7 Medical Law Review 103–34.

---

[91] 'Informed Consent to Medical Treatment and the Impotence of Tort' in SAM McLean (ed), *First Do No Harm* (Ashgate Aldershot 2006).

Kennedy, Ian, *Treat Me Right* (OUP Oxford 1998) ch 9.

Kennedy, Ian, 'The Fiduciary Relationship and its Application to Doctors' in P Birks (ed), *Wrongs and Remedies in the Twenty-first Century* (Clarendon Press Oxford 1986) 111–40.

Skegg, PDG, 'English Medical Law and "Informed Consent": An Antipodean Assessment and Alternative' (1999) 7 Medical Law Review 135–65, 138.

Stapleton, Jane, 'Cause in Fact and the Scope of Liability for Consequences' (2003) 119 Law Quarterly Review 388–425.

Teff, Harvey, 'Consent to Medical Procedures: Paternalism, Self-Determination or Therapeutic Alliance' [1985] 101 Law Quarterly Review 432–53.

6

CONFIDENTIALITY

1. CENTRAL ISSUES

1. Doctors are under a duty to respect their patients' confidentiality for two reasons. First, information about a person's health is paradigmatically private, and secondly, without a guarantee of confidentiality, patients may be unwilling to provide information which might be vitally important in diagnosing and treating them.

2. The Data Protection Act 1998 provides that sensitive personal data must be processed fairly and lawfully. Normally the patient's consent is necessary, but there are a number of exceptions to this, such as the use of data for research and audit.

3. The legal duty of confidentiality is not absolute. The reality of medical treatment is that information will often have to be shared between a number of healthcare professionals. Information can also be disclosed where the public interest in disclosure outweighs the public interest in respecting confidentiality, for example, because there is a risk of serious harm to others.

4. Genetic information raises a number of complex issues:

(a) First, the inherently shared nature of genetic information poses particular challenges for a model of confidentiality which has traditionally stressed the privacy of an individual's health records. One person's diagnosis may reveal information about her close family members.

(b) Secondly, genetic tests are often predictive rather than diagnostic. This means that third parties, such as employers and insurers, might have compelling reasons for wanting to find out about a person's risk of future ill health.

(c) Thirdly, DNA databases might be useful for the police, the NHS, and commercial organizations.

2. INTRODUCTION

Unlike patient autonomy, which is a relatively recent preoccupation of medical law and ethics, a doctors' duty to respect their patients' confidentiality has its origins in the first codes of medical ethics. The Hippocratic Oath, for example, states that:

whatsoever things I see or hear concerning the life of men, in my attendance on the sick or even apart therefrom, which ought not to be noised abroad, I will keep silence thereon, counting such things to be as sacred secrets,

and patient confidentiality also receives unqualified protection in the modern version of the Oath, the Declaration of Geneva:

I will respect the secrets which are confided in me, even after the patient has died.

In this chapter, we begin by examining the ethical justifications for protecting patient confidentiality. We then consider various different legal sources of the duty of confidence. Next, we flesh out the exceptions to the duty of confidence, and the remedies available for its breach. We then look at some of the special issues raised by genetic information. Finally, we look at patients' rights to gain access to their medical records.

3. WHY RESPECT CONFIDENTIALITY?

Both deontological (duty-based) and teleological (consequentialist) reasoning can be used to justify the existence of a duty of confidence between patients and doctors (for a full description of what is meant by these terms, see further Chapter 1 p. 11). First, information about a person's health and medical treatment is paradigmatically private, and it could therefore be argued that she should have the right to control who has access to it. For example, the Medical Research Council's guidance on confidentiality states:

Respect for private life is a human right, and the ability to discuss information in confidence with others is rightly valued. Keeping control over facts about one's self can have an important role in a person's sense of security, freedom of action, and self-respect.[1]

Secondly, optimum medical care can be provided only if a patient feels able to be honest with her doctor, and this in turn will be possible only if the patient believes that her doctor is under a duty not to disclose personal, and perhaps embarrassing information. If patients being treated for drug addiction, mental illness or HIV infection, for example, believed that their medical notes might be seen by future employers, there would be a powerful disincentive towards seeking medical care and advice.

In the next extract, Raanan Gillon explains how both consequentialist reasoning and respect for autonomy justify the protection of patient confidentiality.

Raanan Gillon[2]

[I]n order to do a good job for their patients doctors often need to have information of a sort that people generally regard as private, even secret. Some of the information is merely embarrassing to discuss, some may be positively harmful to the patients or others if it is divulged. Doctors routinely ask a series of questions about bodily functions that people would not dream of discussing with anyone else. When a patient's medical problems may relate to genitourinary functions a doctor may need to know about that patient's sexual activities, sometimes in detail. When a patient's problems are psychological a doctor may need to know in great detail about the patient's experiences, ideas and feelings, relationships past and present, even in some contexts about the person's imaginings and fantasies. In genetics contexts investigations may demonstrate non-paternity— that is, that the putative father of a patient's child is not the genetic father.

Such intrusive medical inquiries are based not on prurience or mere inquisitiveness but on the pursuit of information that is of potential assistance to the doctor in treating and helping the

[1] Personal Information in Medical Research (MRC 2000).

[2] 'Confidentiality' in Helga Kuhse and Peter Singer (eds), *A Companion to Bioethics* (Blackwell Oxford 1998) 425–31, 426–7.

patient. Nonetheless many patients are unlikely to pass on this information unless they have some assurances of confidentiality.

Quite apart from the medical benefits to the patient, maintenance of confidentiality may in some circumstances benefit the health of others. In the context of transmissible diseases, especially sexually transmissible diseases, so long as the patient continues to trust his or her doctor the doctor is left in a position of being able to educate and influence the patient in ways that can reduce the likelihood of the disease being passed on. As soon as confidentiality is broken the trusting relationship is likely to be undermined and the opportunity to help reduce the spread of disease is lost.

Thus the primary moral justification of medical confidentiality seems to be that it produces better medical consequences . . .

Quite apart from such consequentialist justifications, medical confidentiality can also be justified from a variety of other moral perspectives. Respect for autonomy, the fundamental value in Kantian ethics, would also seem to support a commitment to confidentiality, at least if autonomy is understood in its contemporary sense of self-determination, or deliberated or thought-out choice for oneself.

Of course, whether or not it is true that patients would be reluctant to be candid with them, if their confidentiality was not protected is essentially an *empirical* question. Interestingly C Jones points out that few people have attempted to find out whether patient trust is, in fact, contingent upon respect for confidentiality. Jones's study did, however, confirm the generally untested assumption that patients might be deterred from seeking treatment if their confidentiality was not respected.

C Jones[3]

The utilitarian justification for maintaining medical confidentiality rests ultimately on a calculation of the effects of confidentiality or disclosure on the behaviour of current and potential future patients. This calculation is often based upon theoretical views of how patients are likely to behave, but in principle it is also open to empirical study: how does the behaviour of patients alter when presented with different standards of confidentiality? Only if there is good reason, grounded in empirical evidence, to believe that patients will be reluctant to disclose potential damaging information in situations where subsequent disclosure is anticipated, could we be confident that the utilitarian basis for confidentiality is justified. Conversely, evidence that patient behaviour is not significantly altered by disclosure practices would fundamentally weaken the utilitarian position.

Surprisingly, such empirical evidence is not readily available, perhaps because ethical questions are commonly considered to be better answered by appeal to theory rather than by practical testing. It is usually assumed that patients consider confidentiality to be important and that they would be less likely to seek treatment if this was not assured; few studies have asked patients directly. This study represents a preliminary attempt to assess the views of patients on this issue . . .

The utilitarian position receives considerable support from the views expressed in this study by patients. They clearly value confidentiality, see it as important in a medical consultation, and recognise that disclosure without consent would be likely to deter some patients from seeking treatment. To this extent it seems that the generally accepted view of the benefits of confidentiality

---

[3] 'The utilitarian argument for medical confidentiality: a pilot study of patients' views' (2003) 29 Journal of Medical Ethics 348–52.

can be justified. However for many people the utility of confidentiality appears to be outweighed by the benefits of disclosure in order to protect third parties. They were prepared to endorse disclosure of information at the same time as recognising that treatment might be impaired as a result.

Although important, confidentiality is clearly not an absolute obligation. The Hippocratic Oath only enjoins doctors to keep secret that 'which ought not to be noised abroad', the implication being that there will be circumstances in which information *should* be 'noised abroad'. The Declaration on Geneva does not appear to be qualified in this way, but the existence of exceptions to the duty of confidence is so well established that it would probably be a mistake to read too much into this.

Most obviously, an absolute duty of confidentiality would make it impossible to provide effective medical treatment. Unless a patient's notes can be read by other healthcare professionals, it would be impossible to provide appropriate diagnostic and therapeutic care. Patients no longer have a one to one relationship with a single doctor, rather medical care is now provided by teams of doctors and nurses, all of whom need to have access to information about the patient's condition. Patients may be referred to specialist consultants, or for additional diagnostic procedures, such as X-rays and scans. If information about the patient's condition could never be shared, the provision of healthcare would grind to a halt. As more people purchase private health insurance, a certain amount of information about patients' medical treatment may also have to be shared with insurers.

In the next extract, Lisa Parker suggests that in practice patient information is increasingly widely shared within the healthcare sector and that the belief that what one tells one's doctor 'will go no further' has always been an illusion.

Lisa S Parker[4]

In a 1982 article declaring confidentiality to be a decrepit concept, physician and bioethicist Mark Siegler noted that structural features of the modern health-care delivery system presented greater threats to patient confidentiality than did third parties with competing interests. Examining the care received by one of his patients during a routine hospital stay, Siegler recognized that nearly one hundred people—members of the health-care team—had access to his patient's medical record . . .

Nevertheless, one function of confidentiality protections is eroded by these routine uses of patient information: . . . patients have lost control of their personal information. Although they may be no more likely to suffer embarrassment or economic loss as information about the course of their illnesses is stored electronically in data banks and routinely analyzed by statisticians for the benefit of others, patients have lost the opportunity to control their informational contribution to this enterprise. Of course, it is not clear that they ever had such control. Patients never could literally 'control' their medical records so as to prevent inadvertent or malicious disclosures of their personal information. Moreover, individual physicians have always drawn anecdotal conclusions from the treatment of individual patients and then applied those conclusions in the treatment of future patients . . . What patients may have lost, then, is the *illusion* that they maintained control of their personal information when disclosing it within the privacy of the physician–patient relationship.

[4] 'Information(al) Matters: Bioethics and the Boundaries of the Public and the Private' (2002) 19 Social Philosophy and Policy 83–112, 89–90.

In the next extract, Lawrence Gostin points out that because patients' notes now contain a great deal of information which can easily be shared and transferred, the protection of confidentiality has become even more important.

Lawrence O Gostin[5]

Only a few generations ago, physicians kept minimal written records about their patients. Physicians usually knew their patients and did not see a need to maintain extensive written reminders of patients' clinical histories. Today, the quantity of health records and the nature of the data they contain have increased substantially. The health records of patients, therefore, contain significant amounts of sensitive information that are available for inspection by many others. . . .

Genomic data present particularly novel and far-reaching privacy concerns, making these data distinct but not unique. The current and likely future proliferation of genetic databases means that holders of these genomic data will possess vast amounts of information. The potential uses of the genetic material are considerable, ranging from clinical, research, and public health applications to determining parentage and providing forensic evidence . . .

The combination of emerging computer and genetic technologies poses particularly compelling privacy concerns. Science has the capacity to store a million fragments of DNA on a silicon microchip . . . This technology can markedly facilitate research, screening, and treatment of genetic conditions. But it may also permit a significant reduction in privacy through its capacity to inexpensively store and decipher unimaginable quantities of highly sensitive data.

As we see later in this chapter, other exceptions to the duty of confidentiality exist, often justified by the 'public interest'. Because the principal justification for *respecting* patient confidentiality is also the public interest, working out whether disclosure is justified in a particular case will often involve a complex balancing exercise between competing interests. For example, if a patient confides in his doctor that he has committed a very serious crime, such as child abuse, should the doctor inform the police? What if the offence is recreational drug use? On the one hand, there is a clear public interest in the prevention and detection of crime, but on the other hand, it is also in the public interest for paedophiles and drug users to seek help. What if a patient is HIV positive, and his wife, who is also the doctor's patient, is unaware of his HIV status? Again, informing the wife might enable her to take preventative measures to ensure that she does not become infected, but simultaneously, deterring people from being tested for HIV by disclosing the test results without their consent might have wider negative implications for public health.

Given the number of variables, it is difficult to draw hard and fast rules about the circumstances which will justify disclosure of confidential information. The lack of clarity that results from this sort of case-by-case balancing exercise undoubtedly makes it difficult for doctors to know exactly when their primary duty of confidentiality will be trumped by competing considerations. To make an already confusing situation worse, the law in this area is especially difficult to understand. This is largely because the legal basis for a duty of confidentiality, and the remedies available for its breach, remain unclear. Added to this, the legal duty of confidence exists in vastly different situations, from duties under the Official Secrets Act to the protection of commercially sensitive information. It is difficult to extrapolate principles which will

---

[5] 'Health Informational Privacy' (1995) 80 Cornell Law Review 451, 489–92.

be applicable in the context of medical information from cases involving government secrets or patented information. Furthermore, some statutes, most notably, the Data Protection Act 1998 clearly have an impact upon medical records, and yet because this was never their principal focus, their application to the doctor–patient relationship can again be ambiguous and confusing.

At the outset, it should however be remembered that not all patient information is equally sensitive. A patient might be very anxious to keep her HIV status private, but be much less concerned about whether a consultant has used an X-ray of her broken foot in a lecture to junior doctors.

Furthermore, it could be argued that the priority given to patient confidentiality within medical law and ethics rests upon an unrealistically individualistic model of medical decision-making. In practice, most patients do not want to keep information about their health secret *from the whole world*. Rather while people might not want their employers or insurers to have access to their medical records, they generally feel more relaxed about discussing their health with people who are close to them. In fact, patients facing difficult medical choices or the diagnosis of serious illness will often want a close family member to be present during discussions with their doctors. In the next extract, Roy Gilbar argues that, in the context of familial relationships, the strict rule of confidentiality should be reconsidered.

Roy Gilbar[6]

While the relationship between patients and employers or insurers is primarily confrontational, with patients anxious to protect their rights and not be discriminated against, the relationship with family members is generally based on care, commitment and mutual responsibility. Consequently, information is in most cases communicated more freely within the family than with other third parties. Even when patients are reluctant to disclose medical information to their family members, this derives from the complex emotional relationship they have with them, and not from a fear that their fundamental rights would be exploited. For the doctor, this means that his/her duty of confidentiality when it concerns family members should be less strict than it is with regard to other third parties. It should also be based on his/her knowledge and understanding of the familial relationship . . .

[P]atients often consider the interests of their relatives and the implications of their decision on their familial relationship, while doctors are willing to involve family members more than the law currently permits to help the patient cope with the bad news. In other words, doctors and patients value the patient's familial relationship as a separate and significant component in this area. Thus, the strict legal rule of medical confidentiality, which is adopted by many lawyers and policy-makers, should be re-considered. . . .

If it is accepted that the gaps between law and practice should be bridged, then it can be argued that a doctor's duty of confidentiality must be qualified when it concerns the family. It must reflect awareness of familial solidarity and mutual responsibility and the reality that family members are inherently involved in the patient's well-being and medical care. In practice, the involvement of the family in the doctor–patient relationship has already received medical recognition. Medical students are currently taught that a patient's illness affects not only the individual patient but also his/her entire family. Doctors in various areas of medicine have learned to accept that the support

[6] 'Medical Confidentiality Within the Family: The Doctor's Duty Reconsidered' (2004) 18 International Journal of Law, Policy and the Family 195, 204–5.

and comfort that family members provide to the patient during all the stages of his/her illness is important, and that the family rather than the individual patient, should be considered as the unit of medical care. This, in many cases, leads to the conclusion that adhering to a strict rule of confidentiality may compromise the interests of the patient instead of promoting them.

But even if we were to accept that patients do not always want to keep information about their health secret from their closest friends or relatives, disclosure should still lie within their control. Not all familial relationships are harmonious and supportive, and a person might have very good reasons for wanting to keep information from her relatives.

4. A DUTY OF CONFIDENTIALITY

In the following sections we examine a number of different sources of the legal duty of confidence.

(a) AT COMMON LAW

The origins of the legal duty of confidence lie in the equitable jurisdiction of the Chancery Division to grant injunctions in order to prevent the infringement of legal and equitable rights. So what gives rise to an enforceable duty of confidentiality? In *Phipps v Boardman*,[7] Lord Upjohn said:

The true test is to determine in what circumstances the information has been acquired. If it has been acquired in such circumstances that it would be a breach of confidence to disclose to another then courts of equity will restrain the recipient from communicating it to another.

In *Stephens v Avery*,[8] Sir Nicolas Browne-Wilkinson VC explained that:

The basis of equitable intervention to protect confidentiality is that it is unconscionable for a person who has received information on the basis that it is confidential subsequently to reveal that information. Although the relationship between the parties is often important in cases where it is said there is an implied as opposed to express obligation of confidence, the relationship between the parties is not the determining factor. It is the acceptance of the information on the basis that it will be kept secret that affects the conscience of the recipient of the information.

And in *AG v Guardian Newspapers (No 2)*,[9] known as the *Spycatcher* case, Lord Bingham explained that the duty of confidence arises from an obligation of conscience:

The cases show that the duty of confidence does not depend on any contract, express or implied, between the parties. If it did, it would follow on ordinary principles that strangers to the contract would not be bound. But the duty 'depends on the broad principle of equity that he who has received information in confidence shall not take unfair advantage of it' . . . A third party coming into possession of confidential information is accordingly liable to be restrained from publishing it

---

[7] [1967] 2 AC 46.   [8] [1988] Ch 449.   [9] [1990] AC 109.

if he knows the information to be confidential and the circumstances are such as to impose upon him an obligation in good conscience not to publish.

In the same case, Lord Goff laid out the necessary conditions for the existence of a duty of confidence:

a duty of confidence arises when confidential information comes to the knowledge of a person (the confidant) in circumstances where he has notice, or is held to have agreed, that the information is confidential, with the effect that it would be just in all the circumstances that he should be precluded from disclosing the information to others. I have used the word 'notice' advisedly, in order to avoid the . . . question of the extent to which actual knowledge is necessary; though I of course understand knowledge to include circumstances where the confidant has deliberately closed his eyes to the obvious. The existence of this broad general principle reflects the fact that there is such a public interest in the maintenance of confidences, that the law will provide remedies for their protection.

Lord Goff went on to suggest three limiting principles. First, that the information must itself be confidential, and must not already be in the public domain. Secondly, there is no duty of confidentiality in relation to useless information or trivia. Thirdly, the duty to respect confidentiality is not an absolute one, and can sometimes be trumped by the public interest in disclosure.

The factors which give rise to a duty of confidentiality are thus both vague and somewhat question-begging: effectively a duty of confidence arises when someone knows, or ought to know, that the information she has acquired is confidential. It is both the *nature* of the information and the *circumstances in which it was disclosed* that create the duty of confidentiality.

For our purposes, however, the position is relatively clear. Medical information will generally be the sort of information which is treated as confidential, and the doctor–patient relationship is plainly one in which a duty of confidence exists. As Boreham J stated in *Hunter v Mann*,[10]

in common with other professional men, for instance a priest and there are of course others, the doctor is under a duty not to disclose, without the consent of his patient, information which he, the doctor, has gained in his professional capacity, save . . . in very exceptional circumstances.

And in *W v Edgell*,[11] a case which we consider in more detail below at p. 341, the existence of a duty of confidence between Dr Edgell and the patient was not in doubt. According to Bingham LJ,

It has never been doubted that the circumstances here were such as to impose on Dr Egdell a duty of confidence owed to W. He could not lawfully sell the contents of his report to a newspaper, as the judge held. Nor could he, without a breach of the law as well as professional etiquette, discuss the case in a learned article or in his memoirs or in gossiping with friends, unless he took appropriate steps to conceal the identity of W. It is not in issue here that a duty of confidence existed.

An alternative basis for the duty of confidentiality at common law would be to characterize it as an aspect of the doctor's duty of care. So a doctor who discloses

---

[10] [1974] QB 767.   [11] [1990] Ch 359.

information which should have been kept private may not have acted as a reasonable doctor, and the patient might therefore be able to bring an action in negligence. This will only be possible, however, if the patient has suffered some sort of damage as a result of this breach, perhaps because the patient was denied insurance coverage after an unwarranted disclosure. But more commonly, the 'harm' from breach of confidentiality will be less tangible and an action in tort much less promising.

It is usually assumed that the duty of confidentiality is owed to the patient, rather than to the hospital treating her. However, the hospital too might have an important interest in ensuring the confidentiality of their patient records. In *Ashworth Hospital Authority v MGN Ltd*,[12] the *Mirror* newspaper had published information about the medical treatment of Ian Brady, one of the Moors murderers. Ian Brady had been keen to publicize what he perceived to be his ill treatment, and had himself attempted to put information about his treatment into the public domain. The hospital obtained an order requiring the newspaper to identify the employee who had 'leaked' Brady's medical notes. On appeal, the House of Lords decided that the security of medical records was of such overriding importance that it was essential that the person who had disclosed them to the newspaper was identified and punished, even if the patient himself did not object to the disclosure. According to Lord Woolf:

while Ian Brady's conduct in putting similar information into the public domain could well mean that he would not be in a position to complain about the publication, this did not destroy the authority's independent interest in retaining the confidentiality of the medical records contained in Ashworth's files. . . .

The care of patients at Ashworth is fraught with difficulty and danger. The disclosure of the patients' records increases that difficulty and danger and to deter the same or similar wrongdoing in the future it was essential that the source should be identified and punished. This was what made the orders to disclose necessary and proportionate and justified. The fact that Ian Brady had himself disclosed his medical history did not detract from the need to prevent staff from revealing medical records of patients. Ian Brady's conduct did not damage the integrity of Ashworth's patients' records. The source's disclosure was wholly inconsistent with the security of the records and the disclosure was made worse because it was purchased by a cash payment.

(b) THE HUMAN RIGHTS ACT 1998

Could a patient's interest in confidentiality be protected by Article 8 of the Human Rights Act 1998, the 'right to respect for private and family life'? Plainly respect for private life could include keeping personal information, such as medical notes, private. Article 8 is not an absolute right, however, and is qualified by 8(2):

(1) Everyone has the right to respect for his private and family life, his home and his correspondence.

(2) There shall be no interference by a public authority with the exercise of this right except such as is in accordance with the law and is necessary in a democratic society in the interests of national security, public safety or the economic well-being of the country, for

---

[12] [2002] 1 WLR 2033.

the prevention of disorder or crime, for the protection of health or morals, or for the protection of the rights and freedoms of others.

There have been a number of cases in which patients have relied upon Article 8 when complaining about the disclosure of medical information. It has not proved especially difficult for individuals to establish that any disclosure of their medical records constitutes a prima facie violation of Article 8. The principal obstacle to a successful claim is that Article 8(2) gives public authorities a fairly broad margin of appreciation *for* justifying disclosure. In *Z v Finland*,[13] for example, Z was married to someone who had been charged with a number of sexual offences. He was HIV positive, and in order to find out when he became aware of his HIV status, the police sought and gained access to Z's medical records. The ECHR held that seizing Z's medical records and ordering her doctors to give evidence did not violate Article 8 because there were good reasons for requiring this information: a legitimate aim was being pursued and the measures taken were not disproportionate.

In view of the highly intimate and sensitive nature of information concerning a person's HIV status, any state measures compelling communication or disclosure of such information without the consent of the patient call for the most careful scrutiny on the part of the court, as do the safeguards designed to secure an effective protection . . .

At the same time, the court accepts that the interests of a patient and the community as a whole in protecting the confidentiality of medical data may be outweighed by the interest in investigation and prosecution of crime and in the publicity of court proceedings, where such interests are shown to be of even greater importance.

However, revealing her identity in the Court of Appeal judgment, and allowing this information to become public after 10 years did amount to a disproportionate interference with her right to respect for her private and family life, and was not supported by any cogent reasons.

Again in *MS v Sweden*, the ECHR found that the need to suppress benefit fraud offered sufficient justification for the disclosure of the applicant's medical records:

The court reiterates that the protection of personal data, particularly medical data, is of fundamental importance to a person's enjoyment of his or her right to respect for private and family life as guaranteed by art 8 of the Convention. . . .

It recognises that, in deciding whether to accept the applicant's compensation claim, the Office had a legitimate need to check information received from her against data in the possession of the clinic. In the absence of objective information from an independent source, it would have been difficult for the Office to determine whether the claim was well founded.

In *A Health Authority v X*, the application of Article 8 to medical records was considered in the context of an application by a Health Authority for disclosure of patient records in order to investigate a GP practice's failure to comply with its terms of service to determine whether disciplinary action should be taken. At first instance Munby J had held that disclosure of a patient's records could be justified but only if there were strict measures in place to protect confidentiality.[14] Disclosure would be

---

[13] (1997) 25 EHRR 371, (1997) 45 BMLR 107.   [14] [2001] 2 FCR 634.

permissible on the express conditions that (a) the documents were to remain confidential and (b) the authority and every other public body or other person to whom the documents might be transmitted was subject to the obligation to take effective and adequate safeguards against abuse. The Court of Appeal agreed both that disclosure would be justified, and that Munby J had acted within his powers by imposing conditions upon that disclosure.

A Health Authority v X[15]

The health authority was concerned about a GP practice's compliance with its terms of service. In particular the authority wished to investigate: (i) The possibility that there had been a serious over-dispensing of medicines; (ii) the completeness of medical records; (iii) whether there had been an inappropriate delegation of responsibility in relation to the medical care of patients; and (iv) the adequacy of the consent sought before performing medical procedures. It sought disclosure of specified case papers (the List A documents) and the medical notes of certain named patients, two of whom refused to consent to such disclosure (the List B documents).

Thorpe LJ

There is obviously a high public interest, analogous to the public interest in the due administration of criminal justice, in the proper administration of professional disciplinary hearings, particularly in the field of medicine. In the application of the authorities which he had cited, Munby J properly ordered the release of the case material, namely the list A documents.

Although the list B documents are separately categorized . . . the list B documents were inextricably connected . . . In those circumstances in my opinion the objection to production fell to be decided in accordance with the principle that determined the application for the release of the list A documents, namely whether the public interest in effective disciplinary procedures for the investigation and eradication of medical malpractice outweighed the confidentiality of the records . . . A balance still had to be struck between competing interests. The balance came down in favour of production as it invariably does, save in exceptional cases. . . .

Without [the power to attach conditions] to an order directing the release of case papers in Children Act proceedings to a third party, the court would be left with a crude choice between directing or refusing release. Striking a balance between competing public interests, often across the interface of distinct justice systems, requires much more sophisticated powers. In my opinion Munby J was correct in law to claim that power and equally correct to proceed to a discretionary exercise of that power having regard to the relevant facts and circumstances in so far as they were revealed to him.

In addition to Article 8(2)'s qualification of the right to privacy, Article 8 has to be put into the balance with Article 10, the right to freedom of expression, and section 12 of the Human Rights Act, which further specifies that 'The court must have particular regard to the importance of the Convention right to freedom of expression.'

Hence, the public interest in a free press is such that any interference with the press's freedom to publish information must be justified. In another context, in *Douglas v Hello!*,[16] Brooke LJ held that

Although the right to freedom of expression is not in every case the ace of trumps, it is a powerful card to which the courts of this country must always pay appropriate respect.

---

[15] [2001] EWCA Civ 2014, [2002] 2 All ER 780.   [16] [2001] 2 All ER 289.

The need to balance the interests protected by Articles 8 and 10 was applied to medical information in *Campbell v MGN Ltd.*[17] The House of Lords had to determine whether the press's freedom to publish information about a celebrity's treatment for drug addiction should take priority over her right to privacy.

Campbell v MGN Ltd[18]

The defendant newspaper published a number of articles about the claimant, Naomi Campbell, a famous fashion model. The articles and accompanying photographs revealed that she was a drug addict; was receiving treatment for her addiction; and was attending Narcotics Anonymous (NA). The claimant accepted that the newspaper had been entitled, in the public interest, to disclose the information that she was a drug addict and that she was receiving treatment for her addiction, because she had previously falsely and publicly stated that she was not a drug addict. However, she brought proceedings against the publishers for breach of confidence and compensation under the Data Protection Act 1998 with respect to the information and photographs relating to her attendance at NA. The judge upheld her claim. This was overturned by the the Court of Appeal. By a 3:2 majority, the House of Lords allowed the claimant's appeal.

Lord Hope

The context for this exercise is provided by articles 8 and 10 of the convention. The rights guaranteed by these articles are qualified rights. Article 8(1) protects the right to respect for private life, but recognition is given in article 8(2) to the protection of the rights and freedoms of others. Article 10(1) protects the right to freedom of expression, but article 10(2) recognises the need to protect the rights and freedoms of others. The effect of these provisions is that the right to privacy which lies at the heart of an action for breach of confidence has to be balanced against the right of the media to impart information to the public. And the right of the media to impart information to the public has to be balanced in its turn against the respect that must be given to private life . . .

Any interference with the public interest in disclosure has to be balanced against the interference with the right of the individual to respect for their private life. The decisions that are then taken are open to review by the court. The tests which the court must apply are the familiar ones. They are whether publication of the material pursues a legitimate aim and whether the benefits that will be achieved by its publication are proportionate to the harm that may be done by the interference with the right to privacy. The jurisprudence of the European Court of Human Rights explains how these principles are to be understood and applied in the context of the facts of each case. Any restriction of the right to freedom of expression must be subjected to very close scrutiny. But so too must any restriction of the right to respect for private life. Neither article 8 nor article 10 has any pre-eminence over the other in the conduct of this exercise . . .

The first question is whether the objective of the restriction on the article 10 right—the protection of Miss Campbell's right under article 8 to respect for her private life—is sufficiently important to justify limiting the fundamental right to freedom of expression which the press assert on behalf of the public. It follows from my conclusion that the details of Miss Campbell's treatment were private that I would answer this question in the affirmative . . .

Looking at the matter from Miss Campbell's point of view and the protection of her article 8 convention right, publication of details of the treatment which she was undertaking to cure her addiction—that she was attending NA, for how long, how frequently and at what times of day she had been attending this therapy, the nature of it and extent of her commitment to the process and

[17] [2004] UKHL 22, [2004] 2 AC 457.   [18] Ibid.

the publication of the covertly taken photographs (the third, fourth and fifth of the five elements contained in the article)—had the potential to cause harm to her.

Baroness Hale

I start, therefore, from the fact—indeed, it is common ground—that all of the information about Miss Campbell's addiction and attendance at NA which was revealed in the *Mirror* article was both private and confidential, because it related to an important aspect of Miss Campbell's physical and mental health and the treatment she was receiving for it. It had also been received from an insider in breach of confidence. . . . But the starting point must be that it was all private and its publication required specific justification . . .

What was the nature of the freedom of expression which was being asserted on the other side? There are undoubtedly different types of speech, just as there are different types of private information, some of which are more deserving of protection in a democratic society than others. Top of the list is political speech. The free exchange of information and ideas on matters relevant to the organisation of the economic, social and political life of the country is crucial to any democracy. . . . Artistic speech and expression is important for similar reasons . . .

But it is difficult to make such claims on behalf of the publication with which we are concerned here. The political and social life of the community, and the intellectual, artistic or personal development of individuals, are not obviously assisted by pouring over the intimate details of a fashion model's private life. . . .

The weight to be attached to these various considerations is a matter of fact and degree. Not every statement about a person's health will carry the badge of confidentiality or risk doing harm to that person's physical or moral integrity. The privacy interest in the fact that a public figure has a cold or a broken leg is unlikely to be strong enough to justify restricting the press's freedom to report it. What harm could it possibly do? Sometimes there will be other justifications for publishing, especially where the information is relevant to the capacity of a public figure to do the job. But that is not this case and in this case there was, as the judge found, a risk that publication would do harm. The risk of harm is what matters at this stage, rather than the proof that actual harm has occurred. People trying to recover from drug addiction need considerable dedication and commitment, along with constant reinforcement from those around them. That is why organisations like NA were set up and why they can do so much good. Blundering in when matters are acknowledged to be at a 'fragile' stage may do great harm.

Notice that the House of Lords found that an obligation of confidence existed because of the *nature* of the information about Ms Campbell's treatment for drug addiction, rather than because of any pre-existing relationship between her and the *Mirror* newspaper. Unlike the cases on breach of confidence which we considered in the previous section, it appears that the right to privacy attaches to *any* paradigmatically private information, regardless of the circumstances in which that information is acquired.

(c) THE DATA PROTECTION ACT 1998

The Data Protection Act 1998 was passed in order to implement an EC directive.[19] Schedule 1 of the Act contains eight Data Protection Principles. The first Data

---

[19] European Directive 95/46/EC on the Protection of Individuals with Regard to the Processing of Personal Data and on the Free Movement of Such Data (known as the Data Protection Directive).

Protection Principle states that all personal data must be processed 'fairly and lawfully'. Processing essentially means doing anything at all with information, so obtaining, storing, disclosing or using information will all be covered by the Act. What does it mean to process data *fairly* and *lawfully*? Obviously to be lawful, processing must meet common law obligations of confidentiality, but the Act itself further defines 'fairness' and 'legality' in a way which is, to say the least, rather confusing. For sensitive personal data, which under section 2(e) includes information about a person's 'physical or mental health or condition', processing will have been fair and lawful provided that (in addition to meeting common law obligations of confidentiality) at least one condition from Schedule 2 of the Act and one from Schedule 3 are satisfied.

Data Protection Act 1998 Schedule 1

1. Personal data shall be processed fairly and lawfully and, in particular, shall not be processed unless—

   (a) at least one of the conditions in Schedule 2 is met, and

   (b) in the case of sensitive personal data, at least one of the conditions in Schedule 3 is also met.

Schedule 2

CONDITIONS RELEVANT FOR PURPOSES OF THE FIRST PRINCIPLE: PROCESSING OF ANY PERSONAL DATA

1. The data subject has given his consent to the processing.

2. The processing is necessary—

   (a) for the performance of a contract to which the data subject is a party, or

   (b) for the taking of steps at the request of the data subject with a view to entering into a contract.

3. The processing is necessary for compliance with any legal obligation to which the data controller is subject, other than an obligation imposed by contract.

4. The processing is necessary in order to protect the vital interests of the data subject.

5. The processing is necessary—

   (a) for the administration of justice,

   (b) for the exercise of any functions conferred on any person by or under any enactment,

   (c) for the exercise of any functions of the Crown, a Minister of the Crown or a government department, or

   (d) for the exercise of any other functions of a public nature exercised in the public interest by any person.

6. (1) The processing is necessary for the purposes of legitimate interests pursued by the data controller or by the third party or parties to whom the data are disclosed, except where the processing is unwarranted in any particular case by reason of prejudice to the rights and freedoms or legitimate interests of the data subject.

   (2) The Secretary of State may by order specify particular circumstances in which this condition is, or is not, to be taken to be satisfied.

Schedule 3

CONDITIONS RELEVANT FOR PURPOSES OF THE FIRST PRINCIPLE: PROCESSING OF SENSITIVE PERSONAL DATA

1.   The data subject has given his explicit consent to the processing of the personal data. . . .

3.   The processing is necessary—

(a) in order to protect the vital interests of the data subject or another person, in a case where—

(i) consent cannot be given by or on behalf of the data subject, or

(ii) the data controller cannot reasonably be expected to obtain the consent of the data subject, or

(c) in order to protect the vital interests of another person, in a case where consent by or on behalf of the data subject has been unreasonably withheld. . . .

8.   (1) The processing is necessary for medical purposes and is undertaken by—

(a) a health professional, or

(b) a person who in the circumstances owes a duty of confidentiality which is equivalent to that which would arise if that person were a health professional.

(2) In this paragraph 'medical purposes' includes the purposes of preventative medicine, medical diagnosis, medical research, the provision of care and treatment and the management of healthcare services.

Under Schedule 2, the data subject must consent to the 'processing' of personal data. There are, however six exceptions to the need to obtain consent contained in Schedule 2, of which three are worth highlighting here. First, data may be processed without consent if it is necessary to protect the vital interests of the data subject. This exception is not confined to situations where the patient's life is in danger, rather it could simply mean that sharing the information is necessary in order to protect her health. It is, however, only justifiable if the processing is *necessary* as opposed to merely convenient.

Secondly, processing without consent might be justifiable under Schedule 2 if it is 'necessary' for functions of a public nature exercised in the public interest, or for the exercise of functions of government departments, or a Secretary of State. Under the National Health Service Act 1977, the Secretary of State for Health is under a duty to 'continue the promotion of a comprehensive health service'. Provided that the processing of patient information was *necessary* for him to fulfil this function, it would appear lawful to use patient records without consent. Here, of course, the problem is what might be meant by 'necessary'. Is the maintenance of comprehensive cancer registries *necessary* for the promotion of a comprehensive health service, for example?

Thirdly, processing without consent is legitimate if it is necessary for the purposes of the data controller's legitimate interests. This might allow disclosure for the purposes of research or audit, and again the crucial question is whether the use of data is *necessary* for these purposes.

Once a condition from Schedule 2 has been satisfied, it is then necessary to turn to

Schedule 3, which contains ten exceptions to the need to obtain the data subject's 'explicit consent' to the processing of sensitive personal data. Here things become slightly clearer because the 8th condition in Schedule 3 is that processing without consent is justifiable if it 'is necessary for medical purposes', and is undertaken by a health professional or a person who owes an equivalent duty of confidentiality. Medical purposes are not confined to treatment, but include 'preventative medicine, medical diagnosis, medical research, the provision of care and treatment and the management of health care services'. Given this expansive list, the only limiting criterion here is again that the processing should be *necessary* for these purposes.

A further exception to the explicit consent requirement is contained in paragraph 3 of Schedule 3 which provides that processing will be fair and lawful if it is in the vital interests of the data subject or another person. Hence, information can be disclosed without consent to protect the health of a third party.

The Data Protection (Processing of Sensitive Personal Data) Order 2000 added a further condition to Schedule 3. This allows for processing which is in the 'substantial public interest' where necessary for the discharge of certain public functions, such as protecting the public against malpractice, or other seriously improper conduct, unfitness or incompetence. Hence disclosure to the General Medical Council (GMC) in relation to an allegation of professional misconduct, or to the Healthcare Commission in the exercise of its clinical governance role, would be permissible without consent. The limiting factors are that the processing must be in the substantial public interest, and again that it must be necessary for discharging the particular public function.

The second Data Protection Principle specifies that information must be obtained only for one or more specified and lawful purposes, and must not be further processed in a way that is incompatible with those purposes. Section 33 contains an exception where the further processing is for the purposes of research. This means that there is no need to obtain specific patient consent to the use of their medical records for research purposes, provided that there is no possibility of identifying the patients, or causing them substantial damage or distress.

The final Data Protection Principle which is relevant for our purposes is the fifth one, which specifies that information must be kept no longer than necessary for the purposes for which it is processed. Again there is an exception for information which is processed for research purposes, which can be kept indefinitely.

In line with the Data Protection Act, the British Medical Association endorses the use of medical information without consent for the purposes of research and audit.

British Medical Association

Research

While it can constitute a justifiable use of personal health information, research should ideally use anonymised data wherever possible. It may be possible to use pseudonyms or other tracking mechanisms for information which cannot be anonymised, thus ensuring accuracy and minimising the use of personal identifiers. Health professionals must make reasonable efforts to ensure that patients understand that their data may be used in research unless they exercise their right to object. Identifiable information should not be used for research purposes if the individual has registered an objection.

Audit

Clinical audit should be carried out by health professionals with clear professional obligations to maintain confidentiality. It is good ethical practice to take steps to inform patients that the quality of care is reviewed through the process of audit and that this might involve looking through a patient's records to produced anonymised audit data. If patients express a refusal to allow their information to be used for audit purposes, this should be respected.

The BMA has no ethical objections to anonymous records being used for clinical audit purposes without consent, provided that the process of removing identifying details is carried out by a member of the health care team involved in treating the patient. Where no additional individual has access to records, no breach of confidentiality can occur. Where access to identifiable information is required by other individuals, for example audit professionals in hospitals, consent to disclosure must be sought. Such consent may be gained by providing patients with information about the fact and purpose of audit, and giving them an opportunity to refuse to allow their records to be disclosed.

If any of these provisions are breached, the Data Protection Act provides for three different remedies. First, under section 10 a data subject can serve a notice requiring the data controller to cease or refrain from processing his personal data. The data subject must establish that the processing is causing, or would be likely to cause substantial damage, either to her or to a third party. Secondly, it is possible to seek compensation under section 13 where the data subject or another has suffered damage and consequent distress as a result of the disclosure. The data controller will, however, have a defence if he can show that he took reasonable care to comply with the Act. Thirdly, under section 14 the court can order the data controller to rectify or destroy inaccurate data.

(d) OTHER STATUTORY PROVISIONS

In certain situations, additional obligations to respect confidentiality are created by statute. For example, the Human Fertilisation and Embryology Act 1990 section 33 imposes extra restrictions upon the disclosure of information held in confidence by the Human Fertilisation and Embryology Authority. The NHS (Venereal Diseases) Regulations 1974[20] provide that information about sexually transmitted diseases can only be communicated to medical practitioners for the treatment and prevention of disease. Under the Abortion Regulations 1991[21] there is a duty to report each termination of pregnancy to the Chief Medical Office, but there are also a number of restrictions upon any further disclosure of this information.

(e) GOOD MEDICAL PRACTICE

As we saw at the outset of this chapter, the duty of confidentiality has been a fundamental ethical obligation since the first attempts to codify medical ethics in Ancient Greece. And more modern guidance to doctors, most notably from the GMC, reinforces the importance of respecting patient confidentiality:

[20] SI 1974/29.   [21] SI 1991/499.

General Medical Council[22]

1   Patients have a right to expect that information about them will be held in confidence by their doctors. Confidentiality is central to trust between doctors and patients. Without assurances about confidentiality, patients may be reluctant to give doctors the information they need in order to provide good care. If you are asked to provide information about patients you must:

- inform patients about the disclosure, or check that they have already received information about it;
- anonymise data where unidentifiable data will serve the purpose;
- be satisfied that patients know about disclosures necessary to provide their care, or for local clinical audit of that care, that they can object to these disclosures but have not done so;
- seek patients' express consent to disclosure of information, where identifiable data is needed for any purpose other than the provision of care or for clinical audit—save in the exceptional circumstances described in this booklet;
- keep disclosures to the minimum necessary; and
- keep up to date with and observe the requirements of statute and common law, including data protection legislation.

Although this guidance does not have the status of law, it is certainly not without teeth. First, given the confusion evident in the various legal sources of the duty of confidentiality, in practice it is the GMC's guidance to the medical profession which will be most useful to doctors faced with a dilemma about whether breaching patient confidentiality would be justifiable. Secondly, breach of the GMC guidelines may lead to disciplinary proceedings, and if found guilty of 'serious professional misconduct', the doctor can be struck off the medical register. The United Kingdom Central Council for Nursing, Midwifery and Health Visiting's *Code of Professional Conduct* sets out similar duties and penalties for nurses, midwives, and health visitors.

Thirdly, breach of the GMC guidelines would be prima facie evidence that the doctor had failed to act as a responsible medical practitioner and was therefore in breach of his duty of care. Proving that a doctor has been negligent should be relatively straightforward where there has been a clear breach of the GMC's rules. As noted earlier, however, the patient will only be able to bring an action in negligence if some sort of damage was caused by the breach of confidence.

In 1997 a review of the use of patient-identifiable information in the NHS, chaired by Fiona Caldicott, was published by the Department of Health. The Caldicott Committee's report advocated greater awareness of the need to respect patient confidentiality, and the introduction of security measures to limit unauthorized disclosures. It laid out six principles,

(1) justify the purpose(s) for which the information is required

(2) do not use patient-identifiable information unless it is absolutely necessary

(3) use the minimum necessary patient-identifiable information

---

[22] Confidentiality: Protecting and Providing Information (GMC 2004) <http://www.gmc-uk.org/standards/default.htm>.

(4) access to patient-identifiable information should be on a strict need-to-know basis

(5) everyone with access to patient-identifiable information should be aware of their responsibilities

(6) understand and comply with the law.

The Report made sixteen recommendations on the use of information in the NHS. These emphasized the need to develop techniques and systems to ensure the confidentiality of patient-identifiable data. It suggested that each health organization should nominate a senior health professional to be responsible for safeguarding the confidentiality of patient information. The Government accepted the Committee's recommendations, and so-called 'Caldicott Guardians' have been in existence since 1999. In 2003 the Department of Health issued a Code of Practice on Confidentiality for NHS Staff which embodies the Caldicott Principles, and lays out detailed guidance on the use of identifiable patient information.[23]

5. INCOMPETENT PATIENTS

If the legal basis for the general duty of confidence is unclear, its application to children and incompetent adults is even more obscure. On the one hand, it seems clear that this fundamental aspect of a doctor's duty towards her patients should be universal. A sweeping exception for all children and incompetent adults would be unacceptably discriminatory. Medical records self-evidently contain confidential information, and if the duty of confidentiality arises from the very nature of the information itself, then it must apply equally to the records of those who lack capacity. For example, in *Venables v News Group Newspapers*,[24] Dame Elizabeth Butler-Sloss P stated that

Children, like adults, are entitled to confidentiality in respect of certain areas of information. Medical records are the obvious example.

But on the other hand, if it is the existence of a confidential *relationship*, or the *expectation* that information will be kept secret which gives rise to a duty of confidence, profoundly incapacitated patients, such as newborn babies or permanently unconscious adults will have no expectation that information about them will be held in confidence. Of course, incapacity is a matter of degree, and a mildly impaired adult, or a teenage child, might have the requisite expectation of confidence.

The House of Lords decision in the *Gilllick* case (which we considered in detail in Chapter 4, p. 233) clearly established that children who have reached an age of sufficient maturity will in certain circumstances have the right to keep information about their medical treatment from their parents. It is, however, unclear whether the child's right of confidentiality against her parents is confined to children who are *Gillick* competent. On the one hand, it might be argued that that was precisely what the House of Lords decided in *Gillick*. But on the other hand, a child may be capable of feeling distressed at the betrayal of a confidence before she possesses the requisite capacity to give an effective consent to medical treatment. Although there is insuffi-

---

[23] Available at <http://www.dh.gov.uk/>.   [24] [2001] 2 WLR 1038.

cient case law to determine the exact parameters of a doctor's duty of confidentiality towards her child patients, it seems likely, as the British Medical Association's guidance suggests, that the familiar best interests test would be invoked in order to determine whether a doctor acted reasonably in either withholding or disclosing information which a non-*Gillick* competent child had asked to be kept private.

British Medical Association[25]

Children who lack the competence to give consent to treatment are also entitled to confidentiality. These patients should be encouraged to allow their parents to be involved but if they cannot be persuaded, doctors must judge whether disclosure to parents is necessary in the child's medical interests.

In all cases involving young people, health professionals should try to persuade them to allow their parents to be informed. Even when the young person is too immature to give consent to the treatment requested, the confidentiality of the consultation should still generally be maintained unless there is an overriding justification for not doing so. The medical duty of confidentiality is not dependent upon the competence of the patient and, unless there are very convincing reasons to the contrary, parents should only be told about their child's request for treatment, medication or advice with permission.

Parents clearly have rights to be informed to the degree necessary to fulfil their parent responsibilities, however, and the right to family life in the European Convention on Human Rights supports parental involvement in decision making. In cases of conflict, the harms of breaching confidentiality must be weighed against the benefits of disclosure. For example it seems likely to be ethically justifiable to disclose information in order to allow a third party to give consent to essential treatment on the child's behalf. Nevertheless, a decision to disclose information against a young person's wishes is a significant one.

Obviously a very young child's right to confidentiality does not involve keeping treatment information from her parents. On the contrary, a child's parents are under a duty to take decisions about her medical treatment, and they can only do this if they are properly informed. The doctor's duty of confidentiality is therefore owed to the family unit of parent(s) *and* child, rather than just to the child herself. Moreover, the parents too may be bound by a duty of confidentiality towards their child. In *Re C (A Minor)(Wardship: Medical Treatment)*,[26] for example, Thorpe LJ said:

The parents undoubtedly owe C a duty of confidentiality, save in so far as C's welfare otherwise requires.

Incompetent adults are undoubtedly also owed a duty of confidentiality, but again, as the GMC guidance makes clear, the need for others to be involved in their care may mean that treatment information will in certain circumstances have to be disclosed to their carers. Usually the patient's agreement should be sought, but where disclosure is 'essential in their medical interests', information may be disclosed to a relevant third party.

---

[25] *Consent, Rights and Choices in Health Care for Children and Young People* (BMA London 2001) paras 4.1, 4.1.3.
[26] [1990] Fam 39.

General Medical Council[27]

28   Problems may arise if you consider that a patient lacks capacity to give consent to treatment or disclosure. If such patients ask you not to disclose information about their condition or treatment to a third party, you should try to persuade them to allow an appropriate
person to be involved in the consultation. If they refuse and you are convinced that it is
essential, in their medical interests, you may disclose relevant information to an appropriate person or authority. In such cases you should tell the patient before disclosing any
information, and where appropriate, seek and carefully consider the views of an advocate
or carer. You should document in the patient's record your discussions with the patient and
the reasons for deciding to disclose information.

In *R (on the application of S) v Plymouth City Council*[28] Hale LJ explained that while an
incapacitated adult did have an interest, albeit 'purely theoretical', in the confidentiality of his medical records, disclosure to his mother was necessary and proportionate.

R (on the application of S) v Plymouth City Council[29]

C was 27 years old, and had serious learning and behavioural difficulties. His mother had opposed
a recommendation from the local social services authority, but had not been shown the documen-
tation upon which their decision had been based. She had made a number of requests to have
access to her son's files, all of which had been refused. C's mother applied for judicial review of the
decisions to refuse her access to the relevant recommendations and reports. Her application was
dismissed by Maurice Kay J, but her appeal to the Court of Appeal was successful.

Hale LJ

[W]hile C's interest in preserving confidentiality is purely theoretical given his lack of capacity, the
mother is entitled to the information she requires in order to seek legal and professional advice
upon the exercise of her functions as nearest relative. . . .

C's interest in protecting the confidentiality of personal information about himself must not be
underestimated. It is all too easy for professionals and parents to regard children and incapacitated adults as having no independent interests of their own: as objects rather than subjects. But
we are not concerned here with the publication of information to the whole wide world. There is a
clear distinction between disclosure to the media with a view to publication to all and sundry and
disclosure in confidence to those with a proper interest in having the information in question. . . .

C also has an interest in having his own wishes and feelings respected. It would be different in
this case if he had the capacity to give or withhold consent to the disclosure: any objection from
him would have to be weighed in the balance against the other interests, although as *W v Egdell*
shows, it would not be decisive. . . .

There is no suggestion that C has any objection to his mother and her advisers being properly
informed about his health and welfare. There is no suggestion of any risk to his health and welfare
arising from this. The mother and her advisers have sought access to the information which her
own psychiatric and social work experts need in order properly to advise her. That limits both the
context and the content of disclosure in a way which strikes a proper balance between the
competing interests.

Degenerative brain diseases, such as Alzheimer's, raise particularly interesting

---

[27] Confidentiality: Protecting and Providing Information (GMC 2004) <http://www.gmc-uk.org/
standards/default.htm>.

[28] [2002] EWCA Civ 388, [2002] 1 WLR 2583.

[29] Ibid.

questions in relation to patient confidentiality. Patients who are suspected of having Alzheimer's disease are often first referred for diagnosis following a request from a relative, rather than because the patient herself is concerned about her symptoms. The clinical assessment will often be based upon descriptions of behaviour given by close relatives, and the diagnosis of Alzheimer's is, in practice, usually given to the patient's principal carer, rather than to the patient herself. As Pucci et al. point out,

At a certain stage of the disease, the patient is completely dependent on a caregiver who, in most cases, is a close relative. The physician cannot do without the interaction with the relative. Thus, it is mandatory to recognise a relationship between the physician and the relative/patient dyad rather than a simple physician/patient one. Within such a relationship the communication of the diagnosis to the relative is necessary.[30]

Clearly absolute respect for patient confidentiality in such circumstances is impractical. The reality of certain degenerative diseases is that the duty of confidentiality is in practice owed to the patient's primary carer. Indeed, Pucci et al.'s research indicated that most relatives of patients suffering from Alzheimer's disease believe that the patient should never be told about the diagnosis, for fear of provoking or aggravating depressive symptoms.[31]

6. DECEASED PATIENTS

Although there are no cases directly on this point, it seems unlikely that the *legal* duty of confidentiality survives a patient's death. Despite this, the Department of Health's Code of Practice and the GMC Guidance both suggest that the *ethical* obligation to respect patient confidentiality continues to exist after the patient has died.

Department of Health[32]
   28. ... [T]he Department of Health and the General Medical Council are in agreement that, whilst there are no clear legal obligations of confidentiality that apply to the deceased, there is an ethical basis for requiring that confidentiality obligations, as outlined in this document, must continue to apply.

General Medical Council[33]
   30. You still have an obligation to keep personal information confidential after a patient dies. The extent to which confidential information may be disclosed after a patient's death will depend on the circumstances. If the patient had asked for information to remain confidential, his or her views should be respected. Where you are unaware of any directions from the patient, you should consider requests for information taking into account:

   • whether the disclosure of information may cause distress to, or be of benefit to, the patient's partner or family;

---

[30] E Pucci et al., 'Relatives' attitudes towards informing patients about the diagnosis of Alzheimer's disease' (2003) 29 Journal of Medical Ethics 51–4, 53.

[31] Ibid, 51.

[32] Confidentiality: NHS Code of Practice (DH 2003).

[33] Confidentiality: Protecting and Providing Information (GMC 2004) <http://www.gmc-uk.org/standards/default.htm>.

- whether disclosure of information about the patient will in effect disclose information about the patient's family or other people;
- whether the information is already public knowledge or can be anonymised;
- the purpose of the disclosure.

If you decide to disclose confidential information you must be prepared to explain and justify your decision.

In the next extract, Jessica Berg explains why it might be important to maintain confidentiality after a patient's death.

Jessica Berg[34]

It is an interesting philosophical exercise to consider whether dead people have interests that survive their death, and, if so, whether they can be 'harmed' or 'wronged' by actions taken after their death. . . . Although it seems obvious that a dead body does not have interests, it is not so clear that a previously living person has no interests that survive death. . . .

Whether or not one accepts the argument that there are interests that survive death, there are clearly interests of the living that must be considered. In fact, these interests seem to form a stronger basis for understanding confidentiality protections in the postmortem context. First, there are the interests of current and future patients in assuming that information they disclose to their physicians will remain confidential.

Second, there are interests of third parties in maintaining the confidentiality of information related to the deceased. . . . Although we have a general moral conviction that people may dispose of their property after death, the obligation to abide by their wishes is a moral obligation to people still living, not to the deceased. Likewise, we might argue that preserving confidentiality after death coincides with our value of confidentiality as a general practice. . . . The practical concern in the context of confidentiality is whether people will be less likely to confide sensitive information to their physician (lawyer, mental health professional, etc.) knowing the possibility of disclosure postmortem. The ethical rule to maintain confidentiality, even postmortem, is premised, at least in part, on the notion that such rule will result in the best consequences . . .

Moreover, there is yet another group of interests that must be considered in this context—those of people now living and their interests in preserving the confidentiality of the specific person who has died. First, blood relatives of the deceased have an interest in controlling information that has implications for their own health (and thus identity). Although the interests of blood relatives in maintaining confidentiality may not supercede the individual's right to control his or her medical information during life, they may well be given greater weight (or at least be less likely to be outweighed) after that person has died.

Second, there are more nebulous interests of third parties in preventing the disclosure of confidential information. The dead live on in the memories of the living. Harms to the memory of the deceased may entail very real harms to people now living who have an interest in preserving the original memory, such as relatives or close friends of the deceased.

---

[34] 'Grave Secrets: Legal and Ethical Analysis of Postmorten Confidentiality' (2001) 34 Connecticut Law Review 81, 90–1, 95–6, 98–9.

7. EXCEPTIONS TO THE DUTY OF CONFIDENTIALITY

As was noted earlier, the duty of confidentiality is not absolute, and a number of exceptions exist which we flesh out in the following sections. At the outset, it is, however, worth noting that breaches of confidentiality do not necessarily involve a doctor *deliberately* deciding to share information about a patient with other people. Rather, inadvertent breaches of confidentiality are, in fact, more common. NHS in-patients spend most of their time on wards, and as a result any conversations they have with their doctors will often be overheard by other patients or healthcare workers. Patients' physical privacy can be protected to some extent by curtains, but it is probably impossible to guarantee the confidentiality of discussions which take place at the patient's bedside. Where there is particularly sensitive information to impart, it might therefore be important to ensure that the patient is given the opportunity to receive it in private.

(a) CONSENT

If the patient explicitly consents to the disclosure of information, then plainly the doctor is no longer under a duty of non-disclosure. This is not strictly speaking an exception to the duty of confidence, rather the patient's agreement to disclosure simply means that no duty of confidence exists. In *C v C*,[35] both parties to divorce proceedings had requested the respondent's doctor to disclose information about his venereal disease, and it was held that disclosure in such circumstances could not amount to a breach of confidence.

More complicated is the question of when a patient could be said to have impliedly consented to disclosure. The British Medical Association has suggested that

In the absence of evidence to the contrary, patients are normally considered to have given implied consent for the use of their information by health professionals for the purpose of providing the care they have come to receive. Information sharing in this context is acceptable to the extent that health professionals share what is necessary and relevant for the episode of care on a need to know basis.[36]

In order to establish that there was implied consent to disclosure, it would, as the General Medical Council's guidance to doctors, and the Department of Health's Code of Practice make clear, be necessary to prove that the patient was aware of the practice of disclosure and given an opportunity to object to it:

General Medical Council[37]

10   Most people understand and accept that information must be shared within the health care

---

[35] [1946] 1 All ER 562.
[36] Confidentiality and disclosure of health information (BMA London 1999).
[37] Confidentiality: Protecting and Providing Information (GMC 2004) <http://www.gmc-uk.org/standards/default.htm>.

team in order to provide their care. You should make sure that patients are aware that personal information about them will be shared within the health care team, unless they object, and of the reasons for this. It is particularly important to check that patients understand what will be disclosed if you need to share identifiable information with anyone employed by another organisation or agency who is contributing to their care. You must respect the wishes of any patient who objects to particular information being shared with others providing care, except where this would put others at risk of death or serious harm.

Department of Health[38]

12 It is extremely important that patients are made aware of information disclosures which must take place in order to provide them with high quality care. In particular, clinical governance and clinical audits, which are wholly proper components of healthcare provision, might not be obvious to patients and should be drawn to their attention. Similarly, whilst patients may understand that information needs to be shared between members of care teams and between different organizations involved in healthcare provision, this may not be the case and the efforts made to inform them should reflect the breadth of the required disclosure. This is particularly important where disclosure extends to non-NHS bodies . . .

14 Patients generally have the right to object to the use and disclosure of confidential information that identifies them, and need to be made aware of this right. Sometimes, if patients choose to prohibit information being disclosed to other health professionals involved in providing care, it might mean that the care that can be provided is limited and, in extremely rare circumstances, that it is not possible to provide certain treatment options. Patients must be informed if their decisions about disclosure have implications for the provision of care or treatment . . .

15 Where patients have been informed of

(a) the use and disclosure of their information associated with their healthcare; and

(b) the choices that they have and the implications of choosing to limit how information may be used or shared;

then explicit consent is not usually required for information disclosures needed to provide that healthcare. Even so, opportunities to check that patients understand what may happen and are content should be taken . . .

If a patient undergoes a medical examination requested by a third party, such as an employer, could it be said that she impliedly consents to the disclosure of the medical report to that third party? The GMC guidance specifies that consent to disclosure in such circumstances must be express and in writing:

Where doctors have contractual obligations to third parties, such as companies or organisations, they must obtain patients' consent before undertaking any examination or writing a report for that organisation. Before seeking consent they must explain the purpose of the examination or report and the scope of the disclosure. Doctors should offer to show patients the report, or give them copies, whether or not this is required by law.[39]

---

[38] Confidentiality: NHS Code of Practice (DH 2003).
[39] General Medical Council Confidentiality: Protecting and Providing Information (GMC 2004) <http://www.gmc-uk.org/standards/default.htm> para 17.

In contrast, *obiter dicta* in the Court of Appeal decision in *Kapadia v London Borough of Lambeth*[40] suggest that the patient's consent to disclosure can be implied from her agreement to undergo the examination. This was a case in which an employee who was claiming that he had been discriminated against on the grounds of disability had refused to consent to the disclosure of a medical report to his employer, without first seeing the report. However, according to Pill LJ, having agreed to the examination, the employee's further consent to the report's disclosure was not required:

On the facts the court knows, the report should, in my judgment, have been disclosed by the doctor to the employers. No further consent was required from the claimant. By consenting to being examined on behalf of the employers the claimant was consenting to the disclosure to the employers of a report resulting from that examination. A practice under which a person who has agreed to be examined in circumstances such as these, but then claims a veto upon disclosure of the report to those who obtained it is not, in my view, a good practice. Indeed it is an impediment to the fair and expeditious conduct of litigation.

This apparent discrepancy between the statement of Pill LJ and the GMC guidance is further evidence that in some circumstances, standards of good medical practice may impose more onerous obligations on doctors than the common law. We encountered another such gap in relation to obtaining informed consent in Chapter 5, p. 309. Doctors would, of course, be well advised to ensure that their conduct meets the more stringent requirements of GMC guidance, and so written consent to the disclosure of a patient's medical report to a third party should normally be obtained.

It might be possible to argue that the patient impliedly consented to the use of medical information for research, teaching and audit purposes, but this might also be justified under the public interest exception discussed in the next section. From the point of view of health care professionals, the public interest justification may be preferable because it would not be necessary either to inform the patient about the use of information, or to give her the right to object.

(b) PUBLIC INTEREST

Probably the most important exception to the duty of confidentiality is where the public interest in disclosure of information outweighs the public interest in protecting patient confidentiality. In *A-G v Guardian Newspapers Ltd (No 2)*,[41] for example, Lord Goff said:

The third limiting principle is of far greater importance. It is that, although the basis of the law's protection of confidence is that there is a public interest that confidences should be preserved and protected by the law, nevertheless that public interest may be outweighed by some other countervailing public interest which favours disclosure. This limitation may apply, as the judge pointed out, to all types of confidential information. It is this limiting principle which may require a court to carry out a balancing operation, weighing the public interest in maintaining confidence against a countervailing public interest favouring disclosure.

And according to Lord Griffiths, in the same case:

---

[40] (2000) 57 BMLR 170.   [41] [1988] 3 WLR 776 at 807.

The courts have, however, always refused to uphold the right to confidence when to do so would be to cover up wrongdoing . . . This approach has been developed in the modern authorities to include cases in which it is in the public interest that the confidential information should be disclosed. This involves the judge in balancing the public interest in upholding the right to confidence, which is based on the moral principles of loyalty and fair dealing, against some other public interest that will be served by the publication of the confidential material. Even if the balance comes down in favour of publication, it does not follow that publication should be to the world through the media. In certain circumstances the public interest may be better served by a limited form of publication perhaps to the police or some other authority who can follow up a suspicion that wrongdoing may lurk beneath the cloak of confidence.

Because the public interest in protecting confidentiality is considerable, only weighty countervailing considerations should be allowed to override the doctor's prima facie duty of confidence, and disclosures should always be kept to the minimum. In the following sections we consider a number of different, though overlapping, public interest justifications for disclosure of confidential information.

(1) PREVENTING HARM TO OTHERS

Where the possibility of harm to others is used to justify disclosure, there should, as the BMA and the GMC guidance makes clear, be a *real* risk of *serious* harm.

British Medical Association[42]
When considering disclosing information to protect the public interest, doctors must:

- consider how the benefits of making the disclosure balance against the harms associated with breaching a patient's confidentiality
- assess the urgency of the need for disclosure
- consider whether the subject might be persuaded to disclose voluntarily
- inform the subject before making the disclosure and seek his or her consent, unless to do so would enhance the risk of harm or inhibit its effective investigation
- reveal only the minimum information necessary to achieve the objective
- seek assurances that the information will be used only for the purpose for which it was disclosed and be able to justify the decision

Non-consensual disclosure is generally only considered justifiable in cases where the threat appears serious and imminent and disclosure is likely effectively to limit or prevent it occurring.

General Medical Council[43]
27   Disclosure of personal information without consent may be justified in the public interest where failure to do so may expose the patient or others to risk of death or serious harm. Where the patient or others are exposed to a risk so serious that it outweighs the patient's privacy interest, you should seek consent to disclosure where practicable. If it is not practicable to seek consent, you should disclose information promptly to an appropriate person or authority. You should generally inform the patient before disclosing the information. If

---

[42] Confidentiality and disclosure of health information (BMA London 1999).
[43] Confidentiality: Protecting and Providing Information (GMC 2004) <http://www.gmc-uk.org/standards/default.htm>.

you seek consent and the patient withholds it you should consider the reasons for this, if any are provided by the patient. If you remain of the view that disclosure is necessary to protect a third party from death or serious harm, you should disclose information promptly to an appropriate person or authority. Such situations arise, for example, where a disclosure may assist in the prevention, detection or prosecution of a serious crime, especially crimes against the person, such as abuse of children.

W v Edgell is a relatively straightforward example of the public interest in disclosure trumping the public interest in protecting confidentiality. The patient had killed five people and wounded two others. A psychiatrist's report indicating that he continued to pose a risk to the public plainly contained information which might enable a serious threat to public safety to be avoided.

W v Edgell[44]

The plaintiff, W, suffered from paranoid schizophrenia. In 1974 he shot and killed five people and injured two others, and was subsequently detained in a secure hospital. In 1986, the plaintiff applied to a mental health review tribunal for release. The Secretary of State refused. W's solicitors commissioned a report from the defendant, Dr Edgell, as an independent consultant psychiatrist. The defendant's report disclosed that the plaintiff had a long standing and continuing interest in home made bombs, and did not accept the view that the plaintiff was no longer a danger to the public. The plaintiff withdrew his application to the tribunal. Dr Edgell contacted the medical director of the hospital, who, having discussed W's case with Dr Edgell, agreed that the hospital should receive a copy of the report in the interests of W's further treatment, and that the Secretary of State should also receive a copy, which he forwarded to the tribunal. When W discovered that the report had been disclosed he issued a writ against E and the recipients of the report seeking (i) an injunction to restrain them from using or disclosing the report, (ii) delivery up of all copies of the report and (iii) damages for breach of the duty of confidence. The judge dismissed W's claim, and his appeal was dismissed by the Court of Appeal.

Sir Stephen Brown P

The balance of public interest clearly lay in the restricted disclosure of vital information to the director of the hospital and to the Secretary of State who had the onerous duty of safeguarding public safety.

In this case the number and nature of the killings by W must inevitably give rise to the gravest concern for the safety of the public. The authorities responsible for W's treatment and management must be entitled to the fullest relevant information concerning his condition. It is clear that Dr Egdell did have highly relevant information about W's condition which reflected on his dangerousness. . . .

In so far as the judge referred to the 'private interest' of W, I do not consider that the passage in his judgment accurately stated the position. There are two competing public interests . . . Of course W has a private interest, but the duty of confidence owed to him is based on the broader ground of public interest.

Bingham LJ

The decided cases very clearly establish (1) that the law recognises an important public interest in maintaining professional duties of confidence but (2) that the law treats such duties not as

[44] [1990] Ch 359.

absolute but as liable to be overridden where there is held to be a stronger public interest in disclosure.

The parties were agreed, as I think rightly, that the crucial question in the present case was how, on the special facts of the case, the balance should be struck between the public interest in maintaining professional confidences and the public interest in protecting the public against possible violence.

There is one consideration which in my judgment, as in that of the judge, weighs the balance of public interest decisively in favour of disclosure. It may be shortly put. Where a man has committed multiple killings under the disability of serious mental illness, decisions which may lead directly or indirectly to his release from hospital should not be made unless a responsible authority is properly able to make an informed judgment that the risk of repetition is so small as to be acceptable. A consultant psychiatrist who becomes aware, even in the course of a confidential relationship, of information which leads him, in the exercise of what the court considers a sound professional judgment, to fear that such decisions may be made on the basis of inadequate information and with a real risk of consequent danger to the public is entitled to take such steps as are reasonable in all the circumstances to communicate the grounds of his concern to the responsible authorities.

While the balancing exercise in *W v Edgell* was relatively straightforward, other situations may be less clear-cut. Exactly how dangerous does a patient have to be before the public interest in disclosure trumps the public interest in protecting confidentiality?

What if the patient has never actually harmed anyone, but has some dangerous thoughts or fantasies? In the US case *Tarasoff v Regents of the University of California*,[45] the patient had confided in his psychotherapist that he intended to harm T. The therapist informed the University police, but did not inform T herself, whom the patient subsequently murdered. T's family successfully sued the University for their employee's failure to protect T. The California Supreme Court held that:

When a therapist determines, or pursuant to the standards of his profession should determine, that his patient presents a serious danger of violence to another, he incurs an obligation to use reasonable care to protect the intended victim against such danger.

No similar case has yet arisen in the UK. Commenting on the likely response to a *Tarasoff*-type case in the UK, Sheila McLean and John Kenyon Mason have suggested:

The probability is that there would be no legal obligation to warn the person at risk but that, should the doctor do so, the breach of confidentiality would be regarded as justified.[46]

If disclosure was routine in such circumstances, there is a danger that patients would be reluctant to share information about their fantasies with their psychiatrists, which in turn makes it more likely that their underlying psychiatric problems would remain untreated. Paradoxically then breaching the confidentiality of potentially dangerous patients might *increase* the risk of them causing harm to others.

Here there is a clear overlap with an issue we consider in more detail in the next chapter, namely the increased focus in mental health law upon reducing the risk

---

[45] 551 P 2d 334 (Cal 1976).
[46] *Legal and Ethical Aspects of Healthcare* (Greenwich Medical Media 2003) 42.

mentally ill individuals might pose to the community. This emphasis upon risk-avoidance necessarily involves sharing information about potentially dangerous patients with a number of different people, such as potential employers, or housing and social service authorities. If such patients realize that they can no longer expect their medical records to be confidential, there is a real danger that they might be deterred from seeking treatment, thus actually *increasing* the risk they might pose to the public.

Particular difficulties also arise in relation to communicable diseases, such as HIV. If a doctor knows that an HIV positive individual has not informed her sexual partner of her HIV status, does the public interest in disclosure trump the public interest in protecting confidentiality? Although alerting the sexual partner of an HIV positive individual may enable one individual to take steps to avoid infection, there is also a strong public interest in encouraging people to come forward for HIV testing and treatment, which might be hampered if disclosure of a positive result was routine. Nevertheless, the GMC suggest that non-consensual disclosure to a sexual partner will sometimes be justifiable.

General Medical Council[47]

22   You may disclose information about a patient, whether living or dead, in order to protect a person from risk of death or serious harm. For example, you may disclose information to a known sexual contact of a patient with HIV where you have reason to think that the patient has not informed that person, and cannot be persuaded to do so. In such circumstances you should tell the patient before you make the disclosure, and you must be prepared to justify a decision to disclose information.

23   You must not disclose information to others, for example relatives, who have not been, and are not, at risk of infection.

What if the HIV positive patient refuses to permit the doctor to inform other health care workers? Again, the GMC advice appears to indicate that in exceptional circumstances, disclosure without consent may be legitimate.

General Medical Council[48]

18   If you diagnose a patient as having a serious communicable disease, you should explain to the patient:

(a)   The nature of the disease and its medical, social and occupational implications, as appropriate.

(b)   Ways of protecting others from infection.

(c)   The importance to effective care of giving the professionals who will be providing care information which they need to know about the patient's disease or condition. In particular you must make sure that the patient understands that general practitioners cannot provide adequate clinical management and care without knowledge of their patients' conditions.

19   If patients still refuse to allow other health care workers to be informed, you must respect

---

[47] *Serious Communicable Diseases Guidance to Doctors* (GMC London 1997) <http://www.gmc-uk.org/standards/default.htm>.
[48] Ibid.

the patients' wishes except where you judge that failure to disclose the information would put a health care worker or other patient at serious risk of death or serious harm. Such situations may arise, for example, when dealing with violent patients with severe mental illness or disability. If you are in doubt about whether disclosure is appropriate, you should seek advice from an experienced colleague. You should inform patients before disclosing information. Such occasions are likely to arise rarely and you must be prepared to justify a decision to disclose information against a patient's wishes.

A further difficult balancing exercise arises where the HIV positive patient is also a healthcare worker. The risk of HIV transmission by healthcare workers is incredibly low—there have been only two reported cases worldwide[49]—and so both the Department of Health and the GMC suggest that only in exceptional circumstances will the public interest in disclosure trump the normally overwhelming public interest in encouraging individuals to be tested and treated for the HIV virus.

Department of Health[50]

10.2 Every effort should be made to avoid disclosure of the infected worker's identity, or information which would allow deductive disclosure. This should include the use of a media injunction as necessary to prevent disclosure of a health care worker's identity. The use of personal identifiers in correspondence and requests for laboratory tests should be avoided and care taken to ensure that the number of people who know the worker's identity is kept to a minimum. Any unauthorised disclosure about the HIV status of an employee or patient constitutes a breach of confidence and may lead to disciplinary action or legal proceedings. Employers should make this known to staff to deter open speculation about the identity of an infected health care worker.

10.3 The duty of confidentiality, however, is not absolute. Legally, the identity of infected individuals may be disclosed with their consent or without consent in exceptional circumstances where it is considered necessary for the purpose of treatment, or prevention of spread of infection. Any such disclosure may need to be justified.

General Medical Council[51]

35 If you know, or have good reason to believe, that a medical colleague or health care worker who has or may have a serious communicable disease, is practising, or has practised, in a way which places patients at risk, you must inform an appropriate person in the health care worker's employing authority, for example an occupational health physician, or where appropriate, the relevant regulatory body. Such cases are likely to arise very rarely. Wherever possible you should inform the health care worker concerned before passing information to an employer or regulatory body.

In X v Y,[52] a newspaper had discovered the identity of two general practitioners who had AIDS, and were continuing to practise. The newspaper had already published an article with the headline 'Scandal of Docs with AIDS'; and it intended to publish further information which would enable the doctors to be identified. The health

[49] Department of Health, *AIDS/HIV infected health care workers guidance on the management of infected health care workers and patient notification* (DH 2003) para 2.2.
[50] Ibid.
[51] *Serious Communicable Diseases Guidance to Doctors* (GMC London 1997) <http://www.gmc-uk.org/standards/default.htm>.
[52] [1988] 2 All ER 648.

authority sought, and was granted, an injunction restraining the defendants from publishing the identity of the two doctors. Rose J took into account the fact that the risk of a GP transmitting the HIV virus to his patients is negligible, and held that:

In the long run, preservation of confidentiality is the only way of securing public health otherwise doctors will be discredited as a source of education, for future individual patients 'will not come forward if doctors are going to squeal on them'. Consequently, confidentiality is vital to secure public as well as private health, for unless those infected come forward they cannot be counselled and self-treatment does not provide the best care. . . .

I keep in the forefront of my mind the very important public interest in freedom of the press. And I accept that there is some public interest in knowing that which the defendants seek to publish (in whichever version). But in my judgment those public interests are substantially outweighed when measured against the public interests in relation to loyalty and confidentiality both generally and with particular reference to AIDS patients' hospital records.

A conflict between the freedom of the press and patients' interest in confidentiality also arose in *H (A Healthcare Worker) v Associated Newspapers Ltd*.[53] H was a healthcare worker, who had been diagnosed as HIV positive, and notified his employers, N Health Authority. N proposed to carry out a 'lookback' exercise, that is, to notify H's patients and offer them advice and an HIV test. Citing evidence that no infected patient had ever been identified by one of these lookback exercises, H claimed that it would be unlawful.

Meanwhile, the *Mail on Sunday* wanted to publish a story about H's action against N. H obtained an injunction restraining the soliciting or publication of any information which might directly or indirectly lead to the disclosure of his identity, or his whereabouts, or his speciality. The Court of Appeal granted orders restraining the publication of information of H's and N's identity, but refused to order that his speciality too should be kept secret. The risk that this would reveal H's identity was too small to justify inhibiting debate 'on what is a matter of public interest'. The Court of Appeal again stressed the importance of maintaining patient confidentiality. Lord Phillips MR stated:

The consequences to H if his identity were to be disclosed would be likely to be distressing on a personal level. More than this, there is an obvious public interest in preserving the confidentiality of victims of the AIDS epidemic and, in particular, of healthcare workers who report the fact that they are HIV positive. Where a lookback exercise follows, it may prove impossible to preserve the identification of the worker but, if healthcare workers are not to be discouraged from reporting that they are HIV positive, it is essential that all possible steps are taken to preserve the confidentiality of such reports.

(2) PREVENTING OR DETECTING CRIME

Both the GMC guidance and the Department of Health Code of Practice specifically mention that disclosure of confidential information may be justified where it would assist in the prevention or detection of a serious crime.

---

[53] [2002] EWCA Civ 195, 65 BMLR 132.

Department of Health[54]

30 Under common law, staff are permitted to disclose personal information in order to prevent and support detection, investigation and punishment of serious crime and/or to prevent abuse or serious harm to others where they judge, on a case by case basis, that the public good that would be achieved by disclosure outweighs both the obligation of confidentiality to the individual patient concerned and the broader public interest in the provision of a confidential service.

31 Whoever authorizes disclosure must make a record of any such circumstances, so that there is clear evidence of the reasoning used and the circumstances prevailing. Disclosures in the public interest should also be proportionate and be limited to relevant details . . .

32 Wherever possible the issue of disclosure should be discussed with the individual concerned and consent sought. Where this is not forthcoming, the individual should be told of any decision to disclose against his/her wishes. This will not be possible in certain circumstances, e.g. where the likelihood of a violent response is significant or where informing a potential suspect in a criminal investigation might allow them to evade custody, destroy evidence or disrupt an investigation.

Section 11 of the Police and Criminal Evidence Act 1984 classifies medical records as 'excluded material' to which the police will not usually be allowed access. An exception exists if the police are investigating a 'serious arrestable offence'.[55] In such cases, the police may obtain a special procedure warrant from a circuit judge, which will require the disclosure of medical records. During a trial, the judge has a discretion to excuse a witness from answering a question when it would involve a breach of confidence, but equally he can order a breach of confidentiality if it is necessary in the interests of justice.

Under section 172 of the Road Traffic Act 1988, a person can be required to give information which may lead to the identification of a driver who is alleged to have committed certain offences. In *Hunter v Mann*,[56] a doctor had treated two people who had been involved in a road accident on the same day as a hit and run accident had occurred. A police officer asked the doctor to disclose the names and addresses of the two people he had treated, but he refused on the grounds that he would be breaching his duty of confidentiality. He was convicted under the Road Traffic Act 1972, and this was upheld on appeal. Boreham J stated that:

May I say, before leaving this case, that I appreciate the concern of a responsible medical practitioner who feels that he is faced with a conflict of duty. That the appellant in this case was conscious of a conflict and realised his duty both to society and to his patient is clear from the finding of the justices, but he may find comfort, although the decision goes against him, from the following. First that he has only to disclose information which may lead to identification and not other confidential matters; secondly that the result, in my judgment, is entirely consistent with the rules that the British Medical Association have laid down.

Often, of course, disclosure justified by the need to prevent serious crime could also be justified by the 'harm to others' exception we have just considered. But the two are

---

[54] Confidentiality: NHS Code of Practice (DH 2003).   [55] Schedule 1.
[56] [1974] QB 767.

not necessarily synonymous. There is a public interest in the detection of crime even when there is no immediate risk of reoffending, and even when the crime itself did not involve physical injury. Obviously, the less serious the criminal offence, the less likely that the public interest in protecting confidentiality will be trumped by the public interest in facilitating the prevention and detection of crime.

The Department of Health Code of Practice gives some guidance on the meaning of serious crime:

Department of Health[57]

The definition of serious crime is not entirely clear. Murder, manslaughter, rape, treason, kidnapping, child abuse or other cases where individuals have suffered serious harm may all warrant breaching confidentiality. Serious harm to the security of the state or to public order and crimes that involve substantial financial gain and loss will also generally fall within this category. In contrast, theft, fraud or damage to property where loss or damage is less substantial would generally not warrant breach of confidence.

Although note that in *Woolgar v Chief Constable of the Sussex Police* the Court of Appeal agreed that the police were entitled to disclose information to a professional regulatory body on public interest grounds, even though, in this case, no charges had been brought against the individual in question.

Woolgar v Chief Constable of the Sussex Police[58]

W, a registered nurse and the matron of a nursing home, was arrested and interviewed by the police following the death of a patient in her care. Although no charges were brought, the matter was referred to the United Kingdom Central Council for Nursing, Midwifery and Health Visiting (the UKCC), the regulatory body for the nursing profession. The UKCC asked the police to release any relevant information. The police practice was to seek authority to disclose from those who had given statements, but W refused to give consent. The police nevertheless indicated that they would listen to the tape of the interview in order to decide whether it should be disclosed to the UKCC. W sought an injunction to restrain the police from disclosing the contents of the interview, but the application was dismissed. She appealed.

Kennedy LJ

Essentially Mr Wadsworth's submission was and is that when the appellant answered questions when interviewed by the police she did so in the reasonable belief that what she said would go no further unless it was used by the police for the purposes of criminal proceedings. The caution administered to her so indicated, and in order to safeguard the free flow of information to the police it is essential that those who give information should be able to have confidence that what they say will not be used for some collateral purpose.

However, in my judgment, where a regulatory body such as the UKCC, operating in the field of public health and safety, seeks access to confidential material in the possession of the police, being material which the police are reasonably persuaded is of some relevance to the subject matter of an inquiry being conducted by the regulatory body, then a countervailing public interest is shown to exist which, as in this case, entitles the police to release the material to the regulatory body on the basis that save in so far as it may be used by the regulatory body for the purposes of its own inquiry, the confidentiality which already attaches to the material will be maintained. . . .

---

[57] Confidentiality: NHS Code of Practice (DH 2003) 35.   [58] [1999] 3 All ER 604.

Putting the matter in convention terms . . . disclosure is 'necessary in a democratic society in the interests of . . . public safety or . . . for the protection of health or morals, or for the protection of the rights and freedoms of others.'

Even if there is no request from the regulatory body, it seems to me that if the police come into possession of confidential information which, in their reasonable view, in the interests of public health or safety, should be considered by a professional or regulatory body, then the police are free to pass that information to the relevant regulatory body for its consideration.

It is also worth noting that in *A Health Authority v X* (considered above p. 323), the Court of Appeal again held that disclosure, subject to conditions, would be justified on the grounds that the administration of disciplinary proceedings was analogous to the administration of criminal justice.

(3) TEACHING, RESEARCH AND AUDIT

Without access to patient information, it would be impossible to train medical staff, conduct clinical research, and carry out audits of patient care. Usually, of course, the patient's consent to the use of their medical notes should be sought. But in certain rare circumstances, disclosure without consent may be legitimate. Initially fitting this within the 'harm to others' exception that we considered earlier might seem unpromising, since the benefits to patients from well trained staff, and properly tested and regulated treatments, although substantial, are not sufficiently direct or immediate that any particular instance of training or audit will avert an immediate risk of death or serious injury.

Remember, however, that the balancing exercise does not just involve looking at the harm that might be averted by disclosure, but also involves taking into account the relative importance of respecting patient confidentiality in the particular case. As we saw, where the identification of someone with HIV might result from disclosure, the public interest in keeping that information private is considerable, but where the disclosure involves the use of medical records in an epidemiological study, with no intention to disclose the patient's identity, or to feed any information back to her, the public interest in maintaining secrecy is reduced, and perhaps will be more readily outweighed by the public interest in improved health care provision.

We saw earlier that the GMC supports the use of patient information without consent for research purposes in certain circumstances, and this approach is also evident in the Medical Research Council's guidance.

Medical Research Council[59]

2.1 General Principles

(1) Personal information of any sort which is provided for health care, or obtained in medical research, must be regarded as confidential. Wherever possible people should know how information about them is used, and have a say in how it may be used. Research should therefore be designed to allow scope for consent, and normally researchers must ensure that they have each person's explicit consent to obtain, hold, and use personal information. In most clinical research this is practicable. . . .

---

[59] Personal Information in Medical Research (MRC 2000).

2.2.1 . . . Based on the ethical and legal advice it has received, the Medical Research Council considers that in some circumstances it is justifiable to use personal information, and disclose it to a limited number of other people without consent.

2.2.2 The principles governing research using information without consent are:

(1) Hospitals and practices involved in research must *develop* procedures for making patients aware that their information may sometimes be used for research, and explaining the reasons and safeguards. If patients object to their information being passed to others, patients should have the opportunity to discuss this with their doctor, and their objections must be respected.

(2) When consent is impracticable, confidential information can be used without consent only if:

- the likely benefits to society outweigh the implications of the loss of confidentiality so that it is clearly in the public interest for research to be done;
- there is no intention to feed the information back to patients or take decisions that affect them, and;
- there are no practicable alternatives of equal effectiveness.

Research must have been planned with confidentiality in mind: from the earliest stages of planning a study, researchers and/or those responsible for patient care should have given careful consideration to whether consent could be made practicable. The judgement that consent is impracticable is never that of the researcher alone: unless an ethics committee concurs, and health professionals agree to take part in the study on this basis, the research cannot take place.

(3) The infringement of confidentiality must be kept to a minimum. Even where there is a strong justification for the study, the design must minimise the volume and sensitivity of the personal information that is disclosed, and the number of people who have access to it before it is coded or anonymised.

For research purposes, it will often be possible to anonymize data. In *W v Edgell*, Bingham LJ implied that concealing the patient's identity would prevent any breach of confidence:

Nor could he, without a breach of the law as well as professional etiquette, discuss the case in a learned article or in his memoirs or in gossiping with friends, *unless he took appropriate steps to conceal the identity of W.* (my emphasis)

More recently, in *R v Department of Health, ex parte Source Informatics*, the Court of Appeal has specifically addressed the question of the confidentiality of anonymized patient information. It decided that disclosing anonymized information cannot amount to a breach of confidence.

R v Department of Health, ex parte Source Informatics Ltd[60]

The applicants obtained information from general practitioners and pharmacists about the drugs which had been prescribed for patients. The information came from prescription forms each of which contained the doctor's name, the patient's name, the date of prescription, the product prescribed and the quantity. For modest payments to general practitioners and pharmacists, all

---

[60] [2001] QB 424.

the information on the prescription forms, except for the patient's identity, was passed on to the applicants. The anonymized information was sold by the applicants to pharmaceutical companies who used it for marketing purposes. The Department of Health issued advice that the anonymization of this information did not remove the duty of confidence owed to patients, and that general practitioners and pharmacists should not participate in the scheme. The applicants applied for judicial review, seeking a declaration that the Department of Health's policy guidance was wrong. Latham J dismissed their application, but their appeal to the Court of Appeal was successful.

Simon Brown LJ

To my mind the one clear and consistent theme emerging from all these authorities is this: the confidant is placed under a duty of good faith to the confider and the touchstone by which to judge the scope of his duty and whether or not it has been fulfilled or breached is his own conscience, no more and no less. One asks, therefore, on the facts of this case: would a reasonable pharmacist's conscience be troubled by the proposed use to be made of patients' prescriptions? Would he think that by entering Source's scheme he was breaking his customers' confidence, making unconscientious use of the information they provide? . . .

In my judgment the answer is plain. The concern of the law here is to protect the confider's personal privacy. That and that alone is the right at issue in this case. The patient has no proprietorial claim to the prescription form or to the information it contains. . . .

If, as I conclude, his only legitimate interest is in the protection of his privacy and, if that is safeguarded, I fail to see how his will could be thought thwarted or his personal integrity undermined. . . . [I]n a case involving personal confidences I would hold . . . that the confidence is not breached where the confider's identity is protected . . .

I would . . . hold simply that pharmacists' consciences ought not reasonably to be troubled by co-operation with Source's proposed scheme. The patient's privacy will have been safeguarded, not invaded. The pharmacist's duty of confidence will not have been breached.

The Data Protection Act 1998 raises another question in relation to anonymization of records. While completely anonymized data is not covered by the legislation, it will often be difficult to ensure that there is no possibility of linking the individual and the information about them. If it remains possible to link the individual and the information, then the Data Protection Act applies to any processing of that information.

Even if the law is clear that the disclosure of anonymized records is not a breach of confidence, the process of anonymization itself undoubtedly involves the 'processing' of sensitive personal data, and will therefore be subject to the Data Protection Act. Under the First Data Protection Principle, this must be done fairly and lawfully. If the patient has not specifically consented to the anonymization, it would have to be established that it was 'necessary' under Schedule 2, and done for 'medical purposes' under Schedule 3.

It is not clear that either requirement is easily satisfied in the *Source Informatics* case. Certainly it would be hard to argue that anonymizing data so that it could be sold to pharmaceutical companies who would use it to increase their profits is 'necessary' for the exercise of public functions under Schedule 2. While it might be possible to argue that it was done for 'medical purposes' under Schedule 3, it could equally plausibly be argued that the *marketing* of medicines is not itself a medical purpose. Moreover, it was not the pharmaceutical companies who were carrying out the anonymization. Rather Source Informatics were doing this purely for financial gain, and it would be very difficult to argue that increasing their profits was a medical purpose. There is a further problem with the application of the Second Data Protection Principle to the *Source Informatics* case. The Second Principle is that data should be obtained for specific purposes, and not used for others. Here patient information was obtained for the purposes of treatment, and then used for commercial purposes by Source Informatics. The Second Data Protection Principle is qualified by section 33, which provides that it will not be breached where the further processing is done for 'research purposes'. Again, it might be possible to argue that Source Informatics were anonymizing the prescription forms for research purposes, but it is also at least arguable that Source Informatic's principal interest in the anonymized data was in fact commercial, and not strictly a 'research purpose'.

The Court of Appeal dealt with this difficulty in a rather unsatisfactory way. Simon Brown LJ appeared sympathetic to counsel's argument that the patients could be taken to have impliedly consented to the anonymization process. But, with respect, implied consent in such circumstances seems unlikely. Unless the patients knew about the proposed use of their prescription forms, and had been given the opportunity to object, it would be difficult to find any justification for inferring that the patient had consented to the anonymization process.

In order to trace the progression of disease, it is sometimes necessary to use coded data, where the patient is not named, but where the code would make it possible to identify the patient. The need to obtain the patient's consent to the use of her records in this sort of epidemiological research is potentially a huge obstacle to the generation of useful data. Cancer registries, for example, hold an enormous amount of information about past patients, and if these historical records could not be used without tracing every patient and retrospectively asking for consent, invaluable research into the causes of cancer would grind to a halt. Moreover, as Michael Ferriter and Martin Butwell explain in the next extract, there would be a danger of 'consent bias' since some people (perhaps those suffering from diseases which attract some sort of stigma) might be less likely than others to give consent, and the data would therefore no longer be representative of the UK population as a whole. Seeking consent could also cause wholly unnecessary alarm to patients who might fear that a request to re-examine their medical records has been prompted by concern for their health.

Michael Ferriter and Martin Butwell[61]

There are whole areas of observational research—epidemiological research using case notes, case registers and disease registers—which do not require direct contact with the patient and where gaining consent may be impractical, impossible or undesirable: impractical because of dealing with such large numbers; impossible because of tracing all the participants; undesirable because in seeking consent the sample may be biased; or in gaining consent, needless anxiety may be caused to participants. . . .

[C]onsent can fundamentally damage research by introducing bias. On a technical level, one of the strengths of carrying out research where hitherto consent has not been needed is its freedom from many such biases. It is acknowledged that certain groups of people are more likely to consent to take part in research than others. For whatever reasons, younger patients, men and

[61] 'Confidentiality and Research in Mental Health' in Christopher Cordess (ed), *Confidentiality and Mental Health* (Jessica Kingsley Publishers London 2001) 159–69, 162, 164.

members of ethnic minorities are all less likely to consent to participate in health research. This leads to a consequent bias in research carried out, problems in generalisation to the wider population as a whole and, ultimately, to the disadvantage of people in less compliant groups. . . .

The crucial question that needs to be asked is: Has anyone ever been harmed by the use of their healthcare data in a case or disease register?

Section 60 of the Health and Social Care Act 2001 was intended to address the fear that strict adherence to the Data Protection Act 1998, and perhaps also to the common law duty of confidentiality, might prove a significant obstacle to invaluable medical research.

Health and Social Care Act 2001 section 60 Control of patient information

(1) The Secretary of State may by regulations make such provision for and in connection with requiring or regulating the processing of prescribed patient information for medical purposes as he considers necessary or expedient—

(a) in the interests of improving patient care, or

(b) in the public interest. . . .

(3) Regulations under subsection (1) may not make provision requiring the processing of confidential patient information for any purpose if it would be reasonably practicable to achieve that purpose otherwise than pursuant to such regulations, having regard to the cost of and the technology available for achieving that purpose. . . .

(7) Before making any regulations under this section the Secretary of State shall, to such extent as he considers appropriate in the light of the requirements of section 61, consult such bodies appearing to him to represent the interests of those likely to be affected by the regulations as he considers appropriate.

Section 60 allows the Secretary of State to make regulations which authorize the disclosure of confidential patient information without consent where it is needed to support essential NHS activity. This power can only be used to support medical purposes that are, first, in the interests of patients or the wider public, and, secondly where consent is not a practicable alternative, and, thirdly, where anonymized information will not suffice. The continuing need for the regulations must be reviewed annually. Section 61 of the Act established a Patient Information Advisory Group to advise the Secretary of State on whether bypassing consent would be appropriate. It explains its role as follows:

Patient Interest Advisory Group[62]

14 The Patient Interest Advisory Group is not content to allow Section 60 powers to be used for the sake of convenience or to make the process of obtaining patient information easier. We require any organisation or individual seeking Section 60 support to demonstrate that there is no other reasonably practicable way, at the current time, of carrying out activities that require patient information. In particular, it must be shown that the activity cannot practicably rely upon patient consent or the use of anonymised data in the near future.

15 Organisations and individuals seeking Section 60 support must also present a robust case to demonstrate that the use of patient identifiable information is in the best interest of patients or, alternatively, serves a wider public good.

---

[62] First Annual Report (DH 2003).

The first regulations passed under section 60 were the Health Service (Control of Patient Information) Regulations 2002. These apply to cancer registries, and to the Health Protection Agency (previously the Public Health Laboratory Service) which deals with communicable diseases and other risks to public health. These Regulations provide that anything done for the purpose of processing confidential patient information shall be taken to be lawfully done despite any obligation of confidence owed in relation to that information. Although note that the Patient Information Advisory Group suggests that where a patient specifically refuses to consent to the use of their information, their wishes should be respected.[63]

In the next extract, L Turnberg explains that section 60 involves a process so 'tortuous and bureaucratic' that it is likely to be of limited usefulness.

L Turnberg[64]

Let me remind you of what is involved in section 60. Where it has not been possible to obtain prior informed consent to pass information on to someone not directly concerned with the care of the patient, or to undertake research using such information, it is necessary to gain permission under section 60. This involves firstly, the approval of a local research ethics committee, then application to officials in the Department of Health, who then pass it on (if it is acceptable to them) to the Patients' Information Advisory Group. If accepted at that stage, there is then a period of two or three months public consultation and if, at the end of that process, the Patients' Information Advisory Group finally accepts a proposal, they make a recommendation to the Secretary of State, who then has to gain the approval of both the House of Commons and the House of Lords. This incredibly bureaucratic and long drawn out process can clearly take many months and imposes many hurdles.

Paula Case criticizes the 2001 Act from a different perspective, arguing that the exception it creates to the principle of patient confidentiality is likely to further undermine patient trust.

Paula Case[65]

Issues surrounding the ownership/permitted uses of medical data are currently of unprecedented importance, given that, at this point in time, patients have higher expectations of autonomy in the doctor–patient relationship than ever, a decline in trust in the healing professions has necessitated increased transparency in medical decision-making, and whilst targets have been set for almost complete coverage of the population by electronic patient records by 2005, recent patient surveys suggest general opposition to opting out from consent requirements for research.

The implications of the new Act for patient trust and the therapeutic relationship will be felt at two levels. First of all, it has been widely anticipated that the therapeutic relationship between doctors and patients will be scarred. Patients apprised of the possibility of disclosure of their records to 'government departments' may be less frank with their doctors with implications for the quality of their health care. That discretion may be exercised so as to protect confidence and to withdraw from the information supply chain as much as possible. Trust in health care institutions is also implicated by the provision in the 2001 Act. Not only might hospitals and relevant

---

[63] PIAG First Annual Report (DH 2003) para 26.

[64] 'Common sense and common consent in communicable disease surveillance' (2003) 29 Journal of Medical Ethics 27–9.

[65] 'Confidence Matters: The Rise and Fall of Informational Autonomy in Medical Law' (2003) 11 Medical Law Review 208–36, 234–5.

government departments be regarded by some as part of the conspiracy to deprive patients of informational autonomy, but the whole system of government and legislation are coloured by these reforms. The fact that Parliament has passed ostensibly contradictory legislation—protecting individual rights with the much applauded Human Rights Act and Data Protection Act, and biting chunks out of those protections in the next legislative breath, might be regarded as damning evidence of untrustworthiness.

Section 60 is a temporary measure, and the intention is that the bypassing regulations will be displaced when both better consent procedures, and more effective anonymization and encryption techniques are developed. It is, however, worth remembering that sophisticated computer systems to encrypt and anonymize data are expensive. Although patient confidentiality is important, when asked, most patients express a willingness to consent to the use of their medical records in research and audit. It could be argued that most patients would prefer the NHS to spend its resources on patient care, rather than on complicated systems to ensure that records are unidentifiable. In the next extract, MPM Richards et al. explain that patients in a breast cancer study seemed relatively unconcerned about the use of their medical notes for the purposes of research.

MPM Richards, M Ponder, P Pharoah, S Everest, and J Mackay[66]

None of those we interviewed had any concerns about confidentiality in relation to the ABC study. We asked if they knew how they had been selected for the study. None did; most simply assumed the researchers would have been told by their GPs or the cancer clinic of their breast cancer. Such possible passing on of information did not cause any concerns. In fact, the sample had been identified through the regional cancer registry but this was not stated in the information given at recruitment. The existence of such a registry was unknown to all but one of the interviewees, who included two nurses and a GP's secretary. The woman who knew of the registry had a close relative who worked in cancer research.

Women were asked how they would feel if their blood sample was passed to other medical researchers for work on other diseases 'such as heart disease or mental illness'. All said they would be quite happy for this to be done. They were further asked what they would feel about their samples going to a commercial company or a drug company for research. Most were also content with this though a couple were a little hesitant. One had concerns over patenting and said she would only agree if it was for a drug that would be available to everyone. She said she thought that cancer research should be done by the government, not private companies. . . .

Our interviews suggest that those who have had breast cancer are pleased to take part in genetic epidemiological research and do not perceive any particular issues related to confidentiality. Furthermore, participants said they were content for their blood samples to be used for other medical research. Most, but not all women, included commercial or drug company research in this.

There are also some practical limits upon the effectiveness of anonymization which cannot be addressed by more advanced techniques. Where a family suffer from a very rare genetic disorder, it will often be impossible to conceal their identity. As Alastair Kent explains:

[66] 'Issues of consent and feedback in a genetic epidemiological study of women with breast cancer' (2003) 29 Journal of Medical Ethics 93–6.

What works for a large scale multicentre clinical trial of a new drug for a common disease may be inappropriate for a study of a very rare genetic disorder requiring samples and case histories from clinicians throughout the UK and often further afield, each of whom may only know of one person or family with the condition in question.[67]

Further powers to bypass patient confidentiality are contained in the Health and Social Care (Community Health and Standards) Act 2003, section 68, which states that any NHS body or person providing health care for an NHS body may be required by the Commission for Health Audit and Improvement (CHAI), often known as the Healthcare Commission, to

provide it with any information, documents, records (including personal records) or other items—

   i. which relates or relate to—

      1. the provision of health care by or for an NHS body, or

      2. the discharge of any of the functions of an NHS body; and

   ii. which the CHAI considers it necessary or expedient to have for the purposes of this Chapter.

Notice that the section makes no reference to the need to obtain the patient's prior consent to disclosure. This is therefore potentially an extremely sweeping exception to the principle of patient confidentiality, and much will depend upon the Healthcare Commission's interpretation of 'necessary or expedient'.

(4) STATUTORY EXCEPTIONS

A number of statutes create specific exceptions to the duty of confidentiality. For example, the Supreme Court Act 1989 allows orders for the discovery of medical records in actions involving claims for personal injury or death. The Public Health (Control of Disease) Act 1984 permits a registered medical practitioner who suspects or has become aware that a patient is suffering from a notifiable disease or food poisoning, to disclose the patient's name, age, sex, and address to the 'proper officer of the local authority'. Under section 10, notifiable diseases means cholera, plague, relapsing fever, smallpox and typhus. This is supplemented by the Public Health (Infectious Diseases) Regulations 1988,[68] which set out further infectious diseases which must be reported, such as tuberculosis, viral hepatitis, whooping cough and yellow fever. The Misuse of Drugs (Notification of and Supply to Addicts) Regulations 1973[69] require doctors to notify the Chief Medical Officer of the identity of any person who they consider or have reasonable grounds to suspect is addicted to any notifiable drug, other than for medical purposes.

---

[67] 'Consent and confidentiality in genetics: whose information is it anyway?' (2003) 29 Journal of Medical Ethics 16–18, 17.
[68] SI 1988/1546.   [69] SI 1973/799.

8. REMEDIES

If a patient discovers an impending breach of confidence, she can apply for an injunction to prevent disclosure. But what if the disclosure has already taken place? If it were possible to bring an action in negligence because the breach of confidence also amounted to a breach of the doctor's ordinary duty of care, then it might be possible to recover damages if, for example, the disclosure has caused economic loss or psychiatric illness. But what if the only 'harm' is the patient's distress? Usually, it is not possible to recover damages for injury to feelings or reputation, but there are exceptions to this rule, such as damages for defamation. It is not entirely clear whether the courts would be willing to award damages for the injured feelings caused by a breach of confidentiality. At first instance in *W v Edgell*, Scott J stated that:

I think [it] open to question whether shock and distress caused by the unauthorised disclosure of confidential information can . . . properly be reflected in an award of damages . . . In my judgment, W would not, even if I had found Dr Edgell to be liable, have been entitled to damages. He would have had to be content with a declaration and an injunction.

The point was not considered in the Court of Appeal. In contrast, in *Cornelius v De Taranto*,[70] a psychiatric report, which contained certain potentially defamatory statements had been circulated without the subject's consent. At first instance, Morland J awarded the claimant £3750 damages, which included £3000 'for the injury to the claimants feelings caused by the unauthorized disclosure of the confidential information':

Morland J
Under art 8 of the Convention for the Protection of Human Rights and Fundamental Freedoms 1950 'everyone has the right to respect for his private and family life' and '(there) shall be no interference by a public authority with the exercise of this right except such as is in accordance with the law and is necessary in a democratic society . . . for the protection of health' . . .

In my judgment, it would be a hollow protection of that right if in a particular case in breach of confidence without consent details of the confider's private and family life were disclosed by the confidant to others and the only remedy that the law of England allowed was nominal damages. In this case an injunction or order for delivery up of all copies of the medico-legal report against the defendant will be of little use to the claimant. The damage has been done. The details of the claimant's private and family life are within the archives of the National Health Service and she has been unable to retrieve them. . . .

In the present case, in my judgment, recovery of damages for mental distress caused by breach of confidence, when no other substantial remedy is available, would not be inimical to 'considerations of policy' but indeed to refuse such recovery would illustrate that something was wrong with the law. . . .

My conclusion is that I am entitled to award damages for injury to feelings caused by breach of confidence. Although it is a novel instance of such a remedy, it is in accord with the movement of current legal thinking.

On appeal, the Court of Appeal did not specifically discuss the question of compensa-

---

[70] (2001) 68 BMLR 62.

tion for breach of confidence, but they left the damages award intact. The Law Commission has recommended that damages should be available for the mental stress caused by a breach of confidence, but their proposals have not been implemented.[71]

As we saw earlier, there is a right to compensation for distress under section 13 of the Data Protection Act 1998, although the scope of this right is limited. The claimant must prove that she has suffered physical, financial or psychiatric damage, and the data controller has a defence if she took all reasonable care to comply with the Act.

9. GENETIC INFORMATION

All of us have a number of defective genes. Because we inherit two copies of each gene, one from each of our parents, we will usually have a normal gene that can compensate for the abnormal one. There are several different ways in which defective genes might cause ill-health. First, if the gene is dominant (an example is Huntington's Disease), a single gene inherited from either parent will cause the disease. Secondly, if the gene is recessive (such as cystic fibrosis and sickle cell anaemia), a person will only develop the disease if they inherit the gene from both parents. People who have only one copy of the gene are known as carriers. They will not develop the disease themselves, but if they reproduce with another carrier, there is a one in four chance that any child they might have will have a double dose of the relevant gene and will therefore suffer from the disease in question. Thirdly, X-linked disorders (such as Duchenne Muscular Dystrophy and haemophilia) involve a mutation on the X chromosome. Women have two X chromosomes, and so they will usually have a second normal X chromosome to compensate for the defective one. Women will usually only be carriers of these diseases, and the risk is to their male offspring. Men have an X and a Y chromosome, and so if they inherit a mutation on the X chromosome, they will develop the disease. Fourthly, chromosomal disorders (such as Down's syndrome) arise when a person has an abnormality in their chromosomes, perhaps because they have too many copies of a particular chromosome.

As Lori Andrews explains in the next extract, genetic test results raise some particularly interesting questions about confidentiality. Because genetic conditions are inherited, a positive genetic diagnosis may reveal that other family members are also at risk. The problem is obviously most acute for identical twins, who share the same DNA. If one twin is diagnosed with a genetic disorder, she cannot avoid knowing that her twin sister has the same condition. For other relatives, the implications of a relative's positive diagnosis may be less certain, but nonetheless significant. As a result, complicated questions arise about whether this information should be kept secret, or shared with other family members.

It is also important to remember that genetic tests are often predictive rather than diagnostic. Let us imagine that a 20-year-old woman tests positive for the mutation which causes Huntington's disease. She will currently be healthy, and may not develop any symptoms for another thirty years. But since the test indicates that she is very

---

[71] Breach of Confidence Report No 110, 1981 Cmnd 838.

unlikely to live to old age, this information would, as Andrews points out, be incredibly useful to insurance companies, which base their calculations of premiums upon actuarial tables that predict a person's life-expectancy. It could also be of interest to her future employers, who may prefer to employ someone with a normal working life-expectancy.

Lori B Andrews[72]

Genetics shares many features with other medical fields, but it also has several unique features that raise concerns about its impact on people's lives. First, genetics often plays a central role in people's lives. Because genes are usually viewed as immutable and essential to the determination of a person's identity, information about genetic predispositions may cause a person to change his or her self-perception and may cause others to treat that person differently. Second, people may undergo genetic testing or therapy without sufficient advance consideration of its potential effects. In most instances, people seek medical services because they are already ill. However, . . . healthy people undergoing testing may not consider the psychological, social, and financial impact of learning genetic information about themselves before they agree to genetic testing . . .

Genetics has another unique feature. Genetic testing of a particular individual also reveals genetic risk information about his or her relatives. A parent and a child have half their genes in common, as do siblings. Cousins share one-quarter of their genes, as do grandparents and grandchildren. The acquisition and disclosure of genetic information raise new and profound questions of 'gen-etiquette', questions about the moral obligations owed to relatives. If a woman learns she has a genetic mutation predisposing her to breast cancer, does she have a moral or even a legal duty to share that information with her sister? What about an estranged cousin? . . .

Genetic information influences people's relationships with third parties, such as insurers and employers. While individuals might want to know their own genetic makeup in order to make important life decisions, such information can also be used against them. . . . The chilling irony of genetic testing is that, even in rare cases where a treatment exists, people may be afraid to get tested for the disorder because their insurer might drop them entirely or an employer may refuse to hire them based on their test results.

DNA test results might also be exceptionally useful to the police by enabling them to maintain a DNA database which could be searched rapidly as soon as new evidence is found at a crime scene. Of course, the public interest in the identification and prosecution of criminals is substantial, but difficult questions arise about whose DNA should be placed on a database, and how long it should be kept. DNA databases might also be useful for research purposes, and to assist the management of health care provision.

Fears have been raised that genetic testing could lead to discrimination against those found to have genetic disorders. Adam Moore describes an extreme example of genetic discrimination in Orchemenos in Greece, where sickle-cell anaemia is particularly common.[73] Researchers tested everyone in the village so that carriers could ensure that they did not marry each other. It was assumed that carriers would choose to marry non-carriers, in order to avoid having children with sickle-cell anaemia. The

---

[72] 'A Conceptual Framework for Genetic Policy: Comparing the Medical, Public Health and Fundamental Rights Models' (2001) 79 Washington University Law Quarterly 221, 225–6, 259–60.
[73] 'Owning Genetic Information and Gene Enhancement Techniques: Why Privacy and Property Rights May Undermine Social Control of the Human Genome' (2000) 14 Bioethics 97–119, 107.

problem was that the non-carriers refused to cooperate. Carriers became a stigmatized subclass, who were forced to marry among themselves, thereby making the situation worse than before.

In addition, the potential for genetic discrimination is exacerbated by the fact that certain genetic traits are particularly associated with different ethnic groups. For example, Askenazi Jews are disproportionately likely to have the BRCA1 or BRCA2 mutations, which increase the risk of developing breast and ovarian cancer, and to carry the gene associated with Tay-Sachs disease.

Let us now turn to consider in more detail the various third parties who might have an interest in acquiring a patient's genetic test results.

(a) INSURERS

On the one hand, it instinctively seems unfair if a genetic test result which is plainly not within her control prevents someone from obtaining insurance, or means that she faces vastly increased premiums. But on the other hand, we should remember that insurance companies already take a person's health and family history into account when setting premiums. Someone with a family history of Huntington's disease will face increased premiums, regardless of whether she has been tested for the Huntington's gene. Moreover, forbidding insurance companies from taking this sort of information into account might also have adverse consequences. If individuals discover that they are likely to suffer from a serious disease, they might purchase a great deal of insurance, whereas individuals with a clean bill of health might not bother buying insurance at all. This phenomenon is known as adverse selection. Plainly it would be very difficult to maintain a market in insurance if only those people who are 'bad' risks choose to insure themselves. In the next extract, the Human Genetics Commission explains further how genetic information might be used and misused by insurance companies.

Human Genetics Commission[74]

7.37 There has been much written about the possible harmful consequences in using genetic information in insurance. It appears to us from our survey of the People's Panel and our consultation that there is a widely held public view that those who are affected by genetic conditions should not feel excluded from the normal benefits of society (employment, participation in public life, and, it might be argued, access to insurance). Over recent decades, the position of disabled people has been steadily improved by legislation designed to enhance their opportunities in society. It would run counter to this commitment were society to allow new classes of persons to grow up which would be subjected to improper discrimination.

7.38 The insurance industry is based on over 200 years of experience of having access to all relevant information. However, this did not take account of the serious social policy and moral justice issues associated with the use of personal genetic information. An individual's genetic makeup is arguably different from other 'relevant information' that is a matter of lifestyle choice such as dangerous sports or driving a sports car . . .

[74] Inside Information: Balancing interests in the use of personal genetic data (HGC 2002) available at <http://www.hgc.gov.uk/>.

7.40 Where insurance is linked to important public goods like house ownership or life insurance, the consequences of failure to obtain cover are immediately apparent. Here applicants or potential applicants cannot join the 'housing ladder' and cannot protect their families from financial disaster if they die prematurely. In such a case it is not unreasonable to balance the moral and social costs to individuals and society against the costs to the insurance industry. We are familiar with the idea that both individual and corporations should be prepared (if not willing) to pay something in order to secure important moral or social goals.

7.41 This is a well-established principle and has been part of our collective morality, and indeed public policy since the nineteenth century . . . No industry can claim immunity from moral and social obligations. Nor can any industry claim that the costs of meeting its moral and social obligations must be discharged by others. Of course these costs are often passed on to consumers and clients, but the primary responsibility of discharging the obligations properly belongs to the agency posing the danger . . .

7.65 Our overall conclusion is that there is now an opportunity for a reasoned dialogue on a long-term approach to the use of personal genetic information in life and health insurance. This needs to be informed by appropriate independent research and analysis. There also needs to be in our view, a more fundamental debate about the merits of moving towards socially-inclusive insurance pooling arrangements which can provide those with an adverse genetic test result with access to affordable insurance. We believe . . . that such measures will be necessary to ensure those individuals, and society, can benefit from advances in genetic testing for healthcare.

Until relatively recently, the question of what insurance companies should and should not be permitted to ask potential purchasers was controlled only by the Association of British Insurers (ABI). The House of Lords Science and Technology committee considered the matter in 2001, and made a number of criticisms of the insurance industry's handling of genetic test results.

House of Lords Science and Technology Committee 5th Report[75]

Paragraph 31   We acknowledge insurers' concerns about the risk of adverse selection and accept, as a principle, that commercial insurance companies should have access to the same information as applicants, where it is relevant and reliable—but only if there are no adverse consequences for society as a whole (for example, by discouraging people from taking tests).

Paragraph 32   It does not appear to be certain, at present, that the information obtained from positive genetic tests is relevant to the insurance industry.

Paragraph 38   We suggest that at present the very small number of cases involving genetic test results could allow insurers to ignore all genetic test results with relative impunity, allowing time to establish firmly their scientific and actuarial relevance.

Paragraph 64   There must be doubts whether the ABI, a trade organisation funded by insurers to represent their own interests, is the right body to regulate the use of genetic test results.

Paragraph 70   We do not believe that legislation denying insurers access to all genetic test results would be appropriate.

[75] 26 March 2001 <http://www.parliament.the-stationery-office.co.uk/pa/cm200001/cmselect/cmsctech/174/17402.htm>.

Paragraph 71 The best way forward for the Government and industry would be a voluntary moratorium on the use of all positive genetic test results by insurers for at least the next two years. During this time more research should be done to establish the actuarial and scientific relevance of genetic test results to the assessment of premiums, and the possible consequences for research and healthcare. If the insurers are unable, or unwilling, to regulate themselves and enforce this moratorium, we recommend that Government enforce its will by legislation. We further recommend that insurers should still consider negative test results in assessing insurance applications throughout any moratorium.

Following additional recommendations from the Human Genetics Commission (HGC), in October 2001 insurance companies in the UK agreed to impose a voluntary five-year ban on the use of positive genetic test results to set insurance premiums. This moratorium was extended in 2005 and will now run until November 2011. The only exceptions, which are intended to limit the problem of adverse selection, are for life insurance cover greater than £500,000 and health insurance (critical illness, income protection or long term care insurance) cover greater than £300,000. For policies above these amounts, positive genetic test results may be used provided that the Genetics and Insurance Committee has approved the test in question. The only test so far approved for this purpose is for Huntington's Disease.

The moratorium on the use of genetic tests applies only to positive results. Negative test results *can* be taken into account. So a person with a family history of early onset Alzheimer's Disease who has found out that she does *not* carry the relevant gene, can ask an insurer to reduce her premium to reflect her reduced risk of premature morbidity.

(b) EMPLOYERS

For a number of reasons, employers also might find genetic test results useful when planning recruitment and promotion. As Alexander Capron explains:

First, an employee who is prone to get sick will generate expenses: medical treatment costs, sick days, and potentially even disability benefits. Second, if the problem might be described as job-related, then the genetic condition could lead directly to workers compensation payments—for instance, a genetic predisposition to a bad back in an employee who has to do a lot of lifting. Finally, employers generally want to avoid hiring persons who are going to be sick a great deal because such persons cannot be relied upon to be present when needed and the expense of training them may thus be wasted if they become totally disabled.[76]

Employers might also be interested in genetic test results which reveal that an individual poses some risk to fellow workers or other relevant people, in part as a result of the fear of litigation. For example, an airline might want to know if any of its pilots have an elevated risk of epilepsy.

While reducing risk to the individual worker by excluding people with a genetic predisposition to a work-related condition may initially appear to be a sensible

[76] 'Which Ills to Bear? Reevaluating the "Threat" of Modern Genetics' (1990) 39 Emory Law Journal 665, 692.

precautionary step, it could be argued that this approach looks at the problem of workplace hazards from the wrong direction. Striving to employ individuals who are more resistant to hazardous workplaces assumes that the working environment could not possibly be made any safer. Yet this will seldom be true. Rather than attempting to exclude those who are particularly susceptible to toxic substances, might it not be preferable to provide an optimally safe working environment for *all* workers?

It might also be argued that this apparently benevolent concern for employees' health is unduly paternalistic. An individual might rationally choose to engage in work that poses a small risk to her health in preference to unemployment, which itself carries a significant risk to health and wellbeing. It also seems rather disingenuous for employers to cite the long-term impact a particular hazard might have upon an individual's future participation in the workforce as grounds for refusing to employ her in the short term. Short-term contracts are now common, and few employees stay in the same workplace for more than a few years.

It has been suggested that genetic discrimination in the workplace should be treated in the same way as other illegitimate discriminatory practices. Indeed, existing anti-discriminatory legislation will offer some fortuitous protection against discrimination where the genetic condition occurs primarily in one sex (such as haemophilia), or in particular racial groups (such as sickle-cell anaemia). Discriminating against individuals who have these genetic traits may amount to a breach of the Sex Discrimination Act 1975 and the Race Relations Act 1976 respectively. An employer or prospective employer would therefore be required to justify treating the individual less favourably than an employee without this condition. The Disability Discrimination Act 1995 may also offer some protection for employees with an adverse genetic test result, as long as the individual is *already* disabled by their condition. The definition of 'disability' under the Act does not cover people who have a predisposition to future ill health. The Data Protection Act 1998 might also offer some protection against employers' unreasonable use of genetic test results. These results are undoubtedly sensitive personal data, and they must therefore be processed fairly and lawfully.

Currently then the protection offered to individuals who are discriminated against on the grounds of genetic test results is rather random and ad hoc. In the next extract, Larry Gostin advocates the specific prohibition of genetic discrimination.

Larry Gostin[77]

Genetic discrimination violates basic tenets of individual justice and is detrimental to public health. Discrimination based upon actual or perceived genetic characteristics denies an individual equal opportunity because of a status over which she has no control. Discrimination based on genetic factors can be as unjust as that based on race, gender or disability. In each case, people are treated inequitably, not because of their inherent abilities, but solely because of pre-determined characteristics. The right to be treated equally and according to one's abilities in all the diverse aspects of human endeavor is a core social value.

Genetic discrimination is harmful not merely because it violates core social values, but also because it thwarts the creativity and productivity of human beings, perhaps more than the disability itself. By excluding qualified individuals from education, employment, government service

---

[77] 'Genetic Discrimination: The Use of Genetically Based Diagnostic and Prognostic Tests by Employers and Insurers' (1991) 17 American Journal of Law and Medicine 109, 112–15.

or insurance, the marketplace is robbed of skills, energy and imagination. Such exclusion promotes physical and economic dependency, draining rather than enriching social institutions. Finally, genetic discrimination also undercuts the Human Genome Initiative's fundamental purpose of promoting the public health. Infusing human and financial resources into the Genome Initiative is justified by the promise of clinical benefits in identifying, preventing and effectively intervening in human disease. If fear of discrimination deters people from genetic diagnosis and prognosis, renders them less willing to confide in physicians and genetic counselors, and makes them more concerned with loss of a job or insurance than with care and treatment, the benefits of genetic data collection will not be fully achieved. . . .

Society's ability to develop and implement ambitious genetic screening and intervention strategies will depend upon the adequacy of safeguards against breaches of confidence and discrimination. . . .

Genomic information may be highly beneficial for patients and health care professionals in areas related to prevention, treatment, diet, lifestyle or reproductive choices. Employers, insurers, educators, police and others, however, will surely come to have access to genomic information. When genomic information is used by social institutions, not to prevent or treat disease, but to deny opportunity, exclude from work or benefits, remove health care coverage or restrict liberty, a whole new dimension to the Genome Initiative becomes apparent. Adverse employment and insurance decisions are particularly hurtful when rendered on the basis of false assumptions regarding the nature, accuracy and predictability of genetic tests. . . .

The course currently charted by the Human Genome Initiative is filled with the promise of unimagined medical advancement for human-kind. The potential harm to human beings by rendering them virtually unemployable or uninsurable may be equally real. Policy makers should consider legal strategies to prevent such genetic discrimination.

Both the UNESCO *Declaration on the Human Genome and Human Rights* and the Council of Europe *Convention on Human Rights and Biomedicine* also propose that genetic discrimination should be specifically prohibited.

UNESCO *Declaration on the Human Genome and Human Rights*
Article 6: no one shall be subjected to discrimination based on genetic characteristics if this has the effect of infringing human rights, fundamental freedoms or human dignity.

Council of Europe *Convention on Human Rights and Biomedicine*[78]
Article 11: Any form of discrimination against a person on grounds of his or her genetic heritage is prohibited.

And separate legislation outlawing genetic discrimination is advocated by the Human Genetics Commission:

Human Genetics Commission[79]
6.30 We have concluded that there are a number of legal and pragmatic reasons why amending the DDA [Disability Discrimination Act] would not be appropriate to address concerns. It would require a major change to the particular definition of disability which underpins the DDA. There is also the difficulty of defining those with a pre-symptomatic genetic condition—would, for example this include those with a family history of a

---

[78] Oviedo, 4.IV.1997.
[79] Inside Information: Balancing interests in the use of personal genetic data (HGC 2002) available at <http://www.hgc.gov.uk/>.

common chronic condition such as heart disease? Even if it were possible to strike the correct balance such that it included those who had had a genetic test and had a high risk of developing a genetic condition, we understand that the burden of proof would be on the individual to show that they were presymptomatic for a condition and had been unfairly discriminated against.

6.31 In the light of our recommendation on separate legislation to address genetic discrimination, we recommend that no further consideration be given to amending the definitions in the Disability Discrimination Act to include protection for those who have a pre-symptomatic genetic condition.

6.32 As we indicate in chapter 2, the principle that no person shall be discriminated against on the basis of genetic characteristics receives more-or-less universal support . . .

6.41 In view of the national and international consensus and developing statutes it appears to us that amending existing UK legislation will not be sufficient to address concerns in the area of insurance and employment, as well as in other potential areas such as education and healthcare . . .

We recommend that the Government consider in detail the possible need for separate UK legislation to prevent genetic discrimination and that this evaluation form part of a long-term policy review on the use of personal genetic information in insurance and employment.

In contrast, Richard Epstein argues that full disclosure should be the norm where there are informational asymmetries between, for example, people who know that they have the gene for Huntington's disease and their employers or insurers. Epstein would even extend this duty of disclosure to potential spouses who, he argues, have a right to know that the person they are marrying will develop a terminal degenerative disease in middle age.

Richard A Epstein[80]

A person who knows that he is at risk for Huntington's disease has a strong incentive to acquire life and health insurance for the condition. This is because the expected payoffs are far greater than the stated premiums, which are based on the life expectancy and health needs of ordinary persons . . .

I think that in the case of Huntington's disease it is immoral for a person to marry (or even take a job) and conceal the condition from the potential spouse or employer. This conclusion is valid in commercial settings as well as in marital ones so long as results in selective knowledge to one side that is denied to the other. When an individual has knowledge that he is at risk of incapacitation, perhaps from family history, then full disclosure should be the norm. . . .

At this point it is critical to note that the plea for privacy is often a plea for the right to misrepresent one's self to the rest of the world . . . No doubt the individual who engages in this type of deception has much to gain. But equally there can be no doubt that this gain exists in all garden variety cases of fraud as well. To show the advantage of the fraud to the party who commits it is hardly to excuse or to justify it, for the same can be said of all cases of successful wrongs. On the other side of the transaction, there is a pronounced loss from not knowing the information when key decisions have to be made. For example, a woman may choose the wrong husband; an employer may pass up a good employee with a strong medical record and a clear

---

[80] 'The Legal Regulation of Genetic Discrimination: Old Responses to New Technology' (1994) 74 Boston University Law Review 1, 10–13.

upward path in favor of a worker who will, in the end, be the source of enormous personal and financial costs. To show that the condition is one for which the speaker is not responsible hardly justifies concealment at all . . .

The person who wants privacy need not apply for the position or the insurance coverage. But he should not be able to have it both ways, and at someone else's expense.

In the US, employers' interest in their employees' health status is intensified by the fact that most people's health insurance is provided by their employers, thus providing a double disincentive to employ anyone with a genetic predisposition to ill health. Not only might a high-risk employee have a shorter or less productive working life, but also their insurance premiums will generally be higher, and so they will be more costly to employ even while they are healthy.

(c) FAMILY MEMBERS

Genetic disease is generally transmitted through procreation, and so the results of genetic tests will often reveal information (albeit often quite imprecise and uncertain) about other family members. If a person finds out that she has a particular genetic condition, she will inevitably also have found out that one or both of her parents passed on the relevant gene(s), and that her siblings have an increased risk of having the same condition. In addition, genetic diagnoses will often rely upon information about other family members. Indeed, the principal reason for having a genetic test in the first place will usually be the existence of a shared family history of a particular condition. And one of the most important initial diagnostic tools will often be to construct a family tree showing which other members of a family had, or might have had, the disease in question. The inherently shared nature of genetic information poses particular challenges for a model of confidentiality which has traditionally stressed the privacy of an individual's health records.

As a result, there are those who have argued that genetic information is in some sense 'communal', and that sharing it between family members is therefore legitimate. Alastair Kent has suggested that this tends to be the view of members of families who are at risk of genetic disease:

Among those living in families where there is a diagnosis of a substantial risk of genetic disease, there is a strongly held view that such information should not be seen as the private property of the individual. Rather it should be seen as family information held in common by all those to whom it applies.[81]

And in the next extract, Katherine O'Donovan and Roy Gilbar argue that while a *legal* duty to share genetic information may not exist, people generally feel under a *moral* obligation to tell other family members about any increased risks they may face.

Katherine O'Donovan and Roy Gilbar[82]

Since most genetic diseases have no cure, the courts are unlikely to justify a breach of confidentiality, let alone impose a duty on doctors to disclose in such circumstances . . .

---

[81] 'Consent and confidentiality in genetics: whose information is it anyway?' (2003) 29 Journal of Medical Ethics 16–18, 17.

[82] 'The Loved Ones: Families, Intimates and Patient Autonomy' (2003) 23 Legal Studies 353, 355, 358.

Yet, in the absence of a complete cure, the availability of genetic information can help family members to avoid risk factors, by, for example, changing their life-style and diet. Such measures can be taken where environmental factors (and not only biological ones) play a significant part in the development of the disease. However, the existence of environmental factors of the disease also means that the ability to predict its onset is very limited. This affects the utility of disclosure to family members, because the likelihood of onset of a disease can be very low. In addition, in such circumstances, it is very difficult to assess the scope of relatives who may be affected by its onset. Hence it is unlikely that the courts will allow a breach of patient's confidentiality where prevention of harm cannot be guaranteed . . .

One response to the challenge this area of genetics poses to law and ethics is to accept a relational definition of autonomy, namely to acknowledge that people face great difficulties to manage their lives when they are socially isolated . . .

Thus, when individuals enter into close relationship and become members of family, they realise that their membership entails some responsibilities. This recognition emerges from the empirical data regarding patients' views about disclosure of genetic information to family members. These studies indicate that patients who receive genetic information from their doctors feel morally responsible for communicating the information to their family members . . .

The argument that intimate relationship implies responsibility is reflected in another study conducted by Lehmann et al. This study reports that 85% of the respondents believe that patients should disclose genetic information to relatives even when the disease is unavoidable and incurable. This suggests that the underlying reason for sharing information within the family does not derive solely from the desire to prevent harm to others, as lawyers argue, but from a strong sense of moral responsibility and from the recognition that medical information has implications in various aspects of family members' lives . . .

The underlying argument of this paper is that human identity has two elements: one is the sense of being separate and the other is a sense of belonging. Individuals and societies are constantly moving between the two, trying to find a reasonable compromise. Calling on individualistic autonomy as the primary value in medical ethics, or on self determination as central to medical law, whilst simultaneously overlooking the patient's identity in relationships with others, is too narrow an approach to the complexities of human lives.

Alissa Brownrigg suggests that five factors should be taken into account when deciding whether disclosure to other family members might be justifiable:

(1) the severity of the disease identified by testing;

(2) the availability of preventive or curative options for that disease;

(3) the accuracy and reliability of the test performed;

(4) the ability of the physician or health care provider to interpret and address issues relevant to the test performed; and lastly,

(5) the protections afforded to the tested individual against discrimination.[83]

First, the severity of the disease is important because breach of confidentiality should be a last resort, and justifiable only if a threatened harm is imminent or serious. Secondly, if there are no available means of treating the disease or preventing its onset, knowing that one faces an increased risk of developing a serious disease may cause

---

[83] Alissa Brownrigg 'Mother still knows best: Cancer-related gene mutations, Familial Privacy and a Physician's Duty to Warn' (1999) 26 Fordham Urban Law Journal 247, 273.

significant distress but without any prospect of averting the risk in question. Moreover, knowing about a genetic predisposition to ill health might have adverse financial consequences, such as increased insurance premiums. Of course, there may be some steps that individuals can take to reduce the risk of serious adverse consequences, even if a complete cure does not exist. Women who discover that they have the BRCA1 gene, which increases the risk of developing breast and ovarian cancer, will be offered routine mammograms which might enable the disease to be diagnosed in its early stages, thus increasing the prospect of a complete cure. Some women have even chosen to have prophylactic double mastectomies in order to eliminate the risk of developing breast cancer.

Genetic information might also be useful for people who are planning to have children. As we shall see in Chapter 14, someone who knows that she is at risk of passing on a serious genetic condition may be able to undergo preimplantation genetic diagnosis in order to ensure that any child she has will not have the particular disease.

Thirdly, the risk of false positives and false negatives should be taken into account. Both can cause significant harm: a false negative result may mean that an individual does not receive the care that she needs, and a false positive result will cause unnecessary distress. If a test's accuracy cannot be relied upon, there are good reasons for not disclosing its results. Fourthly, genetic test results are complex and difficult to interpret. Unless doctors have a good understanding of how to interpret and use genetic data, again disclosure might not be appropriate. Finally, where a genetic test might reveal a person's susceptibility to debilitating illness, it may make it difficult to obtain insurance or employment, and unless anti-discriminatory measures are in place, again this may militate against disclosure.

In essence, these factors are relevant to whether disclosure to a family member fits within the public interest exception which we considered earlier, that is there must be a real risk of serious harm to others which could be averted by non-consensual disclosure. The BMA guidance on disclosing genetic information to family members adopts this sort of model: disclosure without consent should be exceptional and must be rigorously justified.

British Medical Association[84]

Genetic information
It is the BMA's advice that in all areas of health care, the doctor's duty of confidentiality to their patients is of fundamental importance and should only be breached for the reasons identified in this guidance. The Association also believes that individuals have moral responsibilities to their relatives, which means that they should at least consider the implications of their actions for their family, and take an informed decision about whether to share the results of genetic tests with their relatives. Health professionals have an important role to play in advising people of the implications of test results for other family members, and in encouraging the sharing of information with those affected. In the BMA's experience, often patients will be willing to share relevant information. However, unless there are overwhelming reasons to override a decision not to inform family members, refusals to do so must be respected.

---

[84] Confidentiality and disclosure of health information (BMA London 1999).

If patients cannot be persuaded to share relevant information with their relatives for whom it has implications, doctors should consider the following points:

- the severity of the disorder
- the level of predictability of the information provided by testing
- what, if any, action the relatives could take to protect themselves or to make informed reproductive decisions, if they were told of the risk
- the level of harm or benefit of giving and withholding the information
- and the reason given for refusing to share the information.

If having considered these factors the doctor feels that the balance lies in favour of making a disclosure against a patient's wishes, he or she must discuss this with the patient before disclosing the information, and must explain the reasons why this is considered to be justified. Wherever possible in such cases it is advisable for information to be passed to family members in a way that does not identify the patient, for example by saying that information has been gained from 'a relative' without naming him or her.

Whether information is to be shared with relatives with or without consent, the process of sharing must be approached with sensitivity to protect family members' rights not to know. Information should not be forced upon an unwilling recipient.

In the next extract, Dean Bell and Belinda Bennett, argue that genetic information should not be treated as a special case, and that a doctor should only divulge an individual's genetic test results to other family members if this disclosure could be justified under the public interest exception we considered above. This would mean that breaching confidence could be legitimate only where it would 'prevent or lessen a serious or imminent threat to the life or health of a relative':[85]

Dean Bell and Belinda Bennett[86]

It is not clear that genetic information is sufficiently different from other medical information to justify the development of an alternative legal framework for that information. As this article has shown, the law protects confidentiality with exceptions provided for certain circumstances. Furthermore, where a patient poses a risk to another individual the courts have accepted that limited disclosures of confidential information may be justified in order to avert that harm. In other words, if the concern is that patients might not advise their relatives of their genetic risk, and that relatives may suffer as a result, the existing law of confidentiality arguably already provides a framework for disclosure to be permitted if the health of another is at risk . . .

The law in relation to confidential information currently contemplates a range of situations in which confidential information may be disclosed (both under statute law as well as common law). There may well be, and arguably probably are, situations involving familial genetic information which would satisfy the requirements for disclosure by a doctor. But such a disclosure would not be subject to a blanket rule: it would depend on a range of factors specific to the case at hand, including the nature of the genetic condition and the precise genetic mutation (itself subject to change over time as the Human Genome Project and related research provides more accurate information about the health risks posed by particular mutations), knowledge which the doctor has about the family member, and so on.

[85] 'Genetic Secrets and the Family' (2001) 9 Medical Law Review 130–61, 132.
[86] Ibid, 130–61, 158–9, 161.

Because one family member's genetic test results will usually just reveal that their relatives have an elevated risk of being predisposed to a particular condition, as Loane Skene points out in the next extract, the 'public interest' exception will very rarely be satisfied. Not only is the risk of suffering the particular disease uncertain, for many genetic conditions there is currently no known cure, and so disclosure would seldom enable this risk to be averted. Furthermore, the 'public interest' exception requires a balancing act to be performed between the public interest in confidentiality, and the harm that might be prevented by disclosure. Since disclosure without consent might dissuade individuals from taking genetic tests, it would be necessary to establish very weighty reasons to justify making an exception from the doctor's primary duty to protect her patient's confidentiality. As a result, Loane Skene disagrees with Bell and Bennett, arguing that genetic information is a special case and that disclosure of familial risk will sometimes be justifiable even where it would not fit within the normal 'public interest' exception.

Loane Skene[87]

When considering genetic information, there are several factors that need to be borne in mind. Firstly genetic conditions generally have a family history. Although a mutation may arise spontaneously, for example from environmental causes, that is the exception. This means that it will often not come as a surprise for blood relatives to learn of the existence of a particular mutation in the family. It is already family knowledge. Genetic registers in fact keep track of family 'pedigrees' showing the incidence of established diagnoses and potential risk of family members.

Secondly, it is the experience of clinicians and counsellors that, in the vast majority of cases, inquirers are happy to involve their blood relatives in the consultation or follow-up process . . . Thirdly, it should be noted that genetic information is of two kinds. There is the fact that a mutation is in the family; and the fact that a particular person has tested positive for the mutation. The information that is familial is the first kind. A person's own genetic status is personal information and should generally be kept confidential in the same way as information concerning the patient's clinical or surgical history. Whether the person chooses to disclose his or her genetic status to family members—or even chooses not to know it at all—is a matter for that person alone . . .

Bell and Bennett suggest that the common law is adequate to protect a doctor who feels compelled to disclose a genetic risk to a relative of the patient without the patient's consent. They base this on the 'public interest' exception to the general confidentiality requirement, which will justify disclosure where there is a serious and imminent risk to the person or a third party (I would add: and the risk is capable of being averted by a warning).

I have some doubts about the adequacy of this little-tested principle in relation to genetic testing . . . The law requires the risk to be serious and imminent. It is difficult to imagine a situation in which a genetic risk would be of this type. Take FAP [Familial Adenematous Polyposis, a type of colorectal cancer], for example, where in my view disclosure is most arguably justified. The risk is serious; it is a potentially lethal condition. The diagnosis is certain. And there is an effective intervention (monitoring and surgery if needed). Yet the risk could not be described as imminent. For these reasons I do not believe the common law exception is sufficient.

In the next extract, Allen Buchanan cautions against treating *all* genetic tests in the same way. Rather, there are genetic conditions, such as hereditary hemochromatosis,

---

[87] Ibid, 162–9, 166, 168–9.

which is a serious condition for which a safe, relatively noninvasive, cheap, and fully effective treatment exists. Here the potential to avert serious harm by non-consensual disclosure is strong. In contrast, hereditary Alzheimer's disease is untreatable, and considerable stigma attaches to its diagnosis. Buchanan argues that genetic conditions thus exist upon a spectrum, with conditions like hemochromatosis at one end, and Alzheimer's at the other. Furthermore, where a condition lies on this spectrum is of course subject to change as more genetic diseases become treatable, thus increasing the number of cases in which doctors will face genuine dilemmas about whether to breach patient confidentiality.

Allen Buchanan[88]

At present, with a few exceptions, diagnosis for genetic diseases outstrips treatment. This is especially true for the genetic tests that currently receive the most extensive media coverage and public discussion, including tests for the BRCA1 and BRCA2 genes, the APO E4 Alzheimer's gene test, and the test for the Huntington's gene. In each of these cases, the medical benefit of testing is very dubious at present because there is no effective treatment for the condition. If all genetic tests were like these, the ethical landscape of genetic testing would be far simpler than it is in fact. . . .

The situation is quite different if there is an effective treatment for a potentially lethal disease that can be detected by a genetic test. In this case, the clinician will reasonably believe that there is a single right course of action, and that the ethical responsibilities of the patient are clear from the perspective of widely accepted and easily defended values.

At present there are few such conditions. Perhaps the clearest case of a lethal late-onset disease that meets this description is hereditary hemochromatosis. If detected early enough, hereditary hemochromatosis has a simple, inexpensive, virtually riskless, and fully effective treatment; yet this disease has devastating effects on the liver, heart, and endocrine system if left untreated . . . It is reasonable to expect that in the future there will be more cases where those who test positive for a serious genetic condition will have the option of a successful treatment . . .

The case of hereditary hemochromatosis, though at this time unusual so far as the efficacy of treatment goes, illustrates the danger of generalizing ethical assumptions that may make sense for diseases for which the prognosis is much bleaker. In the case of this relatively common genetic disease, . . . it is much more difficult to dismiss the notion that patients have a responsibility to inform relatives that they are at risk. . . .

The fundamental point here is that it is necessary to think in terms of a continuum of tests for genetic disorders, with hereditary hemochromatosis at one end of the spectrum and Huntington's disease and Alzheimer's disease at the opposite extreme. On the left end of this spectrum, we have a disease that is cheaply, safely, and effectively treatable; on the right, we have those for which there presently is no effective treatment. . . . Depending upon where a test lies on the spectrum, different ethical judgments about the responsibilities of patients and clinical geneticists will apply.

It is also important to recognize that disclosure might jeopardize the relatives' right *not* to know about any predisposition they might have to genetic disease. Where test results cannot lead to a cure, but might instead cause depression and despair, and make it difficult for an individual to purchase insurance, an individual may have very good reasons for preferring to remain in ignorance about her susceptibility to an

[88] 'Ethical Responsibilities of Patients and Clinical Geneticists' (1998) 1 Journal of Health Care Law and Policy 391, 395–7.

incurable disease. There is no cure, people with the gene are guaranteed to develop the symptoms in middle age, and it is an extremely unpleasant degenerative and terminal disease. Although testing may reveal that an individual is unaffected, and hence remove a huge source of anxiety, it is equally likely that she will discover that she is destined for a short, painful and distressing future. We should not perhaps be surprised that take-up of genetic tests within families who know that there is a risk that they may have the gene which causes Huntington's Disease has been extremely low: fewer than 15 per cent of at-risk individuals have opted to take the test.[89]

It is also important to note that it is not only direct disclosure which might threaten the right not to know. Simply alerting relatives to the existence of information, and asking them whether they wish to receive it, in itself reveals to them that there is something to worry about.

The right 'not to know' is enshrined in a number of international documents. Article 10.2 of the *European Convention on Human Rights and Biomedicine* states:

Everyone is entitled to know any information collected about his or her health. However, the wishes of individuals not to be so informed shall be observed.

And Article 5c of the UNESCO Declaration on the Human Genome similarly provides that:

The right of every individual to decide whether or not to be informed of the results of genetic examination and the resulting consequences should be respected.

In the next extract, R Andorno defends the idea of a right not to know one's genetic status against a number of criticisms.

R Andorno[90]

Several criticisms have been formulated against the formal recognition of a right not to know one's genetic status. The main practical objection is that this right is not feasible because, in order to decide not to receive some information, the person should previously be informed of the possibility of having a particular health risk. Now, this is precisely what the individual wanted to avoid.

A most fundamental objection is that, according to a long and well established philosophical tradition, knowledge is always good in itself and therefore a 'right to remain in ignorance' appears as a contradiction; that is, as an irrational attitude, which is incompatible with the notion of 'right'. . . .

The right not to know would be also contrary to the recent evolution of the doctor–patient relationship, which tends to abandon the old paternalism that allowed the doctor not to tell the truth to the patient. Moreover, the claim not to know would be contrary to the doctor's 'duty to disclose' risks to patients. Therefore such a claim would represent a return to a paternalistic attitude given that it puts people in a state of ignorance, depriving them of choice. . . .

The main thesis of this paper is that the claim for not knowing one's genetic status, far from being contrary to *autonomy*—understood as an individual's self determination—may be indeed considered a legitimate expression of this basic bioethical principle. In other words, the choice of not knowing the results of genetic tests does not fall into a paternalistic attitude because the

---

[89] David Craufurd et al., 'Uptake of Presymptomatic Predictive Testing for Huntington's Disease' (1989) 334 Lancet 603, 604.

[90] 'The right not to know: an autonomy based approach' (2004) 30 Journal of Medical Ethics 435–9.

challenge to medical paternalism is precisely based on the idea that people should be free to make their own choices with respect to information. If we understand autonomy in this wider sense, then the decision not to know should be, at least in principle, as fully respected as the decision to know.

Thus, the possibility to choose not to know the results of genetic tests may constitute an *enhancement of autonomy*, because the decision to know or not to know is not taken out of the hands of the patient by the doctor . . .

One has to recognise however that the refusal to be informed about one's genetic status may in some cases be problematic, because genetic information is not only an individual, but also a family affair. Tests results may alert family members about a serious risk, giving them the opportunity of changing their life plans, or eventually of preventing or treating a disease. The familial nature of genetic information has even led some ethicists to argue that the concept of 'genetic privacy' is a contradiction in terms.

Similarly, Graeme Laurie agrees that a right not to know is an important aspect of personal autonomy, and explains how it might operate in different contexts.

Graeme Laurie[91]

To disclose genetic information to someone who has not expressed a desire to know can be disrespectful in two ways.

First, furnishing an individual with information that she has actually said she does not want to receive disrespects her wishes and is an affront to her as an autonomous person. The pivotal ethical principle of respect for autonomy surely requires that we respect her wishes.

Second, even if no wish has been expressed, we cannot ignore the spatial privacy interests which are also compromised. Giving unwanted information requires the recipient to take into account factors by which she was previously unrestrained, and it coerces her into self-reflection and re-evaluation of self. Control of information about ourselves must be an essential part of any concept of ourselves as autonomous persons, but 'control' should not be limited merely to control of who has access to that information. It should also include the facility not to accept the information ab initio. A concept of 'control' which is wide enough to encompass this notion permits us to retain a private sphere that is truly our own. Furthermore it allows us to maintain that unsolicited revelations of personal information are an invasion of that sphere, even when such revelations about ourselves are made to ourselves . . .

The precise content of the 'right' not to know will be context specific. For example, in the familial milieu, it might include a right not to be given information about a relative's diagnosis or a right not to be required to take part in linkage studies in order to build up an overall family profile. In the context of insurers and employers, it would certainly include a right not to be required to undergo testing and would probably also include a right to resist disclosure of test results if these were required simply to further the interests of third parties. Finally, in the context of a state request for access to genetic information, the right could be used to challenge the legitimacy of a screening programme—for how can population screening be justified if no cure or effective treatment is available for the target condition . . .

Yet irrespective of context—and in each case—the kernel of the right not to know is the concept of respect for an individual privacy interest in not being subjected to unwarranted information about themselves.

---

[91] 'In Defence of Ignorance: Genetic Information and the Right not to Know' (1999) 6 European Journal of Health Law 119–32, 124, 128–9.

(d) THE POLICE

If the DNA of every citizen were recorded and stored on a central police database, the identification of criminals from biological traces left at the scene of a crime would be much more straightforward. But while a central record of every citizen's DNA which could be scanned quickly and accurately would be useful, it is almost certainly both impractical and ethically dubious. Universal testing would be expensive. And clearly a population-wide database would be useful only if people could be compelled to give samples. A police database which relied only upon samples given voluntarily would, for obvious reasons, be of limited use. However, forcing individuals to give samples without consent might be said to violate their rights to privacy and bodily autonomy.

More plausible are databases of DNA taken from people who have already been arrested or convicted of offences. Samples are regularly taken from both groups, and the costs of retaining the results for future use would be relatively low. But should a distinction be drawn between those who have been convicted of offences, and those who have been acquitted or released without charge? And should we distinguish between serious and trivial offences? On the one hand, only including the results of people who have been convicted (perhaps further restricted to convictions for serious offences) will reduce the size, and therefore the usefulness of the database. But on the other hand, unless there has been a conviction, keeping a person's DNA on police records implies that some suspicion still attaches to them, and might appear to undermine the principle that people must be presumed innocent unless proven guilty.

The position in the UK is fairly clear. The Police and Criminal Evidence Act 1984 was amended in 2001 to provide that DNA samples can be retained from all suspects, regardless of whether they have been convicted of an offence provided that they are used only for purposes related to the prevention and detection of crime.

Police and Criminal Evidence Act 1984 section 64(1A)

Where—(a) fingerprints or samples are taken from a person in connection with the investigation of an offence, and (b) subsection (3) below does not require them to be destroyed, the fingerprints or samples may be retained after they have fulfilled the purposes for which they were taken but shall not be used by any person except for purposes related to the prevention or detection of crime, the investigation of an offence or the conduct of a prosecution.

Whether or not section 64(A) is compatible with the Human Rights Act 1998 came before the House of Lords in the following case.

R (on the application of S) v Chief Constable of South Yorkshire[92]

The police lawfully took fingerprints and DNA samples from claimants in two separate cases after each had been arrested and charged. Neither had previous convictions. One of the claimants was acquitted and proceedings against the other were discontinued. The defendant chief constable decided to retain the fingerprints and DNA samples taken from the claimants. The claimants each applied for judicial review, contending, inter alia, that s 64(1A) of the 1984 Act infringed their rights to respect for their private life under art 8(1). The Divisional Court held that the retention of the fingerprints and DNA samples of individuals who had not been convicted of a criminal

---

[92] [2004] UKHL 39, [2004] 4 All ER 193.

offence did not contravene the right under art 8(1). The Court of Appeal held the claimants' rights under art 8(1) had been infringed, but that that interference was justified under art 8(2) as being in accordance with the law and necessary in a democratic society for the prevention of crime. The claimants appeal to the House of Lords was dismissed. The majority held that the retention of DNA samples was not a breach of art 8(1), but that even if it were it would be justifiable under 8(2).

Lord Brown

Given the carefully defined and limited use to which the DNA database is permitted to be put— essentially the detection and prosecution of crime—I find it difficult to understand why anyone should object to the retention of their profile (and sample) on the database once it has lawfully been placed there. The only logical basis I can think of for such an objection is that it will serve to increase the risk of the person's detection in the event of his offending in future. But that could hardly be a legitimate objection, nor, indeed, is it advanced as such. Such objections as were suggested, however, seem to be entirely chimerical. First, the fear of an Orwellian future in which retained samples will be reanalysed by a mischievous state in the light of scientific advances and the results improperly used against the person's interest. If, of course, this were a valid objection it would apply no less to samples taken from the convicted as from the unconvicted and logically, therefore, it would involve the destruction of everyone's samples. But no such abuse is presently threatened and if and when it comes to be then will be the time to address it . . .

The second suggested objection is to the retention of profiles obtained from those at one time reasonably suspected of crime but subsequently acquitted or not proceeded against, the objection being that they are thereby stigmatised as properly belonging to the same group as the convicted. This to my mind is an equally unrealistic objection. Mr Gordon QC (for the appellants) was quite unable to suggest in whose eyes they would be stigmatised. . . .

In short, it seems to me that the benefits of the larger database brought about by the now impugned amendment to PACE are so manifest and the objections to it so threadbare that the cause of human rights generally (including the better protection of society against the scourge of crime which dreadfully afflicts the lives of so many of its victims) would inevitably be better served by the database's expansion than by its proposed contraction. The more complete the database, the better the chance of detecting criminals, both those guilty of crimes past and those whose crimes are yet to be committed. The better chance too of deterring from future crime those whose profiles are already on the database. And these, of course, are not the only benefits. The larger the database, the less call there will be to round up the usual suspects. Instead, those amongst the usual suspects who are innocent will at once be exonerated. Were these appellants to succeed in their challenge, the cause of justice would be seriously impeded.

In the next extract, Lord Justice Sedley, writing extra-judicially, argues that the current position, where samples are retained only from those, both innocent and guilty, who happen to have come into the hands of the police is unfair, and that Parliament should instead give serious thought to the creation of a population-wide database.

Stephen Sedley[93]

My argument is that the case is growing for a national database holding the DNA profile of everyone living in or entering the country.

The present system, sanctioned by legislation, is that the police may take and keep a DNA

---

[93] An extract from a lecture, ' "Rarely pure and never simple": the law and the truth', delivered in 2004 at Leicester University and published under the title 'Short Cuts' (2005) 27 *London Review of Books*.

sample from everyone they arrest, whether or not the person is charged or convicted. This has the unfortunate effect of putting the innocent on a par with the guilty. It draws a not very logical line between innocent people who have and have not passed through the hands of the police. But it does not follow that the law should be moved back to what it once was, so as to require the police to destroy their DNA records of everyone not eventually convicted. What follows no less logically is that the taking and retention of an individual's DNA profile should not depend at all on whether he or she happens to have come into the hands of the police. . . .

It can be, in fact, something rather worse than a fortuity. We know that there is an ethnic imbalance in arrests for certain types of offence, as well as in the use of stop and search powers. This . . . has the unacceptable consequence that members of some ethnic minorities face a disproportionately high chance of getting on to the police DNA database without being convicted of anything. A universal and uniform database will at least resolve this problem. . . .

The need for independent corroborative evidence does not diminish but grows with an increased use of DNA profiling. Each of us must have innocently left our DNA—perhaps a hair or a fingerprint—in places which will one day be the scene of a crime. Suspicion—proof even more so—has to be based on more than such coincidences. But where at present the only identifiable DNA will belong to people who have been arrested, with the associated risk that only the usual suspects will fall under suspicion, a universal database will ensure that the process of elimination starts from the full range of potential suspects. . . .

There is, in other words, no gain without risk; but in a society disturbed not only by serious crime but by the possibility of people being mistakenly acquitted or convicted of it, the potential gain represented by a comprehensive national DNA register is considerable; and the risks, so long as they are confronted, are controllable.

(e) OTHER DNA DATABASES

In 1998 Iceland granted a US biotechnology company called deCODE an exclusive licence to build a database of all Icelanders' medical records, including genetic test results, and the right to commercial exploitation of the database for 12 years. Although participation is not compulsory, the database operates on an 'opt out' basis, so unless Icelanders specifically object, their medical records and genetic test results will be held in the database. Consent can be presumed, it was argued, because coding techniques are in place to minimize the chances of individuals being identifiable. Critics have, however, argued that it will be difficult to ensure that individuals cannot be identified from genetic data and medical records in a country with only 290,000 inhabitants.[94] The intention is in part to provide information which will help to improve prediction, diagnosis and treatment of disease, and to manage health services more cost-efficiently, but as Merz et al. point out in the following extract, it is principally a commercial venture, which has made some Icelanders suspicious about the use of their personal data.

Jon F. Merz, Glenn E. McGee, and Pamela Sankar[95]

The reasons why 20,000 Icelanders have opted out of the HSD [Health Service Database] are not

---

[94] Vilhjálmur Árnason Coding and Consent: Moral Challenges of the Database Project in Iceland (2004) 18 Bioethics 27–49.

[95] ' "Iceland Inc."?: On the ethics of commercial population genomics' (2004) 58/6 Social Science and Medicine 1201–9.

known, but we can imagine several. For example, citizens might be concerned about violations of their medical privacy. The retrospective data collection will be performed by an estimated 300 trained medical transcriptionists, who will be assigned to sites throughout the country to access, abstract, and encode hundreds of thousands of medical records. While these transcriptionists may be contractually bound to maintain confidentiality of what they see, this systematic, comprehensive exposure and coding of 15 years of past medical records of nearly all citizens will nonetheless comprise an unparalleled invasion of privacy. In a nation of only 270,000 inhabitants, all of whom use the same medical care system, half of whom live in the capital Reykjavik, and most of whom are related to one another, the likelihood of a transcriptionist encountering information of personal interest is high. . . .

While consent for legitimate centralized governmental collection and use for public health purposes would globally be deemed unnecessary, the fundamental, exclusive, and principal commercial research purpose of the HSD suggests that failure to secure express permission from citizens to collect and use their data for exclusive commercial research purposes violates international ethical standards . . .

In conclusion, we believe that the major ethical concerns posed by the HSD arise because its primary purpose is commercial, and only secondarily does it support legitimate governmental operations.

In the UK, the Biobank initiative is a smaller scale attempt to track a representative sample of the population.[96] Following two pilot studies, from 2006 it will collect a blood sample, lifestyle details and medical histories from half a million volunteers aged between 40 and 69 who will be recruited from GP practices by trained nurses. The information will be stored and anonymized, and then the participant's future medical records will be tracked for up to 30 years. The intention is to generate data which will be useful for research into the causes of common diseases, such as cancer, heart disease and stroke, and for public health purposes. Participants in the project give consent to any future project for which the data is used. Anonymized information held by Biobank will be accessible to commercial bodies and academic/scientific users.

10. ACCESS TO MEDICAL RECORDS

The question of patients' access to their medical records was first considered in the following case, in which the Court of Appeal held that access to medical records could be denied where that would be in the best interests of the patient, but did not consider in any detail whether there might be a common law right of access to medical records.

R v Mid Glamorgan Family Health Services Authority, ex parte Martin[97]
The applicant had had psychological problems, and as a young man he had received treatment from doctors and assistance from a female social worker with whom he fell in love. She was taken off his case and from the late 1960s he had repeatedly requested access to his medical records. The health authority had refused, but as a compromise had proposed that the records could be

---

[96] See further JV McHale 'Regulating Genetic Databases: Some Legal and Ethical Issues' (2004) 12 Medical Law Review 70–96.
[97] [1995] 1 WLR 110.

disclosed to the applicant's medical adviser for him to consider whether the information was likely to cause him harm. He challenged this decision on the grounds that it breached the European Convention on Human Rights.

Nourse LJ

[A] doctor, likewise a health authority, as the owner of a patient's medical records, may deny the patient access to them if it is in his best interests to do so, for example if their disclosure would be detrimental to his health. . . .

[T]he doctor's general duty, likewise the health authority's, is to act at all times in the best interests of the patient. Those interests would usually require that a patient's medical records should not be disclosed to third parties; conversely, that they should usually, for example, be handed on by one doctor to the next or made available to the patient's legal advisers if they are reasonably required for the purposes of legal proceedings in which he is involved. . . .

Evans LJ

The record is made for two purposes which are relevant here: first, to provide part of the medical history of the patient, for the benefit of the same doctor or his successors in the future; and secondly, to provide a record of diagnosis and treatment in case of future inquiry or dispute. Those purposes would be frustrated if there was no duty to disclose the records to medical advisers or to the patient himself, or his legal advisers, if they were required in connection with a later claim. Nor can the duty to disclose for medical purposes be limited, in my judgment, to future medical advisers. There could well be a case where the patient called for them in order to be able to give them to a future doctor as yet unidentified, eg in case of accident whilst travelling abroad.

But the present case is not one where the records are required for medical purposes, or in connection with any dispute or projected litigation. . . .

To release the records to the applicant himself, when there are grounds for supposing that they might cause harm to his physical or mental health, would be to risk causing or aggravating the kind of injury which previously they undertook to prevent or cure. These are valid reasons, in my judgment, for holding that any common law right of access is limited to this extent.

In the next extract, Dermot Feenan criticizes the decision in *Martin* on the grounds that the Court of Appeal did not give sufficient weight to the applicant's right to see his records.

Dermot Feenan[98]

The framing of the exception in terms only of detriment to the patient seems insufficient protection of a patient's interests in personal health information. The sufficiency of the exception may be tested by reference to analogous law, comprising persuasive Commonwealth and American dicta and British legislation . . .

It is easy to understand why [Australian and American] courts require more than simply the doctor's view of potential detriment. There appears to be an implicit acknowledgement by them of the danger of paternalistic bias by the doctor regarding information disclosure. Aside from judicial precedent, mounting empirical evidence undermines doctors' assertions designed to restrict or obstruct information disclosure on the basis that patients would be unable to deal with harmful information . . . It is also acknowledged that unless the exception is carefully circumscribed it may swallow up the primary principle of information disclosure . . .

---

[98] 'Common Law Access to Medical Records' (1996) 59 Modern Law Review 101.

The exception in *Martin* also falls short of similar policy encapsulated in British freedom of information legislation. In the Access to Health Records Act 1990, which gives a statutory right of access to health records, section 5(1)(a) provides that access shall not be given where in the opinion of the holder of the record . . . information is '*likely* to cause *serious harm* to the physical or mental health of the patient'. This section makes clear the gravity of the harm and its likelihood. These criteria reflect the fact that the purpose of the legislation, which was to establish a right of access to health records, was not to be circumscribed too easily . . .

It seems that the Court of Appeal in *Martin* simply accepted the opinion of the consultant psychiatrist and, thence, respondents' solicitors, that disclosure would be detrimental to the patient. As the above common law dicta and legislation show, detriment alone ought to be insufficient. Since it is plausible that this issue may arise again before courts in England and Wales . . ., it seems that it would be appropriate to require that a doctor bears the onus of justifying non-disclosure on the basis that such disclosure would be likely to cause serious harm to the patient and that such harm could not reasonably be prevented through counselling with the patient.

The Access to Medical Reports Act 1988 establishes a right of access to reports prepared by doctors for employers, potential employers and insurers. Anyone seeking such a report must notify the subject, who has a right to withhold consent. If the subject consents to the report, she can, before it is issued, demand to see its contents, and insist that inaccurate or misleading information is amended. If the practitioner is not prepared to amend the report, the subject can attach a statement explaining her position.

There are a number of exceptions to the subject's access to the report. Any parts which reveal information about a third party need not be disclosed. And if the doctor believes that disclosure would be likely to cause serious harm to the physical or mental health of the individual, or would reveal the doctor's intention to, for example, suggest further investigations, again the doctor need not disclose the report. This latter therapeutic exception in section 7(1) is very widely drawn; in particular, notice that it is a subjective test. All that is necessary is that the doctor is of the opinion that disclosure would cause harm.

Access to Medical Reports Act 1988 section 7

(1) A medical practitioner shall not be obliged to give an individual access . . . to any part of a medical report whose disclosure would in the opinion of the practitioner be likely to cause serious harm to the physical or mental health of the individual or others or would indicate the intentions of the practitioner in respect of that individual.

(2) A medical practitioner shall not be obliged to give an individual access . . . to any part of a medical report whose disclosure would be likely to reveal information about another person, or to reveal the identity of another person who has supplied information to the practitioner about the individual, unless—

(a) that person has consented; or

(b) that person is a health professional who has been involved in the care of the individual and the information relates to or has been provided by the professional in that capacity.

Another potential limitation upon the Act's effectiveness is that it applies only to reports prepared by medical practitioners who are responsible for the subject's clinical care.[99] This does not appear to include doctors who are employed directly by the employer or insurer. Moreover, the Act applies to *written* reports, and it is not clear whether an oral disclosure of the subject's state of health would be covered. Although there is a right to apply to the court to ensure compliance, the Act does not provide for compensation in the event of its breach.

Patients also have a right of access to information under section 7 of the Data Protection Act 1998. In order to claim access to information, the data subject must make a request in writing; pay the specified fee (of up to £10); and supply information which confirms his identity and helps to locate the particular information. Information must then be supplied promptly, within 40 days or less. If the data controller fails to supply the relevant information, a court can order him to do so.

Exactly what are 'data subjects' entitled to under the Act? First, they can ask whether their personal data is being processed by the data controller; secondly, they can ask for a description of the data and the purposes for which it is being processed and the identity of its recipients; and thirdly, where possible, for a copy of any information held.

The right of access to health records under the Data Protection Act is not absolute, however. Under the Data Protection (Subject Access Modification) (Health) Order 2000,[100] data which might otherwise have to be disclosed can be withheld if it would be likely to cause serious harm to the physical or mental health of the data subject or any other person, or would lead the data subject to identify another person (other than a health professional who has been involved in the care of the data subject) who has not consented to the disclosure of his or her identity.

Personal data which is processed only for research purposes is also exempt from the right of access provided that the data is not processed to support measures or decisions with respect to particular individuals, is not done in such a way as would be likely to cause the patient substantial damage or distress, and the results do not identify the patient. Under section 31, regulatory agencies, such as the Healthcare Commission, and bodies which protect the public against malpractice, such as the GMC, can also claim exemption.

Of course the Data Protection Act 1998 must now be read in the light of the Freedom of Information Act 2000 which provides another route for access to information held by public bodies. Personal information is, however, exempt from the Freedom of Information Act's provisions both in relation to the patient's own access to her health records and to third parties seeking access to them. It is only non-personal health information, such as an NHS trust's policy decisions, which might be subject to requests under the Freedom of Information Act.

Clearly one situation in which a patient might want access to her medical records is if she is contemplating an action in negligence. Under section 33 of the Supreme Court Act 1981, she can apply for a court order which will require the relevant doctor or hospital to disclose her records or notes. There must be a real prospect of litigation before disclosure will be ordered. A patient cannot use section 33 in order to engage in a 'fishing expedition' in the hope that some evidence of negligence might emerge. In

---

[99] Section (2)1.   [100] SI 2000/413.

addition, limitations can be imposed upon disclosure. The patient herself has no right to see her records, rather the court may restrict disclosure to the patient's legal and/or medical advisers. And there is also the familiar public interest exception to disclosure, although this is probably unlikely to be engaged when the patient is seeking disclosure of her medical records to her legal adviser.

11. CONCLUSION

Despite the origins of the legal duty of confidence being somewhat opaque, doctors are unquestionably under a duty to respect their patients' confidentiality. The duty is not an absolute one, however. On the contrary, in a wide range of situations, the duty to respect confidentiality is suspended or modified. For example, patient notes have to be shared among healthcare professionals; information can be disclosed where there is a serious risk of harm to others; and patient records can be used for epidemiological research and clinical audit. Most exceptions to the duty of confidentiality could be justified on 'public interest' grounds, but it must be admitted that the existence of a 'public interest' exception to the duty of confidence does not offer very clear guidance to doctors about when disclosure of patient information is justifiable. Essentially, the public interest exception requires the merits of disclosure in a particular case to be weighed against the general public interest in the maintenance of patient confidentiality.

Not only is the 'public interest' exception both vague and potentially extremely broad, but also the legal rules which govern the duty of confidentiality are rather confusing. For example, the Human Rights Act protects privacy, and while privacy and confidentiality are clearly similar, they are not the same thing. The duty of confidentiality does not offer general protection for all personal information, instead it simply prevents the *redisclosure* of information that was originally disclosed within a confidential relationship. Hence viewing the question of confidentiality through the lens of the Human Rights Act may have a distorting effect upon the basic legal principles which underpin the duty of confidence.

Genetic information gives rise to some increasingly complex questions about the limits and extent of the duty of confidentiality. At present, there are limits upon our capacity to detect susceptibility genes, but in the future, it will be possible to find out with ever greater specificity about one's risk of future ill-health. Prenatal susceptibility screening may also enable potential parents to find out a great deal of information about their offspring's future health. Normally, however, it is only acceptable to carry genetic tests out on a child where there would be an immediate therapeutic advantage. N Wexler gives the extreme example of a woman in the US who requested genetic testing for Huntington's disease for her two children, on the grounds that she only had enough money to send one to Harvard![101]

---

[101] N Wexler 'Clairvoyance and caution: repercussions from the Human Genome Project' in DJ Kevles and L Hood (eds), *The Code of Codes: Scientific and Social Issues in the Human Genome Project* (Harvard UP 1992) 211–43, 233.

There is, perhaps, an inevitable tension between an individualistic model of confidentiality, in which a person's health information is regarded as paradigmatically private, and the inherently shared nature of genetic information. Since I share half of my DNA with my first degree relatives, I cannot avoid learning something about them, and vice versa, if I undergo genetic testing. Whether or not that should translate into a *right* to shared familial information is, as we have seen, extremely controversial.

My own view would be that this is yet another issue where it might be important to distinguish between moral and legal duties. The evidence undoubtedly indicates that people who find out that they have a gene associated with a particular condition generally feel under a *moral* duty to communicate that information to relevant relatives. But there is a danger that imposing a *legal* obligation of disclosure, either upon the person who has been tested or upon her doctor, might act as a disincentive to undergo genetic testing.

Our capacity to diagnose genetic disease currently far outstrips our capacity to treat it, so at present, breaching confidentiality by disclosing genetic information to relatives would seldom fit within the public interest exception of preventing serious harm to others. In the future, however, as it becomes possible to successfully treat more genetic diseases, there will be increasing pressure on the principle of confidentiality in the context of genetic disease, and the balancing exercise between the public interest in disclosure and the public interest in confidentiality will become even more finely balanced and complicated.

12. FURTHER READING

BELL, DEAN and BENNETT, BELINDA, 'Genetic Secrets and the Family' (2001) 9 Medical Law Review 130–61.

CASE, PAULA, 'Confidence Matters: The Rise and Fall of Informational Autonomy in Medical Law' (2003) 11 Medical Law Review 208–36.

FEENAN, DERMOT, 'Common Law Access to Medical Records' (1996) 59 Modern Law Review 101.

General Medical Council, *Confidentiality: Protecting and Providing Information* (GMC 2004) <http://www.gmc-uk.org/standards/default.htm>.

GILBAR, ROY, 'Medical Confidentiality Within the Family: The Doctor's Duty Reconsidered' (2004) 18 International Journal of Law, Policy and the Family 195.

Human Genetics Commission, Inside Information: Balancing interests in the use of personal genetic data (HGC 2002) available at <http://www.hgc.gov.uk/>.

JONES, C, 'The utilitarian argument for medical confidentiality: a pilot study of patients' views' (2003) 29 Journal of Medical Ethics 348–52.

LAURIE, GRAEME, 'In Defence of Ignorance: Genetic Information and the Right not to Know' (1999) 6 European Journal of Health Law 119–32.

LAURIE, GRAEME, *Genetic Privacy: A Challenge to Medico-Legal Norms* (CUP Cambridge 2002).

McHALE, JV, 'Regulating Genetic Databases: Some Legal and Ethical Issues' (2004) 12 Medical Law Review 70–96.

McLEAN, SHEILA and MASON, JOHN KENYON, *Legal and Ethical Aspects of Healthcare* (Greenwich Medical Media, 2003) ch 3.

O'DONOVAN, KATHERINE and GILBAR, ROY, 'The Loved Ones: Families, Intimates and Patient Autonomy' (2003) 23 Legal Studies 353.

SKENE, LOANE, 'Genetic Secrets and the Family' (2001) 9 Medical Law Review 162–9.

7

MENTAL HEALTH LAW

1. CENTRAL ISSUES

1. Mental health law is distinctive because it authorizes both detention and compulsory treatment.

2. Most mentally ill patients are not, however, subject to compulsory powers. Among hospital inpatients, only a small minority are 'sectioned', and the majority are admitted informally. 'Informal' patients do not have access to the same protections as detained patients, even when they are not, in practice, free to leave. The recent judgment of the ECHR in the *Bournewood* case will require a change in the law to ensure that compliant, incapacitated patients are offered more protection against de facto detention.

3. Usually patients are detained because they pose a risk to themselves or others, and/or because this is the only way to ensure that they

receive appropriate treatment. In recent years, increasing and unwarranted emphasis has been placed upon the risk mentally ill people pose to others.

4. It is possible to treat a mentally disordered patient without consent for her mental disorder, even if she is competent and refusing treatment. This exception to the principle of patient autonomy has been interpreted surprisingly broadly by the courts.

5. The patient's right to challenge her detention is protected by Article 5 (the right to liberty) of the Human Rights Act.

6. The 'care in the community' policy has not been an overwhelming success, and the new draft legislation will create further difficulties through its introduction of community treatment orders.

2. INTRODUCTION

In this chapter we attempt a broad overview of mental health law in the UK. There are arguments for and against including a chapter on mental health law in a medical law textbook. On the one hand, mental health law is a subject in its own right, and a single chapter is undoubtedly incapable of doing full justice to its breadth and complexity. Yet on the other hand, for a medical law textbook to exclude any discussion of the regime which governs the treatment of mentally ill patients would appear to mirror the misguided belief, described by Tom Campbell and Chris Heginbotham in the next extract, that the mentally ill are not really like other patients. In my view the risks of oversimplification and omission are probably outweighed by this latter concern.

Tom Campbell and Chris Heginbotham[1]
Persons with mental illnesses are made to suffer a range of unnecessary deprivations which result

---

[1] *Mental Illness: Prejudice, Discrimination and the Law* (Dartmouth Aldershot 1991) 7, 9–10.

from crude and erroneous assumptions about mental illnesses which lead us to lump their victims together in a pariah class of sub-humans. People with a history of mental illness repeatedly experience the frustration and insult caused by a lack of respect for them as individuals and the absence of humane consideration for their situation.

While a mental illness can happen to any member of society, its natural effects are such that its victims rarely achieve or sustain economic security or social influence. Social attitudes accelerate and reinforce this downward spiral through social and economic exclusion. Mental illness thus routinely brings with it membership of a wronged, insulted and excessively deprived class of persons . . .

To be perceived or classified as 'mentally ill' is to be vulnerable to all manner of disadvantages which are not defensible on the basis of what it is to have a mental illness, or mistaken assumptions about the general distribution of certain characteristics amongst the mentally ill as a group, together with serious overestimations of the significance of those features of mental illnesses which are relevant to differential treatment, all engender indefensible responses to particular individuals with mental illnesses and are reflected in social policies relating to the rights and interests of mentally ill people.

Moreover, these responses are directly or indirectly related to attitudes of distaste, fear and dislike of 'the mentally ill' as a class. These unreasonable hostile reactions to people with mental illnesses bring deprivations and disadvantages that would not be tolerated if they were inflicted on other citizens. The result is that mental illness discrimination exacerbates the often already unfortunate plight of those with mental illnesses. Thus, schizophrenia or depression can bring pain, misery and the incapacity to participate in normal social life. Not only are these sufferings and difficulties insufficiently recognized and tackled, but the situations of those affected are made worse by additional socially imposed disadvantages in the fields of employment, social welfare, financial services, health care and civil liberties.

We begin with a short history of mental health policy, tracing the rise and fall of asylums and the more recent emphasis, first, upon care in the community, and more recently still, upon risk-avoidance. Next we consider the various stages involved in the treatment of mental illness, starting with a definition of mental disorder and a description of how patients are admitted to the mental health system.

In Chapter 4, we looked at the concept of mental incapacity, and it is critically important to remember that mentally ill people are not necessarily incapable of making medical decisions. Recall the patient in *Re C*,[2] who suffered from paranoid schizophrenia, and yet was found to be capable of deciding that he did not want his gangrenous leg amputated. Competent mentally ill patients should generally have the same rights to refuse medical treatment as other competent adults, but there are some important exceptions, and we consider when mentally ill patients can be treated without consent. Finally we look at discharge from the mental health system, and the availability of care in the community.

The fundamental legal difference between mental health law and other areas of medical law is that it authorizes the detention and compulsory treatment of people suffering from mental illness. This is radically out of line with the principle of patient autonomy which, as we have seen, now dominates medical law. Patients suffering from treatable infectious diseases are not routinely detained and treated without

---

[2] [1994] 1 All ER 819, [1994] 1 WLR 290.

consent, so why should it be possible to detain and compulsorily treat people with mental health problems? There are three possible justifications:

(1) It might enable them to gain access to treatment. Where a mentally ill patient is also incapable of giving valid consent to treatment, the only way for her to obtain the treatment she needs is to treat her without consent. However, as we have seen, mentally ill people are not necessarily also mentally incapacitated, and for competent mentally ill patients, other justifications are necessary.

(2) It could be argued that detention and treatment without consent are sometimes necessary to protect the patient from herself. Someone who is suicidal, for example, might subsequently be glad that she was prevented from taking her own life.

(3) Alternatively, it might be argued that detention and compulsory treatment are necessary to protect the public from dangerous mentally ill patients.

As we shall see later, this latter idea that the public needs protection from people with psychiatric problems has been in the ascendancy in recent years. It is, however, extremely controversial because it essentially amounts to *preventative detention*, that is detaining people not because they have been found guilty of a criminal offence, but because there is perceived to be a *risk* that they *might* cause harm to others. Not only does this create an exception to some basic principles of criminal justice, but it could also be argued that mental illness creates no greater risk of violence than drinking too much, for example, and that the principle of preventative detention, if applied consistently, should result in the routine compulsory detention and treatment of aggressive binge drinkers.

Before we begin our overview of mental health law and policy in the UK, it should be noted that this chapter has been written at a time of enormous flux. It had been apparent for some time that the Mental Health Act 1983, which essentially simply updated and in parts reproduced the Mental Health Act 1959, was in need of reform, and this need became more pressing in the light of the incorporation of the European Convention on Human Rights through the Human Rights Act 1998. The Mental Health Act 1983 was the subject of the first declaration of incompatibility with the Human Rights Act, and the lack of fit between the two pieces of legislation has proved to be a rich source of litigation.

An Expert Committee, chaired by Genevra Richardson, was established in 1998, and its review of the Mental Health Act was submitted to the Department of Health the following year.[3] Also in 1999, the Fallon Committee's report into concerns about poor practices at Ashworth Special Hospital was published.[4] It had focused on the treatment of people with personality disorders. These reports led to the publication of two separate green papers, followed in 2000 by one combined white Paper, and in 2002 by a draft Mental Health Bill. This first Bill was subjected to overwhelming and near-universal criticism. Both the British Medical Association and the Royal College

---

[3] *Review of the Mental Health Act: Report of the Expert Committee* (DoH London 1999).
[4] *Report of the Committee of Inquiry in the Personality Disorder Unit, Ashworth Special Hospital* (DoH London 1999).

of Psychiatrists argued that the proposed legislation was unworkable. The 2002 Bill was then withdrawn, and a new Bill was introduced in 2004 which attempted to accommodate some of the criticisms levelled at the earlier Bill. A joint select committee was appointed to scrutinize the 2004 Bill, and its report was published in 2005.[5] At the time of writing, the government has issued its response to the joint committee's report, and has indicated that it accepts some of their criticisms of the Bill, but not others.[6] The Mental Health Bill was included in the Queen's speech in 2005, and will be introduced to parliament in 2005/6. It is not known when any new Act would come into force, but given the need to draft a new Code of Practice, the new statute is unlikely to repeal the 1983 Act until 2007, at the earliest.

At the time of writing, the final version of the Bill has not yet been published, but it is likely that it will reproduce the 2004 Bill, with some modifications in the light of the joint committee's report. In this chapter, we will look at both the Mental Health Act 1983, which since 1990 has been accompanied by a regularly updated Code of Practice, and its probable replacement. Obviously the Bill is likely to be subject to further amendment during its passage through parliament, and so references to the content of the draft Bill should be treated cautiously. The full text of the new Act will be available on the Office of Public Sector Information website.[7]

It is also worth remembering that, as we saw in Chapter 4, reform of the law on mental incapacity proceeded separately from these troubled mental health law reforms, and culminated in the Mental Capacity Act 2005, discussed in Chapter 4. While mental incapacity and mental illness are by no means synonymous with each other, there are obvious areas of overlap—such as the criteria for treatment without consent—which might usefully have been combined.

At the outset, it should be noted that the very existence of 'mental illness' is doubted by commentators in what is often referred to as the 'anti-psychiatry' movement. These critics, such as Thomas Szasz and Erving Goffman, have argued that psychiatry is not concerned with treating the sick, but instead with controlling and coercing unusual or inconvenient members of society. And of course, as Szasz explains in the next extract, if there is no such thing as mental illness, a special set of laws governing the treatment of the mentally ill is also unnecessary.

Thomas Szasz[8]

The term 'mental illness' is a metaphor. More particularly, as this term is used in mental hygiene legislation, 'mental illness' is not the name of a medical disease or disorder, but is a quasi-medical label whose purpose is to conceal conflict as illness and to justify coercion as treatment.

If 'mental illness' is a bona fide illness—as official medical, psychiatric, and mental health organizations, such as the World Health Organization, the American and British Medical Associations, and the American Psychiatric Association, maintain—then it follows, logically and linguistically, that it must be treated like any other illness. Hence, mental hygiene laws must be

[5] Joint committee on the Draft Mental Health Bill—First Report, 2005, <http://www.publications.parliament.uk/pa/jt/jtment.htm>.

[6] *Government Response to the Report of the Joint Committee on the Draft Mental Health Bill 2004* (DoH London 2005) <http://www.dh.gov.uk/assetRoot/04/11/52/68/04115268.pdf>.

[7] <http://www.opsi.gov.uk/legislation/index.htm>.

[8] *Law, Liberty and Psychiatry: An Inquiry into the Social Uses of Mental Health Practices* (Routledge & Kegan Paul London 1974) xi–xii, 17, 251.

repealed. There are no special laws for patients with a peptic ulcer or pneumonia; why, then, should there be special laws for patients with depression or schizophrenia?

If, on the other hand, 'mental illness' is, as I contend, a myth, then, also, it follows that mental hygiene laws should be repealed . . .

In short, all those who draft and administer laws pertaining to involuntary psychiatric interventions should be regarded as the adversaries, not the allies, of the so-called mental patient. Civil libertarians, and, indeed, all men and women who believe that no one may be justly deprived of their liberty except upon conviction of a crime, should oppose all forms of involuntary psychiatric interventions . . .

When I assert that mental illness is a myth, I am not saying that personal unhappiness and socially deviant behaviour do not exist; but I am saying that we categorize them as diseases at our peril.

The expression 'mental illness' is a metaphor which we have come to mistake for a fact. We call people physically ill when their body-functioning violates certain anatomical and physiological norms; similarly, we call people mentally ill when their personal conduct violates certain ethical, political, and social norms. This explains why many historical figures, from Jesus to Castro, and from Job to Hitler, have been diagnosed as suffering from this or that psychiatric malady . . .

We should guard against . . . the discomfort that the mental patient's behaviour may cause us. If intense enough, it may justify intolerance toward personal idiosyncrasies and so-called aberrations of behavior. And yet, labeling conduct as sick merely because it differs from our own may be nothing more than discrimination disguised as medical judgment.

3. A SHORT HISTORY OF MENTAL HEALTH LAW AND POLICY

There is a very long history of subjecting people who have been classified as 'mad' to special treatment. As early as 1324, the Royal Prerogative gave the King jurisdiction over the freedom and property of 'idiots'. Compulsory detention has been possible for hundreds of years although it used to be the preserve of poor law officers, and Justices of the Peace, rather than doctors. The Vagrancy Act 1744, for example, enabled two or more Justices of the Peace to direct a constable, church warden or overseer of the poor to apprehend

those who by Lunacy or otherwise are furiously mad or so far disordered in their Senses that may be dangerous to be permitted to go Abroad,

so that they could

be safely locked in some secure place . . . (and if necessary) to be there chained . . . for and during such time only as the lunacy or madness shall continue.

Private asylums existed to accommodate richer mad people, but generally the vast majority of those who were considered insane were classified as paupers, and kept in poorhouses. Conditions in both were appalling. Beatings, whippings and rape were common, and prolonged restraint was the norm. A select committee established in 1877 proposed a number of reforms, such as the provision of a system of asylums at public expense; a requirement that two medical certificates accompany an application to detain an individual; and a system of independent inspection of asylums. From the Lunacy Act 1890 onwards, a series of statutes brought such a system into being.

But while it had been hoped that greater legal regulation would improve the treatment of the mentally ill, in practice little changed, and in 1924 the government set up a Royal Commission to make further recommendations for reform. The Mental Treatment Act 1930 was intended to reduce the stigma associated with mental illness, a shift that had its origins in the changing attitudes to people with mental health problems which were prompted by the return of 'shell-shocked' soldiers from the First World War. It also represented a shift towards 'medicalism', with admission decisions taken by psychiatrists, rather than lawyers. As treatments for mental illnesses became available, psychiatrists' social standing had improved because their role was increasingly like that of conventional doctors, and less like that of gaolers. The Percy Commission was set up to consider further reform in the 1950s, and its report culminated in the passage of the Mental Health Act 1959. It emphasized voluntary rather than compulsory admission to hospital, and short-term rather than permanent detention. Although based upon the 1959 Act, the Mental Health Act 1983 attempted to offer more legal safeguards in order to protect the rights of mentally ill patients. We consider it, and its draft successor, in more detail below.

From the nineteenth century onwards there have been dramatic shifts in attitudes towards institutionalizing people with mental illnesses. In 1850, there were 7,140 inpatients, by 1930 there were nearly 120,000 inpatients, and by 1954 this figure had risen to 148,000. Asylums were believed to offer humane and decent surroundings for some of the most marginal members of society. They also undoubtedly facilitated greater social control and surveillance of the insane.[9]

Then in the second half of the twentieth century there was a dramatic turn away from the incarceration of people suffering from mental illnesses. Even for those patients who are not capable of living independently, in patient treatment has increasingly been provided in psychiatric wards in general hospitals, and not in asylums. Now the number of psychiatric hospital beds is around 33,000.[10] Several reasons are commonly given for this move towards decarceration. First, it might be part of a broader trend in social policy away from institutional solutions to social problems; financial support for the poor, for example, is increasingly supposed to be a temporary measure to facilitate their independence, rather than encouraging permanent dependency. Secondly, community care is often perceived to be cheaper than keeping a patient in an institution, and in an overburdened NHS, the pressure to save money is considerable. Thirdly, the discovery of widespread abuse of mentally ill people within institutions meant that asylums were no longer seen as places of safety. Fourthly, the development of drugs, such as tranquillizers, contributed to an increasingly *medical* model of insanity, where it is regarded as a disease that can be effectively managed, if not cured, and sufferers thereby enabled to lead relatively normal lives. Finally, the discovery that mental illness is in fact much more common than had been previously

---

[9] See further, Michel Foucault, *The Birth of the Clinic: An Archaeology of Clinical Perception* (Penguin London 1973).
[10] <http://www.publications.parliament.uk/pa/jt/jtment.htm> para 183.

realized contributed to the view that a diagnosis of mental disorder did not justify locking someone up.

A growing emphasis on community care is evident in mental health policy from the 1960s onwards, but while the number of hospital beds declined, other services were not put in place to replace inpatient care. It had been assumed that mentally ill people would be cared for in the home, and readily reintegrated into the community, but this assumption proved to be hopelessly over-optimistic. It has not been easy for people with mental illnesses to find jobs and accommodation, and their families are not always either able or willing to provide the care that they need.

Many commentators have analysed mental health law as if it were a pendulum swinging between legalism, with an emphasis upon legal protections, and medicalism, where the medical profession is left to determine how individual patients should be treated. This distinction is described by Phil Fennell in the following extract:

Phil Fennell[11]

Nowhere is the tension between autonomy and paternalism more evident than in relation to the treatment of mentally disordered patients. Debate about these questions in the mental health sphere has, until comparatively recently, revolved around two organizing concepts. On the one hand has been legalism, which has emphasized the need to put limits on the power of mental health professionals and the rights of patients to respect for their autonomously expressed wishes. On the other has been that of medicalism which stresses that the safeguards for the individual rights of patients are not so cumbersome as to impede medical interventions aimed at serving those same patients' best interests.

As Nicola Glover-Thomas explains, legal constraints not only protect patients' rights, but also help to legitimate psychiatric practice.

Nicola Glover-Thomas[12]

A person is detained due to his mental condition, rather than his illegal activities, thereby providing the potential for compromising individual autonomy. To avoid this possible abuse the law is used to establish a formal framework in which decisions are made. This framework provides a mechanism for inspecting the validity of decisions to detain and treat individuals. Such decisions need to be justified because once they have been legitimated for therapeutic purposes, it becomes increasingly difficult to establish oppressive activity. Psychiatric practice must be seen to be subject to social, moral and political control. Legal scrutiny provides the final opportunity to protect patient rights. Clearly, the law acts as a mechanism of control because it establishes a framework in which care decisions are made and incorporates legal safeguards surrounding detention, treatment and other coercive aspects of the legislation. The formation of these safeguards protects both the patient and those working within the psychiatric field. They legitimate psychiatric practices because they ensure the decisions are made in a procedurally sound way. . . . The existence of a formal legal framework allows the public to accept decisions, which overtly remove rights from individuals. The need for psychiatrists to seek second medical opinions and to obtain opinions from other professionals allows psychiatric practice to be seen as accountable and legitimate.

[11] 'Inscribing Paternalism in the Law: Consent to Treatment and Mental Disorder' (1990) 17 Journal of Law and Society 29–51, 29.
[12] *Reconstructing Mental Health Law and Policy* (Butterworths London 2002) 34–5.

4. WHAT IS MENTAL ILLNESS?

Mental illness is common: it is estimated than one in six adults in the UK will suffer from some sort of mental illness each year. Some mental disorders are mild and relatively easy to live with, whereas others can be fatal. Mental illness is often more difficult to diagnose than physical illness. Unlike an X-ray of a broken bone, it will not always be possible to establish precisely what is wrong with a person's mental health. Instead psychiatrists attempt to diagnose mental disorders through the patient's own description of her symptoms, and through observing her behaviour.

Insofar as illness means abnormal functioning, in order to define mental illness it might first be necessary to have some idea of what normal mental wellbeing consists in. Yet as we all know, this would be incredibly difficult to pin down. Sadness, anger and frustration are all normal facets of the human condition, and hardly evidence of mental illness. On the other hand, depression can be an extremely debilitating condition which is capable of interfering with its sufferers' ability to lead a normal life at least as much as any physical illness.

Because mental health law can sanction involuntary detention and compulsory treatment, including treatment with powerful mind-altering chemicals, it is obviously crucial that there should be clear criteria defining the conditions which can trigger these drastic consequences. It is also important to remember that labelling someone as mentally ill or mentally disordered will often carry more stigma, and result in more discriminatory treatment, than the diagnosis of a physical condition, so again a clear definition and accurate diagnosis are especially important.

(a) DEFINING MENTAL DISORDER UNDER THE 1983 ACT

Under the 1983 Act, the statutory definition of mental disorder is contained in section 1(2):

Mental Health Act 1983 section 1

(1) The provisions of this Act shall have effect with respect to the reception, care and treatment of mentally disordered patients, the management of their property and other related matters.

(2) In this Act—

- 'mental disorder' means mental illness, arrested or incomplete development of mind, psychopathic disorder and any other disorder or disability of mind and 'mentally disordered' shall be construed accordingly;

- 'severe mental impairment' means a state of arrested or incomplete development of mind which includes severe impairment of intelligence and social functioning and is associated with abnormally aggressive or seriously irresponsible conduct on the part of the person concerned and 'severely mentally impaired' shall be construed accordingly;

- 'mental impairment' means a state of arrested or incomplete development of mind (not amounting to severe mental impairment) which includes significant impairment of intelligence and social functioning and is associated with abnormally aggressive or seriously irresponsible conduct on the part of the person concerned and 'mentally impaired' shall be construed accordingly;

- 'psychopathic disorder' means a persistent disorder or disability of mind (whether or not including significant impairment of intelligence) which results in abnormally aggressive or seriously irresponsible conduct on the part of the person concerned;

(3) Nothing in subsection (2) above shall be construed as implying that a person may be dealt with under this Act as suffering from mental disorder, or from any form of mental disorder described in this section, by reason only of promiscuity or other immoral conduct, sexual deviancy or dependence on alcohol or drugs.

Section 1(2)'s definition of mental disorder is extremely broad, since it covers not only mental illness and psychopathic disorder, but also any 'arrested or incomplete development of mind' and 'any other disorder or disability of mind'. It is not therefore necessary for someone with a mental disorder to be behaving abnormally. In contrast, mental impairment, severe mental impairment and psychopathic disorders are defined in part with reference to abnormally aggressive or seriously irresponsible conduct. Indeed a patient can only be categorized as psychopathic (psychopathy is an outdated term for what is now referred to as personality disorder) if he is behaving aggressively or irresponsibly. Other than the degree of severity, there is little difference between the definition of mental impairment and severe mental impairment. The distinction is only important in the context of section 3 of the 1983 Act, which authorizes compulsory detention. Someone with non-serious mental impairment and psychopathy can be confined under section 3(2)(b) only if treatment is available which 'is likely to alleviate or prevent a deterioration of his condition' (we come back to this 'treatability' criterion later at p. 404). In contrast, a person with severe mental impairment can be confined even if treatment is not available.

The reason for specifying in section 1(3) that no one should be treated as mentally disordered 'by reason only of promiscuity or other immoral conduct, sexual deviancy or dependence on alcohol or drugs' is that, in the past, 'lunatic' asylums were regularly used to deal with marginal people, or those whose conduct was judged immoral. For example, section 1 of the Inebriates Act 1898 permitted the detention of habitual drunkards. 'Feeble-minded' unmarried women who gave birth while on poor relief could be confined to an asylum under section 2 of the Mental Deficiency Act 1913 because becoming pregnant outside of marriage was, at that time, believed to offer evidence of both moral depravity and mental defectiveness.

There is, however, an interesting interaction between the definition of psychopathy, and section 1(3). Sexual deviancy, promiscuity and alcohol abuse could be 'seriously irresponsible conduct' for the purposes of section 1(2), and yet section 1(3) specifically excludes those whose only misbehaviour relates to their immoral conduct, sexual deviancy or dependence on alcohol or drugs. This issue arose in *R v Mental Health Review Tribunal, ex parte Clatworthy*.[13] The applicant had been convicted of indecent offences against young children and was detained under the Mental Health Act 1983. The diagnosis of his psychopathic disorder had been made solely on the basis of his

---

[13] [1985] 3 All ER 699.

sexual deviancy, and Mann J therefore held that, since this had to be discounted under section 1(3), he should be discharged.

The mixture of medical and social criteria in section 1(2) makes it difficult to know whether it is for professionals to determine what mental disorder means, or whether the statute is simply employing an ordinary language definition. For example, someone could be defined as mentally impaired because there is something wrong with her mind (which sounds like a medical condition, that might need to be diagnosed by a psychiatrist), or because she is behaving aggressively (which sounds like a social definition, that could be readily identified by a lay person). In *R v Trent MHRT, ex parte Ryan*,[14] a case in which the court had to decide whether a number of offences of indecent assault against children amounted to seriously irresponsible conduct, Nolan LJ suggested that the definition of pyschopathy rests on both clinical and non-clinical criteria:

it seems to me in the first place that although the question whether in a clinical sense the applicant suffers from a psychopathic disorder is a diagnostic and medical question, the definition in section 1(2), which I have quoted, imports questions which are not strictly of a clinical or medical nature, because part of the definition (the latter part) consists of the words, 'which results in abnormally aggressive or seriously irresponsible conduct on the part of the person concerned'.

No doubt whether the conduct is the result of the disorder is again a medical question. Whether it amounts to seriously irresponsible or abnormally aggressive behaviour seems to me . . . to raise questions other than of a purely clinical nature. . . . The fact that medical evidence is involved in the definition is of course in itself no reason why it should not be decided by the members of the Tribunal in the light of their own expertise and examination of the patient.

The vast majority (around 98 per cent) of people who are detained within the mental health system are categorized as mentally ill, but under section 1(2) of the Act, this receives no further definition. Does this mean that it is a matter for clinical judgment, or that the words are used in their ordinary language sense? In a 1974 case, the Court of Appeal tended towards the latter interpretation:

W v L[15]

Shortly after they were married, the husband began to exhibit symptoms of mental disorder by perpetrating occasional senseless acts of cruelty on domestic animals—he put a cat in the oven, cut its throat, and had hanged one dog and strangled another. He had also threatened his wife with violence. Although the experts were satisfied that the husband was suffering from a 'psychopathic disorder', the question whether he was also suffering from a 'mental illness' arose.

Lawton LJ

The facts of this case show how difficult the fitting of particular instances into the statutory classification can be. Lord Denning MR and Orr LJ have pointed out that there is no definition of 'mental illness'. The words are ordinary words of the English language. They have no particular medical significance. They have no particular legal significance. How should the court construe them? The answer in my judgment is . . . that ordinary words of the English language should be construed in the way that ordinary sensible people would construe them. That being, in my judgment, the right test, then I ask myself, what would the ordinary sensible person have said

---

[14] Unreported 4 Oct 1991 (Transcript on LEXIS).   [15] [1974] QB 711.

about the patient's condition in this case if he had been informed of his behaviour to the dogs, the cat and his wife? In my judgment such a person would have said: 'Well, the fellow is obviously mentally ill'. If that be right, then, although the case may fall within the definition of 'psychopathic disorder' . . ., it also falls within the classification of 'mental illness'.

In the next extract Brenda Hoggett criticizes Lawton LJ's adoption of what she famously described as the 'man-must-be-mad' test:

Brenda Hoggett[16]
It is impossible not to think of this as the 'man-must-be-mad' test. It simply adds fuel to the fire of those who accuse the mental hygiene laws of being a sophisticated machine for the suppression of unusual, eccentric, or inconvenient behaviour (and in this country without due process of law). It pays scant regard to the painstaking efforts of psychiatrists to distinguish mental health from mental illness by means of carefully described deficiencies, not in behaviour, but in mental functioning. It draws no recognisable distinction between illness and personality disorder. It tells us nothing about why some people who are cruel to animals should be regarded as responsible for their actions and some should not . . .

[L]ay people's understanding of mental illness is notoriously limited or faulty. It would make more sense to focus on the commonly accepted medical meaning of the phrase.

Does the public have a clear and consistent idea of what mental illness consists in? Certainly it should be recognized that the acceptability of behaviour varies across different cultures and at different times. In the past homosexuality, for example, was classified as a mental illness, and was treated with drugs, psychotherapy and electric aversion therapy.

It is important to remember that, other than the stigma of being so defined, no consequences automatically flow from being categorized as mentally disordered, rather it is a first step in the process of invoking formal powers under the Act. Further criteria must also be satisfied before such steps can be taken, and we consider these in the next section, after we have looked at the new definition of mental disorder in the draft Bill.

(b) DEFINING MENTAL DISORDER UNDER THE DRAFT MENTAL HEALTH BILL

The draft Mental Health Bill's definition of mental disorder is much shorter:

'Mental disorder' means an impairment of or a disturbance in the functioning of the mind or brain resulting from any disability of disorder of the mind or brain.

It must be admitted that this is exceptionally broad, and could potentially apply to many more people than the 1983 Act's definition. Indeed the Royal College of Psychiatrists has suggested that the Bill's definition might include patients suffering from multiple sclerosis, Parkinson's disease, learning disability, or even dependence on alcohol or nicotine.[17]

---

16 *Mental Health Law* (4th edn Sweet & Maxwell London 1996) 32.
17 *Reform of the Mental Health Act 1983: Response to the draft Mental Health Bill and consultation document* (RCP 2004).

Initially the draft Bill did not contain any exclusions, such as that contained in section 1(3) of the Mental Health Act 1983, which prevents individuals from being categorized as mentally disordered solely because of promiscuity or other immoral conduct, sexual deviancy or addiction. But following criticism from the joint committee on the draft Mental Health Bill,[18] the Government has accepted that a specific exclusion on the grounds of substance misuse, such as dependence on alcohol or drugs, should be inserted into the Bill.[19]

The joint committee had also recommended that where the person was suffering from a learning disability or a communicative disorder such as autism:

they should only be subject to compulsory powers if they also display seriously aggressive or severely irresponsible behaviour as a result of their condition, and if such treatment as is properly and reasonably required can only be provided to such patients under conditions of compulsion.[20]

But this was not accepted by the Government on the grounds that to have a condition which applied only to patients with a certain sort of disorder would be discriminatory.[21]

Again, it is important to remember that simply being defined as mentally disordered does not necessarily mean that someone will be subject to the formal powers contained in the Bill, rather it is a necessary but certainly not a sufficient condition. The other conditions are to be found elsewhere in the Bill (see below).

5. ADMISSION TO THE MENTAL HEALTH SYSTEM

Around 250,000 people each year are admitted to the mental health system. 90 per cent of these are admitted informally under section 131 of the 1983 Act (see below). The remaining 10 per cent are compulsorily detained or 'sectioned', and most of these are detained for no more than a month for the purposes of assessment. Because compulsory detention poses a greater threat to a patient's civil liberties than informal admission, both academic commentary and litigation has tended to focus upon the small group of formally admitted patients. It is however important to bear in mind that the vast majority of patients do not enter the mental health system through the exercise of compulsory powers, and so do not have access to the various protective measures which accompany formal detention. When we take into account the fact that most people who suffer from mental illness do not receive inpatient treatment in hospital, it becomes clear that compulsorily detained patients represent a tiny percentage of those with mental health problems. Interestingly, then, 'mental health law' has little application to the vast majority of mentally ill individuals in society.

---

[18] Joint Committee on the Draft Mental Health Bill—First Report, 2005, <http://www.publications.parliament.uk/pa/jt/jtment.htm>.

[19] *Government Response to the Report of the Joint Committee on the Draft Mental Health Bill 2004* (DoH London 2005) <http://www.dh.gov.uk/assetRoot/04/11/52/68/04115268.pdf>.

[20] Joint Committee on the Draft Mental Health Bill—First Report, 2005, <http://www.publications.parliament.uk/pa/jt/jtment.htm>.

[21] *Government Response to the Report of the Joint Committee on the Draft Mental Health Bill 2004* (DoH London 2005) <http://www.dh.gov.uk/assetRoot/04/11/52/68/04115268.pdf>.

(a) VOLUNTARY ADMISSION UNDER THE 1983 ACT

Under section 131 of the 1983 Act, anyone who 'requires treatment for mental disorder' (defined in section 1(2) considered above) may be admitted informally:

Mental Health Act 1983 section 131

(1) Nothing in this Act shall be construed as preventing a patient who requires treatment for mental disorder from being admitted to any hospital or [registered establishment] in pursuance of arrangements made in that behalf and without any application, order or direction rendering him liable to be detained under this Act, or from remaining in any hospital or [registered establishment] in pursuance of such arrangements after he has ceased to be so liable to be detained.

(2) In the case of a minor who has attained the age of 16 years and is capable of expressing his own wishes, any such arrangements as are mentioned in subsection (1) above may be made, carried out and determined even though there are one or more persons who have parental responsibility for him (within the meaning of the Children Act 1989).

Section 131 does not appear to cover admission for assessment rather than treatment. In *R v Kirklees MBC, ex parte C*[22] the Court of Appeal suggested that the patient's voluntary admission to hospital for assessment would be lawful at common law, in the same way as a person's admission to hospital for an operation:

Lloyd LJ

I agree with Miss Lawson that s 131 of the Act does not in terms cover the case of a patient who is admitted for assessment, despite the definition of patient which covers, as I have said, a person appearing to suffer from mental disorder, as well as a person actually so suffering. Mr Spencer QC for the council did not contend otherwise. It may seem odd that whereas in Part II of the Act there is provision for compulsory admission for assessment (s 2) and compulsory admission for treatment (s 3), s 131 is confined to voluntary admission for treatment. . . . But whatever the explanation, nothing turns on the absence of any provision covering voluntary admission for assessment, as distinct from treatment; for s 131 does not create or purport to create any new power, nor does it confer any new immunity. It merely preserves and confirms what was there before . . .

So far as I have been able to ascertain, there has never been any doubt that an adult patient may be lawfully admitted to hospital for assessment, provided he or she consents, just as he or she may be fully admitted to hospital for an operation. The reason is not hard to see. Although this is in appearance a claim for judicial review, on the ground that the applicant's life record, as it has been termed, has been adversely affected, it is in reality a claim for damages for false imprisonment. But it has always been a defence to a claim for false imprisonment that the victim has consented. If, therefore, the applicant had been of full age and sound mind, and had consented to her admission for assessment, the hospital would have had a complete answer to a claim for damages for false imprisonment. It could not possibly be argued that s 131 had by inference deprived the hospital of that immunity . . .

The only remaining question is whether it makes any difference that W was not an adult at the time of her admission, but a minor. The answer is that it could make no difference provided always the council is competent to consent on her behalf, and did in fact consent . . .

In the end, this was a very straightforward case. W was admitted to an open ward . . . as an

---

[22] [1993] 2 FLR 187.

informal patient with the consent of the council acting in loco parentis. The purpose of the admission was for assessment . . . There is nothing in the Mental Health Act 1983 or in the previous law which suggests to me that the council's conduct was in any way illegal.

Usually informal admission is possible because the patient herself is willingly seeking treatment, and in such cases there are clear advantages in avoiding the use of formal powers. If a patient's liberty is not restricted, it is less likely that her relationship with her doctors will be compromised. Voluntarily admitted patients may be more likely than detained patients to cooperate with any treatment plan, and may find the experience of hospitalization less distressing.

Of course, it is possible that the patient will come under pressure, perhaps from her family, to agree to informal admission, and, in practice, she may not have anywhere else to go. It is also possible for an informally admitted patient to subsequently be formally detained under section 5 of the 1983 Act. Once in hospital, as Phil Fennell explains in the next extract, informally admitted patients are, therefore, not necessarily free to leave.

Phil Fennell[23]

What does informal status mean? It does not entitle the patient to leave the hospital at will, contrary to the impression given by the Code of Practice on the Mental Health Act 1983 which affirms the importance of informal patients understanding 'their right to leave hospital'. The 'right' is subject to significant limitations. Under the 1983 Act, doctors have the power to detain any in-patient for up to 72 hours and mental health nurses can detain psychiatric in-patients for up to six hours pending an application for their compulsory admission . . . For informal patients truly to understand their 'right' to leave, hospitals would have to tell them that it may be removed by decisions of doctors or nurses to restrain them from leaving hospital.

Even if there were an unlimited right for informal patients to leave hospital, to speak of mentally incapacitated patients having it makes little sense. There may be nowhere else capable of providing the care which the patient needs, he may have no home to go to and be too dependent to survive in sheltered accommodation. Any hospital or nursing home accepting responsibility for looking after mentally incapacitated informal patients thereby assumes a duty of care towards them. That duty of care extends to preventing them from leaving when to do so would put them at risk. Not being detained does not make an informal patient 'freer'. Paradoxically it may make them less free, because if formally detained, they would have access to statutory safeguards such as review of detention by a mental health review tribunal, the right to a second opinion if treated for mental disorder without consent, and the benefit of the complaints jurisdiction of the MHAC [Mental Health Act Commission].

In the next extract, Michael Cavadino draws upon his interviews with patients at an NHS psychiatric hospital which he calls 'Fardale' in order to examine whether informal patients' stays in hospital are genuinely voluntary.

Michael Cavadino[24]

It seems uncomfortably true that the very informality of informal admission can make it easier to detain [informal] patients illegally, since greater legal formality can make abuse easier to monitor

---

[23] 'Doctor Knows Best? Therapeutic Detention under Common Law, the Mental Health Act and the European Convention' (1998) 6 Medical Law Review 322–53, 332–3.
[24] *Mental Health Law in Context* (Dartmouth Aldershot 1989) 77, 79–80, 87–8.

and thereby deter it . . . Another uncomfortable possibility is that the simplicity of the procedures for formal detention since 1959 has led to patients being made aware that they can be taken to hospital with little difficulty whether they like it or not, and that in some cases it has been this knowledge and not any desire to cooperate that has led the patient to enter hospital informally.

So it is certainly *possible* for a patient to be informal but nevertheless 'coerced' in a very real sense into accepting hospitalization . . .

[T]here is little empirical evidence that patients are typically or routinely coerced into *entering* hospital in the first place against their express wishes, although it does happen sometimes. But what about after admission? It is possible for patients to enter hospital voluntarily or acquiescently but at some later stage to be prevented from leaving, or be subjected to some other forcible control, which would normally be incompatible with informal admission. This can happen if patients are restrained from leaving hospital by force or threat of force; or led to believe that they are not free to leave; or locked in a side-room; or denied access to their clothes; or given medical treatment such as drugs by force or threat of force; or if the patient demands discharge and is not allowed to take it. Such occurrences were by no means uncommon in Fardale . . .

On the question of whether they would like to leave hospital, a substantial minority of the informal patients (38 per cent) said that they would . . . So why were so many patients still in hospital informally who would rather leave? . . . Of the informal patients who expressed a desire to leave, 14 per cent did indeed believe that they were not free to leave hospital . . . But in most cases, patients perceived other constraints as being more important. Foremost among these other constraints was lack of accommodation, or suitable accommodation, outside the hospital . . .

It seems, then, that although there are indeed *some* informal patients who stay in hospital because they feel coerced to do so, factors such as lack of accommodation are of much greater importance than the fear of legal or extra-legal force—certainly in the eyes of the patients themselves.

There are other times when patients are informally admitted to hospital not because they have willingly gone into hospital, but because they are too incapacitated to express a preference. The Percy Commission, whose Report formed the basis of the Mental Heath Act 1959 had recommended that compulsory powers should not be used for such patients:

We consider compulsion and detention quite unnecessary for a large number, probably the great majority, of the patients at present cared for in mental deficiency hospitals, most of whom are childlike and prepared to accept whatever arrangements are made for them. There is no more need to have power to detain these patients in hospital than in their own homes or any other place which they have no wish to leave . . .

We therefore recommend that the law and its administration should be altered, in relation to all forms of mental disorder, by abandoning the assumption that compulsory powers must be used unless the patient can express a positive desire for treatment, and replacing this by the offer of care, without deprivation of liberty, to all who need it and are not unwilling to receive it.[25]

Notice that section 131 states that nothing in the Act prevents a patient from '*being* admitted' (my emphasis) to hospital, implying that there is no need for informal patients to actively and voluntarily admit themselves. Rather, the decision to

[25] *Report of the Royal Commission on the Law Relating to Mental Illness and Mental Deficiency 1954–1957* (1957) (Cmnd 169) 100–1, paras 289–91.

admit the patient to hospital can be taken by others, but the patient's compliance means that compulsory detention is unnecessary.

While informal admission in such circumstances might be convenient for the medical team, it potentially leaves the patient without any of the formal protections which apply to compulsorily detained patients. For example, it is only necessary to obtain a second opinion before giving a patient electro-convulsive therapy (ECT) if the patient has been compulsorily admitted. In contrast, an informal patient can be given ECT whenever her doctor believes it to be in her best interests. Moreover, because, in theory at least, informal patients can leave hospital at any time, they do not have a right of appeal to the Mental Health Review Tribunal (MHRT), which as we see later, has the power to order a patient's discharge. This issue arose in the *Bournewood* case.

R v Bournewood Community and Mental Health NHS Trust, ex parte L[26]

The patient, L, who was 48, was autistic and profoundly mentally retarded. He was unable to speak and his level of understanding was severely limited. He had lived in a mental hospital for over 30 years, but in 1994 went to live with paid carers. On a visit to a day centre, he had become agitated and was admitted to hospital informally. His carers were denied access to him, on the grounds that he might want to leave if he saw them. The consultant psychiatrist said that if L tried to leave, he would have been compulsorily detained, but the NHS trust argued that so long as L was not trying to leave the hospital, he could continue to be detained informally under section 131 without his consent. The Court of Appeal decided that L had been compulsorily detained. A majority (3:2) in the House of Lords overturned this and found that L had not been detained. As we see below, a subsequent appeal to the ECHR was successful.

Lord Goff

There can be no doubt that the decision of the Court of Appeal has caused grave concern among those involved in the care and treatment of mentally disordered persons. . . . I am able to summarise the position which has arisen following the Court of Appeal's judgment as follows. First and foremost, the effect of the judgment is that large numbers of mental patients who would formerly not have to be compulsorily detained under the Act of 1983 will now have to be so detained. Inquiries by the Commission suggest that 'there will be an additional 22,000 detained patients resident on any one day as a consequence of the Court of Appeal judgment plus an additional 48,000 admissions per year under the Act.' This estimate should be set against the background that the average number of detained patients resident on any one day in England and Wales is approximately 13,000. . . .

It is obvious that there would in the result be a substantial impact on the available resources; the Commission recorded that the resource implications were likely to be considerable, not only for the mental health services and professionals who have to implement the Act, but also for Mental Health Review Tribunals and for the Commission itself. . . .

[L's] readmission, as such, did not constitute a deprivation of his liberty. As Dr. Manjubhashini stated in her affidavit, he was not kept in a locked ward after he was admitted. And the fact that she, like any other doctor in a situation such as this, had it in her mind that she might thereafter take steps to detain him compulsorily under the Act, did not give rise to his detention in fact at any earlier date. Furthermore his treatment while in hospital was plainly justified on the basis of the common law doctrine of necessity.

[26] [1998] 3 WLR 107.

Lord Steyn (dissenting)

[F]ewer than 10 per cent of mentally disordered patients cared for in hospitals and mental nursing homes are admitted under the provisions of the Mental Health Act 1983. The rest of this group can be sub-divided into two sub-groups: the first and larger sub-group consists of patients capable of consenting to admission, who have so consented; the second sub-group comprises compliant but incapacitated patients, i.e. patients who are incapable of giving consent but do not express unwillingness to be admitted. Diagnostically there is usually no or virtually no difference between patients in the second sub-group (compliant incapacitated patients) and patients compulsorily admitted under the Act of 1983. If considerations of financial resources are put to one side, there can be no justification for not giving to compliant incapacitated patients the same quality and degree of protection as is given to patients admitted under the Act of 1983 . . .

Counsel for the trust and the Secretary of State argued that L was in truth always free not to go to the hospital and subsequently to leave the hospital. This argument stretches credulity to breaking point. The truth is that for entirely bona fide reasons, conceived in the best interests of L, any possible resistance by him was overcome by sedation, by taking him to hospital, and by close supervision of him in hospital. And, if L had shown any sign of wanting to leave, he would have been firmly discouraged by staff and, if necessary, physically prevented from doing so. The suggestion that L was free to go is a fairy tale . . . In my view L was detained because the health care professionals intentionally assumed control over him to such a degree as to amount to complete deprivation of his liberty . . .

The general effect of the decision of the House is to leave compliant incapacitated patients without the safeguards enshrined in the Act of 1983. This is an unfortunate result. . . . Given that such patients are diagnostically indistinguishable from compulsory patients, there is no reason to withhold the specific and effective protections of the Act of 1983 from a large class of vulnerable mentally incapacitated individuals. Their moral right to be treated with dignity requires nothing less.

It is noteworthy that, despite being decided in 1998, the House of Lords in the *Bournewood* case did not mention the Human Rights Act 1998, which was due to come into force in 2000. While Article 5, below, is most directly relevant, stopping L from seeing his carers might also have amounted to an interference with his right to respect for his private and family life (protected by Article 8).

Article 5 Right to Liberty and Security

(1) Everyone has the right to liberty and security of person. No one shall be deprived of his liberty save in the following cases and in accordance with a procedure prescribed by law: . . . .

(e) the lawful detention of persons for the prevention of the spreading of infectious diseases, of persons of unsound mind, alcoholics or drug addicts or vagrants; . . . .

(4) Everyone who is deprived of his liberty by arrest or detention shall be entitled to take proceedings by which the lawfulness of his detention shall be decided speedily by a court and his release ordered if the detention is not lawful.

L's case was then taken to the European Court of Human Rights. On his behalf it was alleged that his treatment had amounted to detention, and that there had been a violation of Article 5(1) (right to liberty and security), and that the procedures available to seek a review of the legality of his detention did not satisfy the requirements of Article 5(4).

HL v United Kingdom[27]
Judgment of the ECHR

[T]he concrete situation was that the applicant was under continuous supervision and control and was not free to leave. Any suggestion to the contrary was, in the Court's view, fairly described by Lord Steyn as 'stretching credulity to breaking point' and as a 'fairy tale' . . . The Court therefore concludes that the applicant was 'deprived of his liberty' within the meaning of Article 5 § 1 of the Convention. . . .

It is recalled that an individual cannot be deprived of his liberty on the basis of unsoundness of mind unless three minimum conditions are satisfied: he must reliably be shown to be of unsound mind; the mental disorder must be of a kind or degree warranting compulsory confinement; and the validity of continued confinement depends upon the persistence of such a disorder . . .

[T]he Court finds striking the lack of any fixed procedural rules by which the admission and detention of compliant incapacitated persons is conducted. The contrast between this dearth of regulation and the extensive network of safeguards applicable to psychiatric committals covered by the 1983 Act is, in the Court's view, significant.

In particular and most obviously, the Court notes the lack of any formalised admission procedures which indicate who can propose admission, for what reasons and on the basis of what kind of medical and other assessments and conclusions. There is no requirement to fix the exact purpose of admission (for example, for assessment or for treatment) and, consistently, no limits in terms of time, treatment or care attach to that admission. Nor is there any specific provision requiring a continuing clinical assessment of the persistence of a disorder warranting detention. The nomination of a representative of a patient who could make certain objections and applications on his or her behalf is a procedural protection accorded to those committed involuntarily under the 1983 Act and which would be of equal importance for patients who are legally incapacitated and have, as in the present case, extremely limited communication abilities.

As a result of the lack of procedural regulation and limits, the Court observes that the hospital's health care professionals assumed full control of the liberty and treatment of a vulnerable incapacitated individual solely on the basis of their own clinical assessments completed as and when they considered fit: as Lord Steyn remarked, this left 'effective and unqualified control' in their hands. While the Court does not question the good faith of those professionals or that they acted in what they considered to be the applicant's best interests, the very purpose of procedural safeguards is to protect individuals against any 'misjudgments and professional lapses' (Lord Steyn). . . .

The Court therefore finds that this absence of procedural safeguards fails to protect against arbitrary deprivations of liberty on grounds of necessity and, consequently, to comply with the essential purpose of Article 5 § 1 of the Convention. On this basis, the Court finds that there has been a violation of Article 5 § 1 of the Convention.

Since the judgment of the ECHR was handed down, the government has indicated that it accepts that additional procedural safeguards are necessary for incapacitated patients who are not formally detained but who are, in effect, deprived of their liberty.[28] In the meantime, its advice is that NHS bodies must ensure that they consider whether any arrangement made for an incapacitated person in fact amounts to a

---

[27] *(Application no 45508/99)* 5 Oct 2004.
[28] *Advice on the decision of the European Court of Human Rights in the case of* HL v UK *(the Bournewood case)* (DoH 2004) <http://www.dh.gov.uk/assetRoot/04/09/79/92/04097992.pdf>.

deprivation of his liberty.[29] Alternatives to admission should always be considered, and any restrictions should be kept to the minimum necessary. Where the deprivation of liberty is essential, consideration should be given to the use of formal powers under the Mental Health Act, while recognizing that this should not be done simply to 'be on the safe side'.[30] The government has also advised that efforts should always be made to help patients retain contact with their family or other carers.[31]

The *Bournewood* case is important for a number of reasons. First, recall that Lord Goff suggested that, even if there were a few occasions when L had in fact been detained, his detention could in any event be justified at common law under the doctrine of necessity. In the next extract, Phil Fennell is critical of this resort to a common law doctrine which, he argues, fails to offer sufficient protection to patients, and gives far too much discretion over detention to the medical profession.

Phil Fennell[32]

Surely if someone's liberty is going to be interfered with, and there is a statutory procedure which gives safeguards to the patient, that procedure should be observed in preference to using common law, which affords fewer external protections? Lord Goff disagreed, viewing admission under the statutory procedures as 'a last resort' . . . Encouraging use of statutory powers only as a 'last resort' risks subversion of the purpose of statutory regulation. Should professionals be able to opt out by relying on the common law? . . .

It is doubtful whether a detention on grounds of common law necessity could satisfy the requirements of Article 5, since it would be carried out on the say-so of the consultant psychiatrist, without the need to present objective evidence to any competent authority of the need for detention.

Secondly, as Lord Goff pointed out, if it was necessary to use formal powers to admit patients such as L, the cost implications would be considerable. Approximately three times as many patients would have to go through the formal admissions process, and thereafter have access to mechanisms both to review their detention, and allow them to apply for discharge. The ECHR's decision may then place a considerable financial burden on the NHS, but, in the view of Ian Bynoe and Anthony Holland scarce resources should be irrelevant when a person's liberty is at stake.

Ian Bynoe and Anthony Holland[33]

[M]ental health law is not practised in a textbook vacuum but largely within a public sector possessing only finite resources. Their availability in a general sense and the services provided in individual cases are therefore likely to influence how legislation is interpreted and applied. The level of in-patient bed occupancy may determine in practice whether or not an application is made for compulsory admission; the demand for scarce accommodation may influence the time when someone will be discharged on leave or from section.

It was vigorously argued in *Bournewood* that the resources required to admit and treat incapacitated patients under the Act rather than informally would severely test local services, consuming a wholly disproportionate share of their limited staff resources. Concerns mainly

---

[29] Ibid.   [30] Ibid.   [31] Ibid.

[32] 'Doctor Knows Best? Therapeutic Detention under Common Law, the Mental Health Act and the European Convention' (1998) 6 Medical Law Review 322–53, 343, 348.

[33] 'Law as a Clinical Tool: Practicing Within and Outwith the Law' in N Eastman and J Peay (eds), *Law Without Enforcement: Integrating Mental Health and Justice* (Hart Publishing Oxford 1999) 89–107, 103.

focused on the additional paperwork associated with use of the Act, extra visits and liaison with and attendance at, hearings and meetings of the hospital's Mental Health Act Managers. In the same case, in the Court of Appeal, the Bournewood NHS Trust Managers opposed the use of the Act, on the ground that if this were required routinely, it would create an unforeseen and intolerable demand for section 117 after-care services. Such an emphasis on services and practices rather than principle is clearly regrettable.

Thirdly, as the ECHR noted, the protections against unwarranted or arbitrary detention under Article 5 should be available to *every* patient who has their liberty restricted. In practice L was certainly not free to leave the ward since his doctors admitted, first, that they would have invoked the power (contained in section 5 of the Act) to detain L if he had tried to leave, and second, that the decision to deprive L of any access to his carers was taken, in part at least, precisely in order to ensure that he did not attempt to leave the hospital.

(b) COMPULSORY ADMISSION UNDER THE 1983 ACT

The 1983 Act provides for the compulsory admission of patients for assessment under section 2, and for treatment under section 3. These compulsory powers are used on about 44,000 occasions each year. At any one time approximately 12,000 patients are detained for treatment in hospital.

Mental Health Act 1983 section 2

(2) An application for admission for assessment may be made in respect of a patient on the grounds that—

(a) he is suffering from mental disorder of a nature or degree which warrants the detention of the patient in a hospital for assessment (or for assessment followed by medical treatment) for at least a limited period; and

(b) he ought to be so detained in the interests of his own health or safety or with a view to the protection of other persons.

(3) An application for admission for assessment shall be founded on the written recommendations in the prescribed form of two registered medical practitioners, including in each case a statement that in the opinion of the practitioner the conditions set out in subsection (2) above are complied with.

(4) . . . a patient admitted to hospital in pursuance of an application for admission for assessment may be detained for a period not exceeding 28 days beginning with the day on which he is admitted, but shall not be detained after the expiration of that period unless before it has expired he has become liable to be detained by virtue of a subsequent application, order or direction under the following provisions of this Act.

Section 3

(2) An application for admission for treatment may be made in respect of a patient on the grounds that—

(a) he is suffering from mental illness, severe mental impairment, psychopathic disorder or mental impairment and his mental disorder is of a nature or degree which makes it appropriate for him to receive medical treatment in a hospital; and

(b) in the case of psychopathic disorder or mental impairment, such treatment is likely to alleviate or prevent a deterioration of his condition; and

(c) it is necessary for the health or safety of the patient or for the protection of other persons that he should receive such treatment and it cannot be provided unless he is detained under this section.

(3) An application for admission for treatment shall be founded on the written recommendations in the prescribed form of two registered medical practitioners, including in each case a statement that in the opinion of the practitioner the conditions set out in subsection (2) above are complied with.

Before we flesh out the meaning of sections 2 and 3, it is also worth noting that there are a few other routes into the mental health system. In an emergency, a patient can be admitted under section 4 on the basis of one medical recommendation that 'it is of urgent necessity for the patient to be admitted and detained under section 2'. Under section 136, if a police officer finds in a public place 'a person who appears to him to be suffering from mental disorder and to be in immediate need of care or control', he can be removed to a place of safety, usually a police station, for 72 hours 'for the purpose of enabling him to be examined by a registered medical practitioner and to be interviewed by an approved social worker and of making any necessary arrangements for his treatment or care'. And under section 5 a voluntarily admitted patient can subsequently be compulsorily detained for up to 72 hours in order to prevent him from leaving hospital, after which the formal powers under section 3 must be invoked.

Applications for section 2 and 3 orders can be made by the patient's nearest relative or, more usually, by an approved social worker, and the application must be supported by two medical practitioners. Under section 2, an individual can be detained for assessment for up to 28 days, after which the patient must either be discharged; admitted as an informal patient; or detained under section 3. Under section 3, individuals can be admitted for treatment, initially for up to six months, and this can then be renewed for a further six months. Thereafter the individual can be detained for up to a year, with the possibility of annual renewal.

Because the compulsory detention of an individual represents a fundamental violation of her freedom, it must be justified according to clear and defensible criteria. These have tended to consist in a combination of preventing the individual from harming herself and/or others, and enabling her to receive treatment: what Bartlett and Sandland describe as 'criteria relating to dangerousness and therapeutic benevolence'.[34]

For example, under sections 2 and 3, the person must be suffering from a mental disorder of 'a nature or degree which warrants admission to hospital' (section 2), or 'which makes it appropriate for him to receive medical treatment in a hospital' (section 3), both of which have a therapeutic intent. But under section 2, detention is permissible if the patient 'ought to be detained' to protect the health or safety of the patient, or to protect other persons, or under section 3, detention must be 'necessary

---

[34] P Bartlett and R Sandland, *Mental Health Law: Policy and Practice* (2nd edn OUP Oxford 2003) 142.

for the health or safety of the patient or for the protection of other persons', both of which focus upon the patient's dangerousness.

It is interesting that the Act uses such a variety of different words, such as 'warrants', 'appropriate' and 'necessary' to justify the use of compulsion. These are clearly not synonyms. Admission for assessment under section is possible if the mental disorder is of a nature or degree which *warrants* admission for assessment, whereas for admission for treatment under section 3, it must both be *appropriate* for treatment to be given in hospital, and *necessary* to detain the patient. Genevra Richardson and Oliver Thorold argue that this lack of clarity is particularly unfortunate given the significance of a finding that detention is justifiable.

Genevra Richardson and Oliver Thorold[35]

The cumulative statutory requirements are commonly understood to mean that compulsory admission should be in some sense a last resort: beneficence may only trump autonomy when there is no alternative . . . Even acknowledging the inherent difficulty of defining the appropriate threshold for compulsory admission, the existing formulations appear needlessly general and provide an inadequate guide to practitioners. Adequate protection for the patient from unjustified compulsion calls for much greater clarity of statutory expression.

In the next extract Jill Peay further suggests that the patient's 'need' to be in hospital may arise not because of the nature of her illness, but as a result of her *attitude* towards treatment.

Jill Peay[36]

Curiously, in clinical terms, 'the need to be in hospital' may not arise. This is not because the illness *can only* be treated in hospital, but because the patient will not *accept* treatment where he is (in the community). Since the only route by which *compulsory* treatment can be legally achieved is via the Act, and since the Act only allows compulsory treatment *in hospital*, such treatment can only be achieved via admission to hospital. Hence, the person is perceived as needing to be in hospital because of his/her attitude to treatment, which may or may not be determined by the illness itself.

Notice that section 3(2)(b) specifies that in the case of psychopathic disorder or mental impairment, the treatment must be 'likely to alleviate or prevent a deterioration of his condition'. This is the so-called 'treatability' requirement: patients with these conditions can only be detained under section 3 if effective treatment is available. The problem is that many psychopathic (now called personality-disordered) patients are not in fact treatable. If detention is only possible for *treatable* psychopathy, then some of the more dangerous mentally disordered individuals could not lawfully be detained. In *R v Canons Part MHRT, ex parte A,*[37] a case in which a patient with a psychopathic disorder refused to participate in group therapy, Roch LJ attempted to flesh out the meaning of the treatability test:

Roch LJ

I would suggest the following principles. First, if a Tribunal were to be satisfied that the patient's

---

[35] 'Law as a Rights Protector: Assessing the Mental Health Act 1983' in N Eastman and J Peay (eds), *Law Without Enforcement: Integrating Mental Health and Justice* (Hart Publishing Oxford 1999) 109–31, 113.
[36] *Decisions and Dilemmas: Working with Mental Health Law* (Hart Publishing Oxford 2003) 38.
[37] [1995] QB 60.

detention in hospital was simply an attempt to coerce the patient into participating in group therapy, then the Tribunal would be under a duty to direct discharge. Second, 'treatment in hospital' will satisfy the 'treatability test' although it is unlikely to alleviate the patient's condition, provided that it is likely to prevent a deterioration. Third, 'treatment in hospital' will satisfy the 'treatability test' although it will not immediately alleviate or prevent deterioration in the patient's condition, provided that alleviation or stabilisation is likely in due course. Fourth, the 'treatability test' can still be met although initially there may be some deterioration in the patient's condition, due for example to the patient's initial anger at being detained. Fifth, it must be remembered that medical treatment in hospital covers 'nursing and also includes care, habilitation and rehabilitation under medical supervision.' Sixth, the 'treatability test' is satisfied if nursing care etc. are likely to lead to an alleviation of the patient's condition in that the patient is likely to gain an insight into his problem or cease to be unco-operative in his attitude towards treatment which would potentially have a lasting benefit.

These 'principles' have been criticized by Peter Bartlett and Ralph Sandland:

Peter Bartlett and Ralph Sandland[38]

While the principles enunciated by Roch LJ appear innocuous enough at first glance, they are problematic. The first principle holds that detention should not be used in order to coerce consent to treatment; yet the fourth principle acknowledges that there may be an initial reluctance to consent based for example on anger at admission, and the sixth principle holds that rendering the patient cooperative in attitude toward treatment is a therapeutic objective. It is, on a practical level, difficult to see how confining a patient through the period of their initial anger with the hope of rendering them cooperative is different from the coercion prohibited by the first principle.

In the next extract, Eric Matthews argues that personality disorders are not treatable because they are not really illnesses at all, and that it is a mistake to deal with personality-disordered individuals as if they were suffering from mental illness.

Eric Matthews[39]

[T]here are some conditions classified as mental disorders . . . in which the harm caused by the disorder is not, or at least not primarily, to the disordered person, but to others. The various sorts of sexual deviation called 'paraphilias', such as paedophilia, represent good examples. These disorders seem to have no parallel among physical illnesses: someone who is physically ill suffers him- or herself, and any harm caused to others (eg through infection) is contingent. But a paedophile does not himself suffer from his paedophilia (except indirectly, in that he suffers social disapproval): those who suffer are the children he abuses . . .

The important distinction here, therefore, is not one between mental and physical *illness*, but between illness in general and a particular kind of mental disorder which is not an illness in any sense. Secondly, precisely *because* these disorders are not illnesses, the question which arises with them is not to do with compulsory *treatment*. Paedophiles are often said to be 'untreatable': but that is rather misleading. They do not *require* treatment in the medical sense, since their condition is not an illness, not something which causes them suffering contrary to their own wishes. It is their personality itself, and the wishes which emanate from it, which are said to be disordered. The treatment which they require is that which would prevent this disordered personality causing

---

[38] P Bartlett and R Sandland, *Mental Health Law: Policy and Practice* (2nd edn OUP Oxford 2003) 152.

[39] 'Mental and Physical Illness—An Unsustainable Separation?' in N Eastman and J Peay (eds), *Law Without Enforcement: Integrating Mental Health and Justice* (Hart Publishing Oxford 1999) 47–58, 54, 58.

harm to others, not something which they would either choose or reject on the basis of their own self-interest . . .

This suggests that what is legally required to deal with such cases is, again, not a 'Mental Health Act', which among other things has the unfortunate effect of reinforcing popular prejudices about the allegedly violent and dangerous character of all mentally ill people . . . Rather we need to address the difficult issues involved in the containment of people who behave in anti-social ways, but who are not what might be called 'rational criminals' whom one might hope to deter by imprisonment or some other standard form of punishment, or who may in some cases be deemed to need to be detained in advance of having committed any offence. The horrendous balancing act involved, between regard for civil liberties and the protection of the vulnerable is, however, a matter for the criminal law, not for mental health legislation.

However, the World Health Organizations' *International Statistical Classification of Diseases and Related Health Problems*, tenth revision (known as ICD-10), does contain a definition of 'dissocial personality disorder':

World Health Organisation[40]

Personality disorder, usually coming to attention because of a gross disparity between behaviour and the prevailing social norms, and characterized by at least 3 of the following:

a.   callous unconcern for the feelings of others;

b.   gross and persistent attitude of irresponsibility and disregard for social norms, rules and obligations;

c.   incapacity to maintain enduring relationships, though having no difficulty in establishing them;

d.   very low tolerance to frustration and a low threshold for discharge of aggression, including violence;

e.   incapacity to experience guilt and to profit from experience, particularly punishment;

f.   marked proneness to blame others, or to offer plausible rationalizations, for the behaviour that has brought the patient into conflict with society.

The Mental Health Act Code of Practice provides further guidance on the use of section 2 and 3.

Mental Health Act Code of Practice[41]
Para 1.1

The detailed guidance in the Code needs to be read in the light of the following broad principles, that people to whom the Act applies (including those being assessed for possible admission) should:

• Receive recognition for their basic human rights under the European Convention of Human Rights;

• Be given respect for their qualities, abilities and diverse backgrounds as individuals and be assured that account will be taken of their age, gender, sexual orientation, social, ethnic, cultural and religious background, but that general assumptions will not be made on the basis of any one of these characteristics;

---

[40] ICD-10 F60.2 (WHO 1992).   [41] (DoH 1999) available at <http://www.dh.gov.uk>.

- Have their needs taken fully into account, though it is recognized that, within available resources, it may not always be practicable to meet them in full;

- Be given any necessary treatment or care in the least controlled and segregated facilities compatible with ensuring their own health or safety or the safety of other people;

- Be treated and cared for in such a way as to promote to the greatest practicable degree their self determination and personal responsibility, consistent with their own needs and wishes;

- Be discharged from detention or other powers provided by the Act as soon as it is clear that their application is no longer justified.

Para 2.6

In judging whether compulsory admission is appropriate, those concerned should consider not only the statutory criteria but should also take account of:

- The guiding principles in chapter 1 [see above];

- The patient's wishes and view of his or her own needs;

- The patient's social and family circumstances;

- The nature of the illness/behaviour disorder and its course;

- What may be known about the patient by his or her nearest relative, any other relatives or friends and professionals involved, assessing in particular how reliable this information is;

- Other forms of care or treatment including, where relevant, consideration of whether the patient would be willing to accept medical treatment in hospital informally or as an outpatient and of whether guardianship would be appropriate;

- The needs of the patient's family or others with whom he or she lives; the need for others to be protected from the patient;

- The burden on those close to the patient of a decision not to admit under the Act.

When the Code was first published in 1990, it advised that section 3 should be used when a patient has been admitted in the past, needs compulsory admission for treatment, and has already been assessed in the recent past. Since 1999 the Code has advised that section 3 may also be appropriate where the patient is thought to need admission for treatment, and has recently been assessed, regardless of whether they have previously been admitted.[42] Effectively this means that 'known' patients are more likely to be admitted under section 3, and are therefore more likely to be detained for longer periods. In the next extract Barbara Hatfield and Valerie Antcliff explain the recent trend towards increased use of detention under section 3 of the Act.

Barbara Hatfield and Valerie Antcliff[43]

The increasing use of detention under the Mental Health Act in England and Wales has been identified both nationally and, in this analysis of activity, in a particular region. . . . The increase in detentions under section 3 is particularly marked and has impacted disproportionately on those with more serious conditions. Whilst this is clearly in keeping with official guidance, it represents an increase in the frequency and amount of coercive power used in respect of those with serious

[42] Mental Health Act Code of Practice (DoH 1999) para 5.3.
[43] 'Detention under the Mental Health Act: balancing rights, risks and needs for services' (2001) 23 Journal of Social Welfare and Family Law 135–53, 147–8.

and enduring mental illnesses. Detentions under the Act involving men have also risen disproportionately.

It seems likely that a number of factors account for these trends. First, the escalation of concerns about violence throughout the 1990s has resulted in pressures upon professionals to minimize risks. This is reflected not only in greater use of detention in hospital, but in the more frequent use of section 3 which permits imposition of services in the community following discharge under section 25A. An emphasis upon the risk of harm to others may also result in higher levels of coercive intervention in relation to men . . .

[I]t has been identified that those detained under section 3 of the Act are more socially vulnerable than those detained under section 2 in terms of lack of employment and lack of an identified relationship partner. Whilst this may be explicable as the consequences of severe mental illness, it means that this group experiences higher levels of vulnerability by virtue of exclusion from these important social domains. This may in turn render individuals less resilient in the face of external stress and more likely to experience crises.

Of course the Mental Health Act must now be read in conjunction with the Human Rights Act 1998. As we saw earlier at p. 399, Article 5 protects the right to liberty. There is an exception in Article (1)(e), which permits the lawful detention of persons of unsound mind, but only according to a procedure prescribed by law, and provided that it is possible to challenge the lawfulness of detention speedily in a court. The requirement that the deprivation of liberty must be 'in accordance with a procedure prescribed by law' means that the law must be clear, and the process through which people may be detained must be known in advance.

In *Winterwerp v The Netherlands* the European Court of Human Rights fleshed out three conditions that apply to the 'unsound mind' exception in Article 5(1)(e):[44]

In the court's opinion, except in emergency cases, the individual concerned should not be deprived of his liberty unless he has been reliably shown to be of 'unsound mind'. The very nature of what has to be established before the competent national authority—that is, a true mental disorder— calls for objective medical expertise. Further, the mental disorder must be of a kind or degree warranting compulsory confinement. What is more, the validity of continued confinement depends upon the persistence of such a disorder.

In short, *Winterwerp* lays down three criteria which must be satisfied:

- There must be objective medical evidence of unsound mind, and
- The unsoundness of mind must warrant compulsory detention, and
- The unsoundness of mind must continue throughout the patient's detention.

Whatever criteria are used to trigger admission to the mental health system, it may be difficult to ensure that they are applied consistently and objectively. For example, research appears to indicate that there is considerable over-representation of black Caribbean people in mental health admissions. In Flannigan et al.'s study of admissions in Southwark in Inner London, 23 per cent of the hospital psychiatric population was Afro-Caribbean, which represented twice the proportion in the general

---

[44] ECHR series A vol 33 (1979).

population.[45] Moreover, this minority ethnic group was also much more likely to be compulsorily admitted to the mental health system. White people were admitted informally in 80 per cent of cases; admitted under compulsory powers in 17 per cent of cases, and in an emergency in 3 per cent of cases.[46] In contrast, black people from the Caribbean were admitted informally in 55 per cent of cases; were compulsorily admitted in 35 per cent of cases, and were admitted using emergency powers in 10 per cent of cases.[47] Whether or not there is a higher incidence of mental health problems within this group, or whether these statistics simply reflect pre-existing discriminatory assumptions, Flannigan's study clearly showed that black people from the Caribbean were more likely to be diagnosed as sufficiently mentally disturbed to justify both admission to the mental health system, and the use of compulsory powers.

(c) ADMISSION UNDER THE DRAFT MENTAL HEALTH BILL

The draft Mental Health Act Bill reproduces some aspects of the present system. It will still be possible to detain someone for assessment for 28 days, and this can be followed by longer periods of detention for treatment, again 6 months in the first instance, with renewals of up to a year possible after two years. But rather than having two separate routes for detention for assessment and treatment, there will be a 'single gateway' to the use of compulsory powers. To be subject to compulsory powers, the following conditions must be satisfied.

Draft Mental Health Bill 2004 clause 9

(2) The first condition is that the patient is suffering from mental disorder.

(3) The second condition is that that mental disorder is of such a nature or degree as to warrant the provision of medical treatment to him.

(4) The third condition is that it is necessary—

  (a) For the protection of the patient from—

    (i) Suicide or serious self-harm, or

    (ii) Serious neglect by him of his health or safety, or

  (b) For the protection of other persons, that medical treatment be provided to the patient.

(5) The fourth condition is that medical treatment cannot lawfully be provided to the patient without him being subject to the provisions of this Part.

(6) The fifth condition is that medical treatment is available which is appropriate in the patient's case, taking into account the nature or degree of his mental disorder and all other circumstances of his case.

(7) The fourth condition does not apply in the case of a patient aged 16 or over who is at substantial risk of causing serious harm to other persons.

(8) For the purposes of this Part, a determination as to whether a patient is at substantial risk

---

[45] C Flannigan, G Glover, S Feeney, J Wing, P Bebbington, and S Lewis, 'Inner London Collaborative Audit of Admissions in Two Health Districts' (1994) 165 British Journal of Psychiatry 734.
[46] Ibid.   [47] Ibid.

of causing serious harm to other persons is to be treated as part of the determination as to whether all of the relevant conditions appear to be or are met in his case.

So in addition to suffering from a mental disorder, it must be of a sufficient nature and degree to warrant the provision of medical treatment. This is intended to ensure that only those with serious mental disorders are covered, although it is important to note that it sets a lower threshold than the 1983 Act, under which the mental disorder had to be of a nature or degree to warrant *admission to hospital*, and not merely to warrant *the provision of treatment*. The joint committee on the Draft Mental Health Bill recommended that:

the second condition for the use of compulsion at clause 9(3) of the draft Bill be amended so as to read the 'mental disorder is of such a nature or degree as to warrant the provision of medical treatment to him under compulsory powers'.[48]

But the government has rejected this, on the grounds that the fourth condition— namely that 'medical treatment cannot lawfully be provided to the patient without him being subject to the provisions of this Part'—would make such an amendment redundant.[49]

Under the draft Bill, it must be necessary to provide medical treatment to protect the patient from suicide or serious self harm or neglect, or to protect others. It is interesting that the risk of harm to one's self must be 'serious' to trigger the use of compulsory powers, but in the case of harm to others, *any* potential harm, serious or otherwise, might qualify. It is hard to see why compulsory powers are justifiable where the patient only poses a risk of causing *trivial* harm to others. Indeed the joint committee recommended

that the criterion at clause 9(4)(b) of the draft Bill be changed to read 'for the protection of other persons from significant risk of serious harm'.[50]

Again, the government disagreed arguing, first, that the wording in the Bill replicates that in the 1983 Act, and that this has not caused any problems, and, second, that the new Act will have to be interpreted in the light of the Human Rights Act, which means that detention has to be a proportionate response to the risk of harm.[51]

According to the fourth condition, it must be impossible to provide treatment lawfully without subjecting the patient to formal powers under the Act, unless the exception in 9(7) is satisfied. This condition is intended to ensure that compulsory powers are not used where treatment could lawfully be provided without them. So, for example, if the patient lacks capacity, treatment in her best interests can be given without invoking powers under the Mental Health legislation. Similarly, if the patient is cooperative, the use of compulsory powers is unnecessary. Importantly, clause 9(7) provides an exception to this condition if the patient is over the age of sixteen, and at a

---

[48] Para 118.

[49] *Government Response to the Report of the Joint Committee on the Draft Mental Health Bill 2004* (DoH London 2005) <http://www.dh.gov.uk/assetRoot/04/11/52/68/04115268.pdf>.

[50] Joint Committee on the Draft Mental Health Bill—First Report, 2005, <http://www.publications.parliament.uk/pa/jt/jtment.htm> para 128.

[51] *Government Response to the Report of the Joint Committee on the Draft Mental Health Bill 2004* (DoH London 2005) <http://www.dh.gov.uk/assetRoot/04/11/52/68/04115268.pdf>.

substantial risk of causing serious harm to other persons. In such cases, the use of compulsory powers would be legitimate even if it would be possible to provide treatment without them. Effectively this means that *unnecessary* compulsion is acceptable if there is a risk of serious harm to others.

It is hard to see why, if there is a less restrictive alternative—perhaps because the patient voluntarily accepts and is fully complying with the treatment plan—compulsion should nevertheless be invoked. In their evidence to the joint committee, King's College London argued that invoking the use of compulsory powers, even when a patient is actually requesting treatment, 'will prove a very effective means of deterring patients from seeking help from mental health services'.[52] The government has accepted that there may be some 'exceptional cases', where despite judging the patient to be at risk of causing harm to others, the risk can be managed without the use of compulsory powers, and it intends to investigate the possibility of amending the draft Bill to accommodate such cases.[53]

The fifth condition specifies that there must be treatment which is 'appropriate'. What does this mean? Many of the joint committee's witnesses believed that 'appropriate' was too vague and ambiguous a term, and in particular, that it does not specify that there has to be any therapeutic element to the treatment. So, for example, simply locking someone up might be 'appropriate' treatment. As a result, the joint committee recommended that this condition should be amended to include a test of therapeutic benefit, as exists in the new Scottish legislation.[54] Under the Scottish Mental Health (Care and Treatment) (Scotland) Act 2003 compulsory powers can only be used where medical treatment 'which would be likely to (i) prevent the mental disorder worsening; or (ii) alleviate any of the symptoms, or effects, of the disorder, is available for the patient'. Again, the government has rejected this proposed amendment, suggesting that it is implicit in the other conditions that compulsion can only be used where it is for a clinical purpose.[55]

There are several important differences between the exercise of compulsory powers under the 1983 Act and the system set up by the draft Mental Health Bill.

First, if detained for assessment under the Bill, a care plan would have to be completed by the patient's clinical supervisor within five days. Secondly, compulsion after 28 days would have to be authorized by a tribunal following examination by two medical practitioners and an approved mental health professional, who might be a social worker or a community pyschiatric nurse. The tribunal would also have the power to amend the care plan, or send the application back for further assessment.

Thirdly, the Bill severs the link between compulsion and admission to hospital. This is intended to address what has been called the 'revolving door' problem, whereby mentally disordered individuals are admitted to hospital for treatment, and later

[52] Joint Committee on the Draft Mental Health Bill—First Report, 2005, <http://www.publications.parliament.uk/pa/jt/jtment.htm> para 146.

[53] *Government Response to the Report of the Joint Committee on the Draft Mental Health Bill 2004* (DoH London 2005) <http://www.dh.gov.uk/assetRoot/04/11/52/68/04115268.pdf>.

[54] Joint Committee on the Draft Mental Health Bill—First Report, 2005, <http://www.publications.parliament.uk/pa/jt/jtment.htm> para 141.

[55] *Government Response to the Report of the Joint Committee on the Draft Mental Health Bill 2004* (DoH London 2005) <http://www.dh.gov.uk/assetRoot/04/11/52/68/04115268.pdf>.

discharged when their condition improves, only to fail to take their medication once released, leading to an inevitable deterioration in their condition such that readmission to hospital becomes necessary. Under the Bill mandatory treatment orders can be made for patients who are living in the community (we consider this point in more detail below at p. 442).

A final important difference is that the dangerousness criterion for detention is emphasized, and the treatability requirement modified, which means that personality disordered individuals could be detained *solely to protect the safety of others*, even if there is *no therapeutic intention*, and *no possible health benefit* for the patient. Treatment does have to be 'available' and 'appropriate' but there is no requirement that the treatment is likely to alleviate the patient's condition, and the condition itself does not have to be treatable. It might even be possible to argue that locking someone up is 'appropriate' treatment.

This latter shift has been heavily criticized, with psychiatrists fearing that they will be forced to detain people purely according to a *dangerousness* test, where there is no *clinical* reason for keeping them in hospital. It also presupposes that it is in fact possible to accurately predict which patients will pose a risk to others if they are not detained. In practice, however, the evidence suggests that it is extremely difficult to accurately predict dangerousness.

The MacArthur project in the US involved 939 people, who were divided into five categories of risk and whose behaviour was monitored for the next twelve months.[56] 63 individuals were categorized as high risk, of whom forty eight were violent in the subsequent year. It is important to remember than almost a quarter of these 'high risk' individuals were not violent, and if they had been detained under a dangerousness standard, the deprivation of their liberty would not have prevented any violence at all. Moreover, in total 176 individuals in the study committed violent acts in the year following assessment, only forty-eight of whom would have been captured by a dangerousness standard which detained only those in risk category 5.[57] To prevent the other 128 violent individuals from harming other people, individuals who fell into the lower risk categories would have to be detained, and in these the predictions of violent behaviour are extremely unreliable. In risk category 3, for example, 74 per cent of individuals were not violent in the year following assessment. If people in this risk category had been compulsorily detained in order to prevent harm to others, in a large majority of cases, the detention would have been wholly unwarranted. Indeed it has been estimated that with current knowledge and skills, between 2,000 and 5,000 people would have to be detained in order to prevent one homicide.[58]

As Nancy Wolff explains in the next extract, there is undoubtedly a (misguided) public perception that mentally ill people pose a risk of harm to others, and that their detention is therefore warranted.

---

[56] J Monahan, HJ Steadman, E Silver, P Appelbaum, P Clark Robbins, EP Mulvey, LH Roth, T Grisson and S Banks, *Rethinking Risk Assessment: The MacArthur Study of Mental Disorder and Violence* (OUP Oxford 2001).

[57] Ibid.

[58] *Evidence Submitted to the Joint Committee on the Draft Mental Health Bill* (RCP 2004) 18.

Nancy Wolff[59]

Implicit in the public's perception of severe mental illness is the notion that not only are persons with these disorders more likely to engage in violent acts, but also that the higher relative risk is evenly distributed across the entire group of disordered individuals. Evidence suggests, however, that the distribution of risk within this population is bimodal forming two subgroups: low risk and high risk. . . . The high risk group is comparatively small . . . Evidence on homicides in England and Wales suggests that 0.05 per cent of persons with severe mental illness pose the greatest risk of homicidal violence. The low risk group is the larger of the two, comprising roughly 90 per cent of persons with severe mental illness. While individuals in the low-risk group have violence profiles that are more like the general population, they may still engage in non-violent criminal or social deviance that arouses the concern of the public and brings them to the attention of law enforcement agencies. Behaviours that deviate from social norms, such as dishevelled and unkempt appearance, talking to oneself, sleeping on public sidewalks, may be interpreted by the public as evidence of menace potential. Guided by fear, the public may misinterpret and overreact to the behaviour or appearance of persons with mental illness, if such indicators of social nuisance confirm stereotypical beliefs . . .

The reality is that homicide and other acts of violence are part of the human experience. Steps can and should be taken to effectively manage homicidal and violent tendencies related to mental illness. But it is sheer fantasy to claim that these tendencies can be managed in ways that eliminate the risk of violence. . . .

If the public remains committed to the perfectability expectation, each violent act committed by a person with a mental illness will be interpreted as potentially avoidable, which could motivate the public to rightfully (a) demand that the government allocate more money to reduce future events through more secure care and supervision of high-risk individuals or (b) support legal reforms that constrain the civil liberties of persons with mental illness. Spending more will simply increase the care and supervision costs per high-risk case and . . . decrease the resources available for low-risk cases, while never attaining the target of zero absolute risk. In all likelihood, however, the cycle of moral panic, community-care backlash, and escalated spending will continue with each inevitable violent event.

In addition to the difficulties in accurately predicting dangerousness, it is not clear that this is a task for which doctors are especially well qualified, nor that this is a role that psychiatrists are keen to assume. In the following extract, Jill Peay suggests that interventions which are designed not to treat the patient, but rather to protect others, are fundamentally alien to the normal therapeutic role of the psychiatrist.

Jill Peay[60]

[I]n mental health practice the law permits practitioners to intervene solely for the safety of other persons and will, where compulsion is used, do the patient harm, if only to the patient's sense of autonomy. Under the Draft Bill 2002, the curious concept of giving medical treatment to a patient who posed a substantial risk of causing serious harm to other persons, solely for the benefit of those other persons, would have built on this role of clinician as dispenser of interventions with no necessary benefit to the patient being treated. Any new law adopting this approach would therefore be likely to be doubly unfamiliar to clinicians, being outside their terms of reference as

---

[59] 'Risk, Response and Mental Health Policy: Learning from the Experience of the United Kingdom' (2002) 27 Journal of Health Politics, Policy and Law 801–32, 806–7, 815–16.
[60] *Decisions and Dilemmas: Working with Mental Health Law* (Hart Publishing Oxford 2003) 173–4.

doctors, and outside their terms of reference as experienced psychiatrists. In such circumstances, would clinicians regard doing good to others (a public health function blurring into custodian) as more important than respecting the principle of autonomy? Similarly, the British Association of Social Workers (BASW) regarded their function under the 1983 Act as critical and in keeping with their professional expertise. However, they have argued that the role of 'approved mental health professional' under the Draft Bill 2002 would, in effect, have required them to act as hired muscle for the Secretary of State and would likely be in breach of the BASW Code of Ethics.

Indeed the Royal College of Psychiatrists, in their written evidence to the joint committee on the Draft Mental Health Bill argue that the emphasis on risk avoidance will cause 'significant damage' to the profession.

Royal College of Psychiatrists[61]

The draft Mental Health Bill suggests that a psychiatrist's primary role relates to public safety rather than the treatment of individual patients. This contrasts with the rest of medicine where the General Medical Council is quite clear about the role of a doctor: 'Make the care of your patient your first concern' and 'Listen to patients and respect their views'. Surveys undertaken amongst trainees demonstrate that if there is a perception of a new law being increasingly coercive, or the role of the psychiatrist moving from that of a doctor (with roles and responsibilities similar to doctors in other branches of medicine) to a role primarily of social control this will exacerbate the recruitment difficulty. Many members of the College have stated they will take early retirement or transfer to branches of psychiatry where the Bill would have little or no impact. It is the College's view that significant damage will be done to the morale of the profession, the esteem in which the profession is held and, consequently, to patient care . . .

Mentally ill patients are more likely to be victims than the rest of the population. This is due both to the vulnerability caused by some illnesses and the stigma of being seen as 'a mental patient'. However it is recognised that there is a tiny minority of patients who, at times, may be dangerous to others.

Every death is a tragedy, for the victim, perpetrator, their family and friends and any professionals involved. The percentage of homicides committed each year by the mentally ill, as a percentage of the total is falling. The following figures are not intended to minimize the importance of each death but may help to put the matter into perspective.

For each citizen killed by a mentally ill person:

* 10 are killed by corporate manslaughter
* 20 by people who are not mentally ill
* 25 by passive smoking
* 125 by NHS hospital acquired infection

The proposed legislation is extremely unlikely to have any impact on suicide or homicide rates. With reference to suicide, recent research demonstrated that even within the high-risk group of in-patients there would need to be 100 patients detained unnecessarily in order to prevent one suicide. With regard to homicide, [Crawford] has shown that with a predictive test with a sensitivity and specificity of 0.8 (far better than anything available currently) 5000 people would need to be detained to prevent one homicide. Szmukler has shown that if the predictive test became even better (0.9) this would still require the detention of 2000 people to prevent each homicide. This

---

[61] *Evidence Submitted to the Joint Committee on the Draft Mental Health Bill* (RCP 2004) 31–4.

emphasises that prevention of homicide and suicide can only ever arise as a secondary benefit from improved mental health care for a population and never via prediction per se of such events.

The starting point in risk reduction is encouraging patients to seek help and talk about their thoughts and feelings . . . It is hard to believe that potential patients will not be deterred from the services if they know that psychiatrists will have a duty to enforce treatment on them, not only in hospital but also in the community, even when they are perfectly able to make decisions for themselves. Patient avoidance will certainly limit effective intervention.

Although note that Peter Bartlett argues that it is impossible to avoid detaining some patients on the grounds that they are dangerous, and that criticism of the draft Bill should focus upon the problematic drafting of its dangerousness criterion for detention, rather than upon its existence.

Peter Bartlett[62]

The concerns [of critics of the Mental Health Bill] are also problematic on theoretical grounds, insofar as they suggest that psychiatry can avoid social control. The reality is that psychiatric treatment in any situation other than by free and competent consent of the patient is by its nature about social control. The vast bulk of people currently confined in psychiatric facilities are categorised as 'mentally ill', and for them there is no requirement of treatability. Most of them are treatable of course, but that does not remove the social control function. They tend to be admitted when their behaviour becomes socially unacceptable; and they are treated until it is no longer unacceptable. Alternatively, they are admitted when they are perceived to be unable to cope or function in society, and treated until they can be discharged, able to do so. When such behavioural features are significant factors in clinical decision-making, doctors are acting as agents of social control . . .

The proper question is therefore not how psychiatrists can cease to be agents of social control: they cannot. The better question, to be asked bluntly, is when the social control is justified. The squeamishness of critics of the government bill to engage with that question does not help. The reality is that we need mental health legislation, and we must therefore choose from a set of criteria of administration, all of which are problematic. The acknowledgement that mental health law is about social control allows that choice to be made in a fashion which acknowledges the individual and social interests at stake, in a way which acknowledges appropriate policy concerns and the need for a system which will actually function in practice . . .

The standards of dangerousness contained in the draft mental health bill are exceptionally badly drafted . . . A patient who is 'at substantial risk of causing harm to other person' . . . is be treated under compulsion even if the compulsion is not necessary. Quite why this unnecessary compulsion is justifiable is at best highly questionable . . .

The question is when social control is justified in a psychiatric crisis. Dangerousness provides a standard where the public interest in intervention is clear, and a properly drafted dangerousness standard may provide the best way forward. The government's approach may be the right one; but a shame about the drafting. If that is the case, the way forward is to engage in a serious debate as to what a proper dangerousness standard should look like.

Bartlett suggests that the rather vague 'risk of harm to others' criterion for detention in the Mental Health Bill should be replaced with a requirement there should be

---

[62] 'The Test of Compulsion in Mental Health Law: Capacity, Therapeutic Benefit and Dangerousness as Possible Criteria' (2003) 11 Medical Law Review 326–52, 328–9, 349, 352.

specific *evidence* of behaviour which gives rise to a real *likelihood* that the patient will cause *serious* bodily harm.

(d) CRIMINALS AND RESTRICTED PATIENTS

Section 37 of the Act permits a court to make a hospital order in respect of anyone who has been found guilty of an offence which is punishable by imprisonment. Before making such an order the court has to be satisfied, first, that the grounds for admission under section 3 are satisfied, and second that:

the court is of the opinion, having regard to all the circumstances including the nature of the offence and the character and antecedents of the offender, and to the other available methods of dealing with him, that the most suitable method of disposing of the case is by means of an order under this section.[63]

Under section 41 of the Act, patients who have committed criminal offences can also be made subject to restriction orders. This means, first, that the medical staff lose the right to determine the patient's movements, and second, that patients are subject to additional control and security. In deciding whether to make a restriction order, the court must take into account the nature of the offence; the offender's past history; the likelihood of re-offending, and of any risk to the public. While subject to a restriction order, it is not possible for the patient/prisoner to be given leave of absence, or be transferred or discharged without the Secretary of State's consent. Although it is possible for restriction orders to be made for fixed periods of time, this is unusual.

The Home Secretary also has the power under section 48 to ensure that remand prisoners or those detained under the Immigration Act 1971 and the Nationality, Immigration and Asylum Act 2002 are transferred to hospital if they are in urgent need of treatment.

6. TREATMENT OF THE MENTALLY ILL

At the outset, it is important to remember that the normal rules which cover consent to medical treatment (considered in Chapter 4) apply to mentally disordered individuals. In short, competent adults have the right to refuse medical treatment, regardless of whether they are suffering from a mental disorder, and those who lack capacity may be treated in their best interests. There are, however, a number of important exceptions which apply only to those who have been formally admitted to the mental health system. Some of these create special protections for compulsorily admitted individuals, while others permit treatment without consent, regardless of the patient's competence.

---

[63] Section 37(2)(b).

(a) TREATMENT UNDER THE MENTAL HEALTH ACT 1983

Under section 57 of the Act, certain types of treatment cannot be given without the patient's consent *and* a second opinion.

Mental Health Act 1983 section 57

(2) Subject to section 62 below, a patient shall not be given any form of treatment to which this section applies unless he has consented to it and

(a) a registered medical practitioner . . . (not being the responsible medical officer) and two other persons . . . (not being registered medical practitioners) have certified in writing that the patient is capable of understanding the nature, purpose and likely effects of the treatment in question and has consented to it; and

(b) the registered medical practitioner . . . has certified in writing that, having regard to the likelihood of the treatment alleviating or preventing a deterioration of the patient's condition, the treatment should be given.

(3) Before giving a certificate under subsection (2)(b) above the registered medical practitioner concerned shall consult two other persons who have been professionally concerned with the patient's medical treatment, and of those persons one shall be a nurse and the other shall be neither a nurse nor a registered medical practitioner.

Section 57 applies to psychosurgery ('any surgical operation for destroying brain tissue or for destroying the functioning of brain tissue'), and leaves open the possibility of other treatments being added by regulations. This has happened only once, when section 57 was extended by regulations to cover 'the surgical implantation of hormones for the purpose of reducing male sex drive', otherwise known as chemical castration.[64] Under section 57, these treatments cannot be given without the patient's consent, so it would not be lawful to carry out psychosurgery or chemical castration on incompetent patients unless such treatment would fit within the emergency exception in section 62 (see below). Section 57 is seldom used. One reason for this is that the surgical implantation of hormones would be unusual: most treatments to suppress a male patient's sex drive take the form of pills, given orally, or injections, neither of which are covered by this section. Such drugs can therefore be given under section 63 (see below) for three months, after which they fall within section 58.

Under section 58, both electro-convulsive therapy (ECT) and the administration of psychiatric medicines for periods longer than three months, require *either* the informed consent of the competent patient, *or* a second opinion from an independent doctor certifying both that the patient lacks capacity, and that the treatment should be given in order to alleviate or prevent deterioration in the patient's condition.

Mental Health Act 1983 section 58

(3) Subject to section 62 below, a patient shall not be given any form of treatment to which this section applies unless—

(a) he has consented to that treatment and either the responsible medical officer or a registered medical practitioner appointed for the purposes of this Part of this Act by

---

[64] Mental Health (Hospital, Guardianship and Consent to Treatment) Regulations SI 1983/893, reg 16.

the Secretary of State has certified in writing that the patient is capable of understanding its nature, purpose and likely effects and has consented to it; or

(b) a registered medical practitioner appointed as aforesaid (not being the responsible
medical officer) has certified in writing that the patient is not capable of understanding the nature, purpose and likely effects of that treatment or has not consented to it
but that, having regard to the likelihood of its alleviating or preventing a deterioration
of his condition, the treatment should be given.

The need for a second opinion under sections 57 and 58 was intended to protect the
interests of detained patients, but in practice, power to determine whether patients
should be given these especially intrusive treatments continues to lie with the medical
profession. In recent years, however, the courts have suggested that the second opinion appointed doctor (SOAD) should not simply rubber stamp the responsible medical officer (RMO)'s judgment. In *Regina (Wilkinson) v Broadmoor Special Hospital
Authority*[65] (a case we look at in detail below at p. 427), the Court of Appeal was
sharply critical of the tendency to regard the SOAD's role as one of review, rather than
independent assessment. According to Simon Brown LJ:

Whilst, of course, it is proper for the SOAD to pay regard to the views of the RMO who has, after
all, the most intimate knowledge of the patient's case, that does not relieve him of the responsibility of forming his own independent judgment as to whether or not 'the treatment should be given'.
And certainly, if the SOAD's certificate and evidence is to carry any real weight in cases where, as
here, the treatment plan is challenged, it will be necessary to demonstrate a less deferential
approach than appears to be the norm.

It is also now clear that SOADs are under a duty to provide reasons for their decisions.
In *Regina (Wooder) v Feggetter*[66] the claimant's RMO decided that he should receive
anti-psychotic medication, despite his refusal to consent. An SOAD provided the
necessary certificate under section 58(3)(b). The claimant, who wanted his delusional
condition to be treated without drugs, argued that the SOAD should provide reasons
for granting the certificate. The Court of Appeal agreed. According to Brooke LJ:

With the coming into force of the Human Rights Act 1998 the time has come, in my judgment, for
this court to declare that fairness requires that a decision by a SOAD which sanctions the violation
of the autonomy of a competent adult patient should also be accompanied by reasons . . . I would
be disposed to grant a declaration that fairness demands that a SOAD should give in writing the
reasons for his opinion when certifying under section 58 of the Mental Health Act 1983 that a
detained patient should be given medication against his will, and that these reasons should be
disclosed to the patient unless the SOAD or the RMO considers that such disclosure would be
likely to cause serious harm to the physical or mental health of the patient or any other person.

An exception to sections 57 and 58 is created by section 62:

Mental Health Act 1983 section 62

(1) Sections 57 and 58 above shall not apply to any treatment—

(a) which is immediately necessary to save the patient's life; or

---

[65] [2002] 1 WLR 419.   [66] [2002] EWCA Civ 554, [2003] QB 219.

(b) which (not being irreversible) is immediately necessary to prevent a serious deterioration of his condition; or

(c) which (not being irreversible or hazardous) is immediately necessary to alleviate serious suffering by the patient; or

(d) which (not being irreversible or hazardous) is immediately necessary and represents the minimum interference necessary to prevent the patient from behaving violently or being a danger to himself or to others. . . .

(3) For the purposes of this section treatment is irreversible if it has unfavorable irreversible physical or psychological consequences and hazardous if it entails significant physical hazard.

This means that, in an emergency, the treatments covered by sections 57 and 58 can be given without a second opinion and/or the patient's consent. Given that the treatments covered by section 57 are rarely used, and will even more seldom be 'immediately necessary', section 62's suspension of the protection contained in section 57 is of little practical importance. The question of whether drugs should be prescribed for longer than three months will also seldom arise in an emergency. Research appears to indicate that section 62 is most commonly used to justify ECT, mainly for female patients suffering from depressive disorders.[67] Although used comparatively infrequently, in practice the principal effect of section 62's suspension of section 58 is that emergency ECT can be administered to a competent, refusing patient without her consent.

Of more practical importance is section 63, which enables treatment to be provided without consent :

Mental Health Act 1983 section 63

The consent of a patient shall not be required for any medical treatment given to him for the mental disorder from which he is suffering, not being treatment falling within section 57 or 58 above, if the treatment is given by or under the direction of the responsible medical officer.

It is important to remember that section 63 applies to *competent* adults. At common law and under the Mental Capacity Act 2005, a patient who lacks capacity can be given treatment for the mental disorder from which she is suffering if it is in her best interests. And obviously, if a competent adult patient is consenting to treatment, then there would be no need to resort to the power contained in section 63. So in practice this section enables treatment for mental disorder to be given to a competent adult *who has refused to consent to treatment*. As Genevra Richardson explains in the next extract, this is radically out of step with the increasingly dominant principle of patient autonomy.

Genevra Richardson[68]

At present the law in England and Wales is unusually inconsistent and discriminatory in the way it deals with questions of competence and patient autonomy with regard to mental disorder. The

---

[67] P Fennell, *Treatment Without Consent: Law, Psychiatry and the Treatment of Mentally Disordered People since 1845* (London Routledge 1996) 199.
[68] 'Autonomy, Guardianship and Mental Disorder: One Problem, Two Solutions' (2002) 65 Modern Law Review 702–23, 707–8, 711.

Mental Health Act 1983 permits a person suffering from a mental disorder of the necessary degree to be detained in hospital and treated for that disorder against her competent wishes. No assessment of competence is required. Although the wishes of the patient may be relevant to the treatment decision taken on her behalf, statute allows that decision to be driven by beneficence and social protection, patient autonomy is only one of a number of factors to be considered. Thus, while the common law grants patient autonomy a central role in relation to both physical and mental disorder, in relation to treatment of mental disorder of sufficient severity statute requires patient autonomy to cede to the values of paternalism and social protection. It was suggested above that the paternalist justification for this statutory approach originated in the now contested belief that mental disorder equates to loss of judgment. It is therefore interesting to note that the statutory powers of compulsion are limited to treatment for mental disorder, compulsory patients can still refuse treatment for physical disorder: judgment, it seems, is lost in relation to treatment for *mental* disorder only . . .

The 1983 Act provides for compulsory treatment for mental disorder only, not for physical disorder. Thus the distinction between mental and physical disorder becomes crucial for the formal patient, because even a formal patient retains the right to receive treatment for physical disorder according to ordinary legal principles. This means that a formal patient who remains competent can refuse treatment for a physical disorder while detained under the Act, while he must accept treatment for mental disorder. Much, therefore, turns on the meaning given to mental disorder and if it is interpreted too generously there is a danger that a competent patient could be forced to accept treatment for a condition which has little or no bearing on his or her mental state.

Medical treatment is defined in section 145 as including nursing, care, habilitation, and rehabilitation under medical supervision. Although not specifically mentioned, it has been assumed that if it is necessary to use force to administer treatment under section 63, then this is also permissible, as part of the patient's medical treatment. In *R v Broadmoor Special Hospital Authority, ex parte S, H and D*,[69] Auld LJ described how both the 1959 and the 1983 Mental Health Acts 'leave unspoken' the necessary incidents of control which must accompany any power to detain patients and treat them compulsorily:

Sections 3 and 37 of the 1983 Act provide for detention, not just for its own sake, but for treatment. Detention for treatment necessarily implies control for that purpose. . . . Both statutes leave unspoken many of the necessary incidents of control flowing from a power of detention for treatment, including: the power to restrain patients, to keep them in seclusion . . ., to deprive them of their personal possessions for their own safety and to regulate the frequency and manner of visits to them.

And in *Tameside and Glossop Acute Services Trust v CH*,[70] a case we consider in detail below, Wall J also took for granted that the power to treat under section 63 was necessarily accompanied by the power to use force in order to ensure that the patient receives the treatment in question:

I am therefore satisfied that the treatment of the defendant's pregnancy proposed by Dr G is within the broad interpretation of s 63 of the Mental Health Act approved by the Court of Appeal in B v Croydon Health Authority: it follows that since the defendant's consent to it is not required,

---

[69] *The Times* 17 Feb 1998.   [70] [1996] 1 FLR 762.

Dr G is entitled, should he deem it clinically necessary, to use restraint to the extent to which it may be reasonably required in order to achieve the delivery by the defendant of a healthy baby.

Obviously the scope of section 63 depends upon the meaning given to treatment 'for the mental disorder from which he is suffering'. In practice, a number of medical procedures which are not straightforwardly directed towards curing the patient's mental illness have been sanctioned under this section, on the grounds that alleviating the symptoms of the disorder, or enabling the patient to receive treatment for her disorder, are all in fact intended to prevent the patient's deterioration.

In *Re KB (Adult) (Mental Patient: Medical Treatment)*[71] Ewbank J said that the force-feeding of an anorexic patient was treatment for her mental disorder.

Ewbank J

[A]norexia nervosa . . . is an eating disorder and relieving symptoms is just as much a part of treatment as relieving the underlying cause. If the symptoms are exacerbated by the patient's refusal to eat and drink, the mental disorder becomes progressively more and more difficult to treat and so the treatment by naso-gastric tube is an integral part of the treatment of the mental disorder itself. It is also said that the treatment is necessary in order to make psychiatric treatment of the underlying cause possible at all . . . feeding by naso-gastric tube in the circumstances of this type of case is treatment envisaged under s 63 and does not require the consent of the patient.

It is, however, clear that force-feeding does not cure anorexia, and, as Penney Lewis explains in the next extract, repeated episodes of force-feeding can in fact make recovery from anorexia less likely.

Penney Lewis[72]

The anorexic's holy grail is control . . . Force-feeding crushes the patient's will, destroying who the patient is. This is the antithesis of what a successful, therapeutic treatment must be . . . The patient may be force-fed up to a more healthy weight and then discharged from hospital, free to return to her previous eating pattern and to lose the weight she has been forced to gain. As her trust has been violated, she may be less likely to seek medical help for her anorexia or for any other medical problem. The gain has been short-term, rather than long-term. The immediate crisis has been averted, but long term damage has been done. Forcing treatment upon a young sufferer of anorexia merely reinforces her lack of self-confidence by taking this decision out of her control, and denies her the capacity for self-directed action which must be developed if she is to recover from this illness. Anorexics who have been force-fed may turn to the more life-threatening behaviour associated with bulimia, including vomiting and laxative abuse. They may be more likely to commit suicide, or to become entrenched in their refusal to eat and thereby become chronic sufferers.

Kirsty Keywood points out that the courts have also been surprisingly disinterested in whether clinicians would characterize force-feeding as 'treatment' for anorexia.

Kirsty Keywood[73]

What is particularly interesting, however, is that the courts' assessment of the patients' best

---

[71] [1994] 2 FCR 1051.

[72] 'Feeding Anorexic Patients Who Refuse Food' (1999) 7 Medical Law Review 21–37, 32–4, 36–7.

[73] 'Rethinking the anorexic body: How English law and psychiatry "think" ' (2003) 26 International Journal of Law and Psychiatry 599–616, 601–11.

interests is focused on the short-term health gains achieved through refeeding, with little thought to the potential long-term consequences of involuntary treatment. Moreover, the courts' assessment fails to parallel the diversity of views in the clinical and ethical literature on the appropriateness of involuntary treatment.

A number of clinicians perceive involuntary treatment as being necessary in a small number of cases in order to preserve life, restore weight, and restore patients' cognitive abilities to a sufficient degree that they may engage meaningfully in psychotherapy, without necessarily damaging the therapeutic alliance between doctor and patient. Others observe that compulsory treatment, with its higher mortality rate at follow up, may well compromise the relationship between doctor and patient and erode further the patient's self-esteem. Indeed, the courts' assessment of the appropriateness of involuntary treatment pays little regard to the consequences of overriding the expressed wishes of the patient diagnosed with anorexia nervosa. Notwithstanding the paucity of evidence that involuntary treatment of anorexia nervosa yields significant benefits to the patient in the long term, it is perhaps surprising that the courts have not given greater consideration to the appropriateness of interventions such as non-consensual nasogastric feeding . . . The courts have traditionally premised their judgments on a set of assumptions about the appropriateness of involuntary intervention in the treatment of anorexia nervosa which find (as yet) no firm empirical support within the domains of evidence-based medicine.

In *B v Croydon HA*[74] the patient's compulsion to self-harm was said to be a symptom of her mental disorder, and hence the Court of Appeal again authorized force-feeding under section 63.

B v Croydon HA[75]

B was a 24 year old woman who suffered from a psychopathic disorder for which the only known treatment was psychoanalytic psychotherapy. One of her symptoms was a compulsion to harm herself. While she was compulsorily detained in hospital under section 3 of the Mental Health Act 1983 she stopped eating and her weight fell to a dangerous level. B sought to restrain the health authority from tube feeding her without her consent. Thorpe J held that tube feeding constituted medical treatment for the mental disorder from which B was suffering and that her consent was not required by virtue of section 63 of the Act of 1983. B's appeal was dismissed with by the Court of Appeal.

Neill LJ

I am satisfied that the words in section 63 of the Mental Health Act 1983 'any medical treatment given to him for the mental disorder from which he is suffering' include treatment given to alleviate the symptoms of the disorder as well as treatment to remedy its underlying cause. In the first place it seems to me that it would often be difficult in practice for those treating a patient to draw a clear distinction between procedures or parts of procedures which were designed to treat the disorder itself and those procedures or parts which were designed to treat its symptoms and sequelae. In my view the medical treatment has to be looked at as a whole, and this approach is reinforced by the wide definition of 'medical treatment' in section 145(1) as including 'nursing' and also 'care, habilitation and rehabilitation under medical supervision.'

In the next extract, Sameer Sarkar and Gwen Adshead highlight the 'striking' anomaly this case reveals between the treatment of those with and without mental disorder.

---

[74] [1995] Fam 133.   [75] Ibid.

Sameer Sarkar and Gwen Adshead[76]

Such decisions reveal striking anomalies in the way that English courts have dealt with treatment refusal in relation to mental and physical disorder. Consider tube-feeding as an example. An ordinary person who decides to starve themselves to death (for example, a prisoner), or a terminally ill person who is not eating during the final stages of life, cannot be force fed against their will. . . .

If, however, food-refusing individuals can be deemed to be suffering from a mental disorder, then they can be force fed, even if they are deemed to be competent. The 'not eating' is understood as a symptom, which is secondary to the mental disorder, and forced feeding is the appropriate treatment for that symptom. This was the case in *B v Croydon Health Authority* where, although B's treatment refusal was deemed to be competent, she could be force fed in the face of her refusal because she was detained for treatment of a mental disorder . . .

In the case of suspected mental disorder, the judiciary appears to abandon autonomy as the overriding value in relation to consent, and instead favour beneficence in the form of treatment intervention.

If categorizing force feeding as treatment for mental disorder is controversial, the following case offers an even more dramatic example of the expansive interpretation given to section 63.

Tameside and Glossop v CH[77]

CH suffered from paranoid schizophrenia and was 38 weeks pregnant. She was detained under section 3 of the Mental Health Act 1983. The fetus was suffering from growth retardation, and the doctors involved in her care believed that to avoid stillbirth, labour should be induced, and that it might become necessary to perform a caesarean section. CH believed the medical staff were a threat to her child and did not want them to proceed.

Wall J

At first blush, it might appear difficult to say that performance of a Caesarian [sic] section is medical treatment for the Defendant's mental disorder:

I am, however, satisfied that on the facts of this case so to hold would be 'too atomistic a view' . . . There are several strands in the evidence which, in my judgment, bring the proposed treatment within s 63 of the Act. Firstly, there is the proposition that an ancillary reason for the induction and, if necessary the birth by Caesarian [sic] section is to prevent a deterioration in the Defendant's mental state. Secondly, there is the clear evidence of Dr M that in order for the treatment of her schizophrenia to be effective, it is necessary for her to give birth to a live baby. Thirdly, the overall structure of her treatment requires her to receive strong anti-psychotic medication. The administration of that treatment has been necessarily interrupted by her pregnancy and cannot be resumed until her child is born. It is not, therefore, I think stretching language unduly to say that achievement of a successful outcome of her pregnancy is a necessary part of the overall treatment of her mental disorder. . . .

I am therefore satisfied that the treatment of the Defendant's pregnancy proposed by Dr G is within the broad interpretation of s 63 of the Mental Health Act approved by the Court of Appeal in *B v Croydon Health Authority*.

---

[76] 'Treatment over objection: minds, bodies and beneficence' (2002) Journal of Mental Health Law 105–18, 114.

[77] [1996] 1 FCR 753.

In the following extract, Andrew Grubb criticizes the 'sheer breadth' of the Tameside decision.

Andrew Grubb[78]

It is clear, therefore, that s. 63 provides a broad and, in practice, quantitatively extensive exception to the common law rule that medical treatment may only be given to a competent adult with consent. Section 63 licences what would otherwise be trespassory touchings . . .

How can induced labour or Caesarean section be 'medical treatment given for [the patient's] mental disorder' under s. 63? It seems incredible that anyone should so regard it. On the face of it the decision in *CH* seems quite wrong . . .

The patient's consultant psychiatrist gave evidence first, that stillbirth (the alternative to the procedures) would lead to a profound deterioration in the patient's mental health; and secondly, that the pregnancy had interrupted the patient's treatment with strong anti-psychotic medication because of the dangers to her fetus . . . Both reasons offered by the judge are questionable. The second is plainly wrong. It is tantamount to saying that any physical condition which impedes the direct treatment of the patient's mental disorder is covered by s. 63 . . .

[T]he most potent argument against Wall J's approach is the sheer breadth of his decision on the scope of s. 63. There will be many, apparently unrelated, physical conditions which could be shown to have an impact on a mentally disordered patient's mental health. All of these, once the psychiatric evidence is there, will now fall within s. 63 and not require the patient's consent. It was not Parliament's intention to licence the treatment of physical conditions which are not a cause or symptoms of the mental disorder. The Government saw s. 63 in far more limited terms covering 'perfectly routine, sensible treatment' . . . Given the exceptional nature of the power of compulsory detention, non-consensual treatment should be restricted to clear cases of 'treatment for the mental disorder', there are considerable dangers in interpreting s. 63 too broadly.

As Ceri Widdett and Michael Thomson suggest in the next extract, it is also interesting to compare *CH with Re C*[79] (see Chapter 4, p. 196), a case in which a paranoid schizophrenic with a gangrenous leg was found competent to refuse potentially life-saving surgery. Thorpe J did not even consider whether section 63 of the Mental Health Act might apply. *Re C* was distinguished in both *Croydon* and *Tameside*, on the grounds that treating C's gangrene 'was not likely to affect his mental condition' (*per* Wall J in *Tameside*), and 'was entirely unconnected with the mental disorder' (*per* Hoffmann LJ in *Croydon*). Widdett and Thomson would, however, contest whether such a sharp distinction exists between *Re C* and *CH*.

Ceri Widdett and Michael Thomson[80]

In *CH* the suggested proximity between the defendant's mental health and her pregnancy may be located within broader stories regarding female instability during pregnancy. . . .

[I]n his evidence to the Court, Dr G asserted that it was in the defendant's interests to give birth to a live child. This position was supported by Dr M—her consultant psychiatrist. Dr M offered a bleak prognosis in the event of a still-birth. The defendant would experience a deterioration of her mental health, facing increasing paranoia and an impeded recovery. Yet the picture if she should have a live-birth differed dramatically:

---

[78] 'Commentary: Treatment without Consent (Pregnancy) Adult' (1996) 4 Medical Law Review 193–8, 194–6.

[79] [1994] 1 All ER 819 [1994] 1 WLR 290.

[80] 'Justifying Treatment and Other Stories' (1997) 5 Feminist Legal Studies 77, 84–8.

The prognosis if she delivers a healthy infant is that she can recover from her psychosis and be able to provide care and support for her child. She will then be in a stable mental condition and rational and free from psychotic symptoms ... The best interests of the patient lie in her producing a healthy child.

Having a child is clearly constructed as curative and normalising ...

For a substantial period of the nineteenth century the female reproductive organs were considered central to any definition of Woman. The reproductive organs were 'the *controlling* organs in the female body'.... Given the centrality of the female reproductive organs they became intimately tied to all aspects of women's heath, particularly ill health ... Typical of this medical discourse is the following extract from one of the numerous guides to women's health of this period:

[Most] diseases will be found, on due investigation, to be in reality, no disease at all, but merely the sympathetic reaction or the symptoms of one disease, namely a disease of the womb.

As a corollary a woman's good health—mental and physical—depended on the proper functioning of her reproductive organs ...

CH's health was intimately tied to bearing a (live) child. More specifically the prognosis for her mental health was polarised by the possible outcomes of her pregnancy. To an extent this poignantly mirrors the phenomenon of hysteria in the last century ... The cause and treatment of hysteria became (obsessively) located in the female reproductive organs ...

In sharp contrast to CH's treatment is Thorpe J's response to C's wish to refuse treatment for gangrene. Thorpe J informed the Court: 'His rejection of amputation seemed to result from sincerely held conviction. He had a certain dignity of manner that I respect.' Even if we remain unconvinced that politically unacceptable nineteenth century discourses are still shaping mental health practice and law, it is clear that women are afforded less respect than men in terms of self-determination, bodily integrity, and autonomy.

Although Widdett and Thomson argue that the courts display much more paternalistic attitudes towards female patients, another possible explanation is that, in fact, C's life was not at risk at the time of the application, whereas both *Croydon* and *Tameside* involved emergency situations, in which the courts have always tended to err on the side of caution when deciding whether to respect refusals of medical treatment (for more discussion of this point, see Chapter 4). Certainly an expansive interpretation of section 63 has been used in cases where the patient is male. In *R v Collins, ex parte Brady*,[81] Ian Brady, one of the Moors murderers who was detained under the Mental Health Act 1983, had gone on hunger strike in order to protest at his treatment. Maurice Kay J held that force feeding could be justified under section 63 as treatment for the mental disorder from which he was suffering.

On any view, and to a high degree of probability, s 63 was triggered because what arose was the need for medical treatment for the mental disorder from which the applicant was and is suffering. The hunger strike is a manifestation or symptom of the personality disorder.

In *R (on the application of B) v Ashworth Hospital Authority*,[82] a slightly different question arose. The House of Lords had to consider whether section 63 only applied

---

[81] [2000] Lloyd's Rep Med 355.   [82] [2005] UKHL 20, [2005] All ER (D) 279 (Mar).

to treatment for the particular type of mental disorder which initially justified the patient's detention. B had been detained on the grounds of mental illness, namely schizophrenia, but while he was in hospital, he was also found to be suffering from a psychopathic disorder. B argued that the decision to place him on a ward for patients with psychopathic disorder was unlawful because this was not the type of mental disorder which had justified his detention. The House of Lords rejected this argument.

Baroness Hale

There are a great many reasons for thinking that section 63 is not so limited. The first is the plain meaning of the words used. The patient's consent is not required for 'any medical treatment' given to him for 'the mental disorder from which he is suffering'. . . . Thus, the natural and ordinary meaning of the words is that the patient may be treated without consent for any mental disorder from which he is suffering, and any treatment ancillary to that; but treatment for any physical disorder can only be given with his consent or under the doctrine of necessity as it applies to patients who lack the capacity to consent. . . .

I conclude that the words of section 63 mean what they say. They authorise a patient to be treated for any mental disorder from which he is suffering, irrespective of whether this falls within the form of disorder from which he is classified as suffering in the application, order or direction justifying his detention.

As I said earlier, compulsory patients are a vulnerable group who deserve protection from being forced to accept inappropriate treatment. But restricting their treatment to that which is designed for their 'classified' disorder is so haphazard as to be scarcely any protection at all. . . . [P]sychiatry is not an exact science. Diagnosis is not easy or clear cut. As this and many other cases show, a number of different diagnoses may be reached by the same or different clinicians over the years. As this case also shows, co-morbidity is very common . . .

It is not easy to disentangle which features of the patient's presentation stem from a disease of the mind and which stem from his underlying personality traits. The psychiatrist's aim should be to treat the whole patient. . . . Once the state has taken away a person's liberty and detained him in a hospital with a view to medical treatment, the state should be able (some would say obliged) to provide him with the treatment which he needs. It would be absurd if a patient could be detained in hospital but had to be denied the treatment which his doctor thought he needed for an indefinite period while some largely irrelevant classification was rectified.

Since the Human Rights Act 1998 came into force, the courts have also had to consider whether treatment without consent might violate a patient's convention rights. Article 3 states that 'no-one shall be subjected to torture or to inhuman or degrading treatment or punishment'. This is an absolute right, with no qualification, and the European Court of Human Rights has fleshed out its application to treatment of the mentally ill in *Herczegfalvy v Austria*:[83]

The court considers that the position of inferiority and powerlessness which is typical of patients confined in psychiatric hospitals calls for increased vigilance in reviewing whether the Convention has been complied with. While it is for the medical authorities to decide, on the basis of recognised rules of medical science, on the therapeutic methods to be used, if necessary by force, to preserve the physical and mental health of patients who are entirely incapable of deciding for themselves

---

[83] (1992) 15 EHRR 437.

and for whom they are therefore responsible, such patients nevertheless remain under the protection of art 3, the requirements of which permit of no derogation.

The established principles of medicine are admittedly in principle decisive in such cases; as a general rule, a measure which is a therapeutic necessity cannot be regarded as inhuman or degrading. The court must nevertheless satisfy itself that the medical necessity has been convincingly shown to exist.

It should, however, be noted that *Herczegfalvy* itself concerned a detained patient who was handcuffed and strapped to his bed, and these measures were said to be a therapeutic necessity:

In this case, according to the psychiatric principles generally accepted at that time, medical necessity justified the treatment in issue, including forcibly administered food and neuroleptics, isolation, and attaching handcuffs to a security bed. Thus, there was no violation of Article 3.[84]

Herczegfalvy v Austria was applied by the Court of Appeal in the following case:

Regina (Wilkinson) v Broadmoor Special Hospital Authority[85]

The claimant was a convicted mental patient compulsorily detained at a secure hospital. His responsible medical officer decided that he should receive anti-psychotic medication, despite his refusal to consent, under sections 58 and 63 of the Mental Health Act 1983. A second opinion doctor was appointed. The claimant sought judicial review of their decision to administer treatment despite his refusal to consent, contending that it infringed his right to life under article 2 of the Convention for the Protection of Human Rights and Fundamental Freedoms, his right not to be subject to degrading treatment under article 3 and his right to privacy under article 8, and that, in order to comply with his right to a fair trial under article 6 and in accordance with the principles of natural justice, he should be entitled to require the two doctors concerned, together with his own medical expert, to attend the hearing to give evidence and be cross-examined.

Simon Brown LJ

If in truth this appellant has the capacity to refuse consent to the treatment proposed here, it is difficult to suppose that he should nevertheless be forcibly subjected to it. [I]ts impact on the appellant's rights above all to autonomy and bodily inviolability is immense and its prospective benefits (not least given his extreme opposition) appear decidedly speculative. Even, moreover, if the appellant is incompetent, the court will need to be satisfied (in the language of the ECtHR in *Herczegfalvy*) 'that the medical necessity has been convincingly shown to exist . . . according to the psychiatric principles generally accepted at the time'.

Hale LJ

What help, if any, does the Human Rights Act give in resolving this question? Under art 3 of the Convention for the Protection of Human Rights and Fundamental Freedoms, 'No-one shall be subjected to torture or to inhuman or degrading treatment or punishment'. This is an absolute right which permits of no qualification or excuse. The European Court of Human Rights has given us some guidance in *Herczegfalvy v Austria* . . .

One can at least conclude from this that forcible measures inflicted upon an incapacitated patient which are not a medical necessity may indeed be inhuman or degrading. The same must apply to forcible measures inflicted upon a capacitated patient . . .

I do not take the view that detained patients who have the capacity to decide for themselves can

---

[84] Ibid.   [85] [2002] 1 WLR 419.

never be treated against their will . . . Given that under the Convention forcible treatment which is not a 'medical necessity' may well be inhuman and degrading, substantial benefit from it would be required for it to be justified . . . Whatever the position before the Human Rights Act, the decision to impose treatment without consent upon a protesting patient is a potential invasion of his rights under art 3 or art 8.

Non-consensual treatment, and any associated use of force or restraint, can only avoid being categorized as inhuman or degrading treatment if it is 'convincingly shown' to be a medical or therapeutic necessity. What does this mean in practice, and in particular how high is the standard of proof? These questions arose in the following case.

Regina (N) v M and Others[86]

The claimant's RMO produced a treatment plan which included anti-psychotic medication by injection. The claimant refused to consent, and obtained an opinion from an independent psychiatrist that she had capacity, was unlikely to be psychotic, and should not be given anti-psychotic medication. A second opinion appointed doctor issued a certificate under section 58(3)(b) of the Mental Health Act 1983 stating that the claimant was suffering from paranoid psychosis or severe personality disorder and required regular anti-psychotic treatment. He also thought that the claimant did not have capacity. The claimant's application for judicial review of the decisions of the responsible medical officer and the second opinion appointed doctor was dismissed, and the Court of Appeal dismissed her appeal.

Dyson LJ

In the light of [Herczegfalvy v Austria], it is common ground that the standard of proof required is that the court should be satisfied that medical necessity has been 'convincingly' shown. . . .

Mr Kelly [for the claimant] submitted that this test is, in effect, the same as the criminal standard of proof. We disagree. It seems to us that no useful purpose is served by importing the language of the criminal law. The phrase 'convincingly shown' is easily understood. The standard is a high one. But it does not need elaboration or further explanation. . . .

It seems to us that there is much to be said for the view that in these cases there is but a single question: has the proposed treatment been convincingly shown to be medically necessary? The answer to that question will depend on a number of factors, including (a) how certain is it that the patient does suffer from a treatable mental disorder, (b) how serious a disorder is it, (c) how serious a risk is presented to others, (d) how likely is it that, if the patient does suffer from such a disorder, the proposed treatment will alleviate the condition, (e) how much alleviation is there likely to be, (f) how likely is it that the treatment will have adverse consequences for the patient and (g) how severe may they be? . . .

Mr Kelly's submission on analysis involves the proposition that, in a case where there is a responsible body of opinion that a patient is not suffering from a treatable condition, then it cannot be convincingly shown that the treatment proposed is medically necessary. We reject this submission. . . . In our judgment, the fact that there is a responsible body of opinion against the proposed treatment is relevant to the question whether it is in the patient's best interests or medically necessary, but it is no more than that. The court has to decide in the light of all the evidence in the case whether the treatment should be permitted.

The right to be free from non-consensual medical treatment might also be protected by Article 8, the right to respect for private and family life. In *X v Austria*,[87] for

---

[86] [2003] 1 WLR 562.　　　　[87] (1980) 18 DR 154, 156.

example, the European Commission explicitly stated that 'compulsory medical inter-vention, even if it is of minor importance, must be considered an interference with this right'. In practice, however, the protection offered by Article 8 is qualified insofar as an interference can be shown to be 'necessary in a democratic society' for, among other things, 'the protection of health'. This as the Court of Appeal explained in *R(N) v M and Others*,[88] means that if the treatment has been convincingly shown to be medically necessary, neither Article 3 nor Article 8 will have been violated, since the interference with the right to respect for private life would be proportionate, and justified within the terms of Article 8(2).

While section 63 is only relevant to the compulsory treatment of *competent* patients, the protection which is superimposed upon it by the Human Rights Act applies equally to *incompetent* patients. Hence if a patient who lacks capacity never-theless manifests a desire not to be treated, treating her against her wishes could amount to inhuman or degrading treatment, and thus would be acceptable only if it could be convincingly shown to be a therapeutic necessity. In the following case, the solitary confinement of an incapacitated patient was held to have been a violation of Article 3.

Keenan v United Kingdom[89]

Following the suicide of her son, K applied to the European Court of Human Rights seeking relief. Her son, X, who had been receiving anti-psychotic medication, had been imprisoned after assault-ing his girlfriend. During his transfer from the prison health care centre to the main prison, X had assaulted two hospital officers and, despite the prison health staff being aware of his mental health problems, he had been subject to solitary confinement. Within 24 hours, he had hanged himself.

Judgment of the ECHR

The Court recalls that ill-treatment must attain a minimum level of severity if it is to fall within the scope of Article 3. The assessment of this minimum is relative: it depends on all the circum-stances of the case, such as the duration of the treatment, its physical and/or mental effects and, in some cases, the sex, age and state of health of the victim . . .

It is relevant in the context of the present application to recall also that the authorities are under an obligation to protect the health of persons deprived of liberty . . . In particular, the assessment of whether the treatment or punishment concerned is incompatible with the standard of article 3 has, in the case of mentally ill persons, to take into consideration their vulnerability and their inability, in some cases, to complain coherently or at all about how they are being affected by any particular treatment . . .

The lack of effective monitoring of Mark Keenan's condition and the lack of informed psychi-atric input into his assessment and treatment disclose significant defects in the medical care provided to a mentally ill person known to be a suicide risk. The belated imposition on him in those circumstances of a serious disciplinary punishment—seven days' segregation in the punishment block and an additional twenty-eight days to his sentence imposed two weeks after the event and only nine days before his expected date of release—which may well have threatened his physical and moral resistance, is not compatible with the standard of treatment required in respect of a

---

[88] [2003] 1 WLR 562.   [89] (27229/95) 10 BHRC 319.

mentally ill person. It must be regarded as constituting inhuman and degrading treatment and punishment within the meaning of Article 3 of the Convention.

Accordingly, the Court finds a violation of this provision.

(b) TREATMENT UNDER THE DRAFT MENTAL HEALTH BILL

The draft Mental Health Bill requires the tribunal to authorize the treatment plan proposed by the patient's clinical supervisor, and the tribunal has the power to veto any planned treatment which appears unwarranted. This significantly extends the remit of tribunals, and to be workable, many more tribunal members will have to be appointed. Of course, the treatment plan is likely to require review and amendment during any prolonged period of compulsion, and it is not yet clear whether any changes will also need to be authorized by the tribunal. If this were the case, the tribunals' already expanded workload might become unmanageable, and more importantly the delay during which authorization is sought might compromise patient care.

The Bill contains a number of special provisions which apply to different types of treatment. ECT, for example, can be given either with the consent of a competent patient, or with the authority of the clinical supervisor, where it is immediately necessary to save the patient's life, or to prevent a serious deterioration in her condition, or to alleviate serious suffering. If ECT is to be given to an incapacitated patient when it is not 'immediately necessary', it must be authorized by the tribunal.

Psychosurgery, and other treatments to be specified in regulations, are categorized as Type A treatments, and are subject to a special regime. Such treatments can only be given to a competent patient with the patient's consent. If a patient cannot consent to Type A treatment, it must only be given if he is not likely to become capable; the treatment is in his best interests, and he is not likely to resist it. Special rules also apply to Type B treatments, which are to be defined in regulations, but do not include either ECT or Type A treatments. Again regulations will specify when Type B treatments can be given without consent.

There is some tension between the draft Bill And the Mental Capacity Act 2005. As we saw in Chapter 4 p. 221, under sections 24 and 25 of the Mental Capacity Act, provided they are valid and applicable, advance directives which specify that an individual does not want further treatment must be honoured. However, under the draft Mental Health Bill an advance refusal *in relation to treatment for mental disorder* will not be binding. Indeed under the original draft Bill, the only criteria to determine whether treatment should be given to incapacitated patients was the recommendation of the clinical supervisor and the approval of the tribunal. The patient's previous wishes were irrelevant. The joint committee recommended that the Bill should provide that, while not binding, advance decisions in relation to future mental health treatment should at least be taken into account, and the government has said that it will try to amend the Bill accordingly.[90]

---

[90] Joint Committee on the Draft Mental Health Bill—First Report, 2005, <http://www.publications.parliament.uk/pa/jt/jtment.htm>.

7. DISCHARGE

Once a patient has been detained, it is important to remember that her detention must continue to be justified by her condition. As we saw earlier, *Winterwerp v Netherlands* made clear that the mental disorder has to be of a kind or degree warranting compulsory confinement, and the validity of continued confinement is contingent upon the mental disorder's persistence. The responsible medical officer (RMO) has an ongoing duty to consider whether the conditions which justified the patient's original detention continue to be satisfied. And in practice, many detained patients are discharged by their RMOs once they are satisfied that the patient is no longer suffering from a mental disorder which necessitates detention for treatment, perhaps because the treatment she has received has been effective.

(a) DISCHARGE UNDER THE 1983 ACT

Detentions under section 2 will automatically lapse after 28 days, and unless the patient is formally detained under section 3, the patient must be discharged. For patients detained under section 3, their detention should automatically be reviewed by the Mental Health Review Tribunal (MHRT) after six months, and thereafter every three years.

Under section 66 of the 1983 Act, a patient who has been admitted to hospital compulsorily under sections 2 or 3 of the 1983 Act has a right to request that the MHRT considers whether they should be discharged. Of course, not all patients will have the capacity to exercise this right, and in *R (on the application of MH) v Secretary of State for Health*[91] the question of whether this differential access to the MHRT might be incompatible with the Human Rights Act arose. MH, a 32-year-old woman with Down's syndrome had been admitted under section 2. She lacked the capacity to appeal to the MHRT herself, and the Court of Appeal found that by failing to provide a mechanism through which the detention of incompetent patients could be referred to the MHRT, Section 2 of the Mental Health Act was incompatible with Article 5(4) of the Human Rights Act.

Buxton LJ

MH, though deprived of her liberty, was in practice unable, as the state knew, to take proceedings in the form of an application to the MHRT that would otherwise be available to her. Therefore the state, in accordance with the spirit of article 5.4, should make that application on her behalf, or otherwise ensure that her case was brought before the MHRT. . . .

I cannot think that the scheme of protection for persons detained in cases of suspected unsound mind can have been intended to exclude, simply because of their mental inability, persons who find themselves in the position of MH. The matter may perhaps be tested by asking what reply the authors of the ECHR would have given had they been asked whether the particular language that they adopted in article 5.4 was intended to exclude from the protection of article 5 a person who,

---

[91] [2004] EWCA CIV 1690, [2004] All ER (D) 64 (Dec).

solely because of lack of capacity to do so, was unable to take proceedings. At least if they were English lawyers I suspect that they would have replied with a testy 'of course not'. . . .

I would therefore declare that section 2 of the Mental Health Act 1983 is incompatible with article 5.4 of the European Convention on Human Rights in that it is not attended by adequate provision for the reference to a court of the case of a patient detained pursuant to section 2 in circumstances where a patient has a right to make application to a Mental Health Review Tribunal but the patient is incapable of exercising that right on his own initiative.

There is a clear parallel here with the *Bournewood* 'gap' considered earlier. As we have already seen, informally admitted patients are, in theory at least, free to leave hospital whenever they like, which means there are no special measures governing their discharge from hospital. In practice, however, as we saw in the *Bournewood* case, incapacitated patients' freedom to leave hospital may be more illusory than real. Following *MH*, the government will also need to consider introducing measures to enable the compulsory detention of an incapacitated individual to be reviewed by an MHRT.

The criteria for the MHRT's decision-making are contained in section 72.

Mental Health Act 1983 section 72

(1) Where application is made to a Mental Health Review Tribunal by or in respect of a patient who is liable to be detained under this Act, the Tribunal may in any case direct that the patient be discharged, and—

    (a) the Tribunal shall direct the discharge of a patient liable to be detained under section 2 above if they are not satisfied—

        (i) that he is then suffering from mental disorder or from mental disorder of a nature or degree which warrants his detention in a hospital for assessment (or for assessment followed by medical treatment) for at least a limited period; or

        (ii) that his detention as aforesaid is justified in the interests of his own health or safety or with a view to the protection of other persons;

    (b) the Tribunal shall direct the discharge of a patient liable to be detained otherwise than under section 2 above if they are not satisfied—

        (i) that he is then suffering from mental illness, psychopathic disorder, severe mental impairment or mental impairment or from any of those forms of disorder of a nature or degree which makes it appropriate for him to be liable to be detained in a hospital for medical treatment; or

        (ii) that it is necessary for the health of safety of the patient or for the protection of other persons that he should receive such treatment; or

        (iii) . . . that the patient, if released, would be likely to act in a manner dangerous to other persons or to himself.

Notice that for continued detention to be justified, the patient has to be suffering from a mental disorder of a *nature or degree* which warrants detention in hospital. An important word here is 'or': a patient might be suffering from a disorder whose *nature* warrants detention in hospital, but to a *degree* which does not. In *R v Mental Health*

Review Tribunal for the South Thames Region, ex parte Smith,[92] the court held that this means that someone might be detained on the grounds that the condition from which they are suffering generally justifies detention, even if at the time of the application, they are not affected to a 'degree' which warrants detention in hospital. The draft Mental Health Bill retains this wording. It has, however, been criticized by Peter Bartlett and Ralph Sandland:

Peter Bartlett and Ralph Sandland[93]

[T]he requirement in *Winterwerp* is for unsound mind sufficient to 'justify' detention, and we would want to argue, as has not been done to date before the European Court, that a test which allows nature 'or' degree permits detention when a person's disorder is of a nature but *not* of a degree to justify compulsory hospitalisation, which is outwith the spirit of the Convention. In our, perhaps optimistic, view, the preferable and Convention-compliant wording must be that the mental disorder in question is of both a nature *and* a degree to warrant detention.

Each MHRT must have at least one legal, medical and lay member, and most will contain just these three individuals. If the MHRT decides that the criteria for admission are not made out, it must order the patient's discharge. Discharge can however be deferred, if arrangements have to be made for the patient's accommodation and/or care. Tribunals do not generally assess the lawfulness of the initial detention, but rather whether the grounds for detention exist at the time of the hearing. If a patient wishes to challenge the legality of her initial detention, she must apply for judicial review, or seek a writ of habeas corpus.

The MHRT must give reasons for its decision. Where there is conflicting evidence, the MHRT must explain, in language that can be understood by the patient herself, why one witness's evidence was preferred. In *R v Ashworth Hospital Authority, ex parte H*,[94] the MHRT ordered the immediate discharge of a patient, despite the fact that five out of six medical reports had been against discharge. The Court of Appeal found that this decision was *Wednesbury* unreasonable, since no reasonable tribunal could have come to this decision in the light of the evidence before it, and furthermore that the tribunal's reasons—namely that it simply preferred the evidence of the one doctor who believed discharge to be appropriate—were insufficient.

In practice, orders for the discharge of patients are comparatively rare. Of over 11,000 hearings each year, orders for discharge are made in approximately 10 per cent of cases,[95] although there does appear to be considerable regional variation in the rates of discharge.

It is possible to appeal against an MHRT decision on a point of law under section 78 of the Mental Health Act 1983. For example in *Bone v Mental Health Review Tribunal*[96] a patient applied under section 78 for the tribunal's decision to be quashed

---

[92] *The Times* 9 Dec 1998.
[93] P Bartlett and R Sandland, *Mental Health Law: Policy and Practice* (2nd edn OUP Oxford 2003) 466.
[94] [2003] 1 WLR 127.
[95] Department of Health, *Mental Health Review Tribunal Report April 1999 to March 2001* (DoH London 2001). See also E Perkins, *Decision-making in Mental Health Review Tribunals* (DoH London 2000) and G Richardson and D Machin, 'A Clash of Values? Mental Health Review Tribunals and Judicial Review' (1999) 1 Journal of Mental Health Law 3.
[96] [1985] 3 All ER 330.

on the grounds that it had erred in law by not giving sufficiently clear reasons for its decision. Because it will allow broader consideration of the issues, tribunals' decisions are more commonly challenged through applications for judicial review, usually on the grounds of illegality.

Recall that under Article 5(4) of the Human Rights Act, anyone who has been compulsorily detained must have a right to challenge the lawfulness of her detention in a court, and the court must decide this issue 'speedily'. The question of how 'speedy' the legal challenge must be to satisfy Article 5(4) arose in the following case.

R (on the application of C) v Mental Health Review Tribunal[97]

C had been detained in hospital under section 3 of the Mental Health Act 1983 and immediately applied to the MHRT for discharge. It was the practice of the MHRT to list hearings of applications for discharge eight weeks after the application had been made. C submitted that the practice was arbitrary, and did not satisfy the Human Rights Act 1998 Sch. 1 Part I Art. 5(4) which specified that the lawfulness of a detention should be determined 'speedily'.

Lord Phillips MR

My conclusion is that the practice of fixing hearing dates eight weeks after the date of application is bred of administrative convenience, not of administrative necessity. There is nothing inconsistent with article 5(4) of the Convention in having a target date of eight weeks maximum. The circumstances of some cases may well require eight weeks' preparation for the hearing. In such cases an eight-week period will not conflict with the requirement of article 5(4) that the decision on the application must be obtained speedily.

When the eight-week target was introduced, I can understand the temptation, and perhaps even the need, initially to list cases so as to make use of the whole of the target period . . . What seems to have occurred is that an eight-week lead time for hearings has become the rule when an application is made by a section 3 patient.

I do not consider lawful a practice which makes no effort to see that the individual application is heard as soon as reasonably practicable, having regard to the relevant circumstances of the case. Such a practice will inevitably result in some applications not leading to the speedy decision required by article 5(4). The present case is an instance of this result.

Similarly, in *R v Mental Health Review Tribunal, ex parte KB*[98] a conjoined application was brought by a number of patients who had waited between 4 and 27 weeks for a hearing. The reasons for the delays included difficulties in preparing reports and in timetabling tribunal hearings. Stanley Burton J found that lack of resources did not offer a defence to the breach of Article 5(4):

Under Article 5(4), it is for the state to ensure speedy hearings of detained patients' applications. The state must establish such Tribunals or courts and provide such resources, as will provide speedy hearings. It is therefore irrelevant to the question whether there has been an infringement of Article 5(4) which government department or other public authority was at fault.

In *R v MHRT, ex parte B*[99] effective case management would have avoided the delay of nine months for a tribunal hearing, and Scott Baker J again held that there had been a breach of Article 5(4):

---

[97] [2002] 1 WLR 176.   [98] [2002] EWHC 639 (Admin).   [99] [2002] All ER (D) 304 (Jul).

A delay does not of itself give rise to a breach of Article 5(4), but it does give rise to the need for an explanation. . . . The delay in this case of eight and a half months is so long as to call for an explanation by the state (represented in this instance by the Tribunal). No adequate explanation has been forthcoming, albeit it is plain that with effective case management the substantive hearing would have taken place a great deal earlier without in any way prejudicing B's right to a fair hearing. I have come to the conclusion that the lawfulness of B's detention was not decided speedily in this case and that therefore there is a breach of Article 5(4) of the ECHR.

The next important question which arises is the burden of proof. In its original form, the Mental Health Act 1983 required the patient to prove that continued detention is no longer justified. In effect, this amounts to a presumption against discharge: if the patient cannot prove that her detention is unjustified, the default position will be that detention continues. However, under the Human Rights Act there should be a presumption in favour of liberty, and it is for those seeking to detain a patient to prove that continued detention is justified.

This issue arose in *R (on the application of H) v Mental Health Review Tribunal*.[100] The Court of Appeal decided that section 72 of the Mental Health Act 1983 was incompatible with Article 5 of the Convention in so far as it imposed the burden of proof on the patient to establish that detention was unjustified, rather than requiring discharge if it cannot be proved that the criteria for admission continue to be satisfied. In response to this case, the wording of the Mental Health Act was amended by the Mental Health Act 1983 (Remedial) Order 2001.[101] Now it is for those who are arguing against the patient's discharge to prove that the patient *does* meet the criteria for detention, and not for the patient to prove that she *does not.*

If the responsible medical officer (RMO) disagrees with the tribunal's decision to order a patient's discharge, is there anything to stop her simply readmitting the patient under section 3? Of course, if circumstances have changed dramatically between the time of the tribunal hearing and the time of readmission, then this might be legitimate. But where there has not been a substantial change of circumstances, RMOs should not attempt to override the tribunal's decision through a new admission.

In *R v East London and the City Mental Health NHS Trust, ex p Von Brandenburg*[102] the patient's discharge had been ordered by an MHRT, but had been deferred for seven days so that suitable accommodation could be found. Six days later, the patient's RMO arranged for his readmission under section 3 of the Mental Health Act 1983. The patient sought judicial review of the decision to readmit him. The House of Lords found that there might be circumstances when it would be lawful to readmit a patient despite a tribunal's decision to discharge her, but that these would depend upon the approved social worker (ASW) forming the reasonable and bona fide belief that she had information not known by the tribunal which put a different complexion on the case. Resectioning is therefore only appropriate where material facts have subsequently come to light, and must not be used by ASWs in order to trump tribunal decisions with which they disagree.

---

100 [2001] EWCA Civ 415, [2001] 3 WLR 512.   101 SI 2001/3712.
102 [2003] UKHL 58 (Transcript on Lexis).

Lord Bingham

[A]n ASW may not lawfully apply for the admission of a patient whose discharge has been ordered by the decision of a mental health review Tribunal of which the ASW is aware unless the ASW has formed the reasonable and bona fide opinion that he has information not known to the Tribunal which puts a significantly different complexion on the case as compared with that which was before the Tribunal. It is impossible and undesirable to attempt to describe in advance the information which might justify such an opinion. I give three hypothetical examples by way of illustration only:

The issue at the Tribunal is whether the patient, if discharged, might cause harm to himself. The Tribunal, on the evidence presented, discounts that possibility and directs the discharge of the patient. After the hearing, the ASW learns of a fact previously unknown to him, the doctors attending the patient and the Tribunal: that the patient had at an earlier date made a determined attempt on his life. Having taken medical advice, the ASW judges that this information significantly alters the risk as assessed by the Tribunal.

At the Tribunal hearing the patient's mental condition is said to have been stabilised by the taking of appropriate medication. The continuing stability of the patient's mental condition is said to depend on his continuing to take that medication. The patient assures the Tribunal of his willingness to continue to take medication and, on the basis of that assurance, the Tribunal directs the discharge of the patient. Before or after discharge the patient refuses to take the medication or communicates his intention to refuse. Having taken medical advice, the ASW perceives a real risk to the patient or others if the medication is not taken.

After the Tribunal hearing, and whether before or after discharge, the patient's mental condition significantly deteriorates so as to present a degree of risk or require treatment or supervision not evident at the hearing.

In cases such as these the ASW may properly apply for the admission of a patient, subject of course to obtaining the required medical support, notwithstanding a Tribunal decision directing discharge.

(b) DISCHARGE UNDER THE DRAFT MENTAL HEALTH BILL

The Bill will allow patients to appeal against their detention at any time during the first 28 days, and again during any further assessment period. Because the new tribunal will have the power to make compulsory treatment orders, which can last for up to six months, any appeal during the 28-day assessment period could result in a treatment order, thus offering patients a disincentive to appealing at all. Questions of natural justice might also arise if the patient's appeal against detention could be heard by exactly the same tribunal as authorized their detention. How likely is this tribunal to overturn its own previous decision? Because the Bill specifies that only the tribunal has the power to authorize discharge, it raises the possibility that patients whose clinical supervisors believe they should be discharged may nevertheless continue to be detained.

8. COMMUNITY CARE

As we have seen, there has been a marked trend away from inpatient care towards what is euphemistically known as 'care in the community'. Community care has two purposes: first to ensure that mentally disordered individuals have access to appropriate treatment, and secondly to exercise some degree of control and supervision over their behaviour. In general it takes the form of primary care provision from GPs, and aftercare services provided to people who have been discharged from hospital.

(a) COMMUNITY CARE UNDER THE 1983 ACT

Section 46 of the National Health Service and Community Care Act 1990 requires local authorities to ensure that a wide variety of services are available to mentally disordered people living in the community. These services are provided by social workers and community psychiatric nurses, often as part of community mental health teams. Section 117 of the Mental Health Act 1983 requires primary care trusts, or health authorities and social service departments, in co-operation with voluntary agencies, to provide aftercare services to those who have been discharged from detention under the Act.

Usually aftercare services involve medical treatment; help with accommodation; and assistance with education and training. Although initially there was some confusion over whether local authorities were entitled to charge patients for services provided under section 117, the House of Lords in *R v Manchester City Council, ex parte Stennett*[103] agreed with the Court of Appeal that the exceptional vulnerability of compulsorily detained patients meant that aftercare services for this class must be provided free of charge, even though it was estimated that this would cost between £30 million and £80 million per year. Since section 117 applies only to previously detained patients, informal patients who leave hospital will not necessarily receive free aftercare services, anther anomaly thrown up by the sharp distinction drawn under the Act between informal and detained patients. The government has said that the new Bill will provide for free aftercare for six weeks after discharge, but thereafter discharged patients will be subject to means-testing, in the same way as informal outpatients.[104]

It is clear that there is a *duty* to provide aftercare services. In *R v Ealing District Health Authority, ex parte Fox*[105] Otton J held that once a tribunal has ordered a conditional discharge, the health authority must ensure that the appropriate arrangements are in place:

a district health authority is under a duty under s 117 of the Mental Health Act 1983 to provide after-care services when a patient leaves hospital, and acts unlawfully in failing to seek to make practical arrangements for after-care prior to that patient's discharge from hospital where such

---

[103] [2002] UKHL 34, [2002] 2 AC 1127.
[104] *Government Response to the Report of the Joint Committee on the Draft Mental Health Bill 2004* (DoH London 2005) <http://www.dh.gov.uk/assetRoot/04/11/52/68/04115268.pdf>.
[105] [1993] 1 WLR 373.

arrangements are required by a mental health review Tribunal in order to enable the patient to be conditionally discharged from hospital.

But what if a health authority cannot find healthcare professionals who are prepared to take responsibility for a patient's treatment after discharge? This was the issue in *Fox*, where no psychiatrist was willing to treat F in the community, and Otton J found that the court could not compel a psychiatrist to act contrary to his clinical judgment:

I agree . . . that it would not be appropriate to make an order of mandamus to compel the health authority at this stage to provide psychiatric supervision in the community for the applicant. I accept his contention that such an order would in effect compel a doctor to supervise a patient against the doctor's will where the doctor's refusal arises from an honestly held clinical judgment that the treatment is not in the patient's best interests or is not in the best interests of the community in which the supervision would take place.

This was followed in *Camden and Islington Health Authority, ex parte K*.[106] Again it had proved impossible to find a psychiatrist willing to supervise the applicant's care in the community, and Lord Phillips suggested that section 117 should not be taken to impose an absolute and unworkable obligation on health authorities:

section 117 imposes on health authorities a duty to provide aftercare facilities for the benefit of patients who are discharged from mental hospitals. The nature and extent of those facilities must, to a degree, fall within the discretion of the health authority, which must have regard to other demands on its budget . . .

I can see no justification for interpreting section 117 so as to impose on health authorities an absolute obligation to satisfy any conditions that a Tribunal may specify as prerequisites to the discharge of a patient. . . . An interpretation of section 117 which imposed on health authorities absolute duties which they would not necessarily be able to perform would be manifestly unreasonable.

Of course, if a patient is no longer sufficiently mentally disordered to justify detention in hospital, then the failure to facilitate her release might amount to a breach of Article 5(4). However, where a patient's release is conditional upon the provision of services, it might, as Lord Phillips suggests, be possible to argue that, in the absence of those services, she continues to be sufficiently mentally disordered to justify detention under Article 5:

If a health authority is unable, despite the exercise of all reasonable endeavours, to procure for a patient the level of care and treatment in the community that a Tribunal considers to be a prerequisite to the discharge of the patient from hospital, I do not consider that the continued detention of the patient in hospital will violate the right to liberty conferred by article 5.

K then appealed to the European Court of Human Rights, which confirmed that there had been no violation of Article 5(1)(e). The ECHR held that:

As events in the present case showed, the treatment considered necessary for such conditional discharge may not prove available, in which circumstances there can be no question of interpreting Article 5 § 1(e) as requiring the applicant's discharge without the conditions necessary for

---

[106] [2001] 3 WLR 553.

protecting herself and the public or as imposing an absolute obligation on the authorities to ensure that the conditions are fulfilled.[107]

R v Secretary of State for the Home Department, ex parte IH[108] was another case in which despite the MHRT finding that the grounds for continued detention were not met, it proved impossible to find a psychiatrist willing to supervise IH in the community, and hence the conditions attached to his discharge could not be met. In these circumstances, the House of Lords found that there had been no violation of Article 5(1)(e) and continued detention remained lawful despite the tribunal's order. Lord Bingham held that:

The duty of the health authority, whether under s 117 of the 1983 Act or in response to the Tribunal's order of 3 February 2000, was to use its best endeavours to procure compliance with the conditions laid down by the Tribunal. This it did. It was not subject to an absolute obligation to procure compliance and was not at fault in failing to do so. It had no power to require any psychiatrist to act in a way which conflicted with the conscientious professional judgment of that psychiatrist.

Care in the community can also be provided via the appointment of a guardian under section 7 of the Act. A guardianship application can be made by an approved social worker or the patient's nearest relative. The patient must be over the age of 16, and two medical practitioners must certify that she is suffering from mental illness, psychopathic disorder, severe mental impairment, or mental impairment of a nature which warrants reception into guardianship, and that it is necessary in the interests of the welfare of the patient or for the protection of other persons that the patient should be so received.[109] The intention is to ensure that the individual has a safe and secure environment, rather than to provide treatment for her disorder; as a result there is no 'treatability' requirement. The nearest relative has a right of veto, so no guardianship application can succeed in the face of their objection, it is however possible to apply to replace the nearest relative, if, for example, the approved social worker believes that the relative is exercising the right of veto unreasonably.

Under section 8, the guardian has certain powers, such as the power to decide where the patient should live; to require access to the patient's place of residence; and to ensure the patient attends hospital for treatment. There is no power to compel the patient to actually receive treatment, however, and no sanctions are available to the guardian if she is unable to exercise her powers. As a result, guardianship orders are effective only where the patient is relatively compliant, when the order is, in practice, probably unnecessary. Unsurprisingly, therefore, guardianship is used comparatively infrequently. Nicola Glover-Thomas explains that:

The guardian's lack of powers has created despondency and led to the growing debate about community treatment orders and the future of community care . . . In practice guardianship has failed to live up to expectations and has not provided a workable community care measure.[110]

---

[107] *Kolanis v United Kingdom* (APP NO 517/02) [2005] All ER (D) 227 (Jun).
[108] [2003] UKHL 59 (Transcript).   [109] Section 7(2).
[110] Nicola Glover-Thomas, *Reconstructing Mental Health Law and Policy* (Butterworths London 2002) 79–80.

One attempt to overcome the difficulty of providing effective care in the community came before the courts in *R v Hallstrom, ex parte W*.[111] The patient had been sectioned, but the intention had been that they would remain on leave from hospital, under section 17. Section 17 is normally used as part of a detained patient's treatment plans in order to facilitate their eventual reintegration into the community. In *Hallstrom*, there had been no intention to detain the patient, and compulsory detention, coupled with the granting of leave under section 17, was operating as a 'long leash', enabling greater supervision, and leaving open the possibility of compulsory treatment. McCullough J held that the criteria for the use of compulsory powers were not satisfied where it was not necessary for the patient to be treated in hospital. This was overruled by the Court of Appeal in *B v Barking, Havering and Brentwood Community NHS Trust*,[112] which held that renewal of a section 3 order while a patient was on leave was possible provided that the patient's treatment required some inpatient care. Extended leave can therefore be used in order to assist the patient's rehabilitation within the community, provided some element of inpatient treatment is envisaged.

In 1995, the Mental Health (Patients in the Community) Act inserted a new section 25A into the 1983 Act. This introduced the possibility of 'aftercare under supervision'. Under a supervised discharge order, the patient can be discharged from hospital but remain supervised within the community. Such patients are assigned to a supervisor who is supposed to ensure that appropriate after-care arrangements are in place, and to a community medical officer who is supposed to make sure that they receive appropriate treatment. Under section 25A(4), supervised discharge orders can only be made where

(a) [the patient] is suffering from mental disorder, being mental illness, severe mental impairment, psychopathic disorder or mental impairment;

(b) there would be a substantial risk of serious harm to the health or safety of the patient or the safety of other persons, or of the patient being seriously exploited if he were not to receive the after-care services to be provided for him under section 117 . . . after he leaves hospital; and

(c) his being subject to after-care under supervision is likely to help to secure that he receives the after-care services to be so provided.

The supervision order may further specify where the patient should live and can require her to attend specific places for treatment or education, with the power to take and convey the patient to hospital if necessary. In practice these orders have been little used because patients who refuse treatment must be brought back to hospital, and re-sectioned if necessary. The orders therefore add little to the existing powers to re-section individuals once the criteria for compulsion are once again met.

(b) THE FAILINGS OF COMMUNITY CARE

The failures of the community care system are well known. Homicides committed by mentally ill people who have been released into the community are commonly

---

[111] [1986] 2 All ER 306.   [112] [1999] 1 FLR 106.

pointed to as evidence of insufficient care and control of mentally disordered individuals living in the community. The media coverage of a few cases in which discharged mental patients have killed strangers has undoubtedly led to public support for measures which impose greater control over mentally disordered individuals. In practice, however, the evidence is equivocal. The Report of the National Confidential Inquiry into Suicide and Homicide by People with Mental Illness found that a third of all homicides were committed by people who had had a diagnosis of mental disorder, and 15 per cent had symptoms of mental illness when they committed the offence.[113] However, mentally ill individuals were in fact less likely to kill a stranger than those who were not mentally ill. Certainly there does not seem to be any connection between community care policies and homicide rates: Taylor and Gunn's 1999 study found that the number of mentally ill persons committing homicides had declined by 3 per cent each year for the past four decades.[114]

It is also perhaps interesting that other factors which are implicated in the homicide statistics, such as alcohol use, do not lead to the same levels of public anxiety and desire for greater surveillance and control of alcohol users. In the next extract, Brenda Hoggett suggests that if dangerousness is really the criterion for preventative detention, it makes no sense to single out dangerous people who happen to be mentally disordered.

Brenda Hoggett[115]

But what about the people who are really dangerous? Society may have a right to protect itself against them, whether or not they are responsible, and even if there is nothing the medical profession can do for them. This should be a very limited category. We should make it quite clear what we mean by dangerousness. We should be sure that the event of danger presented is sufficient to justify the level of intervention. And we should be able to separate those who are dangerous from those who are not with a higher degree of reliability than we can at present. Mental disorder as such is not the criterion. There are plenty of sane people who are dangerous, and plenty of insane people who are not. If we are going to deprive people of either proportionality or the normal principles of guilt and innocence in order to protect society against serious risk, we should be concentrating on the accurate identification and discovery of that risk and on nothing else.

In any event, people with mental health problems who receive inadequate care in the community are in fact much more likely to harm themselves than others, and the suicide rate of people who have been discharged from hospital is high. Too often patients living in the community 'fall through the net' and do not receive appropriate treatment.

---

[113] *Safety First: Five Year Report of the National Confidential Inquiry into Suicide and Homicide by People with Mental Illness* (DoH 2001).

[114] P Taylor and J Gunn, 'Homicides by People with Mental Illness: Myth and Reality' (1999) 174 British Journal of Psychiatry 9.

[115] *Mental Health Law* (4th edn Sweet & Maxwell London 1996) 131.

(c) COMMUNITY CARE UNDER THE DRAFT
MENTAL HEALTH BILL

One of the central reforms introduced by the draft Mental Health Bill is the possibility of compulsion in the community, under which patients may be placed under a duty to make themselves available for treatment. These will only be available if the patient has already been formally admitted to hospital at least once. Community Treatment Orders (CTOs) are intended to ensure that patients receive necessary treatment in the least restrictive environment, so that an individual judged to be in need of compulsory treatment does not necessarily have to be detained in hospital for that treatment to be provided.

CTOs have, however, been subject to a number of criticisms. First, it has been suggested that patient trust, and in particular a patient's willingness to seek out psychiatric services will be compromised by the prospect of compulsion in the community. In the next extract Fiona Caldicott et al. point out that compulsion in the community is rejected for physical illnesses on the grounds that patients might avoid contact with health services, and they question why similar arguments are not accepted in the context of mental illness.

Fiona Caldicott, Edna Conlan, and Anthony Zigmund[116]

Patients rightly fear the associated reduction in their autonomy and the increased stigma of being made subject to such an order, where patients suffering from physical illnesses are not compulsorily medicated in the community. Patients ask why it is that any prospective deterioration in their condition through failure to follow medical advice should be subject to compulsion? If the answer seeks justification in the risk that such failure poses a danger to the well-being of others, why is it that diabetics or epileptics who fail adequately to follow a prescribed medical regime should nonetheless still be able, for example, to drive their cars (until such time as their licence is removed based on a report from their doctor), without them being removed to hospital for forcible administration of a sticky bun or insulin (as appropriate) or of an anti-convulsant? Were this the case, is it not likely that even more patients suffering from disorders that might bring them within the ambit of state control would find ways to avoid contact with the medical profession in order never to risk being subject to such coercive care? In summary, such a response runs a high risk of being anti-therapeutic. If the argument is so readily understood in respect of HIV and sexually transmitted diseases (ie that we need confidentiality if patients are to volunteer themselves for treatment and thereby reduce the aggregate risk and extent of suffering) why is it seemingly so hard to understand that marking out those with mental disorders as suitable for subjection to a coercive regime is likely, in the short term in respect of that patient and in the long term in respect of the body of patients, to reduce overall patient compliance? . . .

It has been strongly argued that a programme of care in the community is likely only to be capable of substantially helping those who are prepared to volunteer for it; the potentially negative impact of a regime of coerced care is all too evident.

Secondly, Judith Laing queries whether community treatment orders will genuinely represent the least restrictive alternative.

---

[116] 'Client and Clinician—Law as an Intrusion' in N Eastman and J Peay (eds), *Law Without Enforcement: Integrating Mental Health and Justice* (Hart Publishing Oxford 1999) 75–88, 79–80.

Judith Laing[117]

The government's assertion that the community treatment order is justified on the basis of providing a less restrictive alternative is also debatable and somewhat 'illusory'. Opponents of compulsory community treatment allege that it is a controlling mechanism and will not be the least restrictive alternative due to the fact that it actually increases the potential for monitoring and controlling people's lives . . . There are also limits as to the type of 'therapy' that can be administered against the patient's will in the community. Inevitably, compulsory treatment in the community will consist of depot medication [an injection which releases a drug slowly over several weeks] and controversial physical treatments such as ECT. It is also argued that compulsory community orders could act as a 'hazard' and a disincentive for patients to seek help . . . Indeed, compulsory community orders may well exacerbate the problems faced by the mentally ill by increasing the stigma directed towards them as well as the discrimination and social exclusion experienced by them.

Thirdly, in the next extract, Patricia Walton, writing from the perspective of an Approved Social Worker (ASW), suggests that, in any event, a patient's refusal to take psychotropic drugs may not be a decision which needs to be treated by compulsion, rather it may be a rational response to the unpleasant side effects of these drugs.

Patricia Walton[118]

ASWs are strongly opposed to compulsion in the community on social and human rights grounds: some people find the drug effects intolerable; some people find relentless awareness of their circumstances intolerable; the risks of suicide and other effects of unwanted long term drug treatment have not been considered; psychiatric treatments can be harmful; the impact of forcible treatment on the family and within the community have not been considered; a person's home should be a safe haven; people ultimately have the right to choose ill health . . . In the experience of ASWs, when people stop taking medication there is often complex interplay of reasons and the thinking around compulsory community treatment takes a simplistic view of this . . . In their experience many, possibly most, people on long-term medication choose to come off it from time to time, to be free of side-effects or to achieve a feeling of autonomy.

Fourthly, it is also important to remember that the criteria for compulsion in the community will inevitably include more people than the 1983 Act. Under the current legislation, patients can only be subject to compulsory treatment orders if it is necessary for them to be *detained in hospital*. If it is no longer necessary to prove that detention is justified before treatment can be given compulsorily, more patients will qualify and, numerically at least, the potential infringement of civil liberties and interference with patients' private lives, will be greater. Indeed the Royal College of Psychiatrists has warned that:

By removing the conditions of needing to be ill enough to warrant admission to hospital patients may become subject to compulsion despite suffering from only very mild illnesses.[119]

Finally, CTOs disproportionately emphasize the compulsory administration of medication, at the expense of other services, such as psychotherapy, and help with housing

---

[117] 'Rights Versus Risk? Reform of the Mental Health Act 1983' (2000) 8 Medical Law Review 210–50, 240.

[118] 'Reforming the Mental Health Act 1983: an approved social worker perspective' (2000) 22 Journal of Social Welfare and Family Law 410–14, 410.

[119] *Evidence Submitted to the Joint Committee on the Draft Mental Health Bill* (RCP 2004) 17.

and employment, which may be equally important in helping patients to function in the community. As Nicola Glover-Thomas suggests in the next extract, it is not clear that the lack of compulsory powers is the principal reason for the failures of the community care policy.

Nicola Glover-Thomas[120]

[T]wo . . . key factors . . . contributed to the failure of community care. One of the most startling oversights has been the disregard of housing provision and its role in the integration of patients into the community. . . . It has been acknowledged that 'adequate housing has a major role to play in community care and is often the key to independent living'. It is essential that released psychiatric patients be provided with an adequate base in the community. Indeed, its importance should not be underestimated. In *The Report into the Care and Treatment of Christopher Clunis* it was observed that Christopher Clunis had been 'treated as . . . single, homeless, and itinerant with no family ties', and the more they treated him as such the more he began to fulfil that role. The improvement of his condition was hampered by spasmodic homelessness resulting in loss of contact with the mental health structure . . .

A second factor which has prevented the effective integration of psychiatric patients into the community is the lack of occupational/employment prospects and the social activity associated with these opportunities. Patients in psychiatric facilities are offered a ready-made social setting, which enables them to improve essential skills for independent living in the community. Opportunities to maintain these skills need to be made available once the patient has been discharged. Regular social activity is an inherent part of the community care policy, for such integration helps to obliterate the social 'outcast' which has commonly been associated with released patients in the past . . . However the clear benefits associated with these occupational opportunities have been threatened, because of the high levels of disability discrimination and ongoing problems with stigma.

9. ALTERNATIVE APPROACHES

As should be evident, there is much dissatisfaction among academic commentators and those working in the mental health field with the turn that the draft legislation has taken. But if the draft Bill is not the best way forward, what alternative approaches might there be? In the next extract, Nigel Eastman and Jill Peay argue that detention and treatment without consent should only be possible (a) if the patient lacks capacity, or (b) under some dangerousness criterion, and that the two routes to admission should be clearly separated in order to avoid stigmatizing those who suffer from mental illness.

Nigel Eastman and Jill Peay[121]

We are not alone in suggesting that thought ought to be given to replacing our current structure of mental health law, possibly with generic legislation separately covering incapacity and dangerousness, and certainly by legislation which puts on an equal footing the treatment of mental and physical disorders. Whilst it has been argued that the discriminatory locus is in attitudes towards

---

[120] *Reconstructing Mental Health Law and Policy* (Butterworths London 2002) 146–7.
[121] 'Afterword: Integrating Mental Health and Justice' in N Eastman and J Peay (eds), *Law Without Enforcement: Integrating Mental Health and Justice* (Hart Publishing Oxford 1999) 197–218, 212, 215.

those with mental disorders and not in the law *per se*, we would argue that the special presence of the law underpins these discriminatory attitudes and sustains discriminatory treatment . . .

Generic dangerousness legislation with tightly drawn criteria based on established behaviour and a clear and present threat is attractive if only because it is likely to make us think seriously abvout the need for protection of the rights of offenders, rather than confusing the advantages of dangerousness legislation with a therapeutic justification. Moreover, since most dangerous people are not mentally ill the balance of any generic legislation would immediately shift the focus of attention away from those suffering from mental disorder . . . Where the evidence is that mentally disordered people are in the aggregate little more dangerous . . . than other citizens and that it is substance abuse that most significantly raises the rate of violence in both patient and comparison groups, it is wrong that the mentally disordered in general should be tainted with an association with these high risk offenders.

Similarly, Michael Gunn advocates separating what he describes as the 'police power' to detain individuals who pose a threat to others, from incapacity, which he agrees should be the only other justification for detention and treatment without consent.

Michael Gunn[122]

An acceptable alternative to the police power of the State would be the right to admit someone not capable of making decisions about treatment for their own mental health. A capacity based alternative would permit a short term admission to assess capacity, where there was uncertainty about the individual's ability to make the relevant decisions. In the case of both bases for compulsory admission there would be the usual procedural protections, such as the requirement that hospitalisation be the least restrictive alternative for provision of the treatment that was deemed necessary. Length of permissible detention would need to be reliant upon the continuing existence of the mental health problem and of either the need for the protection of others or the incapacity of the person admitted (dependent upon the basis for the original detention).

What treatment and care can be provided once a person has been admitted might be justifiable on two streams. Where the person is admitted on the basis of the police power, such treatment only as to reduce the risks to others that the person presents would be permissible. Where the person is admitted on the basis of incapacity, the treatment should be aimed at (a) making the person capable where possible, and (b) in the interim, providing him or her with treatment that is necessary whether for his or her mental or physical needs (necessary being determined by the time scale of incapacity and whether it is possible to wait for capacity to be acquired/recovered) . . .

If my argument were to be followed, capacity would be central, where the police power was not being used. . . . [The Government's proposed reforms] potentially involve long term incarceration without the subject having been found guilty of a crime, but on the basis of predicted (and then presumed) dangerousness. If justifiable, it must be by analogy with quarantine laws, that is the removal of a person from an environment where he or she will cause significant harm that can only be prevented by that removal. This places enormous reliance upon the accuracy of dangerous prediction, a subject of considerable controversy.

The government disagrees with these suggestions on the grounds that they would fail to capture competent patients who might pose a risk to themselves, until such patients

---

[122] 'Reform of the Mental Health Act 1983: The Relevance of Capacity to Make Decisions' (2000) Journal of Mental Health Law 39–43, 41, 43.

were so ill that they lacked capacity.[123] But of course the government's position is seriously inconsistent with the rules governing the treatment of physically ill individuals, who are permitted, while they are competent, to refuse treatment even if that refusal will lead to their death. Moreover, as we saw in Chapter 4, the right to refuse treatment exists 'notwithstanding that the reasons for making the choice are rational, irrational, unknown or even non-existent'.[124] In contrast, the implication of the government's position is that it should be possible for competent patients, who happen to be mentally ill, to be detained and treated without consent, in order to protect them from themselves.

10. CONCLUSION

It is, in my view, hugely regrettable that reform of the Mental Health Act has proceeded almost entirely separately from the reform of the law relating to mental capacity, which we considered in Chapter 4. There is undoubtedly considerable overlap between the group of patients who lack decision-making capacity and those who suffer from mental illness. So for many mentally ill patients, it will be legitimate, both at common law and under the Mental Capacity Act 2005, to treat them without their consent according to the doctor's view of where their best interests lie. Protecting such patients from themselves is clearly justifiable. But for the sub-group of mentally ill patients who are competent, paternalism needs some further justification beyond the fact that the patient may pose a risk to themselves. As we saw in Chapter 4, competent patients who want to refuse life-saving treatment undoubtedly pose a risk to themselves, but this does not justify treating them without consent.

Is there something special about mental illness which justifies riding roughshod over the principle of patient autonomy? On the one hand, it is clear that some mental disorders create self-destructive desires, such as the desire to end one's life, which might be effectively treated by appropriate medication and/or therapy. On the other hand, the dependency and helplessness which result from *physical* illness can also lead to the desire to end one's life, and yet provided the patient remains competent, treatment without consent would plainly be unlawful. *Either* we have to argue that *all* patients who pose a risk to themselves lack capacity, *or*, to be consistent, we should have to rethink our commitment to respecting competent refusals of life-saving treatment. The compromise position embodied in the current and future mental health legislation, which permits *competent* mentally ill people to be treated without consent for their mental disorders, discriminates between identically situated patients on the grounds of mental illness, and on that basis alone, is seriously problematic.

Finally, it is to be hoped that any new Mental Health Act does not reproduce the draft Bill's profoundly misguided emphasis upon the risk mentally disordered individuals pose to others. It is undoubtedly true that there is a very small sub-set of mentally disordered people who are likely to be violent, but this is, of course, equally

---

[123] *Government Response to the Report of the Joint Committee on the Draft Mental Health Bill 2004* (DoH London 2005) <http://www.dh.gov.uk/assetRoot/04/11/52/68/04115268.pdf>.
[124] *Re T* [1993] Fam 95, *per* Lord Donaldson MR.

true of the population as a whole. A tiny minority of people, whether they are mentally ill or not, are simply more likely to commit violent offences than the rest of us. But our capacity to predict in advance who these people are is not sufficiently accurate to justify the deprivation of liberty. And, in any event, the propensity to violence appears to correlate at least as much with substance abuse and drunkenness than it does with mental illness.

11. FURTHER READING

Bartlett, Peter, 'The Test of Compulsion in Mental Health Law: Capacity, Therapeutic Benefit and Dangerousness as Possible Criteria' (2003) 11 Medical Law Review 326–52.

Bartlett, P and Sandland, R, *Mental Health Law: Policy and Practice* (2nd edn OUP Oxford 2003).

Campbell, Tom and Heginbotham, Chris, *Mental Illness: Prejudice, Discrimination and the Law* (Dartmouth Aldershot 1991).

Eastman, N and Peay, J (eds), *Law Without Enforcement: Integrating Mental Health and Justice* (Hart Publishing Oxford 1999).

Fennell, Phil, *Treatment Without Consent: Law, Psychiatry and the Treatment of Mentally Disordered People since 1845* (Routledge London 1996).

Fennell, Phil, 'Inscribing Paternalism in the Law: Consent to Treatment and Mental Disorder' (1990) 17 Journal of Law and Society 29–51.

Fennell, Phil, 'Doctor Knows Best? Therapeutic Detention under Common Law, the Mental Health Act and the European Convention' (1998) 6 Medical Law Review 322–53.

Glover-Thomas, Nicola, *Reconstructing Mental Health Law and Policy* (Butterworths London 2002).

Gunn, Michael, 'Reform of the Mental Health Act 1983: The Relevance of Capacity to Make Decisions' (2000) Journal of Mental Health Law 39–43.

Laing, Judith, 'Rights Versus Risk? Reform of the Mental Health Act 1983' (2000) 8 Medical Law Review 210–50.

Lewis, Penney, 'Feeding Anorexic Patients Who Refuse Food' (1999) 7 Medical Law Review 21–37.

Peay, Jil, *Decisions and Dilemmas: Working with Mental Health Law* (Hart Publishing Oxford 2003).

Richardson, Genevra, 'Autonomy, Guardianship and Mental Disorder: One Problem, Two Solutions' (2002) 65 Modern Law Review 702–23.

Widdett, Ceri and Thomson, Michael, 'Justifying Treatment and Other Stories' (1997) 5 Feminist Legal Studies 77.

8

CLINICAL RESEARCH

1. CENTRAL ISSUES

1. Animal experiments usually precede trials involving human subjects. To obtain a licence from the Home Office, researchers have to establish that the use of animals is necessary, and must try to minimize animal suffering.

2. International codes of research ethics, such as the Nuremberg Code and the Helsinki Declaration, have established universally applicable principles of good research practice.

3. All research protocols must first be approved by an ethics committee.

4. Consent to participation in research must be both informed and voluntary. In particular, it is important to ensure that, when patients are enrolled in clinical trials, they understand that they are taking part in an experiment, rather than receiving treatment which their doctor believes to be in their best interests.

5. For incompetent subjects, consent must be sought from their 'representative', and a number of other protections exist to ensure that researchers only use people who lack capacity when the research could not be done on competent adults.

6. Some groups have routinely been excluded from clinical trials, and while this may be prompted by paternalistic concern for their welfare, the consequence is that it is impossible to know whether treatments are either safe or effective for members of these excluded groups.

7. Carrying out research in developing countries raises a number of distinctive and complex ethical issues.

2. INTRODUCTION

Without research medical progress would be impossible. New treatments can be tested on animals, but animal experiments will not always be able to fully predict the impact a treatment will have on humans. The toxicity of thalidomide, for example, had been investigated in animals, and yet its capacity to cause birth defects was not detected. Research on human subjects is the only way in which we can satisfactorily establish the effectiveness and safety of medical treatment. But while we all want the medical care that we receive to have been rigorously tested, serving as a research subject may pose risks to an individual's health. The principal question raised by the regulation of experiments involving human subjects is how to balance the competing interests of society (which wants all of its medical treatment to have been proved safe and effective), and the individual research subject (who does not want to be exposed to increased health risks).

Although research on human subjects is not the only time when medical law has to weigh the interests of society against the welfare of individuals—another example might be the duty to report contagious diseases—this balancing exercise offers a particularly good example of the conflict between deontological (duty-based) and teleological (consequentialist) reasoning that we considered in Chapter 1. If we adopt a strict utilitarian perspective, conducting research on a comparatively small number of people—with or without their consent—in order to benefit the rest of society through the provision of effective medical treatment might be justifiable, even if it poses a considerable risk to the health of the small pool of research subjects. In contrast, a deontological approach, such as that adopted by Hans Jonas in the next extract, would condemn any course of action that disregarded the rights, dignity and integrity of the individual research subject, regardless of the benefits to the rest of society. This would offend Kant's categorical imperative (see further p. 12), because we would be treating these individuals solely as a means to an end, and not as ends in themselves. Indeed Jonas would go further and say the subjects of experiments are treated as 'things'.

Hans Jonas[1]

What is wrong with making a person an experimental subject is not so much that we make him thereby a means (which happens in social contexts of all kinds), as that we make him a thing . . .

Mere 'consent' (mostly amounting to no more than permission) does not right this reification. The 'wrong' of it can only be made 'right' by such authentic identification with the cause that it is the subject's as well as the researcher's cause—whereby his role in its service is not just permitted by him, but *willed* . . . Ultimately, the appeal for volunteers should seek this free and generous endorsement, the appropriation of the research purpose into the person's own scheme of ends . . .

Let me say only in conclusion that if some of the practical implications of my reasonings are felt to work out toward a slower rate of progress, this should not cause too great dismay. Let us not forget that progress is an optional goal, not an unconditional commitment, and that its tempo in particular, compulsive as it may become, has nothing sacred about it. Let us also remember that a slower progress in the conquest of disease would not threaten society, grievous as it is to those who have to deplore that their particular disease be not yet conquered, but that society would indeed be threatened by the erosion of those moral values whose loss, possibly caused by too ruthless a pursuit of scientific progress, would make its most dazzling triumphs not worth having.

Both extreme utilitarianism and its opposite are unattractive and caricatured moral positions. In practice, most people adopt some sort of mixed approach, which takes into account both individual rights *and* the common good. We do not want to sacrifice some human beings' lives for the benefit of others, but at the same time we do not want to stifle medical progress by refusing to allow any experiments on human subjects. All attempts to regulate research therefore try to effect this sort of compromise between the need to promote medical progress by conducting research on humans, and the need to protect the wellbeing and integrity of individual research subjects.

Aside from people (such as Christian scientists) who would reject all medical interventions, everyone benefits from living in a society in which drugs and other treatments have been properly tested. It might therefore be argued that we are all

---

[1] 'Philosophical Reflections on Experimenting with Human Subjects' (1969) 98 Daedalus 219–47.

under a *moral* obligation to incur some inconvenience or slightly increased risk to our health by participating in medical research. If we wish to benefit from experiments on humans, but are not actually willing to take part in them ourselves, are we 'free-riding' on the sacrifices of others? We will consider this question in more detail later.

When thinking about how research on humans should be regulated, it is also important to remember that there are more interests at stake than just the individual research subject's concern for her own health, and society's interest in medical progress. As Paul McNeill explains in the next extract, the researcher herself has considerable *self-interest* in devising, carrying out and publishing interesting research. Her reputation, career progression and ability to secure funding in the future will largely depend upon whether she has conducted experiments which have yielded significant and publishable results. The desire for self-advancement creates a powerful incentive towards both going ahead with research despite an ethics committee's reservations, and falsifying results. Regulations must therefore minimize the risk that unethical research takes place in the first place, and ensure that unethical or fraudulent research practices are detected and condemned.

Paul M McNeill[2]

While society, or at least some individuals within it, *may* benefit from research, there are very direct and tangible benefits for the researcher. [Paul] Ramsey wrote that 'it is not only that medical benefits are attained by research but also that a man rises to the top in medicine by the success and significance of his research'. For this reason the scientist cannot be regarded as a disinterested party. The researcher's interest in his or her own advancement and standing may be an added pressure to cut corners and act in ways that are unsafe . . .

Instances of blatant disregard for subjects' welfare have understandably gained the most attention. However, it is likely that more harm has been caused (in total) by researchers who mean no harm but are unaware of the extent of risk to their patients. Their bias towards achieving the goals of their research may lead them to minimise, in their own thinking, the risks inherent in their research and give a disproportionate value to the research enterprise . . .

Scientists are as capable as any other group of pursuing their own interests to the exclusion of the interests of others.

Not only is the reputation of the researcher at stake, but sponsors of research—such as pharmaceutical companies—will, as Solomon Benatar points out, have considerable financial interests in the results of experiments on human subjects.

Solomon Benatar[3]

Clinical research has become a burgeoning activity in recent years, largely stimulated by the pharmaceutical industry's interest in new drugs with high marketing profiles . . . In industrialised countries . . . the major interest in large profitable markets for drugs has led to the proliferation of research on 'me too' drugs (with only marginal potential advantages [over existing drugs]) that may allow market niches to be captured. There is also a drive to develop 'lifestyle drugs' for improving the quality of life and alleviating the symptoms of old age. The desire to make vast sums of money from medicinal drugs can be viewed as a modern version of the gold rush. Why make

---

² *The Ethics and Politics of Human Experimentation* (CUP Cambridge 1993).
³ 'Avoiding Exploitation in Clinical Research' (2000) 9 Cambridge Quarterly of Healthcare Ethics 562–5, 562–3.

drugs for sick people who cannot afford them when one can make drugs for people with resources who seek marginal improvements or those who are well and will pay for the possibility of a healthier old age. Proliferation of clinical research, much of it promotional and of dubious scientific value, follows.

The World Trade Organization's TRIPS[4] Agreement imposes a minimum 20-year period of patent protection, allowing pharmaceutical companies a monopoly over the production and marketing of new drugs for at least 20 years. If a new medicine has been proved to be safe and effective in the treatment of a particular condition, the profit which can be made from its worldwide prescription will be phenomenal. The pharmaceutical industry is now one of Britain's principal manufacturing sectors, spending around £3 billion each year on research and development.[5]

In the UK, unlike research on animals[6] and on embryos,[7] there is no primary legislation governing the conduct of research on human subjects; nor is there a body of common law setting out the principles under which it is legitimate to experiment on human beings. Instead, trials on humans are regulated by a variety of national and international regulations and guidelines. In addition to international codes of research ethics, it is also important to remember that regulations in one country may exert indirect, but nevertheless significant control over research carried out in other countries. For example, the US licensing authority (the Food and Drug Administration, or FDA) insists that all drugs—except those used to treat life-threatening conditions—must have been subjected to placebo-controlled trials. As a result, pharmaceutical companies who wish to market their products in the exceptionally lucrative US market will have to comply with US regulations, even if the research in fact takes place elsewhere.

In this chapter, we begin with a brief summary of the rules governing experiments on animals, which will usually precede trials involving human subjects. Next we look at what is meant by 'research'. It is important to remember that not all medical research consists in the testing of new treatments or drugs. Epidemiological research, for example, may just involve tracking the incidence of a particular condition in the population, and thus raises different, and perhaps fewer ethical issues.

We then turn to examine the various international ethical codes, and the guidelines and regulations that exist in the UK, and we examine the role of ethics committees in authorizing and monitoring research. The subject's voluntary and informed consent to participation is widely believed to be what justifies exposing her to the risks inherent in a research trial, and we consider what qualifies as sufficiently 'voluntary' and 'informed' consent. If consent is a necessary precondition of ethical research, we also investigate whether, and in what circumstances, it would be legitimate to carry out research on those who *cannot* give consent.

We then examine whether the benefits and burdens of research participation are evenly distributed, drawing particular attention to the special issues raised when research is conducted in developing countries. Next, we review the question of publication ethics—could there be a duty to disseminate one's research findings, and

---

[4] Trade Related Aspects of Intellectual Property Rights.   [5] See further <http://www.abpi.org.uk>.
[6] Animals (Scientific Procedures) Act 1968.   [7] Human Fertilisation and Embryology Act 1990.

should unethical research ever be published? Finally, we look at the arrangements for compensation when individuals sustain injuries as a result of their participation in research.

3. ANIMAL EXPERIMENTS

In the UK, all research involving laboratory animals is regulated by the Animals (Scientific Procedures) Act 1986, which put into effect the requirements of a European directive.[8] The Act defines 'protected animals' as all non-human vertebrates and the common octopus; insects such as fruit flies are also commonly used in research but are not protected by the legislation.

Before any experiment can be carried out on a protected animal, a licence must first have been obtained from the Home Office. Licences will be issued only when the scientific objectives cannot be achieved without using animals; and experiments must minimize animal suffering. The Home Office employs an inspectorate, consisting of doctors and veterinarians, to advise on all applications for licences.

Under section 3 of the Act, the laboratory, the individual researcher and the project itself must each be separately approved.

Animals (Scientific Procedures) Act 1986
3. No person shall apply a regulated procedure to an animal unless—

   (a) he holds a personal licence qualifying him to apply a regulated procedure of that description to an animal of that description;

   (b) the procedure is applied as part of a programme of work specified in a project licence authorising the application, as part of that programme, of a regulated procedure of that description to an animal of that description; and

   (c) the place where the procedure is carried out is a place specified in the personal licence and the project licence.

These three authorizations will be granted only if:

- the individual researcher has the necessary skills and training (Personal Licence); and

- the object of the research cannot be achieved in other ways and the likely benefits of the research justify any likely distress to the animals (Project Licence); and

- the laboratory has the necessary facilities and staff to house and care for the animals properly (Certificate of Designation).

To obtain a Personal Licence, the individual researcher must have been on an approved training course covering the law and ethics of animal research; the basics of caring for animals; and ways of recognizing symptoms of illness or distress. The Personal Licence will specify both the techniques and the species of animal which the individual is entitled to use.

[8] 86/609/EEC.

To obtain a Certificate of Designation, a laboratory must meet strict Home Office criteria on staffing, veterinary care, and the quality of housing, lighting, ventilation and temperature control. Each laboratory must have a 'Named Veterinary Surgeon' and a 'Named Animal Care and Welfare Officer', both of whom are responsible for protecting the health and welfare of the animals within the laboratory.

Before applying for a Project Licence, the researchers must first have been subject to a local ethical review process. Once the project has been approved locally, an application can be made to the Home Office. Under section 4(3) of the Act, the Secretary of State can only issue licences for certain research purposes, and the need to use protected animals must be justified under section 5(5).

Animals (Scientific Procedures) Act 1986

4 (3) A project licence shall not be granted for any programme unless the Secretary of State is satisfied that it is undertaken for one or more of the following purposes—

(a) the prevention (whether by the testing of any product or otherwise) or the diagnosis or treatment of disease, ill-health or abnormality, or their effects, in man, animals or plants;

(b) the assessment, detection, regulation or modification of physiological conditions in man, animals or plants;

(c) the protection of the natural environment in the interests of the health or welfare of man or animals;

(d) the advancement of knowledge in biological or behavioural sciences;

(e) education or training otherwise than in primary or secondary schools;

(f) forensic enquiries;

(g) the breeding of animals for experimental or other scientific use. . . .

5(4) In determining whether and on what terms to grant a project licence the Secretary of State shall weigh the likely adverse effects on the animals concerned against the benefit likely to accrue as a result of the programme to be specified in the licence.

(5) The Secretary of State shall not grant a project licence unless he is satisfied—

(a) that the purpose of the programme to be specified in the licence cannot be achieved satisfactorily by any other reasonably practicable method not entailing the use of protected animals; and

(b) that the regulated procedures to be used are those which use the minimum number of animals, involve animals with the lowest degree of neurophysiological sensitivity, cause the least pain, suffering, distress or lasting harm, and are most likely to produce satisfactory results.

(6) The Secretary of State shall not grant a project licence authorising the use of cats, dogs, primates or equidae unless he is satisfied that animals of no other species are suitable for the purposes of the programme to be specified in the licence or that it is not practicable to obtain animals of any other species that are suitable for those purposes.

All relevant previous research must be identified and evaluated in order to avoid unnecessary duplication of existing results. The project must use the smallest number of animals necessary to meet the objectives of the research, and the Home Office will only grant a licence if the likely benefits of the project outweigh the likely adverse effects on the animals.

Note that section 5(5)(b) of the Act requires that the animals chosen for experiments must be of the lowest neurophysiological sensitivity required to meet the stated objectives. Most of the animals used in experiments in the UK are rodents (84 per cent). Birds and fish are used in 5 per cent and 7 per cent of experiments respectively. Under section 5(6) of the Act, specific justification is required for the use of cats, dogs, horses, and non-human primates. In practice, these animals are used in fewer than 1 per cent of all experiments. Regulations have prohibited the use of great apes, such as gorillas and chimpanzees. Almost all animals used in experiments are bred especially for the purposes of research in order to ensure that they are free from any infection or disease. Increasingly animals used in research have been genetically modified: in 2002 25 per cent of all procedures involved genetically modified animals.

For complex licence applications, such as those involving primates, the Home Office may refer the project to the Animal Procedures Committee (APC), a committee of scientific, legal and ethical experts set up by section 19 of the Act to provide advice on especially controversial legal and ethical issues.[9] As well as advising on individual applications, the APC also publishes guidance on more general ethical issues. In 2003 the APC issued a detailed report examining how the cost/benefit assessment, which underpins the justification for animal experiments under the Act, should work in practice:

Animal Procedures Committee[10]

3.1 The Animals (Scientific Procedures) Act 1986 requires that cost–benefit assessments, including assessments of scientific validity, be made case-by-case. These cost–benefit assessments operate on the assumption that animal experiments *can*, at least potentially, be scientifically valid and that benefits can result. Some anti-vivisectionist positions challenge this assumption absolutely. If such categorical denials of scientific validity are accepted, the Act, and with it the cost–benefit assessment, becomes redundant, since *no* animal experiments can be justified . . .

At one extreme, an absolute, categorical position that all animal experiments are scientifically invalid is untenable. However, so too is the opposite categorical position, that the validity of using animals in experiments is a forgone conclusion and should not be questioned. The case that animal experiments can produce scientifically valid results is clear, strong and sustainable, but cannot be construed as an absolute case that every potential use of animals is scientifically valid and fail safe. Nor, moreover, does the case that valid extrapolations can be made from animal experiments necessarily imply that the use of animals is the only or best means of achieving the particular objectives.

Scientific validity is a necessary, but not a sufficient, condition for animal experiments to be judged acceptable according to the cost–benefit assessment required under the Act. It is a condition capable of being fulfilled, but has to be judged case-by-case and subjected to detailed critical evaluation . . .

3.2 This will involve asking practical, scientific questions about the choice and design of animal

⁹ See further <http://www.apc.gov.uk/>.

¹⁰ *Review of Cost–Benefit Assessment in the Use of Animals in Research* (APC 2003) available at <http://www.apc.gov.uk/>.

studies, in order to determine whether and how far the proposed use of animals is reliable and relevant to the objectives or questions being asked. More widely, it should also involve asking whether and how far the proposed use of animals is the most appropriate approach—including whether it is appropriate to use animals at all.

The Home Office issues detailed statistics each year on the use of animals in experiments in the UK.[11] Although the number of animals used for research has halved in the last twenty five years, in 2002 over 2.73 million procedures involving animals took place, a rise of about 110,000 (4.2 per cent) on 2001.

In what circumstances, if any, is it acceptable to use animals in research? Opinion on this question is deeply divided, as Lyle Munro explains.

Lyle Munro[12]

Experimentalists claim that as there is no satisfactory alternative, the use of animals is essential to human health. The antivivisectionists maintain that the researcher's case is deeply flawed and that the availability of cruelty free alternatives renders animal experimentation morally reprehensible. Neither side is willing to compromise since each perceives the other's position as evil. That it is no exaggeration to use the term 'evil' is borne out by the language of vilification that continues to be used by some of the protagonists in the controversy.

In contrast, Richard Ryder suggests that scientists do not necessarily dismiss animal welfare arguments, but rather are caught in a dilemma: is it ever acceptable to cause pain to animals in order to try to eliminate a source of human suffering?

Richard D Ryder[13]

As scientists we acknowledge that the human species is but one of many species. We know that other animals often behave as we do when in pain and that their nervous systems and their biochemistry are similar to our own. We know that nonhumans are related to us through evolution and that, therefore, it is inconsistent to put our own species on a moral pedestal entirely separate from all the others. How can it be moral to cause pain or misery to monkeys, dogs, or rats, if it is immoral to do this to humans? There are no *rational* grounds for asserting this. If it is wrong to experiment painfully upon unconsenting humans, it must, logically speaking, be wrong to do likewise to nonhumans. We cannot, with consistency argue that nonhumans are so like us that they produce valid experimental results and then claim that they are morally different. We should remember simply this: pain is pain regardless of species.

I have said that the trade-off problem is central to ethics. The work of the animal experimenter whose research is strictly therapeutic in its objectives and aimed specifically and sincerely at the alleviation of painful illness is a striking example of this problem. Such scientists are caught on the horns of this dilemma; in their quest to reduce pain are they justified in causing pain?

The critical issue is whether humans are entitled to use animals for their own ends, and one obvious point of comparison is with the food industry. If killing animals for food is morally acceptable (and obviously not everyone agrees that it is), then surely it must also be legitimate to use animals in potentially valuable scientific experiments?

[11] <http://www.homeoffice.gov.uk/docs/animalstats.html>.

[12] 'From Vilification to Accommodation: Making a Common Cause Movement' (1999) 8 Cambridge Quarterly of Healthcare Ethics 46–57, 47.

[13] 'Painism: Some Moral Rules for the Civilized Experimenter' (1999) 8 Cambridge Quarterly of Healthcare Ethics 35–42, 41–2.

Of course many opponents of animal experiments are also vegetarians or vegans, but there are those that would argue that laboratory animals suffer more than those bred for food, and that the two should therefore be treated differently. This claim is hard to sustain, however, given the nature of intensive factory farming and the strict controls that now govern the treatment of animals used in experiments. Battery chickens, or veal calves lead restricted and distressing lives, whereas Home Office guidance states that no animal experiments must inflict prolonged distress on animals. It is also no longer lawful to use animals for 'trivial' research, such as the testing of cosmetics or tobacco products.[14]

In the next extract, David Thomas argues that, because animals can feel pain and cannot give consent, it would be more accurate to draw an analogy between animal experiments and research involving people who lack capacity.

D Thomas[15]

[T]here is an ethical overlap between the way we treat food animals and the way we treat lab animals. However, the much more pertinent comparator is non-consensual experiments on people . . .

[W]hy should the fact (if this is what it is) that A has more value than B mean that A is at liberty to cause pain to B for A's benefit? This is the crucial gap in logic which pro-vivisectionists rarely address. Let us accept for the sake of argument that it was provable that the human species was more important than other species—whether because people generally (though not always) have greater capacity for rational thought, may have greater self awareness, are better able to empathise, or have more sophisticated culture. It is not explained why those attributes mean that we can cause pain to those we relegate further down the hierarchy of value. And, if cruel exploitation of *other* species is justified on a relative value basis, then, logically, so must cruel exploitation *within* our species. Some people, indisputably, have greater capacity for rational thought, have greater self awareness, are better able to empathise, or have a deeper cultural appreciation than other people. However, most people do not conclude that the more endowed are for that reason entitled to cause pain to the less endowed for their own benefit. . . .

Experiments on animals and non-consensual experiments on people are obvious comparators because both involve physical and psychological suffering for an unwilling, sentient victim. In each case consent is neither sought nor presumed and the victim is not the intended beneficiary.

However, society treats the two cases very differently. This is because ethical sleight of hand is deployed. Different ethical principles are applied to the two types of experiment.

With non-consensual experiments on people, a *deontological* approach is taken. The prevailing view is that such experiments are *inherently* wrong, whatever the potential benefits to others . . . With animals, by contrast, the approach is a kind of *utilitarianism*. The law allows scientists to cause pain to animals if *others* might benefit.

In the next extract, RG Frey further suggests that it may be preferable to carry out experiments on non-sentient human subjects than on sentient animals.

RG Frey[16]

The truth is, I think, that some human lives have fallen so far in value, quality, richness, and scope for enrichment that some animal lives exceed in value those human lives. Anencephalic infants and

---

[14] *Guidelines on the Operation of the Animals (Scientific Procedures) Act 1986* (Home Office 2000).
[15] 'Laboratory animals and the art of empathy' (2005) 31 Journal of Medical Ethics 197–202.
[16] 'Pain, vivisection, and the value of life' (2005) 31 Journal of Medical Ethics 202–4.

people in permanently vegetative states are cases in point. It was comforting in the past to think that all human lives were more valuable than any animal life, but the quality of life of a perfectly healthy dog or cat must vastly exceed the quality of any human life that has ceased to have experiences of any sort, that has ceased to have in essence any sort of content. I am not a speciesist but the capacities and scope for enrichment of a life of a normal adult human arguably exceeds that of any rodent found in our labs, with arguably higher quality and value. To confine our judgments about humans and rodents only to the issue of whether they can feel pain and suffer . . . strikes me as ignoring all the capacities and abilities that go toward enriching a life and so toward giving it a quality and value. This strikes me as precisely something that we must not do.

If we have to experiment . . ., then which life do we use? We use that life of lower quality, and we have a non-speciesist way of determining which life that is . . . How can we justify an experiment on a perfectly healthy rodent with an experiential life as opposed to an anencephalic infant with, so far as we know, no experiential life at all?

In 2002 the House of Lords Animals in Scientific Procedures Select Committee published a report which lays out the arguments for and against animal experimentation:

House of Lords Animals in Scientific Procedures Select Committee[17]

4.4 The main criticisms levelled against the use of animals in research are:

- research on animals is unethical. Harm should not be caused to any animal unless it is for the ultimate benefit of that particular animal;

- research on animals is ineffective. Diseases manifest themselves in different ways in animals than in humans. New compounds (for example, new pharmaceutical products) may be beneficial to certain animals, but have no effect on humans. Similarly, compounds which might have been beneficial to humans have in the past been ruled out because they have produced negative results in animals;

- animal research is harmful to human health, because it diverts money away from non-animal research, and some drugs have serious side-effects which are not discovered until the drug is administered to patients. A number of witnesses argued that animal research provides misleading information, and is responsible for the growing trend in drug-related doctor-induced illness ('iatrogenesis');

- there is a record of failure in modelling disease. Induced conditions, such as artificially induced Parkinson's Disease caused by chemical or physical lesions in the brains of mice, are not good models of naturally occurring conditions. Equally, drugs which have been effective in combating stroke in animals have been ineffective in humans;

- some animal research is trivial; some is used to develop products which duplicate existing ones; and some is of little relevance—retrospective analyses show that some animal research is never cited in the literature;

- animal use continues largely through habit, scientific inertia, and the availability of funding from pharmaceutical companies and research councils. If the same amount of money and intellectual effort had been invested in non-animal methods over the years, scientists would have discovered similarly effective drugs.

4.5 Scientists and industry have countered that animal research is effective. The Department of Health, which spends approximately £6 billion each year on pharmaceuticals, asserts

---

[17] <http://www.publications.parliament.uk/pa/ld200102/ldselect/ldanimal/150/150.pdf>.

unequivocally that: 'Properly regulated animal research is absolutely essential to the discovery of new treatments as well as to the assessment of safety and efficacy of medicines'.

4.6 In particular those in favour of animal research argue that:

- animals are used to develop an understanding of normal, healthy biological systems;

- animals are used as models for humans. Animal research helps scientists to understand the mechanisms of diseases and compounds, as well as their specific effects. Humans would of course be better models and human volunteers are always used in later stages during clinical trials. Experimenting on humans at the early stages of drug development is unacceptable, so the best available models—animals—should be used instead;

- many mammals are physiologically very similar to humans: they have similar vital organs— brain, heart, lungs, liver, kidneys—and process toxins in the liver in similar, though not identical, ways. . . .

- the usefulness of animal models is illustrated by the similarity of the veterinary and human pharmacopoeias, and the same drugs are often used to treat the same diseases;

- research on animals is often carried out for the overall benefit of other animals; . . .

- animal experiments continue to be used because they have produced, and continue to pro- duce, extensive and beneficial advances in science: 'Virtually every medical achievement of the last century has depended directly or indirectly on research in animals'.

The House of Lords Select Committee endorsed the use of animals *where necessary*:

On balance, we are convinced that experiments on animals have contributed greatly to scientific advances, both for human medicine and for animal health. Animal experimentation is a valuable research method which has proved itself over time.[18]

It also specifically endorsed what has become known as the 3Rs approach, explained in the following extract:

House of Lords Animal in Scientific Procedures Select Committee[19]

1.12 In 1959, two British scientists, the zoologist William Russell and the microbiologist Rex Burch, published *The principles of humane experimental technique*, a study of the ethical aspects of animal research commissioned by the Universities Federation for Animal Welfare (UFAW). They said that all animal experiments should incorporate, so far as is possible, the Three Rs: replacement, reduction and refinement. They have been defined as:

- Replacement of conscious, living vertebrates by non-sentient alternatives;

- Reduction in the number of animals needed to obtain information of a given amount and precision; and

- Refinement of procedures to reduce to a minimum the incidence or severity of suffering experienced by those animals which have to be used.

1.13 The Three Rs are widely accepted by the international scientific community—almost all those who use animals have said in evidence that they agree with the principle that reduction, refinement, and replacement should take place wherever possible. Many of those who disagree with the use of animals in scientific procedures also agree with the principle of the Three Rs, but

---

[18] Para 4.8.
[19] <http://www.publications.parliament.uk/pa/ld200102/ldselect/ldanimal/150/150.pdf>.

are concerned that they are not always implemented. Some anti-vivisectionists dispute the Three Rs concept on the basis that both reduction and refinement tacitly acknowledge that animals should continue to be used.

4. WHAT IS RESEARCH?

(a) USE OF ANONYMOUS DATA OR SAMPLES

A great deal of medical research is carried out without making direct contact with individual patients. Epidemiology, for example, is 'the study of the occurrence and distribution of diseases and other health-related conditions in populations'. Originally it just referred to the study of epidemics, but now it involves analysis of the prevalence and distribution of particular medical conditions, in order to test hypotheses about suspected causes of disease and relevant risk factors.

Major difficulties would be posed if patients had to give informed consent to the use of information from their medical notes. The process of tracking down every patient and asking their permission would be so time-consuming that this sort of research would not be viable. Because the health benefits of large scale surveys using existing data are considerable, and the infringements of individuals' autonomy and privacy are slight, the preferred solution—as we see later in this chapter—has generally been to allow some research to take place despite the lack of consent. Ideally the patient's agreement to the use of information gathered during her treatment should be sought, but if it would be impossible to obtain consent, then provided the information has been adequately anonymized, and there is no intention to feed the results back to individual patients, researchers do not have to seek consent.

(b) INNOVATIVE THERAPY

It is not always easy to tell the difference between treatment and research. Most medical knowledge is tentative: very few treatments have been proved to be 100 per cent effective. Given that almost all medical treatment is conducted under conditions of uncertainty, and that doctors are continuously learning from the outcomes of their patients' treatment, what justification could there be for treating 'research' as though it were wholly separate from the normal combination of treatment and information gathering?

Ordinary medical treatment, as we saw in Chapter 3, must satisfy the *Bolam* test, as modified in *Bolitho*: that is, it must reach a standard of care which is both accepted as proper by a responsible body of medical opinion, and capable of withstanding logical analysis. This means that doctors must only give their patients established treatments that have already been properly tested. In certain circumstances, however, a doctor might act reasonably by offering a patient treatment which has not been rigorously tested on humans. For example, if all orthodox treatments have been exhausted, and the patient's condition is extremely serious, it might be acceptable to try a treatment which has not yet been licensed for use in humans. Certainly the Helsinki Declaration (see below, p. 473) endorses the use of unproven treatment where no other options exist:

Helsinki Declaration[20]

> 32 In the treatment of a patient, where proven prophylactic, diagnostic and therapeutic methods do not exist or have been ineffective, the physician, with informed consent from the patient, must be free to use unproven or new prophylactic, diagnostic and therapeutic measures, if in the physician's judgement it offers hope of saving life, re-establishing health or alleviating suffering. Where possible, these measures should be made the object of research, designed to evaluate their safety and efficacy. In all cases, new information should be recorded and, where appropriate, published.

Research is different from innovative therapy in one crucial respect: namely that the primary purpose of research is to generate new scientific knowledge by testing a hypothesis, rather than to offer the patient individualized care. But while innovative therapy is not, strictly speaking, research, it might nevertheless be important to ensure that extra care is taken when obtaining consent to treatment that has not been fully tested on humans. Applying the principles which govern the provision of information prior to medical treatment (considered in full in Chapter 5), we could say that the fact that treatment is experimental is a 'material fact', non-disclosure of which would be negligent. If the patient is incompetent, other additional safeguards—such as the court declaration which was sought and granted in *Simms v Simms*—might be necessary.

Simms v Simms[21]

An eighteen year old boy and a sixteen year old girl (the patients) were at the advanced stage of vCJD (variant Creutzfeldt-Jakob disease—the human form of BSE—a rare and fatal neurode-generative disorder). As a result of the disease, which caused increasing neurological damage, the patients had become helpless and mentally-incapacitated, with a severely limited enjoyment of life. Both were bound to die. There was no cure and no recognized effective drugs capable of prolonging life or arresting the continuing neurological deterioration. Medical research had, however, identified a treatment (PPS) which inhibited the progress of a similar disease in mice. The treatment was untested on humans, and so its efficacy and risks were unknown. Nevertheless, the patients' parents wanted their children to receive it, and applied for a declaration that the treatment would be in their best interests, and hence lawful.

Dame Elizabeth Butler-Sloss P

To the question 'Is there a responsible body of medical opinion which would support the PPS treatment within the United Kingdom?' the answer in one sense is unclear. This is untried treatment and there is so far no validation of the experimental work done in Japan. The 'Bolam test' ought not to be allowed to inhibit medical progress. And it is clear that if one waited for the 'Bolam test' to be complied with to its fullest extent, no innovative work such as the use of penicillin or performing heart transplant surgery would ever be attempted. I do however have evidence from responsible medical opinion which does not reject the research . . .

---

[20] World Medical Association, Declaration of Helsinki: Ethical Principles for Medical Research Involving Human Subjects (6th version adopted at the 52nd WMA General Assembly, Edinburgh, Scotland, Oct 2000) available at <http://www.wma.net/e/policy/b3.htm>.

[21] [2003] 1 All ER 669.

Where there is no alternative treatment available and the disease is progressive and fatal, it seems to me to be reasonable to consider experimental treatment with unknown benefits and risks, but without significant risks of increased suffering to the patient, in cases where there is some chance of benefit to the patient. A patient who is not able to consent to pioneering treatment ought not to be deprived of the chance in circumstances where he would have been likely to consent if he had been competent . . .

The chance of improvement is slight but not non-existent. The families ought to regard that possibility as unlikely but not impossible, since no one knows the outcome. There is, from the medical evidence, a possibility of arresting the disease temporarily, and the possibility of prolonging the life of these two patients to some extent, although whether that be in weeks, months or years is impossible to tell . . .

I think it is reasonable, at this stage of my judgment, to put into the balance that, if there is a possibility of continuation of a life which has value to the patient and the patient is bound to die sooner rather than later without the treatment, these two young people have very little to lose in the treatment going ahead. I am satisfied it is a reasonable risk to take on their behalf . . .

Although this cannot be a research project, there would be an opportunity to learn, for the first time, the possible effect of PPS on patients with vCJD and to have the opportunity to compare it with the treatment about to be given to patients in Japan.

(c) THE DIFFERENCE BETWEEN NON-THERAPEUTIC AND THERAPEUTIC RESEARCH

Medicines can only be licensed for use after extensive clinical trials. First animal trials must have shown that there is a reasonable likelihood that the new drug will work, and that it is unlikely to have unacceptable side-effects. After satisfactory evidence from animal trials has been gathered, there are usually then three phases of trials on humans. Phase I trials commonly involve a small number of healthy volunteers, who are given the drug so that researchers can study its toxicity, and the way in which it is absorbed. Next, in a phase II trial, the drug is given to a group of people suffering from the condition which it is intended to treat in order to evaluate its effectiveness, and the existence of any side-effects. Finally phase III trials will involve monitoring a larger group of subjects who take the medicine under supervision for an extended period of time. After licensing, the drug will continue to be monitored closely before it can be categorized as an 'established' medicine, and although no longer strictly research, this might be referred to as a phase IV trial.

Normally phase I trials are non-therapeutic, whereas the subjects recruited for phase II and III trials will often be patients who may hope to receive some health benefit from participation. For certain new treatments, it would plainly be unethical to begin trials in healthy volunteers. An obvious example would be the use of very toxic drugs, such as chemotherapeutic agents, in cancer treatment. While the risks associated with these drugs may outweigh the benefits for patients with cancer, there could be no justification for imposing them upon healthy volunteers. Hence, some trials will have to involve patients from the outset.

Despite the apparent clarity of the distinction between therapeutic research, which might also benefit the subject, and non-therapeutic research, where there will be no direct benefit, a number of commentators, such as Robert Levine, have questioned whether it is appropriate to treat them differently, because even therapeutic trials will invariably also involve non-therapeutic procedures, such as additional blood tests.

Robert J. Levine[22]

Every clinical trial has some components that are non-therapeutic. When we evaluate entire protocols as either therapeutic or non-therapeutic, as required by the Declaration of Helsinki, we end up with what I call the 'fallacy of the package deal.' Those who use this distinction typically classify as 'therapeutic research' any protocol that includes one or more components that are intended to be therapeutic; therefore, the non-therapeutic components of the protocol are justified improperly according to the more permissive standards developed for therapeutic research.

Practical difficulties in drawing a bright-line boundary between therapeutic and non-therapeutic research are particularly important given that, as Simon Verdun-Jones and David Weisstub explain, the principal legal consequence of labelling research 'therapeutic' appears to be to weaken the protection available to vulnerable subjects. Patients who are incompetent, whether as a result of age or mental incapacity, can be enrolled in a research trial relatively easily if the trial can be described as 'therapeutic', even if it contains elements which are quite obviously non-therapeutic. If the research is instead categorized as non-therapeutic, it must pose no more than minimal risk. There is then a danger that researchers might exaggerate the likelihood of a direct benefit to research subjects—what Lars Noah refers to as 'benefit creep'[23]—in order to avoid the more restrictive rules which govern non-therapeutic research. Given that research which is described as 'therapeutic' can legitimately expose incompetent subjects to *more than minimal risk*, Simon Verdun-Jones and David Weisstub argue that it is critically important that a researcher's claim that an experiment is 'therapeutic' should be rigorously investigated.

Simon Verdun-Jones and David Weisstub[24]

One of the most critical *legal consequences* of identifying a research protocol as being primarily non-therapeutic is that there is a significant legal barrier to the involvement of those research subjects whose capacity to give an informed consent to participation is in doubt. Such subjects generally belong to one or more of the following groups, whose members have historically been regarded as being particularly vulnerable in the context of non-therapeutic experimentation: children, the elderly, the mentally disordered, the developmentally disabled, and prisoners . . .

Since the classification of an experiment as either therapeutic or non-therapeutic will profoundly affect the legal and ethical restrictions that apply, a high standard must be met before an experiment should be classified as *therapeutic* . . . [A]n element of uncertainty is, by definition, inherent in all experiments. However, 'possible', 'hypothetical', or 'speculative' benefits should not be sufficient in the present context. Rather, a therapeutic benefit must be 'likely', 'probable' or 'reasonably foreseeable'. If this standard cannot be achieved, then the experiment must be classi-

---

[22] 'International Codes of Research Ethics: Current Controversies and the Future' (2002) 35 Indiana Law Review (2002) 557.

[23] 'Informed Consent and the Elusive Dichotomy between Standard and Experimental Therapy' (2002) 28 American Journal of Law and Medicine 361.

[24] Simon N Verdun-Jones and David N Weisstub, 'Drawing the Distinction between therapeutic research and non-therapeutic experimentation: Clearing a way through the definitional thicket', 88–110 in David N Weisstub (ed), *Research on Human Subjects: Ethics, Law and Social Policy* (Elsevier Oxford 1998).

fied as *non-therapeutic*. It is important to emphasize that it is not the desired purpose or objective of an experiment, but rather its reasonably expected effect on individual research subjects, which should influence research ethics committees in making this crucial assessment.

A further problem with the therapeutic/non-therapeutic distinction is that the whole point of doing the trial in the first place is that no-one actually *knows* whether the treatment which is under investigation will work, there is just the *chance* that it might. To say that a trial is therapeutic implies that it is known in advance that participants will benefit, when any potential benefit is, in fact, necessarily speculative.

Randomized controlled trials (RCTs), discussed in the next section, highlight another problem in categorizing research as therapeutic or non-therapeutic. In a placebo-controlled RCT, there is a 50 per cent chance that the patient will receive no treatment at all. Could such a trial be properly described as 'therapeutic'? On the one hand, there is a chance that the patient will be in the active arm of the study and will receive a treatment which has some chance of working, but it is at least as likely that the patient will receive no direct health benefit at all.

(d) RANDOMIZED CONTROLLED TRIALS

While it is worth noting that some of the most important medical breakthroughs—such as the discovery of penicillin—were the result of luck, rather than well planned clinical trials, randomized controlled trials (RCTs) are considered to be the 'gold standard' in medical research.

The purpose of research is to discover whether a new treatment works, and while this might sound straightforward, researchers have to ensure that their results are not distorted by positive results which are caused by factors other than the treatment which is being studied. For example, a proportion of patients would probably have recovered anyway, regardless of whether they received effective treatment.

In an RCT, the research participants are randomly allocated, usually by computer, to either the control or the active arm of the study. Those in the active arm are given the new treatment, while those in the control group are given either an inert placebo or, as we see later, the best available treatment. In both groups, it can be anticipated that some of patients' conditions will improve regardless of whether they have received any treatment, so researchers will be interested in whether more of the patients in the active arm are showing signs of improvement than in the control group.

An RCT is also supposed to minimize what is known as the 'placebo effect'. Many people report an improvement in their condition after receiving a new 'treatment', even if they have in fact been given an inert substance, such as a sugar pill. If—say—1000 patients are allocated to each arm of the study, and 600 in the active arm experience some improvement, while 300 in the control group also appear to have been helped, it has been suggested that this tells us that the new treatment has actually worked in 300 subjects.

Two central ethical dilemmas are posed by RCTs. First, while they offer the best way to establish whether a new treatment actually works, randomly allocating a patient to the active or control arm of the study is radically at odds with a doctor's normal duty to decide what treatment would be best for the individual patient. If a doctor believes that drug X is the optimum treatment for a patient's condition, enrolling that patient in an RCT clearly breaches the doctor's duty to place the interests of the research subject above the interests of science. As a result, an RCT will only be ethical if there is what is known as 'equipoise', that is, as Alex John London explains, genuine uncertainty about which treatment is best.

Alex John London[25]

In its most basic formulation equipoise represents a state of genuine and credible doubt about the relative therapeutic merits of some set of interventions that target a specific medical condition. The requirement that equipoise exist as a necessary condition for the moral acceptability of a clinical trial comparing these interventions is motivated by two interlocking ideas. First, when equipoise obtains it is morally permissible to allow an individual's medical treatment to be assigned by a random process because there is no sufficiently credible evidence to warrant a judgment that one intervention is superior to the other(s). Second, clinical trials that are designed to break or disturb equipoise provide information that will enable the medical community to improve its existing clinical practices. The requirement is thus seen as a way to reconcile the need to improve the state of medical knowledge and clinical practice with the duty to ensure that the welfare of individual subjects is not knowingly sacrificed for the welfare of future patients of greater scientific understanding.

This conflict between the duty to protect participants' wellbeing and the need to obtain scientifically valuable results is thrown into particularly sharp focus when working out when a trial should be stopped. Preliminary results may appear to show that subjects receiving the new treatment are doing better than those in the control group. At this point, there are two good reasons for stopping the trial. First, it might be in the best interests of the individual subjects for the trial to be halted so that all patients can receive the new treatment. Secondly, the state of equipoise which justifies research on human subjects may have been lost, because the researcher now has some evidence that the new treatment works.

Stopping the trial in the early stages will, however, reduce the scientific validity of the results. There is a higher risk of error, and treatment which has been inadequately tested may endanger the health of future patients. The interests of science and society are therefore served by continuing the research until statistically significant results have been obtained, although this will inevitably sometimes conflict both with the researcher's duty to place the welfare of subjects above the interests of science, and with the equipoise requirement.

The second ethical dilemma raised by RCTs is whether it is ever possible to give informed consent to participation. A patient cannot be told whether they have been allocated to the active or the control arm of the test, because this would invalidate the results. Since an RCT is dependent upon the patients in the control group not knowing what treatment they will receive, their consent could never be *fully* informed. Defenders of RCTs might nevertheless argue that the patient gives informed consent to random allocation, and to being part of an experiment in which they know they will not be told the results of that random allocation until after the trial has ended

[25] 'Equipoise and International Human Subjects Research' (2001) 15 Bioethics 312–32.

(e) THE USE OF PLACEBOS

Giving the control group a placebo is relatively uncontroversial where there is no known treatment for the condition from which the participants suffer, which means that there is equipoise between the new treatment and no treatment at all. As Claire Foster explains in the next extract, more difficult questions arise where effective treatment already exists, and the researcher instead wants to find out whether a new treatment might be better.

Claire Foster[26]

[T]o decide whether or not a trial should be placebo controlled rests on whether we tend to be more goal-based or duty-based in our thinking. The goal-based approach is to conduct placebo controlled trials wherever possible, only avoiding them when there is likelihood of real harm. The assumption is that the placebo controlled trial is the better trial scientifically. Arguments which have been raised against that view are (i) that this entails a too-simplistic interpretation of the placebo effect; and (ii) that a placebo controlled trial only shows a treatment's efficacy against nothing, it does not show its merits relative to other treatments. The latter problem can be overcome by including active arms in a placebo-controlled trial.

The duty-based approach, which will more often conclude that a trial should not be placebo controlled, would not do so for scientific reasons. Rather, the view is that it is simply wrong to deny treatments, if there are any, to patients who after all expect to be treated. For it is one thing to establish that, for scientific reasons, a trial needs a placebo arm. It is another for an individual researcher to be in equipoise about that placebo arm. For the duty-based approach to be satisfied, the researcher needs to be entirely happy that her patient will receive a placebo instead of an active treatment.

Because a placebo-controlled trial may deprive research subjects of appropriate treatment, it would appear to offend the fifth principle of the Helsinki Declaration, namely that 'In medical research on human subjects, considerations related to the well-being of the human subject should take precedence over the interests of science and society'. The Helsinki Declaration's solution to this problem is to ensure that patients in the control group are given the 'best current treatment' for the particular condition. Not only does this protect the wellbeing of research subjects, but it has also been suggested that it leads to more useful results: researchers will be able to establish whether or not the new treatment is better than existing treatments, rather than just proving that it is better than nothing.

Helsinki Declaration[27]

29. The benefits, risks, burdens and effectiveness of a new method should be tested against those of the best current prophylactic, diagnostic, and therapeutic methods. This does not exclude the use of placebo, or no treatment, in studies where no proven prophylactic, diagnostic or therapeutic method exists.

Some commentators have, however, questioned whether a blanket prohibition on

---

[26] *The Ethics of Medical Research on Humans* (CUP Cambridge 2001).
[27] World Medical Association, Declaration of Helsinki: Ethical Principles for Medical Research Involving Human Subjects (6th version adopted at the 52nd WMA General Assembly, Edinburgh, Scotland, Oct 2000) available at <http://www.wma.net/e/policy/b3.htm>.

placebo-controlled trials where treatment already exists is justified. Placebo-controlled trials will usually produce more scientifically reliable results than those with an active control because difference between the new drug and a placebo will usually be more pronounced than that between a new drug and the best standard treatment. Statistically significant proof of efficacy can therefore be obtained more quickly, using fewer research participants. Particularly when testing new treatments for relatively minor conditions, such as headaches or hayfever, it would seem unduly paternalistic to insist that the control group should receive the best standard treatment. In the next extract, Franklin Miller and Howard Brody argue that provided the subjects have given informed consent, and that they will not be exposed to excessive risk if they are given a placebo, such trials are not inherently unethical.

Franklin G Miller and Howard Brody[28]

Physicians in clinical practice have a duty to promote the medical best interests of patients by offering optimal medical care. In RCTs, however, physician-investigators are not offering personalized medical therapy for individual patients. Rather, they seek to answer clinically relevant scientific questions by conducting experiments that test the safety and efficacy of treatments in *groups* of patients. The process of treatment in RCTs differs radically from routine clinical practice. Treatment is selected randomly, not by an individualized assessment of what is best for a particular patient . . .

Owing to these fundamental differences in purpose and process, the ethics of clinical trials is not identical to the ethics of clinical medicine. Specifically, the obligations of physician-investigators are not the same as the obligations of physicians in routine clinical practice. Investigators have a duty to avoid exploiting research participants, not a therapeutic duty to provide optimal medical care. Accordingly, enrolling patient volunteers in placebo-controlled trials that withhold proven effective treatment is not fundamentally unethical as long as patients are not being exploited. Patients may be seeking medical benefits by enrolling in clinical trials; however, they are not being exploited if:

- they are not being exposed to excessive risks for the sake of scientific investigation; and
- they understand that they are volunteering to participate in an experiment rather than receiving personalized medical care directed at their best interests . . .

Consider a placebo-controlled trial of a new treatment for allergic rhinitis [hayfever]. There exist proven effective treatments for this condition. Nonetheless, it is difficult to see what could be morally wrong about a short-term trial comparing a novel treatment for allergic rhinitis with a placebo. Trial participants randomized to placebo may be more likely to suffer from mild to moderate discomfort associated with untreated allergic rhinitis. But individuals with this condition often forgo treatment, and short periods without treatment pose no risks to health. . . . If it is ethically justifiable to conduct a placebo-controlled trial of a new treatment for allergic rhinitis, then *what counts ethically is not denial of treatment but lack of substantial risk to participants* . . .

Just as it is ethically justifiable to conduct non-therapeutic studies that pose some, but not excessive, risks of harm without the prospect of medical benefit, so it can be ethical to use placebo controls in scientifically valuable RCTs that involve withholding proven effective treatment, provided that the risks are not excessive and participants give informed consent.

[28] 'What Makes Placebo-Controlled Trials Unethical?' (2002) 2 American Journal of Bioethics 3–9.

In response to this sort of criticism, the World Medical Association issued a 'clarification' to principle 29 of the Helsinki Declaration in October 2001, suggesting that placebo controlled trials might be legitimate even where effective treatment exists if (a) there are compelling scientific reasons; or (b) if the subjects would not thereby be exposed to any risk of serious or irreversible harm.

Helsinki Declaration (Clarification)[29]

The WMA is concerned that paragraph 29 of the revised declaration of Helsinki has led to diverse interpretations and possible confusion. It hereby affirms its position that extreme care must be taken in making use of a placebo-controlled trial and that in general this methodology should only be used in the absence of existing proven therapy. However, a placebo-controlled trial may be ethically acceptable, even if proven therapy is available, under the following circumstances:

- Where for compelling and scientifically sound methodological reasons its use is necessary to determine the efficacy or safety of a prophylactic, diagnostic or therapeutic method, or

- Where a prophylactic, diagnostic or therapeutic method is being investigated for a minor condition and the patients who receive placebo will not be subject to any additional risk of serious or irreversible harm.

(f) SHAM SURGERY

So far we have assumed that the most invasive experiments involving human subjects are trials of new medicines. In a placebo-controlled drugs trial, patients in the active harm may be exposed to the risks and benefits of the new treatment, while those in the control arm are deprived of the opportunity of receiving the new treatment, but are subjected to no extra risk. Where a course of medical treatment—such as surgery—is more intrusive, conducting a randomized controlled trial would involve carrying out a sham procedure on patients in the control group which *does* expose them to some additional risks. Could this ever be ethical?

The issue has arisen recently in the context of trials of fetal tissue grafting for patients suffering from Parkinson's disease. Experiments in animals, and preliminary trials on 300 human subjects, had appeared to indicate that intercerebral transplants of fetal tissue could substantially improve the condition of sufferers of Parkinson's disease. Because these initial trials involving humans had not been RCTs, it was impossible to tell how much of this improvement was due to the placebo effect. This is an acute problem for a disease such as Parkinson's where patients' subjective accounts of their progress are particularly important. The only way to eliminate the distortions caused by the placebo effect would be to carry out sham surgery on a control group, and compare their results with those of patients who had been given fetal tissue grafts. Patients receiving sham surgery have a hole drilled in their skull, and are exposed to the risks inherent in undergoing any surgical procedure, with no expectation of any benefit at all. Because the sole purpose of sham surgery is to generate useful

---

[29] World Medical Association, Declaration of Helsinki: Ethical Principles for Medical Research Involving Human Subjects (6th version adopted at the 52nd WMA General Assembly, Edinburgh, Scotland, Oct 2000) available at <http://www.wma.net/e/policy/b3.htm> Clarification (Oct 2001).

information, some commentators have condemned these trials for putting the interests of science above the welfare of individual research subjects.

On the other hand, it might be argued that unless surgical techniques are properly tested on humans, future patients are likely to be exposed to potentially ineffective and/or unsafe treatment. Carrying out sham surgery on a small number of patients might then benefit thousands of people in the future, and prevent the NHS from wasting resources on inadequately tested and potentially useless or dangerous surgery. While this argument makes good sense from a utilitarian perspective, does it involve sacrificing the interests of a few individuals in order to benefit society as a whole?

The preferred solution to this problem has not been a blanket prohibition of sham surgery. Rather, as RL Albin explains in the next extract, their use has to be rigorously justified, and the risks to subjects must be minimized. In particular, extra care should be taken when obtaining informed consent to ensure that the research subjects actually understand what is meant by randomization, and are fully aware that they may be about to undergo a surgical procedure which will expose them to some risks, with no chance of improving their condition. Because sham neurosurgery obviously exposes subjects to more than minimal risk, it should be particularly difficult to justify carrying out such experiments on incompetent patients.

RL Albin[30]

[I]t is common for surgical techniques to be introduced into clinical practice without rigorous evaluation. The result can be exposure of substantial numbers of patients to procedures that incur significant risks and have no benefit. In addition to becoming a public health hazard, inadequately evaluated surgical methods can consume valuable societal resources . . . This is not a theoretical concern. There are abundant examples of widely adopted surgeries that were abandoned subsequently for lack of efficacy . . .

Use of sham surgery is unattractive because the increased risk to control subjects is not accompanied by any possibility of benefit. In some cases, however, sham surgery controls are strongly preferred on scientific grounds and may be necessary to answer the key questions. Sham surgery controls cannot be prohibited absolutely but their use must be balanced carefully against the safety of research subjects.

Because of the necessity of minimising risk for research subjects, sham surgery controls should not be the default method of constructing human clinical trials involving surgical interventions. Sham surgery controls should be used only with careful justification and I believe that these circumstances will be rare. When is sham surgery justified? I propose formal criteria as a decision aid.

First, all the general standards for ethical conduct of clinical trials must be satisfied . . .

Second, there cannot be reasonable alternative research designs. There must be a legitimate and substantiated concern about placebo effects or other forms of potential bias that cannot be defused by use of an alternative design . . .

Third, there must be procedure for minimising the risk–benefit ratio . . . The major risks associated with grafting are the danger of infection resulting from introduction of foreign material, the risk of intracerebral haemorrhage from introduction of the injection cannulae, the risk of general anaesthesia, and the risk from the use of potentially toxic anti-rejection drugs. The sham procedure was designed to avoid these risks. No tissue was injected . . . general anaesthesia and

[30] 'Sham surgery controls: intercerebral grafting of fetal tissue for Parkinson's disease and proposed criteria for use of sham surgery controls' (2002) 28 Journal of Medical Ethics 322–5.

anti-rejection drugs were not used . . . If no sham procedure avoiding the major risks of the intervention can be established, then sham surgery controls should be abandoned.

Fourth, the minimum necessary number of subjects should be enrolled . . .

Fifth, there should be an exceptionally vigilant, independent safety monitoring board.

The first placebo-controlled study of fetal tissue grafts in Parkinson's patients took place in the US. Forty patients were recruited, and all of them had four tiny holes drilled into their foreheads. Half of them received fetal tissue grafts, and half received nothing. Three patients in the control group said their symptoms had improved. In two thirds of the patients who received transplants, the fetal tissue took hold and started to produce the missing neurochemical dopamine, which is necessary for the brain to generate both walking and speaking functions.[31]

5. INTERNATIONAL ETHICAL CODES

The first national code of research ethics was promulgated in Germany in 1900 when the Prussian Minister of Religious, Educational and Medical Affairs issued a directive which provided that research should only be carried out on competent adults, who had given consent after a proper explanation of the possible adverse consequences. Further rules were issued in Germany in 1931 which prohibited risky experiments involving children, and specified that research on humans was only legitimate where there had been previous tests on animals, and where informed consent had been given. Ironically, it was the grotesque corruption of the German medical profession under the Nazis that led to the first international code of research ethics.

(a) THE NUREMBERG TRIALS

The discovery of what had been done in the name of medical research during the Second World War resulted in the prosecution of twenty German doctors and three scientists at Nuremberg.[32] Some of the defendants were eminent and internationally renowned physicians. Others, according to the prosecutor Telford Taylor, were 'the dregs of the German medical profession'.[33] The trial was conducted by the Allied Forces, and the judges were American lawyers appointed by the Military Governor of the American zone. Sixteen defendants were found guilty, seven, including Karl Brandt who was Hitler's physician, were hanged.

Many of the experiments carried out in the concentration camps were directed towards the 'war effort'. In Dachau, victims were forced to remain outdoors without clothing for 9–14 hours, or were kept in tanks of iced water for 3 hours at a time, in order to find out the best way to rewarm German pilots who had parachuted into the North Sea. Also at Dachau, 1,200 inmates were deliberately infected with malaria in order to test new immunization and treatment options. At Ravensbrueck, battle

---

[31] Peter A Clark, 'Placebo Surgery for Parkinson's Disease: Do the Benefits Outweigh the Risks?' (2002) 30 Journal of Law, Medicine and Ethics 58.

[32] Trials of War Criminals before the Nuremberg Military Tribunals, *United States v Karl Brandt.*

[33] Telford Taylor, *Opening Statement of the Prosecution* 9 Dec 1946.

conditions were simulated by making incisions which were then contaminated with glass, woodshavings, or bacteria. Russian prisoners of war at Buchenwald were given poisons and their reactions were observed. Some died immediately, others were killed so that autopsies could be performed. Vaccines for diseases such as typhus, smallpox, and cholera were tested by deliberately infecting both a group of prisoners who had been given the vaccine, and the members of a control group who had not been immunized, and who were obviously likely to develop fatal diseases as a result. Because mass surgical sterilization would be too costly and time-consuming, the Nazis were keen to develop techniques that could sterilize large numbers of people, ideally without them noticing. Several thousand women were sterilized by injection, and men were castrated using X-rays.

In the next extract, Telford Taylor, one of the prosecutors at Nuremberg lays out some of the accusations against the Nazi scientists.

Telford Taylor[34]

A sort of rough pattern is apparent on the face of the indictment. Experiments concerning high altitude, the effect of cold, and potability of processed sea water have an obvious relation to aeronautical and naval combat and rescue problems. The mustard gas and phosphorus burn experiments, as well as those relating to the healing value of sulfanilamide for wounds, can be related to air-raid and battlefield medical problems. It is well known that malaria, epidemic jaundice and typhus were among the principal diseases which had to be combated by the German Armed Forces and by German authorities in occupied territories. To some degree, the therapeutic pattern outlined above is undoubtedly a valid one, and explains why the Wehrmacht, and especially the German Air Force, participated in these experiments. Fanatically bent upon conquest, utterly ruthless as to the means or instruments to be used in achieving victory, and callous to the sufferings of people whom they regarded as inferior, the German militarists were willing to gather whatever scientific fruit these experiments might yield.

But our proof will show that a quite different and even more sinister objective runs like a red thread through these hideous researches. We will show that in some instances, the true object of these experiments was not how to rescue or to cure, but how to destroy and kill. The sterilization experiments were, it is clear, purely destructive in purpose. The prisoners at Buchenwald who were shot with poisoned bullets were not guinea pigs to test an antidote for the poison; their murderers really wanted to know how quickly the poison would kill . . .

Mankind has not heretofore felt the need of a word to denominate the science of how to kill prisoners most rapidly and subjugated people in large numbers. This case and these defendants have created this gruesome question for the lexicographer. For the moment we will christen this macabre science *thanatology*, the science of producing death. The thanatological knowledge, derived in part from these experiments, supplied the techniques for genocide, a policy of the Third Reich, exemplified in the 'euthanasia' program, and in the widespread slaughter of Jews, Gypsies, Poles, and Russians. This policy of mass extermination could not have been so effectively carried out without the active participation of German medical scientists.

Arthur Caplan points out an interesting comparison between the Nazis' willingness to sacrifice some individuals' lives in order to save others and the Allies' similar preparedness to knowingly sacrifice some conscripts' lives for the greater good.

---

[34] Telford Taylor, *Opening Statement of the Prosecution* 9 Dec 1946.

Arthur Caplan[35]

Many who conducted lethal experiments or actively engaged in genocide argued that it was reasonable to sacrifice the interests of the few in order to benefit the majority. The most distinguished of the scientists who was put on trial, Gerhard Rose, the head of the Koch Institute of Tropical Medicine in Berlin, said that he initially opposed performing potentially lethal experiments to create a vaccine for typhus on camp inmates. But he came to believe that it made no sense not to risk the lives of 100 or 200 men in pursuit of a vaccine when 1000 men a day were dying of typhus on the Eastern front. What, he asked, were the deaths of 100 men compared to the possible benefit of getting a prophylactic vaccine capable of saving tens of thousands? Rose, because he admitted that he had anguished about his own moral duty when asked by the Wehrmacht to perform the typhus experiments in a concentration camp, raises the most difficult and most plausible moral argument in defense of lethal experimentation.

The prosecution encountered some difficulty with Rose's argument. The defense team for Rose noted that the Allies themselves justified the compulsory drafting of men for military service throughout the war, knowing many would certainly die, on the grounds that the sacrifice of the few to save the many was morally just.

An expert witness in the Nuremberg trial, Andrew Ivy, proposed three basic principles to govern research on humans:

- Consent must be voluntary.
- There should have been previous experiments on animals.
- Trials should be conducted by responsible and medically qualified individuals.

The Nuremberg Code, which the Court set out in its final judgement, expands these into 10 principles:

Nuremberg Code[36]

The great weight of the evidence before us is to the effect that certain types of medical experiments on human beings, when kept within reasonably well-defined bounds, conform to the ethics of the medical profession generally. The protagonists of the practice of human experimentation justify their views on the basis that such experiments yield results for the good of society that are unprocurable by other methods or means of study. All agree, however, that certain basic principles must be observed in order to satisfy moral, ethical and legal concepts:

1. The voluntary consent of the human subject is absolutely essential.
This means that the person involved should have legal capacity to give consent; should be so situated as to be able to exercise free power of choice, without the intervention of any element of force, fraud, deceit, duress, over-reaching, or other ulterior form of constraint or coercion; and should have sufficient knowledge and comprehension of the elements of the subject matter involved as to enable him to make an understanding and enlightened decision . . .

2. The experiment should be such as to yield fruitful results for the good of society, unprocurable by other methods or means of study, and not random and unnecessary in nature.

---

[35] 'How did Medicine go so wrong' 53–92 in Arthur L Caplan (ed), *When Medicine went Mad: Bioethics and the Holocaust* (Human Press Totowa NJ 1992).
[36] '*Trials of War Criminals before the Nuremberg Military Tribunals under Control Council Law No. 10*', vol 2, 181–2. US Government Printing Office (Washington, DC 1949).

3. The experiment should be so designed and based on the results of animal experimentation and a knowledge of the natural history of the disease or other problem under study that the anticipated results will justify the performance of the experiment.

4. The experiment should be so conducted as to avoid all unnecessary physical and mental suffering and injury.

5. No experiment should be conducted where there is an a priori reason to believe that death or disabling injury will occur; except, perhaps, in those experiments where the experimental physicians also serve as subjects.

6. The degree of risk to be taken should never exceed that determined by the humanitarian importance of the problem to be solved by the experiment.

7. Proper preparations should be made and adequate facilities provided to protect the experimental subject against even remote possibilities of injury, disability, or death.

8. The experiment should be conducted only by scientifically qualified persons. The highest degree of skill and care should be required through all stages of the experiment of those who conduct or engage in the experiment.

9. During the course of the experiment the human subject should be at liberty to bring the experiment to an end if he has reached the physical or mental state where continuation of the experiment seems to him to be impossible.

10. During the course of the experiment the scientist in charge must be prepared to terminate the experiment at any stage, if he has probable cause to believe, in the exercise of the good faith, superior skill and careful judgment required of him that a continuation of the experiment is likely to result in injury, disability, or death to the experimental subject.

Although the publication of the Nuremberg Code had tremendous symbolic resonance, its impact upon medical practice was limited. In part, this is because doctors assumed that it was specifically addressing the abuses of Nazism, and, as a result, that it had limited relevance for the medical profession in general. Most of the defendants at Nuremberg were guilty of murder, and if the Code was simply directed towards ensuring that doctors did not murder their patients, its impact upon the conduct of ordinary clinical experiments would clearly be minimal.

The Code's scope is, however, wider than this: the permissible limits of medical research were also on trial. For example, the first principle in the Nuremberg Code— that the voluntary consent of the human subject is absolutely essential—would be redundant if the defendants' only crimes had been murder, where the consent of the victim is never a defence. Rather the Code is laying out the conditions under which *any* clinical research involving human subjects is acceptable.

It is also worth noting that the United States' enthusiasm for prosecuting German doctors and scientists who had carried out brutal and inhuman experiments on concentration camp inmates did not extend to similarly abusive behaviour by Japan in the 1930s and 1940s. Between 1930 and 1945, Japan conducted extensive trials of biological warfare in a site in China known as Unit 731.[37] It has been estimated that

---

[37] See further SH Harris, *Factories of Death: Japanese Biological Warfare 1932–45 and the American Cover-Up* (Routledge London 1994).

over 3,000 people died as a result of exposure to germs such as anthrax, cholera, and typhoid, and following experiments involving being dehydrated, frozen, or given transfusions of horse blood. At the end of the war, the US gave Japanese experimenters immunity from prosecution in return for information about biological warfare. A Soviet military tribunal did prosecute twelve personnel from Unit 731, but the trial and the code it proposed received virtually no publicity.

Although there have not been research abuses on the scale of those conducted in the Nazi concentration camps since the Nuremberg trials, exploitative medical research did not start and stop with the Nazis. On the contrary, there were plenty of examples of unethical research prior to the Second World War. In the eighteenth and nineteenth centuries, for example, experiments would often be carried out on orphans, prostitutes, and other 'expendable' social groups. There have also been many incidences of exploitation since the end of the Second World War. In the 1960s and 1970s, a number of important articles and books were published which drew attention to the lack of external control over experiments performed on humans. Henry Beecher's article 'Ethics and Clinical Research', which appeared in the *New England Journal of Medicine* in 1966,[38] and Maurice Pappworth's book *Human Guinea Pigs*, published in 1967,[39] both gave details of extensive violations of the principles encapsulated in the Nuremberg Code. For example, in the US, between 1932 and 1972 the United States Public Health Services carried out the now infamous Tuskegee study, in which effective treatment for syphilis was withheld from 400 poor and uneducated black men without their knowledge or consent, so that the disease's progression could be observed.

(b) THE HELSINKI DECLARATION

In 1954, the Eighth General Assembly of the World Medical Association drafted a set of principles to be followed in research involving human subjects. This document was redrafted in the early 1960s and adopted at the Eighteenth World Medical Association assembly in Helsinki in 1964. The Helsinki Declaration has since been revised six times, most recently in Edinburgh in 2000.[40]

In contrast to the Nuremberg Code's insistence that no research should take place if the subject herself has not given informed consent, the Helsinki Declaration specifies that a substitute decision-maker may give consent on behalf of incompetent subjects. Initially the Helsinki Declaration drew a distinction between therapeutic and non-therapeutic research. Since then, the terms 'therapeutic' and 'non-therapeutic' have been removed, but it continues to treat 'medical research combined with medical care' differently from 'pure' research. In 1975, the Helsinki Declaration was amended to include the recommendation that all research projects should be assessed by an independent committee.

---

[38] HK Beecher, 'Ethics and clinical research' (1966) 274 New England Journal of Medicine 1354–60.
[39] MH Pappworth, *Human Guinea Pigs: Experimentation on Man* (Beacon Press Boston 1967).
[40] World Medical Association, Declaration of Helsinki: Ethical Principles for Medical Research Involving Human Subjects (6th version adopted at the 52nd WMA General Assembly, Edinburgh, Scotland, Oct 2000) available at <http://www.wma.net/e/policy/b3.htm>.

Helsinki Declaration[41]

5. In medical research on human subjects, considerations related to the well-being of the human subject should take precedence over the interests of science and society . . .

10. It is the duty of the physician in medical research to protect the life, health, privacy, and dignity of the human subject.

11. Medical research involving human subjects must conform to generally accepted scientific principles, be based on a thorough knowledge of the scientific literature, other relevant sources of information, and on adequate laboratory and, where appropriate, animal experimentation. . . .

13. The design and performance of each experimental procedure involving human subjects should be clearly formulated in an experimental protocol. This protocol should be submitted for consideration, comment, guidance, and where appropriate, approval to a specially appointed ethical review committee, which must be independent of the investigator, the sponsor or any other kind of undue influence . . .

15. Medical research involving human subjects should be conducted only by scientifically qualified persons and under the supervision of a clinically competent medical person.

17. Physicians should abstain from engaging in research projects involving human subjects unless they are confident that the risks involved have been adequately assessed and can be satisfactorily managed. Physicians should cease any investigation if the risks are found to outweigh the potential benefits or if there is conclusive proof of positive and beneficial results.

18. Medical research involving human subjects should only be conducted if the importance of the objective outweighs the inherent risks and burdens to the subject. This is especially important when the human subjects are healthy volunteers.

(c) THE CIOMS GUIDELINES

In 1982, in response to the concern that research was being carried out in developing countries in order to save money and to avoid restrictive regulations, the World Health Organization (WHO) and the Council for International Organizations of Medical Sciences (CIOMS) published their *International Ethical Guidelines for Biomedical Research Involving Human Subjects*. These have since been updated twice, most recently in 2002. Their purpose is

to indicate how the ethical principles that should guide the conduct of biomedical research involving human subjects, as set forth in the Declaration of Helsinki, could be effectively applied, particularly in developing countries, given their socioeconomic circumstances, laws and regulations, and executive and administrative arrangements.

In short, they are designed to address the practical difficulties in implementing universally applicable ethical standards in countries with vastly different standards of health care provision. At the heart of the CIOMS Guidelines are three basic ethical principles: respect for persons, beneficence and justice:

---

[41] World Medical Association, Declaration of Helsinki: Ethical Principles for Medical Research Involving Human Subjects (6th version adopted at the 52nd WMA General Assembly, Edinburgh, Scotland, Oct 2000) available at <http://www.wma.net/e/policy/b3.htm>.

Council for International Organizations of Medical Sciences (CIOMS)[42]

Respect for persons incorporates at least two fundamental ethical considerations, namely:

(a) respect for autonomy, which requires that those who are capable of deliberation about their personal choices should be treated with respect for their capacity for self-determination; and

(b) protection of persons with impaired or diminished autonomy, which requires that those who are dependent or vulnerable be afforded security against harm or abuse.

Beneficence refers to the ethical obligation to maximize benefits and to minimize harms. This principle gives rise to norms requiring that the risks of research be reasonable in the light of the expected benefits, that the research design be sound, and that the investigators be competent both to conduct the research and to safeguard the welfare of the research subjects. Beneficence further proscribes the deliberate infliction of harm on persons.

Justice refers to the ethical obligation to treat each person in accordance with what is morally right and proper . . .

In general, the research project should leave low-resource countries or communities better off than previously or, at least, no worse off. It should be responsive to their health needs and priorities in that any product developed is made reasonably available to them, and as far as possible leave the population in a better position to obtain effective health care and protect its own health.

Justice requires also that the research be responsive to the health conditions or needs of vulnerable subjects. The subjects selected should be the least vulnerable necessary to accomplish the purposes of the research.

As we shall see later, the Guidelines advocate the universal applicability of certain basic ethical standards, while recognizing that there may be times when superficial aspects of these general principles may need to be modified in order to take account of diverse cultural values.

(d) THE INTERNATIONAL CONFERENCE ON HARMONISATION OF TECHNICAL REQUIREMENTS FOR REGISTRATION OF PHARMACEUTICALS FOR HUMAN USE

The International Conference on Harmonisation of Technical Requirements for Registration of Pharmaceuticals for Human Use (ICH) brings together the regulatory authorities of Europe, Japan and the United States, as well as experts from the pharmaceutical industry. Its purpose is to make recommendations on ways to achieve greater harmonization of regulations in order to reduce the need to duplicate trials of new medicines. To facilitate the mutual acceptance of data generated during clinical trials by regulatory authorities in the three regions, the ICH has published a number of guidelines on the conduct of clinical trials, including a general *Guideline for Good Clinical Practice*, and some specific guidance on trials involving geriatric and paediatric populations.

---

[42] *International Ethical Guidelines for Biomedical Research Involving Human Subjects* <http://www.cioms.ch/>.

The International Conference on Harmonisation of Technical Requirements for Registration of Pharmaceuticals for Human Use[43]

2.1 Clinical trials should be conducted in accordance with the ethical principles that have their origin in the Declaration of Helsinki . . .

2.2 Before a trial is initiated, foreseeable risks and inconveniences should be weighed against the anticipated benefit for the individual trial subject and society. A trial should be initiated and continued only if the anticipated benefits justify the risks.

2.3 The rights, safety and well-being of the trial subjects are the most important considerations and should prevail over interests of science and society.

2.5 Clinical trials should be scientifically sound, and described in a clear, detailed protocol.

2.6 A trial should be conducted in compliance with the protocol that has received prior independent ethics committee (IEC) approval. . . .

2.9 Freely given informed consent should be obtained from every subject prior to clinical trial participation.

(e) IMPACT OF INTERNATIONAL CODES

Unless they have been incorporated into the laws of individual nations, none of these international codes are legally binding. Certain principles are, however, common to all of these international documents, and the practical requirements which emerge from them could, perhaps, be summarized as follows:

1. Before the research starts:

→ it must be established that the research is scientifically valid

→ the risks must be proportionate to the benefits

→ the research protocol should have been approved by an ethics committee

→ if competent, the subject must give informed consent

→ if incompetent, other protections must be in place

2. During the research:

→ the experiment must be stopped if there is a risk of injury or death

→ the experiment must be stopped once equipoise has been lost

→ the subject must be free to withdraw from the trial at any time

3. After the research has finished:

→ the subject should have access to information about the trial, and to treatment which has been proved to be effective as a result of the trial

→ research findings should be disseminated

→ subjects who have been injured as a result of the trial should be appropriately compensated.

[43] Guideline for Good Clinical Practice E6 (1996).

To be ethical, research must satisfy the requirements of good scientific practice. Unless research will produce valid and accurate results, there could be no justification for imposing its risks upon research subjects. Risks to participants must also be reasonable in relation to the anticipated benefits from the research. For a number of reasons, however, this principle is rather imprecise. First, the word 'reasonable' is itself ambiguous: if a strict utilitarian interpretation is adopted, it might justify research in which a very small number of subjects' health is sacrificed in order to carry out research capable of benefiting millions of people. Recall that this was the justification given by some of the Nazi doctors for conducting research directed towards saving thousands of German soldiers' lives. Secondly, because the outcome of the research is necessarily unknown, the researcher will rarely be in a position to *know* exactly what risks and benefits might flow from the research. If she already knows the answer to this question, then carrying out further experiments on humans would be scientifically pointless, and hence unethical. The rule that the risks must be proportionate to the anticipated benefits therefore requires informed *guesswork* rather than absolute certainty.

There is also a danger that invoking a risk/benefit calculation in order to justify research on human subjects may be dangerously misleading. If told that the risks of participation in a research trial are outweighed by its benefits, subjects might not appreciate that this calculation is necessarily speculative. Because, of course, if researchers were in fact certain that a particular benefit would accrue to research subjects, the trial would be redundant, and therefore unethical. Since we know that most people volunteer to participate in research as a result of perceived self-interest, unwittingly exaggerating the probability that the subject will benefit from participation may mean that her consent is less than fully informed. And even if participation in research *might* benefit the individual subject, it is important to remember that this will never be the trial's principal purpose. On the contrary, any anticipated benefit to individual research subjects will be incidental to its primary aim, which is to produce generalizable knowledge.

6. REGULATION OF RESEARCH IN THE UK

(a) GUIDELINES

In the UK, a variety of bodies have issued guidance on good practice in research. The first was the Medical Research Council (MRC), which issued a statement in 1963 entitled *Responsibility in Investigations on Human Subjects*. Its latest general set of *Guidelines for Good Clinical Practice in Clinical Research* was published in 1998, and is accompanied by a variety of other documents which are intended to offer guidance and advice on the conduct of high quality and ethically sound research.[44] Guidelines have also been issued by, among others, the Department of Health; the Royal College of Physicians; the Royal College of Psychiatrists; the Royal College of Paediatrics; and

---

[44] Available at <http://www.mrc.ac.uk/>.

the General Medical Council. With some slight variations, these guidelines reproduce the basic ethical principles contained in the various international documents we considered in the previous section.

Medical Research Council[45]

2.1 Clinical trials should be conducted in accordance with the ethical principles that have their origin in the Declaration of Helsinki and are consistent with GCP [good clinical practice].

2.2 Before a trial is initiated, foreseeable risks and inconveniences should be weighed against the anticipated benefit for the individual trial participant and society. A trial should be initiated only if the benefits justify the risks.

2.3 The rights, safety and well-being of the trial participants are the most important consideration and should prevail over interests of science and society.

General Medical Council[46]

5. Because the benefits of the research are not always certain and may not be experienced by the participants, you must be satisfied that the research is not contrary to their interests. In particular:

• you must be satisfied that, in therapeutic research, the foreseeable risks will not outweigh the potential benefits to the patients. The development of treatments and furthering of knowledge should never take precedence over the patients' best interests;

• in non-therapeutic research, you must keep the foreseeable risks to participants as low as possible. In addition the potential benefits from the development of treatments and furthering of knowledge must far outweigh any such risks;

• before starting any research you must ensure that ethical approval has been obtained from a properly constituted and relevant research ethics committee . . .

• you must conduct research in an ethical manner and one that accords with best practice;

• you must ensure that patients or volunteers understand that they are being asked to participate in research and that the results are not predictable;

• you must obtain and record the participants' consent; save in exceptional circumstances where specific approval not to obtain consent must have been given by the research ethics committee;

• respect participants' right to confidentiality;

• you must complete research projects involving patients or volunteers, or do your best to ensure that they are completed by others, except where results indicate a risk that participants may be harmed or no benefit can be expected;

• you must record and report results accurately.

(b) ETHICS COMMITTEES

In 1967 the Royal College of Physicians (RCP) issued a report which stated that hospitals' responsibility for the safety and ethical acceptability of research could be

---

[45] *Guidelines for Good Clinical Practice in Clinical Research* (MRC, Apr 1998).
[46] *Research: The Role and Responsibilities of Doctors* (GMC 2002) available at <http://www.gmc-uk.org/>.

discharged if projects had first been approved by a group of doctors. A year later, the then Ministry of Health sent a notice to regional and area health authorities, and to boards of governors of hospitals, asking them to set up research ethics committees (RECs). More detailed guidance was issued in 1975, including the recommendation that all RECs should include at least one lay member.

From the outset, the duties of RECs in the UK were, on the one hand, to maintain ethical standards of practice in research and protect subjects from harm; and on the other hand, to promote and facilitate research. Julia Neuberger's study of the practice of ethics committees, published in 1992, found that committees were confused by the obvious tension between the duty to critically review research, and the duty to ensure that researchers were not unduly hindered.[47]

Neuberger also found considerable variation in the practices of RECs. The size of committees varied, as did how often they met and how long they took to review each research protocol. There was inadequate lay representation, and a substantial minority of committees did not contain a GP, a nurse, or a pharmacologist. Only one committee had ever conducted a spot-check on an ongoing project. Hardly any proposals (as few as 1 per cent) were rejected, and Neuberger concluded that ethics committees were essentially *advisory* bodies, with no power to insist upon compliance with any of their recommendations:

However hard they work, however thorough their examination of research protocols on a case-by-case basis, however much better constituted and trained, and however well supported they may be administratively, unless they have the power to ensure that all research is submitted to them and to stop research that they regard as unethical, they will not be taken sufficiently seriously. For these reasons and others, this report . . . recommends that there should be proper legislation.[48]

A centralized system of research ethics committees was set up by Department of Health Guidance in 1991. But particular problems continued to exist when a research project involved hospitals in different regions of the UK, when seeking approval from a series of different committees, each with their own idiosyncratic procedures and priorities, was so time-consuming and costly that many potentially valuable research projects had to be abandoned. This problem was addressed in 1997 by the setting up of multi-centre research ethics committees (MRECs). At first, MRECs could only authorize research projects if five or more different NHS regions were involved, now they can authorize trials taking place in two or more places.

LRECs continue to have a role in considering distinctively *local* issues. So once ethical approval has been given by the MREC, the protocol is referred back to an LREC for consideration of 'pertinent local issues'. Initially there was some confusion over what counted as a 'local issue', and so the system continued to be subject to delays, with some LRECs persisting in turning down applications on the grounds of more general ethical concerns. Furthermore, for certain sorts of research, such as observational studies on patients with very rare genetic diseases who are geographically dispersed throughout the country, the need to gain additional LREC approval in

---

[47] *Ethics and Health Care: The Role of Research Ethics Committees in the UK* (King's Fund London 1992).
[48] Ibid, 8.

every location was a considerable burden. Lewis et al. describe one such research project where, in addition to the MREC's authorization, LREC approval also had to be sought from fifty-three different committees.[49]

The new governance arrangements for research in the UK were therefore partly a response to the recognition that the procedures and powers of ethics committees were offering a far too fragmented, inconsistent and ineffective system for ensuring that high quality and ethically sound research is carried out in the UK. The Central Office for Research Ethics Committees (COREC), now part of the National Patient Safety Agency, was set up in 2000, to improve and coordinate the organization of RECs.[50] COREC now coordinates applications for ethics committee approval, offers training to REC members and is intended to develop common standards.

Additionally, as we see in the next section, a European directive came into force in 2004, implemented in the UK by the Medicines for Human Use (Clinical Trials) Regulations 2004, with the aim of standardizing the regulation of medical research throughout the European Union,[51] including the systems for ethical review of research protocols.

Regulation 12 of the Medicines for Human Use (Clinical Trials) Regulations 2004 specifies that the favourable opinion of an ethics committee is a precondition of any clinical trial. Under Regulation 15(5), an ethics committee is required to take into account various matters, including

- the anticipated risks and benefits of the trial;
- the procedure for obtaining informed consent;
- where relevant, the justification of research on persons incapable of giving informed consent;
- the provision of compensation in the event of injury or death;
- the arrangements for rewarding or compensating investigators and trial subjects.

Regulation 15(10) also sets a time limit of 60 days between receipt of a valid application and the issuing of the REC's opinion, unless the trial involves gene therapy, somatic cell therapy, or a medicinal product containing a genetically modified organism, in which case longer time limits (of up to 180 days) apply.

The new Regulations retain the dual system of local and multicentre ethics committee approval, but they attempt to reduce delays by ensuring that local issues are dealt with within strict time limits by a small number of local committee members. Local issues are now defined in the governance arrangements as:[52]

---

[49] Julia C Lewis, Susan Tomkins, and Julian R Sampson, 'Ethical approval for research involving geographically dispersed subjects: unsuitability of the UK MREC/LREC system and relevance to uncommon genetic disorders' (2001) 27 Journal of Medical Ethics 347–51.

[50] <http://www.corec.org.uk/>.

[51] *On the approximation of the laws, regulations and administrative provisions of the Member States relating to the implenetation of good clinical practice in the conduct of clinical trials on medicinal products for human use.* Directive 2001/20/EC 4 Apr 2001, Official Journal 2001 L121: 34–41.

[52] *Research Governance Framework for Health and Social Care* (DoH 2001).

- The suitability of the local researcher
- The appropriateness of the local research environment and facilities
- Specific issues relating to the local community, such as the need for information to be translated.

While the new system will undoubtedly speed up the cumbersome process of ethics committee approval, and will ensure that committees are adequately funded, the priority given to the needs of researchers may still be in tension with the duty to protect the wellbeing of research subjects. As we saw earlier, Article 5 of the Helsinki Declaration demands that the 'well being of the human subject should take priority over the interests of science and society'. While this commitment to subjects' well-being is reproduced in the governance arrangements, it appears to be the responsibility of *researchers* and not ethics committees, to ensure that participants' welfare is protected.

Research Governance Framework for Health and Social Care[53]

3.12.2 Research ethics committees and their members must act in good faith and provide impartial and independent advice within their remits and terms of reference. Their primary responsibility is to ensure that the research respects the dignity, rights, safety and well-being of individual research participants. They should also work efficiently to facilitate the good conduct of high quality research that offers benefits to participants, services and society at large. Unjustified delay to such research is itself unethical.

3.12.8 NHS research ethics committees require researchers working in the NHS to keep them informed of the progress of a study. . . . However, the principal investigator and his or her employer, the research sponsor and the care organisation, and not the research ethics committee, are responsible for ensuring that a study follows the agreed protocol and for monitoring its progress.

It is also perhaps significant that the first principle in the governance arrangements states that the research ethics committee's duty is to '*enable* relevant research of good quality' (my emphasis). Ethics committees are also specifically charged with '*reassuring the public*' that research subjects are offered adequate protection. Their purpose is therefore in part to foster a positive public image of medical research.

Cave and Soren point out that the directive too was 'industry led', and that one of its principal purposes is to ensure that Europe is an attractive destination for researchers planning potentially profitable clinical trials.[54] Again, there may be a conflict of interest between RECs' duty to critically review research protocols and their responsibility for promoting public confidence in research.

In addition, a number of further problems with the system for ethical review remain. First, there has sometimes been some confusion over whether RECs are supposed to judge the scientific validity of research, as well as whether it is ethically sound. Following their review of the operation of ethics committees in 2005, the Department of Health reiterated that RECs should decide whether the protocol is

---

[53] DoH 2001.
[54] E Cave and S Holm, 'New governance arrangements for research ethics committees: is facilitating research achieved at the cost of participants' interest' (2002) 28 Journal of Medical Ethics 318–21.

ethically acceptable, with appropriate specialists judging whether the research has any scientific merit before the question of whether it meets appropriate ethical standards is considered.[55]

Secondly, P Wainwright and J Saunders dispute the assumption that local issues require fresh consideration by a local *ethics* committee. They argue that whether proposed research is *ethical* is not something that is necessarily subject to local variation.

P Wainwright and J Saunders[56]

[T]here is an inherent tension in the idea that there can be local ethical issues (as opposed, one must presume, to 'central ethical issues') that render a study ethically sound in one place and not in another. The intention in this article is to argue that there are no such things as local ethical issues and that the review of matters currently described as 'locality issues' should not be the responsibility of a research ethics committee . . .

It would of course be unethical to allow an incompetent investigator to run a clinical trial at a particular centre. It would also be unethical to present the local ethnic community, many of whom do not speak English, with information and consent materials printed only in English . . . They are of course unethical, but the ethical standard is one that is set at the national or international level, and not at the local. . . .

We have argued in this paper that the only questions of research ethics relating to studies reviewed by RECs are central issues: the REC reviews the ethics of the study. It would be unethical to allow incompetent researchers to conduct research in inadequate facilities, but this is not a question of the ethics of research. The competence of the investigator and the suitability of the facilities are empirical questions that the REC is not competent to address and these are issues that should be outside the responsibility of the REC.

Thirdly, in response to criticisms made by Neuberger and others that lay members were often in a minority on committees, and that meetings tended to be dominated by scientists and doctors, the role of the lay members has been strengthened in recent years: the Department of Health's guidelines state that a layperson must be the chair or the deputy chair, and the RCP guidelines specify that lay members should be 'persons of responsibility and standing who will not be overawed by medical members'. Yet the role of the lay members of ethics committees remains unclear. They are not appointed *in order to* represent the interests of society, or the interests of research subjects. Rather they are simply members of the public who must express their *own* opinion, which may turn out to be very pro-science. If the lay members' purpose is to ensure that the interests of research subjects are adequately represented, then it might be important to recruit people with experience of participating in research. Analogously, if the lay members are also supposed to represent the interests of the community, it might be appropriate to ensure that committees include representatives of patient groups. Where the research project involves members of particular social groups, such as students, junior NHS employees, or the elderly, it might also be important to seek the views of relevant representatives.

[55] *Report on the Future Operation of Research Ethics Committees* (DoH 2005) available at <http://www.dh.gov.uk>.
[56] 'What are local issues? The problem of the local review of research' (2004) 30 Journal of Medical Ethics 313–17.

Fourthly, because of their access to the original protocol, RECs are particularly well placed to monitor researchers' adherence to the ethical standards upon which the REC's approval was based. In practice, however, RECs exercise comparatively little ongoing scrutiny of research once the initial protocol has been approved. While progress reports must be submitted, the committee's role is largely confined to collecting information volunteered by the researchers, rather than investigating the extent to which there has been compliance with the original protocol. If deviations from the protocol are likely to go unnoticed, and unpunished, researchers have no incentive to ensure scrupulous compliance. Perhaps unsurprisingly, studies have indicated that there are divergences from the research plan in as many as a quarter of all projects.[57]

(c) MEDICINES FOR HUMAN USE (CLINICAL TRIALS) REGULATIONS 2004

In 2001 the European Parliament issued Directive 2001/20/EC on the approximation of the laws, regulations and administrative provisions of the Member States relating to the implementation of good clinical practice in the conduct of clinical trials on medicinal products for human use.[58] In the UK, the Directive led to the Medicines for Human Use (Clinical Trials) Regulations 2004, which came into force in May 2004.

A clinical trial is defined in Regulation 2(1):

Medicines for Human Use (Clinical Trials) Regulations 2004 reg 2(1)
'clinical trial' means any investigation in human subjects, other than a non-interventional trial, intended—

(a) to discover or verify the clinical, pharmacological or other pharmacodynamic effects of one or more medicinal products,

(b) to identify any adverse reactions to one or more such products, or

(c) to study absorption, distribution, metabolism and excretion of one or more such products.

Regulation 28 states that 'No person shall conduct a clinical trial or carry out the functions of the sponsor of a trial . . . otherwise than in accordance with the conditions and principles of good clinical practice.' This effectively confirms that the various international codes of research ethics should have legally binding force. Good clinical practice (GCP) is fleshed out in Schedule 1, Part II.

Medicines for Human Use (Clinical Trials) Regulations 2004 Schedule 1 part II
1. Clinical trials shall be conducted in accordance with the ethical principles that have their origin in the Declaration of Helsinki, and that are consistent with good clinical practice and the requirements of these Regulations.

2. Before the trial is initiated, foreseeable risks and inconveniences have been weighed against the anticipated benefit for the individual trial subject and other present and future patients. A trial should be initiated and continued only if the anticipated benefits justify the risks.

---

[57] T Smith, EJH Moore, and H Tunstall-Pedoe, 'Review by a local medical research ethics committee of the conduct of approved research projects, by examination of patients' case notes, consent forms, and research records and by interview' (1997) 314 British Medical Journal 1588.

[58] *Official Journal* L 121, 01/05/2001 P. 0034–0044.

3. The rights, safety, and well-being of the trial subjects are the most important considerations and shall prevail over interests of science and society.

4. The available non-clinical and clinical information on an investigational medicinal product shall be adequate to support the clinical trial.

5. Clinical trials shall be scientifically sound, and described in a clear, detailed protocol.

6. A trial shall be conducted in compliance with the protocol that has a favourable opinion from an ethics committee.

7. The medical care given to, and medical decisions made on behalf of, subjects shall always be the responsibility of an appropriately qualified doctor or, when appropriate, of a qualified dentist.

8. Each individual involved in conducting a trial shall be qualified by education, training, and experience to perform his or her respective task(s).

9. Subject to the other provisions of this Schedule relating to consent, freely given informed consent shall be obtained from every subject prior to clinical trial participation.

10. All clinical trial information shall be recorded, handled, and stored in a way that allows its accurate reporting, interpretation and verification.

11. The confidentiality of records that could identify subjects shall be protected, respecting the privacy and confidentiality rules in accordance with the requirements of the Data Protection Act 1998 and the law relating to confidentiality.

12. Investigational medicinal products used in the trial shall be—

    (a) manufactured or imported, and handled and stored, in accordance with the principles and guidelines of good manufacturing practice, and

    (b) used in accordance with the approved protocol.

13. Systems with procedures that assure the quality of every aspect of the trial shall be implemented.

In addition to ethics committee approval, under Regulation 17, every clinical trial must now have a clinical trial authorization issued by the licensing authority, which in the UK is the Medicines and Healthcare products Regulatory Agency or MHRA (we consider the work of the MHRA in more detail in the next chapter when we look at the licensing of medicines). The MHRA has the power to suspend or prohibit a clinical trial either generally, or at a particular site, either if it has grounds for believing that the conditions set out in the original request for authorization are no longer satisfied, or if it receives information raising doubts about the conduct, safety or scientific validity of the trial. Regulations 32–5 provide for notification, within strict time limits, of actual and suspected serious adverse events. Sponsors are required to provide an annual list of all serious adverse events, and a report on the safety of the trial's subjects. Regulations 49 and 50 create a number of offences. For example, it is an offence to start a clinical trial without a favourable ethics committee opinion.

The Regulations also contain detailed provisions on obtaining informed consent from competent patients and the circumstances in which research on incompetent subjects is legitimate. We consider these in the next sections in the context of a more detailed discussion of the role of consent in research.

7. CONSENT TO PARTICIPATION IN RESEARCH

(a) THE COMPETENT SUBJECT

(1) VOLUNTARINESS

Because the research subject will commonly be exposing herself to some increased risk, without necessarily gaining any benefit in return, it has been suggested that we should be particularly concerned to ensure that her consent has been given voluntarily. In part, this might involve making sure that she was fully informed about the nature of the research trial, and we consider the question of informed consent in the following section. But it might also be important to ensure that external factors had not exerted so much pressure on her that she felt she had no other option but to agree to take part. Choosing to 'volunteer' for research is only truly voluntary if it would have been possible for the subject to refuse.

In this section, we begin by looking at whether offering to pay research subjects might unduly influence their decisions. Next we consider the special vulnerability of patients. Finally, we look at other 'vulnerable' groups, such as prisoners and medical students.

(a) Payments

Paying people to participate in research has been criticized for a number of reasons. First, in the next extract, Paul McNeill argues that the offer of money may prove irresistible, especially for the poorest sections of society.

Paul McNeill[59]

It is clearly not possible to remove all risks. An experiment would not be an experiment if it was known in advance that the experimental procedure was safe. For this reason, those who volunteer for research should be those who clearly understand the extent and the nature of that risk. Comprehension of the risk is important. Furthermore, I claim that subjects should not be induced to disregard or downplay an appreciation of that risk by the offer of a financial reward . . .

The reason that inducement is particularly of concern is that those most susceptible to inducement may be the least able to assess the aims and technical information relating to the research and to decide on whether or not the risk is worth taking. It is already the poor and socially disadvantaged who volunteer for most research yet it is typically the better off members of society who benefit from research. The offering of financial inducement simply exacerbates this inequity and adds further to the risks for those disadvantaged people . . .

The basis of my argument against inducement is that it encourages people to expose themselves to risk of harm. This encouragement is greater for the impecunious. The difficulty is acute when the experiment has a clear potential for harm such as experimenting with chemical compounds (drug research) and other medical research . . .

[F]inancial inducement to take part in research can be justified where there is no known, and very little likelihood of harm. The case against inducement is much more persuasive where there is

---

[59] 'Paying People to Participate in Research: Why Not?' (1997) 11 Bioethics 391–6.

a risk of harm to the subjects. There is something repugnant about offering money to relatively poor people, impecunious students, travellers and others, to take part in research, which, by its nature, exposes them to risks of harm. The poor in our societies already have higher risks of poor health and other adverse life events. Inducement to take part in experimentation should not be allowed when it adds to those risks.

Not only could the lure of money persuade poor people to volunteer for research, but it might also offer an incentive to misrepresent characteristics—such as depression or drug use—which would otherwise disqualify someone from participation, thus increasing the health risks to which they are exposed. In the next extract, JP Bentley and PG Thacker draw on empirical research which suggests that while payments do not 'blind' individuals to risk, they do increase subjects' willingness both to participate in research, and to conceal information about 'restricted activities'.

JP Bentley and PG Thacker[60]

With respect to willingness to participate, both risk level and monetary payment had a significant effect; with higher levels of risk and lower levels of payment leading to lower willingness ratings. . . . Without payment, respondents' willingness to participate decreased and their willingness to participate without payment was influenced only by risk level, with higher risk levels leading to lower willingness ratings.

This study suggests that monetary payment increases respondents' willingness to participate in research regardless of the level of risk; higher levels of payment make respondents more willing to participate, even if the study is relatively risky. However, higher monetary payments, at least in this study, did not appear to blind respondents to risks . . .

Monetary payments appeared to influence respondents' propensity to neglect to tell researchers about restricted activities they have engaged in either before or during a study, with higher payment levels leading to a higher propensity to neglect to tell. . . . Risk level appeared to influence respondents' propensity to neglect to tell researchers about experiencing negative effects, with respondents in the low risk group having the highest propensity to neglect to tell.

This study also showed that higher levels of monetary payment may influence subjects' behaviours regarding concealing information about restricted activities. If such activities were actually engaged in, the results of the hypothetical studies may have been distorted (that is, alcohol, caffeine, medications, herbal products may all affect the pharmacokinetics of a study drug). However, findings from this study suggest that this effect may be more likely to occur in lower risk studies.

Secondly, the 'taint' of money is thought by some to contaminate the ethical virtue of altruistic participation. Tod Chambers, for example, argues that 'the gift of one's own health should not be thought of as a commodity'.[61] Third it is sometimes argued that payments will skew subject selection, and thereby undermine the validity of research findings. Poorer sections of society, such as students, are often overrepresented in research projects, while richer groups, such as wealthy middle-aged businessmen tend to be underrepresented.

---

[60] 'The influence of risk and monetary payment on the research participation decision making process' (2004) 30 Journal of Medical Ethics 293–8.
[61] 'Participation as Commodity, Participation as Gift' (2001) 1 American Journal of Bioethics 48.

Against this, it could be argued, first, that since participation in medical research will often be time-consuming, inconvenient and uncomfortable, without payments it might be difficult to recruit sufficient numbers of subjects. Second, it is not clear why being paid to assume the burdens of research participation is necessarily more problematic than paying people to do other unskilled and unpleasant employment which may pose some risk to a person's health. (We encounter this point again in Chapter 12 when we consider payment for living organ donation.) In the next extract, Martin Wilkinson and Andrew Moore argue that inducements are not necessarily coercive.

Martin Wilkinson and Andrew Moore[62]

Consider the following argument for allowing inducements. Some researchers would find it worthwhile to pay inducements in order to attract enough subjects. Those who would accept this reward would not do so unless it were worth while to them. As a result of offering the reward, the researchers get the subjects they want. As a result of participating, the subjects get the reward they want. Both are better off. No one is worse off. Inducement is thus a good thing.

This seems to us to be a good argument, which at least makes a *prima facie* case for inducement. It has the same structure as an argument justifying wages for work, or any other market transactions. Many people would not work if they were not paid; in that sense wages are inducements. Few people think that, as a result, it is wrong to offer wages. Those that do have concerns about the existing wage system usually object that wages are too *low*, not that they are too high, or that they are offered at all. . . .

If badly off people were in some way coerced into participating as subjects, then their autonomy would be infringed upon and their consent invalidated. Coercion is paradigmatically a case of the denial of autonomy, since it consists in the deliberate imposition of one person's will on another. However, coercion usually takes the form of threats, which restrict people's options. Inducements are offers, not threats, and they expand people's options.

Thirdly, the offer of experimental treatment to desperately ill patients, and the 'therapeutic misconception' (considered in the next section), will often offer a much more powerful incentive than money for agreeing to participate in research, and for misrepresenting one's disqualifying characteristics. A research subject who has been paid is probably *more* likely to have given fully informed consent to her participation in a research trial than a patient who is mistakenly under the assumption that her doctor is treating her in her best interests.

The compromise position adopted in the various ethical guidelines is that payment is acceptable provided it is at a fairly modest level, and hence unlikely to overbear an individual's will.

General Medical Council[63]

14 You must not offer payments at a level which could induce research participants to take risks that they would otherwise not take, or to volunteer more frequently than is advisable or against their better interests or judgement;

In the next extract, Christine Grady defends this idea that modest payments to research subjects compensate for the inconvenience and discomfort to which they

---

[62] 'Inducement in Research' (1997) 11 Bioethics 373–89.
[63] *Research: The Role and Responsibilities of Doctors* (GMC 2002) available at <http://www.gmc-uk.org/>.

will be exposed, without interfering with the voluntariness of their decision to participate.

Christine Grady[64]

Presumably, most subjects attracted to research by money, or subjects who choose to participate in research partly because of the money, do have the freedom to refuse. Prospective subjects are reminded of their right to exercise this freedom in the process of obtaining informed consent. They are advised that participation is their choice and they have the right to refuse or withdraw at any time without penalty. In addition, many people who are attracted to research because of the money (including students, people looking for a little extra money, or even the 'professional guinea pig') generally do have additional options for obtaining money, usually from other full or part-time unskilled jobs. Perhaps they select research participation because it has more flexible hours, is time limited, or seems more interesting or easier . . . Perhaps the potential for undue induce-ment—in the sense that money literally makes research an offer than one cannot refuse—is a worry when a person is economically destitute and truly has no other options for acquiring comparable amounts of money. . . .

Money is also believed capable of inappropriately distorting people's judgments and motiv-ations . . . [O]ffers of money could cause potential participants to misrepresent something about themselves in order to gain or maintain enrolment in a study and receive the money. Misrepresen-tation may not only jeopardize the participant's informed consent, but possibly also his or her well-being as well as the integrity of the study . . . Presumably, however, the larger the sum of money involved, the greater the potential for distorting judgment or promoting potential partici-pants to life or ignore risks. Commentators and common wisdom have argued that limiting the amount of payment offered for research participation minimizes the possibility that money will distort judgment and push people towards deception. Payment as recognition of the research participant's contribution and calculated according to some regularly applied and locally accept-able standard (per day, visit, or procedure) is likely to be more modest and less likely to distort judgement than amounts designed solely to attract subjects and outperform the competition in terms of recruitment.

In contrast, writing from a Canadian perspective, Trudo Lemmens and Carl Elliott suggest that the compromise position in which subjects are paid, but not much, is disingenuous. They argue that it would be better to straightforwardly admit that the researcher is *employing* the research subject. This would enable these 'employees' to benefit from protective legislation—such as health and safety rules—which would prevent them from being exposed to unreasonable risks.

Trudo Lemmens and Carl Elliott[65]

Should we be worried that healthy people are being paid to enroll in research studies? Bioethicists cannot decide and so the issue has dropped into a regulatory vacuum. US and Canadian regula-tions and guidelines frown on paying research subjects, but they do not prohibit it. They allow researchers to pay subjects, but discourage them from paying very much, lest subjects be 'unduly influenced' or 'coerced' into enrolling in a study against their better judgement. Some guidelines or statutes suggest that 'compensation for loss and inconvenience is acceptable', but other pay-ment is not. Given this sort of waffling, it is no wonder that Institutional Review Boards (IRBs)

---

[64] 'Money for Research Participation: Does it Jeopardize Informed Consent' (2001) 1 American Journal of Bioethics 40–4.
[65] 'Justice for the Professional Guinea Pig' (2001) 1 American Journal of Bioethics 51–3.

are baffled. How much are researchers allowed to pay a research subject undergoing a bron-choscopy? How much for a simple blood drawing? What is it worth to go without sleep for 36 hours, or to be exposed to malaria, or to try an experimental antipsychotic drug?

In the world that regulatory bodies have created, healthy subjects take part in studies because of the money, yet researchers have to pretend that the subjects are motivated by something other than money. Research subjects cannot negotiate payment, since payment is not supposed to be the focus of the transaction . . .

It is time to stop pretending that the relationship between for-profit, multibillion-dollar corporate entities and healthy volunteers is the same as the relationship between an academic physician-investigator and sick patients. We have argued that research studies on healthy subjects—unlike research on sick patients—are best characterized as a kind of labor relation. If regulatory bodies realized this, they would be in a far better position to protect these subjects from exploitation. Labor-type legislation could give research agencies the clout of occupational health and safety agencies by giving them the power to conduct inspections and ensure that 'working' conditions are safe. Collective negotiations and unionization could give research participants a stronger voice in arguing for good working conditions. Research participants could negotiate standards of payment based on the level of discomfort they are asked to undergo, the number and types of procedures, the duration of the studies and other factors. . . .

Are there dangers to this kind of shift? Yes, absolutely. The most serious danger is that the payment argument could be hijacked to defend even more commercialization of the research enterprise and even more exploitation of vulnerable subjects . . . The current regulatory system is even more dangerous. Ethical guidelines and regulations ought to protect healthy research subjects from exploitation. But instead, the current regulatory scheme prohibits subjects from receiving a fair wage and denies them the legal resources available to other high-risk workers.

(b) Patients

One of the principal problems faced when enrolling patients into clinical research trials is the 'therapeutic misconception'. This is the problem that individuals might not understand that they are taking part in research which is designed to yield generalizable knowledge, and not to meet their individual health needs. Of course, the danger that research subjects will wrongly assume that they are receiving treatment which their doctor believes to be in their best interests exists only when a new treatment is being tested on people who suffer from the condition which it is designed to alleviate. For obvious reasons, healthy volunteers are much more likely to realize that they have consented to take part in an experiment. Paradoxically, then, it may be easier to gain informed consent when the research is clearly non-therapeutic.

Standard consent forms may exacerbate this problem by setting out what the study intends to achieve for future patients. Confusion between the goals of the research and what patients hope for themselves is then inevitable. Nancy King advocates a much blunter approach:

When benefit cannot reasonably be expected, the consent form should say, 'You will not benefit'.[66]

Terminally ill patients are an especially vulnerable group, particularly if none of the standard treatments have worked, and they have been told that no more can be done

---

[66] Nancy MP King, 'Defining and Describing Benefit Appropriately in Clinical Trials' (2000) 28 Journal of Law, Medicine and Ethics (2000) 332, 334

for them. In such circumstances, enrolling in a trial of an experimental new drug may appear to offer their best hope of recovery. Of course, their desperation to try anything does not necessarily vitiate their consent, but it does suggest that researchers should be careful not to overstate the likelihood that the patient will receive a direct health benefit.

The doctor–patient relationship is based upon trust, and it is often difficult for patients to understand that their doctor might be suggesting a course of action which is not necessarily in their best interests. Certainly, there is evidence that some research subjects do not realize that they have taken part in an experiment, even when they have apparently given informed consent. For example, Katie Featherstone and Jenny L Donovan interviewed participants in a research trial who clearly found it very hard to believe that they had really been allocated treatment randomly.

Katie Featherstone and Jenny L Donovan[67]

There were a number of factors that contributed to the men's struggle to understand . . . Allocation according to randomisation appeared to some to be very haphazard. It was difficult for these men to believe that such a haphazard procedure was reasonable, particularly when they had completed so many questionnaires about their symptoms and undergone clinical tests, some of which were very invasive. The men reasoned that the data from the questionnaires and clinical tests must be useful, not just for research purposes, but also for clinicians to make individualised treatment decisions—hence the unacceptability of randomisation. . . .

[E]ven when trials adhere to strict informed consent procedures and ensure that 'simple language' is used, this does not guarantee that subjects will fully understand the implications of participation and that they may still have unrealistic treatment expectations. . . . It has been suggested that potential trial participants should be informed specifically about the components of research that constitute a change from the standard doctor–patient relationship— randomisation and blinding.

It is common for patients to feel grateful to the medical team involved in their care, and so if asked to participate in a research trial, refusal may not feel like a realistic option. Patients have ongoing relationships with their doctors, and as a result, they may be concerned that a refusal might jeopardize their future care. In the next extract, Franz J Ingelfinger draws attention to the fact that illness often increases patients' vulnerability and dependency, and hence makes it even harder for them to object to participation in research.

Franz J Ingelfinger[68]

Incapacitated and hospitalized because of the illness, frightened by strange and impersonal routines, and fearful for his health and perhaps life, he is far from exercising a free power of choice when the person to whom he anchors all his hopes asks, 'Say, you wouldn't mind, would you, if you joined some of the other patients on this floor and helped us to carry out some very important research we're doing?' When 'informed consent' is obtained, it is not the student, the destitute bum, or the prisoner to whom, by virtue of his condition, the thumb screws of coercion are most

[67] 'Why don't they just tell me straight, why allocate it?' The struggle to make sense of participating in a randomized controlled trial (2002) 55 Social Science and Medicine 709–19.
[68] 'Informed (But Uneducated) Consent' (1972) 287 New England Journal of Medicine 466.

relentlessly applied; it is the most used and useful of all experimental subjects, the patient with disease.

(c) Other vulnerable groups

It is worth noting that the category of people who are considered vulnerable when obtaining consent to participation in research extends far beyond those who may be unable to give a valid consent to medical treatment. Medical students or junior employees, for example, may feel pressure to agree to participate in their teachers' or employers' research projects. The Helsinki Declaration requires researchers to be particularly cautious if the subject is in a dependent relationship to her.

Helsinki Declaration[69]

23. When obtaining informed consent for the research project the physician should be particularly cautious if the subject is in a dependent relationship with the physician or may consent under duress. In that case the informed consent should be obtained by a well-informed physician who is not engaged in the investigation and who is completely independent of this relationship.

Similarly, the General Medical Council guidance instructs doctors that they must

ensure that no real or implied coercion is used on participants who are in a dependent relationship to you, for example, medical students, a junior colleague, nurse in your practice or employee in your company.[70]

For medical students and employees, this means that consent should normally be obtained by an independent doctor.

In the eighteenth and nineteenth centuries, prisoners were often used as research subjects. This was partly done because of their low social status, and partly for reasons of convenience: follow-up studies are obviously facilitated if the research subjects can be guaranteed to remain in the same place for many years. However, the abuses the Nazis perpetrated upon concentration camp inmates undoubtedly changed the perception that prisoners can be treated as an expendable resource. On the contrary, prisoners are now categorized as a particularly vulnerable group for the purposes of obtaining consent to participation in research.

Small financial rewards may be disproportionately attractive in prison where the opportunities for earning money are limited. Boredom too might encourage prisoners to enrol in scientific studies. It is not, however, clear that a prisoner who is willing to take part in research in order to relieve the monotony of prison life, or to earn a small amount of extra money, has necessarily been coerced. Perhaps more importantly, prisoners may wrongly believe that agreeing to take part in research might lead to early parole or other privileges, and as a result may not feel that refusal is a realistic option. In the UK, there is no blanket ban on conducting research on prisoners, but the voluntariness of a prisoner's consent should be subject to particular

---

[69] World Medical Association, Declaration of Helsinki: Ethical Principles for Medical Research Involving Human Subjects (6th version adopted at the 52nd WMA General Assembly, Edinburgh, Scotland, Oct 2000) available at <http://www.wma.net/e/policy/b3.htm>.

[70] General Medical Council, *Research: The Role and Responsibilities of Doctors* (GMC 2002) para 8.

scrutiny. As we saw in Chapter 4, in *Freeman v Home Office*,[71] a case involving treatment rather than research, the Court of Appeal suggested that:

where, in a prison setting, a doctor has power to influence a prisoner's situation and prospects a court must be alive to the risk that what may appear, on the face of it, to be a real consent is not in fact so.

Because of their special vulnerability, it would therefore be difficult to justify carrying out any research on prisoners unless the fact of a person's incarceration was directly relevant to the research. An example might be psychological studies involving the impact of imprisonment on depression.

(2) INFORMATION

As we saw in Chapter 12, treating someone without their consent may constitute a battery. For consent to ordinary medical treatment to be valid, the patient must have been informed 'in broad terms' about the nature of the medical procedure.[72] So if someone has not been told that they are participating in a research trial, any apparent consent could be invalid, either because there has been fraud which vitiates their consent, or because they have agreed to a procedure which is materially different from that which is actually carried out.

The rule that competent subjects must give their fully informed consent to participation in research is common to all of the various guidelines and codes governing experiments on human subjects from Nuremberg onwards. Indeed it is widely believed that the informed consent of the subject is what justifies imposing the risks of research participation upon individuals.

Helsinki Declaration[73]

22 In any research on human beings, each potential subject must be adequately informed of the aims, methods, sources of funding, any possible conflicts of interest, institutional affiliations of the researcher, the anticipated benefits and potential risks of the study and the discomfort it may entail. The subject should be informed of the right to abstain from participation in the study or to withdraw consent to participate at any time without reprisal. After ensuring that the subject has understood the information, the physician should then obtain the subject's freely-given informed consent, preferably in writing. If the consent cannot be obtained in writing, the non-written consent must be formally documented and witnessed.

Similarly, Schedule 1 Part 3 of the Medicines for Human Use (Clinical Trials) Regulations 2004 specify that the research subject must have given 'informed consent'.

Medicines for Human Use (Clinical Trials) Regulations 2004 Schedule 1 Part 3
CONDITIONS WHICH APPLY IN RELATION TO AN ADULT ABLE TO CONSENT OR WHO
HAS GIVEN CONSENT PRIOR TO THE ONSET OF INCAPACITY

    1.   The subject has had an interview with the investigator, or another member of the investigat-

---

[71] [1984] QB 524.
[72] *Chatterton v Gerson* [1981] QB 432.
[73] World Medical Association, Declaration of Helsinki: Ethical Principles for Medical Research Involving Human Subjects (6th version adopted at the 52nd WMA General Assembly, Edinburgh, Scotland, Oct 2000) available at <http://www.wma.net/e/policy/b3.htm>.

ing team, in which he has been given the opportunity to understand the objectives, risks and inconveniences of the trial and the conditions under which it is to be conducted.

2. The subject has been informed of his right to withdraw from the trial at any time.

3. The subject has given his informed consent to taking part in the trial.

4. The subject may, without being subject to any resulting detriment, withdraw from the clinical trial at any time by revoking his informed consent.

5. The subject has been provided with a contact point where he may obtain further information about the trial.

But what does it mean to give 'informed consent'? How much information does an individual have to be given before their consent can be considered 'informed'? The GMC guidance fleshes out this requirement.

General Medical Council[74]

19 You must ensure that any individuals whom you invite to take part in research are given the information which they want or ought to know, and that is presented in terms and a form that they can understand. You must bear in mind that it may be difficult for participants to identify and assess the risks involved. Giving the information will usually include an initial discussion supported by a leaflet or sound recording, where possible taking into account any particular communication or language needs of the participants. You must give participants an opportunity to ask questions and to express any concerns they may have.

As we saw earlier, a particular problem is raised when the subject gives consent to participation in an RCT: because an RCT will only yield reliable results if the subject *does not know* whether they are in the control group or not: their consent is therefore inevitably based upon less than full information. It is also particularly hard for subjects to understand the idea of randomization. Patients often appear to believe that they will benefit from participation in a trial, even where they have been informed that there is a fifty-fifty chance that they will not receive any treatment at all.

Moreover, although we might agree that researchers must tell subjects about the risks involved in participation before their consent can be considered fully informed, there will inevitably be grey areas, where the relevance of particular sorts of information is less clear. Do participants need to know about the funding arrangements for the research, for example? Must they be informed about any personal or financial benefit that the researcher hopes to receive as a result of this trial? Should they be told if the researcher has been paid to recruit subjects? How much should the researcher disclose about their own motivation in carrying out the research, or their qualifications for doing so?

Because gaining the subject's informed consent is a necessary precondition of participation in a research trial, there is also a danger that researchers will assume that the provision of information only has to happen at one fixed moment before the trial begins. But to be valid, the subject's consent to participation must be fully informed *throughout* the trial, and researchers may therefore be under a duty to ensure that subjects are provided with information that emerges after the trial has begun, so that

---

[74] *Research: The Role and Responsibilities of Doctors* (GMC 2002) available at <http://www.gmc-uk.org/>.

their decision to *continue* to participate is also properly informed. But this raises an obvious problem—if researchers must fully disclose their preliminary findings about the risks and benefits of a new treatment, subjects may exercise their right to withdraw from the trial before statistically significant data have been gathered.

Under Schedule 1 of the Medicines for Human Use (Clinical Trials) Regulations 2004 the subject's informed consent should normally be formally recorded on a signed, written consent form, or if the subject is unable to write, consent should be given orally in the presence of at least one witness and recorded in writing. It is important to remember that a signed consent form is not the same thing as a binding contract between the subject and the researcher. The existence of a signature on a consent form does not guarantee that the subject has given informed consent to participation. Nor does it force the subject to keep her side of the 'bargain': subjects must always be free to withdraw from the research project, without being subject to any penalty at all.

It is also worth noting that there is an important difference between providing information and ensuring that patients fully *understand* the information that they have been given. Evidence that patients are sometimes unaware that they have taken part in research, despite their signature on a written consent form which unambiguously states that the procedures are part of a research project, shows that simply providing information will not always be sufficient to ensure that the subject's consent is adequately informed. As Jay Katz explains in the following extract, gaining properly informed consent is a much more time-consuming and expensive exercise than the common practice of simply offering research subjects a printed sheet of information.

Jay Katz[75]

I shall argue that respect for individual autonomy and for self-determination, which informed consent is intended to safeguard, will remain hollow aspirations until the nature and quality of the conversations between physician-investigators and patient-subjects about participation in research are radically transformed. . . .

Research is not entirely a voyage into the utterly unknown. When a clinical trial is contemplated, considerable information, though not yet scientifically validated, is generally available to suggest that experimental treatments may promise to be beneficial. Thus, in situations in which the experimental treatment is compared with existing standard therapy, all kinds of known or conjectured evidence has accumulated about their respective merits. Patient-subjects generally remain ignorant of most, if not all, of these complexities of knowledge and ignorance . . .

The investigators who appear before patient-subjects as physicians in white coats create confusion. Patients come to hospitals with the trusting expectation that their doctors will care for them. They will view an invitation to participate in research as a professional recommendation that is intended to serve their individual treatment interests. It is that belief, that trust, which physician-investigators must vigorously challenge so that patient-subjects appreciate that in research, unlike therapy, the research question comes first. This takes time and is difficult to convey. It can be conveyed to patient-subjects only if physician-investigators are willing to challenge the misperceptions that many patients bring to the invitation . . .

Thus, recruitment of subjects will prove to be more time consuming. Completion of research

---

[75] 'Human Experimentation and Human Rights' (1993) 38 Saint Louis University Law Journal 7.

may also be delayed and, if too many patients refuse, selection bias will make some research impossible to conduct. Not only may scientific progress be impeded but physician-investigators' self-interests in recognition and advancement of their careers may be jeopardized.

(b) THE INCOMPETENT SUBJECT

If the consent of the subject is what makes research morally acceptable, where does this leave individuals who are unable to give legally valid consent to treatment? As we saw in Chapter 4, there are three categories of patients who are unable to consent to medical treatment: children, mentally incapacitated adults, and unconscious patients. (For a full account of the law governing the treatment of incompetent patients, see pp. 203–48.) Recall that parents usually give consent to their child's treatment, subject to the courts' power to overrule parental decision-making in order to protect the child's best interests. Mentally incapacitated adults can normally be treated by doctors in their best interests, although court approval is necessary in a small sub-set of cases, such as non-therapeutic sterilization. An unconscious patient may be given treatment that is immediately necessary to preserve their life or health.

None of these rules would appear to facilitate incompetent patients' participation in medical research. Since taking part in an experiment involves being exposed to a procedure whose effect is, by definition, uncertain, it will not usually be in the best interests of a patient. It is, however, important to remember that a blanket ban on research involving patients who lack capacity might also be inappropriate. If no trials can ever take place involving children and mentally incapacitated or unconscious adults, members of these groups will have access only to inadequately tested treatments. Children absorb drugs differently from adults, and so simply giving them a reduced dose of a medicine which has been tested on adults is likely to be either ineffective or unsafe. In the next extract, Paul Miller and Nuala Kenny explain that shielding children from the dangers of research might itself cause children significant harm.

Paul B Miller and Nuala P Kenny[76]
Ironically, the protective impulse to shield children entirely from the harms of research participation has the potential to cause them significant harm. History tells of the dangerous consequences of presuming treatments tested on adults to be safe and efficacious for children . . . For scientific and ethical reasons, children should receive wherever possible only those treatments that have been adequately evaluated on children. . . . Reliance on the results of research involving adults as the knowledge base from which to develop the care of children may make the provision of such care unnecessarily dangerous.

Moreover, as Lainie Friedman Ross points out, we allow parents to subject their children to other sorts of risks, such as being a passenger in a car or taking part in sporting activities.

---

[76] 'Walking the Moral Tightrope: Respecting and Protecting Children in Health-Related Research' (2002) 11 Cambridge Quarterly of Healthcare Ethics 217–29, 218–19.

Lainie Friedman Ross[77]

[Paul] Ramsey's position was that children should never participate as research subjects in 'non-therapeutic research' (that is, research which has no direct benefit for the children-subjects). Ramsey argued that for research to be moral, the subject must give his informed consent. Since the child cannot give informed consent, his parents must act as his surrogate. . . . Ramsey argues that parents cannot give informed consent for their child's participation in activities which do not directly benefit the child. This is not the case. Parents often take their children on self-serving errands and excursions. . . .

The argument that parents can only consent to activities which directly benefit their child holds parents to a best interest standard. This standard has been criticized because it permits too much state intervention and does not allow for parents to balance the needs of the child with the needs of other family members. . . .

Parental authorization of a child's participation in research of minimal risk and harm does not necessarily treat the child solely as a means. Rather, parents who value participation in social projects will try to inculcate similar values into their child. . . .

Many activities in a typical child's life, in fact, will present greater risks and harms, including such routine activities as participation in contact sports and traveling as a passenger in the family car . . . Parents are morally and legally authorized to decide which risks their child can take and in what settings. Parental authorization or prohibition of a child's participation in this type of research, then, is not abusive or neglectful. . . .

Given the minimal amount of risk which the proposed research entails, the child's participation will not interfere with the child's developing personhood even if she is forced to participate against her will. Their decision to override their child's dissent is not abusive; parents legitimately override their child's decisions in many daily activities. This is one way in which parents steer their child's development into the person she will become.

In other words, a child's participation in minimal risk research which offers no direct therapeutic benefit, even if she dissents, is consistent with the modified principle of respect. Although parents should always consider their child's opinion in their decisionmaking, parents ought to have final decisionmaking authority about whether their child participates in such research.

Since some mental illnesses impede their sufferers' decision-making capacity, it will only be possible to test drugs which might improve the lives of people with these sorts of conditions if research is carried out upon patients who cannot give consent. Emergency medicine often involves treating patients who have lost consciousness, and are therefore unable to consent to treatment. Again excluding such patients from research would inhibit the development of new techniques to address severe, life-threatening conditions.

If a blanket ban on incompetent subjects' participation in research is not justified, when might it be permissible to carry out research on individuals who cannot give consent? Although slightly different rules apply depending upon the reason for a person's inability to consent, some common principles can be detected:

- It must be impossible to do the research on individuals who *are* able to consent to participation.

---

[77] 'Children as Research Subjects: A Proposal to Review the Current Federal Regulations Using a Moral Framework' (1997) 8 Stanford Law and Policy Review 159.

- The research must be likely to benefit either the individual subject, or other members of the group to which the subject belongs.
- Efforts should be made to gain the subject's assent to participation, and any evidence that the subject does not wish to participate should be decisive.
- Where the research is non-therapeutic, unless the circumstances are exceptional, it should pose no more than a minimal risk to the subject.

The 'minimal risk' condition exists in most guidelines on the ethics of experiments involving incompetent subjects, yet its meaning is inherently unclear. It has been suggested that the likelihood of harm or discomfort from a minimal risk procedure should be no greater than that encountered in daily life, or during routine medical examinations. But this too is alarmingly vague because the extent to which individuals encounter discomfort or the risk of harm during their daily lives varies dramatically. Sick children, for example, may experience very high levels of pain and discomfort, but presumably we would not want to say that intrusive non-therapeutic experiments can legitimately be carried out on children whose existing quality of life is very low. Conversely, some mentally incapacitated adults will find any disruption to their routine frustrating and confusing, and so a procedure which might be of 'minimal risk' to a competent adult could present higher risks for some incompetent patients. The emphasis upon *risk*, as opposed to the burdens of participation is also unfortunate. A procedure, such as a bone marrow biopsy, may present almost no risk to an individual's health, but it may nevertheless be extremely painful and uncomfortable.[78]

Because the benefits from non-therapeutic research accrue to society, rather than to the individual subject, in the absence of the subject's freely given consent, such research might appear to contradict the basic principle that the well being of the subject should take precedence over the interests of science and society. To expose incompetent subjects to risks *solely* in order to advance scientific knowledge might be to treat such individuals merely as means, rather than as ends in themselves. If non-therapeutic research on those who cannot give consent does offend the Kantian imperative (see Chapter 1), it will do so regardless of whether the risk to the subject is minimal or substantial.

It could, however, be argued that the difficulties raised by incompetent patients' participation in research result from an over-emphasis upon consent as the justification for carrying out experiments on human subjects. Where consent cannot be gained from the individual subject, the principal ethical justification for enrolling them in a research trial is absent, and hence their participation is inherently problematic. Yet an alternative approach might view research participation as a valuable social activity, which should be equally available to all members of society.

Research subjects benefit from participation not only when there is a chance of receiving more effective treatment for a condition from which they are suffering. Indirect benefits—such as diversion from monotonous routine; the opportunity for social interaction; and the sense of satisfaction from engaging in socially useful activity—may be just as important, and perhaps particularly so where individuals' mental

---

[78] Penney Lewis, 'Procedures that are Against the Medical Interests of Incompetent Adults' (2002) 22(4) Oxford Journal of Legal Studies 575–618.

impairments restrict their capacity to lead rich and fulfilling lives. While it is obviously important to ensure that vulnerable populations are not exploited by researchers, and that individuals' wishes are respected even if they are unable to give legally valid consent, recognizing the possibility of non-health benefits to participants might allow non-therapeutic research to be justified as being in an incompetent individual's best interests. As we saw in Chapter 4, in relation to the medical treatment of incompetent patients, 'best interests' is not necessarily confined to clinical need, but might also encompass psychological and emotional benefits.

In the following extract, Penney Lewis argues that non-therapeutic research on incompetent patients can only be justified by engaging in a utilitarian calculation in which the gains to society are allowed to justify infringing the rights and dignity of the individual subject. The conditions laid out in the various guidelines may appear to reduce the practical impact of this violation, by ensuring that incompetent subjects are only used as 'a means to an end' in certain tightly circumscribed circumstances, but it would seem difficult to square carrying out non-therapeutic research on incompetent adults with both the first principle in the Nuremberg Code: 'The voluntary consent of the human subject is absolutely essential', and the original text of Principle 5 of the Helsinki Declaration: 'Concern for the interests of the subject *must always* prevail over the interests of science and society' (my emphasis). Interestingly, the most recent version of the Helsinki Declaration contains a subtle weakening of this rule: 'in medical research on human subjects, considerations related to the well-being of the human subject *should* take precedence over the interests of science and society' (my emphasis).

Penney Lewis[79]

In the context of non-therapeutic research, the existence of an international 'consensus', supporting the participation of incompetent persons, is used to avoid providing a justification for a utilitarian calculation that allows the use of vulnerable members of society in order to benefit others. Hiding the choice does not make it go away. It remains, and facing it will better protect the incompetent, even if the choice is made in favour of the utilitarian approach. What then is the choice to be made? In order to avoid objectifying incompetent persons, and invading their dignity interests, some diminution in scientific progress will occur—primarily in the diseases and conditions of the incompetent, which will impose costs on future incompetents . . .

Alternatively, we might be willing to sacrifice the interests of incompetent persons to a certain extent, in order to obtain the societal and individual gains associated with the research projects and transplants that could then proceed . . .

Non-therapeutic research has in effect been privileged over other procedures such as organ transplantation and sterilization, in the sense that the utilitarian approach has been applied only to it. One pragmatic reason is that in the latter two cases, the best interests test has been available, and therefore the utilitarian approach is not needed in the same way that it is for non-therapeutic research. Moreover, there are powerful groups in society pushing for research to proceed, while organ donation has no such lobby. Individuals who want transplants to proceed do not possess sufficient power to provide the societal interest that has succeeded in gaining such a 'consensus' around lowish risk non-therapeutic research on incompetent persons . . .

[79] Penney Lewis, 'Procedures that are Against the Medical Interests of Incompetent Adults' (2002) 22 Oxford Journal of Legal Studies 575–618.

Judicial approval is generally considered desirable for organ and tissue donation from incompetents and for their non-therapeutic sterilization. It is not, however, encouraged for the approval of non-therapeutic research with incompetent subjects. To obtain judicial approval for all research projects would be overly burdensome on both the judiciary and the research community. A separate system has evolved of research ethics committees, which approve research projects. These committees may be more willing than judges to engage in utilitarian balancing of the interests of society against the interests of the incompetent prospective research subject.

Regardless of the means, if we are willing to encroach on the interests of incompetents for reasons related to societal good, then there is no principled reason why this should be the case solely for non-therapeutic research.

Let us now turn to the rules contained in the Medicines for Human Use (Clinical Trials) Regulations 2004 Schedule 1. There are some differences between the rules covering children, adults and emergencies, but before we consider these separately, let us first consider the need to obtain consent from the incompetent person's 'legal' representative, which is common to all three situations.

(a) Seeking a representative's consent

Under Schedule 1 Parts 4 and 5 of Medicines for Human Use (Clinical Trials) Regulations 2004, where a person cannot give consent to participation, consent must be obtained from their 'legal representative'. Usually, it is envisaged that someone will act as a potential research subject's legal representative by virtue of their relationship with her. For a child, the personal legal representative should be a person with parental responsibility. The personal legal representative of an adult should be the person with the closest personal relationship with the potential subject, who is herself capable of giving consent.

There will, however, be situations in which finding a suitable personal legal representative will be impossible, either because there is no-one who is sufficiently close to the patient able or willing to take on this role; or in an emergency, identifying and contacting a close friend or relative in time, may not be feasible. In such circumstances the regulations stipulate that the patient's doctor should fulfil the role of the 'professional legal representative', unless she is 'connected with the conduct of the trial'. This will disqualify not only the principal researcher and those on her team, but also anyone who provides health care under the direction or control of members of the investigating team, whether in the course of the trial or otherwise. If the patient's doctor has any connection with the trial, the health care trust must nominate someone else.

Once a personal or professional legal representative has been identified, her consent to the subject's participation in the clinical trial should be sought. She is expected to base her decision on the subject's 'presumed will', hence the desirability of the finding a personal legal representative who has a good understanding of the subject's probable views. The legal representative should be given an opportunity to understand the objectives, risks, and inconveniences of the trial, and the conditions under which it is to be conducted. They should be informed that their decision should be based on what the potential subject would have wanted herself, and that they can withdraw consent to the subject's participation at any time. Independent advice about their role should be made available. Where a professional legal representative has been appointed, subject to the duty to respect patient confidentiality, she may consult any-one who might be able to help her determine the potential subject's presumed will.

The legal representative is also responsible for ensuring that the subject's continued participation remains appropriate. This will be comparatively straightforward where the personal legal representative is a close friend or relative, who will be aware of any changes in the subject's circumstances. Where a professional legal representative has been appointed, this sort of informal review will not be possible and specific arrangements should be in place to ensure that the legal representative regularly re-evaluates the subject's continued participation.

(b) Children

If a child is ill, and there is no standard treatment available for her condition, enroll-ing her in a research trial in which she might receive an experimental new treatment could be consistent with her doctor's ordinary duty of care. But where the research is non-therapeutic, and by definition, *not* in the child's best interests, should children ever be used as research subjects? As we saw in the previous section, under the Medicines for Human Use (Clinical Trials) Regulations 2004 someone with parental responsibility, or in an emergency, a professional legal representative, must give informed consent to a child's participation in research. In addition, under Schedule 1 Part 4, a number of other conditions must be satisfied:

Medicines for Human Use (Clinical Trials) Regulations 2004 Schedule 1 Part 4
CONDITIONS AND PRINCIPLES WHICH APPLY IN RELATION TO A MINOR . . .

6. The minor has received information according to his capacity of understanding, from staff with experience with minors, regarding the trial, its risks and its benefits.

7. The explicit wish of a minor who is capable of forming an opinion and assessing the informa-tion referred to in the previous paragraph to refuse participation in, or to be withdrawn from, the clinical trial at any time is considered by the investigator.

8. No incentives or financial inducements are given—

    (a) to the minor; or

    (b) to a person with parental responsibility for that minor or, as the case may be, the minor's
        legal representative, except provision for compensation in the event of injury or loss.

9. The clinical trial relates directly to a clinical condition from which the minor suffers or is of such a nature that it can only be carried out on minors.

10. Some direct benefit for the group of patients involved in the clinical trial is to be obtained from that trial.

11. The clinical trial is necessary to validate data obtained—

    (a) in other clinical trials involving persons able to give informed consent, or

    (b) by other research methods.

The Royal College of Paediatricians' guidance confirms that parents should be able to consent to their children's participation in research where the risks are 'sufficiently small'.

Royal College of Paediatrics[80]

These guidelines are based on six principles:

- Research involving children is important for the benefit of all children and should be supported, encouraged and conducted in an ethical manner
- Children are not small adults; they have an additional, unique set of interests
- Research should only be done on children if comparable research on adults could not answer the same question
- A research procedure which is not intended directly to benefit the child subject is not necessarily either unethical or illegal
- All proposals involving medical research on children should be submitted to a research ethics committee
- Legally valid consent should be obtained from the child, parent or guardian as appropriate. When parental consent is obtained, the agreement of school age children who take part in research should also be requested by researchers.

Research with children is worthwhile if each project:

- has an identifiable prospect of benefit to children
- is well designed and well conducted
- does not simply duplicate earlier work
- is not undertaken primarily for financial or professional advantage
- involves a statistically appropriate number of subjects
- eventually is to be properly reported.

Parental consent will probably not be valid if it is given against the child's interests. This means that parents can consent to research procedures that are intended directly to benefit the child, but that research that does not come into this category can only be validly consented to if the risks are sufficiently small to mean that the research can be reasonably said not to go against the child's interests. Even when it is not legally required, researchers should obtain the assent or agreement of school age children to their involvement in the research, and should always ensure that the child does not object.

Clearly there might be a conflict of interest if parents could be paid to enrol their children in research trials. As a result, any incentives or financial inducements to the child, or to anyone with parental responsibility, are ruled out by the Medicines for Human Use (Clinical Trials) Regulations 2004.

If the potential child subject is over the age of 16, or *Gillick* competent, as we saw in Chapter 4, she may be able to give a valid consent to medical treatment. Section 8 of the Family Law Reform Act 1969, which gives 16- and 17-year-olds a statutory right to consent to treatment does not specifically mention research. Interestingly, however, Regulation 2 of the Medicines for Human Use (Clinical Trials) Regulations 2004 defines 'minor' as 'a person under the age of 16 years' and 'adult' as 'a person who has attained the age of 16 years'. For *Gillick* competent children under the age of 16, both

---

[80] 'Child Health: Ethics Advisory Committee Guidelines for the ethical conduct of medical research involving children' (2000) 82 Archives of Disease in Childhood 177–82.

their consent *and* that of their parents should be sought for the child's participation in a research trial.

(c) Adults

Again, in addition to the consent of their personal or legal representative, a number of additional conditions and principles are laid out in the 2004 Regulations.

Medicines for Human Use (Clinical Trials) Regulations 2004 Schedule 1 Part 4
CONDITIONS AND PRINCIPLES WHICH APPLY IN RELATION TO AN INCAPACITATED ADULT

6. The subject has received information according to his capacity of understanding regarding the trial, its risks and its benefits.

7. The explicit wish of a subject who is capable of forming an opinion and assessing the information referred to in the previous paragraph to refuse participation in, or to be withdrawn from, the clinical trial at any time is considered by the investigator.

8. No incentives or financial inducements are given to the subject or their legal representative, except provision for compensation in the event of injury or loss.

9. There are grounds for expecting that administering the medicinal product to be tested in the trial will produce a benefit to the subject outweighing the risks or produce no risk at all.

11. The clinical trial relates directly to a life-threatening or debilitating clinical condition from which the subject suffers.

Note that the Medicines for Human Use (Clinical Trials) Regulations 2004 specify that research involving incapacitated adults will be acceptable only if 'the clinical trial relates directly to a life-threatening or debilitating clinical condition from which the subject suffers'. This limiting criterion is clearly directed towards ensuring that incompetent individuals are not used where it would be possible to recruit competent subjects. However, it could be argued that the requirement that the study must be concerned with the disorder from which the patient suffers pays too little attention to the preferences and wishes of incompetent adults. An incompetent person might wish to take part in non-therapeutic research to investigate a condition from which a number of close family members suffer, in preference to research which is only likely to benefit unknown individuals who share her own mental disorder.

It is important to remember that adults who lack the capacity to consent to medical treatment exist on a spectrum from those who are permanently insensate and wholly unaware of their own existence (such as patients in a persistent vegetative state), to those whose cognitive impairments are only slightly more severe than those of adults who fall just on the other side of the legal 'cut-off' point for decision-making capacity. Individuals in this latter group, while unable to give a valid consent to medical treatment, are nevertheless able to express their desire or unwillingness to participate in research. Just as with minors, the Medicines for Human Use (Clinical Trials) Regulations 2004 provide that the subject's desire not to participate must be considered. The GMC guidance goes further and suggests that their wishes should be decisive.

General Medical Council[81]

48. Research into conditions that are not linked to incapacity should never be undertaken with adults with incapacity if it could equally well be done with other adults. It should be limited to areas of research related to the participants' incapacity or to physical illnesses that are linked to their incapacity. If you involve this group of people in research you must demonstrate that:

- it could be of direct benefit to their health; or
- it is of special benefit to the health of people in the same age group with the same state of health; or
- that it will significantly improve the scientific understanding of the adult's incapacity leading to a direct benefit to them or to others with the same incapacity; and
- the research is ethical and will not cause the participants emotional, physical or psychological harm; and
- the person does not express objections physically or verbally.

49. You must also ensure that participants' right to withdraw from the research is respected at all times. Any sign of distress, pain or indication of refusal irrespective of whether or not it is given in a verbal form should be considered as implied refusal.

It is important to remember that incompetent patients who are capable of expressing an opinion will generally be familiar with limitations upon their capacity to make decisions for themselves. If an incompetent person is used to being treated or detained without consent, she may have no reason to believe that her reluctance to take part in research would be respected. As we saw earlier, it is difficult for *all* patients to understand the difference between treatment and research, and this problem may be even more acute for mentally incapacitated individuals. Simply stating that research should not be carried out *against* the wishes of an incompetent adult presupposes both that such patients will understand that they have more robust rights to refuse to participate in research than they do for treatment, and that they will be both able and willing to make their feelings known.

Section 30 of the Mental Capacity Act 2005 provides that 'intrusive research carried out on, or in relation to, a person who lacks capacity to consent to it is unlawful' unless a number of conditions are satisfied. These include, under section 31, that the research could not be carried out on adults with capacity; that the research poses no more than minimal risk, and that either the subject or others with her condition will benefit from the research. The Act does not apply to research which is covered by the Medicines for Human Use (Clinical Trials) Regulations 2004. Because the definition of 'clinical trial' in regulation 2 is extremely broad—all research involving medicinal products is covered—the 2005 Act's scope is limited.

(d) Emergencies

In an emergency, the requirement to obtain a third party's consent will normally involve seeking the views of a professional legal representative. Even if a personal legal

---

[81] *Research: The Role and Responsibilities of Doctors* (GMC 2002) available at <http://www.gmc-uk.org/>.

representative is available, she may be severely traumatized. In such trials, it might be appropriate for suitable professional legal representatives to be nominated at the outset of the trial.

Where a professional legal representative has been appointed in an emergency, review of the appropriateness of continued participation is especially important. It might also be appropriate for the role of legal representative to be transferred subsequently to an individual who is closely connected with the subject. Alternatively, if the subject recovers competence, she has the right to decide whether or not to continue participation in the trial, and the legal representative will have no further role.

Since the 2004 Regulations came into force it became apparent, following the experience of researchers involved in a large international trial investigating cardiac arrest—who had found it impossible to include UK patients—that the process of appointing and consulting a legal representative is unworkable in the context of emergency medicine.[82] As a result, the Medicines and Healthcare products Regulatory Agency (MHRA) will consult on a proposal to amend the regulations so that an incapacitated person can be entered into a clinical trial involving emergency treatment before consent is obtained from her legal representative. This exception to the requirement for prior consent will be subject to strict safeguards.[83]

Research involving emergency medicine is obviously important if care is to improve. However, as we saw in Chapter 4, patients who have been temporarily incapacitated in an emergency can be given medical treatment only if it is necessary to save their lives, or to prevent grave permanent injury. Hence, unless participation in a particular research trial offers the best chance of saving a person's life, or averting serious injury, it would be very difficult to justify enrolling them in a trial without their consent.

Certainly the GMC guidance makes clear that research into emergency medicine can only be justified where it is self-evidently therapeutic. The doctor must genuinely believe that participation in the trial offers her patient a chance of receiving potentially life-saving treatment which is at least as good, or better than that offered by other available treatments.

General Medical Council[84]

51. In an emergency where consent cannot be obtained, treatment can be given only if it is limited to what is immediately necessary to save life or avoid significant deterioration in the patient's health. This may include treatment that is part of a therapeutic research project, where the risks of the new treatment are not believed to exceed the known risks of standard treatment. If, during treatment, the patient regains capacity, the patient should be told about the research as soon as possible and their consent to continue should be sought.

---

[82] Hansard 18 Jan 2005: Column 32WS.
[83] Ibid.
[84] *Research: The Role and Responsibilities of Doctors* (GMC 2002) available at <http://www.gmc-uk.org/>.

8. FACILITATING PARTICIPATION IN RESEARCH

(a) THE BENEFITS OF PARTICIPATION

So far, we have concentrated on the special vulnerability of research subjects, and discussed the sort of safeguards that should be in place in order to protect people from being pressurized into taking part in research. Because the outcome of research is, by definition, uncertain, our assumption has been that research participants are exposed to some risks without necessarily receiving any health benefits in return. But this view of participation in clinical trials as a burden, such that we ought to take extra care to ensure that consent is both real and informed, has been challenged in recent years as a result of the recognition that being a research subject might sometimes hold out the possibility of very great benefits.

The catalyst for this shift in emphasis has been the AIDS pandemic. Before AZT was licensed for use in humans, anyone diagnosed as HIV positive could expect to die from an AIDS-related illness within a comparatively short space of time. Patients knew, however, that research into drugs which might be capable of delaying the onset of AIDS was ongoing. Unsurprisingly, there was no shortage of volunteers for these studies. For some cancer patients too, access to 'cutting-edge' treatment is available only to participants in clinical trials. If the important issue for individuals becomes access to the benefits of taking part in clinical research, rather than protection from its dangers, rather different ethical issues are raised. We might, for example, need to ensure that there is fair and equitable distribution of places in research trials.

In the next extract, Rebecca Dresser explains the role of patient advocacy groups in promoting research participation, and draws attention to the danger that they may over-estimate the benefits of research participation.

Rebecca Dresser [85]
During the 1980s, HIV/AIDS activists became major figures in biomedical research . . . Eventually, other patient advocacy organizations became more active in the research arena. Advocates persuaded government officials to ease the rules governing patients' access to investigational medications for a variety of serious, life-threatening conditions. . . .

[Patient] advocates tend to stress the positive dimensions of biomedical research. In much advocacy communication, there is a failure to clearly distinguish between partially tested experimental interventions and proven medical care. Consistent with this approach, advocates often portray study participation as the way to obtain cutting-edge therapy.

This failure to draw a clear line between investigational interventions and established clinical care affects the perceptions of patients and of the general public. It can promote the therapeutic misconception—a phenomenon that occurs when people do not understand the aims and methodological requirements of biomedical research. The primary purpose of research is to gain knowledge that will improve care for future patients, not to deliver treatment tailored for an individual patient. When research and treatment are confused, patients may enrol in research studies

---

[85] 'Patient Advocates in Research: New Possibilities, New Problems' (2003) 11 Washington University Journal of Law and Policy 237, 240–1.

without a good understanding of the trade-offs involved. Such patients may have an unrealistic hope for personal benefit without recognizing the risks and uncertainties accompanying their participation in the studies.

Patient advocates may also promote the therapeutic misconception at a broader level. For example, patient advocates often suggest that research can end the suffering and deprivation inflicted by illness. The general message is that with more funding for research, cures are destined to emerge. Although this feel-good message may lift the spirits of people coping with disease and injury, and aid with fundraising, it may also promote public misunderstanding of the research process. There is no question that research can lead to health care improvements. Almost always, however, it takes many years and many false starts before effective practical applications become available. But advocates too often downplay this part of research; instead, they equate support for research with support for imminent improvements in treatment.

(b) EXCLUSION FROM RESEARCH

A number of different groups within society have traditionally been underrepresented among research subjects. Most notable, perhaps, has been the exclusion of women who, in part because of their longer life expectancy, actually represent the majority of health care consumers. Obviously, if a disease (such as prostate cancer) occurs only in men, it would be inappropriate to recruit female subjects. But, for a number of reasons, women have also been excluded from research into conditions which affect both sexes.

First, it has been suggested that women's physiology is different from that of men, and that this might complicate results, and lead to less 'clean' data. Because women's hormonal profiles vary dramatically over the life cycle, more women would have to be recruited, thus increasing the costs of the research. Of course, women's reproductive physiognomy is only a complicating factor if the male body is regarded as the norm. Of more practical importance, there is also a central paradox in this justification for women's exclusion. If the female body reacts differently to treatment, and hence might distort a study's results, then dosages of a treatment which have only been tested on men are likely to be either ineffective or unsafe for female patients. Despite being undertested in women, most drugs are prescribed to both sexes, and it is therefore unsurprising that evidence has indicated that women are more likely than men to report adverse drug reactions.

A second reason for excluding women of reproductive age is the possibility that they might become pregnant during the trial, thus exposing the fetus to the unknown toxicity of the treatment in question, and the researchers to the possibility of liability for prenatal injury.

In the next extract, Marie Fox criticizes the neglect of women's health needs which results from gender bias in research design.

Marie Fox [86]

Although the justifications for explicit exclusions are generally couched in the rhetoric of protecting women and their unborn children, the issue which looms largest for those sponsoring or

---

[86] 'Research Bodies: Feminist Perspectives on Clinical Research' in S Sheldon and M Thomson (eds), *Feminist Perspectives on Health Care Law* (Cavendish London 1998) 115–34.

conducting trials is likely to be fear of liability for any teratogenic impact . . . Again feminist lawyers have challenged this rationale, arguing that there is potentially greater liability if unsafe products are marketed, since pharmaceutical companies do not bar women, including women of child-bearing capacity, from purchasing or being prescribed such drugs . . . Other reasons for the exclusion of women from clinical protocols may be less marked. First, in scientific literature there is a particularly marked tendency to define and perceive the male as generically human, and the female as a special subgroup. This is related to a second factor, the dearth of female scientific researchers, which is largely glossed over in the bioethics literature. . . . A third crucial factor accounting for the exclusion of women relates to the gender identity of those funding medical research. In Britain most funding is provided by the pharmaceutical industry, while the remainder comes from the Medical Research Council, private charities and health departments. Thus, the choice of problems for study in medical research is substantially determined by the same group— of mainly white, middle-class men—who conduct the research. Given this, inevitably the allocation of resources for biomedical research has been enormously skewed toward the health needs of this group . . .

The relative neglect of women's health needs raises issues of justice, as well as calling into question the scientifically dubious practice of marketing drugs and procedures which have been inadequately tested for their impact on women. Since the choice and definition of problems for research is influenced by the under-representation of women at all stages of the research process, research on conditions specific to females receives low priority, funding and prestige. Even breast cancer is not a major research priority, despite being the most prevalent form of cancer. Less politicised diseases, such as dysmenorrhoea or incontinence in older women, fare much worse in funding terms . . . Moreover, certain diseases which affect both sexes are wrongly labelled as male diseases . . . This is particularly true of heart disease, the primary killer of women and men in the West.

While there might be good reasons for not recruiting women who are trying to conceive onto trials of experimental drugs, a blanket ban on women's participation seems unwarranted, and it might be fairer to ask women whether there is a chance that they might become pregnant during the trial, and to believe them if they say that there is no risk of conception.

While restricting pregnant women's participation in research seems readily understandable, it is important to remember that a blanket ban might also be inappropriate. If no drugs are ever tested on pregnant women, it will never be possible to find out if they can safely be taken during pregnancy. This is why so many medicinal products contain a warning that they should not be used by pregnant woman. Most of these warnings are not designed to protect women and their fetuses from drugs which are known to be harmful, rather they simply indicate that they have not been proved to be safe, because no studies have been carried out. It is important to remember that abstaining from using any medicines during pregnancy is not necessarily an option for some pregnant women. A woman who suffers from severe depression, for example, and might be likely to harm herself if she stops taking anti-depressants is faced with an invidious dilemma. She must either carry on taking a medicine which has not been proved safe during pregnancy, or risk the potentially serious consequences of stopping her medication.

Other groups have also tended to be underrepresented in research, with obvious implications for their access to safe and effective medical treatment. For a number of reasons elderly people have often been excluded. Researchers have been concerned, first, that it would be difficult to ensure that elderly subjects rigorously adhered to the research protocol; secondly, that long term follow-up might be impeded by the subjects' deaths; and thirdly, that subjects might suffer from multiple disorders which could distort the results. But not only is research on older subjects essential in order to improve the quality of care available to the elderly, it is also a mistake to assume that all elderly people are equally infirm or close to death. On the contrary, many old people are healthier and more independent than younger adults. Moreover, elderly subjects are less likely to have work and family commitments which could interfere with participation in research.

One solution to the problem of unjust exclusion, embodied in the Research Governance Framework, has been to require researchers to justify any recruitment restrictions in their protocols.

Research Governance Framework For Health And Social Care[87]

2.2.7 Research and those pursuing it should respect the diversity of human culture and conditions and take full account of ethnicity, gender, disability, age and sexual orientation in its design, undertaking, and reporting. Researchers should take account of the multi-cultural nature of society. It is particularly important that the body of research evidence available to policy makers reflects the diversity of the population.

(c) A DUTY TO PARTICIPATE?

A further issue missed by the prevailing emphasis on protecting research subjects from exploitation is the question of whether users of health care services might in fact be under a duty to share in the burdens of research participation. It is certainly true that these burdens are not distributed evenly across society. Most experiments are carried out on people who are ill. Among healthy volunteers, certain groups—in particular students, junior medical staff and the unemployed—are overrepresented, while others—such as wealthy individuals in full time employment—will very seldom participate.

Uneven recruitment of research subjects gives rise to two distinct problems. First, it might be argued that the risks associated with participation in research should be distributed fairly across society, and that it is unjust for certain sections of society to bear a disproportionate burden. Since the sort of financial rewards which persuade students or the unemployed to volunteer are unlikely to act as an incentive to those who do not currently participate in research, we might have to think in terms of some sort of *duty* to enrol as a research subject. We could, for example, view serving as a research subject as one aspect of the duties we assume under a 'social contract', in which we accept some restrictions upon our individual autonomy in return for the benefits of living in a safe and cohesive community. Indeed the Research Governance Framework suggests that:

All those using health and social care services should give serious consideration to invitations to become involved in the development or undertaking of research.[88]

---

[87] DoH 2001.
[88] *Research Governance Framework For Health And Social Care* (DoH 2001) para 3.4.1.

Even if there could be no *legal* duty to participate in research, it might be argued that anyone who wants to have access to well-tested medical treatments is under a *moral* duty to serve as a research subject. But Arthur Caplan would go much further; he argues that, in certain circumstances, it might be appropriate for a hospital to refuse to treat those who are unwilling to take part in clinical research.

Arthur L Caplan[89]

Modern medicine is a vast social enterprise in which certain benefits are produced at the cost of various burdens, which include the need to conduct medical research. If individuals consciously, knowingly, and continuously accept the benefits of medical care by seeking out physicians and hospital personnel when they are ill, then they would seem to meet the conditions for being bound by the principle of fair play. If the only way the knowledge and skills utilized in modern medicine can be generated is through research involving human subjects, then those who accept the fruits of such research would appear to be under a duty to bear the burdens of research when called upon by the group to do so.

The principle of fair play can, I believe, be used to generate the moral foundation for broader public participation in biomedical research. Few patients are innocent bystanders, unwilling recipients of medical care. Most actively seek out the highest quality care they can possibly receive, and in so doing, cement their status as obligated participants in an ongoing cooperative enterprise . . .

The only morally acceptable means of achieving this end is for the [teaching hospital] to simply exclude those persons who knowingly accept the benefits of a cooperative activity, but renege on their obligation to bear the costs associated with producing the benefits. Medical institutions which clearly and forthrightly identify themselves to patients as research institutions would be within their rights to exclude persons who refuse to participate in any form of research if they wish to do so.

John Harris also believes that we may have an obligation to participate in research. According to Harris, whether or not a research subject stands to benefit from participation should not be confined to the narrow question of whether her health will be directly improved. Instead he argues that we all benefit from living in a society in which medical research is ongoing, and that participation should no longer be regarded as a supererogatory act, but, like jury service and taxation, as one of a number of mandatory contributions to the public good which we accept as the price of living in a civilized society.

John Harris[90]

We all benefit from the existence of the social practice of medical research. Many of us would not be here if infant mortality had not been brought under control, or antibiotics had not been invented. Most of us will continue to benefit from these and other medical advances. . . . Since we accept these benefits, we have an obligation in justice to contribute to the social practice which produces them. We may argue that since we could not opt out of advances that were made prior to our becoming capable of autonomous decision making we are not obliged to contribute. It may, however, still be unfair to accept their benefits and implies also that we will forgo the fruits of any

[89] 'Is There an Obligation to Participate in Biomedical Research' in Stuart F Spicker, Ilai Alon, Andre de Vries, and H Tristram Engelhardt (eds), *The Use of Human Beings in Research* (Kluwer Dordrecht NL) 1988 229–48.
[90] 'Scientific research is a moral duty' (2005) 31 Journal of Medical Ethics 242–8.

future advances. Few, however, are willing to do so, and even fewer are really willing to forgo benefits that have been created through the sacrifices of others when their own hour of need arises! . . .

We all also benefit from the knowledge that research is ongoing into diseases or conditions from which we do not currently suffer but to which we may succumb. It makes us feel more secure and gives us hope for the future, for ourselves and our descendants, and for others for whom we care. If this is right, then I have a strong general interest that there be research, and in all well founded research; not excluding but not exclusively, research on me and on my condition or on conditions which are likely to affect me and mine. All such research is also of clear benefit to me. A narrow interpretation of the requirement that research be of benefit to the subject of the research is therefore perverse. . . .

If it is right to claim that there is a general obligation to act in the public interest, then there is less reason to challenge consent and little reason to regard participation as actually or potentially exploitative. We do not usually say: 'are you quite sure you want to' when people fulfil their moral and civic obligations. We do not usually insist on informed consent in such cases, we are usually content that they *merely* consent or simply acquiesce. When—for example, I am called for jury service no one says: 'only attend if you fully understand the role of trial by jury, due process, etc in our constitution and the civil liberties that fair trials guarantee'.

Secondly, the de facto exclusion of certain groups from medical trials mean that we cannot be sure that medical treatment will be either safe or effective when given to members of the excluded group. If new drugs are principally tested on young, healthy students, their impact upon middle-aged men with sedentary lifestyles may be uncertain. Research which only proves that a medical treatment works in a small subset of the population to which it will eventually be provided is perhaps also then *methodologically* unsound.

9. PUBLICATION ETHICS

(a) SHOULD UNETHICAL RESEARCH BE PUBLISHED?

If unethical research has yielded useful information, should it be published, or used by future researchers? Data generated by the Dachau hypothermia experiments, for example, has been cited in subsequent research, but its use remains extremely controversial. On the one hand it might be argued that once unethical research has actually taken place, and produced results which might save lives, a refusal to disseminate this information will lead to even more suffering than has already occurred. Precautions could be taken to ensure that the researcher does not benefit from publication: names could be withheld, for example, and the results could be accompanied by an indictment of the researcher and her methods.

But on the other hand, allowing unethical research to be published sends a rather confusing message to researchers. If it is impossible to disseminate research unless it has met certain standards, researchers have a powerful incentive to ensure that they comply with these basic ethical principles.

The various international codes contain a presumption against the publication of unethical research, but they all fall short of imposing an absolute prohibition. Paragraph 27 of the Helsinki Declaration, for example, states that research which con-travenes its guidance *should* (as opposed to *must*) not be published.[91] And the CIOMS Guidelines suggest that although unethical research should not normally be pub-lished, 'careful consideration' may be necessary where publication could have wider health benefits.

CIOMS[92]
Commentary on Guideline 2: Ethical Review Committees
Unless there are persuasive reasons to do otherwise, editors should refuse to publish the results of research conducted unethically, and retract any articles that are subsequently found to contain falsified or fabricated data or to have been based on unethical research. Drug regulatory author-ities should consider refusal to accept unethically obtained data submitted in support of an application for authorization to market a product. Such sanctions, however, may deprive of benefit not only the errant researcher or sponsor but also that segment of society intended to benefit from the research; such possible consequences merit careful consideration.

In the next extract, Florencia Luna argues that research which seriously breaches basic ethical principles should not be published, but where the breaches of ethical guidelines are less serious, publication may be warranted.

Florencia Luna[93]
When a manuscript containing unethical research is submitted to a journal, the editor has, at least, three options: (a) publish the unethical research, (b) publish it with an explicit condemnation of the methods used; (c) reject the article on moral grounds.

The rationale for publishing unethical research (option a) is that the experiments were done, the data are valuable and that nothing can be done for those victims (e.g. neither health nor dignity nor life can be restored to the victims) and other people might be saved by using the data. In this way, the subjects' undeserved sacrifice may help humanity or science . . .

Option (b) can be found in the argument Jay Katz proposes in a letter to the *New England Journal of Medicine* 'it would be unfortunate if data "improperly obtained" were not published. Such an editorial policy would maintain the low visibility of "unethical experimentation" '. And he asks to include in the section on methods a clear statement of how consent was given so they could be subject to our collective scrutiny . . .

Behind this idea of public scrutiny seems to lie the idea of publicly punishing the authors of such unethical research. . . . On the other hand, even if we do accept the idea of punishing the authors, would it not be more effective—in the academic world—*not* to publish an article than to publish it . . . Publishing might be rightly seen as a *reward*. It implies a positive judgment and it is one of the main goals for scientists, one of the conditions for success.

The third option, then, is to reject the article on moral grounds . . . However, there is a possible objection to this strong position against not publishing unethical research. There are investigations which we will easily agree on their being unethical . . . but there are others where their unethical character is less clear . . .

[91] World Medical Association, Declaration of Helsinki: Ethical Principles for Medical Research Involving Human Subjects (6th version adopted at the 52nd WMA General Assembly, Edinburgh, Scotland, Oct 2000) available at <http://www.wma.net/e/policy/b3.htm>.

[92] *International Ethical Guidelines for Biomedical Research Involving Human Subjects* <http://www.cioms.ch/>.

[93] 'Vulnerable Populations and Morally Tainted Experiments' (1997) 11 Bioethics 256–64.

I would suggest, then, a *combined policy*. For those cases where there are serious ethical problems—where basic human rights are not respected, where there is not adequate informed consent,
no voluntariness of the subjects, I would support a strong policy . . . For dubious cases, where the
risk assessment can be doubted or where there are suspicions of ethical problems, a policy . . . may
be appropriate which will allow a rebuttal and a serious discussion of the ethical problems
suspected.

(b) THE DUTY TO PUBLISH

If information gathered during research is not published, research subjects will have
been exposed to some risks without any corresponding benefits to scientific knowledge. While the risks associated with the therapeutic components of research might
be justified by the anticipated health gains for individual participants, the only justification for the risks which flow from non-therapeutic procedures is the prospect of
generating valuable information. If results are not published, the information produced will have no social value, and the original justification for carrying out the
research will have been lost.

When asked why they agreed to take part in research, many subjects cite the prospect of helping future patients. If the participants had known in advance that a
particular trial's results would not be published, and would therefore have no
practical benefit, it seems likely that many of them would have refused to take part.

It is also important that both negative and positive results are published. While
positive results (which prove that a new treatment works) may be more interesting
and newsworthy than negative results (which show that a new treatment is ineffective
or harmful), unless negative results are also published, there is a danger that other
researchers may instigate identical and futile trials, thereby exposing a new set of
research subjects to wholly avoidable risks. Researchers may therefore be under a duty
to ensure that a trial's results are properly disseminated, regardless of whether they are
positive or negative, and indeed principle 27 of the Helsinki Declaration confirms that
'negative as well as positive results should be published or otherwise publicly
available'.[94]

But while unpublished research may fail to fulfil the moral requirement that
researchers only carry out research where there is a realistic prospect of obtaining
valuable information, this is not translated into an enforceable legal duty to disseminate one's findings. On the contrary, research ethics committees do not attempt to
monitor the extent to which researchers publish their results. Alarmingly, studies
appear to indicate that the *majority* of clinical trials do not result in published
papers.[95]

[94] World Medical Association, Declaration of Helsinki: Ethical Principles for Medical Research Involving
Human Subjects (6th version adopted at the 52nd WMA General Assembly, Edinburgh, Scotland, Oct 2000)
available at <http://www.wma.net/e/policy/b3.htm>.
[95] Judit Pich, Xavier Carné, Joan-Albert Arnaiz, Begoña Gómez, Antoni Trilla and Juan Rodés, 'Role of a
research ethics committee in follow-up and publication of results' (2003) 361 The Lancet 1015–16.

10. RESEARCH IN DEVELOPING COUNTRIES

At the outset, it is important to acknowledge that drawing a distinction between 'developed' and 'developing' countries is itself controversial. Not only does it over-emphasize economic development, at the expense of other social and political factors which are relevant to the provision of health care, it also implies that nations can easily be divided into two categories, when in fact a spectrum exists. South Africa, for example, sits rather uneasily in the category of 'developing countries', and yet South Africa's experience of the AIDS pandemic has been comparable with that of some of the poorest African nations.

Moreover, within some countries the standard of medical care varies dramatically. In poorer nations, there are often vast differences between the quality of medical care in cities, and that which is available in rural areas. I shall employ the terms 'developed' and 'developing' here because these are the terms most commonly used in the relevant literature, but it should be noted that this is simply a convenient shorthand, and the important distinction is between richer countries, which have well developed systems for testing and providing high quality health care to their populations, and poorer countries, where the system for delivering medical care is inadequate to meet the whole population's health needs.

Inadequate health care, and the resulting high rates of disease, disability and premature mortality, are a major problem in the world's poorest nations. Less than 10 per cent of the $50–60 billion spent on medical research each year is devoted to diseases which account for 90 per cent of the global disease burden. Research into low-cost treatments for diseases, such as malaria and tuberculosis, which principally affect the populations of very poor countries is desperately needed. It would therefore be a mistake to ban all externally sponsored research which addresses those countries' distinctive health needs.

However, the adverse publicity, and potentially crippling legal actions, that sponsors of research face when trials go wrong in developed countries offer a compelling incentive for companies to conduct research in places where they are much less likely to be held to account for engaging in dangerous research practices. In the next extract, Benjamin Mason Meier explains how the governments of poor countries are themselves sometimes complicit in ensuring that researchers face comparatively few obstacles when planning clinical trials.

Benjamin Mason Meier[96]
National regulation of human experimentation differs dramatically between developed and developing, particularly African, nations. Many African nations lack any legislative protections for subjects of medical research. To a large degree, this legislative vacuum is intentional. While governments of these nations are desperate to bring medical research to their dying populations, their nations cannot afford such research without subsidies from multinational pharmaceutical corporations. To court these pharmaceutical corporations, African nations vie to minimize regulation on the conduct of medical research. They fear that legislation, and resulting lawsuits, could

[96] 'International Protection of Persons Undergoing Medical Experimentation: Protecting the Right of Informed Consent' (2001) 20 Berkeley Journal of International Law 513.

have a chilling effect on beneficial research efforts. As a result, African nations have shown great reluctance to impose any restrictions on human research, thereby creating a medical 'race to the bottom' at the expense of human rights and human life.

For example, although the Ivory Coast submits all human research protocols to a 'Research Committee' for review and approval, the government lacks any 'special requirements for obtaining informed consent from the human subjects.' Even where these ethical review boards review research protocols, corruption often prevents these boards from protecting the interests of experimental subjects. While this corporate-friendly environment benefits transnational corporations, it does so to the detriment of African citizens. This lack of effective regulation has given a perverse incentive to scientists in developed countries to conduct human trials in Africa when they cannot get approval for such research at home . . .

No single international legal standard guides physicians in obtaining the consent of their subjects. Rather, human experimentation is guided only by a host of informal guidelines, and individual nations lack the capacity to punish physicians for human experimentation in violation of those guidelines. The diversity of these modern guidelines creates problems in the regulation of international experimentation, where physicians from developed countries simply capitalize on those developing countries adhering to the least protective informal guidelines.

Because the risk of exploitation is undoubtedly real, the principal task for regulations must therefore be to ensure that high quality research capable of improving the lives of people in the world's poorest nations is encouraged, while also ensuring that these countries do not become the pharmaceutical industry's 'sweat shop'.

Most codes of ethics suggest that western companies should only carry out research in poorer countries where that research is likely to benefit the host nation. The Helsinki Declaration provides that:

Medical research is only justified if there is a reasonable likelihood that the populations in which the research is carried out stand to benefit from the results of the research.[97]

Similarly, the Nuffield Council on Bioethics' report on *The ethics of research related to healthcare in developing countries* suggested that externally sponsored research should 'fall within the ambit of the national priorities for research related to health care in developing countries'.[98]

It is also important to recognize that incentives to participation in research may work differently in extremely poor countries. Not only might comparatively small sums of money be disproportionately attractive, but also simply taking part in a research trial holds out the possibility of receiving medical care that might not otherwise be available. Regular contact with a team of health care professionals will enable any unrelated medical condition to be diagnosed and treated more speedily than normal. The offer of any medical care at all, as the Nuffield Council on Bioethics explains, offers a considerable incentive to participation.

Nuffield Council on Bioethics[99]

6.30 Guaranteed healthcare or a payment offered to individuals on condition that they take

[97] World Medical Association, Declaration of Helsinki: Ethical Principles for Medical Research Involving Human Subjects (6th version adopted at the 52nd WMA General Assembly, Edinburgh, Scotland, October 2000) available at <http://www.wma.net/e/policy/b3.htm>.
[98] Nuffield Council on Bioethics, *The ethics of research related to healthcare in developing countries*, Apr 2002.
[99] Ibid.

part in a research project could be considered to be exploitative if otherwise there is a very low probability of receiving such a benefit. This contrast in benefits, depending on whether an individual enrols in research is particularly important in developing countries ... Research ethics committees should bear this in mind when assessing whether it is acceptable to conduct research projects which may involve more than minimal risk. In such circumstances special care should be taken when determining the nature of additional healthcare to be offered to participants as an inducement.

In some developing countries, it may be usual practice for decisions—such as whether to participate in research—to be taken by the leader of the community, or a senior family member, rather than by the individual herself. Does respect for cultural differ-ence demand that consent should be sought from this authority figure, or is the duty to obtain the individual subject's free and informed consent a universal moral requirement?

The CIOMS Guidelines recommend that seeking consent from someone other than the research subject may sometimes be advisable in order to show appropriate respect for a community's cultural traditions, but that it could never replace the additional need to obtain the subject's own consent.

CIOMS[100]
Commentary on Guideline 4: Individual informed consent
In some cultures an investigator may enter a community to conduct research or approach pro-spective subjects for their individual consent only after obtaining permission from a community leader, a council of elders, or another designated authority. Such customs must be respected. In no case, however, may the permission of a community leader or other authority substitute for individual informed consent.

The Nuffield Council on Bioethics further recommends that where an individual does not wish to participate in research, despite the community leader's agreement, researchers have a duty to facilitate their non-participation.

Nuffield Council on Bioethics[101]
6.22 We recommend that, in circumstances where consent to research is required, genuine consent to participate in research must be obtained from each participant. In some cultural contexts it may be appropriate to obtain agreement from the community or assent from a senior family member before a prospective participant is approached. If a prospective participant does not wish to take part in research this must be respected. Researchers must not enroll such individuals and have a duty to facilitate their non-participation.

Another ethical problem that arises when research is carried out in developing coun-tries is the extent of the researchers' obligations towards the community after the trial is over. Should researchers be under a duty to make treatments which have proved to be effective available to all of the participants in the trial, or to the wider community as well? If the research subjects have benefited from better general healthcare during

---

[100] *International Ethical Guidelines for Biomedical Research Involving Human Subjects* <http://www.cioms.ch/>.
[101] *The ethics of research related to healthcare in developing countries*, Apr 2002.

the trial, is there an obligation to continue to provide this level of care once the trial has ended?

While it might seem unfair to carry out trials in poor countries if there is no prospect that the community itself will ever benefit from the research, it would be difficult to compel drugs companies to assume responsibility for all of the future health needs of developing countries. Forcing external sponsors of research to make completely open-ended commitments to supply expensive new drugs to the whole community might represent a significant disincentive to locating potentially valuable research in poorer countries.

In 2004 the World Medical Association (WMA) added a note of clarification to the Helsinki Declaration, which falls short of mandating that drugs must be made available to research participants after the trial is over, but recommends that post-trial access is one factor that ethics committees should take into account when judging whether a proposed trial is ethical.

The WMA hereby reaffirms its position that it is necessary during the study planning process to identify post-trial access by study participants to prophylactic, diagnostic and therapeutic procedures identified as beneficial in the study or access to other appropriate care.

Post-trial access arrangements or other care must be described in the study protocol so the ethical review committee may consider such arrangements during its review.[102]

In 1997 an article by Peter Lurie and Sidney Wolfe was published in the *New England Journal of Medicine* in which they criticized fifteen clinical trials, involving 12,000 HIV positive women in nine countries, which were designed to test whether low-cost treatments might be effective in reducing perinatal (i.e. mother to baby) transmission of the HIV virus.[103] These studies had been designed by, among others, the World Health Organization and UNAIDS, a United Nations agency which coordinates efforts to combat the spread of AIDS.

In developing countries, perinatal transmission of the HIV virus is a major public health problem. Nearly 2000 HIV infected children are born every day, 90 per cent of them in Africa. And this is despite the existence of an effective means of preventing transmission during pregnancy, which is now standard treatment in the West. The treatment, which is known as the 076 protocol, involves oral and intravenous doses of the antiretroviral drug zidovudine (commonly known as AZT) to pregnant women throughout pregnancy, and during childbirth; abstaining from breastfeeding; and the provision of AZT to babies for six weeks after birth. On its own, the 076 protocol reduces transmission rates from 25 per cent to 8 per cent, and delivery by caesarean section can further reduce the risk of infection. When all possible precautions are taken, only about 1 per cent of infants born to HIV positive mothers will themselves be infected.

Despite HIV infection in infancy effectively being a preventable disease in the West, there are several reasons why it is impossible to offer the 076 protocol in most

---

[102] Bryan Christie 'WMA says trial participants must have access to best treatment when a trial ends' (2004) 329 British Medical Journal 876.

[103] P Lurie and SM Wolfe 'Unethical trials of interventions to reduce perinatal transmission of the human immunodeficiency virus in developing countries' (1997) 337 New England Journal of Medicine 853–6.

developing countries. First, it is prohibitively expensive, costing approximately one hundred times more than the average *per capita* health expenditure in many of the world's poorest countries. Secondly, it requires the intensive provision of health services throughout pregnancy and after childbirth. Such services will often simply be unavailable in poor countries. For example, early pregnancy testing is essential, and it must be possible to provide AZT intravenously during childbirth. Thirdly, in countries without clean water supplies, abstaining from breast feeding will in fact represent a greater threat to infant health than that posed by HIV transmission.

The controversial trials that were the subject of the *New England Journal of Medicine* article were directed towards addressing this problem by testing whether a simpler and cheaper course of treatment could nevertheless reduce transmission rates. The studies were randomized controlled trials, in which one group of HIV positive pregnant women received a short course of AZT during the last four weeks of pregnancy, and a control group received a placebo. Following positive preliminary results from a trial in Thailand, in which perinatal transmission rates among breastfeeding women were halved (19 per cent of babies in the control group were infected, compared with 9 per cent of the babies whose mothers received the short course of AZT), the research was halted. Controversy continues, however, over whether these trials should ever have taken place.

In short, the problem was that the control group was given a placebo despite the existence of effective treatment to prevent perinatal HIV transmission. And it has been estimated that before the trials were stopped, over 1000 babies in the control group became infected with the HIV virus. This would appear to conflict with two basic ethical principles.

First, Principle II(3) of the version of the Helsinki Declaration which applied in 1997 appeared to permit placebo controlled trials only where no treatment exists.

In any medical study, every patient—including those of a control group, if any—should be assured of the *best proven* diagnostic and therapeutic method. This does not exclude the use of an inert placebo where no proven diagnostic or therapeutic method exists. (my emphasis)

Using a placebo control in these HIV trials deprived the patients in the control group of the 'best proven' treatment to prevent the perinatal transmission of the HIV virus, namely the 076 protocol. Secondly, could it really be said that a state of equipoise existed over which treatment was best for the patients? Because the 076 protocol had already been *proved* to be extremely effective, it might be argued that the requisite uncertainty in the scientific community which justifies imposing risks on research subjects was absent.

Lurie and Wolfe accused researchers of exploiting subjects by withholding treatment which is provided as standard in developed nations. Deviating from the duty to provide a control group with the 'best proven' treatment was criticized on the grounds that it introduces a double standard in research, whereby subjects in rich countries are guaranteed a higher level of care than those from poorer nations. Not only does this offend basic egalitarian principles, it also offers a compelling incentive for sponsors of research trials to locate them in countries where subjects can legitimately be offered a lower standard of care.

P Lurie and SM Wolfe[104]

Acceptance of a standard of care that does not conform to the standard in the sponsoring country results in a double standard in research. Such a double standard, which permits research designs that are unacceptable in the sponsoring country, creates an incentive to use as research subjects those with the least access to health care.

What are the potential implications of accepting such a double standard? Researchers might inject live malaria parasites into HIV-positive subjects in China in order to study the effect on the progression of HIV infection, even though the study protocol had been rejected in the United States and Mexico. Or researchers might randomly assign malnourished San (bushmen) to receive vitamin-fortified or standard bread. One might also justify trials of HIV vaccines in which the subjects were not provided with condoms or state-of-the-art counseling about safe sex by arguing that they are not customarily provided in the developing countries in question. These are not simply hypothetical worst-case scenarios; the first two studies have already been performed, and the third has been proposed and criticized . . .

Residents of impoverished, postcolonial countries, the majority of whom are people of color, must be protected from potential exploitation in research. Otherwise, the abominable state of health care in these countries can be used to justify studies that could never pass ethical muster in the sponsoring country. . . .

It is time to develop standards of research that preclude the kinds of double standards evident in these trials. In an editorial published nine years ago in [this] *Journal*, Marcia Angell stated, '*Human subjects in any part of the world should be protected by an irreducible set of ethical standards.*' Tragically, for the hundreds of infants who have needlessly contracted HIV infection in the perinatal-transmission studies that have already been completed, any such protection will have come too late.

In contrast, supporters of the trials argued that local solutions to the burden of disease should be sought, and that research capable of having practical application in poor countries should not be stopped in order to ease Western consciences. No women in the control group was actually any worse off than she would have been if she had not enrolled in the trial, and using a placebo control meant that statistically significant results could be obtained more quickly. It was further argued that the 076 protocol had only been proved effective in well-nourished populations with a low incidence of anaemia. Since AZT can exacerbate anaemia, it was necessary to test it against a placebo in order to ascertain its effectiveness in populations in which anaemia and malnutrition are common. Because this requirement that a control group must be given the 'best proven' treatment appeared to hamper research into cheaper alternatives, several commentators suggested that it should be replaced by a duty to give the control group the 'best attainable' or 'best current' treatment.

Both the revised Helsinki Declaration, and the CIOMS Guidelines now specifically address the use of placebo controls where effective treatment is known to exist.

Helsinki Declaration[105]

29 The benefits, risks, burdens and effectiveness of a new method should be tested against those of the best current prophylactic, diagnostic, and therapeutic methods.

---

[104] Ibid.

[105] World Medical Association, Declaration of Helsinki: Ethical Principles for Medical Research Involving Human Subjects (6th version adopted at the 52nd WMA General Assembly, Edinburgh, Scotland, Oct 2000) available at <http://www.wma.net/e/policy/b3.htm>.

CIOMS[106]

Commentary on Guideline 11: Choice of control in clinical trials

An exception to the general rule is applicable in some studies designed to develop a therapeutic, preventive or diagnostic intervention for use in a country or community in which an established effective intervention is not available and unlikely in the foreseeable future to become available, usually for economic or logistic reasons. The purpose of such a study is to make available to the population of the country or community an effective alternative to an established effective intervention that is locally unavailable. . . . [T]he scientific and ethical review committees must be satisfied that the established effective intervention cannot be used as comparator because its use would not yield scientifically reliable results that would be relevant to the health needs of the study population. In these circumstances an ethical review committee can approve a clinical trial in which the comparator is other than an established effective intervention, such as placebo or no treatment or a local remedy . . .

Ethical review committees will need to engage in careful analysis of the circumstances to determine whether the use of placebo rather than an established effective intervention is ethically acceptable. They will need to be satisfied that an established effective intervention is truly unlikely to become available and implementable in that country. This may be difficult to determine, however, as it is clear that, with sufficient persistence and ingenuity, ways may be found of accessing previously unattainable medicinal products, and thus avoiding the ethical issue raised by the use of placebo control.

In the debates over the ethical legitimacy of these trials, the prohibitive cost of optimum treatment was often taken for granted. It is, however, important to remember that, while it may have cost a lot to develop, AZT is not in fact expensive to manufacture, and could be made cheaply by pharmaceutical companies in poor countries. In part, the reason why developing countries cannot afford to provide the 076 protocol is that the TRIPS Agreement allows one company to hold the global patent on a drug like AZT for at least twenty years, during which time no generic equivalent may be produced. Permitting poor countries to manufacture generic versions of expensive patented drugs might offer a more ethically defensible solution to the problem of unaffordable medicines than permitting a double standard in research ethics.

In response to pressure from African countries, in 2001 the World Trade Organization issued a *Declaration on the TRIPS Agreement and Public Health* which allows developing countries to seek a waiver on public health grounds from the TRIPS Agreement. The new agreement states that the TRIPS Agreement

can and should be interpreted and implemented in a manner supportive of WTO members' right to protect public health and, in particular, to promote access to medicines for all.

But, as Paquita de Zulueta explains, it remains to be seen whether this Declaration will substantially improve access to new medicines in developing countries.

Paquita de Zulueta[107]

Following the 076 study, anti-retroviral prophylaxix to reduce maternal–fetal transmission has

---

[106] *International Ethical Guidelines for Biomedical Research Involving Human Subjects* <http://www.cioms.ch/>.

[107] 'Randomised Placebo-Controlled Trials and HIV-Infected Pregnant Women in Developing Countires: Ethical Imperialism or Unethical Exploitation' (2001) 15 Bioethics 289–311.

been whittled down, or changed, such that cheaper, simpler and reasonably effective regimes suitable for breast feeding populations have been found . . . Yet these regimes are not being implemented in those countries that need them most. A number of factors contribute to this, the most relevant being the lack or resources and political will . . .

Arguably at this stage little significant progress can be made in further efforts to find a cheaper, simpler prophylactic regime without over-compromising efficacy. In addition, it is easy to forget that the most effective way of reducing paediatric AIDS is by primary prevention in women of reproductive age . . .

The well-developed resource-rich nations now have the uncomfortable choice of either accepting the status-quo: the gross inequity between the rich and the poor nations, and the relentless progress of this devastating and widespread disease, or recognising that this terrible state of affairs creates an ethical imperative for mounting an international strategic resonse. If we accept a global ethics and a common humanity, then the devastation of Africa by this pandemic is everybody's problem . . .

Despite the bleak picture, there are hopeful signs . . . Drugs companies have agreed to reduce the costs of some of their drugs for distribution in poorer countries . . . The debt burden has been removed from some poorer nations. Political remedies have been suggested, such as the clearance of national debt, the supply of pharmaceuticals at very low cost, the offer of aid contingent on democratic reform, the ban of sales of weapons of war, and so on. The facilitation of poorer countries to manufacture drugs should not be unduly constrained by patent law (particularly, Trade Related Aspects of Intellectual Property Rights or TRIPS). Sadly, but unsurprisingly, many of these promises have not, as yet, been translated into solid action; the Western governments and powerful pharmaceutical companies still seem to be dominated by the mercenary motto of 'business as usual'.

While these HIV trials may have been especially controversial, the ethical dilemmas raised by conducting AIDS-related research in developing countries extend far beyond this one example. HIV vaccine trials, for example, must be conducted in populations that are particularly at risk from contracting all the various forms of the HIV virus. Not only do most new infections now occur in developing countries, but there are also different strains of the HIV virus, some of which are prevalent only in certain parts of the world.

Trials of HIV vaccines raise exceptionally difficult ethical questions. For a new vaccine to be proved effective, it is necessary to test it in a population in which new infections are likely to be occurring, and to establish that the rate of infection in the vaccinated group is lower than that of the control group. This immediately introduces a conflict of interest for researchers since it is in the interests of their study that members of the control group are not universally successful in preventing HIV infection through behaviour modification. Yet it would obviously be unethical to withhold information about preventative measures from the control group.

There is also the danger that participants in a vaccine trial may wrongly believe themselves to be protected against the HIV virus, and as a result may engage in riskier behaviour than they would otherwise, thus in fact *increasing* their risk of infection. As we saw earlier, people taking part in research trials do not always understand the concept of randomization, so they may not fully grasp that being allocated to the control group will mean that they receive no protection at all against transmission.

Furthermore, participants may not realize that even if they are in the 'active' arm of the trial, the vaccine has not yet been proved effective in preventing transmission of the HIV virus, and so should not be relied upon as a precautionary measure.

11. COMPENSATION FOR INJURIES

If a subject did not consent to her participation in a research trial, she could—in theory—bring an action in battery (see further Chapter 5 p. 262). However, because a person who takes part in a research project will usually have signed a consent form first, it will be difficult for her to establish that she was not informed 'in broad terms'[108] about the nature of the trial.

If a subject suffers injury during a research trial, she might be able to claim that the researcher, who would undoubtedly owe her a duty of care, was in breach of that duty. This might happen in two ways. First, a person could be injured as a result of negligence in the design or execution of the research project. Secondly, the information provided to the subject, although sufficient to avoid a charge of battery, may have been inadequate, and amount to a breach of the researcher's duty of care. In this latter situation, the research subject will have to establish that she would not have consented to take part in the research trial if she had been provided with the relevant information, and hence would not have suffered whatever injury has materialized as a result of her participation.

Where it is the design of the research project that caused the subject's injuries, could the members of the REC also be liable for failing to notice that the protocol itself was defective? It could be argued that it is foreseeable that negligent approval of a dangerous research project will cause injury, and that there is a relationship of proximity between the REC and the research subjects. But would it be fair, just and reasonable to impose liability on the members of the REC? There have been no cases in which injured research subjects have sued REC members, and such actions are improbable given the much deeper pockets of other potential defendants, such as the NHS and/or a pharmaceutical company. The Department of Health did address this concern in its 1991 *Guidelines on Local Research Ethics Committees*, and its advice was that there would be little chance of a successful claim against an REC member:

Legal advice available to the Department of Health is that there is little prospect of a successful claim against an LREC member for a mishap arising from research approved as ethical by the LREC. Any such claim would lie principally against the researcher concerned and against the NHS body under the auspices of which the research took place.[109]

As we saw in Chapter 3, victims of medical mishaps face numerous obstacles when bringing actions in negligence, and this will be equally true for individuals who have been injured during research rather than treatment. It has, however, been argued that people injured during research trials should not have to overcome all of the hurdles that the tort of negligence places in the path of those seeking compensation for

---

[108] *Chatterton v Gerson* [1981] QB 432.
[109] Department of Health, *Guidelines on Local Research Ethics Committees* (DoH 1991) para 2.11.

injuries sustained during ordinary medical treatment. The Pearson Commission, for example, advocated a 'no fault' compensation scheme for people injured during medical research, drawing an analogy with the statutory compensation offered to people injured by vaccination programmes. The community as a whole benefits from both vaccination and research, and should therefore offer adequate compensation for the small proportion of the population who will suffer injuries as a result. Their proposal was never implemented, but for two reasons, people who have been injured as a result of their participation in a research trial are in fact unlikely to have to resort to an ordinary action in negligence.

First, the various guidelines and codes which govern research specify that clear and fair arrangements for compensation in the event of injury or loss should exist before the trial begins. In the UK, under Regulation 15(5) of the Medicines for Human Use (Clinical Trials) Regulations 2004, RECs must be adequately reassured that adequate insurance and indemnity arrangements exist for the treatment and compensation of subjects who are injured, disabled or killed as a result of their participation in the research.

Secondly, the adverse publicity that would result from a court action in which a pharmaceutical company was sued for injuries inflicted on a research subject represents a powerful incentive towards the making of *ex gratia* payments. Certainly the Association of the British Pharmaceutical Industry (ABPI)'s guidelines recommend that compensation should be paid, even if the victim cannot establish negligence. Not having to prove fault will undoubtedly make it easier to obtain compensation, but it should be remembered that the subject still has to establish causation, which will often—as we saw in Chapter 3—be a significant obstacle, particularly where the subject is a patient whose pre-existing condition offers another plausible explanation for any deterioration in their condition. The ABPI also suggest that compensation might be reduced or excluded where a patient suffering from a serious disease was warned of the risk of an adverse reaction before enrolling in the trial.

Association of the British Pharmaceutical Industry[110]

  1.2 Compensation should be paid when, on the balance of probabilities, the injury was attributable to the administration of a medicinal product under trial or any clinical intervention or procedure provided for by the protocol that would not have occurred but for the inclusion of the patient in the trial.

  1.7 For the avoidance of doubt, compensation should be paid regardless of whether the patient is able to prove that the company has been negligent in relation to research and development of the medicinal product under trial or that the product is defective and therefore, as the producer, the company is subject to strict liability in respect of injuries caused by it.

  4.1 The amount of compensation paid should be appropriate to the nature, severity and persistence of the injury and should in general terms be consistent with the quantum of damages commonly awarded for similar injuries by an English court in cases where legal liability is admitted.

  4.2 Compensation may be abated, or in certain circumstances excluded, in the light of the

---

[110] Clinical Trial Compensation Guidelines, ABPI, 1991.

following factors (on which will depend the level of risk the patient can reasonably be expected to accept):

4.2.1 the seriousness of the disease being treated, the degree of probability that adverse reactions will occur and any warnings given;

4.2.2 the risks and benefits of established treatments relative to those known or suspected of the trial medicine.

12. CONCLUSION

Throughout this chapter, we have seen that there is generally assumed to be a sharp distinction between research and ordinary medical treatment. In particular, in relation to research, there is undoubtedly a duty to obtain 'informed consent', whereas, as we saw in Chapter 5, the judiciary has been hostile to the introduction of the 'doctrine of informed consent' for routine medical treatment. People who volunteer to take part in research are regarded as more vulnerable and dependent, and in greater need of clear and frank information than patients. Is this special concern for research subjects justified?

On the one hand, the long history of the abuse of research subjects should undoubtedly alert us to the need to have protective mechanisms in place to ensure that vulnerable individuals do not end up taking part in research without knowing that this is what they are doing, or without being given the option of refusal. Yet on the other hand, it is worth remembering that the decision to consent to treatment will also sometimes be a difficult decision, which requires an individual to balance risks and benefits, some of which may be uncertain and speculative. Rather than viewing research subjects as uniquely vulnerable and in need of a great deal of sensitively provided information, perhaps we should acknowledge that patients too are often faced with complex decisions, and with information which may be difficult for them to understand and evaluate.

A final interesting distinction between patients and research subjects is the insistence, in the Helsinki Declaration, that any control group should be assured of the 'best current treatment'. Again, this draws a sharp distinction between participants in research and patients. Within the NHS at least, patients are indubitably *not* assured of the best current treatment. Rather, it is generally accepted that limited resources mean that sometimes less than optimal treatment may have to be provided in order to ensure that the NHS can continue to run a comprehensive health service. As we saw in Chapter 2, the reality of rationed health care is that patients are deprived of beneficial treatment. If it is absolutely clear that patients do not have the right to demand the 'best current' treatment, is it anomalous that participating in research gives subjects precisely this right?

13. FURTHER READING

CAVE, E and HOLM, S, 'New governance arrangements for research ethics committees: is facilitating research achieved at the cost of participants' interest' (2002) 28 Journal of Medical Ethics 318–21.

FOSTER, CLAIRE, *The Ethics of Medical Research on Humans* (CUP Cambridge 2001).

FOX, MARIE, 'Research Bodies: Feminist Perspectives on Clinical Research' in S. Sheldon and M Thomson (eds), *Feminist Perspectives on Health Care Law* (Cavendish London 1998) 115–34.

HARRIS, JOHN, 'Scientific research is a moral duty' (2005) 31 Journal of Medical Ethics 242–8.

LEWIS, PENNY, 'Procedures that are Against the Medical Interests of Incompetent Adults' (2002) 22(4) Oxford Journal of Legal Studies 575–618.

MCNEILL, PAUL M, *The Ethics and Politics of Human Experimentation* (CUP Cambridge 1993).

WEISSTUB, DAVID N (ed), *Research on Human Subjects: Ethics, Law and Social Policy* (Elsevier Oxford 1998).

9

PRODUCT LIABILITY AND THE REGULATION OF MEDICINES

1. CENTRAL ISSUES

1. Before any new medicine can be put into general circulation, it must have a marketing authorization.

2. European regulation is increasingly important in relation to the licensing and marketing of medicines, and it has two aims: to harmonize consumer protection regimes and to facilitate the free movement of goods.

3. The difficulty in using negligence to compensate patients for drug-related injuries is demonstrated by the case of thalidomide. Thalidomide had caused extremely disabling and sometimes fatal injuries, but it would have been extremely difficult to prove that its manufacturer had been negligent.

4. Strict liability for injuries caused by defective products was introduced by the Consumer Protection Act 1987, in response to a European directive. So far, there has been comparatively little litigation, but it is noteworthy that, while at first, the courts appeared to equate liability under the Act with negligence, a more robust, albeit only first instance judgment has reasserted that liability under the Act does not require proof of fault.

5. Causation represents a significant obstacle to recovery for drug-related injuries, in part because patients who take medicines are already ill, and in part because injuries may only manifest themselves many years later, when it might be difficult to identify the manufacturer whose drug caused the injuries.

6. In the future, pharmacogenetics is likely to transform the way in which medicines are prescribed, by enabling doctors to know *in advance* whether a drug is likely to suit an individual patient.

2. INTRODUCTION

In this chapter, we consider the regulation of medicines. Although the availability of safe and effective pharmaceutical drugs is not the only factor that has contributed to increased life expectancy in the last hundred years—better sanitation and nutrition have also been vitally important—there is no doubt that the increasing availability of effective medicines has significantly improved public health.[1] The development of penicillin, antibiotics, and vaccines against diseases such as tuberculosis (TB) and polio, means that it is now comparatively rare for people living in the world's richest

[1] Jasper Woodcock 'Medicines—The Interested Parties' in R Blum et al. (eds), *Pharmaceuticals and Health Policy: International Perspectives on Provision and Control of Medicines* (Croom Helm London 1981) 27–35, 27.

countries to die from infectious diseases, and it is the degenerative diseases of old age, such as cancer and heart disease, which have become the most common causes of death. But while medicines have undoubtedly helped to transform the health of people living in the west, their availability in poorer countries continues to be inadequate.

The pharmaceutical industry is driven by profit, and it is in Europe and the US where huge profits can be made from successful drugs. An effective treatment for depression or obesity, for example, is likely to generate much higher profits than a cure for a 'neglected disease', such as malaria or sleeping sickness. A 2002 *British Medical Journal* editorial spelled out the problem.

British Medical Journal[2]

[O]ut of 1393 new drugs marketed between 1975 and 1999, only 16 were for neglected diseases, yet these diseases accounted for over 10% of the global disease burden. In contrast, over two thirds of new drugs were 'me too drugs' (modified versions of existing drugs), which do little or nothing to change the disease burden . . .

When it comes to the world's most neglected diseases, however, these present absolutely no market opportunities. Without such opportunities, there is no incentive for the pharmaceutical industry to invest in drug research and development. The patients have no purchasing power, no vocal advocacy group is pleading for their needs, and no strategic interests—military or security— are driving concern about these conditions.

For example, sleeping sickness, which claims thousands of lives annually in Africa, can be considered as a most neglected disease. Current drug treatments are in scarce supply, difficult to administer, and often toxic. Melarsoprol, which was developed over 50 years ago, kills up to 10% of people who are given the drug, and in some regions drug resistance means it is ineffective in a third of patients. An effective, less toxic drug, has been developed—eflornithine—but the company that developed it stopped its production in 1995, citing commercial failure. African patients could not afford to buy the drug. Eflornithine became available again five years later in the United States, when it was found to reduce unwanted facial hair in women.

The injustice of American women depilating their faces while thousands in Africa were dying of a treatable illness finally led the original makers to restart production of the drug.

The drive to provide a pharmacological solution to an ever increasing number of problems is sometimes referred to as 'medicalization'. The menopause can be 'treated' with hormone replacement therapy; medication now exists for behavioural difficulties in children; and drugs are increasingly used to combat conditions such as baldness, obesity, anxiety and sexual impotence.

The research and development of new drugs involves enormous financial investment. On average it takes between ten and twelve years and costs £800 million to develop a new medicine.[3] For every 10,000 compounds which are synthesized, tested, and developed, only one or two will ultimately reach the market,[4] and 90 per cent of compounds which get as far as the preclinical development stage will fail before

---

[2] 'The world's most neglected diseases' (2002) 325 British Medical Journal 176–7.

[3] Zosia Kmietowicz, 'Regulations are stifling development of new drugs' (2004) 328 British Medical Journal 600.

[4] Richard Sykes, *New Medicines, The Practice of Medicine, and Public Policy* (Nuffield Trust London 2000) 65.

launch.[5] The money invested in these failures inevitably increases the price of success-ful drugs. In order to recoup their investment, pharmaceutical companies are allowed to hold the patent on any new drug for twenty years, that is they have the right to prevent others from making or selling an identical product.[6] Of course, some of this patent term will expire while the drug is being tested, and so in reality firms may enjoy only ten years of 'on the market' patent protection. Nevertheless, generic versions of drugs, which are much more affordable, cannot be produced until this period is over. For example, despite the discovery of drugs (such as AZT) which are capable of substantially delaying the onset of AIDS, people in the world's poorest countries who become infected with the HIV virus are still likely to die within a few years because patent protection means that the drugs are simply unaffordable.

Although intellectual property rights undoubtedly raise the price of medicines, and hence might not appear to be in the interests of consumers, the pharmaceutical industry has argued that, without them, investing in research and development would be so risky that the development of innovative medicines would be stifled. This sort of argument is disputed in the next extract by Graham Dukes who argues that the pharmaceutical industry's commercial accountability to shareholders takes priority over its accountability to communities.

MN Graham Dukes[7]

Two definitions of industry accountability predominate: commercial duty to shareholders; and duty to the community.

In the commercial sense, a pharmaceutical company is obliged to deliver a sound return on investment for shareholders. That return must be adequate to reward investors but also be suf-ficient to attract new capital when needed. From this point of view, the pharmaceutical industry has done very well. Throughout periods of economic stagnation and even recession over the past 30 years, it has remained highly and increasingly profitable. Mergers have hardly ever taken place because of failing companies; the strong have simply linked up with the even stronger.

From the broad social point of view, the pharmaceutical industry has a duty to supply com-munities with good drugs at an affordable price, and to provide reliable information on them . . . The much-repeated argument from pharmaceutical companies, that high drug prices are mainly attributable to research costs, merits cautious scrutiny. With publicly available data, we can ascertain that costs of advertising and promotion generally much exceed research expenditure. Furthermore, industrial research usually benefits from public support, either in the form of tax breaks or as direct scientific input. . . .

Ideals about public health and welfare coexist with an increasingly vigorous commercial and competitive creed, and can be overshadowed by it. A fair proportion of people in any western country today have an interest in the financial well-being of the drug industry, either as workers, investors, or as pensioners indirectly dependent on the industry's performance on the stock mar-ket. The difficulty arises when financial performance is at all dependent on practices that might seem to betray the industry's broader duty to contribute positively to health care. The constant flow of new drugs, including many which contribute little or nothing new to health care, promo-tional pressure on doctors to prescribe new drugs (generally more costly than the previous

---

[5] Ibid.

[6] Patent Act 1977 s 25(1). World Trade Organization (WTO) Agreement on Trade-Related Intellectual Property Rights (TRIPS), Art 33.

[7] 'Accountability of the pharmaceutical industry' (2002) 260 The Lancet 1682–4.

product), and the setting of prices at the highest level which a market will bear can all be criticised from society's point of view.

For a number of reasons, medicines are unlike other products. First, purchase decisions are generally not taken by the consumers themselves, but by their professional advisers. Secondly, any medicine which is powerful enough to cure disease or alleviate symptoms will also be strong enough to cause adverse side effects, in at least some consumers, and these can sometimes be extremely serious and/or unpleasant. If complete safety is unattainable, deciding when a medicine is safe *enough* involves complex risk/benefit calculations. For example, chemotherapy has extremely unpleasant side effects, which would not be worth putting up with in a medicine which cured a comparatively trivial condition, such as hayfever, but which might be outweighed by the possible benefit of curing cancer. Thirdly, the cultural and symbolic significance of medicines is amply demonstrated by the placebo effect, which we considered in the previous chapter. It is clear that the powerful belief on the part of both doctors and patients in the therapeutic value of medicines can itself have a significant effect upon a patient's health.

The role of regulation in this area is complex. First, since the rules only apply to medicines, a clear definition of what counts as a medicine is necessary. Secondly, it is important to ensure that drugs are both safe and effective, and next we examine the licensing process in the UK. Thirdly, we consider the increasing standardization of the regulation of medicines within the European Union. Fourthly, if the entire NHS budget is not to be swallowed up by the spiralling costs of medicines, it is important to ensure that the drugs which are prescribed in the NHS are affordable, and we look briefly at limits which are placed upon the prescribing of medicines. Finally, we consider the law's response to defective medicines, examining in turn the role of contract, negligence and statute, most notably the Consumer Protection Act 1987.

At the outset it is worth noting that government policy in this area will be influenced by a number of competing factors, which may pull in rather different directions. On the one hand, the government has an interest in containing costs within the NHS, which might lead it to consider restricting access to new and expensive drugs. Yet, the government will also be concerned to improve patient care, and in contrast that might mean expanding access to effective medicines. Because the pharmaceutical industry is phenomenally profitable, and a major employer, the government has a further clear interest in ensuring that the UK is an attractive location for such companies, by, for example, making sure that its product liability regime does not stifle innovation. Yet at the same time, the government's concern for patient safety might lead it to favour a strict liability regime for all drug-related injuries.

3. WHAT IS A MEDICINE?

(a) DEFINING MEDICINAL PRODUCTS

In practice, it will sometimes be difficult to determine whether something, such as a food supplement or a herbal remedy, is a medicine. Because the Medicines Act 1968 applies only to medicinal products, it is obviously important to be able to tell whether a particular product needs a marketing authorization (see below) before it can be sold. This is a job for the Medicines and Healthcare products Regulatory Agency (MHRA), previously the Medicines Control Agency (MCA). And as we can see from the following case, the courts will be slow to interfere with the Agency's determination of whether or not something is a medicinal product.

R v Medicines Control Agency, ex parte Pharma Nord[8]

The applicants had marketed melatonin tablets in the UK. The MCA informed manufacturers, importers, distributors and retailers of unlicensed melatonin that, in its view, melatonin was a medicinal product and should only be supplied on prescription. The applicants argued that melatonin was similar to vitamin pills, which were freely on sale in the UK without the need for a licence. The applicants applied for judicial review arguing that the MCA's reasons for classifying melatonin as a medicinal product were inadequate and not in accordance with EC Directive 65/65. Recognizing that they were unlikely to succeed in proving *Wednesbury* unreasonableness, they sought a full trial on the merits of whether melatonin should be considered a medicinal product. Collins J refused to exercise his discretion to transfer the case to the civil courts, and the Court of Appeal dismissed the applicant's appeal.

Lord Woolf MR

1. Under European and domestic law it is the MCA which has the initial heavy responsibility of protecting the public against the dangers to health which can result from the unlicensed marketing of medicinal products. It is also the MCA's equally important initial responsibility to decide what is or is not a medicinal product. Unless it determines that a substance is a medicinal product there is no action which it can lawfully take to control its use.

2. The decisions of the European Court make it clear that, in coming to a decision on the facts as to whether a product is medicinal, there is scope for a not insignificant element of policy to enter into the determination . . .

4. The determination of the facts and the application of the policy in a case such as this are not ideally suited to the adversarial processes of the courts. If the case was one where the MCA could not reasonably have come to the decision which it did so that the outcome was one which is conventionally determined on applications for judicial review, the position would be different. However, in this case the MCA is in a better position to evaluate the evidence than a judge. It has accumulated experience in relation to other products which a court lacks. It is an expert body. The MCA has to develop a consistent policy between similar products. The issues are . . . ones in relation to which the court should be wary of becoming involved . . .

6. . . . [W]here what is involved is reasonably regarded by the MCA as a medicinal product, I do not consider that, as a matter of discretion, the civil courts should readily exercise their discretionary declaratory jurisdiction to reinvestigate the facts in civil proceedings against the wishes of the MCA.

So how does the Agency decide whether a product is a medicine? 'Medicinal products' are defined in the Codified Pharmaceutical Directive[9] as follows:

- Any substance or combination of substances presented for treating or preventing disease in human beings or animals.

---

[8] (1998) 44 BMLR 41.   [9] 2001/83/EEC.

- Any substance or combination of substances which may be administered to human beings or animals with a view to making a diagnosis or to restoring, correcting or modifying physiological function in human beings or animals is likewise considered a medicinal product.

The two limbs of this test refer to *presentation* and *function*. In short, if a product is either *marketed* for the treatment or prevention of disease, or *used* for diagnostic purposes, or to alter physiological function, it is a medicinal product. Either is sufficient for a product to qualify as a medicinal product.

When determining whether a product has been 'presented' for the treatment of disease, the MHRA will consider any claims—both explicit and implicit—made for it, and will look at the presentation of the product as a whole, including its labelling, packaging and advertising.[10] Also relevant will be the form the product takes and the way it is to be used: in effect, does it *look like* a medicine? Claims that a product relieves symptoms, such as stress or anxiety, will be regarded as medicinal claims.[11] And the reference to 'prevention' means that products which claim to 'protect against' disease will similarly be treated as medicinal products.[12] Claims that a product 'helps to maintain a healthy lifestyle', in contrast, have not been regarded by the MHRA as medicinal claims.[13]

The second limb refers to the medicinal purpose of the product. Here it is enough that the product contains active ingredients which have a physiological effect. It is not necessary for the product to also be presented as a medicine. Hence, a herbal remedy which has a known active ingredient in a therapeutic dose will fall within the definition, even if it does not claim to be a medicine.

(b) LIFESTYLE DRUGS AND THE PROBLEM OF ENHANCEMENT

When we think about medicines, we generally assume that people take them when they are unwell, in order to restore their health or alleviate their symptoms. Yet in recent years there has been increasing interest in biomedical enhancements which might be taken not to restore normal functioning, but rather to improve upon it. It is by no means easy to draw a line between enhancements and ordinary medical treatment. Many modern medicines are intended to reverse some of the symptoms of ageing, such as forgetfulness, wrinkles, baldness, and sexual dysfunction. Are these 'enhancements', or attempts to restore 'normal' functioning?

Treatments for recognized disorders can often also be used by people who want to feel 'better than well'.[14] Viagra can be used to treat impotence, but it could also be taken by people who want to enhance their sexual performance. Let us imagine that scientists discover an effective treatment for memory loss. This might be regarded as necessary medical treatment for patients with Alzheimer's Disease, but what if it was prescribed to students to improve their performance in examinations, or obtained by

---

[10] MHRA, *A guide to what is a medicinal product* (MHRA Guidance Note 8, 2003) para 15.
[11] Ibid, para 16.   [12] Ibid.   [13] Ibid, para 17.
[14] Carl Elliott, *Better than Well: American Medicine meets the American Dream* (Norton New York 2003); Peter Kramer, *Listening to Prozac* (Penguin New York 1994).

international chess players in order to gain a competitive advantage?[15] In all three cases, the drug *enhances* memory function, but its social acceptability depends upon the context in which it is taken. In the next extract, Peter Conrad and Deborah Potter discuss how difficult it can be to draw a distinction between therapy and enhancement.

Peter Conrad and Deborah Potter[16]

[T]he therapy–enhancement line is a thin one. As we know from our studies of medicalization a wide range of conditions or behaviours can be defined as a medical problem, as some kind of disorder in need of treatment. We also know that conditions can move in and out of medical jurisdiction. Medical definitions can change; new medical diagnoses can be developed which will justify certain types of enhancement as therapy. In the US in recent years the diagnosis of Adult ADHD [Attention Deficit Hyperactivity Disorder] has become popular, for which Ritalin is often prescribed. Many 'successful' adults have approached their physicians with problems of personal disorganisation, inability to finish projects and difficulty with concentration or focus. Some have diagnosed themselves as having ADHD and sought treatment from physicians . . ., we have termed this the 'medicalization of underperformance' and raised the issue of whether Ritalin for adults is a treatment or an enhancement . . .

In a sense, we can see biomedical enhancement as a double temptation: the object itself is tempting (eg several inches of height, younger features or improved performance) *and* the bio-medical route to the enhancement is a temptation as well (eg a rapid road to improvement, a technological strategy, a medical solution). . . . The key to enhancement, however, is that only some are enhanced. There is no edge if it is universal . . .

The social forces driving biomedical enhancement are strong . . . Science and medicine work to create new treatments for human problems, some of which may become enhancements . . . Prozac was first introduced for the clinically depressed and soon was promoted for making individuals better than well; it is likely that Alzheimer treatments may lead to memory enhancements for the rest of us . . .

Biomedical enhancements do not involve hard work, in fact they are something of a techno-logical fix. It seems likely most people do not . . . consider runners who raise their aerobic ability and run marathons in under three hours unnatural. Indeed we admire such individuals for their fortitude. They have achieved their enhancement through diligence and hard work, exemplary characteristics in our culture. If women could enhance their breasts at the gym or children increase their height by working out, would unnaturalness be an issue at all? . . . [W]e might note that our society has adopted a sort of 'pharmaceutical Calvinism' when it comes to taking medications. This entails a belief that it is better to achieve an objective naturally than with drugs or medications; this includes pleasure, sexual satisfaction, mental stability and bodily fitness. Using drugs is an inferior and even suspect way of reaching a goal. But what is natural resides in the social definition, not in the phenomenon.

It is important to recognize that what we consider to be 'normal functioning' is itself socially constructed and culturally variable. As Carl Elliott explains, the pharma-ceutical industry has learned that to sell new drugs successfully, it is sometimes first necessary to 'sell' the existence of the disease which they are intended to treat.

---

[15] Peter Conrad and Deborah Potter, 'Human growth hormone and the temptations of biomedical enhancement' (2004) 26 Sociology of Health and Illness 184–215, 186.

[16] Ibid, 200, 203–5.

Carl Elliott[17]

The pharmaceutical industry . . . has learned that the key to selling psychiatric drugs is to sell the illnesses they treat. Antidepressants are a case in point. Before the 1960s, clinical depression was thought to be an extremely rare problem. Drug companies stayed away from depression because there was no money to be made in antidepressants. So when Merck started to produce amytriptaline, a tricyclic antidepressant, in the early 1960s, it realised that in order to sell the antidepressant it needed to sell depression.

Forty years later, of course, it is now clear to everyone that the market for antidepressants was not a shallow one at all: that it was, in fact, a tremendously lucrative market, as the remarkable success of Prozac and its sister drugs have demonstrated. The notion of 'clinical depression' has expanded tremendously to include many people who might once have been called melancholic, anxious, or alienated. . . .

This does not mean that drug companies are simply making up diseases out of thin air, or that psychiatrists are being gulled into diagnosing well people as sick. No one doubts that some people genuinely suffer from, say, depression, or attention-deficit/hyperactivity disorder, or that the right medications make these disorders better. But surrounding the core of many of these disorders is a wide zone of ambiguity that can be chiseled out and expanded. Pharmaceutical companies have a powerful financial interest in expanding categories of mental disease, because it is only when a certain condition is recognized as a disease that it can be treated with the products the companies produce.

Using the example of anti-baldness medication, Ray Moynihan et al. describe the process of industry-sponsored medicalization.

Ray Moynihan, Iona Heath, David Henry, and Peter C Gøtzsche[18]

There's a lot of money to be made from telling healthy people they're sick. Some forms of medicalising ordinary life may now be better described as disease mongering: widening the boundaries of treatable illness in order to expand markets for those who sell and deliver treatments. Pharmaceutical companies are actively involved in sponsoring the definition of diseases and promoting them to both prescribers and consumers. The social construction of illness is being replaced by the corporate construction of disease . . .

The medicalisation of baldness shows clearly the transformation of the ordinary processes of life into medical phenomena. Around the time that Merck's hair growth drug finasteride (Propecia) was first approved in Australia, leading newspapers featured new information about the emotional trauma associated with hair loss. The global public relations firm Edelman orchestrated some of the coverage but largely left its fingerprints off the resulting stories. An article . . . in the *Australian* newspaper featured a new 'study' suggesting that a third of all men experienced some degree of hair loss, along with comments by concerned experts and news that an International Hair Study Institute had been established. It suggested that losing hair could lead to panic and other emotional difficulties, and even have an impact on job prospects and mental wellbeing. The article did not reveal that the study and the institute were both funded by Merck and that the experts quoted had been supplied by Edelman.

So how should doctors respond to patients' requests for so-called 'lifestyle' drugs? In

---

[17] Carl Elliott, *Better than Well: American Medicine meets the American Dream* (Norton New York 2003) 123–4.
[18] 'Selling sickness: the pharmaceutical industry and disease mongering' (2002) 324 British Medical Journal 886–91.

the next extract, the British Medical Association (BMA) suggests that improving a person's quality of life can sometimes be a legitimate use of NHS resources. The contraceptive pill, for example, which is available free of charge on prescription, does not treat any sort of disease, but rather enhances women's quality of life by enabling them to control their fertility.[19] However, the BMA also advises that patients do not have the right to be provided with any drug which they believe will improve their quality of life, especially since all medicines carry some risks and these may be less acceptable where there is no clinical indication for prescribing the drug in question.

British Medical Association[20]

It is generally accepted that doctors should prescribe medication only if they consider it necessary for the patient, but views of what is 'necessary' differ. More frequent request from patients for what have been termed 'lifestyle drugs', such as antiobesity drugs, antidepressants, and hair loss treatments, illustrate the way in which perceptions of 'clinical need' have changed. Although there are certainly those for whom antidepressants and appetite suppressants are clinically indicated and cannot be considered as lifestyle drugs, for many others they are seen as a quick and easy solution. When in search of a quick fix, it is easier to take medication than to spend time and energy on diet and exercise, or to spend time exploring, through counselling, the root of anxiety or depression.

What constitutes a lifestyle drug has been the subject of debate in the medical literature. It is defined in the Concise Oxford Dictionary as: 'a pharmaceutical product characterised as improving quality of life rather than alleviating or curing disease'. Improving quality of life is, however, a legitimate aim of the health service, so the fact that oral contraceptives fall within this definition does not mean they should not be prescribed within the NHS. Where the boundary lies between what is and what is not acceptable to prescribe with NHS funding, however, is a matter for debate. Until clear guidance is issued, cases should be considered on an individual basis. . . . In addition to the financial considerations, there are also questions of safety. There are inherent risks with virtually all medication and part of the doctor's role is to balance those risks against the anticipated benefits for the patient. When the drug is not clinically indicated, the benefits the patient will, or believes he or she will, derive need to be weighed against the risks. Doctors must be willing to justify their decisions to prescribe in these circumstances; patient demand or preference, on its own, is unlikely to provide sufficient justification.

4. LICENSING

Thalidomide had been marketed in the late 1950s as a remedy for morning sickness in pregnancy. Clinical trials had given no indication of its propensity to cause birth defects, and its UK manufacturers, Distillers, claimed that it could 'be given with complete safety to pregnant women and nursing mothers without adverse effect on mother or child'.[21] Unfortunately, this claim proved to be false, and between 1956 and 1961 12,000 children were born in over thirty countries with very severe limb defects.

---

[19] See further, Silvia Pezzini, 'The Effect of Women's Rights on Women's Welfare: Evidence from a Natural Experiment' (2005) 115 The Economic Journal C208.

[20] *Medical Ethics Today: The BMA's handbook of ethics and law* 2nd edition (BMA London 2004) 458–9.

[21] Pamela Ferguson, *Drug Injuries and the Pursuit of Compensation* (Sweet & Maxwell London 1996) 5.

One-third of these 'thalidomide' babies died within a month. Before the 1960s, there had been remarkably few restrictions upon the marketing of medicines. There was, for example, no legal requirement upon pharmaceutical companies to prove the safety and efficacy of new medicines before putting them into circulation. Unsurprisingly, the thalidomide tragedy led to increased interest in regulating the safety of medicines, resulting in the Medicines Act 1968, which was intended to provide an effective system for the licensing and monitoring of drugs.

In 1998 the Medical Devices Agency was set up to regulate medical devices (such as intra-uterine contraceptives and pacemakers), and in 2003 it was merged with the Medicines Control Agency to form the Medical and Healthcare products Regulatory Agency (MHRA), which is responsible for regulating both drugs and devices. In this chapter, we will focus on medicines. The rules covering medical devices are slightly narrower in scope, and the onus is placed on the manufacturer, rather than the MHRA, to ensure that the device complies with the various safety requirements.

(a) MARKETING AUTHORIZATION

Under regulations 17–21 of the Medicines for Human Use (Clinical Trials) Regulations 2004, authorization must be sought from the MHRA before a new medicine can be tested in a clinical trial. Schedule 3 of the Regulations sets out the information which must be submitted before a clinical trial can be authorized, such as summaries of the chemical, pharmaceutical and biological data on the active substance and the finished product, and summaries of the non-clinical pharmacology and toxicology data on that product, if available.

Only when trials have indicated that the drug is reasonably safe and effective can a drug company apply for what used to be known as a product licence, and is now referred to as a marketing authorization. Before any medicinal product (including generic equivalents of established drugs) can be made available for public use, under section 7(2) of the Medicines Act, it must have a marketing authorization.

Medicines Act 1968 section 7(2)

Except in accordance with a licence granted for the purposes of this section (in this Act referred to as a 'product licence') no person shall, in the course of a business carried on by him, and in circumstances to which this subsection applies,

(a) sell, supply or export any medicinal product, or

(b) procure the sale, supply or exportation of any medicinal product, or

(c) procure the manufacture or assembly of any medicinal product for sale, supply or exportation.

Although the Secretary of State for Health is formally responsible for the licensing of medicines, in practice this role is undertaken by the MHRA, with advice from the Medicines Commission and the Committee on the Safety of Medicines (CSM). Section 19 specifies a number of factors which it should take into account when deciding whether to grant a marketing authorization.

Medicines Act 1968 section 19

(1) ... in dealing with an application for a product licence the licensing authority shall in particular take into consideration—

(a) the safety of medicinal products of each description to which the application relates;

(b) the efficacy of medicinal products of each such description for the purposes for which the products are proposed to be administered; and

(c) the quality of medicinal products of each such description, according to the specification and the method or proposed method of manufacture of the products, and the provisions proposed for securing that the products as sold or supplied will be of that quality.

(2) In taking into consideration the efficacy for a particular purpose of medicinal products of a description to which such an application relates, the licensing authority shall leave out of account any question whether medicinal products of another description would or might be equally or more efficacious for that purpose.

Notice that one factor which is *not* relevant is the price of the medicinal product. So the fact that a medicine is prohibitively expensive is not a good reason to deny it a marketing authorization. Of course, it might subsequently be decided that an expensive new medicine cannot be prescribed within the NHS, but provided that it meets the threshold levels of safety, effectiveness and quality, it should be granted a marketing authorization. Also irrelevant to the basic assessment of a drug's safety is the question of whether other medicines are equally or more effective than this new one.

When applying for a marketing authorization, the pharmaceutical company must submit full details of the research which has been carried out, and the results obtained, including any adverse reactions. The manufacturer must also provide information about the manufacturing process and quality control mechanisms, and must indicate how the drug will be marketed by, for example, submitting any leaflets to be supplied with the product, or specimen containers. All this information will then be analysed by the CSM. It is perhaps worth noting that the CSM bases its advice to the MHRA principally upon information submitted by the manufacturer. Once granted, a marketing authorization lasts for five years, after which a manufacturer must apply for its renewal.

If a manufacturer is applying for a marketing authorization for a generic medicine, it is not necessary to supply the MHRA with such full information if it can be demonstrated that the product is essentially similar to a product which is already in circulation.[22] In *In Re Smith Kline*[23] the applicant company, which had held the patent on a drug called 'cimetidine' for nearly 20 years, did not want the MCA to rely upon its research when considering other companies' applications to manufacture generic versions of its product. Smith Kline argued that this was confidential information. The House of Lords held that the MCA was under a duty to protect the public, and that when considering applications for product licences for generic versions of a drug, it was necessary to compare the information supplied in the later application with that in the original application, in order to ensure that both products were similar,

---

[22] EEC Art 4.8 of Council Directive (65/65/EEC) as amended by Council Directive (87/21/EEC).
[23] [1990] 1 AC 64.

safe, effective and reliable. The MCA therefore had a right and a duty to make use of all the information obtained by it under the Act.

In *Organon v Department of Health and Social Security*,[24] the Court of Appeal had to consider whether it was appropriate for the CSM to take into account not only a drug's safety when taken in the recommended dose for its intended purpose, but also its toxicity following overdose.

Organon v Department of Health and Social Security[25]

As a result of reports of adverse reactions, the CSM proposed to suspend Organon's licence to manufacture an antidepressant called mianserin under section 28(g) of the Medicines Act 1968, which provides that a licence can be suspended on the grounds 'that medicinal products of any description to which the licence relates can no longer be regarded as products which can safely be administered for the purposes indicated in the licence'. Organon wanted to submit evidence to the CSM that mianserin was less toxic than other antidepressants, and hence less likely to be fatal if a patient took an overdose. Initially, the CSM ruled that it was only entitled to take account of the drug's safety when taken for the purposes indicated in the licence, and hence evidence of toxicity following the drug's misuse was not relevant. The Divisional Court disagreed and held that the risks a drug posed if it was misused should be relevant to an assessment of its safety, and this decision was upheld by the Court of Appeal.

Mustill LJ

[O]ne must ask what test is to be applied when deciding whether Mianserin can 'safely' be 'administered' for the purpose of alleviating symptoms of depression. For my part, I doubt whether much is to be gained by considering the meaning of the word 'safety' in isolation: indeed, I doubt whether it is possible to do so. Thus, a drug which creates few hazards if marked with appropriate warnings and recommendations may be much more dangerous if these are omitted. Again, there is no absolute standard of safety. Very few drugs are entirely free from the risk of inducing adverse side effects in some patients. The question must always be whether the degree of risk is sufficiently low to be acceptable, and this cannot be addressed without an appreciation of the benefits to be gained from taking a risk of that degree. . . .

It strikes me as plain, and this much was virtually conceded, that however sympathetically paragraph (g) is read, administering the drug for the purposes of alleviating the symptoms of depression cannot be stretched to include the taking of the drug for the purpose of suicide . . .

I do not, however, believe that this is the right approach to the Medicines Act, the object of which is to promote public health and safety, and which should, if at all possible, be construed in a way favourable to the attainment of that object. To read paragraph (g) in the narrow sense for which the Authority contends, and which the words at first sight themselves seem to indicate, would work in the opposite direction. This would entail that if the Authority discovered, after the grant of a licence, that although in the intended dosage the drug remained acceptably safe, nevertheless if taken in even moderate excess it was potentially lethal, it would be beyond the Authority's jurisdiction even to consider whether the original risk/benefit analysis should be reconsidered, with a view to variation, suspension or cancellation of the licence. This result strikes me as so absurd that it cannot have been within the contemplation of Parliament. It must therefore be taken that the references to 'administered' and 'purposes' extend beyond circumstances which involve strict compliance with the intended use of the drug, and that the risks attaching to misuse can properly be brought into account.

---

[24] *The Times* 6 Feb 1990 (transcript available on Lexis).   [25] Ibid.

There remains the question whether the Licensing Authority is entitled to pay regard to the risks associated with the use of other drugs intended for the same purpose. I believe the answer to be plain. . . . Imagine, for example, that there are two drugs, A and B, which confer much the same benefits, but at a risk which is greater for A than for B, how could the Licensing Authority, as the guardian of public health, properly debar itself from taking the extra risk of A into account when making the choice between licensing one drug, or the other, or both, or neither? . . . I do not intend to suggest that the Licensing Authority will in every case find it necessary or even helpful to engage in the task of making comparisons with other drugs. Simply that to rule out such considerations in every case is not in accordance with the requirements of section 28.

A special exception from the need to obtain a marketing authorization exists for herbal remedies. Under section 12 of the Medicines Act 1968, herbal remedies which contain only plant materials are exempt from the requirement to obtain a marketing authorization if either the herbal remedy was made up on the premises from which it was supplied and prescribed after a one-to-one consultation (s 12(1)); or, if it is a pre-prepared over-the-counter remedy, it is not sold under any brand name and does not make any written therapeutic claims (s 12(2)). Over-the-counter herbal remedies which *do* make therapeutic claims must have a marketing authorization.

From October 2005 the UK must implement a European directive, the Traditional Herbal Medicinal Products Directive, by establishing a registration scheme for authorizing manufactured over-the-counter traditional herbal medicines (to be known as the Traditional Herbal Medicines Registration Scheme or THMRS).[26] The purpose of the directive is to ensure free movement of herbal medicinal products, and to set up a route for the registration of traditional herbal remedies, which do not meet the criteria for a marketing authorization under the Medicines Act.

Under the terms of the directive, manufacturers will have to demonstrate safety and quality, but not efficacy. Evidence of efficacy is seldom available for herbal medicines because randomized controlled trials, which as we saw in the previous chapter are the 'gold standard' in clinical research, are seldom carried out. Applicants must submit a review of safety data and an expert report on quality, in addition to evidence of at least thirty years of traditional use, fifteen of which should have been in the EU. It is assumed that some level of efficacy will exist if the remedy has been used for this length of time. In exceptional circumstances, registration will be possible even if the product has not been in use in the EU for fifteen years, but it will still be necessary to prove that it has been used elsewhere for at least thirty years. The product label must inform the consumer that the basis for registration is traditional use, rather than rigorous clinical trials, with the following warning:

The safety and efficacy of the product rely exclusively on information obtained from its long-term use and experience.

In order to avoid the submission of duplicate evidence, the Committee for Herbal Medicinal Products (CHMP), which is part of the European Medicines Evaluation Agency (EMEA), will develop a European positive list of ingredients. Establishing that a product contains an ingredient which is on the indicative list does not necessarily

---

[26] The Traditional Herbal Medicinal Products Directive (2004/24/EC) Official Journal of the European Union L136/85.

mean that an application for registration will be successful, but it will mean that applicants do not need to submit detailed evidence of safety or traditional use. Evidence of quality will still be necessary. Section 12(1) of the Medicines Act will continue to offer an exemption for herbal medicines that are made up on the premises and sold after a one-to-one consultation.

(b) CLASSIFICATION OF MEDICINES

In addition to deciding whether to grant a marketing authorization, the MHRA also classifies medicines into one of three categories:

(a) prescription only medicines (POM);

(b) suppliable by a pharmacist without prescription (P);

(c) general sale list medicines, which can be sold over the counter and do not need to be dispensed by a pharmacist (GSL).

A European directive specified the factors which should be taken into account when deciding whether a medicine should be prescription-only, and these were inserted into section 58A(2) of the Medicines Act 1968. The MHRA must consider whether the medicine:

(a) is likely to present a direct or indirect danger to human health, even when used correctly, if used without the supervision of a doctor or dentist; or

(b) is frequently and to a very wide extent used incorrectly, and as a result is likely to present a direct or indirect danger to human health; or

(c) contains substances or preparations of substances of which the activity requires, or the side-effects require, further investigation;

(d) is normally prescribed by a doctor or dentist for parenteral administration [that is, intravenously or by injection].

Section 58A(3) also specifies that the Secretary of State should take into account whether a medicine is likely, if incorrectly used, to present a substantial risk of medicinal abuse, lead to addiction or be used for illegal purposes.

Medicines can be reclassified, if they no longer appear to pose the requisite danger to human health. Where self-medication is safe, as is the case in relation to treatments for colds or hayfever, for example, there are obvious advantages in enabling individuals to purchase medicines for themselves. This will save the NHS money, both through the costs of the medicine itself and by eliminating the need to make an appointment with a GP in order to obtain a prescription, and will often be more convenient for patients. In recent years, partly in response to an EU directive,[27] an increasing number of prescription-only medicines have been reclassified in the UK. Of course, one consequence of this is that the leaflets supplied with medicines become even more important, since they may represent the only information the patient receives about how to take the medicine safely. The most high-profile recent

---

[27] Council Directive 92/26/EEC *Classification for the supply of medicinal products for human use.*

reclassification of a medicine was for the post-coital contraceptive pill, known colloquially as the 'morning after pill'. In 2000 the MCA and the CSM agreed that the risks posed by post-coital contraception did not justify its prescription-only status, so it was re-classified as a pharmacy-available medicine.[28] In the following extract, David Prayle and Margaret Brazier evaluate this trend towards the reclassification of medicines.

David Prayle and Margaret Brazier[29]

The result of European intervention and the radically altered attitude of British regulators to categorising medicines is this: more and more medicines of greater potency are available for purchase in pharmacies and in ordinary retail outlets.

Three principal motivations for change can be identified. First, the Pharmaceutical Society, representing and regulating pharmacists, pressed for greater availability of medicines in pharmacies, ie changes from POM to P status. Making more medicines available over the counter in pharmacies was perceived as an extension of the pharmacist's professional role . . . Second, the government has sought to promote change, partly as an integral element in its general policy of deregulation but also to drive down costs in the NHS drug budget. When a medicine moves to P status it is hoped more and more patients will simply purchase the product themselves, saving the cost to the NHS of certain prescriptions and saving expensive general practitioner (GP) time.

Third, the pharmaceutical industry has an obvious and powerful interest in reclassification. Increased sales of P and GSL medicines can be expected, particularly as such medicines, unlike POM medicines, can be advertised to the general public. As a number of previously profitable POM medicines reach the stage when patent protection expires, the manufacturer must seek means of combating competition from generic copies. Altering the medicine's status to P and enthusiastically advertising the product under its tried and tested brand name is a useful strategy to maintain, if not increase sales figures.

A brave new world of more open access to medicines beckons. Should it be applauded?

A restrictive approach to access to medicines restricts individual autonomy. The longer the list of POM medicines, the less able individuals are to control their own health status via self-diagnosis and self-medication . . . Reducing the list of POM medicines might be seen as enhancing autonomy. The flaw in this approach derives from the anomalous P category of medicines. They can be purchased, but only from a pharmacy under the supervision and control of a pharmacist. Persons seeking a P medicine must in theory submit to an interrogation from the pharmacist (or his assistant) about their familiarity with the drug, their medical history and their potential use of the product. This 'consultation' may well take place before an audience of other customers . . .

What justification can there be for allowing a 'retailer' to police his customers' purchasing habits? . . .

[T]he heart of the question becomes: are medicines different from other consumer goods? Why should paracetamol be policed in a way alcohol is not? Why should aspirin be treated differently from insecticide. It may be argued that the answer should be that medicines are no different from other goods. In that case, the whole edifice of the regulation of medicines needs re-thinking.

---

[28] The Prescription Only Medicines (Human Use) Order was laid before Parliament on 11 Dec 2000.
[29] 'Supply of medicines: paternalism, autonomy and reality' (1998) 24 Journal of Medical Ethics 93–8, 94–5, 98.

(c) POST-LICENSING REGULATION

Regulation does not cease once a product has been licensed. Regulations specify the information which much be provided with a medicine, such as instructions for use, contra-indications, and warnings about side-effects.[30] Leaflets supplied with medicines must contain information about its active ingredients; indications for its use; warnings about the product's interaction with other substances, such as alcohol, and about any effect it might have on the user's capacity to drive or operate machinery. Dosage instructions, such as how the medicine should be taken, and how frequently, must also be included, and if appropriate, what should be done in the event of an overdose.[31] The advertising of medicines is also strictly controlled. Prescription-only medicines cannot be marketed directly to the public (unlike in the US), and there are restrictions on the contents of advertisements to doctors.[32]

The manufacturer is under a duty to keep a record of all adverse drug reactions (ADRs) reported to it, and the MHRA will also record all reported side-effects. The 'yellow card scheme' enables GPs, nurses, midwives, health visitors and, since 2005, patients to report ADRs electronically.[33] Drugs are divided into two groups for the purposes of the yellow card scheme: new drugs (denoted by a black triangle) are monitored closely for a minimum of two years, during which time *all* suspected ADRs should be reported. For established drugs, only serious suspected ADRs must be reported. Other areas of special interest have been identified, for which all suspected ADRs should be reported, such as reactions in children and the elderly. In 1996, following the identification of serious cases of liver toxicity associated with a traditional Chinese medicine, the yellow card scheme was extended to include unlicensed herbal products. Monitoring ADRs from herbal remedies has proved particularly difficult, however, since patients appear to be less likely to consult their doctor if they suspect an adverse reaction.

Approximately 18,000 ADR reports are made each year, mostly by GPs, including about 440 reported deaths.[34] Companies must have adequate procedures for the speedy recall of products, if this should become necessary.[35] The mere existence of an adverse reaction does not, however, mean that a medicine has become unacceptably unsafe. As Pamela Ferguson explains, it may be necessary to balance the risks to a minority of patients against the benefits the drug may have for the majority, and in some circumstances a more appropriate response might be to give a more specific warning about contra-indications for the medicine's use.

Pamela Ferguson[36]

It is clearly not realistic to expect current pre-marketing tests to detect any but the most common adverse reactions. If more stringent procedures were introduced, involving many more people in

---

[30] Medicines (Labelling) Regulations 1976 SI 1976/1726, as amended.

[31] Medicines (Leaflets) Regulations 1977 SI 1977/1055, as amended.

[32] Medicines (Advertising) Regulations 1994, SI 1994/1932, as amended.

[33] <http://www.yellowcard.gov.uk/>.

[34] Andrew Tucker and David Taylor, *Health, Wealth and Medicines for All* (King's Fund London 2000) 17.

[35] Medicines (Standard Provisions for Licences and Certificates Regs (SI 1971/972) Sch 1 I(6), as amended by Medicines (Standard Provisions for Licences and Certificates Regs (SI 1992/2846).

[36] Pamela Ferguson, *Drug Injuries and the Pursuit of Compensation* (Sweet & Maxwell London 1996) 38.

clinical trials over longer periods, this would increase the cost of drug development and greatly delay the marketing of new, and possibly highly beneficial, drugs. . . .

While more could be done to improve *post*-marketing detection methods, thereby limiting the amount of harm which a drug may cause, this inevitably means that some patients will have been injured in the interim. A question also remains as to how the licensing authority should most appropriately respond once it becomes aware of an adverse reaction. It may decide that the safest course is to withdraw the product's licence but, except in the most extreme of cases where the benefits themselves are questionable and are greatly outweighed by the risks, this deprives those patients who had benefited from the drug.

(d) THE IMPACT OF REGULATION

Obviously the stricter the licensing requirements, the less straightforward it is to introduce new medicines. So a stringent regulatory framework may increase patient safety, but at the cost of stifling innovation, which in turn may mean that patients are denied access to beneficial medicines. In the next extract, Harvey Teff points out that it is difficult to measure the health gains or losses that result from licensing decisions. He also suggests that regulators will inevitably be risk averse, since the damage to their reputation should they license another thalidomide would be catastrophic, whereas any risk to public health through *not* licensing a potentially beneficial medicine will be much less visible.

Harvey Teff[37]
Regulatory requirements are undeniably among the factors which inhibit drug innovation, though to what extent and with what consequences is far from clear . . .

[I]t seems plain that one cannot measure with any precision how far regulation has inhibited the development and introduction of valuable new drugs, let alone whether any fall in innovation has on balance been detrimental to health. Nor can one *know* how many major therapeutic disasters have been averted by a particular level of regulation. Similarly, on the reasonable hypothesis that relaxing controls encourages an increase in the production of marginally less safe and effective, as well as useless, drugs, one would not be able to assess with any accuracy the harmful effects—in terms of the failure of patients to obtain more beneficial treatment, and wasted expenditure by the industry—still less balance such costs against the supposed benefits in terms of innovation.

Several key concepts, such as 'safety', 'efficacy' and 'innovation' itself are so open-ended that bold assertions about appropriate levels of regulation have to be treated with caution. Thus there can be no absolute level of drug safety, since the risk of using a drug has to be calculated in the light of such considerations as the seriousness of the illness, the condition of the patient and the proposed length of treatment; while we cannot, by definition, be precise about the *chronic* toxicity of substances which have been on the market for only a short period. Most, if not all, drugs cannot be effective unless they are also powerful enough to be potentially harmful. Nor, at a broader level of inquiry, can the issue of what constitutes 'safety' for drugs be satisfactorily determined without reference to possible alternative modes of treatment and prevention, or, for that matter, to what are deemed socially acceptable levels of risk in general. . . .

[37] 'Regulation under the Medicines Act 1968: A continuing prescription for health' (1984) 47 Modern Law Review 303–23, 303, 308–11.

[T]he regulator tends to unduly risk averse. In the context of pharmaceuticals, he has little or nothing to lose by refusing, or at least delaying, the grant of a licence; everything to lose if he approves a thalidomide. Thus where guidelines are bound to be arbitrary to some extent—how many species of animals should be tested, over what period of time, for what risks—the regulator is prone to err on the side of caution, to indulge in a kind of 'defensive licensing'.

John Abrahams would disagree, arguing that the pharmaceutical industry has sufficient influence over the licensing authority to ensure that the regulator gives them 'the benefit of the doubt'.

John Abraham[38]

Pharmaceutical firms have well-oiled lobbying strategies to capture regulatory agencies: more subtly, industry can penetrate into the heart of regulatory political subculture via the so-called revolving door . . . In the UK, a large proportion of scientists in the British drug regulatory authority started their careers in industry, and many move back there . . .

Regulatory capture is especially important because the risk–benefit assessment of drugs has a high degree of technical uncertainty, which is inherent in toxicology, clinical trials, and epidemiology. Therefore, it is crucial to know how far regulators are willing to give the manufacturer the benefit of scientific doubt about safety and efficacy of their product. Indeed, regulators too often consistently award industry the benefit of scientific doubt when reviewing products.

For the past 50 years, industry has been quick to ward off regulation it perceives to be contrary to its interests by threatening that such regulation will have damaging results for the nation's export trade, balance of payments, or employment. Too often, regulatory agencies have accepted these threats uncritically. . . .

Furthermore, mergers within the industry, which are undertaken to increase profits, probably have far more detrimental effects on employment than drug regulation. For example, in 2001, the merger of Glaxo Wellcome with SmithKlineBeecham (now GlaxoSmithKline) is estimated to have resulted in many thousands of job losses.

5. EUROPEAN REGULATION

European regulation of the pharmaceutical industry has become increasingly important in recent years. Its two principal aims are to protect consumer safety, and to harmonize the regulatory regimes throughout Europe in order to facilitate the free movement of goods. We look at the impact of the European directive on product liability later in this chapter, but other Europe-wide regulations apply to licensing, marketing, and advertising.

There has been progressive harmonization of rules on labelling and package leaflets,[39] advertising,[40] and the reporting of adverse side effects.[41] These directives have amended the UK's regulations. The European Agency for the Evaluation of Medicinal Products (commonly known as the European Medicines Evaluation Agency or EMEA) was established in 1993. And a new European system for the authorization of medicinal products was set up in January 1995. It offers two routes for the licensing of medicinal products:

---

[38] 'The pharmaceutical industry as a political player' (2002) 360 The Lancet 1498–502.
[39] Directive 92/27/EEC.   [40] Directive 92/28/EEC.   [41] Directive 75/319/EEC.

(a) A centralized procedure with applications made directly to a sub-committee of EMEA, formerly the Committee for Proprietary Medicinal Products (CPMP), now the Committee for Medicinal Products for Human Use (CHMP), which advises the Commission on whether to issue a European marketing authorization.[42] Use of this procedure is compulsory for products derived from biotechnology, and optional for other innovative medicinal products. For products authorized under the centralized procedure, national licensing authorities must report all adverse reactions to EMEA, which will then notify other states' licensing authorities.

(b) The decentralized or 'mutual recognition' procedure is applicable to the majority of conventional medicinal products.[43] Applications are made via the licensing procedures in individual member states, but all other EU countries have agreed to the mutual recognition of these national marketing authorizations. Member states are entitled to object to the mutual recognition of another country's marketing authorization on the grounds that the product poses a risk to public health, although they do not have the final say, and ultimately it is for the Commission, on the advice of the CPMP, to determine whether the State has grounds to refuse to approve a product that has received a marketing authorization in another Member State.

The centralized procedure is clearly attractive to manufacturers since it potentially speeds up the process of approval and reduces bureaucracy. At the same time, it inevitably reduces national control over the licensing process. One interesting side-effect of the decentralized mutual recognition procedure is that it effectively places European regulatory agencies in competition with each other. A drug company seeking to market a new drug throughout Europe can obtain a marketing authorization in any EU country, and so, as Tamara Hervey and Jean McHale explain in the next extract, it will tend to choose the one which appears to have the speediest and least demanding licensing regime. Unsurprisingly, approval times for new medicines have been dropping throughout Europe, but as Hervey and McHale warn, this may not be in the best interests of patients.

Tamara Hervey and Jean McHale[44]

There are two problems with decentralised procedures. If they leave a great deal of discretion to the Member States . . ., then the aim of creating a single market in pharmaceuticals is effectively compromised, and any benefits of such a single market (to the industry, and ultimately to patients as consumers) may not be reaped. Moreover, a system where mutual recognition of national authorisations is compulsory runs the risk that the least demanding regulatory regime sets the standards. Such a 'race to the bottom' is not appropriate for products such as pharmaceuticals, where the risks to human life and health are fundamental if regulatory mechanisms are not properly applied and enforced. . . .

Faster agencies are more popular with industry; the benefits to patients of slower, more painstaking, product assessment are not factored into the system.

---

[42] Directive 93/41/EEC Council Regulation (EEC) No 2309/93.   [43] Directive 93/39/EEC.
[44] *Health Law and the European Union* (CUP Cambridge 2004) 297–8.

Efforts to harmonize the regulation of medicines also exist outside of the EU. For example, the International Conference on Harmonisation (ICH), launched in 1990, attempts to harmonize certain technical requirements imposed upon the pharmaceutical industry in US, Europe and Japan.[45] The first ICH steering committee re-affirmed its:

commitment to increased international harmonisation, aimed at ensuring that good quality, safe and effective medicines are developed and registered in the most efficient and cost-effective manner. These activities are pursued in the interest of the consumer and public health, to prevent unnecessary duplication of clinical trials in humans and to minimise the use of animal testing without compromising the regulatory obligations of safety and effectiveness.

Mutual recognition arrangements also exist between the EU and Switzerland, Canada, Australia, and New Zealand. Again these are intended to facilitate trade by eliminating the need to undergo duplicate testing and scrutiny of new products.

6. FUNDING

In the next extract, Peter Davis develops the idea that the pharmaceutical market is distinctive. Not only is the regulator of medicines simultaneously the principal purchaser, but also consumers do not generally make purchase decisions themselves. The decision to purchase a medicine is made instead by the patient's doctor, who is also insulated, to some degree, from cost considerations. In recent years changes to NHS funding (discussed in Chapter 2) mean that GPs have become more aware of the costs of the medicines that they prescribe, but they are still not spending their own money. Given this rather indirect connection between consumers and purchasers of medicines, competition in the pharmaceutical market tends to depend upon product differentiation, rather than price. As we have seen, for the first twenty years of their life, medicines also benefit from patent protection, which means that there will often be a monopoly supplier of a drug that may be capable of saving lives. Pharmaceutical companies are inevitably able to exploit the market distortions created by this position of power.

Peter Davis[46]

In extreme cases an important drug may only be produced by a single company. Barriers to entry from potential competitors are presented by exclusive patent rights, the establishment of brand loyalty among doctors and the start-up costs of innovation, production and promotion. On the demand side there are also marked departures from standard market conditions. In the first place, there is considerable inequality of information, with patients rarely understanding the complex dimensions of the drugs they are taking. Further, decisions about purchases are usually made on behalf of a patient by an agent (the doctor). Finally, the state is in a position as principal funder to exert considerable monopsony power. Market failure is also in evidence. The industry is highly innovative, but only invests where it can see a market return. Hence, the health problems of groups that have low effective demand—either because of their small size or because of low incomes—

---

45 See further <http://www.ich.org>.
46 *Managing Medicines: Public Policy and Therapeutic Drugs* (Open UP Buckingham 1997) 135.

are less likely to attract the interest of the industry. There are even examples of drugs that a company has actually developed but then finds to be insufficiently commercially viable to take to the marketing stage (so-called 'orphan' drugs). Finally, because therapeutic drugs have the power to heal, to alleviate suffering and even to save lives, an important moral dimension intervenes in the usual play of market forces . . .

[L]evels of therapeutic drug use do not reflect in any straightforward way the distribution of health need in the community; they are also influenced by the propensity of lay people to resort to medical care in time of need, by the availability of potential treatments and, above all, by professional norms of 'appropriate' patterns of care. These variations reflect differences in culture, in traditions of professional training and belief, and in health system structure.

This is not to deny that health need has an absolutely decisive and primary influence on aggregate patterns of drug consumption. But there is also a degree of elasticity about the relationship between health need and pharmacological treatment, an elasticity that gives a certain latitude to the shaping of lay and professional patterns of care and that introduces a further element of indeterminacy in the attempts of governments to manage their pharmaceutical budgets.

Although it has increased in recent years,[47] the UK's expenditure on medicines remains comparatively modest. A 2001 study found that the UK spent £124 a year per person on medicines, compared with £139 in Germany, £187 in France, £301 in Japan, and £355 in the US.[48] On average, each UK citizen receives nine prescription items per year.[49]

While it is true that many new medicines are expensive, their use does not necessarily represent a net drain on NHS resources. If effective drugs can avoid the need for surgery; facilitate day surgery; reduce the number of hospital admissions, and the average length of a hospital stay, then they may in fact *save* the NHS money. Moreover, by reducing ill-health, and its associated costs, medicines have the capacity to increase the UK's gross domestic product (GDP). A study in the US attempted to calculate the economic value of eradicating disease. It found that eliminating deaths from heart disease would generate $48 trillion, and curing cancer would be worth $47 trillion. More realistically, reducing the death rate from either of these diseases by 20 per cent would be worth approximately $10 trillion, which is more than the US's annual GDP.[50]

Nevertheless, however great the benefits—both economic and social—of modern medicines, cost containment has become essential within the NHS, and various techniques are currently used to reduce prescribing costs. First, generic versions can be substituted for branded medicines once the patent has expired. There has been considerable progress in changing prescribing habits, and more than half of all drugs supplied to patients are now unbranded generic versions.[51] Twenty years ago, the figure was 20 per cent. Secondly, drugs can be reclassified into over-the-counter medicines, so that the patient pays the full cost herself. As we saw earlier, there is a

[47] Department of Health, *Introduction to the 1999 PPRS* (DoH 2002).
[48] ABPI, *The Cost of Medicines: Good Value for Patients* (ABPI 2001).
[49] Andrew Tucker and David Taylor, *Health, Wealth and Medicines for All* (King's Fund London 2000) 21.
[50] Richard Sykes, *New Medicines, The Practice of Medicine, and Public Policy* (Nuffield Trust London 2000) 138.
[51] ABPI, *The Cost of Medicines: Good Value for Patients* (ABPI 2001).

trend in this direction, particularly for fairly low-cost medicines, such as cold and hayfever remedies.

Thirdly, co-payments from patients (known in the UK as the prescription charge) raise some additional revenue,[52] and might additionally act as a disincentive towards excessive consumption of pharmaceutical drugs. When the Labour government abolished prescription charges in 1965, the number of NHS prescriptions—which had been stable at around 240 million per year since 1952—rose to over 300 million.[53] When prescription charges were reintroduced three years later, they were accompanied, for the first time, by extensive exemptions. Approximately 80 per cent of medicines are currently prescribed to groups who are exempt from payments, such as children and the elderly, and so the impact of prescription charging on the overall cost of medicines to the NHS is now relatively small. Although 60 per cent of prescribed medicines in fact cost *less* than the prescription charge,[54] in some cases the real cost of the prescribed treatment is much higher. On average, the cost of each medicine prescribed to an NHS patient is £10, so medicines prescribed to non-exempt patients are still subsidized by the NHS.[55]

Moreover, because the decision to prescribe is made by the doctor and not by the patient, prescription charges do not have a straightforward deterrent effect. Indeed, if a doctor believes that a prescribed medicine is appropriate, the patient's failure to pick up the prescription in order to avoid incurring the charge is likely to have a negative impact upon her health. In the next extract, Mandy Ryan and Stephen Birth argue that if, as the evidence suggests, prescription charges actually deter people from seeing their doctor in the first place, their adverse effect upon patient health will be even more significant.[56]

Mandy Ryan and Stephen Birch[57]

The above estimates imply that the policy of regular and frequent increases in the real charge for NHS prescribed drugs has been associated with a significant reduction in the rate of utilisation of prescribed drugs among non-exempt patients . . . As a result of the charge increases, the distribution of prescribed drugs has been distorted by the impact of the charge. Need, or ability to benefit, as a means of sharing scarce resources has been compromised by consideration of ability and willingness to pay within the non-exempt group . . .

The revenue consequences of the charges policy suggest that the Government has been successful in generating resources that can be devoted to other aspects of the primary care sector. Although the often cited rationale for the charges policy is to raise additional funds for health care provision *from those patients able to pay more,* estimates based on this analysis imply that around 66% of the funds generated by the charges policy accrues from the reduction in utilisation of the service.

It should not be assumed that reduced utilisation by non-exempt groups represents frivolous or

[52] Andrew Tucker and David Taylor, *Health, Wealth and Medicines for All* (King's Fund London 2000) 40.

[53] David Taylor and Alan Maynard, *Medicines, the NHS and Europe: Balancing the Public's Interest* (Kings Fund London 1990) 10.

[54] ABPI, *The Cost of Medicines: Good Value for Patients* (ABPI 2001).

[55] Ibid.

[56] See also Rainer Winkelmann, 'Copayments for prescription drugs and the demand for doctor visits—Evidence from a natural experiment' Health Economics (2004) 1081–9.

[57] 'Charging for Health Care: Evidence on the Utilisation of NHS Prescribed Drugs' (1991) 33 Social Science and Medicine 681–7, 685–6.

unwarranted use of the service that is deterred by increasing charges. . . . As a consequence charges may be inhibiting, as opposed to promoting improvements in the efficiency of use of scarce health care resources . . .

Delays in consulting GPs may lead to increased probabilities of referral for diagnostic procedures or hospital admissions. Similarly any increase in morbidity may lead to reductions in government revenues resulting from the reduction in the tax base if work absence due to illness increases.

In contrast, Richard Sykes offers a more positive assessment of co-payments.

Richard Sykes[58]

Greater sharing of the cost of medicines by patients would relieve pressure on national drug budgets, allow focus on priority areas, and create headroom for innovation. Giving people an incentive to ration consumption of healthcare may also help to keep costs down. The arrival of additional funding sources would break up the current monopsony position of government and will lead inevitably to greater plurality in both finance and provision of healthcare. . . .

Cost sharing is an important feature of many national health systems. This is especially true for pharmaceuticals . . . The rationale for cost sharing is not just concerned with raising revenues, but is equally about encouraging patients to be responsible users of health services . . .

Patient contribution to the costs of medicine may also help to address an important cause of treatment failures—non-compliance with treatment regimes—which is a significant cause of inefficiency in health systems. . . . Patient compliance is an important issue because lack of adherence to treatment regimes has been reported as the main cause of non-response to medication, leading to poorer health outcomes and increased costs. Measuring the extent of non-compliance is complicated, but studies indicate that rates of compliance are remarkably low (i.e. some studies suggest that as few as 40 per cent of patients are fully compliant) and possibly worsening. There is a range of approaches for improving compliance with treatment regimes . . ., some of the most successful strategies involve offering financial incentives. . . .

Assuming the UK does not want to move towards a general healthcare system supported by insurance, patient co-payments could still be operated effectively . . . Conditions and products could be allocated into categories depending on severity and impact. Clearly the so-called 'lifestyle' products could be put into a low or non-reimbursement category. In other cases, there will be conditions where some groups of patients do get partial or full reimbursement. The determination should be made on clinical need and benefit rather than costs.

The reality is that products to treat conditions (mis)labelled as 'lifestyle' are less and less likely to receive reimbursement, but under present arrangements in the UK this also effectively means that most patients are denied access to them at all. Whilst the NHS should continue to provide essential care, some mechanism will increasingly be needed to allow patients ready access to the medicines they want outside NHS funding. British patients will want to exercise choice through an alternative mechanism for obtaining certain medicines subject only to the grant of a product licence.

Fourthly, government can restrict the profits made by the pharmaceutical industry. In the UK this is done via the Pharmaceutical Price Regulation Scheme, a voluntary agreement reached between government and the pharmaceutical industry, which restricts companies' profits from NHS sales to a maximum of 21 per cent.

---

[58] Richard Sykes, *New Medicines, The Practice of Medicine, and Public Policy* (Nuffield Trust London 2000) 193–6.

Fifthly, as we saw in Chapter 3, certain medicines may be 'blacklisted' from NHS supply by the Secretary of State for Health, and will therefore only be available via private prescription, where the patient pays the full price of the drug. Restrictions on the Secretary of State's power to exclude certain medicines from NHS coverage are contained in Article 7(3) of a European directive 89/105, known as the Transparency Directive:

Any decision to exclude an individual medicinal product from the coverage of the national health insurance system shall contain a statement of reasons based on objective and verifiable criteria.[59]

This provision formed the basis of an appeal by Pfizer against the Secretary of State's decision to severely restrict NHS access to the anti-impotence drug Viagra. In *R (on the application of Pfizer Ltd) v Secretary of State for Health*,[60] the Court of Appeal endorsed the Secretary of State's right to make what it categorized as an essentially *political* decision about the relative importance of treatment for erectile dysfunction. The Court of Appeal also said that the provisions of Article 7(e) would be satisfied provided the criterion on which the decision had been based was published, as this one had been, and served a legitimate aim (here, cost containment in the NHS). Buxton LJ explained that:

For the criteria to be 'verifiable', all that is necessary is that they should be published and available, in particular to would-be importers, to satisfy themselves that they do not contain disguised restrictions on intra-Community trade. And the measures are 'objective' . . ., if they are based on a legitimate aim, that of improving the economics of the state health system.

Cost containment measures which aim to restrict clinical discretion face powerful opposition from both the medical profession and the pharmaceutical industry. Strategies which emphasize the need to improve the quality and consistency of prescribing decisions are more likely to be successful. In Chapter 3 we considered the role of NICE, the National Institute for Clinical Excellence, in promoting fair and consistent access to drugs throughout the NHS. NICE appraises new or costly medicines in order to assess their clinical and cost effectiveness, and to decide whether they should be available within the NHS, and if so, whether access should be restricted to certain specified categories of patients. Unsurprisingly, both patient groups and the pharmaceutical industry engage in sustained lobbying of NICE, and drug companies will generally exercise their right of appeal if NICE decides to restrict NHS patients' access to one of their medicines.

In the following extract John Hutton and Alan Maynard warn that it may be impossible for NICE to properly evaluate the cost-effectiveness of a new drug *before* it is marketed, because the data which is necessary for adequately assessing cost-effectiveness will generally not exist until the product has been in general use for sometime. But if NICE were to wait until this information was available, access to potentially valuable medicines would be delayed.

---

[59] Directive 89/105, Art 7(3).   [60] [2002] EWCA Civ 1566, 70 BMLR 219.

John Hutton and Alan Maynard[61]

Once a drug or medical device is licensed and has marketing approval, doctors are free to prescribe its use and the NHS will cover the costs. In the case of drugs, manufacturers are free to set the initial price (subsequently price rises require approval) within the indirect constraint of the Pharmaceutical Price Regulation Scheme, which governs the overall level of profits that companies can make from sale to the NHS. The process by which a previously licensed product can be removed from the list of drugs covered by NHS expenditure is very restrictive . . . Control over the use of drugs has to be exercised through influencing the prescribing behaviour of doctors . . .

The basic principles underlying the NICE appraisal process are that best practice can be determined in a way which is applicable across the whole system; that guidelines should be based on the best available clinical and economic evidence; and that appraisal should take place before a technology is marketed . . .

The potential for conflict between these understandable aims when implementing a system of economic evaluation of new pharmaceuticals is considerable. Many of these problems arise because of the inherent differences between clinical and economic evaluation . . . The requirement to produce evidence of cost-effectiveness before the market launch of a new pharmaceutical imposes immediate restrictions on the type of economic evaluation possible (and also the nature of the clinical data available). The preferred source of data for an economic evaluation is generally considered to be a naturalistic or pragmatic trial. Definitions vary but the essential characteristic is that the data on health care resource use and clinical effectiveness are observed in a routine care environment, with the study design having minimal impact on the way care is delivered. A further desirable characteristic is that the study should be properly comparative with the new treatment being compared to the most common existing treatment approach and the most cost-effective existing treatment approach—the two by no means being guaranteed to coincide. Such data are not available, by definition, before a product is marketed and in routine use. . . .

This concern over obtaining reliable evidence before approving products for general use implies further delays in the marketing of new pharmaceuticals. From the societal perspective there is a risk of delaying the benefits of effective drugs by trying to avoid unproductive expenditure on products that are not cost-effective.

In Chapter 2, we saw that the gap between demand for healthcare services and the NHS's capacity to supply them is likely to widen, as the population lives longer and as more expensive treatments become available. Beyond the fairly modest prescription charge, with its widespread exemptions, there has, as yet, been little interest in the question of whether patients should be expected to contribute towards the costs of their medicines. This may change, however, as more so-called 'lifestyle' or enhancement drugs become available. Viagra, for example, is available on an NHS prescription to certain categories of patient, but there are limits to how many pills each patient can be prescribed. Men who meet the relevant clinical criteria can purchase additional pills by obtaining private prescriptions from their doctors. This sort of mixed approach to prescribing is likely to become more common as patients increasingly demand greater access to drugs which the NHS cannot afford to provide.

[61] 'A NICE Challenge for Health Economics' (2000) 9 *Health Economics* 89–93, 89–91.

7. PRODUCT LIABILITY

No drug is 100 per cent safe, most will occasionally produce adverse drug reactions (ADRs). Some of these are common and fairly minor, and will generally have been discovered during clinical trials. Consumers can then be warned about potential side-effects when the drug is marketed. Other drug reactions are rare and unpredictable, and may be extremely serious. It is likely that these will only be discovered *after* a drug is put into circulation. During clinical trials, a new drug may be tested on between one and five thousand people. If a particular side-effect occurs in one patient in a thousand, it is unlikely that the connection between the medicine and these symptoms will have been picked up during the trial. If the reaction is rarer still, it may not come to light until many years after the drug is first used in patients. Furthermore, as we saw in the previous chapter, certain groups—such as the elderly—are routinely excluded from clinical trials, even though they may be among the ultimate consumers of the medicine being tested. As a result, it is likely that ADRs which particularly affect these excluded groups will not be detected during clinical trials.

In this section, we consider the various avenues open to a patient who believes that she has been injured by a medical product.

(a) CONTRACT

Contractual remedies are of limited relevance to consumers who suffer drug-related injuries. It would be very unusual for a contract to exist directly between the consumer of a medicine and its manufacturer. And when a drug is prescribed under an NHS prescription, there will be no contract with either the pharmacist, or the doctor who wrote the prescription. In *Pfizer Corporation v Minister of Health*[62] Lord Reid had to consider whether there had been a sale when outpatients were provided with prescription drugs on payment of the charge, then 2s (shillings):

in my opinion there is no sale in this case. Sale is a consensual contract requiring agreement expressed or implied. In the present case there appears to me to be no need for any agreement. The patient has a statutory right to demand the drug on payment of 2s. The hospital has a statutory obligation to supply it on such payment. And if the prescription is presented to a chemist he appears to be bound by his contract with the appropriate authority to supply the drug on receipt of such payment. There is no need for any agreement between the patient and either the hospital or the chemist, and there is certainly no room for bargaining. Moreover the 2s. is not in any true sense the price: the drug may cost much more and the chemist has a right under his contract with the authority to receive the balance from them. It appears to me that any resemblance between this transaction and a true sale is only superficial.

And in *Appelby v Sleep*,[63] Lord Parker CJ stated:

The first thing that is clear is that there will have been no sale by the chemist to the patient, the person presenting the prescription. Not only has that been so held [in *Pfizer v Ministry of Health*],

---

[62] [1965] 2 WLR 387.   [63] [1968] 1 WLR 948.

but it is clearly the case, because the patient is not paying for the medicine or drugs, and that is so even if there is a prescription charge.

It is only when drugs are supplied privately, or when medicines are bought over the counter, that a contractual remedy for a defective medicine is possible.

If the consumer does have a contract, either with the pharmacist or with a doctor dispensing a private prescription, then the ordinary rules of contract law apply. If the product does not correspond with its description, or is not of satisfactory quality, there might be a breach of the Sale of Goods Act 1979.[64] Liability does not require proof of fault on the part of the supplier. It would be relatively straightforward to establish a breach of one of these sections for what are known as manufacturing defects, such as the contamination of a particular batch of medicines. But since most drugs have some side effects, it will be difficult to establish that a medicine which has caused an adverse reaction has breached the implied condition of satisfactory quality.

One complicated question raised by the application of contract law to the sale of medicines relates to sections 14(2B) and 14(3) of the Sale of Goods Act, under which goods must either be fit for the purpose for which they are commonly supplied, or if the buyer makes known the particular purpose for which they are being bought, that they are reasonably fit for that purpose. How much information about the consumer's condition must the pharmacist obtain in order to assess whether the medicine is fit for its purpose? If a consumer has a contraindication for taking a particular medicine, such as high blood pressure or diabetes, then arguably that medicine is not fit for the purpose for which she has bought it. Pharmacists who fail to inquire whether a medicine which has been bought over the counter is fit for the purpose for which the particular consumer has purchased it might then find themselves strictly liable for any consequent injuries.

(b) NEGLIGENCE

The manufacturer of a medicine could be liable in negligence if the consumer can prove that she was owed a duty of care, and that the manufacturer's breach of that duty caused her injury. Since *Donoghue v Stevenson*,[65] it is uncontroversial that manufacturers owe the ultimate consumers of their products a duty to take reasonable care to ensure that the product is safe, so establishing the existence of a duty of care will be straightforward. However, difficulties might arise for the consumer in proving first, that there was a breach of that duty, and, second, that the breach caused her injury.

In order to determine whether the manufacturer has breached its duty, it is necessary to work out what standard of care the pharmaceutical industry owes to the consumers of its products. The manufacturer's duty is simply to exercise such care as is reasonable in all the circumstances. Factors relevant to this assessment include the magnitude of risk, the probability of harm, the burden of taking precautions to prevent the risk materializing, and the utility of the defendant's conduct. Manufacturers are certainly not under a duty to ensure that every drug is completely safe for every potential consumer. All medicines present some risks: aspirin, for example, is

---

[64] Sections 14(2) and 14(3), as amended.   [65] [1932] AC 562.

generally considered to be safe and effective, yet it will cause serious adverse effects in a minority of consumers.

Three different types of product defect might be identified: manufacturing defects, design defects, and the failure to give adequate warnings. It will be relatively straight-forward to prove that there has been a breach of duty when the patient's injury was caused by a manufacturing defect, perhaps because of an error made during the manufacturing process. Failure to ensure that medicines leave the manufacturer's premises in a fit state for human ingestion will generally indicate that there has been negligence on the part of the manufacturer.

Design defects are rather more complicated. Plainly, manufacturers have a duty to design medicines safely, but particular difficulties arise if an unforeseen adverse side effect subsequently emerges, as happened with thalidomide. The claimants would have to prove that the risk of injury was foreseeable, and that supplying the product in the light of this risk was unreasonable. Not only will it be very difficult for claimants to gain access to the information necessary to prove this, but also research trials cannot be expected to discover every possible side-effect in every possible consumer. The benefits of new medicines mean that it will generally be reasonable to put them into circulation once experiments indicate that they meet an acceptable threshold level of safety. It would not be reasonable to expect manufacturers to have identified all potential ADRs before marketing a new drug: this would stifle innovation; unreasonably delay the availability of potentially valuable new medicines; and require vastly increased rates of participation in clinical trials. If, as was the case with thal-idomide, the pharmaceutical company could not reasonably have been expected to know that it would cause devastating birth defects if taken at a particular time in pregnancy, then there could be no negligence.

Manufacturers might also be liable for defective warnings. No drug is completely safe for all possible users, and a manufacturer will generally have acted reasonably if he took reasonable steps to alert consumers to the risk of some side-effect, or to con-tra-indications for taking the medicine in question. Prescription drugs are a rather special case in that it is not necessary for them to be made safe for *anybody* who might use them. Unlike products which can be bought over the counter, it should be possible to ensure that a drug is not prescribed to those individuals for whom it will be unsafe. If, for example, the manufacturer categorically states in the information it has pro-vided to doctors that medicine X should never be taken by anyone with high blood pressure, the manufacturer would be able to avoid liability if someone with high blood pressure subsequently suffers injuries after being prescribed medicine X.

In the US, this is known as the 'learned intermediary' rule: that is, it is for the doctor to determine whether to prescribe a particular drug to her patient, and to give appropriate warnings. A patient will generally rely upon her doctor's advice, and a manufacturer's package insert is unlikely to override assurance from her GP that she can safely take the medicine which she has been prescribed. Of course, doctors might make prescribing errors, and be liable in negligence if they either fail to take reason-able care in determining whether a drug is suitable, or fail to explain how to take the medicine safely. This would be a straightforward clinical negligence action, and the principles which we considered in Chapter 3 would apply.

If the patient's claim is that a failure to warn her of possible side effects caused her injury, then even if she succeeds in establishing a breach of the manufacturer's duty of care, she will come up against the vexed problem of proving causation in 'failure to warn' cases, which we considered in detail in Chapter 5, p. 290. In short, the problem is that she must prove that she would not have been injured if she had been properly informed, and in this context, this means that she must establish that she would not have taken the drug in question if she had been warned of the particular side effect. Let us imagine that a patient was not warned about a 0.1 per cent risk of hair loss associated with taking a particular anti-depressant. Even if she had in fact been warned, she might have judged that the benefits of alleviating her depression out-weighed this very small risk of losing her hair. But after this risk has materialized, and with the benefit of hindsight, she now knows for certain that she is the one of the unfortunate minority who will suffer hair loss. In these circumstances, how reliable is her evidence that, if she had known about this tiny risk, she would have chosen not to take the drug?

As we saw earlier, there is no contract between a pharmacist and a patient receiving an NHS prescription. The pharmacist will, however, owe the patient a duty of care. If she negligently dispenses the wrong drug, or the wrong dosage, she could be liable for any resulting injury. In *Prendergast v Sam and Dee Ltd*,[66] a doctor had written a prescription for Mr Prendergast, an asthmatic suffering from a chest infection, which included Amoxil tablets. The pharmacist misread the doctor's unclear handwriting, and dispensed Daonil instead, a drug used in the treatment of diabetes. As a result of taking an excessive dose of Daonil, Mr Prendergast suffered permanent brain damage. He sued both the doctor and the pharmacist, and both were found to have been negligent. Despite the unclear handwriting, the pharmacist should have realized that it was extremely unlikely that the doctor had meant to write Daonil on the prescrip-tion. The prescription was for a short course of Amoxil, to be taken three times a day. Diabetics would usually be on continuous courses of Daonil, which is taken only once a day. The dosage would also have been unusually high for Daonil, and since Mr Prendergast paid for his prescription, the pharmacist should have realized that he was not diabetic (diabetics are entitled to free medicines). The Court of Appeal refused to overturn the judge's apportionment of liability: the pharmacist was liable to pay 75 per cent of Mr Prendergast's damages, and the doctor 25 per cent.

Might it also be possible for an injured patient to bring an action against the regulatory authorities for their failure to ensure that a drug was safe enough? Liability for breach of statutory duty is extremely unlikely, since it seems implausible that Parliament intended to create an action for damages for any breach of the Medicines Act 1968, which was clearly passed in order to protect public health, and not to provide redress to individual patients. In a negligence action, it would be necessary for the claimant to establish that there is a relationship of proximity between the regula-tory agency and the injured patient, and that it would be fair, just and reasonable to impose a duty in these circumstances. Proving the existence of a proximate relation-ship between the MHRA or the CSM and the person who has been injured would be

---

[66] *The Times* 14 Mar 1989 (transcript on Lexis).

difficult. And in working out whether a duty of care would be reasonable, the courts will take into account the purpose of the power granted to the public body, which is again to protect the public in general, and not either to offer a remedy to individuals, or to effectively indemnify the pharmaceutical industry against liability for defective medicines.

Two cases can be contrasted here. *In Re HIV Haemophiliac Litigation,*[67] the Court of Appeal refused to strike out a claim in negligence against the Department of Health by haemophiliacs who had been infected with the HIV virus following blood transfusions, while admitting that such actions will seldom succeed:

where, as here, foreseeability by a defendant of severe personal injury to a person such as the plaintiff is shown, and the existence of a proximate relationship between plaintiff and defendant is accepted, the plaintiff is well on his way to establishing the existence of a duty of care. He may still fail to do so if it is held that imposition of such a duty on the defendant would not in all the circumstances be just and reasonable, but it is by no means clear to me at this preliminary stage that the department's submissions on that aspect must prevail.[68]

The case was settled before a full consideration of whether a duty existed or not took place. But in any event, the relationship between the relatively small number of haemophiliacs in the UK and the authorities responsible for the safety of blood transfusions is perhaps distinguishable from a case in which a patient claims that the MHRA or the CSM owed them a duty of care, as we can see from the following case.

Smith v Secretary of State for Health (on behalf of the Committee on Safety of Medicines)[69]
Amanda Smith contracted chickenpox when she was six years old, and was given an aspirin tablet on two consecutive days. Her condition worsened, and she was diagnosed with Reye's syndrome. A month later, her parents discovered that the CSM had advised that aspirin should not be given to children under the age of twelve, except on medical advice. The status of warnings on aspirin was to be changed, and junior aspirin was going to be reclassified as a Pharmacy Medicine. The claimant became permanently disabled with spastic tetraplegia, frequent epileptic convulsions, lack of speech and had to be carried or pushed everywhere. The claimant brought an action for negligence. She argued that the Secretary of State for Health or the Committee on Safety of Medicines was liable for failure to issue public warnings immediately after it had decided to change its advice on aspirin.

Morland J
In my judgment, such discretionary/policy decisions are not justiciable in private law cases. Indeed, in my judgment, it would be contrary to the public interest to allow them to be so. Although often there is a narrow line between discretionary/policy decisions and operational decisions, the decisions of the CSM . . ., are well on the discretionary/policy side of the line. . . .

In my judgment, no common law duty was owed by the CSM or the Secretary of State in respect of the decisions allegedly negligent, even if there was fault in failing to stick to the original timetable. In my judgment, the reasons for that were discretionary/policy and not justiciable.

I wish to make it clear that I am not asserting that the Secretary of State or the CSM could never be liable at common law for breach of duty of care to an individual member of the public from a failure to exercise or a improper exercise of statutory powers and duties: for example, if the

---

[67] (1990) 41 BMLR 171.   [68] Per Bingham LJ.   [69] [2002] EWHC 200 (QB), 67 BMLR 34.

Secretary of State had delayed implementation of the CSM 29/30 May decision until after a bye-election in a marginal constituency where there was a large aspirin factory; or if the CSM had postponed its May meeting until the end of June because it clashed with the Epsom Derby meeting.

Even if a claimant were to succeed in establishing that a regulatory authority owed her a duty of care, proving that it had breached its duty would not be straightforward. If the CSM's duty is to act in accordance with a responsible body of medical opinion, given that it is composed of medical experts, proving that their collective judgment represented a breach of their duty of care would be exceptionally difficult.

(c) CONSUMER PROTECTION ACT 1987

As should be clear, both contract and negligence suffer from significant defects as mechanisms for compensating people who have been injured by defective products. The thalidomide disaster was a particularly potent example of the inadequacies of existing common law remedies. Widespread sympathy for the thalidomide victims led to increasing interest in strict liability, through which the manufacturer, rather than the consumer, would bear the risk of its product causing injury.

In 1985 the European Union adopted a directive[70] which was intended to harmonize European product liability regimes, both in order to remove the distorting impact differing standards of legal liability within the EU were having upon competition, and to ensure that consumers throughout Europe enjoy equal protection against dangerous products. For a number of reasons, the directive has been only partially successful in achieving harmonization. First, certain aspects of the directive, most notably the controversial development risks defence, which we discuss below at p. 568, were optional, and their take-up has varied across Europe.[71] Secondly, because it does not replace liability under a country's domestic civil law regime, similar strict liability statutes throughout Europe co-exist with vastly different systems of tort liability for personal injuries. As Jane Stapleton explains:

despite the vaunted claim that the Directive was aimed at the approximation of product regimes across Member States, in a real sense, it has merely added onto existing regimes a further level of disparate rules varying, for example, according to which options in the Directive were implemented and what local rules exist in relation to non-pecuniary loss.[72]

Thirdly, the implementing legislation has to be applied by national courts, whose interpretations of the provisions in the directive may vary considerably. For example, if there are national variations in consumer expectations, the directive's definition of defect (which relies upon what consumers generally are entitled to expect) may lead to varying levels of consumer protection.[73]

---

[70] *Products Liability* 85/374/EEC.

[71] Member States were also given the option to include unprocessed game and agricultural produce, and to impose financial ceilings on liability.

[72] Jane Stapleton, 'Products Liability in the United Kingdom: The Myths of Reform' (1999) 34 Texas International Law Journal 45, 47.

[73] Geraint Howells, *Comparative Product Liability* (Dartmouth Aldershot 1993) 196.

Of course, harmonization does not necessarily dictate the introduction of strict liability. It would have been possible to introduce an EU-wide fault-based system instead. So why did the Commission favour a strict liability regime? First, as Hans Claudius Taschner points out in the next extract, the Commission argued that strict liability promotes loss-spreading: rather than the costs of injuries falling on individual consumers, they will be borne by manufacturers, who are better able to spread the cost by insurance, and by raising prices, so the costs are ultimately borne by all consumers. Secondly, it was argued that justice demands that consumers should not have to bear their own losses if they cannot discharge the onerous burden of proving negligence.

Hans Claudius Taschner[74]

The crucial problem of product liability is that the producer did not act negligently when manufacturing the defective product. . . . The problem is that the product defect was unavoidable. . . . In numerous decisions manufacturers of various products have admitted that they would like to be able to produce a totally defect-free product line but that this would be impossible.

The question of product liability is therefore who should bear the consequences of damage resulting from unavoidable defects: the victim, society at large, or the relatively small group of product users, one of whom unfortunately used a defective product. There are only three available solutions to the problem of product liability: first is liability for fault, or negligence, which is regarded as the classical solution; second is a no-fault system or compensation by the state as established in New Zealand; or third is liability independent of fault. The classical solution leads to the conclusion that the consequences of defective products must be borne by the victim like an Act of God. According to the New Zealand no-fault system, neither the victim nor the producer, but society at large should absorb the cost of damages. The necessary funds to compensate the victim in such a collectivist system are raised from contributions to the social security budget or by taxes. This arrangement has not been adopted by the EC on the grounds of incompatibility with its traditional economic system.

The Commission developed the third- and last-mentioned solution whereby the economic loss suffered by the victim, his damage, is transferred to the producer, at least provisionally. The producer insures himself and passes on the cost of the insurance premiums to all users of his products, one of which, having a manufacturing defect, has caused damage. The producer does this by including those costs in his general production costs which leads to a slight increase in the final product price. This so-called 'insurance solution' avoids the arbitrary character of the classical solution, as well as the collectivist aspect of the no-fault scheme. The only way to transfer the economic loss of the victim to all non-damaged users of non-defective products easily is to provide for liability independent of fault. It is not a question of condemning the manufacturer by the imposition of this kind of liability or of punishing him by requiring payment of damages from his profit.

As we see later, however, the directive does include a number of 'defences', which inevitably limits its capacity to protect consumers. Jane Stapleton argues that by trying to protect both consumers *and businesses*, the directive is a classic example of 'Euro-fudge'.

---

[74] 'Harmonization of Product Liability Law in the European Community' (1999) 34 Texas International Law Journal 21, 28–9.

Jane Stapleton[75]

The Directive did not result from some perceived bottom-up forensic pressure from claims. Rather, the engine of this reform was social and political. In particular, the concern of the public in these countries had been galvanized by the disaster caused by the unforeseen side effects of the Thalidomide pregnancy drug. Meanwhile, by the late 1970s, the European Commission was keen to promote consumer protection measures to show Europeans that the 'common market' was not there simply to serve big business. It proposed very pro-consumer draft Directives in 1976 and 1979. Yet there remained intense concern within the European Parliament and the Council that substantial exculpatory provisions be included in any future Directive.

As a result, the Directive is one of the high-water marks of Euro-fudge and textual vagueness. The point is that the Directive tries to square a circle: it uses the rhetoric of 'strict liability,' and yet, in Articles 6(2) and 7(e), it seems to provide solid protection for reasonable businesses, a compromise demanded by the UK Government of Margaret Thatcher.

The directive was given effect in the UK by the Consumer Protection Act 1987 (CPA). There are some differences in wording between the directive and the CPA, but in *Commission v UK*,[76] the European Court of Justice (ECJ) found that there was no evidence that the UK courts were interpreting the Act in a way that is inconsistent with the directive, though this may have been because there had been virtually no cases. Moreover, the ECJ were influenced by the fact that section 1 of the CPA specifically states that the provisions in the relevant part of the Act were passed in order to comply with the directive, and should be construed accordingly.

In *A v National Blood Authority*,[77] a case we consider in detail later, Burton J relied upon the judgment in *Commission v UK*,[78] and section 1 of the CPA as evidence that the Act must be interpreted consistently with the directive. In the spirit of consistency, he decided to go straight to the directive and apply it directly:

in so far as the wording of the CPA, in relation to matters which have been the subject matter of particular issue in this case, differs from the equivalent articles in the directive, it should not be construed differently from the directive; and consequently the practical course was to go straight to the fount, the directive itself.

The Act imposes strict liability on manufacturers and, in certain circumstances, suppliers for defective products which cause physical injury, or property damage greater than €500. Pure economic loss is not covered. Any claim must be brought within three years of the discovery of the damage or injury, with a long-stop of ten years from when the product was first put into circulation. This ten-year time limit is intended to make it easier for manufacturers to insure against liability, because no claims are possible more than ten years after a product is first marketed. It will inevitably leave some people who suffer drug-related injuries uncompensated, however, since some adverse reactions take many years to manifest themselves. Of course, an action in negligence may be possible after the ten-year limit has expired (limitation periods in relation to negligence actions were considered in Chapter 3, p. 150).

The Act only applies to products put into circulation *after* it came into force on the 1 March 1988. Because it applies only to *new* products, it might have been expected

---

[75] 'Bugs in Anglo-American Products Liability' (2002) 53 South Carolina Law Review 1225, 1230–2.
[76] [1997] AER (EC) 481.　　　[77] [2001] 3 All ER 289.　　　[78] [1997] AER (EC) 481.

that there would be comparatively little litigation immediately following the Act's introduction. But the paucity of litigation has nonetheless been surprising—certainly the evidence does not bear out Lord Griffiths (writing extra-judicially) et al.'s prediction in 1988:

We have little doubt that, once it is no longer necessary to prove negligence, there will be a significant increase in product liability litigation in England.[79]

In the next extract Jane Stapleton analyses possible explanations for the Act's limited impact.

Jane Stapleton[80]

If, in practice, the Directive only imposes stricter liability on producers in relatively peripheral cases one might have predicted that its impact on the overall pattern of products liability in the United Kingdom would be small. This was indeed what some of us predicted. But even sceptics have been surprised at how very little effect this new cause of action has had in practice. That this has been a Europe-wide phenomenon was confirmed by the reports from Member States given to a review conference at the Centre de Droit de la Consommation in Louvain-la-Neuve (Belgium) in 1995, ten years after the adoption of the Directive and by the official ten-year review mandated by the Directive itself.

In short, the findings have been that there has been no perceptible, or at least no reported, impact on insurance premiums, research and development activity, product innovation in general, or product-caused injury rates . . .

The truth is that the revolution in the products field that manufacturers feared and consumer advocates hoped the Directive would produce has simply not happened. What is the reason for this lack of impact? . . .

In my view, the most convincing explanation for this no-significant-impact phenomenon is simply that the new law scarcely advances the position of the consumer at all . . . Save in a few peripheral contexts, no greater liability is imposed by the Directive than already exists under the other two main causes of action available to victims of defective products. Certainly, the tenor of the Member State reports at the Louvain-la-Neuve conference was that other domestic causes of action were proving adequate. One might be forgiven for asking, if this is the case, why (apart from Euro-window-dressing) was such energy wasted on such a 'reform' as the Directive? . . .

As to lessons to be learnt by consumer advocates, the most painful ones by far for them to accept are first, the failure of the Directive, both doctrinally and in practice, to advance significantly the position of the victim of defective products; and second the inadequacy of the European Community law-making machine to deliver much more than a diluted 'lowest common denominator' in the field of consumer protection. Unless and until these failures are acknowledged and the causes for them understood, the future of consumer protection reforms in European countries is bleak.

In the last few years, there have been a handful of claims under the Act, though at the time of writing, none have reached the House of Lords. Only one case involving a medicine has been heard by the English courts, and this failed to get as far as a full consideration of the Act itself.

---

[79] Lord Griffiths, Peter De Val, and RJ Dormer, 'Developments in English Product Liability Law: A Comparison with the American System' (1988) 62 Tulane Law Review 353, 375.

[80] 'Products Liability in the United Kingdom: The Myths of Reform' (1999) 34 Texas International Law Journal 45, 63–5, 67.

XYZ and Others v Schering Health Care Ltd[81] involved a group action by claimants who had taken different brands of the Combined Oral Contraceptive (COC), and who claimed to have suffered various cardio-vascular injuries (which come under the collective description of Venous-thromboembolism, VTE). They argued that the pills they took were defective under the Consumer Protection Act 1987 and/or the Product Liability Directive. Their claims followed a 'pill scare' in 1995. The CSM had written to doctors stating that three unpublished studies into the safety of COCs had indicated 'around a twofold increase in the risk' of VTE. The defendants claimed that there is no increased risk and that the CSM's warning was misjudged.

Both the defendants and the claimants agreed that the action under the CPA could only proceed if there was in fact a twofold increase in the risk of VTE. After an extraordinarily lengthy analysis of the evidence, Mackay J concluded that:

there is not as a matter of probability any increased relative risk of VTE carried by any of the third generation oral contraceptives supplied to these Claimants by the Defendants as compared with second generation products containing Levonorgesterel.

Because the claimants' case had failed on this preliminary issue, it was not necessary for Mackay J to consider the application of the Consumer Protection Act. At the time of writing, a multi-party action involving more than a thousand children who claim to have been injured by the Measles-Mumps-Rubella (MMR) vaccine is underway,[82] but has not yet proceeded to a full hearing.

(1) WHO CAN BE LIABLE?

Under section 2, a number of actors may be jointly and severally liable under the Act. This means that an injured consumer can choose to sue any of the various possible defendants, each of whom may be liable for the total loss. It would then be up to the losing defendant to recoup his losses from the other possible defendants. By increasing the number of potential defendants, the likelihood that a consumer will be able to find a solvent one is thereby increased.

Those who can be strictly liable for defective products include producers, importers into the European Union, and 'own-brand' suppliers (in relation to medicines, this might mean *Boots* could be liable for defects in their own-brand painkillers, for example). Under section 2(3) suppliers will be liable if they are unable to identify the producer. It is clear that a pharmacist is a supplier. Doctors might also be suppliers if they actually provided the medicine, as commonly happens in hospitals. To absolve themselves of responsibility, both supplying doctors and pharmacists should therefore keep detailed records of the manufacturers of the drugs which they supply. This may be both difficult and expensive, particularly if the medicines are generic drugs, or have been supplied in an emergency. Furthermore, as a result of the Act's limitation period, these records must be kept for ten years.

---

[81] [2002] EWHC 1420 (QB).
[82] See, eg, *Re MMR and MR Vaccine Litigation (No 12); Sayers and Others v Smithkline Beecham plc and Others* [2005] EWHC 539 (QB).

(2) WHAT IS A PRODUCT?

Medicines and medical devices are unquestionably 'products' for the purposes of the Act, but until fairly recently, it was unclear whether human body tissues or fluids would be covered. In *A v National Blood Authority*,[83] it was accepted by both parties that blood was a product under the Act, and it therefore seems probable that gametes (that is, sperm and eggs) might also be subject to the Act's provisions. Whether or not whole organs could be described as 'products' is as yet unclear.

(3) WHAT IS A DEFECT?

An action can only lie if the product is 'defective', and the definition of defect under section 3 of the Act is, to say the least, rather confusing.

Consumer Protection Act 1987

3 (1) Subject to the following provisions of this subsection, there is a defect in a product for the purposes of this Part if the safety of the product is not such as persons generally are entitled to expect; and for those purposes 'safety', in relation to a product, shall include safety with respect to products comprised in that product and safety in the context of risks of damage to property, as well as in the context of risks of death or personal injury.

(2) In determining for the purposes of subsection (1) above what persons generally are entitled to expect in relation to a product all the circumstances shall be taken into account, including—

(a) the manner in which, and purposes for which, the product has been marketed, its get-up, the use of any mark in relation to the product and any instructions for, or warnings with respect to, doing or refraining from doing anything with or in relation to the product;

(b) what might reasonably be expected to be done with or in relation to the product; and

(c) the time when the product was supplied by its producer to another; and nothing in this section shall require a defect to be inferred from the fact alone that the safety of a product which is supplied after that time is greater than the safety of the product in question.

The Act does not distinguish between manufacturing, design or failure to warn defects. It simply states that a product is defective if its safety is not such as persons generally are entitled to expect. This definition of defect will apply easily and straight-forwardly to manufacturing defects, where the product is less safe than it should have been because of a mistake in the production process. As Griffiths et al. explain:

The standard against which such defects are to be judged is the 'perfect' example of the product in question. Thus, the standard is effectively set by the manufacturer.[84]

But in the context of medicinal products, manufacturing defects are extremely rare. Usually patients who have been injured by a medicine will want to allege either that its design was defective, or that they were inadequately warned about a particular risk, and in both cases, working out what level of safety 'persons generally' are entitled to expect becomes much more complicated. Indeed Jane Stapleton has argued that a consumer expectation test is inherently unhelpful:

[83] [2001] 3 All ER 289.

[84] Lord Griffiths, Peter De Val, and RJ Dormer, 'Developments in English Product Liability Law: A Comparison with the American System' (1988) 62 Tulane Law Review 353, 377.

The core theoretical problem with the definition, however, is that it is circular. This is because what a person is entitled to expect is the very question a definition of defect should be answering.[85]

In relation to new or complex products, such as medicines, consumers may have no clear expectations about the level of safety which they are entitled to expect. Of course, it could be argued that consumers never actually *expect* to be injured by a particular product,[86] so that *any* product which causes injury is defective. The test is an objective one, however: it is what consumers are *entitled* to expect, and people are not entitled to expect that medicines will never cause any unwanted side effects. On the contrary, it is to be expected that medicines which are powerful enough to alter physiological function will occasionally cause adverse reactions.

Pamela Ferguson suggests another reason why the consumer expectation test applies particularly awkwardly to pharmaceutical products:

While one can accept that consumers may develop certain expectations as to the safety of most consumer goods, pharmaceutical drugs and devices are in a different position since they have to pass strict requirements, laid down by government bodies, before they can be marketed. It is arguable that a consumer should not expect a product which has satisfied the standards imposed by such bodies to be any safer than in fact it is.[87]

In short, if the CSM has decided, after scrutinizing all the available evidence, that a medicine is sufficiently safe, it might seem odd for a court to subsequently decide that consumers are entitled to expect it to be safer. Remember, however, that the CSM simply judges whether the risk/utility balance is acceptable in the light of *existing* information. Rare side effects will seldom be detected during clinical trials, and so a particular adverse reaction may not come to light until the drug has actually been used by a large number of people for several years.

Section 3(2) sets out a number of factors which are relevant to what consumers generally are entitled to expect, such as, under section 3(2)(a), any warnings provided with the product. Of course, the existence of a warning does not necessarily lead to the conclusion that a product is not defective. Given the relatively low cost of warnings, there is a danger that manufacturers might warn of every conceivable risk in the hope of avoiding liability. This would be undesirable, because the danger signal imparted by warnings is likely to be diluted if they become ubiquitous and over-inclusive. Moreover, it should not be possible for manufacturers of manifestly unsafe products, which could have been made safer, to avoid liability by warning of the risk the product presents. Rather warnings should only absolve a manufacturer of liability if avoiding the existence of the risk was not a realistic option.

Also relevant under section 3(2)(b) is what might reasonably be expected to be done with the product. Plainly this means that injuries caused by taking an overdose will not be covered by the Act. A more difficult question is the extent to which it is reasonable to expect consumers to take medicines *exactly* according to the manufacturer's instructions. Recall that at p. 547 Richard Sykes drew attention to studies which suggest that as many as 60 per cent of patients fail to comply with the directions

---

[85] *Product Liability* (Butterworths London 1994) 234.   [86] Ibid, 235.
[87] Pamela Ferguson, *Drug Injuries and the Pursuit of Compensation* (Sweet & Maxwell London 1996) 116.

for a medicine's use. Because it can reasonably be expected that a patient will forget to take a pill, for example, or leave too short a time between doses, a medicine should be safe enough even if there is some slight deviation from the packet's instructions. If non-compliance might lead to very serious adverse consequences, then a very clear warning would be necessary, and this would then bring it within section 3(2)(a).

Section 3(2)(c) specifies that a product is not to be considered defective simply because a better product is subsequently put into circulation. So a product's defectiveness must be judged according to prevailing safety standards at the time when it was supplied (as we saw in Chapter 3, an analogous rule applies in negligence actions). This seems fair if we are assessing the degree to which a manufacturer is *at fault*. However, liability under the Act is supposed to be *strict*, in which case the question of whether it would have been reasonable to expect the manufacturer to reach higher safety standards than the norm should not perhaps be relevant.

A different sort of approach to the question of whether a product is defective would be to adopt a straightforward risk/benefit calculation: are the risks which the product presents justified by its benefits? So, for example, aspirin causes some risk of adverse side effects in a very small minority of patients, but given its overwhelming health benefits for other patients, persons generally are not entitled to expect that aspirin can safely be taken by every possible consumer. In contrast, thalidomide might have alleviated morning sickness, but the risks of premature death and severe disability are far too grave to justify its use in relieving nausea in early pregnancy, and adopting a risk/benefit approach, it would therefore be categorized as a defective product. Interestingly, there has been some interest in using thalidomide to slow the rate at which brain tumours grow. For gravely ill patients, who are very unlikely to object to the condition that they do not become pregnant while taking it, the benefits of thalidomide may outweigh its risks.

The availability of alternative products would also be relevant to this sort of risk/benefit calculation. Let us imagine that a new contraceptive pill will cause a very undesirable side-effect, such as blindness, in 0.01 per cent of consumers. Not only might we want to weigh the risk of blindness against the benefit of effective contraceptive protection, but it would also be relevant that other contraceptive pills exist which do not have this undesirable side effect. If, however, a drug which carried a similar risk was the *only* effective cure for AIDS, it might be reasonable to accept a 0.01 per cent risk of blindness.

In the following extract James Henderson and Aaron Twerski argue that a risk/benefit approach is much more straightforward for courts to apply than the consumer expectation test.

James A Henderson and Aaron D Twerski[88]

[T]he consumer expectations test asks: how much safety does the reasonable consumer have a right to expect? . . . On any view, consumer expectations provide an incoherent standard with which to answer the question of: how much safety? For example, what is a court to do when it concludes that a design feature disappoints reasonable expectations of safety, but it is clear to the

---

[88] 'What Europe, Japan and Other Countries can Learn from the New American Restatement of Products Liability' (1999) 34 Texas International Law Journal 1, 18–19.

court that correcting the feature will introduce risks of a different sort, to a different group of consumers whose reasonable expectations will be disappointed by the new design? Viewing each claim of design defect in isolation, consumer expectations would appear to allow both claims, notwithstanding that they are contradictory.

Equally troubling are those cases in which consumer expectations regarding product safety are—perhaps because the relevant risks are obvious—below the levels of safety of which reasonable design technology is capable. Even if reasonable consumers would want greater safety, and be willing to pay for it, they have no rational basis to expect it when the risks are obvious or the manufacturer has a bad reputation. One response might be that consumers have a right to expect reasonable design safety, determined on the basis of risk-utility analysis. But this response simply replaces consumer expectations as an independent test with the risk-utility test with which consumer expectations are here being contrasted.

In addition to these conceptual problems, it must be added that courts must be able to implement a test for design defectiveness, whatever its content. As earlier observed, the consumer expectations test relies heavily on intuition in its application. This reliance reflects the fact that the test is quite vague. Indeed, its vagueness approaches the level captured by the infamous dictum (in an altogether different substantive context): 'I know it when I see it.' Vagueness of this magnitude undermines courts' ability to make decisions at all. . . .

Of course, no legal rule can eliminate entirely the need for judicial discretion. But compared with consumer expectations, risk-utility analysis more clearly identifies the factual data relevant to determination of design defectiveness.

So how has the consumer expectation test worked in practice? Before Burton J's important judgment in *A v National Blood*, considered below, in three first instance judgments and in one judgment in the Court of Appeal, the courts appeared to suggest that what consumers were entitled to expect depended upon the *reasonableness* of the defendant's conduct. This looks very like an assessment of whether the defendant was *negligent*.

In *Richardson v LRC*,[89] a condom had failed inexplicably. Ian Kennedy J held that although users did not expect condoms to fail, persons generally were not entitled to expect any contraceptive to be 100 per cent effective. He reached this conclusion after extensive discussion of the testing procedures adopted by the defendants. But if the level of safety people are entitled to expect cannot be measured without reference to the *reasonableness* of the defendant's conduct, 'strict liability' may be indistinguishable from negligence.

Similarly, in *Worsley v Tambrands*[90] a woman developed toxic shock syndrome, a rare but potentially fatal condition associated with tampon use. She had read the leaflet, which was included with the box of tampons, but her husband had thrown it away before she became ill. As a result, she did not immediately recognize the symptoms, and her condition worsened. Ebsworth J appeared to argue that the manufacturer had *taken reasonable care* to warn the consumer of the risk associated with tampon use.

As a matter of common sense, that which persons generally are entitled to expect in relation to the product, is that the box contains an unambiguous and clear warning that there is an association

---

[89] [2000] PIQR P164.   [90] [2000] PIQR P95.

between TSS and tampon use and directs that menstruating woman to the internal leaflet for full details. . . .

TSS is a rare but potentially very serious condition which may be life threatening, but it is necessary to balance the rarity and the gravity. That balance is reasonably, properly and safely struck by the dual system of a risk warning on the box and a full explanation in the leaflet if the former is clearly visible and the latter is both legible and full.

And in *Foster v Biosil*[91] Cherie Booth QC, sitting as a recorder, held that the claimant had to establish some defect in the breast implant, not merely that it had failed in circumstances which were unsafe and contrary to what persons generally might expect. It is implicit in her judgment that the claimant had to produce evidence of some shortcoming in the design or manufacture of the product, which effectively means proving that the manufacturer had not taken reasonable care.

Finally, in *Abouzaid v Mothercare*,[92] a case involving a child injured by an elasticated strap on a baby's fleece sleeping bag, the Court of Appeal specifically stated that what the defendant could have done differently was relevant to what consumers generally were entitled to expect:

I have come to the conclusion that, though the case is close to the borderline, the product was defective within the meaning of the Act. . . . Members of the public were entitled to expect better from the appellants. . . . It is not necessary for the Court to determine precisely what more should have been done. It is clear that more could have been done.

This trend towards a negligence-based interpretation of defect was interrupted by the decision of Burton J in *A v National Blood Authority*.

A and Others v National Blood Authority[93]

The 114 claimants had been infected with Hepatitis C [a chronic viral infection of the liver] through blood transfusions which had used blood products obtained from infected donors. During the period when most of the claimants were infected, the risk of such infection through blood transfusions, though known to the medical profession, was impossible to avoid, either because the virus itself had not yet been discovered or because there was no way of testing for its presence in blood. The claimants brought actions against the authorities responsible for the production of blood and blood products under the Consumer Protection Act 1987. They succeeded in establishing that the infected blood was defective under Article 6, and that the defendants could not invoke the development risks defence in Article 7(e).

Burton J

The question to be resolved is the safety or the degree or level of safety or safeness which persons generally are entitled to expect. The test is not that of an absolute level of safety, nor an absolute liability for any injury caused by the harmful characteristic. In the assessment of that question the expectation is that of persons generally, or the public at large. The safety is not what is actually expected by the public at large, but what they are entitled to expect. . . . The court decides what the public is entitled to expect . . . Such objectively assessed legitimate expectation may accord with actual expectation; but it may be more than the public actually expects, thus imposing a higher standard of safety, or it may be less than the public actually expects. Alternatively the public may have no actual expectation—eg in relation to a new product . . .

---

[91] (2000) 59 BMLR 178.   [92] Per Pill LJ.   [93] [2001] 3 All ER 289, 60 BMLR 1.

Conclusions on Article 6 (Defect)

It is not seriously argued by the defendants, notwithstanding some few newspaper cuttings which were referred to, that there was any public understanding or acceptance of the infection of transfused blood by Hepatitis C. Doctors and surgeons knew, but did not tell their patients unless asked, and were very rarely asked. It was certainly, in my judgment, not known and accepted by society that there was such a risk . . .

It is quite plain to me that the directive was intended to eliminate proof of fault or negligence. I am satisfied that this was not simply a legal consequence, but that it was also intended to make it easier for claimants to prove their case, such that not only would a consumer not have to prove that the producer did not take reasonable steps, or all reasonable steps, to comply with his duty of care, but also that the producer did not take all legitimately expectable steps either. . . .

I conclude therefore that avoidability is not one of the circumstances to be taken into account within article 6. I am satisfied that it is not a relevant circumstance, because it is outwith the purpose of the directive, and indeed that, had it been intended that it would be included as a derogation from, or at any rate a palliation of, its purpose, then it would certainly have been mentioned; for it would have been an important circumstance.

The claimants had become infected with Hepatitis C from blood transfusions at a time when it was known that a percentage of all blood was infected, but reliable tests to identify infected blood had not yet been devised. In deciding whether the infected blood was defective, Burton J asked himself what consumers were entitled to expect, and explicitly declined to take into account whether the defendants had acted reasonably:

The Claimant does not have to be concerned with the producer's conduct at all. He does not have to adduce, or rebut, evidence about how the process or choice which led to the product having the characteristic complaint. He has only to persuade the court that a product with that characteristic fell below the level of safety that persons generally are entitled to expect as the Community standard.

Crucially then Burton J found that the avoidability of the harmful characteristic was not relevant to what consumers might reasonably expect. Also irrelevant were the costs, difficulty or impracticability of taking precautionary measures, and the benefit to society or the utility of the product. The public, Burton J found, expected blood to be free from infection:

[The blood products in this case] were defective because I am satisfied that the public at large was entitled to expect that the blood transfused to them would be free from infection. There were no warnings and no material publicity, certainly none officially initiated by or for the benefit of the defendants, and the knowledge of the medical profession, not materially or at all shared with the consumer, is of no relevance. It is not material to consider whether any steps or any further steps could have been taken to avoid or palliate the risk that the blood would be infected.

So whether or not ensuring all blood was infection-free was in practice attainable did not affect the consumer's expectation that blood products would be safe. Although Burton J recognized that the public's *actual* expectations might be too high or too low, and that the test is an objective one of what they are *entitled* to expect, here the public's *actual* and unreasonable expectations were allowed to determine the definition of defectiveness. The consequence of his judgment is that consumers may legitimately expect 100 per cent safety, even if this is a completely unreasonable and impractical expectation. And applying Burton J's judgment in a subsequent case, Field J held that 'the avoidability of the risk of harm is not a relevant circumstance'.[94]

In the context of HIV infected blood, Andrew Grubb and David Pearl have however argued that consumers *do* take into account what might reasonably be done to avoid the risk of infection:

If a reasonable person has any expectation about the safety of blood, it will be that the blood has been tested to the usual extent currently employed.[95]

The central problem is that a consumer expectation test which excludes consider-ations of what the defendant could reasonably have done to avoid the risk has an air of artificiality about it, particularly when the test is what people generally are *entitled* to expect. Are consumers really entitled to expect a wholly unattainable level of safety? Yet once we start to take into account the *reasonableness* of the defendant's actions, the inquiry begins to look indistinguishable from the sort of reasoning the court might adopt in a negligence action.

One way out of this apparent impasse would be to categorize blood as an unavoid-ably unsafe product. In *A v National Blood Authority* Burton J accepted that unavoid-ably unsafe products, such as knives or alcohol, would not be defective under the Act:

There are some products, which have harmful characteristics in whole or in part, about which no complaint can be made. The examples that were used of products which have obviously dangerous characteristics by virtue of their very nature or intended use, were, on the one hand knives, guns and poisons and on the other hand alcohol, tobacco, perhaps foie gras. . . . Drugs with advertised side-effects may fall within this category.

Where a product is unavoidably unsafe, and the danger is generally known, con-sumers are not entitled to expect 100 per cent safety. Burton J rejected this solution to the problem of infected blood, however, in part because consumers had not been warned about the risk of infection, and so the danger was not generally known.

In his judgment Burton J adopted a rather curious distinction between standard products, which are as the producer intended, and non-standard products, which differ from the standard product. This is analogous to the distinction between manu-facturing defects, where the product is not as the producer intended, perhaps because it was contaminated during the manufacturing process, and design defects, where the product is as the producer intended, but because of some intrinsic problem in its design, it turns out to be defective. Of course, the language of manufacturing and design defects applies rather awkwardly to blood, which is neither manufactured nor designed, and this may be why Burton J chose to talk instead about standard and non-standard products:

Thus a standard product is one which is and performs as the producer intends. A non-standard product is one which is different, obviously because it is deficient or inferior in terms of safety, from the standard product: and where it is the harmful characteristic or characteristics present in

[94] *Bogle v McDonald's* [2002] EWHC 490 (QB) (transcript on Lexis).
[95] *Blood Testing, AIDS and DNA Profiling* (Jordan and Sons Bristol 1990) 144.

the non-standard product, but not in the standard product, which has or have caused the material injury or damage.

Infected blood was, in his view, a non-standard product. He then had to ask himself

whether the public at large accepted the non-standard nature of the product i.e., they accept that a proportion of the products is defective (as I have concluded they do not in this case).

It is not clear whether he would have reached the same conclusion on this point and on the question of whether blood is unavoidably unsafe if the people undergoing blood transfusions had been warned of the risk of infection.

In the next extract, Richard Goldberg argues that a risk/benefit approach might have made sense in *A v National Blood Authority* since it would have allowed the utility of blood to be weighed against the unavoidable risk of infection.

Richard Goldberg[96]

It is arguable that all medicinal products carry a risk of adverse reactions, even in a minority of consumers, and that these consumers are not necessarily entitled to expect that the products will be risk free. Despite the emphasis on consumer expectation in Burton J's judgment, there is an inherent logic in addressing the problems of defective medicinal products by weighing the risks against the anticipated benefits and against the 'costs' of not using the product, such as the risk of disease.

In the US, what are known as 'blood shield statutes' have generally been adopted to exempt blood products from strict liability regimes. In part, this is because a risk/benefit analysis suggests that where the utility of a product is great, and is not achievable by a substitute product, and where the risk of infection is known and unavoidable, strict liability for infection would be unreasonable. Writing before the judgment in *A v National Blood*, Andrew Grubb and David Pearl assumed that a similar outcome would be likely under the Consumer Protection Act.

Andrew Grubb and David Pearl[97]

The utility of blood, ie the obvious benefits to patients coupled with the absence of any less dangerous alternative to blood which could be substituted for it, are likely to lead a court to the conclusion that blood is not defective. . . .

The inapplicability of the 1987 Act to the transmission of HIV through blood or blood products should come as no surprise since, even in the jurisdictions where strict liability originates, the US courts usually do not impose strict liability where infection is transmitted through blood. The great utility of blood or blood products in the treatment of patients has led almost all courts not to apply strict liability in this area.

(4) DEFENCES

Section 4 of the Consumer Protection Act provides a number of defences. Most of these can be dealt with very briefly. First, it is a defence if the defect is attributable to compliance with a statutory obligation. An (unlikely) example might be if the

---

[96] 'Paying for Bad Blood: Strict Product Liability after the Hepatitis C Litigation' (2002) 10 Medical Law Review 165–200, 174.

[97] *Blood Testing, AIDS and DNA Profiling* (Jordan and Sons Bristol 1990) 151–4.

manufacturer intended to warn of a particular side effect, but the licensing authority refused to agree to this. Secondly, the defendant will escape liability if he can prove that the product was never supplied to another, or was not supplied in the course of a business. Thirdly, there may be a defence if the defect was not present when the product was supplied.

Fourthly, contributory negligence applies, and so a patient who takes the wrong dose of a drug which subsequently causes injury may be responsible in whole or in part for her own injuries. It should perhaps be noted that the application of contributory negligence to a strict liability regime is rather complicated. If damages are to be apportioned according to the degree of fault of the parties, how might this work when the defendant has not necessarily been at fault at all? Where the claimant has behaved irresponsibly, but the defendant is blameless, does apportionment mean that the claimant's damages must be reduced by 100 per cent? In practice, the application of contributory negligence just means that the claimant's damages will be reduced according to the extent to which their injury was caused by their blameworthy conduct.

The most important and controversial defence is known as the development risks or 'state of the art' defence and is contained in section 4(1)(e):

[I]t shall be a defence . . . that the state of scientific and technical knowledge at the relevant time was not such that a producer of products of the same description as the product in question might be expected to have discovered the defect if it had existed in his products while they were under his control.

The UK Act's version of the development risks defence is slightly different from that in Article 7(e) of the directive:

The producer shall not be liable as a result of this Directive if he proves: . . . that the state of scientific and technical knowledge at the time when he put the product into circulation was not such as to enable the existence of the defect to be discovered.

The UK's defence thus appears to be broader in scope than that of the directive since the relevant state of knowledge is that of 'producer[s] of products of the same description'. Hence a manufacturer could have a defence under the CPA if other producers were equally ignorant of the way to detect the defect in question, even if the defect was in fact discoverable, whereas under the directive, there would only be a defence if the defect was undiscoverable. It was this inconsistency which prompted the European Commission to bring infringement proceedings against the UK. As we saw earlier, the European Court of Justice found that section 4(1)(e) was capable of being interpreted in accordance with Article 7(e), and this is precisely what Burton J did in *A v National Blood*:

Although the United Kingdom Government has not amended s 4(1)(e) of the CPA so as to bring it in line with the wording of the directive, there is thus binding authority of the Court of Justice that it must be so construed.

This defence was included in order to accommodate the fear that liability for undiscoverable defects would be likely to impede innovation within the pharmaceutical industry. In particular, it was thought that strict liability for unknowable risks would make it impossible to obtain liability insurance. The defence is optional, and although most countries have chosen to include it, some, such as Luxembourg and Finland, have not. In Spain and Germany it does not apply to medicines, and in France it does not apply to products derived from the human body. This uneven take-up of the defence means that its impact upon insurance will be reduced, since manufacturers will in any event have to insure against liability in countries where the defence is unavailable.

Clearly, the development risks defence has little impact upon manufacturing defects. Rather, it is in relation to design defects, and failures to warn, that a manufacturer might seek to rely upon evidence that the risk in question was not discoverable when the product was put into circulation. The question of discoverability is, as Charles Pugh and Marcus Pilgerstorfer point out, of critical importance.

Charles Pugh and Marcus Pilgerstorfer[98]

When a defect in a product is known in the sense of it being in the bank of scientific and technical knowledge, it will usually be because it has previously been discovered. In such circumstances the defence is clearly not available to a producer—the fact that the defect has been discovered is conclusive proof of its discoverability . . .

A more difficult situation is where the defect is not known but is arguably discoverable. The strictness of liability imposed by the Directive as a whole is dependent upon whether, on a proper construction of Art.7(e), the focus is on the simple ability to discover the defect, or whether the Court enquires into how reasonable it was for the defect to have been discovered. . . .

It should be recalled that the purpose of ascertaining the state of relevant knowledge is not necessarily to decide whether the defect itself was known (if that were shown, it would be the end of the enquiry) but rather to see whether that knowledge would have enabled the defect to be discovered . . .

There is an additional limit on what knowledge is relevant for the purposes of Article 7(e). Knowledge must be accessible in what has become known as the 'Manchurian' sense. [In *Commission v UK*] the ECJ held that it was 'implicit in the wording of article 7(e) that the relevant scientific and technical knowledge must have been accessible at the time when the product in question was put into circulation'. The much debated example given by the Advocate General is of an academic in Manchuria publishing in a local scientific journal in Chinese which does not go outside the boundaries of the region. In such cases the defence will remain available notwithstanding that the total world body of scientific and technical knowledge might have enabled the defect to be discovered. The relevant body of knowledge on which to focus is 'accessible knowledge'. . . .

Once the relevant knowledge has been ascertained, the next stage in the Court's enquiry into the availability of the Article 7(e) defence is to consider the discoverability of the defect. The presence of this second criterion puts it beyond doubt that it is insufficient for the producer to show simply that the defect was not 'known' at the time the product was put into circulation. A producer must go further and show that the relevant knowledge was not such as to 'enable the existence of the defect to be discovered'.

If the defence only applies to completely undiscoverable risks, its impact will be minimal. Usually the tools to discover the existence of a risk will exist, even if it would not have occurred to anyone to use them. For example, in the case of thalidomide, an

[98] 'The Development Risk Defence: Knowledge, Discoverability and Creative Leaps' (2004) 4 Journal of Personal Injury Law 258–69.

animal did exist which would display the same teratogenic effect when thalidomide was administered during pregnancy. But no-one had any reason to believe that thalidomide should be tested on pregnant rabbits. Rather it was assumed that, because thalidomide had no adverse effects on women, and there had been no sign of any problems when it was tested on rats, it would not be toxic for the human fetus.

To have any teeth, the defence must protect manufacturers where the risk *was* discoverable, but only by extraordinary means. In essence, this means that manufacturers will not be liable where they took reasonable care to establish whether the product posed a risk to consumers. This looks very like the standard of care in negligence. Indeed, in the House of Lords debate on the Act, Lord Scarman pointed out that:

If you introduce the 'state of the art' defence, you are really introducing negligence or fault by the back door.[99]

Not only does the development risks defence appear to introduce a negligence-type test of what it is reasonable to expect from a manufacturer, but also the evidence which would be necessary to refute such a claim is likely to involve claimants in precisely the sort of protracted and expensive litigation which the Consumer Protection Act was intended to simplify.

If the development risks defence is in practice synonymous with the duty to take reasonable care, the Act's principal advantage for injured consumers is that, once it has been established that the product in question was defective, the burden of proof of reasonable care is shifted to the defendant.

The development risks defence has been extremely controversial. For many academic critics, the defence's ability to neutralize the impact of strict liability is regrettable. As Christopher Newdick explains, unforeseen risks are precisely the sort of defects which are most likely to occur in medicines. If manufacturers have a defence for such risks, the impact of strict liability on the pharmaceutical industry will be minimal.

Christopher Newdick[100]

It will be recalled that it was the tragedy of thalidomide that gave rise to the debate concerning strict liability in this country. Ironically, however, it is the future victims of an accident of precisely this form that would most seriously be prejudiced by a state of the art defence. The pharmaceutical industry in this country has not generally been accused of irresponsible or unreasonable behaviour. By its very nature it works in an area in which unforeseeable accidents are inevitable, where fault is usually absent and known risks frequently judged acceptable as regards the few, in the interests of the many. In additions, their actions have the approval of an official licensing body. These factors would effectively be sufficient to guarantee that, unless a special exception were made to such a defence, the pharmaceutical industry would be its principal beneficiary.

Jane Stapleton questions why we should treat unforeseeable design errors more leniently than equally blameless manufacturing errors:

---

[99]   414 HL Deb col 1427.
[100]   'Strict Liability for Defective Drugs in the Pharmaceutical Industry' (1985) 101 Law Quarterly Review 405–31, 408.

We still have no principled explanation of why, for example, it is fair to hold a manufacturer strictly liable for some product flaws he could not discover (for example, some manufacturing errors), but not fair to do so in relation to a different set of product flaws he could not discover (namely, unforeseeable design dangers).[101]

The development risks defence does have its supporters, however. Christopher Hodges, for example, points out that defence's positive impact upon innovative practices is, in the long run, likely to serve the interests of patients as well as manufacturers.

Christopher Hodges[102]

It is the essence of innovation that the risks which may be encountered in the use of a product cannot reasonably be identified or quantified at the time at which it is marketed—either fully or, in some cases, at all. Of course, one approach might be to require producers to test products fully before marketing them. But that would be unrealistic. First, testing usually includes testing in use by real humans in real life situations . . . there must be a limit to the duration and cost of such an exercise. With medicines, the limit is effectively prescribed by regulation, taking into account ethical constraints on repetitive or excessive testing. If testing were required to continue until all possible risks which might occur with use of a product had not been identified, few producers could afford to innovate and consumers would not benefit from advances in science and technology. Research would stagnate if denied practical application and commercial advantage . . .

The encouragement of innovation has become a major aim of the European Union's policy to develop growth and competitiveness and to decrease unemployment . . . On this basis, citizens and industry are not viewed as distinct groups which are in conflict, but as part of an integrated system where the principal concern is the ultimate benefit of EU citizens. On this basis, it is entirely appropriate that responsible citizens should share some of the risks involved in developing products if they wish to participate in the benefits. . . .

The basic problem with the defence is that a literal concept of *undiscoverability* is an unworkable test. The truth is that *any* defect can be discovered prior to marketing given sufficient testing. Such testing simply requires time and money. . . . The issue, however, is how much testing it is reasonable to expect the producer of an innovative product to undertake pre-marketing. Community policy recognises ethical, commercial and social limitations on the extent of pre-market testing . . .

At the time at which a product is placed on the market, it may well be discoverable that it has certain defects which are as yet unidentified or unquantified but which would be discovered given further testing.

Burton J's judgment in *A v National Blood Authority* may have come as a surprise to academic commentators who had assumed that the development risks defence meant that liability under the Act would in practice be indistinguishable from negligence, in that manufacturers who had taken reasonable care would be able to avoid liability for defective products.

---

[101] 'Bugs in Anglo-American Products Liability' (2002) 53 South Carolina Law Review 1225, 1241.
[102] 'Development Risks: Unanswered Questions' (1998) 61 Modern Law Review 560–70, 561.

A and Others v National Blood Authority[103]
Burton J
[I]t is common ground here that the existence of the defect in blood generally, ie of the infection of blood in some cases by Hepatitis virus notwithstanding screening, was known, and indeed known to the defendants. . . .

Conclusions on Article 7(e) (development risks defence)
[T]he risk ceases to be a development risk and becomes a known risk not if and when the producer in question . . . had the requisite knowledge, but if and when such knowledge were accessible anywhere in the world outside Manchuria. Hence it protects the producer in respect of the unknown. . . .

[O]nce the problem is known by virtue of accessible information, then the non-standard product can no longer qualify for protection under art 7(e).

In the light of my construction of art 7(e), and the conclusion that the risk of Hepatitis C infection was known, the art 7(e) defence does not arise.

In *A v National Blood Authority*, the defendants knew about the existence of the risk of infection, but they did not know how to detect it in individual bags of blood. The only way in which it would have been possible to ensure that no recipients of blood transfusions became infected with the Hepatitis C virus would have been to stop carrying out blood transfusions, which would have breached the National Blood Authority's obligation to supply blood, and would lead to a much greater risk to public health than the comparatively small risk of Hepatitis C infection. In short, the National Blood Authority almost certainly *had* exercised reasonable care.

Nevertheless, Burton J held that once the manufacturer knew of the existence of a defect, it was a known risk and the development risks defence could not apply, even if there was no known way of avoiding the risk in question. If the development risks defence is confined to *unknown* risks, and has no application to *known but unavoidable* risks, its scope is significantly more restrictive than most people had assumed.

Geraint Howells and Mark Mildred point out that Burton J

certainly did not fit the stereotype of a judge intoxicated by a negligence-based world view. Rather he displayed a reformist zeal to show that he appreciated that the Directive was intended to make a break with the past and introduce a new form of civil liability.[104]

In the next extract Jane Stapleton argues that Burton J's 'reformist zeal' was misplaced.

Jane Stapleton[105]
In short, the court in the Hepatitis C case was determined to give the Directive 'work to do' in the United Kingdom; that is to give it a wider ambit of entitlement than existed elsewhere in the English law of obligations. It was eager to avoid a construction that would 'not only be toothless but pointless.' The trial judge seems to have thought this required an adoption of the construction urged by the claimants. In my view, this was mistaken. For example, it would still be consistent with the pro-consumer purpose of the Directive, as selected by the judge, that the Directive was

---

[103] [2001] 3 All ER 289, 60 BMLR 1.
[104] 'Infected Blood: Defect and Discoverability. A First Exposition of the EC Product Liability Directive' (2002) 65 Modern Law Review 95–106, 98.
[105] 'Bugs in Anglo-American Products Liability' (2002) 53 South Carolina Law Review 1225, 1249–50.

aimed merely at leveling up other Member States to the level of consumer protection already in place in the United Kingdom. In any case, the Directive did unequivocally make a number of improvements to the position of the UK consumer that did not require the court to adopt the claimants' construction.

In my view, the 'reformist zeal' of the trial judge in the Hepatitis C case simply preferred the heroic rhetoric of the claimants' cause.

A v National Blood is a difficult case. On the one hand, it is hard not to feel sympathy for the claimants, who had already had the misfortune to be in need of blood transfusions, from which they were unlucky enough to contract a potentially life-threatening illness. Yet on the other hand, the National Blood Authority was also in a difficult position. In two important respects, the National Blood Authority is unlike a manufacturer of a defective product, and so an Act which was designed to apply to manufacturers who have put defective products into circulation may apply somewhat awkwardly to this sort of public body.

First, the manufacturer of a product, such as a medicine, is not under a *legal duty* to supply that medicine. If the manufacturer has any doubts about a product's safety, on the contrary, its duty would be to ensure that it is not put into circulation. The National Blood Authority, in contrast, is under a *duty* to supply blood. It was not open to them to stop all blood transfusions in the UK while they worked out how to identify this new strain of Hepatitis. Secondly, as we saw earlier, the purpose of the CPA was to facilitate loss-spreading. Rather than the loss falling on the unlucky victim, it would be transferred to the manufacturer, and the assumption was that manufacturers would be able to spread the loss among all consumers by raising the prices of its product. Again, the National Blood Authority does not have the option of transferring the costs of damages to the consumers of its products.

Even if, on balance, it is thought fair for the National Blood Authority to bear the costs of the claimant's injuries, as opposed to the claimants' themselves, it is perhaps ironic that, in the field of medical law, the only successful action under the CPA has not been against the deep pockets of the pharmaceutical industry, but rather against an integral part of the financially overstretched NHS.

(5) CAUSATION

Regardless of whether or not it is necessary to prove fault in relation to a defective drug, the problem of establishing causation will remain. In Chapter 3 p. 140, we looked at causation in negligence actions in detail. In short, the 'but for' test applies, and the claimant must prove that 'but for' the defendant's negligence, she would not have suffered her injuries. As we can see from *Loveday v Renton*, this is by no means straightforward.

Loveday v Renton[106]
A child claimed that she had suffered permanent brain damage after being vaccinated against whooping cough (pertussis). She sued the doctor who had administered the vaccine. Stuart-Smith LJ split the question of causation into two parts. First, there was the general question about

---

[106] [1990] 1 Med LR 117.

whether the whooping cough vaccine *could ever cause* brain damage, and second, there was the question of whether it *had in fact caused* the specific injury to this plaintiff. Following a four month trial, and having heard evidence from nineteen expert witnesses, Stuart-Smith LJ was not satisfied that the vaccine could in fact ever cause permanent brain damage.

Stuart-Smith LJ

[W]hen I embarked on the consideration of the preliminary issue, I was impressed by the case reports and what was evidently a widely held belief that the vaccine could, albeit rarely, cause brain damage . . . But . . . I have become more and more doubtful that this is so. I have now come to the clear conclusion that the Plaintiff fails to satisfy me on the balance of probability that pertussis vaccine can cause permanent brain damage in young children. It is possible that it does; the contrary cannot be proved. But in any event the Plaintiff's claim must fail.

There are a number of reasons why causation causes particular difficulties in product liability cases. People who take medicines are generally ill, and it may therefore be difficult to prove that any deterioration in their condition is caused by the drug they took, and not by their pre-existing illness, or some other agent. Many typical adverse drug reactions are indistinguishable from conditions which occur spontaneously, and it will be very difficult to *prove* that the patient's symptoms were caused by a particular medicine.

In addition, patients will often take a number of different medicines, either simultaneously, or over a period of time. Pinpointing which drug was responsible for their injury is therefore difficult, and exacerbated by the fact that it might be a combination of one or more drugs which triggered the patient's reaction. If each taken singly would be safe, could any manufacturer be said to be responsible for a reaction caused by the drugs' interaction with each other? In the next extract, Pamela Ferguson discusses the various practical difficulties which a claimant may face in trying to prove causation.

Pamela Ferguson[107]

In respect of pharmaceutical products, it is their very nature which leads to causation difficulties. Drugs are intended to be consumed and to have a biological effect. The action of any drug in the body of a particular individual can never be predicted with complete accuracy. Many symptoms which may be ascribed to an adverse effect of a medication may actually be due to the natural progression of an underlying disease or illness. Drugs are absorbed at varying rates by different persons, they may be metabolised and excreted differently. A drug may interact with others which are being taken by a patient, or with foodstuffs. Studies have shown that many people who are neither ill nor taking any medication perceive that they are suffering from 'symptoms'. Had such people been receiving drug therapy, they might have attributed their symptoms to the treatment.

A person who is injured by a car which has faulty brakes or by an exploding kettle is at least aware that the car or the kettle was 'involved' in causing the injury . . . This is in contrast to the position with pharmaceutical drugs which may leave little or no trace once consumed . . . [W]hile some people do suffer from immediate allergic reactions to drugs, in the majority of cases . . ., the injuries which are alleged to have been caused by these drugs took several months, or in some cases years, to become manifest.

---

[107] Pamela Ferguson, *Drug Injuries and the Pursuit of Compensation* (Sweet & Maxwell London 1996) 121–2.

It should also be remembered that, as we have seen, patients often fail to follow prescribing instructions. Proving that the patient's deterioration was caused by taking the medicine, when there is a significant chance that the patient did not take it in the recommended way, may be particularly difficult.

In the next extract, Mark Mildred discusses the different types of evidence which might be used to prove causation, all of which may be of limited assistance to a claimant.

Mark Mildred[108]

The problem [of causation] is posed in its most acute form by the proposition that there is no pharmaceutical product which is known to cause a unique side effect or injury. The problem then becomes sorting out any such side effect or injury caused by the product from those occurring in nature . . . What types of evidence are available to help the search for the plausibility of the existence of a cause and effect relationship?

They fall into four categories. The first is biochemical evidence whereby experimental scientists can demonstrate a biological or chemical reaction in a test tube. This evidence can provide a theoretical proof of an effect observed in humankind but no more. It can supplement but not replace other evidence.

The second type, animal evidence, is of equally limited value. Laboratory animal body systems are so different from those of primates that it is almost always possible for defendants to argue that for either dose-related or endemic reasons a positive result in animal work cannot be extrapolated to humans. Its main value is that negative results in all animals at all levels may tend to exclude the plausibility of a cause and effect relationship in humans.

Epidemiological evidence is the evidence gained from looking at numbers of people who have been exposed to a particular product or products. The best evidence comes from studies where two groups of people, matched as closely as possible, are compared with a view to seeing whether the incidence of a medical condition, for example, is higher in the group exposed to the product under scrutiny than in the group not so exposed . . . The plaintiff's problem here is that he has no control over the research which has been done and therefore it is unlikely that the perfectly designed study to test the causal connection which he must prove will exist. Further, there are ethical problems in commissioning studies once a causal connection between product and condition is suspected. . . .

Despite the shortcomings it is likely, in a contested product liability action, that it is by reference to epidemiological evidence that the claim stands or falls. It was, for example, by a concerted and profound criticism of the epidemiology in . . . *Loveday and Renton* that the defendants prevailed on the issue of causation.

Although the law focuses narrowly on the question of whether there is adequate scientific proof of a causal link between the medicine taken by the claimant and her injuries, the wider policy question is who should bear the burden of medical uncertainty?[109] Because of the overwhelming practical difficulties in proving

---

[108] 'Representing the plaintiff in drug product liability cases' in Geraint Howells (ed), *Product Liability, Insurance and the Pharmaceutical Industry: An Anglo-American Comparison* (MUP Manchester 1990) 24–36, 27–8.

[109] Robert Lee, 'Vaccine Damage: adjudicating scientific dispute' in Geraint Howells (ed), *Product Liability, Insurance and the Pharmaceutical Industry: An Anglo-American Comparison* (MUP Manchester 1990) 52–67, 60.

causation, the answer would seem to be that the burden of uncertainty will generally lie with the person who claims to have been injured by a defective medicine.

Even if it is clear that the patient's injuries were caused by taking a particular drug, it might be difficult to prove which manufacturer produced the drug in question. Once a drug can be produced generically, many different manufacturers will be producing an identical product, and by the time the patient's injury materializes, it may be impossible to prove which company manufactured the drug that was in fact taken by this patient. Additionally, patients may have taken the same drug manufactured by a number of different companies for several years, in which case it will be virtually impossible to identify the manufacturer of the medicine which actually caused the injury in question.

In the US, a number of novel strategies have been adopted by the courts in order to assist claimants who might be defeated by evidential difficulties in identifying the correct defendant. Probably the most well known emerged from the case of *Sindell v Abbott Laboratories*,[110] and is referred to as 'market-share liability'. It is explained by Pamela Ferguson in the following extract:

Pamela Ferguson[111]
The market share theory requires a plaintiff to demonstrate that the defendants were responsible for a substantial share of the drug market. Each defendant must then show that it did not produce the particular drug which was responsible for the plaintiff's injury (it has been held that a manufacturer who had 10 per cent of the DES [diethylstilbestrol] market did not have a sufficiently large 'market share' to be subject to this form of liability). Each manufacturer which fails to demonstrate this is liable to pay a percentage of the compensation awarded to the plaintiff, and this percentage is dependant on the share of the market for which the company was responsible at the relevant time (that is, at the time when the plaintiff's injury or loss occurred). A defendant may bring other producers of the drug into the action as co-defendants.

In essence, market share liability means that the defendants are held liable for creating a *risk of harm*. Would the English courts be likely to adopt such an approach? Until *Fairchild v Glenhaven Funeral Services*,[112] the short answer would almost certainly have been 'no'. As we saw in Chapter 3, in cases such as *Hotson v East Berkshire Area Health Authority*[113] and *Wilsher v Essex Area Health Authority*[114] the courts have been adamant that the claimant must prove on the balance of probabilities, that her injuries were caused by *this* defendant.

In *Fairchild*, the House of Lords took a more flexible approach to causation. The claimants had suffered mesothelioma as a result of exposure to asbestos in the workplace, but they had worked for a number of companies during their lifetimes, and none could prove which employer had caused their illness. The House of Lords found that each of the employers had increased the risk to the workers, and causation was established against all of them.

It is not clear whether this would help people who suffer injuries after taking a drug which is manufactured by several companies. As we saw in Chapter 3, in *Gregg v*

---

110 (1980) 607 P 2d 924.
111 *Drug Injuries and the Pursuit of Compensation* (Sweet & Maxwell London 1996) 140–1.
112 [2002] UKHL 22, [2003] 1 AC 32.   113 [1987] AC 750.   114 [1988] AC 1074.

Scott,[115] the House of Lords endorsed the traditional approach to causation in medical cases, and seemed reluctant to extend the *Fairchild* exception. And in *Fairchild* itself, Lord Hoffmann distinguished the market share approach adopted in *Sindell*:

The case bears some resemblance to the present but the problem is not the same. For one thing, the existence of the additional manufacturers did not materially increase the risk of injury. The risk from consuming a drug bought in one shop is not increased by the fact that it can also be bought in another shop.

Nevertheless, he described the market share approach adopted in *Sindell* as 'imaginative', and suggested that such cases should 'be left for consideration when they arise'.

Although holding defendants liable in the absence of proof that their product actually caused the claimant's injuries might initially appear to be a measure which protects consumers' interests, it is important to remember that pharmaceutical companies will have to insure against the possibility of market share liability. Inevitably, this means their premiums will increase and that the costs of medicines will rise.

Where the causal link between the defendant's product and the claimant's injury is tenuous, and may in fact never have existed at all, in reality what is being proposed is a kind of 'rough justice' between manufacturers as a class, and victims of injuries. In such circumstances, it might be preferable to admit that this is essentially a no-fault compensation scheme, paid for by the pharmaceutical industry, rather than fudging the issue of causation.[116]

(6) VACCINE DAMAGE

Special state compensation exists for patients who are disabled as a result of vaccination. Vaccines are different from ordinary medicines in that the intention is not just to benefit the individual child who is immunized, but also to contribute towards the public health goal of eliminating certain diseases through population-wide immunization. Indeed it has been argued that vaccination programmes are inherently unethical because the intervention is performed on an asymptomatic individual, who bears the risk associated with the vaccine but who may not actually benefit from it.[117] In the next extract, Angus Dawson refutes this argument, suggesting that individuals who are vaccinated do benefit from the public good of 'herd protection'.

Angus Dawson[118]
The first concern is that preventive programmes focus on interventions that are performed upon asymptomatic individuals. The worry here is that where such an intervention carries *any* risk of harm it is harder to justify the exposure on individuals to such risk when they do not have the disease itself. . . . If the intervention carries any risk of harm (or perhaps just inconvenience) then all are subject to this, and any of the individuals may potentially be harmed, whilst only a few unidentifiable individuals will benefit. The concern might then be raised that individuals are being 'sacrificed' for the good of the population. . . . [I]f potential participants are clearly informed of

---

[115] [2005] UKHL 2 (transcript on Lexis).

[116] Pamela Ferguson, *Drug Injuries and the Pursuit of Compensation* (Sweet & Maxwell London 1996) 146.

[117] P Skrabanek, 'Why is Preventive Medicine Exempted from Ethical Constraints?' (1990) 16 Journal of Medical Ethics 187–90.

[118] 'Vaccination and the Prevention Problem' (2004) 18 Bioethics 515–30, 519–21, 524.

the relevant facts, then it is unlikely that they will consider it worth participating as the benefits for them as individuals are unclear: at best any such benefits are likely to be distant and small, but more likely they are probably non-existent (whilst any potential harms will clearly exist) . . .

I wish to argue that [this] is incorrect, for two reasons. The first is that at least some individuals do benefit from the programme. The individual beneficiaries are the ones who otherwise would have become infected with the relevant disease. Whilst it is true that such individuals are only likely to be a subgroup in the vaccinated population, and that it is impossible to identify them in advance, we can be sure that at least some individuals will certainly benefit. However, far more importantly and decisively . . ., I will argue that *all* individuals in fact benefit from such programmes (at least once herd protection exists in the relevant population). This benefit is related to the share that each person has in the existence of herd protection as a public good.

Although childhood vaccination is not compulsory in the UK, there are a number of vaccinations that are recommended. Before they start school, most children in the UK have received twenty-seven doses of vaccine.[119] Because vaccination involves the injection of small quantities of active, infectious agents in order to trigger the body's immune response, the existence of rare but serious adverse reactions is unsurprising. While the existence of a causal link between vaccination and some side effects has been widely accepted, others—in particular, the putative connection between the MMR vaccine and autism—are heavily disputed.

It would be very difficult for an individual who suffers a severe adverse effect following routine vaccination to establish that either the doctor who performed the vaccination or the manufacturer of the vaccine had been negligent. Even if some doctors have questioned the safety of certain vaccines (such as, most recently, the MMR vaccine), to establish that the doctor who performed one of the recommended vaccinations had been negligent, it would be necessary to prove that the vaccination was not supported by a responsible body of medical opinion. Since the vast majority of doctors strongly support all of the recommended vaccinations, this will be impossible, unless the child has some special characteristics which make vaccination unwise. Similar difficulties would be present in an action against the vaccine's manufacturer, who will be able to argue that it is impossible to expect absolute safety from a vaccination programme. And following the Court of Appeal's decision in *Loveday v Renton*, even if the manufacturer could be said to have breached its duty of care, proving causation would be exceptionally difficult. An action against the Department of Health, on the grounds that it recommends childhood vaccination, would also be very unlikely to succeed.

Yet if vaccination programmes pose a risk of injury to a small number of people which is believed to be outweighed by the enormous public health benefits of universal immunization, it would seem fair to offer some compensation to the small group of individuals whose health is compromised for the greater good. Of course, the cost/benefit calculation will not always favour vaccination. The chance of being exposed to the smallpox virus, for example, is now so small that the risk of harm from vaccination is no longer justified.

In the 1970s, the Pearson Commission recommended that a special strict liability

---

[119] Stephanie Pywell, 'A Critical Review of the Recent and Impending Changes to the Law of Statutory Compensation for Vaccine Damage' (2000) 4 Journal of Personal Injury Law 246–56.

scheme should be set up to compensate those who suffer injuries following vaccination. This proposal was never implemented, and instead an 'interim' scheme was introduced by the Vaccine Damage Payments Act 1979. As amended, the Act continues to apply today.

Under section 1, a person who has been severely disabled as a result of vaccination against diptheria, tetanus, whooping cough, poliomyelitis, measles, rubella, tuberculosis, smallpox, mumps, Haemophilus type b infection (hib), or meningitis C, is entitled to a sum of £100,000 (increased from £40,000 in 2000). Applicants must have been vaccinated in the UK since 1948 (and in the case of smallpox, before 1971). Under section 3(1), claims must be made before the claimant's twenty-first birthday (this was increased from a six-year time limit in 2000). 'Severe disability' is defined in section 1(4) as 60 per cent disablement (this was reduced in 2000 from 80 per cent). And under section 3(5), the causal link between the vaccine and the disability has to be proved, on the balance of probabilities.

The Scheme is funded from the Social Security budget, and claims are made initially to the Department of Work and Pensions. If the claim is rejected, under section 4 the claimant can appeal to an independent tribunal. There is no further appeal to a court, although the Secretary of State is empowered to reverse the Tribunal's decision.[120]

The scheme has not been an overwhelming success, and there have been comparatively few successful claims. As might have been expected, the majority of claims were made in the first few years after the scheme was set up. Between 1989 and 1999, only forty-four awards were made, thirty-two of which were made after appeals.[121] Rates of success vary between different vaccines: a high proportion of claims resulting from the single measles vaccine are successful, compared with low rates for the MMR vaccine.[122] Success rates also appear to vary considerably in different parts of the country.

It remains to be seen whether the reduction in the disability threshold in 2000 will make it any easier for claimants to receive compensation. In any event, it could plausibly be argued that setting any threshold level of disablement is unfair, regardless of the level at which it is set. Even if it were possible to evaluate the extent of a child's disablement with this sort of precision, why should a child who suffers 59 per cent disablement receive nothing, while a child with 60 per cent disablement might be entitled to £100,000? A sliding scale which compensated a child according to the extent of her disablement, without any minimum threshold level, might be fairer.

Moreover, the sum of £100,000, while undoubtedly substantial, will not necessarily be sufficient to meet all of the child's needs throughout his life, especially if the vaccine caused severe brain damage. It is certainly much less than an award in tort, where full compensatory damages are the norm, and brain-damaged children can receive many millions of pounds. On the other hand, as is pointed out in the following

---

[120] SI 1999/2677.
[121] Stephanie Pywell, 'The Vaccine Damage Payment Scheme: A Proposal for Radical Reform' (2002) 9 Journal of Social Security Law 73–93, 81.
[122] Ibid, 83.

extract, children who receive lump sum payments under the Act are treated more generously than most disabled children.

Patrick Atiyah[123]

A very small proportion of children suffer severe brain damage as a result of vaccination, in particular, vaccination against whooping cough. It is difficult to establish causation with any certainty because small children not infrequently develop convulsions for the first time in the first two years of life, and only some of these attacks follow routine vaccinations . . . [V]accination is a classic case of the 'free-rider' problem much discussed by economists. The benefit to each individual child of being vaccinated may not be very great in view of the fact that most other children are likely to be vaccinated, and that the risk of infection has been thus greatly reduced; yet if the parents of all children reasoned in this way, vaccination would decline and the diseases in question would spread more widely again, with greater risk to all. Further, the main beneficiary from vaccination is often not the vaccinated child but other younger children with whom he or she comes into contact: whooping cough is most dangerous for very young babies, prior to the normal age for vaccination; by the time a child is vaccinated it is normally past the age at which the disease could prove fatal. There is thus a case for arguing that young children who are vaccinated before they are old enough to understand the issues are being used for the benefit of others.

The imposition of strict liability on drug manufacturers does not meet the problem because it is not clear that the product is defective. . . . However, the political pressure on this issue was so great that the Government felt forced to announce some concession even before the [Pearson] Commission reported, and it promised a lump sum payment . . . to any child who could be shown to have suffered severe injury as a result of a vaccination against any one of a large number of ailments. . . .

Why should children disabled in this particular way be treated so generously in a financial sense, as compared with other disabled children? The OPCS Disability Survey estimated that there were some 136,000 children under 16 in the four most serious disability categories; and the Pearson Commission estimated that 90% of severely disabled children were suffering from congenital defects. Why does a very small number of vaccine-disabled children have a better claim to financial support than other disabled children? It appears that in this case, as in some others, preferential treatment for a small group was the result of a well conducted political campaign which played on public sympathy for particularly heart-rending cases.

8. PHARMACOGENETICS

Before we leave the regulation of medicines, it is worth highlighting a new development which has the potential to transform the way in which medicines are prescribed. Currently drugs are developed and prescribed for the whole population, even though we know that patients respond to drugs in different ways. A medicine which is effective for some patients may not work for others. Treatments for conditions such as diabetes, depression and asthma may be effective in only 60 per cent of patients, and for some treatments for cancer, the figure is as low as 25 per cent.[124] In addition, some patients will suffer adverse reactions, and others may need a higher or lower dose than

---

[123] Peter Cane, *Atiyah's Accidents Compensation and the Law* (6th edn Butterworths London 1999) 89–90.
[124] Nuffield Council on Bioethics, *Pharmacogenetics: Ethical Issues* (Nuffield Council on Bioethics London 2003) 18.

normal. This means that doctors often have to engage in a 'trial and error' process, until a medication programme which works effectively for the individual patient is discovered. The delays this causes are particularly significant in relation to antidepressants, which often have to be taken for up to six weeks before any therapeutic effect becomes noticeable. The 'trial and error' approach to the prescription of antidepressants may then mean that patients spend many months in a depressed state waiting to find a medicine that will relieve their symptoms. Obviously, if it were possible for doctors to know in advance whether or not a medicine would be likely to suit a particular patient, it would be possible to ensure that patients receive effective medication immediately, and do not undergo useless or dangerous treatment.

Because part of this variation in response to drugs is thought to be due to genetic differences which affect the way in which drugs are absorbed and metabolized, genetic testing is now seen as a route towards what is often referred to as 'pharmacogenetics'. Prescribing would be preceded by a genetic test, which would ideally reveal whether the drug would be likely to work, what dose would be appropriate, and whether the patient would be likely to suffer any adverse reactions. In practice, pharmacogenetics would be likely to identify genotype *groups* for whom particular medicines would be effective, or for whom they pose unacceptable risks of adverse side effects.

In their report into the ethical issues raised by pharmacogenetics, the Nuffield Council on Bioethics suggested that in the future the MHRA might be likely to require the use of a pharmacogenetic test as a condition of issuing a licence for a medicine's use.[125] Drugs which have been withdrawn from circulation because of adverse reactions might be reinstated for use only in population subgroups for whom they may be effective without posing a risk of unacceptable side effects. As well as improving patient care, reducing prescribing errors has the potential to save NHS resources. Pharmacogenetics could also transform the clinical trial process, since participants could be selected for whom the drug would be likely to be both safe and effective. Indeed it has been estimated that within five years, at least 50 per cent of clinical trials will be preceded by the genetic testing of participants.[126]

Nevertheless there are a number of problems associated with pharmacogenetics. First, if clinical trials were redesigned so that a drug was only tested on a genetically selected subgroup, there could be no guarantee that it would be safe for a patient with a different genotype. Second, as OP Corrigan points out in the next extract, although genes undoubtedly affect the metabolism of medicines, other factors—such as the patient's age, sex, diet or exposure to other drugs—will also have an impact. Genetic tests alone cannot establish exactly what medicine will work effectively, in what dose, and with what side effects, leading Corrigan to argue that more effort should be put into identifying non-genetic reasons for variable responses to medicines.

OP Corrigan[127]

[T]he likelihood that pharmacogenetics can make a substantial impact on the reduction of the incidence of serious adverse drug reactions is also highly debatable. The [Nuffield] report accepts

---

[125] Ibid, xvi.   [126] Ibid, 22.
[127] 'Pharmacogenetics, ethical issues: review of the Nuffield Council on Bioethics Report' (2005) 31 Journal of Medical Ethics, 144–8.

the premise that pharmacogenetics will be an effective mechanism for reducing the incidence of adverse drug reactions, a claim about benefit that has underpinned much of the ethical impetus for pharmacogenetics research. Although the report acknowledges that ADRs can be caused by various factors other than genetic variation, it fails to mention the importance of other variables such as age or sex, to name only two. A recent study of ADRs in the elderly has shown that serious ADRs are predictable, and that more than two thirds of ADRs are therefore preventable. In other words, the problem of ADRs could be radically reduced if other non-genetic based prescribing interventions were adopted.

Thirdly, the information tests which might reveal whether a drug would be likely to work for a particular patient will rarely come in the form of a 'yes/no' answer, but rather are more likely to suggest the *probability* of success and safety. And this means it will be necessary to decide what probability of effectiveness justifies treatment. If a genetic test reveals that the only available treatment for a patient's condition has a 30 per cent chance of working, does this justify prescribing it? And should the choice lie with the patient or the doctor?

Fourthly, pharmacogenetics will involve a massive expansion of genetic testing, which will raise important questions about confidentiality, discrimination, and the patients right 'not to know' information which is inadvertently discovered during testing. These issues were considered in detail in Chapter 6.

Fifthly, the ability to target drugs more effectively will not necessarily simply reduce NHS expenditure on drugs. Rather, if there is a dramatic reduction in the quantity of drugs prescribed, pharmaceutical companies will face a correspondingly massive reduction in their profits, unless, as seems likely, they respond by increasing the price of drugs in order to cover both the reduction in demand, and the costs associated with developing these new pharmacogenetic tests. If the cost of medicines rises, there would not necessarily be any net reduction in prescribing costs.

Sixthly, if pharmacogenetics reveals that a particular drug is only likely to be effective in a very small proportion of patients, then there may be little incentive for pharmaceutical companies to invest resources in developing it. Instead, drug companies might concentrate their research and development on drugs which will work for the majority of patients, leaving others with unusual diseases or unusual genetic reactions—which incidentally might correspond with membership of minority ethnic groups—with no effective treatment.

Finally, as Johannes Van Delden et al. point out in the next extract, there is of course the danger that genetic tests will reveal that there is no effective treatment for a particular patient. Being identified as hard, or even impossible to treat may have devastating implications for patients. Obtaining health insurance, for example, would prove very difficult for such individuals. This in turn, as Van Delden et al. suggest, might prompt individuals to refuse genetic testing, with the result that the doctor cannot know whether the patient is in the subgroup for whom a medicine is unsuitable or dangerous. By exposing the patient to the possibility of a serious adverse reaction, would the doctor be in breach of her duty of care, or should the patient herself be considered responsible for her resulting injuries?

Johannes Van Delden, Ineke Bolt, Annemarie Kalis, Jeroen Derijks and Hubert Leufkens[128]

The first problem that might occur in genotyping is that by testing the patient it might be revealed that the patient is a non-responder for all available drug options. The patient turns out to be an 'orphan' for whom genotyping provided no advantage, but only the knowledge that he probably cannot be treated. . . . [S]omeone might turn out to be a non-responder for multiple drugs, which might give him the label 'hard to treat'. Therefore, some patients might not want to be tested for pharmacogenetic profiles, as they do not want to gain knowledge that might put them in a disadvantageous position.

This leads to the question of what a physician should do if a patient refuses to be genotyped. He could give the patient the 'bulk drug', but by doing so he in fact gives the patient a suboptimal treatment. Besides, he knowingly increases the risk of potentially dangerous side-effects by not testing the patient. If such side effects emerge, who can then be considered to be responsible for them, the physician or the patient?

The Nuffield Council on Bioethics' report considered this problem, and argued that the way in which pharmacogenetics are presented to the public will inevitably affect people's willingness to undergo pre-treatment genetic testing.

Nuffield Council on Bioethics[129]

A question arises regarding whether patients will have the option to receive treatment without taking an associated test. It cannot be assumed that patients will be keen to take a pharmacogenetic test, even if it will improve the likelihood of their receiving a safe and effective treatment. Such an aversion may be irrational, but may be based on a legitimate fear that information produced by the test could make it difficult to obtain insurance, or that it might indirectly reveal information about a medical condition which cannot be effectively treated.

The situation regarding patient choice is complicated. Health professionals are able to prescribe medicines to patients who do not have the characteristics for which the medicine was licensed, but they will be held accountable for problems that arise as a result. This is called 'off-label' prescribing. Where a pharmacogenetic test is part of the licence conditions of a medicine, it is unlikely that a health professional would wish to prescribe the medicine without the test, particularly if this would mean putting the patient at risk of an adverse reaction, or subjecting the patient to a medicine that might have very little beneficial effect. However, where tests are not part of the licence conditions, the information they provide may be just one factor among many in deciding whether to prescribe a medicine. If an individual has a low likelihood of response, but there are no alternative treatments and the adverse events associated with the medicine are not substantial, the medicine might be prescribed without making use of the test. . . .

The public perceptions of pharmacogenetics are important in part because resistance to pharmacogenetic testing could lead to patients not receiving the best care. Patients might not be given the most beneficial medicines if these may only be prescribed with a genetic test they refuse to take. Even more serious is the possibility that a medicine may be administered without an associated pharmacogenetic test, and result in a serious, predictable and avoidable adverse reaction. We think it likely that the acceptance of pharmacogenetics will depend not only on which tests are introduced and for which purposes they are used, but also on the way they are presented to the public at large and to individual patients.

---

[128] 'Tailor-Made Pharmacotherapy: Future Developments and Ethical Challenges in the Field of Pharmacogenomics' (2004) 18 Bioethics 303–21, 314–15.

[129] Nuffield Council on Bioethics, *Pharmacogenetics: Ethical Issues* (Nuffield Council on Bioethics London 2003) xxii, 7.

9. CONCLUSION

The regulation of medicines, once they are ready to be marketed, cannot be viewed in isolation from the rules which govern the stages before medicines can be licensed for general use. It is worth noting that when we considered the regulation of clinical research in the previous chapter, it was similarly apparent that European law is playing an increasingly dominant role. This is interesting, because in many of the other areas of medical law that we consider in this book, aside from the impact of the incorporation of the European Convention on Human Rights via the Human Rights Act, European law is of comparatively little importance. In relation to issues such as abortion, euthanasia, organ transplantation, and stem cell research, for example, there are vast differences between the laws in different European countries. And even when common principles, such as the European Convention on Human Rights apply, Member States often have a wide margin of appreciation in their interpretation.

When regulating the pharmaceutical industry and access to medicines, however, there is increasing European harmonization. Why is this? One obvious answer is that here we have been concerned with the regulation of a *market*, rather than with *sensitive ethical issues*. Protecting consumers and promoting economic growth are familiar aims for European regulation, whereas balancing the rights and wrongs of complex ethical dilemmas has usually been left to individual nation states.

In the next few years, it will be interesting to see whether the courts are faced with more claims under the Consumer Protection Act 1987. Burton J's thoughtful, albeit idiosyncratic, decision surprised many commentators, and its implications are currently uncertain. In particular, it is not clear whether Burton J's claimant-friendly reading of both the definition of defectiveness, and the development risks defence, might encourage more litigation.

It will also be important to keep track of two other new important developments in this area. First, how will the NHS (and NICE) react to the increasing availability of so-called 'lifestyle' or enhancement drugs? Will these be available on the NHS, or by private prescription, or not at all? Would there be anything 'wrong' with students taking memory-enhancing drugs, which were originally designed for Alzheimer's patients? Should such drugs be available to anyone who wants them, provided that they are willing to pay? Secondly, pharmacogenetics may have a number of important implications. Will personalized medicine improve patient care, or might it lead to the categorization of both patients and diseases, so that pharmaceutical companies can concentrate their investment into both the most profitable patient-types and the most common diseases, leaving others without effective care?

10. FURTHER READING

Dawson, Angus, 'Vaccination and the Prevention Problem' (2004) 18 Bioethics 515–30.

Elliott, Carl, *Better than Well: American Medicine meets the American Dream* (Norton New York 2003).

Ferguson, Pamela, *Drug Injuries and the Pursuit of Compensation* (Sweet & Maxwell London 1996).

Goldberg, Richard, 'Paying for Bad Blood: Strict Product Liability after the Hepatitis C Litigation' (2002) 10 Medical Law Review 165–200.

Hervey, Tamara and McHale, Jean, *Health Law and the European Union* (CUP Cambridge 2004) ch 8.

Howells, Geraint (ed), *Product Liability, Insurance and the Pharmaceutical Industry: An Anglo-American Comparison* (MUP Manchester 1990).

Howells, Geraint and Mildred, Mark, 'Infected Blood: Defect and Discoverability. A First Exposition of the EC Product Liability Directive' (2002) 65 Modern Law Review 95–106.

Newdick, Christopher, 'Strict Liability for Defective Drugs in the Pharmaceutical Industry' (1985) 101 Law Quarterly Review 405–31.

Nuffield Council on Bioethics, *Pharmacogenetics: Ethical Issues* (Nuffield Council on Bioethics London 2003).

Prayle, David and Brazier, Margaret, 'Supply of medicines: paternalism, autonomy and reality' (1998) 24 Journal of Medical Ethics 93–8.

Sykes, Richard, *New Medicines, The Practice of Medicine, and Public Policy* (Nuffield Trust London 2000).

Teff, Harvey, 'Regulation under the Medicines Act 1968: A continuing prescription for health' (1984) 47 Modern Law Review 303–23.

10

ABORTION

1. CENTRAL ISSUES

1. Underlying the question of abortion's legality are two issues. First, what is the fetus's moral status? And, secondly, should a pregnant woman's right to autonomy include the right to terminate an unwanted pregnancy?

2. The principal purpose of the Abortion Act 1967 was to enable doctors to act lawfully by terminating their patients' unwanted pregnancies. As a result, the Act entrusts the medical profession with considerable discretion over abortion decision-making.

3. The most commonly used 'ground' for abortion is that continuing the pregnancy poses a greater risk to the woman's physical or mental health than termination. This is subject to a twenty-four week time limit. Improvements both in fetal imaging techniques and in neonatal survival rates are placing increasing pressure on the twenty-four week time limit.

4. Abortion on the grounds of serious fetal abnormality is lawful until birth. Doctors again have considerable discretion in determining what counts as a sufficiently serious handicap.

2. INTRODUCTION

In this chapter we consider one of the most contentious medical procedures: the termination of pregnancy. We begin with a necessarily brief survey of the ongoing debate over abortion's moral legitimacy. Should pregnant women have the right to terminate their unwanted pregnancies, or do fetuses have a right to life which should 'trump' women's reproductive freedom? As will be obvious, there is never likely to be agreement on the morality of abortion. Nevertheless, despite the absence of anything remotely resembling consensus, abortion has been legal in (most of) the UK for almost 40 years. We then examine the current legal position, and consider how the Abortion Act 1967, as amended, works in practice. Obviously the conflict between the interests of the fetus and those of the pregnant woman could be framed in terms of 'rights', and so we also consider the impact of the Human Rights Act 1998.

In certain circumstances, the legality of abortion has proved to be especially controversial, and we investigate these cases separately. In particular, in recent years there has been considerable interest, first, in whether abortion on the grounds of fetal abnormality amounts to a type of eugenics, and secondly, in whether technological developments which enable very premature babies to survive mean that we should rethink the time limits within which abortion is legal. Finally, we highlight some differences between the regulation of abortion in the UK and in other countries.

Before I begin, a brief note about terminology: in this chapter, I will not describe pregnant women as 'mothers', and nor will I use the term 'unborn child' to refer to a fetus. This is because, until birth, there is no mother and there is no child. Motherhood and childhood only begin after a child has been born. In the context of abortion, the fetus may never become a child and the pregnant woman may not become a mother.

3. THE ETHICS OF ABORTION

In what circumstances, if any, is it legitimate for a woman to terminate an unwanted pregnancy? Instinctive responses to this question will lie somewhere upon a spectrum which has 'never' at one end, and 'whenever she likes' at the other, with most people falling somewhere in between, believing that abortion is *sometimes*, but *not always* justifiable. Towards the restrictive end of the spectrum, it might be argued that abortion is legitimate where the woman's life is in danger, or perhaps when she is pregnant as a result of an act of rape and/or incest. At the more permissive end, it might be contended that abortion should be available upon request, at least during the earliest stages of pregnancy.

But while an instinctive response to the legitimacy of abortion may be a useful starting point for further investigation, as we saw in Chapter 1, the requirement to give reasons, or to justify one's moral views is an important feature of ethical reasoning. Fortunately, in relation to abortion, there is a rich philosophical literature from which to draw. At the risk of drastic over-simplification, three different strands of analysis are worth identifying.

- An emphasis on the moral status of the fetus, and in particular upon its personhood, or potential personhood.
- An emphasis upon the physical invasiveness of pregnancy, and upon the degree of self-sacrifice which would be forced upon women if they were compelled to continue an unwanted pregnancy.
- A compromise position in which abortion is permitted, but only in certain restricted circumstances which are designed to offer the fetus some protection.

Let us take each of these positions in turn.

(a) THE MORAL STATUS OF THE FETUS

First, opponents of abortion, like John Finnis, have tended to concentrate on the fetus's moral status, arguing that its personhood, or alternatively its future or potential personhood, should lead us to be extremely reluctant to tolerate its destruction.

John Finnis[1]
I have been assuming that the unborn child is, from conception, a person and hence is not to be

---

[1] 'The Rights and Wrongs of Abortion: A Reply to Judith Thomson' (1973) 2 Philosophy and Public Affairs, 117–45.

discriminated against on account of age, appearance or other such factors insofar as such factors are reasonably considered irrelevant where respect for basic human values is in question. [Judith Jarvis] Thomson argues against this assumption, but not, as I think, well. She thinks . . . that the argument in favor of treating a newly conceived child as a person is merely a 'slippery slope' argument, rather like (I suppose) saying that one should call all men bearded because there is no line one can confidently draw between beard and clean shavenness. . . . It is discouraging to see her relying so heavily and uncritically on all this hoary muddle. . . .

[At conception] two sex cells, each with only twenty-three chromosomes, unite and more or less immediately fuse to become a new cell with forty-six chromosomes providing a unique genetic constitution . . . which thenceforth throughout its life, however long, will substantially determine the new individual's makeup. This new cell is the first stage in a dynamic integrated system that has nothing much in common with the individual male and female sex cells, save that it sprang from a pair of them and will in time produce new sets of them. To say that *this* is when a person's life began is not to work backwards from maturity, sophistically asking at each point 'How can one draw the line *here*?' Rather it is to point to a perfectly clear-cut beginning to which each one of us can look back . . . Judith Thomson thinks she began to acquire human characteristics' 'by the tenth week' (when fingers, toes etc. became visible). I cannot think why she overlooks the most radically and distinctively human characteristic of all—the fact that she was conceived of human parents.

This sort of argument has been disputed by others, such as Mary Ann Warren, who contend that while the fetus may be human, it is not yet a person, and that its potential to become a person cannot justify giving it primacy over the rights of an actual person, namely the pregnant woman.

Mary Ann Warren[2]

What characteristics entitle an entity to be considered a person? . . . I suggest that the traits which are most central to the concept of personhood . . ., are, very roughly, the following:

   (1) Consciousness . . ., and in particular the capacity to feel pain.

   (2) Reasoning (the *developed* capacity to solve new and relatively complex problems);

   (3) Self-motivated activity . . .

   (4) The capacity to communicate . . .

   (5) The presence of self-concepts, and self-awareness . . .

We needn't suppose that an entity must have *all* these attributes to be properly considered a person . . . Neither do we need to insist that any one of these criteria is necessary for personhood . . .

All we need to claim, to demonstrate that a fetus is not a person, is that any being which satisfies *none* of (1)–(5) is certainly not a person. I consider this claim to be so obvious that I think anyone who denied it, and claimed that a being which satisfied none of (1)–(5) was a person all the same, would thereby demonstrate that he had no notion at all of what a person is—perhaps because he had confused the concept of personhood with that of genetic humanity. . . .

[I]f (1)–(5) are indeed the primary criteria of personhood, then it is clear that genetic humanity is neither necessary or sufficient for establishing that an entity is a person . . . [A] fetus is a

---

[2] 'On the Moral and Legal Status of Abortion' (1973) 1 The Monist 43–61.

human being which is not yet a person, and which therefore cannot coherently be said to have full moral rights. . . .

We have seen that a fetus does not resemble a person in any way which can support the claim that it has even some of the same rights. But what about its *potential*, the fact that if nurtured and allowed to develop naturally it will probably become a person? . . . It is hard to deny that the fact that an entity is a potential person is a strong prima facie reason for not destroying it; but we need not conclude from this that a potential person has a right to life . . . But even if a potential person does have some prima facie right to life, such a right could not possibly outweigh the right of a woman to obtain an abortion, since the rights of any actual person invariably outweigh those of any potential person, whenever the two conflict.

Warren's criteria for personhood are themselves controversial. Philip Abbott, for example, points out that the test for 'personhood' advocated by philosophers such as Warren would exclude not only fetuses, but also a significant proportion of children and incapacitated adults.

Philip Abbott[3]

What makes one a person (or human in the moral sense)? Warren suggests five 'traits' . . . Note how deftly Warren plies her trade. A fetus *might* be able to feel pain, but surely he or she is unable to reason, especially with *developed* capacity. What is shocking about this criterion (2) is that a two-year old may fail to meet it. What this means . . ., and let us be direct about this, is that we must restrain our emotions and come to regard an infant as not a person at all but a mere clump of genetic humanity. Are not then the comatose patient, the schizophrenic, the catatonic, the unaided mute, the paraplegic in danger of slipping into that awful category 'genetic human'.

We must ask what the consequences are of this collapsing humanity, this clarification of the 'confusion' over the genetic and the moral senses of humanity . . . There are very few general laws of social science, but we can offer one that has a deserved claim: *the restriction of the concept of humanity in any sphere never enhances a respect for human life*. It did not enhance the rights of slaves, prisoners of war, criminals, traitors, women, children, Jews, blacks, heretics, workers, capitalists, Slavs, Gypsies. The restriction of the concept of personhood in regard to the fetus will not do so either. . . .

[Warren] approached the question 'what is human?' in terms of 'what characteristics must an entity have in order to claim rights?' . . . To be human in any moral sense is to have the ability to be a holder of rights. To be a holder of rights one must pass a test of independence in order to establish that one is in a position to claim those rights.

While in legal terms at least, it is clear that a person with rights exists after birth but not before, in the next extract, Ranaan Gillon argues that it is not evident that a newborn baby is a morally different entity to a fetus immediately prior to birth.

Raanan Gillon[4]

UK law, like that of many other jurisdictions, is explicit that a fetus is not legally speaking a person and does not have the legal rights of persons including the right to life enjoyed by (natural) persons, whereas a born child is a person and does have a right to life. While in practical terms the simple criterion of birth is generally easy to apply and corresponds to a stage when what was

---

[3] 'Philosophers and the Abortion Question' (1978) 6 Political Theory 313–35.
[4] 'Is there a "new ethics of abortion"?' (2001) 26 suppl II Journal of Medical Ethics ii5–ii9, ii8.

previously hidden and private inside another human being is now a revealed, public, and clearly separate social entity, as a criterion for moral differentiation of a human being's intrinsic moral status it seems highly implausible. Essentially it is a criterion of what might be dubbed biological geography, asserting that a human being does not have a right to life if it lies north of a vaginal introitus but has a right to life once it has passed south and has (entirely) emerged from the vagina. What morally relevant changes can there have been in the fetus in its passage from inside to outside its mother's body to underpin such a momentous change in its intrinsic moral status?

(b) THE PREGNANT WOMAN'S RIGHT TO SELF-DETERMINATION

A second line of argument (exemplified below by Judith Jarvis Thomson and Eileen McDonagh) analyses abortion from the perspective of the pregnant woman, pointing out the physical invasiveness of carrying a pregnancy to term, and arguing that restrictions on women's access to abortion effectively compel them to exercise a wholly unprecedented degree of self-sacrifice. Margaret Olivia Little explains the starting point for this argument particularly well:

To be pregnant is to be *inhabited*. It is to be *occupied*. It is to be in a state of physical intimacy of a particularly thorough-going nature. The fetus intrudes on the body massively; whatever medical risks one faces or avoids, the brute fact remains that the fetus shifts and alters the very physical boundaries of the woman's self.[5]

Of course, the fetus is not a malicious intruder: it is occupying the woman's body through no fault of its own. However, the claim being made on this line of analysis is that the state does not have the right to force the woman to continue in this relationship of unparalleled intimacy without her consent. Margaret Olivia Little draws an analogy with sexual intimacy which may be a source of pleasure with consent, but a profound violation without it.[6]

Eileen L McDonagh[7]
A woman who seeks an abortion . . . is explicitly saying 'no' to pregnancy; she does not consent to the condition in her body resulting from a fertilized ovum and later a fetus. The key issue in the abortion debate, therefore, is not merely a woman's right to exercise her right of choice as an isolated individual, but rather her right to consent to what a separate entity, the fetus, does to her when pregnancy results from its presence and implantation in her uterus . . .

[T]he fetus harms a woman not only in medically abnormal pregnancies threatening her health or life, but in all pregnancies, including medically normal ones, if a woman does not consent to the condition of pregnancy. Pregnancy is a condition constituting massive transformations of a woman's body and liberty, and, thus, constitutes serious harm without her consent.

The massive effects of a fetus on a woman's body correspond to the level of injury justifying the use of deadly force, if a woman does not consent to those effects. If a born person were to affect another born person's body in even a fraction of the ways a fetus affects a woman's body, the

---

[5] 'Abortion, Intimacy, and the Duty to Gestate' (1999) 2 Ethical Theory and Moral Practice 295–312.
[6] Ibid.
[7] 'My Body, My Consent: Securing the Constitutional Right to Abortion Funding' (1999) 62 Albany Law Review 1057.

magnitude of the injury would be easy to recognize. Imagine a born person who injected into another's body, without consent, hormones 400 times their normal level, or someone who, without consent, took over the blood system of another to meet her own personal use, or someone who, without consent, grew a new organ in that person's body. . . .

Some may object that if a woman consents to sexual intercourse (action X), then by extension she has consented to pregnancy (condition Y) as a foreseeable consequence of sexual intercourse. However . . . [m]oral responsibility for a condition and consent to a condition must be distinguished. A person who consents to an action that has the foreseeable risk of a subsequent condition may be held morally responsible for that condition, should it occur, but that person is not presumed by law to have consented to the condition itself. . . . A woman who voluntarily engages in sexual intercourse (action X), may be partially morally responsible for the condition of pregnancy (condition Y), should it occur, but it does not follow that she is legally required to consent to that condition. . . .

Generally, when a person creates a risk, it does not follow that the person consents to injuries occurring subsequent to the risk. Thus, if a person consensually creates a risk that she will be mugged by walking down an alley alone, late at night, responsibility for causing the risk does not constitute consent to the injury of mugging that may be subsequent to that risk . . . In addition, even if a woman is contributorily negligent in creating the risk that a fetus will harm her, she nevertheless retains the right to self-defense to stop the fetus from harming her.

Some may object that the fetus has no intention of affecting a woman's body and no ability to control its effects upon her; therefore, some argue that the fetus is 'innocent.' Because of this innocence, they argue, the fetus cannot be responsible for injuring a woman. . . . Yet even if a party is innocent of affecting another's body, those effects can nevertheless constitute injury. The law recognizes that both involuntary and voluntary acts can cause harm and injury to other people, and that the nonvoluntary characteristic of action does not give the perpetrator of that action any right to inflict harm or injury. To advance women's rights . . . requires identifying sources of harm characteristically relegated to scenes that are 'private, consensual, and naturalized.' In the last quarter century, women have succeeded in gaining recognition that nonconsensual sexual relations, including those in marriage, constitute serious harm and warrant state assistance for terminating that harm. Jurisprudential resources may now extend those guarantees to pregnancy itself. As argued here, a woman's consent to sexual intercourse can be disentangled from her right to consent to pregnancy; pregnancy need not be depicted as a naturalized condition precluding a woman from calling upon the state to protect her bodily integrity and liberty from nonconsensual effects resulting from the fetus . . .

The woman's right to an abortion is not, on this view, necessarily dependent upon proving that the fetus is not a person. Rather, as Judith Jarvis Thomson argues in the next extract, even if the fetus *is* a person, it might be argued that pregnant women have the right to use self-defence in order to protect themselves from the physical invasion of an unwanted pregnancy.

Judith Jarvis Thomson[8]

I propose, then, that we grant that the foetus is a person from the moment of conception. How does the argument go from here? Something like this, I take it. Every person has a right to life. So the foetus has a right to life. No doubt the mother has a right to decide what shall happen in and to her body; everyone would grant that. But surely a person's right to life is stronger and more stringent

---

[8] 'A Defence of Abortion' (1971) 1 Philosophy and Public Affairs 47.

than the mother's right to decide what happens in and to her body, and so outweighs it. So the foetus may not be killed; an abortion may not be performed.

It sounds plausible. But now let me ask you to imagine this. You wake up in the morning and find yourself back to back in bed with an unconscious violinist. A famous unconscious violinist. He has been found to have a fatal kidney ailment, and the Society of Music Lovers has canvassed all the available medical records and found that you alone have the right blood type to help. They have therefore kidnapped you, and last night the violinist's circulatory system was plugged into yours, so that your kidneys can be used to extract poisons from his blood as well as your own. The director of the hospital now tells you, 'Look, we're sorry the Society of Music Lovers did this to you—we would never have permitted it if we had known. But still, they did it, and the violinist is now plugged into you. To unplug you would be to kill him. But never mind, its only for nine months. By then he will have recovered from his ailment, and can safely be unplugged from you.' Is it morally incumbent on you to accede to this situation? No doubt it would be very nice of you if you did, a great kindness. But do you *have* to accede to it? What if it were not nine months, but nine years? Or longer still? What if the director of the hospital says, 'Tough luck, I agree, but you've now got to stay in bed, with the violinist plugged into you, for the rest of your life. Because remember this. All persons have a right to life, and violinists are persons. Granted you have a right to decide what happens in and to your body, but a person's right to life outweighs your right to decide what happens in and to your body. So you cannot ever be unplugged from him.' I imagine you would regard this as outrageous, which suggests that something really is wrong with that plausible-sounding argument I mentioned a moment ago.

In this case, of course, you were kidnapped; you didn't volunteer for the operation that plugged the violinist into your kidneys. Can those who oppose abortion on the ground I mentioned make an exception for a pregnancy due to rape? Certainly. They can say that persons have a right to life only if they didn't come into existence because of rape; or they can say that all persons have a right to life, but that some have less of a right to life than others, in particular, that those who came into existence because of rape have less. But these statements have a rather unpleasant sound. Surely the question of whether you have a right to life at all, or how much of it you have, shouldn't turn on the question of whether or not you are the product of a rape.

A related argument draws attention to the common assumption that deciding to have an abortion is a more difficult and serious moral choice than deciding to carry a pregnancy to term, even though motherhood undoubtedly involves an extraordinarily demanding and long-lasting commitment. Through the presumptions that women seeking abortion need counselling, and conversely, that women who are about to become mothers do not, motherhood is assumed to be an easy and natural choice for all women, whereas, as Reva Siegel explains, rejecting motherhood is sometimes seen as evidence of 'unseemly egoism'.

Reva Siegel[9]

Legislators may condemn abortion because they assume that any pregnant woman who does not wish to be pregnant has committed some sexual indiscretion properly punishable by compelling pregnancy itself. Popular support for excusing women who are victims of rape or incest from the proscriptions of criminal abortion laws demonstrates that attitudes about abortion do indeed rest on normative judgments about women's sexual conduct. . . .

---

[9] 'Reasoning from the body: A historical perspective on abortion regulation and questions of equal protection' (1992) Stanford Law Review 261.

If legislators assume that women are 'child-rearers,' they will take for granted the work women give to motherhood and ignore what it takes from them, and so will view women's efforts to avoid some two decades of life-consuming work as an act of casual expedience or unseemly egoism. Thus, they will condemn women for seeking abortion 'on demand,' or as a mere 'convenience,' judging women to be unnaturally egocentric because they do not give their lives over to the work of bearing and nurturing children—that is, because they fail to act like mothers, like normal women should.

But the idea that women always have the moral right to decide for themselves whether they want to become a mother is disputed by Rosalind Hursthouse, who contends that motherhood is intrinsically good. Hursthouse analyses abortion from the perspective of 'virtue ethics' (considered in Chapter 1, p. 20), and argues that a woman who rejects motherhood without a compelling or 'virtuous' reason for doing so, is acting wrongly.

Rosalind Hursthouse[10]

The fact that the premature termination of a pregnancy is, in some sense, the cutting off of a new human life, connects with all our thoughts about human life and death, parenthood and family relationship, must make it a serious matter. To disregard this fact about it, to think of abortion as nothing but the killing of something that does not matter, or as nothing but the exercise of some right or some rights one has, or as the incidental means to some desirable state of affairs, is to do something callous and light-minded, the sort of thing that no virtuous and wise person would do . . .

The familiar facts support the view that parenthood in general, and motherhood and childbearing in particular, are intrinsically worthwhile, are among the things that can be correctly thought to be partially constitutive of a flourishing human life. If this is right, then a woman who opts for not being a mother (at all, or again, or now) by opting for abortion may thereby be manifesting a flawed grasp of what her life should be, and be about—a grasp that is childish, or grossly materialistic, or shortsighted, or shallow.

I say '*may* thereby': this *need* not be so. Consider, for instance, a woman who has already had several children and fears that to have another will seriously affect her capacity to be a good mother to the ones she has—she does not show a lack of appreciation of the intrinsic value of being a parent by opting for abortion. Nor does a woman who has been a good mother and is approaching the age at which she may be looking forward to being a good grandmother. Nor does a woman who discovers that her pregnancy may well kill her, and opts for abortion and adoption. Nor, necessarily, does a woman who has decided to lead a life centred around some other worthwhile activity or activities with which motherhood would compete . . .

But some women who choose abortion rather than have their first child, and some men who encourage their partners to choose abortion, are not avoiding parenthood for the sake of other worthwhile pursuits, but for the worthless one of 'having a good time', or for the pursuit of some false vision of the ideals of freedom or self-realisation.

[10] 'Virtue Theory and Abortion' in Daniel Statman (ed), *Virtue Ethics* (Edinburgh University Press Edinburgh 1997) 227–44.

(c) A COMPROMISE POSITION?

Thirdly, a middle ground exists which acknowledges both that the fetus's potential personhood is a good reason to afford it some protection, and that the pregnant woman has a legitimate interest in self-determination. This 'third way' would protect the woman's right to terminate her pregnancy, but only in certain circumstances. This is consistent with almost every country's regulation of abortion: abortion is permitted within parameters—such as time limits—which are supposed to indicate the seriousness of fetal destruction. Ronald Dworkin, for example, argues that most people share the belief that all human life is *intrinsically* valuable, such that its destruction is always a very bad thing. However, it does not follow from this that all forms of human life should have rights. One can believe that a painting by Vermeer is intrinsically valuable, and that it would be a bad thing for it to be destroyed, but this does not mean that the painting has a *right* not to be destroyed. Dworkin's argument is that most people share a deep belief in the sanctity of human life, and therefore always regard abortion as a morally serious matter. Disagreement over abortion, according to Dworkin, results from people's different ideas about what is required by respect for human life. When the human fetus's interest in continued survival conflicts with the human pregnant woman's interest in making important decisions about her body and her life, respect for human life's intrinsic value does not tell us which should take priority.

Ronald Dworkin[11]

[D]iscussions of abortion almost all presume that people disagree about abortion because they disagree about whether a fetus is a person with a right to life from the moment of its conception, or becomes a person at some point in pregnancy, or does not become one until birth. And about whether, if a fetus is a person, its right to life must yield in the fact of some stronger right held by pregnant women. . . .

[T]his account of the abortion debate, in spite of its great popularity, is fatally misleading. . . . The detailed structure of most conservative opinion about abortion is actually inconsistent with the assumption that the fetus has rights from the moment of conception, and the detailed structure of most liberal opinion cannot be explained only on the supposition that it does not . . .

[E]ven those conservatives who believe that the law should prohibit abortion recognize some exceptions. It is a very common view, for example, that abortion should be permitted when necessary to save the mother's life. Yet this exception is . . . inconsistent with any belief that a fetus is a person with a right to live. Some people say that in this case a mother is justified in aborting a fetus as a matter of self-defense; but any safe abortion is carried out by someone else—a doctor—and very few people believe that it is morally justifiable for a third party, even a doctor, to kill one innocent person to save another.

Abortion conservatives often allow further exceptions. Some of them believe that abortion is morally permissible . . . when pregnancy is the result of rape or incest. The more such exceptions are allowed, the clearer it becomes that conservative opposition to abortion does not presume that the fetus is a person with a right to life. It would be contradictory to insist that a fetus has a right to life . . . that ceases to exist when the pregnancy is the result of a sexual crime of which the fetus is, of course, wholly innocent.

---

[11] *Life's Dominion* (HarperCollins London) 1993.

On the other side, a parallel story emerges. . . . A paradigm liberal position on abortion has four parts. First, it rejects the extreme opinion that abortion is morally unproblematic, and insists, on the contrary, that abortion is always a grave moral decision . . . Second, abortion is nevertheless morally justified for a variety of serious reasons . . . Third, a woman's concern for her own interests is considered an adequate justification for abortion if the consequences of childbirth would be permanent and grave for her or her family's life. . . . The fourth component in the liberal view is the political opinion . . . that at least until late in pregnancy, . . . the state has no business intervening even to prevent morally impermissible abortions, because the question of whether an abortion is justifiable is, ultimately, for the woman who carries the fetus to decide. . . .

The truth is that liberal opinion, like the conservative view, presupposes that human life itself has intrinsic moral significance, so that it is in principle wrong to terminate a life even when no one's interests are at stake.

4. THE LAW

(a) THE CRIMINAL LAW

Until 1803, abortion was governed by the common law. It was a criminal offence only after 'quickening' (the moment when the woman can first feel the fetus moving inside her, which is normally about 16–18 weeks into the pregnancy).

Bracton[12]
If one strikes a pregnant woman or gives her poison in order to procure an abortion, if the foetus is already formed or quickened, especially if it is, he commits homicide.

Coke[13]
If a woman be quick with childe, and by a potion or otherwise killeth it in her wombe; or if a man beat here, whereby the child dieth in her body, and she is delivered of a dead child, this is a great misprision, and no murder.

Blackstone[14]
Life . . . begins in contemplation of law as soon as an infant is able to stir in the mother's womb. For if a woman is quick with child, and by a potion, or otherwise, killeth it in her womb; or if any one beat her, whereby the child dieth in her body, and she is delivered of a dead child; this, though not murder, was by the ancient law homicide or manslaughter. But at present it is not looked upon in quite so atrocious a light, though it remains a very heinous misdemeanor.

Since Lord Ellenborough's Act of 1803, abortion has been regulated by statute. Under the 1803 Act abortion became a felony throughout pregnancy, and the death penalty was introduced for abortion after quickening. Abortion was the subject of a number of statutory reforms during the nineteenth century, such as the abolition of capital punishment in 1837. As a result of increasing medical knowledge, it had become apparent that 'quickening' did not mark a special moment in the development of the growing fetus, and the 1837 Offences Against the Person Act removed the distinction between abortions before and after 'quickening'.

---

[12] *De Legibus et Consuetudinibus Angliae* (On the Laws and Customs of England) thirteenth century.
[13] *Institutes of the Laws of England* seventeenth century.
[14] *Commentaries on the Laws of England*, vol 1 (1765).

It is a nineteenth-century statute which continues to apply to abortion today. Statutory defences do now exist, but under sections 58 and 59 of the Offences Against the Person Act 1861, the maximum sentence for a woman who intentionally procures her own miscarriage is life imprisonment, and anyone who assists her could be imprisoned for up to five years.

Offences Against the Person Act 1861
Section 58
Every woman, being with child, who, with intent to procure her own miscarriage, shall unlawfully administer to herself any poison or other noxious thing, or shall unlawfully use any instrument or other means whatsoever with the like intent, and whosoever, with intent to procure the miscarriage of any woman, whether she be or not with child, shall unlawfully administer to her or cause to be taken by her any poison or other noxious thing, or shall unlawfully use any instrument or other means whatsoever with the like intent, shall be guilty of felony.

Section 59
Whosoever shall unlawfully supply or procure any poison or other noxious thing, or any instrument or thing whatsoever knowing that the same is intended to be unlawfully used or employed with intent to procure the miscarriage of any woman, whether she be or not be with child, shall be guilty of a misdemeanor.

The critical ingredients of the offences under sections 58 and 59 are, first, that someone must *do* something with a poison or instrument or other noxious thing, and, secondly, that they must *intend* to procure a miscarriage. Notice also that the first limb of section 58 applies only to women who are in fact 'with child'. A woman could not be convicted of the full offence under section 58 unless she was actually pregnant. A woman who mistakenly believes that she is pregnant could, nevertheless, be guilty of *conspiring* to procure an abortion, as was the case in *R v Whitchurch*.[15] Other people can be guilty 'whether she be or not with child', provided that they believe her to be pregnant, and intend to cause her to miscarry.

It is also important to note that sections 58 and 59 refer to poison or instruments being used *unlawfully*. On one interpretation, the word 'unlawfully' is wholly redundant here: since the purpose of these sections is to create a criminal offence, it goes without saying that the act described is *unlawful*. But a more plausible explanation is that the offence is only committed where the abortion is carried out *unlawfully*, meaning of course that it might be possible to lawfully procure an abortion. Because it has never been doubted that doctors are entitled to carry out life-saving surgery, even if its consequence will be the termination of pregnancy, it is likely that the word 'unlawfully' is intended to create an exception—akin to the one in the Infant Life Preservation Act 1929—for terminations performed to preserve the pregnant woman's life. This was certainly the interpretation preferred by Macnaghten J in his summing up to the jury in *R v Bourne*. Moreover, he interpreted this exception to justify abortions not only where the pregnant woman was in imminent danger of death, but also where the effect of carrying the pregnancy to term might be to 'make the woman a physical or mental wreck'.

---

[15] (1890) LR 24 QBD 420.

R v Bourne[16]

A fourteen year old girl had become pregnant following a violent rape. With the consent of her parents, Aleck Bourne, obstetrical surgeon at St Mary's Hospital, performed an abortion. Mr. Bourne was charged under s. 58 of the Offences Against the Person Act, 1861, with unlawfully procuring her miscarriage. His defence was that, in the circumstances of the case, the operation was not unlawful, because in his opinion the continuance of the pregnancy would probably cause serious injury to the girl.

Macnaghten J

This is the second case at the present session of this Court where a charge has been preferred of an offence against this section, and I only mention the other case to show you how different the case now before you is from the type of case which usually comes before a criminal court. In that other case a woman without any medical skill or medical qualifications did what is alleged against Mr. Bourne here; she unlawfully used an instrument for the purpose of procuring the miscarriage of a pregnant girl; she did it for money . . . She used her instrument, and, within an interval of time measured not by minutes but by seconds, the victim of her malpractice was dead on the floor.

The case here is very different. A man of the highest skill, openly, in one of our great hospitals, performs the operation. Whether it was legal or illegal you will have to determine, but he performs the operation as an act of charity, without fee or reward, and unquestionably believing that he was doing the right thing, and that he ought, in the performance of his duty as a member of a profession devoted to the alleviation of human suffering, to do it. . . .

[I]n my view the proviso that it is necessary for the Crown to prove that the act was not done in good faith for the purpose only of preserving the life of the mother is in accordance with what has always been the common law of England with regard to the killing of an unborn child. No such proviso is in fact set out in s. 58 of the Offences Against the Person Act, 1861; but the words of that section are that any person who 'unlawfully' uses an instrument with intent to procure miscarriage shall be guilty of felony. In my opinion the word 'unlawfully' is not, in that section, a meaningless word. I think it imports the meaning expressed by the proviso in s. 1, sub-s. 1, of the Infant Life (Preservation) Act, 1929 [that 'no person shall be found guilty of an offence under this section unless it is proved that the act which caused the death of the child was not done in good faith for the purpose only of preserving the life of the mother.'] and that s. 58 of the Offences Against the Person Act, 1861, must be read as if the words making it an offence to use an instrument with intent to procure a miscarriage were qualified by a similar proviso.

What then is the meaning to be given to the words 'for the purpose of preserving the life of the mother' . . . I think those words ought to be construed in a reasonable sense, and, if the doctor is of opinion, on reasonable grounds and with adequate knowledge, that the probable consequence of the continuance of the pregnancy will be to make the woman a physical or mental wreck, the jury are quite entitled to take the view that the doctor who, under those circumstances and in that honest belief, operates, is operating for the purpose of preserving the life of the mother. . . .

It is an observation that appeals to one's common sense that it must be injurious to a girl that she should go through the state of pregnancy and finally of labour when she is of tender years. Then, too, you must consider the evidence about the effect of rape, especially on a child, as this girl was . . . You are the judges of the facts and it is for you to say what weight should be given to the testimony of the witnesses; but no doubt you will think it is only common sense that a girl who for nine months has to carry in her body the reminder of the dreadful scene and then go through the pangs of childbirth must suffer great mental anguish, unless indeed she be feeble-minded or

16 [1939] 1 KB 697.

belongs to the class described as 'the prostitute class,' . . . But in the case of a normal, decent girl brought up in a normal, decent way you may well think that Dr. Rees was not overstating the effect of the continuance of the pregnancy when he said that it would be likely to make her a mental wreck, with all the disastrous consequences that would follow from that.

Following *R v Bourne*, it was apparent that an abortion could lawfully be performed if the pregnant woman's mental health was endangered by her unwanted pregnancy. And some doctors were evidently prepared to interpret this 'mental wreck' exception rather broadly, and terminate the pregnancies of women who were distressed, rather than mentally ill. Because such doctors were risking prosecution, their fees tended to be high, and so these safe, 'legal' abortions were inaccessible to the majority of women, who continued to rely on the services of illegal abortionists. Although exact figures are unavailable, at least 100,000 illegal abortions took place each year prior to abortion's partial decriminalization in 1967. Some of these 'backstreet' abortionists' practices were extremely dangerous, and mortality rates were high.

Although it is now of minimal practical relevance, brief mention should also be made of a further criminal statute. Under the Infant Life (Preservation) Act 1929 it is an offence to destroy the life of a child capable of being born alive, unless the act is done in good faith for the purpose only of preserving the life of the mother. The purpose of this Act was to close a legal loophole. In 1929, it was unlawful to kill a fetus *in utero*, and it was murder to kill a child which had been fully born and was living without any connection with its mother. However, no protection was afforded to the child while it was in the process of being born and before it had been completely separated from its mother. Until the Infant Life (Preservation) Act was passed, killing the child during childbirth was not an offence.

Infant Life (Preservation) Act 1929, section 1(1)

[A]ny person who, with intent to destroy the life of a child capable of being born alive, by any wilful act causes a child to die before it has an existence independent of its mother, shall be guilty of felony, to wit, of child destruction, and shall be liable on conviction thereof on indictment to penal servitude for life:

Provided that no person shall be found guilty of an offence under this section unless it is proved that the act which caused the death of the child was not done in good faith for the purpose only of preserving the life of the mother.

In 1929 a child was presumed to be 'capable of being born alive' at 28 weeks, but since 1929 the age at which a fetus is able to breathe independently had dropped steadily, and the time limit the 1929 Act imposed on lawful abortions had correspondingly reduced. In *Rance v Mid-Downs Health Authority*,[17] Mr and Mrs Rance brought an action in negligence after Mrs Rance gave birth to a boy with spina bifida. They argued that Mrs Rance should have been given the opportunity to terminate the pregnancy. Brooke J held that since the diagnosis was only possible at 26 weeks—at which point the fetus would be capable of being born alive—an abortion would have been unlawful under the 1929 Act.

The 1929 Act is, however, no longer relevant in determining whether a proposed

---

[17] [1991] 1 QB 587.

abortion is lawful. The Abortion Act 1967 was amended in 1990 to provide that no offence under the Infant Life (Preservation) Act is committed provided that the pregnancy is terminated in accordance with the provisions in the 1967 Act.

Abortion Act 1967, section 5(1)

No offence under the Infant Life (Preservation) Act 1929 shall be committed by a registered medical practitioner who terminates a pregnancy in accordance with the provisions of this Act.

(b) THE ABORTION ACT 1967

(1) THE BACKGROUND TO LEGALIZATION

In order to understand the form that abortion's legalization took in the UK, it is important to realize that the Abortion Act 1967, which provides limited statutory defences to the criminal offences described above, was not enacted in order to provide women with the *right* to terminate their unwanted pregnancies. Rather, the principal factor behind public and parliamentary support for legalization was concern about the high mortality rates caused by illegal abortions, especially among the poor. Inadequate contraception—the pill only became widely available during the 1960s—meant that unwanted pregnancies were common. Poor women were therefore faced with an invidious choice between giving birth to a child for whom they would be unable to provide adequate care, or resorting to an illegal and often dangerous abortion. In *R v Scrimaglia*,[18] a case in which a 'backstreet' abortion took place *after* legalization, the then Lord Chief Justice commented that 'one of the objects, as everyone knows, of the new Act was to try to get rid of the back-street insanitary operations'.

In 1966, it was clear that the law was not preventing women from terminating their unwanted pregnancies, instead it was ensuring that large numbers of abortions were performed in unhygienic surroundings, using dangerous techniques. Successful prosecutions were rare: the women themselves would seldom be prepared to give evidence against illegal abortionists, and the police were often reluctant to prosecute. The law was, in short, utterly ineffective.

Although, as we have seen, some doctors were prepared to perform abortions, the possibility of prosecution served as a powerful deterrent, even if the woman's circumstances were truly desperate and continuing the pregnancy might lead to her suicide, or her mental or physical collapse. Despite the alarmingly high numbers of avoidable deaths caused each year by botched illegal abortions, the procedure's dubious legality inhibited most doctors from offering women safe legal abortions. Unsurprisingly, the medical profession resented the criminal law's interference with their freedom to act in the best interests of their patients. Abortion, then, was not legalized in order to enhance women's reproductive autonomy, rather the Abortion Bill's principal purpose was to enable doctors to act lawfully in assisting women who were driven to distraction by the prospect of yet another mouth to feed. In the next extract, Sally Sheldon argues that supporters of the Abortion Bill appeared to share their

---

[18] (1971) 55 Cr App R 280.

opponents' belief that women could not be trusted to make the decision to terminate their pregnancies for themselves.

Sally Sheldon[19]

[In] the parliamentary debates preceding the introduction of the Abortion Act . . . [t]he doctor is talked of as a 'highly skilled and dedicated', 'sensitive, sympathetic' member of a 'high and proud profession' which acts 'with its own ethical and medical standards' displaying 'skill, judgement and knowledge'. The woman who experiences an unwanted pregnancy, on the other hand, is portrayed as someone who is fundamentally incapable of taking such an important decision for herself—either because she is downtrodden and driven to desperation (in the language of the reformers) or, for the opponents of reform, because she is selfish and morally immature. The first of these two images is summed up in the following quotation taken from the parliamentary debates, which is typical of the rhetoric deployed by the reformers. Lord Silkin . . . told the House of Lords . . .

There is the woman who already has a large family, perhaps six or seven children . . . There is the question of the woman who loses her husband during pregnancy and has to go out to work, and obviously cannot bear the strain of doing a full day's work, and looking after a child. There is the woman whose husband is a drunkard or a ne'er-do-well, or is in prison serving a long term, and she has to go to work.

On the other side of the debate, the opponents of reform portrayed the woman as selfish, feckless and irresponsible. Jill Knight, a Conservative MP, was one of the leading opponents of reform . . . She reveals an image of women seeking abortion as selfish, treating babies 'like bad teeth to be jerked out just because they cause suffering . . . simply because it may be inconvenient for a year or so to its mother.' She later adds that a 'mother might want an abortion so that a planned holiday is not postponed or other arrangements interfered with.' The ability and willingness of the woman to make a serious decision regarding abortion, considering all factors and all parties, is dismissed. Rather, she will make a snap decision for her own convenience. The task of the law is thus perceived essentially as one of responsibilization: if the woman seeks to evade the consequences of her carelessness, the law should stand as a barrier. . . .

These constructions of women are of more than historic interest, as the form of regulation adopted by the Abortion Act is fundamentally predicated upon them.

Given this background, the form that legalization took is not surprising. As we see below, abortion is not available upon request. Rather, abortion continues to be proscribed by the Offences Against the Person Act 1861 (and in Scotland by the common law), but the Abortion Act 1967 provides that abortion will be lawful (in England, Scotland and Wales, the Act does not apply in Northern Ireland), and no offence will have been committed, if the criteria laid out in the Act are met. We consider these in more detail below, but they are, in short, that two doctors agree that the woman's circumstances satisfy one of the four statutory 'grounds' for abortion; that the abortion is carried out by a registered medical practitioner in an approved place; and that it is notified within seven days to the Chief Medical Officer of the Department of Health. Although the basic substance of the legislation remains unaltered since 1967,

---

[19] 'The Abortion Act 1967: A Critical Perspective' in Ellie Lee (ed), *Abortion Law and Politics Today* (Macmillan London 1998) 43–58.

the Abortion Act was amended in 1990 by the Human Fertilisation and Embryology Act.

(2) THE GROUNDS FOR ABORTION

The statutory defences to the criminal offences in the Offences Against the Person Act are contained in section 1 of the Abortion Act 1967, as amended:

Abortion Act 1967 section 1(1)

Subject to the provisions of this section a person shall not be guilty of an offence under the law relating to abortion when a pregnancy is terminated by a registered medical practitioner if two registered medical practitioners are of the opinion, formed in good faith:

(a) that the pregnancy has not exceeded its twenty fourth week and that the continuation of the pregnancy would involve risk, greater than if the pregnancy were terminated, of injury to the physical or mental health of the pregnant woman or any existing children of her family; or

(b) that the termination is necessary to prevent grave permanent injury to the physical or mental health of the pregnant woman; or

(c) that the continuance of the pregnancy would involve risk to the life of the pregnant woman, greater than if the pregnancy were terminated; or

(d) that there is a substantial risk that if the child were born it would suffer from physical or mental abnormalities as to be seriously handicapped.

(2) In determining whether the continuance of a pregnancy would involve such risk of injury to health as is mentioned in paragraph (a) or (b) of subsection (1) of this section, account may be taken of the woman's actual or reasonably foreseeable environment.

Let us investigate the meaning of this section in more detail.

(a) Unsuccessful terminations

There is an unfortunate ambiguity in the first sentence of section 1. It appears to suggest that the defence only exists 'when a pregnancy is terminated'. Does this mean that the defence does not exist where the pregnancy is *not* terminated? Because the 1861 Act criminalizes anything done with the *intent* to procure a miscarriage, a literal interpretation of section 1 might leave unsuccessful terminations in an awkward lacuna: A person can be guilty of an offence under the 1861 Act even if the woman's pregnancy is not terminated, but the defence only exists if the pregnancy *is* terminated. A similar problem arises if the woman having the abortion turns out not to have been pregnant. The doctor could still be charged under the 1861 Act for *attempting* to procure a miscarriage, but no defence would exist if there had not in fact been a pregnancy to terminate.

The issue was considered by the House of Lords in the *Royal College of Nursing of the United Kingdom Respondent v Department of Health and Social Security*[20] (discussed in more detail below). A majority held that it would be 'absurd' and 'cannot have been the intention of Parliament' that anyone taking part in an unsuccessful

---

[20] [1981] AC 800.

termination would be unable to rely upon the defences contained in the Abortion Act and would therefore be guilty of an offence under the Offences Against the Person Act 1861. As Lord Edmund-Davies explained:

Were it otherwise the unavoidable conclusion is that doctors and nurses could in such cases be convicted of what in essence would be the extraordinary crime of attempting to do a lawful act.

He then quoted with approval from Smith and Hogan's *Criminal Law*:

the legalisation of an abortion must include the steps which are taken towards it. Are we really to say that these are criminal until the operation is complete, when they are retrospectively author-ised, or alternatively that they are lawful until the operation is discontinued or the woman is discovered not to be pregnant when, retrospectively, they become unlawful? When the conditions of the Act are otherwise satisfied, it is submitted that [the doctor] is not unlawfully administering, etc., and that this is so whether the pregnancy be actually terminated or not.

Hence, it seems likely that a doctor who unsuccessfully attempted to terminate a pregnancy within the terms of the Abortion Act 1967 would have a defence to the criminal offence contained in section 59 of the Offences Against the Person Act.

(b) The need for medical approval

Notice that the Act does not entitle a woman to decide to terminate an unwanted pregnancy, even if her circumstances clearly fit within the statutory grounds. Instead what matters is the two doctors' opinion that an abortion would be lawful. It is also worth noting that the statute does not even specify that the section 1(1) conditions have to actually be satisfied. The legality of an abortion rests wholly upon whether the doctors have formed the *opinion*, in good faith, that the woman's case fits within the statutory grounds, not upon whether those grounds in fact *exist*. So an abortion would be legal even if the woman's circumstances did not satisfy the statutory grounds provided that the two doctors who authorized her termination had acted in good faith. Doctors performing abortions will therefore only fail to be protected by the defence in section 1(1) if there is evidence that they did not act in good faith.

There has been one successful prosecution since the Act came into force. In *R v Smith*,[21] the evidence indicated that the doctor had failed to carry out an internal examination and had made no inquiries into the pregnant woman's personal situation. He was convicted on the grounds that he had not, in good faith, attempted to balance the risks of pregnancy and termination. The Court of Appeal appeared to indicate that a doctor will have acted in good faith if he complies with accepted medical practice: 'good faith' thus seems to be synonymous with the *Bolam* test (discussed in Chapter 3).

R v Smith[22]

Miss Rodgers sought her GP's advice about terminating her pregnancy. He referred her to a pregnancy advice centre, who referred her to Dr. Smith's specialist abortion clinic in Harley Street. She saw Dr Smith for about fifteen minutes. The doctor made no internal examination, and asked no questions about her medical history, but he did ask why she wanted an abortion. She told him

---

[21] [1974] 1 All ER 376.   [22] [1973] 1 WLR 1510 CA.

she was not in love and was frightened at the idea of childbirth. There was no suggestion of the need for a second opinion or for further inquiries. Miss Rodgers did not see a second doctor, and no inquiries or investigations were made into her personal history, her family background, or her actual or future environment.

Scarman LJ

The [Abortion] Act (though it renders lawful abortions that before its enactment would have been unlawful), does not depart from the basic principle of the common law as declared in *R. v. Bourne*, namely, that the legality of an abortion depends upon the opinion of the doctor. It has introduced the safeguard of two opinions: but, if they are formed in good faith by the time when the operation is undertaken, the abortion is lawful. Thus a great social responsibility is firmly placed by the law upon the shoulders of the medical profession. . . .

[t]he sequence of events was such as to call for very careful consideration as to whether it was possible to believe that Dr. Smith had formed in good faith, or at all, the opinion necessary to give him the protection of the Abortion Act. Had he, or had he not, abused the trust reposed in him by the Act of Parliament? The burden was on the prosecution to prove beyond reasonable doubt that he had. All this was faithfully explained to the jury by the recorder. We quote only one passage towards the end of the summing up:

> . . . If two doctors genuinely form an opinion in each case that they deal with that the risk of continuance is more than the risk of termination, it does not matter whether they are right or wrong in that view. If they form that opinion genuinely and in good faith, that in fact comes within the Act, and there is no guilt attached to it. You have to wonder in the case of Dr. Smith whether such a view could genuinely be held by a medical man. . . . The only indication on the case notes about any danger to her mental or physical health was the word 'depressed,' 'not willing to marry and depressed.' Those are the only words about it on the case notes. You have to ask yourselves, was there any balancing of the risks involved in allowing the pregnancy to continue and allowing the pregnancy to be terminated, or was this a mere routine abortion for cash? That is what you have to consider. Was a second opinion even contemplated as a necessity in this case of Miss Rodgers? If, on the very first interview when the girl was seen by Dr. Smith, the very first interview he had with her, he offered to operate on her the next morning, was there any real contemplation or thought that a second opinion was necessary?

Further evidence that the statute's purpose is to protect medical discretion rather than women's rights comes from the inherent vagueness of the statutory grounds. The Act does not, for example, specify that abortion is legal where the pregnancy has resulted from an act of rape or incest. This ambiguity was deliberate. David Steel's Abortion Bill did initially contain more specific clauses, such as one which permitted abortion where the woman was pregnant as a result of rape, but these were opposed by both the British Medical Association and the Royal College of Obstetricians and Gynaecologists. While doctors will invariably allow rape victims to terminate their pregnancies, a definitive list of situations in which abortion is lawful was rejected in part because it would erode medical discretion, and might give women the impression that in certain circumstances abortion would be an entitlement. Sir George Baker P's judgment in *Paton v British Pregnancy Advisory Service Trustees*[23] (for the facts of this case, see its discussion below at p. 618), explains very clearly that, under the 1967 Act, it

[23] [1979] QB 276.

is doctors rather than pregnant women who bear principal responsibility for deciding whether a pregnancy should be terminated.

Sir George Baker P

My own view is that it would be quite impossible for the courts in any event to supervise the operation of the Abortion Act 1967. The great social responsibility is firmly placed by the law upon the shoulders of the medical profession . . . The two doctors have given a certificate. It is not and cannot be suggested that the certificate was given in other than good faith and it seems to me that there is the end of the matter in English law. . . .

This certificate is clear, and not only would it be a bold and brave judge . . . who would seek to interfere with the discretion of doctors acting under the Abortion Act 1967, but I think he would really be a foolish judge who would try to do any such thing, unless, possibly, where there is clear bad faith and an obvious attempt to perpetrate a criminal offence.

In the next extract, Sally Sheldon criticizes the Abortion Act's delegation of abortion decision-making to doctors, arguing that the decision *whether* to terminate a pregnancy is not necessarily a question which requires *clinical* expertise.

Sally Sheldon[24]

The Abortion Act is fundamentally underpinned by the idea that reproduction is an area for medical control and expertise and that the doctor is the most appropriate expert to deal with abortion . . .

The granting of such power to doctors in the field of abortion is often justified by the argument that abortion is essentially a medical matter. However, the actual decision whether or not a given pregnancy should be terminated is not normally one that requires expert medical advice, or the balancing of medical criteria. Further, the doctors' decision-making power is not, according to the terms of the Abortion Act, contained within a narrow, limited medical field. In judging whether or not abortion could be detrimental to the mental or physical health of the pregnant woman, under s. 1(2) of the Act, 'account may be taken of the pregnant woman's actual or reasonably foreseeable environment.' The woman's whole lifestyle, her home, finances and relationships are opened up to the doctor's scrutiny, so that he may judge whether or not the patient is a deserving case for relief. The power given to doctors here far exceeds that which would accrue merely on the basis of a technical expertise . . .

The law clearly aims to protect medical autonomy and discretion rather than to grant substantive rights to the woman, even where she is in the most extreme circumstances . . . [T]he law serves to grant woman and doctor together some rights against the state, but grants the woman no right to privacy or autonomy *vis-à-vis* the doctor.

In the following sections we look at the four different grounds for abortion contained in section 1(1) in more detail.

(c) The 'social' ground

Abortion Act 1967 section 1(1)(a)

that the pregnancy has not exceeded its twenty fourth week and that the continuation of the pregnancy would involve risk, greater than if the pregnancy were terminated, of injury to the physical or mental health of the pregnant woman or any existing children of her family;

---

[24] Sally Sheldon, *Beyond Control: Medical Power and Abortion Law* (Pluto London 1997).

I The time limit

Section 1(1)(a), often referred to as the 'social ground', is the only one which imposes a time limit. As we saw earlier, following the 1990 amendment to the Abortion Act 1967 the Infant Life (Preservation) Act no longer applies, and so the other three grounds for abortion are—in theory at least—available until birth. Obviously, the existence of a time limit means that it is important to know the moment at which a pregnancy begins. When calculating the length of a pregnancy that is being carried to term, the convention is to treat the first day of the pregnant woman's previous period as the relevant start date, even though conception would usually have occurred about two weeks later. The reason for this is that fertilization and implantation are processes that take place imperceptibly over several days. Fertilization may not begin until a few days after sexual intercourse, and will usually take several hours; implantation again takes several days and will not usually start until at least six to seven days after fertilization began. It is therefore impossible to detect the moment at which the fertilized ovum attaches itself to the wall of the uterus, and the woman can be considered pregnant. Dating the pregnancy from the woman's previous period allows doctors to calculate the length of gestation with greater precision.

For the purposes of the Abortion Act, however, using this convenient fictional 'start date' is more problematic. Insofar as section 1(1)(a) consists in a defence to a criminal offence, any ambiguity must be construed in favour of the defendant, that is the pregnant woman and/or her doctor. It would seem unfair to deny a woman an abortion when she was, as a matter of fact, 22 weeks pregnant, but the date of her previous period fell outside the 24-week limit. Rather, the better interpretation is probably that the pregnancy began when, according to medical judgement, implantation is likely to have occurred. This undoubtedly introduces a margin of uncertainty, but again, if a borderline case were to arise, the ambiguity would have to be construed in favour of the pregnant woman and her doctors.

In practice, 88 per cent of abortions take place during the first 12 weeks of pregnancy, and 60 per cent in the first 9 weeks.[25] Only a tiny minority (around 1 per cent) takes place after the nineteenth week of pregnancy,[26] so the introduction of a 24-week time limit for what is known as the 'social' ground has had minimal practical impact, especially since the Infant Life Preservation Act had already been interpreted as imposing a 24-week time limit upon abortion. But it is also important to remember that women do not have the *right* to an abortion up to 24 weeks, rather doctors have the *power* to carry out terminations if they believe the grounds in the Act are satisfied. Very few obstetricians are, in practice, prepared to carry out abortions for 'social' reasons late into the second trimester. Medical discretion, therefore, generally leads to an earlier time limit than that specified in the statute, and a woman will often find it difficult to obtain an abortion under this ground after about the sixteenth week of pregnancy.

Advances in neonatal medicine which mean that premature babies born before 24 weeks' gestation are now capable of survival, coupled with developments in

---

[25] *Abortion Statistics 2004* (DoH 2005) <http://www.dh.gov.uk/assetRoot/04/11/66/35/04116635.pdf>.
[26] Ibid.

visualization techniques, such as ultrasound, which can now show fetal movements in considerable detail, have given rise to renewed interest in the time limits for abortion. In the first extract, Deborah Kirklin discusses the role of medical imaging and illusion in the abortion debate.

D Kirklin[27]

The latest developments in fetal ultrasound technology, made public by a group called *Create*, and first introduced to the wider UK public by the *Evening Standard* . . ., have evoked a flood of responses from the public, pro-life and pro-choice campaigners, and politicians, re-igniting the debate about abortion in the UK and elsewhere. The focus of the *Evening Standard* articles, on the smiling, walking, and waving babies that the images purport to show, was echoed throughout the worldwide media coverage that followed. In July 2004, Sir David Steel, sponsor of the 1967 Abortion Act, publicly stated that the *Create* images led him to believe it was time to review the legal time limit for abortions. . . .

What interests me here is the powerful role that biomedical imaging, and the human artifice it involves, can play in influencing the nature, timing, and tone of this debate. The ultrasound technology involved is without doubt impressive. A computer is used to simulate the 3D appearance of the fetus in the womb by combining a series of 2D images and then filling in any gaps; the 4D images are generated by using the simulated 3D images to produce a rapidly changing sequence of images, an illusion of fetal movement is thereby created. . . . What is not immediately apparent when viewing the video clips is that these video clips are in fact video loops, with the same movement shown again and again. Thus the waving fetus is an illusion created by showing the movement of the fetus' arm, from left to right across its body, over and over again. The smiling fetus, who appears to coyly smile then relax its mouth before coyly smiling again, is also an illusion. We do indeed see the fetus draw back its lips but instead of seeing what happens next, the illusion of smiling is created by the loop presentation of the images.

I am not pointing this out in order to deny the possibility that fetuses are capable of making the movements that these video clips purport to show, a proposition that I find totally plausible. Nor am I suggesting that the producers and distributors of these images set out intentionally to deceive those accessing them. I am, however, very interested in the potential for medically and scientifically generated images to create illusions of this sort, whether intentionally or unintentionally.

Below John Wyatt argues that developments in neonatal medicine since 1967 have inevitably affected attitudes towards late abortion.

John Wyatt[28]

In 1967 when the Abortion Act came into force in Britain, the scientific understanding of fetal development and behaviour was rudimentary. The fetus was shrouded in mystery. . . . Twenty years later we have discovered that babies have a range of sophisticated abilities with well developed sensory perception in all systems: vision, hearing, touch, taste and smell. They also have a wide range of learning capacities (including even the ability to imitate facial expressions). . . .

The first fetal movements are seen at seven weeks and over twenty different movement patterns have been described up to 16 weeks including hand–face contact, startle and sucking and swallowing movements. . . .

In 1967 long term survival of preterm babies born before thirty-two weeks was unusual and

---

[27] 'The role of medical imaging in the abortion debate' (2004) 30 Journal of Medical Ethics 426, 426.
[28] 'Medical paternalism and the fetus' (2001) 27 Journal of Medical Ethics ii15–ii20.

twenty-eight weeks seemed an absolute barrier. Since then the prospects for very premature babies have been transformed by the development of specialised intensive care techniques and a huge investment in neonatal research and training. . . . Survival at twenty-three and twenty-four weeks of gestation is now commonplace and occasional survival at twenty-two weeks and less than 500g birthweight has been described. . . .

Medical practice in modern perinatal centres can have a paradoxical element. In one part of the hospital a huge concentration of resources, human expertise, parental concern and professional dedication is devoted to ensuring the survival of babies born as early as twenty-three to twenty-four weeks. In an adjacent part of the hospital agonised discussions about the possibility of feticide in a much more mature fetus are taking place. Hospital staff may feel deeply uneasy about raising the option of feticide when a major abnormality is detected in the third trimester . . . Although late feticide is performed relatively rarely, the juxtaposition of this practice with neonatal intensive care units inevitably poses ethical conflicts for health professionals.

The development of neonatal intensive care is predicated on the belief that even tiny, immature and uniquely vulnerable babies deserve the very best care and that professionals have an ethical duty to act in each baby's own interests even at considerable cost to society. If there is no responsibility to consider fetal interests until delivery, then it must be explained why the moment of birth in itself leads to a transformation of our ethical responsibilities.

In contrast, Sally Sheldon argues that reliance on viability as the cut-off point for lawful abortion might have negative consequences for women's access to abortion services.

Sally Sheldon[29]

The adoption of viability as the cut-off point for abortions was heralded as a victory for pro-choice campaigners, as it currently ensures an upper limit which is high in comparison to other Western abortion laws. However, the effect of the 1990 debates has been to entrench in the public—and parliamentary—consciousness that abortion is permissible prior to viability, but should be forbidden after this point. This is a notion which future campaigns may find hard to dislodge. . . . While the present state of medical science makes it impossible to sustain neo-natal life at much less than twenty-four weeks of gestational development for reasons of lung development, it is surely not inconceivable that this limit will be gradually pushed downwards. If this happens, pro-choice groups will face a particularly bitter struggle to try and separate out the legitimacy of abortion from the notion of viability.

More immediately, the concentration on viability as the decisive factor obscures other considerations . . . [and] shifts the focus of decision-making away from women who make complex evaluations of their particular circumstances, and of the *social* sustainability of new life. . . .

The other worrying trend, highlighted during the [1990] debates . . . is the use of medical knowledges to support the construction of the foetus as a separate individual . . . During the 1990 parliamentary debates, the Society for the Protection of Unborn Children (SPUC) sent each MP a plastic replica of a foetus at twenty weeks of gestation. Although various MPs expressed their distaste at this strategy . . ., not one commented on what I would see as the most worrying aspect of this tactic: that the foetus is represented in total abstraction from the body of the woman that carried it . . . [T]he foetus is not and cannot exist without the body of the pregnant woman which

[29] 'The Law of Abortion and the Politics of Medicalisation' in J Bridgeman and S Millns (eds), *Law and Body Politics: Regulating the Female Body* (Dartmouth Aldershot 1995).

actively nourishes and supports it. Its representation as a free-floating and separate entity embodies a fundamental deceit.

II The risk to health

For an abortion to be lawful under section 1(1)(a), continuing the pregnancy must pose a risk, greater than if the pregnancy were terminated, of injury to the physical or mental health of the pregnant woman or her children. And under section 1(2) the doctor is specifically directed to take account of the woman's actual or reasonably foreseeable environment. In 2004 95 per cent of all abortions were authorized on the grounds that the pregnancy posed a risk to the pregnant woman's own health, and 3 per cent because of a risk to her children.[30] For two reasons, this ground is very easily satisfied. First, the Royal College of Obstetricians and Gynaecologists suggest that its reference to health is normally assumed to refer to the World Health Organization's definition of 'health' as 'a state of physical and mental well-being, not merely an absence of disease or infirmity'. This means that the abortion only needs to be necessary in order to promote the woman's mental wellbeing, rather than to prevent her from suffering physical or psychiatric harm. The mental wellbeing of a woman who does not want to be pregnant is, almost by definition, promoted by allowing her to have an abortion. Secondly, given that pregnancy and childbirth are invariably more risky than termination, an abortion will usually also promote the woman's *physical* wellbeing.

Under this ground, an abortion can also be authorized if carrying the pregnancy to term would cause a risk of injury to the physical or mental health of any existing children of the pregnant woman's family. The section does not specify that the potentially affected children have to be her biological offspring, it is enough that they are children living in her family. Usually, of course, having another brother or sister does not pose a direct risk to a child's health. Rather, it could be argued that by over-stretching the family's financial resources and diverting the mother's attention away from the care of her existing children, the arrival of a new baby may have an adverse effect upon their health.

(d) Prevent grave permanent injury

Abortion Act 1967 section 1(1)(b)
that the termination is necessary to prevent grave permanent injury to the physical or mental health of the pregnant woman.

An abortion may be lawful under section 1(1)(b) if it is necessary to prevent grave permanent injury to the pregnant woman's physical or mental health, or to prevent a risk to her life. 'Grave permanent injury' is not defined in the statute, but there seems to be no doubt that this ground will only be satisfied if the woman's condition is extremely serious. In the House of Lords debates in 1990, Lord Mackay described this as 'a stiff legal test to cover special situations'. It is also worth noting that abortion is not necessarily lawful under this ground just because the pregnancy is exposing the pregnant woman to the risk of grave permanent injury. Instead, the abortion must

---

[30] *Abortion Statistics 2004* (DoH 2005) <http://www.dh.gov.uk/assetRoot/04/11/66/35/04116635.pdf>.

be 'necessary' to prevent this injury materializing. If the injury could be prevented *without* aborting the fetus, then abortion would not be justified under this section.

(e) Risk to the pregnant woman's life
Abortion Act 1967 section 1(1)(c)
that the continuance of the pregnancy would involve risk to the life of the pregnant woman, greater than if the pregnancy were terminated.

Under section 1(1)(c), doctors must decide that continuing the pregnancy poses a greater risk to the pregnant woman's life than abortion. It is not necessary that abortion should *remove* the risk to the pregnant woman's life, rather abortion merely has to *reduce* the risk. An abortion may not save a terminally ill woman's life, but it might nevertheless pose less risk to her health than carrying a pregnancy to term and going through childbirth. Recall that in *R v Bourne*, risk to life was broadly interpreted to encompass situations in which the pregnancy would 'make the woman a physical or mental wreck'. For the purposes of section 1(1)(c), however, an elastic interpretation of 'risk to life' would not be appropriate because it would render this section synonymous with section 1(1)(a), and therefore redundant as a separate ground.

(f) The fetal abnormality ground
Abortion Act 1967 section 1(1)(d)
that there is a substantial risk that if the child were born it would suffer from physical or mental abnormalities as to be seriously handicapped.

Approximately 1 per cent of all abortions in England and Wales are carried out solely under section 1(1)(d), which permits abortion until birth where there is a substantial risk that the resulting child would be born seriously handicapped.[31] Access to abortion under this ground depends upon two doctors agreeing that a particular handicap is 'serious', and that the risk of it materializing is 'substantial'. Again notice the doctors' wide discretion to decide whether a particular abnormality meets the threshold level of seriousness, and how substantial the risk is of it occurring. This flexibility means that doctors might, for example, refuse to perform very late abortions unless the disability is so grave that the fetus would be likely to die shortly after birth.

In deciding whether a fetus's abnormality is sufficiently serious, the Royal College of Obstetricians and Gynaecologists have recommended that doctors take into account the probability that effective treatment will be available; the probable degree of self-awareness and ability to communicate with others; the suffering that would be experienced; and the extent to which the person might be dependent upon others. There is no definitive list of conditions which justify abortion, or of conditions which do not, and so there are inevitably discrepancies between different doctors' definitions of 'serious handicap'.

The question of what might count as a serious handicap was raised in an application for judicial review by Joanna Jepson in 2003 following her discovery that, in 2001 in Birmingham, an abortion had been carried out on a fetus with a cleft palate after 24

---

[31] *Abortion Statistics 2004* (DoH 2005) <http://www.dh.gov.uk/assetRoot/04/11/66/35/04116635.pdf>.

weeks gestation.[32] Her argument was the debates in Parliament prior to the passage of the 1990 amendments to the Abortion Act, which as we have seen permitted abortion for abnormality up until birth, made clear that third trimester abortions would be justifiable only for extremely serious conditions, and not for minor abnormalities like cleft palate. West Mercia police launched an investigation following her complaint, but no prosecution was instigated. It was this failure to prosecute which prompted Joanna Jepson's legal action. Jackson J initially granted her leave to apply for judicial review, on the grounds that the case raised an issue of public importance, but admitted that she would face considerable obstacles at the full hearing:[33]

For my part, having listened to the competing submissions of counsel, it does seem to me that the claimant in these proceedings faces substantial evidential hurdles and substantial legal hurdles. There will be arguments about standing and there will be considerable legal debate about whether, in the light of the advice received from the Royal College of Obstetricians and Gynaecologists, the decision not to prosecute can be challenged . . . Nevertheless, I am persuaded, having listened to the submissions of counsel, that this case does raise serious issues of law and issues of public importance which cannot be properly or fully argued in the context of a permission application.

West Mercia police then conceded that their initial investigation may not have been sufficiently thorough, and the case was reopened under a different team of officers, who referred it to the Crown Prosecution Service (CPS). In 2005, the CPS determined that the doctors who authorized the abortion had acted in good faith. According to the Chief Crown Prosecutor:

This complaint has been investigated most thoroughly by the police and the CPS has considered a great deal of evidence before reaching its decision. The issue is whether the two doctors who had authorised the termination were of the opinion, formed in good faith, that there was a substantial risk that if the child were born it would suffer from such physical and mental abnormalities as to be seriously handicapped. I consider that both doctors concluded that there was a substantial risk of abnormalities that would amount to the child being seriously handicapped. The evidence shows that these two doctors did form this opinion and formed it in good faith. In these circumstances I decided there was insufficient evidence for a realistic prospect of conviction and that there should be no charges against either of the doctors.[34]

It is worth pointing out that under section 1(1)(d) there only need be a substantial *risk* of handicap, so an abortion could be justified under this section even if the fetus turns out not to suffer from any disability provided that there was a substantial risk that it might have done. What might be meant by 'substantial' risk? If there is a one in four chance that a child would have a particular genetic disease, such as cystic fibrosis, does this count as a 'substantial risk', or must the risk of abnormality be greater to be categorized as 'substantial'? The statute itself is not clear.

How might section 1(1)(d) apply to genetic tests which are increasingly able to predict *future* susceptibility to disease? Is a fetus which has the gene that causes Huntington's disease (a fatal adult-onset condition) at *substantial risk* of suffering

---

[32] *Jepson v The Chief Constable of West Mercia Police Constabulary* [2003] EWHC 3318.

[33] Ibid.

[34] 'CPS decides not to prosecute doctors following complaint by Rev Joanna Jepson' CPS Press Release, 16 Mar 2005 <http://www.cps.gov.uk/news/pressreleases/117_05.html>.

from such abnormalities as to be *seriously handicapped*? If the child must be seriously handicapped from birth, many genetic diagnoses will not satisfy section 1(1)(d), and abortion would instead only be lawful within the first 24 weeks of pregnancy under section 1(1)(a). Alternatively it could be argued that simply knowing that one has the gene which causes a fatal and incurable disease which will be likely to lead to one's premature death is itself a serious handicap.

The fetal abnormality ground is especially controversial. In the next extract, Simo Vehmas argues that once a woman has decided to have a baby, it is not legitimate for her to reject a particular fetus on the grounds that it does not have the characteristics she requires. We will encounter similar arguments in Chapter 14 p. 844 when we look at preimplantation genetic diagnosis.

Simo Vehmas[35]

It is a common belief that children with cognitive impairments inevitably pose an overwhelming economic or emotional burden for their families due to the special attention the child requires. This belief, however, is based more on prejudices than reality . . . When considering the parenting of a child with a cognitive impairment, people seem to forget the fact that *every* child is more or less a burden to her parents. Children without impairments may cause stress to their parents due to problems (e.g., drug and alcohol abuse and eating disorders) which children with cognitive impairments usually do not get involved in. Families of children with cognitive impairments do not necessarily experience any more difficulties than families with so-called normal children—their problems are just different . . .

Often . . . social and cultural factors contribute more to the well-being or ill-being of families than the child's impairment in itself. Families which receive support from their societies and communities are, despite a child's impairment, likely to cope better than families which are emotionally and financially on their own . . .

The reason why parents view a disabled child as a problem is often a result of the fact that they generally tend to anticipate 'the birth of a usual perfect baby'.

A conscious decision to procreate should bring about conscious assent to assuming obligations as a parent. That is, conscious assent to parenthood means committing oneself to acting and evaluating one's actions and decisions in the light of the project of parenthood. One dimension of parenthood is committing oneself to caring for any kind of child. Parents who rejected their child who became seriously disabled due, for example, to a car accident, would probably be considered as acting morally wrongly *as parents*. . . .

[I]t is against the project of parenthood to qualify one's commitment to nurture one's child on the basis of her potential competence . . .

It is true that parents generally wish their future child to conform more or less to some culturally formed ideal. This means that parents characteristically prefer having a good-looking, healthy and intellectually average (or, preferably, above average) child instead of an ugly, sickly and intellectually subaverage child. But to perform parental tasks well, the parents' commitment to care for their child has to be unconditional, which means that the commitment holds even if the child turns out to be ugly, sickly and intellectually subaverage.

---

[35] 'Parental Responsibility and the Morality of Selective Abortion' (2002) 5(4) Ethical Theory and Moral Practice 463–84.

Although note the BMA's analysis of the difficulties women face in making the decision to terminate a pregnancy after a diagnosis of fetal abnormality.

British Medical Association[36]

At whatever stage fetal abnormality is diagnosed, women and their partners need good quality information about the implications of the result and the options open to them. Women will then need time and support to allow them to come to terms with the situation before deciding how to proceed. The vast majority of these pregnancies will be wanted and the decision of whether to terminate a pregnancy in such circumstances is never easy. The fact that parents decide to terminate an affected pregnancy does not mean that they do not experience an intense sense of loss and bereavement. Very little research has been undertaken into the way parents make decisions following the diagnosis of severe fetal abnormality. This is partly because of the relatively small number of patients involved but also because of the inherent difficulty of obtaining valid consent and parents' active co-operation at what is inevitably a time of great distress. As such there is very little information available about how women are counselled following diagnosis, what information and support they receive and how this affects the type and quality of decisions made. In a review of the research evidence available, however, Helen Statham reports that parents frequently speak of feeling 'numb' and 'deeply shocked' when given the information. She says: 'Once a diagnosis has been made, parents experience deep shock at the loss of what they had believed previously was a normal pregnancy, whatever the abnormality and whatever the decision they subsequently make. In shock, and experiencing symptoms of acute grief including anger, despair, guilt, inadequacy, sleeping and eating difficulties they have no choice but to make decisions about the management and outcome of the pregnancy.'

Sally Sheldon and Stephen Wilkinson criticize the fetal abnormality ground from a different perspective, arguing that it is difficult to find a defensible reason for treating abortion on the grounds of fetal abnormality differently from other sorts of abortion. They consider three possible justifications for maintaining section (1)(1)(d) as a separate ground, first, the interests of the child-to-be; secondly, allowing the pregnant woman to conceive a non-disabled child instead; and, thirdly, protecting the pregnant woman's interests. The only logical justification for allowing women to terminate pregnancies where the fetus is disabled is—they suggest—to protect the woman's *own* interests, in which case this ground for abortion is functionally indistinguishable from section (1)(1)(a).

Sally Sheldon and Stephen Wilkinson[37]

The 'Foetal Interests Argument' attempts to justify s.(1)(1)(d) by claiming that termination actually benefits the disabled foetus, by saving it from a life of suffering. It claims that termination in these circumstances can thus be thought of as a kind of foetal euthanasia. . . . The first [objection] is that it only applies to a very narrow range of cases. These are cases where the likely alternative to termination is a resultant child whose quality of life is not merely low, but negative: that is, she would, quite literally, be better off dead, or better off never having been born. Whilst we are happy to grant, for the sake of argument, that there are cases where any resultant child will have a negative quality of life (for example, a child suffering from Tay-Sachs disease) many actual

---

[36] *Abortion Time Limits: A Briefing Paper from the BMA* (BMA 2005) <http://www.bma.org.uk/ap.nsf/Content/AbortionTimeLimits>.

[37] 'Termination of pregnancy for reason of foetal disability: are there grounds for a special exception in law?' (2001) 9 Medical Law Review 85–109.

foetal impairments are indisputably not like this. For in most cases, the resultant child will have a quality of life which, although arguably less good than it would have been without impairment, is still positive overall and therefore a 'life worth living'. . . .

The second problem with the 'Foetal Interests Argument' is one of maintaining law's internal coherence. . . . In a series of . . . cases, the courts have held that, in order for treatment to be withdrawn from impaired neonates, the question to be asked is whether the child's future quality of life will 'demonstrably' be 'so awful that in effect [it] must be condemned to die'. . . . The gulf between the standards applied in these cases and in s.(1)(1)(d) of the Abortion Act can be clearly illustrated by taking the example of Down's syndrome. Routine pre-natal testing now predicts a large number of likely cases of Down's syndrome, and termination is then offered under s.(1)(1)(d). However, in the case of *Re B (A Minor)(Wardship: Medical Treatment)* the courts held that it would be unlawful to withhold treatment . . . from a child suffering from Down's syndrome.

The second argument for s.(1)(1)(d) is the 'Replacement Argument' . . . On this view, it is acceptable to 'trade off' the life of one foetus against that of another in a utilitarian way, their status being such that killing one solely in order to generate an increase in the general good is permissible . . . So we should remain aware of what lies behind the 'Replacement Argument': the view that the foetus has a very low moral status indeed—so low that it can be permissibly killed for purely utilitarian reasons.

The first [objection] . . . is that it assumes something which cannot simply be assumed: that the woman in question will at least try to become pregnant again . . . Admittedly, we cannot guarantee that each particular aborted foetus will be 'replaced' by another non-disabled foetus from the very same mother. However, viewing the situation holistically, it is likely that, if we allow abortion for reason of foetal disability, a *group* of mostly non-disabled fetuses will come to exist which would not otherwise exist . . . A second . . . more serious objection [is that] if the fetuses in question really do have very low status, such that they can be killed for purely utilitarian reasons, then it is not clear why *special* provisions covering disability are required. . . . With that assumption in place . . . we have a justification not for having a special exception for disabled fetuses but rather for a much more permissive policy across the board.

Even if section (1)(1)(a) more accurately describes the reason for aborting an abnormal fetus, a time limit is attached to the so-called 'social ground'. Maintaining fetal abnormality as a separate ground might therefore be desirable in order to allow for the tiny number of abortions carried out in the third trimester of pregnancy following the discovery of a grave fetal abnormality, without provoking the vigorous opposition which would be likely to defeat any proposal to remove the time limit from section (1)(1)(a).

(3) OTHER RESTRICTIONS UPON ACCESS TO ABORTION

(a) Personnel

Section 1 of the Abortion Act specifies that abortion will only be lawful if it is carried out *by* a medical practitioner. Terminations carried out by nurses or by the woman herself would therefore be unlawful. This restriction has particular significance for the regulation of what are known as medical (as opposed to surgical) abortions. Early in pregnancy, the 'abortion pill' mifepristone (commonly known as RU486) can be used to dislodge the embryo from the lining of the uterus. These medical abortions are increasingly common, and approximately 19 per cent of all abortions are now carried out in this way.[38]

If the woman herself takes the abortion pill, and—as happens in approximately 3 per cent of cases—miscarries before she returns to hospital for the insertion of a prostaglandin pessary has she terminated the pregnancy herself? We would normally say that a person who takes a pill is the principal cause of that pill's consequences. In relation to euthanasia, a doctor who hands a patient a lethal drug has not killed her, rather this would be a case of assisted suicide. Analogously, if a woman takes a pill which causes her to miscarry, has she terminated her own pregnancy, and hence committed an offence under the Offences Against the Person Act 1861, to which the Abortion Act offers no defence?

The question of whether women who take the abortion pill might be terminating their own pregnancies has never been considered by a court. Nurses' involvement in non-surgical abortions has, however, been approved by a majority of the House of Lords. In the following case, they decided that nurses could actively participate in terminating pregnancies, provided that a registered medical practitioner is supervising the entire procedure. Women's own involvement in medical terminations might be justified on similar grounds provided that they are supervised by a medical practitioner, who retains responsibility throughout.

Royal College of Nursing v Department of Health and Social Security[39]

The Department of Health and Social Security (DHSS) had issued advice that medical induction (where the pregnancy is terminated by inducing contractions) could properly be said to be 'termination by a registered medical practitioner' provided it was decided on and initiated by him and provided he remained throughout responsible for its overall conduct and control in the sense that acts needed to bring it to its conclusion were done by appropriately skilled staff acting on his specific instructions, but not necessarily in his presence. The Royal College of Nursing sought a declaration that the circular was wrong in law. They succeeded in the Court of Appeal, but by a 3:2 majority, the House of Lords reversed this decision.

Lord Diplock

What limitation . . . is imposed by the qualifying phrase: 'when a pregnancy is terminated by a registered medical practitioner'? In my opinion in the context of the Act, what it requires is that a registered medical practitioner, whom I will refer to as a doctor, should accept responsibility for all stages of the treatment for the termination of the pregnancy. The particular method to be used should be decided by the doctor in charge of the treatment for termination of the pregnancy, he should carry out any physical acts, forming part of the treatment, that in accordance with accepted medical practice are done only by qualified medical practitioners, and should give specific instructions as to the carrying out of such parts of the treatment as in accordance with accepted medical practice are carried out by nurses or other members of the hospital staff without medical qualifications. To each of them, the doctor, or his substitute, should be available to be consulted or called on for assistance from beginning to end of the treatment. In other words, the doctor need not do everything with his own hands; the requirements of the subsection are satisfied when the treatment for termination of a pregnancy is one prescribed by a registered medical

---

[38] *Abortion Statistics 2004* (DoH 2005) <http://www.dh.gov.uk/assetRoot/04/11/66/35/04116635.pdf>.
[39] [1981] AC 800.

practitioner carried out in accordance with his directions and of which a registered medical practitioner remains in charge throughout.

(b) Conscientious objection

Abortion Act section 4 (1):

no person shall be under any duty, whether by contract or by any statutory or other legal requirement, to participate in any treatment authorised by this Act to which he has a conscientious objection.

Under section 4 of the Act, medical personnel have a right of conscientious objection to participation in the provision of abortion services, unless the abortion is necessary to prevent grave permanent injury to the physical or mental health of a pregnant woman, or to save her life. Section 4 not only protects doctors who believe abortion is always wrong, but could also be used by doctors who are willing to perform abortions in the early stages of pregnancy, but who 'conscientiously object' to late abortions.

While the right is not limited to doctors, and nurses could undoubtedly refuse to assist during surgery, administrative staff are unlikely to be able to claim exemption. In *Janaway v Salford Heath Authority*[40] the House of Lords rejected a medical receptionist's claim that she had been wrongfully dismissed for refusing to type a letter of referral for an abortion. Lord Keith held that participation 'in its ordinary and natural meaning referred to actually taking part in treatment administered in a hospital or other approved place in accordance with section 1(3), for the purpose of terminating a pregnancy'.

'Taking part in treatment', however, is still rather vague. Does a doctor who certifies that the woman's circumstances satisfy the statutory grounds (on what is now known as the 'blue form') 'participate' in her treatment? In *Janaway v Salford Heath Authority*,[41] the House of Lords specifically declined to express an opinion, and left open the question of whether a GP's right of conscientious objection could extend to refusing to sign what was then the 'green form'. Lord Keith said:

It does not appear whether or not there are any circumstances under which a doctor might be under any legal duty to sign a green form, so as to place in difficulties one who had a conscientious objection to doing so. The fact that during the 20 years that the Act of 1967 has been in force no problem seems to have surfaced in this connection may indicate that in practice none exists. So I do not think it appropriate to express any opinion on the matter.

Although the statute itself is unclear, referring a pregnant woman to another doctor is probably not 'participating' in her treatment. Certainly in *Barr v Matthews*,[42] Alliott J suggested that 'once a termination of pregnancy is recognized as an option the doctor invoking the conscientious objection clause should refer the patient to a colleague at once'. The Royal College of Obstetricians and Gynaecologist's most recent guidelines advise doctors with a conscientious objection to abortion that they should refer a patient who requests abortion to another doctor:

Practitioners cannot claim exemption from giving advice or performing the preparatory steps to

[40] [1989] AC 537.   [41] Ibid.   [42] (2000) 52 BMLR 217.

arrange an abortion where the request meets the legal requirements. Such steps include referral to another doctor, as appropriate.

Doctors are not obliged to publicize their conscientious objections to abortion, so women will not usually know in advance whether or not their doctor is a conscientious objector. As a result, it is possible that some women mistake their doctor's lack of cooperation as an indication of their ineligibility for termination, rather than an expression of his moral convictions. In *Saxby v Morgan*,[43] for example, although the claimant's action in negligence ultimately failed, she had been told by her doctor that her pregnancy was too far advanced for him to refer her for a termination, despite being between 18 and 19 weeks' pregnant, and so clearly within the time limits in the Abortion Act.

While a woman whose doctor has a conscientious objection to abortion clearly has the right to seek another doctor's assistance, this will tend to delay her abortion. And locating another medical practitioner will not always be straightforward. Women living in rural areas, for example, may not easily be able to find an alternative medical practitioner. Of course, no doctor working in a private abortion clinic will have a conscientious objection to abortion, so women who are able to find and afford private treatment will be unaffected by the Abortion Act's conscience clause.

(c) Places

Under section 1(3) of the 1967 Act, except in an emergency, 'any treatment for the termination of pregnancy' must be carried out in a National Health Service Hospital, or in a place approved for the purposes of the Act by the Department of Health. There are currently seventy-eight approved abortion clinics in the UK. Regulations provide that special approval is necessary to perform an abortion after 20 weeks in an abortion clinic, and that pregnancies of 24 weeks or more can only be terminated in NHS Hospitals.

The development of the abortion pill, RU486 raises two obvious difficulties here. First, if taking the pill is 'treatment for the termination of pregnancy', it must happen in an NHS Hospital or an approved place. There is no *clinical* reason why medical abortions should have to take place in hospital. Could women therefore be prescribed RU486 in their GP's surgeries? Section 1(3A) of the 1967 Act was added in 1990 to allow the Secretary of State for Health to approve classes of places where the treatment consists 'primarily in the use of such medicines as may be specified'. In theory, then, it would be possible for all GPs' surgeries to be approved for the purposes of medical abortion. However, this has not yet happened and the abortion pill must be dispensed and taken in an NHS hospital or other approved place. It would also, of course, be *possible* for women to take the pill in their own homes, but clearly this would be prohibited by section 1(3).

Secondly, after the woman takes the abortion pill, she must wait between 36 and 48 hours (during which time she may miscarry), before returning to the hospital where a prostaglandin pessary will normally be inserted in order to ensure that the pregnancy has been terminated. For up to two days, then, the drug is acting to terminate her

---

[43] [1997] 8 Med LR 293.

pregnancy and may in fact do so. If 'treatment for the termination of pregnancy' is occurring throughout this period, the woman would have to remain in hospital. In practice, women are routinely sent home after being observed for a couple of hours, so it is only the taking of the pill which seems to be classified as 'treatment'.

(d) Emergencies

Abortion Act 1967 section 1(4)

Subsection (3) of this section, and so much of subsection (1) as relates to the opinion of two registered medical practitioners, shall not apply to the termination of pregnancy by a registered medical practitioner in a case where he is of this opinion formed in good faith that the termination is immediately necessary to save the life or to prevent grave permanent injury to the physical or mental health of the pregnant woman.

Under this provision, emergency abortions do not have to be performed in an NHS Hospital or other approved place, and may be carried out without seeking a second doctor's opinion. A similarly worded provision in section 4 means that doctors cannot invoke the conscientious objection clause where the abortion is necessary to save the woman's life or prevent grave permanent injury.

(e) Reporting

All terminations must be notified to the Chief Medical Officer of the Department of Health (or in Wales, the Chief Medical Officer of the Welsh Assembly) within 14 days. In addition to notifying the Department of Health of the grounds on which the abortion has been authorized, and the length of gestation, the notification form also records information such as the woman's age and marital status, her place of usual residence, and the outcome of any previous pregnancies. This data allows detailed Abortion Statistics to be produced each year.[44]

(4) A THIRD PARTY'S RIGHTS (OR LACK OF THEM)

(a) Men

As we have seen, final authority over whether a pregnancy may lawfully be terminated rests with the two medical practitioners who have, in good faith, decided that the woman's circumstances fit within the statutory grounds. Given that the decision is constructed as a *medical* one, taken by a doctor in his patient's best interests, it is unsurprising that the pregnant woman's sexual partner has no right to obstruct medical discretion and prevent her from obtaining an abortion. In *Paton v Trustees of the British Pregnancy Advisory Service*,[45] a husband sought an injunction to restrain the defendants from terminating his estranged wife's pregnancy. Sir George Baker P rejected his application, and Mr Paton then took his case to the European Commission of Human Rights,[46] where his submission that he had standing to protect his unborn child's right to life was dismissed. The European Commission also rejected his

---

[44] Available at <http://www.dh.gov.uk>. At the time of writing the most recent statistics are *Abortion Statistics 2004* (DoH 2005) <http://www.dh.gov.uk/assetRoot/04/11/66/35/04116635.pdf>.
[45] [1979] QB 276.   [46] *Paton v United Kingdom* [1980] 3 EHRR 408.

claim that his right to respect for his private and family life, guaranteed by Article 8 of the European Convention on Human Rights, had been violated. Instead, the Commission found that the pregnant woman's right to respect for *her* private life prevailed, and Mr Paton's claim was described as 'manifestly ill-founded'.

Paton v British Pregnancy Advisory Service Trustees[47]

Mrs Paton, the second defendant, obtained a medical certificate entitling her to a lawful abortion within the terms of the Abortion Act 1967. Her husband, the plaintiff, sought an injunction to restrain his wife and the first defendants, a charitable organisation, from causing or permitting an abortion to be carried out upon the wife without his consent.

Sir George Baker P

The first question is whether this plaintiff has a right at all. The foetus cannot, in English law, in my view, have a right of its own at least until it is born and has a separate existence from its mother . . . [T]here can be no doubt, in my view, that in England and Wales the foetus has no right of action, no right at all, until birth. . . .

The father's case must therefore depend upon a right which he has himself. . . . [T]his plaintiff must, in my opinion, bring his case, if he can, squarely within the framework of the fact that he is a husband. . . .

My own view is that it would be quite impossible for the courts in any event to supervise the operation of the Abortion Act 1967. The great social responsibility is firmly placed by the law upon the shoulders of the medical profession . . . The two doctors have given a certificate. It is not and cannot be suggested that the certificate was given in other than good faith and it seems to me that there is the end of the matter in English law. The Abortion Act 1967 gives no right to a father to be consulted in respect of a termination of a pregnancy. True, it gives no right to the mother either, but obviously the mother is going to be right at the heart of the matter consulting with the doctors if they are to arrive at a decision in good faith . . . The husband, therefore, in my view, has no legal right enforceable in law or in equity to stop his wife having this abortion or to stop the doctors from carrying out the abortion. . . .

Today the only way [counsel for Mr Paton] can put the case is that the husband has a right to have a say in the destiny of the child he has conceived. The law of England gives him no such right; the Abortion Act 1967 contains no such provision. It follows, therefore, that in my opinion this claim for an injunction is completely misconceived and must be dismissed.

In *C v S*,[48] Robert Carver applied for an injunction to restrain Oxfordshire Health Authority and his former girlfriend, who was between 18 and 21 weeks pregnant, from terminating her pregnancy, on the ground that the foetus was a 'child capable of being born alive' within the meaning of section 1(1) of the Infant Life (Preservation) Act 1929. His claim was rejected on the basis of evidence that this foetus was not capable of being born alive, but Lord Donaldson MR nevertheless suggested that if the question of his right to be heard had arisen, 'we should have had to have given very considerable thought to the words of Sir George Baker P in *Paton v British Pregnancy Advisory Service Trustees*'. Despite the failure of his legal action, Mr Carver did manage to persuade his former girlfriend to have the baby and to hand it over to him after the birth.

In 1997 a Scottish man attempted to prevent his wife from having an abortion.

---

[47] [1979] QB 276.   [48] [1988] QB 135.

Initially, after an *ex parte* hearing, Mr Kelly was granted an interim interdict (injunction) preventing the abortion from taking place. After hearing legal arguments, the Lord Ordinary withdrew the injunction, and Mr Kelly took his action to the Inner House, where it was again rejected.[49] Just before it was to be decided whether Mr Kelly should be granted leave to appeal to the House of Lords, he abandoned his case, and Mrs Kelly had an abortion in England.

It would be possible for the woman's sexual partner to notify the police if he believed that there had not been compliance with the Abortion Act 1967. However, because the statute gives doctors very broad discretion to determine the legitimacy of abortion, this strategy would be unlikely to succeed.

(b) Other interested parties

Aside from the putative father, other third parties might be interested in trying to prevent a woman from having an abortion, an obvious example being anti-abortion pressure groups, such as the Society for the Protection of the Unborn Child (SPUC). Usually such groups attempt to influence women's abortion decisions by distributing anti-abortion literature, or dispensing anti-abortion advice to pregnant women. On one occasion however, an anti-abortion pressure group sought a court injunction in order to try to prevent an abortion taking place. The case arose after an obstetrician, Professor Philip Bennett, had revealed in a press interview that a woman who was expecting twins had asked him to terminate one twin. Considerable media interest was generated by this story, and—on the assumption that the woman's request had been prompted by her straitened financial circumstances—SPUC approached the hospital where Professor Bennett worked, wishing to offer the pregnant woman a substantial sum of money so that she would be able to continue with the pregnancy. The Hospital refused to pass on their offer, and SPUC applied to the High Court, where they were initially granted an interlocutory injunction preventing the Hospital from carrying out an abortion until after the full hearing, which was due to take place the following morning. Later that day, it was revealed that the abortion had already taken place, and SPUC's application for judicial review was withdrawn.

SPUC's claim had been that the Hospital was under a duty to inform the pregnant woman about their offer of financial assistance, since—they argued—this was a relevant factor when considering the woman's 'actual or reasonably foreseeable circumstances' under section 1(2) of the Abortion Act. Although this argument was never fully considered, it is unlikely that it would have succeeded given that, first, under the Act it is the *doctors*, rather than the pregnant woman herself, who are entitled to take into account the woman's circumstances, and, second, that doctors have considerable clinical discretion in deciding whether abortion is appropriate. As Sally Sheldon points out in the next extract, the emphasis upon medical discretion within British abortion law has at times worked to protect the freedom of women seeking abortions.

Sally Sheldon[50]

If SPUC had succeeded in restraining this termination pending the giving of certain information to

---

[49] *Kelly v Kelly* [1997] SLT 896.
[50] 'Multiple Pregnancy and Re(pro)ductive choice' (1997) 5(1) Feminist Legal Studies 99–106.

[the pregnant woman], it would have set a very dangerous precedent. The idea that it is the anti-choice groups who should dictate what information should be given to women considering abortion cannot fail to alarm. The spectre is raised of the kinds of measures deployed in the United States where, in some states, women have been subjected to dissuasive counselling or forced to watch anti-choice material before deciding on termination in the name of the right to make an informed choice. However, this spectre seems unlikely to haunt British women. In this country, the approach taken by the courts has been one of protecting a broad space for medical discretion and refusing to second-guess the decisions made within it.

(5) THE HUMAN RIGHTS ACT 1998

It would of course be possible to frame the abortion issue in terms of rights, and in the context of the Human Rights Act, to pit the woman's right to respect for her private and family life under Article 8 against any right to life which the fetus might have under Article 2. The fetus is not a legal person and so it seems likely that it is not protected by Article 2. The case law of the European Commission, as we saw in *Paton v UK*, has tended to decide abortion cases by prioritizing the woman's right to respect for her private and family life under Article 8. More recently, in *Vo v France*,[51] the ECHR decided that, at the European level, there was no consensus on the moral status of the fetus. The only common ground was that the fetus was a member of the human race. Its capacity to become a person meant that it should be protected as a matter of human dignity, but did not make it a person with a right to life which would be protected by Article 2.

5. ABORTION IN PRACTICE

(a) NHS PROVISION

In recent years, the proportion of abortions which are funded by the NHS has increased dramatically, and in 2004 82 per cent were publicly funded, of which 51 per cent were carried out in specialist private clinics.[52] But it is also important to note that there is considerable variation in NHS provision of abortion, with some health authorities funding a minority of the terminations performed in their region, and others funding almost all of them.

(b) THE INCIDENCE OF ABORTION

In 1969—the first full year in which the Abortion Act was in operation—49,829 abortions were notified to the Department of Health. By 2004, 185,415 abortions were performed on resident women in England and Wales, and 8,760 abortions were performed on non-resident women.[53] The number of abortions performed has generally risen steadily each year since the Act came into force in 1968. One exception was 1998,

---

[51] (2005) 40 EHRR 12.
[52] *Abortion Statistics 2004* (DoH 2005) <http://www.dh.gov.uk/assetRoot/04/11/66/35/04116635.pdf>.
[53] Ibid.

where as a result of a widely publicized 'pill scare', the number of abortions rose very sharply, only to fall again the following year.

6. SPECIAL SITUATIONS

(a) INCOMPETENT PATIENTS

As we saw in Chapter 4, patients who lack the capacity to consent to their medical treatment can be given treatment which is in their best interests. Accordingly, it is possible for minors or women who are mentally incapacitated to have their pregnancies terminated, if this is judged to be in their best interests. Unlike sterilization, abortion has not been treated as a 'special case' for which court approval is necessary. In *Re SG*, Sir Stephen Brown P decided that, since the Abortion Act 1967 already specifies the circumstances in which abortion will be lawful, a further court declaration will usually be unnecessary.

Re SG (Adult Mental Patient: Abortion)[54]

The applicant, a woman of twenty-six, was severely mentally handicapped with the mental age of a seven or eight year old. She was looked after at home by her parents with some outside assistance. When she was found to be pregnant, her general practitioner and a consultant gynaecologist recommended an abortion as a matter of urgency. The applicant by her father and next friend applied for a declaration that it would be lawful to terminate the pregnancy despite her inability to give consent by reason of mental incapacity. In the alternative, she also issued a summons seeking a declaration that such a declaration was not required.

Sir Stephen Brown P

I have no doubt on the facts of this case that, if a declaration such as was considered in the case of *Re F* is required as a matter of good practice, I should make it, but in the light of the present state of law I accept the submissions of the Official Solicitor that it is not necessary that the specific approval of the High Court should be a condition precedent to the carrying out of a termination of pregnancy. I consider that the Abortion Act 1967 provides fully adequate safeguards for the doctors who are to undertake this treatment. Accordingly, I am prepared to indicate that in my judgment a formal declaration is not required for this particular treatment. However, it is important that I should also make it clear that the conditions of s 1 of the Abortion Act 1967 must be complied with.

In the handful of cases which have come before the courts, there has been disagreement over whether abortion is, in fact, in the best interests of the pregnant minor or incompetent adult. Although women who lack capacity are not able to give a valid consent to an abortion, they may nevertheless have a preference which should be taken into account. Despite the decisions in cases such as *Re R* and *Re W* (considered in Chapter 4 at p. 239), which suggest that a minor's refusal to consent to medical treatment can be overridden by the courts, it is very difficult to imagine that the courts would sanction the performance of an abortion on a fourteen year old girl against her wishes. And we can see from *Re B*, extracted below, that the wishes of a

[54] [1991] 2 FLR 329.

minor, and likewise of an adult woman who lacks capacity, will be relevant to an assessment of her best interests.

Re B (Wardship: Abortion)[55]

B, who was twelve years old and had normal intelligence and understanding for a girl of her age, wished to have her pregnancy terminated. She was supported by her grandparents, with whom she lived, and the putative father who was aged sixteen. The local authority, making her a ward of court, applied for leave to have her pregnancy terminated. B's natural mother opposed the application on the grounds that she did not believe in abortion.

Hollis J

The court, in its wardship jurisdiction, has been called in in this case to make the decision on the principle that the interests of the ward are first and paramount. Thus, it seems to me that the ward's wishes are not decisive but are, in my view, a part of the evidence which it is important to take into consideration. The mother's wishes, as the natural parent, are also of importance. . . . If the mother's view is to prevail, it means that this girl will be forced to continue with her pregnancy against her own expressed wishes. One can easily imagine what a mental turmoil she may thus suffer. She may have to leave school for an extended period, not least to avoid adverse comment there, she may reject the baby when born, she will have to face the traumatic considerations as to what should happen to the baby after birth.

There is, of course, the possibility that having felt the baby in her arms she will want to keep it, which the mother herself agrees would be impractical. There, thus, might follow a traumatic period for the ward when a decision is come to, possibly through the courts, as to whether the baby should be adopted or cared for by other members of the extended family . . .

In the end, I came to the clear conclusion that it would be in the ward's best interests to have her pregnancy terminated and that, having balanced all the risks, a continuance of the pregnancy would involve risk to the ward greater than if the pregnancy were terminated, of injury to her physical and mental health.

It is, however, important to remember that a child's or an incapacitated woman's own views on abortion will not be decisive. In *Re SS*, below, the woman's preference for a termination was ignored on the grounds that an abortion at this advanced stage of pregnancy was not in her best interests. This case is particularly troubling because Wall J admitted that his decision would almost certainly have been different if the hearing had taken place as soon as the hospital became aware of S's desire to have an abortion. A wholly avoidable delay in bringing legal proceedings therefore deprived her of the opportunity to have her preference respected, and she was forced to carry her unwanted pregnancy to term, and to go through childbirth against her wishes.

Re SS (An Adult: Medical Treatment)[56]

The applicant, S, was twenty-four weeks pregnant. She was thirty-four years old and suffered from schizophrenia, and was detained under the Mental Health Act 1983 at a psychiatric hospital. She applied to the court seeking two declarations: (i) that she lacked the capacity to make a decision about the termination of her pregnancy; and (ii) that it was, in the existing circumstances, in her best interests to undergo a termination of the pregnancy. Having a termination at such a late stage of the pregnancy involved going into labour and effectively giving birth to the dead foetus. Expert medical evidence viewed such an option as likely to be equally stressful and upsetting in its

[55] [1991] 2 FLR, 426.   [56] [2002] 1 FLR 445.

own way as a normal delivery followed by the removal of the child, even if that was S's preferred option. Dr M, instructed by the Official Solicitor, reported that S wanted a termination because she could not cope with looking after a baby, and that she would kill herself if she did not have a termination. S already had four children; the eldest three lived with her husband and S had no contact with them; the fourth had been given up for adoption.

Wall J

It is . . . in my judgment . . . significant that none of the professional witnesses is able to say that a termination now is likely to be less traumatic and damaging to the applicant's physical and mental health than a normal delivery followed by the removal of the child. It must follow that there is no positive professional evidence that a termination now is in the applicant's best interests. . . .

I am, firstly, influenced by the nature of the procedure . . . which it would be necessary for the applicant to undergo, and which would undoubtedly be extremely traumatic. It would also require the applicant's co-operation and active participation, which she might well not provide. I think it unlikely that she would have any real understanding of what was happening. I contrast that with the fact that the applicant has had four children, and that labour in each case has been straightforward. The birth process, therefore, is likely to be much less traumatic than a termination of pregnancy at nearly 24 weeks.

I recognise, however, this is only one aspect of the problem. If the pregnancy is not terminated, the applicant will be obliged to carry a child (which she does not want) to term, and it is very likely that the child will be removed at birth. There is also a risk of harm to the foetus during the pre-birth period, coupled with the stress of the events which are likely to follow the birth. . . .

[W]hilst the risk of deliberate self-harm or harm to the foetus cannot be ruled out (a) there is no obvious evidence of self-harm (as opposed to self-neglect) in the applicant's medical history, and (b) medical and nursing supervision should reduce the risk of it occurring. The applicant has previously had a child removed from her care either at birth or shortly afterwards, and placed for adoption. I do not underestimate the stress of that process. However, there is no evidence that it caused a radical deterioration in her mental or physical health. It is for these reasons . . . that I came to the conclusion that, on a fine balance, the continuation of the pregnancy carried the lesser detriment to the applicant, and that, accordingly, a termination of pregnancy in these circumstances was not in her best interests.

This is sufficient to deal with the case. I am, however, extremely concerned that the court was presented with this application little more than twenty-four hours before the statutory deadline, when the hospital had been aware of the applicant's pregnancy, and her expressed (albeit fluctuating) wish to undergo a termination since her admission at the beginning of August 2001 . . .

I do not wish to appear critical of any of the doctors in this case, and I have not investigated the matter in sufficient depth to enable me to reach specific conclusions, even if it were appropriate for me to do so. Several points, however, are clear to me. The first is that had this case been placed before the court in mid August 2001 the result would, I am confident, have been quite different. The nature of the procedure to terminate the pregnancy required at 23+ weeks has been a powerful factor in my decision. Had the case been heard at an earlier stage in the pregnancy, the balance might well have shifted the other way.

(b) THE BOUNDARY BETWEEN CONTRACEPTION
AND ABORTION

Postcoital contraception, such as the 'morning-after' pill, works by preventing the implantation of a fertilized egg. If a woman is considered to be pregnant as soon as fertilization occurs, then preventing a fertilized egg from implanting would trigger an extremely early abortion, and this could be lawful only if the conditions set out in the Abortion Act have been satisfied. Two doctors would have to certify that, in their opinion, one of the statutory grounds exists, for example, and the procedure would have to be reported to the Department of Health. Plainly this would make the use of postcoital contraception extremely time-consuming and inconvenient.

As we saw earlier, the Offences Against the Person Act 1861 defines abortion as 'procuring a miscarriage', so an offence would only be committed if the morning-after pill causes a woman to 'miscarry'. Miscarriage must be the antonym of 'carriage', a word that seems to imply that the fertilized egg must have attached itself to the pregnant woman's body. The legislation itself is silent on the meaning of miscarriage, leading Glanville Williams to suggest that 'there is, therefore, nothing to prevent the courts interpreting the word "miscarriage" in a way that takes account of customary and approved birth control practices'.[57] In a written answer to Parliament when the morning after pill was licensed for use in 1983, the Attorney General explained that the words in the 1861 statute should be presumed to have been used 'in their popular, ordinary or natural sense':

> it is clear that, used in its ordinary sense, the word 'miscarriage' is not apt to describe a failure to implant . . . Likewise, the phrase 'procure a miscarriage' cannot be construed to include the prevention of implantation.[58]

It seems to be settled medical opinion that pregnancy occurs when the fertilized egg implants in the woman's uterus (which as we saw earlier, will normally be between six and seven days after fertilization began), rather than when the sperm starts to fertilize the egg. Pregnancy tests reveal the presence of the hormone human chorionic gon-adotrophin (hCG) which is released only once implantation has begun. It is therefore impossible to tell whether or not an egg has been fertilized unless and until it implants itself. Approximately 75 per cent of all naturally fertilized eggs will be lost before the woman's next period, and it would be counter-intuitive to describe these losses as miscarriages. Rather, until a pregnancy test reveals that a fertilized egg has attached itself to her uterus, we would not consider a woman to be pregnant.

Adopting implantation as the defining feature of pregnancy is also consistent with the rules governing assisted reproduction. If eggs have been fertilized in a petri dish, common sense clearly dictates that implantation and not fertilization has to be the test for pregnancy. This is confirmed by section 2(3) of the Human Fertilisation and Embryology Act 1990 which states that:

> For the purposes of this Act, a woman is not to be treated as carrying a child until the embryo has become implanted.

---

[57] G Williams, *Textbook on Criminal Law* (Stevens and Son London 1983) 294.   [58] Ibid.

Remember that the first limb of section 58 applies only to women who are 'with child'. Under the second limb, however, doctors can commit an offence even if the woman is not in fact pregnant, provided that they believe her to be pregnant, and intend to cause her to miscarry. During the 72 hours after sexual intercourse within which the morning-after pill must be taken, the dominant medical understanding is that there can be no pregnancy. If a woman cannot be pregnant 72 hours after sexual intercourse, she herself could not commit an offence under the first limb of section 58, and proving that a doctor or pharmacist *intended* to procure a miscarriage under the second limb would likewise be impossible.

Despite the widespread belief that the use of postcoital contraception does not constitute an offence under the Offences Against the Person Act 1861, the matter has come before the courts on two occasions. First, in *R v Dhingra*, a doctor was charged under section 58 of the 1861 Act after fitting a woman with an IUD eleven days after he had had sexual intercourse with her. Wright J held that there could not have been a miscarriage, and hence no offence had been committed under section 58.

R v Dhingra[59]

The defendant doctor had fitted his secretary, Miss Fortey, with an IUD as a post-coital contraceptive. He was charged with an offence under section 58 of the 1861 Act.

Wright J

[W]hat is the position in law? It turns, as it seems to me, upon the true construction in section 58 of the word 'miscarriage'. Does it have the wider meaning of any external interference with the process of reproduction from the time of fertilization; or does it have the narrower meaning of the displacement from the woman's womb, and subsequent loss of, an established pregnancy? It is this more restricted meaning that is used by the medical profession in modern times . . .

[T]he adoption of the wider definition of 'miscarriage' seems to me to lead to the consequence that an offence under this Section might be committed by anyone who inserted an IUCD in a woman, in the course of routine contraceptive precautions, with the intention of preventing a pregnancy at any time in the future.

A like consideration would seem to me to apply to the administration of any contraceptive pill containing the hormone progestogen, which operates in a similar way, whether that pill was taken pre- or post-coitally. Such an interpretation is so startling, so much in variance with what is ordinarily understood to be the purpose of section 58, and would so interfere with what is by now the well-established practices of the medical profession in the family planning field, that I would be intensely reluctant to adopt this wider construction of the section unless forced to do so by incontrovertible arguments. . . .

Further still, and finally, as this is a Criminal Statute, if there are two otherwise equally acceptable constructions of this particular section, I am satisfied that I should adopt that which is more favourable to the defendant.

I have come to the conclusion that I should adopt the narrower interpretation of this part of section 58, and hold that the word 'miscarriage' in this context relates to the spontaneous expulsion of the products of pregnancy. I further hold, in accordance with the uncontroverted evidence that I have heard, that a pregnancy cannot come into existence until the fertilized ovum has become implanted in the womb . . .

It follows from this—and I so hold—that the insertion of an intra-uterine contraceptive device

[59] Unreported, 25 Jan 1991.

before a pregnancy has become established, with the intention of preventing the successful implantation in the uterine wall of any fertilized ovum that may result from a prior act of sexual intercourse, does not amount to an offence under section 58 of the Offences Against the Person Act 1861.

Secondly, when regulations (which we considered in Chapter 9) were introduced allowing the morning-after pill to be dispensed by pharmacists without the need for a prescription, in *R (on the application of Smeaton) v Secretary of State for Health*, the Society for the Protection of the Unborn Child (SPUC) sought to challenge them. They argued that the morning-after pill is an abortifacient, and so women and pharmacists would be committing offences under the Offences Against the Person Act. In a long and wide-ranging judgment, Munby J dismissed their claim. His reasons can be summarized as follows. First, because miscarriage is not defined in the 1861 Act, it should be used in its ordinary sense, which is the termination of an established pregnancy. Before implantation, there is no pregnancy, and there can therefore be no miscarriage. Secondly, because other contraceptives, such as the pill and intra-uterine devices (IUDs) may also work by inhibiting the implantation of a fertilized egg, if SPUC's arguments were to be accepted, every method of contraception, except the condom, might involve the commission of a criminal offence. This would mean that 34 per cent of all women between the ages of 16 and 49 (approximately 4.5 million women) would potentially be guilty of criminal offences. Thirdly, complying with the conditions set out in the Abortion Act would delay the use of the morning-after pill, which would mean that it was less effective, and would, in practice, lead to an increase in the number of abortions.

R (on the application of Smeaton) v Secretary of State for Health[60]

John Smeaton, on behalf of SPUC claimed that the morning-after pill was an abortifacient, rather than a contraceptive. They argued that the meaning of miscarriage in 1861 included the prevention of implantation, and so post-coital contraception could amount to a criminal offence under sections 58 and 59 of the 1861 Act. Since the conditions laid out in the Abortion Act are not met when the morning-after pill is dispensed, no defence is available.

Munby J

I have made it clear that the court cannot concern itself with moral or religious issues. But that does not mean that I can blind myself to the social realities, which underlie this case, nor to the social implications were I to find in favour of SPUC. . . . Here I merely outline two of the salient features of this aspect of the case. The first is this. . . . On the logic of its own case SPUC's challenge, and the allegations of serious criminality *inter alia* by the woman concerned, are not simply to the morning-after pill. They extend to *any* chemical or device which operates, or may operate, by impeding, discouraging or preventing the natural process at any time after fertilisation has started, alternatively has completed. They extend to *any* drug or device which may operate in that way, even if it may also operate in a way which impedes, discourages or prevents the process of fertilisation. The medical profession and female members of the public have for years been operating on the basis that the use, prescription and supply of such chemicals and devices is legal and involves no potential criminality. The pill has been available since the 1960s and the morning-after pill since the early 1980s. That position has remained unchallenged until sought to be

[60] [2002] Criminal Law Review 664.

reopened in these proceedings. The other is this. Making Levonelle available from pharmacists without a prescription means that it can be obtained more quickly following intercourse when a woman knows or suspects that her regular method of contraception has failed, particularly during weekends and public holidays. If SPUC were to succeed in this challenge, the result would be, as I have said, that Levonelle could be prescribed only by doctors who had complied with the requirements of the Abortion Act 1967. This in turn would mean that:

- Levonelle would tend to be administered either not at all or at a later stage, when the expert evidence is that it is less effective and more likely to operate post-fertilisation.

- There would inevitably be an increase in the number of abortions as conventionally understood, a result which . . . SPUC would presumably not welcome.

[T]he correct approach can be set out in the form of four propositions:

(i) the 1861 Act is an 'always speaking' Act;

(ii) the word 'miscarriage' is an ordinary English word of flexible meaning which Parliament in 1861 chose to leave undefined;

(iii) it should accordingly be interpreted as it would be *currently* understood;

(iv) it should be interpreted in the light of the best current scientific and medical knowledge that is available to the court . . .

[T]here is in truth no substantial dispute as to the current meaning of the word 'miscarriage' . . . miscarriage is the termination of . . . a post-implantation pregnancy. Current medical—and, indeed, I would add, current lay and popular—understanding of what is meant by 'miscarriage' plainly excludes results brought about by IUDs, the pill, the mini-pill and the morning-after pill. . . .

Finally, it is not irrelevant to note that my decision accords with social realities. I am declaring licit—not criminal—that which has in fact been the daily practice of countless people in this country for many, many years.

There would in my judgment be something very seriously wrong, indeed grievously wrong with our system—by which I mean not just our legal system but the entire system by which our polity is governed—if a judge in 2002 were to be compelled by a statute 141 years old to hold that what thousands, hundreds of thousands, indeed millions, of ordinary honest, decent, law abiding citizens have been doing day in day out for so many years is and always has been criminal. I am glad to be spared so unattractive a duty . . .

I have to say that I cannot see that it is any part of the responsibilities of public authorities—let alone of the criminal law—to be telling adult people whether they can or cannot use contraceptive devices of the kind which I have been considering. . . .

Government's responsibility is to ensure the medical and pharmaceutical safety of products offered in the market place and the appropriate provision of suitable guidance and advice. Beyond that, as it seems to me, in this as in other areas of medical ethics, respect for the personal autonomy which our law has now come to recognise demands that the choice be left to the individual.

(c) SELECTIVE REDUCTION

Fetal reduction, or the selective termination of one or more fetuses, is a much more complex procedure than complete termination, and it has only become possible in the last twenty years as a result of advances in ultrasonography. In practice selective reduction of multiple pregnancies is rare, and the limits which the HFEA places on the number of embryos that can be transferred to a woman's body in one IVF treatment cycle (see Chapter 14 p. 806) should reduce still further the number of selective reductions. In 2004, 64 selective terminations took place.

Initially it was unclear how the Offences Against the Person Act 1861 and the Abortion Act 1967 would apply to a procedure in which one or more fetuses are destroyed but the woman continues to be pregnant. This confusion has been addressed by a further amendment to the Abortion Act effected by The Human Fertilisation and Embryology Act 1990.

Abortion Act 1967 section 5(2)

For the purposes of the law relating to abortion, anything done with intent to procure a woman's miscarriage (or, in the case of a woman carrying more than one foetus, her miscarriage of any foetus) is unlawfully done unless authorised by section 1 of this Act and, in the case of a woman carrying more than one foetus, anything done with intent to procure her miscarriage of any foetus is authorised by that section if—

(a) the ground for termination of the pregnancy specified in subsection (1)(d) of that section applies in relation to any foetus and the thing is done for the purpose of procuring the miscarriage of that foetus, or

(b) any of the other grounds for termination of the pregnancy specified in that section applies.

Since section 5(2) specifies that the ordinary Abortion Act grounds apply equally to selective reduction, one or more fetuses can be destroyed if, for example, there is a risk to the woman's mental or physical health, or if there is a substantial risk that a child would be born seriously handicapped.

The application of section 1(1)(a), the so-called 'social' ground, to selective reduction is unproblematic given the considerable difficulties commonly encountered in caring for twins, triplets, and higher order multiple births. But another indication for selective reduction, namely improving the chances of survival of the remaining fetuses, is not covered by a literal interpretation of section 1 of the Abortion Act. Such abortions would only be lawful if a slightly more elastic interpretation were accepted, and improving the chances that one or more babies will survive were taken to be necessary to avert a risk to their mother's mental wellbeing, or alternatively to reducing the risk that the child, if born, would be at substantial risk of suffering from a serious handicap.

(d) THE LIVING ABORTUS

The vast majority of abortions are performed when the fetus is not capable of surviving outside of the pregnant woman's body. Hence, removing the fetus from the woman's uterus inevitably leads to its death. But although abortion and fetal destruction are normally indistinguishable, they are not necessarily so. If the fetus is born alive, it has an existence separate from its mother, and the pregnant woman could not insist upon its destruction. Where the fetus might be viable, abortion normally involves killing the fetus while it is still inside the woman's body, prior to its removal.

In practice, a tiny number of abortions involve deliberate feticide, and in most of these, the fetus has an abnormality so serious that it would be likely to die shortly after birth. An example might be anacephalus, where the fetus is born with virtually no brain. The question of whether it is right for doctors to deliberately kill such a fetus prior to its delivery has not been especially controversial because the baby will in any event die during or immediately after birth. Much more complicated ethical dilemmas will be raised if it becomes possible for fetuses to survive independently at earlier stages in pregnancy.

During the second half of the twentieth century, dramatic progress in neonatal medicine steadily reduced the age at which a fetus became viable. Babies have survived after as little as 22 weeks' gestation, but this is very unusual, and the risk that the baby will be seriously disabled is extremely high. In one of the largest studies of extremely premature babies, of all those born at 22 weeks' gestation, 84 per cent died in the delivery room, 14 per cent died in the neonatal intensive care unit, and 1 per cent survived to discharge.[61] Of the two children who survived to discharge, one had severe disability and one had mild disability at 6 years of age.[62]

It is not clear whether there is some absolute limit to the age at which a premature baby is capable of surviving independently. Before about 21 weeks, the fetus's lungs are solid and breathing would be impossible. A fetus that could not breathe could only survive outside of the pregnant woman's body if scientists were able to develop some sort of 'artificial womb' which could simulate the uterine environment until the baby became capable of independent life.

If this becomes possible, it will clearly raise some very complicated questions for abortion law. If a fetus at 12 weeks' gestation could be transferred to an artificial womb to continue its development, does abortion cease to be synonymous with fetal destruction? Could we say that a woman has the right to the fetus's removal from her body, but not the right to its death? Artificial wombs might enable the partners of pregnant women to both respect their partner's decision not to continue with the pregnancy *and* to bring up the child which is gestated artificially. Given that the conflict between fetal life and women's self-determination has proved so intractable, the prospect of artificial wombs might seem superficially appealing since they would allow us to respect women's reproductive autonomy without destroying fetal life. In the next extract, Judith Jarvis Thomson extends her 'violinist' analogy (described earlier at p. 592) to argue that the woman's right to detach the fetus from her body does not give her the right to insist upon its death.

Judith Jarvis Thomson[63]

[W]hile I am arguing for the permissibility of abortion in some cases, I am not arguing for the right to secure the death of the unborn child. It is easy to confuse these things in that up to a certain point in the life of the foetus it is not able to survive outside the mother's body; hence removing it from her body guarantees its death. But they are importantly different. I have argued that you are not morally required to spend nine months in bed, sustaining the life of that violinist; but to say this is by no means to say that if, when you unplug yourself, there is a miracle and he

---

[61] EPICure <http://www.nottingham.ac.uk/human-development/EPICure/> (July 2005).
[62] Ibid.   [63] 'A Defence of Abortion' (1971) 1 Philosophy and Public Affairs 47.

survives, you then have a right to turn round and slit his throat. You may detach yourself even if this costs him his life; you have no right to be guaranteed his death, by some other means, if unplugging yourself does not kill him . . . [T]he desire for the child's death is not one which anybody may gratify, should it turn out to be possible to detach the child alive.

If it becomes possible to gestate a fetus in an artificial womb, a number of difficult questions would arise. What, for example, would the child be told about the circumstances of their birth? If the legal definition of 'mother' is the woman who gives birth to a child, would children gestated artificially be motherless? Would only fetuses whose putative 'fathers' were offering to care for them be transferred to artificial wombs? If so, what should happen if the man changes his mind before 'birth'? If all aborted fetuses were to be artificially gestated, we would be creating massive numbers of orphaned newborn babies.

7. ABORTION IN OTHER COUNTRIES

There is insufficient space to provide a detailed survey of abortion laws throughout the world. Instead we briefly consider the law in Northern Ireland, Ireland, and the United States. It is, however, worth noting that there is enormous cross-national variation in the regulation of abortion. Despite European harmonization across many legal issues, there is no consistency in the regulation of abortion in Europe. Abortion is available upon request in the first trimester in some countries (such as the Netherlands), and illegal unless necessary to save the pregnant woman's life in others (such as Ireland). Moreover, within different countries abortion laws have changed dramatically in order to reflect shifts in political and religious affiliations. For example, the liberal abortion regime that existed in Poland prior to the break-up of the Soviet bloc was replaced by a much more restrictive system, in part as a result of the power the Catholic Church acquired through its role in the anti-Soviet *Solidarity* movement.

In countries which prohibit or severely restrict access to abortion, women who can afford it may travel abroad to terminate their unwanted pregnancies (over 6,000 Irish women have abortions in England each year). If abortion 'tourism' is impracticable, women may resort to illegal and often unsafe abortions (there are an estimated 610,000 unsafe abortions in Nigeria each year, resulting in 20,000 deaths).

(a) NORTHERN IRELAND

The legal status of abortion in Northern Ireland is unclear. The Abortion Act 1967 does not apply, and so there are no *statutory* defences to sections 58 and 59 of the Offences Against the Person Act 1861. However, as we saw earlier, *R v Bourne* indicates that a defence may nevertheless exist if the pregnancy is endangering the pregnant woman's life, and for this purpose, it is sufficient if the consequence of carrying the pregnancy to term would be to leave her a 'mental wreck'. Thus individual doctors must decide, on a case by case basis and with the potential threat of criminal prosecution, whether a woman's circumstances are such that continuing with the pregnancy would leave her a 'mental wreck'. Court rulings in Northern Ireland have confirmed that there are circumstances in which abortion will not be a criminal offence, but because there is no specific statutory defence, the parameters within which abortion may lawfully be performed remain unclear.[64] The only cases that have arisen have involved girls and women who have either lacked capacity or been threatening suicide. In all these cases, the authorities caring for them have sought the court's approval for the termination of pregnancy, and medical opinion has been unanimous that abortion was in the girl or woman's best interests.

The first case to consider the lawfulness of abortion in the abstract was *Re Family Planning Association of Northern Ireland*.[65] This was a case brought by the Family Planning Association of Northern Ireland which had asked the Department of Health for Northern Ireland for guidance on when abortion could be lawfully performed. Initially Kerr J rejected their application on the grounds that the medical profession was not unclear about the law, which was governed by the *Bourne* exception—restrictively interpreted—to the Offences Against the Person Act 1861. This was, however, overturned on appeal. The Court of Appeal held that the Department of Health, Social Services and Public Safety could not be compelled to issue guidelines on abortion, but suggested it would be prudent to do so

Fewer than one hundred abortions are performed in Northern Ireland each year, and most of these follow the detection of a serious fetal abnormality. Women from Northern Ireland who wish to terminate their pregnancies commonly travel to England, and over 1200 women do so each year.[66] In addition to being extremely inconvenient, this will inevitably delay their abortions. Moreover, since Northern Irish women are not entitled to NHS abortions, poorer women may find it impossible to afford the trip to a private English clinic in order to terminate their unwanted pregnancies.

The Family Planning Association of Northern Ireland has campaigned for the extension of the Abortion Act 1967 to Northern Ireland, but as Eileen Fegan and Rachel Rebouche explain in the following extract, this strategy may have a number of disadvantages. Not only is the scheme set up by the Abortion Act itself the subject of substantial criticism among feminists for its emphasis on medical paternalism, but also cultural differences between Northern Ireland and the rest of the UK might mean that the terms of the Act would in fact be interpreted in a much more restrictive fashion.

Eileen Fegan and Rachel Rebouche[67]

However, without a prior shift in Northern Irish culture and abortion discourse, extension of the 1967 Abortion Act could cause further problems. Most immediately, there are practical as well as ideological problems particular to the context of Northern Ireland. Apart from the strategic inconsistency of endorsing a model British feminists and pro-choice activists have long sought to reform, it puts Northern Irish women at the mercy of a medical profession that has been seen to be

---

[64] *Northern Health and Social Services Board v F & G* [1993] NILR 268; *Northern Health and Social Services Board v A* [1994] NIJB 1; *Western Health and Social Services Board v CMB*, 29 Sept 1995, unreported; *Down Lisburn Health and Social Services Board v CH & LAH*, 18 Oct 1995, unreported.

[65] [2003] NIQB 48.

[66] *Abortion Statistics* 2004 (DoH 2005) <http://www.dh.gov.uk/assetRoot/04/11/66/35/04116635.pdf>.

[67] 'Northern Ireland's Abortion Law: The Morality of Silence and the Censure of Agency' (2003) 11 *Feminist Legal Studies* 221–54, 239–40, 251–2.

largely conservative in their attitudes concerning abortion. Even after the High Court declaration in 1993 (in *Re K*) that a termination for a minor was legal, no doctor could be found to perform it within the region. This is in sharp contrast to the liberal approach to the provisions of the 1967 Abortion Act taken by doctors in Great Britain. In addition, the communal culture of the jurisdiction may be enough to prevent many, particularly rural, women from attempting to access abortion near home. . . . The introduction of the Abortion Act against what is seen as a polarised and emotionally charged cultural backdrop might even give way to a more restrictive interpretation of the 1967 Act than is currently experienced in the rest of the UK. . . .

In Northern Ireland many forms of cultural intimidation discourage the disclosure of pro-choice views. . . . Despite progress on many controversial issues, this leaves pro-choice feminism in Northern Ireland 'feeling' very much like an underground movement. . . . It would seem that even if we choose to stay silent on abortion and women's agency as a controversial issue on cultural grounds, there are already signs that this largely patriarchal culture will not endure indefinitely. Women and men are expressing attitudes which differ from those traditionally identified with Northern Ireland: there is a growing secularisation of society, men and women are rethinking gender roles; and sexual mores are changing.

(b) IRELAND

Abortion is illegal in Ireland except where the pregnancy poses a real and substantial risk to the pregnant woman's life. Ireland's abortion law consists in both constitutional and legislative provisions. Not only does the Offences Against the Person Act 1861 apply, but also the Irish Constitution was amended in 1983 by Article 40.3.3 which provides that the 'unborn' and the pregnant woman have an equal right to life. Hence, unless the pregnant woman's life is in danger, the fetus's right to life must take priority.

As in Northern Ireland, women from the Republic of Ireland will commonly travel to private English (or Welsh or Scottish) clinics in order to terminate their unwanted pregnancies, and over 6,200 women do so each year.[68] The legality of this practice was called into question in the case of *Attorney General v X*.

Attorney General v X[69]

A fourteen year old girl had become pregnant after being raped by a schoolfriend's father. She and her mother travelled to England so that she could have an abortion. Before they left, her father had contacted the Irish police to enquire whether a fetal tissue sample should be preserved as DNA evidence which might be used in prosecuting the rapist. In response, the Irish Attorney General sought, and was initially granted an injunction to restrain X from travelling abroad to obtain an abortion. Costello J held that under Irish law (article 40.3.3. of the Constitution) the prohibition on abortion extended to a restriction on the right to travel abroad in order to obtain an abortion, that the danger to the mother's life (which might justify the abortion) was not in the instant case sufficiently probable (the danger of suicide) as to outweigh the certainty of death of the foetus. This was overturned on appeal when the Irish Supreme Court held that the risk to X's life was great and outweighed the destruction of the unborn life.

---

[68] Available at <http://www.dh.gov.uk>. At the time of writing the most recent statistics are *Abortion Statistics 2004* (DoH 2005) <http://www.dh.gov.uk/assetRoot/04/11/66/35/04116635.pdf>.
[69] [1992] 2 CMLR 277.

O'Flaherty J

I believe that the law in this State is that surgical intervention which has the effect of terminating pregnancy bona fide undertaken to save the life of the mother where she is in danger of death is permissible under the Constitution and the law. The danger has to represent a substantial risk to her life though this does not necessarily have to be an imminent danger of instant death. The law does not require the doctors to wait until the mother is in peril of immediate death. I believe the instant case to come within this principle.

Egan J

In my opinion the true test should be that a pregnancy may be terminated if its continuance as a matter of probability involves a real and substantial risk to the life of the mother. The risk must be to her life but it is irrelevant, in my view, that it should be a risk of self-destruction rather than a risk to life for any other reason. The evidence establishes that such a risk exists in the present case.

The question of whether it is acceptable to offer advice on arranging abortions in England, Wales, or Scotland came before the European Court of Justice in *Open Door Counselling Ltd v Ireland*.[70] The Irish Supreme Court's decision to uphold an injunction granted by the High Court restraining the applicants from providing such assistance to pregnant women was challenged by women who worked in the Dublin Well Women centre and by women of childbearing age on the grounds that it restricted their rights under Article 10 to impart and receive information. The ECHR noted that states enjoyed a wide margin of appreciation in relation to moral questions 'particularly in an area such as the present which touches on matters of belief concerning the nature of human life'. The question then was whether the restriction on the provision of information was justified because it pursued the legitimate aim of 'the protection of morals of which the protection in Ireland of the right to life of the unborn is one aspect'. By a majority the ECHR held that the restriction on the provision of information was disproportionate since non-directive counselling did not necessarily lead to the termination of fetal life, the information was in any event available elsewhere, and there was some evidence that the absence of information might pose a risk to women's health.

In response to the X case, a referendum in 1992 led to a constitutional amendment which limits the State's ability to stop a woman from travelling abroad for an abortion. In the same referendum, voters decided that there should be a limited right to receive information on abortion services in England, and a proposal that suicide risk should be excluded as a ground for life-saving abortion was rejected. A further referendum was held in 2002, and by a very narrow margin, voters again rejected the Government's proposal that the risk of suicide should cease to offer a justification for the termination of pregnancy.

(c) THE UNITED STATES

In *Roe v Wade*,[71] the US Supreme Court recognized for the first time that a woman's freedom to choose whether to bear a child was a fundamental constitutionally protected liberty, which the state could restrict only in order to promote a compelling

---

[70] *The Times* 5 Nov 1992 (ECHR).   [71] 410 US 113 (1973).

state interest. The right to privacy, the Supreme Court held, 'is broad enough to encompass a woman's decision whether or not to terminate her pregnancy'. Prior to viability, the state did not have a compelling interest in fetal life, and hence restrictions on a woman's right to decide to terminate her pregnancy would be unconstitutional. The decision in *Roe v Wade* has never been overturned, and yet its scope has been significantly narrowed by subsequent decisions of the Supreme Court. Anti-abortion campaigners have had some success in persuading state legislatures to pass regulations which in practice restrict women's access to abortion, and the constitutionality of these has been tested by the Supreme Court on a number of occasions.

In *Webster v Reproductive Health Services*,[72] the Supreme Court weakened the notion of a constitutionally protected right to choose abortion. It held that restrictions on women's right to choose abortion would be unconstitutional only if they imposed an 'undue burden', and even then, they might be justified by important state interests. Three years later, in *Planned Parenthood v Casey*,[73] the Supreme Court upheld all but one of the restrictions (such as a mandatory 24-hour waiting period, and a parental consent requirement for minors) that a Pennsylvania statute had imposed upon women's access to abortion. Only the spousal notification requirement was rejected on the grounds that, given the proportion of women who may fear assault at the hands of their sexual partner, it did represent an 'undue burden' on women's right to choose abortion. The State, it was argued in *Casey*, had a 'profound interest in potential life', and was therefore entitled, throughout pregnancy, to:

take measures to ensure that the woman's choice is informed, and measures designed to advance this interest will not be invalidated as long as their purpose is to persuade the woman to choose childbirth over abortion, provided that they do not impose an 'undue burden on the right'.

In the following extract, Syliva Law argues that by permitting states to place obstacles in the path of women choosing abortion, the Supreme Court in *Casey* effectively overturned *Roe v Wade*:

Sylvia A Law[74]

Many times over the past few months I have been puzzled when sophisticated people . . . ask me whether the Supreme Court will overrule Roe v. Wade. This surprises me because, like Justices Blackmun and Scalia, I believe that the Supreme Court effectively overruled Roe in 1989. . . .

From a pro-choice point of view, one plausible assessment of the Casey decision is that it represents the worst of all possible worlds. The joint opinion affirmed a woman's 'fundamental constitutional right' to abortion, but simultaneously allowed the state to adopt measures that effectively curtail many women's exercise of the abortion right. This curtailment hits hardest those women who are most vulnerable, i.e. the poor, the unsophisticated, the young, and women who live in rural areas.

The twenty-four-hour waiting requirement sends a powerful message that is degrading, condescending, and paternalistic to all women. It assumes that women make rash decisions, and reinforces negative stereotypes about women. It imputes women's competence as moral and practical decision-makers. Just as seriously, the impact of the twenty-four-hour waiting

---

[72] 492 US 490 (1989).   [73] 112 S Ct 2791 (1992).

[74] 'Abortion Compromise: Inevitable and Impossible' (1992) University of Illinois Law Review 921, 931, 940–1.

requirement will be sharply differentiated on lines of class, age, sophistication, and geography. . . . Abortions will be later, more costly, and more intrusive, but women will eventually obtain them. . . .

A compromise that says the rich and sophisticated can have abortions but the poor and naive cannot should be rejected as hostile to our most fundamental commitments to equal treatment. Regulatory programs such as that adopted in Pennsylvania sabotage widely shared values. They make abortion more costly, more dangerous, and later in the pregnancy term. All of this is directly contrary to the concerns of those who seek to protect fetal life, as well as those who are pro-choice.

States have further sought to restrict access to abortion by banning certain abortion procedures, particularly those used in abortions carried out later in pregnancy. A termination carried out in the final trimester of pregnancy may involve the fetus being killed *in utero* before being delivered in the normal way. While not a medical term, these late abortions have been emotively described as 'partial birth' abortions. In 2000 by a narrow (5–4) majority, in *Stenberg v Carhart*, the US Supreme Court struck down Nebraska's 'partial birth' abortion law on two grounds.[75] First, the Nebraska legislature had failed to include an exception where this type of abortion was necessary to preserve the woman's health. The statute's exclusion clause applied only if the abortion procedure was necessary to save the woman's life but this was held to be too narrow. Secondly, the wording of the statute was insufficiently precise, and that insofar as its ambiguity might lead doctors to fear prosecution or imprisonment, the statute placed an 'undue burden upon a woman's right to make an abortion decision'. Hence, since *Stenberg*, it seems clear that to be constitutional any ban on a particular abortion procedure must satisfy these two requirements: first, there must be no ambiguity or vagueness about the procedure which it bans, and secondly, the law must contain a health exception not limited to instances where the woman's life is at risk.

Steps to restrict access to abortion have also happened at federal level. The Partial Birth Abortion Act 2003 attempted to prohibit a particular procedure used in late abortions. The statute defines a partial birth abortion as a procedure in which a physician intentionally delivers a living fetus through the cervix until, in a breach position, only the head remains in the uterus, or, in a head-first presentation, the entire fetal skull is outside the body of the woman and the physician 'perform[s] an overt act that he knows will kill the partially delivered living fetus'. The statute includes an exception for any 'partial birth abortion that is necessary to save the life of a mother whose life is endangered by a physical disorder, physical illness, or physical injury'. It is not clear that this legislation complies with the two limitations on abortion bans articulated in *Stenberg*. First, 'partial birth abortion' is not a medical term, and so it may not be entirely clear to doctors what they are and are not allowed to do. Although intended to apply to third trimester abortions, arguably the Act could also apply to vacuum aspiration procedures which commonly take place in the first trimester of pregnancy. In addition to not satisfying Justice O'Connor's first requirement for a constitutional abortion ban, this lack of clarity might have a chilling effect

---

[75] *Stenberg v Carhart* US 120 S Ct 2597, 147 L.Ed.2d 743 (2000).

on doctors' willingness to perform lawful abortions and thus further restrict women's access to abortion. Secondly, the Act only permits doctors to carry out the banned procedure where it is necessary to save the woman's life, and this is too narrow to qualify as a sufficient health exception.

The background to this progressive narrowing of the right to abortion in the US has been an exceptionally acrimonious battle over the legitimacy of abortion. Unlike in Britain, a candidate's views on abortion are often a crucial electoral issue, and nominations to the Supreme Court have similarly been decided on the basis of a judge's track record on abortion. A hard-core minority of anti-abortion campaigners have murdered doctors and set fire to clinics. And this fear of reprisals for carrying out abortions has led to a marked unwillingness among gynaecologists to provide abortion services. In the next extract Marlene Gerber Fried describes how abortion in the US may be legal but also substantially unavailable, particularly to poorer women, teenagers, and women living in rural areas.

Marlene Gerber Fried[76]

The impact of eroding access to abortion has been felt most severely by low-income women, young women, and women of color, who comprise a disproportionate number of the poor. Access has been undermined primarily through denial of public funding for abortion, parental involvement laws, and the loss of abortion services.

Public funding, an absolute necessity if all women are to have access to abortion rights, was lost in 1976, just three years after *Roe v Wade*. The Hyde Amendment, which prohibits federal Medicaid funding except in cases of life endangerment, has been renewed by Congress every year since. Most states have followed the federal precedent and prohibit the use of state funds for abortions . . .

Publicity surrounding the murders of doctors and clinic workers has made the public at large sharply aware of the extreme vulnerability of abortion providers. In fact, clinics and providers have been targets of violence since the early 1980s . . . These acts included death threats, stalking, attacks with chemicals, arson, bomb threats, invasions and blockades. While federal legislation such as the Freedom of Access to Clinic Entrances Act will certainly help, anti-abortionists are increasingly turning to harassment of individual doctors and their families, picketing their homes, following them, circulating 'Wanted' posters.

The provider shortage has only recently come to public attention, although it represents a major threat to abortion rights . . . While the overall numbers are themselves very disturbing, of even greater concern is the very uneven distribution of services. Nine out of ten abortion providers are now located in metropolitan areas . . . Ninety four per cent of nonmetropolitan counties have no services. . . .

Anti-abortion activists aim also to cut off the supply of potential future providers. They have targeted medical students, generating understandable concerns about taking up practice in such a dangerous and marginalized field . . .

Few medical students are being trained in abortion techniques, despite the fact that abortion is the most common obstetrics surgical procedure. Almost half of graduating obstetrics and gynecology residents have never performed a first-trimester abortion . . .

---

[76] 'Abortion in the United States—Legal but Inaccessible' in R Solinger (ed), *Abortion Wars: A Half Century of Struggle, 1950–2000* (University of California Press Berkeley 1998) 208–26, 212, 214–15.

Another area in which the anti-abortion movement has had considerable legislative and ideological success is the restriction of abortion for young women. Parental involvement laws requiring either parental consent or notification before minors can obtain abortions affect millions of young women.

8. CONCLUSION

It is commonly remarked that English law's medicalization of abortion has effectively depoliticized the issue. If the decision to terminate a pregnancy is taken by a woman's *doctor*, on the grounds that pregnancy poses *a risk to health*, it becomes very difficult to challenge both individual abortion decisions, and the rules governing access to abortion. Partly this is because of the confidentiality that attaches to the doctor/patient relationship and partly because of the trust and confidence that most people have in the medical profession. In recent years, however, there has been increasing political and media interest in the question of access to abortion.

Perhaps oddly, one of the principal areas of concern has been the time limit in section 1(1)(d) of the Abortion Act. If babies can survive at 22 weeks, it has been suggested that permitting abortion for 'social' reasons up until 24 weeks is anomalous. But the reality is that fewer than 1 per cent of all abortions take place between 20 and 24 weeks, and most of these would probably fit within the fetal abnormality ground, and so be unaffected by any reduction of the time limit in section 1(1)(a). Reducing the time-limit would, in practice, have virtually no impact upon the *number* of abortions carried out each year in the UK, so any proposed change in the law would be largely symbolic.

It is also important to think about *why* women have late abortions. There are three main reasons. First, the results from prenatal tests, such as the 18- to 20-week anomaly scan, may not be available until around the twentieth week of pregnancy. Secondly, a woman's circumstances may have changed drastically since she became pregnant. Her partner may have left her, or died, and she may feel unable to bring his child into the world. Thirdly, a woman may not realize she is pregnant until relatively late in pregnancy. This may be because she is very young or leads a chaotic life, and does not recognize the symptoms of pregnancy; or it may be because she is using a form of contraceptive, such as the progesterone-only pill, which can result in her periods stopping altogether. Reducing the time limit for abortion might mean that women who fall into one of these categories would be forced to continue a now unwanted pregnancy to term.

Finally, it is worth pointing out that there is currently a vast gap between the theory and the practice of abortion law. Students studying abortion law for the first time are often surprised to learn both that women do not have the right to terminate their unwanted pregnancies, and that abortion is still, prima facie, a criminal offence. This surprise is understandable, given that, in practice, abortion is available upon request in England, Scotland and Wales within at least the first 13 weeks of pregnancy, and perhaps up to about 16 weeks. So while academic criticism of abortion law based upon its excessive medicalization is, in my view, persuasive and important, the reality is that women *do* make their own abortion decisions, and that the medical profession will very seldom interfere with their 'right' to do so.

A further possible reform of abortion law would therefore be to bring the legislation into line with the reality that abortion *is* available upon request. Yet, as in other European countries, any future 'right' to abortion on request would almost certainly be confined to the first 12 or 14 weeks of pregnancy. In practice then, such a step might make it *more difficult* for women who need access to abortion after 13 weeks, since they would have to fit within a special medical exception (such as that the pregnancy poses a grave risk to their health), rather than, at present, simply having to shop around for a provider who is willing to help them. Oddly then, the status quo, despite being peculiarly paternalistic and outdated, may in practice serve women's needs rather better than some of the plausible legislative alternatives.

Nevertheless, it is surely time to recognize that it no longer makes any sense for the regulation of what is now a straightforward and common medical procedure to consist in a set of defences to the criminal offence of terminating pregnancy. It is perhaps worth considering whether Munby J's reasons for rejecting the use of criminal law in relation to postcoital contraception might be equally apposite in relation to abortion. Recall that in *Smeaton* he said,

I have to say that I cannot see that it is any part of the responsibilities of public authorities—let alone of the criminal law—to be telling adult people whether they can or cannot use contraceptive devices of the kind which I have been considering. . . .

Government's responsibility is to ensure the medical and pharmaceutical safety of products offered in the market place and the appropriate provision of suitable guidance and advice. Beyond that, as it seems to me, in this as in other areas of medical ethics, respect for the personal autonomy which our law has now come to recognise demands that the choice be left to the individual.

9. FURTHER READING

BMA, *Abortion Time Limits: A Briefing Paper from the BMA* (BMA 2005) <http://www.bma.org.uk/ap.nsf/Content/AbortionTimeLimits>.

JACKSON, EMILY, *Regulating Reproduction* (Hart Publishing Oxford 2001) ch 3.

JACKSON, EMILY, 'Abortion, Autonomy and Prenatal Diagnosis' (2000) 9 Social and Legal Studies 467–94.

KIRKLIN, D, 'The role of medical imaging in the abortion debate' (2004) 30 Journal of Medical Ethics 426.

LEE, ELLIE (ed), *Abortion Law and Politics Today* (Macmillan London 1998).

LEE, ELLIE (ed), *Abortion: Whose Right?* (Hodder & Stoughton London 2002).

SHELDON, SALLY, *Beyond Control: Medical Power and Abortion Law* (Pluto London 1997).

SHELDON, SALLY and WILKINSON, STEPHEN, 'Termination of pregnancy for reason of foetal disability: are there grounds for a special exception in law?' (2001) 9(2) Medical Law Review 85–109.

SHELDON, SALLY, 'Unwilling Fathers and Abortion: Terminating Men's Child Support Obligations?' (2003) 66 Modern Law Review 175–94.

Special issue of the *Journal of Medical Ethics* (2001) 26 suppl II.

11

LIABILITY FOR OCCURRENCES
BEFORE BIRTH

1. CENTRAL ISSUES

1. At common law, the fetus cannot be owed a duty of care, but a child's action for prenatal injuries crystallized at birth when the child 'inherited' her damaged body. This is also the position under the Congenital Disabilities (Civil Liability) Act 1976. With the exception of injuries sustained in road traffic accidents, mothers cannot be held liable for injuring their children *in utero*.

2. Under English law, it is generally assumed that children cannot have an action for 'wrongful life', that is where their claim is that, but for the defendant's negligence, they would not have been born.

3. Parents can bring an action for 'wrongful conception', usually following negligent sterilization or negligent post-sterilization advice.

The question of whether parents should be entitled to damages to cover the unwanted child's maintenance costs is extremely controversial.

4. In a series of recent cases, the courts have held that the maintenance costs of a healthy child are unrecoverable, but that parents are entitled to recover for the additional costs associated with caring for a disabled child. The House of Lords has recently suggested that a 'conventional award' of £15,000 should be made to acknowledge that there has been a wrongful interference with the mother's reproductive autonomy, but it is as yet unclear whether this applies only where the mother is disabled, or whether it extends to other wrongful conception cases.

2. INTRODUCTION

In this chapter, we consider the possibility of liability, either to the child herself or to her parents, for events which occur before birth. If a child is born suffering from an abnormality which is attributable to another person's conduct, she might want to claim damages. There are a number of different ways in which a child's health can be adversely affected before she is born. Before a child is even conceived, it is possible that her parents' capacity to give birth to a healthy baby might be impaired, an example might be exposure to toxic substances which damage sperm or egg cells. Negligence during IVF treatment, before the embryo is transferred to the woman's body, might also result in the birth of a disabled child. And of course the child might have sustained injuries while *in utero*. All of these actions will usually be brought under the Congenital Disabilities (Civil Liability) Act 1976, but we also briefly consider the possibility of an action at common law for prenatal injuries because it is still theoretically possible (if unlikely) that a child born before the 1976 Act came into force could have an action for an injury caused prenatally.

A different sort of claim which a child might bring is much more controversial, and raises some complex philosophical problems. In what are often referred to as 'wrongful life' actions, a disabled child is claiming that if the defendant had not been negligent, her parents would have been able to avoid her birth, an example might be where negligent prenatal testing deprived the mother of the opportunity to terminate her pregnancy.

Turning to actions which the parents might bring, we can divide these into 'wrongful conception' and 'wrongful birth' claims. A 'wrongful conception' action might lie if the parents want to claim that the defendant's negligence led them to *conceive* an unwanted child; examples include carrying out a sterilization operation negligently, or offering the patient misleading information about its success. In such cases, the mother might want to claim for the pain and discomfort of pregnancy and childbirth, and expenses such as maternity clothes. Much more difficult is the question of whether the parents should also be able to claim for the costs of the child's upbringing. In recent years, the House of Lords has considered this question in depth on two occasions.

A 'wrongful birth' action involves the claim that the child's *birth* (as opposed to her conception) was the result of the defendant's negligence. For example, negligent prenatal testing might mean that the pregnant woman is not offered the option of termination, and she might therefore argue that, but for the defendant's negligence, her disabled child's birth would have been avoided.

This terminology is in such common usage that it will be adopted in this chapter, however it is worth noting Harvey Teff's criticism of phrases such as 'wrongful life' and 'wrongful birth'. As we shall see later in this chapter, their implication that the claimant is 'impugning life itself' may be one of the reasons why these cases have proved to be so problematic.

Harvey Teff[1]

These labels ['wrongful life' and 'wrongful birth'] are unfortunate not least in their bizarre, even macabre, overtones. One is not instinctively attracted to the cause of someone who appears to be impugning life itself. This aside, the terms are neither immediately intelligible nor readily distinguishable from each other. Though both signify claims for damages when negligent conduct has resulted in a child being born, they conceal a host of different legal and social implications, depending both on the circumstances leading up to the birth and on its consequences. Thus 'wrongful life', 'wrongful birth' and other expressions canvassed by courts and commentators are potentially a source of considerable confusion.

---

[1] 'The Action for "Wrongful Life" in England and the United States' (1985) 34 International & Comparative Law Quarterly 423–41, 425.

3. ACTIONS BY THE CHILD

In this section, we consider two ways in which a child might claim that they have been harmed before birth. First, we look at claims in respect of injuries suffered prenatally, and secondly, we look at the much more controversial question of whether life itself could ever amount to a compensatable harm.

(a) PRENATAL INJURY

Since 1976, recovery for injuries sustained before birth has been covered by statute. Because it is still theoretically possible that a child born before the Congenital Disabilities (Civil Liability) Act came into force could bring an action for prenatal injury which has not manifested itself until much later in life, we first consider the possibility of liability at common law.

(1) AT COMMON LAW

There are three ways in which a child might be harmed before birth. First, injuries might be sustained *in utero*; secondly, it is possible for a child to be harmed as a result of something that happened to her parents before she was conceived; and third, the child could be stillborn.

(a) Occurrences *in utero*

A fetus is not a legal person, which means that it cannot be owed a duty of care. Nor is it possible for a fetus to suffer damage which is compensatable in tort: no damages could be paid to a fetus. In *Paton v BPAS*,[2] a case we considered in the previous chapter, Sir George Baker P was emphatic on this point:

The foetus cannot, in English law, in my view, have any right of its own at least until it is born and has a separate existence from the mother. That permeates the whole of the civil law of this country . . .

[I]t was universally accepted, and has since been accepted, that in order to have a right the foetus must be born and be a child . . . [T]here can be no doubt, in my view, that in England and Wales, the foetus has no right of action, no right at all, until birth.

On the other hand, applying the 'neighbour' principle, it is plainly foreseeable that negligent conduct might cause injuries to a developing fetus, and result in a child being born disabled. In the following extract, PJ Pace lays out the different ways in which this dilemma might be resolved.

PJ Pace[3]

In considering whether a right of action is to be granted in such circumstances, there are at least four possible approaches which can be, and in other jurisdictions have been, adopted. The first, a fiction applied in Civil Law jurisdictions and based upon Roman law, is that a child *in utero*, if

---

² [1979] QB 276.   ³ 'Civil Liability for Pre-Natal Injuries' (1977) 40 Modern Law Review 141.

subsequently born alive, is deemed as if already born if that would be to its advantage. The second involves attributing to the child *in utero* legal personality which, in the absence of a live birth, would have important implications for both opponents and proponents of abortion. The third, and biologically unsound view is that the unborn child is merely a part of his mother and, therefore, there can be no action on his behalf, but only on behalf of his mother, if she, while pregnant, sustained injuries through another's negligence. The fourth approach takes the view that, since the tort of negligence is incomplete unless and until damage is suffered by the plaintiff, that tort is in fact completed on the live birth of the injured infant, at which time the infant has legal personality and is able to sue through his next friend, albeit that injuries were inflicted on the infant while he was *in utero*.

In 1993, in *Burton v Islington Health Authority*, the courts adopted the fourth solution: the *child* only suffers damage when she is born, and acquires legal personality. The duty of care is said to 'crystallize' at birth when the child acquires legal personhood, and inherits her damaged body.

Burton v Islington Health Authority; De Martell v Merton and Sutton Health Authority[4]

The mother of the claimant (then referred to as a plaintiff) in the first action underwent a gynaecological operation in September 1966 while pregnant, which led to her child being born with numerous abnormalities. In the second action, a child alleged negligence by medical staff when his mother was in labour resulting in him being born disabled. Because both children were born before the Congenital Disabilities (Civil Liability) Act 1976 came into force, the cases had to be decided according to the common law. The Court of Appeal determined that both children did have a cause of action.

Dillon LJ

To say that the plaintiff suffered his injuries the moment after his birth rather than in the period leading up to his birth involves a legal fiction. But the fiction is that which denies the living creature which became the plaintiff a persona in the period prior to birth. It is that legal fiction which the health authority relies upon in denying liability to the plaintiff. It is not open to the health authority to deny liability on the ground that the organism that they injured was not in law the plaintiff and yet to deny responsibility for the defects with which the plaintiff was born on the ground that they inflicted them before birth. In law and in logic no damage can have been caused to the plaintiff before the plaintiff existed. The damage was suffered by the plaintiff at the moment that, in law, the plaintiff achieved personality and inherited the damaged body for which the health authority (on the assumed facts) was responsible. The events prior to birth were mere links in the chain of causation between the health authority's assumed lack of skill and care and the consequential damage to the plaintiff.

A similar approach is evident in other areas of the law. For example, child protection laws do not apply to a fetus, and so no steps to protect a child can be taken until she is born alive. This question arose in *Re F*, extracted below. Although the Court of Appeal held that the local authority could not protect the fetus while still *in utero*, it would acquire the power to take the child into care as soon as it was born.

Re F (in utero)[5]

A local authority was concerned that a pregnant woman, who was mentally disturbed and led

---

[4] [1993] QB 204.   [5] [1988] Fam 122.

what was described as a 'nomadic' existence, would not take sufficient care or seek appropriate medical attention during childbirth. They sought to make the fetus a ward of court in order to ensure that the mother attended hospital for the child's birth. Hollings J refused their application on the grounds that the court had no wardship jurisdiction over a fetus. On appeal, the Court of Appeal agreed.

May LJ

Even though this is a case in which, on its facts, I would exercise the jurisdiction if I had it, in the absence of authority I am driven to the conclusion that the court does not have the jurisdiction contended for . . .

Secondly, I respectfully agree with the judge below in this case that to accept such jurisdiction and yet to apply the principle that it is the interest of the child which is to be predominant is bound to create conflict between the existing legal interests of the mother and those of the unborn child and that it is most undesirable that this should occur.

Next, I think that there would be insuperable difficulties if one sought to enforce any order in respect of an unborn child against its mother, if that mother failed to comply with the order. I cannot contemplate the court ordering that this should be done by force, nor indeed is it possible to consider with any equanimity that the court should seek to enforce an order by committal.

Balcombe LJ

Approaching the question as one of principle, in my judgment there is no jurisdiction to make an unborn child a ward of court. Since an unborn child has, ex hypothesi, no existence independent of its mother, the only purpose of extending the jurisdiction to include a foetus is to enable the mother's actions to be controlled. Indeed, that is the purpose of the present application.

In relation to inheritance too, a fetus cannot inherit property, and yet if a child beneficiary is *en ventre sa mère* when a testator dies, the gift will crystallize at birth. This principle derives from a well-established civil law rule that an unborn child will be deemed to be born whenever her interests require it. In *C v S*[6] (a case we considered in the previous chapter, in which a man sought to prevent his pregnant girlfriend from having an abortion), Heilbron J summarized the law as follows:

The authorities, it seems to me, show that a child, after it has been born, and only then in certain circumstances based on his or her having a legal right, may be a party to an action brought with regard to such matters as the right to take, on a will or intestacy, or for damages for injuries suffered before birth. In other words, the claim crystallises on the birth, at which date, but not before, the child attains the status of a legal persona, and thereupon can then exercise that legal right.

Similarly criminal law will allow responsibility for acts which took place before a child's birth to crystallize once the child is born. Homicide is the killing of a person, which means that someone who kills a fetus cannot be guilty of either manslaughter or murder. But what if the child is born alive, but injuries which were sustained *in utero* subsequently cause her death? In *Attorney-General's Reference No 3 of 1994*,[7] the House of Lords held that there is no need for the person who died to have been a legal person at the time when the injuries which caused death were inflicted, and hence a conviction for manslaughter would be possible. Lord Hope explained that:

[6] [1988] QB 135.   [7] [1998] AC 245.

For the foetus, life lies in the future, not the past. It is not sensible to say that it cannot ever be harmed, or that nothing can be done to it which can ever be dangerous. Once it is born it is exposed, like all other living persons, to the risk of injury. It may also carry with it the effects of things done to it before birth which, after birth, may prove to be harmful. It would seem not to be unreasonable therefore, on public policy grounds, to regard the child in this case, when she became a living person, as within the scope of the mens rea which B had when he stabbed her mother before she was born.

(b) Occurrences pre-conception

Negligence before a child is conceived might also lead to birth of a disabled child. An example might be if a negligently performed abortion weakens the pregnant woman's ability to safely carry and deliver a child, or if either parent was exposed to chemicals or radiation which damage their reproductive organs. No such case has ever been brought before the English courts, but it is possible that the same approach would be adopted, and the child would be said to sustain the injuries in question when she is subsequently born alive. Of course, if the child who suffers damage has not yet even been conceived, in practice it will be difficult to establish that the defendant owed her a duty of care to prevent her from being born disabled. She is undoubtedly a less foreseeable claimant than if she is *in utero* when she sustains her injuries.

Particularly difficult factual issues will arise when the conduct which caused the injuries happened a very long time before the claimant was conceived. An example of this would be the drug diethylstilbestrol, which was taken by pregnant women in the 1950s in order to prevent miscarriage. In fact, it caused a variety of injuries, both to the pregnant woman and the fetus she was carrying at the time, but importantly it also affected any female fetuses' reproductive organs, thereby injuring *their* future children. Thus, children might be born disabled as a result of a drug taken by their *grandmothers*. In practice, identifying the defendant and proving causation would be exceptionally difficult where the alleged negligence took place several decades before the claimant's birth. And there might also be policy reasons for restricting liability to subsequent generations, in order to avoid the possibility of unquantifiable and indefinite future liability. Certainly the Law Commission had reservations about liability in such circumstances, and under the Congenital Disabilities (Civil Liability) Act 1976, discussed below, a duty is owed only to the children of the person who was affected by the occurrence.[8]

(c) When the child is stillborn

There can be no action on behalf of a stillborn child. Death is a precondition of any action under the Fatal Accidents Act 1976, and because a stillborn child has never been a legal person, it cannot be said to have died for the purposes of the Act. Any claim for a negligently caused stillbirth would be by the mother, who might—depending on the circumstances—have an action for personal injury, and by the father, if he could be said to have suffered psychiatric injury, perhaps as a result of

---

[8] Report no 60 *Report on Injuries to Unborn Children* (1974) Cmnd 5709.

witnessing the stillbirth, or its immediate aftermath.[9] (We consider the possibility of a third party recovering damages for psychiatric injury in Chapter 3 p. 113.)

(2) CONGENITAL DISABILITIES (CIVIL LIABILITY) ACT 1976

The Congenital Disabilities (Civil Liability) Act 1976 replaces any common law action for prenatal injuries for all births from 22 July 1976. It was amended by the Consumer Protection Act 1987 so that it also applies to children whose injuries are caused by defective products (see further Chapter 9).

Congenital Disabilities (Civil Liability) Act 1976, section 1

(1) If a child is born disabled as the result of such an occurrence before its birth as is mentioned in subsection (2) below, and a person (other than the child's own mother) is under this section answerable to the child in respect of the occurrence, the child's disabilities are to be regarded as damage resulting from the wrongful act of that person and actionable accordingly at the suit of the child.

(2) An occurrence to which this section applies is one which—

(a) affected either parent of the child in his or her ability to have a normal, healthy child; or

(b) affected the mother during her pregnancy, or affected her or the child in the course of its birth, so that the child is born with disabilities which would not otherwise have been present.

(3) Subject to the following subsections, a person (here referred to as 'the defendant') is answerable to the child if he was liable in tort to the parent or would, if sued in due time, have been so; and it is no answer that there could not have been such liability because the parent suffered no actionable injury, if there was a breach of legal duty which, accompanied by injury, would have given rise to the liability.

(4) In the case of an occurrence preceding the time of conception, the defendant is not answerable to the child if at that time either or both of the parents knew the risk of their child being born disabled (that is to say, the particular risk created by the occurrence); but should it be the child's father who is the defendant, this subsection does not apply if he knew of the risk and the mother did not.

(5) The defendant is not answerable to the child, for anything he did or omitted to do when responsible in a professional capacity for treating or advising the parent, if he took reasonable care having due regard to then received professional opinion applicable to the particular class of case; but this does not mean that he is answerable only because he departed from received opinion. . . .

(7) If in the child's action under this section it is shown that the parent affected shared the responsibility for the child being born disabled, the damages are to be reduced to such extent as the court thinks just and equitable having regard to the extent of the parent's responsibility.

---

[9] *Alcock v Chief Constable of South Yorkshire* [1992] 1 AC 310 and *White v Chief Constable of South Yorkshire* [1999] 2 AC 455.

Section 4

(3) Liability to a child under section 1 [1A] or 2 of this Act is to be regarded . . . as liability for personal injuries sustained by the child immediately after its birth.

Section 1(5) is an attempt to codify the common law test for the standard of care owed by professionals. A doctor will not be liable for injuries sustained *in utero* if he exercised reasonable care in the light of 'the then received professional opinion'.

Notice that under section 4(3) the Act adopts the common law 'fiction' that the injuries are sustained immediately after birth, when the child becomes a legal person, and the duty of care 'crystallizes'. The Act also confirms the common law position that there can be no liability to a child who is stillborn. Under section 1(1), the action only arises if the child is born, and 'born' is defined in section 4(2) as 'born alive (the moment of a child's birth being when it first has a life separate from its mother)'.

Under section 1(2)(a) and 1(2)(b) the Act applies both to pre-conception occurrences which affect either parent's ability to have a healthy child, and to injuries sustained during pregnancy and childbirth. Section 1(4) provides that there is no liability for pre-conception risks if the parent knew of the risk of the child being born disabled, although this does not apply if the father is the defendant and he knew of the risk but the mother did not. This might arise if the child's father had a disease, such as syphilis, which would be likely to cause his child to be born disabled. If in such circumstances, he knew of the risk of infection but did not inform the child's mother, the child could still have an action against her father. This sort of scenario resembles an action for 'wrongful life', because *this* child could not have been born without her injuries. The act which led to her creation was also the act which caused her disabilities. These could have been avoided only if she had not been conceived. Given the Law Commission's acceptance of an action by a child in these circumstances and their simultaneous rejection of 'wrongful life' actions, the implicit acceptance of a wrongful life claim against a father in section 1(4) is almost certainly unintentional.

The same is true of section 1(2)(a), under which a child could have an action when one of her parents' ability to have a normal healthy child has been affected. In such cases, it would not have been possible for this child to have been born healthy, and therefore her claim is that, as a result of the defendant's negligence, it was impossible for her to come into existence other than in a disabled state. This again looks rather like a 'wrongful life' claim.

Under section 1(3) the duty owed to a child under the Act is a derivative one, and exists only when a duty is already owed to one of the child's parents. The parent does not actually have to have suffered actionable injury, but the defendant must have been in breach of a duty of care owed to the parent. This has a number of consequences. First, where the child suffers injuries because of a decision taken by the pregnant woman, for example to refuse caesarean delivery, the child could have no claim under the Congenital Disabilities Act 1976. Any claim is contingent upon establishing that there was a breach of a duty owed to the mother, and a doctor who respects his patient's refusal of medical intervention acts properly, and is clearly not in breach of his duty of care. Moreover the defences of *volenti non fit injuria* and contributory negligence apply. If the parent's claim would have been defeated by the defence of *volenti*, then the child can have no action for her injuries. And if the child's injuries are partly attributable to the defendant's fault, and partly attributable to her parent's behaviour, then under section 1(7) any damages must be reduced according to the extent to which the parent is responsible for the child being born disabled.

Secondly, because the child's action arises through the duty owed to her parents, the problem of liability to second- or third-generation claimants is resolved. It is only possible to recover for prenatal injuries if the defendant owed a duty of care to the claimant's parents, and this would obviously not be the case when the claimant's *parent* was *in utero* when the injuries which eventually led to the claimant's injuries occurred.

Thirdly, it is also worth noting that under section 1(2)(b), liability for prenatal injuries will exist only when the occurrence *affected the mother* during her pregnancy. Much turns on what is meant here by 'affected'. If it is narrowly construed to mean 'injured', then there will be times when the fetus suffers injuries but the pregnant woman does not. For example, an X-ray during pregnancy may have no effect at all on the pregnant woman, but could injure the developing fetus. Inadequate use of monitoring equipment will also not generally affect the pregnant woman, but could cause the child to be born disabled. On the other hand, if, as Adrian Whitfield suggests, 'affected' simply means 'involved', then provided the defendant owed a duty of care to the pregnant woman in relation to the act which injured the fetus, and she was in some sense 'involved' in the relevant act, the child will have a cause of action.[10]

The 1976 Act was amended in 1990 by the Human Fertilisation and Embryology Act, which added section 1A and section 4(4)(A):

Section 1A

(1) In any case where—

    (a) a child carried by a woman as the result of the placing in her of an embryo or of sperm and eggs or her artificial insemination is born disabled,

    (b) the disability results from an act or omission in the course of the selection, or the keeping or use outside the body, of the embryo carried by her or of the gametes used to bring about the creation of the embryo, and

    (c) a person is under this section answerable to the child in respect of the act or omission,

the child's disabilities are to be regarded as damage resulting from the wrongful act of that person and actionable accordingly at the suit of the child. . . .

(3) The defendant is not under this section answerable to the child if at the time the embryo, or the sperm and eggs, are placed in the woman or the time of her insemination (as the case may be) either or both of the parents knew the risk of their child being born disabled (that is to say, the particular risk created by the act or omission).

Section 4(4A)

In any case where a child carried by a woman as the result of the placing in her of an embryo or of sperm and eggs or her artificial insemination is born disabled, any reference in section 1 of this Act to a parent includes a reference to a person who would be a parent but for sections 27 to 29 of the Human Fertilisation and Embryology Act 1990.

---

[10] 'Actions Arising from Birth' in A Grubb with J Laing (eds) *Principles of Medical Law* (2nd edn OUP Oxford 2004) 789–851, 807.

The purpose of section 4(4)(A) is to ensure that a child will have an action where it is the sperm or egg donor whose capacity to conceive a normal, healthy child was affected before conception.

Section 1A extends liability under the Act to occurrences during fertility treatment, when the embyro is being stored *in vitro*. A child whose disability results from the negligent selection or storage of embryos will have an action under the Act. If the parents knew of the risk that their child would be born disabled, there is no liability. An example might be if all of the embryos created during a cycle of IVF were affected by a genetic disorder, and the parents agreed to the transfer of embryos which they knew to be affected.

The application of the 1976 Act to cases where the child is born disabled as a result of negligent selection of embryos again raises the complicated question of whether this might in fact involve a 'wrongful life' claim. In these cases, the negligent selection did not *cause* the child's disabilities, which exist because the child is genetically abnormal. Rather the negligent selection caused *this child to exist*, and the child's claim must be that if the doctors had exercised proper care and skill, she would never have existed at all. This is undoubtedly a wrongful life claim. It is not clear that the legislature intended to create a statutory wrongful life action for children born following negligent embryo selection, and yet they appear to have done so.

(3) 'MATERNAL' LIABILITY/IMMUNITY

Under section 1(1) of the Congenital Disabilities (Civil Liability) Act 1976, liability under the Act is confined to people 'other than the child's own mother', so a child cannot bring an action against her mother for injuries sustained *in utero*. Allowing a child to sue her mother would, the Law Commission argued, create additional stress within the family.[11] Moreover, mothers of disabled children are often unable to work full time, and will therefore rarely have sufficient funds to pay compensation to their children. And since a mother is normally already responsible for her child's care, any damages she might be ordered to pay would in practice often be paid to herself.

An exception is, however, created in section 2 if the child's injuries were caused by her mother's negligent driving.

Congenital Disabilities (Civil Liability) Act 1976, section 2

A woman driving a motor vehicle when she knows (or ought reasonably to know) herself to be pregnant is to be regarded as being under the same duty to take care for the safety of her unborn child as the law imposes on her with respect to the safety of other people; and if in consequence of her breach of that duty her child is born with disabilities which would not otherwise have been present, those disabilities are to be regarded as damage resulting from her wrongful act and actionable accordingly at the suit of the child.

The reason for the driving exception to maternal immunity is clear. Compulsory road traffic insurance means that the pregnant woman will benefit from her own liability, since this will enable damages to be paid *by her insurance company* to her child which will, in practice, be paid to her, to assist her in caring for her disabled child.

---

[11] Report no 60 *Report on Injuries to Unborn Children* (1974) Cmnd 5709.

Fathers are not exempt. The Law Commission argued that there were fewer ways in which a father's conduct might injure the developing fetus. Indeed the most likely possibility is an assault on the mother, and there would not seem to be any good policy reasons to exclude liability in such circumstances.

Because the Act so clearly provides for maternal immunity, with the exception of road traffic accidents, it also seems unlikely that any court would find a mother liable at common law for causing prenatal injury, unless the injuries were caused by negligent driving

(b) 'WRONGFUL LIFE'

The essence of a wrongful life claim is that the child alleges that, but for the defendant's negligence, she would not have been born and the damage—i.e. her wrongful life—would have been avoided. In these cases, it is not claimed that the defendant's action caused the child's disability, but rather that she failed to give her parents the option not to give birth to this particular child. A wrongful life action might arise in a number of different situations. First, before conception, the child's parents might be negligently advised that they are not at risk of passing on a genetic disorder. Secondly, as we saw earlier, negligence during IVF treatment might result in an embryo which is likely to be born disabled being transferred to the woman's uterus. Third, negligent care during pregnancy might mean that the fetus's abnormality is not detected, and the pregnant woman is deprived of the option of termination.

The issue has arisen in only one English case, *McKay v Essex AHA*, and the Court of Appeal rejected the possibility that life itself could be compensatable damage.

McKay v Essex Area Health Authority[12]

Mrs McKay came into contact with rubella when she was less than two months pregnant. She sought medical advice, but her blood samples were mislaid, and she was wrongly informed that she had not been affected by rubella, and that she need not consider an abortion. Mary McKay was born seriously disabled as a result of rubella infection during pregnancy.

Stephenson LJ

In this case we are unanimously of the opinion that the infant plaintiff's claim for what has been called 'wrongful life' discloses no reasonable cause of action. . . .

[T]his child has not been injured by either defendant, but by the rubella which has infected the mother without fault on anybody's part . . . The only right on which she can rely as having been infringed is a right not to be born deformed or disabled, which means, for a child deformed or disabled before birth by nature or disease, a right to be aborted or killed; or, if that last plain word is thought dangerously emotive, deprived of the opportunity to live after being delivered from the body of her mother. The only duty which either defendant can owe to the unborn child infected with disabling rubella is a duty to abort or kill her or deprive her of that opportunity . . .

This analysis leads inexorably on to the question: how can there be a duty to take away life? . . .

There is no doubt that this child could legally have been deprived of life by the mother's undergoing an abortion with the doctor's advice and help. So the law recognises a difference between the life of a foetus and the life of those who have been born. But because a doctor can lawfully by statute do to a foetus what he cannot lawfully do to a person who has been born, it does not follow that he is under a legal obligation to a foetus to do it and terminate its life, or that the foetus has a legal right to die . . .

To impose such a duty towards the child would, in my opinion, make a further inroad on the sanctity of human life which would be contrary to public policy. It would mean regarding the life of a handicapped child as not only less valuable than the life of a normal child, but so much less valuable that it was not worth preserving . . .

Added to that objection must be the opening of the courts to claims by children born handicapped against their mothers for not having an abortion . . .

Finally, there is the nature of the injury and damage which the court is being asked to ascertain and evaluate.

The only loss for which those who have not injured the child can be held liable to compensate the child is the difference between its condition as a result of their allowing it to be born alive and injured and its condition if its embryonic life had been ended before its life in the world had begun. But how can a court of law evaluate that second condition and so measure the loss to the child? Even if a court were competent to decide between the conflicting views of theologians and philosophers and to assume an 'after life' or non-existence as the basis for the comparison, how can a judge put a value on the one or the other, compare either alternative with the injured child's life in this world and determine that the child has lost anything, without the means of knowing what, if anything, it has gained? . . .

To measure loss of expectation of death would require a value judgment where a crucial factor lies altogether outside the range of human knowledge and could only be achieved, if at all, by resorting to the personal beliefs of the judge who has the misfortune to attempt the task. If difficulty in assessing damages is a bad reason for refusing the task, impossibility of assessing them is a good one. A court must have a starting point for giving damages for a breach of duty. . . .

I am happy to find support for this view of the matter in the Law Commission Report on injuries to Unborn Children and the Congenital Disabilities (Civil Liability) Act 1976.

Ackner LJ

I cannot accept that the common law duty of care to a person can involve, without specific legislation to achieve this end, the legal obligation to that person, whether or not in utero, to terminate his existence. Such a proposition runs wholly contrary to the concept of the sanctity of human life . . .

The disabilities were caused by the rubella and not by the doctor . . . What then are her injuries, which the doctor's negligence has caused? The answer must be that there are none in any accepted sense. Her complaint is that she was allowed to be born at all, given the existence of her pre-natal injuries. How then are her damages to be assessed? Not by awarding compensation for her pain, suffering and loss of amenities attributable to the disabilities, since these were already in existence before the doctor was consulted. She cannot say that, but for his negligence, she would have been born without her disabilities. What the doctor is blamed for is causing or permitting her to be born at all. Thus, the compensation must be based on a comparison between the value of non-existence (the doctor's alleged negligence having deprived her of this) and the value of her existence in a disabled state.

But how can a court begin to evaluate non-existence, 'the undiscovered country from whose bourn no traveller returns?' No comparison is possible and therefore no damage can be established which a court could recognise.

Griffiths LJ

To my mind, the most compelling reason to reject this cause of action is the intolerable and insoluble problem it would create in the assessment of damage. The basis of damages for personal injury is the comparison between the state of the plaintiff before he was injured and his condition after he was injured. This is often a hard enough task in all conscience and it has an element of artificiality about it, for who can say that there is any sensible correlation between pain and money? Nevertheless, the courts have been able to produce a broad tariff that appears at the moment to be acceptable to society as doing rough justice. But the whole exercise, difficult as it is, is anchored in the first place to the condition of the plaintiff before the injury which the court can comprehend and evaluate. In a claim for wrongful life how does the court begin to make an assessment? The plaintiff does not say, 'But for your negligence I would have been born uninjured.' The plaintiff says, 'But for your negligence I would never have been born.' The court then has to compare the state of the plaintiff with non-existence, of which the court can know nothing; this I regard as an impossible task.

The Court of Appeal gave a number of reasons for their 'firm conclusion that our law cannot recognize a claim for "wrongful life" '.[13] First, it would be contrary to public policy for a doctor to owe a child a duty of care to ensure that she did not exist, since this would undermine the sanctity of human life. Secondly, such actions could mean that doctors would be under a duty to persuade pregnant women to terminate their pregnancies. Thirdly, the law did not recognize being born as damage: life, however gravely disabled, was better than the alternative. Fourthly, assessing the quantum of damages in such a case would be impossible. Tort damages are intended to put the claimant in the position she would have been in if the tort had not been committed. But since the claimant would not have existed if the defendant had not been negligent, this would be impossible, because no-one knows what non-existence is like.

There are some tensions at the heart of this reasoning. On the one hand, the Court of Appeal was anxious to stress that being born could not constitute damage because the law will always treat life as beneficial. But on the other hand, all three judges argued that it is simply impossible to compare existence and non-existence. Surely we can only reach the first conclusion if we *have* compared the two outcomes, and decided that life is in fact better than non-life?[14] It is also perhaps a little misleading to suggest, first, that the law is incapable of comparing existence and non-existence, and, second, that if such a comparison is made, existence must always be preferred. When decisions about the non-treatment of severely disabled neonates are taken, the courts have sometimes undoubtedly decided that a profoundly handicapped life is worse than no life at all. In *Re J (A Minor) (Wardship: Medical Treatment)*, a case we consider in Chapter 16, Taylor LJ said:

Despite the court's inability to compare a life afflicted by the most severe disability with death, the unknown, I am of the view that there must be extreme cases in which the court is entitled to say: 'The life which this treatment would prolong would be so cruel as to be intolerable.'[15]

In the next extract, Mark Strasser contrasts the courts' refusal to entertain

---

[13] *Per* Griffiths LJ.
[14] Harvey Teff (1985) 34 International & Comparative Law Quarterly 423–41, 433.
[15] [1991] Fam 33.

comparisons between existence and non-existence in relation to wrongful life actions with their lack of concern over such existential questions when it comes to actions for 'wrongful death'.

Mark Strasser[16]

Yet, if it is impossible to say whether it would be better to be alive than not to exist, then it would seem that wrongful death actions should not be recognized, since it would be impossible to establish that the individual had been harmed by having had her life end prematurely. After all, the person might have been benefited by having received her 'just' rewards earlier rather than later.

The claim here is not that courts or legislatures should deny recovery for wrongful death in those instances in which it seemed 'reasonable' to believe that the person had not been harmed because she had gone to heaven. Nor is the claim that an evil individual should receive more compensation for wrongful death because it seemed 'reasonable' to believe that he had been forced to go to hell prematurely. Rather, it is merely that considerations of whether there is an afterlife and what such a life would be like do not affect or preclude recovery in other areas of tort and there is no reason that analogous considerations should have such a role in the wrongful life context. . . .

[T]here is no requirement to establish the value of existence for use in the relevant calculation of damages for wrongful death awards, so there should be no such requirement for the calculation of wrongful life awards either.

It might also be argued that difficulty in assessing damages is not usually a good reason for denying a remedy at all in the law of tort. Indeed the courts are familiar with setting monetary awards for personal injuries, such as blindness or the loss of a limb, which obviously cannot ensure that the victim is returned to the position she was in before she was injured. Similarly, any sum awarded to compensate for a person's pain and suffering cannot return her to a pain-free existence, and will again inevitably be arbitrary. Instead of offering precise compensation, damages are simply intended to acknowledge that a claimant has suffered harm which is attributable to the defendant's negligence, and that she is therefore entitled to a financial award to offer some redress for both the pecuniary and non-pecuniary consequences of her injuries. Put like this, it seems less obvious that 'wrongful life' actions must fail.

It is also doubtful whether recognizing a duty in these circumstances would compel doctors to urge pregnant women to have abortions. Rather the duty would be to give women sufficient information in order to make an informed choice about the option of abortion, which is consistent both with the Abortion Act 1967, and with a doctor's ordinary duty of care towards her pregnant patient.

In the following extract, Robert Lee criticizes the Court of Appeal's judgment in *McKay* for excessive legalism, arguing that the court's decision to frame the issues in a certain way made their rejection of Mary McKay's claim inevitable. He also suggests that an alternative and less legalistic way of formulating the question in *McKay* might have led to a different outcome.

---

[16] 'Wrongful Life, Wrongful Birth, Wrongful Death and the Right to Refuse Treatment: Can Reasonable Jurisdictions Recognize all but one?' (1999) 29 Missouri Law Review 29, 67, 70.

Robert Lee[17]

We see in the case of wrongful life that the very categorization of problems assists in the determination of outcomes . . . Thus the process of legal classification confers the attribute of significance on certain facts alone. We see a narrowing of this focus as the particular elements of the tort are then considered. It is this which allows the Court of Appeal in *McKay* to isolate the duty as that of terminating another's existence. In so framing the duty the court implicitly denies an alternative analysis: that the duty is to inform as to likely handicap, and since the mother is the only person who ought to be permitted to decide on behalf of the foetus, then in order to be meaningful, the information must be imparted to the mother. Failure to fulfil this duty may give rise to actionable damage on the part of the child. The latter interpretation respects autonomy in so far as this is possible, and leaves choices concerning pregnancy and childbirth vested in the woman. The interpretation of duty actually adopted denies choice by placing the continuing control over informed decisions in the hands of the (predominantly male) medical profession under the supervision of their legal counterparts. . . .

In order to satisfy the demands of the legal concepts of damage and causation, the plaintiff finds it necessary to assert the preferability of non-existence over life. This is a legal fiction which conceals a far more basic assertion—that handicapped children need financial support.

Harvey Teff makes a similar point about the judges' use of language, arguing that the very term 'wrongful life' may be to blame for the court's summary dismissal of a claim that might have been dealt with more sympathetically if it had been described differently.

Harvey Teff[18]

The emotive labels 'wrongful life' and 'wrongful birth' have themselves contributed to the revulsion, colouring judicial reaction by their implicit denigration of life. When the issues are depicted primarily in metaphysical or theological terms, there is a tendency for courts to retreat in the face of such daunting comparisons as the relative value of life and non-existence. Yet a straightforward description of the culpable conduct prompting such suits suggests that both the parents and children concerned have ample justification for seeking legal redress. Thus children have been born with severe physical and mental handicaps, and sometimes with fatal afflictions, because negligent failure to detect or advise parents about serious genetic defects and infections has effectively ruled out the avoidance or termination of pregnancy. If in describing such traumatic events we employ terminology suggestive of familiar legal categories, such as 'negligently inflicted injury', or 'absence of informed consent', the terms of the debate are immediately altered. . . . [T]he main danger is that exclusive or undue concentration on the theme that such actions represent a denial of the value of life conveys a very partial and misleading picture of what is at stake.

It is scarcely surprising that the characterization of 'birth' and 'life' as 'wrongful' has often prompted judicial hostility, if not sheer incredulity. . . . The widespread condemnation of 'wrongful life' actions thus affords a striking example of symbolic affirmation. Yet in such actions the child is manifestly not decrying birth or life *as such*. Rather he is making an undeniably powerful appeal to our sense of justice. He is asserting that he has been subjected to some particular disabling

---

[17] 'To be or not to be: Is that the question? The claim of wrongful life' in Robert Lee and Derek Morgan (eds), *Birthrights: Law and Ethics at the Beginnings of Life* (Routledge London 1989) 172–94, 188–9.

[18] 'The Action for "Wrongful Life" in England and the United States' (1985) 34 International & Comparative Law Quarterly 423–41, 427–8.

condition, typically because of the negligent conduct of a professionally qualified defendant, whose potential liability for inflicting comparable injuries on a live person would be beyond dispute.

As is clear from Stephenson LJ's judgment, the Court of Appeal in *McKay* assumed that there could also be no action for wrongful life under the Congenital Disabilities (Civil Liability) Act 1976, and this was certainly the Law Commission's intention. Their report claimed that:

Such a cause of action, if it existed, could place an almost intolerable burden on medical advisers in their socially and morally exacting role. The danger that doctors would be under subconscious pressure to advise abortions in doubtful cases through fear of an action for damages is, we think, a real one.[19]

Section 1(2)(b) specifies that the occurrence to which the Act applies must have led to the child being 'born with disabilities which would not otherwise have been present'. So the assumption behind the Act is that, but for the occurrence, this child would have been born normal and healthy. Since in a wrongful life action, it is impossible for the child to have been born without the disabilities in question, it seems clear that it would be impossible for someone in Mary McKay's position to bring a wrongful life action under the Act.

However, as we saw earlier, the 1976 Act does, probably unintentionally, carve out a wrongful life action where the child is born disabled because of negligent selection of embryos during fertility treatment. No such cases have come before the courts, but it would be interesting to see whether the courts would be troubled by the fact that the child would be claiming that non-negligent selection would have prevented her birth.

In some other countries, wrongful life actions have had slightly more success. In the US, although most states do not permit actions for wrongful life, there have been some notable exceptions, such as *Curlender v Bio-Science Laboratories*,[20] where a child recovered damages after negligent pre-natal testing failed to detect that she had Tay-Sachs disease.

When wrongful life actions have succeeded, the courts have tended to concentrate on the fact that the claimant's disabled existence is in part attributable to the defendant's negligence, and have tended to downplay the existential problem which dominated the judgments in *McKay*, namely that the child's claim is that they should not have been allowed to be born. A wrongful life action brought following the failure to diagnose rubella during pregnancy succeeded in France in 2000 in the controversial *Perruche* case,[21] discussed in the next extract, but legislation passed shortly afterwards (known as the *loi anti Perruche*) has nullified its precedent value.[22]

In the *Perruche* decision, as Anne Morris and Severine Saintier explain in the following extract, the *Cour de Cassation* was adamant that it was compensating Nicolas for his disabilities, and not for his birth. And it could plausibly be argued that the child is not seeking damages for her very existence, but rather for the disabilities

---

[19] Report no 60 *Report on Injuries to Unborn Children* (1974) Cmnd 5709 para 89.
[20] 106 Cal App 3d 811 (1980).
[21] *Cass Ass Plen* 17.11.00 JCP G2000, II-10438, 2309.
[22] For discussion, see Anne Morris and Severine Saintier, 'To Be or Not to Be: Is That the Question? Wrongful Life and Misconceptions' (2003) 11 Medical Law Review 167–93.

which inevitably—as a result of the defendant's negligence—accompany it. In essence, as Shifrin points out:

> Even if that plaintiff could not have been born and enjoyed the benefits of life without his particular, concomitant burdens, it does not follow that he should be the one to foot the bill for these burdens.[23]

The child in a wrongful life action is not necessarily claiming that she would have been better off if she had never existed, instead even if life itself must always be deemed to be a benefit, it is perfectly possible for that benefit to co-exist with the costs that flow from being born disabled. People, as the California Supreme Court observed in *Curlender* can undoubtedly be both benefited and harmed at the same time:

> The reality of the 'wrongful life' concept is that such a plaintiff both *exists* and *suffers* due to the negligence of others.[24]

Anne Morris and Severine Saintier[25]

The acceptance of the child's right to compensation in *Perruche* was criticised as offending against the principle of human dignity. It was claimed that the distinction between the birth of a healthy and a disabled baby, in awarding compensation only for the latter devalues disabled lives and encourages eugenics. To condemn the Court for compensating Nicolas for being born is, however, to misconstrue the basis of the decision. Sargos, adviser to the court, . . . insisted that it is *not* for being born that the child seeks compensation, but for his disabilities and their consequences. The *Cour de Cassation* accepted that argument: since the child exists, the issue is not his birth but his disabilities. Some have argued that to accept that disabilities constitute 'harm' places a negative value on the life of a disabled child and is contrary to the principle of human dignity. For Sargos, refusing to compensate the child is equally contrary to human dignity. Compensation gives him the means to protect his dignity, and enhances that dignity by giving him, personally, the right to claim. It would be worse to allow only the parents to claim because that defines the child purely as a loss (or burden) to them and denies him the right, as any other legal person, to claim compensation for his injury . . .

  In France, as in Britain, compensation is meant to place the victim in the position he was in prior to the tort and this is assessed by comparing his status before and after the fault. In a wrongful life claim had the fault not occurred the claimant would not exist, thus the comparison required is said to be between life and non-existence and that cannot be assessed, not least because to view non-existence as preferable is a paradox, giving death a positive value and life a negative value. Leaving aside the metaphysical considerations, the problems in wrongful life claims are not that different from other cases. In many cases of physical injury compensation cannot put the victim in the position he was in prior to the damage, rather it aims to give the victim, as far as money can, a 'normal' life or at least to ameliorate the effects of the tort. Similarly, compensation in a wrongful life claim could be aimed at ameliorating the consequences of the tort (living an impaired life) and providing the child with an improved quality of life.

As we see below, where negligent prenatal testing deprived the pregnant woman of the

---

[23] Seana Valentine Shiffrin, 'Wrongful Life, Procreative Responsibility and the Significance of Harm' (1999) 5 Legal Theory 117–48, 135.

[24] 106 Cal App 3d 811, 830 (1980).

[25] 'To Be or Not to Be: Is That the Question? Wrongful Life and Misconceptions' (2003) 11 Medical Law Review 167–93, 185–6.

option of termination, she herself might have an action for the 'wrongful birth' of the resulting disabled child. Of course, it could be argued that the duty to give information which enables a pregnant woman to exercise her right to seek a termination is owed only to the mother, and not to the fetus. But if the mother can claim damages for the wrongful birth of a disabled child, why would it be contrary to public policy to allow the child herself—who is, after all, the one who suffers *physical harm* as a result of the doctor's negligence—to bring an action for her own injuries? This point has been made forcefully by Tony Weir:

> To assert that one cannot owe a duty to a foetus to kill it is plausible enough, but the plausibility fades a bit when one has to admit that a duty to kill the foetus may well be owed to the mother: if a duty is owed to one of the affected parties, why not to the other?[26]

Usually, of course, the existence of the mother's claim will mean the courts' rejection of wrongful life suits will make little practical difference, since the family as a whole will benefit from any damages received by the mother. If the mother is dead, however, the absence of the child's freestanding action might cause problems, since the child's needs undoubtedly survive her mother's death. Analogously, if the child has been adopted, or taken into care, she may not benefit from any damages that are paid to her mother. Furthermore, since the mother will only be under a legal duty to support the child during her minority, damages paid to the parents will generally not compensate for the costs which would be incurred after the child is 18 years old.

The courts' rejection of wrongful life actions can also be contrasted with the acceptance of a child's action for prenatal injury. In both cases, the defendant's negligence leads to the birth of a disabled child, but in the latter case recovery is straightforward because the defendant *caused* the injury itself. Although there is clearly an important factual difference between the two claims, it does not necessarily seem fair that children whose injuries result from negligent prenatal testing should have to bear all of the financial costs associated with their disabilities, whereas children who are injured *in utero* can receive full compensation for their losses.

As Deana Pollard points out in the following extract, the difference between these two claims is likely to become increasingly blurred as it becomes possible to offer *treatment* following accurate prenatal diagnosis. If negligent prenatal testing deprived a fetus of the opportunity of an effective cure for their condition, so that their disabilities could, in fact, have been prevented before birth, it might be possible to argue that the doctor in fact *caused* those injuries.

Deana A Pollard[27]

Juxtaposed to the majority rule in wrongful life cases is a universal rule that a child may state a claim for prenatal negligence causing injury to itself. The current analytical paradigms thus make a harsh distinction between prenatal harm to the fetus, resulting in injury, and failure to diagnose pre-existing defects, resulting in the birth of a child with disorders. The former is analyzed as general malpractice, whereas the latter is analyzed as a 'wrongful life' action. The analytical distinction is based on the concept that but for the negligence in prenatal injury cases, no injury would have occurred to the fetus. Comparatively, in regards to wrongful life claims, the underlying

---

[26] 'Wrongful life—nipped in the bud' (1982) 41 Cambridge Law Journal 225, 227.
[27] 'Wrongful analysis in wrongful life jurisprudence' (2004) 55 Alabama Law Review 327.

premise is that but for the negligence, the defect still would occur in the child because it pre-existed the malpractice. . . .

However, genetic testing and prenatal medical intervention are rapidly advancing. It is now sometimes the case that early detection of genetic defects provides an opportunity for the mother and/or fetus to undergo medical treatment to prevent the defect's manifestation at birth. In these cases, the claim is not that life itself was wrongful but rather that but for the doctor's negligent failure to detect the defect, medical intervention could have minimized or could have prevented the defect from manifesting at birth. Current wrongful life analysis is rendered obsolete by such cases involving negligent genetic testing, which are more akin analytically to prenatal malpractice, as causation arguably exists between the malpractice and the defect.

So far, we have assumed that the defendant in a wrongful life action will be a doctor who gave negligent advice about the likelihood that this child would be born disabled, and in this context, as we have seen, a number of commentators have questioned the courts' refusal to entertain such claims. But of course if it were to be accepted that an action should lie when a child claims that her birth ought to have been avoided, should children also be able to sue their parents for bringing them into the world in an impaired state? Could a child sue her mother for choosing not to undergo prenatal tests, for example, or for not having an abortion if an abnormality is detected?

Certainly, in *McKay* Stephenson LJ appeared to assume that actions against mothers for not aborting disabled fetuses would be the logical corollary of permitting children to bring 'wrongful life' actions against doctors:

Added to [the sanctity of life] objection must be the opening of the courts to claims by children born handicapped against their mothers for not having an abortion.

And the point was conceded by counsel for the plaintiffs who had:

accepted that if the duty of care to the foetus involved a duty on the doctor, albeit indirectly, to prevent its birth, the child would have a cause of action against its mother, who had unreasonably refused to have an abortion.[28]

With respect, this seems doubtful. As we saw earlier, the Congenital Disabilities (Civil Liability) Act 1976 prevents children from suing their mothers for prenatal injuries, unless these were caused by negligent driving, when compulsory insurance will be available to cover the damages. Since it would be impossible for parents to obtain insurance to cover 'wrongful life' claims, it seems highly improbable that the courts would seek to punish a parent who elected to bring up a disabled child, especially since the reality would generally be that the parents would be paying damages to *themselves*.

4.   ACTIONS BY THE PARENTS

Again, there are two sorts of action that parents might have where their child is born injured as a result of another's negligence. First, we consider actions when negligence led to the child's *conception*, usually because one of the parents had undergone a

---

[28] *Per* Ackner LJ.

sterilization operation which, for some reason, failed to achieve sterility. Secondly, we consider claims for wrongful *birth*, which arise where the defendant's negligence prevented the mother from avoiding the child's birth.

(a) 'WRONGFUL CONCEPTION'

If a woman becomes pregnant following a negligently performed sterilization operation, or is given negligent advice about her or her partner's sterility, there are three possible outcomes. First, she might miscarry or the baby might be stillborn, in which case an action for her pain and suffering would be uncontroversial, although the sum would be relatively modest. Secondly, she could decide to terminate the pregnancy. Again, a claim for the costs of an abortion, and any associated discomfort, stress or loss of income would be straightforward, and the award would also be fairly small. The third possibility is that the woman carries the pregnancy to term and gives birth to a live baby. In this third scenario, if the patient can establish that their sterilization operation was negligently performed, or that they were given negligent pre- or post-operative advice, their claim will be for damages to compensate them for the 'wrongful conception' of a child that they did not want.

(1) CAN THERE BE RECOVERY FOR WRONGFUL CONCEPTION?

Although in practice there is little difference between the claims, it is worth noting that an action for wrongful conception might be brought in contract or in tort.

(a) Contract

If a sterilization operation is carried out in the private sector, the patient will have a contract with the clinic or hospital in which they are treated. If the sterilization is unsuccessful, and the patient subsequently becomes pregnant, an action in contract is possible. In practice, however, as we saw in Chapter 3, the courts will only imply into the contract a duty to exercise reasonable care in carrying out the sterilization, and in giving pre- and post-operative advice. There will certainly not be an implied guarantee that sterility will be achieved. As a result, cases brought in contract law will generally be indistinguishable from the negligence actions we consider in the next section

In *Eyre v Measday*,[29] the Court of Appeal rejected the argument that the doctors' statements that vasectomy and female sterilization were 'irreversible' amounted to implied guarantees of sterility. Slade LJ explained:

in my opinion, in the absence of any express warranty, the court should be slow to imply against a medical man an unqualified warranty as to the results of an intended operation, for the very simple reason that, objectively speaking, it is most unlikely that a responsible medical man would intend to give a warranty of this nature. Of course, objectively speaking, it is likely that he would give a guarantee that he would do what he had undertaken to do with reasonable care and skill; but it is quite another matter to say that he has committed himself to the extent suggested in the present case.

[29] [1986] 1 All ER 488.

This was followed in *Thake v Maurice.*

Thake v Maurice[30]

Mr and Mrs Thake had had five children, and they contracted with the defendant surgeon to perform a vasectomy operation on Mr Thake, for which they paid £20. The defendant explained that, subject to an uncertain possibility of surgical reversal, the operation was irreversible. He did not warn them that there was a small risk that the operation, even if successful, might spontaneously reverse itself in the future. This risk materialized. By the time Mrs Thake realized that she was five months pregnant with the couple's sixth child, it was too late for her to terminate the pregnancy. The Thakes brought an action for breach of contract, breach of collateral warranty, misrepresentation and breach of the defendant's contractual duty of care. The Court of Appeal (Kerr LJ dissenting) rejected the claim for breach of warranty, but nevertheless found that the failure to warn of spontaneous reversal had been negligent.

Neill LJ

Both the plaintiffs and the defendant expected that sterility would be the result of the operation and the defendant appreciated that that was the plaintiffs' expectation. This does not mean, however, that a reasonable person would have understood the defendant to be giving a binding promise that the operation would achieve its purpose or that the defendant was going further than to give an assurance that he expected and believed that it would have the desired result. Furthermore, I do not consider that a reasonable person would have expected a responsible medical man to be intending to give a guarantee. Medicine, though a highly skilled profession, is not, and is not generally regarded as being, an exact science. The reasonable man would have expected the defendant to exercise all the proper skill and care of a surgeon in that speciality; he would not in my view have expected the defendant to give a guarantee of 100 per cent success.

   Accordingly, though I am satisfied that a reasonable person would have left the consulting room thinking that Mr. Thake would be sterilised by the vasectomy operation, such a person would not have left thinking that the defendant had given a guarantee that Mr. Thake would be absolutely sterile.

(b) Tort

As we saw in Chapter 3, there are several stages to an action in tort. The defendant must owe the claimant a duty of care; the duty must be breached; and the breach must cause damage, which is not too remote. As we see below, wrongful conception cases have proved to be a rather special case, however, because the courts have been concerned that the application of the ordinary rules of tort law would have unpalatable consequences.

I The existence of a duty of care

A person who is sterilized is unquestionably owed a duty of care. Whether a duty is owed to their partner is slightly more complicated. If a woman's sterilization goes wrong, her partner's loss will be purely economic. In such cases, it would be necessary to establish that there was a proximate relationship between him and the doctor who carried out his sexual partner's sterilization. This would generally only be possible if he was within the doctor's contemplation at the time of the operation, because he was the patient's husband or partner.

If it is the man's vasectomy that does not work, his partner might be said to suffer physical injury as well as financial losses. Although the physical injury element of her claim is not governed by the restrictive rules which cover pure economic loss, it seems clear that the courts will not find that a doctor owes a duty to all future sexual partners of a patient undergoing sterilization, but only to women who are within the doctor's contemplation when the operation is carried out.

In *Goodwill v British Pregnancy Advisory Service*,[31] Mr MacKinlay had had a vasectomy, arranged by the defendants, four years before he began having a sexual relationship with Mrs Goodwill. Although initially successful, the vasectomy had spontaneously reversed itself. Mrs Goodwill became pregnant, and sued the defendants for loss of income, and for the costs of bringing up her daughter. She argued that the defendants had owed *her* a duty of care to give Mr McKinlay proper advice about the permanency of sterility. Her claim was struck out as an abuse of process:

[T]he defendants were not in a sufficient or any special relationship with the plaintiff such as gives rise to a duty of care. I cannot see that it can properly be said of the defendants that they voluntarily assumed responsibility to the plaintiff when giving advice to Mr MacKinlay. At that time they had no knowledge of her, she was not an existing sexual partner of Mr MacKinlay but was merely, like any other woman in the world, a potential future sexual partner of his, that is to say a member of an indeterminately large class of females who might have sexual relations with Mr MacKinlay during his lifetime. I find it impossible to believe that the policy of the law is or should be to treat so tenuous a relationship between the adviser and the advisee as giving rise to a duty of care.[32]

II Breach of duty

Once a duty of care has been established, it is necessary to work out whether the duty has been breached. This might be the case where the operation was *performed* negligently, or where a doctor offered negligent *advice* about the operation's success, perhaps because post-vasectomy sperm samples were not properly tested.

It is now extremely unlikely that any case would be brought in which a doctor failed to warn either a male or a female patient of the risk that the operation may not succeed. Since the mid-1980s, it has been known that there is a small chance that a vasectomy will spontaneously reverse itself several years later, even when initial sperm samples indicated that the operation had been successful.[33] In *Newell v Goldenberg*[34] the court held that no competent body of medical opinion would have omitted to inform a patient of this small risk of vasectomy reversal, and the failure to give an appropriate warning was therefore negligent. Similarly, there is a small risk that the most common type of female sterilization will fail to achieve sterility, and the Royal College of Obstetricians and Gynaecologists now recommends full and frank disclosure of this risk.[35] A doctor who failed to draw either of these risks to the patient's attention would undoubtedly be in breach of her duty of care, and so any future claims would almost certainly be settled out of court.

---

[31] [1996] 1 WLR 1397.   [32] *Per* Peter Gibson LJ.

[33] See further E Jackson, *Regulating Reproduction* (Hart Publishing Oxford 2001) 28–9.

[34] [1995] 6 Med LR.

[35] Royal College of Obstetricians and Gynaecologists, *Male and Female Sterilisation* (RCOG London 1999).

For the same reason, it is unlikely that any action would reach court based upon a failure to explain to a vasectomy patient that birth control should continue to be used until two negative sperm samples have been taken. The only remaining scenario in which a statement about sterility might lead to litigation is where the parents were given inaccurate test results (as happened in *Mcfarlane*, below), either as a result of negligent testing, or negligent interpretation of the results.

III Causation

While it is sexual intercourse, rather than the failed sterilization that actually *causes* a pregnancy, having unprotected sex will not amount to a *novus actus interveniens* (an act which breaks the chain of causation), unless the patient knows that the steriliza- tion has failed. In *Sabri-Tabrizi v Lothian Health Board*,[36] for example, S knew that her sterilization operation had failed. The court found that her decision to nevertheless expose herself to the risk of pregnancy was unreasonable, and did constitute a *novus actus interveniens*.

It is also now clear that the pregnant woman has no duty to mitigate her loss by having an abortion, or by having the child adopted. Lord Steyn in *McFarlane*, discussed below, robustly rejected both possibilities:

I cannot conceive of any circumstances in which the autonomous decision of the parents not to resort to even a lawful abortion could be questioned. For similar reasons the parents' decision not to have the child adopted was plainly natural and commendable. It is difficult to envisage any circumstances in which it would be right to challenge such a decision of the parents.

IV What losses can be compensated?

Once the existence of a duty of care towards a patient undergoing sterilization, and perhaps his/her partner has been established, it is undoubtedly foreseeable that any breach of that duty might lead to pregnancy, and the birth of an unwanted child. Could this amount to compensatable damage? Pregnancy and childbirth are natural processes, which would not normally be described as 'injuries'. But because they can be painful and risky, it has not proved difficult to persuade the courts that an unwanted pregnancy and delivery is a personal injury for which compensation can be sought. Auld LJ considered the question in *Walkin v South Manchester Health Authority*:[37]

the failure of the attempt to sterilise the patient was not itself a personal injury. It did her no harm; it left her as before. . . . However, it seems to me that the unwanted conception, whether as a result of negligent advice or negligent surgery, was a personal injury in the sense of an 'impairment'. . . . The resultant physical change in her body resulting from conception was an unwanted condition which she had sought to avoid by undergoing the sterilisation operation. It seems to me that the unwanted conception, whether as a result of negligent advice or negligent surgery, was a personal injury in the sense of an 'impairment', . . .

This was confirmed by the House of Lords in *McFarlane*.[38] Lord Steyn explained:

Counsel for the health authority argued as his primary submission that the whole claim should fail because the natural processes of conception and childbirth cannot in law amount to personal

---

[36] [1998] BMLR 190.   [37] [1995] 1 WLR 1543.   [38] [2000] 2 AC 59.

injury . . . [E]very pregnancy involves substantial discomfort and pain. I would therefore reject the argument of the health authority on this point.

And Lord Clyde agreed that:

natural as the mechanism may have been, the reality of the pain, discomfort and inconvenience of the experience cannot be ignored. It seems to me to be a clear example of pain and suffering such as could qualify as a potential head of damages.

There are also certain costs associated with pregnancy, such as maternity clothes and loss of income, and these too have been recoverable on the grounds that they are consequential economic losses. The costs of the child's upbringing are also of course foreseeable, but as we see below, their recovery in tort has proved to be much more controversial.

The issue was first raised in *Udale v Bloombsury AHA*[39] and it was decided that the maintenance costs of a healthy child were not recoverable on grounds of public policy. Children, according to Jupp J, were a 'blessing', and their birth should be an occasion for joy not litigation. It would also, he reasoned, be undesirable for a child to learn that her birth had been a mistake. This was overruled by the Court of Appeal in *Emeh v Kensington and Chelsea AHA*,[40] a case involving the birth of a disabled child, where it was held that public policy did not justify a blanket prohibition on the recovery of maintenance costs. The Court of Appeal did not specify whether their judgment applied only to disabled children, so post-*Emeh*, it appeared that the costs of a child's upbringing were in principle recoverable.

A number of judges expressed regret or surprise that a doctor who made a mistake during the treatment of a patient undergoing sterilization might be liable for the full costs of any resulting child's upbringing, but until 1999, this appeared to be the law.[41] And, of course, awards could be very high indeed. In *Benarr v Kettering*,[42] for example, following a negligently performed vasectomy, damages were awarded to cover the child's future private education.

Then in 1999 in *McFarlane v Tayside Health Board* the House of Lords considered the issue for the first time, and while Mrs McFarlane was entitled to damages for the pain and inconvenience of pregnancy (Lord Millett dissented on this point), the Lords unanimously held that the maintenance costs of a normal, healthy child were not recoverable. It is an important and complicated case, and unsurprisingly it has been followed by a number of other cases which have tested its application to slightly different sets of facts, one of which also reached the House of Lords.

McFarlane v Tayside Health Board[43]

Six months after Mr McFarlane had undergone a vasectomy operation, the surgeon negligently informed him that his sperm counts were negative and that he no longer needed to take contraceptive precautions. A year and a half later, Mrs McFarlane became pregnant and gave birth to their fifth child, Catherine. She sued Tayside Health Board. A majority of the House of Lords found that

---

[39] [1983] 1 WLR 1098.   [40] [1985] 2 WLR 233.
[41] *Allen v Bloomsbury Health Authority* [1993] 1 All ER 651, *per* Brooke J; *Jones v Berkshire Health Authority* (2 July 1986) (unreported) *per* Ognall J.
[42] (1988) 138 NLJ 179.   [43] [2000] 2 AC 59.

she was entitled to general damages for the pain, suffering and inconvenience of pregnancy and childbirth, but the Lords were unanimous that the McFarlanes were not entitled to be compensated for the costs associated with Catherine's upbringing.

Lord Slynn

It is to be remembered on this part of the case that your Lordships are concerned only with liability for economic loss. It is not enough to say that the loss is foreseeable as I have accepted it is foreseeable. . . . It is to be remembered that in relation to liability the House has recognised that in respect of economic loss in order to create liability there may have to be a closer link between the act and the damage than foreseeability provides in order to create liability . . .

The doctor undertakes a duty of care in regard to the prevention of pregnancy: it does not follow that the duty includes also avoiding the costs of rearing the child if born and accepted into the family. Whereas I have no doubt that there should be compensation for the physical effects of the pregnancy and birth, including, of course, solatium for consequential suffering by the mother immediately following the birth, I consider that it is not fair, just or reasonable to impose on the doctor or his employer liability for the consequential responsibilities, imposed on or accepted by the parents to bring up a child. The doctor does not assume responsibility for those economic losses. If a client wants to be able to recover such costs he or she must do so by an appropriate contract.

Lord Steyn

It is possible to view the case simply from the perspective of corrective justice. It requires somebody who has harmed another without justification to indemnify the other. On this approach the parents' claim for the cost of bringing up Catherine must succeed. But one may also approach the case from the vantage point of distributive justice. It requires a focus on the just distribution of burdens and losses among members of a society. If the matter is approached in this way, it may become relevant to ask commuters on the Underground the following question: Should the parents of an unwanted but healthy child be able to sue the doctor or hospital for compensation equivalent to the cost of bringing up the child for the years of his or her minority, i.e. until about 18 years? My Lords, I am firmly of the view that an overwhelming number of ordinary men and women would answer the question with an emphatic 'No'. And the reason for such a response would be an inarticulate premise as to what is morally acceptable and what is not. . . . Instinctively, the traveller on the Underground would consider that the law of tort has no business to provide legal remedies consequent upon the birth of a healthy child, which all of us regard as a valuable and good thing.

My Lords, to explain decisions denying a remedy for the cost of bringing up an unwanted child by saying that there is no loss, no foreseeable loss, no causative link or no ground for reasonable restitution is to resort to unrealistic and formalistic propositions which mask the real reasons for the decisions. And judges ought to strive to give the real reasons for their decision. It is my firm conviction that where courts of law have denied a remedy for the cost of bringing up an unwanted child the real reasons have been grounds of distributive justice. That is, of course, a moral theory. It may be objected that the House must act like a court of law and not like a court of morals. That would only be partly right. The court must apply positive law. But judges' sense of the moral answer to a question, or the justice of the case, has been one of the great shaping forces of the common law. What may count in a situation of difficulty and uncertainty is not the subjective view of the judge but what he reasonably believes that the ordinary citizen would regard as right . . .

Relying on principles of distributive justice I am persuaded that our tort law does not permit parents of a healthy unwanted child to claim the costs of bringing up the child from a health authority or a doctor. If it were necessary to do so, I would say that the claim does not satisfy the requirement of being fair, just and reasonable.

Lord Hope
The Child-rearing Costs
This is a claim for economic loss. . . . It is not difficult to see that in such cases a very substantial award of damages might have to be made for the child's upbringing. Awards on that scale would be bound to raise questions as to whether it was right for the negligent performance of a voluntary and comparatively minor operation, undertaken for the perfectly proper and understandable purpose of enabling couples to dispense with contraceptive measures and to have unprotected intercourse without having children, to expose the doctors, and on their behalf the relevant health authority, to a liability on that scale in damages. It might well be thought that the extent of the liability was disproportionate to the duties which were undertaken and, consequently, to the extent of the negligence.

As to the law, it has not been suggested that the costs of rearing the child are too remote, in the sense that they were not a reasonably foreseeable consequence of the defender's negligence. For my part, I would regard these costs as reasonably foreseeable by the wrongdoer. But in the field of economic loss foreseeability is not the only criterion that must be satisfied. There must be a relationship of proximity between the negligence and the loss which is said to have been caused by it and the attachment of liability for the harm must be fair, just and reasonable . . .

There are benefits in this arrangement as well as costs. In the short term there is the pleasure which a child gives in return for the love and care which she receives during infancy. In the longer term there is the mutual relationship of support and affection which will continue well beyond the ending of the period of her childhood.

In my opinion it would not be fair, just or reasonable, in any assessment of the loss caused by the birth of the child, to leave these benefits out of account. Otherwise the pursuers would be paid far too much. They would be relieved of the cost of rearing the child. They would not be giving anything back to the wrongdoer for the benefits. But the value which is to be attached to these benefits is incalculable. The costs can be calculated but the benefits, which in fairness must be set against them, cannot. The logical conclusion, as a matter of law, is that the costs to the pursuers of meeting their obligations to the child during her childhood are not recoverable as damages.

Lord Clyde
But in attempting to offset the benefit of parenthood against the costs of parenthood one is attempting to set off factors of quite a different character against themselves and that does not seem to me to accord with principle. At least in the context of the compensation of one debt against another, like requires to be offset against like. . . . A parent's claim for the death of a child is not offset by the saving in maintenance costs which the parent will enjoy. . . . Furthermore, in order to pursue such a claim against the risk of such a set-off, a parent is called upon in effect to prove that the child is more trouble than he or she is worth in order to claim. That seems to me an undesirable requirement to impose upon a parent and further militates against such an approach. Indeed, the very uncertainty of the extent of the benefit which the child may constitute makes the idea of a set-off difficult or even impracticable. . . .

But that the pursuers end up with an addition to their family, originally unintended but now, although unexpected, welcome, and are enabled to have the child maintained while in their custody free of any cost does not seem to accord with the idea of restitution or with an award of damages which does justice between both parties. . . .

There is no issue here of mitigation of damages. But while it is perfectly reasonable for the pursuers to have accepted the addition to their family, it does not seem to me reasonable that they should in effect be relieved of the financial obligations of caring for their child. That seems to me to be going beyond what should constitute a reasonable restitution for the wrong done. . . .

In the present case we are concerned critically with a claim for an economic loss following upon allegedly negligent advice. In such a context I would consider it appropriate to have regard to the extent of the liability which the defenders could reasonably have thought they were undertaking. It seems to me that even if a sufficient causal connection exists the cost of maintaining the child goes far beyond any liability which in the circumstances of the present case the defenders could reasonably have thought they were undertaking.

Furthermore, reasonableness includes a consideration of the proportionality between the wrongdoing and the loss suffered thereby. . . . Counsel for the respondents sought to stress the modesty of the likely level of award in the present case. But once it is accepted that the cost of private education may be included in appropriate cases, a relatively much more substantial award could be justified.

Lord Millett

I do not consider that the present question should depend on whether the economic loss is characterised as pure or consequential. The distinction is technical and artificial if not actually suspect in the circumstances of the present case, and is to my mind made irrelevant by the act that Catherine's conception and birth are the very things that the defenders' professional services were called upon to prevent. In principle any losses occasioned thereby are recoverable however they may be characterised. . . .

I am also not persuaded by the argument that the remedy is disproportionate to the wrong. True, a vasectomy is a minor operation, while the costs of bringing up a child may be very large indeed, especially if they extend to the costs of a private education. But it is a commonplace that the harm caused by a botched operation may be out of all proportion to the seriousness of the operation or the condition of the patient which it was designed to alleviate . . .

There is something distasteful, if not morally offensive, in treating the birth of a normal, healthy child as a matter for compensation . . .

In my opinion the law must take the birth of a normal, healthy baby to be a blessing, not a detriment. In truth it is a mixed blessing. It brings joy and sorrow, blessing and responsibility. The advantages and the disadvantages are inseparable. Individuals may choose to regard the balance as unfavourable and take steps to forgo the pleasures as well as the responsibilities of parenthood. They are entitled to decide for themselves where their own interests lie. But society itself must regard the balance as beneficial. It would be repugnant to its own sense of values to do otherwise. It is morally offensive to regard a normal, healthy baby as more trouble and expense than it is worth . . .

It does not, however, follow that Mr and Mrs McFarlane should be sent away empty handed. . . . They have suffered both injury and loss. They have lost the freedom to limit the size of their family. They have been denied an important aspect of their personal autonomy. Their decision to have no more children is one the law should respect and protect. They are entitled to general damages to reflect the true nature of the wrong done to them. This should be a conventional sum which should be left to the trial judge to assess, But which I would not expect to exceed £5000 in a straightforward case like the present.

Although their conclusion on recovery for maintenance costs was unanimous, as Brooke LJ in pointed out in the Court of Appeal judgment in *Parkinson* (considered below), the Law Lords certainly did not speak with one voice:

Our task has been made more difficult because the five members of the House of Lords spoke with five different voices.

In a subsequent case, one of them, Lord Steyn, revealingly described the task of discussing the judgments in *McFarlane* as 'gruesome'.[44]

All of the Law Lords agreed that an unwanted pregnancy could be treated as a species of personal injury. In addition to allowing a claim for the physical damage associated with pregnancy, this also means that consequential financial losses, such as the cost of maternity clothes, will be recoverable. In contrast, although they also could be said to be a foreseeable consequence of the personal injury of pregnancy and childbirth, the majority treated the costs of Catherine McFarlane's upbringing as pure economic loss. Lord Millett dissented on this point, referring to the distinction drawn between consequential and pure economic losses as 'technical and artificial if not actually suspect in the circumstances of the present case'.

Readers who are familiar with tort law may remember that special rules cover the recovery of pure economic loss. In short, the three stage *Caparo v Dickman*[45] test applies:

(1) the loss should be foreseeable;

(2) there must be a relationship of sufficient proximity between the doctor and their patient;

(3) it should be fair, just and reasonable to impose a duty of care in these circumstances.

Of course, the birth of a child, and the costs of her upbringing, are foreseeable consequences of negligently advising a patient that sterility has been achieved. And it is equally axiomatic that there will be a relationship of sufficient proximity between the doctor who performed the sterilization and the patient. Although Mrs McFarlane was not herself being treated, she was undoubtedly identifiable by Mr McFarlane's doctors as someone who would be likely to suffer loss if Mr McFarlane's operation went wrong. A majority of the House of Lords rejected the McFarlane's claim on the third limb of this test, namely that imposing liability on the health authority for the costs of a healthy child's upbringing would not be fair, just, and reasonable. A number of different reasons were given for this conclusion.

First, some of the Law Lords suggested that it would be unfair to compensate the parents for the costs of rearing a child, unless these could be reduced in order to reflect the benefits that the child would bring to her parents. But they refused to embark upon this sort of balancing exercise on the grounds that it was either impossible and/or unseemly. Lord Hope, for example, argued that while the costs of a child's upbringing can be calculated, 'the benefits, which in fairness must be set against them, cannot'. For Lord Millett, the crucial point was not that it was impossible to weigh the benefits of raising children against the costs, but that society must always regard the balance as beneficial because it would be 'morally offensive' to do otherwise.

---

[44] *Rees v Darlington Memorial Hospital NHS Trust* [2003] UKHL 52, [2003] 4 All ER 987.
[45] [1990] 2 AC 651.

The Lords thus appeared to assume that this sort of offset calculation was necessary but either impossible or offensive. But is it really true that damages would have to be reduced in order to reflect the benefits the child brings to her parents? Two analogies, while imperfect, are instructive here. First, and this point was acknowledged by Lord Clyde in *McFarlane*, when parents bring an action for the death of their child, their damages are not reduced in order to reflect the money that they will save by *not* having to pay for the child's upkeep. Secondly, the child support which an absent parent must pay to the caring parent in order to contribute towards their child's upbringing is not reduced in order to reflect the benefits the principal carer gains from the child's company. Again, an offset calculation would be unthinkable. Why then, given that in other contexts the law will not engage in a cost/benefit calculation in order to reduce sums payable to a child's parents, is such an exercise essential, but impossible, following negligent sterilization?

Further, as Lord Clyde points out, an offset rule is normally dependent upon comparing like with like. Hence, financial damages might be reduced in order to take account of any financial benefit the claimant received. But in relation to wrongful birth, the House of Lords appears to assume that damages for the *economic* costs of bringing up a child would have to be reduced in order to take account of the *emotional* benefits of the child's companionship. A trade-off between incommensurate goods is unusual. We would not normally say that an employee's damages for being rendered unfit to work should be reduced in order to reflect the benefits he enjoys from being able to spend more time with his family. Lord Clyde gave the example of a mineworker rendered unfit for work underground. If he claims damages for loss of earnings, the defendant is not entitled to offset 'the pleasure and benefit which he may enjoy in the air of a public park'. In *McFarlane*, the underlying fear seems to be that parents who are, in the end, delighted by the child's existence would be *unjustly enriched* if they were able to deflect all of her maintenance costs onto the NHS.

Even if it were accepted that an offset calculation is necessary, it might also be argued that the question of whether an unplanned child's birth represents a net 'gain' for a family is a question of fact. It may be true that most people, most of the time, consider that the advantages of having a child, even if she was initially unwanted, outweigh the disadvantages. But this will not always be the case. For some families, the birth of another child might be a disaster. As we see below, in his dissenting judgment in the Court of Appeal in *Rees v Darlington Memorial Hospital NHS Trust*,[46] Waller LJ gave an example of a poor single mother with four children, who knows that a fifth will lead to her mental breakdown, and who has no support from her family. If the birth of an unwanted child provokes the mother's physical or mental collapse, she may be able to prove that the advantages of having another child have not, in fact, outweighed the disadvantages. Yet the law will not allow her to bring forward such evidence, because it has already decided that, in Lord Millett's words, 'society itself must regard the balance as beneficial'.

Given that the claimants in 'wrongful conception' cases have attempted to remove the possibility of conception permanently through invasive surgery, it is plain that, at

---

[46] [2002] 2 WLR 1483.

the time of the operation at least, they believed that the disadvantages of having another baby outweighed any joy that the child might bring. The patient was sterilized precisely in order to avoid the 'benefits' of parenthood. It is perhaps odd that the law insists that such people should view the failure of their surgery as a 'blessing', and an occasion for joy. If the benefits of parenthood always outweigh its disadvantages, it is unclear why anyone would want to be sterilized in the first place.

Secondly, both Lord Hope and Lord Clyde were concerned that the size of any claim in damages for a child's upbringing would be disproportionate to the degree of fault. It is clear from *Benarr v Kettering*, for example, that a child's maintenance costs will sometimes be very high indeed, and if recoverable, an NHS trust might have to pay vast damages for a relatively minor lapse of judgment. Moreover, not only would compensating parents for the costs of private education for the whole of a child's life lead to some extremely high awards, but it would also result in invidious distinctions between the damages available to different families since wealthy parents would receive much more money for their unwanted children than poor parents.

Lord Millett, rightly in my view, objected to this argument on the grounds that damages in tort are not intended to correspond to the *gravity* of fault, but rather to put the claimant in the position they would have been if the negligent act had not occurred. This inevitably leads invidious differences in the size of awards: a rich businessman who loses the ability to work will receive a much higher award than an unemployed man who has suffered identical injuries.

Thirdly, Lord Steyn based his judgment upon considerations of distributive justice. If children cannot claim for 'wrongful life', he reasoned that it would be unfair to allow parents to claim for 'wrongful conception'. Lord Steyn was reluctant to attempt to squeeze his rejection of the McFarlane's claim into existing principles of tort law. Instead, he admitted that his was principally a moral judgment, and he specifically appealed to public opinion, or more precisely to London commuters:

it may become relevant to ask of the commuters on the Underground the following question: 'Should the parents of an unwanted but healthy child be able to sue the doctor or hospital for compensation equivalent to the cost of bringing up the child for the years of his or her minority, i.e. until about 18 years?'

For Lord Steyn, then, it is the *instincts* of the public which should determine the question, although if forced to fit this moral judgment within the existing negligence framework, he said he would argue that 'the claim does not satisfy the requirement of being fair, just and reasonable'. In the next extract, Robin Oppenheim is sceptical about the difference Lord Steyn appears to draw between distributive justice and fairness under the *Caparo* test.

Robin Oppenheim[47]

Before analysing the approach of the courts to [distributive and corrective justice] principles, it is worth seeking to define more closely what they mean. Honore explains the principle of corrective justice as follows:

---

[47] 'The "Mosaic" of Tort Law: The Duty of Care Question' (2003) Journal of Personal Injury Law 151–71, 164, 166.

[I]t requires those who have without justification harmed others by their conduct to put the matter right. This they must do on the basis that the harm-doer and harm-sufferer are treated as equals, neither more deserving than the other. The balance must be restored.

Distributive justice is concerned with the just distribution of burdens and losses, including risks, within a community. This may require members of a community to bear the risk of harm to others even where they are not at fault . . . It may require the imposition of vicarious liability. It may also limit the application of the corrective justice principle.

If the issue is simply one of fairness, then distributive justice brings nothing to the analysis at the policy assessment stage that the third limb of the Caparo test does not already provide. . . . Indeed, it is arguable, reading the judgments in McFarlane that the application of the distributive justice principle provides an apparently respectable vehicle for reasoning that judges are supposed to abjure, namely making decisions on the basis of judicial perception of what public policy dictates. . . .

The law's primary concern should be corrective justice. The courts are ill-equipped to start making judgments, at very least without evidence, as to what the hypothetical person would regard as an ideal solution of distributive justice. It assumes a hypothetical person who is, in truth a judicial cipher, in order to create a uniformity of view where perhaps none exists (as perhaps signified by the continuing legal debate as to the rights and wrongs of . . . McFarlane).

A final underlying reason for the Lords' rejection of the McFarlane's claim was, I would suggest, less explicitly articulated. Underlying their unease about the possible consequences of recovery may have been the concern that scarce NHS resources should not be diverted to the parents of healthy children. In recent years, as we saw in Chapter 2, there has been increasing judicial recognition that the NHS is financially overstretched. Given that rationing of acute medical treatment is now inevitable, the House of Lords may have been alarmed at the prospect that the NHS might have to pay potentially very large sums of money for the private education and maintenance costs of a healthy child. This was certainly Tony Weir's principal objection to the post-*Emeh* case law:

For the fourteen years since *Emeh* the National Health Service, short of resources for curing the sick, has been disbursing large sums of money for the maintenance of children who have nothing wrong with them.[48]

In their more recent judgment in *Rees*, considered below, the House of Lords explicitly discussed the question of whether compensating parents for the birth of a healthy child is an appropriate use of public resources. But while it is clearly undoubtedly true that Tayside Health Board has more pressing demands upon its budget than Catherine McFarlane's upkeep, it is not normally open to a court to deny a claimant damages because the defendant could deploy the money more effectively elsewhere.

In *McFarlane* Lord Millett made an interesting suggestion which was not taken up by any of the other judges, namely that the McFarlanes should be entitled to a conventional sum of £5,000 to compensate for the wrongful interference with their freedom to limit the size of their family. In part, this proposal may have been prompted by the fact that 'full' damages in a case such as this would be an

---

[48] 'The Unwanted Child' (2000) 59 Cambridge Law Journal 238–41, 238.

inappropriate use of scarce NHS resources. As we see below, Lord Millett's novel compensatory award was greeted with much more enthusiasm by the House of Lords in *Rees*, considered below.

Of course it was inevitable that issues which were not directly dealt with by the judgments in *McFarlane* would rear their head in subsequent litigation. On a comparatively minor point, in *Greenfield v Irwin*,[49] the mother had been in full-time employment and sought to recover loss of earnings not just around the time of the birth, but during the subsequent years when she would be caring for the baby at home. While *McFarlane* had not directly addressed future loss of earnings, the Court of Appeal decided that these costs were in fact part of the costs of raising the child, and since *McFarlane* applied, they were not recoverable. May LJ, for example, stated that:

there seems to me to be no material distinction between the costs of caring for and bringing up a child held to be irrecoverable in McFarlane and the mother's claim for loss of earnings in this appeal.

Laws LJ also appeared to be concerned that to allow recovery in such circumstances would not be compensation, but the 'conferment of a financial privilege':

It is to be noted that if this lady were to obtain the damages she seeks, she would happily be in a position whereby she would look after her much loved child at home, yet at the same time in effect would receive the income she would have earned had she stayed at work. In my judgment that is not just compensation; it is the conferment of a financial privilege, which has nothing to do with just compensation.

Of more importance, in *McFarlane* the House of Lords did not state whether their judgment would have been the same if Catherine McFarlane had been born disabled. Lord Steyn had suggested that 'in the case of an unwanted child, who was born seriously disabled the rule may have to be different', and Lord Clyde pointed out that 'it has to be noted in the present case we are dealing with a normal birth and a healthy child'. Unsurprisingly, it was not long before the question of whether *McFarlane* applied to disabled children came before the courts in *Parkinson v St James and Seacroft University Hospital NHS Trust*.[50]

Parkinson v St James and Seacroft University Hospital NHS Trust[51]

Angela Parkinson, who already had four children and did not think she could cope with a fifth, underwent a sterilization operation. The sterilization was negligently performed, and she subsequently became pregnant. During the pregnancy, Mrs Parkinson was advised that the child might be born disabled, but she chose not to have an abortion. The Parkinson's fifth child, Scott, suffered from a serious behavioural disorder. It was accepted that his disability was not caused by the defendant's breach of duty. The family's resources were severely overstretched: they were living in a cramped two bedroom house, and Scott's birth meant that Mrs Parkinson was unable to return to paid employment. The pregnancy placed an intolerable strain on the Parkinson's marriage, and they separated before Scott was born. At first instance Longmore J held that Mrs Parkinson could

49 [2001] 1 WLR 1279.   50 [2001] 3 WLR 376.
51 [2001] EWCA Civ 530, [2002] QB 266.

recover the costs of providing for Scott's special needs, and his judgment was upheld by the Court of Appeal.

Brooke LJ

  (i) the birth of a child with congenital abnormalities was a foreseeable consequence of the surgeon's careless failure to clip a fallopian tube effectively;

 (ii) there was a very limited group of people who might be affected by this negligence, viz Mrs Parkinson and her husband (and, in theory, any other man with whom she had sexual intercourse before she realised that she had not been effectively sterilised);

(iii) there is no difficulty in principle in accepting the proposition that the surgeon should be deemed to have assumed responsibility for the foreseeable and disastrous economic consequences of performing his services negligently;

 (iv) the purpose of the operation was to prevent Mrs Parkinson from conceiving any more children, including children with congenital abnormalities, and the surgeon's duty of care is strictly related to the proper fulfilment of that purpose;

  (v) parents in Mrs Parkinson's position were entitled to recover damages in these circumstances for 15 years between the decisions in Emeh's case and McFarlane's case, so that this is not a radical step forward into the unknown;

 (vi) for the reasons set out in (i) and (ii) above, Lord Bridge of Harwich's tests of foreseeability and proximity are satisfied, and . . . an award of compensation which is limited to the special upbringing costs associated with rearing a child with a serious disability would be fair, just and reasonable;

(vii) if principles of distributive justice are called in aid, I believe that ordinary people would consider that it would be fair for the law to make an award in such a case, provided that it is limited to the extra expenses associated with the child's disability.

I can see nothing in any majority reasoning in McFarlane's case to deflect this court from adopting this course, which in my judgment both logic and justice demand. . . . [I]n my judgment it would not be fair, just and reasonable to award compensation which went further than the extra expenses associated with bringing up a child with a significant disability.

What constitutes a significant disability for this purpose will have to be decided by judges, if necessary, on a case by case basis. The expression would certainly stretch to include disabilities of the mind (including severe behavioural disabilities) as well as physical disabilities. It would not include minor defects or inconveniences, such as are the lot of many children who do not suffer from significant disabilities.

Hale LJ

Not surprisingly, their Lordships [in *McFarlane*] did not go into detail about what is entailed in the invasion of bodily integrity caused by conception, pregnancy and childbirth. But it is worth while spelling out the more obvious features. Some will sound in damages and some may not, but they are all the consequence of that fundamental invasion. They are none the less an invasion because they are the result of natural processes. They stem from something which should never have happened. And they last for a great deal longer than the pregnancy itself. Whatever the outcome, happy or sad, a woman never gets over it. I do not, of course, forget the serious consequences for many fathers, and will return to these later, but there are undoubted and inescapable differences between the sexes here . . .

From the moment a woman conceives, profound physical changes take place in her body and continue to take place not only for the duration of the pregnancy but for some time thereafter. Those physical changes bring with them a risk to life and health greater than in her non-pregnant state. Those risks vary according to the age, state of health, and other characteristics of the woman, and of the unborn child. . . . Along with those physical changes go psychological changes. Again these vary from woman to woman. Some may amount to a recognised psychiatric disorder, while others may be regarded as beneficial, and many are somewhere in between. . . .

Along with these physical and psychological consequences goes a severe curtailment of personal autonomy. Literally, one's life is no longer just one's own but also someone else's. One cannot simply rid oneself of that responsibility. The availability of legal abortion depends upon the opinions of others. Even if favourable opinions can readily be found by those who know how, there is still a profound moral dilemma and potential psychological harm if that route is taken. Late abortion brings with it particular problems, and these are more likely to arise in failed sterilisation cases where the woman does not expect to become pregnant. . . .

Continuing the pregnancy brings a host of lesser infringements of autonomy related to the physical changes in the body or responsibility towards the growing child. The responsible pregnant woman forgoes or moderates the pleasures of alcohol and tobacco. She changes her diet. She submits to regular and intrusive medical examinations and tests. She takes certain sorts of exercise and forgoes others. She can no longer wear her favourite clothes. She is unlikely to be able to continue in paid employment throughout the pregnancy or to return to it immediately thereafter.

The process of giving birth is rightly termed 'labour'. It is hard work, often painful and sometimes dangerous. It brings the pregnancy to an end but it does not bring to an end the changes brought about by the pregnancy. It takes some time for the body to return to its pre-pregnancy state, if it ever does, especially if the child is breast fed. There are well known psychiatric illnesses associated with childbirth and the baby blues are very common . . .

Quite clearly, however, the invasion of the mother's personal autonomy does not stop once her body and mind have returned to their pre-pregnancy state. . . .

Parental responsibility is not simply or even primarily a financial responsibility . . . The primary responsibility is to care for the child. The labour does not stop when the child is born. Bringing up children is hard work. . . .

The obligation to provide or make acceptable and safe arrangements for the child's care and supervision lasts for 24 hours a day, seven days a week, all year round, until the child becomes old enough to take care of himself. . . .

Of course, most pregnancies are not caused wrongfully. But this case proceeds on the basis that this one was. The whole object of the service offered to the claimant by the defendants was to prevent her becoming pregnant again. They had a duty to perform that service with reasonable care. They did not do so. She became pregnant as a result. On normal principles of tortious liability, once it was established that the pregnancy had been wrongfully caused, compensation would be payable for all those consequences, whether physical or financial, which are capable of sounding in damages. . . .

A majority of their Lordships in McFarlane's case clearly recognised that on normal principles the claim would be allowable . . .

At the heart of it all is the feeling that to compensate for the financial costs of bringing up a healthy child is a step too far. A child brings benefits as well as costs; it is impossible accurately to calculate those benefits so as to give a proper discount; the only sensible course is to assume that they balance one another out. . . .

The true analysis is that this is a limitation on the damages which would otherwise be recoverable on normal principles. There is therefore no reason or need to take that limitation any further than it was taken in McFarlane's case. This caters for the ordinary costs of the ordinary child. A disabled child needs extra care and extra expenditure. He is deemed, on this analysis, to bring as much pleasure and as many advantages as does a normal healthy child. Frankly, in many cases, of which this may be one, this is much less likely. The additional stresses and strains can have seriously adverse effects upon the whole family, and not infrequently lead, as here, to the break-up of the parents' relationship and detriment to the other children. But we all know of cases where the whole family has been enriched by the presence of a disabled member and would not have things any other way. This analysis treats a disabled child as having exactly the same worth as a non-disabled child. It affords him the same dignity and status. It simply acknowledges that he costs more . . .

Whatever the commuter on the Underground might think of the claim for Catherine McFarlane, it might reasonably be thought that he or she would not consider it unfair, unjust or disproportionate that the person who had undertaken to prevent conception, pregnancy and birth and negligently failed to do so were held responsible for the extra costs of caring for and bringing up a disabled child.

It is of critical importance to remember that this is not a case in which the child's disability was *caused by* the defendant's negligence. If a botched sterilization operation not only failed to achieve sterility, but also damaged the patient's reproductive organs and impaired her ability to give birth to a healthy child, then the child would have a straightforward action under the Congenital Disabilities (Civil Liability) Act 1976.

In *Parkinson*, the defendant's negligence did not cause the child's disability, rather it caused the child, who just happened to be disabled, to be conceived. Because there is always a small risk—in *Parkinson* it was put at between one in 200 and one in 400— that a child might be born suffering from a congenital abnormality, the birth of a disabled child is a foreseeable consequence of any negligent sterilization operation.

It should however be noted that the maintenance costs of a healthy child are obviously much more foreseeable than the statistically less likely possibility that a child will be born disabled, and extra costs thereby incurred.[52] It is also true that the maintenance costs of a disabled child are likely to be higher than those of a normal healthy baby, and since crucially we are not concerned with cases in which the defendant *caused* the disability, the concern forcefully expressed in *McFarlane* about the damages potentially being wholly disproportionate to the degree of fault must apply even more compellingly on the facts in *Parkinson*.

Furthermore, recall that several of the judgments in *McFarlane* argued that the benefits of the child's existence had to be put into the balance with the costs, but that this calculation was either unseemly or impossible. Surely, as Alasdair Maclean points out in the next extract, the same must be true when the child is born disabled.

Alasdair Maclean[53]

Unless one is prepared to argue that having a disabled child is not – as a matter of policy—a

[52] Laura CH Hoyano, 'Misconceptions about Wrongful Conception' (2002) 65 Modern Law Review 883–906, 891.

[53] 'An Alexandrian approach to the knotty problem of wrongful pregnancy: *Rees v Darlington Memorial Hospital NHS Trust* in the House of Lords', [2004] 3 Web JCLI <http://webjcli.ncl.ac.uk/2004/issue3/maclean3.html>.

blessing, which might be interpreted as devaluing the disabled, then the [offset] calculation is no more possible for the birth of a disabled child than it is for the birth of a healthy child. The costs arising from the disability are simply additional maintenance costs and, if the detriments cannot be weighed against the benefits then simply increasing the detriments cannot change that: if x cannot be balanced against y then nor can x be balanced against y + z.

At times the Court of Appeal appeared less than enthusiastic about the judgment in *McFarlane*. In particular, Hale LJ's powerful exegesis of the physical and psychological invasions of pregnancy and motherhood indubitably applies just as compellingly to the birth of a healthy child. Nevertheless *McFarlane* was binding upon them, and so the important question was whether Scott's disabilities meant that Angela Parkinson's case could be distinguished. The Court of Appeal decided that the cases were different, and the extra costs incurred as a result of the child's disability were recoverable.

The Court of Appeal was keen to emphasize that their decision did not imply that the birth of disabled children is not a 'blessing', rather it simply acknowledges that they will often cost more than healthy children.

Plainly, there may be additional costs associated with raising a disabled child, but arguably the extent to which an unwanted child will be a serious burden will often depend more upon whether her family has sufficient resources and support, than on whether the child is born disabled. For example, a rich couple may be able to afford additional childcare, and be able to accommodate a disabled child's special needs with ease, whereas a single mother with no income and inadequate accommodation may find an additional healthy child an overwhelming burden.

Three problems of interpretation remained after the Court of Appeal's decision in *Parkinson*. First, what counts as a disability for these purposes? The Court of Appeal suggested that the disability must be 'significant', and Hale LJ argued that the test should be the same as that in the Children Act 1989:

how disabled does the child have to be for the parents to be able to make a claim? The answer is that the law has for some time distinguished between the ordinary needs of ordinary children and the special needs of a disabled child. Thus, for the purposes of the services to be provided under Part III of the Children Act 1989, . . . 'a child is disabled if he is blind, deaf or dumb or suffers from mental disorder of any kind or is substantially and permanently handicapped by illness, injury or congenital deformity or such other disability as may be prescribed' . . . I see no difficulty in using the same definition here.

The child's disability must therefore meet some threshold level of seriousness before the extra costs associated with it are recoverable. But while we can be certain that parents are not entitled to recover the additional costs incurred as a result of a relatively minor abnormality, such as short-sightedness, it seems likely that future courts might have to address precisely what counts as a significant disability for these purposes.

Secondly, for there to be recovery, the Court of Appeal stressed that the child's disability must be a foreseeable consequence of the defendant's negligence. In *Parkinson*, they reasoned that it was foreseeable that a proportion of children will suffer from congenital abnormalities, and hence Scott's disabilities were a foreseeable result of the negligent sterilization. The Court of Appeal did not confine recovery to disabilities that were present at conception. Hale LJ stated:

I conclude that any disability arising from genetic causes or foreseeable events during pregnancy (such as rubella, spina bifida, or oxygen deprivation during pregnancy or childbirth) up until the child is born alive, and which are not novus actus interveniens, will suffice to found a claim.

But what if the child *subsequently* becomes disabled: are her extra needs also a foreseeable consequence of the defendant's negligence? This question arose in *Groom v Selby*.[54] Ms Groom had undergone a sterilization operation following the birth of her second child, and after having suffered two miscarriages. When the operation was performed, Ms Groom was in fact in the very early stages of another pregnancy. When she subsequently went to her doctor complaining of abdominal pains, and having missed a period, the doctor failed to test for pregnancy, and simply prescribed antibiotics. Pregnancy was eventually diagnosed when Ms Groom was 12 weeks pregnant, but by this stage, she did not feel able to have an abortion. It was admitted that the doctor's failure to carry out a pregnancy test was negligent, and that this had deprived Ms Groom of the opportunity to terminate the pregnancy. Ms Groom's daughter, Megan, was born prematurely, and subsequently developed meningitis complicated by brain abscesses.

Although strictly speaking this was a 'wrongful birth' rather than a 'wrongful conception' claim, the question for the court was when the disability must have been caused in order to fit within the *Parkinson* exception to *McFarlane*. The doctor contended that Megan was a healthy child at birth, and hence *McFarlane* and not *Parkinson* applied, thus ruling out recovery for the additional costs associated with Megan's disabilities. However, the Court of Appeal held that Megan could not properly be described as a 'healthy child' at birth because the bacteria which was responsible for her meningitis was already present on her skin. Brooke LJ stated that:

We are concerned in the present case with a child whose severe handicap arose from the normal incidents of conception, intra-uterine development and birth. Her prematurity (which made her particularly vulnerable) was not due to any new intervening event and her exposure to the bacterium which proved her downfall occurred during the process of birth.

Hale LJ agreed:

There will always be borderline cases in the application of any principle. In *Parkinson*, Brooke LJ and I were also agreed on the source of the disability: it must be genetic or arise from the processes of intra-uterine development and birth. That was what the doctor negligently failed to prevent. Megan's meningitis was 'bad luck', in the sense that many newborn babies do not succumb to such infections. But it arose from the process of her birth during which she was exposed to the bacterium in question.

Since the birth of a premature child who developed meningitis as a result of her exposure to bacteria during the normal birth process was a foreseeable consequence of the doctor's admitted negligence, Ms Groom was entitled to recover damages for

---

[54] [2001] EWCA Civ 1522, (2001) 64 BMLR 47.

the extra costs associated with Megan's disability. Interestingly, Brooke LJ expressly declined to take considerations of distributive justice into account in this case:

I see no need to have recourse to principles of distributive justice in this case. I think that lay people might be equally divided in opinion if asked to decide what was fair in such a complex case. This shows how it may not be appropriate to use all the recent tests propounded by the House of Lords in every difficult case of this kind.

Thirdly, what if it is not the child but the parent who is disabled? This issue has arisen twice since *Parkinson*. We can deal with the first case, *AD v East Kent Community NHS Trust*,[55] fairly briefly. This case involved a mentally disabled woman, A, who had become pregnant, while living on a mixed psychiatric ward, by a man who was also in the defendant's care. A gave birth to a healthy daughter, C, and A's mother, Mrs A, agreed to look after C for the foreseeable future. The Court of Appeal dismissed A's claim. She herself had suffered no loss. Mrs A was providing her services voluntarily, which meant that she too could not have an action in her own right.[56] Moreover Judge LJ argued that:

it would be invidious to attempt to put a money value on the benefit that she will derive from the joy of having her healthy granddaughter living with her and growing up in her home.

The second case, *Rees v Darlington Memorial Hospital NHS Trust*, requires rather more scrutiny.

Rees v Darlington Memorial Hospital NHS Trust[57]
In 1995 the claimant, who was severely visually handicapped and feared that her lack of sight would prevent her from being able to look after a child, underwent a sterilization operation. The operation was carried out negligently at a hospital managed by the defendants. The claimant subsequently conceived, and in 1997 gave birth to a healthy child. She claimed damages not only for the pain and discomfort of pregnancy and childbirth, but also for the additional costs incurred as a result of her disability.

By a 2 to 1 majority, the Court of Appeal allowed recovery on the grounds that the claimant's case could be distinguished from *McFarlane* because *McFarlane* only applied to healthy parents.[58] It is, however, worth noting Waller LJ's powerful dissenting judgment, in which he argued that whether the birth of an unwanted child is a 'disaster' will often depend more upon the resources and support available to the mother than on whether she happens to be disabled:

Waller LJ (dissenting)
If one takes the facts to be that a woman already has four children and wishes not to have a fifth; and if one assumes that having the fifth will create a crisis in health terms, unless help in caring for the child was available. She cannot recover the costs of caring for the child which might alleviate the crisis, as I understand McFarlane's case. I would have thought that her need to avoid a breakdown in her health was no different from the need of someone already with a disability, and indeed her need might be greater depending on the degree of disability. Does she, or ordinary

---

[55] [2002] EWCA Civ 1872, [2003] 2 FCR 704.
[56] Following the House of Lords judgment in *Hunt v Severs* [1994] 2 All ER 385.
[57] [2003] UKHL 52, [2003] 4 All ER 987.   [58] [2002] 2 WLR 1483.

people, look favourably on the law not allowing her to recover but allowing someone who is disabled to recover?

If one were to add that the lady with four children was poor, but the lady with a disability was rich—what then? It would simply emphasise the perception that the rule was not operating fairly. One can add to the example by making comparisons between possible family circumstances of the different mothers. Assume the mother with four children had no support from husband, mother or siblings, and then compare her with the person who is disabled, but who has a husband, siblings and a mother all willing to help. I think ordinary people would feel uncomfortable about the thought that it was simply the disability which made a difference.

On appeal, because of the importance of the issue, and the possibility of revisiting its recent judgment in *McFarlane*, seven Law Lords heard the case. The House of Lords unanimously declined to revisit their judgment in *McFarlane*, so despite its recent rejection by the High Court of Australia,[59] *McFarlane* remains good law in the UK. But the Law Lords disagreed over whether the present case could be distinguished from *McFarlane*. By a 4 to 3 majority the House of Lords held that it could not: the child was healthy, so *McFarlane* applied and there could be no recovery for any of the costs associated with the child's upbringing. The dissenting judges would have allowed Karina Rees to recover for the extra costs associated with her disability.

It should, however, be noted that the majority also added a very significant 'gloss'.

Lord Bingham

The policy considerations underpinning the judgments of the House [in *McFarlane*] were, as I read them, an unwillingness to regard a child (even if unwanted) as a financial liability and nothing else, a recognition that the rewards which parenthood (even if involuntary) may or may not bring cannot be quantified and a sense that to award potentially very large sums of damages to the parents of a normal and healthy child against a National Health Service always in need of funds to meet pressing demands would rightly offend the community's sense of how public resources should be allocated. . . .

Subject to one gloss, therefore, which I regard as important, I would affirm and adhere to the decision in McFarlane.

My concern is this. Even accepting that an unwanted child cannot be regarded as a financial liability and nothing else and that any attempt to weigh the costs of bringing up a child against the intangible rewards of parenthood is unacceptably speculative, the fact remains that the parent of a child born following a negligently performed vasectomy or sterilisation, or negligent advice on the effect of such a procedure, is the victim of a legal wrong. . . .

I can accept and support a rule of legal policy which precludes recovery of the full cost of bringing up a child in the situation postulated, but I question the fairness of a rule which denies the victim of a legal wrong any recompense at all beyond an award immediately related to the unwanted pregnancy and birth. . . .

To speak of losing the freedom to limit the size of one's family is to mask the real loss suffered in a situation of this kind. This is that a parent, particularly (even today) the mother, has been denied, through the negligence of another, the opportunity to live her life in the way that she wished and planned. I do not think that an award immediately relating to the unwanted pregnancy and birth gives adequate recognition of or does justice to that loss. I would accordingly support the suggestion favoured by Lord Millett in McFarlane that in all cases such as these there be a

---

[59] *Cattanach v Melchior* [2003] HCA 38.

conventional award to mark the injury and loss, although I would favour a greater figure than the £5,000 he suggested (I have in mind a conventional figure of £15,000) and I would add this to the award for the pregnancy and birth. This solution is in my opinion consistent with the ruling and rationale of McFarlane. The conventional award would not be, and would not be intended to be, compensatory. It would not be the product of calculation. But it would not be a nominal, let alone a derisory, award. It would afford some measure of recognition of the wrong done. And it would afford a more ample measure of justice than the pure McFarlane rule.

Lord Nicholls

I have heard nothing in the submissions advanced on the present appeal to persuade me that this decision by the House [in McFarlane] was wrong and ought to be revisited. On the contrary, that the negligent doctor or, in most cases, the National Health Service should pay all the costs of bringing up the child seems to me a disproportionate response to the doctor's wrong. It would accord ill with the values society attaches to human life and to parenthood. The birth of a child should not be treated as comparable to a parent suffering a personal injury, with the cost of rearing the child being treated as special damages akin to the financially adverse consequences flowing from the onset of a chronic medical condition.

But this is not to say it is fair and reasonable there should be no award at all except in respect of stress and trauma and costs associated with the pregnancy and the birth itself. An award of some amount should be made to recognise that in respect of birth of the child the parent has suffered a legal wrong, a legal wrong having a far-reaching effect on the lives of the parent and any family she may already have. The amount of such an award will inevitably have an arbitrary character. I do not dissent from the sum of £15,000 suggested by my noble and learned friend Lord Bingham of Cornhill in this regard. To this limited extent I agree that your Lordships' House should add a gloss to the decision in McFarlane v Tayside Health Board.

Lord Millett

I still regard the proper outcome in all these cases is to award the parents a modest conventional sum by way of general damages, not for the birth of the child, but for the denial of an important aspect of their personal autonomy, viz the right to limit the size of their family. This is an important aspect of human dignity, which is increasingly being regarded as an important human right which should be protected by law. The loss of this right is not an abstract or theoretical one. As my noble and learned friend Lord Bingham of Cornhill has pointed out, the parents have lost the opportunity to live their lives in the way that they wished and planned to do. The loss of this opportunity, whether characterised as a right or a freedom, is a proper subject for compensation by way of damages.

The award of a modest sum would not, of course, go far towards the costs of bringing up a child. It would not reflect the financial consequences of the birth of a normal, healthy child; but it would not be meant to. They are not the proper subject of compensation for the reasons stated in McFarlane. A modest award would, however, adequately compensate for the very different injury to the parents' autonomy.

Lord Steyn (dissenting)

In the present case the idea of a conventional award was not raised at first instance or in the Court of Appeal. For my part it is a great disadvantage for the House to consider such a point without the benefit of the views of the Court of Appeal. And the disadvantage cannot be removed by calling the new rule a 'gloss'. It is a radical and most important development which should only be embarked on after rigorous examination of competing arguments . . .

No United Kingdom authority is cited for the proposition that judges have the power to create a remedy of awarding a conventional sum in cases such as the present. There is none. It is also noteworthy that in none of the decisions from many foreign jurisdictions, with varying results, is there any support for such a solution. This underlines the heterodox nature of the solution adopted.

Like Lord Hope I regard the idea of a conventional award in the present case as contrary to principle. It is a novel procedure for judges to create such a remedy. There are limits to permissible creativity for judges. In my view the majority have strayed into forbidden territory. It is also a backdoor evasion of the legal policy enunciated in McFarlane. If such a rule is to be created it must be done by Parliament. The fact is, however, that it would be a hugely controversial legislative measure. It may well be that the Law Commissions and Parliament ought in any event, to consider the impact of the creation of a power to make a conventional award in the cases under consideration for the coherence of the tort system.

I cannot support the proposal for creating such a new rule.

Lord Hope (dissenting)

The award of a conventional sum is familiar in the field of damages for personal injury. . . . This is the means by which the court arrives, as best it can, at a figure for the damage suffered which is incapable of being calculated arithmetically . . . But financial loss does not present the same problem. It is capable of assessment in money. So it has never been the practice to resort to a conventional sum as a means of compensating the claimant for that part of the loss that falls under the head of special damages.

A majority of the House of Lords recognized that non-recovery in *McFarlane* was itself an exception to the ordinary rules of tort law, and that carving out exceptions to exceptions should be avoided. On the normal principles of tort law, the claimant should be able to recover all of the reasonably foreseeable consequences of the doctor's negligence, including the costs associated with the child's upbringing. But for two reasons, the majority in *Rees* explained that the law has refused to countenance the prospect of giving damages for the costs of a healthy baby. First, the birth of a healthy baby is said to be a blessing, and it has been held that it would be contrary to public morality to regard it as a loss compensatable by damages. Secondly, although parents in these circumstances have the detriment of additional costs, they also experience the benefit of bringing up a child. Fair compensation for the detriment associated with having a child should, it has been argued, take account of this benefit, and yet the courts have held that it is impossible or undesirable to calculate benefit and detriment in this way. As a result, the preferred solution has been not to allow the payment of any damages at all.

But the new gloss added by the majority in *Rees* is based on the view that, while accurate compensation in these circumstances is both inappropriate and impossible, the parents in these cases have undoubtedly been wronged: they have been deprived of their freedom to control the size of their family. As a result, the majority of the House of Lords advocated what they described as a modest 'conventional award', which would not be intended to compensate for the actual loss suffered by the claimants, but rather to offer some recognition of the wrong done to them. The figure proposed by Lord Bingham, and accepted by the rest of the majority in this case, was £15,000. In short, the majority in *Rees* decided that it did not want to compensate Karina Rees according to ordinary negligence principles because this would give her too much money. Instead, it preferred to compensate her according to its own novel scheme, which would acknowledge that she had been wronged, without giving her exorbitant damages.

It could be argued that the majority in *Rees* was attempting to find a judicial solution to some of the problems clinical negligence poses for the NHS. Patients who are treated negligently do deserve some recognition that they received inadequate care, which may have caused them harm, inconvenience, discomfort or financial loss. But at the same time, giving them full compensation for all of their losses undermines the capacity of the NHS to provide adequate healthcare to the rest of the population. Hence, the problem of clinical negligence can be simply stated. By giving a handful of negligently treated patients full compensation, it becomes more difficult to guarantee universal access to comprehensive health services, free at the point of use. In these circumstances, it could be argued that it would be more sensible for patients who are the victims of inadequate treatment to receive a standard notional award, which recognizes that a wrong has been done to them, but does not attempt to provide full compensation. Not only might this reduce the actual sums payable, but crucially it avoids the legal costs incurred by the process of setting individualized compensatory payments, such as the need to employ two sets of expensive expert witnesses.

But while moving towards a standardized compensation scheme within the NHS would undoubtedly have many merits, it is at least arguable that the introduction of such a radical departure from the existing tort system should be a matter for parliament. This was certainly the view of the dissenting judges in *Rees*. In his vehement dissenting judgment, Lord Steyn argued that the majority had gone beyond the limits of permissible judicial creativity.

Following *Rees*, the status of the Court of Appeal judgment in *Parkinson* is a little uncertain.

Three of the Law Lords specifically approved of the Court of Appeal's decision in *Parkinson*. Lord Hutton, for example, said:

In my opinion the decision of the Court of Appeal in *Parkinson* was right . . . in my opinion it is fair, just and reasonable to award damages for the extra costs of bringing up a disabled child.

Similarly according to one of the dissenting judges, Lord Hope:

A disabled child is likely to need extra care and the provision of this care is likely to mean extra expenditure . . . I consider that, as a matter of legal policy, the Court of Appeal were right to hold that in principle these extra costs are recoverable.

And Lord Steyn, who also dissented from the majority's conclusions, expressly confined *McFarlane* to the birth of a healthy child:

The legal policy on which *McFarlane* was based is critically dependent on the birth of a healthy and normal child. That policy does not apply where the child is seriously disabled physically and/or mentally.

In contrast, three of the other Law Lords were critical of the *Parkinson* decision, and would have also applied the conventional award in cases where the child was born disabled. Lord Bingham, with whom Lord Nicholls agreed, offered a number of criticisms of the Court of Appeal's judgment in *Parkinson*.

Lord Bingham

I would for my part apply this rule also, without differentiation, to cases in which either the child or the parent is (or claims to be) disabled:

(1) While I have every sympathy with the Court of Appeal's view that Mrs Parkinson should be compensated, it is arguably anomalous that the defendant's liability should be related to a disability which the doctor's negligence did not cause and not to the birth which it did.

(2) The rule favoured by the Court of Appeal majority in the present case inevitably gives rise to anomalies such as those highlighted by Waller LJ in his dissenting judgment [see above p. 677].

(3) It is undesirable that parents, in order to recover compensation, should be encouraged to portray either their children or themselves as disabled . . .

(4) In a state such as ours, which seeks to make public provision for the consequences of disability, the quantification of additional costs attributable to disability, whether of the parent or the child, is a task of acute difficulty.

Similarly, Lord Scott said that he had 'some doubts' about the Court of Appeal's conclusion on foreseeability in *Parkinson*.

Lord Scott

The possibility that a child may be born with a congenital abnormality is plainly present to some degree in the case of every pregnancy. But is that a sufficient reason for holding the negligent doctor liable for the extra costs, attributable to the abnormality, of rearing the child? In my opinion it is not. Foreseeability of a one in 200 to 400 chance does not seem to me, by itself, enough to make it reasonable to impose on the negligent doctor liability for these costs. It might be otherwise in a case where there had been particular reason to fear that if a child were conceived and born it might suffer from some inherited disability. And, particularly, it might be otherwise in a case where the very purpose of the sterilisation operation had been to protect against that fear. But on the facts of Parkinson I do not think the Court of Appeal's conclusion was consistent with McFarlane.

Lord Millett did not express an opinion either way, on the grounds that

it is not necessary for the disposal of the present appeal to reach any conclusion whether *Parkinson* was rightly decided, and I would wish to keep the point open.

Given this equivocation, and the lack of consensus in the Lords on whether the parents of disabled children should now receive the conventional award, or, following *Parkinson*, damages to compensate for the additional costs associated with the child's disability, further litigation involving disabled children is inevitable.

A factual variation which has yet to be considered post-*McFarlane* is where the sterilization operation was carried out privately, and an action could therefore be brought in contract. It is not clear what difference, if any, this might make. Certainly it has long been assumed that the choice of action is in practice immaterial, since the courts will simply imply into a contract a duty to take reasonable care both in carrying out the operation and in providing appropriate and accurate information.[60] Lord Slynn in *McFarlane* did suggest that 'If a client wants to be able to recover such [maintenance] costs he or she must do so by an appropriate contract', but it would seem highly improbable that any clinician would enter into a contract which provided for the full recovery of maintenance costs if the operation did not succeed. Nevertheless, one of the reasons for refusing recovery cited in *Rees* would clearly not apply if the operation took place in the private sector. Lord Bingham, for example, had argued that there was:

a sense that to award potentially very large sums of damages to the parents of a normal and healthy child against a National Health Service always in need of funds to meet pressing demands would rightly offend the community's sense of how public resources should be allocated.

Finally, it is important to note that although most 'wrongful conception' cases have involved negligent sterilizations, or the giving of negligent advice about a sterilization operation's success or permanency, it is also possible that the negligent provision of other sorts of contraceptive treatment might lead to an unwanted conception. This happened in *Richardson v LRC*,[61] a case we considered briefly in Chapter 9 when we looked at product liability. In *Richardson*, the claimant had become pregnant after a condom burst inexplicably, and she brought an action under the Consumer Protection Act 1987, including a claim for the costs of maintaining her child. Her claim was rejected by Ian Kennedy J, in part because *McFarlane* had excluded the possibility of recovering the costs of a healthy child's upbringing:

It is the policy of the law, albeit subject to the precise terms of any contract, to exclude from a claimant's claim the costs of the upbringing of an uncovenanted child. That is equally applicable whether the claim is laid in negligence or a breach of a statutory duty.

(2) SHOULD THERE BE RECOVERY FOR WRONGFUL CONCEPTION?

Damages in tort can only be recovered where the type of loss was foreseeable. Plainly, the costs of a child's upbringing are a foreseeable consequence of negligent sterilization. Furthermore, tort damages are intended to put the claimant in the position they would have been in if the tort had not been committed. As we have seen, if ordinary principles of tort law are applied to these cases, the costs of the child's upbringing would appear to be recoverable. Moreover, in the next extract Alasdair Mullis argues that the considerations which commonly inform the courts' decisions in negligence actions, such as the possibility of the 'floodgates' opening and the availability of insurance, would also point in favour of allowing recovery.

Alastair Mullis[62]
Where someone decides for whatever reason that he or she does not want any more children and has a sterilisation to achieve that end he or she should be entitled to rely upon the doctor exercising all reasonable skill in the conduct of the operation and in giving related advice. Where

---

[60] CR Symmons, 'Policy Factors in Actions for Wrongful Birth' (1987) 50 Modern Law Review 269–306, 271.
[61] [2000] PIQR P164.
[62] 'Wrongful Conception Unravelled' (1993) 1 Medical Law Review 320–35, 333–4.

the doctor fails to exercise the required level of skill the patient should be entitled to recover damages to put him in the position he was in prior to the operation, so far as that is possible. The patient ordered his affairs in a particular way relying on the skill of the doctor, the doctor should, therefore, compensate him for any loss he suffers as a result of that reasonable reliance . . .

Secondly, there is the 'floodgates question'. Traditionally, the courts have been concerned to avoid imposing liability where to do so would involve making the defendant liable to an indeterminate number of people, in an indeterminate amount, for an indeterminate period of time. It is argued that generally, at least, there is no such risk here. First, the number of potential plaintiffs is in the usual case limited to two and they can recover once only. Secondly, in most of these cases the woman will become pregnant fairly soon, usually within a year, after the operation. Finally, the amounts awarded have not usually been excessive and will of course be limited to the first child.

Thirdly, the courts have in a number of cases considered the insurance position. In wrongful conception cases, as in other cases of medical negligence, the loss will not be borne by the doctor himself . . . The parents, however, will not only be unlikely to insure against the risk of pregnancy but they may well be unable to do so. It is surely better, given this background, that the loss should fall on the health authority.

Yet an exception has been carved out in *McFarlane*, and *Parkinson* offers a limited exception to that exception. *Rees* complicates matters further by permitting a novel non-compensatory award, and it is not clear whether this will now apply in *all* 'wrongful conception' cases, or only those in which the mother is disabled.

Is this situation satisfactory? As we can see from the following extracts, the general consensus among academic critics would appear to be 'no'. Even commentators who support the result in *McFarlane*, such as Tony Weir, would accept that the reasoning is 'uneasy'.

Tony Weir[63]

For the fourteen years since *Emeh* the National Health Service, short of resources for curing the sick, has been disbursing large sums of money for the maintenance of children who have nothing wrong with them. To give but a single example out of very many: in 1993 the Lambeth Health Authority had to pay Mrs Cort no less than £140,679 ('James might not have been planned, but I wouldn't give him up for the world'). The House of Lords has now put an end to that . . .

The result in *McFarlane* is quite right, and we should not be surprised if the reasoning is uneasy: whenever it enters the family home the law of obligations—not just tort, but contract and restitution as well—has a marked tendency to go pear-shaped.

In the next extract, Laura Hoyano criticizes Lord Steyn's appeals in *McFarlane* to distributive justice and the 'inarticulate premises' of London commuters.

Laura Hoyano[64]

Distributive justice has become yet another label, without pretending to intellectual rigour. The transmogrification of the man on the Clapham omnibus is not limited to a change of public transport, as he is no longer just a convenient measure for the standard of care expected on non-experts, but also the gatekeeper for negligence law itself. . . . Appeals to commuters on the Underground to decide duty of care issues allow the courts to avoid confronting the sharp edges of tort policy—deterrence, external scrutiny of professional standards of competence, cheapest cost

---

[63] 'The Unwanted Child' (2000) 59 Cambridge Law Journal 238–41, 238, 241.
[64] 'Misconceptions about Wrongful Conception' (2002) 65 Modern Law Review 883–906, 904–6.

avoidance of the risk, insurability against loss, other modes of loss-spreading—and whether carving out *ad hoc* exceptions to well-established legal principles is a matter for parliamentary rather than judicial action. Ultimately, it is Parliament, and not the courts, who are accountable to the commuters on the Underground. Lord Lloyd's prophecy in *Marc Rich* that the law of negligence risks disintegrating into a series of isolated decisions without any coherent principles at all, with the retreat from *Anns* turning into a rout, is fast becoming a reality. The waste of resources, both of the courts and the litigants appearing before them, in trying to divine the meaning of precedents set in this fashion is illustrated all too graphically by the post-*McFarlane* cases . . .

How much time is there between stops on the London Underground, to allow those passengers to assimilate the evidence, weigh up all the factors, and look down the track to future implications of their decision—as is the duty of the judiciary? Not only might London commuters not represent public opinion in the country as a whole, but they might not produce a clear majority, particularly in a complex case. With the utmost respect to Lord Steyn, it is not satisfactory for tort law to be based upon an 'inarticulate premise as to what is morally acceptable and what is not' . . .

Distributive justice . . . permits the judiciary to abdicate its responsibility to identify and explain intellectually rigorous and coherent principles as the basis for decisions, in favour of an empirically untested appeal to public opinion, yielding unpredictable results which invite reversal at every level of appeal, depending on each judge's subjective and avowedly instinctive notions of what justice requires. Thus distributive justice is no more illuminating—and arguably less—than the public policy which the Law Lords were anxious to eschew . . .

The 'wrongful conception' cases demonstrate that distributive justice can be just as unruly a horse as public policy for the courts to ride.

Nicky Priaulx is similarly critical of the approach adopted in *Rees*, arguing, first, that it undermines the decision in *McFarlane*, and, secondly, that it does not offer adequate compensation for the interference with a woman's reproductive autonomy.

Nicky Priaulx[65]

What becomes clear . . . is that neither the majority nor the minority approaches [in *Rees*] are capable of achieving the aim that their Lordships had hoped for: adherence to the *McFarlane* legacy. Quite simply, *McFarlane* no longer stands as good law in the light of *Rees*. If healthy children constitute a benefit serving to outweigh all of the detriments of parenthood, then surely a conventional award overcompensates parents? Both approaches, whether an exception based on disability allowing additional costs or the majority approach of the conventional award constitute significant inroads into the *McFarlane* judgment. Nevertheless, while these illustrate forcefully that their Lordships have changed course it is certainly not a turn in the right direction . . .

But, one might ask, what of this conventional award? . . . While some might welcome this type of development and regard it as curative of the *McFarlane* legacy, it is argued that this scheme of 'compensation' pays nothing more than lip service to the principle of reproductive autonomy. On reflection, the award *is* best described as a gloss on *McFarlane*. Not only is the award derisory in a financial sense, certain to leave women for the greater part reliant upon their own resources in caring for the products of negligence, but so too must their Lordships' 'respect for autonomy' be seen in a similar light. How does the assumption that *all* parents are identically situated, with the same impact on their lives through the birth of an unplanned child illustrate respect for the notion of *individual* autonomy.

---

[65] 'That's One Heck of an "Unruly Horse"! Riding Roughshod over Autonomy in Wrongful Conception' (2004) 12 Feminist Legal Studies 317–31, 327, 329.

While Alasdair Maclean supports the 'gloss' in *Rees*, he too recognizes that it may 'end up pleasing no one'.

Alasdair Maclean[66]

The beauty of [the conventional] award is that it makes no unjustly arbitrary distinction between the claimants, all of whom will receive the same award. It will also make it considerably easier to come to an out of court settlement since there will be no need to haggle over the projected expenses of raising a child or the impact of a disability on those costs. It is, however, a bold but risky strategy. It is bold because, with one stroke, it destroys the knotty tangle weaved by the courts' ill-considered use of distributive justice. It is risky because it may end up pleasing no one, except perhaps the NHS. Given the potential costs involved in raising a child, the parents of a healthy child may still feel hard done by. Disabled parents may feel aggrieved because the comparatively small award is unlikely to meet the additional costs incurred because of their disability. Those in favour of a full award in line with corrective justice principles may feel that the solution fails to do justice and those who believe *McFarlane* was a wholly just decision may feel that the judgment has been undermined.

Peter Cane suggests that the triad of cases, *McFarlane*, *Parkinson*, and *Rees*, illustrate the difficulties in case-by-case judicial law making. It was, he argues, inevitable that *McFarlane* left the way open for an action in relation to a disabled child, and that in turn the question of whether the mother's disability makes a difference would also arise.

Peter Cane[67]

The real problem here is not the majority's solution [in *Rees*]—about the wisdom and fairness of which people might disagree—but the fact that the court in *McFarlane* apparently did not see *Parkinson* or *Rees* coming. What this sequence of cases shows is that if the Law Lords (and their successors on the U.K. Supreme Court) are to take their law-making function seriously—as they seem (to their credit) inclined to do—they must, at least, be prepared to contemplate the possibility that it may be dangerous to consider individual cases too much in isolation and on their precise facts. If the increasingly popular notion of 'distributive justice' is to earn its keep, it must force judges beyond the mantra of treating like cases alike to thinking hard about the criteria of likeness—which involves, at least, comparing and contrasting the case before the court with cases not before the court. Stumbling from one set of facts to the next is, as *Rees* shows, a formula for confusion and instability in the law.

And finally Robin Oppenheim suggests that an alternative route for deciding these cases would be under the Human Rights Act 1998. If the decision in *McFarlane* interferes with a person's legitimate family planning decision, and therefore violates Article 8 (respect for private and family life), it could be justified only if it was proved to be both proportionate and *necessary* under Article 8(2).

Robin Oppenheim[68]

The point of departure should be as Hale L.J. suggests in *Parkinson*, that a wrongful conception or

---

[66] 'An Alexandrian approach to the knotty problem of wrongful pregnancy: *Rees v Darlington Memorial Hospital NHS Trust* in the House of Lords', [2004] 3 Web JCLI <http://webjcli.ncl.ac.uk/2004/issue3/maclean3.html>.

[67] Peter Cane, 'Another Failed Sterilisation' (2004) 120 Law Quarterly Review 189–93, 190–1.

[68] 'The "Mosaic" of Tort Law: The Duty of Care Question' (2003) Journal of Personal Injury Law 151–71, 169–70.

birth claim involves an invasion of bodily integrity. This raises issues that can be addressed under Article 8 of the Convention, which provide respectively for the right to respect for a person's private and family life and home. . . .

It is eminently arguable that the ability to regulate one's own fertility and plan the size of one's family, in the context of loss of autonomy and bodily integrity that unwanted pregnancy entails, falls within the ambit of this bundle of rights and where negligent advice has the consequence of disrupting that ability when conception takes place there is an infringement of Article 8(1). . . .

If the limited recovery rule laid down by McFarlane is treated on the facts of a given case as an infringement of Article 8(1), the court must then go on to consider whether it fits within any of the restrictions under Article 8(2) that are necessary in a democratic society, namely whether it is a legitimate aim answering a pressing social need and applied proportionately. The only relevant exception is probably Article 8(2) on the basis that it was necessary 'for the protection of health or morals'. If society recognises a social entitlement to family planning, it is arguably not morally offensive to adjudicate upon the economic consequences of claims relating to the failure of family planning services and advice. It is difficult to see how non-recognition of a claim for economic loss could be said to be necessary for the protection of health or morals, as required by Article 8(2). There is no pressing social need for the restriction.

(b) 'WRONGFUL BIRTH' (NEGLIGENT PRENATAL TESTING OR ADVICE)

In a wrongful birth action, the parents' claim is that the defendant's negligence led not to their child's *conception*, but to her *birth*. This might happen in a number of different ways. First, before conception, there might have been negligent genetic counselling which wrongfully suggested to the parents that they were not at risk of passing on a genetic disease. If they had been properly advised, they would have been able to avoid the birth of their disabled child, perhaps by deciding not to have children, or by employing preimplantation or prenatal genetic testing. Of course, as the number of genetic tests increases, complex questions are likely to arise about when a doctor has a duty to advise a particular couple that they should undergo genetic testing, either if they seek advice before conceiving, or during pregnancy. It will, for example, be necessary to determine what sort of risk factors might trigger a duty to recommend genetic testing.

Secondly, negligence during IVF treatment—most likely when a couple are undergoing preimplantation genetic diagnosis or screening (PGD/PGS, see Chapter 14 p. 840 for a description)—might lead to the birth of a disabled child who would not have existed if the embryos had been properly screened. Thirdly, where there has been negligence in offering prenatal tests, or in interpreting or communicating their results, the mother might argue that she was deprived of the option of termination.

When the claim is that a woman was deprived of the opportunity of terminating a pregnancy, an action will only lie if an abortion would in fact have been lawful. In *Rance v Mid-Downs HA*,[69] Mrs Rance had not been told about a suspected abnormality, which turned out to be spina bifida. She claimed that if she had been properly informed, she would have terminated the pregnancy, and her severely disabled son,

[69] [1991] 1 QB 587.

John, would not have been born. However, in 1983 an abortion at 26 weeks (which is when John's abnormality was first suspected) would have been unlawful, and so even if Mrs Rance had been told that her baby would have spina bifida, she would not have been able to prevent his birth. Applying the 'but for' test, her loss could not be attributed to the defendant's negligence. The time limits in the Abortion Act 1967 have since been amended by the Human Fertilisation and Embryology Act 1990, and, as we saw in the previous chapter, an abortion on the grounds of fetal abnormality may now be lawful up until birth. Provided that the disability is serious, it is unlikely that the illegality of an abortion would now block a mother's claim for wrongful birth following negligent prenatal testing.

The facts which give rise to a wrongful birth action on the part of the parents will generally be indistinguishable from those which might prompt the child to bring a 'wrongful life' action. Since wrongful life actions are generally unlikely to succeed, it is therefore the child's mother, and not the child herself, who will normally sue when the claim is that proper care would have avoided the birth of a disabled child. The one exception might be the limited 'wrongful life' exception which, as we saw earlier, appears to exist in the Congenital Disabilities Act 1976, when it is the negligent *selection* of embryos that caused the child's disabilities.

Rand v East Dorset HA[70] was the first wrongful birth action to be decided post-*McFarlane*. Negligent prenatal screening had failed to detect that the fetus had Down Syndrome. Newman J concluded that the House of Lords had not ruled out compensation for the extra costs associated with a child's serious disability. His judgment was subsequently followed in *Hardman v Amin*,[71] a case in which a GP had negligently failed to diagnose his pregnant patient's rubella infection, leading to the birth of her severely handicapped son. Henriques J held that *McFarlane* did not affect recovery for the wrongful birth of a disabled child. In any event, he believed that commuters on the Underground would accept the premise that the defendant should be responsible for the costs of a child's disability where it was his fault that the child was born disabled:

If the commuters on the underground were asked whether the costs of bringing up Daniel (which are attributable to his disability) should fall on the claimant or the rest of the family, or the state, or the defendant, I am satisfied that the very substantial majority, having regard to the particular circumstances of this case, would say that the expense should fall on the wrongdoer.

With respect, it is perhaps worth noting that the 'wrongdoer', Dr Amin, would not, of course, be paying the damages himself.

A similar approach was adopted in *Lee v Taunton and Somerset NHS Trust*.[72] The couple believed themselves to be at risk of having a disabled child has a result of their epilepsy medication. A high resolution ultrasound was performed during pregnancy, but it failed to detect the fetus's spina bifida. Toulson J again suggested that commuters on the Underground would not regard the birth of a disabled child as a blessing, and nor would they regard it as unjust that a negligent doctor should be required to compensate the parents for failing to given them the option of preventing the child's birth.

---

[70] (2000) 56 BMLR 39.   [71] (2000) 59 BMLR 58.   [72] [2001] 1 FLR 419.

Toulson J

I do not believe that it would be right for the law to deem the birth of a disabled child to be a blessing, in all circumstances and regardless of the extent of the child's disabilities; or to regard the responsibility for the care of such a child as so enriching in the ordinary nature of things that it would be unjust for a parent to recover the cost from a negligent doctor on whose skill that parent had properly relied to prevent the situation.

If the matter were put to an opinion poll among passengers on the Underground, I would be surprised if a majority would support such a view. . . .

The fact remains that in all the cited cases, before and after McFarlane, of birth of a disabled child after alleged negligence in failing to detect foetal abnormalities which would have led to a termination of the pregnancy, the courts have recognised the claimant's right to claim damages for the cost of meeting the child's special needs. . . . I have considered whether the decision in McFarlane should lead to a different conclusion in this type of case, and I do not believe so.

Toulson J also discussed whether the compensation should cover *all* of George's maintenance costs, rather than just those which were attributable to his spina bifida.

Toulson J

George was incapable of being born other than severely disabled. That being so, to try to separate the consequences of George's existence and George's disabled existence is metaphysically impossible and practically unreal. If George's birth was not a deemed blessing, I cannot see a barrier to Mrs Lee recovering the full costs of his maintenance, except for the important fact that she was wanting to bear a healthy child. If, following a termination of her pregnancy with George, she had continued with her attempts and had been successful, she would have incurred the costs of bringing up a healthy child in any event.

In a wrongful birth action, allowing only the additional costs associated with the child's disability arguably would make more sense because the pregnancy itself is wanted, and the parents would in any event have incurred the costs of caring for a healthy child. It is therefore *only* the special costs associated with the disability, and not the ordinary maintenance costs of a normal child, which are attributable to the defendant's negligence.

It should also be noted that parents in wrongful birth cases cannot claim for the pain and discomfort of pregnancy, because these are not attributable to the defendant's negligence. In a wrongful birth case, the mother would have suffered the same pain and discomfort if the child had been normal and healthy.

5. CONCLUSION

The uncertainties which remained after the House of Lords' judgment in *McFarlane* made it inevitable that cases such as *Parkinson* and *Rees* would follow, in order to test whether slight variations on the facts would enable claimants to recover the maintenance costs of children conceived as a result of another's negligence. Interestingly, neither *Parkinson* nor *Rees* has clarified the scope of *McFarlane*, which continues to be opaque, to say the least. Following the decision in *Rees*, two critical questions remain unanswered. First, the status of the exception to *McFarlane* in *Parkinson* is now uncertain. The House of Lords were split over whether *Parkinson* had been rightly decided, and that question will inevitably rear its head again in the next few years.

Secondly, is the conventional award in *Rees* confined to cases in which the mother is disabled, or might it apply to all wrongful conception cases? Certainly the justifications given for it do not appear to be confined to *disabled* parents: in Lord Millett's words there had been a 'denial of an important aspect of . . . personal autonomy, viz the right to limit the size of their family', and Lord Bingham said that 'the real loss suffered in a situation of this kind . . . is that a parent, particularly (even today) the mother, has been denied through the negligence of another, the opportunity to live her life in the way that she wished and planned'. But if the conventional award were to apply to a case like *McFarlane*, then surely the courts would be admitting that the birth of a child is not always a blessing, and the whole foundation of the judgment in *McFarlane*, despite their Lordships' apparent support for it in *Rees*, starts to look a little unstable.

It is impossible to predict how any future cases involving, first, a disabled child, and second, a healthy child born to healthy parents, will be decided. Should another wrongful conception case reach the House of Lords, it will, however, be interesting to see whether Baroness Hale is on the panel. In her judgments in the Court of Appeal in both *Parkinson* and *Rees*, her dissatisfaction with the decision in *McFarlane* is evident. Recall her extraordinarily detailed description of the physical and emotional invasiveness of pregnancy, childbirth and motherhood. In *Rees*, a number of their Lordships admitted that the principal loss in these cases is an interference with the woman's reproductive autonomy, but none went quite so far as Hale LJ, as she then was, did in *Parkinson*.

In relation to 'wrongful life' actions, it is often assumed that the door closed on them over twenty years ago in *McKay*. Yet, for two reasons, I think this assumption may be premature. First, the judgments placed considerable emphasis upon the sanctity of human life, and while this would undoubtedly still be a relevant factor, it may exert less pull over the judiciary now than it did in 1982. Since then, numerous cases have explored the question of when life-prolonging treatment becomes futile, or is not in the patient's best interests. If, as the Court of Appeal assumed in *McKay*, life must *always* be preferred to non-existence, it would be impossible to justify withdrawing life-sustaining treatment from a living patient.

Secondly, there has been surprisingly little litigation under the Congenital Disabilities (Civil Liability) Act 1976, but if/when a claimant brings an action under section 1A(2)(b), the court may be forced to address an inconsistency between the 1976 Act and the Court of Appeal's judgment in *McKay*. In such a case the claimant would be claiming that negligence in the process of embryo selection resulted in a genetically abnormal embryo being transferred to the woman's body. The disabled child would have to argue that non-negligence would have prevented her birth, and the courts would have to grapple with what would appear to be a statutory action for wrongful life.

6. FURTHER READING

CANE, PETER, 'Another Failed Sterilisation' (2004) 120 Law Quarterly Review 189–93.

JACKSON, EMILY, *Regulating Reproduction* (Hart Publishing Oxford 2001) 25–41.

HOYANO, LAURA, 'Misconceptions about Wrongful Conception' (2002) 65 Modern Law Review 883–906.

LEE, ROBERT, 'To be or not to be: Is that the question? The claim of wrongful life' in Robert Lee and Derek Morgan (eds), *Birthrights: Law and Ethics at the Beginnings of Life* (Routledge London 1989) 172–94.

MACLEAN, ALASDAIR, 'An Alexandrian approach to the knotty problem of wrongful pregnancy: *Rees v Darlington Memorial Hospital NHS Trust* in the House of Lords' [2004] 3 Web JCLI <http://webjcli.ncl.ac.uk/2004/issue3/maclean3.html>.

MORRIS, ANNE and SAINTIER, SEVERINE, 'To Be or Not to Be: Is That the Question? Wrongful Life and Misconceptions' (2003) 11 Medical Law Review 167–93.

MULLIS, ALASTAIR, 'Wrongful Conception Unravelled' (1993) 1 Medical Law Review 320–35.

PACE, PJ, 'Civil Liability for Pre-Natal Injuries' (1977) 40 Modern Law Review 141.

PRIAULX, NICKY, *The Harm Paradox: Tort Law and the Unwanted Child in an Era of Choice* (UCL Press London 2006).

SYMMONS, CR, 'Policy Factors in Actions for Wrongful Birth' (1987) 50 Modern Law Review 269–306.

TEFF, HARVEY, 'The Action for "Wrongful Life" in England and the United States' (1985) 34 International & Comparative Law Quarterly 423–41.

12

ORGAN TRANSPLANTATION

1. CENTRAL ISSUES

1. Organ transplantation is successful and cost-effective, but there is an acute shortage of organs available for transplant, and the gap between supply and demand is widening.

2. Under the new legislation, the Human Tissue Act 2004, consent to cadaveric donation is necessary, either from the deceased person, or from her nominee, or from the highest ranking qualified relative.

3. This consent-based model will not dramatically increase the pool of cadaveric organ donors. Other options include moving towards an 'opt-out' system, where consent is presumed; offering either financial or non-financial incentives; and treating dead people's organs as a public resource.

4. In recent years, the number of living organ donors has increased. Regulation of living organ donation is directed towards ensuring that the donor has given informed consent, and that no money has changed hands.

5. Xenotransplantation, that is animal-to-human transplantation, could potentially solve the organ shortage, but it raises a number of difficult ethical issues. Currently the most compelling objection to xenotransplantation is the unknown and possibly unknowable risk of cross-species infection.

2. INTRODUCTION

For two reasons, the first attempts to transplant organs from one person's body into another were inevitably unsuccessful. First, before it became possible to suppress the recipient's immune system, any foreign tissue would automatically be rejected. Secondly, because organs deteriorate rapidly as soon as a person's cardio-respiratory system stops working, it also used to be very difficult to ensure that organs taken from cadavers 'survived' the transplant process. The first recipients of transplanted organs were usually selected because they were in the final and inevitably fatal stages of acute organ failure, and they generally died within a matter of days or weeks.

The first successful organ transplant was a live kidney transplant, between identical twins, which took place in Boston in 1954. In the UK, the first successful transplant involved a similar operation six years later in Edinburgh. Since the 1960s, techniques for maintaining the quality of organs before and during transplantation have improved dramatically, and immunosuppressant therapy can minimize the problem of rejection. The prognosis for transplant patients is now extremely good. After one year, 82 per cent of heart transplants, 94 per cent of living donor kidney transplants, and 87 per cent of cadaveric kidney transplants will still be functioning well.[1] Of course, transplant surgery sometimes fails, and immunosuppressant drugs may have a negative impact upon a person's health. But from the point of view of patients, a transplant will commonly represent the optimum treatment for organ failure. Heart and liver transplants are often life-saving. The availability of dialysis means that kidney failure is not necessarily life-threatening, but being dependent on dialysis is so unpleasant that kidney transplant patients often benefit from a much improved quality of life.

Because alternative treatments for patients with organ failure, such as dialysis, are expensive, transplantation will also often represent a net gain for the NHS. Successful kidney transplantation is much cheaper than providing dialysis to a patient with renal failure. The average cost of dialysis is £21,000 per patient per year.[2] The cost of a kidney transplant is £17,000 per patient per transplant, and the immunosuppression required by a patient with a transplant costs around £5,000 per patient per year.[3] After one year, each kidney transplant therefore saves the NHS £16,000 per year. The cost benefit of kidney transplantation compared to dialysis over a period of nine years (the median graft survival time) is then £128,000.[4] Restoring otherwise sick and dependent patients to better health clearly also has advantages for their families, and for society in general.

In short, transplantation surgery is a successful and often cost-effective therapeutic option. The chief problem, as is well known, is that there are insufficient organs available for transplant, and this problem is exacerbated by improvements in transplant technology which expand the pool of potential recipients to include older patients, as well as those previously thought too ill to undergo such a major operation. Ironically, artificial organs have in fact exacerbated the organ shortage because, while not yet effective enough to offer permanent replacements, they allow transplant teams to temporarily 'bridge' patients who would otherwise die, enabling them to be put on the organ donor waiting list until a human organ becomes available. The pool of possible recipients therefore continues to grow steadily, while the pool of potential organ donors remains too small to satisfy this demand. Indeed the number of cadaveric organs available for transplant has actually declined in recent years, due at least in part to a reduction in mortality rates from road traffic accidents.

The median waiting time for a kidney transplant is 500 days. Given waiting times of over a year, unsurprisingly mortality rates on the organ donor waiting list are high: up to 30 per cent of patients on the waiting list will die before an organ becomes available. This understates the scale of the problem, however, because some patients are never put on the waiting list, even though they might benefit from an organ transplant, because the doctors involved in their care recognize that it is unlikely that they would become eligible for a transplant in time. The chief ethical issue raised by organ transplantation then is how to increase the number of organs, either from dead donors, or from alternative sources of supply, such as live donors or animals.

---

[1] <http://www.uktransplant.org.uk/ukt/statistics/statistics.jsp> (July 2005).
[2] UK Transplant Factsheet, *The Cost Effectiveness of Transplantation* (UK Transplant, 2005) <http://www.uktransplant.org.uk/ukt/newsroom/fact_sheets/cost_effectiveness_of_transplantation.jsp>.
[3] Ibid.   [4] Ibid.

There is, it seems, widespread public support for organ transplantation. Opinion polls consistently indicate that at least 70 per cent of the population would want their organs to be used to save others in the event of their death. Although some people claim to have religious objections to organ donation, scholars from all the major religions have endorsed transplantation on the grounds that the imperatives of healing and saving life may sometimes trump other considerations, such as a proscription of the mutilation of corpses. A 1995 Fatwa, for example, stated that giving and receiving organs is compatible with Islam.[5] Yet despite broad public approval of transplantation, comparatively few people carry organ donor cards (20–30 per cent), or are registered on the organ donor register (20 per cent). There is therefore a desperate shortage of organs available for transplant. The paradox of this situation is pointed out by Sheila McLean:

We have the doctors ready, willing and able to undertake the surgery, we have people dying with usable organs and we apparently have a compliant public. Why then is the programme so strapped?[6]

It should, however, be noted that there are some voices of dissent who would contest the widespread assumption that increasing the number of organ transplants would be a self-evidently desirable end.[7] Although transplant surgery is often cost-effective, heart transplants continue to be extremely expensive, and this raises some of the questions about the appropriate allocation of scarce NHS resources which we considered in Chapter 2. Discussions of the ethical issues arising from organ transplantation often leave out the financial costs of surgery, and instead appear to assume that a shortage of organs is the only barrier to a hugely increased transplant programme, as if the NHS has a bottomless capacity to perform complex and expensive transplant surgery.

At the time of writing, the law relating to organ transplantation is in a state of flux. The Human Tissue Act 2004 is due to come into force in 2006. Because it will repeal the previous legislation (the Human Tissue Act 1961 and the Human Organ Transplants Act 1989), in this chapter we will concentrate upon the new Act. The principal factor behind this new legislation was the retained organs scandal at Bristol Royal Infirmary and Alder Hey Children's Hospital. It became apparent that many children's organs had been retained without parental knowledge, let alone consent.[8] For reasons of space, in this chapter we focus only upon the parts of the Act which deal

---

[5] For discussion of Muslim attitudes towards organ donation, see Clare Hayward and Anna Madill, 'The meaning of organ donation: Muslims of Pakistani origin and white English nationals living in North England' (2003) 57 Social Science and Medicine 389–401; and Sahin Aksoy, 'A Critical Approach to the Current Understanding of Islamic Scholars on Using Cadaver Organs Without Permission' (2001) 15 Bioethics 461–72.

[6] 'Transplantation and the "Nearly Dead"; The Case of Elective Ventilation' in S Mclean (ed), Contemporary Issues in Law, Medicine and Ethics (Dartmouth Aldershot 1996) 143–61, 146.

[7] Barbara Koenig, 'Dead Donors and the "Shortage" of Human Organs: Are We Missing the Point?' (2003) 3 American Journal of Bioethics 26–7; RC Fox and J Swazey, Spare parts: Organ replacement in American Society (OUP Oxford 1992).

[8] See further, M Brazier, 'Organ retention and return: problems of consent' (2003) 29 Journal of Medical Ethics 30–3; Brazier, 'Human Tissue Retention' (2004) 72 Medico-Legal Journal 39; John Harris, 'Law and regulation of retained organs: the ethical issues' (2002) 22 Legal Studies 527–49; Brazier 'Retained organs: ethics and humanity' (2002) 22 Legal Studies 550–69.

with organ transplantation, although it is worth noting that David Price has suggested that '[t]he focus of current concern, the retention of organs and tissue following post-mortem, threatens to appreciably skew what will ultimately be extensive legislative changes embedded for at least the medium term'.[9]

The Act sets up a new Human Tissue Authority (HTA),[10] which will, as part of the review of arm's length bodies, be merged with the Human Fertilisation and Embryology Authority (whose role we consider in Chapters 13 and 14) to form the Regulatory Authority for Tissues and Embryos (RATE). This is expected to happen in 2008. Until then the HTA will operate autonomously, but the two bodies will work closely together to ensure a smooth transition to the new Authority.

The HTA will issue licenses for the storage and use of tissues. Most organs that are used in transplantation cannot be stored for any length of time, and so it is only when tissue, such as bone marrow, is banked for future use in transplantation that the licensing regime becomes relevant. Because we concentrate on solid organ donation in this chapter, the licensing process will not be discussed in any detail.[11] Of more importance are the Codes of Practice which the HTA will issue to cover issues such as consent, donation and removal of tissue. At the time of writing, these have been published in draft form only, for the purpose of public consultation. I will refer to the draft Codes of Practice, but it should be remembered that the final Codes of Practice may be different. They will be available from the HTA's website.[12]

In this chapter, we first consider cadaveric donation, looking first at who may become a donor, and which organs may be taken. We then turn to the definition of 'brain death', which has enabled organs to be taken from donors whose hearts are still beating. The system of organ retrieval in the UK is then summarized, and we look at the consent-based model adopted in the Human Tissue Act 2004. Because of the shortage of organs from cadavers, a number of possible strategies to increase the number of cadaveric donors have been canvassed and we evaluate these in turn.

Next we look at living organ donation. We analyse the legitimacy of performing such a serious operation on someone solely in order to benefit a third party. Could a person give valid consent in such circumstances, and could it ever be appropriate to take an organ from a child or an incompetent adult? We discuss the restrictions placed on living organ donation in the Human Tissue Act, and we look at the controversial question of whether offering financial incentives to living donors would be an acceptable way to increase the number of volunteers. Finally, we consider the ethical, practical and legal obstacles to transplanting animal organs into human recipients.

---

[9] 'From Cosmos And Damian To Van Velzen: The Human Tissue Saga Continues' (2003) 11 Medical Law Review 1.
[10] <http://www.hta.gov.uk>.   [11] See further <http://www.hta.gov.uk>.
[12] <http://www.hta.gov.uk>.

3. DEAD DONORS

(a) WHO CAN BE A DONOR?

It is important to remember that comparatively few people die in circumstances which make it possible to use their organs for transplantation. A person's organs must be healthy, which will generally rule out people who die from degenerative diseases such as cancer. Potential donors will often be people who have suffered massive head injuries but whose other organs are unlikely to have been damaged. In order to reduce damage to the organs, it is preferable to remove them from a person who has died while on an artificial ventilator. UK Transplant carried out an audit of all potential donors in 2003/4 and found that of all the patients who die while connected to an artificial ventilator, only 7 per cent have been diagnosed as brain-stem dead with no medical contraindications to organ donation.[13] Of these 1,379 patients, only 621 become solid organ donors. An average of 3.5 organs can be taken from each cadaver, so obtaining organs from these 758 unused but suitable potential donors undoubtedly has the potential to massively increase the number of transplants.

Obviously attempts must be made by the transplant team to ensure that the potential donor does not have any genetic condition or infectious disease which could jeopardize the recipient's health. It will, for example, be important that to obtain as full a family and social history as possible, and to carry out such tests as are practicable. Guidance is provided by the Department of Health's *Guidance on the microbiological safety of human organs, tissues and cells used in transplantation.*[14] Because organs must be transplanted quickly, however, there are limits on how thorough such investigation can be, and this means that some risk of disease transmission is probably inevitable. In seeking the recipient's consent to transplantation, it is of course necessary to ensure that she is properly informed about this small residual risk.

While diagnostic tests can, of course, be carried out before transplantation to test for the HIV virus, the problem is that an HIV test only shows that a person did not have the virus between 3 and 6 months previously. This means that there will always be a chance that the donor might have been in the 'window period' before seroconversion when he or she died. The Department of Health's guidance suggests that efforts should be made to ensure that there has been no evidence of high-risk activity, such as being paid for sex, injecting drugs, having homosexual sex, or sex with someone from a specified list of countries in Africa.[15]

(b) DEFINITION OF DEATH

If organs can only be removed once someone has died, and if they must be removed as soon as possible after death, accurately pinpointing the moment of death is vitally

---

[13] *Potential Donor Audit* (UK Transplant 2005) <http://www.uktransplant.org.uk/ukt/statistics/potential_donor_audit/potential_donor_audit.jsp>.

[14] Department of Health 2000 <http://www.dh.gov.uk>.

[15] *Guidance on the microbiological safety of human organs, tissues and cells used in transplantation.* Department of Health 2000 <http://www.dh.gov.uk>.

important. The problem, however, is that death is usually a process which takes place over a period of time: a person's organs do not all stop functioning at the same moment, but rather they fail progressively once the brain has irreversibly died. Brain death itself involves two distinct changes which do not always happen simultaneously: one is the permanent loss of consciousness (caused by death of the upper brain), and the other is the loss of the brain's ability to regulate other bodily functions such as breathing (caused by death of the lower brain).

Throughout history, definitions of death have attempted to designate some point at which a person's loss of bodily functions becomes irreversible. In the past, a body could not be conclusively considered dead until putrefaction had begun. This changed in the nineteenth century, when death started to be diagnosed once a person had stopped breathing and their heart had stopped beating. During the twentieth century, medical progress undermined these tests because in some circumstances it became possible to revive someone whose heart had stopped beating. If someone is successfully resuscitated, then plainly they were not dead despite their temporary absence of heart function. The invention of the artificial ventilator also made it necessary to decide whether a diagnosis of death could ever be made while someone's heartbeat was being maintained artificially. If such patients are alive, then the decision to remove them from the ventilator is much more controversial than it would be if they have already been diagnosed as dead.

Pressure to rethink the definition of death also, of course, came from developments in transplant surgery. As we have seen, loss of cardio-respiratory function will cause irreversible damage to a person's organs. Organs will generally only be suitable for transplant if death can be diagnosed following irreversible brain death, instead of waiting for the donor's heart to stop beating. Although cardio-respiratory function cannot be maintained indefinitely once someone's brain has died, continuing to ventilate a person who has been diagnosed as brain dead enables doctors to remove organs while the heart is still beating. Of course it is vitally important that these 'heart beating donors' must first have been satisfactorily diagnosed as dead: in Hans Jonas's words, 'the patient must be absolutely sure that his doctor does not become his executioner'.[16]

The first attempt to define death using cessation of brain function took place in France in 1959 when a group of neurosurgeons described a condition in which there was no detectable brain activity: they called this 'death of the central nervous system', and although they did not address the question of whether this was the same as death, they concluded that removing a patient whose central nervous system had died from a ventilator would be justified despite their artificially maintained heartbeat.

Debate over the need for a new definition of death continued during the 1960s, and brain death was formally defined in 1968 by an Ad Hoc Committee of the Harvard Medical School, whose report *A Definition of Irreversible Coma* opened with the following statement:

Our primary purpose is to define irreversible coma as a new criterion for death. There are two

[16] *Philosophical Essays: From Ancient Creed to Technological Man* (Prentice Hall Englewood Cliffs, NJ 1974) 131.

reasons why there is a need for a definition: (1) Improvements in resuscitative and supportive measures have led to increased efforts to save those who are desperately injured. Sometimes these efforts have only partial success, so that the result is an individual whose heart continues to beat but whose brain is irreversibly damaged. The burden is great on patients who suffer permanent loss of intellect, on their families, on the hospitals, and on those in need of hospital beds already occupied by these comatose patients. (2) Obsolete criteria for the definition of death can lead to controversy in obtaining organs for transplantation.[17]

The concept of brain death has now been adopted by most Western countries. In Japan, however, brain-stem death has proved exceptionally controversial, in part because of cultural attitudes towards death and the special relationship which is believed to exist between ancestral spirits and the living, and in part because there is simply less trust in the medical profession. Indeed the surgeon who performed the first heart transplant in Japan in 1968 was charged with murder. In 1997, brain death was recognized in Japan, but only when the patient has specified in writing that she wishes to donate her organs after death, and her family does not wish to overrule her wishes. Unless both these conditions are satisfied, brain dead patients are not considered legally dead. In the first three years following this change in the law, organs were procured from only nine brain dead donors.[18]

In the UK there is no statutory definition of death. Rather, the diagnosis of death is regarded as a matter of clinical judgement. Since the late 1970s, brain-stem death, or the irreversible loss of brain-stem function has been treated as the definitive criterion for diagnosing death. Following recommendations from the British Transplantation Society and the Royal Colleges the criteria for establishing death are now contained in the Department of Health's *Code of Practice for the Diagnosis of Brain Stem Death*:[19]

Death entails the irreversible loss of those essential characteristics which are necessary to the existence of a living human person. Thus, it is recommended that the definition of death should be regarded as 'irreversible loss of the capacity for consciousness, combined with irreversible loss of the capacity to breathe'. The irreversible cessation of brain stem function (brain stem death) . . . will produce this clinical state and therefore brain stem death equates with the death of the individual.

The Department of Health's Code of Practice states that the diagnosis of brain stem death must be made by at least two registered medical practitioners, and to avoid conflicts of interest, neither of these should be a member of the transplant team.[20] Although death can only be pronounced following two sets of brain stem tests, the legal time of death is when the first test indicates brain stem death.[21]

In *Re A*,[22] the parents of a 2-year-old boy who had been diagnosed as brain stem dead did not want him to be removed from the ventilator. Two sets of brain stem tests had been carried out, the first on 21 January, and the second on 22 January. The doctors sought, and were granted a declaration that they could lawfully disconnect the

---

[17] Ad Hoc Committee of the Harvard Medical School to Examine the Definition of Death (1968) 205(6) Journal of the American Medical Association 85–8, 85.

[18] See further Margaret Lock, *Twice Dead: Organ Transplants and the Reinvention of Death* (University of California Press Berkeley 2002).

[19] Department of Health, *Code of Practice for the Diagnosis of Brain Stem Death* (HSC 1998/035), para 1.

[20] Ibid, para 3.3.   [21] Ibid.   [22] [1992] 3 Med LR 303.

ventilator. Endorsing the Code of Practice's definition of death, Johnson J stated: 'I have no hesitation at all in holding that A has been dead since . . . January 21.'

Because organ transplantation depends so heavily upon public goodwill, it is especially important that the public accepts that brain-stem death is not an especially 'early' diagnosis of death. In 1980, a Panorama TV programme questioned the validity of brain-death criteria, leading to an immediate and sharp reduction in the number of organs becoming available for transplant: it took 15 months for organ procurement rates to recover.

It has been difficult for the public to accept that a person whose heart is still beating, and who appears to be breathing, albeit with mechanical assistance, is really dead, and this confusion is undoubtedly exacerbated by the fact that the person will still be connected to what is commonly known as a *life*-support machine. A warm, breathing body certainly does not look dead, and relatives often find the concept of organ retrieval prior to cessation of heart and lung function disturbing. There has also, of course, been the concern that death was being redefined in order to serve the needs of transplant surgeons. Youngner, for example, argues that:

we have identified a group of severely injured and dying persons who are so 'beyond harm' that we feel justified in killing them in order to obtain their organs. Since we would rather not think that we are killing them, we simply gerrymander the line between life and death to include them in the latter category.[23]

In the next extract, Peter Singer argues that the concept of brain death is 'at best, rather odd' and considers the reasons why it has nevertheless proved to be relatively uncontroversial.

Peter Singer[24]

The idea that someone is dead when their brain is dead is, at best, rather odd. Human beings are not the only living things in the world. All living things eventually die, and we can generally tell when they are alive and when they are dead. Isn't the distinction between life and death so basic that what counts as dead for a human being also counts as dead for a dog, a parrot, a prawn, an oyster, an oak, or a cabbage? . . .

[T]o be 'brain dead' is something that can only happen to a being with a brain. It can't happen to a cabbage, nor to an oak, and not really to an oyster either. And though it would in theory be possible, no-one talks about 'brain death' in the case of dogs or parrots either. 'Brain death' is only for humans. Isn't it odd that for a human being to die requires a different concept of death from that which we apply to other living beings?

The question is a vital one, in every sense of the term. When warm, breathing, pulsating human beings are declared to be dead, they lose their basic human rights. They are not given life support. If their relatives consent . . ., their hearts and other organs can be cut out of their bodies and given to strangers. The change in our conception of death that excluded these human beings from the moral community was one of the first in a series of dramatic changes in our view of life and death. Yet, in sharp contrast to other changes in this area, it met with virtually no opposition? How did this happen? . . .

[23] Stuart Youngner, 'Some must die' in SJ Youngner, RC Fox and LJ O'Connell (eds), *Organ Transplantation: Meanings and Realities* (University of Wisconsin Press Madison 1996) 50.
[24] *Rethinking Life and Death: The Collapse of our Traditional Ethics* (OUP Oxford 1994) 20, 22, 32, 35.

In summary, the redefinition of death in terms of brain death went through so smoothly because it did not harm the brain-dead patients and it benefited everyone else: the families of brain-dead patients, the hospitals, the transplant surgeons, people needing transplants, people who worried that they might one day need a transplant, people who feared that they might one day be kept on a respirator after their brain had died, taxpayers and the government. . . .

The picture I have been presenting of brain death up to now suggests that it is a convenient fiction. It was proposed and accepted because it makes it possible for us to salvage organs that would otherwise be wasted, and to withdraw medical treatment when it is doing no good.

It has also been suggested that medical techniques which increasingly enable brain-stem function to be maintained artificially cast doubt upon the continued validity of brain stem-death as the principal criterion used to diagnose death. As Kerridge et al. suggest in the following extract, people who have been diagnosed as brain dead can have some bodily functions maintained artificially for increasingly long periods of time. If brain dead patients can 'survive' on a ventilator for several months, are they really dead?

IH Kerridge, P Saul, M Lowe, J McPhee, and D Williams[25]

When the concept of brain death was first introduced it was argued that death of the brain stem inevitably implied the imminent death of the whole body . . . This argument is no longer tenable as medical therapy and intensive care have become increasingly sophisticated at replacing brain stem function, and we now know that bodies with a dead brain stem may be kept alive for prolonged periods of time. Brain dead pregnant women have been maintained for months and later given birth to healthy infants and brain dead children have been reported to survive for up to 14 years with ventilatory and nutritional support. In other words brain stem criteria can still be used to define prognosis, although the timing of death depends upon provision or withdrawal of intensive care.

Suggestions that the brain stem is the supreme regulator of the body seem both biologically and philosophically simplistic . . . Furthermore the heart, the liver, the kidneys, and other organs are all required to maintain bodily integrity, and loss of the functions of any of these organs will result in eventual disintegration of the organism without artificial support. Many individuals who are clearly alive depend upon technology such as pacemakers, dialysis machines or even ventilators to live. Whether there is a 'supreme regulator' therefore seems open to question. This argument may also be confused by the fact that the functions of the kidneys, heart, and lungs can be replaced by technological means, whereas that of the brain stem cannot. This is, however, very dependent upon technology; indeed aspects of brain stem function can now be replaced and it seems likely that more progress might be made in this area . . .

There is also some evidence that the brain continues to regulate some bodily functions in patients who meet the criteria for brain death . . . Patients who satisfy brain-death criteria may also respond to painful stimuli (such as surgical excision)—suggesting the existence of integrated neurological function at a brain level and many may exhibit spontaneous or reflect movements. . . .

Organ transplantation requires the use of living tissue for the purposes of transplantation . . . It has been suggested by critics of brain-death that the concept was introduced, not because its proponents really believed that such patients were dead, but as a 'convenient fiction' that allowed the development of organ transplantation.

[25] 'Death, dying and donation: organ transplantation and the diagnosis of death' (2002) 28 Journal of Medical Ethics 89–94, 90–1.

Perhaps it should be admitted that it is impossible to define the moment of death with any certainty or precision, and that the important task therefore is to determine at what point *in the process of dying* organ retrieval becomes legitimate. The rule that organs may only be retrieved once a person is dead is intended to foster public trust in the transplantation system. But it is at least arguable that the certainty implied by this 'dead donor' rule misrepresents the ambiguity of death.[26] Indeed, Truog and Robinson have suggested that we should straightforwardly admit that it is legitimate to retrieve organs from the 'imminently dying', with their consent.[27] They argue:

that sometimes the harm of dying is sufficiently small that patients should be allowed to voluntarily accept that harm if it makes organ donation possible.

In Truog and Robinson's view, we should be:

shifting the key ethical question from 'Is the patient dead?' to 'Are the harms of removing life sustaining organs sufficiently small that patients or surrogates should be allowed to consent to donation?'

Julian Savulescu would agree:[28]

Since I believe we die when our meaningful mental life ceases, organs should be available from that point, which may significantly predate brain death. At the very least, people should be allowed to complete advance directives that direct that their organs be removed when their brain is severely damaged or they are permanently unconscious.

In the next extract, M Potts and DW Evans criticize these sorts of argument on the grounds that taking organs from living patients, even if they are imminently dying, would involve doctors killing their patients.

M Potts and DW Evans[29]

We contend that Truog and Robinson's arguments for the moral acceptability of organ procurement once the dead donor rule is eliminated are unsuccessful, and that the unacceptability of such transplantation should lead to changes in current policy. . . . Removing a vital organ, such as the heart, directly causes the death of the patient, and is not merely allowing the effects of disease or injury to take their course. It is the organ removal surgery that kills the donor. . . .

Truog and Robinson's proposals that unpaired vital organs be removed from 'brain dead' and other classes of patients can be seen as the endorsement of killing people for their organs. One difficulty with this is that once utilitarian considerations are used to justify killing ventilator/dependent patients who are dying, those same considerations could also be used to justify killing non-ventilator/dependent patients or patients who are not dying.

Another major problem with doctors being involved in killing patients is that such a practice by medical professionals fundamentally distorts the nature of medicine itself. . . .

Currently, the statement on organ donor cards asserts that organs may be taken 'after my death'. We believe that such wording should be changed to reflect the fact that 'brain dead'

[26] Elyssa R Koppelman, 'The Dead Donor Rule and the Concept of Death: Severing the Ties That Bind Them' (2003) 3(1) American Journal of Bioethics 1–9, 4.

[27] RE Truog and WM Robinson, 'Role of brain death and the dead-donor rule in the ethics of organ transplantation' (2004) 31 Critical Care Medicine 2391–6.

[28] J Savulescu, 'Death, us and our bodies: personal reflections' (2003) 29 Journal of Medical Ethics 127–30.

[29] 'Does it matter that organ donors are not dead? Ethical and policy implications' (2005) 31 Journal of Medical Ethics 406–9.

individuals are not dead in the usual understanding of what death is. Explanatory literature accompanying organ donor cards should be frank that a 'brain dead' donor's heart is beating during part of the organ removal surgery. There should be open public discussion and debate on the determination of death instead of the current domination of the orthodox . . . 'brain stem death' position. Pluralism on the issue of the determination of death should be publicly acknowledged.

In the following extract, Torbjörn Tännsjö suggests that the search for *one* definition of death is futile. The circulatory and respiratory criterion makes sense in some circumstances, because the logical conclusion of accepting brain death as the definitive and *only* diagnosis of death is that we should be prepared to bury a person who was still breathing and whose heart was still beating. For practical reasons, such people have to be disconnected from life-support before burial or cremation, and hence the question of whether we would bury a warm, breathing body does not arise. However, in theory at least, the brain-stem criterion would appear to permit this.

In contrast, the brain stem criterion seems more appropriate in the context of organ donation, when most organs have to be removed before heart and lung function ceases. Tännsjö's argument is therefore that we should admit that there are *two* separate criteria for defining death: one for death of the person and one for death of the body. Brain death means that the *person* has died, whereas the *body* is only dead when it has ceased to function as a unified organism.

Torbjörn Tännsjö[30]

For a person (or a self) to 'die' is for this person (or self) to *cease to exist*. A criterion of when this has taken place is the brain death criterion. When the brain is dead there is no consciousness anymore and the person is gone. For a body to 'die' is *ceasing to function as one unified organism* . . . And the circulatory-respiratory criterion is a fairly good criterion if we want to ascertain whether a body has . . . died . . .

We can now define death of a person as the point at which the person in question ceases to exist. This happens when there is too little psychological continuity and connectedness left over. If there is no consciousness at all, then there is no person at all. And we can define the death of the body as the point at which the body ceases to function as a unified organism. This means that bodies, in contradistinction to persons, often continue to exist after their death. There are dead bodies, but there are no dead persons. . . .

But could it not be objected that to have a beating heart is to be a person? I do not think that this is a plausible move. First of all, it could simply be rejected on linguistic grounds. Most of us would not call someone without a working brain, someone whose brain had irreversibly ceased to exist, a 'person'.

Secondly, and more importantly, even if some would do so, they would still have to admit that something of importance was gone once someone's brain had ceased to exist. In particular, even those who reject the brain-death criterion do typically accept that we stop ventilating people whose brains have irreversibly ceased to function. What they object to as manipulative is merely the saying that these people are 'dead'.

When the body is dead (as well as the person to whom it used to belong), we have more license in our dealings with it, but we are still not allowed to do anything that may seem offensive . . .

When the person is gone (and no earlier), it is appropriate to take (vital) organs from her living

---

[30] 'Two concepts of death reconciled' (1999) 2 Medicine, Health Care and Philosophy 41–6, 43–4.

body for transplantation purposes. The reason that in some cases this should be done while his or her body is still alive is, of course, that otherwise the transplantation will fail.

Patients in a persistent vegetative state, or anencephalic infants, have permanently lost the capacity for consciousness, that is, their upper brain is dead, but their lower brain continues to function normally. Because a person is only categorized as brain dead when the *whole* brain has stopped functioning, such patients are undoubtedly still alive. There are those who argue that the current definition of death is too restrictive, and that some patients whom we now treat as alive—such as patients in a persistent vegetative state, or anencephalic infants—should instead be regarded as dead.

Anencephalic babies are born with the congenital absence of the cerebral cortex and major parts of the skull. Most are stillborn, and of those who are born alive, 95 per cent will die within a week. Anencephalic babies will never achieve consciousness, but they do have a functioning brain stem. For an anencephalic infant's organs to be suitable for use in transplantation, she must first have been placed on a ventilator. Would this be lawful? Because there is no chance that an anencephalic baby will recover, it will not be in *her* best interests to be connected to an artificial ventilator. Since ventilation is started only to benefit a third party, does it involve using the baby *solely* as a means to an end? Of course, there may be some emotional value to the parents from the knowledge that their inevitably doomed child was able to save another baby's life, but again, the benefit here is to a third party, and not to the anencephalic infant herself.

A further problem is that it is impossible to diagnose death using brain stem tests in anencephalic newborn babies, and the Royal Medical Colleges have confirmed that:

Organs for transplantation can be removed from anencephalic infants when two doctors who are not members of the transplant team agree that spontaneous respiration has ceased.[31]

Because cessation of cardiorespiratory function causes rapid deterioration of the organs, the organs of anencephalic babies may be unsuitable for use for transplantation. The solution advocated by John Robertson is to suggest that when the capacity for sentience is irrevocably absent, the minimum criteria for personhood no longer exist, despite the presence of a functioning brain stem.

John Robertson[32]

Because public confidence that organ donation does not harm or slight the interests of donors is crucial for our voluntary system of organ procurement, it is with much trepidation that I raise the question of altering the dead donor rule in order to facilitate organ procurement . . .

A major reason for the requirement that the organ donor be dead is to protect the donor from being harmed by organ removal. If the donor is dead, taking his organs will not harm him. In contrast, if he or she is alive, it is assumed that removing organs will kill or otherwise injure the donor.

This view of the dead donor rule, however, assumes that the live donor has interests in continued

---

[31] Conference of Medical Colleges and Faculties of the United Kingdom (1988), Working party on Organ Transplantation in Neonates (DHSS London).

[32] 'Relaxing the Death Standard for Organ Donation in Pediatric Situations' in Deborah Mathieu (ed), *Organ Substitution Technology: Ethical, Legal and Public Policy Issues* (Westview Press Boulder Colorado 1988) 69–76, 69–74.

living and in not being physically injured. Whereas this assumption is true in most instances and thus should be strictly followed, it may not apply to situations of irreversible coma, near-dead pediatric patients and anencephalics . . . Such patients, though legally still alive, may no longer have interests in living or in avoiding physical harm that should be respected . . .

A major societal concern in such near-death situations is restricting the proposed practice to organ sources that clearly lack interests at the time of removal, thus preventing the practice from spilling over to incompetent patients who retain interests in avoiding pain, death, and undignified treatment . . .

Although often presented as a slippery slope problem, this concern is more accurately viewed as a problem of loose categorization. The danger in accepting a category of living human subjects who lack interests and thus may be used as an organ source is that this category will not be defined carefully and strictly enough to confine the practice to those for whom it is justified. . . .

[But] critiera for defining anencephaly can . . . be tightened, and diagnostic safeguards built in to assure that it is a true case of anencephaly. . . . The mere risk of error and mistake should not prevent such schemes if reasonably right safeguards and procedures for applying the criteria have been adopted . . .

A second major societal concern arises from the symbolic or cultural meaning of using people in this way. . . . But . . . when parents find meaning in donating organs at a time of tragedy from an infant who is not harmed by the donation and another person and family gain immeasurably, one may reasonably view the entire transaction as respectful of human needs and dignity.

Treating the destruction or absence of the cerebral cortex as evidence of death would, of course, increase the pool of potential organ donors. In the next extract, WF May employs a slippery slope argument (see further Chapter 1) to argue against redefining death in order to increase the pool of organ donors.

WF May[33]

One should judge the patient dead only because the patient is dead and not because other users of organs are hovering nearby.

To invoke the need for organs as a reason for declaring a specific class of people dead creates a runaway, imperial argument, difficult to limit. Under the press of one kind of exigency or another, one could redefine death to include anencephalics, and then perhaps the next time, hydrocephalics, microcephalics, and so on, denying any independent and firm boundaries to mark off the dead from the dying or the vegetative. . . .

An opportunistic redefinition of death would eventually produce other unfortunate results. It would lead patients to distrust doctors and hospitals, and would weaken the readiness of families to donate the organs of truly dead patients. Convenience and utility should not justify enlarging the kingdom of the dead. While, historically the need for organs and the development of the technology for perfusing and successfully transplanting them supplied the *occasion* for reflection on the criteria for determining death, the need for healthy organs should not influence the standards for determining that a patient or a class of patient is dead. That decision should rest solely on the patient's condition.

---

[33] *The Patient's Ordeal* (Indiana UP 1991) 176–7.

(c) TYPE OF TRANSPLANT

Donor cards allow people to specify which organs they are prepared to donate for use. The reason for this is that it is judged preferable to allow people to 'opt-out' of donating certain organs (commonly hearts or corneas), if this will increase the probability that they will volunteer to donate other organs, such as kidneys or lungs.

It would, in theory, be possible to transplant ovarian or testicular tissue from a cadaver into a living person. Any child the recipient conceived would then be genetically related to the deceased donor. The question of whether this could ever be acceptable was considered by the HFEA in 1994. Although the HFEA had 'no objection in principle' to the use of eggs from adult female cadavers, it also decided that it would not currently approve their use in infertility treatment due to concern about the possible negative impact upon children of learning about their genetic origins.[34]

In recent years, the possibility of transplanting limbs and faces has raised some new ethical dilemmas. Limb transplantation might enable amputees and others who currently have to rely upon prosthetic limbs, to lead a more normal life. The first human hand transplant took place in France in 1998. Currently the Royal College of Surgeons has recommended that more research is necessary before facial transplantation should go ahead,[35] but in the future, it might be used to treat people who have been seriously disfigured by burns or other injuries.

A number of distinctive ethical issues are raised by these new sorts of transplant. First, while the side-effects and risks of taking immunosuppressant drugs for the rest of one's life will often be worth assuming when the alternative to transplantation is death, or very severely impaired existence, as Donna Dickenson and Guy Widdershoven explain the next extract, the risk/benefit calculation is less clear when the alternative is an otherwise normal and healthy life without the use of, say, a hand. Secondly, the long-term impact, both physiological and psychological, of receiving another person's hand, limb or face remain unknown. For example, Dickenson and Widdershoven point out that people tend to feel intuitively less comfortable both about the prospect of donating hands after death, and about receiving such a visible part of another's body, than they do about organs which they have never seen.

Donna Dickenson and Guy Widdershoven[36]

Unlike life-saving transplants, the benefits of limb transplants do not self-evidently surpass the burdens. The risks of lifelong immunosuppressive medication, as well as the possible development of melanomas and other cancers, mean that a limb transplant may actually shorten life . . .

The most obvious benefit of most other organ transplants, saving life, does not apply to limb transplants. The nearest similarity is to restoration of function, for example, through corneal transplants. However, artificial limbs currently provide a better level of function than the limb transplants so far performed, which does not hold for corneal transplants. . . .

It might be argued that hand allografts entail the transposition of an organ with personal qualities from one person to another. This goes beyond the issue of the hand's visibility, though that

---

[34] Human Fertilisation and Embryology Authority, *Donated Ovarian Tissue in Embryo Research and Assisted Conception* (London 1994 HFEA).

[35] Royal College of Surgeons of England, *Facial Transplantation. Working Party Report.* Nov 2003.

[36] 'Ethical Issues in Limb Transplants' (2001) 15 Bioethics 110–24, 112–13, 122–4.

too is an issue . . . Likewise, it may be conceivable that the intimacy which the hand can express is transformed as a result of transplantation, necessarily having an emotional impact on those who are intimately related to both donor and recipient. It is indeed unsettling to think that the hand with which one has once been intimate may now stroke another body. Even more than the issue of bodily integrity, the issue of personal identity seems to require extensive communication with close relatives in the case of limb transplantation . . .

The hand, as an expression of both agency and intimacy, occupies a different place in our moral sensibility than internal organs. Again, this is not a reason for absolutely prohibiting hand transplants, if those intimate with both donor and recipient consent, but it is a reason for thinking that the decision is not down to the individual donor or recipient alone.

In the next extract, Rhonda Gay Hartman discusses some of the special issues raised by face transplants.

Rhonda Gay Hartman[37]

Presently, facial transplant is intended as a procedure for persons severely disfigured by burn, accident, or disease. Yet, what about people suffering from a vascular birthmark or a botched face-lift? . . . Disfigurement—as with defect or deformity—is a social construction shaped by cultural forces, and, thus, subjective elements shaped by social and cultural norms accompany any determination of facial disfigurement . . . Certainly, the specter looms that someone facially disfigured as a result of choosing to undergo numerous cosmetic surgeries may want to undergo facial transplant. . . .

Whether the prospective transplant recipient should have input concerning donor tissue likewise merits consideration. Unlike receipt of a solid organ that is internal to the body, receiving donor tissue for face transplant involves an external, visual component for the recipient and for others to whom the recipient attaches importance. Given that the human face is both intrinsic and instrumental to selfhood, the recipient arguably should have a say about the donor tissue . . .

The psychological impact on the recipient following the procedure is also germane. It is at least imaginable that a recipient of a facial transplant could experience psychological shock equal to or exceeding that of the original disfigurement. The nature of the psychological shock carries implications apart from difficulty in adjustment and adaptability, such as a recipient perceiving a stranger's presence engrafted onto one's self and, thus, feeling foreign to one's self or even violated. . . .

Complicating this could be the confusion experienced by family members, who may have difficulty adjusting psychologically to the person post-surgery, viewing him as if he were a stranger. For example, they might perceive the presence of an intruder (donor) and thereby feel confused and less connected to and emotionally distant from the recipient. This lack of responsiveness to the recipient could deepen his sense of isolation and frustrate his already difficult psychological adjustment at a time when emotional support is most needed.

While face and limb transplants almost certainly do raise slightly different issues from the transplant of internal organs, intuitive distaste or discomfort alone does not offer a good reason to prohibit these sorts of transplants. In particular, it is worth reminding ourselves that people reacted similarly to the first organ transplants. There was, for example, widespread concern that having another person's heart would be psychologically disturbing.

---

[37] 'Face Value: Challenges of Transplant Technology' (2005) 31 American Journal of Law and Medicine 7.

(d) AUTHORIZATION OF REMOVAL

If an inquest might have to be held, or a post-mortem examination required, the consent of the coroner is necessary before any part of the body may be removed. This will of course delay organ retrieval, and in practice may mean that organs will be unavailable for use in transplantation.

(1) BEFORE THE HUMAN TISSUE ACT 2004

Under the previous legislation (the Human Tissue Act 1961), there were two rather complicated ways in which the removal of organs for transplant could be authorized. First, the deceased person could request that her organs be used for transplant, perhaps by carrying an organ donor card. Secondly, if the deceased had not requested that her organs be used, the person lawfully in possession of the body could authorize removal, if having made such reasonable enquiry as was practicable, there was no reason to believe that the deceased had expressed an objection, or that the surviving spouse or any surviving relative objected. If the deceased had requested that her organs be used for transplantation, there was therefore no formal need to seek agreement from the donor's relatives. In practice, however, both for compassionate reasons and in order to avoid the negative publicity that would be likely to follow if relatives' wishes were ignored, partners and/or family members were always consulted, even if the donor had already made her wishes clear.

(2) THE HUMAN TISSUE ACT 2004

The new Act undoubtedly clarifies and simplifies the process of authorizing removal of organs for transplantation. Under section 1, no organ can be taken without 'appropriate consent'.

(a) Adults

For adults appropriate consent can, under section 3, be obtained in three different ways.

Section 3

(6) Where the person concerned has died . . . 'appropriate consent' means—

(a) if a decision of his to consent to the activity, or a decision of his not to consent to it, was in force immediately before he died, his consent;

(b) if—

(i) paragraph (a) does not apply, and

(ii) he has appointed a person or persons under section 4 to deal after his death with the issue of consent in relation to the activity,

consent given under the appointment;

(c) if neither paragraph (a) nor paragraph (b) applies, the consent of a person who stood in a qualifying relationship to him immediately before he died.

So if the deceased consented to organ transplantation, by carrying a donor card or being registered on the organ donor register, the doctors would act lawfully in retrieving her organs. The deceased's consent does not have to be in writing, and if there is no donor card, or the deceased is not on the organ donor register, other efforts should be made to find out whether the deceased had expressed her wishes about organ donation. Paragraph 14 of the draft Code of Practice states that:

if no records are held, an approach should be made to the relatives or other relevant persons by a transplant co-ordinator or a member of the team caring for the patient until their death, or via a joint approach, to establish any known wishes of the deceased.[38]

If the deceased's wishes are not known, but she has appointed someone under section 4 to deal with consent, then the appointed person's consent will be sufficient. A person might want to nominate a representative to give consent in order to ensure that the decision is taken by someone who knows her wishes, rather than leaving it to whoever turns out to be the highest ranking qualified relative at the time of her death.

Section 4 lays out the process for nominating a representative:

Section 4

(1) An adult may appoint one or more persons to represent him after his death in relation to consent for the purposes of section 1. . . .

(3) An appointment under this section may be made orally or in writing.

(4) An oral appointment under this section is only valid if made in the presence of at least two witnesses present at the same time.

(5) A written appointment under this section is only valid if—

(a) it is signed by the person making it in the presence of at least one witness who attests the signature,

(b) it is signed at the direction of the person making it, in his presence and in the presence of at least one witness who attests the signature, or

(c) it is contained in a will of the person making it.

(6) Where a person appoints two or more persons under this section in relation to the same activity, they shall be regarded as appointed to act jointly and severally unless the appointment provides that they are appointed to act jointly.

(7) An appointment under this section may be revoked at any time. . . .

(9) A person appointed under this section may at any time renounce his appointment.

(10) A person may not act under an appointment under this section if—

(a) he is not an adult, or

(b) he is of a description prescribed for the purposes of this provision by regulations made by the Secretary of State.

Where the deceased person had not given consent and had either not nominated someone to give proxy consent, or under sections 3(7) and 3(8) their nominee is unable to consent, or 'it is not reasonably practicable to communicate with [their

---

[38] Human Tissue Authority (HTA), *Code of Practice 2: Donation of organs, tissues and cells for transplantation* (HTA 11 July 2005) <http://www.hta.gov.uk/consult/codes/code2/>.

nominee] within the time available' then consent can be sought from someone in a qualifying relationship.

Qualifying relationships are defined in section 27(4) and are ranked, so that the consent of a spouse or partner should be sought first, and that of a parent or child only if no spouse or partner is available to consent, and that of a brother or sister only if no spouse, partner, parent or child can give consent, and so on. The full hierarchy is as follows:

(a) spouse or partner;[39]

(b) parent or child;

(c) brother or sister;

(d) grandparent or grandchild;

(e) child of a brother or sister;

(f) stepfather or stepmother;

(g) half brother or half sister;

(h) friend of long standing.

Of course, because organs must be retrieved as quickly as possible after death, it may not always be feasible to contact the person highest in the hierarchy of qualifying relatives, or they may not wish to make the decision, or may lack the capacity to do so. In such circumstances, paragraph 24 of the draft Code of Practice suggests that:

In circumstances where a person in a qualifying relationship does not wish to deal with the issue of consent, or is not able to do so, the principles applied to the ranking of qualifying relationships can be waived and the next person in the ranking approached. This is also the case if the activity for which consent is sought is such that it would not be practicable to communicate with the most relevant ranking person within the time available.[40]

Section 27(5) states that 'Relationships in the same paragraph of subsection (4) should be accorded equal ranking', so where there is both a parent and a child, either is able to give consent. And under section 27(7):

If the relationship of each of two or more persons to the person concerned is accorded equal highest ranking . . . it is sufficient to obtain the consent of any of them.

This means that if the deceased has both an estranged spouse and a new partner, the consent of the estranged spouse would be sufficient, even if her current partner objects. Similarly, where the deceased has no spouse or partner, but several children, any one of them can give consent, even if all of the other children are opposed to organ retrieval. In the next extract, David Price points out some practical difficulties which may result from this.

---

[39] Partner is defined in s 54(9): 'For the purposes of this Act, . . . a person is another's partner if the two of them (whether of different sexes or the same sex) live as partners in an enduring family relationship.'

[40] Human Tissue Authority (HTA), *Code of Practice 2: Donation of organs, tissues and cells for transplantation* (HTA 11 July 2005) <http://www.hta.gov.uk/consult/codes/code2/>

David Price[41]

One might wish to dispute the correctness of the pecking order established by the [Human Tissue] Act, but the most important aspect of the scheme is that where the consent of one qualifying relative has been given, no one of a lesser 'rank' *nor anyone of the same rank* can veto that consent. Whilst it was conceded that parents might frequently disagree, as might a person's existing partner and his or her estranged spouse, the existing scheme was justified by the Government on the basis that requiring the consent of all, or a majority, would be unworkable, and that in practice where one such relative objected a decision might be made not to take, store or use the tissue in any event, despite the legitimacy of so doing. The contrast with the previous law is, at least theoretically, very marked. Under the 1961 Act the objection of *any* surviving relative would be sufficient to veto removal and use of the tissue. The framework under the new Act consequently makes even more pressing the need for a system to record a person's *objections* to the taking and use of tissue after death, as one relative who objects on the basis of personal knowledge about the individual's reservations might be 'overruled' by another consenting relative of the same or higher class. However, no such mechanism currently exists or is established by the Act. Whilst there is no means of de-enfranchising a specific relative from giving a consent after one's death, the Government considers that the ability to appoint a 'nominated relative', thus by-passing that individual, obviates such a need. This is dubious. Just because one can identify a person who one knows one does not want to make such decisions does not mean that one inevitably knows someone who one does!

It is important to remember that under the Human Tissue Act 2004, it is *lawful* to take organs where an appropriate consent exists, but not *obligatory*. As before, it is likely that the relatives' views will be taken into account even if the deceased has made her wishes known. Paragraph 15 of the HTA's draft Code of Practice suggests that, in such circumstances, health professionals should try to encourage the family to respect the deceased's wishes, but in the face of continued objection, it may not be appropriate to proceed:

If the family, or those close to the deceased, object to the donation for whatever purpose, when the deceased has explicitly consented, health professionals should seek to discuss the matter sensitively with the family, encouraging them to recognise the wishes of the deceased, and making clear that they do not have the legal right to veto or overrule the deceased wishes. Health professionals need to consider each case individually and whether, in extreme cases, it would be appropriate not to proceed with organ donation in the face of continued objection of the bereaved family.[42]

Analogously, where a nominated representative has consented to donation, but relatives object, paragraph 46 of the draft Code of Practice suggests that, despite being lawful, retrieval may not be appropriate:

As with consent given by the deceased before they died, the consent of the nominated representative cannot be overridden by other individuals, including family members. It would be advisable, nevertheless, to ensure that appropriate consultation and discussion takes place between the health professionals involved and all interested family members and others who are close to the

---

[41] The Human Tissue Act 2004 (2005) 68 Modern Law Review 798–821.

[42] Human Tissue Authority (HTA), *Code of Practice 2: Donation of organs, tissues and cells for transplantation* (HTA 11 July 2005) <http://www.hta.gov.uk/consult/codes/code2/>.

deceased. Even when consent has been given, it may not always be appropriate to proceed if there is sustained objection from others.[43]

And even where one of the highest ranking qualifying relative has given consent, the views of other relatives are certainly not irrelevant. Paragraphs 25 and 26 of the draft Code of Practice address this scenario:

If a spouse consents to use for donation, but other family members object strongly, the benefits of carrying out the activity will need to be considered against the distress and resentment that would be caused by going ahead in the face of strong opposition. This will be especially sensitive where people in equally ranked qualifying relationships disagree. . . .

It should be remembered that obtaining appropriate consent only enables the activity to be lawfully carried out should it be decided to do so – it does not mean that it has to be carried out. The aim should be to reach an agreed position by inclusive discussion, where possible; this will need careful explanations of the options and the potential benefits of transplantation. It is thus not the intention that the ranking provision in the Act should be used to impose one family member's wishes over others where there are overwhelmingly strong objections that might outweigh any benefit.[44]

So while the deceased's family do not have a legal right of veto, in practice doctors may be reluctant to retrieve organs where relatives object, both for compassionate reasons and from the more pragmatic desire to avoid the bad publicity which might result from ignoring the wishes of recently bereaved and distraught relatives.

It could, however, be argued that giving relatives any say over what happens to a person's body after her death is inconsistent with the now-dominant principle of patient autonomy: why should a family member who has absolutely no say over a person's medical treatment during her life be able, in practice, to *overrule* her decision to donate her organs? On the other hand, Margaret Lock suggests that it is families, rather than donors, who make the greatest sacrifice when organs are taken from a dead body:

[W]e encourage the idea that donation is a selfless act, but it can also be thought of as the giving away of something no longer of any use . . .: it takes virtually no effort to sign a donor card. But donor families make a much greater emotional sacrifice. They must usually come to terms with the fact that someone dear to them has been transformed, in the space of a few hours, and often through a violent encounter, from a healthy individual into an irrevocably damaged entity, suspended between life and death. To give selflessly under these circumstances requires courage, as well as faith in the ICU staff and in the truth of their assessments.[45]

So why do 40 per cent of relatives object to transplantation?[46] UK Transplant's audit of potential donors found that the most common reasons given are religious beliefs and wanting to be with the deceased when the ventilator is switched off (23 per cent); that the family do not know what the individual would have wanted (20 per cent);

[43] Ibid.   [44] Ibid.
[45] Margaret Lock, *Twice Dead: Organ Transplants and the Reinvention of Death* (University of California Press Berkeley 2002) 373.
[46] *Potential Donor Audit* (UK Transplant 2005) <http://www.uktransplant.org.uk/ukt/statistics/potential_donor_audit/potential_donor_audit.jsp>.

that they do not want surgery to the body (20 per cent); and that they feel the deceased has suffered enough (19 per cent).[47]

(b) Children

Where the deceased is a child, organ retrieval will be lawful if there is appropriate consent under section 2(7):

Section 2

(7) Where the child concerned has died . . . 'appropriate consent' means—

  (a) if a decision of his to consent to the activity, or a decision of his not to consent to it, was in force immediately before he died, his consent;

  (b) if paragraph (a) does not apply—

   (i) the consent of a person who had parental responsibility for him immediately before he died, or

   (ii) where no person had parental responsibility for him immediately before he died, the consent of a person who stood in a qualifying relationship to him at that time.

Hence a mature minor's consent will be sufficient for organ retrieval to be lawful (see Chapter 4 for analysis of when a child will have capacity to make her own medical decisions). Just as with adults, even where the child's wishes are known, perhaps because she is carrying an organ donor card, retrieval should not go ahead without discussion with her family, whose wishes must also be taken into account. Paragraph 18 of the draft Code of Practice states that:

The position for a child, who before they died was competent to reach a decision and gave their consent for organ or tissue donation to take place following their death, is no different from that of an adult. Their consent is sufficient to make lawful the removal, retention or use of tissue for that purpose. Clearly, in any case where a child has given consent to donation, especially if the child has self-registered on the Organ Donor Register, it will be essential to discuss this with the child's family and take their views and wishes into account before deciding how to proceed.[48]

Where the child has not made her views about organ donation known, or lacks capacity, consent can be obtained from anyone with parental responsibility, or if no-one has parental responsibility, someone in the highest ranking qualifying relationship (using the above list) can give consent.

(3) LIABILITY FOR UNLAWFUL REMOVAL

The previous legislation did not provide for any penalty—either civil or criminal—in the event of its breach. It was not clear, therefore, what sanctions there might be if a person's organs were taken and used for transplant purposes either without her consent, or in the face of a relative's objection. Section 5 of the Human Tissue Act 2004 now provides that anyone who takes organs without appropriate consent

---

[47] *Potential Donor Audit* (UK Transplant 2005) <http://www.uktransplant.org.uk/ukt/statistics/potential_donor_audit/potential_donor_audit.jsp>.

[48] Human Tissue Authority (HTA), *Code of Practice 2: Donation of organs, tissues and cells for transplantation* (HTA 11 July 2005) <http://www.hta.gov.uk/consult/codes/code2/>.

commits an offence, unless he reasonably believes that he did in fact have appropriate consent. The maximum penalty is three years imprisonment.

(e) SYSTEM FOR REMOVAL AND ALLOCATION

UK Blood and Transplant (formerly UK Transplant) is a special health authority set up to oversee transplantation arrangements in the UK. Its responsibilities include maintaining the national transplant waiting list; matching and allocating organs; transporting organs to recipient centres and maintaining the organ donor register. It also promotes organ donation and transplantation, and maintains transplant coordinator services.

Once a patient is identified as a potential organ donor, the local donor coordinator should be contacted. Donor coordinators are responsible for ascertaining the views of the potential donor's relatives or carers, and may contact UK Blood and Transplant order to find out whether the donor is on the organ donor register. Once agreement to organ donation has been obtained, the donor coordinator will notify UK Blood and Transplant, which maintains a national database of all potential organ recipients. When the appropriate recipient has been identified, the donor coordinator liaises between the surgical teams responsible for both the donor and the recipient's care. Specialist recipient coordinators then oversee the recipients' care, both pre- and post-transplant.

In the UK, there are different systems of allocation for different organs. For livers, hearts, and lungs, the UK is divided into seven or eight zones, depending upon the organ. Once an organ becomes available, first priority is given to any patient in the UK whose need is categorized as 'super-urgent' because they are in imminent danger of death (i.e. they will die within three days without a transplant). If there are none of these, the organ will then be offered within the zone where the donor is being maintained. If there are no appropriate local recipients, the organ will become available nationally, at which point there is a rota between the different zones. If, for example, zone A gets an organ on one occasion, it will then go to the bottom of the list for the next available organ.

In contrast, for kidneys there is a priority-rated list created by a points system. This gives first priority to paediatric recipients, and takes into account a range of other factors, such as the patient's tissue type, time spent on the waiting list, and geographical distance. The process is done automatically by computer, and the kidney will be offered to the recipient who has the most 'points'.

Cadaveric organ donation is anonymous. The donor's family will be told that the transplant (or transplants) have taken place, but they are not told anything about the recipient. Nor can the recipient find out any information about the donor.

Because the whole organ transplant programme depends so heavily upon public goodwill, both from donors themselves, through expressing their willingness to donate, and from relatives, through their agreement to the donation, it is especially important that the criteria used to distribute organs are fair. If allocation decisions are perceived to be unacceptable, public support for organ transplantation might diminish and the shortage of organs would be likely to be exacerbated. The provision of liver transplants to alcoholics has, for example, proved to be particularly controversial. Unlike the shortage of financial resources in the NHS which we considered in Chapter 2, decisions about organ distribution take place in the context of *absolute* scarcity, there are simply insufficient organs to enable everyone who needs a transplant to receive one. This means that whatever criteria are used to select recipients, it is inevitable that some people will die because *other* people received the available organs.

(f) THE SHORTAGE OF ORGANS

UK Blood and Transplant issues detailed statistics on transplant activity in the UK.[49]

Year	Cadaveric donors	Cadaveric transplants	Waiting list	Living donors
1992	876	2591	5124	126
2003/4	772	2394	7236	460

As is clear from the above table, there are more people on the waiting list for transplants than there are available organs, and this gap between supply and demand is widening. When reforming the law on transplantation, as we have seen, the government opted to stick closely to a consent model for transplantation, and it is not clear that this will have much impact on donation rates. So how might it be possible to increase the number of cadaveric organs available for transplant? In the next sections, we consider a number of possible strategies.

(1) IMPROVED COORDINATION

It has been suggested that some potential cadaveric donations are lost because the organ procurement system is inefficient. Transplant coordinators tend to be based in the few large transplant centres in the UK, and it is the responsibility of medical teams working in other hospitals to contact them should a potential organ donor be identified. In contrast in Spain, following the introduction of a new transplant coordinator network in 1990, every major hospital with an intensive care unit, not just those which also have a transplant unit, has a coordinating transplant team consisting of medical staff who *also* work in intensive care. This means that organ procurement and intensive care are much more effectively integrated, and hence health care professionals who have no direct experience of organ transplantation are nevertheless very well informed about the procedures involved in obtaining organs for transplant. While improving coordination could not eliminate the organ shortage, the effect on procurement rates appears to have been extremely positive: in Spain, 33.6 organs are obtained per million population, in the UK the equivalent figure is 13.2.

Of course, there might be other reasons—such as increased publicity—why Spain's transplant rates have increased over this period. And although the integration of organ procurement and intensive care may have advantages, there might be dangers in

---

[49] At the time of writing, the web address is still <http://www.uktransplant.org.uk/> but this may be changed after the merger.

blurring the roles of carer and organ procurer. Intensive care unit (ICU) staff should always have the treatment of patients, rather than the procuring of organs, as their first priority. As Sheila McLean points out, 'medical ethics require that the doctors seeking to harvest organs should be different from those involved in the care of the patient'.[50]

Nevertheless, there would seem to be obvious benefits in ensuring that hospitals have closer links with transplant units. It is also crucially important that the first discussion with relatives in an intensive care unit—which, by definition, has to take place at a moment of extreme stress—is made sympathetically, by an experienced and well informed health care professional.

(2) ELECTIVE VENTILATION

In May 1988, the Royal Devon and Exeter Hospital introduced a new protocol designed to enable organs to be taken from potential donors who were dying outside of intensive care units. Once identified, and with the agreement of the relatives, such patients would be transferred to an ICU and 'electively ventilated' to ensure that their organs would be suitable for transplant. The relatives were told that the patient would be very unlikely to recover, and were asked to agree both to organ donation and to the patient's transfer to an ICU to enable organ donation to proceed after the patient's death. During the next 19 months, the number of organs available for transplant increased by more than 50 per cent. Obtaining organs from people who would other- wise be unsuitable donors has clear health benefits for patients on the transplant waiting list, but for a number of reasons, it is not clear whether elective ventilation is either legally or ethically justifiable.

First, beds in ICUs are scarce and expensive. Is it acceptable to transfer a dying patient to a high dependency unit when this is done not for her own good, but in order to ensure that her organs will be capable of benefiting others? Commonly there are not enough beds in an ICU for every patient who might need one, and it would seem unreasonable to deprive a patient who might recover of treatment in order to ventilate someone who will die in any event. Of course, this argument only rules out elective ventilation if the potential organ donor would *always* be depriving another patient of access to an intensive care bed. While this might often be the case, there could be circumstances in which a dying patient could be placed in a bed that would otherwise be unused in order to ensure that her organs would be available to others after her death. Might it in fact be unethical to leave a bed empty when its use might save several lives? Moreover, because transplantation is more cost-effective than, say, dialysis, a substantial increase in the number of organs available for transplant would save the NHS money, and thus might offset the costs of elective ventilation, and enable more intensive care beds to be provided.

Secondly, elective ventilation is arguably unlawful. As we saw in Chapter 4, because unconscious patients are incompetent, doctors are under a duty to treat them in their best interests. Placing a patient who is not expected to recover on a ventilator in order to ensure that her organs are suitable for transplant is not done to benefit her, but

---

[50] Sheila McLean, 'Transplantation and the "Nearly Dead"; The Case of Elective Ventilation' in S Mclean (ed), *Contemporary Issues in Law, Medicine and Ethics* (Dartmouth Aldershot 1996) 143–61, 149.

rather to benefit third parties on the organ transplant waiting list. Indeed, as JK Mason points out in the next extract, ventilating a patient where there is no intention to benefit her could be an assault.

It has been suggested that elective ventilation is 'not against' the best interests of the incompetent patient. An analogy could be drawn with non-therapeutic research on incompetent patients (see further Chapter 8, p. 495), where it is judged lawful to carry out procedures that carry no more than a minimal risk on incompetent adults in order to benefit others. However, it is thought that there is a small risk that once placed on a ventilator, the patient who would otherwise have died might instead lapse into a permanent coma or a persistent vegetative state. If there is a small risk that elective ventilation might induce permanent coma or a persistent vegetative state, JK Mason argues that it would not necessarily be a 'minimal risk' procedure, and might in fact be 'against' the best interests of the patient.

JK Mason[51]

The practice of 'elective ventilation' is a far more controversial way of extending the source of organs beyond the intensive care unit (ICU) and into the medical and geriatric wards. . . . There is no way in which invasive non-consensual treatment of a dying and incurable patient can be regarded as being in his or her best interests; it follows that elective ventilation must involve an assault or trespass to the person . . .

The 'best interests' test must also apply to the ethical parameters. It cannot be in the patient's best interest to prolong his dying by invasive medicine. We can be doing him no good—and we *may* be doing him harm. Looked at in this way, there can be no starker example of using a patient as a means and offending a basic Kantian imperative . . .

The possibility must also be considered that the criminal law may be infringed in so far as an assault by way of medical invasion of the body is decriminalised only on the grounds that it is for the patient's good. . . . There is concern for the consequent misuse of the ICU—which is there to save lives rather than to prepare for death—and the possible denial of scarce therapeutic resources to needy patients. It is impossible to generalise about such matters which depend on the individual circumstances and on agreement between the intensivists and the transplant surgeons. All would accept that the therapeutic role of the ICU is paramount and that no person being electively ventilated should come between the emergency patient and his or her treatment.

It is prognosis, however, that raises the gravest doubts as to the validity of the process . . . [There are] three possible untoward outcomes: the patient may develop some other condition while under intensive care, such as sepsis, which invalidates him as a donor; the patient may recover sufficiently to be discharged from hospital; or the patient may stabilise in the persistent vegetative state. It is this last possibility which raises the greatest fears and it is, probably, the least unlikely of the three scenarios to develop. The production of a persistent vegetative state in a person who was close to a peaceful natural death could only be described as a clinical disaster which, if publicised, could be catastrophically detrimental to the whole transplantation programme.

While it would be difficult to argue that treatment which prolonged the process of dying was in the best interests of the patient, it might, however, be possible to establish that the patient was so strongly committed to being an organ donor during her

---

[51] 'Contemporary Issues in Organ Transplantation' in S Mclean (ed), *Contemporary Issues in Law, Medicine and Ethics* (Dartmouth Aldershot 1996) 117–41, 120–1.

lifetime that elective ventilation would allow her final wishes about the fate of her body to be fulfilled. Might it further be possible to argue that elective ventilation would be lawful if the patient had executed an advance directive requesting that all steps, including elective ventilation, are carried out in order to enable her organs to be used in transplantation? The problem here is that, as we saw in Chapter 4 p. 222, it is only advance *refusals* which are binding upon doctors. An advance request might be indicative of the patient's wishes, but would have no legal force. Moreover, if elective ventilation is in fact unlawful, the patient's request would be irrelevant.

A final possible justification for elective ventilation would be to argue that the patient is in fact already dead when ventilation is begun. If brain stem tests are confirmatory, the patient will always have in fact died sometime before the tests confirm that she is in fact dead. In the Exeter Protocol, ventilation was begun only *after* spontaneous respiratory arrest, and the doctors therefore argued that they ventilated the patient *at the moment of death*, even though death would be confirmed later once brain stem tests had been carried out. If the patient is *already* dead, then there is no duty to act in her best interests, and procedures designed to maximize the chance that her organs could be used successfully would not necessarily be unlawful. This argument is, however, extremely controversial. Treating patients who are 'nearly dead' as though they are already dead might have disastrous consequences for patients' trust in their doctors. And if elective ventilation sometimes induces the persistent vegetative state (in which patients are plainly still alive), it would be difficult to argue that such patients were dead when ventilation began. Certainly, the Department of Health's legal advice was that elective ventilation is unlawful. Paragraph 4.3 of the *Code of Practice for the Diagnosis of Brain Stem Death*[52] states that:

Very occasionally it may be considered certain that death will inevitably occur shortly, as in the case of gross cerebral trauma or cerebral haemorrhage, but brain stem death has not been established. In these cases artificial ventilation of the patient should not be undertaken solely to preserve organ function. The Health Departments have been advised that ventilation in these circumstances is unlawful. It cannot be demonstrated to be for the benefit of the patient (and may indeed run the risk of causing serious harm) and thus is not in the best interest of the patient. The agreement of the relatives to elective ventilation does not alter the legal position.

(3) NON-HEARTBEATING DONORS

In recent years there have been a small but increasing number of non-heartbeating donors (NHBD). In 2003/4, there were seventy three NHBDs, an increase of 20 per cent on the previous year.[53] In practice, this means that patients who die of cardiac arrest on general wards, or in accident and emergency departments, or those who are declared dead on arrival at hospital, might still be potential donors. It is only kidneys and livers that can be taken from non-heartbeating donors. Death is diagnosed using cardiac criteria, rather than brain-stem tests, and after death has been confirmed, the organs are cooled using an in situ perfusion technique. The Human Tissue Act 2004 confirms the legality of cold perfusion techniques. Under section 43, if part of a body is or may be suitable for use for transplantation, it is lawful to take the minimum

---

[52] Department of Health 1998, para 1.   [53] <http://www.uktransplant.org.uk/>.

necessary steps for the purpose of preserving the part for use for transplantation, until it has been established that consent for transplantation has not been, and will not be, given.

The British Transplantation Society has indicated that NHBD is acceptable where the potential donor indicated their wish to donate, and the organ donation procedure has been discussed with and agreed by relatives prior to the donor's death. Since they are less accustomed than intensive care units with the procedures involved in organ transplantation, it is important that staff working in accident and emergency departments, and ordinary medical wards are aware of the possibility of using kidneys or livers from such patients, so that the transplant coordinator can be notified without delay. It is also necessary to ensure that the potential recipients have been adequately informed about the increased risk of a poorer outcome in cases when organ retrieval takes place *after* the donor's heart has stopped beating.

(4) ALLOWING CONDITIONAL DONATION

In July 1998, a man who was unconscious and in a critical condition was admitted to an ICU in the North of England. His relatives agreed to organ donation in the event of his death, but only on condition that the organs went to white recipients. In this instance, the person on the waiting list who was most urgently in need of a liver transplant was white, and without the organ he would have died within 24 hours. The two people who were at the top of the kidney transplant points system also happened to be white. Because the condition would have made no difference in this case, the organs were accepted and two kidneys and a liver were successfully transplanted into three different individuals.

Unsurprisingly, the case received a great deal of publicity, and the Department of Health set up an investigation.[54] The panel established that the three organs went to the same people who would have received them if no condition had been attached, so no one was in fact disadvantaged. But the panel also concluded that it had been wrong for the organs to have been accepted in the first place. The panel recommended that organs must not be accepted if the donor or the family wish to attach conditions about the recipient. This guidance has since been formalized by the Department of Health, and it is clear that the prohibition on conditional donation applies to *all* conditions, and not just those grounded in racism or any another sort of prejudice.

Although conditional donation in a case such as this is plainly morally objectionable, the issue is made more complicated by the presence of identifiable individuals on a waiting list who might die if a suitable organ is turned down on moral grounds. The liver recipient in this case would have died within 24 hours if this organ was not accepted, making it extremely unlikely that an alternative non-conditional organ would have become available in time to save his life. It would surely be understandable if he was prepared to put his interest in continued life over society's preference for unconditional altruism.

It is also worth remembering that cadaveric donation is anonymous. In practice

---

[54] An Investigation into Conditional Organ Donation <http://www.doh.gov.uk/organdonation/report.htm>.

then, the organ could be accepted with the condition attached, and the condition could then be ignored. Because the organs do not *belong* to the family, it is certainly very difficult to imagine what sort of remedy they might have if they discovered that the organ had in fact been given to someone who did not satisfy their condition. The argument that ignoring relatives' wishes might have an adverse impact upon donation rates also seems comparatively weak in this sort of case.

It might further be argued that there is an inconsistency between the rules on living organ donation, where donation is normally to a specified individual, and cadaveric donation which must be unconditional. And as TM Wilkinson points out in then next extract, it is hard to see what would be wrong with allowing directed donation to a close friend or relative after death. Of course, it would rarely be possible for cadaveric donation to be directed to a specific individual because most organ donors are not aware of their impending sudden death. But it is possible to imagine circumstances in which a person knows that she is going to die, and in which she expresses a preference that one of her organs should be used to treat a close relative with acute organ failure.

TM Wilkinson[55]

Is it really so bad to attach a condition to an organ donation? Of course it was bad in the case of the racist. The motive there was some mix of hatred and contempt and there is nothing to be said for it. But what about the condition that an organ go to a relative? There seems nothing morally wrong about agreeing to donate a kidney, say, on condition that it go to a sibling, whether the donation is to be from a living person or a dead one . . .

Setting aside a special concern for one's nearest and dearest, let us consider the panel's explanation of what is wrong with attaching a condition to a donation. The panel claims that conditional donation 'offends against the fundamental principle that organs are donated altruistically and should go to patients in the greatest need'. Altruism in its normal sense refers roughly to a non-self interested concern for the interests of others. Importantly, a wide variety of other-regarding motives can be regarded as altruistic, such as a special concern for children, or the deaf, or the poor. 'Altruism' . . . does not require, for example, that actions be motivated out of adherence to a greatest happiness principle or, saliently here, a greatest needs principle. Consequently, there need be nothing non-altruistic about conditional donation. Wanting organs to go to a child—although also apparently opposed by the panel—is not a violation of altruism any more than donating to a children's charity is . . .

What remains of the panel's argument? Here is one way to take their argument: it is wrong to accept organs if one would then be in the position of not being free to allocate them to the person in greatest need. That principle needs much more elaboration and defence than can be wrung out of the panel's report, especially since its effect could be to cause some to die with no gain to anyone else. Even if the principle is sound, it does not support the unconditional rejection of conditional donation, because it does not justify rejecting conditional offers that would lead to the organs going to those in greatest need anyway . . . Conditional offers could be accepted on the understanding that the organs would only be used when satisfying the condition coincided with allocating to the person in greatest need.

---

[55] 'What's not wrong with conditional organ donation?' (2003) 29 Journal of Medical Ethics 163–4.

(5) REQUIRED REQUEST

It has been suggested that some doctors find it difficult to ask distressed relatives about organ donation. If doctors do not mention the possibility of donation, potentially life-saving organs may be lost, and individuals who could have benefited from those organs may lose their lives. To try to eliminate this risk, most US states have introduced a system called 'required request'. Rather than leaving the question of whether or not to ask distressed relatives about donation to the discretion of individual doctors, medical practitioners are instead under a *duty* to bring up the question of organ donation.

The chief ethical problem with required request legislation is its interference with clinical discretion. If we can imagine circumstances in which asking the relatives to consent to organ donation might cause grave harm or distress, we should have to include a 'professional privilege' exception. And indeed it seems clear that even where required request legislation exists, some relatives are still not asked about donation because the medical team judges that such a request would be inappropriate in the circumstances. In practice, it appears that relatives are not approached in up to 20 per cent of cases in the US.

Of course, the counter-argument might be that where a balance has to be struck between causing distress to the relatives of a dying person, and saving the lives of patients waiting for organ transplants, avoiding death should *always* take priority over upsetting grieving relatives. Wherever the balance lies, it is not in fact clear that a shift towards required request would actually make much difference in practice. Studies appear to indicate that most potential organ donors *are* identified and that their relatives *are* asked about organ donation.[56] In UK Transplant's audit of potential donors, solid organ donation was discussed with the next of kin in 86 per cent of cases.[57]

(6) PRESUMED CONSENT

Organ donation in the UK is an 'opt-in' system, where individuals are able to volunteer to become organ donors, and if they have not done so, under the Human Tissue Act 2004, their nominated representative or a qualified relative may give appropriate consent. Opt-in systems are commonly contrasted with 'opt-out' systems, often called 'presumed consent', where it is assumed that every potential donor is willing to donate their organs, but people who object to donation are able to 'opt out' by formally registering their unwillingness to donate. Certainly on the basis of the evidence, this assumption seems warranted: when asked, most people do say that they would be willing to donate. But for a few practical reasons, there might be difficulties in moving towards an unqualified presumed consent system.

First, the assumption behind presumed consent is that the public is sufficiently well-informed about the organ transplantation system that any failure to register an

---

[56] D Gentleman, J Easton, and B Jennett, 'Brain death and organ donation in a neurosurgical unit: audit of recent practice' (1990) 301 BMJ 1203.

[57] *Potential Donor Audit* (UK Transplant 2005) <http://www.uktransplant.org.uk/ukt/statistics/potential_donor_audit/potential_donor_audit.jsp>.

objection in fact reflects someone's willingness to donate, rather than their lethargy or lack of knowledge. Secondly, it has been argued that the term 'presumed consent' is misleading, because the reality is that such a system permits organs to be taken *without* consent.[58] Failing to register an objection is not synonymous with consent, and in practice, presumed consent may simply be a more sympathetic way to describe a system in which organs are, in the absence of a recorded objection, treated as a public resource (see below p. 728). Thirdly, it would be necessary to maintain a large, centralized database on which objections could be recorded, and amended if people change their minds. It would further be necessary to ensure that this database could be rapidly and accurately accessed as soon as a potential donor is identified.

A number of countries have adopted presumed consent laws, but in most of these the relatives continue to be consulted about organ transplantation. Taking organs in the face of a relative's vigorous objection would probably be counter-productive because of the adverse publicity it would generate. In France, for example, doctors always ask for familial consent to organ donation, and the presumed consent policy exists only on paper.[59] Nevertheless, as English and Somerville suggest in the following extract, changing the default position may subtly influence relatives' attitudes towards donation, and lessen the decision-making burden.

V English and A Sommerville[60]

Although legislation covering transplantation is usually characterised as being based on either explicit consent ('opt in') or presumed consent ('opt out'), this oversimplification fails to recognise the nuances that can radically alter the way the system operates in practice. In fact, these are merely two ends of a spectrum with strict explicit consent at one extreme and strict presumed consent at the other. With the former, organs can only be used if the donor has specifically authorised it and with the latter organs can be freely used unless the deceased has formally registered an objection. In practice very few, if any, systems operate at either end of the spectrum . . . In Belgium, which is usually held up as the model for presumed consent legislation, relatives are still consulted before organs are removed and have the option to veto the donation although they rarely do so. . . .

Given that most people, when asked, express willingness to donate their organs after their death, there are reasonable grounds for presuming that they probably really do wish to donate. The current law, however, presumes they do not . . .

Arguably, simply changing the default position could have huge benefits. Not least for relatives themselves who, at a time of emotional upheaval and bereavement, may not relish being asked to decide in the absence of any indication of the wishes of the deceased. One of the advantages of a presumed consent system is that the main burden of making this decision is lessened for the relatives although they would still be involved . . .

The possibility of relatives refusing donation when the deceased person actually wished to donate has already been mentioned. The opposite can also happen. Currently, individuals who strongly object to donation lack any formal mechanism for registering that objection and the decision to donate may ultimately be made by distant relatives. Under the opt in system, there are

---

[58] CA Erin and J Harris, 'Presumed consent or contracting out' (1999) 25 Journal of Medial Ethics 365–6.

[59] Bernard Teo, 'Is the adoption of more efficient strategies of organ procurement the answer to persistent organ shortage in transplantation?' (1992) 6 Bioethics 113–29, 127.

[60] 'Presumed consent for transplantation: a dead issue after Alder Hey?' (2003) 29 Journal of Medical Ethics 147–52.

no guarantees that relatives will not act contrary to the strongly held views of a deceased person, either through lack of knowledge or lack of agreement with them. In this way, an opt out system where objections can be registered and must be respected, would enhance individual autonomy for those who do not want to be donors.

Certainly the evidence suggests that introducing a system based upon presumed consent invariably leads to a significant increase in the number of organs available for transplant.[61] In the next extract, Kennedy et al. discuss the dramatic increase in the number of kidneys available for transplant which followed the introduction of a presumed consent system in Belgium.

I Kennedy, RA Sells, AS Daar, RD Guttmann, R Hoffenberg, M Lock, J Radcliffe-Richards, N Tilney and the International Forum for Transplant Ethics[62]

In the case of Belgium there is well documented and convincing evidence that a change in the law from contracting in to contracting out in 1986 led to an increase in organ supply. Staff at the organ-transplantation centre in Antwerp were strongly opposed to the new law and retained a contracting in policy accompanied by enhanced public and professional education; by contrast, at Leuven the new law was adopted. In Antwerp, organ donation rates remained unchanged; in Leuven they rose from 15 to 40 donors per year over a 3-year period. In the whole country organ donation rose by 55% within 5 years despite a concurrent decrease in the number of organs available from road-traffic accidents. Citizens who wish to opt out of the scheme may register their objection at any Town Hall; since 1986 less than 2% of the population have done so. Use of a computerised register has simplified ascertaining the existence of any objection. In Belgium, despite the existence of this law, doctors are encouraged to approach the relatives in all cases and practitioners may decide against removing the organs if in their opinion this would cause undue distress or for any other valid reason. Less than 10% of families do object compared with 20–30% elsewhere in Europe. . . . It would seem from the Belgian experience that relatives may be reluctant to take a personal decision about the removal of organs, but they find it easier to agree if they are simply confirming the intention of the dead person. If this is so, a contracting out system has a moral benefit of relieving grieving relatives of the burden of deciding about donation at a time of great psychological stress.

A change in the law thus achieves the dual effect of increasing the supply of organs and lessening the distress of relatives. Those who have moral objections to it must produce convincing evidence that the harm that would follow such a change would outweigh these clear benefits.

The BMA advocates a system which it calls 'presumed consent with safeguards'.[63] This would allow organs to be removed after the individual's death if consent can be presumed because there is no evidence from the non-donor register, or volunteered by the family, that the individual objected to his or her body, or any specific part of the body, being used for transplantation after death. If, however, the individual has not expressed any views about donation while alive but it is apparent that to proceed with the donation would cause major distress to a first degree relative or long-term partner, the donation should not proceed. Close relatives would thus retain a right of veto, but

---

[61] See further, Kenneth Gundle, 'Presumed Consent: An International Comparison and Possibilities for Change in the United States' (2005) 14 Cambridge Quarterly of Healthcare Ethics, 113–18.

[62] 'The case for "presumed consent" in organ donation' (1998) 351 The Lancet, 1650–2.

[63] BMA Medical Ethics Committee, *Organ donation in the 21st century: time for a consolidated approach* (BMA 2000).

the difference would be in the nature of the approach to the relatives. Family members would not be asked to give permission for organ donation. Rather, they would be told that the individual had not registered an objection to donation while alive and that unless they object—either because they are aware of an unregistered objection by the individual or because it would cause a close relative or long-term partner major distress—the donation will proceed.

British Medical Association[64]

The BMA's reasons for supporting presumed consent are set out below.

- It is reasonable and appropriate to assume that most people would wish to act in an altruistic manner and to help others by donating their organs after death.

- Studies show that the majority of people would be willing to donate but only a small number of these are on the NHS Organ Donor Register or carry a donor card. While this level of apathy exists, people will continue to die while waiting for donor organs.

- Given that the majority of people would be willing to donate, there are good reasons for presuming consent and requiring those who object to donation to register their views.

- A shift to presumed consent would prompt more discussion within families about organ donation.

- It is more efficient and cost-effective to maintain a register of the small number who wish to opt out of donation than of the majority who are willing to be donors.

- With such a shift, organ donation becomes the default position. This represents a more positive view of organ donation which is to be encouraged.

- Despite the acknowledged difficulties of obtaining meaningful data about the success of presumed consent in other countries, the BMA believes that, as one part of a broader strategy, a shift to presumed consent is likely to have a positive effect on donation rates.

In the light of the concerns over the lack of consent to the use of tissue raised by the organ retention scandals at Bristol and Alder Hey,[65] it is probably unsurprising that the government chose to maintain a consent-based 'opt-in' system in the Human Tissue Act 2004.

(7) MANDATED CHOICE

Would it instead be possible to require every individual to decide whether or not they want their organs to be available for transplantation after their death? Mandated choice would be analogous to other non-optional public duties, such as filling in the electoral register or paying taxes. Like a presumed consent system, it would require the maintenance and updating of an easily accessible database. As P Chouhan and H Draper explain in the next extract, it would also require extensive public education.

---

[64] Ibid.
[65] See further, Margaret Brazier, 'Organ retention and return: problems of consent' (2003) 29 Journal of Medical Ethics 30–3; Brazier 'Human Tissue Retention' (2004) 72 Medico-Legal Journal 39; John Harris, 'Law and regulation of retained organs: the ethical issues' (2002) 22 Legal Studies 527–49; Brazier, 'Retained organs: ethics and humanity' (2002) 22 Legal Studies 550–69.

P Chouhan and H Draper[66]

Mandated choice requires competent adults to decide whether they wish to donate their organs after their deaths. Individuals are free to choose whether to donate, and even which organs they would like to donate: what they are not permitted to do is to fail to register their wishes. Individuals can also choose to let their relatives have the final say. Unless they are granted this right, however, the relatives have neither power nor opportunity to veto an individual's decision, whether it was for or against decision . . .

A move to mandated choice would also have to be accompanied by extensive public education so that when making their choices, people are sufficiently informed about both the need for choice and the implications of their decision. Finally, choices, though binding would also be revocable: indeed, people could change their minds as often as they wish, and the most recent choice would prevail. . . . To avoid coercion, registered choices would be confidential and no privileges would accrue from the particular choice made.

(8) INCENTIVES

(a) Financial incentives

Financial incentives to cadaveric donation could not operate as a straightforward sale, in the same way as payments to living donors (considered below at p. 744). When the organs are retrieved, the donor is dead and is therefore unable to receive money in return for their donation. Instead there are a number of other possibilities. First, people could receive a payment in return for their *agreement* to donate their organs after death. However, since very few of us are ever likely to be suitable organ donors, money would generally be paid to non-donors. Moreover, in order to protect patient autonomy it would have to be possible for people to change their minds about donation after they had been paid, which would obviously leave the system open to abuse. A second possibility is that the payment could be made to a nominated individual after donation has taken place. Thirdly, money could be offered directly to the relatives in return for their agreement to the donation. An example might be an offer of financial assistance with funeral expenses.

In 1999 Pennsylvania introduced a controversial and experimental plan to pay $300 towards the funeral costs of families who consented to the donation of their relatives' organs. The plan was never implemented, but in response to this proposal, Siminoff and Mercer carried out a study of 600 US families who had been asked to donate organs. 23.8 per cent found the 'funeral incentive' proposal offensive, while 25 per cent did not; 20.3 per cent said that they would have appreciated the offer, but interestingly, 92.5 per cent of families who had refused to donate stated that such an offer would have made no difference to their decision.[67]

Of course, the prospect of any financial incentives to organ donation will come up against the arguments against commodification of the human body, which we consider in more detail below in relation to living donors. In the next extract, AL Caplan explains why he finds the offer of cash for body parts offensive.

---

[66] 'Modified mandated choice for organ procurement' (2003) 29 Journal of Medical Ethics 157–62, 158.
[67] Laura Siminoff and Mary Beth Mercer, 'Public Policy, Public Opinion, and Consent for Organ Donation' (2002) 11 Cambridge Quarterly of Healthcare Ethics 377–86.

AL Caplan[68]

No factual support has been advanced for the hypothesis that payment will increase cadaver donation . . . There is no empirical evidence that families raise the issue of money or compensation at the time when they are faced with requests or decisions about making organs and tissues available for transplantation. What factual evidence there is lends support to the opposite conclusion—that significant numbers of Americans would be angered, offended and insulted by offers of money or financial rewards for the organs and tissues of their deceased loved ones. . . .

If the only way US society, or any other, can find to pay for the uncompensated costs of medical care or funerals for the indigent is to offer cash for their body parts, such a society has no right to call itself humane, decent, or fair . . .

Financial incentives reduce people to merchandise. Offering bribes, permitting cash rebates, setting estate discounts, or paying for funerals contingent on a favorable decision about procurement says that medicine is willing to commodify the body to whatever extent it takes to allow more transplants to be done. . . .

Calls for markets, compensation, bounties, or rewards should be rejected because they convert human beings into products, a metaphysical transformation that cheapens the respect for life and corrodes our ability to maintain the stance that human beings are special, unique, and valuable for their own sake, not for what others can mine, extract, or manufacture from them. Nor will markets do what their proponents hope. The inevitable opposition such proposals will encounter from many religious leaders means any increase in lives saved attributable to cash prizes will be swamped by the number of lives lost when those who refuse to see the human body as available for sale decline to participate in anything having to do with transplants.

Another solution is proposed by Nicole Gerrand. She suggests that organ donation is more accurately described as an act of charity rather than a gift. Gifts are usually made to specified individuals, and in many social situations, gift-giving is effectively obligatory. In contrast, a charitable act, like organ donation, is intended to benefit people who are not known to the actor, and it is supererogatory. Redefining organ donation as an act of charity would, she argues, enable us to revisit the role of incentives. She points out that there tend to be few objections to the existence of financial incentives towards charitable acts, such as ensuring donations are tax deductible.[69]

Nicole Gerrand[70]

If it is more accurate to describe organ donation as a charitable act, rather than an act of gift-giving, then this may affect some aspects of the current organ procurement procedure . . . [T]here may be scope to review the role of incentives, since it is acceptable for charitable donations to be tax deductible. There could be incentives to assist a potential donor (someone who has agreed to donate her organs after her death) during her lifetime, such as health or life insurance policies, or alternatively, if the payment was made when the organs were retrieved (after the donor had died) then the benefit, in whatever form, would go to the donor's family . . .

The salient features of acts of charity—that they are supererogatory, should be performed voluntarily, and be motivated by altruism—all seem familiar. These are the same features that were argued at the beginning of the transplant era to be necessary to ensure a morally acceptable organ procurement procedure.

---

[68] *Am I my Brother's Keeper? The Ethical Frontiers of Biomedicine* (Indiana UP 1997) 96–8, 100.
[69] 'The Notion of Gift-Giving and Organ Donation' (1994) 8 *Bioethics* 127–50.
[70] Ibid, 132, 147.

(b) Non-financial incentives

Other possible incentives might include giving those who have indicated their willingness to donate priority if they ever need an organ themselves. If signing up to the organ donor register might have future health benefits for the potential donor, then 'opting-in' rates might be expected to increase. Insofar as apathy rather than disapproval of transplantation is the principal reason why people do not take steps to register their agreement to donation, and given that the steps necessary to indicate one's willingness to donate are clearly not arduous, Rupert Jarvis argues that an appeal to the reciprocity of organ donation might be a cheap and effective way to increase donation rates.

Rupert Jarvis[71]

I suggest that legislation governing organ donation be amended such that all and only those who identify themselves as potential donors (perhaps by a card similar to the one currently in use, or by registration on a central computer) are eligible themselves to receive transplant organs . . .

This contract . . . trades a—if not *the*—central interest in remaining alive, against one's *post mortem* interest in not having one's organs removed. This latter is at best *de minimis*: my interests in my organs after death can hardly be said to be enormous. We are presented, then, with what appears to be a thoroughly attractive option: by sacrificing our minimal *post mortem* interests we guarantee our inclusion on the waiting list for the donor organ which might save or vastly improve the quality of our own life.

Adoption of this scheme would, I suggest, address the problem of shortage on two fronts simultaneously. Firstly, by excluding those who do not elect to join the scheme, it will reduce legitimate demand for donor organs. It should be noted that the reduction thus effected will probably be minimal, which is surely a good thing, in that it seems preferable that supply be matched to demand by increasing supply rather than by eliminating demand.

Secondly, and more importantly, the supply of donor organs would at the same time increase as a result of an upturn in the number of potential donors. It hardly seems fanciful to suggest that the vast majority of people would elect to join the scheme, since it is so clearly in their interests to do so, with the potential gain (life) being infinite and the potential loss (*post mortem* dissection which, depending on the manner of their death, they might well have to undergo anyway) being zero.

Moreover, this alignment of the individual's self-regarding interests with the public good is a strength as far as the scheme's likely successful implementation is concerned. Given a moderate version of the social contract theorist's premise, that people tend to act in what they perceive to be their own best interests, it follows that a scheme under which acting in one's best interests is concomitant with, and necessarily entails acting in, the best interests of the population at large will inevitably tend to promote the public good.

But, as Ranaan Gillon explains, it would almost certainly be unethical and impracticable to make willingness to donate the *only* relevant factor when allocating organs to potential transplant recipients. Rather, a points system for allocation, like that used by UK Transplant, which takes into account a range of factors such as immediacy of clinical need and time spent on the waiting list could be weighted such that willing

---

[71] 'Join the club: a modest proposal to increase availability of donor organs' (1995) 21 Journal of Medical Ethics 199–204, 202–3.

donors received a slightly higher ranking than similar candidates who would not be prepared to have their own organs used for transplantation.

Ranaan Gillon[72]

So far as volunteers are concerned there seems little doubt that they would benefit from the scheme ... Indeed if the rejuvenated supply of organs became sufficiently augmented by the scheme, even non-volunteers for organ donation would benefit.

In the absence of such an enormous increase in organ supply, however, the non-volunteers would clearly lose out and stand to benefit less than at present, if the proposal were accepted. They would be deliberately put at the bottom of the queue for transplanted organs, even in particular situations where their need for, and the extent and probability of their potential benefit from, such transplants would be greater than the needs and benefits of the pre-volunteers who would be given priority.

Here seems to be the Achilles heel of Mr Jarvis's proposal. For even if such non-volunteers can properly be said to have only themselves to blame for their predicament; even if they can properly be said to have deliberately and autonomously made their choice and rejected the opportunity to give themselves priority for receipt of transplanted organs; even if they can properly be said to have been selfish, and/or inconsiderate and/or foolish, even immoral, in refusing to pre-volunteer their own organs, nonetheless there is an important countervailing moral tradition in medicine. It is that patients should be given treatment in relation to their medical need, and that scarce medical resources should not be prioritised on the basis of a patient's blameworthiness ...

Fault, past or present, is widely rejected as a 'morally relevant inequality' by currently accepted substantive principles of distributive justice for scarce medical resources. Attractive though Mr Jarvis's proposal may otherwise be, it does seem to entail reversing this moral norm. If past or present fault thus became an accepted criterion for distributive justice for scarce medical resources, a very steep 'logical slippery slope' would have been created.

If the fault and/or inconsiderateness of not previously volunteering his or her organs for transplantation were to justify withholding scarce life-saving resources from a patient, then all other prior faults and inconsiderateness of equal or greater weight could, logically, also be regarded as morally relevant and potentially justificatory for withholding scarce life-saving medical resources from patients. Such a prospect hardly bears contemplation.

It should also be remembered, first, that most of us are unlikely ever to need an organ transplant, and secondly, that people are notoriously reluctant to contemplate their own morbidity. The remote possibility that one might in future suffer acute organ failure and be likely to die without an organ transplant may not seem sufficiently pressing to prompt people to take steps to register their willingness to donate. Instead, a more effective way to penalize 'free-riders' would be to incorporate priority for willing donors as part of a presumed consent system. As Stephanie Eaton argues below, the presumption would be (a) that the deceased person had consented to donation, and (b) that she was not a free-rider. It would be for those who did not want their organs to be used after their death to register their objection, and they would be warned that 'opting-out' *might* reduce their likelihood of being allocated an organ if they ever needed one.

---

[72] 'On giving preference to prior volunteers when allocating organs for transplantation' (1995) 21 Journal of Medical Ethics 195–6, 196.

Stephanie Eaton[73]

Of course, the priority of the clinical over the moral may mean that in practice there is seldom or never a disadvantage as a consequence of free-riding. But the value of the concept of 'free-riding' lies less in its application by doctors to specific cases than in the *political* possibilities it brings forward. Its usefulness lies in the fact that it promotes a discourse which leads to a greater acceptance of the presumption of consent and it may also make decisions easier for families of potential donors.

If it is agreed that most people would consent to benefiting from transplant technology and that free-riding is a morally precarious position to hold, it is possible to arouse people's awareness to the moral consequences of the stance which they are taking when they choose to opt-out. Where people still choose to opt-out knowing that this constitutes free-riding, they should be made aware that they may be disadvantaged in the future if they should ever become potential recipients of organs . . .

Publicity that promotes the idea that an opted-out person may be less likely to receive a transplant if he or she ever needs one, forces opters-out to reconsider their own moral standards. It is hoped that the unease that will be felt when opting-out is acknowledged as being a form of free-riding will have the consequence that few people will choose to opt out . . . Where a person has not made a declaration stating that he or she wishes to opt out, and where it is believed that he or she would not have refused the benefits of transplant technology for him or herself, it can safely be assumed that he or she would have consented to be a donor, given the charitable—and not unreasonable—assumption that this person is not a free rider. Given this assumption, and the obligations which result from being a member of a community of interdependent potential donors and recipients, a decision that infers the consent of that person to donate organs is possible.

(9) A DUTY TO DONATE? ORGANS AS A PUBLIC RESOURCE?

If it were possible to take organs from any dead body without the need for consent, many lives could be saved. In the next extract, HE Emson argues that, once dead, a person's organs should be treated as a public resource, to be distributed to those in need of them.

HE Emson[74]

In my opinion any concept of property in the human body either during life or after death is biologically inaccurate and morally wrong. The body should be regarded morally as on loan to the individual from the biomass, to which the cadaver will inevitably return . . .

I am deeply concerned with the right of the person to govern disposal of their body after death, when separation of body and soul is irrevocably complete and the individual is incapable of reconstitution. The person no longer exists, the soul has departed, and the individual who was but is no longer has no further use for the body which has been part of him or her during life. The concept of the right of a person to determine before death, the disposal of their body after death, made sense only when there was no continuing use for that body. It makes neither practical nor moral sense now, when the body for which the dead person no longer has any use, is quite literally a vital resource, a potential source of life for others . . .

If this argument is correct, then it is even more morally unacceptable for the relatives of the deceased to deny utilisation of the cadaver as a source of transplantable organs. Their only claim

---

[73] 'The subtle politics of organ donation: a proposal' (1998) 24 Journal of Medical Ethics 166–70, 168.

[74] 'It is immoral to require consent for cadaver organ donation' (2003) 29 Journal of Medical Ethics 125–7, 126–7.

upon it is as a temporary memorial of a loved one, inevitably destined to decay or be burned in a very short time. To me, any such claim cannot morally be sustained in the face of what I regard as the overwhelming and pre-emptive need of the potential recipient . . . The need of the potential recipient, the benefit which may accrue to him or her, to me trumps and surpasses all other considerations. . . .

In my opinion, the human cadaver, at the point at which life departs, should become a resource for those who may benefit from donation of its organs . . .

In this situation, the idea of consent and its corollary, refusal are not morally applicable. One may be able to give or refuse consent to a procedure which affects oneself, but organ donation affects no one physically; no human person is involved as donor. To grant the right and power of consent to an individual who may be affected emotionally, is to elevate the possible emotional affect of one person, as more important than the physical life of another. The imbalance of benefit is too great to permit of this, and I find it morally unacceptable.

Alternatively it could be argued that we are under a duty to donate our organs after death, equivalent to the duty of easy rescue, explained by JL Nelson in the next extract.

JL Nelson[75]

[T]here is a strong presumption that refusing to save another person's life when doing so is virtually costless to the person in a position to act, is seriously wrong. . . .

I think that people typically have duties to provide organs to others, should the opportunity arise, and indeed, duties to reconsider and possibly refigure their attitudes about themselves and others insofar as those attitudes threaten their inclinations to be organ providers. Or, to put it a bit more carefully, since it seems a bit strained to think of dead people having duties, I think that removing organs from the dead typically neither harms nor wrongs them, and that therefore we the living have a prima facie duty to support the retrieval of useful organs, both from our own dead bodies, and from those of others. If we find ourselves repulsed or otherwise distressed by this prospect, we have a derivative duty: to seek to revamp our attitudes.

John Harris further points out that since the human body never remains intact for very long after death, objections to organ donation are intrinsically irrational, and, in any event, must be of less importance than the interest of potential recipients who might die without replacement organs.

John Harris[76]

All the moral concern of our society has so far been focused on the dead and their friends and relatives. But there are two separate sets of individuals who have moral claims upon us, not just one. There is the deceased individual and her friends and relatives on the one hand, and the potential organ or tissue recipient and her friends and relatives on the other. Both have claims upon us, the claims of neither have obvious priority. If we weigh the damage to the interests of the deceased and her friends, and relatives if their wishes are overriden against the damage done to would be recipients and their friends and relatives if they fail to get the organs they need to keep them alive, where should the balance of our moral concern lie? . . .

I have never doubted that there is a real sense in which individuals may have some interests that survive their death and hence there are some senses in which an individual's interests are still in

[75] JL Nelson, *Hippocrates' Maze: Ethical Explorations of the Medical Labyrinth* (Rowman & Littlefield NY 2003) 119.
[76] 'Organ procurement: dead interests, living needs' (2003) 29 Journal of Medical Ethics 130–4, 130, 133.

play after death. While such interests deserve some respect, they are relatively weak when compared with the interests of living persons who exist to be harmed in person by the neglect of their interests . . .

My point is that it is surely implausible to think that having one's body remain whole after their death is an objective anyone is entitled to pursue at the cost of other people's lives! It is implausible to the point of wickedness, not least because the objective is irrational and impossible of achievement . . . No dead body remains intact; the worms . . . or the fire and eventually dust claim it . . . The alternatives are not burial intact or disintegration. There is no alternative which does not involve disintegration.

Given the irrationality of the aim, it is difficult to defend a right to pursue such an aim when it is clear that doing so costs lives.

In the next extract, Aaron Spital suggests that 'conscription' of cadaveric organs would not only save lives, but would also have a number of other advantages over consent-based systems.

Aaron Spital[77]

The most important advantage of conscription is that under this plan, the efficiency of organ procurement should approach 100%, which would dramatically increase the number of organs available for transplantation. . . . Another advantage of conscription is that this system would be much simpler and less costly than other approaches to organ procurement. Under this plan there would be no need to search for the best approach for obtaining consent, no need for expensive, labor-intensive educational programs designed to encourage more people to say yes, no need to train requestors to obtain and document consent, no need to maintain donor registries, and no need for complex regulatory mechanisms to prevent abuse as would be required were financial incentives allowed.

A third advantage of conscription is that because permission from the family would no longer be sought, this plan would eliminate the added stress that devastated families now endure when asked to consider organ donation in the midst of the grief and shock that follow the sudden death of a loved one. Furthermore, delays in organ recovery that result from the current need to wait for family approval, and that jeopardize the quality of organs, would be eliminated.

A final advantage of conscription is that, in contrast to other approaches to organ procurement, it satisfies the principle of distributive justice, which refers to equitable sharing of burdens and benefits by members of the community. Under conscription, all people who die with usable organs would contribute to the cadaveric organ pool—there would be no more 'free riders'—and all people would stand to benefit should they ever need an organ transplant. This contrasts with our current system in which people can refuse to donate and yet compete equally for an organ with generous people who choose to give.

Against this, W Glannon argues that we do have an important interest in what is done to our bodies after our death, and that this outweighs the interests of those in need of organs.

W Glannon[78]

Because the body is so closely associated with who we are, we can have an interest in what is done

---

[77] 'Conscription of Cadaveric Organs for Transplantation: A Stimulating Idea Whose Time Has Not Yet Come' (2005) 14 Cambridge Quarterly of Healthcare Ethics 107–12, 108.
[78] 'Do the sick have a right to cadaveric organs?' (2003) 29 Journal of Medical Ethics 153–6, 154.

to it even after we cease to exist. The fact that my body is mine and is essential to my life plan means that I have a deep interest in what is done to it. If it is treated in a way that does not accord with my wishes or interests, then in an important respect this can be bad for me and I can be harmed. The special relation between humans and their bodies can make it wrong for others to ignore the expressed wish that one's organs not be harvested at death, despite their viability for transplantation.

Negative rights have more moral force than positive rights. The right not to be interfered with puts a stronger moral obligation on others than does the right to be aided by them . . . Given the special relation between humans and their bodies, the moral importance of individual autonomy in having a life plan, and that what happens to one's body after death is part of such a plan, the negative right to bodily integrity after death outweighs any presumed positive right of the sick to receive organs from those who did not consent to cadaver donation. This deontological constraint can be sustained despite the utilitarian good that would result from the transfer of organs from the dead to those who are dying from organ failure.

4. LIVE DONORS

(a) THE ETHICAL ACCEPTABILITY OF LIVING ORGAN DONATION

In part as a response to the continuing shortage of cadaveric organs, there has been increasing interest in obtaining certain non-vital organs from living donors. The health risks to living donors are, in the case of kidney donation, comparatively small. It has been estimated that the increased risk of mortality from living with only one kidney is 0.03 per cent, which is 'equivalent to driving back and forth to work 16 miles a day'.[79] The risk of morbidity (ill-health) is greater, with 2 per cent of kidney donors experiencing major morbidity, and 10–20 per cent experiencing minor morbidity. Risks from living liver donation are higher, with mortality rates of 0.5–0.1 per cent, and morbidity rates of 40–60 per cent.[80]

Success rates in living organ donation are higher than when cadaveric organs are used. In part, this may be because the organ is taken from a healthy living person, rather than from someone who has died. But perhaps more importantly, the timing of the transplant can be controlled. When a cadaveric organ becomes available, the operation has to take place as soon as possible after the donor's (usually sudden) death. From the recipient's point of view, this may be less than ideal: she will have virtually no opportunity to prepare for the operation, and it may take place when she is unwell. When an organ is taken from a living donor, however, the transplant team can ensure the operation is carried out when the recipient is in the best possible health.

Despite the obvious advantages in increasing the pool of potential organ donors to

[79] James F Blumstein, 'The use of financial incentives in medical care: the case of commerce in transplantable organs' in A Grubb and MJ Mehlman (eds), *Justice and Health Care: Comparative Perspectives* (John Wiley & Sons Chichester 1995) 9–39, 34.

[80] James Neuberger and David Price, 'Role of living liver donation in the United Kingdom' (2003) 327 British Medical Journal 676–9.

include living persons, the practice remains controversial. Unlike cadaveric donation, living organ donation does pose real, albeit small, health risks to the donor. One study found that 15 per cent of live donors believed that donation had had a negative impact upon their health,[81] and another that approximately 4 per cent regretted their decision to donate.[82] Of course this means that the vast majority of donors did not regret their decision, and that most did not believe that there had been any negative impact upon their health. And most studies appear to show that donors commonly experience increased self-esteem and feelings of well-being.[83] Not only are the risks involved in kidney removal comparatively low, but also there will often be substantial non-clinical benefits to the donor herself. Watching someone one loves suffer is itself a miserable experience, and being able to alleviate their suffering or save their life is likely to have advantages for the donor as well as the recipient.

Interestingly, there appears to be a gender imbalance both among living organ donors, who are more likely to be female, and among recipients, the majority of whom are male.[84] A German study found that mothers were the most frequent donors (27 per cent), followed by wives (19 per cent), fathers (13 per cent), sisters (12 per cent), and husbands (11 per cent).[85] It is not clear why this difference exists, although possible explanations have included men's greater capacity to resist family pressure, and their higher wage earning capacity, which may mean that sparing time for donation and recuperation is perceived to be easier for female family members.

But while the altruistic act of the *donor* might be laudable, in the next extract Carl Elliott argues that both *recipients* of live organs and *doctors* who perform living organ retrieval are encouraging the donor's self-sacrifice, and that this is more problematic.

Carl Elliott[86]

To get at what is troubling about a person who knowingly and willingly consents to a harmful medical procedure, it is necessary to look not simply at the person making the decision to participate, but beyond him to the other people involved in and affected by the exchange . . .

And while it is admirable to risk harm to oneself, it is not admirable to encourage another person to risk harm to himself for one's own benefit . . .

Accepting a sacrifice of great magnitude is not mere passive acquiescence, devoid of any moral import. If I allow someone else to risk his life or health for my sake, I am endorsing his self-sacrifice and agreeing to profit by it . . . What would we think of a person who would take advantage of a donor's willingness to take life-threatening risks? . . .

---

[81] LR Schover, SB Streem, N Boparai, K Duriak, and AC Novick, 'The Psychosocial Impact of Donating a Kidney: Long Term Follow-up from a Urology Based Center' (1997) 157 Journal of Urology 1596–601. See also the study by M. Walter et al., 'Quality of life of living donors before and after living donor liver transplantation' Transplantation Proceedings, volume 35, issue 8, Dec 2003, 2961–3, which indicated that 10 per cent of living liver donors were having difficulty coping with psychological symptoms.

[82] EM Johnson, MJ Remucal, and AJ Matas, 'Living Kidney Donation: Donor Risks and Quality of Life' (1997) Clinical Transplantation 231–40.

[83] RG Simmons, SD Klein, and RL Simmons, *Gift of Life: the Social and Psychological Impact of Organ Transplantation* (Wiley New York 1977) at 176–87.

[84] N Biller-Andorno, 'Gender imbalance in living organ donation' (2002) 5 Medicine, Health Care and Philosophy 199–204, 201.

[85] Noted in N Biller-Andorno, 'Gender imbalance in living organ donation' (2002) 5 Medicine, Health Care and Philosophy 199–204, 201.

[86] 'Doing harm: living organ donors, clinical research and *The Tenth Man*' (1995) 21 Journal of Medical Ethics 91–6, 93.

If an ailing patient were to take advantage of a healthy donor's self-sacrifice, it might well be understandable, but it would not be morally admirable. It would not be the sort of behaviour that we would aspire to and want to encourage.

That a person's decision to harm himself deeply affects a circle of people far beyond him seems so obvious a part of ordinary life that it seems almost trite to emphasize it here. . . . If I pay another person to harm himself for my sake . . ., I must recognize that my actions might very likely damage his family and friends very much. And even while I might defend that person's right to make the decision to harm himself, I would feel very awkward trying to defend myself against the criticism of his family and friends, whose resentment most of us could readily understand.

Finally, it is important to realize that the doctor is not a mere instrument of the patient's wishes. Analyses of living organ donation . . . are often simplified needlessly by a failure to acknowledge outright that the doctor is also a moral agent who should be held accountable for his actions. . . . This shifts the moral balance of the problem in an important way, because while we admire the person who *undergoes* harm to himself for the sake of another, we do not necessarily admire the person who *inflicts* harm on one person for the sake of another. And the latter is what the doctor must do.

As a result of these concerns, it has been suggested that we should not resort to using living donors until we have *exhausted* all possible means of increasing the number of cadaveric organs available for transplant. In addition to avoiding unnecessary health risks to living donors, there are, as Arthur Caplan explains, concerns about the genuineness of a live donor's consent to donation. We return to the question of consent later.

Arthur L Caplan[87]

There are two distinct schools of thought about the morality of asking donors to face grave risks, albeit with a low probability of occurrence, in order to obtain an organ or part of an organ for someone in need of a transplant. Some, who might be termed 'absolutists,' claim that the imposition of serious risk by physicians upon a person for any non-therapeutic purpose is immoral. Imposing mortal risk violates the moral precept against doing harm, which is seen to strongly bind physicians.

Others, who might be termed 'proportionists,' object to living donation only if the imposition of harm or risk seems disproportionate to the benefit that will be attained. Small risks might be acceptable in the service of near certain benefits but great risks for unknown benefits would not be acceptable. The test of the morality of imposing risk or harm is proportionality—whether the benefits are so certain and of a kind that the benefits manifestly outweigh the risks of harm.

Other experts are not so much worried about the imposition or assumption of risk in donation. They believe each individual should be free to make decisions about how much risk and what sorts of risk they wish to face. Instead, this group is concerned that it is simply not possible for a living donor to give true, voluntary, informed consent to donation. . . .

In order to provide valid consent a person must have all relevant information and the opportunity to reflect upon and ask questions about the information from those who will provide objective answers. Transplant centers and other transplant personnel may face problems in providing 'objective' information to prospective donors because those involved in seeking donors have an inherent conflict of interest. They cannot both advocate for the best interests of patients who need transplants and simultaneously protect the best interests of prospective donors. . . .

[87] 'Am I My Brother's Keeper?' (1993) 27 Suffolk University Law Review 1195, 1198–200.

Finally, many critics of live donation worry that the environment in which live donation takes place makes it impossible for anyone to give free and voluntary consent. Family members will ordinarily feel extraordinary pressures to 'volunteer.' The realization that one could be blamed for the failure to help a spouse, a sibling, or a child may be so frightening that potential donors see themselves as having no choice.

But while it is almost certainly preferable to use cadaveric organs, as we have seen, demand massively outstrips supply, and will probably continue to do so. Two conclusions follow from this. First, that we should probably bear in mind that there are good reasons for looking closely at mechanisms, such as presumed consent or financial incentives, which might increase the pool of potential cadaveric donors, because these could reduce the need to resort to living organ donation, and thus have health benefits not only for the recipients of the organs, but also for potential live donors, whose services would no longer be needed. Secondly, if it is almost certainly inevitable that we will continue to have to pursue alternatives to cadaveric donation, we will need to think about the circumstances in which live organ donation should be permitted.

(b) TYPE OF TRANSPLANT

Obviously, it is only possible for living organ donors to donate non-vital organs, such as kidneys, lobes of the lung or liver segments. Most living organ donation involves kidneys (in 2003/4, there were 450 living donor kidney transplants and ten living donor liver transplants).[88] A difficult ethical question about the limits of autonomous decision-making arose in the US in 1998 when a man sought to donate his *second* kidney to his daughter after the first transplant had failed.[89] The operation would not have killed Mr Patterson, but it would have left him dependent upon dialysis for the rest of his life, unless, of course, he himself was able to obtain a kidney transplant. Unlike ordinary living kidney transplants, the donor in this situation faces a dramatic and substantial risk to his own health. It might therefore be argued that carrying out this operation conflicts with the doctor's duty to do no harm, and it might be predicted that very few doctors would contemplate carrying out an operation this risky purely in order to benefit a third party.

(c) LIVE TRANSPLANTATION IN THE UK

In the UK, there has been a steady increase in the use of living donors, particularly for kidney transplants: now approximately 25 per cent of all kidney transplants involve living donors. Live transplantation in the UK is regulated by both the common law and the Human Tissue Act 2004, but it is first worth briefly mentioning the previous legislation.

[88] <http://www.uktransplant.org.uk/ukt/statistics/transplant_activity_report/current_activity_reports. jsp/ukt/tx_activity_report_2004_uk_pp6–10.pdf>.

[89] Ryan Sauder and Lisa S Parker, 'Autonomy's Limits: Living Donation and Health-Related Harm' (2001) 10 Cambridge Quarterly of Healthcare Ethics 399–401.

(1) BEFORE THE HUMAN TISSUE ACT 2004

The law which governed living organ transplants before the Human Tissue Act 2004 (the Human Organ Transplants Act 1989) was passed in response to the widely publicized discovery that a private London hospital had purchased kidneys from poor Turkish citizens and transplanted them into wealthy private patients. The Act's principal purpose was to prohibit trafficking in organs, and it attempted to do this both by direct prohibition on payments and advertising, and by making it more difficult to donate an organ to anyone other than a genetic relative. Non-genetically related donors had to be separately assessed by the Unrelated Live Transplant Regulatory Authority (ULTRA), to ensure that the donor's consent was free and uncoerced.

The problem with this system was that it confused altruism with biological relatedness. The Human Organ Transplant Act 1989 presumed that the motivation was altruistic when people are genetically related, and assumed that genetically unrelated donors are necessarily more susceptible to coercion and pressure. Neither assumption is warranted. The Act treated spouses and long-term partners in the same way as strangers, when in fact one is perhaps *more* likely to want to donate a kidney to one's spouse than to one's nephew or uncle, for example.

As Choudhry et al. explain, the Act also ignored the very real possibility that a related donor might feel coerced by pressure from other family members, or might simply feel that their familial obligations leave them no option but to agree to donation:

there is endless scope for subtle pressure within families and among friends, as is recognised by the transplant teams who try to assess the willingness of related donors. Although the family is idealised as an intimate sphere were relatives act willingly and selflessly to promote each other's interests, it may be characterised by relationships of power and subordination that can be abused, making consent more apparent than real. In addition, even in the absence of unequal power relationships, affective bonds between family members are open to manipulation or exploitation, creating the potential for pressures to consent to organ donation.

Ironically, potential organ donors who have *no* emotional ties to a particular recipient may be better able to make an entirely free and uncoerced decision to donate.

Walter Glannon and Lainie Friedman Ross go further and argue that it is only organ donation to a stranger which can properly be described as altruistic. In the context of parent-to-child donation, they argue that donation is effectively non-optional, and while it may be a beneficent act, it is not an altruistic one.

Walter Glannon and Lainie Friedman Ross[90]

In contrast to the stranger who donates an organ altruistically without any obligation, there are distinctive expectations and obligations on us when we stand in certain relationships to others. These include our children, parents, siblings, friends, and benefactors, though the types of obligation will vary across these relationships. The obligations these relationships entail generally function as constraints on people's behaviour, restricting what they can and cannot do. Parents, for example, are obligated to meet the basic needs and promote the best interests of their

---

[90] 'Do Genetic Relationships Create Moral Obligations in Organ Transplantation?' (2002) 11 Cambridge Quarterly of Healthcare Ethics 153–9, 155–6.

children . . . ., their duty to meet their child's needs in general is not optional . . . Given that altruism consists in purely optional actions presupposing no duty to aid others, any parental act that counts as meeting a child's needs cannot be altruistic. . . .

Few would blame an anonymous individual who considered and then decided not to donate to a stranger. But family members who decide not to donate to their siblings, parents, or children are viewed with contempt. This is because of the moral obligations we expect of those who stand in intimate relations with others. An altruistic donor has no obligation to donate. The decision to donate goes beyond the obligatory and permissible to the supererogatory, and a decision not to donate does not invite or warrant moral criticism because there is no moral basis on which to criticize not performing an act that would have been beyond the call of duty. In contrast, the family member who is a potential donor has a prima facie obligation to donate because of the nature of relationships within the family.

It is perhaps odd, as Martyn Evans indicates in the next extract, that a statute which was intended to promote altruistic donation in practice outlawed the purest form of altruism, namely living organ donation by strangers, who stand to gain no personal benefit from saving an unknown individual's life.

Martyn Evans[91]

Any 'genetic-relative' restriction clearly debars virtually the whole of humanity from the opportunity of such fraternity and love in any given case of need for an organ. It seems therefore perverse to emphasise this altruism and then grossly to circumscribe its opportunities for expression.

Moreover it might be thought that altruism receives its highest expression in the absence of personal relationships—that is, when there can be no question of even emotional self-interest. The gift of an organ to a complete stranger, whose identity is concealed from the donor and from whom the donor's identity is concealed, seems worthy of the highest respect. Any formal restriction to related donors would rule out altruism of this supreme kind.

While the previous legislation banned payments and advertising and placed restrictions upon who could become a live organ donor, it did not regulate the question of consent to donation. This was instead covered by the common law. To some extent this is replicated in the Human Tissue Act 2004. The Act covers consent to the *use* and *storage* of tissue taken from the living, but its *removal* continues to be dealt with by the common law, which we consider in the next section.

(2) CONSENT TO THE REMOVAL OF TISSUE AT COMMON LAW

As we saw in Chapter 4, the criminal law places limits upon the extent to which an adult can consent to the infliction of harm. Although the increased risk of morbidity from living with only one kidney is low, nephrectomy is a serious operation done under general anaesthetic, and as a result, carries with it a small risk of death or irreversible harm. Nevertheless, it has been accepted that competent adults may lawfully consent to organ donation. Indeed the Law Commission has declared that:

there is no doubt that once a valid consent has been forthcoming, English law now treats as lawful donation of regenerative tissue, and also non-regenerative tissue that is not essential to life.[92]

---

[91] 'Organ donations should not be restricted to relatives' (1989) 15 Journal of Medical Ethics 18–19.
[92] Law Commission Consultation Paper No 139, *Consent in the Criminal Law* (HMSO 1995) para 8.32.

Because the living organ donor is undergoing non-therapeutic surgery, it is, however, especially important that their consent is fully informed and voluntary.

In the next extract, Ryan Sauder and Lisa Parker point out that many living donors will feel that they have no choice but to offer to donate an organ to a desperately sick relative, and that feeling compelled to donate may be incompatible with freely given consent.

Ryan Sauder and Lisa S Parker[93]

Frequently, a prospective donor, particularly a parent or sibling of the prospective recipient, will experience the decision to donate as automatic. They frequently report feeling that they had no choice but to donate, and proceed to offer their organs willingly and without hesitation, sometimes even before hearing of the risks involved in such a donation. Disclosure of risks frequently has no effect on the decision to donate. These decisions hardly seem to meet the traditional requirements of informed consent. Failing to take risks of an intervention into account when deciding whether to consent to it, and feeling compelled to consent, are typically hallmarks of a failure of the informed-consent process. Yet we are reluctant to suggest that these prospective donors are not making autonomous decisions to donate and, consequently, that their decisions (and organs) should not be accepted.

In addition to full disclosure of the risks to their own health, potential living organ donors should also be given frank information about the possibility that the transplant might not work, and should be advised about the emotional impact of an unsuccessful donation. If the recipient's need for a transplant results from a genetic condition, more than one family member may require the same transplant, and donors should therefore be advised that they may be able to act as a donor only once.

Because of the emphasis on informed consent, could organs ever be taken from those who lack the capacity to consent? In the case of children, although parents normally consent to their minor children's medical treatment, in the case of sibling-to-sibling organ donation, parents would be faced with a particularly difficult conflict of interest. How could they separate their responsibility for the interests of the potential donor child from their equally compelling concern for the interests of the potential recipient, and for their own interests? As with other especially controversial procedures, court approval should be sought. It seems likely that the courts would be prepared to authorize bone marrow donation, if it could be demonstrated that saving a sibling's life would hold out the possibility of emotional, psychological and social benefit to the child donor. But whether a court would ever be prepared to authorize the removal of a non-regenerative organ, such as a kidney, is another matter.

There were some *obiter* comments about organ donation in *Re W (A Minor)*.[94] The Court of Appeal suggested that the Family Law Reform Act 1969, which gives minors of 16 and 17 years of age the right to consent to medical treatment, would not apply to organ donation procedures because, 'so far as the donor is concerned, these do not constitute either treatment or diagnosis'.[95] Instead, until the age of 18, 'the

[93] 'Autonomy's Limits: Living Donation and Health-Related Harm' (2001) 10 Cambridge Quarterly of Healthcare Ethics 399–401, 403.

[94] [1993] Fam 64.   [95] *Per* Lord Donaldson.

jurisdiction of the court should always be invoked'.[96] Until such a case arises, it is not clear whether the courts would ever be prepared to authorize such an operation.

There have been instances of child organ donation in the US. In *Hart v Brown*,[97] for example, the court was satisfied that the psychological benefit to the donor from her identical twin sister's survival and continued companionship, justified the risks of donation.

At common law, the position of incompetent adults is similar. Again, the decision to remove tissue from an incompetent adult should be taken by the court, applying the best interests test. In the Court of Appeal judgement in *Re F (Mental Patient: Sterilisation)*, a case we consider in detail in Chapter 4, Neill LJ suggested that court approval should be sought before an incompetent person could act as an organ donor, and that the court would have to satisfy itself that the donation was 'necessary' in an incompetent adult's best interests.

There are, however, some operations where the intervention of a court is most desirable if not essential. In this category I would place operations for sterilisation and organ transplant operations where the incapacitated patient is to be the donor. The performance of these operations should be subject to outside scrutiny. The lawfulness of the operation will depend of course on the question whether it is necessary or not, but in my view it should become standard practice for the approval of the court to be obtained before an operation of this exceptional kind is carried out.[98]

In *Re Y (Mental Patient: Bone Marrow Donation)*,[99] bone marrow donation was authorized, on the grounds that this would also be in the donor's social or emotional interests. But in the same case, Connell J doubted whether similar reasoning could justify organ donation:

It is doubtful that this case would act as a useful precedent in cases where the surgery involved is more intrusive than in this case, where the evidence shows that the bone marrow harvested is speedily regenerated and that a healthy individual can donate as much as two pints with no long term consequences at all.

As yet, no cases have arisen and so it is unclear whether there would ever be circumstances in which a court would be satisfied that solid organ donation was in the best interests of an incompetent adult.

Again, in the US there have been cases in which the courts have authorized organ donation from incompetent adults. In *Strunk v Strunk*,[100] the court approved kidney donation from an incompetent adult on the grounds that his brother's death would have caused him psychological and emotional injury greater than any risk associated with the removal of one of his kidneys.

(3) THE HUMAN TISSUE ACT 2004

Under section 33(1) and (2), taking an organ from a living person for the purposes of transplantation (regardless of whether they are related to each other or not) is an offence, unless the requirements in sections 33(3) and 33(5) are satisfied. These are, under section 33(3), that no payment for reward has been given in contravention of

---

[96] *Per* Nolan LJ.   [97] (1972) 289 A 2d 386 (Conn Sup Ct).   [98] *The Times* 8 Dec 1988.
[99] [1997] Fam 110.   [100] (1969) 445 SW 2d 145.

section 32 (see below), and that such other conditions and requirements as may be specified in regulations are satisfied (see below). Section 33(5) offers a defence if the person who takes an organ reasonably believes that the transplant satisfies the section 33(3) requirements.

(a) Consent

Under section 1 of the Act, there must be 'appropriate consent' to the use of human tissue for transplantation. For competent adults, under section 3(2) 'appropriate consent' means 'his consent'. Paragraph 7 of the HTA's draft Code of Practice specifies that consent should be an ongoing process, in order to ensure that the donor has been properly informed:

Appropriate consent from an adult means his or her consent given when competent to do so. The seeking and giving of consent should usually be part of the ongoing conversation with the donor, rather than a one-off event. Therefore, good practice would be that, where possible, the donor's consent to the proposed procedure should be sought well in advance, when there is time to respond to any questions and provide adequate information. Practitioners should also check, before the procedure starts, that consent is still given.[101]

The draft Code of Practice also contains detailed guidance on the information which should be provided as part of the consent process:

Human Tissue Authority
33. Practitioners must always remember that the decision to donate an organ rests solely and entirely with the potential donor who is entitled to change their mind at any time before the operation. Potential donors must be given as much time as they need to make a decision and to ensure that all their concerns are answered and to make a decision.

34. To enable this, the potential donor must be provided with sufficient information by the practitioner in order for them to reach an informed decision. This should include:

- any information on surgical procedures and medical treatments to which a donor may be subjected and the risks involved in both the short and long term;
- the potential advantages for the recipient and that a positive outcome for the recipient cannot be guaranteed;
- the risks involved with the procedure, the chances of success and any possible side effects;
- information regarding tests for transmissible microbiological diseases, such as HIV, hepatitis B and C, HTLV (human T-cell lymphotropic virus) or other such diseases;
- the requirement for anonymity in non-directed and paired donations;
- what counselling services are available;
- the right to withdraw consent at any time;
- the consequences of the withdrawal of consent, especially if it is withdrawn late in the process;
- their right to be free of any kind of coercion or threat against them or anyone else (for

[101] Human Tissue Authority (HTA), *Code of Practice 2: Donation of organs, tissues and cells for transplantation* (HTA 11 July 2005) <http://www.hta.gov.uk/consult/codes/code2/>.

example, family or friends) and that consent deemed to be given under any such pressure will not be validated by the independent assessor;

- the illegality and consequences for someone who has been, or will be offered, given or in receipt of any type of payment or any other benefit for providing human tissue for a transplant. This would include such benefits as any promise of promotion, better work, better housing for themselves or for a member of their family, or the promise of preferential medical treatment;

- reimbursement for expenses or loss of earnings that are reasonably attributable to and directly result from organ donation may be made; and

- and whether they wish to make arrangements for life insurance.

The Act does not rule out the possibility of transplantation from incompetent adults and children, but any such transplants would have to be approved by the HTA and comply with regulations to be published by the Department of Health. Paragraph 46 of the HTA's draft Code of Practice suggests that:

Donation of whole or part organs by incompetent adults or children will be exceedingly rare. Should such a case arise, advice should be sought from the Human Tissue Authority about how to proceed.

It is also likely that, as a matter of good practice, the legality of any decision to remove an organ from an incompetent adult should first be confirmed by a court.

Living donation from children is not ruled out. Indeed, under section 2(3) of the Act, children who have sufficient maturity to consent to such a serious operation (see Chapter 4) might be able to make their own decision to donate an organ:

Section (2)

(3) Where—

  (a) the child concerned is alive,

  (b) neither a decision of his to consent to the activity, nor a decision of his not to consent to it, is in force, and

  (c) either he is not competent to deal with the issue of consent in relation to the activity or, though he is competent to deal with that issue, he fails to do so,

  'appropriate consent' means the consent of a person who has parental responsibility for him.

Where the child herself wishes to consent to donation, and is competent to do so, particular care should be taken to ensure that her decision is voluntary. Under paragraph 11 of the draft Code of Practice:

Good practice would be to consult the child's family and to involve them in the process of the child making a decision. It is also important to establish that a child's consent is voluntary and that they have not been unduly influenced by anyone. Consent for donation should be confirmed in writing and signed by the child in the presence of a witness who can attest the signature.[102]

---

[102] Human Tissue Authority (HTA), *Code of Practice 2: Donation of organs, tissues and cells for transplantation* (HTA 11 July 2005) <http://www.hta.gov.uk/consult/codes/code2/>.

Where the child lacks capacity or does not wish to make a decision, anyone with parental responsibility could give consent, but this alone would not be sufficient for the transplant to go ahead. Paragraph 9 of the draft Code of Practice states that:

Children will be considered as living organ donors only in extremely rare circumstances and this should go ahead only with the consent of the HTA.[103]

In addition, at common law, court approval should also be sought in the form of a declaration from the Family Division.

(b) Restrictions on live donation

The restrictions upon who may donate organs are not contained in the Act itself, but will be fleshed out in regulations. At the time of writing the regulations have not been published, but it seems likely that they will specify various protective mechanisms to ensure that consent is voluntary. ULTRA will be subsumed within the Human Tissue Authority, which will be responsible for deciding whether a proposed living donation should go ahead.

The Act does not specify that HTA approval is necessary for every living organ transplant, but paragraph 31 of the HTA's draft Code of Practice provides that:

The HTA must be satisfied that all legal requirements have been met before the transplant can take place.

All living organ donations—not just those between non-genetically related individuals—will now be independently assessed. Usually this will be done by independent assessors, rather than by the Authority itself. Paragraph 47 of the draft Code of Practice specifies that independent assessors will be appointed to act as the representatives of the HTA. They should be NHS consultants, or of equivalent standing; should not be working in the field of organ transplantation; and should have been trained and accredited by the HTA.[104] Under paragraph 48, these independent assessors are trained to consider for approval all living organ donations for transplantation that fall into the following categories:

Directed:

- Genetically related
- Emotionally related
- paired (the decision in these cases should be made by the HTA until practice is established as routine);

non-directed:

- domino
- altruistic (the decision in these cases should be made by the HTA until practice is established as routine).

Directed donation means that the donor's organs are to be donated to a specified individual. In non-directed donation, the recipient's identity is not known to the

---

[103] Ibid.   [104] Paras 55 and 56.

donor. Note that the Code treats *emotionally* related donors in the same way as genetically related donors, and therefore removes the anomaly in the previous legislation whereby it was more straightforward to donate an organ to a nephew than it was to one's spouse or long term partner. Paired donation takes place when someone volunteers to donate to someone they know, but they turn out to be a poor tissue match. In such circumstances, donor and donee may be paired with another similar couple so that each recipient can receive a well matched organ.

Non-directed donation include 'domino' transplants, where the primary purpose of the donation is the medical treatment of the donor. Because it is more straightforward to carry out heart and lung transplants than to transplant lungs alone, someone who is in need of a lung transplant might receive the heart and lungs from a cadaveric donor. In such circumstances, the recipient's own heart might become available for transplant into another person. This would, of course, be a living unrelated transplant, but, unlike most living donation, the donor is undergoing the operation *for her own benefit*, and so fewer ethical difficulties arise.

So how will the independent assessor decide whether a living organ transplant should go ahead? Paragraph 52 of the draft Code of Practice states that:

[T]he responsibility of the independent assessor is to interview the donor and, in some cases, the recipient on more than one occasion in order to provide a report on the proposed procedure which will include the following six points:

- Be satisfied that a registered medical practitioner has given the donor an explanation of the nature of the medical procedure for, and the risks involved in, the removal of the organ in question, and any other wider implications—for example, the risks to both donor and recipient and the effect upon children and any other dependent relatives.

- Be satisfied that the donor understands the nature of the medical procedure and the risks, as explained by the registered medical practitioner, and consents to the removal of the human tissue in question.

- Be satisfied that the donor's consent to the removal of the human tissue in question was not obtained by coercion or the offer of an inappropriate inducement.

- Be satisfied that the donor understands that she or he is entitled to withdraw consent at any time and understands the consequences of withdrawal for the recipient.

- In cases of organ donation, be satisfied that the donor–recipient relationship is as stated. This will usually require documentary and/or photographic evidence.

- Be satisfied that there were no difficulties in communicating with the donor and/or recipient and, if so, how they were overcome. Any interpreter used should have no personal involvement with either party to the transplant, have some understanding of medical matters and speak the donor's and recipient's language fluently or, in the case of someone with a speech or hearing disability, be experienced in the manner of communication required.

Under paragraph 53, the independent assessor must certify that he is satisfied that all the requirements have been met. This report will be valid for 6 months, after which a further report will become necessary, in case the circumstances have changed.

Note that entirely altruistic living donation, where donor and recipient are strangers, will now be possible but paragraph 71 states that because this is a new type of donation, advice must always be sought from the HTA, which will closely monitor this sort of donation. In addition, paragraph 73 of the draft Code of Practice specifies that all would-be altruistic, non-directed living donors must be interviewed by an independent consultant psychiatrist who must address the following issues:

- Make clear to the donor the meaning of non-directed organ donation. This must give clear and unambiguous instruction that under no circumstances will either the recipient or the donor know the other's identity.

- Be satisfied that a registered medical practitioner has given the donor an explanation of the nature of the medical procedure for, and the risks involved in, the removal of the organ in question, and any other wider implications—for example, the risks to both donor and recipient and the effect upon children and any other dependent relatives.

- Be satisfied that the donor understands the nature of the medical procedure and the risks, as explained by the registered medical practitioner, and consents to the removal of the organ in question.

- Be satisfied that the donor's consent to the removal of the organ in question was not obtained by coercion or the offer of an inducement.

- Be satisfied that the donor understands that he or she is entitled to withdraw consent at any time.

- Be satisfied that the donor has no evidence of current or past mental illness that affects his or her ability to donate altruistically with full, informed consent.

- Be satisfied that there were no difficulties in communicating with the donor and/or recipient and, if so, how they were overcome. Any interpreter used should have no personal involvement with either party to the transplant, have some understanding of medical matters and speak the donor's and recipient's language fluently or, in the case of someone with a speech or hearing disability, be experienced in the sort of communication required.

The psychiatrist's assessment will then be passed to a panel of the HTA, which must decide whether the transplant should go ahead.

(c) Payment

Section 32 of the 2004 Act continues the prohibition of payment for human organs.

Section 32 Prohibition of commercial dealings in human material for transplantation

(1) A person commits an offence if he—

    (a) gives or receives a reward for the supply of, or for an offer to supply, any controlled material;

    (b) seeks to find a person willing to supply any controlled material for reward;

    (c) offers to supply any controlled material for reward;

    (d) initiates or negotiates any arrangement involving the giving of a reward for the supply of, or for an offer to supply, any controlled material;

    (e) takes part in the management or control of a body of persons corporate or unincorporate whose activities consist of or include the initiation or negotiation of such arrangements.

Under sections 32(8) and (10), the prohibition covers both cadaveric and living organ donation. Notice that it is not just organ traffickers who would commit an offence under section 32(1). Recipients of organs too could face prosecution, as could anyone involved in arranging an organ sale. The maximum penalty for offences under section 32(1) is three years imprisonment. Under section 32(2), it is also an offence to publish or distribute an advertisement for the sale of an organ, and the maximum penalty is 51 weeks imprisonment.

Under section 32(6)(a) payment to the holder of a licence (that is, the hospital) in money or money's worth is not to be considered a reward if it 'is in consideration for transporting, removing, preparing, preserving, or storing controlled material'. This means that covering the costs associated with the transplantation process is not to be treated in the same way as a payment *for* an organ. Similarly, under section 32(7)(a), 'any expenses incurred in, or in connection with, transporting, removing, preparing, preserving or storing the material' are not to be treated as a reward.

Section 32(7)(c) permits payments to living organ donors to cover 'any expenses or loss of earnings incurred by the person from whose body the material comes so far as reasonably and directly attributable to his supplying the material from his body'. So a living organ donor could reasonably expect to receive compensation for time that she has to take off work during the organ donation process, and for associated expenses, such as travel costs. The reference to expenses or loss of earnings makes it clear that any such payments are not to be seen as payment for the organ itself, or even compensation for the inconvenience of donation, but rather must simply cover financial costs which are directly attributable to the donation.

(d) WHAT, IF ANYTHING, WOULD BE WRONG WITH A MARKET IN ORGANS?

Trafficking in organs is banned in the UK. A number of reasons are commonly put forward for maintaining a prohibition on the sale of organs.

First, it is argued that there is something intrinsically wrong with commodifying the human body, and that it would be either impossible or degrading to put a value on human body parts. Secondly, commercialization of organ transplantation is believed to undermine the principle that donation should be altruistic. Thirdly, in many parts of the world, living donors are paid for their organs. Wealthy patients have travelled to countries such as India, Iraq, Estonia, Moldova, Turkey, and Ukraine for transplant surgery, which depends upon the payment of relatively modest sums to local volunteers (in Iraq, one study found that donors were paid approximately $500,[105] and in India, payments of £360–£610 have been reported).[106] In the next extracts, existence of a flourishing market in organs in developing countries is cited as evidence that it is only poor and marginalized people who would agree to donate their organs for money.

---

[105] Michael M Friedlaender, 'The right to sell or buy a kidney: are we failing our patients?' (2002) 359 The Lancet 971–3, 971.
[106] Ganapati Mudur, 'Kidney trade arrest exposes loopholes in India's transplant laws' (2004) 328 BMJ 246.

G Berlinguer[107]

The truth of the matter is that, as far as human organs are concerned, the traffic always takes place between the South and the North of the world, or between the poor who sell and the rich who buy . . . [I]n the twenty-first century, the North could attempt to treat its more seriously ill by importing and using organs from members of the poorer classes, in particular from the under-developed countries. Supplies would be more than sufficient, as bodies are the only goods that these countries produce in abundance.

Madhav Goyal, Ravindra L Mehta, Lawrence J Schneiderman, and Ashwini R Sehgal[108]

We found widespread evidence of the sale of kidneys by poor people in India despite a legal ban on such sales. In a one month period, we were easily able to identify and interview more than 300 individuals who sold a kidney. Selling a kidney did not lead to a long-term economic benefit for the seller and was associated with a decline in health status.

Our quantitative findings, along with those of previous qualitative studies, undercut 5 key assumptions made by supporters of the sale of kidneys. First, although paying people to donate may have increased the supply of organs for transplantation, the financial incentive did not supplement underlying altruistic motivations. Only 5% of participants said wanting to help a sick person was a major factor in their decision to sell. Second, selling a kidney did not help poor donors overcome poverty. Family income actually declined by one third, and most participants were still in debt and living below the poverty line at the time of the survey. Third, regardless of these poor economic outcomes, sellers arguably have a right to make informed decisions about their own bodies. However, most participants would not recommend that others sell a kidney, which suggests that potential donors would be unlikely to sell a kidney if they were better informed of the likely outcomes. Fourth, safeguards such as eliminating middlemen or having an authoriza-tion committee did not appear to be effective. Middlemen and clinics paid less than they promised, and the authorization committees did not ensure that donations were motivated by altruism alone. Fifth, nephrectomy was associated with a decline in health status. Previous qualitative reports suggest that a diminished ability to perform physical labor may explain the observed worsening of economic status. . . .

A majority of donors were women. Given the often weak position of women in Indian society, the voluntary nature of some donations is questionable. In fact, 2 participants said that their husbands forced them to donate. . . .

The sale of kidneys by poor people in India does not lead to a tangible benefit for the seller. The value of paying for donations must be reexamined in light of these findings. Although patients with kidney failure deserve access to optimal treatment, such treatment should not be based on the exploitation of poor people.

Fourthly, some people believe that financial incentives may overbear a person's will, and thus cast doubt upon the voluntariness of their consent. EB Brody, for example argues that:

In countries without legal prohibition of organ selling, recruitment campaigns have used selling techniques which effectively negate informed consent among the poorest citizens for whom the possibility of a one-time financial gain of previously unimaginable proportions is so irresistible as

---

[107] *Everyday Bioethics: Reflections on Bioethical Choices in Daily Life* (Baywood Publishing New York 2003) 101.
[108] 'Economic and Health Consequences of Selling a Kidney in India' (2002) 288 JAMA 1589–93.

to obviate rational judgement. Financial incentives in these circumstances are tantamount to coercion.[109]

Fifthly, donation does involve some pain, discomfort and risk, and there are those who are troubled by the prospect of people assuming some risk to health in return for financial reward. Finally, a free market in organs would mean that only rich people would be able to afford to buy them, thus disrupting the principle that scarce health care resources should be distributed according to need rather than ability to pay.

Not all of these arguments withstand logical analysis. For example, it is not strictly true that it would be impossible to put a value on a human organ, nor that doing so is inevitably degrading. Tort law routinely quantifies the loss of various body parts. Victims of criminal injuries are paid damages, without any assumption that such damages undermine the intrinsic value of the human body. Secondly, even if poor people do find the offer of money in return for a kidney especially attractive, this must be equally true of many other sources of income which may pose some risk to a person's health (often much greater than the small risk of living with one kidney). Yet few people would argue that we should pay soldiers, and others whose jobs may pose a risk to their life or health, extremely modest wages in order to ensure that they have not signed up for a career in the army because of the lure of the salary. Indeed, such a suggestion would seem self-evidently both paternalistic and unfair.

Thirdly, it is clear that a black market in human organs already exists, and Radcliffe-Richards et al. argue that it is this, rather than a regulated market, which poses the greatest risk to organ donors.

J Radcliffe-Richards, AS Daar, RD Guttmann, R Hoffenberg, I Kennedy, M Lock, RA Sells, N Tilney[110]

The commonest objection to kidney selling is expressed on behalf of the vendors: the exploited poor, who need to be protected against the greedy rich. However, the vendors are themselves anxious to sell, and see this practice as the best option open to them. . . . To this argument it is replied that the vendors' apparent choice is not genuine. It is said that they are likely to be too uneducated to understand the risks, and that this precludes informed consent. It is also claimed that, since they are coerced by their economic circumstances, their consent cannot count as genuine.

Although both these arguments appeal to the importance of autonomous choice, they are quite different. The first claim is that the vendors are not competent to make a genuine choice within a given range of options. The second, by contrast, is that poverty has so restricted the range of options that organ selling has become the best, and therefore, in effect, that the range is too small. . . .

If our ground for concern is that the range of choices is too small, we cannot improve matters by removing the best option that poverty has left, and making the range smaller still. . . . The only way to improve matters is to lessen the poverty until organ selling no longer seems the best option; and if that could be achieved, prohibition would be irrelevant because nobody would want to sell.

The other line of argument may seem more promising, since ignorance does preclude informed consent. However, the likely ignorance of the subjects is not a reason for banning altogether a

---

[109] *Biomedical Technology and Human Rights* (Unesco 1993) 100.
[110] 'The case for allowing kidney sales' International Forum for Transplant Ethics (1998) 351 The Lancet 1950–2.

procedure for which consent is required. In other contexts, the value we place on autonomy leads us to insist on information and counselling, and that is what it should suggest in the case of organ selling as well. . . .

[A]ll the evidence we have shows that there is much more scope for exploitation and abuse when a supply of desperately wanted goods is made illegal. It is, furthermore, not clear why it should be thought harder to police a legal trade than the present complete ban.

Furthermore, even if vendors and recipients would always be at risk of exploitation, that does not alter the fact that if they choose this option, all alternatives must seem worse to them. Trying to end exploitation by prohibition is rather like ending slum dwelling by bulldozing slums: it ends the evil in that form, but only by making things worse for the victims. If we want to protect the exploited, we can do it only by removing the poverty that makes them vulnerable, or, failing that, by controlling the trade. . . .

The weakness of the familiar arguments suggests that they are attempts to justify the deep feelings of repugnance which are the real driving force of prohibition, and feelings of repugnance among the rich and healthy, no matter how strongly felt, cannot justify removing the only hope of the destitute and dying.

Fourthly, as we saw in Chapter 4, the principle of patient autonomy means that we let people assume considerable risks to their own health by refusing life-sustaining treatment, and that they are entitled to exercise this choice for irrational reasons or even for no reason at all. Is it then unduly paternalistic to prevent someone from incurring a less serious risk to health which might save someone's life?

Fifthly, nor is it clear that paid organ donation is incompatible with altruism: we would permit a mother to donate a kidney to her son if he has kidney failure, but what if the son's condition is instead a rare form of cancer, and optimum treatment is expensive and only available abroad. We would forbid this mother from selling a kidney in order to pay for her son's life-saving treatment, even though her motivation is just as altruistic as the mother whose son happens to have renal failure.

Sixthly, as Stephen Wilkinson points out, there is something wrong with the argument that we should not allow paid organ donation because it is risky. If this is true, then unpaid organ donation is equally risky, and presumably should also be prohibited:

No matter how dangerous paid donation is, it needn't . . . be any more risky than unpaid donation, since the mere fact of payment doesn't *add* any danger. So if paid donation is wrong because of the danger to which the donor is subjected, then free donation must also be wrong on the very same grounds. Free donation, though, is not wrong; on the contrary, we tend to regard it as commendable, heroic even. Therefore paid donation isn't wrong either—or, if it is wrong, it's wrong because of something other than the danger to which the donor is subjected.[111]

Seventhly, allowing payments for organs does not necessarily mean embracing a completely free market. Instead, it would be possible for payments to be made by the NHS rather than individual recipients, and for the organs to then be distributed according to need. Because the cost savings of transplantation are so enormous—recall that the average kidney transplant will save the NHS £128,000—payments to donors could

---

[111] Stephen Wilkinson, *Bodies for Sale: Ethics and Exploitation in the Human Body Trade* (Routledge London 2003) 108.

still be cost-effective. In the next extract, Charles Erin and John Harris suggest that it is possible to contemplate an 'ethical market' in organs.

Charles A Erin and John Harris[112]

There is a lot of hypocrisy about the ethics of buying and selling organs and indeed other body products and services . . . What it usually means is that everyone is paid but the donor. The surgeons and medical team are paid, the transplant coordinator does not go unremunerated, and the recipient receives an important benefit in kind. Only the unfortunate and heroic donor is supposed to put up with the insult of no reward, to add to the insult of the operation . . .

The bare bones of an ethical market would look like this: the market would be confined to a self-governing geopolitical area such as a nation state or indeed the European Union. Only citizens resident within the union or state could sell into the system and they and their families would be equally eligible to receive organs. Thus organ vendors would know they were contributing to a system which would benefit them and their families and friends since their chances of receiving an organ in case of need would be increased by the existence of the market. (If this were not the case the main justification for the market would be defeated.) There would be only one purchaser, an agency like the National Health Service (NHS), which would buy all organs and distribute according to some fair conception of medical priority. There would be no direct sales or purchases, no exploitation of low income countries and their populations (no buying in Turkey or India to sell in Harley Street). The organs would be tested for HIV, etc, their provenance known, and there would be strict controls and penalties to prevent abuse.

Prices would have to be high enough to attract people into the marketplace but dialysis and other alternative care does not come cheap. Sellers of organs would know they had saved a life and would be reasonably compensated for their risk, time, and altruism, which would be undiminished by sale. We do not after all regard medicine as any the less a caring profession because doctors are paid. So long as thousands continue to die for want of donor organs we must urgently consider and implement ways of increasing the supply. A market of the sort outlined above is surely one method worthy of active and urgent consideration.

Finally, insofar as the offer of money might persuade someone to volunteer to be a live organ donor, we should, as J Harvey explains, perhaps be equally or even more concerned about non-financial pressure, such as that exerted within families. If a person's consent can only be considered voluntary if they could realistically have said 'no', it is not obvious that payment is any more coercive than familial obligations.

J Harvey[113]

Now I think there is financial pressure when the potential donor is in poverty. And perhaps it may be argued that this alone is sufficient for banning all paid-for donations. But then, in consistency, the same reasoning should be applied to related donors: since *some* of them are open to heavy psychological and emotional pressure (for example, perhaps by being the submissive and 'guilt'-ridden offspring of an extremely domineering and now ailing parent), then all donations from relatives should be forbidden. This course is not advocated in connection with related donors. Rather, the difficult task of distinguishing between truly vulnerable relatives and those not vulnerable is undertaken. This would point to our attempting the analogous task in the case of paid for donations, namely the task of distinguishing between the truly financially vulnerable and those not so.

112 'An ethical market in human organs' (2003) 29 Journal of Medical Ethics 137–8.
113 'Paying organ donors' (1990) 16 Journal of Medical Ethics 117–19.

5. XENOTRANSPLANTATION

Although whole organ transplants from animals to humans are still at the experimental stage, other sorts of animal tissues have been used in human medicine for some time. Pig heart valves, for example, can be processed so that they act like inert material rather than living tissue, and they have been inserted into human patients for more than thirty years.

There have also been examples of animal-to-human whole organ transplants, but none have been successful, with maximum survival times of a few months. In the most (in)famous case, a baboon heart was transplanted into a 14-day-old neonate, known as 'Baby Fae', and she died within three weeks. Her parents were poor and uneducated, and the consent form they signed appeared to overstate the likely benefits from the transplant. It suggested that:

Long-term survival with appropriate growth and development may be possible following heart transplantation . . . this research is an effort to provide your baby with some hope of immediate and long term survival.[114]

In the next extract, Jeffrey Barker and Lauren Polcrack explain that the history of experimentation in xenotransplantation is not 'ethically promising'.

Jeffrey H Barker and Lauren Polcrack[115]
The history of xenotransplantation as an experimental procedure is not ethically promising. Xenotransplantation in human beings is not a new phenomenon, and throughout its history there have been serious ethical lapses in obtaining informed consent. Many early xenotransplant recipients were unconscious and therefore never consented to the procedure; many were poor and uneducated. Some were prisoners, some were children. The first cardiac xenotransplantation subject (in 1964) was a deaf-mute who never consented to the procedure, and the consent form signed by his step-sister did not mention a non-human organ. Throughout the history of xenotransplantation, the medically, ethically and socially vulnerable have been used as experimental subjects.

The first documented xenotransplantation involving a human host occurred in 1902, when a pig kidney was used in the case of a young woman suffering from end-stage renal failure. Early in the twentieth century, kidneys were transplanted into humans from rabbits, pigs, lambs, goats, macaques, chimpanzees, marmosets and baboons. In each case, however, the transplant failed, and in most cases the patient died as a result.

The principal reason for pursuing research into xenotransplantation is that it would enable many more patients to receive organs that might save their lives. If we could breed animals for their organs, in the same way as we breed them for food, the organ shortage might disappear. Not only would this benefit the thousands of patients currently on the organ waiting list, but it could potentially eliminate the risks to health incurred by living organ donors.

---

[114] Jeffrey H Barker and Lauren Polcrack, 'Respect for persons, informed consent and the assessment of infectious disease risks in xenotransplantation' (2001) 4 Medicine, Health Care and Philosophy 53–70, 59.
[115] 'Respect for persons, informed consent and the assessment of infectious disease risks in xenotransplantation' (2001) 4 Medicine, Health Care and Philosophy 53–70, 56–7.

The question of *which* animal species should be chosen as the source of organs for transplant is also controversial. For a number of reasons, primates have been rejected and pigs appear to be the most likely source. First, chimpanzees and other primates, such as orangutans, are endangered species. Secondly, primates are much 'closer' to humans: they look more like us and we do not eat them. Although note that Marie Fox suggests such reasoning is morally arbitrary.

Marie Fox[116]

Certainly, given that pigs and primates are alike in the morally relevant respects, since both species are sentient, intelligent and sociable, the real reason to distinguish them seems not to rest on mental ability or capacity for suffering but on practical or emotional grounds. . . . [B]y permitting use of certain animals, but not others, as research tools and potential organ donors, law reflects the moral arbitrariness in our response to them.

Thirdly, the chance of zoonosis, that is cross-species disease transmission, seems to be more likely between more closely related species. Fourthly, pigs breed much more quickly than primates, and the organ supply could therefore be replenished more quickly. Finally, pig organs are about the same size as human organs.

Despite the obvious advantages in locating a potentially unlimited supply of transplantable organs, there are several reasons why xenotransplantation continues to be extremely controversial. These can be categorized as either practical problems, such as the risk of rejection and disease transmission, and ethical problems, such as animal welfare considerations. We consider these in turn, before looking at the current regulation of xenotransplantation in the UK.

(a) PRACTICAL PROBLEMS

(1) REJECTION

The first major obstacle to successful xenotransplantation is the likelihood that the animal's organ will be rejected immediately. Although immunosuppressant therapy can now largely counterbalance the risk of rejection in human-to-human transplants, much larger doses might be necessary in animal-to-human transplants, and if given in sufficient quantities these drugs will destroy a person's immune system, and themselves cause death. The use of animal organs will often also prompt what is known as a hyper-acute rejection reaction within minutes or hours of the transplant, and this cannot be adequately controlled by existing immunosuppressants. Instead, a more promising solution to the problem of rejection is to introduce human genes into the animal's genome, thus suppressing the gene which causes hyper-acute rejection. Such animals might then be cloned in order to increase the supply of suitable organs. There has been some success in creating transgenic pigs, and experiments involving primates appear to indicate that the rejection of organs from transgenic pigs can be controlled

---

[116] 'Re-thinking Kinship: Law's Construction of the Animal Body' (2004) 57 Current Legal Problems 469–93, 476–7.

using drugs. Recently survival times of 5 and 8 weeks have been reported in baboons which have received hearts from transgenic pigs.[117]

(2) RISK OF INFECTION

Progress in minimizing the risk of hyper-acute rejection means that the most pressing danger currently presented by xenotransplantation is the possibility of cross-species infection. Variant Creutzfeldt-Jakob disease (vCJD), the human form of bovine spongiform encephalitis (BSE) or 'mad cow' disease, is a dramatic example of cross-species disease transmission. Some people also believe that HIV and AIDS originated in primates. The risk of infection from transplantation is even greater since placing an animal organ inside a human body provides a particularly easy and direct way for a disease to cross the species barrier.

In particular, it is thought that some viruses, such as the porcine endogenous retrovirus (PERV), which is harmless to pigs, and incorporated into the pig genome, would be impossible to eliminate from transgenic pigs, and might be able to cross the species barrier and cause cancer, or irreversible damage to the human immune system. Any risk of cross-species infection would, of course, be exacerbated if the recipient is taking immunosuppressive drugs which reduce her ability to fight any new virus.

It is important to remember that if a disease crosses the species barrier, the risk of infection is faced not only by the recipient herself, but also by her close contacts and the rest of society, which as we can see in the next sections, raises a number of complicated ethical issues.

(a) Impact upon the recipient and her close contacts

Could someone give a valid consent to receiving an animal's organ in the light of the risk of cross-species infection? The first problem here is whether their consent could ever be adequately informed. Insofar as the risks of cross-species infection cannot be known with any certainty before trials in humans have begun, and perhaps for some considerable time afterwards, it would be impossible to give a potential recipient full disclosure of the risks associated with xenotransplantation. As the Nuffield Report into the ethics of xenotransplantation explains:

It is not possible to predict or quantify the risk that xenotransplantation will result in the emergence of new human diseases. But in the worst case, the consequences could be far-reaching and difficult to control. . . . Put bluntly, it may be possible to identify any infectious organism transmitted by xenografting only if it causes disease in human beings, and after it has started to do so.[118]

Since the first patients to receive xenografts will be doing so as part of a clinical trial, the more stringent duties of disclosure that apply when obtaining a subject's consent to participation in a research trial apply (see further Chapter 8). If there is an

---

[117] CGA McGregor, GW Byrne, WR Davies, K Oi, VP Rao, HD Tazelaar, RC Walker, CJ Gostout, and JS Logan, 'Cardiac xenotransplantation: Early success in the orthotopic position' (2005) 24 The Journal of Heart and Lung Transplantation, S95.

[118] Nuffield Council on Bioethics, *Animal-to-Human Transplants: The Ethics of Xenotransplantation* (Nuffield Council on Bioethics London 1996) paras 10.25, 6.14.

unknown and unquantifiable risk to the recipients' health, it is arguable that they could never give sufficiently informed consent to xenotransplantation.

A second problem comes from the principle that participants in therapeutic research trials should be assured of the best current treatment (see Chapter 8). Initially at least, allografts (human-to-human transplants) will continue to be the best treatment for individuals with acute organ failure. It might be argued that xenotransplantation trials should therefore only recruit patients who would, for some reason, not be eligible for a human organ transplant. Patients who are not on the organ donor waiting list might be offered a xenograft on the grounds that this could have a greater chance of success than the treatment—i.e. nothing—which would otherwise be available to them.

Related to this, if the first participants in clinical trials are asked to choose between immediate death or the unknown risks associated with xenotransplantation, it is of course readily understandable that they would opt to receive an animal organ. But being faced with such an invidious choice leads Sheila McLean to suggest that 'there must be questions about whether or not the vulnerability of the patients likely to be involved in early trials would cast doubt upon their competence or capacity to consent'.[119]

Of course, if trials were confined to potential organ recipients who are unable to wait for a human organ, or too sick to be placed upon the organ donor register, success rates of xenografts are likely to be lower than we might expect if comparatively healthy and robust patients were also included.

A further issue is the restrictions which would have to be placed on xenograft recipients. It would be necessary to monitor their health for the rest of their lives. Recipients would not be allowed to give blood or themselves donate organs. They might have to agree to autopsy after death, and if infection occurred, very serious restrictions might have to be placed upon their liberty. It is also possible that their present and future sexual partners would have to be monitored, and that, at least at first, their freedom to have children might be restricted, and they would be told to use barrier methods of contraception. Recipients could be asked to consent in advance to these limitations, and if the alternative is death, it is understandable that a person might be willing to give up some civil liberties in order to obtain a potentially life-saving transplant. But in the next extract, Jeffrey Barker and Lauren Polcrack question whether it would be possible to give fully informed consent to such serious curtailment of one's future liberty.

Jeffrey H Barker and Lauren Polcrack[120]

[T]here are significant concerns with regard to the individual informed consent of the potential xenograft recipient. The recipient must understand as completely as possible the risks to him or herself, to his or [her] contacts, and the risks to society at large, and must be willing to move forward despite those risks. The immediate contacts of the potential recipient must also consent to the probable risks. Any clinical trials of xenotransplantation would require long-term—and probably lifetime—monitoring and surveillance of recipients and their contacts, with the possibil-

---

[119] 'Xenotransplantation: A Pig in a Poke?' (2004) 57 Current Legal Problems 443–68, 464.
[120] 'Respect for persons, informed consent and the assessment of infectious disease risks in xenotransplantation' (2001) 4 Medicine, Health Care and Philosophy 53–70, 66.

ity of lifetime quarantine should serious xenosis occur. All recipients would need to be registered and monitored in order to protect public health. Truly informed consent to these types of radical changes in personal freedom would be difficult to obtain.

If third parties, such as sexual partners, would be subject to surveillance and restrictions upon their liberty, should their consent also be necessary? Informing them about the recipient's medical treatment would not only represent a breach of confidentiality, but also, as Sheila McLean points out in the next extract, it would be most unusual to give a third party a right of veto over another's medical treatment. McLean further highlights the difficulties in enforcing the sort of surveillance regime which many people think would be necessary following the first xenografts.

Sheila McLean[121]

If the consent of third parties is an essential prerequisite to a xenograft, then they are placed in the unusual position of being able, by refusal, to prevent the potential recipient from accepting a therapy which may be of benefit. Secondly, it is unclear just how such agreements [to restrict liberty] could be policed; agreement pre-transplant does not guarantee compliance post-transplant, yet compliance is presumably of the highest order of significance otherwise it would not be required in the first place. What, for example, would be done if a recipient decided not to use barrier contraception? It must be doubted whether or not the state could effectively enter the bedroom and prevent this from happening . . . To continue with this example, it must be asked what would be the state's authority should an individual xenotransplant recipient or the partner of one become pregnant. Could the state compel a pregnancy termination, and if so on what grounds—ethical or legal? In other words, if the surveillance regime is necessary—as seems to be generally agreed—then there are serious concerns about its enforceability. Indeed the UKXIRA working party which drafted the surveillance document noted that any attempt to require rather than invite patients to agree to the limitations to be imposed on their future life would be likely to run contrary to the terms of the Human Rights legislation, in particular Article 8.

(b) Impact upon society

Although it is clearly the recipient of an animal organ who is most immediately at risk from cross-species infection, transmission to others may be possible, and hence xenotransplantation also poses as yet unquantifiable risks to public health. Since it will never be possible to conclusively determine that no such risk exists, we instead have to determine whether the degree of risk is acceptable.

Interestingly, xenotransplantation reverses the usual risk/benefit calculation of participation in a research trial. Generally, as we saw in Chapter 8, the research subject assumes some risk to her own health and wellbeing for the benefit of scientific knowledge. Although the subject may hold out some hope of obtaining a health benefit from the trial, this is not the principal purpose of the research, which is instead to benefit society through the development of effective treatments. In xenotransplantation, the benefit may be to the individual recipient, since it is likely that she would die soon without a transplant. The risk, however, may be to society as a whole through the introduction of animal viruses into the human population. Unlike the individual research subject, it would be impossible to obtain the *public*'s informed consent

---

[121] 'Xenotransplantation: A Pig in a Poke?' (2004) 57 Current Legal Problems 443–68, 459.

before a clinical trial began. Instead Jeffrey Barker and Lauren Polcrack advocate greater public participation in the decision to go ahead with clinical trials.

Jeffrey H Barker and Lauren Polcrack[122]

Xenografts put at risk not only the recipient but those directly associated with the recipient, including caregivers and family members. They also put at risk the public at large by creating the distinct possibility of introducing new or modified pathogens into the human species, pathogens whose virulence, infectivity and mode of retransmission, and potential for treatment are all highly uncertain . . .

Where there is a significant risk to the public, as we believe there is in xenotransplantation, there must be a public process for informing and educating the public, and for ascertaining the willingness of the public to encounter, to consent to these risks. This process of 'collective informed consent' requires not merely public education but active public participation in the decision-making process.

A further problem, as Sykes et al. explain in the next extract, is that 'xenotourism' is likely to mean that it will be very difficult for any country to successfully eliminate the risks posed by xenotransplantion.

Megan Sykes, Anthony d'Apice and Mauro Sandrin[123]

The potential risks of xenotransplantation will not be confined to the country in which the transplant is performed. Even the most assiduous safety efforts of any nation or group of nations may be ineffective in the absence of internationally agreed regulations and monitoring procedures for xenotransplantation. This problem arises because patients are mobile and could receive a xenograft in one country, which may or may not have appropriate regulatory and monitoring processes, and later leave that country and enter another without ever having to state that they are the recipient of a xenograft. In ethical terms, the principle of justice requires all nations to bear their fair share of responsibility regarding the control of infectious disease risks.

At present, no country's immigration authorities routinely ask a question that would reveal that a particular person is a xenograft recipient. The scale of such 'casual' xenotourism is likely to be small. However, there is a risk that entrepreneurial xenotransplanters may deliberately set up business in countries with minimal or no regulation and set about attracting foreigners with organ failure to come to be transplanted and then return home. The absence of questioning about xenotransplantation upon re-entry, and the absence of a mechanism for bringing such patients into surveillance programs in their home countries almost guarantee that such patients will avoid surveillance when they return home.

(b) ETHICAL PROBLEMS

(1) REVULSION

Many people are repelled by the idea of transplanting animal organs into human beings. For some, this will be prompted by their religious beliefs. In Judaism, for example, the pig is not considered fit for human consumption, and the use of pig

---

[122] 'Respect for persons, informed consent and the assessment of infectious disease risks in xenotransplantation' (2001) 4 Medicine, Health Care and Philosophy 53–70, 65.
[123] 'Position Paper of the Ethics Committee of the International Xenotransplantation Association' (2003) 10 Xenotransplantation 194–203.

organs for transplantation might be similarly unacceptable. In order to accommodate these strongly held views, in any future regulation of xenotransplantation there would undoubtedly be a conscientious objection clause, similar to that in the Abortion Act, so that doctors did not have to participate in xenotransplantation; and patients too would be reassured their refusal to accept an animal organ would not affect their eligibility for a human organ. Provided that no-one is compelled to take part in xenotransplantation against their wishes, it would seem inappropriate for some people's instinctive revulsion to be allowed to determine whether xenotransplantation goes ahead, especially since potential recipients' lives may be at stake.

There have also been suggestions that introducing human genes into pigs, and animal organs into humans threatens to blur the barriers between the species. Jason Scott Robert and Françoise Baylis have, for example, suggested that while:

[s]cientifically, there might be no such thing as fixed species identities or boundaries. Morally, however, we rely on the notion of fixed species identities and boundaries in the way we live our lives and treat other creatures.[124]

This leads them to conclude that:

All things considered, the engineering of creatures that are part human and part nonhuman animal is objectionable because the existence of such beings would introduce inexorable moral confusion in our existing relationships with nonhuman animals and in our future relationships with part-human hybrids.[125]

Of course, barriers between the species are constantly evolving, albeit slowly. We share about 98.5 per cent of our DNA with chimpanzees, and so basing moral status upon biology is fraught with difficulty. Moreover, pig heart valves have been used to treat humans for many years, and there would seem to be no doubt that patients who have received them continue to be members of the human species. Perhaps, as Henry T Greely suggests in the following extract, it is a question of degree.

Henry T Greely[126]

[A]fter a few early reports of patient qualms, the use of pig heart valves for medical procedures now raises little concern. Apart from pragmatic fear of the passage of disease and some animal rights concerns that are quite distinct from issues of chimerism . . . other plausible single organ xenotransplants into human beings seem unlikely to be heavily controversial. On the other hand, if it were feasible to transplant a chimpanzee brain into a human, or if a human were given a large number of organs from nonhuman sources, people might worry whether the resulting organism was really human . . .

Chimeras made by moving human parts into nonhuman beings would raise concerns when they are significant enough to raise the question of the possible humanity of the recipient. In both cases the 'importance' of the parts—brains and gametes are more important than heart valves or skin—and the number of parts moved—transplanting five visceral organs would be more troubling than transplanting one—seems significant. So do the uses of such part-human, part-nonhuman chimeras. Making a chimera of a human and a nonhuman is much less controversial when done for medical purposes than if such a creature were made for entertainment or 'art'. The

---

[124] 'Crossing Species Boundaries' (2003) 3 American Journal of Bioethics 1–13, 6.
[125] Ibid, 9.
[126] 'Defining Chimeras . . . and Chimeric Concerns' (2003) 3 American Journal of Bioethics 17–20, 19.

acceptability of totally nonhuman chimeras might also depend on their uses—chimeras as human food might raise special concerns for some because they are eaten.

(2) ANIMAL RIGHTS

It is often said that if we are prepared to breed and kill animals for food, we should logically also accept xenotransplantation, especially since the purpose of breeding animals for their organs (saving lives) would seem to be more valuable and of more immediate benefit than the production of meat. This simple analogy between meat-eating and xenotransplantion has, however, been challenged for a number of reasons. First, Robin Downie has argued that:

whereas the eating of animal flesh may or may not be ethically right, it is 'natural' in the sense that many other animal species in fact do it and (as has been claimed by some) human beings are biologically carnivorous or at least omnivorous. On the other hand, the transplant of animal tissue into human beings is 'unnatural'.[127]

Of course, as Downie himself admits, all medical interventions, including most obviously human-to-human organ transplants, are also 'unnatural'. Downie therefore goes on to suggest that the insertion of human genes into animals and then transplanting their organs into humans is 'profoundly different from previous medical interventions'. This is, of course, a subjective judgement, and it is not clear why xenotransplantation is necessarily any more 'profoundly unnatural' than, say, in vitro fertilization or stem cell research.

Secondly, donor animals would have to be bred and raised in isolation in completely barren and sterile surroundings, and genetic modification might further impair their quality of life. Would this represent a more substantial interference with their welfare than happens when they are bred for their meat? Possibly, although it should be remembered that the conditions in 'battery farms', and the techniques used to produce veal and foie gras are hardly conducive to animals' wellbeing. Of course the inhumane treatment of animals by the food industry does not necessarily justify inhumane treatment in pursuit of organ transplantation. But insofar as the goal of xenotransplantion would be to save the lives of people who would otherwise die due to the shortage of human organs, there would seem to be no reason to be more squeamish about animal welfare where the goal is transplant retrieval than where the goal is to produce cheap chicken or foie gras.

A better analogy might be with the use of animals in research, when it is common for animals to be specially bred to take part in experiments, and to subsequently be killed. In animal experiments, we are using animals in order to further scientific knowledge and to improve the medical treatments that are available to humans. The benefits to individuals may be less direct and immediate than they would be if xenotransplantation were to be successful, but the ethical issues are similar.

Just like experiments on animals and non-vegetarianism, xenotransplantation rests upon the assumption that it is ethically acceptable to kill other species in order to save human lives. This is, according to commentators such as Peter Singer, an example of

---

[127] 'Xenotransplantation' (1997) 23 Journal of Medical Ethics 205–6, 206.

speciesism (that is, favouring one's own species and devaluing other species), which is said to be as morally objectionable or racism or sexism.

Peter Singer[128]

The idea of using animals as a source for organ donation is an example of speciesism, premised as it is on the idea that animals are things for us to use as best suits our own interests, without much concern for the interests of the animals themselves. Perhaps the easiest way to see this is to ask yourself the following question: why should we be prepared to accept the use of organs from animals, but not be prepared to take them from human infants who are, and always will be, less intellectually developed than the nonhuman animals. . . .

What kind of ethic can tell us that it is all right to rear sentient animals in barren cages that give them no decent life at all, and then kill them to take their organs, while refusing to permit us to take the organ of a human being who is not, and never can be, even minimally conscious? Obviously a speciesist ethic . . . My objection is not that we value the life of a normal, self-aware human being, one with a vivid awareness of the future and a desire to continue to be around next week, next month and next year, ahead of the life of an animal who lacks self-awareness and is incapable of any such future-orientated desires. Such an evaluation can be defended, without invoking an arbitrary preference for our species. My objection is to the fact that we disregard the interests of nonhuman animals by ranking them as less worthy of our concern and respect than *any* member of our species, no matter how limited in capacities and potential. . . .

In a world that needlessly rears several billion animals in factory farms each year and then kills them to satisfy a mere preference of taste, it is difficult to argue persuasively against the rearing and slaughter of a few thousand animals so that their organs can be used to save people's lives. That, however, is not a reason for using animals: it is, rather, a reason for changing our views about animals. In a better world, a world that cared properly for the interests of animals, we would do our utmost to avoid choices that pit the essential interests of animals against our own . . . This might involve more effective ways of obtaining organs from humans who are brain dead, or cortically dead. It might involve the development of artificial organs. Or it might involve using our limited medical resources to educate people in looking after the organs with which they were born.

Why do we think that human beings' lives are more valuable and important than animals' lives? Often some appeal is made to distinctively human qualities, such as sentience, consciousness, and the capacity for reason. But as Singer explains, the problem here is that not all human beings possess these characteristics—patients in a persistent vegetative state or anencephalic infants, for example, do not—whereas they are possessed to some degree by animals such as chimpanzees and dolphins. If it is these qualities, and not species membership per se, that count morally, then as Jonathan Hughes points out, two possible consequences follow. Either we should refuse to contemplate using animals which possess the relevant characteristics as xenograft sources. Or we should also be prepared to take organs from human beings who have irrevocably lost the capacities in question.[129]

---

[128] 'Xenotransplantation and Speciesism' (1992) 24 Transplantation Proceedings 728–32.
[129] RG Frey, 'Medicine, animal experimentation, and the moral problem of unfortunate humans' (1996) 12 Social Philosophy and Policy 181–211.

Jonathan Hughes[130]

Justification for both medical and culinary uses of animals typically appeal to the different mental capacities of humans and other animals. Imposing harms on animals in order to benefit humans is acceptable, it is argued, because the harms and benefits that humans are capable of experiencing are greater than those that can be experienced by other animals. The physical pains suffered by animals, according to this argument, are less significant than those suffered by humans, because animals are less sensitive, or because they lack the capacity for fearful anticipation or distressing memory which amplify the effects of physical pain in humans. And death matters less for animals, it is argued, because animals have less to lose than humans in the form of potential for future pleasures and satisfactions, or because the loss of these things matters less to creatures who lack our capacity to foresee, desire and plan for them. Both the Nuffield and Department of Health reports appeal to arguments of this kind in order to justify xenotransplantation, citing the different capacities of different species in support of the view that it is acceptable to use pigs, but not primates, as xenograft donors . . .

Unfortunately for the reports, this kind of argument is vulnerable to a well-known objection. The problem is that capacities for pleasure and pain, fulfilment and suffering vary not only between but within species, including humans. So while it is true that the capacities of a normal adult exceed those of a pig, the same cannot be said for all humans. There are many whose mental capacities are severely and tragically impaired, and it follows that if we are prepared to take organs from animals on the grounds of their limited capacities we should also be prepared to take the organs of those humans whose capacities are similarly restricted. Or conversely, if we insist that we should *not* take organs from such humans, then consistency demands that we refrain also from taking the organs of animals with similar or greater capacities.

Against this, AL Caplan argues that humans do matter more morally because of their relationships with others.

AL Caplan[131]

Severely retarded children and those born with devastating conditions such as anencephaly have never had the capacities and abilities that confer a greater moral standing on humans as compared with animals. Should they be used as the first donors and recipients in xenografting research instead of primates?

The reason they should not has nothing to do with the properties, capacities and abilities of children or infants who lack and have always lacked significant degrees of intellectual and cognitive function. The reason they should not be used is because of the impact using them would have upon other human beings, especially their parents and relatives. A severely retarded child can still be the object of much love, attention, and devotion from his or her parents. These feelings and the abilities and capacities that generate them are deserving of moral respect. Animals do not appear to be capable of such feelings.

If a human mother were to learn that her severely retarded son had been used in lethal xenografting research, she would mourn this fact for the rest of her days. A baboon, monkey, dog or pig would not. . . . Relationships and the impact of action on others count in ethics; and since this is less true or not at all true for animals, a bright chimp does not have greater moral standing than a severely retarded young boy, even if their intrinsic capacities are such that the chimp can do more than the boy. . . .

---

[130] 'Xenografting: ethical issues' (1998) 24 Journal of Medical Ethics 18–24, 23.
[131] *Am I my Brother's Keeper? The Ethical Frontiers of Biomedicine* (Indiana UP 1997) 111.

Humans have, or at least have the potential if they are children, to do more than feel pain or experience pleasure. They experience more than animals do because they exist in social relationships with others that confer meaning and significance upon even the most deformed, disabled, or damaged member of this species. Given the choice between the need to kill a pig and the need to kill a child, the choice seems obvious, even if the child is retarded, mentally ill, or a newborn without consciousness. Why? Because the death of the child not only means the loss of the potential that the child might have had but also has an adverse impact on the child's relatives and family and an even wider negative impact on human beings who assign value, if only symbolic, to the rules and customs that protect their own lives and those of their children. Pigs do not construct such systems and do not live in accordance with such symbols, and these facts are morally relevant when life hangs in the balance.

It might also be argued that we should not address the question of xenotransplantation's ethical legitimacy in isolation from other possible solutions to the shortage of organs, especially since human organs are, at least for the foreseeable future, likely to offer recipients better health prospects than animal organs. For example, we could massively increase the availability of organs if we moved away from a consent model for cadaveric donation, and instead treated the organs of the recently dead as a public resource. This would, admittedly, offend some people's desire to control what happens to their bodies after death, and it could cause distress to their relatives. But animal rights advocates might argue that these harms are relatively trivial when compared with the harm endured by a sentient animal, which is bred in an entirely sterile environment and then killed for its organs.

(c) XENOTRANSPLANTATION IN THE UK

Following two major reports from the Nuffield Council on Bioethics[132] and the Advisory Group on the Ethics of Xenotransplantation set up by the government,[133] there is currently a moratorium on clinical trials involving humans. Both reports concluded that there is as yet insufficient information about animal viruses, such as PERV, and their capacity to spread to the human population. But both reports also agreed that once trials involving primates establish that xenotransplantation meets some threshold level of safety, the possible benefits to humans outweigh animal welfare considerations. In principle, then, both reports concluded that xenotransplantation is ethically acceptable.

The Nuffield Council on Bioethics and the Government's Advisory Group recommended that a National Standing Committee should be set up to continue to monitor new scientific developments, and to ensure that proper ethical standards were maintained. This led to the establishment in 1997 of the Xenotransplantation Interim Regulatory Authority (UKXIRA). In the UK, any clinical trial involving human subjects must not only receive local research ethics committee approval (see Chapter 8), but it must also be scrutinized by UKXIRA, and have the prior written approval of the

[132] *Animal-to-Human Transplants: The Ethics of Xenotransplantation* (Nuffield Council on Bioethics London 1996).

[133] *Animal Tissue into Humans: A Report by the Advisory Group on the Ethics of Xenotransplantation* (DoH 1997).

Secretary of State for Health.[134] Because the Home Office has responsibility for the Animal (Scientific Procedures) Act 1986, considered in Chapter 8, which protects the welfare of animals used in scientific experiments, permission to remove tissues from animals for transplant into humans would also have to be obtained from the Home Office. UKXIRA issued guidance on proposals, which must contain a full risk assessment and demonstrate that the risks to human health are acceptable. So far, only a handful of applications has been received, and none has been approved. In the light of the Nuffield and Department of Health Reports, it is unlikely that any trials will go ahead until there is some shift in the evidence base which demonstrates that the risks of cross-species infection have been controlled.

6. CONCLUSION

As life expectancy increases, the number of people experiencing organ failure will inevitably rise, and the shortage of organs available for transplantation, which we have examined in this chapter, looks set to continue. Persuading more people to expressly consent to the use of their organs after death, and increasing the number of living donors will save some lives, but will not eliminate the ever-widening gap between supply and demand.

How could this problem be solved? It is not yet clear whether the ethical and clinical difficulties raised by xenotransplantation can be satisfactorily addressed. In the next chapter, we will encounter another possible 'solution' to the organ shortage, namely the possibilities opened up by stem cell research. Again, it is as yet unclear whether some of the claims made for the clinical application of stem cell research are realistic. In the short to medium term, then, it is inevitable that people will die while waiting for organs that could save their lives.

It could plausibly be argued that it is extraordinary that we routinely burn or bury organs which could have been used to save lives. Of course, taking organs without the consent of the deceased person, or in the face of their relatives' objections might cause offence and distress, but it is worth remembering that the cost of avoiding this offence and distress is the certain death of identifiable individuals with acute organ failure.

Perhaps regrettably, the emphasis upon patient autonomy and the need for consent has spilled over into the treatment of our bodies after death. I do not mean to suggest that there is no value in respecting an individual's wishes after her death. For many people, exercising control over what happens to their resources and their bodies after they have died is of critical importance. But, in relation to testamentary freedom, the deceased's wishes are not always decisive. If I choose to leave all of my assets to a donkey sanctuary, when this will leave my dependants destitute, my choice can be overridden. In relation to organ donation, could it be argued that the decision to have one's organs burned or buried, when they could be used to save lives, is similarly unfair or immoral? Here we have yet another interesting example of the difference between legal and moral duties. It would be difficult (though perhaps not impossible)

---

[134] HSC 1998/126.

to argue that I have a *legal* duty to donate my organs after death, but the *moral* duty of easy rescue—that is the duty to save a life when to do so would be virtually costless— seems to me to be unarguable.

7. FURTHER READING

Brazier, Margaret, 'Retained organs: ethics and humanity' (2002) 22 Legal Studies 550–69.

Emson, HE, 'It is immoral to require consent for cadaver organ donation' (2003) 29 Journal of Medical Ethics 125–7.

English, V and Sommerville, A, 'Presumed consent for transplantation: a dead issue after Alder Hey?' (2003) 29 Journal of Medical Ethics 147–52.

Erin, Charles A and Harris, John, 'An ethical market in human organs' (2003) 29 Journal of Medical Ethics 137–8.

Fox, M and McHale, J, 'Xenotransplantation: the ethical and legal ramifications' (1998) 6 Medical Law Review 42–61.

Glannon, Walter and Friedman Ross, Lainie, 'Do Genetic Relationships Create Moral Obligations in Organ Transplantation?' (2002) 11 Cambridge Quarterly of Healthcare Ethics 153–9.

Harris, John, 'Organ procurement: dead interests, living needs' (2003) 29 Journal of Medical Ethics 130–4.

Hughes, Jonathan, 'Xenografting: ethical issues' (1998) 24 Journal of Medical Ethics 18–24.

Human Tissue Authority <http://www.hta.gov.uk>.

Kerridge, IH, Saul, P, Lowe, M, McPhee, J, and Williams, D, 'Death, dying and donation: organ transplantation and the diagnosis of death' (2002) 28 Journal of Medical Ethics 89–94.

Mason, JK, 'Contemporary Issues in Organ Transplantation' in S Mclean (ed), *Contemporary Issues in Law, Medicine and Ethics* (Dartmouth Aldershot 1996) 117–41.

McLean, Sheila, 'Transplantation and the "Nearly Dead"; The Case of Elective Ventilation' in S Mclean (ed), *Contemporary Issues in Law, Medicine and Ethics* (Dartmouth Aldershot 1996) 143–61.

McLean, Sheila, 'Xenotransplantation: A Pig in a Poke?' (2004) 57 Current Legal Problems 443–68.

Nuffield Council on Bioethics, *Animal-to-Human Transplants: The Ethics of Xenotransplantation* (Nuffield Council on Bioethics London 1996).

Potts, M and Evans, DW, 'Does it matter that organ donors are not dead? Ethical and policy implications' (2005) 31 Journal of Medical Ethics 406–9.

Price, David, 'From Cosmos And Damian To Van Velzen: The Human Tissue Saga Continues' (2003) 11 Medical Law Review 1.

Price, David, The Human Tissue Act 2004 (2005) 68 Modern Law Review 798–821.

Wilkinson, Stephen, *Bodies for Sale: Ethics and Exploitation in the Human Body Trade* (Routledge London 2003) ch 7.

13

EMBRYO AND STEM CELL RESEARCH

1. CENTRAL ISSUES

1. Some believe that an embryo is a person from the moment of conception. More common is the view that its potential to become a person means that the early human embryo should be treated with 'respect'.

2. In the UK, embryo research is regulated by the Human Fertilisation and Embryology Act 1990, and by the Human Fertilisation and Embryology Authority (HFEA).

3. The 1990 Act appeared to define 'embryo' in a way that did not obviously include embryos created through CNR, the process used to clone Dolly the sheep, but the House of Lords has adopted a purposive approach to statutory interpretation, and CNR is clearly a licensable activity.

4. No research can be carried out on an embryo beyond 14 days.

5. Most experiments use surplus embryos which are donated by couples undergoing IVF treatment, but the legislation allows for the creation of embryos specifically for the purposes of research, provided that the HFEA's licence committee is satisfied that the creation of embryos is necessary.

6. Research must be necessary or desirable for one or more of the statutory purposes, and the use of embryos must be necessary. This means it would not be possible to obtain a licence if the research could be carried out on tissue taken from adults, or on animals.

2. INTRODUCTION

Until relatively recently, it was not possible to create human embryos outside of a woman's body, and so the question of what protection, if any, should be afforded to the earliest stages of a new human life were inextricably bound up with the issue of abortion. Now that eggs can be fertilized *in vitro*, new and difficult questions arise about how the resulting embryos should be treated. In this chapter our focus is upon whether, and in what circumstances, research on human embryos might be acceptable. In order to answer these questions, the potential benefits that may flow from embryo research have to be weighed in the balance with the embryo's moral status, whatever that might be. Some people believe that the respect due to a human embryo will always be incompatible with carrying out experiments upon it, regardless of the potential health benefits, while others believe that properly regulated embryo research is a legitimate scientific endeavour.

Some of the terminology used in this chapter will be unfamiliar to law students, and so at the outset, it is worth noting the meaning of a few key terms. When an egg (*oocyte*) is fertilized by a sperm, a single cell *zygote* is formed. This will then begin the process of cell division. After approximately 4–5 days, a *blastocyst* is formed, which will contain 50–150 cells. At the blastocyst stage it is possible to distinguish between the outer shell or *trophoblast* and the *inner cell mass*. The trophoblast will become the placenta. The inner cell mass at this stage contains *stem cells*. These are *undifferentiated* cells, that is it is not yet possible to know which will become the skin, or bones, or brain, or blood, etc. As we will see later, scientists have been able to extract these stem cells, and, in the future, they believe that it will be possible to control this process of *differentiation* in order to reprogramme stem cells to become specialized tissue.

Initially research on embryos was principally directed towards improving assisted conception techniques, however it is now thought that stem cell research might hold out the possibility of treatments for a wide range of degenerative diseases. Indeed, one of the key themes to which we will keep returning in this chapter is that science moves so quickly that new ethical and legal dilemmas are continuously emerging, and any regulatory system will inevitably struggle to keep up. It is also worth noting that this sort of research increasingly takes place within a global scientific community. Very restrictive rules in one country will not prevent research from taking place, but will instead encourage scientists to travel abroad to places with more liberal regulations.

In this chapter, we begin by examining the philosophical debates over the embryo's moral status. Next we look at regulation in the UK, where embryo research is regulated by the licensing system set up in the Human Fertilisation and Embryology Act 1990 and by the Human Fertilisation and Embryology Authority's licensing decisions. At the end, we briefly consider some other countries' approaches to embryo research.

3. WHAT IS THE MORAL STATUS OF THE EMBRYO?

Deciding upon the embryo's moral status is not just an abstract question of philosophy, theology or morality. As Maureen Junker-Kenny explains in the next extract, because the embryo's status determines how we should treat it, this is a question of enormous *practical* importance.

Maureen Junker-Kenny[1]

It should have become clear by now that definitions of personhood are not lofty philosophical speculations but have an immediate practical significance. The question of personhood is a philosophical one in which we state our self-understanding as humans. Whom do we accept as a member of our species who is entitled to protection and care?

Any definition of the beginning and end of human personhood is caught up in a hermeneutical circle. We define its starting point because we want to act in a certain way, and we act according to how we have defined it. If we consider the moment of implantation in the uterus, or the presence of brain activity, or the ability to communicate, as the starting-point for ascribing personhood, we are free to use the embryo prior to this stage in any way we consider useful.

Each definition has a practical intent. Once we ascribe human life and personhood to an entity,

---

[1] 'The Moral Status of the Embryo' in N Messer (ed), *Theological Issues in Bioethics: An Introduction with Readings* (Darton, Longman and Todd London 2002) 8–75, 71–2.

we want to protect it. If one wants to give maximum protection, one has to use a minimal definition, such as the new genetic unity created by egg and sperm. A maximal definition of human life, such as the ability to communicate, or to act independently, offers minimal protection to the stages prior to these competencies and after they have been lost . . .

It is therefore a *practical* decision at what developmental stage we attribute human person-hood to the embryo, foetus, or newborn, and it is in the interest of the earliest possible protection of 'the weakest link in the chain of the human species' if one states that this new genetic unity is a person.

(a) IS THE EMBRYO A PERSON?

Because any embryo which is used in research will be destroyed or allowed to perish, if an embryo is a person, research would obviously be unacceptable. While the law is clear that a legal person only exists after a child has been born, some religions, most notably Roman Catholicism, do believe that a person comes into being at conception:

Catechism of the Catholic Church

2270 Human life must be respected and protected absolutely from the moment of conception.

2274 Since it must be treated from conception as a person, the embryo must be defended in its integrity, cared for, and healed, as far as possible, like any other human being.

2275 It is immoral to produce human embryos intended for exploitation as disposable biological material.

Interestingly, Catholicism has not always advocated protecting embryos as if they were people from the moment of conception. Until the nineteenth century, *ensoulment* was believed to be the point at which the developing fetus achieved humanity, and this took place some time after fertilization. Male fetuses were ensouled at 40 days, and female fetuses at 80 days.

Now, according to the Vatican at least, it is fertilization which is critical. It is however worth noting that fertilization does not happen instantly. In normal sexual reproduction, fertilization may not begin until a few days after sexual intercourse, and it can take up to 30 hours for a sperm to fertilize an egg. Implantation—which is when the fertilized egg attaches itself to the woman's body—will not start until about 6 or 7 days later, and will again take several days to complete.

Moreover, an embryo will not autonomously become a baby, rather this collection of cells will perish unless subsequently implanted in a woman's uterus and carried for at least 5 months. These are substantial prerequisites: most fertilized eggs fail either to implant or to complete their development, and the vast majority of this natural wastage remains unnoticed. Even if a fertilized egg does implant, some of its cells will divide to form the placenta and umbilical cord, which are discarded at birth: this material is obviously not a 'person'. And up to about 14 days after fertilization begins, an embryo may split and become two embryos (which will, if born, be identical twins), so the early human embryo is not necessarily one identifiable human being, but may become two different ones.

It should be noted that not all Catholics disapprove of all research on embryos. In the next extract, Margaret Foley offers a different Catholic perspective.

Margaret Foley[2]

Those who stand within the Catholic tradition tend to look to the reality of stem cells and, what is more relevant in this instance, to the realities of the sources of cells for current research: human embryos . . . A case can be made both against and for such research, each dependent on different interpretations of the moral status of the embryo . . . First, significant numbers of Catholics . . . make the case *against*. They hold that human embryos must be protected on a par with human persons, at least to the extent that they ought not be either created or destroyed merely for research purposes . . . On the other hand, a case for human embryo stem cell research can be made on the basis of positions developed within the Roman Catholic tradition. Growing numbers of Catholic moral theologians, for example, do not consider the human embryo in its earliest stages (before development of the primitive streak or implantation) to constitute an individualized human entity with the settled inherent potential to become a human being. In this view the moral status of the embryo is therefore not that of a person, and its use for certain kinds of research can be justified. Since it is, however, a form of life, some respect is due to it; for example, it should not be bought and sold. Those who make this case prefer a return to the centuries-old Catholic position that a certain amount of development is necessary in order for a conceptus to warrant personal status. Embryologic studies now show that fertilization (conception) is itself a process (not a moment), and provide warrant for the opinion that in its earliest stages (including the blastocyst stage, when the inner cell mass is isolated to derive stem cells for purposes of research) the embryo is not sufficiently individualized to bear the moral weight of personhood.

Most religions believe that it is important to treat the human embryo with respect, but this is not always incompatible with research. According to the Chief Rabbi's evidence to the House of Lords Select committee on Stem Cell Research, in certain circumstances Judaism would allow the respect due to the early human embryo to be trumped by the benefits which might flow from research:

In Jewish law neither the foetus nor the pre-implanted embryo is a person; it is, however, human life and must be accorded the respect due to human life. Personhood, with its attendant rights and responsibilities begins at birth. Prior to birth, we have duties to both the embryo and the foetus, but these may, in certain circumstances, be overridden by other duties, namely those we owe to persons.[3]

In particular, given Judaism's clear mandate to promote life and health, as Laurie Zoloth points out in the next extract, it would be likely to sanction research into new techniques, such as stem cell therapies, which hold out the hope of curing serious disease and disability.

Laurie Zoloth[4]

Whereas moral status of embryonic tissue is the threshold question for many religious traditions, the Jewish position is that this is of secondary importance to the debate, to be noted after the life-saving consequences of this technology are established . . . The task of healing in Judaism is not

[2] 'Roman Catholic Vies on hES Cell Research' in S Holland, K Lebacqz, and Laurie Zoloth (eds), *The Human Embryonic Stem Cell Debate: Science, Ethics and Public Policy* (MIT Press Cambridge, Mass 2001) 113–18, 115–16.

[3] *Stem Cell Research Report*, Feb 2002 <http://www.parliament.the-stationery-office.co.uk/pa/ld200102/ldselect/ldstem/83/8305.htm> para 4.19.

[4] 'The Ethics of the Eighth Day: Jewish Bioethics and Research on Human Embryonic Stem Cells' in S Holland, K Lebacqz, and Laurie Zoloth (eds), *The Human Embryonic Stem Cell Debate: Science, Ethics and Public Policy* (MIT Press Cambridge, Mass 2001) 95–111, 98, 100, 102.

only permitted, it is mandated; if stem cells can save a life, then not only can they be used, they must be used . . . Furthermore, it is mandated to use the best methods available as soon as they are proved efficacious and not dangerous to the patient. Paradoxically, it might violate rabbinic premises to *stop* research if such research is life saving.

Of course, the argument that the embryo is (or might be) a person is not always necessarily made from a faith perspective. In the next extract, Christopher Tollefsen suggests that killing is such a serious moral wrong, that the burden should be on those who wish to destroy embryos to prove conclusively that they are *not* persons.

Christopher Tollefsen[5]

If research is permitted on some X, whatever X is, then this would seem to require a public and explicit determination that X is not a person. . . .

First, I think that if I have shown that there is a genuine argumentative stasis, this should lead to a moral conclusion . . . that it is simply wrong to create and perform research upon embryos. To destroy embryos one acknowledges *might* be persons, even if one also thinks they might not be persons, is to be willing to kill persons . . .

The second point is to address an objection regarding spare embryos. Spare embryos, simply put, are a problem. There are lots of them, they are doing no good, and it seems one way or another their inevitable fate that they die without coming to term. If they are going to die anyway, why should their deaths not do some good? And indeed, won't we end up killing them one way or another?

The best I can do in reply to this objection is to suggest a way in which spare embryos might best, and with the most possible dignity meet their fate . . . I suggest we view them in a way parallel to those who are in need of an organ transplant which they are unlikely to get, but who are presently receiving extraordinary life preserving treatment . . . I think that if efforts to find donor wombs, so to speak, for homeless embryos have failed, that they should be removed from the cryogenic life support, not with the intention of killing, but with a view to mitigating the costs, for the embryos, and for society, incurred by their preservation.

Many people will be unsatisfied with this. Arthur Caplan, for example, has suggested that 'even if you believe that an embryo is a person, however, and should not be used in any research that would cause its destruction, you still must consider the promise that the therapies from embryonic stem cells hold for those who are paralyzed, burned, dying of liver and pancreas failure, brain injured and suffering from many, many other diseases and injuries. Their moral interests count too.' But for that matter, think of all the good we could attain through experimental research conducted on the elderly, or dying infants and children. Contrary to an influential strand of utilitarian thought, I deny that the destruction of some persons should be brought about for the benefit of other persons . . .

[T]he standards which must be met to permit killing must be pretty high—where there is reasonable doubt, where there is room for reasonable persons to disagree, the default position, it seems to me, should not be permissive.

And in the next extract, Søren Holm suggests that the standard liberal claim that embryos lack the criteria we associate with personhood, and that research is therefore justified may prove too much. In particular, it could also be used to defend research

---

[5] 'Embryos, Individuals, and Persons: An Argument Against Embryo Creation and Research' (2001) 18 Journal of Applied Philosophy 65–77, 68, 74–5.

on young babies or adults suffering from dementia, on the grounds that they too lack qualities such as consciousness or the capacity to reason.

Søren Holm[6]

By far the most common pro-stem cell argument is that derivation of human embryonic stem cells is morally innocuous because human embryos have no moral status. By analyzing their characteristics, we can see that they are not persons and that it is not wrong to kill them . . .

One main problem with this argument is that it proves far too much. . . . The standard argument proves too much in a number of directions. First, and perhaps most important, it justifies the (nonpainful) killing and use of any prepersonal human entity from the fertilized egg to the prepersonal infant. Such a killing can be justified by any kind of net benefit to others. In the current context, it can therefore just as easily justify the killing of infants for their stem cells as it can the destruction of embryos for the same purpose. There is no in principle difference between the two killings.

Second, it places no restrictions on the use of biological material from prepersonal human entities that can justify the destruction of these entities, as long as those uses are beneficial. The derivation of a new and effective antiwrinkle cream can therefore be a perfectly acceptable justification for the production and destruction of embryos.

(b) THE ARGUMENT FROM POTENTIAL

Even if we accept that an early human embryo is not a person, it could instead be argued it has the potential to become a person if carried in a woman's body for at least five months. And some would argue that the embryo's special moral status derives from its potential to become a person. John Marshall, for example, suggests that there will never be any consensus on when personhood is acquired, and that it is instead the embryo's *potential* to become a person which leads him to argue against embryo research.

John Marshall[7]

Why then do I oppose experimentation of the kind that I have defined, namely experiments which lead to the destruction of the entity? It is because I regard the potential to become a human person as of tremendous importance, particularly in our society where there is a certain ambivalence about, and paradoxical attitude towards, life. In opposing experimentation I recognize and do not hide the fact that some advances in knowledge will be lost, but I do assert that those advances are not so great as the scientists would have us believe. I do not therefore hold that the gain is commensurate with the loss. This really is the basis of the argument.

In summary, I argue that each person has to decide in their own mind at what point in the development of this entity one is going to accord to it the status of a person. It is no use looking to the scientist or the philosopher or anybody else to give the answer. It is a judgement which individuals have to make because it is a philosophical-cum-theological judgement about which there has not been revelation, and to which one just has to apply one's mind and thought, using the broad principles with which one guides one's ethical conduct. If one comes to the decision that a

---

[6] 'The Ethical Case against Stem Cell Research' (2003) 12 Cambridge Quarterly of Healthcare Ethics 372–83.

[7] 'The case against experimentation' in A Dyson and J Harris (eds), *Experiments on Embryos* (Routledge London 1990) 55–64, 63–4.

person comes into a being at a certain stage, then clearly this will affect one's attitude towards experimentation. On the other hand, one can conclude that this is a question which cannot be decided universally, and that each person will have their own view. On this argument, because the entity has the potential to become a person, one affirms that it should *not* be interfered with, that *nothing* should be done that prevents it realizing that potential, and things *can* be done which will help it to attain that potential. Therefore one opposes experimentation.

In the next extract, John Harris explains that one of the difficulties with the argument from potential is that gametes (sperm and eggs) also have the potential to become a new human life. If the embryo is special because it has the potential to become a human being, then since egg and sperm have the potential to become an embryo, logically they must also have the potential to become a human being.

John Harris[8]

There are two sorts of objections to the 'potentiality argument' for the moral significance of the embryo. The first is simply that the fact that an entity can undergo changes that will make it significantly different does not constitute a reason for treating it as though it had already undergone those changes. We are all potentially dead, but no-one supposes that this fact constitutes a reason for treating us as if we were already dead.

The second objection is simply that if the potentiality argument suggests that we have to regard as morally significant anything which has the potential to become a fully fledged human being and hence have some moral duty to protect and actualize all human potential, then we are in for a very exhausting time of it. For it is not only the fertilized egg, the embryo that is potentially a full fledged adult. The egg and the sperm taken together but as yet ununited have the same potential as the fertilized egg. For something, or some things, have the potential to become a fertilized egg and whatever has the potential to become an embryo has whatever potential the embryo has.

Of course, as Massimo Reichlin points out, the embryo is clearly a significant step further on in the process of becoming a person than a spermatazoa or an unfertilized egg.

Massimo Reichlin[9]

The argument from potential does not have a good press in today's bioethical debate . . . Most scholars are unsatisfied with this argument, some believing that it does not suffice in order to provide an effective foundation of the respect owed to the human embryo or fetus, many more believing that it proves too much, and that, once we should allow that it works in ruling out abortion and experimentation on preimplantation embryos, we must be prepared to hold that it does rule out contraception too . . .

It is . . . important to preserve the distinction between potentiality and possibility; as we shall see in detail, this distinction can be expressed in Aristotelian terms as that between *active* potentiality—which means a being's inherent capacity to autonomously develop itself—and *passive* potentiality—which only implies the capacity to undergo modifications from external agents. The case of human gametes shows an even more remote sense of potentiality, since what we have in the gametes is not an individual's capacity to undergo modifications, but rather the possibility that two entities unite in order to form a new individual which is distinct from the two originals . . . It

[8] 'On the moral status of the embryo' in A Dyson and J Harris (eds), *Experiments on Embryos* (Routledge London 1990) 65–81, 70.
[9] 'The Argument from Potential: A Reappraisal' (1997) 11 Bioethics 1–23, 1–2, 4–5.

should thus be regarded as seriously misleading to say that an unfertilized ovum is a potential person.

Moreover, the conflation of potentiality and possibility seems to involve a naïve view of fertilization as the mere addition of material with no qualitative increase. As Singer and Wells put it, 'Everything that can be said about the potential of the embryo can also be said about the potential of the egg and sperm when separate but considered jointly' . . . The idea that the event of conception could be something just like 'considering jointly' the egg and sperm seems to simply overlook the fact of the 'biological roulette' through which a new member of the species (what the gametes were not) is formed, and one with an altogether new genetic identity. This makes a 'decisive difference' from an ontological viewpoint. . . . While it can be discussed whether this suffices in order to affirm the presence of a person, fertilization is surely *the* moment (or *the* process, if you consider that it takes a number of hours) of the beginning of a new biological individual: no other moment before this can legitimately make such a claim.

But while it is clearly true that most human gametes have the potential to be a person only in a rather remote sense, Peter Singer and Karen Dawson argue that the embryo *in vitro* resembles egg and sperm more than an embryo *in vivo*, since both require human intervention before their potential to become a baby can be realized.

Peter Singer and Karen Dawson[10]

[B]efore the advent of IVF, in every instance in which we knew of the existence of a normal human embryo, it would have been true to say that, unless it was deliberately interfered with, it would most likely develop into a person. The process of IVF . . . leads to the creation of embryos which cannot develop into a person unless there is some deliberate human act (the transfer to the uterus) and which even then, in the best of circumstances, will most likely not develop into a person.

The upshot of all this is that IVF has reduced the difference between what can be said about the embryo and what can be said about the egg and sperm, considered jointly. Before IVF, any normal human embryo known to us had a far greater chance of becoming a child than any egg plus sperm prior to fertilization taking place. But with IVF, there is a much more modest difference in the probability of a child resulting from a two-cell embryo in a glass dish, and the probability of a child resulting from an egg and some sperm in a glass dish . . .

We noticed earlier that whereas the embryo inside the female body has some definite chance of developing into a child unless a deliberate human act interrupts its growth, the egg and sperm can only develop into a child if there is a deliberate human act. In this respect the embryo in the laboratory is like the egg and sperm, and not like the embryo in the human body. This is of fundamental importance for the notion of potential, because lurking in the background of discussions of the embryo's potential is the idea that there is a 'natural' course of events, governed by the 'inherent' potential of the embryo. We have seen, however, that this notion of 'natural' development, not requiring the assistance of a deliberate human act, has no application to the IVF embryo. Hence those who wish to use the potential of the IVF embryo as a ground for protecting it cannot appeal to this notion of natural development; and for this reason, they find themselves in difficulty in explaining why the embryo in the laboratory has a potential so different from that of the egg alone, or the egg and sperm considered jointly.

Unless a woman agrees to have an embryo transferred to her uterus, and someone else agrees to perform this transfer, that embryo has no future.

---

[10] 'IVF technology and the argument from potential' in P Singer et al. (eds), *Embryo Experimentation* (CUP Cambridge 1990) 76–89, 78, 87.

A different sort of problem with the argument from potential is that if we were to accept that an early human embryo's potential to become a human being rules out its deliberate destruction, certain types of contraception (such as the IUD or the morning after pill), which prevent the implantation of newly fertilized eggs, should also be prohibited. Indeed the ordinary oral contraceptive pill will also sometimes work by preventing implantation, so its legitimacy too might be in doubt. Similarly, IVF treatment involves the creation of embryos which will never be implanted, and which will have to be destroyed or allowed to perish. If we believe that postcoital contraceptive techniques and IVF treatment, both of which routinely result in the destruction of embryos, are permissible, it is hard to see why potentially life-saving research on identical embryos should be prohibited. In the next extract, John Harris goes so far as to argue that anyone who accepts normal sexual reproduction, which inevitably involves the creation and destruction of embryos, should, logically, also accept research on human embryos.

John Harris[11]

I make two appeals to consistency, or to parity of reasoning, that I believe show that no one who either has used or intends to use sexual reproduction as their means of procreation, nor indeed anyone who has unprotected heterosexual intercourse . . . can consistently object on principle to human embryo research nor to the use of embryonic stem cells for research or therapy. . . .

We now know that for every successful pregnancy that results in a live birth many, perhaps as many as five, early embryos will be lost or will 'miscarry' (although these are not perhaps 'miscarriages' as the term is normally used because this sort of very early embryo loss is almost always entirely unnoticed). Many of these embryos will be lost because of genetic abnormalities, but some would have been viable.

How are we to think of the decision to attempt to have a child in the light of these facts? One obvious and inescapable conclusion is that God and/or nature has ordained that 'spare' embryos be produced for almost every pregnancy and that most of these will have to die in order that a sibling embryo can come to birth. Thus, the sacrifice of embryos seems to be an inescapable and inevitable part of the process of procreation. It may not be intentional sacrifice, and it may not attend every pregnancy, but the loss of many embryos is the inevitable consequence of the vast majority (perhaps all) pregnancies.

Given that decisions to attempt to have children using sexual reproduction as the method (or even decisions to have unprotected intercourse) inevitably create embryos that must die, those who believe having children or even running the risk of conception is legitimate cannot consistently object to the creation of embryos for comparably important moral reasons. . . .

I am saying that we do as a matter of fact and of sound moral judgment accept the sacrifice of embryos in natural reproduction, because although we might rather not have to sacrifice embryos to achieve a live healthy birth, we judge it to be defensible to continue natural reproduction in the light of the balance between the moral costs and the benefits. And if we make this calculation in the case of normal sexual reproduction we should, for the same reasons, make a similar judgment in the case of the sacrifice of embryos in stem cell research.

Finally, the possibility of human cloning adds a new dimension to the potentiality argument. As we shall see later, cell nuclear replacement (the technique which was

[11] 'Stem Cells, Sex, and Procreation' (2003) 12 Cambridge Quarterly of Healthcare 353–71, 353, 362–3, 365.

used to create Dolly the sheep) means that, in theory at least, *any cell* could become a new human being.

(c) THE COMPROMISE POSITION

Most people believe that embryos are in some important sense 'special', but would fall short of according them the same status as people. An embryo is clearly a member of our species, but this does not require us to treat a four cell embryo as if it had the same rights and entitlements as a person. The 1984 Warnock Report, which we consider below, embodied this compromise position. It admitted that the instrumental use of the early human embryo will inevitably offend those who believe that a person comes into being immediately after fertilization, but that that offence has to be put into the balance with the benefits which may flow from embryo research. The Warnock Committee recommended that embryo research should be permitted provided that the embryo is not simply treated as a resource for scientists, but is instead accorded proper 'respect'. The compromise view embodied in the Warnock Report formed the basis of the Human Fertilisation and Embryology Act 1990, which is intended to safeguard scientific progress within restrictions which are designed to indicate that the early human embryo has some intrinsic moral importance, and should not be used frivolously or unnecessarily.

More recently, Baroness Warnock has suggested that the report's use of the word 'respect' to describe the treatment of embryos used in research was 'foolish'.

Mary Warnock[12]

I regret that in the original report that led up to the 1990 legislation we used words such as 'respect for the embryo'. That seems to me to lead to certain absurdities. You cannot respectfully pour something down the sink—which is the fate of the embryo after it has been used for research, or if it is not going to be used for research or for anything else.

I think that what we meant by the rather foolish expression 'respect' was that the early embryo should never be used frivolously for research purposes. That is perfectly exemplified by the regulations that are brought in and the licensing provisions that are looked after by the HFEA. It is the non-frivolity of the research which is conveyed by such expressions as 'respect for' or 'protection for' the embryo.

In contrast, Karen Lebacqz argues that it is possible to treat an embryo which is to be used in research with respect:

Karen Lebacqz[13]

I believe that one can indeed speak meaningfully of respecting embryos or embryonic tissue, and that criteria for such respect can be established. Specifically, the tissue must not be treated cavalierly, but as an entity with value . . . To approach something with awe or reverence means that we never become hardened to its intrinsic value, its value apart from us. I suggest that the embryo should not be used cavalierly.

---

[12] Hansard 5 Dec 2002: col 1327.
[13] 'On the elusive nature of respect' in S Holland, K Lebacqz, and Laurie Zoloth (eds), *The Human Embryonic Stem Cell Debate: Science, Ethics and Public Policy* (MIT Press Cambridge, Mass 2001) 9–62, 150, 159.

An entity is treated cavalierly if it is demolished without any sense of violation or loss; if it is treated as only one of many and easily replaceable; if its existence is made the butt of jokes or disrespectful stereotyping. Thus, to require that a blastocyst not be treated cavalierly is to require that it be treated as an entity with incredible value; as something precious which cannot be replaced by any other blastocyst, whose existence is to be celebrated and whose loss is to be grieved.

Regardless of whether the word 'respect' is useful or foolish in the context of embryo research, as John Robertson explains in the next extract, the compromise position is not concerned to protect individual human embryos, since these will ultimately be destroyed, but is instead directing towards protecting the *symbolic* value of human life.

John A Robertson[14]

Denial of the early embryo's inherent moral status and of the correlative moral duty not to destroy embryos does not, however, mean that the human embryo is perceived as being without value, or that it may then be treated like any other excised human tissue. An object or thing can be invested with meaning, even if it lacks rights or interests in itself, as occurs with religious objects, monuments, works of art or even parts of nature. Many people, for example, reject the view that the embryo is a person but believe that the embryo is different from ordinary human tissue because of the unique potential it has to develop into a new human being. Sometimes described as 'special respect', this attitude towards human embryos shows or symbolizes our respect for human life generally.

The desire to make a symbolic commitment to non-rights-bearing entities, such as human embryos, depends on the entity and the context involved. In the context of *in vitro* fertilization (IVF) treatment, for example, the generation of more embryos than can be safely transferred to the uterus is widely accepted as not being unduly disrespectful of human life, because it enables children to be born to infertile couples. Similarly, destroying embryos that are left over from IVF procedures to develop cell-replacement therapies should also be ethically acceptable, for the goal of treating disease and saving life justifies the symbolic loss that arises from destroying embryos in the process. By contrast, selling human embryos or using them in cosmetic-toxicology testing seems to be disrespectful of the symbolic meaning that many people attach to embryos because those uses fulfil no life-affirming or other important purpose.

The House of Lords Select committee on Stem Cell Research[15], whose report we consider in detail later in this chapter also supported the compromise position, arguing that it is only legitimate to use embryos in research if they are 'handled sensitively'. In the next extract Roger Brownsword discusses three possible reasons for this.

Roger Brownsword[16]

Why should the [House of Lords Select] Committee emphasise the need for human tissue to be handled sensitively? At least three considerations spring to mind. First, the insensitive handling of such material can cause offence—one only has to recall the notorious Kelly case where removed body parts were incorporated in so-called works of art. From a utilitarian standpoint, there is

---

[14] 'Human embryonic stem cell research: ethical and legal issues' (2001) 2 Nature Reviews Genetics 74–8, 75.

[15] Department of Health, 2002, Cm 5561.

[16] 'Bioethics today, bioethics tomorrow: stem cell research and the "dignitarian alliance" ' (2003) 17 Notre Dame Journal of Law, Ethics and Public Policy 15, 48.

good reason to avoid occasioning such gratuitous distress. Secondly, if the way in which the tissue is handled deviates from the expectations of the donors, this will be a matter that concerns rights theorists (who will detect departures from the terms of the consent given) but also to utilitarians who will fear that bad publicity might interfere with the donation of embryos needed for utility-yielding research. Thirdly, insofar as the tissue contains information about the genetic make-up of any individuals who do have moral status, then both utilitarians and rights theorists will be concerned, the former about the consequential disutility and the latter about breaches of privacy and confidentiality.

One important dimension of the compromise position is that alternatives should always be pursued in preference to embryo research. The destruction of human embryos is therefore permissible only where there are no other ways of carrying out the research. In the next extract, Gene Outka argues that there should always be a certain reluctance or disquiet over the prospect of using human embryos in research.

Gene Outka[17]

One thus regards research, even on excess embryos, as something to which one only reluctantly acquiesces. This attitude begins in sympathy for those who view their own infertility as an affliction they seek to overcome. It continues in allowing unprecedented *in vitro* technology that sometimes triumphs over this affliction. But such technology brings with it one foreseeable and lamentable outcome, namely, the presence of embryos to be discarded or frozen in perpetuity. One welcomes neither infertility nor excess embryos. The attitude concludes in a desire that one day there will no longer be a need to destroy embryos. That is, one looks forward to a time when it is possible to reprogram adult stem cells so that embryos are no longer required as a source. One further hopes that this time comes quickly, that the establishment of cell lines will make the use of donated embryos a transitional matter. In short, to destroy embryos *never* should leave one at ease or become simply unproblematic, a permanently acceptable part of routine procedures.

(d) MORE ROBUST ARGUMENTS IN FAVOUR OF EMBRYO RESEARCH

As we saw in the previous section, most people adopt consequentialist reasoning in order to justify embryo research: do the good consequences from permitting research outweigh the symbolic harm of disposing of early human life? There are, however, those who believe that the reverence for human embryos upon which this compromise position rests makes little sense. In the next extract Helga Kuhse and Peter Singer argue that embryos do not possess the qualities which ground our respect for persons—such as consciousness and sentience—and that would therefore be legitimate to use them as a resource for experimentation up to the point at which they can feel pain, which would be much later than the current fourteen day limit.

Helga Kuhse and Peter Singer[18]

We believe the minimal characteristic need to give the embryo a claim to consideration is sentience, or the capacity to feel pleasure or pain. Until that point is reached, the embryo does not

---

[17] 'The Ethics of Human Stem Cell Research' (2002) 12 Kennedy Institute of Ethics Journal 175–213, 201.
[18] 'Individuals, humans and persons: The issue of moral status' in P Singer et al. (eds), *Embryo Experimentation* (CUP Cambridge 1990) 65–75, 73–4.

have any interests and, like other non-sentient organisms (a human egg, for example), cannot be harmed—in a morally relevant way—by anything we do. We can, of course, damage the embryo in such a way as to cause harm to the sentient being it will become, if it lives, but if it never becomes a sentient being, the embryo has not been harmed, because its total lack of awareness means that it never has had any interests at all. . . .

Finally, we point to a curious consequence of restrictive legislation on embryo research. In sharp contrast to the human embryo at this early stage of its existence, non-human animals such as primates, dogs, rabbits, guinea pigs, rats and mice clearly can feel pain, and thus often are harmed by what is done to them in the course of scientific research. We have already suggested that the species of a being is not, in itself relevant to its ethical status. Why, then, is it considered acceptable to poison conscious rabbits in order to test the safety of drugs and household chemicals, but not considered acceptable to carry out tests on totally non-sentient human embryos? It is only when an embryo reaches the stage at which it may be capable of feeling pain that we need to control the experimentation that can be done with it. At this point the embryo ranks, morally, with those non-human animals we have mentioned . . .

At what point, then, does the embryo develop a capacity to feel pain? Though we are not experts in this field, from our reading of the literature, we would say that it cannot possibly be earlier than six weeks, and it may well be as late as eighteen or twenty weeks. While we think we should err on the side of caution, it seems to us that the fourteen-day limit . . . is too conservative. Even if we were to be very, very cautious in erring on the safe side, a twenty-eight-day limit would provide sufficient protection against the possibility of an embryo suffering during experimentation.

In contrast, John Marshall suggests that using the embryo's capacity to experience pain as the cut-off point treats embryos in the same way as we treat animals, thus denying their 'peculiarly human' status.

John Marshall[19]

Some of those who advocate experimenting on human embryos propose as a cut-off point emergence of the ability to feel pain . . . No experiment should be carried out which would involve inflicting pain. This may be axiomatic but immediately raises another question. If it is simply that pain must not be inflicted, then a technical advance which enabled the embryo or fetus to be anaesthetised, as are human beings after birth, would remove the cut-off point. Experiments could then presumably continue to a new cut-off point determined by some other criterion.

The ability of the human embryo to feel pain cannot be taken as a satisfactory cut-off point for experiment. Apart from the prognostic difficulty in establishing where to place that point, the use of this criterion is in effect an evasion of the real issue. Experiments on and slaughter of animals are permitted provided that pain is not caused. To allow experiments on embryos before they are considered capable of feeling pain would be to adopt the same criterion as we do for animals. Is this in fact what we are doing by proposing that experiments on the human embryo should be allowed up to the point at which it might feel pain? Are we denying it any status that is peculiarly human?

The use of this criterion is a form of escapism. By saying that pain must not be inflicted, which appears as a praiseworthy moral stance, the fact escapes notice that no answer is being given to the important question of the status of the human embryo. If the embryo is thought to be a person, in the sense of someone who cannot be used as a means to an end, the fact that what is being done

---

[19] 'Experiment on Human Embryos: Sentience as the cut-off point?' in GR Dunstan and MJ Seller (eds), *The Status of the Human Embryo: Perspectives from Moral Tradition* (OUP Oxford 1988) 58–61, 58, 60–1.

can be done without pain becomes an irrelevance. The question, what is being done, must be faced. Is what is being done compatible with the status of the embryo as a person or potential person?

In the next extract, Julian Savulescu defends stem cell research on human embryos from an alternative perspective. Even if the embryo *is* a person, Savulescu argues that stem cell research is likely to be of such overwhelming benefit that it would justify killing a few innocent 'persons' for the greater good of everyone.

Julian Savulescu[20]

I and others have argued that an embryo is a collection of human cells, but is not yet a human being or person in the sense that it would be wrong to kill it. But let us grant that the embryo is a person. Would that make ES research wrong?

I will call the cannibalization claim the following:

It is impermissible to kill one innocent person, A, for the purpose of saving the life of another innocent person B.

I will argue that it is acceptable to kill one person for the purposes of saving others. That is, that there is nothing necessarily wrong with cannibalization. . . .

The fundamental flaw in the cannibalization objection to ES cell research is that it ignores the fact that the research stands to benefit everyone, at all ages. It is not concerned with sacrificing one healthy person who would otherwise die to treat sick people. It is about reducing the risk of death to us all—we are all, even embryos, potential recipients of this intervention. . . .

To employ the Rawlsian veil of ignorance again, I would prefer a world in which I have some chance of being snuffed out as an embryo but a much higher chance of having my fatal diseases successfully treated as an embryo, foetus, child or adult . . .

Detractors of ES research may claim that there are no 'therapies'. We are still at the research stage. So we are killing embryos for no reduction in risk to *anyone*.

The fact that ES cell therapy is at the research stage means that we have to factor in how likely it is that successful treatments will result and how great their benefits will be. . . .

Even if the technology is still at the experimental stage, it may be in all future people's interests for the experiments to be run. Indeed if ES cell therapy is useful in very common diseases like heart disease, stroke, diabetes and so on, then tens if not hundreds of millions of people are potential candidates in the next generation alone. When we then add that all future generations are potential candidates, then potentially billions of people are candidates. It would be rational to undertake such experimentation even if there were only a remote chance of it being successful . . .

We are all at risk of death and serious disability. ES cell technology stands to benefit everyone: embryos, children and adults. It is this property which makes it reasonable to kill some embryos to conduct ES cell research even if the embryo is a person . . .

Opponents of ES cell research will likely remain unconvinced. They will argue that whatever the benefits, intentionally killing embryos is failing to 'respect human dignity' . . .

Is it respecting of human dignity to allow people to wither in nursing homes, unable to swallow, speak or move while all the time embryos are destroyed? What more twisted version of respect for human dignity could there be? It is ES cell research, like organ transplantation, that is respectful of human dignity in its reverence for the lives of the living.

---

[20] 'The Embryonic Stem Cell Lottery and the Cannibalization of Human Beings' (2002) 16 Bioethics 508–29, 513, 515, 521, 526–7, 529.

Against this, Søren Holm argues that the promise of stem cell therapy may not be as great as is often claimed.

Søren Holm[21]

Another type of pro-stem cell argument tries to bypass the question of moral status by showing that stem cell derivation is justified on direct consequentialist grounds. If the good that can be attained is of a sufficient magnitude, then it can outweigh the killing of a certain number of human entities. It is justified to sacrifice some for the benefit of others . . .

This kind of argument may again prove too much—for instance, that it is also justified to sacrifice some adults if the benefits to others are sufficient.

It does, however, also suffer from another problem caused by the embryonic state of present stem cell research. The benefits that are put into the balance to justify the sacrifice are mainly the therapeutic potential promised by stem cell therapy. The public presentation of the benefits of stem cell research has often been characterized by the promise of huge and immediate benefits. As with many other scientific breakthroughs, the public has been promised real benefits within five to ten years (i.e., in this case, significant stem cell therapies in routine clinical use). Several of the five to ten years have now elapsed, and the promised therapies are still not anywhere close to routine clinical use. . . . It is likely that many of the current sufferers from some of the conditions for which stem cell therapies have been promised will be long dead before the therapies actually arrive.

3. REGULATION IN THE UK

(a) THE BACKGROUND TO THE HUMAN FERTILISATION AND EMBRYOLOGY ACT 1990

Research into the possibility of *in vitro* fertilization started in the 1950s. The birth of the first IVF baby in 1978 (see further Chapter 14) prompted the government to assemble a committee, chaired by Mary Warnock, to consider how embryo research and fertility treatment should be regulated. On the question of embryo research, the Committee was divided, and the minority issued a formal expression of dissent.

The Warnock Report was published in 1984, and as we see in the next chapter, a private member's Bill, the Unborn Children (Protection) Bill, which would have banned all embryo research was introduced in 1985. It was very nearly passed: on its second reading 238 MPs voted in favour, and 66 against. Only lack of parliamentary time prevented the Bill from becoming law. The following year, the Unborn Children (Protection) Bill was reintroduced, and despite commanding a significant parliamentary majority, it once again failed to become law.

Following a government consultation paper and a White paper, the Human Fertilisation and Embryology Bill was introduced in 1989, and became law the following year. By the end of the 1980s, public and parliamentary attitudes to embryo research had changed. In part this was a result of greater understanding of exactly what embryo research involves. A six-cell embryo is invisible to the naked eye, and even by the two-hundred cell stage, it is still no bigger than a pin-head. The Act itself

---

[21] 'The Ethical Case against Stem Cell Research' (2003) 12 Cambridge Quarterly of Healthcare Ethics 372–83.

embodied the majority of the Warnock committee's compromise position restricting the circumstances in which embryo research is permissible. Let us now examine the legislation in detail.

(b) THE DEFINITION OF AN EMBRYO

The Human Fertilisation and Embryology Act 1990 appears to contain a statutory definition of the word 'embryo':

Human Fertilisation and Embryology Act 1990 section 1

(1) In this Act, except where otherwise stated—

    (a) embryo means a live human embryo where fertilisation is complete, and

    (b) references to an embryo include an egg in the process of fertilisation.

The reason for including eggs which are 'in the process of fertilization' is so that these also come within the statutory regime. It would obviously be undesirable if there were no limits upon what could be done to an egg *while* it was being fertilized.

When the Act was passed, its drafters could not have anticipated the problems which would be caused by the wording of section 1(1)(a). The central difficulty emerged after the announcement in 1997 that an adult sheep had been successfully cloned. Dolly the sheep had been created through a technique known as cell nuclear replacement (CNR). As shown in the diagram below, this involved removing the nucleus from an egg, and inserting a cell from an adult sheep into this denucleated egg. An electric current was then used to trick it into beginning the process of cell division, which is the earliest stage of new human life.

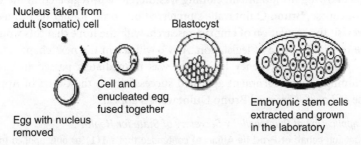

This process undoubtedly leads to the creation of embryos, but it does not involve fertilization, and so would not appear to fall within the statutory definition in section 1(1)(a). The reason for this gap is not that the drafters of the 1990 legislation had failed to anticipate the possibility of cloning. Rather they had assumed that cloning might only become possible using already *fertilized* eggs, in which case any cloned embryos would fall within the definition in section 1. Under section 3(3)(d), the Act specifically prohibits:

replacing a nucleus of a cell of an embryo with a nucleus taken from a cell of any person, embryo or subsequent development of an embryo.

And this would be effective to prevent cloning if the nucleus from the adult cell was placed in an embryo, instead of in an unfertilized egg as happens in CNR.

This apparent gap between the statutory wording and the procedure involved in Dolly's creation was the subject of a judicial review action brought by Bruno Quintavalle, on behalf of the Pro-life Alliance. The applicant claimed that the definition of 'embryo' in the 1990 Act did not cover embryos created by CNR. He further claimed that even if embryos created by CNR were classified as embryos for the purposes of the Act, section 3(3)(d) prohibited their creation. This latter argument was given short shrift by the judiciary: the words 'replacing a nucleus of a cell of an embryo' are clear and unambiguous, they cannot be read as including replacing the nucleus of an egg cell.

The fertilization point is rather more complicated. As we will see in the next chapter, the 1990 Act provides that nobody may produce an embryo outside of a woman's body except in pursuance of a licence granted by the HFEA. But if a cloned 'embryo' is not an embryo for the purposes of the statute, cloning is not a licensable activity, and would not be subject to any of the statutory protections we consider below, such as the 14-day time limit.

Of course, Bruno Quintavalle was not the first person to notice the lack of fit between section 1 of the Human Fertilisation and Embryology Act and CNR, but it had been assumed that because it was so plainly Parliament's intention that *all* embryos should fall within the regulatory framework set up by the 1990 Act, a purposive interpretation of these words would be sufficient to bring CNR within the HFEA's licensing regime.[22] At first instance, however, Bruno Quintavalle succeeded. The government had argued that the subsection should be read as if it read: 'a live human embryo where [if it is produced by fertilisation] fertilisation is complete', but Crane J held that the words were not sufficiently ambiguous to allow him to ignore their clear meaning. Following his judgment, cloning was therefore unregulated in the UK. This was not, of course, Bruno Quintavalle's preferred outcome. Rather he wanted parliament to revisit the regulation of embryo research, with the hope that this would result in a more restrictive piece of legislation. As we will see in the next chapter, following Crane J's judgment, emergency legislation was immediately passed to ban reproductive cloning. The government appealed successfully to the Court of Appeal, and the House of Lords dismissed Bruno Quintavalle's appeal.

R (on the application of Quintavalle) v Secretary of State for Health[23]

The claimant (on behalf of Pro-Life Alliance) contended that s 1(1)(a) only applied to embryos which were the product of fertilization and not to those created by CNR since in 1990 the creation of live human embryos by that method was unknown to Parliament. He argued that such embryos fell outside the regulatory scope of the Act. The judge at first instance agreed, but the Court of Appeal reversed his ruling. The House of Lords dismissed the claimant's appeal.

Lord Bingham

It is not often that Parliament has to frame legislation apt to apply to developments at the advanced cutting edge of science.

The solution recommended and embodied in the 1990 Act was not to ban all creation and

---

[22] See further Aurora Plomer, 'Beyond the HFE Act 1990: The Regulation of Stem Cell Research in the UK' (2002) 10 Medical Law Review 132.

[23] [2003] UKHL 13, [2003] 2 All ER 113.

subsequent use of live human embryos produced in vitro but instead, and subject to certain express prohibitions of which some have been noted above, to permit such creation and use subject to specified conditions, restrictions and time limits and subject to the regimes of control briefly described . . . above. The merits of this solution are not a matter for the House in its judicial capacity. It is, however, plain that while Parliament outlawed certain grotesque possibilities (such as placing a live animal embryo in a woman or a live human embryo in an animal), it otherwise opted for a strict regime of control. No activity within this field was left unregulated. There was to be no free for all.

It is against this background that one comes to interpret s 1(1)(a). . . . Can Parliament have been intending to distinguish between live human embryos produced by fertilisation of a female egg and live human embryos produced without such fertilisation? The answer must certainly be negative, since Parliament was unaware that the latter alternative was physically possible. This suggests that the four words ['when fertilisation is complete'] were not intended to form an integral part of the definition of embryo but were directed to the time at which it should be treated as such. . . . The somewhat marginal importance of the four words is in my opinion indicated by the fact that s 1(1)(b) appears to contradict them . . . The essential thrust of s 1(1)(a) was directed to such embryos, not to the manner of their creation, which Parliament (entirely understandably on the then current state of scientific knowledge) took for granted. . . .

Does the creation of live human embryos by CNR fall within the same genus of facts as those to which the expressed policy of Parliament has been formulated? In my opinion, it plainly does. An embryo created by in vitro fertilisation and one created by CNR are very similar organisms. The difference between them as organisms is that the CNR embryo, if allowed to develop, will grow into a clone of the donor of the replacement nucleus which the embryo produced by fertilisation will not. But this is a difference which plainly points towards the need for regulation, not against it. . . .

Is the embryo created by CNR different in kind or dimension from that for which the Act was passed? Plainly not: as already pointed out, the organisms in question are, as organisms, very similar. While it is impermissible to ask what Parliament would have done if the facts had been before it, there is one important question which may permissibly be asked: it is whether Parliament, faced with the taxing task of enacting a legislative solution to the difficult religious, moral and scientific issues mentioned above, could rationally have intended to leave live human embryos created by CNR outside the scope of regulation had it known of them as a scientific possibility. There is only one possible answer to this question and it is negative.

Lord Steyn

The long title of the 1990 Act makes clear, and it is in any event self-evident, that Parliament intended the protective regulatory system in connection with human embryos to be comprehensive. This protective purpose was plainly not intended to be tied to the particular way in which an embryo might be created. The overriding ethical case for protection was general. Not surprisingly there is not a hint of a rational explanation why an embryo produced otherwise than by fertilisation should not have the same status as an embryo created by fertilisation. It is a classic case where the new scientific development falls within what Lord Wilberforce called 'the same genus of facts' and in any event there is a clear legislative purpose which can only be fulfilled if an extensive interpretation is adopted. As Lord Bingham has demonstrated the makeweight arguments based on the difficulty of applying some regulatory provisions to the new development cannot possibly alter the clear legislative purpose. In the result I would either treat the restrictive wording of s 1(1) as merely illustrative of the legislative purpose or imply a phrase in s 1(1) so that it defines embryo as 'a live human embryo where [if it is produced by fertilisation] fertilisation is complete'.

If it is necessary to choose I would adopt the former technique. It fits readily into s 1(1) since the words of s 1(1)(b) plainly make otiose the words 'where fertilisation is complete' in s 1(1)(a). Treating the latter as merely illustrative requires no verbal manipulation.

For my part I am fully satisfied that cell nuclear replacement falls within the scope of the carefully balanced and crafted 1990 Act.

Lord Millett

Now whatever may be the status of an organism created by CNR before its single cell has split into two, once it has reached the two-cell stage it is an embryo in every accepted sense of that term. In the case of a human embryo, it is a live human organism containing within its cell or cells a full set of 46 chromosomes with the normal potential to develop and, if planted in a woman, to become a foetus and eventually a human being. While there may or may not be good reasons for distinguishing between the different processes by which embryos may be created when it comes to regulating their creation, no one has been able to suggest a reason why Parliament should differentiate between the different processes when it comes to regulating their subsequent use. . . .

These considerations indicate to my mind that Parliament intended to make comprehensive provision for the protection of human embryos however created, and that the failure of particular provisions to capture embryos produced by a process not involving fertilisation is not because Parliament intended to leave them unregulated but because Parliament did not foresee the need to deal with them.

With this introduction I can turn to the wording of s 1(1). The definition in para (a) is in part circular, since it contains the very term to be defined. It assumes that the reader knows what an embryo is. The purpose of the opening words of the paragraph is not to define the word 'embryo' but rather to limit it to an embryo which is (i) live and (ii) human. These are the essential characteristics which an embryo must possess if it is to be given statutory protection. The important point is that these characteristics are concerned with what an embryo is, not how it is produced. . . .

The concluding words of the paragraph ('where fertilisation is complete') have a different function. They do not describe the essential characteristics of an embryo, and do not form part of the definition of the word 'embryo'. They merely indicate the stage of development which an embryo must reach before it qualifies for protection. They are obviously inapplicable to embryos created by a process which does not involve fertilisation, and accordingly say nothing about the status of such embryos.

Paragraph (b) is likewise inapplicable to embryos created by a process which does not involve the use of a fertilised egg. . . . Its evident purpose was to bring the protection of the Bill forward by some 30 hours from the completion of the process of fertilisation to its beginning. . . .

This construction does not require words to be written into the section. There is no gap to be filled by implication. Nor is it a matter of updating the meaning of the word embryo by reference to subsequent developments. It is simply a matter of giving the opening words of para (a) their natural meaning, recognising the function of the concluding words, and confining their operation to the case where they are capable of application. Once it is accepted that the embryo is defined by reference to what it is and not by reference to the process by which it is created, all need for updating falls away. The result is to bring within the regulatory scope of the Act embryos produced by a process which was unknown to Parliament when the Act was passed. But such embryos are in all respects save the method of their creation indistinguishable from other embryos. They are alive and human, and accordingly possess all the features which Parliament evidently considered make it desirable to regulate their use for treatment or research. A construction which allowed for the regulation of embryos produced by fertilisation and not of embryos produced without fertilisation would not only defeat the evident purpose of Parliament to make comprehensive provision for the creation and use of human embryos but would produce an incoherent and irrational regulatory code. While this could be the inevitable result of legislation enacted at a time of rapid technological development, a construction which leads to this result should not be adopted where it can be avoided.

There was a difference between the Court of Appeal and the House of Lords' judgments in Quintavalle. The Court of Appeal's view was that it was of such importance that *all* embryos are covered by the legislation, that this must have been what Parliament had intended. A strained interpretation of the statutory language was therefore permissible in order to uphold Parliament's clear and unambiguous intention. In contrast, in dismissing Bruno Quintavalle's appeal, the House of Lords did not admit to having had to strain the language in the statute. Instead it was argued that embryo is an ordinary word of the English language—and that cloned embryos are undoubtedly embryos within this ordinary language meaning. Section 1(1)(a) was not intended to offer a special statutory redefinition of the word 'embryo'. Rather the normal meaning of the word embryo (which would undoubtedly include embryos created through CNR) must have been taken for granted by the statutory draftsman because the definition is 'a live human *embryo* where fertilisation is complete', which itself contains the word it is supposed to define, with no further elaboration. The important words in this phrase, according to Lord Millett, are 'live' and 'human'— this is the *sort* of embryo that is regulated by the statute—so dead and/or animal embryos are plainly not covered.

The House of Lords also appeared to be assisted by looking at what parliament did *not* intend when passing section 1(1)(a). Its purpose, they argued, was *not* to distinguish between different ways in which embryos might be created, because at that time it did not occur to anyone that they could be created without fertilization having taken place. So the phrases 'when fertilisation is complete' and 'an egg in the process of fertilisation' were directed towards the *time* at which an embryo would be subject to the regulatory control of the statute, and not to the *manner* in which embryos whose creation and use is controlled by the Act are created.

In the next extract, Andrew Grubb argues that it is not strictly true to say that Parliament did not anticipate CNR, and did not have any intention about how such embryos should be regulated, since section 3(3)(d) does appear to attempt to ban the only sort of cloning thought possible in 1990.

Andrew Grubb[24]

[T]he Law Lords sought to interpret the 1990 Act according to what Parliament had intended at the time of its passing but as applied to scientific developments of the present day. Central to their view that Parliament could be taken to have included CNR embryos within the regulatory framework of the 1990 Act was one assumption of fact. The CNR technique was unknown at the time the Act was passed. This is only partially—if at all—true. The precise technique of replacing the nucleus of an egg was not known in the sense that it was not, apparently, contemplated as a means of cloning. But, the concept of CNR *was* known. Parliament itself knew of the CNR technique when applied to the cell of an embryo. That is precisely what section 3(3)(d) contemplates. In the

---

[24] Commentary (2003) 11 Medical Law Review 135–8, 138.

light of section 3(3)(d) it is, in my view, somewhat disingenuous to argue that Parliament had never heard of CNR. It had, but only contemplated the technique's application to replacing the nucleus of a cell as part of an embryo. CNR, where the nucleus of an egg is replaced, does not require an imaginative quantum leap from what was known to be possible . . .

[T]he Law Lords saw Parliament's purpose relevant to the appeal as seeking to bring within the regulatory framework of the 1990 Act all activities involving the creation or use of embryos . . . As counsel for the applicant argued, one could equally see that Parliament in section 3(3)(d) had another purpose: to ban cloning. It simply did not use adequate words to achieve it. In other words, the legislative interpretation of the Law Lords achieves what Parliament did not intend in 1990, namely the regulation of embryo cloning—at least for research purposes. The latter is, of course, now seen as desirable because of the potential therapeutic benefits which may ensue from ES cell research but it was certainly not contemplated by Parliament in 1990. If one had a crystal ball, it might show that Parliament would not have permitted cloning for that purpose either but which is now, as a result of the Law Lords' decision, conveniently permitted under the 1990 Act subject to a licence from the HFEA. Now that would be judicial legislation rather than interpretation!

(c) THE UK'S RESTRICTIONS ON EMBRYO RESEARCH

The restrictions placed upon embryo research, discussed in the following sections, are intended to embody the compromise position embodied in the Warnock report, namely to ensure that valuable scientific research can take place within limits which are designed to show proper 'respect' for the early human embryo. Embryos may not be persons, but they are 'not nothing', and must be treated appropriately, and used only when necessary.

Responsibility for ensuring that research on embryos only takes place within these limits lies with the HFEA's research licence committee. This is a committee made up of HFEA members who scrutinize—with the assistance of advice from peer reviewers and from the HFEA's inspection team—each licence application in order to decide whether it fits within the limits set out in the legislation. Licences are normally granted for three years, although for novel projects, twelve month licences are the norm so that the licence committee has the opportunity to monitor the researchers' progress before deciding whether to renew the licence.

(1) THE FOURTEEN-DAY LIMIT

Under the Act, no research can be carried out on an embryo after 14 days.

The Human Fertilisation and Embryology Act 1990 section 13

(3) A licence cannot authorise

(a) keeping or using an embryo after the appearance of the primitive streak

(4) For the purposes of subsection (3)(a) above, the primitive streak is to be taken to have appeared in an embryo not later than the end of the period of fourteen days beginning with the day when the gametes are mixed, not counting any time during which the embryo is stored.

The primitive streak, which is the first sign of what will become the spinal column, emerges at about 14 days, and was chosen by the Warnock committee as 'one reference point in the development of the human individual'.[25] It is not the emergence of the primitive streak itself which represents the upper time limit for research, however. No experiments may be carried out after fourteen days, even if the primitive streak has not yet emerged. In the following extract Mary Warnock explains why the fourteen day limit was chosen.

Mary Warnock[26]

Fourteen days was decided on as the limit because of the great change in the development of the embryo heralded by the development of the primitive streak. It is only after that that an individual exists with its own now quickly developing central nervous system, its own limbs, its own brain. Even though before that an embryo has a genetic individuality, it has no pattern of human identity, any more than human tissue has. The history of each person who is born can be traced back to the development of the primitive streak and not before. Before that there could have been two or three people formed of the same material. It is because of the enormous change that comes at this stage of development that scientists generally prefer to think of the embryos as actually beginning to exist at this stage. Before that there is the egg and the sperm, and the *conceptus*, that which comes from their conjunction. All these, egg sperm and conceptus are human (that is, they differ from the eggs, sperm and conceptus of other animals) and are of course alive, but are not yet distinct embryos.

Bernard Williams suggests that the fourteen day limit does not reflect some relevant characteristic in the embryo itself, but is instead simply a reasonable regulatory response to a slippery slope argument against embryo research. The limit could equally well, Williams implies, have been drawn slightly earlier or later, but that does not undermine the value of choosing to draw a line somewhere.

Bernard Williams[27]

Warnock starts from a moral assumption that the Committee takes us to share: 'Every one agrees that it is completely unacceptable to make use of a child or an adult as the subject of research procedures which may cause harm or death'. . . . Granted this assumption, the question of embryo experiment . . . immediately raises the matter of the slippery slope. Is there any line that it can be sensible or appropriate to draw between experiment on a neonate, which is rejected, and experiment on an early embryo? What would be involved in drawing such a line? . . .

The Warnock Report is extremely clear that its recommended time limit of fourteen days for such experiment is indeed a regulatory line; though it bears a rough relation to a salient developmental feature, it is not intended to be an approximation to some characteristic which might be thought in itself relevant to the issue of experiment, such as sentience.

Is drawing a line in this way reasonable? Can it be effective? The answer to both these questions seems to me to be 'yes, sometimes', and, as that unexciting reply suggests, there is not a great deal to be brought to deciding them beyond good sense and relevant information. It may be said that a line of this kind cannot possibly be reasonable since it has to be drawn between two adjacent cases in the range, that is to say, between two cases that are not different enough to distinguish. The answer is that they are indeed not different enough to distinguish if that means that their

[25] Warnock para 11.22.

[26] 'Experimentation on human embryos and fetuses' in H Kuhse and P Singer, *A Companion to Bioethics* (Blackwell Oxford 1998) 390–6, 394.

[27] 'Types of moral argument against embryo research' in The Ciba Foundation, *Human Embryo Research: Yes or No?* (Tavistock London 1986) 184–94, 187, 190.

characteristics, unsupported by anything else, would have led one to draw a line there. But though the line is not, in this sense, uniquely reasonable, it is nevertheless reasonable to draw a line there. This follows from the conjunction of three things. First, it is reasonable to distinguish in some way unacceptable cases from acceptable cases; second, the only way of doing that in these circumstances is to draw a sharp line; third, it cannot be an objection to drawing the line just here that it would have been no worse to draw it somewhere else—if that were an objection, then one could conclude that one had no reason to draw it anywhere, and that is a style of argument that led to the death of Buridan's ass, who (it will be remembered) died of starvation between two piles of hay because neither pile had any characteristic that drew him to it rather than to the other.

Many other countries, such as Australia, Japan and Singapore, have also adopted a fourteen day limit. Currently there is little pressure from scientists to extend this limit because at present it has proved impossible to keep an embryo alive *in vitro* beyond about nine days. If, or perhaps when this becomes feasible, scientists may argue more vigorously that the fourteen day limit is an arbitrary cut-off point, capable of stifling valuable research.

(2) THE SOURCES OF EMBRYOS

There are two possible sources of embryos for use in research. First, research might be carried out on embryos that are left over after a couple have had fertility treatment. During an ordinary IVF cycle, as many eggs as possible will be fertilized in order to give a couple the best chance of achieving a pregnancy. This means it is common for couples to produce more embryos than the two (or in rare circumstances three) that may be transferred in one treatment cycle. Some of these embryos will not be suitable for use in treatment, and will either be destroyed or donated to research. Other spare embryos will commonly be frozen for use in future treatment. Once a couple has decided that they do not wish to use their frozen embryos for their own treatment, they may choose to have them destroyed, or they may opt to donate them for the treatment of others, or for use in research. Most embryo research in the UK is carried out on spare IVF embryos, which are donated by couples who have undergone fertility treatment.

Secondly, embryos could be specifically created for use in research. Obviously, this would require donated sperm and ova. There are certain circumstances in which scientists might prefer to create research embryos instead of using spare IVF embryos. For example, where a new fertilization technique is being developed, it might be important to try this on embryos which will not be transferred to a woman's body in order to ensure that embryos created in this way appear to develop normally. This was the case with ICSI (Intra-Cytoplasmic Sperm Injection), in which a single sperm is injected into an egg: the first embryos created through ICSI could not be used in treatment because it was important to see if they developed normally before using this new technique on patients. A second example might be if scientists want to create embryos with particular characteristics, such as a genetic disease, when sperm and eggs from people who are likely to pass on the condition might be used. Thirdly, because reproductive cloning is unlawful, all embryos that are created for therapeutic cloning—discussed below—are inevitably research-only embryos.

Is there a moral difference between conducting research on spare IVF embryos and creating embryos with the express purpose of carrying out experiments upon them? Clearly many people believe so. But why? In the next extract, Sharyn Roach Anleu suggests that the distinction is intended to limit the floodgates of scientific ambition.

Sharyn Roach Anleu[28]

[T]his distinction between 'spare' and 'needed' embryos reflects a pragmatic concern that the absence of formal limits would open the 'floodgates' for scientists to develop thousands of embryos and to engage in large-scale research less connected with treating infertility than with eugenics or their own career enhancement. The assumption is that, if medical scientists acted in their own interests, they would produce many embryos, most of which would never be implanted, and most of the research would not be oriented to alleviating infertility. Creating the category of 'spare' embryos is a mechanism to (i) ensure medical scientists consider interests other than their own; and (ii) restrict the number of embryos, regardless of whose interests they most cherish. Such a distinction is defining the law and delineating the boundaries of medical scientists' work by controlling the availability of resources for experimentation.

A different sort of argument, evident in the House of Lords Stem Cell Research Committee[29] report is that where the initial intention is to create a baby, the embryo is less instrumentalized than where the sole intention is to create an embryo in order to use it in research.

House of Lords Stem Cell Research Committee[30]

4.27 The creation of embryos (whether by IVF or CNR) for research purposes raises difficult issues. Some argue that, if an embryo is destined for destruction, it is more honest to create it specifically for the purpose of research than to use one created for reproductive purposes. But most of those who commented on this issue regarded it as preferable to use surplus embryos than to create them specifically for research. They took the view that an embryo created for research was quite clearly being used as a means to an end, with no prospect of implantation, whereas at the time of creation the surplus embryo had a prospect of implantation, even if, once not selected for implantation (or freezing), it would have to be destroyed. We agree that for this reason it is preferable to use surplus embryos for research purposes if the same results can be achieved with them. It is currently unavoidable that there should be some surplus embryos from IVF treatment, although desirable that the numbers should be reduced as more effective techniques are developed.

In contrast, Erik Parens argues that it is unusual to base an entity's moral status upon the intention of its creator.

Erik Parens[31]

One ethical intuition that seems to motivate the discarded-created distinction is that whereas the act of creating an embryo for reproduction is respectful in a way that is commensurate with the moral status of embryos, the act of creating an embryo for research is not . . . In this view, the

---

[28] 'The Legal Regulation of Medical Science' (2001) 23 Law and Policy 417–40, 427.
[29] *Stem Cell Research Report*, Feb 2002 <http://www.parliament.the-stationery-office.co.uk/pa/ld200102/ldselect/ldstem/83/8305.htm>.
[30] Ibid.
[31] 'On the ethics and politics of embryonic stem cell research' in S Holland, K Lebacqz, and Laurie Zoloth (eds), *The Human Embryonic Stem Cell Debate: Science, Ethics and Public Policy* (MIT Press Cambridge, Mass 2001) 37–50, 44.

moral status of the embryo (and thus the moral status of research on it) is a function of the intention of its maker. The problem with this intuition is that it is difficult to see what the intention of the maker of something has to do with the moral status of that thing once it has come into being. We do not think, for example, that the moral status of children is a function of their parents' intentions at the time of conception. If what something is obliges us to treat it some ways and not others, how it came to being is usually thought to be morally irrelevant.

The distinction between spare IVF embryos and research-only embryos is embodied in the Council of Europe's Convention on Human Rights and Biomedicine, Article 18(2) of which states that 'the creation of human embryos for research purposes is prohibited', and a number of other countries, such as Canada and Australia, expressly prohibit the creation of research embryos.

In contrast, in the UK both the use of spare IVF embryos and the creation of research embryos is permissible (the UK government has not yet signed the Convention on Human Rights and Biomedicine). Under Schedule 2(3)(1) of the 1990 Act, a research licence may authorize 'bringing about the creation of embryos *in vitro*'. But this does not mean that scientists in the UK are free to create as many research embryos as they like. There is no numerical limit upon the creation of embryos for research purposes in the Act, but in deciding whether to grant a licence, the HFEA's licence committee must be satisfied that the creation of embryos is *necessary*. The Warnock report was against the 'manufacture of large numbers of embryos',[32] and it seems clear that the HFEA treats the creation of research embryos as exceptional, requiring special justification. Between 1991 and 1999 over 53,000 embryos which were no longer needed for *in vitro* fertilization treatment were used in research, while only 118 embryos were specifically created in the course of research.[33] The matter was considered again by the House of Lords Stem Cell Research Committee which concluded that the creation of research-only embryos should be permitted only where there is a 'demonstrable and exceptional need'.

House of Lords Stem Cell Research Committee[34]

4.28 There may, however, be some research needs for embryos that cannot be met by the use of surplus embryos, for example when the research is concerned with the act of fertilisation itself. Two examples of such research that were licensed by the HFEA are: to test techniques of freezing eggs, which are very fragile, in order to assess the normality of an embryo created from an egg that has been thawed and fertilised; and the development of Intra-Cytoplasmic Sperm Injection. This procedure involves the direct injection of a sperm into an egg as a means of securing fertilisation by immature sperm. It was necessary to create an embryo to test the effectiveness of the technique and demonstrate its safety. The very small number of embryos created over the last ten years suggests that in practice there is little demand to create embryos by IVF for research. **The Committee believes that embryos should not be created specifically for research purposes unless there is a demonstrable and exceptional need which cannot be met by the use of surplus embryos.**

[32] Warnock para 12.5.

[33] House of Lords Stem Cell Research Committee, *Stem Cell Research Report*, Feb 2002 <http://www.parliament.the-stationery-office.co.uk/pa/ld200102/ldselect/ldstem/83/8305.htm> para 4.26.

[34] *Stem Cell Research Report*, Feb 2002 http://www.parliament.the-stationery-office.co.uk/pa/ld200102/ldselect/ldstem/83/8305.htm.

In response, the Government considered that this end was clearly being met by the HFEA's current case-by-case licensing procedure.

Government response to the House of Lords select committee on stem cell research[35]
The legislation and arrangements for ethical approval of research involving the creation of embryos for research have been in place since 1990. We believe that the existing provisions of the 1990 Act are working well and are sufficiently stringent to achieve what the Select committee is seeking.

Each research proposal is scrutinised by the HFEA on a case by case basis. The Government will require the HFEA to continue to do this and expects the Authority to give particular attention to any projects that involve the creation of embryos.

(3) THE PURPOSES OF RESEARCH: STEM CELL RESEARCH AND THERAPEUTIC CLONING

A further restriction on the use of embryos in research is that they can be used only for certain purposes. The restrictions are contained in Schedule 2 of the Act:

The Human Fertilisation and Embryology Act 1990 Schedule 2(3)

(1) A licence under this paragraph may authorise any of the following—

  (a) bringing about the creation of embryos *in vitro*, and

  (b) keeping or using embryos

(2) A licence under this paragraph cannot authorise any activity unless it appears to the Authority to be necessary or desirable for the purpose of

  (a) promoting advances in the treatment of infertility,

  (b) increasing knowledge about the causes of congenital disease,

  (c) increasing knowledge about the causes of miscarriage,

  (d) developing more effective techniques of contraception, or

  (e) developing methods for detecting the presence of gene or chromosome abnormalities in embryos before implantation,

  or for such other purposes as may be specified in regulations.

(6) No licence under this paragraph shall be granted unless the Authority is satisfied that any proposed use of embryos is necessary for the purposes of the research.

It is important to remember that scientists are not entitled to a licence just because they want to do research that falls within one of the specified purposes. In addition to receiving the approval of an external ethics committee, licences can be granted only if the licence committee is satisfied that the research is 'necessary or desirable' for one of these purposes, *and* that the proposed use of embryos is 'necessary' (sometimes referred to as the necessity principle). All research licence applications are peer-reviewed, and the reviewers are asked to confirm both that the research is necessary or desirable for one of the specified purposes, and that the use of embryos is necessary. The peer reviewers must confirm, and the licence committee must be satisfied that the

---

[35] Department of Health (2002) Cm 5561.

research could not be done *without* using human embryos. This means that if it were possible to conduct the research on animals or on tissue taken from adults, for example, the licence committee could not be satisfied that the use of embryos was *necessary*, and no licence could therefore be granted.

Notice that Schedule 2(3)(2) builds in the possibility of the statute's revision by regulations which can extend the purposes for which embryo research may be carried out. The original purposes in the 1990 Act did not cover embryonic stem cell (ES) research. Stem cells are undifferentiated cells which are capable of becoming specialized differentiated cells. In adults, stem cells allow us to regrow damaged tissue—such as burnt or broken skin. It is generally thought that adult stem cells may be able to form a relatively limited number of cell types. The inner cell mass of the early human embryo instead contains stem cells which possess remarkable plasticity. The first embryonic stem cells are totipotent, which means that they can become *every* cell in the human body, and even a whole new human organism. Later on, embryonic stem cells become pluripotent, which means they are capable of differentiating into several different types of cell in the human body. Stem cells are also immortal: they can continue to divide indefinitely without losing their genetic structure. In 1998, researchers at the University of Wisconsin published a paper explaining how they had, for the first time, derived and cultured human embryonic stem cells which would be capable of lasting indefinitely.[36]

Scientists think that it may become possible to trick these stem cell lines into differentiating into different types of tissue, which could then be used to repair damaged tissues or organs. When coupled with cell nuclear replacement (CNR), considered above, the possibilities become more remarkable still. Therapeutic cloning would involve the extraction of embryonic stem cells from cloned embryos. If the embryo from which embryonic stem cells are removed was cloned from the person with a damaged organ, the replacement tissue would be a perfect genetic match, and there would be no possibility of rejection.

For example, imagine that I need some replacement tissue—perhaps because I have a degenerative brain disease such as Parkinson's. If the cloned embryo is created from my skin cell, the stem cells and any brain tissue grown as a result will be genetically identical to me. This removes the problem of rejection, and the need for a recipient of replacement tissue to suppress their immune systems by taking immuno-suppressant drugs. If this process were to become relatively straightforward, it potentially offers a solution to the organ shortage we considered in the previous chapter: anyone whose organs had failed could simply use therapeutic cloning in order to produce genetically compatible replacement tissue.

More recently, in experiments involving mice, scientists have been able to create gametes from stem cells.[37] The possibilities this raises are truly extraordinary. Infertile men and women would no longer have to resort to treatment with donated gametes since their own gametes could be created artificially. It might even be possible for doctors to enable a woman to create her own 'sperm'. Artificial gametes might then

---

[36] JA Thomson et al., 'Embryonic stem cell lines derived from human blastocysts' (1998) 282 Science 1145–7.
[37] See further G Testa and J Harris, 'Ethics and Synthetic Gametes' (2005) 19 Bioethics 146.

enable a lesbian couple to have a child that is a mixture of their genes, in the same way as in normal heterosexual reproduction.

In 1998, the HFEA and the Human Genetics Advisory Commission (HGAC)[38] undertook a public consultation on human cloning and stem cell research.[39] Their report recommended that new regulations should extend the purposes for which embryo research could be carried out in the UK. Following their report, the Government set up an expert group, chaired by the Chief Medical Officer, Professor Sir Liam Donaldson, to assess the possible benefits of stem cell research, and to advise whether regulations should extend the purposes for which the HFEA might issue licences for research involving human embryos. The CMO's Expert Group's report was published in 2000.[40] It reviewed the scientific evidence, and argued that the potential benefits of this sort of research justified the use of embryos as a source of stem cells. It also recommended that before licensing any stem cell research project, the HFEA should satisfy itself that there are no other means of meeting the objectives of the research, and that individuals whose eggs or sperm are used to create the embryos to be used in research should give specific consent to their use in a research project to derive stem cells.

Following the CMO's Expert Group's endorsement of stem cell research, the Government brought forward regulations extending the purposes for which research on human embryos could be lawfully undertaken, subject to the individual project receiving a licence from the HFEA. Schedule 2's research purposes now include the possibility of carrying out stem cell research into the treatment of serious diseases.

Human Fertilisation and Embryology (Research Purposes) Regulations 2001
Further purposes for which research licences may be authorised

2.—(1) The Authority may issue a licence for research under paragraph 3 of Schedule 2 to the Act for any of the purposes specified in the following paragraph.

(2) A licence may be issued for the purposes of—

(a) increasing knowledge about the development of embryos

(b) increasing knowledge about serious disease, or

(c) enabling any such knowledge to be applied in developing treatments for serious disease.

Unsurprisingly, there was disquiet that such a controversial issue was decided without full parliamentary scrutiny. As a result, although the House of Lords passed the regulations, it added an amendment that a select committee should be set up to consider the question of stem cell research. Setting up a select committee *after* rather than before legislative reform is, of course, unusual. Because of the contentiousness of the issue, the HFEA chose not to issue any licences under the new regulations until the select committee had concluded its deliberations. The committee's report was

---

[38] Now the Human Genetics Commission (HGC).
[39] Cloning Issues in Reproduction, Science and Medicine (Dec 1998).
[40] *Therapeutic Cloning—Stem Cells: Medical Progress with Responsibility 2000* <http://www.doh.gov.uk/cegc/stemcellreport.htm>.

published in February 2002.[41] In the light of its approval of stem cell research, the first licences were granted soon afterwards by the HFEA. By August 2004, one-third of the thirty research projects licensed in the UK involved stem cell research.[42]

And following the House of Lords' decision in *Quintavalle*, considered above p. 778 it is clear that the HFEA also has the power to issue licences for the creation of human embryos using CNR for research purposes. The first CNR licence was issued in August 2004, and at the time of writing there are two research projects involving the creation of embryos through CNR in the UK. In 2005, the researchers who were granted the first CNR licence announced that they had successfully cloned four human embryos, one of which survived for five days.[43] At the time of writing, no stem cell lines have been extracted from CNR embryos in the UK, but the South Korean team, who produced the first cloned human embryo for research purposes, have managed to extract 11 stem cell lines from CNR embryos created from skin cells taken from patients affected by disease or spinal injury.[44]

Opponents of stem cell research often argue forcefully that research should concentrate upon the use of adult stem cells, in preference to those taken from embryos. The House of Lords select committee discussed this question at length, and as Roger Brownsword explains in the next extract, advocated a 'dual track' approach.

Roger Brownsword[45]

During the House of Lords' debate on the Regulations, it was forcibly suggested that new research was coming through to challenge the ruling view that adult stem cells have a relatively limited and specialised range. And, as the Select committee sat, evidence was regularly adduced to add plausibility to the possibility that adult stem cells might be much more plastic than is generally assumed. If the claims for the potency of adult stem cells are made out, the objection runs, surely it would be better to direct research into this channel rather than into hES [human embryonic stem] cells. . . .

The Select committee could have dealt with this issue quite shortly. It could have simply said, for example, that the weight of scientific evidence presented to the Committee overwhelmingly supported a 'dual track' complementary approach to stem cell research, with work being conducted on both adult and hES cells. Moreover the Committee had evidence from a number of leading international *adult* stem cell researchers, each of whom subscribed to the dual track approach. Equally, the Select committee could have kept the issue at arm's length by pointing out that the necessity principle, which is at the heart of the legal framework, means that the HFEA will have to keep this issue under review anyway—in a sense, the operative question is not whether the Select committee judges that research on hES cells is a poor investment of scientific resources, it is whether the HFEA is persuaded that the research can be done in no other way. Taking this approach, the Committee could have made the point that, if the proponents of one track adult

[41] *Stem Cell Research Report*, Feb 2002 <http://www.parliament.the-stationery-office.co.uk/pa/ld200102/ldselect/ldstem/83/8306.htm>.

[42] HFEA, *Thirteenth Annual Report 2003/4* <http://www.hfea.gov.uk/HFEAPublications/AnnualReport/HFEA_ARA_03_04.pdf>.

[43] M Stojkovic, P Stojkovic, C Leary, VJ Hall, L Armstrong, M Herbert, M Nesbitt, M Lako, and A Murdoch, 'Derivation of a human blastocyst after heterologous nuclear transfer to donated oocytes', Reproductive BioMedicine Online 19 May 2005 <http://www.rbmonline.com>.

[44] Hwang et al., 'Patient-Specific Embryonic Stem Cells Derived from Human SCNT Blastocysts', Science 19 May 2005 <http://www.sciencemag.org>.

[45] 'Stem Cells, Superman, and the Report of the Select committee' (2002) 65 Modern Law Review 568–87, 573–4.

stem cell work are right, it will soon become clear that research on embryos is unnecessary and the HFEA will decline to issue licences for such hES cell research. However, the Committee eschews such short responses, dedicating a whole chapter to a detailed and extremely careful consideration of the relative advantages and limitations of research-leading-to-therapy focused on, respectively, adult and embryonic stem cells. One of the most interesting points made here is that, even if research is focusing on adult stem cells, 'ES cells provide the only realistic means at present of studying the mechanisms and control of the processes of differentiation and dedifferentiation' . . . At the end of this discussion, the Committee concludes that, whilst recent research on adult stem cells looks promising and should be strongly encouraged by funding bodies and Government, the dual track approach is essential if maximum medical benefit is to be obtained.

Although broadly supporting the extension of the research purposes, the select committee did comment on some potential problems which might arise under the Regulations. First, what counts as a 'serious' disease? The House of Lords select committee suggested that an indicative list might be helpful, but this was rejected by the government. Nevertheless it is possible that in the future the HFEA may have to make some difficult judgements about whether a particular condition meets the threshold level of seriousness. Secondly, the use of the word 'disease' is perhaps unfortunate given that stem cell therapies might be used to treat people who have suffered serious *injuries*, such as damage to the spinal cord. Thirdly, does the first purpose— 'increasing knowledge about the development of embryos'—cover what is known as basic research, where scientists are in fact simply learning how human stem cells behave and differentiate.

House of Lords Stem Cell Research Committee[46]

8.8 'Serious disease' is not a term that is defined in other statutes (although in other contexts there are references to 'serious disability') and we believe that it would be helpful to have a clearer indication of what it is intended to cover. It is uncertain whether it means serious for the individual or serious for society (the debates suggested that Ministers had the former in mind); and whether it is wide enough to encompass serious injury (to the spinal cord, for example) as well as disease. Moreover, if research properly directed at serious disease later proves to have a useful secondary application for 'non-serious' disease, that application should not be ruled out by the fact that the initial research must be relevant to serious disease. We accept that an exhaustive list of serious diseases would be difficult to frame satisfactorily and might involve making invidious distinctions. It would be less difficult to include in the Regulations an indicative list which gave some central examples while making clear that it was not exhaustive. A further possibility would be for the Department of Health or the HFEA to issue non-statutory guidance on the matter. We consider that this last possibility would be the most flexible and would meet the need best. **We invite the Department of Health to examine with the HFEA the possibility of drawing up indicative guidance as to what constitutes serious disease for the purposes of the Regulations.** . . .

8.15 It is not for us to express an authoritative view on the interpretation of the Regulations. However, it is in the nature of the science that, before research into ES as well as adult

[46] *Stem Cell Research Report*, Feb 2002 <http://www.parliament.the-stationery-office.co.uk/pa/ld200102/ldselect/ldstem/83/8306.htm>.

stem cells can lead to therapeutic applications, there must be basic research; and, given that the Regulations explicitly recognise the development of treatments for serious diseases as one of the new purposes, it would be perverse if basic research were not implicitly incorporated. The Committee confidently believes that Parliament cannot have intended to will the therapeutic end without also willing the necessary means to that end and has no doubt that the HFEA should consider applications made under the Regulations in accordance with the legal advice it has received. Nevertheless, to put the matter beyond any possible doubt, when the Government bring forward legislation they should consider making express provision for such basic research as is necessary as a precursor for the development of cell-based therapies.

Government response to the House of Lords select committee on stem cell research[47]

In both Houses, Health Ministers made clear that they did not believe that guidance in the form of lists of what constituted serious disease would be either helpful or practical.

The Government remains of the view that as every licence application is to be examined by the HFEA on a case by case basis such a list is unnecessary. To date there is no doubt that the types of disease that are being researched under licence from the HFEA—Parkinson's and other neural diseases and pancreatic tissue—are 'serious'. However, we will review this with the HFEA as and when the number of research applications increase.

It is interesting to note that the House of Lords select committee Report went on to express some reservations about the claims being made for stem cell research and therapeutic cloning. It suggested that the sort of individualized treatment described above would be both difficult and expensive. But despite its scepticism about the revolutionary potential of embryonic stem cell research, the House of Lords select committee concluded that research into differentiation was essential in order to work out how it might be possible to grow new tissue, either from embryonic or adult stem cells in the future.

House of Lords Stem Cell Research Committee[48]

5.9   The majority scientific view presented to the Committee was that for practical reasons CNR is unlikely to provide a general basis for therapies in the foreseeable future. We were told that individualised treatments using the patient's own cells would be difficult and expensive and would require a continuing supply of human eggs, which is unlikely to be forthcoming on a large scale. Some medical charities and patients' support groups argued that female members of a patient's family would be prepared to donate eggs for altruistic motives, and this is no doubt true in some cases. Opponents of CNR argued that it would be difficult to avoid pressure being brought to bear on potential donors, although that is a problem that has up to now been dealt with successfully in the United Kingdom by strict regulation of gamete donation, including a prohibition on payment. As a response to these problems it has been suggested that CNR might be used to generate a bank of ES cells from which the best 'match' with the patient could be selected to minimise the risk of immune rejection. Several thousand ES cell lines generated by this process would be required. Whether this is a realistic possibility remains to be seen.

[47] Department of Health (2002) Cm 5561.
[48] *Stem Cell Research Report,* Feb 2002 <http://www.parliament.the-stationery-office.co.uk/pa/ld200102/ldselect/ldstem/83/8306.htm>.

5.10 However, even if CNR does not become a general basis for therapies in the foreseeable future, it still has significant potential as a research technique since it would provide a powerful approach to studying the process of dedifferentiation. In producing Dolly the sheep CNR has shown that dedifferentiation of adult cells is possible and gave a major impetus to research into that process . . .

5.14 The Committee concludes that, even if CNR is not itself used directly for many stem cell-based therapies, there is still a powerful case for its use, subject to strict regulation by the HFEA, as a research tool to enable cell-based therapies to be developed. However, as with embryos created by IVF for research, CNR embryos should not be created for research purposes unless there is a demonstrable and exceptional need which cannot be met by the use of surplus embryos.

Government response to the House of Lords select committee on stem cell research[49]

The Government believes strongly that no single source of stem cells should be worked on exclusively, but wishes to see research move forward on adult, cord blood, fetal and embryonic cell lines. We are pleased that the Select Committee endorses this approach and recognises that we are not dealing with a choice between one source of cells and another.

The application of ES cells to research aimed at understanding cell development and the processes that control cell differentiation will be crucially important. Such research will help us understand early embryo development as well as providing the knowledge needed to move towards cell-based treatments for serious disease.

The Government is convinced, as was the Select Committee, that embryonic stem cell research will be an essential component of stem cell research for the foreseeable future.

As the House of Lords select committee points out, therapeutic cloning would require a continuing supply of human eggs, from which the nucleus could be removed in order to insert one of the patient's own cells. Egg donation is uncomfortable, intrusive, carries a small risk to health, and women are not paid. Given that there is a shortage of donated eggs for use in fertility treatment, is there likely to be an endless supply available for stem cell research, or for therapeutic cloning? Of course, the creation of artificial gametes, discussed earlier, might offer a solution, and in the next extract, Søren Holm suggests that another possibility would be to use non-human eggs.

Søren Holm[50]

If stem cells are to be produced from embryos that are not 'spare' after IVF, the ova for this production must come from women. In the initial research phase the number of ova needed will be relatively small, but for stem cell therapy the number may become very large. If, for instance, a specific therapy is based on nuclear replacement from the intended recipient in order to ensure perfect immunological compatibility, at least one ovum will be needed for each patient (and probably more since the techniques for nuclear replacement are unlikely to become 100% effective any time soon).

This raises general problems concerning how we can ensure that the ova are obtained without coercion or exploitation of the ova donors, sellers or providers, but also more specific questions about how a new practice of non-reproduction related ova procurement would influence the status of women in society. . . .

---

[49] Department of Health (2002) Cm 5561.
[50] 'Going to the Roots of the Stem Cell Controversy' (2002) 16 Bioethics 493–507, 499–500.

One way of solving the problem of shortage of ova, and the potential ethical problems in using women as donors of ova for these purposes is to use ova from other species (eg bovines) in the creation of stem cells by means of nuclear replacement techniques.

It is, as yet, unknown whether the use of ova from other species is technically possible, and if possible whether the stem cells produced would be functionally and immunologically equivalent to stem cells produced using human ova . . .

The additional ethical problems created by this source of ova can, however, be argued to be small as long as the resulting embryos are only used for stem cell production and not for reproductive purposes.

On some lines of argument the ethical problems may actually be less than if human ova are used, since it could be argued that the embryos produced are not really human embryos. If the moral status of human embryos is based in their being human, then the moral status of these 'less than human' embryos could be argued to be less important.

One of the arguments against therapeutic cloning is the 'slippery slope' claim that it might assist the perfection of techniques which could be used in reproductive cloning. Of course, if reproductive cloning is believed to be acceptable, then this is unproblematic; but as we will see in the next chapter, many people believe that it would be morally wrong to produce a cloned baby. In the UK, this slippery slope concern has not prevented the HFEA from licensing the creation of CNR embryos on the grounds, first, that it believes that there are sufficient protections under UK law to prevent reproductive cloning, and, second, that the fact that a practice *might* be misused in another country does not offer sufficient justification for restricting potentially beneficial research in the UK.

It has been suggested that therapeutic cloning, if successful, will lead to a new sort of regenerative medicine. Most people in the West now die as a result of degenerative diseases, such as heart disease and cancer. If it became possible to replace new tissue when required, these techniques might substantially interfere with the human body's natural degeneration. This prompts John Harris to consider a world in which aging, and even death, might no longer be inevitable. If cloned human embryonic stem cells, appropriately reprogrammed, could be used for the constant regeneration of organs and tissue, might we significantly extend the life span?

John Harris[51]

This brings us to the central issue: would substantially increased life expectancy or even immortality be in fact a benefit or a good? There are people who regard the prospect of immortality with distaste or even horror; there are others who desire it above all else. In that most people fear death and want to postpone it as long as possible, there is some reason to suppose that the prospect of personal immortality would be widely welcomed. But it is one thing to contemplate our own personal immortality, quite another to contemplate a world in which increasing numbers of people were immortal, and in which we and all or any future children would have to compete indefinitely with previous generations for jobs, space and everything else . . .

To come down to earth, there is no doubt that immortality would be a mixed blessing, but we should be slow to reject cures for terrible diseases even if the price we have to pay for those cures is increasing life expectancy and even creating immortals. Better surely to accompany the

---

[51] 'The Ethics and Justice of Life-extending Therapies' (2002) 55 Current Legal Problems 65–95, 80, 94.

scientific race to achieve immortality with commensurate work in ethics and social policy to ensure that we know how to cope with the transition to parallel populations of mortals and immortals . . . As and when the numerical balance of these parallel populations seems set to shift dramatically towards significant and problematic numbers of immortals some hard decisions will have to be taken.

On the one hand, the possibility of producing replacement tissue for people whose bodies were degenerating might appear to give rise to some complex ethical issues. For example, these techniques are likely to be expensive, and so significantly increased life expectancy might initially be available only to a small minority of very rich people, raising questions of distributive justice. If in time, regenerative medicine became more widely available, what impact would significantly increased lifespans have for the world and its resources?

On the other hand, it could be argued that finding cures for diseases such as cancer and heart disease is just part of the normal process of scientific development, and that just as the discovery of cures for infectious diseases increased life-spans dramatically during the twentieth century, so we should not be surprised if average life-spans continue to increase as medical knowledge becomes more sophisticated. It could also be argued that there is already an enormous difference between rich and poor people's life spans. In the UK, average life expectancy is now around 80 years, but for homeless people it is around 45 years. In some African countries, the average life span has been dropping as a result of the AIDS pandemic, and in some countries is now as low as 35. Regenerative medicine would not then pose uniquely difficult questions about distributive justice.

(4) CONSENT

One important prerequisite to the use of embryos in research is that the gamete providers should have specifically donated them to research. Without such consent, even if the gamete providers do not want the embryos to be stored for use in their own treatment or donated to others, embryos must be allowed to perish. Under Schedule 3(1) of the 1990 Act, consent to an embryo's use in any project of research must be in writing. Schedule 3(3) specifies that the person giving consent must have been given a suitable opportunity to receive counselling, and must be provided 'with such relevant information as is proper'. Consent can be withdrawn under Schedule 3(4) at any time until the embryo has been used for the purposes of any project of research.

New consent issues are raised by the possibility of extracting stem cell lines from embryos, since these lines are potentially immortal and might be useful to scientists (and in the future, pharmaceutical companies and doctors) for many years to come. The point was considered by the House of Lords Select committee:

House of Lords Stem Cell Research Committee[52]

8.33 The Committee recommends that the HFEA ensures that the implications arising from the 'immortality' of stem cell lines are fully covered in obtaining informed consent from

---

[52] *Stem Cell Research Report*, Feb 2002 <http://www.parliament.the-stationery-office.co.uk/pa/ld200102/ldselect/ldstem/83/8306.htm>.

donors giving embryos for the potential establishment of ES cell lines for research. To prevent future restrictions in using ES cell lines (and therefore minimise the need to generate new ES cell lines) the HFEA should not permit ES cell lines to be generated from donated embryos unless informed consent places no specific constraint on their future use. Where parents wish to restrict the type of research which can be undertaken, for example specifically for reproductive purposes, the embryos donated should be used for purposes other than the generation of ES cell lines.

Government response to the House of Lords select committee on stem cell research[53]

The Government agrees that it would be both undesirable and unworkable for conditional consents to be applied to the derivation of ES stem cell lines. These cell lines can survive indefinitely and conditions on the donations could, as the Select Committee suggests, open up all sorts of unwelcome possibilities. The Government agrees that if potential donors wish to place constraints on how ES cells derived from their donated embryo are used, then it would not be appropriate to accept their embryos for such research and the HFEA should not allow this.

It is essential that donors giving embryos for stem cell research should be given thorough and appropriate information. They need to understand that any stem cell lines created may continue indefinitely and be used in many different research projects.

The Government agrees with the Committee that the HFEA should ensure that all of the implications have been fully explored with potential donors.

The HFEA and the Medical Research Council have jointly contributed towards a standard consent form to the use of embryos for stem cell research. This stresses, among other things, that the couple will not benefit, medically or financially, from any discoveries made during research on their cells. In order to ensure that future treatments are not hampered by the restrictive terms of the original consent, it is not possible for people donating embryos for stem cell research to specify that their stem cell lines are only ever to be used for research purposes. People can consent only to their possible future use in both research and treatment. The UK stem cell bank, set up in 2002, receives every stem cell line recovered by researchers, and the HFEA will not grant licences for stem cell research unless the researchers have made a commitment to deposit each stem cell line with the bank.[54] People donating embryos for stem cell research must be informed of the intention to bank any stem cell lines derived from their embryos.

(5) INCONSISTENCY WITH ABORTION?

Obviously people who have moral objections to abortion will invariably also object to embryo research. And the existence of some inconsistencies between abortion law and the rules governing embryo research has been pointed out both by those who object to the destruction of embryos, and by those who would advocate a more permissive regime. For example, anti-abortionists might argue that if embryos are protected when they are 14 days old, it is illogical to permit the destruction of fetuses at 23 weeks for 'social' reasons. Others might say that if a woman can abort a fetus during the first 24 weeks of pregnancy because termination promotes her best interests, it makes little sense to prohibit potentially life saving research on 16-day-old embryos.

---

[53] Department of Health (2002) Cm 5561.   [54] <http://www.ukstemcellbank.org.uk/>.

Certainly the House of Lords Science and Technology Committee suggested that given the legality of abortion, a ban on embryo research would be 'difficult to justify':

It would be difficult to justify an absolute prohibition on the destruction of early embryos while permitting abortion in a relatively wide range of circumstances post-implantation—indeed well after the emergence of the primitive streak and into the foetal stage of development.

5. INTERNATIONAL PERSPECTIVES

The UK's regulation of embryo research is one of the most liberal regimes in the world. Even countries with fairly permissive regimes, such as the Netherlands, do not currently permit the creation of embryos for research purposes. Towards the other end of the spectrum, Austria, Ireland, Latvia, and Poland have legislation prohibiting human embryonic stem cell research. Germany permits research only if it is done for the benefit of the particular embryo. Since embryos are destroyed after experiments have been carried out, in practice this amounts to a ban on embryo research. In 2002, however, the German Bundestag decided to allow stem cell lines to be imported, provided that the stem cell lines had already been in existence at the time, in order to ensure that the import of stem cells did not contribute to the destruction of more embryos.[55]

The lack of any consensus in Europe on the morality of embryo research means that there are a variety of different regulatory regimes. Article 18 of the Council of Europe's Convention on Human Rights and Biomedicine, which has been signed by only a handful of states, simply says that:

Where the law allows research on embryos in vitro, it shall ensure adequate protection of the embryo.

As Carlos Romeo-Casabona explains in the next extract, it is very difficult to see what this means.

Carlos Romeo-Casabona[56]
The differing approaches in the EU show the lack of legal consensus. . . . The varying legal approaches adopted are: (i) to establish broad provision for both the creation and the use of human embryos for research (United Kingdom and probably The Netherlands); (ii) to provide broad legal provision for the use of surplus frozen embryos (this will be the case following forthcoming legislation in France); (iii) to provide a restrictive legal framework for the use of surplus frozen embryos (Spain, as the embryos are not biologically capable of use for reproduction); (iv) to strictly prohibit the use and freezing of embryos (Germany, but the importation of stem cells has recently been allowed by a new law) . . .

The above summary is intended to provide only a brief description of the legal solutions currently in existence. However, it is sufficiently illustrative to show the lack of any minimal points of consensus. . . .

---

[55] See further Samantha Halliday, 'A Comparative Approach to the Regulation of Human Embryonic Stem Cell Research in Europe' (2004) 12 Medical Law Review 40–69.

[56] 'Embryonic Stem Cell Research and Therapy: The Need for a Common European Legal Framework' (2002) 16 Bioethics 557–67.

The first paragraph of Article 18 [Council of Europe Convention on Human Rights and Bio-medicine] establishes that the states taking part in the convention could authorise experimentation upon human embryos by law. It implies that the decision to authorise or forbid such research rests with the state (by the use of an express legal provision). The only obligation imposed is that if research is permitted, the law has to guarantee adequate protection of the embryo (again, by an express legal provision). In other words, the law must include some type of guarantee which provides adequate protection. However, it is extraordinarily difficult to see what form such protection should take, since the use of an embryo for research is usually incompatible with its role in reproduction.

In the next extract, Samantha Halliday argues that while EU regulation of stem cell research is infeasible, by setting out rules which apply to EU funded research, greater harmonization may be possible.

Samantha Halliday[57]

[T]he European Union may be able to achieve some degree of *de facto* regulation by setting out rules in relation to EU funded embryonic stem cell research. Recently the Commission proposed guidelines to be applied to research involving human embryos and human embryonic stem cells funded by the European Union under the Sixth Framework programme . . .

According to the Commission's guidelines, funded research must comply with the necessity principle and only research conducted upon supernumerary embryos created prior to 27 June 2002 and stem cells derived from those embryos will be eligible for funding. In relation to permissible research purposes, the proposal states that the research must serve one of two particularly important research aims, either increasing scientific knowledge in basic research or increasing medical knowledge for the development of diagnostic, preventative or therapeutic methods to be applied to humans. Embryos must have been donated in accordance with national law, with the explicit, informed consent of the donor and without inducement. . . . The guidelines also require participants to do their best to make newly derived stem cell lines available to the scientific community on a non-profit making basis . . .

In its explanatory memorandum the Commission sets out the rationale for EU funding of embryonic stem cell research—namely that collaborative research at EU level will reduce the number of embryos destroyed by avoiding duplication of research and that the funding will encourage exchange of results and expertise between scientists in the different Member States, hopefully enabling progress to be made more quickly. To that end, the Commission has also announced its intention to publish a call for proposals to establish a European stem cell registry, which should ensure transparency and facilitate access to cells throughout the European Union.

Whilst the Commission's proposed guidelines for funding embryonic stem cell research do not amount to regulation of such research at an EU level, they will be influential in informing debate at the national level and the practical impact of the funding allocated to this type of research could provide a real impetus for harmonisation.

Of course, one difficulty with these funding rules is that they are more restrictive than the UK's regulatory regime, and so scientists who want to carry out research on embryos created expressly for that purpose will apply for a licence in the UK, and any resulting stem cell lines would not be eligible for inclusion in any EU-wide registry.

In the US, privately funded embryo research is regulated only at state level, with

---

[57] 'A Comparative Approach to the Regulation of Human Embryonic Stem Cell Research in Europe' (2004) 12 Medical Law Review 40–69, 66–7.

considerable variation between different states. In some states embryo research is completely prohibited, while in others there is no explicit regulation and therefore little control over what takes place in private research institutions. California has the most liberal regulatory regime, having passed legislation specifically permitting stem cell research and the creation of embryos using CNR. As a result, much of the US's stem cell research now takes place in California. At federal level, the only control on embryo research is through funding, with no federal funding for any research which involves the destruction of embryos.

As in Germany, a compromise was reached on research involving stem cell lines which had already been created. There can now be federal funding for research on human embryonic stem cells, but only if they were derived from stem cell lines established before President George Bush's announcement on the 9 August 2001. The rationale was that there should be no federal support for research which involves the destruction of human embryos but that, if the embryo had already been destroyed, there was no objection to using the stem cells which had been extracted from it. In the next extract, John Robertson defends this at first sight rather disingenuous distinction between the use and the derivation of stem cells.

John A Robertson[58]

Recognition of the use versus derivation distinction now informs federal funding law in the United States . . . As long as some jurisdictions permit destructive embryo research to occur, ES cell lines might be derived that could be used for research in countries that themselves ban the derivation of human ES cells by embryo destruction. This is because the cell lines would have been derived independently of the later decision to use them for research.

The distinction between use and derivation is neither cynical nor disingenuous for it reflects the basic distinction in the ethics of complicity between causing an immoral or wrongful act to occur and benefiting from it once it has occurred. One who intends or causes an immoral act to occur is responsible or has complicity in a causative sense, and may be held responsible for the event. Conversely, one who does not proximately cause a wrongful event is not morally responsible for its occurrence even if he or she later benefits from it.

In 2005 the US House of Representatives approved a bill that would overturn President Bush's policy on human embryonic stem (ES) cell research. The Stem Cell Research Enhancement Act of 2005 would allow an extension of federal funding for research using stem cells derived from surplus embryos donated by patients undergoing IVF. It would not, however, allow funds for research on embryos which have been created specifically for research. It seems likely that the Senate will pass the Act, but if the majority is less than two-thirds, President Bush would be able to use his veto to prevent it from becoming law.

---

[58] 'Human embryonic stem cell research: ethical and legal issues' (2001) 2 Nature Reviews Genetics 74–8, 76.

6. CONCLUSION

Regulating a fast-moving area of science is inevitably a difficult task. Perhaps the clearest illustration of this is the 1990 Act's rather unfortunate 'definition' of the word 'embryo', which, as we have seen, applied rather awkwardly to a technique which was discovered six years after the Act was passed.

The government intends to reform the 1990 Act. At the time of writing, a consultation paper is expected in 2005, which will probably lead to new legislation within a couple of years. So what can we expect from a new Act? It seems unlikely that the government will either dismantle the licensing regime or remove some of the basic restrictions upon the use of embryos, since these are almost certainly responsible for maintaining public confidence. In 2003, a MORI opinion poll found that 70 per cent of the public supported the use of human embryos for medical research to find treatments for serious diseases, and for fertility research.[59] The UK's regulatory regime has also been widely copied by other countries.

Any new Act would therefore build upon the successful features of the current regime, while attempting to fill the various 'gaps' which have emerged since 1990. Certainly, it might be important to redefine the 'embryo', so that embryos created by techniques other than fertilization are clearly included. In addition, the creation of animal/human hybrids or chimeras might be useful for research purposes, and yet this would be prohibited by the 1990 Act, which permits the use of animal gametes only for the purpose of testing the fertility of sperm, and specifies that any embryo thus created must be destroyed no later than the two cell stage. A new piece of legislation might relax this restriction, while ensuring that any such embryos are not used for reproductive purposes.

It would also be important for a new Act to be flexible enough to respond to as yet unforeseen developments. This might be done by building in the possibility of reform via regulations, as happened in the case of the research purposes in Schedule 2 of the 1990 Act. Alternatively, the statute could delegate decision-making power to the regulatory authority. The government has already announced that the new legislation will merge the Human Tissue Authority (whose role we considered in the previous chapter) and the HFEA, to create the Regulatory Authority for Tissues and Embryos (RATE).

Finally, it is worth noting that when the 1990 Act was passed, fertility treatment and embryo research were equally novel and controversial, and there were good reasons to subject both to a special licensing regime. Now the situation is rather different. IVF treatment has become a routine medical procedure, while embryo research remains extremely controversial. Perhaps any new legislation will acknowledge this by softening the regulatory regime in relation to fertility treatment, while recognizing that public confidence in embryo research continues to depend upon both a rigorous licensing procedure and the ongoing monitoring of individual research projects.

---

[59] See further <http://www.mori.com/polls/2003/amrc.shtml> (Aug 2005).

7. FURTHER READING

BROWNSWORD, ROGER, 'Stem Cells, Superman, and the Report of the Select Committee' (2002) 65 Modern Law Review 568–87.

DYSON, A and HARRIS, J (eds), *Experiments on Embryos* (Routledge London 1990).

HALLIDAY, SAMANTHA, 'A Comparative Approach to the Regulation of Human Embryonic Stem Cell Research in Europe' (2004) 12 Medical Law Review 40–69.

HARRIS, JOHN, 'The Ethics and Justice of Life-extending Therapies' (2002) 55 Current Legal Problems 65–95.

HARRIS, JOHN, 'Stem Cells, Sex, and Procreation' (2003) 12 Cambridge Quarterly of Healthcare 353–71.

HOLM, SØREN, 'The Ethical Case against Stem Cell Research' (2003) 12 Cambridge Quarterly of Healthcare Ethics 372–83.

House of Lords Stem Cell Research Committee, *Stem Cell Research Report*, Feb 2002 <http://www.parliament.the-stationery-office.co.uk/pa/ld200102/ldselect/ldstem/83/8305.htm>.

Human Fertilisation and Embryology Authority <http://www.hfea.gov.uk/Research>.

MULKAY, MICHAEL, *The Embryo Research Debate: Science and the Politics of Reproduction* (CUP Cambridge 1997).

SAVULESCU, JULIAN, 'The Embryonic Stem Cell Lottery and the Cannibalization of Human Beings' (2002) 16 Bioethics 508–29.

SINGER, P et al. (eds), *Embryo Experimentation* (CUP Cambridge 1990).

14

ASSISTED CONCEPTION

1. CENTRAL ISSUES

1. The provision of assisted conception services is regulated by the Human Fertilisation and Embryology Act 1990 and the Human Fertilisation and Embryology Authority (HFEA). In addition to the rules set out in the Act itself, the HFEA publishes a Code of Practice, which contains more detailed guidance, and which can be regularly updated in response to new developments. The Act contains particularly strict rules relating to both consent and confidentiality. Controversially, the Act insists that clinicians must not provide a woman with treatment services unless they have considered the welfare of any child that might be born as a result.

2. Anonymity used to be the norm when donated gametes were used, but there has been a recent change in the law, and donors must

now be identifiable. Donors cannot be paid, although egg-sharing schemes represent substantial indirect payment.

3. Preimplantation genetic diagnosis (PGD) is generally used to prevent the birth of a child who would be born with a very serious illness. More controversially, PGD can, in certain circumstances, be used to find out if the child would be a compatible bone marrow donor for a sick older sibling, or to discover whether the child might be likely to develop a serious disease later in life.

4. Reproductive cloning is illegal in the UK. In part, this is because it is currently insufficiently safe to attempt in humans. Some people also believe that it would be unethical to clone human beings.

2. INTRODUCTION

In this chapter, we tackle a vast and potentially unwieldy subject: the regulation of assisted conception techniques. The birth of Louise Brown, the first baby created by *in vitro* fertilization, in Oldham on 25 July 1978 was undoubtedly one of the most important scientific breakthroughs of the twentieth century. Of course, assisted conception did not 'begin' in 1978. Donor insemination, for example, has a much longer history: the first reported case took place towards the end of the nineteenth century. Nevertheless, the possibility of creating and storing embryos *in vitro* has been particularly significant because it has facilitated the subsequent development of a wide variety of other techniques, such as preimplantation genetic diagnosis (see below p. 840).

We begin by looking at the regulation of assisted conception in the UK, which involves a detailed look at the legislation—the Human Fertilisation and Embryology Act 1990—and the work of the Human Fertilisation and Embryology Authority

(HFEA). We break this down into analysis of the licensing procedures, through which clinics are inspected and authorized to perform certain procedures; access to treatment; consent to the use of gametes (sperm and eggs); gamete donation; rules governing the parentage of children; and preimplantation genetic diagnosis. Finally, we briefly examine the as-yet unrealized possibility of human reproductive cloning, which is currently illegal in the UK. As we shall see, debate rages over whether cloning, if it should ever become sufficiently safe, would be an acceptable way to reproduce. In the next chapter we turn to surrogacy.

Initially 'test-tube' babies, as they were then known, were perceived to be unnatural and disturbing. But because infertility is a common problem—about one in seven couples will experience some difficulty in conceiving[1]—it was not long before the public recognized that these new techniques had the potential to alleviate the considerable suffering experienced by couples who discover that they cannot have children naturally. Of course, it should be remembered that not everyone who receives fertility treatment will become pregnant. The average success rate of IVF treatment in women under the age of 35 is 27.6 per cent, with considerable variations between different clinics, some of which achieve success rates of 59 per cent while others' success rates are as low as 10 per cent.[2] But even though fertility treatment offers no guarantee of success, now 1.5 per cent of children born in the UK were conceived *in vitro*,[3] and most people know at least one family which has been created with medical assistance. Anxiety about the propriety of interfering with human reproduction has largely subsided, and there is broad public acceptance of reproductive technologies, at least when they are used to relieve infertility in heterosexual couples. Nevertheless, as Ruth Deech points out in the next extract, because the use of assisted conception affects our understandings of family and kinship, it is unsurprising that new techniques continue to be controversial.

Ruth Deech[4]

The deployment of assisted reproductive technology (ART) affects assumptions which we bring to the understanding of family life and also to the very understanding of family life itself. It goes to the heart of our beliefs about the family, marriage and humanity. Every announcement of a new development in the techniques of assisted reproduction is accompanied by an element of publicly expressed fear, as well as elation at the happiness it might bring. That fear relates to the maintenance of the family as we know it with its own power structure and ability to influence the future. On the one hand, the enablement of birth to an otherwise childless couple represents the creation of a traditional nuclear family. On the other, the ability of gay and single women of all ages to conceive, and the use of ART for convenience purposes, has led some to worry about the creation of family forms that are widely disapproved, and a feeling that acceptance of them is being imposed. With the introduction of genetic engineering, there is a popular fear of loss of reproductive choice, as well as its extension in ways that are unpopular. Freedom to reproduce as one wills has not, however, been a universal principle of civilized society. There have always been restraints, designed to achieve certain fundamental purposes. The age of consent for sexual

---

[1] *The HFEA Guide to Infertility and Directory of Clinics* (HFEA 2005).
[2] Ibid.   [3] Ibid.
[4] 'The HFEA—10 Years On' in J Gunning and H Szoke (eds), *The Regulation of Assisted Reproductive Technology* (Ashgate Aldershot 2003) 21–38, 25.

intercourse and to marriage, the number of children regarded as the optimum, arrangement of marriages, prohibited relationships, tolerance of cohabitation, contraception, abortion, adultery and homosexuality, attitudes to female employment outside the home and to childcare have all fluctuated from time to time and from society to society, as our major influences on the shaping of the next generation. In a democratic society most or all of these factors have been regulated by law. So ART too takes its place as a major factor in reproductive abilities, as important in shaping the family and as necessary to regulate as other factors.

It is also worth noting that there are still those who oppose assisted conception on grounds of principle. As Laura Purdy explains, somewhat paradoxically, opposition to reproductive technologies comes both from conservative religious groups and from feminists.

Laura Purdy[5]

Some people oppose assisted reproduction in principle. This opposition may arise from conservative premises or feminist ones . . .

Conservative objections can be traced to two basic facts. One is that assisted reproduction often separates sex and reproduction. The other is that assisted reproduction radically alters traditional assumptions and relationships. Resistance to separating sex and reproduction is generally based either on some version of natural law theory or on explicit religious principle . . . Because natural law theory tends either to commit the naturalistic fallacy or beg questions, it cannot provide a strong moral basis for prohibiting the separation of sex and reproduction. Religious principle is, in turn, an unacceptable basis for social policy in pluralistic societies, although individuals who adhere to the relevant religion are free, other things being equal, to order their lives according to it. Assisted reproduction does alter traditional ways of doing things, but unless one posits the dubious premise that traditional ways are always best, it does not follow that innovations should be rejected wholesale.

Feminist objections can be traced to the fear that assisted reproduction will help men to subjugate women. Feminists emphasize that social pronatalism leads many women to undertake costly and potentially risky procedures to remedy infertility that would not otherwise trouble them. Furthermore, since men still run society, and are especially prominent in science and medicine, women's quest for help with reproduction adds to men's power over them. A few feminists have claimed that if additional techniques, such as ectogenesis or cloning, were perfected, men might seek to eliminate women from society altogether . . . Feminists also see assisted reproduction as precluding social reforms that would prevent infertility and provide alternative satisfactions for the infertile. These claims raise genuine concerns that need to be evaluated on a case by case basis; however, given the implausible nature of the underlying premise (that men as a group want to subjugate or eliminate women) it would not make sense to reject assisted reproduction in principle on these grounds. . . .

Women's consent might also be questioned on feminist grounds. Pronatalism is pervasive in human society, as is the attitude that women who do not have children are necessarily unfulfilled, or even worthless. . . . The onus of barrenness is so great that some women will even undertake IVF when it is their husbands who suffer from a reproductive problem. Although these points suggest that women considering IVF should have lengthy counselling, they do not support a ban on

    [5] 'Assisted Reproduction' in H Kuhse and P Singer (eds), *A Companion to Bioethics* (Blackwell Oxford 1998) 163–72, 163–4, 166.

the practice. Doing so 'to protect women against themselves' would treat women as legal incompetents, damaging women more than unwise reproductive treatments.

Before we look at the regulation of assisted conception in detail, it is worth noting that at the time of writing the slow process of reforming the 1990 legislation has begun. The House of Commons Science and Technology Committee produced a report in 2005 which sharply criticized the legislation and the HFEA.[6] The Committee itself was deeply divided and half of its members refused to sign the final report. In the light of this report, and advice from other relevant bodies, the Department of Health will then produce its own consultation document, the results of which are likely to lead to a white paper setting out proposals for reform. It has already been announced that as part of the drive to reduce the number of 'arms length bodies' (often referred to as quangos), the HFEA will be merged with the new Human Tissue Authority, whose role we considered in Chapter 12, to form RATE (the Regulatory Authority for Tissues and Embryos). New legislation to set up this amalgamated body, and to lay out its functions, is therefore likely in the next few years.

3. REGULATION OF ASSISTED CONCEPTION

In 1982, four years after the birth of Louise Brown, the Committee of Inquiry into Human Fertilisation and Embryology, chaired by Mary Warnock, an academic philosopher, was commissioned to make recommendations on the regulation of fertility treatment and embryo research.[7] Its report was published in 1984, and although it was debated in the House of Commons shortly afterwards, the Human Fertilisation and Embryology bill, which was based upon the Warnock Committee's recommendations, was not introduced to parliament until 1989. In the meantime, a number of private members' bills were put forward which would have prohibited embryo disposal, and thereby effectively prohibited all IVF treatment and research. In the mid-1980s, the Unborn Children (Protection) Bill, for example, initially commanded a parliamentary majority of 172, and only failed to become law because of effective delaying tactics deployed by the Bill's opponents.

By the time the Human Fertilisation and Embryology Bill finally came before Parliament, hostility towards embryo destruction appeared to have softened, and there was greater acceptance of both infertility treatment and embryo research. Towards the end of the 1980s, clinicians from the Hammersmith Hospital announced the first successful cycles of preimplantation genetic diagnosis, which had enabled couples who were at risk of passing on a serious X-linked disease (these are diseases, such as Duchenne muscular dystrophy, which generally only manifest themselves in boys) to start a pregnancy in the knowledge that their child would not be born seriously handicapped. Undoubtedly, this contributed to increased public sympathy for assisted conception techniques. The Human Fertilisation and Embryology Act was

---

[6] *Human Reproductive Technologies and the Law*, Fifth Report (2005) paras 101, 107 available at <http://www.publications.parliament.uk/pa/cm200405/cmselect/cmsctech/7/7i.pdf>.
[7] Report of the Committee of Enquiry into Human Fertilisation and Embryology (1984).

passed in 1990, and came into force the following year. We consider its provisions in detail below.

(a) THE HUMAN FERTILISATION AND EMBRYOLOGY AUTHORITY

Section 5 of the Human Fertilisation and Embryology Act set up the Human Fertilisation and Embryology Authority (HFEA). The HFEA took over from the Voluntary (and then Interim) Licensing Authority which was established by the Royal College of Obstetricians and Gynaecologists and the Medical Research Council in 1985, following the publication of the Warnock Report. Currently the HFEA has eighteen Members, more than half of whom must be 'lay' members, that is they must not be clinicians or scientists.[8] The HFEA has a number of different functions. It polices the provision of fertility treatment and the carrying out of embryo research (see further Chapter 13) by inspecting clinics and granting licences for particular treatments or research projects, and by maintaining a register of information about provision and outcomes of treatment. The HFEA also has a role in the formation of policy. Under section 25, it must maintain a Code of Practice (at the time of writing in its sixth edition), which gives guidance to clinics about the proper conduct of licensed activities.

There are obvious advantages in using a regularly updated Code of Practice, rather than primary legislation, to regulate such a fast-moving area of clinical practice and research. A good example of the sort of flexibility offered by this model of regulation is the changes in the rules governing the number of embryos that may be transferred in each cycle of IVF. The health risks associated with all multiple pregnancies, but especially higher order multiples such as triplets and quadruplets, are extremely serious. As a result, HFEA policy has progressively lowered the number of embryos which can be transferred in any one cycle, and the hope is that single embryo transfer will eventually become the norm. In the 6th Code of Practice, the rule is that women who are under the age of 40, or using donated eggs, or undergoing aneuploidy screening (which increases the chance of a successful pregnancy) should have no more than two embryos transferred. Women over the age of 40 using their own eggs may have a maximum of three embryos transferred. If this sort of rule had to be contained in primary legislation, rather than a regularly updated Code of Practice, the ability to respond promptly to a continually shifting evidence base would be lost. The legal status of the Code of Practice is, however, a little unclear. A breach of the Code is not an offence, but may be taken into account by a licence committee when deciding whether to vary or revoke a licence.

The HFEA is also responsible for advising the Secretary of State for Health on, among other things, the need for new primary legislation. Under section 7 of the Act, it must produce an Annual Report to the Secretary of State for Health, describing the activities it has undertaken in the past twelve months, and its work programme for the following year. These Reports are laid before Parliament by the Minister.

---

[8] See further <http://www.hfea.gov.uk/AboutHFEA/HFEAMembers> (Aug 2005).

The full Authority meets nine times each year, currently three of these meetings are held in public. It also has a number of sub-committees, such as the Ethics and Law Committee and the Scientific and Clinical Advances Group, which advise the main Authority on policy decisions. In recent years, the HFEA has increasingly engaged in public consultation exercises, using a wide variety of different techniques.

(b) LICENSING

One of the HFEA's most important purposes is to control the activities of licensed clinics and research centres. Sections 3 and 4 of the Human Fertilisation and Embryology Act 1990 provide that the creation, use and storage of embryos, and the storage and use of gametes,[9] can only be carried out under a licence granted by the HFEA. Carrying out any of these activities without a licence is a criminal offence.[10]

It is perhaps worth asking why fertility treatment is subject to this special regulatory regime. A number of reasons might be put forward, not all of which are convincing. First, there are some health risks associated with treatments like IVF, such as the risk of ovarian hyperstimulation syndrome (OHSS), but other medical treatments with serious side-effects are not subjected to this sort of regulatory framework. And in any event, some of the dangers posed by IVF—e.g. the risk of OHSS or of multiple births—exist for unlicensed treatments, such as the prescription of fertility drugs. Another second possible explanation is the special *moral* concern for embryos created outside of the female body. But of course, this justification does not apply to some licensed treatments, such as donor insemination.

Thirdly, it might be argued that the creation of children through artificial means itself raises ethical dilemmas, such as who should be permitted to have access to treatment. Fourthly, because most treatment takes place in the private sector, regulation might be directed towards restraining the excesses of a completely free market in fertility treatment.

A final explanation is that the form regulation takes in the UK reflects the particular set of circumstances which existed when the legislation was passed in 1990. In 1989, when the Bill was drafted, professional bodies, such as the Royal Colleges of Obstetricians and Gynaecologists, had not yet produced their own guidance on the proper conduct of fertility services. Given the novelty and ethical controversy involved, it seemed sensible to consolidate the rules on best practice within a licensing regime.

Under section 11 of the Act, the HFEA can grant three different types of licence: for treatment services; storage of gametes and embryos; and research on embryos (see Chapter 13). Once an application for a licence has been received by the HFEA, an inspection team made up of employees of the HFEA and independent inspectors, will visit the premises and prepare a report for the licence committee. Licences are granted by licence committees, currently made up of five Authority members, at least one of which must be a lay member. Licences can be granted for a maximum of three years, although shorter periods might be used where more regular monitoring is considered

---

[9] There is an exception under s 4(1)(b) if artificial insemination is carried out using the woman's (live) partner's sperm, when no licence is necessary.
[10] Section 41.

necessary. Centres are normally inspected annually, with full inspections taking place once every three years prior to licence renewal. A programme of unannounced inspections is also in place, some of which are random, and some targeted at clinics where there has been cause for concern in the past.

Centres are under a duty to report incidents and 'near misses' to the HFEA. These are monitored and where the HFEA believes that the incident reveals a risk which might occur again, an anonymized 'Alert' will be issued to all licensed centres notifying them of the risk in question. Centres are not penalized for reporting incidents. On the contrary, the HFEA encourages them to do so as part of the trend towards learning from mistakes and near misses, which we explored in detail in Chapter 3. Given that the HFEA's system for recording and learning from incidents is much more well developed than the health service as a whole, it is worth noting that the rate of incidents, or adverse events (approximately 1 per cent) is lower in the assisted conception sector than in other areas of the health service, where it has been estimated that approximately 10 per cent of treatments result in some sort of adverse event.

Sections 12–15 of the Act specify a number of standard licensing conditions which will automatically be attached to each licence. We will look at some of these in detail below, but they include, under section 12(c), that the consent provisions contained in Schedule 3 are complied with; under section 13(5), that account has been taken of the welfare of any child that might be born; and under section 14(2), that the statutory storage periods for gametes are not exceeded. In addition, licence committees may attach specific Conditions to an individual centre's licence, (these are often used to prevent breaches of the Code or the Act), and make Recommendations (which are generally suggestions for improving practice within the centre).

The Licence itself is granted to a Nominal Licensee, which may be a hospital trust. Under section 16(2), each licence application must also designate a Person Responsible (PR), whom the licence committee must consider a suitable person to supervise the activities authorized by the licence, and in particular, under section 17, to ensure that suitable practices are used, and the conditions of the licence complied with. Until the *Attorney General's Reference (2 of 2003)*,[11] it was not clear whether the PR might be vicariously criminally liable for offences committed by his staff. In this case, the senior embryologist had been guilty of extremely serious misconduct, but the Court of Appeal decided that the PR had not vicariously committed an offence.

Section 18 deals with the revocation and variation of licences. A licence can be revoked or varied if misleading information was provided in the licence application; or if the premises are no longer suitable; or if the PR has failed to discharge his responsibilities or comply with directions; or if there has been any other material chance in circumstances. Revocation, but not variation, is also possible if the licence committee is not satisfied that the PR or the nominal licensee are suitable people to discharge their duties, or if the PR dies or is convicted of an offence under the Act. Section 19 sets out the procedure for refusing, varying or revoking a licence. Notice must be given to the PR and the nominal licensee, who then have an opportunity to

---

[11] [2004] EWCA Crim 785.

make representations within 28 days, with a further appeal possible to the Authority, and after that to the High Court.

As a public body, decisions of the Authority and its licence committees are judicially reviewable. Licensing decisions must therefore be lawful (that is, licence committees must act within their statutory powers) and rational (that is, not *Wednesbury*[12] unreasonable). Committees must take into account relevant factors, and disregard irrelevant considerations. But, as we can see from the following case, provided the Authority has not exceeded or abused the powers vested in it by Parliament, its substantive decisions will not be open to challenge via judicial review.

R (on the application of Assisted Reproduction and Gynaecology Centre) and Another v Human Fertilisation and Embryology Authority[13]

At the time of Mrs H's treatment, the HFEA's Code of Practice stated that 'No more than three eggs or embryos should be placed in a woman in any one cycle, regardless of the procedure used.' Mr Taranissi, director of the Assisted Reproduction and Gynaecology Centre, argued that it would be appropriate to make an exception to the 3-embryo rule in Mrs H's case because of her particular treatment needs. The question was referred to a licence committee which decided that to transfer more than three embryos in Mrs H's case would not be acceptable, and would be a breach of the Code of Practice, which might in turn lead to the revocation of the Centre's licence. Mr Taranissi and Mrs H applied for judicial review of this decision.

Wall J (reading the judgment of the Court of Appeal)

This is an area of rapidly developing scientific knowledge and debate, in which the Authority, as the licensing body established by Parliament, makes decisions and gives advice. It is not the function of the court to enter the scientific debate, nor is it the function of the court to adjudicate on the merits of the Board's decisions or any advice it gives. Like any public authority, the Board is open to challenge by way of judicial review, but only if it exceeds or abuses the powers and responsibilities given to it by parliament . . .

The members thought that future treatment for Mrs H was likely to fail but that, if she did succeed in becoming pregnant, there would be a higher risk of multiple pregnancy if five embryos had been transplanted rather than three. The Authority therefore considered that the possible marginal improvement in the chances of pregnancy were outweighed by the albeit small risk of multiple pregnancy. Two scientists may disagree over that proposition, but in our judgment it is impossible to describe it as irrational. . . .

Disagreements between doctors and scientific bodies in this pioneering field are inevitable. The United Kingdom, through the Act, has opted for a system of licensing and regulation. The Authority is the body which is empowered by parliament to regulate. Like any public authority, it is open to challenge by way of judicial review, if it exceeds or abuses the powers and responsibilities given to it by parliament; but where, as is manifest here from an examination of the facts, it considers requests for advice carefully and thoroughly, and produces opinions which are plainly rational, the court, in our judgment, has no part to play in the debate, and certainly no power to intervene to strike down any such decision. The fact that the appellants may disagree with the Authority's advice is neither here nor there.

It is worth noting that the HFEA's ability to regulate fertility services is by no means

---

[12] The test is whether no reasonable body could have come to the same decision: *Wednesbury Corporation v Minister of Housing and Local Government* [1966] 2 QB 275.

[13] [2002] EWCA Civ 20, *Independent* 6 Feb 2002 CA.

comprehensive. The Act does not, for example, cover every intervention which is
directed towards alleviating infertility. The prescription of super-ovulatory hormones,
for example, does not require a licence from the HFEA. Donor insemination can also
be undertaken privately, without a licence, provided the sperm is not 'stored'. This
means that it is possible for an 'introduction' agency, like ManNotIncluded,[14] which
simply 'introduces' would-be recipients to potential sperm donors, and uses couriers
to transport the sperm from donor to recipient, to operate lawfully outside of the
HFEA's regulatory control. If at any time the agency itself actually *stored* the donors'
sperm, a licence would be necessary. This situation may change as a result of the EU
Tissues and Cells Directive, due to be implemented in 2006, which attempts to
regulate *all* uses of tissue such as sperm, not just their storage.[15]

In addition, as Margaret Brazier points out in the following extract, the HFEA
exercises little control over the market in fertility services: the prices charged for
treatment are outside of its regulatory ambit. Nor, of course, can the HFEA control
the provision of treatment services in other countries. As a result, if a particular
service is not readily available in the UK, wealthy would-be patients can seek
treatment abroad.

Margaret Brazier[16]

The most profound change in regulating reproductive medicine since Warnock is, I would argue,
the dramatically increased role of commerce. Warnock based its recommendations in relation
both to fertility treatment and research on the supposition that fertility services would be integrated into the NHS . . . The enormous commercial potential of developments in reproductive
medicine was hardly foreseen . . . Yet debate on commodification and commercialisation is at the
forefront of debate today. A fertility 'industry' has developed to provide treatment on a profit
making basis both to British citizens and 'procreative tourists' escaping more prohibitive regimes
elsewhere in Europe. Pressure to pay gamete donors and surrogates continues.

The reproduction business, even in the United Kingdom, is set to spawn two rather different
sorts of market. The first, which effectively exists today, is the market in fertility services. The
private sector, involving both private licensed fertility clinics and the companies who will seek to
develop both new fertility treatments and therapeutic cloning, necessarily operates on a profit-
making basis. They have a vested interest in the expansion of their business. The more treatment
cycles a woman undergoes, the more people who seek treatment, the greater the profit to a clinic.
In the early years of the reproduction revolution, feminist critics voiced considerable concern
about the potential exploitation of women in the name of science. Such criticism has been more
muted of late but regulators need to be vigilant to ensure that their stated aim of 'safety first' is
comprehensively met by the fertility industry . . .

The second sort of reproduction market, existing only in embryo this side of the Atlantic,
involves trade in gametes and uteruses . . . The debate in the United Kingdom has only just begun.
The proponents of markets may commend their advantages, but all concede that markets must be
regulated as such. Allowing the development of a market in gametes or surrogacy within a system

---

[14] <http://www.mannotincluded.com>.

[15] Directive 2004/23/EC of the European Parliament and of the Council of 31 March 2004 on setting
standards of quality and safety for the donation, procurement, testing, processing, preservation, storage and
distribution of human tissues and cells.

[16] 'Regulating the Reproduction Business?' (1999) 7 Medical Law Review 166–93.

in no sense designed to police such a market could undermine the good work British regulators have done so far.

Another nightmare awaits the HFEA and its counterparts in Continental Europe. Each national jurisdiction has sought to fashion a scheme of regulation acceptable to its own culture and community. However those wealthy enough to participate in reproduction markets can readily evade their domestic constraints. If I can order sperm on the internet, or hire a surrogate mother from Bolivia, are British regulators wasting their time? The international ramifications of the reproductive business may prove to be a more stringent test of the strength of British law than all of the difficult ethical dilemmas that have gone before.

(c) THE CONSCIENCE CLAUSE

As with the Abortion Act 1967, section 38(1) of the Human Fertilisation and Embryology Act 1990 provides that doctors with a conscientious objection to treatment or research can refuse to participate in its provision:

No person who has a conscientious objection to participating in any activity governed by this Act shall be under any duty, however arising, to do so.

The burden of proof of conscientious objection lies with the person claiming to rely upon it.[17] It seems likely that nursing staff too have a right to exclude themselves from the provision of fertility treatment. Whether or not administrative staff, such as receptionists, are entitled to conscientiously object to activities governed by the Act is unclear, and would depend upon whether they could be said to be 'participating' in any of the activities governed by the Act.

A person can invoke section 38 to exclude themselves from *any* activity governed by the Act, they do not have to object to the Act itself. Would it be possible, therefore, for a clinician to 'conscientiously object' to the treatment of lesbians or single women? Michael Freeman has argued that this does not amount to a conscientious objection, but is instead 'rooted in prejudice', and that, in such circumstances, the clinician is not objecting to the *activity* in question, but to the sexual orientation or lifestyle of a would-be patient.[18]

(d) REGULATING ACCESS TO TREATMENT

In the UK there are two ways in which access to fertility treatment is restricted. First, the Act provides that treatment services must not be provided unless account has been taken of the welfare of any child who may be born as a result. This oddly worded provision amounts in theory, if not in practice, to a child-welfare filter upon access to treatment. Secondly, NHS funding for fertility treatment is patchy and often inadequate, and private treatment is expensive. As a result, access to treatment is often contingent upon a person or couple's ability to fund their own treatment. Let us look at these two restrictions in turn.

---

[17] Section 38(2).
[18] 'Medically Assisted Reproduction' in A Grubb with J Laing (eds), *Principles of Medical Law* (2nd edn OUP Oxford 2004) 639–738, 687.

(1) SECTION 13(5)

The Human Fertilisation and Embryology Act contains no formal restrictions upon access to treatment, so any individual, regardless of their age, sexual orientation, or marital status, can legally receive fertility treatment in the UK. But it is worth noting that when the Bill was being debated, an amendment that would have restricted access to treatment services to married couples was defeated by only one vote. Given the extent of parliamentary hostility to the creation of 'fatherless' children, a concession was needed. This took the form of an amendment, introduced into the Lords, which subsequently became section 13(5):

Human Fertilisation and Embryology Act 1990 section 13(5)

A woman shall not be provided with treatment services unless account has been taken of the welfare of any child who may be born as a result of the treatment, (including the need of that child for a father), and of any other child who may be affected by the birth.

The section's specific mention of the child's 'need for a father' must be read in the light of the provisions governing paternity which, as we see below, contemplate the birth of children who will have no legal father. Children born to single or lesbian women treated in licensed clinics with donated sperm are legally father*less*, hence clinics' duty to consider their child's *need for a father* translates into a statutory obligation to take into account the undesirability of single or lesbian motherhood.

For many reasons, section 13(5) is a rather unsatisfactory provision. The direction to take account of the child's 'need for a father' seems particularly outdated in the light both of the increasing proportion of children who are now brought up by single parents, and, of recent changes to adoption legislation, which mean that single people or homosexual couples are now eligible to adopt.[19] Nor is it supported by the evidence, which in fact suggests that children conceived using donor insemination by women without male partners are, if anything, doing better than similarly conceived children who are being brought up by married couples.[20] And, of course, it is also true that the existence of a potential father-figure when assisted conception services are sought offers no guarantee of his presence, either when the child is born, or throughout her childhood.

If interpreted literally, section 13(5) is also rather puzzling because it instructs a clinician to base his decision as to whether to attempt to bring a child into the world in part upon a consideration of that child's welfare. Given that, as we saw when we looked at 'wrongful life' actions in Chapter 11, the law will generally assume that existence is preferable to non-existence, it is difficult to see how a clinician could decide that a child would be benefited by not being born. In practice, the section has not been interpreted literally, and is instead used to check whether there is any reason to believe that prospective patients would be inadequate parents. But this interpretation too is not without difficulty.

It must, for example, be admitted that clinicians do not have access to much

---

[19] Adoption and Children Act 2002.

[20] C Murray and S Golombok, 'Solo mothers and their donor insemination infants: follow-up at age 2 years' (2005) 20 Human Reproduction 1655–60.

information when making this statutory 'child welfare' assessment, and nor do they have any special expertise in evaluating future parenting ability. The HFEA's Code of Practice gives guidance on the interpretation and implementation of section 13(5). This has recently been updated, and whereas before the HFEA recommended that patients' GPs should be routinely contacted and invited to notify the clinic if they have any reason to doubt their adequacy as parents, now the HFEA advises centres that they should only contact third parties, such as GPs and social services departments, if they have cause for concern.

A further problem is that it is almost impossible to police section 13(5) effectively. It is a standard licensing condition that account must be taken of the welfare of any child that might be born, but it would be very difficult to prove that the clinic had erred in this assessment. If account was not properly taken of the welfare of any child, and a future child's welfare suffered as a result, it is not clear who, if anybody, would be able to bring an action against the clinic for non-compliance with section 13(5).

Section 13(5) has also been criticized for placing an unfair burden upon infertile individuals who are, it must be admitted, not necessarily any more likely to pose a risk to their children than fertile people, who can obviously reproduce without anyone scrutinizing their future parenting ability.[21] In the next extract, Gillian Douglas argues that section 13(5) is unacceptably discriminatory.

Gillian Douglas[22]

If we return to the original motivation of those members of both Houses of Parliament who forced the inclusion of s.13(5) in the first place, it seems to be working quite well. It enables centres to justify turning away those whom they would probably have turned away anyway, but under the guise of concern for the prospective child's welfare. Provided a couple appear 'normal', they will be subject to no real scrutiny, and thus their privacy and their autonomy are respected. . . .

But it is not satisfactory to have a statutory provision used in this way to sanction what ultimately amounts to discrimination. It is one thing to reach a conclusion not to treat a person, after having investigated their circumstances, motivation etc, and decided that they would place a child at risk, and quite another to rule out whole groups of people absolutely, based on what may be nothing more than 'gut feeling' (as one clinician put it when explaining the centre's refusal to take unmarried couples for insemination treatment) or disapproval. There is no evidence which shows that single women make worse parents than a heterosexual couple, or that older mothers are worse than younger ones. The basis of the attitude must therefore derive from what it perceived to be social acceptability—or simply stereotyped views of what is perceived to be appropriate family life. One need not appeal to arguments based on a right to reproduce to suggest that it is unfair to leave it to what may frequently come down to the personal whim of the clinician in charge as to whether a person is lucky enough to be accepted for treatment at a particular clinic. . . .

Another possibility would be to make the assessment of the potential child's welfare a real one, by requiring a detailed scrutiny along the lines of adoption law. Again, this presents problems. First it would mean requiring people *really* to justify their desire for a child and to prove their fitness to parent to a third party . . . But it would be even more discriminatory to require those

---

[21] See, eg, Emily Jackson 'Conception and the Irrelevance of the Welfare Principle' (2002) 65 Modern Law Review 176–203.

[22] 'Assisted Reproduction and the Welfare of the Child' (1993) Current Legal Problems 53.

who need assisted reproduction to justify themselves, while those who require no treatment, or even other sorts of fertility treatment, need not. Secondly, the question of whether one can predict the risk to a child's welfare, even from a detailed scrutiny of the parents and household the child will live in, is not straightforward. . . . Even if such assessments could be carried out, it is unlikely that medical staff would be in a position to make judgements on them. They simply do not have the appropriate skills.

The House of Commons Science and Technology Committee's 2005 report robustly criticized section 13(5) and recommended its abolition in future legislation:

House of Commons Science and Technology Committee[23]

The requirement to consider whether a child born as a result of assisted conception needs a father is too open to interpretation and unjustifiably offensive to many. It is wrong for legislation to imply that unjustified discrimination against 'unconventional families' is acceptable. . . .

The welfare of the child provision discriminates against the infertile and some sections of society, is impossible to implement and is of questionable practical value in protecting the interests of children born as a result of assisted reproduction. We recognise that there will be difficult cases but these should be resolved by recourse to local clinical ethics committees. The welfare of the child provision has enabled the HFEA and clinics to make judgements that are more properly made by patients in consultation with their doctor. It should be abolished in its current from. The minimum threshold principle should apply but should specify that this threshold should be the risk of unpreventable and significant harm. Doctors should minimise the risks to any child conceived from treatment within the constraints of available knowledge but this should be encouraged through the promotion of good medical practice not legislation.

It would be possible for a disgruntled would-be patient to apply for judicial review of a decision to refuse treatment in an NHS hospital. There has been only one such case, and it predated the 1990 Act. In *R v Ethical Committee of St Mary's Hospital (Manchester), ex parte Harriott*,[24] an application for judicial review of a consultant's decision to remove a woman from the waiting list for IVF treatment was rejected. The clinic had discovered that the applicant had been turned down for adoption on the grounds of her previous convictions for prostitution. Schiemann J said that:

if the committee had advised, for instance that the IVF unit should in principle refuse all such treatment to anyone who was a Jew or coloured [*sic*], then I think the courts might well grant a declaration that such a policy was illegal.

But in this case:

it is not, and could not be, suggested that no reasonable consultant could have come to the decision to refuse treatment to the applicant.[25]

Although no such challenges have yet been brought, by placing an additional obstacle in the path of single and lesbian women seeking treatment services, section 13(5) is arguably inconsistent with the Human Rights Act 1998, most notably with Article 8 (right to respect for private and family life); Article 12 (the right to found a family)

---

[23] *Human Reproductive Technologies and the Law Fifth Report* (2005) paras 101, 107 available at <http://www.publications.parliament.uk/pa/cm200405/cmselect/cmsctech/7/7i.pdf>.
[24] [1988] 1 FLR 512.   [25] Ibid at 519.

and Article 14 (the right not to be discriminated against in exercising one's convention rights).

The question of Article 12's application to access to fertility services has arisen in the following case.

R v Secretary of State for the Home Department, ex parte Mellor[26]

The applicant was serving a life sentence for murder. He and his wife, who was now aged twenty-five, wanted to start a family, and he applied to the Secretary of State for permission to have access to facilities for artificial insemination. He was concerned that by the time he was released his wife, who would then be thirty-one, might be too old to conceive. The Secretary of State's policy was that the grant of facilities for artificial insemination to prisoners was made only in exceptional circumstances. Since there were none in this case, permission was refused. His application for judicial review was refused, and his appeal dismissed by the Court of Appeal.

Lord Phillips MR

I can summarise the conclusions that I derive from [previous] decisions as follows. (i) The qualifications on the right to respect for family life that are recognised by article 8(2) apply equally to the article 12 rights. (ii) Imprisonment is incompatible with the exercise of conjugal rights and consequently involves an interference with the right to respect for family life under article 8 and with the right to found a family under article 12. (iii) This restriction is ordinarily justifiable under the provisions of article 8(2). (iv) In exceptional circumstances it may be necessary to relax the imposition of detention in order to avoid a disproportionate interference with a human right. (v) There is no case which indicates that a prisoner is entitled to assert the right to found a family by the provision of semen for the purpose of artificially inseminating his wife. . . .

It does not follow from this that it will always be justifiable to prevent a prisoner from inseminating his wife artificially, or indeed naturally. The interference with fundamental human rights which is permitted by article 8(2) involves an exercise in proportionality. Exceptional circumstances may require the normal consequences of imprisonment to yield, because the effect of its interference with a particular human right is disproportionate. . . .

The Secretary of State does not refuse to facilitate a prisoner to provide semen for the artificial insemination of his wife in all circumstances. He responds to requests for such a facility according to a policy. . . .

A policy which accorded to prisoners in general the right to beget children by artificial insemination would, I believe, raise difficult ethical questions and give rise to legitimate public concern. . . .

By imprisoning the husband the state creates the situation where, if the wife is to have a child, that child will, until the husband's release, be brought up in a single parent family. I consider it legitimate, and indeed desirable, that the state should consider the implications of children being brought up in those circumstances when deciding whether or not to have a general policy of facilitating the artificial insemination of the wives of prisoners or of wives who are themselves prisoners . . .

I would simply observe that it seems to me rational that the normal starting point should be a need to demonstrate that, if facilities for artificial insemination are not provided, the founding of a family may not merely be delayed, but prevented altogether.

The Court of Appeal thus held that Article 12 was engaged, but that it was subject to

---

[26] [2001] EWCA Civ 472, [2001] 3 WLR 533.

the same limiting factors as Article 8, and in this case the restriction on the prisoner's ability to found a family was justified since this was an inevitable and legitimate consequence of imprisonment. It is, however, noteworthy that the decision in the case might have been different if the applicant had sought permission to store sperm samples prior to receiving treatment for cancer, when a refusal would not have delayed his capacity to found a family, but prevented it altogether.

(2) FINANCIAL RESTRICTIONS ON ACCESS

Infertility treatment is expensive—one cycle of IVF can cost around £3,000—and its availability within the National Health Service is patchy. In 2003, guidance issued by the National Institute for Clinical Excellence (NICE), whose role we considered in detail in Chapter 2, recommended that each infertile couple should be entitled to up to three cycles of IVF at public expense.[27] The government initially agreed to fund one cycle per couple, although even this has proved difficult to implement with 36 per cent of primary care trusts (PCT) reporting waiting times of over a year.[28]

Before the NICE guidelines were published, most health authorities did not pay for any infertility treatment, and in these areas couples are now confined to their one free cycle. A few health authorities did fund up to three cycles of treatment per couple, and couples in these regions may get a second or third chance if their first NHS cycle does not succeed (thus preserving the postcode lottery), although there is some evidence that many PCTs which previously provided up to three cycles of IVF are now intending to reduce their provision to one cycle.

It is also important to note that the NICE guidelines restrict access to free treatment to *infertile* couples: lesbians and single women, whose inability to conceive without assistance is not the result of biological dysfunction, will still have to pay the full costs of their treatment themselves. In the next extract, JR McMillan argues, first, that providing fertility treatment to single and lesbian women may in fact be *more* cost effective (a criterion which is usually important to NICE) than treating infertile women, since the chances of achieving a successful pregnancy may be higher. And, secondly, that by confining NHS funded treatment to heterosexual couples, NICE has made a social judgement about who *deserves* to have access to publicly funded fertility treatment.

JR McMillan[29]

If pregnancy is the outcome that matters for cost effectiveness then there is no obvious reason why publicly funded fertility treatment should not be provided to lesbians and single women. . . . In fact it might be that lesbians and single women are more cost effective to treat than infertile heterosexual couples because they are less likely to have a physiological cause for their unwanted childlessness. . . .

[B]y recommending that publicly funded fertility treatment should be available to heterosexual couples and not, by implication, to single women and lesbians, the guideline does make social

---

[27] <http://www.nice.org.uk/pdf/CG011niceguideline.pdf>.
[28] Kevin Barron, 'When will the full NICE guidelines on infertility treatment be implemented?' 4 April 2005 Bionews <http://www.bionews.org.uk/commentary.lasso?storyid=2512>.
[29] 'NICE, the draft fertility guideline and dodging the big question' (2003) 29 Journal of Medical Ethics 313–14.

judgments. The guideline says that 'for the purposes of investigation, infertility should be defined as failure to conceive after regular unprotected sexual intercourse for two years in the absence of any reproductive pathology'. This definition rules the majority of lesbians and single women out of consideration.

The NICE guidelines further restrict access to women under the age of 40 in order to reflect the rapid decline in fertility, and hence success rates, once women reach the age of 40.

Individual health authorities who fund additional cycles of treatment may set their own criteria, such as a lower age limit, or a requirement that the couple should have no existing children, either natural or adopted. In *R v Sheffield AHA, ex parte Seale* Auld LJ rejected an application for judicial review of Sheffield Area Health Authority's refusal to fund treatment for women over the age of 35.[30] He held that health authorities were entitled to make decisions on the basis of the financial resources available, and given that infertility treatment is generally less effective in women aged over 35 years, it proved impossible to establish that the health authority's policy was illegal or irrational.

(e) REGULATING THE USE OF GAMETES AND EMBRYOS

(1) CONSENT TO THE USE OF GAMETES

Consent to the storage and use of one's gametes (that is, sperm and eggs) must be voluntary and fully informed. Consent must state what is to be done with the gametes in the event of the donor's death or incapacity, and must specify the maximum period of storage, if this is to be less than the statutory storage period of ten years. This ten-year limit can be extended for individuals whose fertility has or is likely to become significantly impaired, for example because they are about to undergo treatment for cancer which will leave them infertile.[31] It is worth noting that under Schedule 3 of the 1990 Act, unlike other much more invasive medical procedures, consent to the creation of an embryo, or to the use of one's gametes in the treatment of others *must* be in writing, and counselling must have been offered.

Human Fertilisation and Embryology Act 1990
Schedule 3 Consents to use of gametes or embryos.

1   A consent under this Schedule must be given in writing and, in this Schedule 'effective consent' means a consent . . . which has not been withdrawn . . .

2   A consent to the storage of any gametes . . . must—(a) specify the maximum period of storage . . . and (b) state what is to be done with the gametes or embryo if the person who gave the consent dies or is unable because of incapacity to vary the terms of the consent or to revoke it . . .

3   (1) Before a person gives a consent under this Schedule—(a) he must be given suitable opportunity to seek proper counselling about the implications of taking the proposed steps, and (b) he must be provided with such relevant information as is proper.

---

[30] [1994] 25 BMLR 1.
[31] The Human Fertilisation and Embryology (Statutory Storage Period) Regulations 1991 SI 1991/1540.

5(1) A person's gametes must not be used for the purpose of treatment services unless there is an effective consent by that person to their being so used and they are used in accordance with the terms of the consent. (2) A person's gametes must not be received for use for those purposes unless there is effective consent by that person to their being so used. (3) This paragraph does not apply to the use of a person's gametes for the purpose of that person, or that person and another person together, receiving treatment services.

The strictness of the rules governing consent to the use of gametes first came before the Court of Appeal in *R v Human Fertilisation and Embryology Authority, ex parte Blood*.[32] Mrs Blood wanted to be inseminated with her deceased husband's sperm. The problem was that, although Mrs Blood claimed that she and her husband had discussed the posthumous use of his sperm, Mr Blood had not given written consent. Sperm samples had been extracted at Mrs Blood's request while her husband was in a coma. Not only was there no effective consent for the purposes of Schedule 3, but it is possible that the doctors who extracted the sperm had acted unlawfully. As we saw in Chapter 4, incompetent patients must be treated in their best interests. Since Mr Blood was not going to recover, the storage of sperm was certainly not in his best *medical* interests. Indeed it is very hard to see how having genetic offspring after one's death could ever be said to be in a patient's best interests.

Without an effective consent, it would have been unlawful for Mrs Blood to use the sperm samples for treatment in the UK, and the Court of Appeal admitted that their continued storage was also 'technically' an offence, although they also said that there could be 'no question of any prosecution being brought in the circumstances'. Mrs Blood applied for permission to export the sperm to Belgium, where treatment would be lawful. The HFEA refused, and she applied for judicial review of this decision. At first instance, despite expressing considerable sympathy for Mrs Blood, Sir Stephen Brown decided that the HFEA had acted within their discretion. On appeal Mrs Blood succeeded. The Court of Appeal took the view that despite the unlawfulness of the sperm retrieval, in exercising their discretion the HFEA had not taken adequate account of Mrs Blood's right under European law to receive treatment in another Member State.[33]

R v Human Fertilisation and Embryology Authority, ex parte Blood[34]

Mr and Mrs Blood had been trying to start a family. Mr Blood contracted meningitis and lapsed into a coma. Mrs Blood asked for samples of his sperm to be collected by electro-ejaculation for use by her at a later date. Her husband died shortly afterwards. Mrs Blood wanted to use the samples in treatment, but the Human Fertilisation and Embryology Authority refused either to give consent to treatment in the UK, or to exercise its discretion to authorise export of the sperm for treatment abroad. The applicant sought judicial review of the HFEA's decision. At first instance, Sir Stephen Brown P refused her application, this was overturned by the Court of Appeal, which invited the HFEA to make their decision again, taking proper account of Mrs Blood's rights under article 59 of the EC Treaty.

Lord Woolf MR

It follows that Mr Blood's sperm should not, in fact, have been preserved and stored. Technically

---

[32] [1996] 3 WLR 1176; [1997] 2 WLR 806 (CA).   [33] EC Treaty Art 59.
[34] [1997] 2 WLR 806.

therefore, an offence was committed by the licence holder as a result of the storage under s 41(2)(b) of the 1990 Act by the licensee. There is, however, no question of any prosecution being brought in the circumstances of this case and no possible criticism can be made of the fact that storage has taken place because Professor Cook . . . was acting throughout in close consultation with the authority in a perfectly bona fide manner, in an unexplored legal situation where humanity dictated that the sperm was taken and preserved first, and the legal argument followed. From now on, however, the position will be different as these proceedings will clarify the legal position. Because this judgment makes it clear that the sperm of Mr Blood has been preserved and stored when it should not have been, this case raises issues as to the lawfulness of the use and export of sperm which should never arise again. . . .

The absence of the necessary written consent means that both the treatment of Mrs Blood and the storage of Mr Blood's sperm would be prohibited by the 1990 Act. The authority has no discretion to authorise treatment in the United Kingdom. . . .

Parliament by the 1990 Act had left issues of public policy as to export to be determined by the authority. It is the authority's decision that, therefore, has to be capable of being justified in relation to art 59. In coming to its decision, the authority was required to take into account that to refuse permission to export would impede the treatment of Mrs Blood in Belgium and to ask whether, in the circumstances, this was justified. . . .

The first reason given by the authority is a correct statement that in this case there has not been compliance with the 1990 Act in relation to storage or use in the United Kingdom. This is the starting point for the subsequent reasoning which is the essence for the explanation why the authority was not prepared to exercise its undoubted discretion to permit export in Mrs Blood's favour. It was a permissible and proper starting point: in giving a particular direction, the authority is using delegated powers, which should be used to serve and promote the objects of the legislation, which clearly attach great importance to consent, the quality of that consent, and the certainty of it. The authority must balance that against Mrs Blood's cross-border rights as a Community citizen . . .

Parliament has delegated to the authority the responsibility for making decisions in this difficult and delicate area, and the court should be slow to interfere with its decisions. However, the reasons given by the authority, while not deeply flawed, confirm that the authority did not take into account two important considerations. The first being the effect of article 59 of the [EC] Treaty. The second being that there should be, after this judgment has been given, no further cases where sperm is preserved without consent. . . .

From the argument before us and those reasons, it is reasonably clear that it was a concern of the authority that if they gave Mrs Blood consent to export, this would create an undesirable precedent which could result in the flouting of the 1990 Act. . . . The fact that storage cannot lawfully take place without written consent, from a practical point of view means that there should be no fresh cases. No licensee can lawfully do what was done here, namely preserve sperm in this country without written consent.

Although the Court of Appeal agreed that the HFEA was entitled to place restrictions upon the export of sperm, any such restrictions had to be justified on grounds of public policy,[35] and the Court of Appeal was not satisfied that the public interest was served by refusing Mrs Blood permission to export the sperm for treatment elsewhere in Europe. Against this, it could be argued that the power to permit the export of gametes under section 24(4) ought to be subject to the presumption that the gametes

---

[35] EC Treaty Arts 56(1) and 66.

must first be obtained and stored in conformity with national law. It would seem curious for the legislation to build in an easy route for the avoidance of its provisions by allowing any UK citizen to export illegally obtained gametes for use abroad.

Nevertheless, following the decision of the Court of Appeal, the HFEA changed its mind on the grounds first, that there could be no precedent set because sperm should never again be taken without consent, and secondly, that they had failed to establish a sufficiently compelling public policy exception to Mrs Blood's cross border rights. Mrs Blood was therefore allowed to export her deceased husband's sperm, and following treatment in Belgium, she has subsequently had two children. As Derek Morgan and Robert Lee point out in the next extract, the Diane Blood case is interesting, not least because Mrs Blood's need for assisted conception services did not result from infertility, but from her husband's death.

Derek Morgan and Robert Lee[36]

The remarkable thing about *Blood* is that it represents the transformation of the technology of assisted conception, in a way in which even the doctors involved in the sperm recovery had present doubts. Originally developed to address one specific cause of infertility in women, blocked fallopian tubes, IVF has moved rapidly from the experimental to the clinical and has come to occupy the domain of the usual, the commonplace, a routine ingredient on the reproductive menu.

Originally seen as a response to the emergent evidence that involuntary childlessness caused by reproductive inability might seriously harm or compromise a woman's physical and mental health, *Blood* illustrates how quickly we are moving along a direction which runs from desire and longing to demands and litigation. The careful, albeit controversial scheme put in place by the Human Fertilisation and Embryology Act less than a decade ago has been shaken to its foundations by someone who has only limited need of the techniques of reproductive medicine.

The underlying philosophy of that legislation was that subject to a system of regulated licences, the supervision of reproductive medicine could, by and large, be left in the charge of clinical specialists. The 'case' of Diane Blood only serves to illustrate not only how far we have moved in terms of human reproduction in the past 30 years, but also that legislative assumptions of 1990 are being cross cut with the articulation of a fresh voice—that of the consumer who comes to the reproductive market with the usual range of assumptions about rights and guarantees. . . . Whether or not that is a good thing is uncertain. What is certain is that it will not be without consequences.

As we have seen, the Court of Appeal in *Blood* assumed that there would be no more cases in which there was no effective consent to the use of gametes. But a few years later, a case arose in which the sperm provider's widow sought to argue that her late husband's alteration of his consent form had been the result of undue influence. The Court of Appeal did not rule out the possibility that an apparently effective consent for the purposes of the Act might be vitiated by undue influence, but this would require proof of more than pressure to alter a consent form:

Centre for Reproductive Medicine v U[37]

Before starting fertility treatment, Mr U had signed a consent form agreeing that his sperm could

---

[36] 'In the Name of the Father? *Ex parte Blood*: Dealing with Novelty and Anomaly' (1997) 60 Modern Law Review 840–56, 855.

[37] [2002] EWCA Civ 565.

be stored and used after his death. He had later changed that aspect of his consent during a consultation with a specialist nursing sister who asked him to change the form because she and the Centre were opposed in principle to the posthumous use of gametes. Mr U died unexpectedly three months later. His widow wanted to use his sperm in further treatment. She argued, unsuccessfully, that the original consent should stand because its withdrawal was the result of undue influence.

Hale LJ

The question is whether the Centre has an effective consent for the continued storage and later use of these sperm. Without such consent it is unlawful for them to continue to keep it. On the face of it the Centre does not have such consent in this case. There could scarcely be a more obvious way of withdrawing consent than changing the very document upon which it is recorded in the presence of a representative of the Centre and authenticating it for her . . .

Hence a Centre having in their possession a form dealing with the matters with which it is required by Schedule 3 to the 1990 Act to deal should be both entitled and expected to rely upon that form according to its letter, unless and until it can clearly be established that the form does not represent a valid decision by the person apparently signing it. The most obvious examples are forgery, duress or mistake as to the nature of the form being signed (non est factum). The equitable concepts of misrepresentation and undue influence may have a part to play but the courts should be slow to find them established in such a way as to supply a centre with a consent which they would not otherwise have.

One other difficulty raised by the consent provisions in Schedule 3 concerns patients who are not able to give an effective consent for the storage of their gametes. Certain medical treatments for cancer, such as orchidectomy (the removal of testicles) and chemotherapy, may leave the patient permanently sterile. In such circumstances, it is routine to retrieve sperm for storage prior to treatment. If the patient being treated is a non-*Gillick* competent child, or is for some other reason incapacitated, sperm retrieval itself might be lawful on the grounds that it would be in the best interests of the patient, but in the absence of an effective written consent, the storage of the retrieved tissue would be unlawful. This defect in the legislation was highlighted in Sheila McLean's Report to Ministers, commissioned after the *Blood* case.

Sheila McLean[38]

There is one set of circumstances in which it might be thought that the written consent requirement could be waived. If it has been possible to ascertain that the 'best interests' exception to the general requirements of the common law can be invoked to permit the removal of gametes then it clearly could be the case that lawfully obtained gametes would still need to be stored before use. If the interests which render the removal lawful are to be vindicated, then it would be anomalous not to permit such storage.

Thus it may be necessary specifically to amend the legislation to provide that the Human Fertilisation and Embryology Authority has the discretion to waive the consent requirements in schedule 3 to the 1990 Act for storage only in such cases. This will be only until that person is deemed competent to reach an independent decision within the terms of schedule 3 to future storage and/or use.

The government accepted the need for reform, although as yet the statute remains

---

[38] *Review of the Common Law Provisions Relating to the Removal of Gametes and of the Consent Provisions in the Human Fertilisation and Embryology Act 1990* (HMSO London 1997) para 2.6.

unamended. Their proposed amendment would allow gametes to be retrieved and stored without consent provided that the storage would be in the patient's best interests. For this to be the case, the individual would have to be temporarily incapacitated, and likely to suffer from impaired fertility. In such circumstances, storage of the temporarily incapacitated individual's gametes would be lawful only until he or she is capable of deciding what should happen to them.

(2) CONSENT TO THE USE OF EMBRYOS

Unless an embryo created *in vitro* is immediately either transferred to a woman's uterus or discarded, it will be frozen and stored. Because it is common for a cycle of IVF treatment to create more than the two (or exceptionally three embryos) which may be transferred to a woman's body in one treatment cycle, tens of thousands of 'spare' embryos are currently in storage. If the couple from whose gametes they were created do not want to use these frozen embryos in future treatment cycles, what should be done with them? The HFEA initially set a maximum storage period of five years. Subsequent regulations have provided that this limit can be extended to ten years with the patients' consent, where the woman being treated is under the age of forty-five. This ten year upper limit can also be exceeded in exceptional cases, where, for example, embryos are frozen because a woman is about to undergo treatment for ovarian cancer, which will leave her without any more eggs.[39]

Of course, it is possible that the gamete contributors will subsequently disagree about the disposal or use of their frozen embryos. How should such disputes be resolved? As we saw in Chapter 10, when an embryo is *in utero*, men have no say over the pregnant woman's decision to have an abortion. But if an embryo has been frozen and is being stored *in vitro*, the practical justifications for giving women sole decision-making authority are less compelling. To some extent, cryopreservation undoubtedly reduces the asymmetry that normally exists between men and women's interest in their fertilized gametes.

Some differences do remain, however. First, it is possible for the embryos to be transferred to the woman's body and carried to term without involving a third party. In contrast, if the male partner wishes to use the embryos in treatment, he must find a woman willing to be implanted with them. Secondly, the use of frozen sperm is now well established, in contrast egg freezing is still in its infancy and success rates are low. This means that a woman who is about to lose her eggs as a result, for example, of treatment for cancer would be advised to freeze *embryos* created with her partner's sperm, rather than her own eggs. If the couple subsequently split up, and the male partner withdraws his consent to their continued storage, until egg freezing becomes more effective, the woman will be in a much worse position than a man in a similar situation, whose sperm will be available for his use with any future partner.

In the United Kingdom the position is relatively straightforward. The Human Fertilisation and Embryology Act 1990 allows for the variation or withdrawal of

---

[39] The Human Fertilisation and Embryology (Statutory Storage Period for Embryos) Regulations 1996, SI 1996/375.

consent to the use or storage of an embryo.[40] Once either gamete provider has withdrawn their consent to its use or continued storage, the embryo must be destroyed or allowed to perish. Hence whichever partner does not want the embryos to be used in treatment effectively has a right of veto. In *Evans v Amicus Healthcare*, the Court of Appeal confirmed that this right of veto persists even if the embryos in storage represent the other gamete provider's only opportunity to have genetically related offspring.

Evans v Amicus Healthcare and Others[41]

Following the discovery that Natallie Evans had ovarian cancer, she and her then partner, Howard Johnston, underwent a cycle of IVF treatment resulting in the storage of six embryos. Ms Evans was then successfully treated for cancer. She could carry a child, but had no more eggs, and so the stored embryos offered her the only opportunity to have a baby that was related to her. The couple then separated, and Mr Johnston wrote to the clinic to notify it of their separation, and to state that the embryos could be destroyed. Ms Evans sought an injunction requiring the second defendant to restore his consent to the use and storage of the embryos, and a declaration that section 12 of and Schedule 3 to the 1990 Act were incompatible with her rights under article 8 of the European Convention on Human Rights. Her claim was dismissed at first instance, and the Court of Appeal dismissed her appeal.

Thorpe LJ

The clear policy of the Act is to ensure continuing consent from the commencement of treatment to the point of implant. Consent may be given subject to conditions. Consent may be varied. Consent may be withdrawn. Against that background the court should be extremely slow to recognise or to create a principle of waiver that would conflict with the Parliamentary scheme . . .

In our judgment therefore, Mr Johnston was entitled by the terms of the Act to withdraw his consent as and when he did. The effect of his withdrawal of consent is to prevent both the use and the continued storage of the embryo fertilised with his sperm. Future treatment of the appellant would not be 'treatment together' with Mr Johnston. . . .

It was held by Wall J and was accepted before us that the refusal of treatment is an interference with, and therefore a failure to respect, Ms Evans' private life . . .

Like Wall J, we agree that the two principles which visibly underpin Schedule 3 to the Act, neither of them objectionable in Convention terms, are the principle of female self-determination and the principle of consent. The two are articulated by requiring mutual consent to the point of implantation, but by thereafter giving the woman full control of the pregnancy. This protects not only the man but the woman from any compulsion to go through with the treatment . . .

The need, as perceived by Parliament, is for bilateral consent to implantation, not simply to the taking and storage of genetic material, and that need cannot be met if one half of the consent is no longer effective. To dilute this requirement in the interests of proportionality, in order to meet Ms Evans' otherwise intractable biological handicap, by making the withdrawal of the man's consent relevant but inconclusive, would create new and even more intractable difficulties of arbitrariness and inconsistency. The sympathy and concern which anyone must feel for Ms Evans is not enough to render the legislative scheme of Sch. 3 disproportionate. . . .

For Ms Evans this is a tragedy of a kind which may well not have been in anyone's mind when the statute was framed. Where, as has happened here, the parties' confidence in each other's commitment proves ill-founded, there is nothing in the legislation to stop the woman trying again

---

[40] Schedule 3 para 2(4).   [41] [2004] EWCA CIV 727, [2004] All ER (D) 309 (Jun).

with another partner or with a donor. In fact, had there been any doubt about the durability of Mr Johnston's commitment, or even time for Ms Evans to reflect a little about the future, different boxes might have been ticked and the present impasse avoided. As Ms Rose accepted, Ms Evans might have chosen to have her eggs frozen (a risky procedure) or to have had her eggs fertilised by the use of donor sperm. What has brought about the present tragedy is Ms Evans' inability, because of the removal of her ovaries, to produce any more eggs for any of these purposes. In such a situation the simple requirement of continuing consent can work hardship of a possibly unanticipated kind.

The House of Lords refused permission to appeal, and Natallie Evans has instead appealed to the European Court of Human Rights. At the time of writing, her case has not yet been heard, but it can be predicted that the ECHR's decision will turn on whether the interference with her private and family life (Article 8), and her right to found a family (Article 12) is justifiable and proportionate, bearing in mind that Mr Johnston too has a right to respect for his private life. Of course without Mr Johnston's consent, the continued storage of these embryos is unlawful. However, an HFEA licence committee has agreed no regulatory action should be taken against the clinic, and that storage should continue until the final determination is made by the ECHR.

Not everyone would agree that men and women should have an equivalent right of veto over the use of embryos created using their gametes. In the next extract, Christine Overall argues that once sperm leaves the man's body, whether during intercourse or IVF treatment, he loses the right to control what happens to it.

Christine Overall[42]

Once their sperm has been used to fertilize a woman's ovum, men do not have a right to determine whether a child will be born. Men who want to control their sperm should be careful where they put it, and should pause to think before they provide their sperm for insemination or for in vitro fertilization—even with women who are their partners.

Men are therefore entitled to exercise reproductive choice at the time that sperm leaves their body and is conveyed to another location—whether a woman's vagina or a test tube; there are no grounds for extending male reproductive freedom beyond this point . . .

Do 'ejaculatory fathers' (ie sperm providers) have any moral rights to control over embryos? How should competing claims from women and men about reproductive rights with respect to embryos be handled . . . Should their location make a difference to our assessment of who should make decisions about embryos? In questions of abortion, the location of the embryo or fetus in a woman's body is crucially significant to her entitlement to decide whether to continue the pregnancy. In the case of cryopreserved embryos, the fact that the embryos are outside of a woman's body does not necessarily make her interest in decision-making about them less than it is when she is pregnant. For the location of the embryos, in a Petri dish or freezer, does not make them independent of a woman's body . . . that is, the woman who provides the eggs from which the embryos are produced, and into whose uterus the embryos may be implanted. The involvement of this woman gives her the entitlement to decide what happens to the embryos . . .

Thus, in cases of disagreement about the disposition of cryopreserved embryos, joint

⁴² 'Frozen Embryos and "Father's Rights": Parenthood and Decision-Making in the Cryopreservation of Embryos' in Joan Callahan (ed), *Reproduction, Ethics and the Law: Feminist Responses* (Indiana UP Bloomington and Indianapolis 1995) 178–98, 182, 190–1, 194–5.

decision-making gives an effective veto to the man, while giving the embryos to the man entails the de facto endorsement of several morally questionable assumptions and practices. Moreover, under these conditions, the woman faces the burden of undergoing IVF once again. Therefore, decision-making about cryopreserved embryos should, in cases of disagreement, be assigned to the woman, who is entitled to choose whether or not they will be implanted in her uterus . . .

The apparent dispute about a four celled organism is at least as much a debate about reproductive control of women.

(3) THE POSTHUMOUS USE OF GAMETES

Despite the Warnock Report's misgivings about the posthumous use of gametes,[43] it is not prohibited by the Human Fertilisation and Embryology Act 1990. Under para 6.24 of the Code of Practice, sperm can only be used posthumously where the man explicitly consented to posthumous use.

Section 28(6)(b) provides that any child born as a result will be legally fatherless. And until 2003, it was not possible to register the deceased father on the child's birth certificate. This was challenged by the redoubtable Mrs Blood who argued that this infringed her right to respect for her private and family life under Article 8 of the Human Rights Act 1998. Her application for judicial review led to the Human Fertil-isation and Embryology (Deceased Fathers) Act 2003, which amended section 28 of the Human Fertilisation and Embryology Act to provide that a deceased father may be registered on his child's birth certificate if he specifically consented to posthumous registration. This provision applies retrospectively, so any child whose deceased father has not been recorded on their birth certificate is now entitled to have their birth re-registered, and a new birth certificate containing the father's details will be issued. Clinics must now contact men who have consented to the posthumous use of stored embryos and gametes to discover whether they would also consent to being registered as the child's father after their death. For obvious practical reasons, such men will not be recognized as the child's father for any other legal purposes, such as inheritance.

(4) GAMETE DONATION

Most people undergoing fertility treatment in the UK use their own gametes, but in some circumstances, treatment with donated sperm or eggs will be necessary. A num-ber of distinctive questions are raised by gamete donation, such as whether gamete donors should be identifiable, and whether they should be paid. It is also worth considering whether the same rules should apply to sperm and egg donors, given that the experience of sperm donation is much less intrusive and risky than the process of egg donation.

(a) Anonymity

Until April 2005, most gamete donation was anonymous. Children born following anonymous donation can be given access to non-identifying information, such as the donor's ethnic origin or occupation, and donors are encouraged to fill in what is

[43] Mary Warnock, *Report of the Inquiry into Human Fertilisation and Embryology*, Cm 9314 (Department of Health and Social Security London 1984) paras 4.4, 10.9.

known as a 'pen-portrait' in which they leave a message to be given to any children conceived using their gametes. It is also possible, once they reach the age of 18 for children to ask the HFEA whether they were born following fertility treatment, and if they are related to a prospective spouse.[44] This latter provision is rather odd. It is clearly intended to prevent incestual sexual relationships, but of course these could exist outside of marriage. It is not possible for an individual who knows that she was born following donor insemination to find out whether she is related to a prospective *non-marital* sexual partner, even if she is intending to have children with him.

The 1990 Act did not specify that donors had to be anonymous, and some patients did choose to use a known donor. This was particularly common for egg donation, where the discomfort and inconvenience of donation means that women might be willing to donate their eggs to a friend or sister but not to an anonymous recipient.

For a long time, anonymity was believed to be in the interests of donors, recipients, and children. It shielded donors from parental obligations, inheritance claims, and unwanted contact with their offspring, and protected the privacy and security of the recipient family. The assumption was that most donation (especially sperm donation) was contingent upon non-identification, and the guarantee of anonymity was directed towards ensuring that there were adequate stocks of donated gametes.

In recent years, some of these justifications for retaining donor anonymity have been challenged. It is increasingly argued that children need to know the identity of their biological parents, and that the interests of offspring should take priority over the interests of donors and parents. This belief in a psychological need to know one's genetic origins is accompanied by a greater understanding of the importance of knowing about inherited genetic conditions. Children born following anonymous gamete donation are unable to give an accurate family medical history to their doctors, and this might compromise their ability to receive optimum health care.

It has also been argued that a child's right to information about her genetic parentage might be protected by Article 8 of the Human Rights Act 1998, and in the following case, it was accepted that Article 8 was engaged, although the full hearing which would determine whether the failure to supply such information was a breach of Article 8 was delayed, and has been superseded by the government's decision to implement regulations abolishing anonymity.

R (on the application of Rose) v Secretary of State for Health[45]

An action was brought by two people, one an adult called Joanna Rose, and one a child whose identity was protected, who had both been conceived using donated gametes. They sought access to non-identifying information, and where possible, identifying information, about their anonymous donors. The Secretary of State's response was that the issues raised by the claimants would be considered following completion of the consultation exercise, which ultimately led to the 2004 regulations. The claimants sought judicial review of that decision, contending that Articles 8 and 14 were engaged. Their application for leave was granted.

Scott Baker J

- Private and family life is a flexible and elastic concept incapable of precise definition.

---

[44] Human Fertilisation and Embryology Act 1990 ss. 31(4)(b), 31(6).
[45] [2002] EWHC 1593 (Admin), [2002] 3 FCR 731.

- Respect for private and family life can involve positive obligations on the state as well as protecting the individual against arbitrary interference by a public authority.

- Respect for private and family life requires that everyone should be able to establish details of their identity as individual human beings. This includes their origins and the opportunity to understand them. It also embraces their physical and social identity and psychological integrity.

- Respect for private and family life comprises to a certain degree the right to establish and develop relationships with other human beings.

- The fact that there is no existing relationship beyond an unidentified biological connection does not prevent article 8 from biting.

These principles lead me to the following conclusions. Article 8 is engaged both with regard to identifying and non-identifying information, albeit in this case the identity of the donors is not directly sought. What is wanted is non-identifying information and a voluntary contact register. I do emphasise, lest there be any doubt about it, that the fact that article 8 is engaged is far from saying that there is a breach of it. . . .

It is to my mind entirely understandable that AID [artificial insemination by donor] children should wish to know about their origins and in particular to learn what they can about their biological father or, in the case of egg donation, their biological mother. The extent to which this matters will vary from individual to individual. In some instances, as in the case of the claimant Joanna Rose, the information will be of massive importance. I do not find this at all surprising bearing in mind the lessons that have been learnt from adoption. A human being is a human being whatever the circumstances of his conception and an AID child is entitled to establish a picture of his identity as much as anyone else. We live in a much more open society than even 20 years ago. Secrecy nowadays has to be justified where previously it did not. The distinction between identifying and non-identifying information is not relevant at the engagement stage of article 8, but it is likely to become very relevant when one comes to the important balancing exercise of the other considerations in article 8(2). . . .

Everyone should be able to establish details of his identity as a human being. That, to my mind, plainly includes the right to obtain information about a biological parent who will inevitably have contributed to the identity of his child. . . .

The evidence before the court satisfies me that article 8 of the Convention is engaged in the circumstances of these claimants. Whether or not there has been a breach of it is, I emphasise again, an entirely different matter and does not fall for consideration by the court at this stage.

The presumption that anonymity is necessary in order to protect the continued availability of donated sperm has also been undermined by several studies which have indicated that a significant proportion of donors, especially among those who donate during their late twenties and thirties, would be willing to be identified. Ken Daniels describes two studies carried out in the UK, one study involved older donors 53 per cent of whom would not mind if their offspring were able to trace them; the other study involved students, only 18 per cent of whom would continue to provide sperm if their offspring could learn their identity.[46] And evidence from countries in which children can gain access to identifying information about the gamete donor, such as

---

[46] K Daniels, 'The Semen Providers' in K Daniels, Ken and E Haimes (eds), *Donor Insemination: International Social Science Perspectives* (CUP Cambridge 1998) 76–104, 94.

Sweden, suggests that it has not dramatically depleted the supply of donated gametes, but rather that it alters the profile of donors, from students to men with families of their own.

Regulations passed in 2004, which came into force in April 2005, removed anonymity for donations after that date. Stocks of anonymously donated sperm could continue to be used until April 2006, but after that date no sperm can be used in treatment unless the donor is prepared to be identifiable. Children born following non-anonymous donation will have access to identifying information about the donor once they reach the age of 18. Anonymity was not removed retrospectively, although it is possible for previous sperm donors to register their willingness to be identified, so some children may be able to have access to identifying information before 2023.

One potential problem with this shift towards identifiable donors is that a child will obviously only be able to apply to the HFEA for identifying information if she knows, or suspects, that she was conceived using donated gametes. If her parents have pre-tended that she was conceived naturally, the child may not have any reason to make an application to receive identifying information about her genetic parent. Evidence appears to indicate that the majority of parents do *not* tell their children that they were conceived using donated gametes. A European study of families where the chil-dren were conceived using donated sperm found that, by the time children reached the age of 12, only 5 per cent of British parents had told their children about their origins. Some were yet to tell them or yet to decide, but 78 per cent of parents had decided never to tell their children, usually because they thought that the information would be difficult for them, and that it might complicate their relationship with their non-genetic parent.[47] Given such high levels of non-disclosure, any right to identify-ing information about the gamete donor may make little difference to the majority of children conceived using donated gametes.

All possible solutions to this problem are themselves undesirable. It would, for example, be possible to record the use of donated gametes on the child's birth certifi-cate, or to inform the child when she reaches the age of 18 that she was conceived using donated gametes. Stigmatizing children by endorsing their birth certificates, or giving them potentially shocking news at the age of 18 would almost certainly not be in the child's best interests. A legal duty to inform children about the use of donated gametes would be out of step with the principle of family law that, unless parents pose a risk of significant harm to their children, they should be free to bring their children up according to their own beliefs and values.

Instead, it is hoped that the removal of anonymity will promote a culture of open-ness, and that patients should be strongly advised of the merits of being frank with their offpsring. Initial evidence from Sweden is not, however, especially encouraging: Gottlieb et al. found that 89 per cent of Swedish parents of children created using donated gametes had not yet told their children about the circumstances of their conception.[48] In the following extract, Lucy Frith describes a different option, namely

---

[47] S Golombok, A Brewaeys, MT Giavassi, D Guerra, F MacCallum, and J Rust, 'The European study of assisted reproduction families: the transition to adolescence' (2002) 17 Human Reproduction 830–40.

[48] Claes Gottlieb, Othon Lalos, and Frank Lindblak, 'Disclosure of donor insemination to the child: the impact of Swedish legislation on couples' attitudes' (2000) 15 Human Reproduction 2052–6, 2053.

a two-track system in which both anonymous and non-anonymous donation is possible. This option was rejected in the UK, in part because it would lead to unfair differences between donor offsprings' access to information.

Lucy Frith[49]

In the future, it might well be that a choice has to be made between a reduced, non-anonymous programme that respects a child's right to know and a much wider, anonymous programme that seeks to benefit a greater number of childless couples.

One possible means of avoiding such a choice would be to adopt what Pennings refers to as a 'double track' policy. Given the lack of conclusive evidence about the effects of donor anonymity, Pennings has suggested a policy that would allow participants to choose between an anonymous or a non-anonymous donation programme. Donors would be able to choose whether they want to be identified and couples would be able to choose between an anonymous or a non-anonymous donor. In Iceland, where such a system already operates, donors can choose to give anonymously or non-anonymously and couples can choose what type of donor to use. This policy also operates at the Sperm Bank of California, for example, where donors can choose whether they want to be 'an identity release donor'.

This type of donation programme would have the advantage of giving parents a greater choice over what they told their children and also of maintaining donor numbers. Such a programme would, though, while widening parental choice, still leave the provision of information at the discretion of the parents. However, as we have seen, unless a non-anonymous programme incorporates a formal mechanism to inform the children this too leaves the decision to the discretion of the parents.

(b) Payment

For many years, the HFEA expressed a preference for altruistic donation, but pragmatically decided that the supply of sperm may depend upon offering a small incentive to donors. However the EU Tissue Directive[50] demands that attempts should be made to promote altruistic donation, and as a result the HFEA has decided that donors should only be compensated for the losses associated with donation, such as travel expenses and loss of earnings. Until the HFEA's recent change of policy, both sperm and egg donors could be paid up to £15 and have reasonable expenses reimbursed. This sum undoubtedly acted as an incentive for low-income men, such as students, but it did not encourage egg donation, which can be risky, and is extremely time-consuming, intrusive, and uncomfortable.

Although potential egg donors would not be attracted by the £15 payment, other more attractive inducements, such as free or reduced fertility treatment, have evolved. Egg-sharing schemes involve a woman who needs IVF treatment agreeing to donate half of the eggs retrieved during one cycle in return for a substantially reduced fee. As we saw earlier, access to infertility treatment on the NHS is patchy and often inadequate, and private treatment is expensive. There is no doubt that egg-sharing schemes involve substantial, albeit indirect, payment for egg donation. And it is perhaps odd that the preference for altruism coexists with legitimate 'payment in kind' of

---

[49] 'Gamete Donation and Anonymity: The legal and ethical debate' (2001) 16 Human Reproduction 818–24, 823.

[50] Directive on Setting Standards of Quality and Safety for the Donation, Procurement, Testing, Processing, Preservation, Storage and Distribution of Human Tissues and Cells (Directive 2004/23/EC).

several thousands of pounds. Egg sharing schemes carry no extra clinical risk, since the donor would be having the egg retrieval in any event. There is of course the possibility that the recipient of the sharer's eggs may be treated successfully, while her own treatment fails, and para 7.32 of the Code of Practice specifies that women should be counselled about this possibility before treatment.

In the United States, egg donors are paid substantial sums of money: reimbursement for expenses, time, risk, and discomfort is typically about $2,000 per donation.[51] Much higher sums—as much as $50,000—have reportedly been paid to models and Ivy League students and graduates.

David Resnik[52]

Feminist theorists have pointed out that egg commercialization could lead to the exploitation of women who receive money for their eggs. Women could be economically compelled to sell their eggs to rich couples in order to pay for education, support a family, and so on . . . In response to this argument it should be mentioned that the entire ART [Assisted Reproductive Technology] industry, indeed, many features of capitalism, pose similar risks to women. Women face the risk of exploitation from surrogate pregnancy, pornography, nude dancing, massage, modelling, and many practices that society already permits. The commodification of eggs may contribute to the exploitation of women, of course, but it is difficult to establish solid evidence for this claim or demonstrate exactly how much commodification increases these socioeconomic risks. Nor is it clear that commodification of oocytes is any more exploitative than other practice society already accepts. Without further evidence relating to the effects of commodification, these socioeconomic risks are also speculative and hypothetical.

Some ethicists have pointed out that allowing the commodification of human tissues could destroy or threaten the gift relationship that currently exists between donors and recipients, which is an important moral value. If human tissues are assigned an economic value, they will no longer be considered gifts and people will sell tissues instead of giving them . . .

The mere fact that an object can be bought or sold need not destroy our ability to transfer that object as a gift. Many commodities that are routinely bought and sold are also given as gifts . . . People have reasons and motives for giving gifts, even when those gifts have commercial value. Of course, commodification may have some impact on the gift relationship: the ability to legally commodify something may encourage people to sell that thing instead of giving it as a gift. But once again, this is a speculative claim for which we have little evidence. . . .

Perhaps the most visionary utilitarian argument against the commodification of human eggs is that this practice threatens the value we place on the human body. By allowing body parts and products to be commodified, we will transform social and cultural attitudes towards the body . . . [But] our society is by no means 'innocent' when it comes to commodifying the body. Indeed many practices that we currently accept place an explicit economic value on the human body or its parts. These include: . . .

- Injury lawsuits which may compensate plaintiffs for bodily damage . . .

- Insurance on particular body parts, such as a dancer's legs . . .

- Selling human hair for wigs . . .

---

[51] Bonnie Steinbock, 'Sperm as Property' in J Harris, John and S Holm (eds), *The Future of Human Reproduction: Ethics, Choice and Regulation* (Clarendon Press Oxford 1998) 150–61, 150.
[52] 'Regulating the Market in Human Eggs' (2001) 15 Bioethics 1–25.

Since our society already accepts many different practices that commodify the body the selling of human eggs only makes a contribution to this overall trend.

(c) Screening

There are certain limits upon who may donate their gametes. The HFEA imposes an upper age limit of 55 for male donors and 35 for female donors, and a lower age limit of 18 for both sexes. These restrictions are relaxed for the storage of an individual's gametes for their own treatment, so a 16-year-old who is about to undergo treatment for cancer could legitimately have his sperm stored for his own future use.

All donated sperm must be frozen to enable the HIV status of the donor to be conclusively established by a further HIV test six months after the donation was made. Egg donors too must be tested for HIV, although nothing can be done to eliminate the risk that the donor was in the pre-seroconversion 'window' between infection and its detectability. Clinics are also expected to give careful consideration to the suitability of donors, taking into account their personal and family medical history, their potential fertility, including whether they have children of their own, and their attitude towards donation. It is, however, impossible to guarantee that the donor's medical history is accurate. Nor is it possible to screen gametes for all hereditary diseases. The only test that the HFEA recommends should be routinely carried out on all donated gametes is for cystic fibrosis.[53] Among population groups with an increased susceptibility to conditions such as Tay-Sachs, thalassaemia and sickle cell anaemia, screening for these conditions is recommended.[54]

It is of course possible that a donor's genetic condition might be detected *after* their gametes have been used in treatment. Where this happens both the donor and the patient must be offered counselling. The HFEA Code of Practice recommends that particular care should be taken in informing a woman who is pregnant as a result of treatment with the donated gametes.[55]

As the number of identifiable genetic conditions increases, and the costs of screening decrease, there will inevitably be pressure upon clinics to carry out more extensive tests on donated gametes. If a child is born suffering from a condition passed on by the gamete donor, it is also possible that the parents and the child herself could argue that failure to screen for the particular disease was a breach of the clinic's duty of care. Such actions would be similar to the 'wrongful birth' and 'wrongful life' litigation that we considered in Chapter 11. It would involve the claim that had the parents been told of the risk of a particular genetic condition, they would have rejected the gametes that were used in their treatment, and the harm, that is the child's birth, would have been avoided. It might also be possible to sue the gamete donor under the Congenital Disabilities (Civil Liability) Act 1976 (which we considered in Chapter 11, p. 646) for intentional or negligent failure to disclose an inherited condition, but as yet no such claims have been made.

(d) Number of offspring

There is a limit on the number of children which can be produced by each donor. This

---

[53] Code of Practice, para 4.13.   [54] Ibid, para 4.14.   [55] Para 4.30.

applies principally to sperm donors, since it is very unlikely that an egg donor would donate sufficient eggs to come anywhere near the upper limit set for gamete donors.

The HFEA has recently amended the way in which it describes the upper limit on the number of offspring each donor can produce. In the past, the limit was described as 'ten live birth events', which could be exceeded in exceptional circumstances, most commonly to create a full sibling for an existing child. There was no upper limit on the number of sibling births. In reality, then, donors could have many more than ten offspring. If each family created using his gametes had two or three children, a sperm donor might easily have twenty-five offspring. The HFEA has therefore decided that the limit would be more clearly expressed as ten *families*. The limit is policed by restricting access to an individual donor's sperm once they get near the upper limit, but this system is inevitably fallible because the sperm may be being used by a number of different centres, and it is possible that they will all report pregnancies within a short space of time, thus exceeding the ten families limit.

Donors are entitled to set a lower limit, if they choose. Usually this has been done where the donor is known to the recipient. A man might decide to donate sperm to his infertile brother's wife, but not be willing for it to be used by anyone else. He would therefore set a limit of one family. At the time of writing, it is not clear whether the removal of anonymity will prompt more men to specify a lower limit than ten families.

(f) PARENTAGE

A further special feature of treatment with donated gametes is the separation of genetic and social parenthood. In such circumstances, how do we determine the identity of a child's legal parents? We consider maternity and paternity separately below. At the outset it is worth noting that while the UK legislation's definition of motherhood is clear and unambiguous, the rules governing paternity are, in contrast, rather confusing.

(1) MATERNITY

At common law, the woman who gives birth to a child has always been considered its mother. In *The Ampthill Peerage Case*,[56] Lord Simon said 'motherhood, although also a legal relationship is based on fact, being proved demonstrably by parturition'.[57] This statement could be interpreted in two different ways. First, it could mean that gestation is the decisive test for motherhood. Secondly, it could be argued that gestation merely *demonstrates* or offers proof that the woman who gives birth is the *genetic* mother of the child. So while usually assumed to mean that legal motherhood always vests in the gestational mother, an alternative interpretation of this common law rule could be that the test for motherhood is in fact genetic relatedness, rather than gestation. Until the development of *in vitro* fertilization techniques, gestation simply constituted irrefutable evidence of the decisive genetic link.[58]

---

[56] [1977] AC 547.   [57] At 577.
[58] JL Hill, 'What does it mean to be a "Parent"? The Claims of Biology as the Basis for Parental Rights' (1991) 66 New York University Law Review 353, 370.

Regardless of any ambiguity at common law, section 27 of the Human Fertilisation and Embryology Act 1990 is clear and unambiguous:

Human Fertilisation and Embryology Act 1990 section 27(1)

The woman who is carrying or has carried a child as a result of the placing in her of an embryo or of sperm and eggs, and no other woman, is to be treated as the mother of the child.

Hence the woman who gives birth is always the child's legal mother. Whether or not a woman has any genetic relationship with her child is irrelevant, so an egg donor could never be treated as the mother of any child born following egg donation.

(2) PATERNITY

In the past proof of biological paternity trumped the common law presumption of paternity within marriage. This meant that if a woman had undergone donor insemination, it was possible for her husband to subsequently deny that he was the child's father, and thereby avoid the duty to pay child support. In theory, the sperm donor would be the children's legal father, although in practice his anonymity would mean that the child had no identifiable father. Now paternity in such cases is covered by section 28 of the Act. Once paternity is established under section 28 it is equivalent in almost every respect to paternity established by DNA tests or through the common law presumption of paternity. The exception, under section 29(1), relates to the succession to dignities, or transmission of titles of honour.

Section 28(6)(a) provides that where a donor's gametes are used in accordance with the consents required in Schedule 3, the donor is not to be treated as the father of the child.[59] Of course, the obverse will also be true: if there has not been compliance with the consent provisions in Schedule 3, the sperm donor will be treated as the child's father. As a result, if a woman inseminates herself at home with fresh sperm from a friend or relative, or obtained using an internet 'introduction agency' such as ManNotIncluded,[60] the sperm donor will be the child's legal father and, under the Child Support Act 1991, will be liable to pay child support until the child reaches the age of 18.

If a child is conceived in a licensed clinic using donated sperm, slightly different rules apply depending upon whether the mother is (a) married; (b) unmarried, but being treated with a male partner; or (c) being treated without a male partner.

(a) Married couples

If the woman receiving treatment is married, the Act provides for two routes which allow her husband to be recognized as the child's father.

Human Fertilisation and Embryology Act 1990 section 28

(2) If—(a) at the time of the placing in her of the embryo or the sperm and eggs or of her insemination, the woman was a party to a marriage, and (b) the creation of the embryo carried by her was not brought about with the sperm of the other party to the marriage, then, subject to subsection (5) below, the other party to the marriage shall be treated as the

---

[59] Section 28(6)(a).   [60] <http://www.mannotincluded.com>.

> father of the child unless it is shown that he did not consent to the placing in her of the embryo or the sperm and eggs or to her insemination (as the case may be).
>
> (5) Subsections (2) and (3) above do not apply—(a) to any child who, by virtue of the rules of common law, is treated as the legitimate child of the parties to a marriage.

First, under section 28(5), the common law presumption of paternity remains intact, and secondly, under section 28(2), her husband will be the child's father unless he can prove that he did not consent to her treatment. This means that if either the mother or 'father' want to deny the husband's paternity of a child conceived following donor insemination, they would have to rebut two presumptions of paternity. First, the common law presumption of paternity could be rebutted by a DNA test that would establish that he is not the biological father of the child. Once the common law presumption is rebutted, the presumption in section 28(2) would come into operation, and the second task would be to prove that, at the time of the insemination, the husband did not consent to his wife's treatment.

In *Re CH (Contact: Parentage)*,[61] the husband had given written consent to his wife's treatment with donor insemination, and he had been registered as the child's father. The couple had subsequently divorced, and the mother sought to prevent her former husband from obtaining a contact order on the grounds that he was not the child's biological father, and so did not benefit from a presumption in favour of contact. Callman J found that this father fitted squarely within the terms of section 28(2), and that it would therefore be contrary to the intentions of Parliament to deny that he was the legal father:

Callman J

This father not only wanted this child to be conceived but gave it his name. Further, the section provides quite plainly in all its parts that it is in fact quite plain that this father, that is MH, is in law the father by Act of Parliament, so that there is no need for presumption in this case. This case has to be distinguished from a stepfather because Parliament has legislated. The birth certificate shows MH as the father. The child, CH, carries the father's surname on its birth certificate. The mother recognises that the father loves this child. She seeks to sever the tie in law between this child and the father on the grounds that he is not biologically the father. That is against the express wishes of Parliament as enshrined by this Act. It certainly offends principles of justice where a couple have for years sought to achieve a pregnancy through fertility treatment and then the mother seeks to sweep away the rights of the legal father by reason of the absence of a biological link. Without this father's consent and participation in the treatment there would have been no child. The mother must recognise that.

(b) Unmarried couples

If the mother is unmarried, her male partner will be the child's father if the couple were provided with the treatment together.

Human Fertilisation and Embryology Act 1990 section 28

> (3) If no man is treated, by virtue of subsection (2) above, as the father of the child but (a) the embryo or the sperm and eggs were placed in the woman, or she was artificially insemin-

---

[61] [1996] 1 FLR 569.

ated, in the course of treatment services provided for her and a man together by a person to whom a licence applies, and (b) the creation of the embryo carried by her was not brought about with the sperm of that man, then, subject to subsection (5) below, that man shall be treated as the father of the child.

On a literal interpretation, the wording of this section is rather puzzling because it is not clear in what sense the partner of a woman undergoing donor insemination is actually being *treated* by the clinic. This question has been considered by the courts on a number of occasions, and it now seems clear that a man will fall within this section if he and his partner jointly requested treatment 'as a couple'. As Wilson J explained in *U v W (Attorney General Intervening)*:

The test in section 28(3)(a) is not whether the man consented either to be deemed in law to be the father of the prospective child or to become legally responsible for him: it is whether the relevant treatment services were provided for the woman and him together . . . In my view what has to be demonstrated is that, in the provision of treatment services with donor sperm, the doctor was responding to a request for that form of treatment made by the woman and the man as a couple, notwithstanding the absence in the man of any physical role in such treatment.[62]

There is an important practical difference between sections 28(2) and 28(3). If a woman is married, the assumption is that her husband is the father of her child and it would be for him to prove otherwise. Conversely if the woman having treatment is unmarried, the onus is on her partner to prove that they were treated together. The law thus presumes paternity within marriage, but unmarried 'fathers' have to take positive steps to establish their paternity.

A complicated factual variation would be if the woman being treated is married, but is seeking treatment with a man who is not her husband. In such a case, the husband would be presumed to be the child's father at common law, and by virtue of section 28(2). Once both presumptions had been rebutted on the grounds first that the husband was not the biological father, and second that he did not consent to her treatment, section 28(3) would come into play, and provided that the services were provided to the woman and her companion 'as a couple', he could be recognized as the child's father.

It is worth noting that these rules do not apply when treatment is provided abroad. In *U v W (Attorney General Intervening)*[63] even though the couple were undoubtedly 'provided with treatment together' in Rome, the male partner could not be recognized as the children's legal father. Wilson J found that the attribution of paternity when a couple are treated together only applied where the 1990 Act's rules governing consent to the donation and use of gametes had been complied with. He laid out the various protections which would not be in place where treatment took place abroad:

Wilson J

Sections 12 and 13 provide for various conditions to be attached to licences for treatment services. One condition is that elaborate confidential records of the treatment must be kept and some of the information relayed to the authority: section 13(2) and (3) and section 12(g). A second is that the authority must be permitted at all reasonable times to inspect the premises and

---

[62] [1998] Fam 29.   [63] Ibid.

the records and to observe activities: section 12(b). A third is that compliance must be made with a set of provisions in Schedule 3 to the Act of 1990 regulating the procedure for obtaining the consent of donors to the use of their gametes: section 12(c). A fourth is that, prior to treatment, account must have been taken of the welfare of any child who may be born as a result of it, including the need of that child for a father: section 13(5). A fifth is that, where a donor's gametes are to be used, the woman to be treated and, where she is being treated together with a man, the man must have been given a suitable opportunity to receive proper counselling about the implications of taking the proposed steps and have been provided with relevant information: section 13(6)(a).

When, as here, treatment had not been carried out under a licence issued by the HFEA, none of these conditions had been satisfied, and hence what Wilson J described as the 'unique' and 'to many, surprising' ascription of non-genetic paternity to unmarried men could not apply.

(c) Single women

Our final category of patients is women who are not being treated 'together' with a man. This will include single women, lesbian couples, and women using their partner's sperm posthumously. Women whose husbands do not consent to their treatment and who can rebut the common law presumption of paternity, will also fall within this group. In all these situations, the child has no legal father.

(d) Disputes about paternity

In practice, husbands and partners are asked to sign consent forms that specify their agreement to being treated as the child's legal father prior to the provision of infertility treatment,[64] so disputes about paternity are uncommon, although as we can see from the following two cases, not unprecedented.

In *Re D*, the House of Lords confirmed that whether a couple were being 'treated together' under section 28(3) should be judged at the time of embryo transfer or insemination, and not when the couple were first accepted for treatment.

Re D (A Child)[65]

A woman who had previously received unsuccessful treatment with donated gametes together with her partner returned to the clinic after their relationship had ended. By this time, she had a new partner. However she did not tell the clinic that she was no longer being treated together with her ex-partner, and the clinic relied upon the consent forms signed previously by her and her ex-partner. Her ex-partner did not know she was receiving further treatment. This treatment was successful, and after the birth of the child her ex-partner applied for parental responsibility and contact orders under the Children Act 1989.

Although initially both parties accepted that he was the child's legal father, this concession was questioned by the court, and clarification was sought. The mother argued that he was not in fact her daughter's legal father. The Court of Appeal agreed, and her ex-partner's appeal to the House of Lords was dismissed. Lord Walker (with whom the other Law Lords agreed) said that he was 'content to adopt the reasoning and conclusions of the Court of Appeal, in the judgment delivered by Hale LJ, as my own'. We therefore include an extract from Hale LJ's judgment before Lord Walker's further observations.

---

[64] Code of Practice, paras 6.34, 6.36.   [65] [2005] UKHL 33, [2005] 2 FCR 223.

Hale LJ (in the Court of Appeal judgment in *Re R (A Child)*[66])

We start from the proposition . . . that s 28(3) is an unusual provision, conferring the relationship of parent and child on people who are related neither by blood nor by marriage. Conferring such relationships is a serious matter, involving as it does not only the relationship between father and child but also between the whole of the father's family and the child. The rule should only apply to those cases which clearly fall within the footprint of the statutory language.

The wording of s 28 makes it clear that the time at which legal paternity is created is the time when the embryo or the sperm and eggs which subsequently result in the birth of the child are placed in the woman . . . Section 28(3) also focuses on the act of placing the embryo or sperm and eggs in the mother, further suggesting that the question whether this is done 'in the course of treatment services provided for her and a man together' should be answered at that time and no other . . .

[I]n this case there is clear evidence that they were no longer being provided with treatment services together at the relevant time.

Lord Walker

I would add three observations. First, the appellant stressed the need for certainty and clarity . . . But important though legal certainty is, it is even more important that the very significant legal relationship of parenthood should not be based on a fiction (especially if the fiction involves a measure of deception by the mother) . . .

Second, my last paragraph does not imply the view that no weight should be given to the perspective (or perception) of medical staff at the clinic. The clinic's perception is one element to be taken into account in answering the factual question which the Court of Appeal posed, following the language of s 28(3). The idea of providing treatment services to two people 'together' does involve a 'mental element' . . . and the perceptions of the medical staff at the clinic are part of that. But they cannot be the decisive element if they are based partly on deception, and if the rest of the evidence shows that at the material time there is no longer any 'joint enterprise' between the woman and her ex-partner.

Third, in common with the Court of Appeal I do not think that the appellant can get any assistance from art 8 of the European Convention for the Protection of Human Rights and Fundamental Freedoms . . . The assertion that B has a right to family life with R (when he is neither her social father nor her biological father) really assumes that which has to be established.

The HFEA has now amended its Code of Practice so that if the male partner does not attend at the time of embryo replacement, his written acknowledgement that the couple are being treated together should be updated immediately before embryo replacement takes place.[67]

A different sort of dispute over paternity arose in *Leeds Teaching Hospital NHS Trust v A*, where Mr B's sperm was used to fertilize Mrs A's eggs by mistake, Mr A had not consented to the treatment which his wife actually received, and hence he was unable to acquire paternity under section 28(2).

Leeds Teaching Hospital NHS Trust v A[68]

In this case, a white woman, Mrs A sought IVF treatment with her eggs and the sperm of her husband, Mr A, who was also white. She subsequently gave birth to mixed race twins because her eggs had been fertilised with the wrong sperm, that of Mr B, whose wife was receiving treatment

---

66 [2003] EWCA Civ 182, [2003] Fam 129.   67 Code of Practice, para 6.36.
68 [2003] EWHC 259, [2003] 1 FLR 1091.

in the same clinic at the time. Although it was agreed that Mr and Mrs A would raise the twins, it was necessary to determine who was the legal father. The question of whether section 28 applied was complicated because, although Mrs A had received treatment with a stranger's sperm, neither couple had consented to this sort of treatment.

Dame Elizabeth Butler-Sloss P

Section 28 potentially applies because this is a case of twins who have been carried by a woman, Mrs A, as the result of the placing in her of an embryo. It is, however, clear to me that the present situation where the sperm of a man has been placed in the eggs of a woman by mistake was not in the minds of those drafting the Bill or in Parliament's mind when it passed s 28 . . .

Looking superficially at s 28(2), it might appear that Mr A could be the legal father of the twins, since, at the time of the placing in Mrs A of the embryo, Mrs A was a party to the marriage with Mr A and the creation of the embryo carried by her was not brought about with the sperm of Mr A. The application of sub-s (2), however, is subject to two provisos. The first is contained in s 28(5) and provides for the common law presumption of legitimacy of a child born to a mother during her marriage. In the present case, that presumption is displaced by the DNA tests which established that Mr B is the biological father of the twins.

The second proviso, contained in sub-s (2) itself, is the requirement of the husband's consent. Subsection (2) applies unless it is shown that Mr A 'did not consent to . . . her insemination'. . . . The question is whether Mr A consented to the insemination of Mrs A by a third person . . .

On the clear evidence provided in the consent forms Mr A plainly did not consent to the sperm of a named or anonymous donor being mixed with his wife's eggs. This was clearly an embryo created without the consent of Mr and Mrs A. . . . I am satisfied that, on the proper interpretation of s 28(2) . . . Mr A did not consent to the placing in his wife of the embryo which was actually placed. Accordingly, s 28(2) does not apply.

In my judgment the twins' rights to respect for their family life with their mother and Mr A can be met by appropriate family or adoption orders . . . Although they lose the immediate certainty of the irrebuttable presumption that Mr A is their legal father, they will remain within a loving, stable and secure home. They also retain the great advantage of preserving the reality of their paternal identity. . . .

I . . . am certain that the truth in this case is more important to the rights of the twins and their welfare than a fictional certainty. This is not a sperm donor case and should not be treated as such when considering the position of the twins. To refuse to recognise Mr B as their biological father is to distort the truth about which some day the twins will have to learn through knowledge of their paternal identity. The requirement to preserve the truth will not adversely affect their immediate welfare nor their welfare throughout their childhood. It does not impede the cementing of the permanent relationship of each of them with Mr A who will act as their father throughout their childhood.

In the following extract, Andrew Bainham discusses some of the important policy questions which arise from these cases (n.b. Bainham is referring to the Court of Appeal's judgment in *Re R*).

Andrew Bainham[69]

We have here two decisions which turn very much on the correct interpretation of highly technical, some would say ill-drafted, legislation. What are the underlying policy considerations and what are the implications of these decisions for our perceptions of what it takes to become a legal parent?

---

[69] 'Whose Sperm is it Anyway?' (2003) 62 Cambridge Law Journal 566–70, 568–70.

First, we might view both as support for the theory of intentional parenthood. In so far as the law is prepared to confer legal parentage on those who lack a genetic connection, it is prepared to do so only on the basis that those concerned intend to become parents together. In each of these cases the *common* intention of the relevant couples was frustrated by unforeseen circumstances.

Second, and alternatively, we might see these decisions as a rather robust defence of the genetic link as the basis for legal parentage. It was in the end the *presence* of the genetic connection between the twins and Mr B in the *Leeds* case which resulted in the conclusion that he was the legal father. It was the *absence* of this connection which produced the opposite conclusion in *Re R*. The original partner was *not* to be fixed with legal parentage in the absence of a clear statutory exception which applied to him. There is, it is submitted, a great deal to be said for the approach of the President in the *Leeds* case which gave legal *parentage* to the genetic father and *parental responsibility* to Mr A, *the social father* who needed the powers and duties associated with raising children . . .

Third, these decisions raise again the question of when precisely the legal relationship of father and child comes into being, if indeed it does at all . . . We might view it as a matter of some concern that there is no systematic attempt to establish paternity in every case of childbirth and certainly no universal right on the part of children to derive, from birth, kinship links from a father which are taken for granted on the maternal side. The child in *Re R*, for example, was left 'fatherless' and without a paternal family. . . .

The United Nation Convention on the Rights of the Child (article 7) has a strongly genetic flavour about its approach to this question since it visualises, as far as possible the right of the child *from birth* 'to know and be cared for by his or her parents', that is to say, surely, the mother and genetic father. Whether legislation which can result in fatherless children . . . can be squared with this fundamental requirement of the UN Convention is open to doubt. In neither of these cases was there any mention of this difficulty.

(g) COUNSELLING

A further standard licensing condition is that all women, and where they are being treated as a couple, all men too, should not be provided with certain treatments—involving the use of donated gametes or of embryos created outside of the body—unless they have been given 'a suitable opportunity to receive counselling'. Counselling is not mandatory, however, and nor is there any duty upon clinics to make it available free of charge.

The Code of Practice fleshes out what is meant by counselling. It distinguishes between three different sorts:[70]

- Implications counselling covers the implications of treatment for the family and children born as a result. Certain special cases are singled out, such as the 'implications' of treatment with donated gametes or embyros.[71]

- Support counselling provides emotional support at times of stress.

- Therapeutic counselling is intended to help people to cope with the consequences of infertility.

It is only implications counselling which must be made universally available. The

---

[70] Para 7.4.   [71] Para 7.15.

others are recognized as potentially beneficial in certain circumstances, such as where individuals are refused treatment or found to be unsuitable donors, but clinics must simply take 'all practicable steps' to offer support in such circumstances, and are therefore not under a legal duty to make such counselling available.

(h) RECORDING AND DISCLOSING INFORMATION

Section 31 of the Human Fertilisation and Embryology Act requires the HFEA to keep a register of information collected from licensed centres about the provision of treatment services, the keeping and use of gametes and embryos, and the outcomes of treatment. By directions, the HFEA can require licence holders to collect information about donors, recipients, treatment services and the children born as a result. Special rules governing the disclosure of this information, and of any other information obtained in confidence by the HFEA, are contained in section 33. These confidentiality provisions are stricter than common law duty of confidence, which we considered in Chapter 6.

(i) PREIMPLANTATION GENETIC DIAGNOSIS (PGD)

(1) WHAT IS (PGD)?

When a newly fertilized egg has started the process of cell division, and is at the 4–10 cell stage, it is possible to remove one or two of its cells without compromising its capacity for normal development. The removed cell(s) can then be tested in order to detect certain genetic abnormalities. Affected embryos are discarded and only unaffected embryos will be transferred to the woman's uterus or frozen for use in future treatment. It is also possible to discover the embryo's sex, and hence avoid the transmission of X-linked conditions, such as haemophilia, which only affect boys. Because females have two X-chromosomes, they will invariably have a 'normal' gene that can correct a defective gene on the other X chromosome. Males, on the other hand, have only one X-chromosome, so if they inherit a defective gene on the X chromosome, they will develop the disease in question.

Preimplantation genetic diagnosis (PGD) is generally used by couples who are at risk of passing on a genetic disorder, and who will often have already had children or pregnancies which were affected by this inherited condition. The European Society of Human Reproduction and Embryology (ESHRE) conducted a large study of over 1,000 cycles of PGD over seven years.[72] Most couples undergoing PGD had already had pregnancies, but fewer than one in four had healthy children.[73] PGD enables such couples to start a pregnancy in the knowledge that the resulting child will not have a particular abnormality, and avoids the need to resort to prenatal diagnosis and abortion.

Preimplantation genetic screening (PGS) involves screening embryos in women who are particularly at risk of aneuploidy (an abnormal number of chromosomes)

---

[72] Frances A Flinter, 'Preimplantation genetic diagnosis' (2001) 322 BMJ 1008–9.   [73] Ibid.

which is likely to lead to non-implantation, or a high risk of spontaneous miscarriage. The risk of aneuploidy increases with age, so PGS is generally used where the patient is older, or has a history of repeated IVF failure or miscarriage.

Removing one cell from a four cell embryo, and testing it is an extremely complex and time-consuming process, requiring considerable technical expertise. It is by no means a common procedure: since the first reported PGD births in 1990, fewer than 5000 cycles have been performed worldwide.

(2) HOW IS PGD REGULATED?

Before a centre can carry out PGD for any disorder, it must obtain a variation to its treatment licence. Where the centre has experienced embryo biopsy practitioners, and the disease is one for which the use of PGD is well established, such as Duchenne Muscular dystrophy, approval will be routine. More complex applications, such as those for late-onset disorders, or for tissue typing (see below), must be individually considered by a licence committee.

So when will the use of PGD be authorized? The HFEA's Code of Practice equates preimplantation diagnosis with current practice in the use of prenatal diagnosis.[74] The Code specifies that PGD should be available only where there is a significant risk of a serious genetic condition being present in the embryo.[75] The seriousness of the condition is a matter for discussion between the people seeking treatment and the clinical team. Preimplantation sex selection is lawful only if it is carried out in order to prevent the transfer of male embryos where there is a risk that the parents will pass on an X-linked disease.

Many genetic conditions self-evidently meet this threshold level of seriousness. If a child is born with Tay-Sachs disease, for example, her nervous system will start to degenerate during her first year of life, and she will die within three or four years. But for a number of reasons, other conditions may be less clear-cut. First, the severity of a disability may depend at least in part upon both the availability of appropriate treatments or services, and the parent's socio-economic circumstances. In the next extract, Søren Holm discusses the difficulty in drawing a line between severe and non-severe conditions.

Søren Holm[76]

[I]t is very difficult to produce a non-arbitrary dividing line between severe and non-severe conditions. . . . It is disabling to be blind and deaf at the same time, and no amount of re-description can change that . . .

There are, however, many conditions where the situation is not nearly as clear. Many conditions are not universally disabling but only disabling in specific circumstances. Severe myopia (near-sightedness) is only marginally disabling in our society, whereas it was a severe disability before the invention of glasses . . . A more serious problem is that severity varies not only historically but according to the precise social context of each affected person. Even if we assume that the physical and psychological manifestations of a given condition are constant, there will be many

---

[74] Code of Practice para 14.21   [75] Ibid, para 14.22
[76] 'Ethical Issues in Preimplantation Diagnosis' in J Harris and S Holm (eds), *The Future of Human Reproduction* (Clarendon Press Oxford 1998).

conditions where the impact on the person with the condition will vary quite markedly. The degree to which for instance a severe case of club foot will affect a person will depend on the kind of family he or she is born into—whether physical or more sedate pursuits are the centre of family life—and the kind of other abilities which the person has. The severity in the global sense of a severe case of club foot is thus not determined by the medical severity of the condition. Two persons with the same medical severity might end up being widely separated on the global severity scale. . . .

It is furthermore unclear whose assessment of severity should count. There will undoubtedly be differences between the general population, politicians, physicians, persons with the condition, and prospective parents in this assessment, both for specific conditions and for the cut-off point. This uncertainty opens the field for pressure groups wanting to have a specific condition classified in a specific way. It is probably most likely that the pressure will be in the direction of labelling more and more conditions as severe, because that would be the only way to get access to preimplanta-tion diagnosis for these conditions. Because of the conceptual ambiguity underlying the original classification of conditions and the original placing of a dividing line it will be difficult to offer principled arguments against a re-classification. It is therefore foreseeable that 'severity creep' will take place over time, and that more and more conditions will be labelled as severe.

Secondly, it is possible to carry out PGD for some adult-onset genetic conditions, such as Huntington's disease, and for an increased susceptibility to certain late-onset diseases, such as breast cancer. The child would be born healthy, but would be at risk of developing a serious disease in later life. In such cases, the parent who is at risk of passing on the relevant gene might be more likely to die or develop an incapacitating disease while the child is still young. Though, of course, such an individual could reproduce naturally, which would give rise to the same situation, but with the chance that the child too would be at risk of developing the disorder in question. In the next extract, John Robertson argues in favour of using PGD for late-onset conditions.

John A Robertson[77]

A logical extension of PGD for Mendelian disorders is its use to avoid the birth of children who are healthy at birth but face a higher than average risk of having cancer or some other serious disease. . . . Ethically, the question is whether the burdens of carrying susceptibility genes is so great for the child and parents that the burdens of IVF and PGD to screen embryos to avoid the affected children are justified. Many couples with these conditions might choose to go childless, rather than subject their child to the monitoring and worries that having known susceptibility genes carry. PGD may now make it possible to establish pregnancies free of the feared susceptibility condition.

The arguments in favour of such a use are similar to the arguments for avoiding the birth of children with a serious autosomal or X-linked condition. Parents have a strong interest in having children who will be healthy and not face the burdens of continued monitoring, prophylactic surgery, or other preventive actions, none of which is guaranteed to prevent the disease. If one accepts that embryos lack rights and interests but deserve special respect, then a plausible case for permitting PGD for this purpose exists. Creating and destroying embryos to have a healthy child does not treat embryos in a cavalier or frivolous way, and thus is consistent with special respect due embryos. The fact that the disease state does not occur until much later in life, unlike

---

[77] 'Extending preimplantation genetic diagnosis: the ethical debate: Ethical issues in new uses of preimplantation genetic diagnosis' (2003) 18 Human Reproduction 465–71.

other Mendelian disorders, should not be morally significant. Having a child with inherited susceptibility to cancer could be a major source of suffering for parents and child, and could well affect a parental decision to reproduce . . .

PGD has also been used by a woman who carried a gene for early onset Alzheimer's disease (AD), and who wished to have a child that would be free of that condition. . . . [A]voidance of a child who will be healthy for a number of years but then in her 30's or 40's will experience AD [or Huntington's disease (HD)] is a substantial, non-trivial reason for employing PGD, as weighty as its use to avoid a child with susceptibility or disease genes. Indeed, the case is even stronger because the diseases tested for are not preventable, as may be the case with susceptibility genes.

The HFEA has licensed PGD for conditions which will not manifest themselves until later in the child's life, such as Huntington's Disease, and has allowed PGD to screen out a gene which leads to the development of a type of bowel cancer (familial adenomatous polyposis or FAP) for which the only treatment is to have large sections of the bowel removed during childhood. It seems likely that the HFEA will soon be faced with applications for other adult-onset and susceptibility genes, such as BRCA1 which increases the risk of breast and ovarian cancer. At the time of writing, the HFEA is therefore planning to carry out a consultation and subsequently formulate a new policy on the use of PGD for such conditions.

Thirdly, it is possible to detect whether embryos are carriers of recessive disorders. These are diseases, like cystic fibrosis, where the defective gene must be inherited from both parents for the disease to manifest itself. Someone who has only one copy of the defective gene will be a carrier of the disease, but will not develop it herself. If she reproduces with another carrier, her offspring will have a one in four chance of receiving a double dose and inheriting the disease, and a fifty-fifty chance of inheriting one gene, and again being a carrier.

If a carrier embryo implants and is successfully carried to term, the resulting child will be free from the particular condition, but might face some difficult reproductive choices in the future if she chooses to reproduce with another carrier. Clearly, testing for carrier status alone would not fit within the HFEA's guidance, although again this issue will be considered in the forthcoming consultation. In practice, however, carrier embryos may be identified during PGD cycles carried out where *both* parents are carriers, and are undergoing PGD in order to avoid the birth of a child with a recessive condition. In such circumstance, decisions about whether to transfer embryos which are revealed to be carriers will then lie within the clinician's discretion, in consultation with the patients.

A further possibility is that would-be patients might want to positively select embryos which are affected by a particular condition, such as achondroplasia (a condition which results in restricted growth) or congenital deafness. Such a case has not yet arisen in the UK, but it seems likely that clinicians could reject such a request under section 13(5) of the Human Fertilisation and Embryology Act 1990, which as we saw earlier, directs clinicians to take account of the child's welfare before providing a woman with treatment services. If a clinician is under a duty to take account of the welfare of any child who may be born when selecting embryos for transfer to the woman's body, she could plausibly refuse to carry out PGD in order to ensure that a child is affected by a seriously disabling condition.

A more complicated question arises if a couple who sought PGD in order to *avoid* the condition in question, in fact only produce affected embryos. Should the clinician be able to refuse their request to have an affected embryo replaced? If, for example, this is the couple's last opportunity to have their own children, they might prefer to have a handicapped child, rather than no child at all.

In the next extract Julian Savulescu would go further. He argues that, unless the child's life would be so impaired as to be not worth living, positively selecting for disability should be permitted.

Julian Savulescu[78]

[S]ome deaf couples have expressed the desire to use prenatal genetic testing of their fetus or in vitro fertilisation and preimplantation genetic diagnosis to select a deaf child. These choices are not unique to deafness. Dwarves may wish to have a dwarf child. People with intellectual disability may wish to have a child like them . . .

Many would see deliberately creating deaf babies as the most perverse manifestation of creating designer babies. Deafness, they would say, is a disability. Deaf people are denied the world of sound, music, and the most fundamental form of human communication. People who claim that deafness represents a unique culture that can be fostered only by being deaf are mistaken. Hearing children of deaf parents can learn to sign, just as children of English parents can learn to speak Chinese as well as English. It is better to speak two languages rather than one, to understand two cultures rather than one . . .

What if a couple has in vitro fertilisation and preimplantation genetic diagnosis and they select a deaf embryo? Have they harmed that child? Is that child worse off than it would otherwise have been (that is, if they had selected a different embryo)? No—another (different) child would have existed. The deaf child is harmed by being selected to exist only if his or her life is so bad it is not worth living. Deafness is not that bad. Because reproductive choices to have a disabled child do not harm the child, couples who select disabled rather than non-disabled offspring should be allowed to make those choices, even though they may be having a child with worse life prospects. . . .

Reproduction should be about having children who have the best prospects. But to discover what are the best prospects, we must give individual couples the freedom to act on their own value judgment of what constitutes a life of prospect. 'Experiments in reproduction' are as important as 'experiments in living' as long as they don't harm the children who are produced. For this reason, reproductive freedom is important. It is easy to grant people the freedom to do what is agreeable to us; freedom is important only when it is the freedom for people to do what is disagreeable to others.

(3) IS PGD ACCEPTABLE?

The use of PGD has been fiercely criticized by commentators such as David King, who argue that it amounts to a new form of free market eugenics.

David King[79]

If preimplantation genetic diagnosis [PGD] becomes more user friendly and genetic prediction

---

[78] 'Deaf lesbians, "designer disability", and the future of medicine' (2002) 325 British Medical Journal 771–3.
[79] 'Preimplantation genetic diagnosis and the "new" eugenics' (1999) 25 Journal of Medical Ethics 176–81, 180–1.

reasonably robust, what are the implications? I believe there are a number of features of PGD which will encourage an expansion of laissez faire eugenics . . .

In summary, in PGD, the combination of the lack of need for abortion and the availability of multiple embryos creates a radically different situation from that of prenatal testing. Allowing selection between a number of embryos, before pregnancy has commenced, creates an entirely different attitude towards reproduction from prenatal testing and abortion, which serves merely to deal with serious mishaps. In PGD, parents adopt a far more pro-active, directing role, choosing their children in a way which is not so far removed from their experience as consumers, choosing amongst different products.

There are a number of reasons why unrestricted free-market eugenics would be highly undesirable. Firstly, selecting the 'best' amongst multiple embryos sets up a new relationship between parents and offspring . . . They are no longer a gift from God, or the random forces of nature, but selected products, expressing, in part, their parents' aspirations, desires and whims . . .

At a social level there are further undesirable consequences. Opening the human gene pool to the winds of social market forces on a large scale might have a number of effects. Clearly, there is likely to be a tendency for parents to select offspring which conform best to social norms, with regard to health and physical ability, appearance and aptitudes. Disabled people have often expressed fears that an expanded free-market eugenics would correspondingly lessen society's tolerance for those with congenital and genetic disorders . . . It is also possible to imagine selection on grounds of IQ, skin colour, physical build and facial features, etc. It does not seem desirable to allow such forces to operate at the level of selection of who is permitted to be born. Rather, we should combat the social forces which lead us to disvalue some individuals and idealise others. . . .

[A] logical consequence of a system of free-market eugenics in societies where large disparities of wealth and social class continue to exist is a gradual polarisation of society into a genetically privileged ruling elite and an underclass.

In contrast, David Resnik argues that there is nothing inherently wrong with 'parental eugenics'.

David Resnik[80]

Is eugenics inherently wrong? To understand this question, we can distinguish between positive and negative eugenics: positive eugenics attempts to increase the number of favourable or desirable genes in the human gene pool, while negative eugenics attempts to reduce the number of undesirable or harmful genes, e.g., genes that cause genetic diseases. We should also distinguish between state-sponsored and parental eugenics: under state-sponsored eugenics programs the government attempts to control the human gene pool; in parental eugenics parents exert control over the gene pool through their reproductive choices.

Parental eugenics occurs every time people select mates or sperm or egg donors. Most people do not find this kind of eugenics to be as troubling as the state-sponsored eugenics programs envisioned by Aldous Huxley or implemented by Nazi Germany. Indeed, one might argue that this kind of eugenics is a morally acceptable exercise of parental rights. Moreover, most parents do not make their reproductive choices with the sole aim of controlling the human gene pool; any effects these choices have on the gene pool are unintended consequences of parental actions. As long as we accept the idea that parents should be allowed to make some choices that affect the composition of the human gene pool, then parental eugenics is not inherently wrong.

---

[80] 'The Moral Significance of the Therapy–Enhancement Distinction in Human Genetics' (2000) 9 Cambridge Quarterly of Healthcare Ethics 365–77, 373–4.

In the next extract, Leon Kass employs slippery slope arguments (see further Chapter 1 p. 27) to suggest that PGD might lead inexorably to a consumerist attitude towards children, with potential parents increasingly able to select the characteristics of their children.

Leon Kass[81]

Make no mistake: the price to be paid for producing optimum or even only genetically sound babies will be the transfer of procreation from the home to the laboratory. Increasing control over the product can only be purchased by the increasing depersonalization of the entire process and its coincident transformation into manufacture. Such an arrangement will be profoundly dehumanizing, no matter how genetically good or healthy the resulting children. And let us not forget the powerful economic interests that will surely operate in this area: with their advent, the commodification of nascent human life will be unstoppable . . .

What standards will guide the genetic engineers?

For the time being, one might answer, the norm of health. But even before the genetic enhancers join the party, the standard of health is being deconstructed. Are you healthy if, although you show no symptoms, you carry genes that will definitely produce Huntington's disease, or that predispose you to diabetes, breast cancer or coronary artery disease? What if you carry, say 40 percent of the genetic markers thought to be linked to the appearance of Alzheimer's disease? And what will 'healthy' and 'normal' mean when we discover your genetic propensities for alcoholism, drug abuse, pederasty or violence? . . .

Once genetic *enhancement* comes on the scene, standards of health, wholeness or fitness will be needed more than ever, but just then is when all pretence of standards will go out of the window . . . Because memory is good, can we say how much more memory will be better? If sexual desire is good, how much more would be better? Life is good, but how much extension of the lifespan would be good for us? . . .

More modest enhancers . . . eschew grandiose goals . . . They pursue not some faraway positive good, but the positive elimination of evils: disease, pain, suffering, the likelihood of death. But let us not be deceived. Hidden in all this avoidance of evil is nothing less than the quasi-messianic goal of a painless, suffering-free and, finally, immortal existence.

The slippery slope claim being made here is that allowing people to test for unpleasant diseases makes it more likely that one day parents will pre-select embryos on the basis of much more trivial characteristics like height or intelligence. But one problem with this argument is that complex characteristics such as these are not purely genetic. Identical twin studies show that there may be some correlation between a person's genetic make-up and characteristics such as intelligence. But if the sole cause were genetic, the correlation would be 100 per cent, which it is not. It is, in any event, far too simplistic to say that there is a single gene *for* these conditions, and it would simply be impossible to devise a genetic test capable of identifying embryos which are likely to result in the birth of clever or tall children. Insofar as PGD is capable of alleviating tremendous suffering, speculative hypothetical risks do not necessarily justify restricting access to a technology which can prevent the birth of children whose lives are likely to be short and/or painful.

[81] *Life, Liberty and the Defense of Dignity: The Challenge for Bioethics* (Encounter Books San Francisco 2002) 131–2.

(4) TISSUE TYPING

A new use for PGD techniques has emerged in recent years. Tissue or HLA (Human Leukocyte Antigen) typing involves taking a cell from an early embryo, in the same way as for PGD, and testing it to see if the resulting child would be a good tissue match for a sick sibling in need of, say, a bone marrow transplant. If the selected embryo is a good 'tissue match', when the baby is born, blood can be taken from her umbilical cord, and can be used to give her sick older sibling a bone marrow transplant. In relation to the guidance considered above, however, an obvious problem arises: there is not necessarily 'a significant risk of a serious genetic condition being present in the embryo', as demanded by the Code of Practice.

When it first considered the issue in 2001, the HFEA initially decided tissue typing could be legitimate in certain circumstances, most notably, the child to be born had to be at risk of suffering from the same genetic disease as their sick older sibling. This meant a distinction was drawn between two couples, the Hashmis, whose son Zain had beta-thalassaemia major, and the Whittakers, whose son Charlie had Diamond Blackfan Anaemia. Each couple wanted to use PGD and tissue typing in order to select an embryo which would be a good tissue match for their sick child. Because Zain Hashmi's condition was genetic, and any future child might also have this disorder, the Hashmis fitted within the HFEA criteria, and so tissue typing could go ahead. In contrast, because Charlie Whittaker's condition was not inherited, the Whittakers were denied access to tissue typing in the UK. They subsequently had treatment in Chicago, and gave birth to a son who proved to be a good tissue match for Charlie.

Following the HFEA's 2001 decision, Josephine Quintavalle, on behalf of a pressure group called CORE (Comment on Reproductive Ethics), brought an application for judicial review. CORE argued that tissue typing was prohibited by section 3(1)(b) of the 1990 Act which states that 'No person shall . . . (b) keep or use an embryo, except in pursuance of a licence'. Tissue typing undoubtedly involves the 'use' of an embryo, and therefore could only be carried out under a licence granted by the HFEA. However, CORE contended that it would not be possible for the HFEA to license tissue typing under Schedule 2, which specifies that a licence 'cannot authorise any activity unless it appears to the Authority to be necessary or desirable for the purpose of providing treatment services'. 'Treatment services' are defined in section 2 as medical, surgical or obstetric services provided 'for the purpose of assisting women to carrying children'. Schedule 2 lists a number of activities which fall within this definition, among them paragraph 1(1)(d) refers to 'practices designed to secure that embryos are in a suitable condition to be placed in a woman or to determine whether embryos are suitable for that purpose'. Does this include PGD and HLA typing?

At first instance, Maurice Kay J interpreted the definition of 'treatment services' narrowly and literally. Since HLA typing was not *necessary* in order to help a woman to bear a child, it did not fall within this definition, and could not therefore be licensed by the HFEA. His decision would not just have prevented the HFEA from licensing HLA typing, however, but would also have made it impossible to license PGD. On appeal, the Court of Appeal unanimously reversed his decision, taking a much more purposive interpretative approach. Its decision was upheld, again unanimously, by the House of Lords.

Quintavalle (Comment on Reproductive Ethics) v Human Fertilisation and Embryology Authority[82]

Mr and Mrs Hashmi's fourth child was born with a blood disorder known as beta thalassaemia major. By the time he was two and a half years old, he was extremely ill, and his life expectancy was uncertain. His condition could be cured by a transplant of stem cells (supplied from blood taken from the umbilical cord) from someone with matching tissue, such as a sibling. Mrs Hashmi had a one chance in four of producing a child with matching tissue. She decided to have another child, in the hope that it would be a tissue match. Her first pregnancy was also affected by beta thalassaemia major, and Mrs Hashmi had an abortion. The next pregnancy resulted in the birth of a healthy son whose tissue did not match that of Zain. Mrs Hashmi sought advice from CARE, one of the largest providers of assisted conception services in the UK. Its director, Simon Fishel, considered that the approval of the HFEA should be sought before proceeding with tissue typing. Following the HFEA's decision to permit tissue typing in these circumstances, Mrs Hashmi had two unsuccessful attempts to have a baby. The HFEA's 2001 decision was then challenged by Josephine Quintavalle on behalf of CORE, on the ground that the HFEA had no power to issue a licence that permitted the use of HLA typing to select between healthy embryos.

Lord Hoffmann

'Suitable' is one of those adjectives which leaves its content to be determined entirely by context . . . The context must be found in the scheme of the 1990 Act and the background against which it was enacted. In particular, one is concerned to discover whether the scheme and background throw light on the question of whether the concept of suitability includes taking into account the particular wishes and needs of the mother. If so, the authority may authorise tests to determine whether the embryo is in that sense suitable for implantation in her womb. It may, but of course it is not obliged to do so. It may consider that allowing the mother to select an embryo on such grounds is undesirable on ethical or other grounds. But the breadth of the concept of suitability is what determines the breadth of the authority's discretion . . .

[T]he licensing power of the authority is defined in broad terms. Paragraph 1(1) of Sch 2 enables it to authorise a variety of activities (with the possibility of others being added by regulation) provided only that they are done 'in the course of' providing IVF services to the public and appear to the authority 'necessary or desirable' for the purpose of providing those services. Thus, if the concept of suitability in sub-paragraph (d) of 1(1) is broad enough to include suitability for the purposes of the particular mother, it seems to me clear enough that the activity of determining the genetic characteristics of the embryo by way of PGD or HLA typing would be 'in the course of' providing the mother with IVF services and that the authority would be entitled to take the view that it was necessary or desirable for the purpose of providing such services . . .

I would therefore . . . hold that both PGD and HLA typing could lawfully be authorised by the authority as activities to determine the suitability of the embryo for implantation within the meaning of para 1(1)(d).

Lord Brown

The critical question, therefore, put compendiously, is whether tissue testing is a practice designed to determine whether an embryo is suitable for placing in a woman (para 1(1)(d)) and necessary

---

[82] [2005] UKHL 28 (transcript on Lexis).

or desirable for the purpose of providing a medical service which itself is to assist a woman to carry the child (s 2(1)). . . .

Initially, I confess to having found some considerable force in the Appellant's argument that PGD screening is one thing, and properly licensable under the 1990 Act, tissue typing a completely different concept and impermissible. It is one thing to enable a woman to conceive and bear a child which will itself be free of genetic abnormality; quite another to bear a child specifically selected for the purpose of treating someone else. One can read into the statutory purpose specified by s 2(1), that of 'assisting women to carry children', the notion of healthy children—only a genetically healthy embryo being 'suitable' for placing in the woman within the meaning of para 1(1)(d). To read into s 2(1), however, the notion that the child will be a suitable future donor for the health of another would be to stretch the statutory language too far. And it may be said to raise ethical questions of a quite different order from those arising out of straightforward PGD screening.

By the end of the argument, however, I had come to the conclusion that Mr Pannick QC's contended for construction of the 1990 Act is to be preferred . . .

The fact is that once the concession is made (as necessarily it had to be) that PGD itself is licensable to produce not just a viable foetus but a genetically healthy child, there can be no logical basis for construing the authority's power to end at that point. PGD with a view to producing a healthy child assists a woman to carry a child only in the sense that it helps her decide whether the embryo is 'suitable' and whether she will bear the child. Whereas, however, suitability is for the woman, the limits of permissible embryo selection are for the authority. In the unlikely event that the authority were to propose licensing genetic selection for purely social reasons, Parliament would surely act at once to remove that possibility, doubtless using for the purpose the regulation making power under s 3(3)(c).

Prior to the House of Lords' decision, in 2004 the HFEA reviewed the evidence and changed its policy. There was, the HFEA found, no evidence that embryo biopsy posed a risk to the future health of children. This was not because evidence had proved conclusively that the procedure was safe, but rather that there have simply been too few children born following embryo biopsy for any definitive conclusions to be drawn about the procedure's safety. The 2004 guidance replaced the 2001 guidance with a new set of criteria to be taken into account by a licence committee faced with an application for PGD and HLA typing. Most importantly, it is no longer be necessary for the recipient child's condition to be inherited, and subsequently, the Fletchers, whose son had the same condition as Charlie Whittaker, have been allowed to use tissue typing in the UK.

Importantly, in 2004 the HFEA made further amendments to its guidance. Whereas in 2001, the HFEA stated that all other treatment options should have been explored (note not *exhausted*), the 2004 guidance states explicitly that PGD and HLA typing must be a last resort, and that the parents must first have attempted to find a match from the worldwide blood banks, which can be searched very quickly.

In addition, the 2001 guidance stated that the intention should be to take cord blood only. But subsequent evidence from haemotologists suggested both that there might be circumstances in which a bone marrow transplant might become necessary, and that extracting bone marrow from a very young child is much less intrusive and painful than adult bone marrow donation. Obviously the HFEA cannot control subsequent decisions about the medical treatment of children born following licensed treatment and so the previous criterion could not, in practice, prevent a bone marrow transplant from taking place if the cord blood transplant did not work. The 2004 policy reflects this by confirming that the HFEA is confident that existing law (which we considered in Chapter 4) is sufficient to protect children against treatment decisions taken by their parents which are not in fact in their best interests. In *obiter* comments in *Quintavalle*, Lord Hoffmann appeared to endorse this reasoning:

Lord Hoffmann

On 21 July 2004 the authority endorsed with amendment the following recommendation of its Ethics and Legal Committee:

> It was acknowledged that the HFEA did not have any power to impose a condition that would prohibit any future attempt to obtain bone marrow. However the committee noted that obtaining bone marrow for the treatment of siblings from children from the age of one year was a relatively routine treatment strategy where no other matched donor was available. The committee also noted that under common law the test for the type of medical procedures that may be performed on a child is very much higher when such treatment is non-therapeutic. Although parents usually give consent to a child's medical treatment, the courts always have the power to overrule their consent where the procedure would not be in the child's best interests.

These reasons appear to be valid. I have no doubt that medical practitioners take very seriously the law that any operation upon a child for which there is no clinical reason relating to the child itself must be justified as being for other reasons in the child's best interests. If the question appears to be doubtful, a ruling from the court may be obtained. The authority is in my opinion entitled to assume that a child conceived pursuant to its licence will, after birth, receive the full protection of the law.

In addition to the arguments against PGD considered in the previous section, tissue typing raises some new concerns, set out in the extract by Wolf et al. below.

Susan M Wolf, Jeffrey P Kahn, and John E Wagner[83]

[W]e know almost nothing about the psychological impact of being conceived to serve as an HLA-matched donor and save a sibling's life. The effects on the donor child are potentially profound. Indeed, if the cord blood transplant fails or the donor child is otherwise repeatedly considered for harvest over a prolonged period of time, there may be a potential for serious effects. The potential may be all the greater if the donor child comes to resist or refuse further procedures, depending on how the family and medical team respond. . . .

Subjecting the child-to-be to the risks of IVF (mainly twin or potentially higher-order multiple gestation) and possible risks of PGD solely to benefit another child with no medical benefit to the child-to-be is troubling. . . .

Moreover, even if one debates whether using PGD solely to conceive an HLA-matched donor may be said to harm the donor child, this use of PGD exclusively to create an opportunity for later harvesting may be wrong on other grounds, such as violating the ethical injunction to respect each individual and avoid using persons as mere means . . .

When PGD is used solely to create a donor and the sibling's disorder is non-heritable, then, the only possible benefit to the child-to-be will be the psychological benefit of saving the sibling. . . .

The donor child is at lifelong risk of exploitation, of being told that he or she exists as an insurance policy and tissue source for the sibling, of being repeatedly subjected to testing and

---

[83] 'Using Preimplantation Genetic Diagnosis to Create a Stem Cell Donor: Issues, Guidelines and Limits' (2003) 31 Journal of Law, Medicine and Ethics 327, 331–3, 335.

harvesting procedures, of being used this way no matter how severe the psychological and physical burden, and of being pressured, manipulated, or even forced over protest. The parents must intend to rear the donor child lovingly with that child's individual best interests governing all medical decisions for the child. . . .

The parents have a profound conflict of commitment, as the donor child's very conception was an effort to save the sibling. Physicians for that sibling similarly have a profound conflict, as their first commitment, both in time and priority is to saving the sibling. The donor child is entitled to a physician with undivided loyalties.

Wolf et al. argue that the child conceived in order to save an older sibling's life is being used solely as a means, and not as an end in herself, thus offending the Kantian imperative which we considered in Chapter 1, p. 12. This would be equally true of attempts to have another child naturally who might be a good tissue match, and yet few people would argue that couples like the Hashmis should be prevented from having further children in the hope that they might be a good tissue match for Zain. And, of course, the child born following HLA typing is, in any event, not used *solely* as a means, since she is not abandoned after the donation, but rather is likely to be loved in her own right as a new and welcome member of the family.

It has also been argued that tissue typing involves a significant step down the slippery slope because, unlike ordinary PGD, the embryo is positively selected because of a *desirable* characteristic, rather than simply screening out serious disease.

On the other hand, it could plausibly be argued that although the psychological risks associated with being conceived in order to be a donor are speculative, we *know* that the impact of early bereavement is overwhelmingly negative. Children conceived naturally in an attempt to find a good tissue match are likely to be born into families which either have, or will soon, experience the death of a child. In the next extract, Sally Sheldon and Stephen Wilkinson argue that child welfare arguments might be mobilized to *support* the use of HLA typing. The child born following tissue-typing is benefited by being a good tissue match for an older sibling since this enables her to be born into a family which is not wracked by bereavement, and to benefit from a relationship with her older sibling, which she would not otherwise have had.

Sally Sheldon and Stephen Wilkinson[84]

Banning the use of PGD and tissue typing to select saviour siblings would lead to the avoidable deaths of existing children. As such, it seems appropriate to assume that the onus of proof rests with the prohibitionists who must demonstrate that these consequences are less terrible than the results of allowing this particular use of PGD . . .

The first prohibitionist argument is that a saviour sibling would be 'a commodity rather than a person' and would be wrongfully treated as a means rather than an end in itself . . . [T]his worry has its philosophical roots in Kant's famous dictum, 'never use people as a means but always treat them as an end'. However . . . this does not work as an argument against saviour siblings. Firstly it relies on a misreading of Kant who counselled not against treating people as means, but rather against treating them *merely* or *solely* as means. . . .

Secondly, this argument fails to say what is wrong with creating a child as a saviour sibling,

[84] 'Hashmi and Whitaker, "An Unjustifiable and Misguided Distinction"' (2004) 12 Medical Law Review 137–63, 146–8.

when creating a child for a number of other 'instrumental' purposes is widely accepted. Given that (for example) attempting to conceive a child in order to provide a playmate for an existing child is seen as reasonable, how would we distinguish this from the reasons advanced by the Hashmis or Whitakers?. . .

A second argument against permitting the deliberate creation of saviour siblings is that to do so would be to step onto a slippery slope towards allowing 'designer babies' . . . Various objections can be made to this sort of claim. Here we will consider just one (which we believe to be decisive): that allowing the selection of saviour siblings would not, or need not, cause us to become 'permissive' about fully-fledged 'designer babies' given appropriate regulation. . . . Indeed, the role of the HFEA is precisely to draw relevant distinctions, to regulate, and to avert an unthinking slide towards ever greater permissiveness . . .

We turn now to the idea that saviour siblings will be psychologically harmed. . . But even if we concede for the sake of argument that it would be hurtful or upsetting for a selected sibling (a) to discover that she had been conceived for the primary purpose of saving the life of an existing child (B), is it really plausible to suppose that A would be less happy than another, randomly selected sibling (C) who was unable to act as a tissue donor? For it could surely be argued that A would benefit from B's company and may well derive pleasure from knowing that she has saved B's life. In contrast, imagine the psychological impact on C, born into a bereaved family, later to discover that she was a huge disappointment to her parents because of her inability to save B's life. . . . [W]e can at least say that it is far from obvious that child welfare considerations should count against, rather than for, the practice of saviour sibling selection.

(5) SEX SELECTION

There are a variety of different ways in which parents might try to control the sex of their offspring. First, there are a number of ineffectual folk remedies, such as having sex at a particular time during the woman's menstrual cycle, or in a particular position. Secondly, preconception sex selection might be accomplished by sperm sorting, which involves separating X and Y sperm, and artificially inseminating the woman with the separated sperm. Until recently, the success rates were relatively low, but a new technique now promises a 91 per cent success rate for selecting girls, and a 70 per cent success rate for boys.[85] Since this involves the use of the woman's partner's fresh sperm, no licence from the HFEA is required. Thirdly, and more successful still is preimplantation sex selection, using PGD. This does need a licence from the HFEA, and given the policy outlined above, is clearly prohibited. Fourthly, women can undergo prenatal sex diagnosis during pregnancy, and abort the fetus if it is the 'wrong' sex. This would be lawful only if it could be established that the pregnant woman's mental or physical health was endangered by carrying the pregnancy to term (see Chapter 10 for a description of abortion law). It seems unlikely that a doctor would knowingly authorize an abortion requested purely on the grounds of the fetus's sex, but it is of course possible that a woman might discover her fetus's sex, and be prompted to seek an abortion ostensibly for other reasons. It is impossible to tell how many sex-selective abortions are carried out in the UK, but in some parts of the world, such as India, despite being illegal, they are extremely common. Finally,

---

[85] Human Fertilisation and Embryology Authority, *Sex Selection: Options for Regulation* (HFEA 2003).

infanticide has been used in the past in some countries when a woman gives birth to a child of the 'wrong' sex.

The legitimacy of sperm sorting and preimplantation sex selection was considered by the HFEA following a major public consultation in 2003. On the one hand, sperm sorting does not involve the destruction of embryos, so it might be said to raise less difficult ethical dilemmas. But on the other hand, it has the same impact as sex selection using PGD on attitudes towards children. In the end, it was this latter argument, and in particular its apparent acceptance by a large majority of the public, which persuaded the HFEA to recommend that sperm sorting should be regulated, and licensable only where it is performed to avoid the birth of a child who would suffer from a serious disability.

Human Fertilisation and Embryology Authority[86]

131. If the argument for regulation rests partly, although not exclusively, on the need to protect the interests of the children who may be born, parental choice alone cannot be allowed to determine whether sex selection may be used. Whilst prospective parents' desire for treatment, and their informed consent to that treatment, are necessary conditions for treatment to take place, these cannot alone be sufficient.

132. The main argument against prohibiting sex selection for non-medical reasons is that it concerns that most intimate aspect of family life, the decision to have children. This is an area of private life in which people are generally best left to make their own choices and in which the state should intervene only to prevent the occurrence of serious harms, and only where this intervention is non-intrusive and likely to be effective . . .

137. Although some people's private motives for wishing to select in favour of a particular sex may be perceived as morally unacceptable, in our view they need not always be so. In our view it is neither possible nor desirable to restrict access to sex selection on such critieria.

139. In our view the most persuasive arguments for restricting access to sex selection tech-nologies, beside the potential health risks involved, are related to the welfare of the children and families concerned. There was considerable alarm among consultation respondents that children selected for their sex alone may be in some way psychologically damaged by the knowledge that they had been selected in this way as embryos. Some consultation respondents expressed concerns that such children would be treated preju-dicially by their parents and that parents would try to mould them to fulfil their (the parents') expectations. Others saw a potential for existing children in the family to be neglected by their parents at the expense of sex-selected children. Additional worries arose from the fact that the desired outcome is by no means guaranteed by the sperm sorting methods under consideration, and were a misdiagnosis to occur, a resulting child of the 'unintended' sex might suffer as a result of their parents' frustrated expectations.

140. Set against this are arguments for the positive benefit of elective sex selection. It might, for example, diminish the numbers of 'unwanted' children or aborted fetuses, the effects of parental disappointment or the threat to the welfare of children in large families where the parents keep trying to conceive a child of a particular sex naturally . . .

141. . . . Whilst it is not clear that the practice of sex selection would always be incompatible

---

[86] Ibid.

with the welfare of the child born as a result there is clearly ample reason to be cautious. . . .

147. In reaching a decision we have been particularly influenced by the considerations set out above relating to the possible effects of sex selection for non-medical reasons on the welfare of children born as a result, and by the quantitative strength of views from the representative sample polled by MORI and the force of opinions expressed by respondents to our consultation. These show that there is very widespread hostility to the use of sex-selection for non-medical reasons. By itself this finding is not decisive; the fact that a proposed policy is widely held to be unacceptable does not show that it is wrong. But there would need to be substantial demonstrable benefits of such a policy if the state were to challenge the public consensus on this issue. In our view the likely benefits of permitting sex-selection for non-medical reasons in the UK are at best debatable and certainly not great enough to sustain a policy to which the great majority of the public are strongly opposed. **Accordingly we advise that treatment services provided for the purpose of selecting the sex of children, by whatever means this is to be achieved, should be restricted under licence to cases in which there is a clear and overriding medical justification.**

Just like in relation to PGD, the HFEA recommended that a line be drawn between medical and social uses of sex selection technology. But of course, this line is not always as clear cut as is sometimes assumed. Some conditions such as autism or attention deficit disorder correlate with sex—both are much more common in boys— but they are not sex-linked disorders. A couple with sons affected by autism might prefer to have a daughter because she is *less likely* to be affected, but it is not clear that they would fit within the HFEA's criteria.

Because sperm sorting is not currently regulated, primary legislation would be necessary to implement the HFEA's recommendations. This has not yet been forth-coming, so at present sperm sorting for social reasons is lawful in the UK, while PGD may only be used to prevent the birth of a child suffering from a serious disease. It is not clear whether the government will seek to bring sperm sorting within the regulatory framework in any new piece of legislation.

So what are the arguments against allowing sex selection for social reasons? First, it is again argued that sex selection embodies a consumerist attitude towards children. Instead of welcoming a child regardless of its gender, would-be parents who want to choose their child's sex are accused of seeking to ensure that their new baby meets their specifications. Secondly, it is thought that the use of sex selection for social reasons is sexist and discriminatory, and in the next extract, Jodi Danis suggests that allowing people to select the sex of their offspring would also have devastating demographic consequences.

Jodi Danis[87]

Predictions about the consequences of this male preference vary, but even the least pessimistic predictions suggest that accurate sex selection would have significant implications on future population demographics. Although natural selection and mortality should result in a slight

[87] 'Sexism and "The Superfluous Female": Arguments for Regulating Pre-Implantation Sex Selection' (1995) 18 Harvard Women's Law Journal 219.

predominance of women in any population, sex selection has already created a population imbalance in India, where there are only ninety-three women for every 100 men. . . .

Some predict that a population in which males significantly predominate, known as a 'high sex ratio society,' would have devastating results for women. A high sex ratio society might value women for their reproductive capacities, but would also be likely to force women to return to traditional roles centered around the home and family. Demographic imbalances would exacerbate existing sex discrimination because women would not have the political power or economic resources to change the status quo. The underrepresentation of women in positions of power would be even more significant. Oppression and violence against women might increase in male-dominated societies, especially if men felt the need to possess a limited resource and to ensure fidelity. . . .

Some commentators predict that the psychological consequences of sex selection would trans-late into exacerbated male privilege. . . . Males, through their greater numbers, would also know that they were selected more often and were thus more desired, increasing their sense of self-worth and self-importance while diminishing the self-esteem of their younger sisters or other girls. . . .

Other negative psychological results might accrue from parents' expectations that having a child of a particular sex will increase their overall happiness: a child who did not exhibit the traits that the parents associated with the gender of their choice (achievement, sweetness, athletic ability) would suffer from parental disappointment . . .

[B]ecause only those in the middle or upper class can afford sex selection technology, and only those in the upper class can afford the more accurate in vitro technology, a higher proportion of boys would be born to the wealthy. This trend might result in the future masculinization of wealth. . . .

We must strive to create a society in which parents value children for their individual character-istics rather than for their sex and where stereotypes do not motivate reproductive choices. Women must feel positive enough about their sex to want to reproduce women, and social reality must evolve to a point where there is no premium attached to maleness. Sex selection technology is directly oppositional to these goals, and certainly promises social regression in the area of sex equality.

Of course, a couple with four sons are not necessarily guilty of discriminating against boys when they say that they hope their next child will be a girl. But it is further argued that even this sort of preference depends upon sexist preconceptions about a child's gender-specific behaviour. A couple with four boys only want a girl, some would argue, because they think that she will be different from their sons. And in the next extract, Jonathan Berkowitz and Jack Snyder argue that this expectation of difference arises from sexist attitudes.

Jonathan Berkowitz and Jack Snyder[88]

[T]o choose a boy or a girl, parents must have preconceived notions, however vague, about the ramifications of having a certain sexed child: notions which are fundamentally sexist as they are predicated upon anticipated gender based behaviour. Preconceptive sex selection is disturbing because it can be used as a vehicle for parents to express spoken or unspoken sexual prejudice . . .

Though it is unsettling that parents may use sex selection to perpetuate their own sexist assumptions, perhaps the most damaging and sexist aspect of pre-conceptive sex-selection is that

---

[88] 'Racism and Sexism in Medically Assisted Conception' (1998) 12 Bioethics 25–44, 32–3.

it forces one to think in terms of sex, to place a value upon sex, and to prefer one sex over another. With rare exception, it is difficult to imagine that anyone in making a decision intentionally chooses the least advantageous route. It is also doubtful that anyone would endure the expense and effort involved with pre-conceptive sex-selection without a perceived potential for gain. Hence, parents will choose the sex of their child based upon the anticipated gain they will acquire by having a child of a particular sex. This forces parents to figure sex into the calculus of a child's worth, to place a value on sex. Furthermore, by making a choice, parents must essentially prefer one sex over another. This emphasis upon sex is in direct conflict with larger societal goals directed against sexism and which urge individuals to be sex-blind. Pre-conceptive sex-selection represents sexism in its purest most blatant form as prior to conception, before parents can possibly know anything about their child, a child's worth is based in large part upon its sex.

But even if we accept that gender stereotypical attitudes towards child-rearing are undesirable, these are plainly not *caused by* a technique such as sperm sorting. Rather parents with sexist attitudes will also inflict them upon any child that they might have naturally.

The principal argument in favour of allowing sex selection for social reasons derives from John Stuart Mill's harm principle (paraphrased in paragraph 132 of the HFEA's report above). Liberty, according to Mill, should be restricted only when its exercise might cause harm to others. *If*, and of course this is a contentious question, sex selection does not harm anyone, then there is insufficient justification for restricting people's reproductive freedom. Of course, critics of sex selection would argue that it does harm others, such as the child herself (see Jonathan Berkowitz and Jack Snyder, above) and society in general (see Jodi Danis, above). But others, such as David McCarthy and John Harris (below), disagree and contend that these harms are far too speculative and fanciful to justify a restriction on freedom.

David McCarthy[89]

If sex selection were widely available, most people considering their reproductive choices would try to address the question of whether they have good reasons to select the sex of their child, and it is almost certain that there would be substantial disagreement. But a different question is what the law on sex selection should be in the face of reasonable disagreement about the merits of sex selection. As in many disputed areas, what is in question is a basic liberty; in this case, the liberty to make one's own reproductive decisions. Some people regard the use others make of reproductive technology (for example contraceptives) to control the number of children they have and at what stage in their lives as frivolous and morally objectionable. Others regard the use of reproductive technology to sex select as frivolous and morally objectionable. And just as there are insufficient grounds for restricting reproductive liberties in the first case, so there are insufficient grounds for restricting reproductive liberties in the second case. The appeals to the liberties of others, harm and social cost are the only kinds of consideration that could justify restricting a basic liberty, but in the context of sex selection these appeals are weak . . .

In a pluralistic democratic society built upon the ideals of free and equal citizenry, there is always a presumption in favour of liberty. The burden of proof is always on those who want to restrict the liberty of others. Defenders of the legality of sex selection are not seeking to restrict anyone's liberty, whereas opponents are. So the burden of proof is on the opponents to show that those whose liberties they propose to restrict cannot reasonably reject this restriction. It is never

---

[89] 'Why sex selection should be legal' (2001) 27 Journal of Medical Ethics 302–7.

sufficient grounds for one group to restrict the liberty of others that it is clear, as they see it, that
the behaviour they are trying to restrict is morally objectionable. What must be established is that
the behaviour they are trying to restrict itself results in something like significant harm to others
or infringement of their basic liberties or significant social costs. In the case of sex selection, I
have argued that no such grounds have been established.

Note also that John Harris points out a certain contradiction between paragraphs 132
and 147 of the HFEA report (see above).

John Harris[90]

At para 132 the HFEA set out and commit themselves to what may be called the liberal
presumption. This is a firm and consistent statement of one of the presumptions of liberal democracies; that the freedom of citizens should not be interfered with unless good and sufficient
justifications can be produced for so doing . . .

   The HFEA in effect rely on the following very limited arguments against gender selection. The
first is set out in paragraph 139 where they say 'in our view the most persuasive arguments for
restricting access to sex selection technologies, beside the potential health risks involved, are
related to the welfare of the children and families concerned.' The HFEA then glosses this concern
for children by noting that, 'children selected for their sex alone may be in some way psychologically damaged by the knowledge that they had been selected in this way as embryos'. This is a very
tendentious and unwarranted way of putting the point. They produce no evidence that children
would be selected for their sex alone. . . . It is very unlikely that children selected for gender would
be selected solely for their gender. Indeed it is difficult to understand what that might mean since
the parents will want a son or a daughter with all that is implied by the terms 'son' or 'daughter'.
The suggestion that sons or daughters would be so unloved and treated so unacceptably badly that
it would cause psychological damage is a piece of reckless speculation. Suffice it to say that for
these highly speculative and fanciful dangers to count against the powerful formulation of the
liberal imperative would be effectively to deny that imperative any weight or role at all. And indeed
this is precisely what the HFEA have done . . . in paragraph 147 . . . Here not only has the liberal
presumption been turned on its head, but the burden of proof has entirely shifted from the
requirement that the State show that its interference is necessary to prevent the occurrence of
serious harms, to the rather feeble requirement that those who wish to exercise liberty must
qualify for this freedom by showing that its exercise provides substantial demonstrable benefits. If
this is to be the case liberty is meaningless and the presumption of liberal democracies is
overthrown.

   The illiberalism of this conclusion and the poverty of the arguments produced to defend and
sustain it make it imperative that this report is not only rejected but that it be recognised for what
it is, an attempt to formalise the tyranny of the majority and to institutionalise contempt for the
principles of liberal democracy.

One rather odd argument in favour of *limited* access to sex selection for social reasons
is that it facilitates 'family balancing'. The American Society for Reproductive Medicine, for example, has argued that it is ethical to help couples to choose the sex of their
babies for reasons of 'gender variety'. Similarly, the House of Commons Science and
Technology Committee found that there was 'no adequate justification for prohibiting the use of sex selection for family balancing'.[91] On this view, where there is an

---

[90] 'Sex Selection and Regulated Hatred' (2005) 31 Journal of Medical Ethics 291–4.
[91] *Human Reproductive Technologies and the Law*, Fifth Report (2005) para 142 available at <http://
www.publications.parliament.uk/pa/cm200405/cmselect/cmsctech/7/7i.pdf>.

uneven number of children of each sex in a family, sex selection might be legitimate. Although it is undoubtedly true that many parents do hope to have children of both sexes, it is not absolutely clear why the preference for one son and one daughter should be any more deserving of respect than a preference for two daughters.

(6) PREIMPLANTATION GENE THERAPY

Currently the only way in which genetic knowledge can be used before implantation is by discarding embryos discovered to have some genetic abnormality. Preimplantation gene therapy is not yet possible, but at some point in the future scientists may be able to alter the genetic make-up of an early embryo. It is, however, unlikely that it would ever be possible to modify multifactorial characteristics such as height, beauty or intelligence via preimplantation gene therapy. Rather, simple gene insertion, which could be used to treat a very limited number of recessive disorders, such as cystic fibrosis, is all that is likely to be possible in the foreseeable future.

It seems likely that preimplantation gene therapy would be subjected to similar regulation as PGD, so that therapeutic intervention to prevent the birth of a child who would suffer from a serious and debilitating disease might be legitimate, while attempts to enhance a normal genotype in order to create a child with particular traits or characteristics would be prohibited. But of course, as we have seen before, the line between therapy and enhancement it not always clear cut. For example, what if it were possible to ensure that babies had a gene that offered immunity from a disease such as malaria? Plainly, in some parts of the world this would radically improve the population's health, but since such a gene is not a normal part of the human genome, it would appear to be an enhancement.

4. HUMAN REPRODUCTIVE CLONING

(a) THE REGULATION OF CLONING IN THE UK

The first cloned mammal was born in the UK in 1996. The birth of Dolly the sheep (named after Dolly Parton because she had been cloned from an adult mammary cell) was not announced until the following year, and this announcement was immediately followed by demands for the complete prohibition of human reproductive cloning.

In the UK, as we saw in the previous chapter when we considered research on embryos, there was initially some confusion over whether cloning by cell nuclear replacement (CNR) was covered by the Human Fertilisation and Embryology Act 1990 (see Chapter 13 p. 777 for a description of what CNR involves). Section 3(3)(d) of the Act prohibits replacing the nucleus of a cell of an *embryo* with a cell taken from another person or embryo, but Dolly was created by replacing the nucleus of an *egg* with a cell taken from an adult sheep. More importantly still, although a licence from the HFEA is necessary to bring about the creation of an embryo, an embryo is defined in section 1(1)(a) as 'a live human embryo where *fertilisation* is complete'. Fertilization does not take place when a cell is cloned, and so the question arose whether a cloned embryo is an embryo for the purposes of the Act. If it is not, then there would be no need to obtain a licence before creating a cloned embryo, with the result that cloning would be completely unregulated.

This apparent lacuna was the basis of an action brought by Bruno Quintavalle, on behalf of the Pro-Life Alliance. We considered the case in full in the previous chapter, but for our purposes, the important point was that, at first instance, Crane J agreed with his argument that cloning lay outside of the HFEA's powers. Until the Court of Appeal reversed his decision, the consequence of Crane J's judgment was that cloning was unregulated in the UK. In response, maverick doctors, such as Severino Antinori, announced their intention to come to the UK to recruit volunteers for their cloning experiments. Unsurprisingly, emergency legislation was immediately laid before parliament, and the Human Reproductive Cloning Act 2001 created a new criminal offence, punishable by up to ten years imprisonment.

Human Reproductive Cloning Act 2001 section 1(1)

A person who places in a woman a human embryo which has been created otherwise than by fertilisation is guilty of an offence.

In the following extract, Andrew Grubb assesses the 2001 Act.

Andrew Grubb[92]

The wording of the Act is very clever. First it obviates the argument accepted at first instance in the Quintavalle case that a CNR embryo is not an 'embryo' under the 1990 Act . . . Secondly, the wording avoids an even greater definitional problem. The 1990 Act covers embryos produced 'by fertilisation'; the 2001 Act covers all others, i.e. those produced 'otherwise than by fertilisation'. As a consequence, there are no loop-holes. Whatever technique is used—whether CNR or some yet to be developed one—the 2001 Act will apply. It therefore covers the currently unforeseen . . .

However, the 2001 Act is not entirely comprehensive. It only prohibits 'plac[ing] in a woman' a cloned embryo. It does not, on its face, prohibit the creation of such an embryo. This apparent lacuna is not a problem in reality since, following the [House of Lords] decision in *Quintavalle*, the creation of such an embryo without a licence from the HFEA would be a criminal offence under the 1990 Act punishable by up to two years imprisonment (ss 3(1) and 41(2) and (4)). . . .

Another difficulty concerns human/animal hybrids. Where such a hybrid is produced through fertilisation using human and animal gametes, this may only be done with a licence from the HFEA (s.4(1)(c)—prohibiting the mixing of human and live animal gametes). However, the 1990 Act does not cover the case where the animal hybrid is produced through CNR: there is no 'mixing' of gametes. Such a procedure would only be regulated by the HFEA if that 'embryo' is seen as a 'human embryo' under the 1990 Act. Also, placing it in a woman would then be a crime under the 2001 Act. Unfortunately, it is far from clear that such an embryo is a 'human embryo'. . . As such, the regulation and control of this remains outwith the legislation.

The House of Lords Select Committee which considered the regulation of stem cell research in the UK (considered in Chapter 13), endorsed the complete prohibition of human reproductive cloning in the UK, and further suggested that international agreement to ban reproductive cloning would be beneficial.

---

[92] 'Commentary: Reproductive Cloning in the UK, The Human Reproductive Cloning Act 2001' (2002) 10 Medical Law Review 327–9, 328–9.

House of Lords Stem Cell Research Committee[93]
Para 5.2

    (a) given the high risk of abnormalities, the scientific objections to human reproductive cloning are currently overwhelming;

    (b) there are further strong ethical objections in addition to those based on the risk of abnormalities, although not all the arguments deployed against reproductive cloning are equally valid. The most powerful are the unacceptability of experimenting on a human being and the familial and child welfare considerations arising from the ambiguity of the cloned child's relationships; and

    (c) the Committee unreservedly endorses the legislative prohibition on reproductive cloning now contained in the Human Reproductive Cloning Act 2001.

Para 7.18

Despite the difficulties, we believe that there would be advantage in seeking to secure international agreement on prohibiting reproductive cloning. It would send a powerful signal of international opposition to the practice; it would put moral pressure on countries not to permit facilities in their jurisdictions to be used for this purpose; and it would afford further reassurance to the public that there was protection against the use of CNR for research purposes becoming a slippery slope to reproductive cloning.

Notice that the Select Committee suggested that there are both scientific and ethical objections to reproductive cloning. In the next section, we consider these in turn.

(b) ARGUMENTS AGAINST REPRODUCTIVE CLONING

(1) PRACTICAL OR SAFETY-BASED ARGUMENTS

The most compelling reason not to allow human reproductive cloning is that it would currently present an unacceptable risk to the health of the pregnant woman and any child that might be born. As we saw in Chapter 8, research involving human subjects is legitimate only once trials in animals have established that there is a reasonable prospect of success, and that it meets a threshold level of safety. The burden of proof lies with the researcher, and although an absolute guarantee that a procedure is risk-free would be impracticable, cloning in animals is not yet sufficiently safe or effective. Dolly was the sole survivor following the successful transplantation of nuclei to 277 enucleated ewe's eggs.[94] Cloning in animals appears to cause high rates of spontaneous late abortion and early postnatal death.[95] There is also some evidence that successfully cloned animals suffer long-lasting deleterious effects—Dolly herself developed arthritis at an abnormally young age, and died prematurely of an unrelated condition. It is thought that when an adult cell is cloned, it is possible that its advanced age will create an increased risk of cancer and other degenerative diseases. Given this backdrop, it would almost certainly be unethical to conduct research into

---

[93] *Stem Cell Research Report*, Feb 2002.
[94] I Wilmut et al., 'Viable offspring derived from fetal and adult mammalian cells' (1997) 385 Nature 810–13.
[95] Y Kato et al., 'Eight calves cloned from somatic cells of a single adult' (1998) 282 Science 2095–8.

human reproductive cloning. A controversial argument is, however, made by John Harris in the next extract. He argues that since sexual reproduction also involves high levels of wastage of embryos, there is no necessary objection to reproductive cloning on safety grounds.

John Harris[96]

The one decent argument against cloning that does command respect is the claim that in the current state of the art cloning would be likely to result in a high failure rate in pregnancy and an unacceptably high rate of birth defects and genetic abnormalities. . . But embryo wastage *per se* cannot be an objection to reproductive cloning, at least for anyone who accepts natural reproduction. Approximately 80 per cent of embryos perish in natural reproduction. But not only is natural reproduction inefficient, it is also unsafe. Around 3–5 per cent of babies born have some abnormality. Natural reproduction not only involves the foreseeable and unavoidable creation of some embryos which will die, but also some embryos which will go on to become very disabled human beings. Many embryos are created so genetically abnormal that they cannot survive. They miscarry or spontaneously abort. But some survive only to die as grossly deformed babies . . .

It is clear that natural sexual reproduction is a method that has a significant risk of failure, death and abnormality. It is however not immediately ruled out as unacceptably unsafe or 'untested' on this account. Indeed it is well tested and remains unsafe. Natural reproduction is of course also dangerous for the mother. It is well established that carrying a child to term is more dangerous for the mother than early abortion and much more dangerous than not having a child at all . . .

One very important conclusion follows from this discussion. It is that for those who accept natural reproduction, there is no objection in principle to reproductive cloning on grounds of inefficiency or lack of safety. . . Even if attempts at reproductive cloning involve the loss of many embryos which will perish in early embryonic development and also involves the creation of other embryos which will become grossly deformed human beings, this is no different from natural reproduction. Both natural reproduction and human reproductive cloning are relevantly similar activities from the point of view of their moral character—the ethics of the respective activities.

This is a striking conclusion. Acceptance of natural reproduction entails acceptance of reproductive cloning, at least from the perspective of the safety and efficiency of the practice.

It is, of course, true that miscarriage happens in nature, but a clinician who *chose* to use a reproductive technique which massively increased the risk of miscarriage might be in breach of her duty of care. It would be difficult to argue that it was acceptable to expose female patients to a hugely elevated risk of miscarriage. As a result, most scientists and clinicians are of the opinion that concerns about safety currently justify a moratorium on reproductive cloning. Given previous experience, however, it seems likely that scientific progress will mean that at some point in the future cloning experiments involving animals will demonstrate an acceptable level of safety and efficacy. Once the safety objection to cloning is removed, we will have to decide whether human reproductive cloning is ethically acceptable.

---

[96] *On Cloning* (Routledge London 2004) 109–10, 112.

(2) ETHICAL ARGUMENTS

A number of different objections to human reproductive cloning have been raised. At the outset, it is probably worth noting that some of these arguments were also deployed following the birth of Louise Brown in 1978 by people who believed that 'test tube babies' were similarly unnatural, would threaten family relationships, and would be the first step upon a very slippery slope. So perhaps the novelty of cloning, like the novelty of IVF in the late 1970s, inevitably prompts hostility, which may soften with familiarity. On the other hand, many would argue that there is in fact something uniquely disturbing about reproductive cloning. Let us look at this claim in more detail.

First, it has been argued that cloning violates the individual's right to her own unique identity. This argument is undermined by the natural existence of identical twins, who have identical DNA, but undoubtedly have separate identities. The human brain is extraordinarily complex and even genetically identical twins are born with different neural connections.[97] These differences increase as their experiences and environment shape their neural development. Having a unique genotype is not, therefore, an essential prerequisite of individual identity. It is also important to remember that the clone and her DNA source will be less alike than monozygotic twins because their uterine environments, childhood experiences and upbringing will be completely different. As Anne McLaren explains in the next extract, given that genetically identical individuals already exist, it is difficult to base an argument against cloning upon the unacceptability of creating such individuals.

Anne McLaren[98]

It has been argued that the unique identity of human beings must be protected; but monozygotic twins are at least as identical genetically as any deliberately cloned human beings would be, while all the important influences of upbringing and environment that make monozygotic twins not identical would ensure that individuals produced by nuclear transfer were still more different from one another and from their donor. If we do not wish to impugn the unique identity of each monozygotic twin, it is hard to base a convincing argument against cloning on this concept.

Secondly, Alexander Morgan Capron argues that even if we acknowledge the likelihood of significant differences between a clone and her DNA source, the *expectation* of similarity will significantly impair the clone's capacity for individuality.

Alexander Morgan Capron[99]

Given the uniqueness of each individual's environmental experience, from the earliest embryonic moment onwards, it's true that if Mozart were cloned, you wouldn't get another Mozart. But, so long as the impulse to act otherwise exists, the failure of the Mozart clones to measure up to expectations is likely to be a source of harm rather than benefit for them, as their makers' expectations—and elaborate plans or fantasies—are disappointed. . . . Were medicine to sanction clon-

---

[97] G Johnson, 'Soul Searching' in M Nussbaum and C Sunstein (eds), *Clones and Clones: Facts and Fantasies about Human Cloning* (Norton New York 1998) 67–70.

[98] 'Commentary on Ethical Aspects of Cloning Techniques' (1998) 7 Cambridge Quarterly of Healthcare Ethics 192–3, 193.

[99] 'Placing a moratorium on research cloning to ensure effective control over reproductive cloning' (2002) Hastings Law Journal 1057.

ing as a legitimate way of getting the child you want, it would exacerbate rather than reduce the drive to regard children as objects to fulfil parental wants rather than as individuals who are entitled to their own, self-directed lives. . . . To the extent that procreation becomes manufacture, the choice to go on with unmediated 'sexual roulette'—free of whatever benefits genetic tinkering or outright cloning might provide—is likely to seem increasingly irresponsible and perhaps even impermissible.

Similarly, the Explanatory Report to the Additional Protocol to the European Convention on Human Rights and Biomedicine, which specifically prohibits human cloning, states that:

As naturally occurring genetic recombination is likely to create more freedom for the human being than a predetermined genetic make up, it is in the interest of all persons to keep the essentially random nature of the composition of their own genes.[100]

In essence, it is argued that clones would be burdened by the anticipation of uncanny similarity between the lives of the 'parent' and her clone. They would not, as Hilary Putnam puts it, be a 'complete surprise' to their parents.

Hilary Putnam[101]

As things stand now . . ., the amazing thing about one's children is that they come into one's life as different—very different—people seemingly from the moment of birth. In any other relationship, one can choose to some extent the traits of one's associates, but with one's children (and one's parents) one can only accept what God gives one to accept. And, paradoxically, that is one of the most valuable things about the love between parent and child: that, at its best, it involves the capacity to love what is very different from one's self. Of course, the love of a spouse or partner also involves that capacity, but in that case loving someone with those differences from oneself is subject to choice; one has no choice in the case of one's children.

But why should we value diversity in this way? One important reason, I believe, is precisely that our moral image of a good family strongly conditions our moral image of a good society . . . Our moral image of the family should reflect our tolerant and pluralistic values, not our narcissistic and xenophobic ones. And that means that we should welcome rather than deplore the fact that our children are not us and not designed by us, but radically Other. . . . What I have been claiming is that the unpredictability and diversity of our progeny is an intrinsic value and that a moral image of the family that reflects it coheres with the moral images of society that underlay our democratic aspirations . . . [P]erhaps one novel human right is suggested by the present discussion: the 'right' of each newborn child to be a complete surprise to its parents.

Whether or not the expectations parents would have for a cloned child are wholly different from the interest many parents already have in their children's inherited characteristics is debatable. Children often find it burdensome to grow up in the shadow of a successful parent or older sibling. Would cloned children be uniquely burdened by parental pressure and unreasonable expectations?

Furthermore, as Julian Savulescu argues in the next extract, the argument that

---

[100] Additional Protocol to the Convention on Human Rights and Biomedicine on the Prohibition of Cloning Human Beings, Explanatory Report (Council of Europe 1998).

[101] 'Cloning People' in J Burley (ed.), *The Genetic Revolution and Human Rights* (OUP Oxford 1999) 1–13, 10–13.

cloned individuals would be treated differently by their parents and by society as a whole does not necessarily mean that we should prohibit their creation. Rather it might instead be argued that we should be concerned to prevent any such discrimination against clones.

Julian Savulescu[102]

[I]n my view, what would make clones' lives problematic is the way in which their parents, peers and society might treat them. Negative attitudes towards clones would be a new form of discrimination—clonism—against a group of humans who are different in a non-morally significant way. To say that creating a clone is an affront to human dignity is like saying that deliberately creating a black person, or a woman, affronts human dignity. The statement itself affronts the dignity of cloned people. Misinformed bigotry is not a reason to prevent cloning, rather a reason to drop the attitudes.

Parents already create families for all kinds of private reasons, in a variety of ways, with and without medical assistance. The role of the cloned child's parents would be the same as all of these parents': to love the child and give it a good upbringing. Whether clones have good or bad lives simply depends on society and how we choose to treat them, not on the facts of their DNA. We should not fear cloning technology, but instead should use it rationally and responsibly. And we should continue to treat other people, including clones, when they arrive, with equal concern and respect, making sure others also do the same.

Cloning is currently unsafe and Antinori is playing Russian Roulette. But if reproductive cloning were in future to become safe and successful, or if we attempt cloning by embryo splitting, there would be no moral reason to ban cloning by law. Morality should be about people and their lives—not about any other individual's feelings of repugnance about them. As we speak up for those affected by racism, sexism, homophobia—so we should protect future clones in society. We have nothing to fear from cloning or biological modification of human beings except ourselves.

Thirdly, a cloned child would be produced by replicating one parent's DNA, and some people are concerned about the impact this might have upon family relationships. Would it be unbearably odd to raise a child who shared the same DNA as one's spouse? As we have seen, the clone and the DNA source are unlikely to be identical, but the prospect is, as Ian Wilmut and Alexander Morgan Capron explain in the next extracts, undeniably unsettling.

Ian Wilmut[103]

My gravest concern is for the child. Making a copy is not treating the child in the way that he or she deserves, not treating the child as an individual.

Using cloning to treat infertility raises first and foremost in my mind concern about family relationships. If my wife and I are infertile, and we decided that I should be cloned, could I have an effective, healthy relationship with someone who is a copy of me? Could my wife? And, importantly, could the child have a good relationship with me? Although I think it eminently possible for one's attitude towards an adopted child to be the same as it is to one's own offspring, I strongly doubt that the same parity of attitude could be achieved in a family in which there was a genetic replica of one of the parents.

[102] 'Equality, cloning and clonism: why we must clone', Bionews 16 May 2005 <http://bionews.org.uk/commentary.lasso?storyid=2571>.

[103] 'Dolly: The Age of Biological Control, Eugenics and Human Rights' in J Burley (ed), *The Genetic Revolution and Human Rights* (OUP Oxford 1999) 119–28, 22–3.

Alexander Morgan Capron[104]

So, what are some of the concerns about reproductive cloning? One issue about asexual reproduction is whether children would be harmed by having only one parent, in a genetic sense of the term. . . . A second issue is whether the relationship between a person who is the source of a somatic cell nucleus and the one or more persons who are that person's clones can even be described in ways that make sense legally, socially, morally, or what have you. Obviously, such relationships don't fit existing categories and raise questions about who is a 'sibling' (as the phrase 'later-born twin' suggests), or who is a 'parent' (the donor of the somatic cell nucleus or his or her own parents, whose sexual act gave rise to the unique genome represented in the clones)? Consider the question of whether there ought to be restrictions on who a clone could wed. My wife and I have nothing but sons. If we wanted to have a daughter, probably our best method would be to clone my wife. Now, suppose we did that and then, tragically, my wife died. Would her clone, who has no biological relationship to me, be a suitable replacement for my now dead spouse (assuming the clone were by then old enough to marry)? She would be the embodiment of the woman I had married, which is exactly the kind of 'replacement' that people who want to use cloning to replace a dead child are talking about.

Fourthly, cloning would also make it possible for women to reproduce without men. Currently, although single and lesbian women can have children, they still need to use men's gametes. Cloning would enable women to reproduce entirely autonomously, prompting inevitable speculation about the future redundancy of men.

Fifthly, it is argued that the random redistribution of genetic material through natural reproduction leads to a healthy genetic diversity among the population, and that this would be compromised by cloning, which simply involves replicating an existing individual's DNA. Of course the clone also inherits mitochondrial DNA from the de-nucleated egg, so her genotype is not completely identical to the DNA source. Moreover, most people will always continue to prefer to reproduce naturally, so cloning is never likely to be so popular that it poses a risk to the health of the human species.

Sixthly, as we can see in the next extract, slippery slope arguments are commonly used to defend a ban on human reproductive cloning.

George J Annas, Lori B Andrews, Rosario M Isasi[105]

Specifically, the argument is that cloning will inevitably lead to attempts to modify the somatic cell nucleus not to create genetic duplicates of existing people, but 'better' children . . . If it succeeds . . . a new species or subspecies of humans will emerge. The new species, or 'posthuman,' will likely view the old 'normal' humans as inferior, even savages, and fit for slavery or slaughter. The normals, on the other hand, may see the posthumans as a threat and if they can, may engage in a preemptive strike by killing the posthumans before they themselves are killed or enslaved by them. It is ultimately this predictable potential for genocide that makes species-altering experiments potential weapons of mass destruction, and makes the unaccountable genetic engineer a potential bioterrorist. It is also why cloning and genetic modification is of species-wide concern and why an international treaty to address it is appropriate. . . .

---

[104] 'Placing a moratorium on research cloning to ensure effective control over reproductive cloning' (2002) Hastings Law Journal 1057.

[105] 'Protecting the endangered human: toward an international treaty prohibiting cloning and inheritable alterations' (2002) 28 American Journal of Law and Medicine 151, 162, 173.

Biotechnology, especially human cloning and inheritable genetic alteration, has the potential to permit us to design our children and to literally change the characteristics of the human species. The movement toward a posthuman world can be characterized as 'progress' and enhancement of individual freedom in the area of procreation; but it also can be characterized as a movement down a slippery slope to a neo-eugenics that will result in the creation of one or more subspecies or superspecies of humans. The first vision sees science as our guide and ultimate goal. The second is more firmly based on our human history as it has consistently emphasized differences, and used those differences to justify genocidal actions. . . .

The greatest accomplishment of humans has not been our science, but our development of human rights and democracy. Science cannot tell us what we should do, or even what our goals are, therefore, humans must give direction to science. In the area of genetics, this calls for international action to control the techniques that could lead us to commit species suicide.

We looked at slippery slope arguments in Chapter 1, and saw that they essentially involve pessimism about our capacity to regulate effectively in order to prevent a practice being put to undesirable uses. The claim that a technique could be abused is not on its own an adequate justification for banning it unless we have also established that it would be impossible or exceptionally difficult to prevent its abuse. This requires *evidence* that it would be impossible to draw a normative distinction between acceptable and unacceptable uses of cloning, or that it would, in practice, be insuperably difficult to police this boundary.

Seventhly, cloning would raise some complicated questions about genetic confidentiality, an issue we considered in detail in Chapter 6. Just like identical twins, a genetic test performed on the DNA source would reveal genetic information about her clone. We saw in Chapter 6 that difficult intra-familial issues are raised by genetic testing, and these would undoubtedly be especially pronounced where an individual had been created by cloning.

Finally, as Michael Shapiro explains, while perhaps not insurmountable, cloning would raise come complex questions about the parentage of the resulting child. Cloning would involve an egg donor, a DNA source, and a gestational mother. These could, of course, all be the same woman, in which case, would the child have only one parent? Alternatively, they might be three different people: would all three be the child's parents? A further possibility is that the DNA source's *own* parents might claim to the parents of their child' s 'delayed twin'.

Michael Shapiro[106]

We are thus at a loss in several ways. As we saw, we are not sure who the clone's lawful parent or parents are to be—because we are not sure how to apply the idea of 'genetic parent' to asexual reproduction. We have already encountered the question whether the source of the nuclear DNA is a genetic parent. Genetic parents have hitherto contributed only half a child's nuclear DNA, plus mitochondria from the ovum. Perhaps this nuclear source is the 'super-parent' because she provides the entire nuclear genetic complement. But her biological role is so unlike that of any prior genetic parent that we are uncomfortable with this also. Then again, as asked earlier, might the nuclear source's own parents be the genetic parents, and perhaps the presumptive custodial

---

[106] 'I want a girl (boy) just like the girl (boy) that married dear old dad (mom): cloning lives' (1999) 9 Southern California Interdisciplinary Law Journal 1, 47–8, 50.

parents? The offspring, after all, is (almost) genetically identical to the nuclear source, who is their child produced by the union of their standard-issue haploid gametes. The offspring is genetically the delayed twin of their child, the nuclear source. Or should we simply ascribe parenthood to the intended custodial parents?

Our impaired ability to interpret foundational concepts through which we order human social life—here, the very concept of a parent—is bound to have its terrifying aspects. This helps explain the alarmist tone of much of the anti-cloning literature.

(c) ARGUMENTS IN FAVOUR OF REPRODUCTIVE CLONING

Despite the extraordinary advances in infertility treatment over the last twenty-five years, there are still people who cannot be helped to reproduce using the existing technologies. The principal argument in favour of reproductive cloning would be that it could expand the options available to alleviate involuntary childlessness. A secondary argument might be that it is easier to control a practice if it is brought within the UK's strict regulatory framework. If cloning (when it becomes safe and effective) is unavailable in the UK, wealthy British citizens who want to produce cloned children will simply travel abroad. If procreative tourism is inevitable, might it be better to allow cloning in this country where it can be regulated and appropriate safeguards imposed?

In the next extract, John Robertson challenges the 'harm to offspring' justification for banning human reproductive cloning.

John A Robertson[107]

Most of the harms said to flow from human cloning focus on the welfare of children who are given the same DNA as another individual. Whether the feared harm is physical safety, individuality, autonomy, instrumentalization, or threats to lineage, all are claims that the child who results is intrinsically or irrevocably harmed by the experience and, thus, that the best policy would be to prevent cloning from occurring to prevent the harm that the resulting child would experience.

Such claims have wide appeal, but they raise a central conceptual problem that calls into question whether preventing harm to offspring ever justifies preventing their birth altogether. The problem arises because, but for the technique in question, the cloned person would not exist. Banning the technique may prevent a child from being born into the circumstances of concern, but it does so, not by assuring that it is born in different circumstances, but by preventing it from being born at all.

Preventing existence as a way to prevent harm to the person who would exist makes sense for that person only if it reasonably appears that once born, the child's existence would be so full of pain and suffering that its interests would be best served by nonexistence. But it is rare that the techniques at issue—whether cloning or other genetic manipulations—would cause harm or suffering to such an extent . . .

If the children whose welfare is at issue are to exist at all, it can only be in the condition which proponents of this argument say justifies preventing their birth.

When carefully analyzed, the alleged harms of cloning tend to be highly speculative, moralistic, or subjective judgments about the meaning of family and how reproduction should occur. Such choices are ordinarily reserved to individuals, free of governmental coercion or definition of what

---

[107] 'Liberty, Identity and Human Cloning' I (1998) 76 Texas Law Review 1371, 1405–7, 1441.

provides reproductive meaning. One need not accept human cloning as a morally acceptable way of family formation. But personal moral opposition alone is not an adequate basis for laws that prohibit others from using a technique that enables them to achieve legitimate goals of having and rearing biologically related children. Given the general presumption in favor of reproductive freedom, a ban on safe and effective human cloning in all circumstances is not justified.

John Harris suggests that the arguments against human reproductive cloning tend to consist in intuitive feelings of revulsion or uneasiness, but he argues that these do not, in themselves, offer sufficient justification for banning a practice.

John Harris[108]

Clearly the birth of Dolly and the possibility of human equivalents has left many people feeling not a little uneasy, if not positively queasy at the prospect. It is perhaps salutary to remember that there is no necessary connection between phenomena, attitudes, or actions that make us uneasy, or even those that disgust us, and those phenomena, attitudes and actions that there are good reason for judging unethical. Nor does it follow that those things we are confident are unethical must be prohibited by legislation or controlled by regulation. These are separate steps which require separate arguments.

   The idea that moral sentiments, or gut reactions, must play a crucial role in the determination of what is morally permissible is tenacious. . . . A recent, highly sophisticated, and thoroughly mischievous example in the context of cloning comes from Leon R Kass. In a long discussion entitled 'The Wisdom of Repugnance' Kass tries hard and thoughtfully to make plausible the thesis that thoughtlessness is a virtue. 'We are repelled by the prospect of cloning human beings not because of the strangeness or novelty of the undertaking, but because we intuit and feel, immediately and without argument, the violation of things that we rightfully hold dear'. The difficulty is, of course, to know when one's sense of outrage is evidence of something morally disturbing and when it is simply an expression of bare prejudice or something even more shameful. The English novelist George Orwell once referred to this reliance on some innate sense of right and wrong as 'moral nose', as if one could simply sniff a situation and detect wickedness. The problem, as I have indicated, is that nasal reasoning is notoriously unreliable, and olfactory moral phil-osophy, its theoretical 'big brother', has done little to refine it or give it a respectable foundation. We should remember that in the recent past, among the many discreditable uses of so-called 'moral feelings', people have been disgusted by the sight of Jews, black people, and indeed women being treated as equals and mixing on terms of equality with others. In the absence of convincing arguments, we should be suspicious of those who use nasal reasoning as the basis of their moral convictions. . . .

   One of the hallmarks of a moral position is the preparedness to deploy evidence and argument in its support.

Some people have argued that the *reason* why cloning is sought might make a difference to its acceptability. Let us imagine, for example, a couple in which the male partner has received treatment for testicular cancer and now produces no sperm at all, and the female partner has been treated for ovarian cancer and has no more eggs. The only way in which they can currently have a child is to use donated sperm and eggs, or to receive an embryo which has been donated by another couple. In both cases the child will be genetically unrelated to them. It seems possible that they might prefer

---

[108] 'Clones, Genes and Human Rights' in J Burley (ed), *The Genetic Revolution and Human Rights* (OUP Oxford 1999) 61–94, 81–2, 85.

to employ cloning, using the DNA from one or other partner, rather than have a genetically unrelated child. Duplication of one partner's DNA is then a *side-effect* of their desire to have a child who will have a genetic connection to at least one of her parents. In contrast, a fertile couple might opt for cloning because they specifically want to duplicate one partner's, or an existing child's DNA. Is this less deserving of respect than the former case? In the following extract, Dena Davis suggests that it is.[109]

Dena Davis[110]

Let me begin by sorting two different kinds of motivations would-be parents might have for resorting to cloning . . . The first motivation I will call *logistical*. For some reason, this couple is having a very difficult time procreating, and cloning offers some unique advantage to them. . . . I call these logistical motivations because the parents' goal here is simply to have a child. The duplicative element of cloning is a side effect, perhaps even one they would avoid if they could. The parents see cloning as the best option from an array of choices: adoption, childlessness, or reproduction with the use of a third party. If we would support the reproductive efforts of these would-be parents *without* cloning . . ., then the additional factor of cloning should not necessarily doom them in our eyes. Cloning brings in new problems and requires additional counselling, but it is not inherently immoral, nor is there a strong likelihood of harm to the child.

In contrast, with *duplicative* motivations it is the genetic replication itself that is the attraction. Some duplicative motivations will not survive exposure to the facts; parents who think they can guarantee a saintly child if they could only get hold of Mother Teresa's DNA are clearly mistaken. Other duplicative motivations are less obviously foolish but more obviously perilous to the child herself. When parents, for example, wish a new genetically identical child to 'replace' a dearly beloved child who has died young, the psychological pitfalls are clear. No child could possible live up to such glorified expectations, and the parents are likely to be frustrated and disappointed that the 'new' child is so different. After all, the second child's experience will be dramatically different from that of her dead sibling, if only because the second child is a younger sibling in a family that has sustained such a tragedy. Thus it is obvious, first, that the parental motivations are based on a mistaken notion of the importance of genetics over environment and, second, that the enterprise is almost certainly doomed to disaster. Health professionals should not find it difficult to refuse to participate in such an endeavour, especially when the couple that wishes to use cloning for duplicative motivations is still able to procreate in other ways.

5. CONCLUSION

A great deal has changed since the 1990 Act was passed. IVF is now a routine medical procedure, and new techniques, such as tissue typing and reproductive cloning, have become the focus of debate and controversy. During the lifetime of this book, the shape of the Human Fertilisation and Embryology Act's successor should become clearer. It seems likely that it will continue the trend towards risk-based and proportionate regulation, with resources focused upon centres which give rise to concern, rather than over-burdening the majority of clinics, which have good rates of compliance, and good success rates.

Following on from this, a risk-based and proportionate approach to the 'welfare of

---

[109] See also John Robertson, 'Two Models of Human Cloning' (1999) Hofstra Law Review 609, 627–8.

[110] *Genetic Dilemmas: Reproductive Technology, Parental Choices and Children's Futures* (Routledge London 2001) 114–16.

the child' assessment would almost certainly lead to an even more minimal assessment procedure than the one recently adopted by the HFEA. All of the evidence suggests that children born following fertility treatment are, if anything, doing better than children conceived naturally.[111] This should not be surprising since the pool of individuals who use assisted conception services are clearly very committed to having children and, due to restrictions on NHS treatment, will additionally also be fairly well off. In contrast, the pool of people who conceive naturally will include individuals who may find parenting difficult, such as children and drug addicts.

Whether or not there will be a move towards greater NHS provision of fertility treatment, beyond the partially implemented NICE guidelines, remains to be seen. While full implementation of the NICE guidelines would, in my opinion, be a very good thing, fertility treatment must, as we saw in Chapter 2, compete for scarce NHS resources in the same way as other equally, and at times undoubtedly more important treatment services. Clearly, unlimited provision of infertility treatment services would not be feasible, but instead I would argue that funding decisions should be fair and transparent, and based upon relevant criteria.

Emily Jackson[112]

It is important to reiterate that I am not arguing that everyone has a right to be provided with the treatment that may be necessary for them to conceive. Plainly there is a crucial difference between negative liberty or freedom from external constraints—which is the sort of freedom sexually active, fertile, heterosexual couples have in relation to reproduction—and positive liberty—that is the positive provision of resources, which might be what infertile people need in order to conceive. Positive rights to resources are always claimed against a background of relative scarcity and there are therefore inherent limitations upon their satisfaction.

Of course, publicly funded fertility treatment cannot be available indefinitely upon request and rationing is clearly inevitable. And, although I believe that treatment should be available within the NHS, I accept that infertility is not life-threatening and that a health authority could legitimately decide to restrict access to publicly funded assisted conception services. Where treatment is available but rationed, criteria such as the chance of a successful outcome and the number of cycles that a patient has already had at public expense may be relevant. What should not be relevant, in my opinion, is a largely perfunctory attempt to judge their parental adequacy.

6. FURTHER READING

BAINHAM, ANDREW, 'Whose Sperm is it Anyway?' (2003) Cambridge Law Journal 566–70.

BRAZIER, MARGARET, 'Regulating the Reproduction Business?' (1999) 7 Medical Law Review 166–93.

---

[111] See, eg, S Golombok, R Cook, A Bish, and C Murray, 'Families created by the new reproductive tecnologies: quality of parenting and social and emotional development of the children' (1995) 66 Child Development 285–98; S Golombok, A Brewaeys, MT Giavassi, D Guerra, F MacCallum, and J Rust, 'The European study of assisted reproduction families: the transition to adolescence' (2002) 17 Human Reproduction 830–40; C Murray and S Golombok 'Solo mothers and their donor insemination infants: follow-up at age 2 years' (2005) 20 Human Reproduction 1655–60.

[112] 'Rethinking the Pre-Conception Welfare Principle' in K Horsey and H Biggs (eds), *Human Reproduction and Embryology: Reproducing Regulation* (UCL Press London 2006).

BURLEY, J (ed), *The Genetic Revolution and Human Rights* (OUP Oxford 1999).

HARRIS, JOHN, 'Sex Selection and Regulated Hatred' (2005) 31 Journal of Medical Ethics 291–4.

HARRIS, J and HOLM, S (eds), *The Future of Human Reproduction* (Clarendon Press Oxford 1998).

HORSEY, K and BIGGS, H (eds), *Human Reproduction and Embryology: Reproducing Regulation* (UCL Press London 2006).

JACKSON, EMILY, *Regulating Reproduction* (Hart Publishing Oxford 2001) ch 5.

JACKSON, EMILY, 'Conception and the Irrelevance of the Welfare Principle' (2002) 65 Modern Law Review 176–203.

McMILLAN JR, 'NICE, the draft fertility guideline and dodging the big question' (2003) 29 Journal of Medical Ethics 313–14.

MORGAN, DEREK and LEE, ROBERT, 'In the Name of the Father? *Ex parte Blood*: Dealing with Novelty and Anomaly' (1997) 60 Modern Law Review 840–56.

MORGAN, DEREK and LEE, ROBERT, *Human Fertilisation and Embryology; Regulating the Reproductive Revolution* (Blackstone London 2001).

SHELDON, SALLY and WILKINSON, STEPHEN, 'Hashmi and Whitaker: An Unjustifiable and Misguided Distinction' (2004) 12 Medical Law Review 137–63.

SHELDON, SALLY, 'Fragmenting Fatherhood: The Regulation of Reproductive Technologies' (2005) 68 Modern Law Review 523–53.

15

SURROGACY

1. CENTRAL ISSUES

1. It is not unlawful to make a surrogacy agreement, but surrogacy contracts are unenforceable.

2. In theory, surrogate mothers cannot be paid and commercial involvement in surrogacy is banned. In practice, payments to surrogate mothers are routinely authorized retrospectively by the courts.

3. The surrogate mother is always the legal mother of the child from birth. Identifying the legal father is rather more complicated. In some circumstances, the surrogate mother's partner will be the father, in others the commissioning father may be recognized as the father from birth.

4. There are two ways in which legal parenthood can be formally transferred to the commissioning couple: parental orders under section 30 of the Human Fertilisation and Embryology Act 1990, and adoption. There is evidence that some commissioning couples do not formally acquire legal parenthood.

5. The government commissioned the Brazier Committee to review the law relating to surrogacy. Its proposals have not yet been implemented. Most importantly, the Brazier Committee recommended that it should no longer be possible to make payments to surrogates, other than expenses reasonably incurred during pregnancy.

6. The question of whether it is acceptable to pay a woman to bear a child continues to be extremely controversial.

2. WHAT IS SURROGACY?

Surrogacy is the practice whereby one woman (the surrogate mother) becomes pregnant with the intention that the child should be handed over to the commissioning couple (or individual) after birth. Surrogacy can simply involve the surrogate mother inseminating herself with the commissioning father's sperm. This is known as 'partial' surrogacy. Alternatively, in 'full' surrogacy an embryo is created *in vitro*, usually using the commissioning couple's egg and sperm, and is transferred to the surrogate mother's uterus. Because *in vitro* fertilization is involved, these arrangements are regulated by the Human Fertilisation and Embryology Authority (HFEA), whose role was considered in detail in the previous chapter. In contrast, self-insemination with fresh sperm can be accomplished without professional assistance, and so in practice, it is difficult to exercise much control over these arrangements, and there is little information about their outcomes.

Surrogacy is not a common way to have children. The Brazier Report, which we examine later, estimated that between 100 and 180 surrogacy arrangements are made in the UK each year, resulting in 50–80 births.[1] Approximately half of all surrogate mothers are initially unknown to the commissioning couple, while friends, sisters, and sisters-in-law are the most common known surrogates.[2] Disputes between surrogate mothers and commissioning couples are unusual. The Brazier Report estimated that disputes occur in 4–5 per cent of cases, which given the small number of births, means that there will seldom be more than one dispute each year.

Despite its rarity, surrogacy undoubtedly throws up some important questions for the law, and raises some particularly contentious ethical dilemmas. There is also intense and often lurid media interest in surrogacy arrangements, such as that generated in 2004 when it was reported that a 43-year-old woman—dubbed 'surrogran' by the tabloid press—had given birth to her grandchildren after acting as a surrogate mother for her infertile daughter.[3]

In this chapter, we begin by describing the regulation of surrogacy, before turning to the controversial questions of whether surrogacy is an acceptable way to have children, and whether the contracts themselves should be enforceable.

3. REGULATION OF SURROGACY

There have been two major reports into the regulation of surrogacy in the UK. Although the principal focus of the Warnock Report, published in 1984, was the regulation of embryo research and fertility treatment, it also considered the practice of surrogacy. While not recommending its complete prohibition, the majority of the Warnock committee was clearly of the view that regulation should be designed to discourage people from entering into surrogacy arrangements. Its recommendations were never fully implemented. Thirteen years later, the government commissioned a report from the Brazier Committee, whose recommendations are described below. While undoubtedly less hostile to surrogacy than the Warnock Committee, the Brazier Committee were nevertheless again concerned that regulation should not appear to either endorse or encourage the practice of surrogacy.

There has also been a shift in the courts' attitudes towards surrogacy. In 1978, in *A v C*[4] one of the first cases involving a surrogacy arrangement to come before the courts, all three judges in the Court of Appeal were unanimous in their condemnation of surrogacy.

A v C[5]
The father and his partner, who was unable to have children, made an arrangement with the mother that, for a fee, she would be artificially inseminated with the father's sperm, and would

---

[1] Margaret Brazier, Alastair Campbell, and Susan Golombok, *Surrogacy: Review for Health Ministers of Current Arrangements for Payments and Regulation* (HMSO London 1998) Cm 4068 para 6.22 (hereafter Brazier).

[2] Tim Appleton, 'Emotional Aspects of Surrogacy: A Case for Effective Counselling and Support' in R Cook, SD Sclater with F Kaganas (eds), *Surrogate Motherhood: International Perspectives* (Hart Publishing Oxford 2003) 199–207, 200.

[3] See further J Tizzard, ' "Surrogran" commentators wrongly assume the worst', Bionews <http://www.bionews.org.uk/commentary.lasso?storyid=1971> (2 Feb 2004).

[4] Note that the case was decided in 1978 but not reported until 1985 [1985] FLR 445.

[5] [1985] FLR 445.

hand over the baby after birth. During the pregnancy, the mother changed her mind. After the child was born she refused to hand it over, but the father and his partner had regular access to the child. Initially the father sought custody of the child, but this was rejected by Comyn J on the grounds that he had acted in a most selfish, irresponsible, and obsessive manner. The father then applied for access, which was granted at first instance. The mother's appeal was allowed by the Court of Appeal.

Ormrod LJ

It is a simple, logical, but totally inhuman proceeding, and shows, in my view, very grave defects in his character and, indeed, in the characters of all three participants, because the lady with whom he was living was definitely involved in the plan, no doubt now to her great regret. One can feel very sorry for her in that she must feel that it was her fault in a sense that the father was in the position in which he was, so that she felt obliged to help him and take part in this most extraordinary and irresponsible arrangement. It is unnecessary to make any more comment on the irresponsibility shown by all three of the adults in this case, which is perhaps only rivalled by the irresponsibility of the person who performed the insemination on the mother. . . .

In this case we have a situation where there is no bond between the father and the child except the mere biological one. There has never been any association, except of the most exiguous character, between the father and the mother. There has never been anything between them except a sordid commercial bargain. . . .

This was a wholly artificial situation from the very beginning which should never have happened and which no responsible adult should ever have allowed to happen.

Cumming-Bruce LJ too condemned the arrangement as 'a kind of baby-farming operation of a wholly distasteful and lamentable kind', and Stamp LJ described it as 'an ugly little drama'. More recently, as we shall see later, the courts have specifically refused to comment on the morality of surrogacy and have instead concerned themselves solely with protecting the children's welfare. For example, in *Re C (A Minor) (Wardship: Surrogacy)*[6]—the Baby Cotton case—Latey J said that the 'difficult and delicate problems of ethics, morality and social desirability' raised by surrogacy were not relevant to his decision about what would be best for this child:

The baby is here. All that matters is what is best for her now that she is here and not how she arrived. If it be said (though it has not been said during these hearings) that because the father and his wife entered into these arrangements it is some indication of their unsuitability as parents, I should reject any such suggestion.

The medical profession's opposition to surrogacy has also softened over time. The British Medical Association (BMA)—which had previously advised doctors to have no involvement with surrogacy—now accepts that surrogacy may be an acceptable treatment of last resort when 'it is impossible or highly undesirable for medical reasons for the intended mother to carry a child herself'.[7]

The HFEA too accepts that there are circumstances in which surrogacy is acceptable, and like the BMA, these are confined to cases in which a woman is unable to bear a child for medical reasons. According to the 6th Code of Practice, paragraph 3.17:

---

[6] [1985] FLR 846.
[7] *Changing Conceptions of Motherhood: The Practice of Surrogacy in Britain* (BMA London 1996).

Treatment centres are expected to consider the use of assisted conception techniques to produce a surrogate pregnancy only where the commissioning mother is unable for physical or other medical reasons to carry a child or where her health may be impaired by doing so.

Surrogacy as a reproductive option for gay and/or single men, or because a woman would prefer, for non-medical reasons, not to become pregnant, remains extremely controversial.

(a) NON-ENFORCEABILITY

It is not an offence to enter into a surrogacy arrangement, but the agreement itself is not enforceable. Section 1B of the Surrogacy Arrangements Act 1985 was inserted by the Human Fertilisation and Embryology Act 1990:

Surrogacy Arrangements Act 1985 section 1B
No surrogacy arrangement is enforceable by or against any of the persons making it.

Hence, the commissioning couple cannot sue the surrogate mother if she refuses to hand over the baby, and nor can she sue them if she does not receive any of the agreed payments, or if they refuse to take the baby after birth. So while it is lawful to enter into a surrogacy contract, none of the parties are bound by any of the obligations it purports to contain. Given that surrogacy agreements are so precarious, it is perhaps surprising that disputes are so rare.

(b) COMMERCIALIZATION

In response to the notorious 'Baby Cotton' case in 1985[8] (considered below p. 889), the Surrogacy Arrangements Act 1985 was passed in order to prohibit commercial involvement in the initiation and negotiation of surrogacy arrangements. It also makes the publication or distribution of advertisements indicating a willingness to take part in surrogacy arrangements a criminal offence.

Surrogacy Arrangements Act 1985 section 2
(1) No person shall on a commercial basis do any of the following acts in the United Kingdom, that is—

    (a) initiate or take part in any negotiations with a view to the making of a surrogacy arrangement,

    (b) offer or agree to negotiate the making of a surrogacy arrangement, or

    (c) compile any information with a view to its use in making, or negotiating the making of, surrogacy arrangements.

(2) A person who contravenes subsection (1) above is guilty of an offence; but it is not a contravention of that subsection—

    (a) for a woman, with a view to becoming a surrogate herself, to do any act mentioned in that subsection or to cause such an act to be done, or

[8] [1985] FLR 846.

(b) for any person, with a view to a surrogate mother carrying a child for him, to do such an act or cause such an act to be done.

(3) For the purposes of this section, a person does an act on a commercial basis (subject to subsection (4) below) if—

(a) any payment is at any time received by himself or another in respect of it, or

(b) he does it with a view to any payment being received by himself or another in respect of making, or negotiating or facilitating the making of, any surrogacy arrangement.

In this section 'payment' does not include payment to or for the benefit of a surrogate mother or prospective surrogate mother.

Section 3

(1) This section applies to any advertisement containing an indication (however expressed)—

(a) that any person is or may be willing to enter into a surrogacy arrangement or to negotiate or facilitate the making of a surrogacy arrangement

(b) that any person is looking for a woman willing to become a surrogate mother or for persons wanting a woman to carry a child as a surrogate.

(2) Where a newspaper or periodical containing an advertisement to which this section applies is published in the United Kingdom, the proprietor, editor or publisher of the newspaper or periodical is guilty of an offence.

But while commercial surrogacy is, in theory, forbidden by section 1, in practice things are rather different, and typically surrogate mothers receive around £10,000–£15,000 for their services. The reason for this gap between theory and practice is that the courts are entitled to authorize payments made in contravention of the ban on commercial surrogacy. If the court considers that it is in the child's best interests to remain with the commissioning couple, as we see later retrospective authorization of any illegal payments is, in practice, relatively straightforward.

There is, of course, an important difference between the courts' willingness to retrospectively authorize illegal parents when it would be in the child's best interests and *prospectively* condoning payments to surrogates. In *Briody v St Helens and Knowsley Area Health Authority*,[9] the Court of Appeal considered whether Mrs Briody's damages for negligent obstetric care, which had left her unable to carry a child, should include the costs of entering into a surrogacy arrangement. Initially, Mrs Briody had intended to employ a surrogate mother in California, and the illegality of the agreement led Ebsworth J to reject her claim. Before the Court of Appeal, Mrs Briody instead claimed for the costs of entering into a lawful surrogacy arrangement in the UK. However Mrs Briody's case was again rejected, in part because the chance of success was 'vanishingly small' (less than 1 per cent), and the court did not think that it would be reasonable to fund a procedure with such a high chance of failure. Hale LJ concluded that 'expenditure on surrogacy in this case is not "reasonable" and the defendant should not be required to fund it'.

---

[9] [2001] EWCA Civ 1010, [2002] QB 856.

(c) THE DIFFERENCE BETWEEN IVF AND PARTIAL SURROGACY

IVF surrogacy arrangements are covered by the Human Fertilisation and Embryology Act 1990 and regulated by the HFEA. As we saw in the previous chapter, under section 13(5) of the Act, before providing a woman with treatment services, the clinician must take account of the welfare of any child who may be born, and any other children who may be affected by the birth. Hence, before providing treatment, a clinician should not only evaluate the impact of the surrogacy arrangement upon the resulting child, but must also take into account the welfare of the surrogate's existing children. Treatment in an assisted conception clinic will often also be subject to supervision by the clinic's independent ethics committee, which may impose its own restrictions upon access to surrogacy. For example, at Bourn Hall, surrogates must be under 40; have had at least one child, and preferably have completed her own family; they should be married, or in a stable relationship; and their partners must be involved in the counselling process.[10]

In contrast, aside from the relatively ineffective prohibitions upon commercial surrogacy, partial surrogacy arrangements remain largely unregulated. There are, for example, no rules governing access to treatment; the use of fresh sperm inevitably raises the possibility of HIV infection; and there is no formal data collection about the incidence and outcomes of surrogate births. There are no standard procedures for screening surrogate mothers and commissioning couples; there are no pre-treatment counselling requirements, or waiting periods prior to conception. And the ban on commercial involvement in surrogacy means that access to professional expertise, such as legal advice, is extremely limited. There are a number of non profit-making organisations, such as COTS (Childlessness Overcome Through Surrogacy),[11] which help to put potential surrogate mothers in touch with would-be commissioning couples, but these currently operate within a regulatory vacuum.

(d) STATUS

When a child is born as a result of a surrogacy arrangement, who are her legal parents? The rules governing the attribution of mother and fatherhood are different and so we deal with each in turn.

(1) MATERNITY

There are three possible ways in which a child's mother could be identified. First, the legal mother could be the woman who gestates the pregnancy and gives birth, this of course would be the surrogate mother. Secondly, legal motherhood could be synonymous with genetic motherhood, so that the woman whose egg was fertilized would be the resulting child's mother. In full surrogacy, this would be the

---

[10] See further Peter Brinsden, 'Clinical Aspects of IVF Surrogacy in Britain' in R Cook, SD Sclater with F Kaganas (eds), *Surrogate Motherhood: International Perspectives* (Hart Publishing Oxford 2003) 99–110.
[11] <http://www.surrogacy.org.uk/>.

commissioning mother, and in partial surrogacy, the surrogate mother. Thirdly, legal motherhood could vest in the woman who intends to raise the child, that is the commissioning mother.

As we saw in the previous chapter, the legal definition of 'mother' in the UK is clear and unequivocal: the woman who gives birth to a baby is its mother.

Human Fertilisation and Embryology Act 1990 section 27(1)

The woman who is carrying or has carried a child as a result of the placing in her of an embryo or of sperm and eggs, and no other woman, is to be treated as the mother of the child.

The law does not distinguish between different types of surrogacy and so the surrogate mother will always be the child's legal mother from birth, regardless of whether she is genetically related to the baby. As the legal mother, the surrogate mother has the right to decide whether to keep the child, or hand it over to the commissioning couple.

The principal merit of the British approach is that it unambiguously identifies the child's legal mother. A genetic test would also promote certainty, although it would obviously lead to different results depending upon the type of arrangement. In partial surrogacy, a genetic test would vest motherhood in the surrogate mother, while in a full surrogacy arrangement, the commissioning mother would (unless a donated egg was used) be the child's legal mother from birth.

A test based solely upon intention would of course be open to dispute and might result in prolonged uncertainty about a child's parentage. It would, however, have certain advantages. If the commissioning couple decide that they do not want the child, perhaps because she is born with disabilities, a test based upon the pre-conception intentions of the parties would hold the commissioning couple to their agreement. The British approach instead puts the surrogate mother in the difficult position of having prima facie legal responsibility for a child that she never wanted, and leaves the commissioning couple with no legal responsibility for a child whose creation they brought about.

It is worth noting that the definition of motherhood differs markedly from the attribution of paternity where it is the *male* partner who is infertile. As we saw in the previous chapter, if a woman's husband or partner is infertile, and she conceives through donor insemination, the male partner's *intention* to become a father is sufficient to enable him to be recognized, from birth, as the legal father.[12] But if a surrogate mother is employed because the female partner cannot carry a child, her intention to become a mother cannot result in her being recognized as the child's mother from birth.

A number of other countries, such as France and Germany, also adopt a uniform gestational test for motherhood. In contrast, some courts in the United States have attempted to vary the definition of motherhood according to the circumstances of the child's conception. So, for example, in *Johnson v Calvert*,[13] the California Supreme Court was faced with two possible mothers, each seeking a declaration of maternity. Following an IVF surrogacy arrangement, Anna Johnson had given birth to a child

---

[12] Human Fertilisation and Embryology Act 1990 s 28.
[13] *Johnson v Calvert* 851 P 2d 776, 782 (Cal 1993).

who had been conceived *in vitro* using Mr and Mrs Calvert's gametes. In the UK, Anna Johnson's gestational role would have been decisive. In contrast, in California Justice Panelli concluded that both women had 'presented acceptable proof of maternity',[14] and he chose to use intention as the factor which tipped the balance in favour of Crispina Calvert, in part because:

a rule recognizing the intended parents as the child's legal, natural parents should best promote certainty and stability for the child.[15]

And he further argued that:

by voluntarily contracting away any rights to the child, the gestator has, in effect, conceded that the best interest of the child is not with her.[16]

Other US courts have employed genetics as the decisive test for maternity. In *Belsito v Clark*,[17] the court criticized the *Johnson* decision for its uncertainty in circumstances when more than one woman 'intends' to raise the child, and the court instead preferred the certainty offered by a genetic test. A different reason for preferring a genetic definition of legal motherhood was offered in *Soos v Superior Court of Maricopa*.[18] The Appellate Court found that an Arizona statute which specified that the gestational surrogate is the legal mother of the child violated the genetic mother's equal protection rights because there was no compelling reason to justify the dissimilar treatment of similarly situated men and women (the child's genetic father and mother).

(2) PATERNITY

Applying the rules governing ascription of legal fatherhood to a surrogacy arrangement is rather complicated. The rebuttable presumption of legitimacy within marriage would lead to the surrogate mother's husband (if she has one) being treated as the legal father of the child from birth. This will be rebuttable by DNA tests establishing that the surrogate mother's partner is not in fact the child's genetic father. DNA tests would (unless donated sperm was used) identify the commissioning father as the child's father.

There is also a rebuttable presumption that the man who is registered as the father on the birth certificate is the child's father.[19] Evidence appears to indicate that registrars in the UK give contradictory advice about who should be registered as the child's father.[20] Some suggest that no name should be recorded, others advise registering the surrogate's husband as the father, and others recommend registering the commissioning father's name.[21] If the surrogate mother registers her partner on the child's birth certificate, the presumption that he is the father could again be rebutted by DNA tests which will show that he is not. In the case of the commissioning father, however, DNA tests will usually confirm his paternity. Since section 111 of the Adoption and

---

[14] Ibid at 782. [15] Ibid at 783. [16] Ibid at 782.
[17] 644 N E 2d 760 (Ohio Com Pl 1994). [18] 897 P 2d 1356 (Ariz App Div 1 1994).
[19] Births and Deaths Registration Act 1953, s 34(2).
[20] Gena Dodd, 'Surrogacy and the law in Britain: Users Perspectives' in R Cook, SD Sclater with F Kaganas (eds), *Surrogate Motherhood: International Perspectives* (Hart Publishing Oxford 2003) 113–20, 115.
[21] Ibid.

Children Act came into force in 2003, the man who is registered on the child's birth certificate automatically acquires parental responsibility for the child, regardless of whether he is married to the child's mother.

Where IVF surrogacy is involved, the statutory definition of 'father' in section 28 of the Human Fertilisation and Embryology Act 1990 might also apply, but this leads to some odd results (see further Chapter 14, p. 833 for a full description of section 28). Section 28 would treat the surrogate mother's husband (if she has one) as the father of the child, provided that he consented to her treatment. If the surrogate has an unmarried partner, he will be treated as the father if the couple were being 'treated together', which seems unlikely.

It would not be possible for a commissioning father to acquire legal paternity via section 28(3) by arguing that *he* is being treated 'together' with the surrogate because section 28(3) only applies where the woman received treatment with another man's sperm. If the surrogate is single, or if her husband does not consent, or if she is not being treated 'together' with her partner, then the child will have no legal father.

The question of the identity of the child's father arose on the rather unusual facts in *Re Q (Parental Order)*,[22] where the child born following a surrogacy arrangement was created using an egg from the commissioning mother and sperm from an anonymous sperm donor. Johnson J applied section 28 of the Human Fertilisation and Embryology Act 1990 to the facts, and decided that this child did not have a legal father:

In the case of a carrying mother who is married, her husband is to be treated as the father of the child unless it is shown that he did not consent to the carrying mother (his wife) taking part in the process. Unless (and until) that consent is shown not to have been given, the consent of the husband of the carrying mother to the making of the order must be obtained. This is the effect of s 28(2).

However, if there is no one treated as father under s 28 either because the carrying mother was unmarried or she was married and her husband did not consent to the process—then one turns to s 28(3). Under that subsection the man whose sperm was donated is specifically excluded . . . The applicant husband is excluded because on the facts of this case he was not 'treated' with the carrying woman.

A good illustration of some of the problems with the UK's approach to paternity following surrogacy is provided by applying it to the infamous American case, *In Re Marriage of Buzzanca*.[23] In his divorce petition, John Buzzanca had asserted that his marriage to Luanne Buzzanca had been childless. Luanne Buzzanca responded by claiming that a surrogate mother (SM) was expecting the couple's first child. Jaycee Buzzanca, who was born six days later, had been conceived using sperm and eggs from anonymous donors (let us call the sperm donor SD and the egg donor ED). The surrogate (SM) and her husband (SH) did not seek to become Jaycee's parents. The question for the court was a complex one. Out of the three plausible candidates for fatherhood (John Buzzanca, SD, SH) and the three possible mothers (Luanne Buzzanca, ED and SM), who are Jaycee's legal parents?

[22] [1996] 1 FLR 369.
[23] 72 Cal Rptr 2d 280 (Ct App 1998), review denied, No S069696, 1998 Cal LEXIS 3830 (10 June 1998).

At first instance, the trial judge reached the rather surprising conclusion that, despite having six possible mothers and fathers, none could be considered Jaycee's legal parents and Jaycee must be judged to be a legal orphan. This was reversed on appeal when the court held that because Mr and Mrs Buzzanca had jointly initiated Jaycee's conception, they were her legal parents and they were both therefore under a duty to contribute to her support. This seems sensible because John Buzzanca had deliberately instigated Jaycee's unconventional conception, and it would seem unfair for the law to allow him to shrug off any legal responsibility for the resulting child. English law might instead have initially identified the surrogate mother's husband as Jaycee's father, and thus absolved John Buzzanca of his responsibility for the life he deliberately created. Legal responsibility for Jaycee's wellbeing could have vested in a man who was not genetically related to her, and who never intended or wanted to become her father.

(e) TRANSFERRING LEGAL PARENTHOOD

Because the surrogate mother will be the child's legal mother from birth, and the commissioning father will only occasionally be the child's legal father, if the commissioning couple want to become the child's legal parents they will either have to apply for a parental order under section 30 of the Human Fertilisation and Embryology Act 1990 or apply to adopt her. Before we consider each route in detail, it is worth noting that the law appears to be adopting what Julie Wallbank refers to as an 'either/or' approach to parenthood. Wallbank argues that the reality is that children conceived through surrogacy arrangements in fact have two mothers, and that ideally the child should be able to have continued relationships with both of them.

Julie Wallbank[24]

If we look to the case law on parental contact we see that when the paramountcy principle is applied in making the contact order there is an overriding presumption that the child's welfare is best secured from her having continued contact with the biological parent . . . It is my view that by continuing to forward the traditional two-parent family as the paradigmatic form for children's welfare and by denying the interested parties an input into the child's life, we merely reify the social standing of children born through surrogacy as somehow deviant. It way well be the time to institute into surrogacy law and social practice the idea that children can and should have knowledge of and contact with all interested parties whether we call them 'mother' 'father' or some other appropriate epithet. . . .

It appears that in the contexts of insemination by donor and adoption, which both implicate third parties, the law has recognised . . . the psychological benefits that accrue to children from having knowledge as to the means of and/or the contributor to their creation. However, this is not the case regarding surrogacy . . . I have suggested a number of reasons [why] the law in relation to surrogacy has offered little guarantee that children will be told of their birth origins and I have argued thus far, that these reasons hinge on the hegemony of the traditional private nuclear family . . .

---

[24] 'Too Many Mothers? Surrogacy, Kinship and the Welfare of the Child' (2002) 10 Medical Law Review 271–94, 286–7, 293–4.

My own proposal is . . . that there should be no need to decide cases based on the either/or approach. The paramountcy principle is not inimical to child sharing, rather, it is the entrenchment of the ideology that children's interests are best served by the private nuclear family that continues to proscribe alternative ways of being a family . . .

We need to centralise the welfare of the child in these cases rather than subordinate it to the adults involved and ensure that the welfare principle encompasses a thorough consideration of the basic need for children to have knowledge of their birth origins and where possible their wider kinship network. Commissioning parents do need to be made aware that surrogacy involves a collaboration with a woman, ie a person and not just the exploitation of a womb. But all the parties involved, the law and society should also be made to see that having and raising children is a community responsibility and that children and adults may well benefit from extending kinship networks beyond the private nuclear family.

(1) SECTION 30 PARENTAL ORDERS

When a court makes a parental order under section 30, the Registrar General will re-register the child's birth. As with adoption, it will not be possible for the public to make a link between entries in the register of births and the parental order register, but once a child reaches adulthood, she will, after being offered counselling, have access to her original birth certificate. Section 30 was inserted at the report stage of the Human Fertilisation and Embryology Bill after a proposal by an MP who had received a complaint from a couple in his constituency who had gone through a full surrogacy arrangement resulting in the birth of twins, and then been informed that they would have to apply to adopt their genetic children. With little opportunity for debate or consultation, the proposal was accepted and section 30, which lays out the minimal criteria for eligibility for a parental order, came into force in November 1994.

Human Fertilisation and Embryology Act 1990 section 30

(1) The court may make an order providing for a child to be treated in law as the child of the parties to a marriage (referred to as 'the husband' and 'the wife') if

   (a) the child has been carried by a woman other than the wife as the result of the placing in her of an embryo or sperm and eggs or her artificial insemination

   (b) the gametes of the husband or the wife, or both, were used to bring about the creation of the embryo and

   (c) the conditions in subsections (2) to (7) are satisfied

(2) The husband and the wife must apply for the order within six months of the birth of the child . . .

(3) At the time of the application and of the making of the order—

   (a) the child's home must be with the husband and the wife

   (b) the husband or the wife or both of them must be domiciled in the U.K. . . .

(4) At the time of the making of the order both the husband and the wife must have attained the age of 18

(5) The court must be satisfied that both the father of the child (including a person who is the father by virtue of section 28), where he is not the husband, and the woman who carried the

child have freely, and with full understanding of what is involved, agreed unconditionally to the making of the order

(6) Subsection (5) does not require the agreement of a person who cannot be found or who is incapable of giving agreement and the agreement of the woman who carried the child is ineffective . . . if given by her less than six weeks after the child's birth

(7) The court must be satisfied that no money or other benefit (other than expenses reasonably incurred) has been given or received by the husband or the wife for or in consideration of—

(a) the making of the order

(b) any agreement required by subsection (5)

(c) the handing over of the child to the husband and the wife, or

(d) the making of any arrangements with a view to the making of the order, unless authorised by the court

Notice that section 30(5) requires the free and informed consent both of the surrogate mother and the child's father (where he is not the man seeking a parental order). Unlike adoption, it is not possible to dispense with their consent on the grounds that it is being unreasonably withheld.

In 1994, guidance was issued to local authorities and health authorities explaining how the section 30 regulations should operate.[25] When a local authority is aware that a child has been, or is about to be born following a surrogacy arrangement, its social services department is required to make enquiries in order to satisfy itself that the child is not at risk of harm as a result of the arrangement. Following the child's birth, if the local authority have reasonable grounds to believe that the child is suffering, or is likely to suffer significant harm, they would be entitled to seek a care order.[26]

Although a report from a Guardian *ad litem*[27] is needed before a parental order can be made,[28] a section 30 application effectively short-circuits some of the more cumbersome aspects of the adoption process. As a result, access to this fast-track procedure is limited. The applicants must be married to each other; at least one of the applicants must be genetically related to the child; conception must not have been by natural intercourse; the child must be living with the applicants; the surrogate and the child's legal father must have given consent; and the court must be satisfied that no money or benefit, other than for expenses reasonably incurred, has been paid, unless authorized by the court. In deciding whether to make a parental order, the court is directed to 'have regard to all the circumstances, first consideration being given to the need to safeguard and promote the welfare of the child'.[29] Since section 30 applications are classified as 'family proceedings',[30] the courts are entitled, if they see fit, to make an alternative order, such as a residence order, or an additional order, such as an order that the child should continue to have contact with the surrogate mother.[31]

---

[25] Parental Orders (Human Fertilisation and Embryology) Regulations 1994, Local Authority Circular LAC (94) 25.

[26] Children Act 1989 s 31(2).

[27] A person appointed by the court to represent the interests of a minor.

[28] Parental Orders (Human Fertilisation and Embryology) Regulations 1994, Local Authority Circular LAC (94) 25.

[29] Parental Orders (Human Fertilisation and Embryology) Regulations 1994, schedule 1(1)(a).

[30] Section 30(8).   [31] Children Act 1989 s 8.

Given that over 40 per cent of all children are now born to unmarried parents, confining access to parental orders to married couples seems a little outdated. In addition, there are two practical problems with the operation of section 30. First, eligibility for a parental order is conditional upon the child *already living with* the commissioning couple. Yet prior to the making of the order, unless they have obtained a residence order, the commissioning couple may have no legal relationship with the child. As we have seen, the woman who gives birth is always the child's legal mother, and, depending on whose name she has registered on the child's birth certificate, the commissioning father may not be recognized as the child's father. Thus section 30 demands that a child should live for a period of time with a couple who might not have any legal relationship with her. Secondly, by leaving the assessment of the reasonableness of any expenses to the *post hoc* discretion of the court, judged on a case by case basis, there is no prospective guidance for people contemplating involvement in surrogacy.

An application for a parental order may be made in the Family Proceedings court. The guardian *ad litem* must first establish that the section 30 criteria are satisfied, and second, must determine whether there is any reason why a parental order would not be in the best interests of the child. Guardians *ad litem* are therefore charged with policing the 'genetic link' and 'no payment' requirements, *and* with protecting the child's welfare. In carrying out their duties, they face two major problems. First, their powers are extremely limited, so in ensuring both that the child was created using the gametes of at least one of the applicants, and that there have been no unlawful payments, they only have access to information provided by the surrogate and the commissioning couple. Secondly, their two duties are not necessarily compatible with each other. Because the child must already be living with the commissioning parents before an application is made, her welfare will seldom be promoted by removing her from a settled home. So even if there has been a blatant contravention of, for example, the 'no payment' rule, the child's interests may still be best served by making a parental order.

Under section 30(7) the court has the power to authorize payments other than expenses reasonably incurred, and the Brazier Committee was unable to find any case in which an application for a parental Order was refused on the grounds that an unacceptably large sum of money had changed hands.[32] In *Re C*, for example, the couple had paid a woman who was in fact claiming benefits £2000 for 'loss of earnings'. Despite finding that the couple had made an unlawful payment, Wall LJ nevertheless judged that a parental order would be in the child's best interests.

Re C (Application by Mr and Mrs X under s 30 of the Human Fertilisation and Embryology Act 1990)[33]

Mr and Mrs X had tried for over twenty years to have a baby without success. Through COTS they were introduced to a surrogate mother (SM) who agreed to undergo artificial insemination using the husband's semen, to carry any child to term and to surrender the child to the couple at birth. The couple agreed to pay the surrogate mother £12,000 to cover her expenses, including a sum for loss of earnings. During the pregnancy it emerged that SM was, in fact, on income support. The

---

[32] Brazier para 5.3.   [33] [2002] EWHC 157 (Fam), [2002] 1 FLR 909.

sum was, nevertheless, paid and the child was duly handed over at birth. When the couple applied for a parental order under section 30, it was initially refused on the grounds that the justices could not be satisfied that the sum paid related to reasonable expenses only.

Wall LJ

The questions which arise, accordingly, are: (1) can the court be satisfied that the sum of £12,000 paid by Mr and Mrs X to SM was for 'expenses reasonably incurred'? And (2) if the answer to that question is 'no', does the court have the power retrospectively to authorise the payment?

The first question is a pure issue of fact, and it is reasonably clear that the answer to it is 'no'. . . .

What is important, I think, is that on all the evidence it is clear that the memorandum was entered into by Mr and Mrs X in good faith, and without any corrupt intent. They were not paying £12,000 to buy a baby. They were paying a figure for expenses which they had been advised was on the high side, but which was not disproportionate.

None the less, it must follow that money other than for 'expenses reasonably incurred' has been given by Mr and Mrs X to SM as a consequence of the memorandum, and that the court cannot make a parental order unless the payments are 'authorised' by the court. . . .

[T]he factors which seem to me to weigh in the scales when considering the degree to which Mr and Mrs X are tainted by the transaction are the following:

(1) The sum of £12,000 required of them was not disproportionate, given the usual figure quoted by COTS and Mr and Mrs X's wish to ensure that SM did not take employment during the pregnancy. . . .

(2) Mr and Mrs X did not know that SM was claiming income support until after it was confirmed that SM was pregnant. At that point it was plainly too late for them to withdraw.

(3) Mr and Mrs X are plainly a genuine couple who have spent many years attempting to conceive a child; they entered into the memorandum in good faith and without any corrupt intent.

(4) If SM was defrauding the Department of Social Security by not disclosing the sums Mr and Mrs X were paying her, the responsibility for that behaviour is hers alone. There is no suggestion that Mr and Mrs X encouraged or aided and abetted her to do so in any way.

(5) It is very clear that C is a much loved and cherished child. It is manifestly in her interests that she should be treated in law as the child of Mr and Mrs X, and that both should have parental responsibility for her.

For all these reasons, I authorised the payment of £12,000 by Mr and Mrs X to SM and make a parental order under s 30 of the Act.

Where the surrogate mother is happy to hand over the child, and the commissioning couple fulfil all the other section 30 criteria, an application for a parental order will be the simplest way for the commissioning couple to acquire legal parenthood. If the surrogate mother does not want the child, unless the commissioning couple would obviously be woefully inadequate parents, it would rarely be in the child's best interests for the parental order to be refused and the child to be taken into the care of the local authority. Hence, provided that the section 30 conditions are satisfied, obtaining a parental order will be relatively straightforward.

There are, however, several different reasons why a commissioning couple might not be able to apply for a section 30 order. They might, for example, not be married to each other, or the surrogate mother might have refused to consent to the making of an order. If, for any reason, the intended parent(s) are ineligible for a section 30 parental order, the only way in which they can acquire legal parenthood is through adoption.

(2) ADOPTION

The adoption process is onerous and time-consuming. In order to be eligible to adopt a child, the criteria in the Adoption and Children Act 2002 must be satisfied, and potential adopters must endure rigorous scrutiny by local authority social workers over a prolonged period of time. If the surrogate mother does not want the child, but for some other reason the couple are ineligible for a parental order, adoption will usually be in the best interests of the child. But where the surrogate mother has changed her mind and an adoption application is made, the situation is much less straightforward. Under section 52(1) of the Adoption and Children Act 2002, the parents must consent to a child's adoption, unless they cannot be found or are incapable of consenting, or the court is satisfied that 'the child's welfare requires that their consent should be dispensed with'.

When should a surrogate mother's consent to adoption be dispensed with by the court? The answer will often depend upon where the child is living. If she is already settled with the commissioning couple, her interests in avoiding disruption may be decisive. On the other hand, if the child is still living with her mother, the courts would be slow to order her removal. Although decided under previous adoption legislation, the question of whether the mother's consent to adoption should be dispensed with arose in *Re MW (Adoption: Surrogacy)*:

Re MW (Adoption: Surrogacy)[34]

The applicants for adoption, a husband and wife, had entered into a surrogacy agreement with the mother for which she was to receive £7500. The child (M) was handed over after birth and had lived with the applicants since then. Subsequently the mother and the applicants disagreed about contact. The mother launched a publicity campaign in the press and on television, publishing photographs of the baby and causing the applicants considerable distress. She opposed the application for adoption of the child, who was by now two and a half years old.

Callman J

In this case nothing but favourable reports have come forward in respect of the applicants and their care of M, except from the mother, who has a vested interest. . . .

It is quite plain that the test to be approached by a judge when he deals with the history of withholding consent is to ask himself whether, having regard to the evidence, and applying the current values of our society, the advantages of adoption for the welfare of the child appear sufficiently strong to justify overriding the views or interests of an objecting parent . . .

I have had no evidence in this case, in any shape or form, of anything other than beneficial consequences flowing from the care lavished upon M. I think the mother now wants to undo what she did but the wish to undo this is for her benefit . . .

To introduce uncertainty, to disturb the present position, is contrary to the welfare and interests of this small boy. . . . I have found that her withholding of consent under the circumstances of this case is not what a reasonably objective parent would want to do for her child. Under the circumstances I am prepared to dispense with the mother's consent in this case, bearing in mind that she had previously given her consent and plainly had entered into this arrangement from the beginning with the advice of a solicitor. . . . The reality is that sad as it is for the mother I must make an adoption order. . . .

[34] [1995] 2 FLR 789.

This mother originally had a possible prospect of seeing her child by agreement, until there has been such a publicity campaign which has caused such anguish to the applicants and also brought M himself into the limelight. Through that very act she has undermined whatever prospects of contact she might have had. It is largely through her own actions. Accordingly I consider this to be one of those cases where there should be no contact during the minority of M to his mother or his half-sister. It is a sad case, but the mother in the last resort has mainly herself to blame about it. The reality is that I have to guard M's interests.

In contrast, in *Re P (Minors) (Wardship: Surrogacy)*, the children had been living with the surrogate mother since birth, and Sir John Arnold held that this factor outweighed the material and other advantages of being brought up by the commissioning couple.

Re P (Minors) (Wardship: Surrogacy)[35]

Mrs P offered her services as a surrogate mother to Mr and Mrs B who agreed to pay a lump sum to adopt the child. Mrs P was inseminated with Mr B's sperm. During her pregnancy she began to have misgivings about giving up the twins, and a few weeks after they were born she decided to keep the children. The local authority applied to the court to make the children wards of court, so that the court could decide where the children should live. By the date of the hearing the twins had been cared for by Mrs P for five months.

Sir John Arnold P

These children have been, up to their present age of approximately five months, with, quite consistently, their mother and in those circumstances there must necessarily have been some bonding of those children with their mother and that is undoubtedly coupled with the fact that she is their mother, a matter which weighs predominantly in the balance in favour of leaving the children with their mother, but there are other factors which weigh in the opposite balance and which, as is said by Mr B through his counsel, outweigh the advantages of leaving the children with their mother and it is that balancing exercise which the court is required to perform. . . .

They are principally as follows. It is said, and said quite correctly, that the shape of the B family is the better shape of a family in which these children might be brought up, because it contains a father as well as a mother and that is undoubtedly true. Next, it is said that the material circumstances of the B family are such that they exhibit a far larger degree of affluence than can be demonstrated by Mrs P. That, also, is undoubtedly true. Then it is said that the intellectual quality of the environment of the B's home and the stimulus which would be afforded to these babies, if they were to grow up in that home, would be greater than the corresponding features in the home of Mrs P. That is not a matter which has been extensively investigated, but I suspect that that is probably true. Certainly, the combined effect of the lack of affluence on the part of Mrs P and some lack of resilience to the disadvantages which that implies has been testified in the correspondence to the extent that I find Mrs P saying that shortage of resources leads to her sitting at home with little E and overeating, because she has no ability from a financial point of view to undertake anything more resourceful than that. Then it is said that the religious comfort and support which the B's derive from their Church is greater than anything of that sort available to Mrs P. How far that is true, I simply do not know. I do know that the B's are practising Christians and do derive advantages from that circumstance, but nobody asked Mrs P about this and I am not disposed to assume that she lacks that sort of comfort and support in the absence of any investigation by way of cross-examination to lay the foundations for such a conclusion. Then it is

[35] [1987] 2 FLR 421.

said, and there is something in this, that the problems which might arise from the circumstance that these children who are, of course, congenitally derived from the semen of Mr B and bear traces of Mr B's Asiatic origin would be more easily understood and discussed and reconciled in the household of Mr and Mrs B, a household with an Asiatic ethnic background than they would be if they arose in relation to these children while they were situated in the home of Mrs P, which is in an English village and which has no non-English connections. . . .

As regards the other factors, they are, in the aggregate, weighty, but I do not think, having given my very best effort to the evaluation of the case dispassionately on both sides, that they ought to be taken to outweigh the advantages to these children of preserving the link with the mother to whom they are bonded and who has, as is amply testified, exercised over them a satisfactory level of maternal care, and accordingly it is, I think, the duty of the court to award the care and control of these babies to their mother.

Under section 95 of the Adoption and Children Act 2002, any payment or reward made in consideration of the adoption of a child is a criminal offence. But if a child has settled with adopters following an adoption procedure tainted by illegality, removing the child from his or her home in order to 'punish' the wrongfulness of the circumstances in which the child was adopted would not necessarily be in the best interests of that child. As a result, illegal payments made in consideration of adoption can again be 'authorized' by the court.

In *Re An Adoption Application (Surrogacy)*,[36] decided under the previous adoption legislation, Latey J argued that the payments that had been made to the surrogate mother had not been made in consideration for the adoption, but instead to compensate for the inconvenience and expense of pregnancy. Nevertheless, he also indicated that even if the payments had been illegal, he would have used his power to authorize them retrospectively. The child was, by the time of the application, nearly two-and-a-half years old, and had spent his entire life with the commissioning couple who were, according to the pre-adoption reports, excellent parents. To remove the child from his settled and happy home in order to deter other people from engaging in similar arrangements would have amounted to a wilful disregard of the child's welfare.

Although not strictly a surrogacy case, similar considerations are evident in *Re AW (Adoption Application)*.[37] An English couple had made an agreement with a pregnant woman in Germany that her child should be handed over to them in return for £1,000. Despite admitting that there were 'grave concerns' about the prospective adopters' behaviour, their health and the state of their marriage, Bracewell J explained that she had no option but to find that the welfare of the child still demanded that she should not be removed:

I am regrettably compelled to the finding that the Bs have sought to tie the hands of this court by presenting a situation whereby A has been in the family for so long that nobody concerned with her welfare can contemplate her removal. Indeed, they have achieved that object.

The central problem, then, is that once a child has settled within a family, it will very rarely be in her best interests to force her to leave, and it would be unacceptable to attempt to 'punish' the parents by depriving the child of her settled home. The point

---

[36] [1987] Fam 81.　　　　[37] [1993] 1 FLR 62.

is well made by Latey J in *Re C (A Minor)(Wardship: Surrogacy)*. This was the famous 'Baby Cotton' case in which a British woman, Kim Cotton, who went on to set up COTS, acted as a surrogate for an American couple.

Re C (A Minor) (Wardship: Surrogacy)[38]

Following a partial surrogacy agreement arranged by an agency between an American couple and a British woman, a child was born in the UK. After birth, the mother left the child in the care of the hospital. The commissioning father commenced wardship proceedings, and asked that care and control of the child be committed to him and his wife. The local authority supported his application.

Latey J

First and foremost, and at the heart of the prerogative jurisdiction in wardship, is what is best for the child or children concerned. That and nothing else. Plainly, the methods used to produce a child as this baby has been, and the commercial aspects of it, raise difficult and delicate problems of ethics, morality and social desirability. These problems are under active consideration elsewhere.

Are they relevant in arriving at a decision on what now and, so far as one can tell, in the future is best for this child? If they are relevant, it is incumbent on the court to do its best to evaluate and balance them.

In my judgment, however, they are not relevant. The baby is here. All that matters is what is best for her now that she is here and not how she arrived. If it be said (though it has not been said during these hearings) that because the father and his wife entered into these arrangements it is some indication of their unsuitability as parents, I should reject any such suggestion. If what they did was wrong (and I am not saying that it was), they did it in total innocence.

It follows that the moral, ethical and social considerations are for others and not for this court in its wardship jurisdiction.

So, what is best for this baby? Her natural mother does not ask for her. Should she go into Mr and Mrs A's care and be brought up by them? Or should some other arrangement be made for her, such as long-term fostering with or without adoption as an end?

The factors can be briefly stated. Mr A is the baby's father and he wants her, as does his wife. The baby's mother does not want her. Mr and Mrs A are a couple in their 30s. They are devoted to each other. They are both professional people, highly qualified. They have a very nice home in the country and another in a town. Materially they can give the baby a very good upbringing. But, far more importantly, they are both excellently equipped to meet the baby's emotional needs. They are most warm, caring, sensible people, as well as highly intelligent. When the time comes to answer the child's questions, they will be able to do so with professional advice if they feel they need it. Looking at this child's well-being, physical and emotional, who better to have her care? No one.

Of course, it would be a mistake to assume that every illegal payment will automatically be authorized by the courts. In *Re C (A Minor) (Adoption Application)*,[39] a couple made an arrangement with a pregnant woman that she would hand over the baby after birth and that, in order to bypass some of the restrictions of adoption law, the husband would pass himself off as the baby's father. The couple paid her various sums of money. Although there were other reasons for rejecting their application for an adoption order, Booth J also considered whether or not he should retrospectively authorize these payments:

---

[38] [1985] FLR 846.   [39] [1993] 1 FLR 87.

But had I to consider whether or not I should authorise the payments that I find to have been made by Mr and Mrs S to the mother in regard to the adoption by them of C, I would have to take into consideration the purpose for which they were made and all the circumstances of the case. I have no doubt at all that they were payments made by Mr and Mrs S for the handing over to them of C, and that they were made with a view to ensuring that the mother would continue to adhere to the false story and to the deceit which would lead, in the end, to their adoption of the baby. To authorise such payments would be to sweep aside the protection given by the Act to children and it would, in effect, amount to ratifying the sale of a child for adoption. I would not, in the circumstances, have considered it right to authorise any of the payments which I find to have been made by Mr and Mrs S to the mother.

(3) INFORMAL TRANSFERS

While parental orders and adoption are the only ways in which the commissioning couple can become the legal parents of the child born following a surrogacy arrangement, this does not mean that every surrogate birth is followed by a formal application for legal parenthood. A child may be handed over by the surrogate mother, and live with the commissioning couple without any legal formalities. For obvious reasons, it is impossible to tell how many unofficial transfers of children take place each year. Worryingly, however, the Brazier Report suggested that 'a substantial proportion of commissioning couples are failing to apply to the courts to become the legal parents of the child'.[40]

As we saw earlier, it is possible that the surrogate mother may have registered the commissioning father's name on the birth certificate, and, since 2003, this means that he will automatically have parental responsibility for the child. If he is not registered on the birth certificate, or if the child was born before 2003, the commissioning father could acquire parental responsibility through a residence or parental responsibility order. Hence, after an informal transfer, the commissioning father may or may not have parental responsibility for the child. The commissioning mother will only have parental responsibility if she has obtained a residence order. It is then possible that the parents will have no formal legal obligations towards 'their' child. Even if the child's parents have obtained parental responsibility, following an informal transfer, this will be shared with the surrogate mother, who will continue to have parental responsibility for the child, even if she has little or no contact with her. The potential for uncertainty and disputes is obvious.

(f) REFORM

There are a number of defects with the UK's existing regulation of surrogacy. First, the prohibition of commercialization has failed to prevent the routine payment of sums of £10,000–£15,000 to surrogate mothers. Secondly, the Human Fertilisation and Embryology Act's definitions of mother and fatherhood apply awkwardly and inappropriately to surrogacy arrangements. Thirdly, the complexity of the rules governing the transfer of legal parenthood undoubtedly deters some commissioning parents from acquiring a formal relationship with 'their' child, and this is clearly not

---

[40] Brazier para 5.7.

in a child's best interests. Fourthly, surrogacy arrangements—especially when they do not involve IVF treatment—remain largely unregulated, and agreements are often made without any professional advice or guidance.

The government appeared to accept the need for reform when it appointed a committee, chaired by Margaret Brazier, to review aspects of the regulation of surrogacy in the UK. The Committee's terms of reference were to consider (a) whether payments (including expenses) to surrogate mothers should be allowed; (b) to examine whether there is a case for the regulation of surrogacy through a recognized body; and (c) to advise whether changes are needed to the Surrogacy Arrangements Act 1985 and/or the Human Fertilisation and Embryology Act 1990. The Brazier Committee's report (hereafter Brazier) was published in 1998, and we consider its content in detail below. As yet, however, there has been no indication that the government intends to implement any of its recommendations.

Brazier advocated the complete prohibition of any payments to surrogate mothers, other than compensation for specific expenses actually incurred as a result of the pregnancy. Surrogacy, it argued, should be 'a fully informed and free act of giving'.[41] A comparison was made with blood, tissue and organ donation, all of which are, in the UK, legitimate only within a 'gift relationship'.[42] Brazier admits that one consequence of eliminating payments for surrogacy may be that 'few women will be willing to undertake such a commitment, except for a relative or close friend',[43] but a drop in the number of surrogacy arrangements is not, according to Brazier, necessarily a bad thing.

Margaret Brazier, Alastair Campbell and Susan Golombok[44]

5.4   We have received accounts from COTS and elsewhere suggesting that payments of £15,000 or more are being made by commissioning couples to surrogate mothers, with a number of payments being in the range of £10,000–£15,000.

5.6   In the 34 cases of surrogacy in which Guardians were involved, payments made to the surrogate were found to range from nothing to £12,000 . . .

5.10 From the evidence reported in paragraphs 5.4 and 5.6, it appears that payments over and above genuine expenses are being made in a substantial proportion of cases. It is also possible that aside from declared payments, additional sums are being given to surrogate mothers . . .

5.11 . . . [I]t is a fundamental belief in our society that children should not be viewed as commodities to be bought or sold. This principle is also enshrined in the law on adoption. Although a theoretical distinction can be made between payment for the purchase of a child and payment for a potentially risky, time-consuming and uncomfortable service, in practice it is difficult to separate the two, and it remains the case that payment other than for genuine expenses constitutes a financial benefit for the surrogate mother . . .

---

[41] Brazier para 4.37.

[42] Richard M Titmuss, *Gift Relationship: From Human Blood to Social Policy* (Allen & Unwin London 1971).

[43] Brazier para 4.37.

[44] *Surrogacy: Review for Health Ministers of Current Arrangements for Payments and Regulation* (HMSO London 1998) Cm 4068.

5.13 In the UK, bodily parts may be donated only as a gift for which no payments are allowed. We believe that surrogacy should be informed by the same values . . .

5.14 It is also our view that financial benefit should not influence a woman's decision to become a surrogate mother. The evidence we have received suggests that in the absence of financial benefit many surrogate mothers would not have entered into the surrogacy arrangement. Although surrogates are also motivated by a wish to help infertile people, many are primarily motivated by payment, particularly those who have no previous connection with the commissioning couple.

5.15 Embarking on a surrogate pregnancy carries with it emotional risks in addition to the physical risks of pregnancy, and these risks may not become apparent until a pregnancy occurs. For example, the surrogate may regret her decision to enter into such an arrangement when she is expected to relinquish the baby, or later in life, perhaps when she enters into a new relationship or finds that she herself is unable to bear another child . . . Given the difficulties faced by potential surrogate mothers in giving fully informed consent, we believe that the prospect of payment further complicates decision-making and results in an increased likelihood of women entering into a surrogacy arrangement when they would not otherwise have done so, particularly women experiencing financial difficulties.

5.16 Surrogacy brings with it other problems as well. The payment of a surrogate by a commissioning couple to bear a child for them creates a potentially exploitative situation, and we wish to minimise the opportunity for exploitation to occur . . .

5.17 We also wish to discourage women from becoming professional surrogates. There is evidence that some women view surrogacy as a form of employment, i.e. as an alternative to working outside the home, and a growing number of surrogates are entering into more than one surrogacy arrangement. In addition to our concerns about the physical and psychological welfare of surrogates who enter into repeated surrogacy arrangements, we also have reservations about facilitating a situation whereby some relatively poor and less educated women are having babies for their wealthier and better educated counterparts . . .

5.19 The concerns regarding the potential risks to children of being born as a result of a surrogacy arrangement are purely speculative. However, in the absence of systematic data on what actually happens to such children, we believe . . . that it is not necessarily in children's best interests to learn that their surrogate mother benefitted financially from their birth or from giving them away to the commissioning couple.

5.20 In addition, we have concerns regarding the psychological consequences of surrogacy for the surrogate mother's own children . . .

5.21 There are also potential advantages for the commissioning couple of limiting payments to genuine expenses, in that they will not be faced with the prospect of telling a teenage child that they paid a large sum of money to the surrogate mother in order for him or her to be born. It might also be expected that surrogacy arrangements founded on altruism rather than on financial benefit would be less likely to break down. The limitation on payments would also prevent surrogate mothers from making increased financial demands on the commissioning couple once a pregnancy is established . . .

5.23 . . . It is our view that women who become surrogates to help infertile couples should not suffer financial loss as a result of their altruistic act. We believe that the payment of genuine expenses does not commercialise surrogacy and thus that the payment of genuine expenses should be allowed.

Notice that in paragraph 5.21 Brazier suggests that altruistic arrangements will be less likely to break down than commercial ones. No evidence to support this claim is cited, and in fact evidence from the US (where surrogacy is commonly practiced on a commercial basis) suggests that arrangements break down even less frequently. Fewer than 1 per cent of US surrogate mothers change their mind, compared with 4–5 per cent in the UK.[45]

Interestingly, as Michael Freeman points out in the next extract, Brazier does not appear to notice a tension between their conclusion that a ban on surrogacy would be undesirable because it would push the practice underground, and their acknowledgement that a ban on payments will in reality mean that very few women come forward to act as surrogates. The unavailability of surrogate mothers, whether it results from an outright ban or a prohibition on payment, will in practice mean that people who need to employ surrogates in order to reproduce will either travel abroad or enter the black market.

Michael Freeman[46]

The [Brazier] Report fails to appreciate that withdrawing remuneration from surrogates will only drive potential surrogates away from regulated surrogacy into an invisible and socially uncontrolled world where the regulators will be more like pimps than adoption agencies. There is every reason to control surrogacy and to guard against perceived problems, but most women will expect to be rewarded. Brazier agrees and believes that surrogacy will rarely be undertaken by strangers once its recommendations are implemented. This prognosis is misplaced: surrogacy will continue; it will probably grow as infertility increases; it will go underground and the fees will become larger. We cannot stop women exercising their autonomy, nor can we persuade them that being paid aggravates their exploitation, when common sense tells them the reverse . . .

If Parliament agrees with Brazier and denies women the opportunity to be financially rewarded for surrogacy services, an unregulated surrogacy with all the evils attendant on such underground activities will emerge. Brazier would prefer surrogacy to have no future. But the Report points to a future in which it may thrive to the detriment of women, of children and of society.

Moreover, as Derek Morgan explains, the internet undoubtedly now facilitates 'procreative tourism' for people seeking to avoid legal restrictions on surrogacy arrangements.

Derek Morgan[47]

One of the most remarkable developments affecting surrogacy since it achieved public visibility has been the use of the internet. It is used to search for and to advertise surrogacy services; to provide information about services; and to record surrogates' and intended parents' own stories about surrogacy arrangements. One of the main uses of the internet for these purposes is to enable people to circumvent domestic legal regimes that are either hostile to or prohibit surrogacy; the internet is a passport for those who would wish to surf as a 'procreative tourist'.

---

[45] L Andrews, 'Beyond Doctrinal Boundaries: A Legal Framework for Surrogate Motherhood' (1995) 81 Virginia Law Review 2343–75, 2351.

[46] 'Does Surrogacy Have a Future After Brazier?' (1999) 7 Medical Law Review 1–20, 10, 20.

[47] 'Enigma Variations: Surrogacy, Rights and Procreative Tourism' in R Cook, SD Sclater with F Kaganas (eds), *Surrogate Motherhood: International Perspectives* (Hart Publishing Oxford 2003) 75–92, 88.

Various regulatory proposals were considered by the Brazier Committee. It rejected the suggestion that all surrogacy arrangements should take place in licensed fertility clinics. Although this would have the advantage of reducing the risk of transmission of HIV and hepatitis, it was rejected on the grounds that surrogacy should not be just another option in the treatment of infertility, but instead 'require(s) a consideration of other factors, much more akin to the dilemmas of adoption than those of infertility'.[48] The Committee were also worried that its routine provision in assisted conception clinics might lead to its premature use as an alternative to failed IVF treatment.[49] A surrogacy licensing authority was also rejected by the Brazier Report on the grounds that the very small number of surrogate births each year do not justify the expense of maintaining a new regulatory agency.

Instead the Brazier Committee's preferred option was a new Surrogacy Act which would require all agencies involved in surrogacy to be registered with the Department of Health (and equivalent bodies in Scotland, Wales and Northern Ireland), and to operate in accordance with a statutory Code of Practice, which would be drawn up by the Department. The Code of Practice would be binding upon registered agencies, but it would also offer guidance on good practice in surrogacy arrangements, which might be helpful when arrangements are made between friends or family members.[50] Relevant parts of this Code could also be incorporated into the HFEA's Code of Practice, meaning that licensed clinics would then be expected to comply with them.[51]

The Code of Practice would also make provision for the compiling of statistics, and for research into the outcomes of surrogacy arrangements.[52] It would contain a list of the expenses which could legitimately be reimbursed by the commissioning couple; specify safe insemination procedures; and have minimum counselling and information requirements. In addition Brazier suggests that the Code might contain a model 'memorandum of understanding' which would define and clarify the parties' expectations:

Margaret Brazier, Alastair Campbell, and Susan Golombok[53]

8.12 The Code should stress the value in all surrogacy arrangements (including intra-familial and other altruistic arrangements) of drawing up a memorandum of understanding, defining and clarifying the expectations of the parties. That memorandum should record the parties' arrangements to secure the future welfare of the child, including agreements about contact between the surrogate and the child and/or what the child is to be told about his or her origins. It should address how pregnancy is to be established and what screening processes pre-conceptually and pre-natally are agreed to safeguard the health of the surrogate and the child.

8.13 Issues relating to the conduct of pregnancy should be addressed, such as any undertaking the surrogate may have offered in relation to smoking, alcohol, diet and anti-natal care. Arrangements for the commissioning couple to keep in contact with and provide support for the surrogate in the course of pregnancy must be spelled out. What arrangements will follow the birth for the child to be entrusted to the couple, and how the couple will acquire

---

[48] Brazier para 6.13.   [49] Ibid, para 6.15.   [50] Ibid, para 7.18
[51] Ibid, para 7.19   [52] Ibid, para 6.26
[53] *Surrogacy: Review for Health Ministers of Current Arrangements for Payments and Regulation* (HMSO London 1998) Cm 4068.

joint parental responsibility in relation to the child should be agreed. What is to happen in certain contingencies such as the detection of fetal abnormality, miscarriage, stillbirth, the birth of a disabled child, or injury to or the death of the surrogate herself should be agreed. Arrangements for the provision of life and disability cover for the surrogate should be included.

8.14 The Code must emphasise the non-contractual nature of any memorandum of understanding while explaining the importance of all parties setting out as clearly as possible their expectations of each other. It may be that when the Code of Practice is drafted a model memorandum of understanding could be appended to it.

Criteria would be set for the selection of both commissioning couples and surrogate mothers—such as Brazier's suggestion that 'the surrogate should have given birth and have living with her at least one child of her own'.[54] According to Brazier, the Code should also stipulate minimum age for surrogate mothers (Brazier advocates 21)[55] and a minimum interval to elapse between pregnancies (Brazier recommends two years).[56] Brazier also suggested that a woman should undergo a surrogate pregnancy only once, unless she is providing a sibling for an existing child.[57] Brazier also advocates raising the minimum age for commissioning couples to 21, and setting a maximum age limit.[58] In addition, it proposes that the commissioning couple must both have lived in the United Kingdom for at least 12 months immediately prior to their application.[59]

Brazier recommends that the Code of Practice should explicitly state that the welfare of the child must be the 'paramount' concern of all parties, and that participation in surrogacy arrangements must be conditional upon establishing that both the surrogate and the commissioning couple have given the requisite consideration to the child's welfare, and to the impact the surrogate pregnancy may have upon the surrogate's own children.[60]

According to Brazier, surrogacy contracts should continue to be unenforceable, and the prohibition on advertising and the involvement of commercial agencies should remain intact. Under the new Act, there would be a revised procedure for granting parental orders to commissioning couples after application to the Family Division of the High Court. Brazier found that the 'current arrangements whereby magistrates may be confronted at random with one or two applications for parental orders are unsatisfactory'. Accordingly, it suggests that approval of a surrogacy arrangement should be given only 'by judges of the highest experience.' Centralizing applications in the Family Division would, they argue, 'result in the development of the necessary expertise by a small group of judges and would allow similarly for a small panel of Guardians to specialise in surrogacy'.[61]

Access to parental orders would be conditional upon *full compliance* with the statutory rules.[62] Courts would no longer be able to retrospectively authorize illegal payments on the grounds that the welfare of the child demands the making of an order.[63] Guardians *ad litem* would be given additional powers to investigate whether unlawful

---

[54] Brazier para 8.8. [55] Ibid. [56] Ibid. [57] Ibid.
[58] Ibid, para 8.4. [59] Ibid, para 7.24. [60] Ibid, para 8.5. [61] Ibid, 7.24.
[62] Ibid, para 7.3. [63] Ibid, para 7.11.

payments had been made, and couples who had made payments other than the expressly permitted and documented expenses would be required to go through the ordinary adoption process in order to acquire legal parenthood.

In addition to their powers to investigate the making of unlawful payments, the powers of guardians *ad litem* would be strengthened to enable them to detect arrangements where there is in fact no genetic link with the 'commissioning' couple. At present there is a suspicion that some women who are already pregnant are persuaded to agree to give up the child at birth under cover of an apparent surrogacy arrangement, and that even when guardians *ad litem* suspect that there was no preconceptual agreement, they are powerless to prevent parental orders being made.[64] The new Act would give judges the power to order DNA tests, and without a genetic link there could be no eligibility for a parental order. Guardians *ad litem* would also be given powers to check criminal records to ensure that neither of the prospective parents has a previous record of offences against children.

Brazier rejected a suggestion that couples who had made illegal payments should be denied access to adoption. Although it accepted that this might be a more effective deterrent, Brazier concluded that where the surrogate mother does not want the child, a ban on adoption would not be in the child's best interests.[65] As we have seen, it is already possible for a child born following a surrogacy arrangement to be handed over to the commissioning couple without any formal transfer of legal parenthood. If adoption were unavailable, the result might be even more children living with 'parents' who do not have any legal responsibility for them. For similar reasons, Brazier rejected the criminalization of unauthorized payments on the grounds first, that the child might be tainted by the criminality of their conception, and second, that it would provide a further incentive for couples to avoid acquiring any formal relationship with their child.

Brazier's compromise solution to the problem of payments is, with respect, rather odd. Currently, in relation to both adoption and parental orders, the prohibition upon payments can be circumvented relatively easily by *post hoc* judicial approval. Brazier's recommendation would remove one mechanism for the subsequent authorization of payments, while leaving the other intact. In practice then, their proposal would not necessarily end the de facto commercialization of surrogacy, but instead would divert more couples towards the adoption process. Since applying for an adoption order is more cumbersome and time-consuming than the section 30 procedure, the consequence might be longer delays and greater public expense, as well as the rather curious implication that the rigours of the adoption process are in some sense a punishment for a couple's non-compliance with the ban on payments.

(g) THE HUMAN RIGHTS ACT 1998

No surrogacy case has ever come before the European Court of Human Rights or the Commission, and so the application of Convention rights to surrogacy arrangements remains unclear. The most obviously relevant rights are Article 8, the right to respect

---

[64] Brazier, para 7.24.   [65] Ibid, para 7.13.

for private and family life, and Article 14, the right not to be discriminated against in exercising one's convention rights. It might, for example, be possible for unmarried couples to argue that section 30's insistence that eligibility for a parental order depends upon the couple being married to each other discriminates against unmarried couples in the exercise of their right to respect for private and family life. In a dispute over who should keep the baby, both the surrogate mother and the commissioning couple might claim that their Article 8 rights are engaged, though it is not clear that this would add anything to the principles which commonly inform the courts' decisions in such cases, namely that priority should be given to the welfare of the child which, as we have seen, normally means that the child will not be removed from a settled home. Article 12, the right to marry and found a family is also unlikely to have much impact upon surrogacy arrangements, since it does not give rise to a *right* to have a child through unconventional means.

4. IS SURROGACY ACCEPTABLE?

For a number of reasons, surrogacy is a more controversial practice than other assisted conception techniques. First, Elizabeth Anderson argues that it is not in the best interests of the child to discover that her gestational mother gave her away in return for money, shortly after her birth. Similarly the Warnock Report suggested that surrogacy was 'degrading to the child . . . since, for practical purposes, the child will have been bought for money'.[66] Because of the small numbers of surrogate births, there is little evidence of the long-term impact of surrogacy arrangements upon children, so these claims are generally speculative. In a related argument, Elizabeth Anderson maintains that the surrogate mother's own children's sense of security might be undermined by witnessing their mother giving away a child to whom she has just given birth. Again, there is little evidence to support or discount this claim.

Elizabeth Anderson[67]

Commercial surrogacy substitutes market norms for some of the norms of parental love. . . For in this practice the natural mother deliberately conceives a child with the intention of giving it up for material advantage. Her renunciation of parental responsibilities is not done for the child's sake, nor for the sake of fulfilling an interest she shares with the child, but typically for her own sake (and possibly, if 'altruism' is a motive, for the intended parents' sakes). She and the couple who pay her to give up her parental rights over her child thus treat her rights as a kind of property right. They thereby treat the child itself as a kind of commodity, which may be properly bought and sold . . .

By engaging in the transfer of children by sale, all of the parties to the surrogacy contract express a set of attitudes towards children which undermine the norms of parental love. They all agree in treating the ties between a natural mother and her children as properly loosened by a monetary incentive. Would it be any wonder if a child born of a surrogacy agreement feared resale by parents who have such an attitude? . . .

The unsold children of surrogate mothers are also harmed by commercial surrogacy. The

---

[66] Warnock para 8.11.
[67] 'Is Women's Labor a Commodity?' (1990) 19 Philosophy and Public Affairs 71–92, 76–8.

children of some surrogate mothers have reported their fears that they may be sold like their half-brother or half-sister, and express a sense of loss at being deprived of a sibling. Furthermore, the widespread acceptance of commercial surrogacy would psychologically threaten all children. For it would change the way children are valued by people (parents and surrogate brokers)—from being loved by their parents and respected by others, to being sometimes used as objects of commercial profit-making.

Secondly, it is often argued that surrogacy is exploitative. This claim has a number of different strands. It might, for example, be argued that the commissioning couple treat the surrogate mother as a means to an end, thus violating the Kantian imperative (which we considered in Chapter 1). Note too that the Kantian imperative can also be violated where an individual chooses to use themselves as a means to another's end. If it is always wrong to treat oneself, or someone else, as a means to an end, then surrogacy arrangements might be said to be morally wrong. The Warnock Report, for example, stated

that people should treat others as a means to their own ends, however desirable the consequences must always be liable to moral objection.[68]

And Elizabeth Anderson makes a similar point:[69]

The application of commercial norms to women's labor reduces the surrogate mothers from persons worthy of respect and consideration to objects of mere use.[70]

Of course, as we have seen before in this book, the Kantian imperative just warns against treating another person *solely* as a means to an end. Provided that the surrogate mother is also treated as a person in her own right, employing her to carry a baby for 9 months does not necessarily offend the Kantian imperative.

A different sense in which surrogacy is accused of being exploitative is the claim that the risk of actual exploitation, chiefly of the surrogate mother, is too great. On this line of argument, offering a woman money to bear a child creates the possibility of exploitation, especially since commissioning couples will usually be richer than surrogate mothers. The Brazier Report, for example, argued that payments to surrogate mothers 'create a danger that women will give a less than free and fully informed consent to act as a surrogate'.[71]

Richard Arneson disagrees, and claims that banning surrogacy in order to protect poor women from choosing surrogacy is both paternalistic and elitist.

Richard Arneson[72]
When the layers of rhetoric in arguments against commercial surrogacy are stripped away, the morally important residual concern is paternalism . . .

Notice that the mere observation that the women who choose commercial surrogacy tend to be poor and to have few if any minimally attractive work options other than surrogacy is not a reason to ban commercial surrogacy unless one believes that these women are choosing incompetently.

---

[68] Warnock para 8.17.
[69] 'Is Women's Labor a Commodity?' (1990) 19 Philosophy and Public Affairs 71–92, 80, 82.
[70] Ibid.   [71] Brazier, i.
[72] 'Commodification and Commerical Surrogacy' (1992) 21 Philosophy and Public Affairs 132–64, 158–60.

No matter how restricted one's life options, the idea that the narrow range of one's options unacceptably constrains one's choice is not a reason to limit further one's range of choice . . .

My point is simply that a concern that some people are forced to choose their lives from an unfairly small menu of options is a reason to expand not restrict the range of options from which these people must choose.

The suspicion that many of the women choosing commercial surrogacy are choosing from ignorance or confused reasoning or in some other less than substantially voluntary way would seem most naturally to justify state aid to foster intelligent and considered decision-making rather than a ban of the practice.

[T]he thought that commercial surrogacy should be banned because the poor working women who mostly choose it are too incompetent to be entrusted to make their own decisions in this sphere has an ugly, elitist sound. Careful empirical work that goes beyond hunches and guesswork would be required before one could take a prohibitionist proposal seriously. Any such calculation of harms and benefits should proceed from the evaluative standpoint of potential surrogates themselves and not simply impute middle-class concerns to them.

Lori Andrews points out that while money may influence a woman's decision to become a surrogate mother, it is seldom her only reason.

Lori Andrews[73]

Certainly, money is a motivation in this realm, as it is in so many other areas of our lives, including other situations in which people are paid to be surrogate parents (such as nannies, workers in daycare centers, foster parents, and teachers in elementary schools). But money is not the deciding factor for women's participation in surrogacy. The fact that women choose to be surrogates rather than choosing to earn that same (relatively low) amount of money in some other way suggests that there are other motivations. Studies have found that some surrogates have been affected by the plight of infertile family members and friends. Others enjoyed parenting and wanted to help infertile couples become parents. Many of the women I interviewed described the tremendous psychic benefits they received from the feeling that they were helping someone meet a joyous life goal. Many viewed themselves as feminists who were exercising reproductive choice and demonstrating an ethic of care. It seems crass not to try to understand the arrangement from the surrogate's vantage point, in which this type of employment is viewed as a higher calling, like being a health care professional or educator, and may consequently be preferable to working as a check-out clerk in a grocery store or at some other minimum wage job.

Even the Brazier Report acknowledges that 'many women have found being a surrogate an emotionally rewarding experience, with no obvious ill effects on them or their families'.[74]

It is also sometimes argued that it is simply not possible for a woman's consent to bear a child for someone else to be fully informed and entirely voluntary, either because before conception it is difficult for a woman to know whether she will be able to hand over a child to whom she has given birth, or because she is unable to resist the offer of a substantial sum of money. Against this, Stephen Wilkinson argues that, provided a woman is given sufficient information, there is no reason to presume that she is necessarily incapable of agreeing to become a surrogate mother.

---

[73] 'Beyond Doctrinal Boundaries: A Legal Framework for Surrogate Motherhood' (1995) 81 Virginia Law Review 2343–75, 2353–4.
[74] Brazier para 4.26.

Stephen Wilkinson[75]

[I]f (as is suggested) it's true that women's emotions are unpredictable, and that surrogates often have regrets, and that there's much that we don't know about surrogacy arrangements, and that direct experience changes women's attitudes to pregnancy and childbirth, then *simply by telling prospective surrogates in some detail about these facts* we go a long way towards making sure that their consents are adequately informed. Consequently, it seems to me that the general consent arguments considered here (most of which are to do with surrogates' consents being insufficiently informed) are weak and don't provide a justification for banning commercial surrogacy or even for morally condemning it . . .

   Specific consent arguments are ones which, rather than asserting that consent is problematic in *all* surrogacy arrangements, claim that it is problematic specifically in *commercial* ones . . . The first is the claim that payment damages consent because it *influences* prospective surrogates resulting 'in an increased likelihood of women entering into a surrogacy arrangement when they would not otherwise have done so'. This, however, won't suffice because there are numerous cases in which payments influence people without invalidating their consents. Indeed, the whole economy is based on people using money to influence each other . . . in ways which in no way rule out free and informed consent . . .

   The second argument relates specifically to the (supposed) fact that commercial surrogacy does, or would, attract mostly poor women. . . . There's undoubtedly a sense in which women who have to choose between poverty and extreme poverty aren't free to decline paid surrogacy. Indeed this is a general point. People who have to choose between *anything* and extreme poverty are (in that respect) unfree . . . [But] unfreedom of this sort doesn't preclude valid consent. One reason for this is that, if it did, then it would be impossible to consent to (for example) lifesaving medical treatments. So not having any acceptable alternatives isn't, in and of itself, enough to render poor surrogates' consent invalid—because it's possible to consent validly *even when* one is unfree in this 'lacking options' sense.

It is interesting that the concern about surrogate mothers feeling pressurized into entering surrogacy arrangements appears to derive principally from the existence of a financial incentive. Social and emotional pressure to agree to bear a child for a distraught friend or family member is seldom presented as an equivalent obstacle to a potential surrogate's free and autonomous decision making, although as Lori Andrews suggests, in practice it may be extremely difficult to refuse a request from a close friend or relative. Interestingly too, it is seldom argued that surrogacy would be less exploitative if the surrogate were paid *more* for her services. Instead unpaid surrogacy is perceived to be less exploitative. The irony of this is pointed out by Lori Andrews in the next extract, and by Marjorie Shultz who argues that this:

smacks all too familiarly of the notion that while men get paid for their efforts, skills and services, women, being women, should do their woman-things out of purity of heart and sentiment.

Lori Andrews[76]

In fact, I am even more concerned about coercion in the unpaid surrogacy situation. If only paid surrogacy is banned, infertile couples will only be able to have a child through this arrangement by

---

[75] *Bodies for Sale: Ethics and Exploitation in the Human Body Trade* (Routledge London 2003) 171–3.
[76] 'Beyond Doctrinal Boundaries: A Legal Framework for Surrogate Motherhood' (1995) 81 Virginia Law Review 2343–75, 2365–6.

pressuring friends or relatives into being a surrogate. A woman in an arm's-length transaction with a stranger, represented by her own lawyer, would likely have more ability to refuse than a friend or relative. Allowing unpaid rather than paid surrogacy furthers the pressures on women to nurture all others and to care for family members. Moreover, it is disturbing that, in most instances, when society suggests that a certain activity should be done for altruism, rather than money, it is generally a woman's activity. This perpetuates the devaluation of women's activities in a society that is based on a market system.

The third objection to surrogacy flows from the argument that reproduction should not be commodified. In the next extract, Margaret Jane Radin argues that converting procreation into an economic transaction would have a negative impact upon children, women and society as a whole.

Margaret Jane Radin[77]

If we permit babies to be sold, we commodify not only the mother's (and father's) baby-making capacities—which might be analogous to commodifying sexuality—but we also conceive of the baby itself in market rhetoric. When the baby becomes a commodity, all of its personal attributes—sex, eye color, predicted I.Q., predicted height, and the like—become commodified as well. This is to conceive of potentially all personal attributes in market rhetoric, not merely those of sexuality . . .

If a capitalist baby industry were to come into being, with all of its accompanying paraphernalia, how could any of us, even those who did not produce infants for sale, avoid subconsciously measuring the dollar value of our children? How could our children avoid being preoccupied with measuring their own dollar value? This makes our discourse about ourselves (when we are children) and about our children (when we are parents) like our discourse about cars.

Concerns about commodification of women and children . . . might counsel permitting only unpaid surrogacy (market-inalienability). Market-inalienability might be grounded in a judgment that commodification of women's reproductive capacity is harmful for the identity aspect of their personhood and in a judgment that the closeness of paid surrogacy to baby-selling harms our self-conception too deeply. There is certainly the danger that women's attributes, such as height, eye color, race, intelligence, and athletic ability, will be monetized. Surrogates with 'better' qualities will command higher prices in virtue of those qualities. This monetization commodifies women more broadly than merely with respect to their sexual services or reproductive capacity. Hence, if we wish to avoid the dangers of commodification and, at the same time, recognize that there are some situations in which a surrogate can be understood to be proceeding out of love or altruism and not out of economic necessity or desire for monetary gain, we could prohibit sales but allow surrogates to give their services. We might allow them to accept payment of their reasonable out-of-pocket expenses—a form of market-inalienability similar to that governing ordinary adoption.

In contrast, Janice Raymond argues that altruistic surrogacy arrangements are just as demeaning for women as commercial exchanges.

Janice Raymond[78]

Surrogacy, situated within the larger context of women's inequality, is not simply about the commercialization of women and children. On a political level, it reinforces the perception and use

---

[77] 'Market-Inalienability' (1987) 100 Harvard Law Review 1849–1937, 1925–6, 1932–3. This article formed the nucleus of a book, *Contested Commodities*, Harvard University Press 1996.

[78] *Women as Wombs: Reproductive Technologies and the Battle over Women's Freedom* (HarperCollins New York 1993) 57–8.

of women as a breeder class and the gender inequality of women as a group. The practice of surrogacy strikes at the core of what a society allows women to be and become. Taking the commerce out of surrogacy but leaving the practice intact on a non-commercial and contractual basis glosses over the essential violation—the social definition of women as breeders. . . .

Proposals that the law keep clear of reproductive exchanges where no money changes hands are based on unreal gender-neutral assumptions. If the harm of surrogacy, for example, is based only on the commercialization and commodification of reproduction, then the reality that *women are always used* in systems of surrogacy gets no legal notice . . .

The focus on altruism essentializes the woman as gift giver and as gift. It sentimentalizes and thus obscures the ways women are medicalized and devalued by the new reproductive technologies and practices. An uncritical affirmation of reproductive gifts and gift givers—of egg donation, or 'special ladies' who serve as so-called surrogate mothers for others, and of reproductive technology itself as a great gift to humanity—fails to examine the institutions of reproductive science, technology and brokering that increasingly structure reproductive exchanges.

Altruistic reproductive exchanges leave intact the status of women as a breeder class . . . Women's bodies are still the raw material for others' needs, desires, and purposes. The normalization of altruistic exchanges may, in fact, have the effect of further promoting the view that women have a duty or obligation to engage in reproductive arrangements free of charge. In the surrogacy context, altruism essentializes the role of women as *mothers for others*. This emphasis on giving has become an integral part of reproductive technological propaganda, but this altruistic pedestal on which women are placed is only one more way of glorifying women's inequality.

Others, such as Michael Freeman, dispute the idea that surrogate mothers need to be protected against entering surrogacy arrangements, and argue that women should have the right to make decisions about their own bodies.

Michael Freeman[79]

[I]t is worth asking what is entailed in the right to liberty. Central to that right, I would argue, is the right to do with your body as you please. On this analysis, the surrogate mother has a right to use her body to give birth to the baby of another. To deny her the decision to become a surrogate thus violates her right to liberty. We can take away liberty-rights. Very few of them are totally unqualified. But the onus rests on those who wish to restrict liberty to put forward sound moral arguments to support limitations on freedom. What arguments can they adduce? The arguments are phrased in various ways (motherhood or woman is dehumanized, children are commodified) . . . But as arguments proferred to buttress limitations on autonomy, they amount to little more than the enforcement of morality for morality's sake . . .

What of the child? Warnock, it will be remembered, thought a surrogacy agreement was 'degrading to the child who is to be the outcome of it since . . . the child will have been bought for money'. This is surely fallacious. The money is paid to the surrogate mother not to compensate her for giving up the child, nor to 'buy' the child. The money is payment for services, it is compensation for the burden of pregnancy. The child may have a right not to be sold, but that is a distortion of what is happening, even in cases of commercial surrogacy . . .

Put simply, a [slippery slope] objection to surrogacy is that if we allow the practice now it will lead to other practices which are inherently undesirable. To an extent this was more than implicit in the Warnock Report, raising the spectre of surrogacy 'for convenience' as an argument against surrogacy even for the infertile. And it is very clearly the fear of some feminists who see a danger

---

[79] 'Is Surrogacy Exploitative?' in Sheila McLean (ed), *Legal Issues in Human Reproduction* (Gower London 1989) 164–84, 170–1, 173–4, 178.

that a woman's attributes (her colour, height, intelligence, 'looks') may be 'monetized', that the market value attracted by potential surrogates will vary according to whether they have what are deemed desirable attributes or not. They fear men bypassing their wives (or partners) and using surrogates (tested for the 'right' qualities) to produce their children . . .

None of this, it has to be argued, is a pleasant scenario . . . But the real question is: how likely is it that the acceptance of surrogacy will lead to these 'horrible' results . . . Critics of surrogacy can point to all sorts of horrible results, but they cannot say these will happen.

5. SHOULD SURROGACY CONTRACTS BE ENFORCEABLE?

As we have seen, in the UK surrogacy contracts are unenforceable. Those who are in favour of their unenforceability, such as Rosemarie Tong and Katherine Bartlett, argue that it would be unconscionable to force the surrogate mother to hand over 'her' child after birth.

Rosemarie Tong[80]
The value of a 'change of heart' period is very important from a feminist point of view. First, it acknowledges a parental relationship whose moral significance traditional philosophy has ignored—namely, the gestational relationship . . . A second advantage of the 'change of heart' period is that it challenges the notion that contracts must be honored no matter what—as if contracts were more important than people . . .

The adoption approach, with its change of heart clause, replaces what strikes me as the *heartless* contract approach. A deal is not always a deal—at least not when one is trading in some of the deepest emotions human beings can ever feel. Any approach that *binds* women to reproductive decisions—as does the contract approach—must be regarded with deep suspicion.

Katharine T Bartlett[81]
[It] would seem unwise either to criminalize surrogacy contracts or to allow specific enforcement of them. Declining the use of courts to enforce private surrogacy arrangements, even while allow-ing parties to make them, would retain, without coercing, the assumption (or ideology) of current law—that, ordinarily, parents will not give up their children. It would affirm that wanting to keep one's children, even where one has previously agreed otherwise, is not pathological or wrong, but rather understandable and defensible. It would also reject the meaning of pregnancy as a calcu-lated choice between bearing a child with whom the mother will have a relationship (without pay) or bearing a child for another (for pay). . . .

Declining to enforce surrogacy arrangements would also disaffirm the notion of 'convenient' childbearing. Some couples may seek surrogacy arrangements not because they are infertile but because they find pregnancy and childbirth undesirable. The reasons may range from wishing not to risk passing on genetic defects to desiring to avoid the health risks, pain, physical distortion, or annoyance of pregnancy. As a wider range of reasons becomes acceptable, the danger to be

---

[80] 'Feminist Perspectives and Gestational Motherhood: The Search for a Unified Legal Focus' in J Callahan (ed), *Reproduction, Ethics and the Law: Feminist Responses* (Indiana UP Bloomington and Indianapolis 1995) 55–79, 72, 75.

[81] 'Re-expressing Parenthood' (1998) 98 Yale Law Journal 293, 333.

avoided is that parenthood will come to be understood as a recreational activity from which adults can experience pleasure dissociated from inconvenience.

Arguments against the enforceability of surrogacy contracts often amount to the claim that an order for specific performance would be oppressive. Surrogacy arrangements are, however, akin to contracts *for services*, in which an individual agrees to surrender some portion of their liberty in return for something, such as an income, that may be more valuable to them. In a contract for services, if either party were to fail to fulfil their obligations under the agreement, the ordinary remedy would be damages, not specific performance.

There are many contracts where specific performance would be oppressive, and this is not generally regarded as grounds for their complete unenforceability. Just as contract law will not generally force an actor who refuses to go on stage to complete his performance, so a surrogate mother would not necessarily be compelled to hand the baby over after birth. A remedy in damages for breach of contract would protect the surrogate mother's 'right' to keep the child, while compensating the commissioning couple for at least some of their losses. It is perfectly plausible for a surrogate mother's right to resile from her undertaking to hand over the child to coexist with the commissioning couple's right to compensation for losses resulting from their misplaced reliance upon the agreement.

However, there are those who would argue that specific performance might be the appropriate remedy when surrogacy arrangements break down. In the next extract, for example, Marjorie Shultz argues that in certain circumstances, the surrogate mother should be compelled to hand over the baby to the commissioning couple.

Marjorie Shultz[82]

Some argue that parenthood is so central to human experience, and that feelings concerning it are so intrinsically unpredictable and uncontrollable, that binding commitments should not be entertained. . . .

Where contractual ordering is accepted, the state neither requires people to make binding commitments, nor bars them from doing so; it allows individuals to choose whether to make such commitments. Persons who believe that feelings about parenthood are too hard to predict need not enter binding agreements. What is really at issue is whether the state ought categorically to prevent anyone from entering such agreements on the ground that preferences may change.

Parenthood is not the only matter about which feelings and preferences change. Enforcement of promises occurs precisely because people change their minds about performing obligations they have assumed . . .

Allowing procreative arrangements to be governed by private agreement implies a willingness to undertake dispute-resolution. Contractual enforcement assumes the availability of appropriate remedies for breach of a promise. . . .

The mother–child bond is significant and fundamental; its disruption seems, to many, unthinkable. It is less frequently noted, however, that if specific performance is denied where a surrogate refuses to surrender the child, an analogous loss is sustained by the father and, indeed, by the adoptive couple. A reproductive agreement creates expectations regarding the opportunity to parent a child; those expectations have vital importance to those who hold them . . . Even more

---

[82] 'Reproductive Technology and Intention-based Parenthood: An Opportunity for Gender Neutrality' (1990) Wisconsin Law Review 297–398, 348–9, 366–7, 384.

emphatically, in a surrogacy example, a particular life actually comes into being because of such an agreement. Once conception has taken place, reliance on the promises made is about as intense and significant as could be imagined. If intentions and the expectations and reliance that result are taken seriously, the unfairness of denying the equitable remedy [specific performance] becomes comparable to the hardship of granting it. Moreover, the intrusiveness and hardship of compelling surrender of the child are somewhat alleviated by the fact that the surrogate has chosen this path at an earlier point in time, thereby setting in motion others' expectations and inducing their irreversible reliance . . . The analysis above suggests that while particular promises regarding reproductive arrangements might be excused or deemed coerced, unconscionable or violative of public policy, others could well be judged enforceable. Combined with the concerns just expressed regarding expectations and reliance, the argument for specific performance in turning over a child born of a surrogate arrangement seems, at least in some instances, to be compelling . . .

In holding that surrogates but not other parties to the arrangement must have an opportunity to change their minds after giving birth, the court reinforces stereotypes of women as unstable, as unable to make decisions and stick to them, and as necessarily vulnerable to their hormones and emotions. . . . In particular, it exalts a woman's experience of pregnancy and childbirth over her formation of emotional, intellectual and interpersonal decisions and expectations, as well as over others' reliance on the commitments she has earlier made.

The law's failure to enforce surrogacy contracts inevitably contributes to their insecurity. It could even be argued that their complete unenforceability may persuade women to become surrogates even if they are not sure that they would want to give up the child after birth. Giving the surrogate mother complete freedom to withdraw from the contract and keep all of the money that she has been paid might also provide the opportunity for extortion. Once conception has occurred the commissioning couple may be vulnerable to threats from the surrogate mother that she intends to keep the baby, or have an abortion, unless she receives more money.

Unlike other domestic agreements that are outside the scope of contract law, surrogacy arrangements are often based upon an entirely illusory relationship of 'trust' or 'friendship' between strangers. And unlike ordinary contracts, surrogacy arrangements are seldom entered into as a result of the trust that results from reputation and/or a pre-existing relationship; or because effective sanctions exist should the other party fail to keep their promise. Clearly people only enter into such patently risky arrangements because their desire for the best-case outcome is so overwhelming.

In Israel, one of the only countries to have introduced a regulatory regime to approve surrogacy arrangements, the surrogate mother is only permitted to renege on her agreement if there has been a change of circumstances, and the welfare of the child would not be damaged. In the next extract, Rhona Schulz points out that the rigorous approval process which precedes any surrogacy arrangement in Israel minimizes the chance that the surrogate mother will in fact change her mind.

Rhona Schulz[83]

The Approvals Committee's guidelines for drawing up the surrogate motherhood agreement start with a clear statement that it is necessary to ensure, so far as is possible, that the birth mother

---

[83] 'Surrogacy in Israel: An Analysis of the Law in Practice' in R Cook, SD Sclater with F Kaganas (eds), *Surrogate Motherhood: International Perspectives* (Hart Publishing Oxford 2003) 35–53, 39–40, 43, 51.

understands the nature of the commitments involved in the agreement and agrees thereto voluntarily and without coercion. A number of the Approvals Committee's requirements are designed to
further this end.

First, the physician who examines the birth mother has to declare that s/he has explained to the
birth mother the consequences and significance of acting as a surrogate ... Secondly, the
Approvals Committee will not consider any application until it is satisfied that the birth mother
has obtained independent legal advice from a lawyer who is an expert in surrogate motherhood
agreements ... Thirdly, the birth mother is interviewed separately by the Approvals Committee
and will be asked questions designed to test whether her consent is voluntary and informed.
Finally, the Approvals Committee's practice is only to approve birth mothers who have previously
given birth ...

The [Israeli] Law effectively denies the surrogate mother the right to renege unless a court is
satisfied that there has been a change in circumstances and that the welfare of the child would not
be damaged thereby. We are not aware of any cases where the birth mother has requested to keep
the child. One reason for this may be the screening by the Approvals Committee. While, of course,
we cannot be sure that there would have been problems if arrangements had gone ahead with the
birth mothers rejected as unsuitable, it seems likely that the Approvals Committee is in a better
position than the intended parents to judge the suitability of the birth mother both because of the
professional skills and experience of the Approvals Committee members and because they are
more likely to be objective. Childless couples, with limited options open to them, perhaps need
protecting against possible rashness and lack of judgement in choosing a birth mother ...

Perhaps the clear-cut nature of the legislation prevents the problem [of the birth mother
wishing to keep the child] from arising because the birth mother knows from the beginning that
there is simply no possibility of reneging and thus avoids developing any attachment to the child.

6. CONCLUSION

It is important to keep the issue of surrogacy in perspective. Surrogacy arrangements
are rare. Most would-be mothers want to give birth to their own children, and so
surrogacy is always likely to be a last resort for women. Surrogacy may be the only
option for men who do not want to reproduce with a female partner, but again,
demand does not seem to be great.

Nevertheless, despite its rarity, surrogacy does raise some complicated legal questions, such as who should be considered the child's parents, and what should happen
if the arrangement breaks down. Banning surrogacy altogether is not a realistic
option, since the arrangements can be made without the involvement of a third party.
If we know that children are going to be born as a result of surrogacy agreements, we
must have mechanisms to resolve important questions about their parentage and
residence.

In this chapter we have seen that surrogacy is currently regulated by a combination
of surrogacy-specific rules, such as the largely ineffective prohibition of commercialization, and provisions, such as the rules governing the attribution of legal parentage,
which apply incidentally and rather awkwardly to the practice of surrogacy.
Furthermore, the combined effect of the various rules governing surrogacy is that
arrangements remain largely unregulated, thus encouraging would-be commissioning

couples and potential surrogates to make agreements without any formal prospective guidance or professional advice. As a result, I would advocate clearer, more facilitative regulation.

Emily Jackson[84]

[T]he law governing surrogacy consists in an incomplete patchwork of provisions which mean that, despite the arrangements' practical and moral complexity, surrogacy is comparatively unregulated. The two official reports into the practice of surrogacy have advocated regulation that is supposed to restrict or even prevent people from engaging in surrogacy arrangements. Hostility to facilitative regulation is based upon two principal misconceptions. First, as we have seen, there is little evidence to support the twin assumptions that surrogacy exploits women and harms children. Second, making it difficult to engage lawfully in surrogacy arrangements is unlikely to lead people who cannot have children in any other way to simply resign themselves to their childlessness. Rather restrictive regulation may be the catalyst for them to travel abroad to find a surrogate mother, or to make unlawful contracts in a regulatory vacuum.

There are several ways in which the law relating to surrogacy could be reformed so it more accurately reflected the intentions of the parties. Much depends upon the status provisions because if intention governs the determination of parenthood, then the commissioning couple simply *are* the child's parents, and there is no need for any rules governing the transfer of legal parenthood. Although this solution would have an appealing simplicity, it might also lack clarity and certainty, and would require some default position in the event of a dispute. A second possibility might be to make surrogacy contracts enforceable, provided that they satisfied various conditions. So contracts which had been made in circumstances of undue influence, or which were oppressive or unconscionable would be unenforceable. The surrogate mother would continue to be considered the child's legal mother at the moment of birth, and if she chose not to perform her side of the bargain by carrying the pregnancy to term and handing the child over, she would be in breach of contract. If this is characterised as a contract for services, it would not be specifically enforceable and she would instead be liable in damages. Although there would be the usual objections to the commercialisation of something as sacred as childbearing, it might be important to recognise that the real danger posed by surrogacy is the creation of a legal framework which encourages would-be surrogates and would-be commissioning couples to have children without the safeguards that can exist within an effective regulatory scheme.

7. FURTHER READING

BRAZIER, MARGARET, CAMPBELL, ALASTAIR, and GOLOMBOK, SUSAN, *Surrogacy: Review for Health Ministers of Current Arrangements for Payments and Regulation* (HMSO London 1998) Cm 4068.

COOK R, SCLATER SD, with KAGANAS, F (eds), *Surrogate Motherhood: International Perspectives* (Hart Publishing Oxford 2003).

FREEMAN, MICHAEL, 'Is Surrogacy Exploitative?' in Sheila McLean (ed), *Legal Issues in Human Reproduction* (Gower London 1989) 164–84.

FREEMAN, MICHAEL, 'Does Surrogacy Have a Future After Brazier?' (1999) 7 Medical Law Review 1–20.

---

[84] Emily Jackson, *Regulating Reproduction* (Hart Publishing Oxford 2001) 315–16.

JACKSON, EMILY, *Regulating Reproduction* (Hart Publishing Oxford 2001) ch 6.

RADIN, MARGARET JANE, 'Market-Inalienability' (1987) 100 Harvard Law Review 1849–937.

WALLBANK, JULIE, 'Too Many Mothers? Surrogacy, Kinship and the Welfare of the Child' (2002) 10 Medical Law Review 271–94.

WILKINSON, STEPHEN, *Bodies for Sale: Ethics and Exploitation in the Human Body Trade* (Routledge London 2003) ch 8.

16

END OF LIFE DECISIONS

1. CENTRAL ISSUES

1. Euthanasia involves a doctor acting deliberately to end a patient's life. Any doctor who kills a patient might be found guilty of murder, which carries a mandatory life sentence.

2. Assisted suicide is also a criminal offence. Suicide itself is no longer a crime, but this does not mean that patients have a *right* to commit suicide.

3. It is lawful to administer a dose of pain-killing drugs which may shorten a patient's life, by virtue of the doctrine of double effect.

4. Competent adults have the right to refuse life-sustaining treatment, which in practice means a right to insist that doctors physically remove them from the ventilator or the feeding tube which is keeping them alive.

5. The principal arguments in favour of legalizing euthanasia and/or assisted suicide are respect for patient autonomy; mercy; the inconsistency of the line the law currently draws between lawful and unlawful life-shortening practices; and the benefits of openly regulating a practice which might otherwise be shrouded in secrecy.

6. The arguments against legalization include respect for the sanctity of human life; the view that palliative care ought to make euthanasia unnecessary; the dangers of ensuring that requests for euthanasia are genuine; the negative impact legalization might have on the doctor–patient relationship; and the dangers of the slippery slope.

7. Some other countries have legalized euthanasia and assisted suicide, but opinion differs over whether this has improved matters for patients, or made things worse.

8. In relation to incompetent patients, the courts have had to decide whether withdrawing or withholding life-saving treatment could ever be in a patient's best interests. Where the incompetent patient's condition is extremely grave, and especially where medical opinion is that life-prolonging measures would be futile, the courts have been prepared to declare that non-treatment would be lawful.

2. INTRODUCTION

(a) CONTROVERSY AT THE END OF LIFE

Although it will happen to all of us at some point in the future, nobody knows what it is like to die. We may have watched life slip away from another person, and some people's religious faith leads them to have certain expectations about what will happen after their body ceases to be alive. But despite its universal inevitability, the process of dying will always remain mysterious to us. As a result, when judging whether death could ever be preferable to continued life, we are all inevitably behind a veil of ignorance.

Interest in whether it might be legitimate to take steps that will speed up the process of dying is not new. A number of Greek and Roman philosophers, among them Seneca, believed that suicide was a rational response to extreme physical and mental deterioration:

I shall not abandon old age, if old age preserves me intact as regards the better part of myself; but if old age begins to shatter my mind, and to pull its various faculties to pieces, if it leaves me, not life, but only the breath of life, I shall rush out of a house that is crumbing and tottering.[1]

For a number of reasons, the question of whether the medical profession should be allowed to assist their patients to die has become more prominent in recent years. First, new life support techniques are capable of significantly prolonging the dying process, leading some patients to fear a protracted and undignified death. Patients who would previously have died can now be kept alive using mechanical ventilators and artificially delivered nutrition and hydration. While these techniques were initially developed to enable potentially curable patients to survive despite a temporary inability to breathe or swallow, they are now able to keep people who have no chance of regaining consciousness alive for many years. New technologies have therefore forced us to think about the circumstances in which it might be legitimate to discontinue life-prolonging medical treatment.

Secondly, although life expectancy has increased dramatically over the last few decades, medical science has not been as successful in extending the period during which we are able to lead healthy, independent lives. If the population as a whole is living longer, a greater proportion of us, now around 70 per cent, will develop one or more of the diseases of old age, such as cancer or dementia, which are characterized by late onset and extended decline.[2] As a result, a growing number of elderly people face the prospect of a protracted period of debilitating ill health. The fear of spending many years entirely dependent upon others, and of losing one's dignity as one's bodily functions fail has prompted an intensification of public interest in euthanasia and assisted suicide.

Thirdly, as we have seen in previous chapters, the principle of patient autonomy has become increasingly dominant within medical law, giving new impetus to the question of whether a patient's right to make decisions about their medical treatment should extend to being able to ask for assistance in dying. Fourthly, when we looked at religious bioethics in Chapter 1, one common theme that seemed to cut across all of the major religions was the idea that life is not ours to dispose of as we wish. As society becomes increasingly secularized, the weight given to the proscription of suicide and euthanasia within religious teachings has correspondingly diminished.

Fifthly, a number of high profile cases, such as that of Dianne Pretty in the UK and Terri Schiavo in the US, have led to intense media interest in end of life

---

[1] Seneca, 58th *Letter to Lucillus* trans RM Gummere in TE Page et al. (eds), *Seneca: Ad Lucilium Epistulae Morales* vol I (Heinemann London 1961) 409.

[2] Agnes van der Heide, Luc Deliens, Karin Faisst, Tore Nilstun, Michael Norup, Eugenio Paci, Gerrit van der Wal, and Paul J van der Maas, 'End-of-life decision-making in six European countries: descriptive study' (2003) 362 Lancet 345–50.

decision-making. Finally, in the years following the identification of the AIDS virus, a number of well-organized lobbying organizations were set up to provide advice for people living with HIV and AIDS, and to campaign on their behalf. Unsurprisingly, control over medical treatment at the end of life has been one of the key issues for AIDS charities.

(b) ORGANIZATION OF THIS CHAPTER

In this chapter, we are concerned with the legal status of practices that may result in life being shortened. We begin with the competent patient, and in order to avoid repetition, this chapter takes for granted that the reader already understands the concept of legal competence (discussed in full in Chapter 4). First, we look at the current law, distinguishing between lawful and unlawful life-shortening practices. Secondly, the arguments for and against the legalization of voluntary euthanasia and assisted suicide are set out, with extracts from both sides of this emotional and acrimonious debate. Next, we examine some other countries' experience with decriminalization. In the second half of this chapter, our focus is the incompetent patient (again, refer back to Chapter 4 for a definition of incompetence). We start with children, discussing the status of non-treatment decisions both in the criminal law, and flowing from the courts' inherent jurisdiction. We close with discussion of the so-called 'conjoined twins case', Re A.[3] In relation to adults, we begin with an analysis of the House of Lords' ground-breaking decision that life-sustaining treatment could be withheld from Tony Bland, a patient in a persistent vegetative state.[4] We then cover developments since the Bland case.

(c) TERMINOLOGY

The word 'euthanasia' comes from the Greek words eu (good) and thanatos (death). In modern usage, it has developed a slightly different meaning. Although most of us would agree that someone who dies peacefully and suddenly in her sleep after a long and healthy life has had a 'good death', we would not say that this was a case of euthanasia. Rather the Oxford English Dictionary's definition is 'a gentle and easy death, the bringing about of this, especially in the case of incurable and painful disease'. We would also usually confine the term 'euthanasia' to cases in which doctors assist patients to die: if someone kills a relative who is in unbearable pain, we would tend to say that this was a 'mercy killing', rather than an example of euthanasia.

In this chapter, I shall use the word 'euthanasia' to refer only to voluntary active euthanasia, that is where a doctor deliberately acts to kill a patient at her request. But it should be noted that some commentators have contrasted active euthanasia with passive euthanasia, by which they mean the deliberate withholding or withdrawal of life-prolonging medical treatment. In this chapter, I shall simply refer to the withdrawal or withholding of treatment, rather than to passive euthanasia.

A further difference is between euthanasia and assisted suicide. In euthanasia, it is

---

[3] [2001] Fam 147 CA.   [4] Airedale NHS Trust v Bland [1993] AC 789 HL.

the doctor's conduct which causes the patient's death. Whereas in assisted suicide, the patient causes her own death, but someone else (usually, but not always a doctor) has helped her, for example by prescribing a lethal dose of drugs.

Finally, it is worth noting that just as in everyday usage we often use elliptical or euphemistic phrases when talking about death (we might speak of someone having 'passed away' or 'passed on', rather than saying that they are dead), we find similar evasive language within the legal and medical communities. Doctors and judges may refer to 'letting nature take its course' or 'not prolonging the dying process', when discussing life-shortening practices, such as the removal of life support or the provision of life-threatening doses of painkillers. The reasons for this should become apparent later in the chapter.

3. THE COMPETENT PATIENT

(a) THE CURRENT LAW

(1) EUTHANASIA

A doctor who deliberately ends the life of her patient is subject to the ordinary criminal law, and will often satisfy both the *actus reus* (proof of conduct, and proof that the conduct caused death) and the *mens rea* (the intention to kill or to cause grievous bodily harm) for the crime of murder. The doctor's motive and the consent of the victim are irrelevant, as is the fact that the patient may be terminally ill and would therefore have died soon without the doctor's intervention. And because murder carries a mandatory life sentence, the fact that the doctor acted for compassionate reasons cannot be taken into account in sentencing.

If someone in unbearable agony is killed by a friend or family member, it may be possible to reduce the charge to one of manslaughter on the grounds of diminished responsibility, thus allowing for some discretion in sentencing. A health care professional is, however, very unlikely to be able to claim that 'he was suffering from such abnormality of mind ... as substantially to impair his mental responsibility'.[5]

Of course, when a doctor hastens the death of a patient who is terminally ill, there may be some evidential difficulty in establishing that it was the doctor's conduct rather than the pre-existing illness that caused the patient's death. To be guilty of murder, the defendant's conduct must have 'contributed significantly' or been 'a substantial cause' of death: it need not, therefore, be the sole reason for the patient's death. If causation cannot be established, the doctor who administered a potentially lethal injection could, as happened to Dr Cox and Dr Moor (see below), be charged with attempted murder.

Despite the possibility that a doctor who has complied with a patient's request to end her life could face life imprisonment, no such case has ever resulted in a conviction for the full offence of murder. As we can see in the following cases, both juries

---

[5] Homicide Act 1957 s 2(1).

and the judiciary have tended to show leniency towards doctors whom they judge to have acted for compassionate reasons.

In *R v Arthur* (discussed in more detail below at p. 973), Farquharson J instructed the jury to 'think long and hard before deciding that doctors of the eminence we have heard . . . have evolved standards which amount to committing crime'. In 1999 Dr Moor was arrested after taking part in a media debate about voluntary euthanasia, during which he admitted to having helped a number of his patients to die painlessly. He was prosecuted for the murder of George Liddell, an 85-year-old man who had been suffering from bowel cancer. Hooper J told the jury:

You have heard that this defendant is a man of excellent character, not just in the sense that he has no previous convictions but how witnesses have spoken of his many admirable qualities. You may consider it a great irony that a doctor who goes out of his way to care for George Liddell ends up facing the charge that he does. You may also consider it another great irony that the doctor who takes time on his day off to tend to a dying patient ends up on this charge.[6]

The jury acquitted Dr Moor, reaching a unanimous verdict in less than an hour.

In *R v Carr*,[7] the patient had been suffering unbearable pain as a result of inoperable lung cancer, and had repeatedly asked Dr Carr, to help him to die. Dr Carr gave him a massive dose of phenobarbitone, and the patient died two days later. Because natural causes could not be ruled out as the cause of death, Dr Carr was charged with attempted murder. Despite the considerable evidence against Dr Carr, and the judge's unfavourable summing-up, the jury acquitted him.

R v Cox is the only case to have resulted in a doctor's conviction for attempted murder. Dr Cox had given Mrs Boyes a dose of potassium chloride which was guaranteed to kill her, so it was difficult to avoid the conclusion that he had intended to end Mrs Boyes' life, especially since potassium chloride is not a painkiller. It is, however, worth noting that Dr Cox was not struck off the medical register by the GMC, and after a formal reprimand, he returned to practice within a year of his conviction.

R v Cox[8]

Lillian Boyes was 70 years old and terminally ill; she had rheumatoid arthritis and had developed gastric ulcers, gangrene and body sores. Her extreme pain could not be controlled by pain-killing drugs. There was evidence that she had repeatedly asked Dr Cox, a consultant rheumatologist who had been treating her for the last 13 years, and others to kill her. Dr Cox administered a lethal dose of potassium chloride, a drug which is not an analgesic, and she died almost immediately. Because her body had already been cremated, it would—in the light of her terminal condition—have been difficult to prove beyond reasonable doubt that it was the injection rather than her illness that had caused her death, Dr Cox was charged with attempted murder, and convicted. He was given a 12-month suspended prison sentence.

Ognall J

There can be no doubt that the use of drugs to reduce pain and suffering will often be fully justified notwithstanding that it will, in fact hasten the moment of death, but please understand this, ladies and gentleman, what can never be lawful is the use of drugs with the primary purpose of hastening

---

[6] C Dyer, 'British GP cleared of murder charge' (1999) 318 British Medical Journal 1306.
[7] *The Times* 30 Dec 1986. [8] (1992) 12 BMLR 38.

the moment of death. . . . [I]n the context of this case potassium chloride has no curative properties . . . it is not an analgesic. It is not used by the medical profession to relieve pain . . ., injected
into a vein it is a lethal substance. One ampoule would certainly kill . . . the injection here was
therefore twice that necessary to cause certain death.

(2) ASSISTED SUICIDE

At common law, suicide was regarded as self-murder, and was a criminal offence. In
his Commentaries, William Blackstone stated that:

The suicide is guilty of a double offence; one spiritual, in invading the prerogative of the Almighty,
and rushing into his immediate presence uncalled for; the other temporal, against the King, who
hath an interest in the preservation of all his subjects.

Obviously, it was only those who had *unsuccessfully* tried to commit suicide who
could actually be prosecuted for their attempted suicide. If the suicide had been
successful, it was the relatives of the deceased who would suffer through the confisca-
tion of property and restrictions placed upon burial rites. In 1961, suicide and
attempted suicide were decriminalized by the Suicide Act.

Suicide Act 1961
Section 1
The rule of law whereby it is a crime for a person to commit suicide is hereby abrogated.

Section 2
  (1) A person who aids, abets, counsels, or procures the suicide of another, or an attempt by
      another to commit suicide, shall be liable on conviction on indictment to imprisonment for
      a term not exceeding fourteen years. . . .

  (4) No proceedings shall be instituted for an offence under this section except by or with the
      consent of the Director of Public Prosecutions.

The decriminalization of suicide means that even if a person's intention to commit
suicide is discovered, the law cannot prevent her from ending her life. The issue arose
in *Re Z (An Adult: Capacity).*[9] Mr Z had informed the local authority that arrangements had been made for Mrs Z to go to Switzerland so that she could be helped to
die. On the question of whether the Court could interfere with Mrs Z's decision,
Hedley J explained that:

Section 1 of the Suicide Act 1961 abrogated the rule that made suicide criminal. It did not make
suicide lawful, much less did it encourage it; it simply removed suicide from being punishable as a
criminal act. It follows inevitably that our law does not penalise the decision of a competent
person to take their own life. Moreover nor does the law prohibit them from so doing. Human
freedom, if it is to have real meaning, must involve the right to take what others may see as unwise
or even bad decisions in respect of themselves; were that not so, freedom would be largely illusory.
It follows that the court has no basis in law for exercising the jurisdiction so as to prohibit Mrs Z
from taking her own life. The right and responsibility for such a decision belongs to Mrs Z alone
. . . In the circumstances here, Mrs Z's best interests are no business of mine. . . . The court is
simply not entitled to interfere whatever views it may have about the decision in question.

[9] [2004] EWHC 2817 (FAM), [2004] All ER (D) 71 (Dec).

But the fact that it is not now unlawful to commit, or attempt to commit suicide does not mean that there is a *right* to do so. The criminal offences of suicide and attempted suicide were not abolished in order to facilitate ending one's life, but rather to protect already distressed relatives from the imposition of additional hardship, and to ensure that people who had unsuccessfully attempted suicide were able to obtain medical treatment for their mental problems, without fearing prosecution.

Despite suicide's decriminalization, under section 2(1) of the Suicide Act 1961, assisting another person to commit suicide is a criminal offence punishable by up to 14 years imprisonment. While there may be sound public policy reasons for proscribing suicide pacts, it is very unusual for assisting a non-crime to itself be a criminal offence. There have been very few prosecutions under section 2(1) of the Suicide Act. Indeed in the last forty-five years, no doctors have actually been prosecuted for assisting a suicide. Nevertheless, it is clearly possible that doctors who prescribe drugs which could be used to commit suicide, or who give advice on lethal doses, may be committing a criminal offence. Similarly a friend or relative who helps someone to commit suicide could be prosecuted under the 1961 Act.

In *AG v Able*, Woolf J held that the supply of a booklet which set out several methods of committing suicide would not necessarily amount to a criminal offence, but could do so if the supplier had the necessary intent that the advice should be used to assist another identifiable person to commit suicide.

AG v Able[10]

The defendants were members of the executive committee of the Voluntary Euthanasia Society, which had published a booklet entitled *A guide to self-deliverance*. The booklet contained one section setting out seven reasons 'Why you should think again', and another which described five separate methods of suicide. The Attorney-General applied for declarations that supply of the booklet to people who might be considering or intending to commit suicide constituted an offence contrary to section 2(1) of the Suicide Act 1961. Woolf J refused to give the declarations sought, holding that whilst there might be circumstances in which supply of the booklet would amount to an offence, without proof of the necessary intent it could not be said in advance that any particular supply would be an offence.

Woolf J

I have no doubt that in the case at least of certain recipients of the booklet, its contents would encourage suicide. Ignorance as to how to commit suicide must by itself be a deterrent. Likewise, the risks inherent in an unsuccessful attempt must be a deterrent. The contents of the booklet provide information as to methods and methods which are less likely to result in an unsuccessful attempt. This assistance must encourage some readers to commit or attempt to commit suicide. This is clearly appreciated by the publishers, thus their care to control the persons to whom the booklet is to be sold and their advice as to the safe-keeping of the booklet.

I, therefore, have come clearly to the conclusion that there could be circumstances in which to supply the booklet could amount to an offence . . .

The fact that the supply of the booklet could be an offence does not mean that any particular supply is an offence . . . Before an offence under section 2 can be proved, it must be shown that the individual concerned 'aided, abetted, counselled or procured' an attempt at suicide or a suicide

[10] [1983] 3 WLR 845.

and intended to do so by distributing the booklet. The intention of the individual will normally have to be inferred from facts surrounding the particular supply which he made. If, for example, before sending a copy of the booklet, a member of the society had written a letter, the contents of which were known to the person sending the booklet, which stated that the booklet was required because the member was intending to commit suicide, then, on those facts, I would conclude that an offence had been committed of at least an attempted offence contrary to section 2 of the Act. However, in the majority of cases, a member requesting the booklet will not make clear his intentions and the supply will be made without knowledge of whether the booklet is required for purposes of research, general information, or because suicide is contemplated . . .

I therefore conclude that to distribute the booklet can be an offence. But, before an offence can be established to have been committed, it must at least be proved: (a) that the alleged offender had the necessary intent, that is, he intended the booklet to be used by someone contemplating suicide and intended that person would be assisted by the booklet's contents, or otherwise encouraged to attempt to take or to take his own life; (b) that while he still had that intention he distributed the booklet to such a person who read it; and, (c) in addition, if an offence under section 2 is to be proved, that such a person was assisted or encouraged by so reading the booklet to attempt to take or to take his own life, otherwise the alleged offender cannot be guilty of more than an attempt.

If these facts can be proved, then it does not make any difference that the person would have tried to commit suicide anyway. Nor does it make any difference, as the respondents contend, that the information contained in the booklet is already in the public domain. The distinguishing feature between an innocent and guilty distribution is that in the former case the distributor will not have the necessary intent, while in the latter case he will.

Given that a person can commit suicide themselves without committing any criminal offence, what reason would there be for choosing to implicate someone else in one's suicide attempt, and thereby exposing them to potential criminal charges? In short, there are two reasons why people might need assistance in committing suicide. First, they may be physically incapable of arranging their own suicide. Secondly, because patients lack expert knowledge, they may need advice on the combination and quantities of drugs needed to achieve a quick and painless death. Simply overdosing on readily available painkillers, for example, will often lead to a prolonged and agonizing death.

In 2002 the impact of the Human Rights Act 1998 upon the proscription of assisted suicide came before the courts in the Dianne Pretty case. While the House of Lords and the European Court of Human Rights agreed that legalized assisted suicide would be compatible with the Human Rights Act, this did not amount to a right to assistance in committing suicide. Although both courts rejected Mrs Pretty's case, there is a slight difference between the judgments in the House of Lords and that of the ECHR. The Lords found that there had been no prima facie violations of any of Mrs Pretty's convention rights, whereas the ECHR was prepared to admit that Article 8 was engaged, but that a complete prohibition of assisted suicide was not a disproportionate response to the state's concern to protect vulnerable members of society.

R (on the application of Pretty) v Director of Public Prosecutions[11]

The claimant, Dianne Pretty, suffered from motor neurone disease, a progressive and degenerative terminal illness, and faced the imminent prospect of a distressing and humiliating death. She was

---

[11] [2002] 1 AC 800 HL.

mentally alert and wanted to control the time and manner of her dying but her physical disabilities prevented her from taking her life unaided. Her husband was willing to help her provided that he would not be prosecuted under section 2(1) of the Suicide Act 1961. The claimant accordingly requested the Director of Public Prosecutions to undertake that he would not consent to Mr Pretty's prosecution. The claimant sought judicial review of his refusal to give such an undertaking on the grounds that it violated her rights under the European Convention for the Protection of Human Rights and Fundamental Freedoms, as incorporated in the Human Rights Act 1998. In particular she claimed that Article 2 protected a right to self-determination, entitling her to commit suicide with assistance; that failure to alleviate her suffering by refusal of the undertaking amounted to inhuman and degrading treatment proscribed by Article 3; that her rights to privacy and freedom of conscience under Articles 8 and 9 were infringed without justification; and that she had suffered discrimination in breach of Article 14, since an able-bodied person might exercise the right to suicide whereas her incapacities prevented her doing so without assistance. She further claimed that section 2 of the 1961 Act was incompatible with the Convention. The House of Lords dismissed her appeal.

Lord Steyn

For [Mrs Pretty] to succeed it is not enough to show that the European Convention allows member states to legalise assisted suicide. She must establish that at least that part of section 2(1) of the 1961 Act which makes aiding or abetting suicide a crime is in conflict with her Convention rights. In other words, she must persuade the House that the European Convention compels member states of the Council of Europe to legalise assisted suicide . . .

The fact is that among the 41 member states—North, South, East and West—there are deep cultural and religious differences in regard to euthanasia and assisted suicide. The legalisation of euthanasia and assisted suicide as adopted in the Netherlands would be unacceptable to predominantly Roman Catholic countries in Europe. The idea that the European Convention *requires* states to render lawful euthanasia and assisted suicide (as opposed to allowing democratically elected legislatures to adopt measures to that effect) must therefore be approached with scepticism . . . [T]he fact is that an interpretation *requiring* states to legalise euthanasia and assisted suicide would not only be enormously controversial but profoundly unacceptable to the peoples of many member states.

If section 2 of the 1961 Act is held to be incompatible with the European Convention, a right to commit assisted suicide would not be doctor assisted and would not be subject to safeguards introduced in the Netherlands . . . In our parliamentary democracy, and I apprehend in many member states of the Council of Europe, such a fundamental change cannot be brought about by judicial creativity. If it is to be considered at all, it requires a detailed and effective regulatory proposal. In these circumstances it is difficult to see how a process of interpretation of Convention rights can yield a result with all the necessary inbuilt protections. Essentially, it must be a matter for democratic debate and decision making by legislatures . . .

The Director of Public Prosecutions may not under section 2(4) exercise his discretion to stop all prosecutions under section 2(1). It follows that he may only exercise his discretion, for or against a prosecution, in relation to the circumstances of a specific prosecution. His discretion can therefore only be exercised in respect of past events giving rise to a suspicion that a crime under section 2(1) has been committed. And then the exercise of this discretion will take into account whether there is a realistic prospect of securing a conviction and whether a prosecution would be in the public interest . . .

The logic of the European Convention does not justify the conclusion that the House must rule that a state is obliged to legalise assisted suicide. It does not require the state to repeal a provision such as section 2(1) of the 1961 Act. On the other hand, it is open to a democratic legislature to introduce such a measure. Our Parliament, if so minded, may therefore repeal section 2(1) and put in its place a regulated system for assisted suicide (presumably doctor assisted) with appropriate safeguards.

Lord Hope

Mrs Pretty is burdened with a misfortune which has attracted widespread sympathy . . . I believe that the decision which she has taken in such extreme circumstances ought not to be criticised.

(a) Article 2

The short point here is whether the Director's refusal to give the undertaking is incompatible with the first sentence of this Article. It provides that everyone's right to life 'shall be protected by law' . . . It does not say that every person has the right to choose how or when to die. Nor does it say that the individual has a right to choose death rather than life . . . The Director's refusal to give the undertaking has not disturbed or interfered with Mrs Pretty's right to life. Nothing that he has done in response to her request is contrary to any law which is designed to safeguard life. On the contrary, his act in declining to give the undertaking to enable Mr Pretty to assist in his wife's suicide is compatible with the opening words of the second sentence of the Article. It provides that no one shall be deprived of his life intentionally . . . [F]or a third person to take active steps deliberately to deprive another of life, even with the consent of the person thus deprived, is forbidden by the Article. The Article is all about protecting life, not bringing it to an end. It is not possible to read it as obliging the state to allow someone to assist another person to commit suicide.

(b) Article 3

The argument with regard to this Article is that Mrs Pretty will inevitably suffer inhuman or degrading treatment if the disease is allowed to run its course . . . It is clear that [The Director] is not directly responsible for the disease or for its consequences. Nothing has been identified that he has done and should be restrained from doing in order to remove or alleviate these consequences.

(c) Articles 8 and 9

I take these two Articles together, as they are both invoked in support of the same argument. This is that they confer a right to self determination through the right to private life . . . The object of these Articles is to protect the individual against arbitrary interference by the public authorities . . .

The way [Mrs Pretty] chooses to pass the closing moments of her life is part of the act of living, and she has a right to ask that this too must be respected. In that respect Mrs Pretty has a right of self-determination. In that sense, her private life is engaged even where in the face of a terminal illness she seeks to choose death rather than life. But it is an entirely different thing to imply into these words a positive obligation to give effect to her wish to end her own life by means of an assisted suicide. I think that to do so would be to stretch the meaning of the words too far . . .

In any event . . . I would hold that the Director's refusal to give the undertaking was not disproportionate to the object of section 2(1), which is to avoid abuse and to protect the weak and the vulnerable.

(d) Article 14

This Article prohibits discrimination in the enjoyment of the rights and freedoms set forth in the Convention . . . The difficulty which [Mrs Pretty] faces is that, for the reasons already stated, her case does not engage any of the other Articles on which she relies. . . .

Section 1 of the Suicide Act 1961 did not create a right to commit suicide. All it did was to abrogate the rule of law which had previously made it a crime to commit suicide. The fact that it provided in section 2(1) that a person who aids or abets another to commit suicide points clearly to the conclusion that decriminalisation, not the creation of a right, was what was intended. There were good reasons for wishing to decriminalise the act itself. The removal of the fear of prosecution and of the stigma was likely to make it easier to deter those who were planning or attempting suicide. Broadly speaking, it was a measure in favour of saving life, with which the provisions of section 2 are entirely in sympathy.

Mrs Pretty then appealed to the European Court of Human Rights. Her claim was rejected on the 29 April 2002 and she died 12 days later.

Pretty v UK[12]
Judgment of the ECHR
The Court is not persuaded that 'the right to life' guaranteed in Article 2 can be interpreted as involving a negative aspect . . . Article 2 of the Convention . . . is unconcerned with issues to do with the quality of living or what a person chooses to do with his or her life . . . Article 2 cannot, without a distortion of language, be interpreted as conferring the diametrically opposite right, namely a right to die; nor can it create a right to self-determination in the sense of conferring on an individual the entitlement to choose death rather than life.

Article 3 . . . may be described in general terms as imposing a primarily negative obligation on States to refrain from inflicting serious harm on persons within their jurisdiction . . . A positive obligation on the State to provide protection against inhuman or degrading treatment has been found to arise in a number of cases . . . The suffering which flows from naturally occurring illness, physical or mental, may be covered by Article 3, where it is, or risks being, exacerbated by treatment . . . for which the authorities can be held responsible. In the present case, it is beyond dispute that the respondent Government has not, itself, inflicted any ill-treatment on the applicant. Nor is there any complaint that the applicant is not receiving adequate care from the State medical authorities . . . There is no . . . act or 'treatment' on the part of the United Kingdom in the present case.

The Court would observe that the ability to conduct one's life in a manner of one's own choosing may also include the opportunity to pursue activities perceived to be of a physically or morally harmful or dangerous nature for the individual concerned . . . The very essence of the Convention is respect for human dignity and freedom. Without in any way negating the principle of sanctity of life protected under the Convention, the Court considers that it is under Article 8 that notions of the quality of life take on significance. In an era of growing medical sophistication combined with longer life expectancies, many people are concerned that they should not be forced to linger on in old age or in states of advanced physical or mental decrepitude which conflict with strongly held ideas of self and personal identity . . .

The applicant in this case is prevented by law from exercising her choice to avoid what she considers will be an undignified and distressing end to her life. The Court is not prepared to exclude that this constitutes an interference with her right to respect for private life as guaranteed under Article 8(1) of the Convention.

The law in issue in this case, section 2 of the 1961 Act, was designed to safeguard life by protecting the weak and vulnerable and especially those who are not in a condition to take informed decisions against acts intended to end life or to assist in ending life. Doubtless the

---

[12] (2002) 35 EHRR 1.

condition of terminally ill individuals will vary. But many will be vulnerable and it is the vulnerability of the class which provides the rationale for the law in question. It is primarily for States to assess the risk and the likely incidence of abuse if the general prohibition on assisted suicides were relaxed or if exceptions were to be created. Clear risks of abuse do exist, notwithstanding arguments as to the possibility of safeguards and protective procedures.

The Court does not consider therefore that the blanket nature of the ban on assisted suicide is disproportionate. The Government has stated that flexibility is provided for in individual cases by the fact that consent is needed from the DPP to bring a prosecution and by the fact that a maximum sentence is provided, allowing lesser penalties to be imposed as appropriate ... It does not appear to be arbitrary to the Court for the law to reflect the importance of the right to life, by prohibiting assisted suicide while providing for a system of enforcement and adjudication which allows due regard to be given in each particular case to the public interest in bringing a prosecution, as well as to the fair and proper requirements of retribution and deterrence.

The Court does not doubt the firmness of the applicant's views concerning assisted suicide but would observe that not all opinions or convictions constitute beliefs in the sense protected by Article 9(1) of the Convention. Her claims do not involve a form of manifestation of a religion or belief, through worship, teaching, practice or observance ... To the extent that the applicant's views reflect her commitment to the principle of personal autonomy, her claim is a restatement of the complaint raised under Article 8 of the Convention.

In addition to the possibility of discretion in sentencing, notice that under section 2(4) of the Suicide Act the Director of Public Prosecutions (DPP) is specifically charged with exercising discretion over whether or not to proceed with a prosecution. This is because, as Hedley J explained in *Re Z (An Adult: Capacity)*,[13] it will not always be in the public interest to prosecute someone who has contravened section 2(1):

it seems to me inevitable that by making arrangements and escorting Mrs Z on the flight, Mr Z will have contravened Section 2(1) above. It follows that in order for Mrs Z actually to be able to carry out her decision, it will require the criminal conduct of another. That said I remind myself of sub-section (4). Although not unique, the provision is rare and is usually found where Parliament recognises that although an act may be criminal, it is not always in the public interest to prosecute in respect of it.

In the *Pretty* case, the DPP took the view that he could only exercise the discretion under section 2(4) once he had all the facts before him, after a police investigation. Similarly, in evidence to the House of Lords Select Committee on Assisted Dying, the Attorney General has argued that to exercise this discretion *before* any suicide takes place would, in effect, amount to the DPP suspending part of the criminal law.[14]

On the other hand, in the context of the Dianne Pretty case, Richard Tur persuasively argues that section 2(4)—which only allows the Attorney General to exercise his prosecutorial discretion *after* the assisted suicide has taken place—violates citizens' right to know in advance if a particular course of conduct will attract criminal sanctions.

---

[13] [2004] EWHC 2817 (FAM), [2004] All ER (D) 71 (Dec).
[14] Assisted Dying for the Terminally Ill Committee, *Assisted Dying for the Terminally Ill Bill—First Report* (2005), 16.

Richard HS Tur[15]

Subsection 2(4) is wholly unnecessary if it is merely to prevent prosecutions for assisted suicide which are not in the public interest or where there is insufficient evidence simply because these cases already fall within general prosecutorial discretion without any need to enact or invoke the specific terms of subsection 2(4).

A more plausible purpose for subsection 2(4) is to limit the scope of subsection 2(1). An important part of the argument is that even the most carefully drafted rules fail to achieve perfect fit. A rule may include some cases which morally should be excluded and it may exclude cases which morally should be included . . . But arguably subsection 2(4) is a legislative attempt so to qualify subsection 2(1) as to avoid injustice without too seriously compromising sanctity of life. If there are any cases at all in which the Director would withhold consent, then the Pretty case would have been a formidable candidate for inclusion, and there must be some such cases or subsection 2(4) is nugatory . . .

But if the Director ever has good reasons for dispensation after the event, these would be equally good reasons for dispensation before the event in all sufficiently like cases . . .

Those responsible for the Suicide Act were fully aware of the imperfectibility of rules. Any rule drafted would be too wide or too narrow. Because of the risks to the vulnerable they opted for a very wide, blanket rule outlawing assisted suicide, conscious of the risk that so wide a rule might well expose morally undeserving individuals to prosecution. . . . [Th]ose responsible for the Suicide Act tried to ameliorate the potential injustice of a widely stated blanket rule criminalizing assisted suicide in a statute decriminalizing suicide itself by empowering the Director to prevent prosecution by withholding consent. This allocates to the Director the unenviable function of making the legal rule fit moral sensitivities at its margins. Though challenging, this seems preferable to the gross injustice and manifest absurdity of unqualified literalism, or the lottery of inscrutable post hoc dispensation.

Our imaginary couple are saying that they choose morally compelling assisted suicide but will implement their choice only if it is non-criminal . . . It is no answer to them to say that they must implement their choice in order to find out and indeed there is a peculiar cruelty or inhumanity in the law saying to them that because they respect the law so much they must endure their sad plight. It thus appears that those most respectful of the law are subjected to the greater distress which is counter intuitive. So the Pretty question . . .—whether the right to life includes a right to die—was entirely the wrong question and it obscured the fact that section 2 as drafted, interpreted, and applied is vulnerable to an argument that there is a right to know in advance what consequences the criminal law attributes to one's conduct . . .

There is something fundamentally wrong in saying to someone like Dianne Pretty, 'Well you have had a miserable time and morally we quite see that you should be allowed the assistance you seek in ending your own life, but you know, the greater good of society requires that you should continue to suffer for fear of being a bad example—hard cases make bad law'. Morally, society simply should not use someone like Dianne Pretty as a means only and not as an end in herself . . .

Indeed the core underlying notion of human rights is that individuals will not be sacrificed to the social good, at least without overwhelming or compelling justification. It is very disappointing that Dianne Pretty was forced by the Courts to pay the price of protecting those who are truly vulnerable.

---

[15] 'Legislative Technique and Human Rights: The Sad Case of Assisted Suicide' (2003) Criminal Law Review 3–12.

(3) PALLIATIVE CARE THAT MAY HASTEN DEATH: THE DOCTRINE OF DOUBLE EFFECT

Recall that in his summing up to the jury in *R v Cox*, Ognall J said that there 'can be no doubt' that doctors are entitled to administer painkilling drugs, notwithstanding the fact that they may simultaneously hasten the moment of death. And, as we can see from the following extracts, this does appear to be an accepted and well-established principle of law. Notice also that these judges refer to painkilling drugs which may 'hasten death' or 'shorten life', rather than admitting that the drugs may *kill* the patient.

R v Adams[16] Devlin J

If the first purpose of medicine, the restoration of health, can no longer be achieved, there is still much for a doctor to do, and he is entitled to do all that is proper and necessary to relieve pain and suffering, even if the measures he takes may incidentally shorten life.

In Re J (Wardship: Medical Treatment)[17] Lord Donaldson

[T]he use of drugs to reduce pain will often be fully justified, notwithstanding that this will hasten the moment of death.

Airedale NHS Trust v Bland[18] Lord Goff

. . . the established rule that a doctor may, when caring for a patient who is, for example, dying of cancer, lawfully administer painkilling drugs despite the fact that he knows that an incidental effect of that application will be to abbreviate the patient's life. Such a decision may properly be made as part of the care of the living patient, in his best interests; and, on this basis, the treatment will be lawful. Moreover, where the doctor's treatment of his patient is lawful, the patient's death will be regarded in law as exclusively caused by the injury or disease to which his condition is attributable.

This principle is often referred to as the doctrine of double effect, which has its origins in Roman Catholic moral theology, and distinguishes between results which are intended, and results which are merely foreseen as likely, but unintended, consequences of one's actions. As a person's disease progresses, they may need steadily increasing doses of painkillers, such as diamorphine, in order to adequately alleviate their pain. When given in sufficient quantities, such drugs may cause respiratory depression and lead to the patient's death. According to the doctrine of double effect, a doctor who intends a good consequence (relieving pain) is not guilty of murder just because he foresees, but does not intend, a bad consequence (death). But while the doctrine of double effect may make sense when a procedure, such as surgery, carries a small risk to the patient's life which is nevertheless worth taking in order to attempt to improve the patient's condition, in the context of palliative care, it has been used to excuse conduct where death is inevitable.

Despite its widespread acceptance, it is possible that the doctrine of double effect may be at odds with the ordinary principles of criminal law. To be guilty of murder, the patient's death does not have to be the *sole* purpose of the defendant's action. Instead, as we can see from the following extract from Lord Steyn's judgment in the

---

[16] Unreported, 8 Apr 1957.   [17] [1991] 2 WLR 140.   [18] [1993] AC 789.

House of Lords in *R v Woollin*,[19] the criminal law is clear that the jury may infer that a person has the requisite *mens rea* for murder if they engage in conduct which is virtually certain to cause death, even if this is not their primary purpose.

Lord Steyn

Where the charge is murder and in the rare cases where the simple direction is not enough, the jury should be directed that they are not entitled to infer the necessary intention, unless they feel sure that death or serious bodily harm was a virtual certainty (barring some unforeseen intervention) as a result of the defendant's actions and that the defendant appreciated that such was the case ... Where a man realises that it is for all practical purposes inevitable that his actions will result in death or serious harm, the inference may be irresistible that he intended that result, however little he may have desired or wished it to happen.

In the next extracts, Glanville Williams and Margaret Otlowski draw attention to this apparent discrepancy between the ordinary meaning of intention in the criminal law and the doctrine of double effect:

Glanville Williams[20]

There is no legal difference between desiring or intending a consequence as following from your conduct, and persisting in your conduct with a knowledge that the consequence will inevitably follow from it, though not desiring that consequence. When a result is foreseen as certain, it is the same as if it were desired or intended.

Margaret Otlowski[21]

It is well established that motive or desire is not normally relevant to preclude the imposition of criminal liability for conduct which causes death in circumstances where those consequences were intended or at least foreseen. Given the significance of this departure from criminal law principles, it is, perhaps, surprising that there has not been a clearer statement of the basis of the exception.

Indeed John Keown argues that the House of Lords' judgment in *Woollin* in fact casts doubt upon the legality of much conventional palliative care:

John Keown[22]

Unfortunately, a ... recent case may cast doubt on the lawfulness of palliative care which doctors foresee will shorten life ... In [*Woollin*], the Law Lords appeared to rule that a consequence foreseen as virtually certain is intended. The implications of this for doctors who foresee that their palliative care will shorten life are disturbing: are such doctors now *prima facie* liable for murder? ...

Woollin is a retrograde step. First, it suggests that doctors engaged in proper palliative care ... intend to kill—a gross misrepresentation of their state of mind ... Secondly, *Woollin* raises wholly unnecessary doubts about the lawfulness of proper palliative care. It is hardly an answer to say that the courts would hopefully provide doctors with a defence such as necessity: doctors providing proper palliative care are, as all agree, doing nothing wrong in the first place; are entitled to work free from the fear of prosecution, and should not have to rely for acquittal on the chance of the judicial application of an ancient, vague and uncertain defence. Thirdly, because of

---

[19] [1999] 1 AC 82 HL.   [20] *Sanctity of Life and the Criminal Law* (Faber London 1957) 286.
[21] *Voluntary Euthanasia and the Common Law* (OUP Oxford 2000) 176.
[22] *Euthanasia, Ethics and Public Policy: An Argument against Legalisation* (CUP Cambridge 2002) 28–9.

the doubts it creates, *Woollin* may have a chilling effect on the provision of much-needed palliative care and leave patients dying in pain and distress. A ruling that hinders good medicine is clearly bad law . . .

The Law Lords appear to have sleepwalked into conflating intention and foresight of virtual certainty, with potentially dire results for palliative care. *Woollin* should be overruled as a matter of urgency.

However it is worth noting that Lord Steyn in *Woollin* does not go so far as to say that where death is inevitable, the inference *must* be irresistible that he intended that result, rather he merely suggests that in such cases the inference *may* be irresistible. Plainly although Lord Steyn envisages circumstances in which intention may be inferred from the inevitability of death, he also implies there will be times when this may not be the case, and an example might plausibly be the provision of palliative care.

Nevertheless, regardless of the precise meaning of intention within the criminal law, when a doctor foresees that the dose of analgesics that she is about to give to a particular patient is likely to cause their death, she must have reached the conclusion that death is an acceptable outcome. If a doctor were to give a healthy patient with a mild headache a life-threatening injection of diamorphine, her conduct would not be excused by the doctrine of double effect. She could not claim that her intention was merely to relieve pain, and that the patient's death was a foreseen but unintended side-effect. Instead, while death may not be the *principal* purpose of a doctor who administers a potentially lethal dose of painkillers, she must have decided that the patient's interest in pain relief now outweighs her interest in continued life. In the next extract, Glanville Williams suggests that it is artificial for doctors to think only about one consequence of their action (relieving pain), while ignoring another (causing death).

Glanville Williams[23]

It is altogether too artificial to say that a doctor who gives an overdose of a narcotic having in the forefront of his mind the aim of ending his patient's existence is guilty of sin, while a doctor who gives the same overdose in the same circumstances in order to relieve pain is not guilty of sin, provided that he keeps his mind steadily off the consequence which his professional training teaches him is inevitable, namely the death of his patient. When you know that your conduct will have two consequences, one in itself good and one in itself evil, you are compelled as a moral agent to choose between acting and not acting by making a judgement of value, that is to say by deciding whether the good is more to be desired than the evil is to be avoided.

Stephen Wilkinson points out a further difficulty with the doctrine of double effect, namely that it relies upon knowledge of the doctor's primary intention.

Stephen Wilkinson[24]

But *how do we know* what is intended and what is not? This question can arise from two different perspectives. First, from the 'first person' perspective, if a doctor administers diamorphine to

---

[23] *Sanctity of Life and the Criminal Law* (Faber London 1957) 286.
[24] 'Palliative care and the doctrine of double effect', in Donna Dickenson, Malcolm Johnson, and Jeanne Samson Katz (eds), *Death, Dying and Bereavement* (2nd edn Sage London 2000) 299–302.

relieve pain, but at the same time would be glad if the patient's death was hastened . . ., she may not be sure herself which effects she intends and which she doesn't. Second, from the 'third person' perspective, how are other professionals, relatives and the public to know what was going on 'in the doctor's head' when she administered the drug? How are they to know what she intends. This problem may render the doctrine unworkable in practice. Furthermore, it also opens up the possibility of health carers abusing the doctrine and using it as a way of 'smuggling in euthanasia by the back door'. In other words, the acceptance of the doctrine might make it possible to kill patients intentionally while *pretending* that their death is an unintended side-effect.

In contrast, Alexander McCall Smith argues that we should be reluctant to deny doctors the moral 'comfort' they may obtain from framing their actions in terms of helping, rather than killing.

Alexander McCall Smith[25]

Doctors know full well what they are doing when they increase a dose of diamorphine, but they need not describe their act, to themselves or to others as an act of killing. This approach has been described as hypocritical, but if it accords with a moral distinction which is meaningful for doctors, then why should they be denied the comfort it affords them? The moral life is possibly more subtly nuanced than some of the proponents of euthanasia would have us believe. We live by moral metaphor, and the metaphor of helping rather than killing, may be a valuable one to those whose duty it is to look after the terminally ill.

Provided that the drugs which caused a patient's death could plausibly be used as painkillers or sedatives, it would in practice be difficult to disprove a doctor's assertion that her principal aim was the relief of suffering. Hence, in *R v Adam*[26] it was possible for the defence counsel to argue that Dr Adams had intended to relieve Mrs Morrell's pain by administering massive doses of morphine and heroin (both of which are commonly employed as analgesics). Many years after Dr Adams's trial for murder, Patrick Devlin, the judge in the case, wrote a book about the issues it had raised. In *Easing the Passing*, he explained how fine the line will sometimes be between lawful palliative care and murder:

If he really had an honest belief in easing suffering, Dr. Adams was on the right side of the law; if his purpose was simply to finish life, he was not . . . A narrow distinction. But in the law, as in all matters of principle, cases can be so close to each other that the gap can only be perceived theoretically.[27]

In contrast, in *R v Cox*, Dr Cox's use of potassium chloride (which has no analgesic properties) effectively ruled out the application of the doctrine of double effect. If Dr Cox had used morphine rather than potassium chloride to kill Lillian Boyes, his assertion that his primary intention was to relieve her suffering would have been considerably harder to refute.

In addition to the administration of large, and potentially fatal, doses of analgesic drugs, palliative care may also involve what is sometimes described as terminal sedation. If someone is unable to breathe or swallow, they may experience intolerable

---

[25] 'Euthanasia: The Strengths of the Middle Ground' (1999) 7 Medical Law Review 194–207, 206–7.
[26] Unreported, 8 Apr 1957.
[27] *Easing the Passing: The Trial of Dr John Bodkin Adams* (Bodley Head London 1985) 209.

distress that cannot be relieved by large doses of conventional painkilling drugs. In such cases, sedative drugs may be given in combination with analgesics in sufficient quantities that the patient is rendered unconscious. Once the patient is dependent upon artificial nutrition and hydration, as we see later, it can be removed, leading inevitably to the patient's death. Provided the principal purpose of giving the sedatives and painkillers is to relieve pain and suffering, despite the doctor's knowledge that the patient will become permanently unconscious and die shortly afterwards, according to the doctrine of double effect, this may be lawful palliative care. From the patient's perspective, however, as Margaret Pabst Battin explains, terminal sedation will be indistinguishable from being given a lethal injection.

Margaret Pabst Battin[28]

It is flatly incorrect to say that all pain, including pain in terminal illness, is or can be controlled. Some people still die in unspeakable agony. With superlative care, many kinds of pain can indeed be reduced in many patients, and adequate control of pain in terminal illness is often quite easy to achieve. Nevertheless, complete, universal, fully reliable pain control is a myth. Pain is not yet a 'thing of the past', nor are many associated kinds of physical distress. Some kinds of conditions, such as difficulty in swallowing, are still difficult to relieve without introducing other discomforting limitations. . . . Severe respiratory insufficiency may mean . . . 'a singularly terrifying and agonizing final few hours'.

[O]f course, the patient can be sedated into unconsciousness; this does indeed end the pain. But in respect of the patient's experience, this is tantamount to causing death: the patient has no further conscious experience and thus can achieve no goods, experience no significant communication, satisfy no goals. Furthermore, adequate sedation, by depressing respiratory function, may hasten death. Thus, although it is always technically possible to achieve relief from pain, at least when the appropriate resources are available, the price may be functionally and practically equivalent, at least from the patient's point of view, to death.

(4) REFUSAL OF TREATMENT

(a) Contemporaneous refusal

As we saw in Chapter 4, competent adult patients have the right to refuse medical treatment, even if their refusal will lead to their death. Although the right is not absolute, there are very few exceptions.[29] For the purposes of this chapter, and as the following quotes from the *Bland* case make clear, the important point is that doctors *must* comply with a competent adult's refusal of life-sustaining medical treatment.

Airedale NHS Trust v Bland[30]
Lord Goff

[I]t is established that the principle of self-determination requires that respect must be given to the wishes of the patient, so that if an adult patient of sound mind refuses, however unreasonably, to consent to treatment or care by which his life would or might be prolonged, the doctors responsible for his care must give effect to his wishes, even though they do not consider it to be in his best interests to do so . . . To this extent, the principle of the sanctity of human life must yield to

---

[28] *The Least Worst Death: Essays in Bioethics on the End of Life* (OUP Oxford 1994).
[29] An example would be s 63 of the Mental Health Act 1983, see further Chapter 7.
[30] [1993] AC 789.

the principle of self- determination . . . On this basis, it has been held that a patient of sound mind may, if properly informed, require that life support should be discontinued.

Lord Mustill

If the patient is capable of making a decision on whether to permit treatment and decides not to permit it his choice must be obeyed, even if on any objective view it is contrary to his best interests. A doctor has no right to proceed in the face of objection, even if it is plain to all, including the patient, that adverse consequences and even death will or may ensue.

Similarly, the British Medical Association's guidance to doctors explains that where a patient is competent, their right to refuse life-sustaining medical treatment must take priority over the doctors' duty to preserve life.

British Medical Association[31]

It is well established in law and ethics that competent adults have the right to refuse any medical treatment, even if that refusal results in their death . . . The patient is not obliged to justify his or her decision but the health team will usually wish to discuss the refusal with the patient in order to ensure that he or she has based that decision on accurate information and to correct any misunderstandings. Where the health team considers that the treatment would provide a net benefit, that assessment should be sympathetically explained to the patient but patients should not be pressured to accept treatment.

The fact that an individual has made a decision which appears to others to be irrational or unjustified should not be taken as evidence that the individual lacks the mental capacity to make that decision. If, however, the decision is clearly contrary to previously expressed wishes or it is based on a misperception of reality such as, for example, believing that the blood is poisoned because it is red, this may be indicative of a lack of the requisite capacity and further investigation will be required.

Patients refusing medical treatment should ideally base their decisions on sufficient accurate information including an awareness of the condition, the proposed treatment, any significant risks or side effects, the probability of a successful recovery, the consequences of not having the treatment and any alternative forms of treatment. Such information should always be offered but, legally, patients are not required to have accepted the offer of information in order for their refusal to be valid. It is important that the patient is given the opportunity to discuss the information if he or she wishes to do so.

One of the clearest illustrations of the robustness of the law's protection of a competent patient's right to insist on the withdrawal of life-prolonging medical treatment is the *Ms B* case. The doctors involved in Ms B's care did not want to comply with her request that she be disconnected from the ventilator that was keeping her alive, but following her finding that Ms B was competent, Dame Elizabeth Butler-Sloss's conclusion that Ms B had to have her refusal of treatment respected, and that in ignoring that refusal the Hospital had been treating her unlawfully, was inevitable. Interestingly, however, the clinicians who had been caring for Ms B were not forced to participate in bringing about her death, and Ms B was transferred to another hospital where she was removed from the artificial ventilator and died.

---

[31] *Withholding and withdrawing life-prolonging medical treatment: guidance for decision making* (2nd edn 2001) paras 9.1–9.3.

Re B (Adult: Refusal of Treatment)[32]

Ms B was tetraplegic, suffering complete paralysis from the neck down . . . She had begun to experience respiratory problems, and was connected to a ventilator. She had repeatedly requested that she be removed from the ventilator, but the clinicians treating her were not prepared to comply with her request. Ms B sought a declaration that she had mental capacity and that, as a result, the Hospital had been treating her unlawfully.

Dame Elizabeth Butler-Sloss P

The general law on mental capacity is, in my judgment, clear and easily to be understood by lawyers. Its application to individual cases in the context of a general practitioner's surgery, a hospital ward and especially in an intensive care unit is infinitely more difficult to achieve . . .

I start with the presumption that Ms B has mental capacity . . . [T]he judicial approach to mental capacity must be largely dependent upon the assessments of the medical profession whose task it is on a regular basis to assess the competence of the patient to consent or refuse the medical/surgical treatment recommended to the patient. If, as in the present case, two experienced and distinguished consultant psychiatrists give evidence that Ms B has the mental capacity to make decisions, even grave decisions about her future medical treatment, that is cogent evidence upon which I can and should rely . . .

It is important to note from the outset, the importance of avoiding generalisations about the possibilities for patients in Ms B's position for capacity to be diminished by one or a number of temporary factors. Rather, the court's task in the instant case is to determine whether in fact Ms B's capacity is affected by any of the factors identified by the Trust . . .

One must allow for those as severely disabled as Ms B, for some of whom life in that condition may be worse than death. It is a question of values and . . . we have to try inadequately to put ourselves into the position of the gravely disabled person and respect the subjective character of experience. Unless the gravity of the illness has affected the patient's capacity, a seriously disabled patient has the same rights as the fit person to respect for personal autonomy. There is a serious danger, exemplified in this case, of a benevolent paternalism which does not embrace recognition of the personal autonomy of the severely disabled patient. I do not consider that either the lack of experience in a spinal rehabilitation unit and thereafter in the community or the unusual situation of being in an ICU for a year has had the effect of eroding Ms B's mental capacity to any degree whatsoever.

I am therefore entirely satisfied that Ms B is competent to make all relevant decisions about her medical treatment including the decision whether to seek to withdraw from artificial ventilation. Her mental competence is commensurate with the gravity of the decision she may wish to make. . . . I would like to add how impressed I am with her as a person, with the great courage, strength of will and determination she has shown in the last year, with her sense of humour, and her understanding of the dilemma she has posed to the Hospital. She is clearly a splendid person and it is tragic that someone of her ability has been struck down so cruelly. I hope she will forgive me for saying, diffidently, that if she did reconsider her decision, she would have a lot to offer the community at large.

In the light of my decision that the Claimant has mental capacity and has had such capacity since August 2001 I shall be prepared to grant the appropriate declarations. I also find that the Claimant has been treated unlawfully by the Trust since August.

---

[32] [2002] 2 All ER 449.

Importantly, the competent patient's reason for refusing treatment is irrelevant. As Lord Donaldson MR said in *Re T (Adult: Refusal of Treatment)*,[33]

the patient's right of choice exists whether the reasons for making that choice are rational, irrational, unknown or even non-existent.

So even if a patient refuses medical treatment *because* they want to die, the doctor is still bound to comply with her wishes. But could a doctor who, for example, removes a feeding tube from a patient whose intention is to end her life, and provides her with assurances that she can be kept comfortable while she dies from lack of nutrition, be said to be assisting her suicide? It seems not. As Lord Goff explained in *Airedale NHS Trust v Bland*:[34]

In cases of this kind [a refusal of treatment], there is no question of the patient having committed suicide nor therefore of the doctor having aided or abetted him in doing so. It is simply that the patient has, as he is entitled to, declined to consent to treatment which might or would have the effect of prolonging his life, and the doctor has, in accordance with his duty, complied with the patient's wishes.

But why is there 'no question' of a patient whose intention is to take their own life, and who happens to be connected to a life-support system, committing suicide by refusing treatment? One possible explanation is that a patient who seeks to end her life through a refusal of life-sustaining treatment is not acting positively to bring about her death. Her 'suicide' is achieved by her failure to consent to treatment. Is it possible to commit suicide by omission? The House of Lords Select Committee on Assisted Dying suggests not:

Nor does the refusal of life-prolonging treatment by a patient constitute suicide, which in law requires a 'positive act'; and a prisoner who refuses food does not in law 'commit' suicide. By the same logic someone who does not take steps to force a person to eat or a patient to receive treatment is not regarded as aiding and abetting suicide.[35]

A different explanation for distinguishing between suicide and the refusal or life-sustaining treatment is offered by Margaret Otlowski, who suggests that social disapproval of suicide leads us 'to tailor our definition of suicide so as to exclude behaviour which is regarded as acceptable'.[36]

Margaret Otlowski[37]
It is difficult to deny that where a patient dies following the refusal of nutrition or hydration the patient's death is self-induced . . . [W]e need to recognize that refusal of treatment may amount to suicide, but must tailor our response to this particular form of suicide so as to take into account the special considerations applying in the medical context . . .

The most satisfactory way in which the legal principles regarding liability for assisted suicide and the refusal of treatment can be reconciled is for the courts to take a broad view of the patient's right to refuse treatment so that the withholding or withdrawal of treatment performed

---

[33] [1993] Fam 95.   [34] [1993] AC 789.
[35] Assisted Dying for the Terminally Ill Committee, *Assisted Dying for the Terminally Ill Bill—First Report* (2005), para 15.
[36] *Voluntary Euthanasia and the Common Law* (OUP Oxford 2000) 69.   [37] Ibid, 71, 75, 81.

in recognition of that right is exempt from criminal liability even though the legal requirements for establishing liability for assisted suicide against the doctor may be present.

If a doctor withdraws life-sustaining treatment knowing that this will lead to their patient's death, might they additionally satisfy both the *actus reus* and the *mens rea* of murder? If the withdrawal of medical treatment is an act done with the knowledge that it will cause the patient's death, then the patient's consent to the doctor's action is irrelevant and the doctor may be guilty of murder. In order to avoid this conclusion, the withdrawal of medical treatment is commonly described as an omission rather than an action.

It is, nevertheless, still possible to commit murder by omission. An omission will only constitute the *actus reus* of murder if the defendant was under a duty to act: an obvious example being a parent whose failure to feed their child leads to her death. Doctors *are*, of course, under a duty to care for their patients, so in theory, if a doctor's failure to provide medical treatment to their patient results in her death, a charge of murder is possible. And if the charge is murder, the patient's consent to the doctor's conduct is irrelevant. Does this mean that doctors who respect their patients' refusals of life-sustaining treatment are potentially subject to prosecution for murder?

Almost certainly not. Because the patient's right to refuse unwanted intervention suspends the doctor's duty to provide medical treatment, the doctor's omission can no longer constitute the *actus reus* of murder. So a doctor who maliciously unplugs a ventilator from a patient who is temporarily unconscious, but expected to make a full recovery, may be guilty of murder because she had a duty to provide life-prolonging treatment. Whereas a doctor who respects a competent patient's refusal of further life-sustaining treatment no longer has a duty to provide that treatment—on the contrary, her duty is to comply with her patient's wishes—and she therefore acts lawfully by removing life support from the patient.

A further reason for treating the withdrawal of life support as an omission is that not starting life-sustaining treatment in the first place is plainly an omission, rather than an action. If doctors could be guilty of murder if they withdraw life-support, but not if they fail to initiate it, there is a clear incentive to withhold such treatment from patients altogether, which is self-evidently undesirable.

Some commentators have, however, questioned the description of the removal of artificial feeding tubes as an omission. Ian Kennedy, for example, says that

> to describe turning off the machine as an omission does some considerable violence to the ordinary English usage. It represents an attempt to solve the problem by logic chopping. Such an approach may demonstrate to the satisfaction of some that no crime is involved, but it is surely most unsatisfactory to rest the response of the law to what is seen as a testing moral and philosophical issue on some semantic sleight of hand.[38]

And Margaret Otlowski similarly suggests that the characterization of a withdrawal of life-support as an omission is dictated by pragmatism, rather than logic:

> [T]he withdrawal of life-support is now fairly well established medical practice, and there is naturally a reluctance to interpret that practice in such a way as to raise the spectre of doctors

[38] *Treat Me Right*, 351.

incurring criminal liability. Indeed, it would seem that every possible effort has been made to interpret the conduct of the doctors in such a way as to sanction their practices and avoid the possibility that this conduct may be criminal.[39]

Further evidence that withdrawing life-prolonging treatment may be inappropriately described as an omission comes from the suggestion that doctors' conscientious objections to treatment withdrawal should be respected. The General Medical Council's guidance to doctors, for example, states that:

Where a decision to withhold or withdraw life-prolonging treatment has been made by a competent adult patient . . . doctors who have a conscientious objection to the decision may withdraw from the care of that patient.[40]

And as we saw earlier, the doctors who had been caring for Ms B were permitted to refuse to participate in the removal of the ventilator which was keeping her alive. Since it is hard to see how a doctor could have a conscientious objection to 'letting nature take its course', it is surely more plausible to admit that doctors whose consciences prompt them to refuse to participate in the withdrawal of life-prolonging treatment are unwilling to *act* deliberately to cause their patients' deaths. This was certainly the perspective of the treating clinicians in *Re B (Adult: Refusal of Medical Treatment)*.[41] In reviewing their evidence, Dame Elizabeth Butler-Sloss P explained that they

could not, however, bring themselves to contemplate that they should be part of bringing Ms B's life to an end by the dramatic *step* of turning off the ventilator. (my emphasis)

In particular, Dr C:

had studied and spent her professional life trying to do her best to improve and preserve life. She did not feel able to agree with simply switching off Ms B's ventilation. She would not have been able to do it. She felt she was being asked to *kill* Ms B. (my emphasis)

While lawyers may defend doctors' actions in withdrawing life-support by pointing out the legal significance of the difference between acts and omissions, doctors themselves are more likely to justify their conduct by drawing a distinction between 'killing' and 'letting die'. So a doctor who withdraws life-support does not kill, she merely lets the patient die. This explanation undoubtedly has intuitive appeal, perhaps because, as Alexander McCall Smith explains, we may instinctively feel that acting deliberately to end someone's life is worse than letting them die.

Alexander McCall Smith[42]

[T]he statement that it is better for a person to die is quite consistent with a principled rejection of euthanasia. It is a statement which people regularly make when they comment on the death of one who has gone through a great deal of suffering or one whose life is reduced to pain and indignity. Death, we say in such circumstances comes as a relief. This is a far cry from saying that one would be prepared to take active steps to end the life of such a person or from saying it would

---

[39] *Voluntary Euthanasia and the Common Law* (OUP Oxford 2000) 163.

[40] *Withholding and Withdrawing Life-prolonging Treatments: Good Practice in Decision-making*, Aug 2002, para 28.

[41] [2002] 1 FLR 1090.

[42] 'Euthanasia: The Strengths of the Middle Ground' (1999) 7 Medical Law Review 194–207, 201–2, 204–5.

be right for anyone else to do so. Statements of this sort express the moral intuitions of ordinary people, who see a distinction between act and omission. This distinction may be explicable in terms of causal potency, or it may be explained in terms of agent identification (an omission being less *my* act than is the case with positive actions). Whatever basis is chosen, the act/omission distinction does express a widespread moral intuition and there is every reason for giving such intuitions a central role in our morality . . .

The criminal law makes the distinction between act and omission because it recognises that there are natural limits to moral obligations, and, further, because it appreciates that to equiparate act and omission liability would be to impose an unreasonable burden on people . . .

There is a further reason why the act/omission distinction makes sense in the context of euthanasia. Again this has to do with the practical realities of the law of homicide. If it is the case—which it is—that we regard the prohibition against killing as a basic moral value, then it is important to ensure that our criminal law embodies a firm rule that all taking of life is punishable as a serious offence . . .

There are strong grounds for the maintaining of a 'deep prohibition' of the taking of human life . . . A deep prohibition recognises that even if there are merits in certain circumstances in the doing of the prohibited act, there are still grounds why, for symbolic reasons, that act should never be performed . . . The prohibition against killing has to be absolute because the making of any exception to it will destabilise the value we currently accord to human life.

In contrast, the authors of the following extracts argue that it is not in fact obvious that letting someone die is *necessarily* less blameworthy than killing them. Rather, as Jonathan Glover suggests, while killing (or acting positively) will *usually* be more reprehensible than letting someone die (or omitting to act), there may be circumstances in which this is not the case. Killing someone in self-defence, for example, is not a criminal offence; whereas a mother who lets her child die from starvation may be guilty of murder.

Jonathan Glover[43]

Sometimes when I do not do something, it would be entirely unreasonable to blame me for this. If someone I have never heard of killed himself last week in Brazil, without my knowing or doing anything about it, I cannot be blamed for it . . . But some omissions are at the other extreme of blameworthiness. A man who will inherit a fortune when his father dies, and, with this in mind, omits to give him medicine necessary for keeping him alive, is very culpable . . . It seems possible that some of the force of the acts and omissions doctrine derives from tacitly thinking of omissions in terms of examples drawn from the non-culpable end of the spectrum. The doctrine certainly seems less plausible where the omission is deliberate and results from a bad motive.

So it is not the simple fact that a doctor lets someone die that makes their act excusable, rather as Dan Brock explains, it is the surrounding circumstances—such as the patient's request and their intolerable distress—that justify the doctor's conduct.

Dan W Brock[44]

Consider the case of a patient terminally ill with ALS [Amyotrophic Lateral Sclerosis] disease. She is completely respirator dependent with no hope of ever being weaned. She is unquestionably competent and persistently requests to be removed from the respirator and allowed to die. Most

---

[43] *Causing Death and Saving Lives* (Penguin Harmondsworth 1977) 95.
[44] Voluntary Active Euthanasia, Hastings Center Report 22 Mar–Apr 1992, 10–22.

people and physicians would agree that the patient's physician should respect the patient's wishes and remove her from the respirator, though this will certainly cause the patient's death. The common understanding is that the physician thereby allows the patient to die. But is that correct?

Suppose the patient has a greedy and hostile son . . . Afraid that his inheritance will be dissipated by a long and expensive hospitalization, he enters his mother's room while she is sedated, extubates her, and she dies. Shortly thereafter the medical staff discovers what he has done and confronts the son. He replies, 'I didn't kill her. I merely allowed her to die. It was her ALS disease that caused her death'. I think this would rightly be dismissed as transparent sophistry—the son went into his mother's room and deliberately killed her. But, of course, the son performed just the same physical actions, did just the same thing, that the physician would have done. If that is so, then doesn't the physician also kill the patient when he extubates her?

I underline immediately that there are important ethical differences between what the physician and the greedy son do. First, the physician acts with the patient's consent whereas the son does not. Second, the physician acts with a good motive—to respect the patient's wishes and self-determination—whereas the son acts with a bad motive—to protect his own inheritance. Third, the physician acts in a social role through which he is legally authorized to carry out the patient's wishes regarding treatment whereas the son has no such authorization. These and perhaps other ethically important differences show that what the physician did was morally justified whereas what the son did was morally wrong. What they do not show, however, is that the son killed while the physician allowed to die. One can either kill or allow to die with or without consent, with a good or bad motive, within or outside of a social role that authorizes one to do so . . . Both the physician and the greedy son act in a manner intended to cause death, do cause death, and so both kill.

The following example offers a further illustration of this point:

Emily Jackson[45]

Imagine a doctor who has two competent adult patients connected to the same artificial ventilator. Patient A wants to continue living, and patient B wants to die. The doctor switches off the machine, and both patients die. In relation to patient A, because the doctor is under a duty to treat her, switching off the machine is characterised as an action, and the doctor might be guilty of murder. But in relation to patient B, switching off the machine is an omission. Exactly the same course of conduct is, in the eyes of the law, simultaneously both an act and an omission. But we cannot tell whether what the doctor did was an act, and hence culpable, or an omission, and hence blameless, unless we take into account extrinsic factors, such as, in this case, the competent patient's request for treatment withdrawal. Thus the morally relevant fact is not whether what the doctor does is an omission or an action, but rather whether the background against which the decision has been taken justifies the doctor's conclusion that life, in these circumstances, should not be artificially prolonged.

It is, however, worth noting that even if we accept that there is no *necessary* moral difference between killing and letting die, it does not follow that they are therefore morally *equivalent*. So, for example, because treating a patient in the face of a competent refusal is a battery, it might make sense to talk about a *right* to refuse unwanted medical treatment. Refusing to respect someone's request to be killed, in contrast, would not violate their bodily integrity.

---

[45] 'Whose Death is it Anyway? Euthanasia and the Medical Profession' (2004) 57 Current Legal Problems 415–42, 425–6.

So far we have been assuming that the question of treatment withdrawal arises when the competent adult has been given the option of life-prolonging treatment, and exercises their right to refuse. But a different scenario is possible. What if the doctor recommends that life-prolonging treatment (such as cardio pulmonary resuscitation) should not be attempted if the patient suffers a respiratory or cardiac arrest? In 2002, in response to concern that hospitals were including DNR (Do Not Resuscitate) orders in the medical notes of competent elderly patients without prior discussion, the British Medical Association, the Resuscitation Council (UK) and the Royal College of Nursing issued a joint statement on decisions relating to cardiopulmonary resuscitation. They preferred the label, 'Do Not *Attempt* Resuscitation' (DNAR) in order to make clear that resuscitation is not always successful. The guidance emphasizes that it is good practice to discuss writing DNAR orders with competent adult patients, and stresses the need for sensitivity. However, in practice, it is difficult to find a sensitive way to ask a patient who has just been admitted to hospital if she would wish to be resuscitated should she suffer a heart attack.

BMA, Resuscitation Council and the RCN

Where no explicit advance decision has been made about the appropriateness or otherwise of attempting resuscitation prior to a patient suffering cardiac or respiratory arrest, and the express wishes of the patient are unknown and cannot be ascertained, there should be a presumption that health professionals will make all reasonable efforts to attempt to revive the patient . . . Although this is the general assumption, it is unlikely to be considered reasonable to attempt to resuscitate a patient who is in the terminal phase of illness or for whom the burdens of the treatment clearly outweigh the potential benefits . . .

People have ethical and legal rights to be involved in decisions that relate to them. Because patients' own views about the level of burden or risk they consider acceptable carry considerable weight in deciding whether treatment is given, it follows that decisions about whether the likely benefits from successful CPR outweigh the burdens should be discussed with competent patients. Thus where competent patients are at foreseeable risk of cardiopulmonary arrest, or have a terminal illness, there should be sensitive exploration of their wishes regarding resuscitation. This will normally arise as part of general discussions about that patient's care. Information should not be forced on unwilling recipients, however, and if patients indicate that they do not wish to discuss resuscitation this should be respected. Where a DNAR order is made and there has been no discussion with the patient because he or she has indicated a clear desire to avoid such discussion, this must be documented in the health records and the reasons given.

(b) Advance directives

There might be circumstances in which a competent adult patient wishes to issue instructions about how they should be treated if they become incompetent. An obvious example might be a Jehovah's Witness who carries a card stating that they would not want to be given a blood transfusion. Provided that the refusal was made when the patient was competent, and provided it covers the situation that has arisen, and provided that the patient did not subsequently change her mind, an advance refusal has the same legal status as a contemporaneous refusal. In theory, then, an advance refusal of life-sustaining medical treatment is binding upon the medical professionals involved in the patient's care. Of course, an advance directive (sometimes called a living will) may not be confined to a refusal of medical treatment. A patient might want to request that certain treatments be made available to them. But just as with contemporaneous decisions, it is only *refusals* that are definitely binding upon medical staff. Patients do not generally have the right to insist upon any particular course of treatment, and this is equally true when the request is made in advance.

The principal justification for complying with an advance refusal is, of course, respect for patient autonomy. Allowing patients to exercise control over their *future* medical treatment significantly broadens the scope of the principle of patient self-determination because autonomy ceases to be the preserve of competent adults. Rather, *previously* competent adults too have a right to have their autonomous choices respected.

In practice, however, while many people may have expressed a vague preference for a quick and painless death, it is very rare for patients to have drawn up advance directives which are precise enough to be legally binding. Within the NHS, medical staff often have insufficient time to discuss a patient's current prognosis, so consultation about hypothetical future scenarios will rarely be feasible. But even where a patient has attempted to specify in advance that they wish to refuse life-prolonging treatment, two related problems arise. First, as I explain more fully below, the conditions which must be satisfied for an advance refusal to be valid in practice create substantial obstacles to their effectiveness. Secondly, because the consequence of relying upon an advance refusal of life-sustaining treatment will be the patient's death, if there is any doubt about its validity, medical staff will tend to err on the side of caution and administer life-support despite an apparent advance refusal of such treatment.

There are sound legal reasons for doctors to act in this way. If, for example, the patient with an advance refusal of mechanical ventilation had in fact had a change of heart before she became incapacitated, a doctor who withholds life-support will be failing to act in a situation in which she has a duty to act positively to save life. The patient will be dead, and, as we saw earlier, the doctor's conduct will satisfy the *actus reus* and *mens rea* for murder. If, on the other hand, the doctor ignores a refusal which turns out to have been valid, she will have committed the tort of battery. So where there is doubt about the validity of an advance refusal, doctors may be faced with the choice between two evils—potentially committing the crime of murder or the tort of battery. Unsurprisingly, medical staff will tend to choose the latter option.

So why might there be doubt about the validity of an advance directive? There are four practical reasons, and one rather more complicated philosophical reason. Let us consider the practical reasons first. Because the patient is now incompetent, it will be very difficult to *prove* that she was competent when she issued the advance directive. Of course, all patients benefit from the presumption of competence (discussed in Chapter 4), so it would be for medical staff to establish that this patient had in fact been incompetent at the time of her advance refusal. However, for the reasons explained above, if there is any doubt about a patient's earlier competence, medical staff have good reasons to err on the side of caution and ignore the refusal.

Secondly, to be binding the advance refusal must apply to the particular situation that has arisen. But of course it is almost impossible to foresee every medical eventuality when making an advance directive. Any lack of 'fit' between the advance refusal and the patient's current predicament will lead to doubt about its validity, and medical staff will therefore again feel justified in ignoring it. In *W Healthcare NHS Trust v H*,[46] there was considerable evidence from H's friends and family members that she had said repeatedly that if the time came when she could no longer recognize her daughters, she did not want to be kept alive. That was now the case, but the Court of Appeal found that this was insufficiently precise to qualify as a binding advance directive. Brooke LJ stated that:

I am of the clear view that the judge was correct in finding that there was not an advance directive which was sufficiently clear to amount to a direction that she preferred to be deprived of food and drink for a period of time which would lead to her death in all circumstances. There is no evidence that she was aware of the nature of this choice, or the unpleasantness or otherwise of death by starvation, and it would be departing from established principles of English law if one was to hold that there was an advance directive which was established and relevant in the circumstances in the present case, despite the very strong expression of her wishes which came through in the evidence.

A third problem is that the patient's prognosis may have changed since she issued her advance refusal. New therapeutic options might have become available, and medical staff may feel unsure whether the patient would have refused life-sustaining treatment if she had known about them. Finally, even if the patient precisely foresaw the events which have led to her current predicament, there is always the possibility that the patient may have changed her mind about refusing life-sustaining treatment. It is certainly not uncommon for severe life-threatening illness to alter a person's attitudes and priorities. If the patient did have a change of heart before the onset of incapacity, the refusal is no longer valid even if the patient failed to formally repudiate it. Because there will invariably be a risk—albeit perhaps a small one—that the advance directive no longer represents the patient's wishes, there is a danger inherent in respecting *any* prospective refusal of life-sustaining treatment.

In *HE v A Hospital NHS Trust*,[47] doubt was cast on the validity of an advance directive, drawn up when the patient was a Jehovah's Witness, because of her decision to abandon her faith. Munby J found that given the existence of this doubt, the burden of proof was on those who sought to uphold the advance directive to establish that it was still valid:

Munby J

No doubt there is a practical—what lawyers would call an evidential—burden on those who assert that an undisputed advance directive is for some reason no longer operative, a burden requiring them to point to something indicating that this is or may be so. It may be words said to have been written or spoken by the patient. It may be the patient's actions—for sometimes actions speak louder than words. It may be some change in circumstances. Thus, it may be alleged that the patient no longer professes the faith which underlay the advance directive; it may be said that the patient executed the advance directive because he was suffering from an illness which has since been cured; it may be said that medical science has now moved on; it may be said that the patient, having since married or had children, now finds himself with more compelling reasons to choose to

---

[46] [2004] EWCA Civ 1324.   [47] [2003] EWHC 1017 (Fam), [2003] 2 FLR 408.

live even a severely disadvantaged life. It may be suggested that the advance directive has been revoked, whether by express words or by conduct on the part of the patient inconsistent with its continued validity. It may be suggested that, even though not revoked, the advance directive has not survived some material change of circumstances. But whatever the reasons may be, once the issue is properly raised, once there is some real reason for doubt, then it is for those who assert the continuing validity and applicability of the advance directive to prove that it is still operative. The burden of proof is on them. And, as I have said, what is required is clear and convincing proof. If there is doubt that doubt falls to be resolved in favour of the preservation of life. So, if there is doubt the advance directive cannot be relied on and the doctor must treat the patient in such way as his best interests require . . .

There is simply no clear and convincing proof that the advance directive is still valid and applicable. The father's evidence having raised doubts—real doubts, not fanciful doubts or mere speculations—those doubts must be resolved in favour of the preservation of life.

Advance directives are not always invalid, however, as we can see from the following case.

Re AK (Medical Treatment: Consent) [48]

AK, aged 19, had suffered from motor neurone disease for the past two and a half years. The patient's physical condition had gradually deteriorated. For the past three months the only motion which he could achieve was a very tiny movement, a millimetre or less, of one eyelid, through which he was able to answer 'yes' or 'no' to questions. He could not initiate communication himself or show any emotion. At some point, this last vestige of movement would be lost, and it would become impossible for his carers to tell if he was in pain. Because motor neurone disease does not affect intellectual capacity, AK could hear, see, feel, think and understand. AK asked that the doctors remove his ventilator two weeks after he lost his ability to communicate. He was aware that this would inevitably result in his death. The doctors treating him sought a declaration that it would be lawful to discontinue life-sustaining treatment in accordance with his wishes.

Hughes J

[A]n advance indication of the wishes of a patient of full capacity and sound mind are [sic] effective. Care will of course have to be taken to ensure that such anticipatory declarations of wishes still represent the wishes of the patient. Care must be taken to investigate how long ago the expression of wishes was made. Care must be taken to investigate with what knowledge the expression of wishes was made. All the circumstances in which the expression of wishes was given will of course have to be investigated. In the present case the expressions of AK's decision are recent and are made not on any hypothetical basis but in the fullest possible knowledge of impending reality. I am satisfied that they genuinely represent his considered wishes and should be treated as such . . .

It is also necessary critically to examine the proposition that consent has been given, particularly where, as here, communications are so painfully difficult. I have sufficiently reviewed the process which has been adopted to indicate that it is plain that AK's consent is free and genuine . . . It might be necessary, depending on the time-scale, for him to be asked whether his wishes remain the same, but at present his express wishes are clear. Given that his express wishes are clear, the conclusion follows from what I have said that once the conditions which he has stipulated arise it will be unlawful to continue invasive ventilation.

---

[48] [2001] 1 FLR 129.

The philosophical objection to advance refusals has been articulated most clearly by Rebecca Dresser and Allen Buchanan. In short, they argue that profound incapacity may sever the 'psychological continuity' between the competent individual who issued the advance directive, and the incompetent person who now requires life support. As Dresser explains:

If little or no psychological connectedness and continuity exist between the individual at the two points in time, then there is no particular reason why the past person, as opposed to any other person, should determine the present person's fate.[49]

Allen Buchanan[50]

There is, however, a much more profound and potentially grave threat to the moral authority of advance directives . . . This is the objection that the very process that renders the individual incompetent and brings the advance directive into play can—and indeed often does—destroy the conditions necessary for her personal identity and thereby undercut entirely the moral authority of the directive . . .

So long as the degree of psychological continuity which we take to be necessary for the preservation of personal identity is present, the advance directive has full moral authority . . . [But] presumably a point is eventually reached at which the degree of psychological continuity between the author of the advance directive and the incompetent individual is so small that the advance directive of the former has no authority at all over the latter.

So, for example, as a healthy university teacher, I may view the prospect of severe dementia with horror, and I might decide that should I become severely demented, and suffer a life-threatening infection, I would not want to be treated with antibiotics. Let us imagine that I execute an unambiguous advance directive to this effect. But once I am demented, and it is clear to my carers that I am able to gain pleasure (which may previously have seemed unimaginable) from my impaired existence, would it be right to deny me antibiotics if I develop a serious, though easily treatable infection?

The idea that the incompetent adult may be so far removed from their previously competent self that they should not be bound by the latter's advance directive is, unsurprisingly, a controversial one. Ronald Dworkin, for example, has said that advance directives express values which we should continue to respect because the now incompetent patient is not just a collection of current interests, but rather is a person with a past.[51] And Nancy Rhoden has argued that the 'notion that a person is one person, and one person only, from birth through old age, despite whatever changes and vicissitudes she might undergo' is 'deeply embedded in our culture'.[52]

Nancy K Rhoden[53]

If we are to make decisions about them as persons, we must view them not only as they are in the present, but also as the persons they were—persons who had strong opinions about how their body, even when insensate, should be treated . . . We must see the person as she, when competent,

---

[49] R Dresser, 'Life, Death, and Incompetent Patients: Conceptual Infirmities and Hidden Values in the Law' (1986) 28 Arizona Law Review 380–1, 373.

[50] 'Advance Directives and the Personal Identity Problem' (1988) Philosophy and Public Affairs 131–54.

[51] Dworkin, 'Autonomy and the Demented Self' (1986) 64 Milbank Q 4, 14 (Supp. II).

[52] 'Litigating Life and Death' (1988) 102 Harvard Law Review 375, 414.   [53] Ibid, 415.

would have imagined herself after incompetency, rather than viewing her from the outside and as she is now . . .

[A]n entirely present-oriented view is a bad way to view even persons who left no living will; it is unlikely that they would want to be viewed just as a body that can experience only physical sensations . . . Considering the patient only in the immediate present divides the patient from her past, her history, her values, and her relationships—from all those things that make her human.

When the Mental Capacity Act 2005 comes into force, it will cover advance refusals of life-sustaining treatment. We deal with the provisions of the Act in detail in Chapter 4. For the purposes of this chapter, it is worth drawing attention to the special rules for advance refusals of life-sustaining treatment contained in section 25(5) and (6). The person who has issued the advance refusal (P) must specifically acknowledge that they intend to refuse treatment even if this puts their life at risk; the decision must be in writing and signed by P or a representative in P's presence, and the signature must be witnessed. This is more exacting than the common law, under which there is no requirement for an advance refusal to be in writing, regardless of the gravity of its consequences, although as we have seen, there are a number of reasons why such an advance refusal might be found not to apply to the situation in which the patient finds herself.

Where there is doubt about the validity or applicability of an advance decision, under section 26(4) an application can be made to the court of protection (again see further Chapter 4) for a declaration. While the court's advice is being sought, under section 26(5) nothing in the advance decision should prevent the provision of life-sustaining treatment or steps to prevent a deterioration in the P's condition.

(b) SHOULD EUTHANASIA AND/OR ASSISTED SUICIDE BE LEGALIZED?

As we have seen, the law draws a bright line between lawful practices which result in a patient's death (withholding/withdrawing life-prolonging medical treatment and providing palliative care which may incidentally shorten life) and unlawful practices which have the same effect (euthanasia and physician assisted suicide). This means that doctors are allowed to help their patients to die provided that they *happen* either to be connected to a ventilator or nasogastric feeding tube, or to require life-threatening doses of painkillers. Some commentators argue that access to medical assistance in dying should not depend upon a patient's fortuitous need for life-support or massive doses of diamorphine. Whereas others believe that there is a fundamental difference between doctors letting their patients die and killing them, and that the integrity of the medical profession demands an absolute prohibition upon doctors acting deliberately to terminate their patients' lives. Who is right?

In this section, we review the arguments for and against legalizing euthanasia and physician assisted suicide.

(1) ARGUMENTS FOR:

(a) Autonomy

It is often assumed that one of the strongest arguments in favour of legalizing euthanasia and assisted suicide is respect for patient autonomy. Throughout this book, we
have seen that the principle of patient self-determination is increasingly dominant
within medical law, and some commentators would argue that a patient's right to
make decisions about their medical treatment should extend to deciding the time and
the manner of their death. It is undoubtedly true that we all have a profound interest
in how we die. To die quickly and painlessly, perhaps at home and surrounded by
people we love, is obviously preferable to a protracted, frightening, and agonizing
death. As Sylvia Law suggests, giving patients some control over how they die
might then appear to be an especially important aspect of respect for autonomous
decision-making.

Sylvia A Law[54]

First, the core of this dilemma is the individual's desire to retain control over his or her body and
life. As Ronald Dworkin explains, 'Death has dominion because it is not only the start of nothing
but the end of everything, and how we think and talk about dying—the emphasis we put on dying
with "dignity"—shows how important it is that life ends appropriately, that death keeps faith with
the way we want to have lived'.

Second, the right to choice is valuable, however that choice is exercised. The dying patient has
lost control of most significant aspects of his or her life. The assurance that assisted death is an
option provides a measure of autonomy and control, however that autonomy is exercised. Indeed,
evidence from medical practice suggests that frank recognition and discussion of the suicide
option sometimes leads depressed patients to reject it. Third, prohibitions on physician-assisted
dying enforce individual isolation and prevent individuals from seeking the help and companionship of others at a critical time. When suicide is allowed, but help in dying is prohibited, the state
denies important associational interests.

Fourth, it is not easy to hasten death in a private, non-violent way. Bans on physician assistance,
therefore, aggravate . . . suffering. It is, of course, possible to jump off a tall building or to leap in
front of an oncoming train. But most terminally ill patients seek a death that is both more private
and less violent. Patients who unsuccessfully attempt to hasten death are often subjected to
serious indignity.

In contrast, John Keown argues that the right to 'choice' is essentially meaningless and
that an emphasis upon individualistic values such as autonomy marginalizes the
impact our actions have upon others.

John Keown[55]

The 'right to choose x' often serves as a slogan with powerful emotional appeal. But crude slogans
are no substitute for rational reflection, and one can hardly sensibly assert a right to choose 'x'
until one has considered whether it is right to choose 'x'; to do otherwise is simply to beg the
question. Is there a 'right to choose . . . paedophilia'? Or a 'right to choose . . . cruelty to animals'?

[54] 'Physician-Assisted Death: An Essay on Constitutional Rights and Remedies' (1996) 55 Maryland Law
Review 292.
[55] *Euthanasia, Ethics and Public Policy: An Argument against Legalisation* (CUP Cambridge 2002) 54.

Does the mere fact that someone *wants* to blind ponies or to have sex with children carry any moral weight? The 'right to choose' only arguably makes any moral sense in the context of a moral framework which enables us to discern what it is *right* to choose and what choices will in fact promote human flourishing. And not only *our* flourishing, but that of others. For we do not live as atomised individuals, as much loose talk about absolute respect for personal autonomy appears to assume, but in community, where our choices can have profound effects not only on ourselves but on others . . . [R]egarding autonomy as the supreme value invites moral pluralism, which easily becomes moral relativism, which is corrosive of moral community.

There are a number of problems with relying exclusively upon the principle of autonomy when arguing for the legalization of euthanasia and assisted suicide. First, few advocates of legalization would allow unrestricted access to medical assistance in dying. On the contrary, it is generally accepted that doctors should only be allowed to help patients to die in certain limited circumstances. The fact that a person wants to die is not, on its own, a sufficient reason for a doctor to give her a lethal injection. Although opinion differs over whether terminal illness should be a prerequisite, most people would agree that a doctor should only comply with a patient's request for euthanasia or assisted suicide if her pain or suffering or distress has become intolerable. These sorts of restrictions are inconsistent with an important feature of respect for autonomous decision-making, namely that:

A mentally competent patient has an absolute right to refuse to consent to medical treatment for any reason, rational or irrational, or for no reason at all, even where that decision may lead to his or her own death.[56]

Secondly, as we saw in Chapter 4, a patient's right to make decisions about their medical treatment is usually confined to a right to *refuse* treatment. Patients do not have the right to demand that their doctor carry out any particular procedure. So while the principle of autonomy requires doctors to respect a competent patient's refusal of life-prolonging medical treatment, it could not *require* doctors to comply with a request for euthanasia or assisted suicide.

In response, advocates of legalization might accept that while patients have a virtually absolute right to refuse unwanted medical treatment, they would not be entitled to demand that their doctors perform euthanasia. Rather, their right would be to *ask* for assistance in dying, a request which a doctor could legitimately turn down, either because she has a conscientious objection or because it would be incompatible with her duty of care. The purpose of legalization, as is explained in the following extracts, would simply be to *allow* doctors to act lawfully when they comply with a patient's request for assistance.

Ronald Dworkin, Thomas Nagel, Robert Nozick, John Rawls, Thomas Scanlon, and Judith Jarvis Thomson[57]
Certain decisions are momentous in their impact on the character of a person's life—decisions about religious faith, political and moral allegiance, marriage, procreation, and death, for example.

[56] *Re MB* 38 BMLR 175, per Butler-Sloss LJ.
[57] In two cases heard by the US Supreme Court at the same time [*Washington et al v Glucksberg* 117 S Ct 2258 (1997) and *Vacco v Quill* 117 S Ct 2293 (1997)], these six distinguished philosophers presented an Amici Curiae Brief for Respondents—referred to as The Philosophers' Brief—to the Supreme Court.

Such deeply personal decisions pose controversial questions about how and why human life has value. In a free society, individuals must be allowed to make those decisions for themselves, out of their own faith, conscience, and convictions . . . Most of us see death—whatever we think will follow it—as the final act of life's drama, and we want that last act to reflect our own convictions, those we have tried to live by, not the convictions of others forced on us in our most vulnerable moment . . .

Since patients have a right not to have life-support machinery attached to their bodies, they have, in principle, a right to compel its removal. But that is not true in the case of assisted suicide: patients in certain circumstances have a right that the state not forbid doctors to assist in their deaths, but they have no right to compel a doctor to assist them. The right in question, that is, is only a right to the help of a willing doctor.

David Orentlicher[58]

Some commentators distinguish the withdrawal of treatment from euthanasia/assisted suicide on the ground that a right to refuse treatment is a negative right to be left alone while a right to euthanasia or assisted suicide would be a positive right to command aid. This argument mischaracterizes the nature of a right to euthanasia or assisted suicide. Such a right would not mean that patients could require physicians to assist suicides or perform euthanasia. Rather, the right would prevent the state from interfering when a patient and physician voluntarily agree on a course of euthanasia/assisted suicide. Physicians would participate in euthanasia/assisted suicide only if they were willing to do so . . . A right to euthanasia or assisted suicide, too, is a negative right to be left alone . . .

Society recognizes a right to be free of unwanted touchings to ensure that individuals have control over their bodies and are able to exercise self-determination. Yet, a right to euthanasia/assisted suicide would also ensure that individuals have control over their bodies and are able to exercise self-determination. We still need to explain why considerations of personal autonomy are more important with respect to treatment withdrawal than euthanasia/assisted suicide.

(b) Mercy

A different sort of argument for legalization could be framed in terms of the principle of beneficence (see further Chapter 1, p. 15). When curing a patient and restoring her to full health is no longer possible—as we saw earlier in the context of palliative care—the doctors' duty to 'do good' encompasses doing whatever they can to relieve her suffering. If the only way that a patient's distress can be relieved is by ending her life, it could be argued that allowing doctors to take this step is compatible with their duty to act beneficently. In addition to helping individual patients whose suffering has become intolerable, the legalization of euthanasia might also benefit a wider class of patients by reassuring them that their doctor will be allowed to help them to die if their condition becomes unbearable. It has been suggested that some patients are so fearful of a protracted, distressing and undignified death that they take their own lives prematurely while they are still capable of doing so. For such patients, the availability of legalized euthanasia would, in fact, prolong their lives.

Using mercy or beneficence, rather than autonomy, as the justification for legalizing euthanasia and assisted suicide might explain the restrictions that it is generally

---

[58] 'The Alleged Distinction between euthanasia and the withdrawal of life-sustaining treatment: conceptually incoherent and impossible to maintain' (1998) University of Illinois Law Review 837, 847–8.

believed should be placed upon its use. A doctor would only be acting beneficently in helping a patient to die if she has reasonable grounds for believing that the patient's life has ceased to be a benefit to her.

(c) Inconsistency of the status quo

Another reason commonly given for legalizing euthanasia and assisted suicide is that the line the law currently draws between lawful and unlawful life-shortening practices is incoherent and morally irrelevant.[59] On this view, if we are prepared to allow doctors to engage in some practices which will end their patients' lives (such as withdrawing life-prolonging medical treatment, or giving life-threatening doses of painkillers), there is no logical reason why we should not also allow doctors to give their patients lethal injections, particularly since dying from starvation or suffocation may be more protracted and distressing (both for the patient and for her carers) than the quick and painless death that would be induced by a single fatal injection. Para-doxically then, the lawful means of hastening a patient's death generally will often result in a less humane and peaceful death than the unlawful means.

Most of us would prefer to die quickly and at home, surrounded by the people we love. Yet none of the lawful means of hastening patient's lives promote this sort of death. On the contrary, the withdrawal of life-sustaining treatment will generally take place in hospital. And where artificial nutrition and hydration is withdrawn, the patient will slowly starve to death, albeit painlessly, over a period of about two weeks. The moment of death is unpredictable, and the patient's family may not be present. If the patient is given life-threatening doses of painkilling drugs—justified by the doc-trine of double effect—it will only be possible to ensure that her loved ones are present at the moment of her death if the doctor admits that which the doctrine of double effect forbids, namely that she knows she is killing her patient rather than merely attempting to relieve her pain. Voluntary euthanasia administered by a single lethal injection, on the other hand, could be given to a patient in her home in the presence of the people she loves. In the Netherlands, where euthanasia is lawful, 48 per cent of cancer patients die at home. And evidence appears to indicate that the bereaved relatives of cancer patients who die as a result of euthanasia cope better with bereavement, and suffer fewer post-traumatic stress reactions than the bereaved of comparable cancer patients who die naturally.[60] The opportunity to say goodbye; being prepared for the time and manner of the death; and having talked openly about dying all appear to have a positive impact upon a family's ability to come to terms with a person's death.

Moreover, as RG Frey argues in the next extract, making the lawfulness of medical assistance in dying contingent upon whether a patient *happens* to be connected to a ventilator or a morphine drip could be said to discriminate against certain patients whose suffering may be equally unbearable, but whose illnesses deprive them of access to the various lawful means of ending their lives.

---

[59] See further E Jackson, 'Whose Death is it Anyway? Euthanasia and the Medical Profession' (2004) 57 Current Legal Problems 415–442.

[60] Nikkie B Swarte et al., 'Effects of euthanasia on the bereaved family and friends: a cross sectional study' (2003) 327 British Medical Journal 189.

RG Frey[61]

It seems little short of incredible that the fact that a terminally ill patient is on a life-support system could so transform cases, morally, when both cases show quite clearly that patient and doctor are acting together to bring about the patient's death at the instigation of the patient . . . Withdrawing feeding tubes and starving the patient to death is permissible, supplying the patient with a pill that produces death is not. Yet both sorts of assistance assuredly produce death, and both sorts involve the patient and doctor acting together to produce that death.

To be prepared to see the patient dead; to take the step that will assuredly produce death; to know as a certainty that death will ensue or be hastened: is this not morally equivalent to intending the patient's death? If so, there is little difference here between the supply of pills and the withdrawal of feeding tubes, so far as intending the patient's death is concerned.

(d) Benefits of regulation

Proponents of this argument for legalization tend to cite evidence which shows that, despite its illegality, doctors *do* help their patients to die. Obviously, because doctors who admit to practising euthanasia may be charged with murder, it is virtually impossible to gather accurate information about their participation in life-shortening practices. However, anonymous surveys consistently show that between 30 and 60 per cent of all doctors have been asked for assistance in dying, and that a significant minority have complied with such requests.[62] Some commentators then suggest that if euthanasia is happening anyway, but being carried out in secret, legalization would enable it to be properly regulated. Not only are doctors currently unlikely to report instances of euthanasia, but the threat of prosecution means that they are deterred from consulting other colleagues. As a result, euthanasia is being practised without safeguards, such as the requirement that a doctor seeks a second opinion, and without the monitoring that might be facilitated by the keeping of accurate records. In the next extract, Margaret Pabst Battin argues that the purpose of legalization in the Netherlands was precisely to enable some control to be exercised over an otherwise secretive practice.

Margaret Pabst Battin[63]

[For] the Dutch . . . bringing euthanasia and related practices out into the open is a way of gaining control. For the Dutch, this is a way of identifying a practice that, in the Netherlands as in every other country, has been going on undercover and entirely at the discretion of the physician. It brings the practice into public view, where it can be regulated by guidelines, judicial scrutiny, and the collection of objective data. It is not that the Dutch or anyone else have only recently begun to practice euthanasia for the dying patient, nor is this a new phenomenon in the last decade or so; rather, the Dutch are the first to try to assert formal public control over a previously hidden

---

[61] 'Distinctions in Death' 17–42 in Gerald Dworkin, RG Frey, and Sissela Bok, *Euthanasia and Physician-Assisted Suicide: For and Against* (CUP Cambridge 1998) 36, 38.

[62] A survey published in the British Medical Journal (BMJ) in 1994 found that 45 per cent percent of doctors had been asked to take active steps to hasten death, and of these, 32 per cent had complied with such a request. [BJ Ward and PA Tate, 'Attitudes Among NHS Doctors to Requests for Euthanasia', (1994) 308 Brit Med J 1132, 1134.] Three hundred GPs were interviewed by the *Sunday Times* in 1998, and 15 per cent admitted to having helped their patients die. Cherry Norton, Doctor Will You Help Me Die?, *Sunday Times*, 15 Nov 1998, 14. In an anonymous poll of 683 surgeons in New South Wales, Australia, 36 per cent admitted that they had administered high doses of painkillers to patients with the intent of bringing about their death. Five per cent said that they had given a patient a single lethal injection on their clear request (news, BMJ, 2001, 323, 1268).

[63] *The Least Worst Death: Essays in Bioethics on the End of Life* (OUP Oxford 1994) 141.

practice and, hence, to regulate it effectively. Both open public discussion and the development of formal mechanisms such as guidelines, hospital protocols, and reporting requirements are seen as crucial in developing a social consensus, understood and accepted by both physicians and patients, about what can and cannot be permitted.

And in the next extract, RS Magnusson draws upon his interviews with health care professionals to argue that the alternative to legalization is not the wholly successful prohibition of euthanasia, but rather euthanasia's illegality will inevitably mean that it is practiced 'underground'.

RS Magnusson[64]

The key to the euthanasia debate lies in how best to regulate what doctors do. Opponents of euthanasia frequently warn of the possible negative consequences of legalising physician assisted suicide and active euthanasia (PAS/AE) while ignoring the covert practice of PAS/AE by doctors and other health professionals. Against the background of survey studies suggesting that anything from 4% to 10% of doctors have intentionally assisted a patient to die, and interview evidence of the unregulated, idiosyncratic nature of underground PAS/AE, this paper assesses three alternatives to the current policy of prohibition. It argues that although legalisation may never succeed in making euthanasia perfectly safe, legalising PAS/AE may nevertheless be safer, and therefore a preferable policy alternative, to prohibition. At a minimum, debate about harm minimisation and the regulation of euthanasia needs to take account of PAS/AE wherever it is practised, both above and below ground . . .

Despite the growing body of statistical evidence, remarkably little is known about the circumstances in which doctors provide covert assistance to die, whether these attempts result in what was perceived to be a good death for the patient, and the long term impact of involvement on health carers themselves. In *Angels of Death: Exploring the Euthanasia Underground*, I reported on 49 detailed, yet pseudonymous interviews with doctors, nurses, and therapists working in HIV/AIDS health care, principally in Sydney, Melbourne, and San Francisco. . . . Despite their mostly good intentions, interviewees painted a troubling picture of covert PAS/AE . . .

For me, the most striking feature of these accounts was the way they betrayed the absence of norms or principles for deciding when it was appropriate to proceed. One doctor injected a young man on the first occasion they met, despite concerns from close friends that the patient was depressed . . . In another case, a patient brought his death forward by a week so as not to interfere with the doctor's holiday plans . . .

It is important to remember that our ability to castigate the Dutch about their rates of non-compliance comes courtesy of the relative transparency created by the Dutch policy of legalisation. If we wish to make ambit claims about slippery slopes, it is only fair to point out that the reporting rate for Britain, Australia, and most other countries, is zero. Nevertheless, even partial compliance with statutory safeguards may represent an improvement on the kinds of clinical decisions that currently occur in secret.

It might also be argued that legalization would facilitate the equal treatment of similarly situated patients. At present, as Charles Baron explains, access to euthanasia is contingent not upon the gravity of a patient's plight, but upon whether her doctor is willing to run the risk of life imprisonment. This inevitably means that it is only available to a small number of patients. It has further been suggested that the class of patients whose relationships with medical professionals are sufficiently close that they

---

[64] 'Euthanasia: above ground, below ground' (2004) 30 Journal of Medical Ethics 441–6, 441–2, 445.

may be able to persuade them to act illegally are likely to be from the more privileged sections of society. Legalization would therefore enable access to euthanasia to depend upon need, rather than upon one's connections with members of the medical profession.

Charles Baron[65]

In March 1996, an Article in the Journal of the American Medical Association revealed that physicians in the State of Washington commit acts of physician-assisted suicide in percentages that rival those in Holland (where euthanasia and physician-assisted suicide are essentially legalized) . . .

The only possible benefit of keeping such activities secret and unmonitored . . . is preventing abuses from being made public. It is an open secret that such technically illegal practices take place, but prosecutions and disciplinary actions involving them have thus far been almost non-existent . . . Potential abuses are left completely without internal or external checks, and such a regime encourages the view that medical personnel may safely consider themselves 'above the law.' Patients are also denied equal protection of the law. Only patients with 'connections' are able to find physicians to assist them in dying—much as only women with 'connections' were able to obtain professional help in terminating pregnancies before abortion was legalized.

(2) ARGUMENTS AGAINST

(a) Sanctity of life

The legalization of euthanasia and assisted suicide would necessarily involve accepting that death can rationally be preferred to life. And according to Luke Gormally, this offends against the principle that all human life is intrinsically valuable.

Luke Gormally[66]

Euthanasiast killing, even when it is voluntary, involves denial of the ongoing worth of the lives of those reckoned to be candidates for euthanasia. It is a type of killing, therefore, which cannot be accommodated in a legal system for which belief in the worth and dignity of every human being is foundational . . . If the claim that a person lacks a worthwhile life is held to make killing lawful, then the state has ceased to recognize the innocent as having binding claims to protection.

The decriminalization of suicide (and attempted suicide, therefore) makes sense if we contemplate the plight of people having to face criminal proceedings after failed suicide attempts. Decriminalization motivated by the desire to ease the plight of such people does not, however, imply that the law takes a neutral view of the choice to carry out suicide. Those who attempt suicide are clearly moved by the (at least transient) belief that their lives are no longer worthwhile. Since just legal arrangements rest on a belief in the ineliminable worth of every human life, the law must reject the reasonableness of a choice which is so motivated.

Hence the law must also refuse to accommodate the behaviour of those who effectively endorse the choice of the suicide: for they too are acting on the view that the person they are helping no longer has a worthwhile life . . .

[I]f we cannot make sense of the claim that euthanasia is a benefit to the person to be killed without relying on the thought that that person no longer has a worthwhile life, then supporters of

---

[65] 'Physician Assisted Suicide should be Legalized and Regulated' (1997) 41 Boston Bar Journal 15.

[66] 'Euthanasia and Assisted Suicide: 7 reasons why they should not be legalized', in Donna Dickenson, Malcolm Johnson, and Jeanne Samson Katz (eds), *Death, Dying and Bereavement* (2nd edn Sage London 2000) 286–90, 285–7.

voluntary euthanasia are buying into a larger package-deal than they perhaps realize. For if one can be benefitted by being killed, is it reasonable to deprive people of that benefit simply because they are incapable of asking to be killed?

The practice of medicine cannot flourish unless doctors are so disposed that they inspire trust in patients, many of whom are extremely vulnerable. Doctors will not inspire trust unless patients are confident that doctors

- are for no reasons disposed to kill them;
- have no inclination to ask whether a patient is worth caring for or treating, rather than asking what care or treatment might benefit the patient

But the practice of euthanasia systematically undermines both of the required dispositions. For it disposes doctors to kill certain of their patients, and it inculcates a disposition to think of some patients as not having worthwhile lives. Since there are no non-arbitrary criteria for determining who has and who has not a worthwhile life, the temptation to categorize the difficult and the unappealing as not having worthwhile lives is very strong for the person who has failed to eschew such discriminatory thinking as a matter of principle.

This sort of argument against legalization often derives from the religious idea that life is not ours to dispose of as we please. For human beings to choose the moment of their death, and to take active steps to bring it about is—on this view—to usurp God's monopoly upon the power to give and to take life. In contrast, in the next extract Margaret Otlowski suggests that this sort of argument is effectively a matter of private faith, and that it should not be allowed to determine public policy.

Margaret Otlowski[67]

Religious arguments will naturally be convincing to those who accept the religious viewpoint but they clearly do not have universal relevance. Religion is a matter of personal commitment, and objections to active voluntary euthanasia based purely on religious views should not dominate the law nor impinge on the freedoms of others. Whilst the convictions of believers must obviously be respected, it must be recognized that in a pluralistic and largely secular society, the freedom of conviction of non-believers must also be upheld . . . Only if the legal prohibition on active voluntary euthanasia is removed will everyone be able to live according to their own convictions; those who oppose active voluntary euthanasia could reject it for themselves, and those who are in favour of the practice are not forced to live against their convictions.

(b) Legalization is unnecessary

For two different reasons, it is sometimes argued that the legalization of euthanasia is unnecessary. First, improvements in palliative care lead some opponents of legalization to contend that no patient should ever have to die in intolerable agony. On this view, the desire for euthanasia is evidence of our failure to provide sufficient hospice places and high-quality palliative treatment to terminally ill patients. If, so the argument goes, all patients were to be given optimum treatment at the end of life, none would request euthanasia, and the question of its legalization would become redundant. This is, to some extent, an empirical argument which depends upon evidence that all suffering at the end of life can be adequately relieved by palliative care.

---

[67] *Voluntary Euthanasia and the Common Law*, 216.

While it is probably true that few patients now have to endure unbearable levels of pain, other distressing conditions, such as the inability to swallow or difficulties in breathing, cannot be relieved by conventional analgesics, and instead the only way to relieve suffering is to sedate the patient into a coma. As we saw earlier, from the patient's point of view, causing death and inducing permanent unconsciousness may be indistinguishable. Furthermore, pain is seldom the principal or the only reason for patients' requests for euthanasia. On the contrary, patients more frequently cite fear of indignity, loss of control and dependency as their reasons for wanting to be helped to die. The Remmelink study into euthanasia in the Netherlands, which we consider below, found that loss of dignity was a much more common reason for requesting euthanasia than unbearable pain. In Oregon, the principal reasons for requesting physician assisted suicide are loss of autonomy; a decreasing ability to participate in the activities that made life enjoyable; and losing control of bodily functions,[68] there have been no cases in which pain was the only reason for requesting assisted suicide.[69] While optimum palliative care may be able to minimize physical pain, it is less clear that it can eradicate the helplessness and mental anguish that many people experience as a result of their bodies' progressive deterioration. Certainly the House of Lords Select Committee on assisted dying found that:

There was a general consensus among our witnesses as regards the limitations of palliative care in relieving patient suffering. The VES [Voluntary Euthanasia Society] took the view that 'no amount of palliative care can address some patients' concerns regarding their loss of autonomy, loss of control of bodily functions and loss of dignity'. . . . The BMA echoed this view, observing that 'there are patients for whom even the best palliative care is not dealing with their pain', adding that 'in spite of excellent palliative care, the position is not necessarily one which those patients regard as beneficial to them'.[70]

The second reason for arguing that the legalization of euthanasia is unnecessary derives from the recognition that, in practice, doctors do help their patients to die. So, according to this line of argument, the status quo enables patients who are in desperate straits to have access to medical assistance in ending their lives, while simultaneously retaining the symbolically important prohibition upon doctors killing their patients. Martha Minow, for example has argued that:

For now, at least, it is better to live with the lie that prohibition prevents the practice than the lie that its approval would not cost all of us, deeply. It is better to live with the lie that prohibition works so that, at the margin, those who engage in it do so with trembling.[71]

This sort of argument rests upon two different assumptions: first, that in individual cases, euthanasia may be justifiable; and secondly, that openly legalizing euthanasia might have negative consequences for society as a whole. Of course, these assumptions initially appear to pull in entirely different directions, and so the argument that

---

[68] Oregon Department of Human Services, *Fifth Annual Report on Oregon's Death with Dignity Act* (2002) <http://www.dhs.state.or.us/publichealth/chs/pas/ar-smmry.cfm>.

[69] Margaret Pabst Battin, *Ending Life: Ethics and the Way we Die* (OUP Oxford 2005).

[70] Assisted Dying for the Terminally Ill Committee, *Assisted Dying for the Terminally Ill Bill—First Report* (2005) para 88.

[71] Martha Minow, 'Which question? Which lie? Reflections on the Physician-Assisted Suicide Cases' (1997) 1 Supreme Court Review 30.

we should retain euthanasia's illegality while acknowledging that some doctors will be prepared to act unlawfully in order to help their patients to die is an attempt to have it both ways. As Yale Kamisar admits:

I do not deny it is hard to defend an absolute prohibition when you not only expect the prohibition to be violated in certain situations, but you can visualize circumstances where you would understand and forgive the person who did so.[72]

It could, of course, be argued that if we accept that euthanasia might be acceptable in some circumstances, retaining its absolute prohibition is disingenuous and hypocritical. If we think that doctors sometimes act properly in helping their patients to die, it seems unreasonable to expect them to expose themselves to the risk of life imprisonment.

(c) Difficulties in ensuring that a request has been made voluntarily

Obviously, if it were to be legalized, it would be of vital importance to ensure that patients' requests for euthanasia had been made voluntarily. For a number of reasons, some commentators have suggested that in practice this represents an insuperable obstacle to legalization. First, as Susan M Wolf explains, euthanasia is generally requested by patients who are extremely distressed, and whose judgement may be distorted by the depression that often accompanies the final stages of debilitating illness. It has therefore been argued that our inability to *guarantee* that a patient's desire to die is genuine—and not, for example, a symptom of their treatable depression—should lead us to be extremely reluctant to comply with patients' requests for euthanasia.

Susan M Wolf[73]

[A]dvocates for legalizing assisted suicide . . . embrace a model that depicts patients as independent rights-bearers making decisions at the end of life free from undue pressure and coercion. Yet there are numerous problems with this vision. First, patients actually exercise little control over end-of-life care . . . In reality, patients are profoundly dependent on health professionals, with many patients reporting that they want their physician to make treatment decisions for them . . . The research shows . . . that depression is even more strongly correlated with requests for assisted suicide than pain is. Yet patients routinely face inadequate diagnosis and treatment of depression. Given these data, a patient requesting assisted suicide may actually be seeking relief from depression or pain . . .

Terminal patients are quite unlike independent rights-bearers freely negotiating in business transactions. Instead, they are profoundly dependent, often at the mercy of health professionals for everything from toileting to life-saving care, and may be experiencing too much pain, discomfort, or depression to make independent and truly voluntary decisions. They may not even know that relief from their depression or pain is available without suicide.

Secondly, because the consequence of euthanasia will be the patient's death, there is no scope for correcting mistaken decisions if, for example, it subsequently emerges

[72] Yale Kamisar, 'Physician Assisted Suicide: The Problems Presented by the Compelling Heartwrenching Case' (1998) 88 Journal of Criminal Law and Criminology 1121, 1144.
[73] 'Pragmatism in the Face of Death: The Role of Facts in the Assisted Suicide Debate' (1998) 82 Minnesota Law Review 1063, 1074–7.

that the patient had in fact been incompetent (perhaps as a result of treatable depression) when they made the decision to die. Nor is there room for the correction of decisions to die made following a mistaken diagnosis of terminal illness. Given the finality of euthanasia and this inevitable risk of error, opponents of legalization have suggested that we could never be sufficiently certain that a person's request for euthanasia had been properly informed and competently made. It has even been argued that the possibility that a miraculous cure might be discovered after the patient's medically-induced death, but before their life would naturally have come to an end, means that all requests for euthanasia are based upon inadequate information. This last point can probably be discounted, however, because medical progress never moves this quickly. As we saw in Chapter 8, a 'miraculous cure' will have undergone years of experiments before it can be tried on human volunteers. The inevitable time-lag between the knowledge that a new treatment exists and it becoming available to patients largely eradicates the risk that an unexpected cure might miraculously become available shortly after a patient had opted for euthanasia.

Thirdly, as we saw in Chapter 6, consultations between patients and their doctors are protected by the principle of patient confidentiality. So while supporters of legalization often suggest that regulation would enable euthanasia to be scrutinized and monitored, in practice, as Daniel Callahan and Margot White argue in the next extract, it might be difficult to exercise much control over doctors' oral discussions with their patients.

Daniel Callahan and Margot White[74]

If it is true, as it indubitably is, that 'decisions about medical treatment are normally made in the privacy of the doctor–patient relationship,' then an obvious question must be asked: how is it possible, or could it ever be possible, to monitor and regulate those decisions regarding physician-assisted suicide that occur within the ambit of that privacy? How can there be oversight of those discussions, decisions, and transactions which must remain secret, and the confidentiality of which is protected by [law]?

There are two possible ways to proceed here: either we can station a policeman in every doctor's office and next to every sickbed to monitor all conversations, or we can depend upon the individual physician to voluntarily reveal that he or she has been part of an agreement to pursue physician-assisted suicide. Since the former course would both violate doctor–patient confidentiality and be utterly impractical, only the latter option is available. But that course means, in effect, that any physician-assisted suicide regulation must, in the end, be physician self-regulated . . .

We submit that maintaining the privacy of the physician–patient relationship and the confidentiality of these deliberations is fundamentally incompatible with meaningful oversight and adherence to any statutory regulations . . . It is not difficult to imagine many circumstances in which either the physician or the patient, or both, would prefer to keep the agreement secret. How can that situation be monitored or regulated? . . . No evidence could establish that a patient is not suffering the severe and unrelenting suffering he claims, or which the doctor subsequently claims the patient claimed.

Of course, the obvious response to all three of these arguments is that we already allow patients to make decisions which will result in their deaths when we respect

---

[74] 'The Legalization of Physician-Assisted Suicide: Creating a Regulatory Potemkin Village' (1996) 30 University of Richmond Law Review 1, 8–11.

their refusals of life-prolonging medical treatment. Patients who are connected to mechanical ventilators may be distressed, and we may wrongly judge them to be competent, yet this inescapable risk of error does not persuade us that we should prevent patients from taking life and death decisions. We do not prohibit doctors from prescribing potentially lethal doses of painkilling drugs on the grounds that a miracle cure might subsequently become available. Nor do we think that the principle of patient confidentiality represents an insurmountable obstacle to our ability to protect vulnerable patients from being coerced into agreeing to the withdrawal of life-prolonging treatment.

(d) Risk of abuse

In a related argument, some commentators are concerned that if euthanasia were readily available, elderly patients would be pressurized into electing a premature death. In the next extract, Margaret Pabst Battin sets out a variety of different ways in which patients might be vulnerable to abuse.

Margaret Pabst Battin[75]

Three conceptually distinct types of abuse can be identified: . . . what we might call interpersonal abuse, professional abuse, and institutional abuse . . . Chief among the varieties of interpersonal abuse, one might expect, would be that occurring in familial situations: the resentful or greedy spouse, or other family member, who manoeuvres a terminally ill patient now perceived as a burden into requesting euthanasia or assistance in suicide. Such pressures might be malevolent, the product of long years of hostility; or, perhaps more likely, they might be the product of the kind of emotional exhaustion familial caregivers often experience in attending to a patient with a lengthy, deteriorative terminal illness . . .

Professional abuse, understood as that range of ways in which professionals, especially phys- icians, might bring a patient who would not otherwise do so to 'voluntarily' request euthanasia or help in suicide, can exhibit most of the features of interpersonal, domestic abuse—suggestion, manipulation, and threats . . .—but it incorporates an additional feature: the weight of profes- sional authority . . . Especially when it is terminal, illness can place a person in a particularly compromised position. Thus 'professional authority' trades on two factors: the greater weight of the physician and the compromised position of the patient. Both factors invite abuse. Given this disparity of power in the physician/patient relationship, physicians are very well aware of their power to influence patient choices . . . The physician's capacity to shape patient choice in eutha- nasia, both by selective control of information and by initial formulation of both the problem and the solution presented for consent, may be influenced not only by malevolent intentions but also by paternalistic ones . . .

Institutional abuse . . . is conceptually distinct in its central feature: it operates by narrowing the range of actual choices open to the patient. It may seem to closely resemble those forms of professional abuse in which the physician shapes the patient's choice by selectively providing information or proposing one rather than another possible course of action for consent, but it functions in a distinct way: it erects barriers so that certain choices can be made only with difficulty or cannot be made at all. It is not only that choices are shaped, but, more importantly, that only certain choices are possible, while other choices are closed off . . . The fear [is] primarily of policies that are financially motivated, seeking to cut costs in medicine by offering less care.

---

[75] *The Least Worst Death: Essays in Bioethics on the End of Life* (OUP Oxford 1994) 167–71.

In some cases then, pressure to opt for euthanasia might come overtly from unscrupulous or greedy relatives. But it is also common for elderly people to perceive themselves to be a burden to their family, and if death were an option, there is a danger that they might request euthanasia for altruistic reasons, despite their own desire to go on living. In the next extract, Hazel Biggs suggests that this desire to avoid becoming a burden to one's family is particularly acute for elderly women, who might be especially at risk from the legalization of euthanasia.

Hazel Biggs[76]

Those who have been involved in caring for the young, the old and the dying are more likely to experience this type of [psychological] pain and this reluctance to become a burden to their carers. Hence many women's perceptions and tolerance of their own illnesses and infirmities are inescapably coloured by their experiences as carers. They know what is involved because they have been responsible for doing it, or have at least supported others who have done it . . .

As a consequence it is easy to postulate that euthanasia may be an option which appears more attractive to women than men, both for themselves when they need care and perhaps advocated by women who are carers and observe the futile suffering of those for whom they must care . . .

[M]any women feel vulnerable and concerned at the prospect of becoming the cared-for rather than the carer because society appears to no longer value them once they reach this state. Legal change to permit euthanasia could be perilous for women in these circumstances.

This study illustrates that statistically, women live longer than men and that often, because of their experience as carers, they appear to be more vociferous than men in calling for the legalisation of euthanasia. . . . Yet if active euthanasia were to be permitted as a right, what is to prevent the endorsement of this *right* being translated into a duty? How long will it be before those who seek euthanasia in order to avoid being a burden lose the right to continue living until the natural end of their lives? The experiences of women in the Cheyenne and Inuit societies who were expected to withdraw from their communities once they had outlived their usefulness as carers, are indicative of the dangers which could flow from laws permitting euthanasia. The introduction of legal euthanasia could alter social and personal expectations of old age beyond recognition, changing it from a time for relaxation and quiet enjoyment of the twilight years to a time for resisting pressure and the expectations of those who perceive that all useful life is over . . .

In the light of this it is arguable that no reform of the law to legalise euthanasia could provide adequate safeguards to protect those who may be vulnerable to pressure to accept euthanasia for themselves. While it is incumbent upon feminists to uphold the principle of autonomy and individual choice it is important that the principle is not endorsed at the risk of placing pressure on those who may prefer to exercise their choice to live.

In addition, it is possible that pressure to opt for an earlier death might come from the medical profession. Luke Gormally argues that since euthanasia would tend to be cheaper than providing adequate palliative care to terminally ill patients, it might appear to offer a particularly cost-effective solution to the NHS's financial crisis.

---

[76] 'I Don't Want to be a Burden! A Feminist Reflects on Women's Experiences of Death and Dying' in S Sheldon and M Thomson (eds), *Feminist Perspectives on Health Care Law* (Cavendish London 1998) 279–95, 292, 294–5.

Luke Gormally[77]

It is very important to bear in mind that a key element in the context of contemporary debates about legalizing euthanasia is the drive to reduce health care costs. One of the conspicuous dangers of legalization is that, before long, euthanasia would be seen as a convenient 'solution' to the heavy demands on care made by certain types of patient. Medicine would thereby be robbed of the incentive to find genuinely compassionate solutions to the difficulties presented by such patients. The kind of humane impulses which have sustained the development of hospice medicine and care would be undermined because too many would think euthanasia a cheaper and less personally demanding solution.

Of course it would be unethical for doctors to try to persuade their patients to choose euthanasia, but Leon Kass and Nelson Lund argue that simply mentioning death as a treatment option might subtly influence patients' choices.

Leon R Kass and Nelson Lund[78]

Many families and physicians will find in the option of electable death an opportunity to relieve themselves of the emotional burdens of caring for difficult or incurable patients. Others will be able to avoid huge economic costs or to achieve financial gain connected to an earlier demise . . . Even when relatives and physicians are not consciously aware that they are succumbing to such temptations, they will be subtly but surely pulled in that direction.

Because the quick-fix of suicide is easy and cheap, it will in many cases replace the use of hospice and other . . . forms of palliative care . . . [A] quick death will often be the most cost-effective 'therapeutic option' and will therefore be ever more frequently employed . . .

Illness . . . invariably means dependence, and dependence means relying for advice on physician and family . . . With patients reduced—helpless in action and ambivalent about life—someone who will benefit from their death need not proceed by overt coercion. Rather, requests for assisted suicide can and will be subtly engineered. To alter and influence choices, physicians and families need not be driven entirely by base motives or even be consciously manipulative. Well-meaning and discreet suggestions, or even unconscious changes in expression, gesture, and tone of voice, can move a dependent and suggestible patient toward a choice for death. Simply by making assisted suicide an option available to gravely ill persons, will we not 'sweep up, in the process, some who are not really tired of life, but think others are tired of them; some who do not really want to die, but who feel that they should not live on, because to do so when there looms the legal alternative of euthanasia is to do a selfish or cowardly act?' Anyone who knows anything at all about the real life of the elderly and the incurable knows that many of them will experience . . . their right to choose physician-assisted death as a duty to do so . . .

When the physician presents a depressed or frightened patient with a horrible prognosis and includes among the options the offer of a 'gentle quick release,' what will the patient likely choose, especially in the face of a spiraling hospital bill or resentful children? The legalization of physician-assisted suicide, ostensibly a measure enhancing the freedom of dying patients, will in fact in many cases be a deadly license for physicians to recommend and prescribe death.

Again, insofar as there is a risk that patients might opt for a course of action that will result in their death out of a sense of obligation, or as a result of more direct pressure,

---

[77] 'Euthanasia and Assisted Suicide: 7 reasons why they should not be legalized', 286–90 in Donna Dickenson, Malcolm Johnson, and Jeanne Samson Katz (eds), *Death, Dying and Bereavement* (2nd edn Sage London 2000) 285, 287.

[78] 'Physician-Assisted Suicide, Medical Ethics and the Future of the Medical Profession' (1996) 35 Duquesne Law Review 395, 406–8.

this must be equally true when death is achieved by treatment withdrawal. If we do think vulnerable patients need to be protected against choosing a premature death against their own wishes, we should in fact probably be *more* concerned about refusals of life-prolonging treatment, where the decision must be respected even if it is wholly irrational, than legalized euthanasia, which would only be available in certain tightly circumscribed circumstances. As David Orentlicher explains,

The law does not limit withdrawals of treatment only to cases in which a patient is irreversibly ill. Patients whose lives could be saved and who could be restored to very good health with the brief use of a ventilator or the transfusion of blood can still refuse the treatment . . . Physicians are free to turn off ventilators not only when the patient will die without the ventilator, but also when the patient might still be restored to very good health . . . If the risks of . . . abuse are reason enough to condemn decisions to shorten a patient's life, they should lead a person to oppose treatment withdrawal as well as euthanasia and assisted suicide.[79]

Even if we were to acknowledge the possibility that patients' might feel pressurized into requesting assistance in dying, it does not necessarily follow that the only appropriate solution is a complete ban on euthanasia and assisted suicide. Rather, unless we have concluded that there is no other feasible way of protecting vulnerable patients, it might be better to investigate regulations which would enable euthanasia to take place only in cases where the request *does* reflect the patient's enduring and genuine desire to die. A blanket prohibition upon a practice is a peculiarly blunt and imprecise way to prevent its abuse, and may underestimate the law's ability to distinguish between real and coerced consent. Moreover, if we know that euthanasia is, in fact, currently practised covertly, any risk of abuse will be magnified by the secrecy and lack of transparency which are the inevitable consequence of its illegality.

(e) Effect on the doctor–patient relationship

One of the strongest arguments against legalization is that it would have a profoundly deleterious impact upon the doctor–patient relationship, and would damage the integrity of the medical profession. There are two interrelated aspects to this argument. First, from the point of view of the patient, it might be argued that knowing their doctors could legally kill them would reduce patient trust. Brian Simpson, for example, has argued that 'for a doctor to kill his own patients involves a peculiarly alarming breach of trust, and one that is dramatically incompatible with the role of a doctor'.[80] Whether or not patients share this assumption that legalization would diminish their trust in the medical profession is, however, unclear. A 2004 opinion poll found that 70 per cent said that the legalization of assisted suicide would not affect their trust in their doctors, while 9 per cent would trust their doctors *more* and 9 per cent would trust their doctors less.[81] We should of course be wary of the results of these sorts of polls, since so much will depend upon the way in which a particular question is framed. A different survey found that 60 per cent of respondents believed

---

[79] 'The Alleged Distinction between euthanasia and the withdrawal of life-sustaining treatment: conceptually incoherent and impossible to maintain' (1998) University of Illinois Law Review 837, 841–2, 845.

[80] AW Brian Simpson, 'Euthanasia for sale?' (1986) 84 Michigan Law Review 807, 809.

[81] Assisted Dying for the Terminally Ill Committee, *Assisted Dying for the Terminally Ill Bill—First Report* (2005) 77.

that elderly people might be more nervous about going into hospital if euthanasia were legalized.[82]

Secondly, from the point of view of the doctor, if 'killing' were to become a treatment option, the ethical foundations of the medical profession would be undermined, and this in turn would reduce patients' willingness to trust their doctors. The GMC took this view in their evidence to the House of Lords Select Committee on Assisted Dying:

a change in the law to allow physician-assisted dying would have profound implications for the role and responsibilities of doctors and their relationships with patients. Acting with the primary intention to hasten a patient's death would be difficult to reconcile with the medical ethical principles of beneficence and non-maleficence.[83]

And in her evidence to the committee, Dr Vivianne Nathanson of the BMA argued that it is difficult to imagine that many doctors would want to effectively specialize in death:

What doctors find it impossible to consider is who would want to provide that service. They find it almost impossible to conceive of a person who would want to spend their life administering lethal injections. Whether such a service could ever be set up, and who would be the people who took part in it, raises very serious questions.[84]

In the next extract, Leon Kass and Nelson Lund suggest that an absolute 'taboo against medical killing' is necessary to preserve patient trust in the medical profession.

Leon R Kass and Nelson Lund[85]

Authorizing physician-assisted suicide would . . . overturn a centuries-old taboo against medical killing, a taboo understood by many to be one of the cornerstones of the medical ethic. This taboo is at least as old as, and is most famously formulated in, the Hippocratic Oath, in which it stands as the first negative promise of professional self-restraint: 'I will neither give a deadly drug to anybody if asked for it, nor will I make a suggestion to this effect' . . . This . . . is a pledge to refrain from practicing euthanasia, even on request, and from assisting or even encouraging a willing patient in suicide.

This self-imposed professional forbearance . . . is rooted in several deep insights into the nature of medicine. First, it recognizes the dangerous moral neutrality of medical technique: drugs can both cure and kill. Only if the means used serve a professionally appropriate end will medical practice be ethical . . . Most importantly, this taboo against euthanasia and assisted-suicide—like the taboos against violating confidentiality and sexual misconduct, enunciated later in the Oath— addresses a prominent 'occupational hazard' to which the medical professional is especially prone: a temptation to take advantage of the vulnerability and exposure that the practice of medicine requires of patients. Just as patients necessarily divulge and reveal to the physician private and intimate details of their personal lives; just as patients necessarily expose their naked bodies to the physician's objectifying gaze and investigating hands; so patients necessarily expose and entrust the care of their very lives to the physician's skill, technique, judgment, and character. Mindful of the meaning of such exposure and vulnerability, and mindful too of their own human

---

[82] Ibid.   [83] Ibid, 42.   [84] Ibid, 43.
[85] 'Physician-Assisted Suicide, Medical Ethics and the Future of the Medical Profession' (1996) 35 Duquesne Law Review 395, 402, 408–10, 418–19, 424.

penchant for error and mischief, the Hippocratic physicians voluntarily set limits on their own conduct, pledging not to take advantage of or to violate the patient's intimacies, naked sexuality, or life itself . . .

For how can you trust a stranger-doctor to be wholeheartedly devoted to your best interests once he has a license to kill? . . . Should physician-assisted suicide become a legal option, it will enter unavoidably—sometimes explicitly, sometimes tacitly—into many a doctor–patient encounter . . . [A] patient's trust in the physician is a necessary ingredient in the therapeutic relationship and, at least indirectly, in the healing process . . . In the increasingly impersonal world of modern medicine, patients must without any direct evidence presume that their care-givers are trustworthy, even before they have shown that they deserve to be trusted. Especially under these conditions, the trust given to each physician stems largely from the trustworthiness attached to the profession as a whole . . .

The taboo against physician-assisted suicide is perhaps even more crucial as protection against physicians' arrogance, namely, their willingness to judge, on the basis of their own private preju-dices and attitudes, whether this or that life is unworthy of continued existence . . .

Decent medical conduct regarding dying patients must . . . depend decisively on the fragile virtue of the medical profession. The age-old rule that sharply separates deliberate killing from letting patients die in appropriate circumstances enables physicians to handle death by abhorring killing. Without that rule, human weakness and professional arrogance will destroy the hard-won ethos of the profession.

Of course, as we have already seen, doctors do sometimes engage in practices which will 'hasten death' or 'shorten life', so this argument relies upon the existence of a sharp distinction between 'killing' and 'letting die'. For those who reject the idea that killing is always necessarily morally worse than letting die, this argument against legalization will be less persuasive.

(f) Slippery slope

We looked at the series of claims involved in slippery slope arguments in Chapter 1 (refer back to pp. 27–8 for a full account). It is important to remember that when someone invokes a slippery slope argument, they are not arguing that there is some-thing intrinsically wrong with doctors helping their patients to die. Of course, they may also believe this to be true, but this would not be a slippery slope argument. Rather, the slippery slope claim is that even if we were to accept that doctors might sometimes act reasonably when they comply with a patient's request for euthanasia, we should nevertheless continue to prohibit euthanasia because sanctioning some compassionate acts of killing would make it very difficult to prevent those with less benevolent motives from ending patients' lives.

Of course, proponents of slippery slope arguments must explain why allowing some cases of voluntary euthanasia would necessarily lead to other less acceptable practices. They might, for example, argue that it would be virtually impossible to adequately police the boundary between acceptable and unacceptable medical kill-ings. Some of the arguments we encountered earlier concerning the difficulty in distinguishing between voluntary and coerced choices might be relevant here. Alter-natively, Carl Schneider has argued that there is 'a psychological aspect of slippery slopes', namely that 'they work partly by domesticating one idea and thus making its nearest neighbor down the slope seem less extreme and unthinkable'.[86] It is this latter type of slippery slope argument which is invoked in the next extract by Dieter Giesen, who argues that allowing doctors to kill their patients would weaken the absolute prohibition upon the taking of innocent life, and that we would all therefore become progressively desensitized to the horror of murder.

Dieter Giesen[87]

Active euthanasia also poses a major threat to the principle of the inviolability of life . . . Recent history shows us that once firm constraints against killing are removed, a general moral decline will result. The German experience of the Nazi euthanasia programme, during which [about] 100,000 disabled persons were killed because they were classified as living 'lives not worth living', demonstrates the potential for perverse thinking and inhuman deeds once the first step upon the slippery slope is taken.

Experience in the Netherlands to date suggests that, in practice, no sharp distinction can be drawn between voluntary and non-voluntary euthanasia. Instead, commentators have documented a continuum of killing, from the (quite rare) paradigm case of informed and rational choice to frequent instances of familial and medical pressure, to the elimination of defenceless newborns, adjudged to be a burden upon society and to the purging of old people's homes . . . With perhaps as many as 8% of all deaths in the Netherlands resulting from active euthanasia, an atmosphere of fear and distrust has been created among the weakest and most vulnerable sections of that society.

In some ways, as Dan W Brock points out, a slippery slope argument is a straight-forward empirical claim: does legalizing euthanasia make involuntary killing more likely?

Dan W Brock[88]

According to this 'slippery slope' worry, although active euthanasia may be morally permissible in cases in which it is unequivocally voluntary and the patient finds his or her condition unbearable, a legal policy permitting euthanasia would inevitably lead to active euthanasia being performed in many other cases in which it would be morally wrong. To prevent those other wrongful cases of euthanasia we should not permit even morally justified performance of it.

Slippery slope arguments of this form are problematic and difficult to evaluate. From one perspective, they are the last refuge of conservative defenders of the status quo. When all the opponent's objections to the wrongness of euthanasia itself have been met, the opponent then shifts ground and acknowledges both that it is not in itself wrong and that a legal policy which resulted only in its being performed would not be bad. Nevertheless, the opponent maintains, it should still not be permitted because doing so would result in its being performed in other cases in which it is not voluntary and would be wrong. In this argument's most extreme form, permitting euthanasia is the first and fateful step down the slippery slope to Nazism. Once on the slope we will be unable to get off . . .

A similar possible slippery slope worry could have been raised to securing competent patients' rights to decide about life support, but recent history shows that such a worry would have been unfounded. It must be relevant how likely it is that we will end with horrendous consequences and

---

[86] C Schneider, 'Rights Discourse and Neonatal Euthanasia' (1988) 76 California Law Review 151, 168.

[87] 'Dilemmas at life's end: a comparative legal perspective' in John Keown (ed), *Euthanasia Examined* (CUP Cambridge 1995) 204.

[88] *Voluntary Active Euthanasia*, Hastings Centre Report 22 Mar–Apr 1992, 10–22 [60–1].

an unjustified practice of euthanasia. . . . Opponents of voluntary euthanasia on slippery slope grounds have not provided the data or evidence necessary to turn their speculative concerns into well-grounded likelihoods.

Given their empirical nature, we might attempt to evaluate whether legalizing euthanasia represents the first step on a slippery slope by examining data from the countries that have gone some way towards legalization. But as we will see again in the next section, the problem is that different (and often flatly contradictory) interpretations of the available data abound. John Keown, for example, has argued that:

the Dutch experience lends weighty support to the slippery slope argument . . . Within a decade, the so-called strict safeguards against the slide have proved signally ineffectual; non-voluntary euthanasia is now widely practised and increasingly condoned in the Netherlands.[89]

In contrast, Helga Kuhse et al.'s confidential survey of 3,000 Australian doctors found that non-voluntary euthanasia is five times more common in Australia, where euthanasia is illegal, than it is in the Netherlands.[90] Australian doctors were far less likely than their Dutch counterparts to discuss the decision to hasten a patient's death with the patient herself, or to seek her consent. And in their study of six European countries, Agnes van der Heide et al. found that non-voluntary euthanasia was more than twice as common in Denmark as it was in the Netherlands, and that:

Ending of life without the patient's explicit request happened more frequently than euthanasia in all countries apart from the Netherlands; this type of doctor-assisted death was the only one recorded in Sweden (0·23% of all deaths).[91]

If patients' lives are ended in the absence of an explicit request with similar or greater frequency in countries which have *not* legalized euthanasia, it is not clear that the legalization of euthanasia in the Netherlands has *caused* any propensity to engage in non-voluntary euthanasia.

Even if we could establish that it would be difficult to draw or police the line between acceptable and unacceptable instances of euthanasia, it is, in my view, not obvious that an absolute prohibition is the optimum regulatory response.

Emily Jackson[92]

The slippery slope argument suggests that although we might be able to distinguish paradigm cases at the top of the moral slope from those at the bottom, it would be very difficult to locate or police the line between acceptable and unacceptable practices towards the middle of the slope. Yet this 'grey area' problem exists whenever we attempt to regulate *anything*. Let us apply slippery slope reasoning to a more mundane regulatory problem. Should I maintain an absolute prohibition on the late submission of essays on the grounds that giving an extension to student A who has

---

[89] 'Euthanasia in the Netherlands: sliding down the slippery slope?' in J Keown (ed), *Euthanasia Examined* (CUP Cambridge 1995) 261–96, 289.

[90] H. Kuhse et al., 'End-of-life Decisions in Australian Medical Practice' (1997) 166 Medical Journal of Australia 191–6.

[91] Agnes van der Heide, Luc Deliens, Karin Faisst, Tore Nilstun, Michael Norup, Eugenio Paci, Gerrit van der Wal, and Paul J van der Maas, 'End-of-life decision-making in six European countries: descriptive study' (2003) 362 Lancet 345–50.

[92] 'Whose Death is it Anyway? Euthanasia and the Medical Profession' (2004) 57 Current Legal Problems 415–42, 430–2.

a very compelling reason—say, the death of a close family member—might make it difficult for me to draw a line between her case and those of students B, C, D, and E who have progressively less persuasive grounds for late submission? An absolute prohibition would relieve me of the difficulty of drawing distinctions between borderline cases: perhaps student C's computer has stopped working, and student D left her essay on the bus. But I do a grave injustice to student A by preferring the simplicity of an absolute ban over the admittedly more time-consuming and complex task of drawing fine distinctions between serious and trivial excuses for late submission. . . .

Nor is it obvious that a blanket ban is the optimum response to concerns about a practice's potential misapplication. If we can imagine circumstances in which euthanasia might be legitimate, prohibiting it completely in order to prevent it being employed in other less compelling situations is a peculiarly blunt approach to regulation, especially since the consequence for patients who do clearly merit access to euthanasia will be a protracted, painful or otherwise intolerable death. It would be more logical to advocate regulations which confine access to euthanasia to patients whose circumstances lie at the top of the moral slope (whatever those might be), and prohibit it in all other cases.

(3) IS LEGALIZATION LIKELY?

In the early 1990s the House of Lords Select Committee on Medical Ethics investigated whether the law should be reformed. It concluded that there should be no change in the law on intentional killing. The committee was persuaded that 'it would be next to impossible to ensure that all acts of euthanasia were truly voluntary and that any liberalization of the law was not abused'. The committee was concerned about pressure being exerted on sick and elderly individuals to request euthanasia, and about the message legalization would send to vulnerable and disadvantaged people about society's attitudes towards them. Since the select committee's view was endorsed by most political parties and by bodies such as the GMC and the BMA, the prospect of legalization looked very remote indeed.

Over a decade later, in 2004 Lord Joffe introduced a second version of his Assisted Dying for the Terminally Ill Bill into the House of Lords. It would have allowed competent adult patients who were terminally ill and experiencing unbearable suffering to request assistance in dying, either directly through euthanasia or by assisting their suicide, and would have provided doctors with a right of conscientious objection. The Bill had no chance of becoming law before the 2005 general election, but it was scrutinized by the House of Lords Select Committee on Assisted Dying, whose report was published in April 2005. The select committee found that there had been a number of developments since the last select committee reported, most notably the legislation enacted in Oregon, the Netherlands, and Belgium.

It recommended that a new bill should be introduced, which would address the issues discussed in their report, but which should again be subjected to committee scrutiny before being put before parliament. In particular, the select committee suggested that any new bill should distinguish between euthanasia and assisted suicide so that the issues could be addressed separately. The House of Lords Committee appeared to have been influenced by their finding that:

where legislation is limited to assistance with suicide, the take-up rate is dramatically less than in places where voluntary euthanasia is also legalised.[93]

The committee also recommended that

in the framing of any future bill consideration should be given to the inclusion of a requirement for any applicant for assistance with suicide or voluntary euthanasia to be given a psychiatric assessment in order both to confirm that the request is based on a reasoned decision and is free from external pressure and that the applicant is not suffering from a psychiatric or psychological disorder causing impaired judgement. In cases where such disorder was apparent, we would expect an applicant to be offered treatment.[94]

The Committee criticized the Bill's reliance upon 'terminal illness' as a qualifying condition, since predictions about how long a patient is likely to live are notoriously unreliable. It also drew attention to the difficulties caused by a subjective criterion such as 'unbearable suffering', and instead recommended a more objective test, such as 'unrelievable' or 'intractable' suffering or distress, which would make access to assisted suicide contingent upon the patient's carers having unsuccessfully attempted to relieve her suffering. Finally, it was the Committee's view that the doctor's right of conscientious objection should extend to referral to another doctor, and that all health care professionals should have their right not to participate in assisted dying respected.

Whether or not a new bill which contains these additional safeguards would have any chance of becoming law is, of course, open to question. But also significant is the BMA's change of position at their annual representative meeting in 2005. While the BMA has previously opposed legalization, it is now explicitly agnostic. A majority of the BMA's representatives backed the statement:

The BMA should not oppose legislation which alters the criminal law but should press for robust safeguards both for patients and for doctors who do not wish to be involved in such procedures.[95]

(c) EXPERIENCE IN OTHER COUNTRIES

It is not possible to provide a comprehensive analysis of the legal status of euthanasia and assisted suicide throughout the world in this chapter. Instead, we look at a handful of countries where euthanasia and/or assisted suicide have been treated more leniently than in the UK. This ranges from overt legalization in the Netherlands, to the de facto toleration of compassionately motivated assisted suicide in Switzerland.

(1) THE NETHERLANDS

(a) The law

Although a statute specifically legalizing euthanasia was not introduced in the Netherlands until 2001, since 1973 the Dutch courts had gradually been developing

---

[93] Assisted Dying for the Terminally Ill Committee, *Assisted Dying for the Terminally Ill Bill—First Report* (2005) 13.
[94] Ibid, 86   [95] <http://www.bma.org.uk>.

exceptions to the express prohibitions on active voluntary euthanasia and assisted suicide that were contained in Articles 293 and 294 of the Dutch Penal Code:

A person who takes the life of another at that other person's express and serious request is punishable by imprisonment for a maximum of 12 years or by a fine (293)

A person who intentionally incites another to commit suicide, assists in the suicide of another, or procures the means to commit suicide is punishable, where death ensues, by imprisonment for a maximum of 3 years or by a fine (294)

Through a series of court decisions, a set of guidelines had emerged which—if followed—served to protect doctors from criminal liability. To some extent, then, the 2001 Statute simply formalized existing practice in the Netherlands.

In 1973 a Dutch court indicated for the first time that euthanasia might be acceptable in certain circumstances. In the *Postma* case[96] a doctor was prosecuted for giving her mother a fatal dose of morphine. Dr Postma's mother had had a cerebral haemorrhage which had left her very seriously disabled. She had unsuccessfully attempted to commit suicide and had repeatedly expressed her desire to die. There was widespread public sympathy for Dr Postma, and although the Leeuwarden District Court convicted her under Article 293, it imposed a symbolic suspended sentence of a week's imprisonment. Furthermore, the Court took the opportunity to indicate that, despite Article 293, euthanasia could be acceptable if performed in certain circumstances: (1) the patient should be incurably ill; (2) the patient should be experiencing unbearable suffering; (3) the patient should have requested that his or her life be terminated; and (4) the termination is performed by the patient's own doctor, or in consultation with him or her.

Following this decision, a number of other cases were brought before the Dutch Courts. In 1981, a case of assisted suicide prompted the Rotterdam Criminal Court to lay down a set of guidelines which would exempt doctors who had helped their patients to die from punishment:[97]

   (i) The patient must repeatedly and explicitly express the desire to die;

  (ii) The patient's decision must be well informed, free and enduring;

 (iii) The patient must be suffering from severe physical or mental pain with no prospect of relief;

 (iv) All other options for care must have been exhausted or refused by the patient;

  (v) Euthanasia must be carried out by a qualified physician;

 (vi) The physician must consult at least one other physician;

(vii) The physician must inform the local coroner that euthanasia has been performed.

These guidelines were then adopted by the public prosecutor's office as the criteria which would determine whether or not cases of euthanasia or assisted suicide would be prosecuted.

---

[96] *Nederlandse Jurisprudentie* 1973 No 183 District Court of Leeuwarden 21 Feb 1973.
[97] *Wertheim, Nederlandse Jurisprudentie* 1982 No 63 Rotterdam Criminal Court.

The first case to come before the Dutch Supreme Court was brought in 1984. In the *Alkmaar* case,[98] Dr Schoonheim had given a lethal injection to a 95-year-old patient who had signed an advance declaration requesting euthanasia if her condition should deteriorate beyond a certain point, and who had more recently expressed a clear and unequivocal wish to die. Dr Schoonheim was initially convicted. On appeal, the Dutch Supreme Court ruled that there had been insufficient investigation of the possibility that the doctor had faced an irreconcilable conflict of duties. They invoked the *nood-toestand* or 'emergency' defence, which applies where the doctor's duty to abide by the law and preserve the life of his patient may be outweighed by his duty to relieve unbearable suffering. The case was referred back to the Court of Appeal in The Hague, and Dr Schoonheim was acquitted. Of course, the *noodtoestand* defence is only cap-able of absolving doctors of criminal liability where the patient's suffering is so extreme that it overrides the doctor's normal duty to preserve life.

The next critically important case to come before the Dutch courts involved a patient whose suffering was purely mental. In the *Chabot* case,[99] a psychiatrist com-plied with a woman's repeated requests for assistance in committing suicide after the death of both of her sons had left her overwhelmingly unhappy. The Supreme Court accepted that there might be circumstances in which the *noodtoestand* defence would apply despite the absence of physical suffering or terminal illness. The Court did, however, suggest that exceptional care would be need to be taken when deciding that a person's mental suffering was both intolerable and incurable. Dr Chabot was con-victed because there was insufficient independent evidence of the gravity of Mrs Boscher's condition, but no punishment was imposed.

More recently, in the *Sutorius* case, the Supreme court dismissed Dr Suturius's appeal against his conviction for assisting the suicide of an 86-year-old man who was not suffering from any medically classifiable physical or psychiatric disorder.[100] The patient, Edward Brongersma, was obsessed with his physical decline and hopeless existence, he was 'tired of life' and had repeatedly expressed his wish to die. The Supreme Court decided that assisting suicide is only lawful if the patient's 'unbearable and hopeless suffering' is linked to a recognizable medical or psychiatric condition. However, no punishment was imposed on Dr Suturius, because it was accepted that he had acted out of concern for his patient.

Prior to 1990, doctors were under a duty to report cases of euthanasia and assisted suicide to the police, who would then investigate whether the guidelines had been followed, and inform the public prosecutor. Now each case is considered by a regional review committee, usually consisting of a lawyer, a doctor, and an ethicist. If the committee is satisfied that the criteria have been fulfilled, the case is closed without informing the public prosecutor, who is now notified only if the committee finds that the doctor did not fulfil the due care criteria.

The Termination of Life on Request and Assisted Suicide (Review Procedures) Act 2001 amended Articles 293 and 294 of the Criminal Code, and came into force on 1 April 2002. Euthanasia and assisted suicide continue to be criminal offences under

---

[98] *Nederlandse Jurisprudentie* 1985 No 106 Supreme Court 27 Nov 1984.
[99] Ibid, 1994 No 656 Supreme Court.
[100] T Sheldon, 'Being "tired of life" is not grounds for euthanasia' (2003) 326 BMJ 71.

Articles 293(1) and 294(1). But exceptions are introduced in Article 293(2) and 294(2), which both now read:

The act referred to in the first subsection shall not be an offence if it is committed by a physician who fulfils the due care criteria set out in Section 2 of the Termination of Life on Request and Assisted Suicde (Review Procedures) Act, and if the physician notifies the municipal pathologist of this act in accordance with the provisions of section 7, subsection 2 of the Burial and Cremation Act.

Under section 2, the requirements of due care are that the physician:

(a) holds the conviction that the request by the patient was voluntary and well-considered,

(b) holds the conviction that the patient's suffering was lasting and unbearable,

(c) has informed the patient about the situation he was in and about his prospects,

(d) and the patient hold the conviction that there was no other reasonable solution for the situation he was in,

(e) has consulted at least one other, independent physician who has seen the patient and has given his written opinion on the requirements of due care referred to in parts (a)–(d), and

(f) has terminated a life or assisted in a suicide with due care.

Two especially controversial aspects of the new law are worth noting. First, the Act specifically allows for advance requests for euthanasia, with section 2(2) providing that doctors may comply with a request in a written declaration provided that the patient was capable of making a reasonable appraisal of his own interests when the request was made. A 2001 study found that cases involving this sort of advanced directive are 'rare'.[101] Secondly, children over the age of 12 may be entitled to request euthanasia or assisted suicide. A doctor is only allowed to comply with a request from a minor between the ages of 12 and 15 with parental consent. For children aged 16 and 17, parents should be consulted, but they do not have a right of veto. In 2001, there were five reported cases of euthanasia involving children.[102]

While the law specifically addresses the possibility of euthanasia for children over the age of 12, it is silent on the question of euthanasia for very severely disabled newborns. In the next extract Eduard Verhagen and Pieter Sauer controversially suggest that provided certain requirements are met, euthanasia in severely disabled neonates can be acceptable. The Groningen Protocol, named after the Dutch hospital which developed these guidelines, lays out five factors which should be satisfied before doctors should proceed with euthanasia in newborn babies:

• The diagnosis and prognosis must be certain;

• Hopeless and unbearable suffering must be present;

• The diagnosis, prognosis and unbearable suffering must be confirmed by at least one independent physician;

---

[101] Tony Sheldon, 'Only half of Dutch doctors report euthanasia' (2003) 326 BMJ 1164.
[102] Ibid.

- Both parents must give informed consent;
- The procedure must be performed in accordance with the accepted medical standard.

Eduard Verhagen and Pieter Sauer[103]

When both the parents and the physicians are convinced that there is an extremely poor prognosis, they may concur that death would be more humane than continued life. Under similar conditions, a person in the Netherlands who is older than sixteen years of age can ask for euthanasia. Newborns, however, cannot ask for euthanasia, and such a request by parents, acting as the representatives of their child, is invalid under Dutch law. Does this mean that euthanasia in a newborn is always prohibited? We are convinced that life-ending measures can be acceptable in these cases under very strict conditions: the parents must agree fully, on the basis of a thorough explanation of the condition and prognosis; a team of physicians, including at least one who is not directly involved in the care of the patient, must agree; and the condition and prognosis must be very well defined. After the decision has been made and the child has died, an outside legal body should determine whether the decision was justified and all necessary procedures have been followed. . . .

Twenty-two cases of euthanasia in newborns have been reported to district attorneys' offices in the Netherlands during the past seven years. Recently, we were allowed to review these cases. They all involved infants with very severe forms of spina bifida. In most cases (17 of the 22), a multidisciplinary spina bifida team was consulted. In the remaining five cases, at least two other independent medical experts were consulted. The physicians based their decisions on the presence of severe suffering without hope of improvement. The decisions were always made in collaboration with, and were fully approved by, both parents. The prosecutor used four criteria to assess each case: the presence of hopeless and unbearable suffering and a very poor quality of life, parental consent, consultation with an independent physician and his or her agreement with the treating physicians, and the carrying out of the procedure in accordance with the accepted medical standard. The conclusion in all twenty two cases was that the requirements of careful practice were fulfilled. None of the physicians were prosecuted.

Given that the national survey indicated that such procedures are performed in fifteen to twenty newborns per year, the fact that an average of three cases were reported annually suggests that most cases are simply not being reported. We believe that all cases must be reported if the country is to prevent uncontrolled and unjustified euthanasia and if we are to discuss the issue publicly and thus further develop norms regarding euthanasia in newborns.

(b) Euthanasia in practice

Despite the requirement in the 1981 guidelines that doctors should report all cases of euthanasia and assisted suicide, there was concern that many doctors were falsely recording that their patients had died of natural causes. As a result, the Remmelink Committee, whose report was published in 1991, was set up to conduct a wide-ranging and anonymous survey into the true incidence of euthanasia in the Netherlands. It found that, in 1990, 9,000 patients had explicitly requested euthanasia or assisted suicide. There had been 2,300 cases of voluntary euthanasia (1.8 per cent of all deaths) and 400 cases of assisted suicide (0.3 per cent of all deaths). Fifty-four per

---

[103] 'The Groningen Protocol—Euthanasia in Severely Ill Newborns' (2005) 352 New England Journal of Medicine 959–62.

cent of all doctors had performed euthanasia or assisted suicide at least once; 34 per cent said that they not yet done so, but that they could imagine circumstances in which they would; 12 per cent said that they could not envisage circumstances in which they would perform euthanasia themselves; 4 per cent said that they would not be prepared to refer a patient to a doctor with a more liberal attitude.

Two findings of the Remmelink Committee have attracted particular attention. First, the study found that doctors failed to comply with the reporting requirements in the majority of cases. As a result, the monitoring and scrutiny which are supposed to result from decriminalization have obviously been hampered. And secondly, in 1,000 cases (0.8 per cent of deaths), the requirement that the patient should have made an explicit and persistent request had not been satisfied. In more than half of these cases, there had been discussions with the patient in which a desire for euthanasia had been expressed. In most of the remaining cases, the patient was very close to death and in a state of unbearable suffering.

The Committee's own conclusion was that euthanasia was not occurring on an excessive scale in the Netherlands. However, opponents of euthanasia have claimed that the study offers compelling evidence of the 'slippery slope'. Other smaller surveys have been carried out subsequently, and these have tended to confirm the findings of the Remmelink Committee. A study of family doctors carrried out by van der Val et al. did, however, find a significantly lower incidence of euthanasia performed without the patient's explicit and persistent request. More recent studies have shown that doctors, and in particular general practitioners, are increasingly willing to report instances of euthanasia. A 2001 survey found that 54 per cent of all cases of euthanasia were reported (the figure for GPs was 60 per cent).[104] The number of requests for euthanasia remained stable at around 9,700, as did the proportion which were accepted (39 per cent). There was also no change in the number of cases in which a patient's life was ended without an explicit request (around 900). In recent years, there appears to be a slight annual decrease in the number of reported cases of euthanasia. In 1999 there were 2216 cases; in 2000 there were 2123; and in 2001, there were 2054. The reasons for this decrease are unclear.

(c) Commentary

Unsurprisingly, there is intense international interest in how legalized euthanasia has worked in practice in the Netherlands. The problem is that commentators cannot agree on the lessons we should learn from the Dutch experience. Some argue that legalization has worked well, and in the next extract, John Griffiths suggests that the Netherlands offers us an example of the benefits which flow from openly regulating euthanasia.

John Griffiths[105]

In . . . invoking the hoary spectre of a 'slippery slope' in apparent criticism not only of the Supreme Court's decision in the *Chabot* case, but of the entire preceding legal development in the Netherlands, [opponents of legalization] appear to overlook some fundamental facts. The Dutch

---

104 Tony Sheldon, 'Only half of Dutch doctors report euthanasia' (2003) 326 BMJ 1164 (31 May).
105 John Griffiths, 'Assisted Suicide in the Netherlands: The Chabot Case' (1995) 58 Modern Law Review 232–48, 247–8.

data on medical practices which shorten life, in the cases of non-competent or of competent but not-consulted patients, are indeed a matter of concern. However, some differentiation is in order. Almost all of the behaviour concerned involves abstaining from or terminating life-prolonging treatment, or administration of heavy doses of painkillers, in circumstances in which remaining life expectancy was (very) short and the doctor's behaviour may, as far as we know, have been entirely appropriate. There is really not a shred of evidence that the frequency of this sort of behaviour is higher in the Netherlands than, for example, in the United States; the only thing that is clear is that more is known about it in the Netherlands. In short, there is no reason to assume . . . a causal relationship between limited legalisation of euthanasia and 'lack of control' over other sorts of medical behaviour.

Looking more specifically at psychiatric patients, where is the feared 'slippery slope'? Anecdotal evidence suggests that psychiatrists have long engaged in practices which amount to assistance with suicide and there is no apparent reason to suppose they do so more often in the Netherlands than in the United States. . . . How much of this goes on, we cannot say. The only thing we can safely say is that, so long as it is underground, it is quite beyond any form of legal or other control . . . [Those] who invoke the metaphor to criticise Dutch legal developments seem quite confused about the direction in which the 'slippery slope' is tilting . . . [T]he Dutch are busy trying to bring a number of socially dangerous medical practices which exist everywhere under a regime of effective societal control . . . They still have a long way to go. But triumphantly pointing out the shortcomings of Dutch control . . ., is to confuse a cure with a disease. The appropriate Dutch response to this sort of criticism is to concede the imperfections, but to point out that working step-by-step towards effective control is surely better than denial.

Others, such as John Keown, warn that there is clear evidence of abuse, and that the Dutch are currently sliding down the slippery slope.

John Keown[106]

[T]he Dutch claim that their guidelines are sufficiently 'precise' or 'strict' to ensure effective control. Th[e] evidence . . . amply demonstrates that the guidelines have conspicuously failed. Despite Dutch representations to the contrary . . . the reality is that the guidelines have been widely breached, and with effective impunity.

More particularly, the evidence points to the following three conclusions. First, voluntary active euthanasia is far from a rarity and is increasingly performed. Rather than being truly a 'last resort', it has quickly become an established part of mainstream Dutch medical practice to which doctors have resorted even when palliative care could have offered an alternative . . .

Secondly, despite the insistent claims by proponents of voluntary active euthanasia, inside and outside the Netherlands, that allowing it subject to 'safeguards' brings it from the shadows and 'into the open' where it can be controlled, the evidence indicates that such claims merit scepticism. The reality is that most cases of voluntary active euthanasia, until recently a substantial majority, have gone unreported and unchecked. In view of the intractable fact that in a clear majority of cases there has not even been an *opportunity* for official scrutiny, Dutch reassurances of effective regulation ring hollow . . . The reassuring picture of the euthanasia landscape portrayed by the Dutch is surreal . . .

Thirdly, the guidelines have not only been ignored in practice, but they have been diluted in theory. The *Chabot* and *Suturius* cases illustrated the expansive interpretation placed by the

---

[106] *Euthanasia, Ethics and Public Policy: An Argument against Legalisation* (CUP Cambridge 2002) 146–7, 149.

courts on 'unbearable suffering' and, as the court decisions condoning the killing of disabled babies show, the requirement of a request in all cases has now been jettisoned . . .

In short, the failure of the Dutch effectively to control voluntary active euthanasia lends weighty support to the empirical slippery slope argument, and their growing approval of non-voluntary active euthanasia illustrates the force of the logical slippery slope argument.

A different argument altogether, expressed here by John Griffiths, Alex Bood and Heleen Weyers, is that distinctive features of Dutch society and, in particular, of the Dutch health care system reduce the international relevance of euthansia's legalization in the Netherlands.

John Griffiths, Alex Bood and Heleen Weyers[107]

A[n] important characteristic of Dutch society concerns the level of confidence in public institutions and in professions. It seems no accident that legalization of euthanasia is conceived in the United States, for example, in terms of the rights of *patients* (with doctors' organizations often prominent in opposition) whereas in the Netherlands the public discussion concerns the scope of the professional discretion of *doctors* (doctors have from the beginning been prominent in the movement for legalization). On the whole, the Dutch seem comfortable with the idea that doctors can be trusted with the discretion to perform euthanasia, so that the public debate largely concerns the boundaries of this professional discretion and the sorts of procedural controls to which it should be subjected.

Interestingly, the House of Lords Select Committee on Assisted Dying drew attention to a survey which found that out of eleven European countries, including the UK, the Dutch had the highest regard for and trust in their doctors.[108] And in the following extract, Herman Nys gives another example of a distinctively Dutch approach to the question of doctors' involvement in end of life decisions, pointing out that despite the legalization of both euthanasia and assisted suicide, it is euthanasia which has from the outset been more common in the Netherlands.

Herman Nys[109]

Unlike the situation elsewhere, one of the most characteristic features of euthanasia practice in the Netherlands is that from the beginning of public discussion until very recently there has been no suggestion of a legal preference for assistance with suicide above euthanasia. On the contrary, killing with request is more common than assistance with suicide. Griffiths suggests a very interesting explanation for the Dutch preference for killing on request. By contrast with the situation in, for example, the United States, the development of euthanasia law began not so much with a demand for 'patient's rights' as with the insistence by doctors, supported after some initial hesitation by the Medical Association, that under limited circumstances euthanasia is a legitimate medical procedure. The issue was legally formulated not so much in terms of what patients have a right to demand as in terms of what doctors are authorised to do.

---

[107] *Euthanasia and Law in the Netherlands* (Amsterdam UP 1998) 304.

[108] Assisted Dying for the Terminally Ill Committee, *Assisted Dying for the Terminally Ill Bill—First Report* (2005) 41.

[109] 'Physician Involvement in a Patient's Death: A Continental European Perspective' (1999) 7 Medical Law Review 208–46, 236.

(2) OREGON

In the United States, a distinction has been drawn between euthanasia—which is illegal throughout the US—and physician assisted suicide, which is a matter for individual states. A decision of the Supreme Court in 1997 confirmed that there is no constitutional right to assisted suicide, but that legalization is not unconstitutional.[110] In a number of States, among them Washington and California, voters have explicitly rejected legalization. Only in Oregon has a majority of the electorate favoured the legalization of assisted suicide. The Death with Dignity Act 1994 was the result, but its introduction was delayed as a result of a number of legal challenges. It came into force in 1998, and in its first year there were fifteen assisted suicides in Oregon (0.05 per cent of all deaths). Since then, the number of assisted suicides has increased, though the numbers remain small. In 2004, there were thirty-seven assisted suicides (0.12 per cent of all deaths).[111] Attempts to block the practice of assisted suicide in Oregon have continued, however, with the Attorney General John Ashcroft attempting to use the Controlled Substances Act (CSA) to prohibit doctors from prescribing lethal doses of federally controlled drugs to their patients. A court has subsequently decided that this use of the CSA would be invalid since it represented an attempt to interfere with Oregon's authority to regulate medical care within its borders,[112] but the US Supreme Court has now agreed to review the Ninth Circuit Court's decision in *Gonzales v Oregon* (Alberto Gonzales took over from John Ashcroft as Attorney General in 2005). The hearing is due to take place at the end of 2005.[113]

The Death with Dignity Act provides that a physician may comply with a competent, terminally ill, adult patient's voluntary request for a prescription of drugs which will allow her to end her life in a humane and dignified manner. The Act only applies to residents of the state of Oregon. The patient must make an initial oral request, followed by a formal written request. At least 15 days after the written request, the patient must repeat their request orally, and a further 48 hours must elapse before the prescription can be filled. The patient's request must be witnessed by two people other than the doctor, at least one of whom must not be a relative, an heir or an employee of the institution in which the patient is receiving care. The patient must be asked to notify her family. A second doctor must confirm the patient's diagnosis and that the patient is competent and acting voluntarily. The patient must have received complete information about her diagnosis, prognosis and alternative treatments, such as hospice care and pain control. If there is any suggestion that the patient is depressed or has a psychiatric disorder, she must be referred to a psychiatrist or psychologist.

As with the Netherlands, supporters and opponents of legalization offer different interpretations of the evidence from Oregon. As Howard Brody has explained,

Data have been published on the first 15 patients to avail themselves of this opportunity. Proponents claim that the data show excellent adherence to all required safeguards and a very limited use of assisted suicide by a small group of terminally ill patients whose suffering could be relieved

---

[110] *Washington et al v Glucksberg* 117 SCt 2258 (1997) and *Vacco v Quill* 117 SCt 2293 (1997).

[111] Oregon Department of Human Services, *Seventh Annual Report on Oregon's Death with Dignity Act* (2004) <http://egov.oregon.gov/DHS/ph/pas/docs/year7.pdf>.

[112] *Oregon v John Ashcroft* Ninth Circuit Court of Appeals (2004) No 02-35587.

[113] Up to date information should be available from <http://www.deathwithdignity.org/law>.

in no other way. Opponents claim that the Oregon law is basically powerless to police or to detect cases which fall outside the legal guidelines; and so we have no idea how many other deaths may have occurred where the guidelines were ignored.[114]

In the next extract, Dan W Brock argues that there has been no evidence of abuse in Oregon since the statute came into force.

Dan W Brock[115]

Both the report of Coombs Lee and Werth and the report of the Health Division of the State of Oregon on the first year of operation of the Death with Dignity Act in Oregon that has made phys-ician-assisted suicide legal under strict guidelines should be reassuring to supporters of the act as well as to many of its opponents. There is no evidence that any of the abuses feared by opponents of the act have materialized in the first year of its operation. It has not led to unsuccessful suicide attempts; to assisted deaths accompanied by distress to the patient; to any influx of out-of-state residents seeking assisted death; to public deaths; to use of assisted death to avoid dealing with difficult symptoms or to reduce the financial costs of end-of-life care; to disproportionate use of assisted death for weak, vulnerable, or disabled patients or for women; or to increased suicide rates in the general population and especially among the young. On the contrary, the authors suggest several good consequences from the Act, including improvements in end-of-life care such as increased use of hospice . . . and several averted suicides or homicides . . .

I believe it should hardly be surprising that both Compassion and the state Health Division found substantial compliance with the Act and no significant abuse of physician-assisted suicide. Slippery slope worries about possible abuse of physician-assisted suicide can never be put fully to rest, but the limited experience in Oregon to date should provide some reassurance.

Against this, Margot White and Daniel Callahan suggest that the lack of any reporting requirements casts doubt upon the reliability of the available evidence.

Margot White and Daniel Callahan[116]

The Oregon law does not require physicians or anyone else to report cases at all whether they follow the guidelines or depart from them. As a result, the probability of generating accurate and complete data about nonvoluntary or involuntary cases would appear to be virtually nil . . . The fact that no evidence is publicly available at this stage suggesting that the feared 'slippery slope' is at hand in Oregon does not alter the overall concern. It makes little sense to note that the abuse doesn't seem to have materialized if there is no mechanism in place for bringing it to anyone's attention or investigating it. If there is lack of clarity about abusive practices, responsibility for correcting this lies not with PAS opponents, but with the drafters of Oregon's Death with Dignity Act who chose to omit any obligations for health care professionals to report unlawful practices and to omit any sanctions for physicians who fail to report PAS cases in the first place.

(3) NORTHERN TERRITORY, AUSTRALIA

The Rights of the Terminally Ill Act 1995 came into force in the Northern Territory of Australia on 1 July 1996. The Act permitted medical practitioners to comply with terminally ill, competent, adult patients' voluntary requests for euthanasia or assisted

---

[114] 'Kevorkian and assisted death in the United States' (1999) 318 British Medical Journal 953–4.

[115] 'Misconceived Sources of Opposition to Physician-Assisted Suicide' (2000) 6 Psychology, Public Policy, and Law 305, 309–10.

[116] 'Oregon's First Year: The Medicalization of Control' (2000) 6 Psychology, Public Policy, and Law 331, 337.

suicide. The patient had to be 'experiencing pain, suffering and/or distress to an extent unacceptable to the patient'.[117] A psychiatrist had to confirm that the patient was not suffering from treatable clinical depression, and a second doctor had to confirm that the patient's condition was terminal. The patient must have been informed about alternatives, such as palliative care and counselling, and the doctor had to be satisfied that the patient had taken into account the effect their decision might have upon their family. Seven days had to elapse between the request and the issuing of a certificate, and the doctor could only comply with the request after a further 48 hours.

Legal challenges to the Act began immediately, and in 1997, the Federal Government passed the Euthanasia Laws Act, which overturned the Rights of the Terminally Ill Act 1995. Euthanasia was therefore only legal in the Northern Territory of Australia between 1 July 1996 and 27 March 1997. Because of the ongoing legal challenges during these 9 months, some doctors may have been reluctant to comply with patients' requests. In total, seven patients made requests under the legislation and four actually died as a result.

(4) BELGIUM

Belgium formally decriminalized euthanasia in 2002.[118] Interestingly, the Belgian Euthanasia Act does not apply to assisted suicide, only euthanasia has been legalized, provided certain conditions are met. To be eligible, patients must be over the age of 18, competent and conscious, and their requests for euthanasia must be explicit, unambiguous, repeated, and durable. The patient must be in a hopeless situation, suffering from persistent and unbearable pain or distress which cannot be alleviated, and must be suffering from a serious and incurable mental or physical disorder. It is the patient who determines whether her suffering is persistent and unbearable, the physician is simply charged with certifying that the patient herself finds her suffering unbearable. The physician must give the patient full information about her condition and the possibilities of palliative care. A second doctor must consult the patient's medical file, examine the patient and confirm that the patient's suffering is unbearable, and that it cannot be alleviated. If the patient is not terminally ill, two additional requirements are imposed. First, the physician must consult two colleagues, one of whom must assess whether the request is voluntary, considered, and repeated, and second, at least a month must elapse between the request and the performance of euthanasia.

Advance directives requesting euthanasia may also be respected, provided certain conditions are satisfied. The directive must be in writing, signed by the patient, and witnessed by two adults, at least one of whom must have no material interest in the patient's death. If the patient is permanently incapable of writing down her request, she can appoint a representative who must have no material interest in her death to do so. A medical certificate certifying that the patient is permanently incapable of writing must be attached.

---

[117] Section 4.
[118] *Loi relative à l'euthanasie* (The Act Concerning Euthanasia), 28 May 2002, in force 23 Sept 2002.

Doctors are not under a duty to comply with a patient's request for euthanasia, on the contrary, they are entitled to refuse on grounds of conscience or for medical reasons. There is, however, a duty to inform the patient or the patient's representative and explain the reasons for their refusal.

The physician must fill in a registration form and deliver it within four working days to a national commission, consisting of sixteen members, eight of whom are doctors, four are lawyers and four 'from groups charged with the problem of incurably ill patients'. If the commission is satisfied that any of the criteria were not satisfied, the file will be sent to the public prosecutor. The commission reports biannually to parliament on the implementation of the legislation. In 2004, 347 cases of euthanasia were reported.[119]

It is also important to bear in mind, as Gastmans et al. explain, that the legalization of euthanasia in Belgium took place within a context in which there is a strong emphasis upon the provision of palliative care, and where the first response to a request for euthanasia will always be prompt extensive investigation of other palliative options.

C Gastmans, F Van Neste, and P Schotsmans[120]

[I]f euthanasia can ever be justified, it is necessary to provide good palliative care for all and to include in the euthanasia law a palliative filter—that is, a compulsory prior consultation with a specialised palliative care team . . .

The starting point of this clinical practice guideline is the principle that everything possible should be done to provide support and assistance to the competent, terminally ill person who asks for euthanasia, and his or her relatives. The aim is that such an active and integral palliative care approach can in many cases displace the request and allow the patient to die in a dignified manner without euthanasia. This means that healthcare institutions should think of palliative care as an active and integral approach employed in the case of every terminally ill patient, rather than seeing it as one alternative alongside euthanasia. . . . The plea for the palliative filter procedure is only credible if a sufficiently strongly developed and accessible palliative care structure exists. In Belgium, the development of palliative care preceded the euthanasia debate. As a result, Belgian palliative care (for example, the Flemish Palliative Care Federation) played a very active role in the Belgian euthanasia debate. The Belgian euthanasia debate itself functioned as a lever that facilitated the further development of palliative care, as is illustrated by the new law on palliative care that was approved at the same time as the euthanasia law. Because of a very fruitful cooperation between palliative care and the Belgian authorities, a unique, comprehensive, legal, and organisational palliative care framework (palliative care at home, support teams in hospitals and nursing homes, palliative care units) was set up nationwide. This specific situation of palliative care in Belgium makes the main argument of this clinical practice guideline (prioritisation of palliative care over euthanasia) a more realistic and plausible one. Because of the close interactions between the development of palliative care in Belgium and the Belgian euthanasia debate, one can conclude that theoretical arguments for or against (legalisation of) euthanasia always have to be understood against the background of the development of palliative care in any particular country.

[119] Assisted Dying for the Terminally Ill Committee, *Assisted Dying for the Terminally Ill Bill—First Report* (2005) 74.
[120] 'Facing requests for euthanasia: a clinical practice guideline' (2004) 30 Journal of Medical Ethics 212–17, 216.

(5) SWITZERLAND

Euthanasia—or 'murder upon request by the victim'—is illegal under Article 114 of the Swiss Penal Code. It is not considered as grave an offence as murder *without* the victim's request, and the actor's motive will be taken into account in sentencing. Assisting suicide is a criminal offence under Article 115 of the Code, but only if the defendant's motive is 'selfish'. Unlike the Netherlands, Article 115 of the Swiss Penal Code does not specify the involvement of a physician, nor does the patient have to be terminally ill or in intolerable pain. The only precondition for the act's legality is that the motive must be unselfish. Thus, provided that the person's motive for assisting the suicide is compassionate, no offence is committed.

A number of organizations offer assistance to patients who want to commit suicide, and these may impose some additional requirements upon patients. EXIT, for example, has around 50,000 members and helps 100–120 patients to die each year. Patients must be over the age of 18; mentally competent; and suffering from intolerable health problems. EXIT will only help Swiss nationals to commit suicide. Dignitas, a smaller organization set up in 1998, has also been prepared to assist non-Swiss residents to die. The number of foreigners travelling to Switzerland in order to be helped to die rose from three in 2000 to ninety-one in 2003. The prospect of Switzerland becoming the destination for 'suicide tourism' has led to a number of proposed bills which would prohibit foreigners from gaining access to assisted suicide, but none have so far become law.

There are no official statistics on the number of assisted suicides each year because the deaths are not differentiated from unassisted suicides. It has, however, been estimated that approximately 1,800 requests for assisted suicides are made each year. Two-thirds of these are turned down. Of the remaining 600 patients, half die of other causes. In total, about 300 suicides are assisted by the Swiss right to die organizations each year, representing around 0.45 per cent of all deaths.

(6) GERMANY

In Germany, assisting suicide is not a crime provided that the person who is about to commit suicide is competent and has made a voluntary choice. However, doctors are obliged to rescue patients who have attempted to commit suicide. As a result, while it is not an offence to give a patient a lethal drug, once the drug has been taken, the physician must attempt to rescue the patient. However, in the *Hackethal* case in 1998,[121] the Supreme Court found that the physician's duty to save a patient's life may be limited if the patient experiences life as a burden from which she wishes to be freed.

---

[121] For discussion see Herman Nys, 'Physician Involvement in a Patient's Death: A Continental European Perspective' (1999) 7 Medical Law Review 208–46, 233.

4. THE INCOMPETENT PATIENT

Incompetent patients, as we saw in Chapter 4, fall into a number of different categories. In this chapter, because our interest is in practices which may result in an individual's life being shortened we are necessarily concerned with a very small subset of incompetent patients. Patients who lack capacity must be treated in their best interests, and usually, of course, it is obvious that prolonging someone's life will be in her best interests. In the remainder of this chapter, we will be considering whether it could ever be in an incompetent patient's best interests not to have her life prolonged, or more radically, whether death could ever be said to be in the best interests of an incompetent patient. By definition, the issue here is not whether the principle of autonomy requires doctors to comply with their patients' requests for assistance in dying. Rather, we are interested in whether the principle of beneficence (or mercy) might ever permit, or even oblige a doctor to engage in conduct which will hasten an incompetent patient's death.

(a) CHILDREN

(1) THE CRIMINAL LAW

As we saw earlier, failing to provide a patient with life-sustaining treatment could satisfy both the *actus reus* and the *mens rea* for murder. An omission can only constitute the *actus reus* of murder if the defendant was under a duty to act. So if a child dies because their doctor has withheld or withdrawn treatment that they were under a duty to provide, criminal charges are possible. If doctors were always under a duty to prolong children's lives, then the non-treatment of severely handicapped neonates would be murder. It is, however, widely agreed that doctors are not obliged to strive to maintain life at all costs. If treatment is futile (that is, it is not going to lead to any improvement in the patient's condition), doctors are generally assumed to be entitled to withhold or discontinue it. As a result, few doctors have been charged with murder, or attempted murder, following the decision to withhold life-prolonging treatment from a child. In *R v Arthur*,[122] a baby with Down syndrome who had developed pneumonia died shortly after Dr Arthur had prescribed a powerful analgesic and 'nursing care only'. The baby's mother had told Dr Arthur that she did not want the baby to survive. Following Farquaharson J's controversial (see Ian Kennedy's comments below) direction to the jury, Dr Arthur was acquitted.

R v Arthur[123] Farquharson J

If a child is born with a serious handicap—for example, where a mongol has an ill-formed intestine whereby that child will die of the ailment if he is not operated on—a surgeon may say: 'as this child is a mongol I do not propose to operate; I shall allow nature to take its course'. No one could say that that surgeon was committing an act of murder by declining to take a course which would save the child . . .

---

[122] (1981) 12 BMLR 1.   [123] Ibid.

Where a child gets pneumonia and is a child with an irreversible handicap whose mother has rejected him, if the doctor said: 'I am not going to give it antibiotics', and by a merciful dispensation of providence he dies, . . . it would be very unlikely, I would suggest, that you (or any other jury) would say that the doctor was committing murder.

Ian Kennedy[124]
A number of serious criticisms can be made of this reasoning. The first concerns the distinction drawn by the judge between allowing the child to die, allowing nature to take its course, and doing some positive act to bring about its death. This distinction between omissions and commissions has, of course, a respectable pedigree in the criminal law, and has provided a full and fascinating life for generations of moral philosophers. But here it is not a good distinction . . . [I]n both law and ethics, the doctor stands in a special relationship to his patient. Once he has embarked on a course of treatment, once the child is in his care, he has a duty to act affirmatively in the interest of his patient. He breaches that duty if he stands by and does nothing in circumstances in which law and ethics indicate that he should act . . .

My second criticism refers to the criteria which have to be satisfied before the doctor may lawfully adopt a policy of sedation and nursing care only. The court offered only two. The first was that the child be irreversibly disabled. This cannot be satisfactory. Given the consequences of the decision, it cannot be denied that such a criterion must be much more carefully defined . . . [I]rreversible disability says nothing about the severity of the disability . . .

The second criterion, that the parents reject the child, seems to me to be most unsatisfactory. The fate of a child, the life of a child, should not, in my view, depend on whether its parents want it. . . . It has never been part of our law or morality that parents may choose death for their children.

In the light of the Court of Appeal judgments in *Re B* and in *Re J* (see below), Ian Kennedy and Andrew Grubb rightly suggest that 'the *Arthur* case can be consigned to legal history for the oddity it is'.[125]

(2) THE BEST INTERESTS TEST

Aside from the criminal law, there are a number of different ways in which a decision about whether a child should be provided with life-prolonging treatment might come before the courts. The parents might refuse to consent to a procedure which is necessary to save a child's life, as was the case in *Re B*. As we saw in Chapter 4, the doctors might then apply to have the child made a ward of court, and if the court decides that treatment is in the child's best interests, the parent's refusal will be overriden.

In Re B (A Minor) (Wardship: Medical Treatment)[126]
B was born suffering from Down syndrome and an intestinal blockage, which required an immediate operation. If the operation were performed, it was probable that B's life expectancy would be 20 to 30 years. Her parents, having decided that it would be kinder to allow her to die rather than live as a physically and mentally handicapped person, refused to consent to the operation. The local authority made the child a ward of court and sought an order authorising the operation to be performed. At first instance, the judge decided that the parents' wishes should be respected and refused to make the order, but this was overturned by the Court of Appeal.

---

[124] *Treat Me Right: Essays in Medical Law and Ethics* (Clarendon Press Oxford 1991) 155–7.
[125] Ian Kennedy and Andrew Grubb, *Medical Law* (3rd edn Butterworths London) 2167.
[126] [1981] 1 WLR 1421 CA.

Templeman LJ

Fortunately or unfortunately, in this particular case the decision no longer lies with the parents or with the doctors, but lies with the court. It is a decision which of course must be made in the light of the evidence and views expressed by the parents and the doctors, but at the end of the day it devolves on this court in this particular instance to decide whether the life of this child is demonstrably going to be so awful that in effect the child must be condemned to die, or whether the life of this child is still so imponderable that it would be wrong for her to be condemned to die. There may be cases, I know not, of severe proved damage where the future is so certain and where the life of the child is so bound to be full of pain and suffering that the court might be driven to a different conclusion, but in the present case the choice which lies before the court is this: whether to allow an operation to take place which may result in the child living for 20 or 30 years as a mongoloid or whether (and I think this must be brutally the result) to terminate the life of a mongoloid child because she also has an intestinal complaint. Faced with that choice I have no doubt that it is the duty of this court to decide that the child must live. The judge was much affected by the reasons given by the parents and came to the conclusion that their wishes ought to be respected. In my judgment he erred in that the duty of the court is to decide whether it is in the interests of the child that an operation should take place. The evidence in this case only goes to show that if the operation takes place and is successful then the child may live the normal span of a mongoloid child with the handicaps and defects and life of a mongol child, and it is not for this court to say that life of that description ought to be extinguished.

Alternatively, the doctors may believe that life-support should be withheld while the parents want treatment to continue, as in *Re C*.

Re C (A Minor) (Medical Treatment)[127]

C was 16 months old and terminally ill. She was very seriously disabled, and had been in intensive care on a ventilator for the past month. Medical opinion was unanimous that she should not continue on indefinite ventilation, which was likely to cause her increasing distress. The doctors proposed to remove C from the ventilator, and not to engage in resuscitation or reventilation if she were to suffer a further respiratory collapse. C's parents were orthodox Jews and could not contemplate consenting to a course of action that would indirectly shorten her life.

Sir Stephen Brown P

The medical evidence is not in dispute. There is no issue in this case that this is a fatal disease and that in real terms this little child is approaching death. She has a desperately tragic existence. She is emaciated. Although she is conscious there is the prospect of increasing suffering as the days go by. The doctors are all of the view that it would be in her best interests that she be removed from ventilation and that in the event of what they believe to be an inevitable respiratory arrest it would follow that she should not be replaced on ventilation which would of itself give rise to increased suffering and distress . . .

In this case I have no doubt on the evidence before me, including the evidence of the parents themselves, that in this desperate situation it is in the best interests of C that she should now be taken off the ventilation presently being administered and that it should not be reimposed or restored if she should suffer a further respiratory arrest. It is a desperately sad situation for all concerned. The anxiety of the doctors as well as the parents can be well understood. Their objective in their profession is to save and to preserve life but, as has been said in earlier cases that

---

[127] [1998] Lloyd's Rep Med 1 Fam Div.

whilst the sanctity of life is vitally important, it is not the paramount consideration. The paramount consideration is the best interests of little C . . . what the court is being asked to do in this case is to exercise its inherent jurisdiction to approve the course of treatment which is now proposed by the doctors and for which they cannot gain the consent of the parents. In other words to seek the court's consent in the absence of the consent of the parents . . . I believe that in this case I should assent to the course which is proposed by the Hospital Trust. I do so with a feeling of grave solemnity because I realise that the parents themselves will be greatly disappointed. It is a sad feature of this matter that there is, in fact, no hope for C, and what has to be considered is her best interests to prevent her from suffering as would be inevitable if this course were not to be taken.

Or there may not be a dispute between the parents and the medical staff involved in their child's care, and the doctors might seek a declaration that it would be lawful to withhold life-prolonging treatment in order to avoid the risk of criminal charges at a later date. Finally, the child might be a ward of court for reasons unconnected with her medical condition, as was the case in *Re J*, so that all important decisions must, in any event, be made by the court.

In Re J (A Minor) (Wardship: Medical Treatment)[128]

J was born prematurely, suffering from severe brain damage. Immediately after birth and on one other occasion since, he had had to be resuscitated and kept on a ventilator, which he had found distressing. The most optimistic prognosis suggested that he had a considerably shortened life expectancy, that he would become a serious spastic quadriplegic, probably without sight, speech or hearing, but he would be able to feel pain. There was a possibility that he might at any time suffer respiratory collapse requiring further resuscitation. The consultant neonatologist recommended that, in the event of further convulsions requiring resuscitation, J should not be revived by means of mechanical ventilation unless it seemed appropriate to those involved in his care. This recommendation had been accepted by the trial judge. The Court of Appeal dismissed the Official Solicitor's appeal.

Lord Donaldson MR

We know that the instinct and desire for survival is very strong. We all believe in and assert the sanctity of human life . . . [V]ery severely handicapped people find a quality of life rewarding which to the unhandicapped may seem manifestly intolerable. People have an amazing adaptability. But in the end there will be cases in which the answer must be that it is not in the interests of the child to subject it to treatment which will cause increased suffering and produce no commensurate benefit, giving the fullest possible weight to the child's, and mankind's, desire to survive.

Taylor LJ

Three preliminary principles are not in dispute. First, it is settled law that the court's prime and paramount consideration must be the best interests of the child. That is easily said but not easily applied. What it does involve is that the views of the parents, although they should be heeded and weighed, cannot prevail over the court's view of the ward's best interests . . . Secondly, the court's high respect for the sanctity of human life imposes a strong presumption in favour of taking all steps capable of preserving it, save in exceptional circumstances. The problem is to define those circumstances. Thirdly, and as a corollary to the second principle, it cannot be too strongly

---

[128] [1991] Fam 33 CA.

emphasised that the court never sanctions steps to terminate life. That would be unlawful. There is no question of approving, even in a case of the most horrendous disability, a course aimed at terminating life or accelerating death. The court is concerned only with the circumstances in which steps should not be taken to prolong life.

Despite the court's inability to compare a life afflicted by the most severe disability with death, the unknown, I am of the view that there must be extreme cases in which the court is entitled to say: 'The life which this treatment would prolong would be so cruel as to be intolerable.' If, for example, a child was so damaged as to have negligible use of its faculties and the only way of preserving its life was by the continuous administration of extremely painful treatment such that the child either would be in continuous agony or would have to be so sedated continuously as to have no conscious life at all . . . In those circumstances, without there being any question of deliberately ending the life or shortening it, I consider the court is entitled in the best interests of the child to say that deliberate steps should not be taken artificially to prolong its miserable life span . . .

At what point in the scale of disability and suffering ought the court to hold that the best interests of the child do not require further endurance to be imposed by positive treatment to prolong its life? Clearly, to justify withholding treatment, the circumstances would have to be extreme . . .

I consider the correct approach is for the court to judge the quality of life the child would have to endure if given the treatment and decide whether in all the circumstances such a life would be so afflicted as to be intolerable to that child. I say 'to that child' because the test should not be whether the life would be tolerable to the decider. The test must be whether the child in question, if capable of exercising sound judgment, would consider the life tolerable.

The test the courts apply when faced with all these applications is the 'welfare principle', that is, the child's best interests must be their paramount concern. So when will it be in a child's best interests to withhold or withdraw life-prolonging treatment? Because it will almost always be in a child's best interests to continue living, only children who are very gravely ill will be plausible candidates for non-treatment. But exactly how we tell whether a child's condition meets the threshold level of gravity is a difficult question, and a number of different approaches are evident in the judgments reproduced above. First, some judges ask whether continued life would be intolerable to *this particular child* (see, for example, the comments of Taylor LJ in *Re J*). The purpose of this 'substituted judgment' test is to remind decision-makers that disabled people may be able to gain pleasure and satisfaction from a quality of life that might seem intolerable to an able-bodied member of the judiciary. But of course, this test is necessarily speculative because it is simply impossible to discover what this particular child would think of their likely quality of life. Secondly, Templeman LJ in *Re B* suggested that the child's life must be 'demonstrably awful' before non-treatment can be contemplated. While this indicates that the child's condition should be extremely grave, as a test for when non-treatment is justified, it is inherently vague. All that the cases reproduced above tell us is that Down syndrome does not lead to a life that is 'demonstrably awful' (*Re B*), while profound brain damage accompanied by paralysis, blindness and deafness does (*Re J*). Where the line should be drawn between these two points of certainty is unclear.

What seems evident, however, is that the courts will tend to be guided by medical evidence on whether life-prolonging treatment should be withdrawn or withheld from a child and will not order doctors to treat contrary to their clinical judgement. In *Re Wyatt*, for example, medical opinion was 'unanimous' that invasive medical treatment would not be in Charlotte's best interests, and Hedley J's conclusion that they should be permitted not to institute aggressive life saving measures was therefore unsurprising.

Re Wyatt (A Child) (Medical Treatment: Parents' Consent)[129]

Charlotte, who was now 11 months' old, had been born prematurely. She suffered from poor kidney function, respiratory difficulties and severe irreversible brain damage. Medical evidence indicated that she could feel pain and distress, but almost certainly not pleasure. The realistic prognosis for her survival for a further 12 months was 5%. The unanimous medical opinion was that it was not in C's best interests to artificially ventilate her in the future. The applicant NHS Trust sought a declaration which would permit them to discontinue invasive and aggressive treatment of C. The parents believed it was their duty to maintain C's life as she was not yet ready to die.

Hedley J

On the basis of the unanimous medical evidence in this case, the issue in all probability is not whether this baby should live or die but how and when she should die. . . .

Charlotte, of course, is a baby. Whilst the sanctity of her life and her right to dignity are to be respected, she can exercise no choice of her own. In those circumstances someone must choose for her. That is usually her parents but here it is the court. That choice must be exercised on the basis of what is in her best interests. It is the understanding and application of that concept that presents the true difficulty in this kind of case.

The court starts with the fundamental principles of the sanctity of life, the best interests of Charlotte which govern choice and her inherent right to respect for her dignity. . . .

It seems to me therefore that in any consideration of best interests in a person at risk of imminent death is that of securing a 'good' death. It would be absurd to try to describe that concept more fully beyond saying that everyone in this case knows what it means—not under anaesthetic, not in the course of painful and futile treatment, but peacefully in the arms of those who love her most. . . .

I do not believe that any further aggressive treatment, even if necessary to prolong life, is in her best interests. I know that that may mean that she may die earlier than otherwise she might have done but in my judgment the moment of her death will only be slightly advanced. I have asked myself: what can now be done to benefit Charlotte? I can only offer three answers: first, that she can be given as much comfort and as little pain as possible; secondly, that she can be given as much time as possible to spend physically in the presence of and in contact with her parents; thirdly, that she can meet her end whenever that may be in what Mr Wyatt called the TLC of those who love her most. Although I believe and find that further invasive and aggressive treatment would be intolerable to Charlotte, I prefer to determine her best interests on the basis of finding what is the best that can be done for her.

Charlotte Wyatt's parents returned to court in 2005, citing evidence that Charlotte's condition had improved and asking for the declarations that non-treatment would be lawful to be set aside. The case was again heard by Hedley J, who continued to be

---

[129] [2004] EWHC 2247 (FAM).

persuaded by the majority of medical opinion, that intensive care measures should not be taken in the future when, as was likely, Charlotte suffered a serious respiratory collapse.

Re Wyatt (No 3) (A Child) (Medical Treatment: Continuation of Order)[130] Hedley J

Whilst there have been very welcome developments, her condition essentially remains grave, indeed as Dr H put it she remains a terminally ill child . . .

All agree that her day to day life is not intolerable and that every effort should be made to enable her to develop such potential as she has to its fullest extent. All also agree that every reasonable step short of major invasive treatment should be employed as necessary to sustain this life. . . .

I turn then to the question of whether or not it would be in Charlotte's best interests in the event of respiratory collapse to attempt aggressive invasive treatment. That is what the parents want and in that they are supported by Dr G at least to the extent of starting such treatment. No one else who feels qualified to do so shares that view. All agree that all treatment should be offered up to but not including invasive intensive care. All agree that Charlotte's present life should be nurtured, developed and protected up to that point. There are three reasons why they will not go the last step. The first is the doubt that she could survive even with full ICU treatment. The second is that even if she did, it would result in a significant deterioration in her condition. Whilst no one could say that if she survived ICU treatment she could never regain what she has now few think she would in fact do so and she would be left in a position similar to that of last October. The third is that the whole experience of ICU treatment would imperil a peaceful death.

After careful and anxious consideration, I find myself convinced by the majority medical opinion . . . I am quite clear that it would not be in Charlotte's best interests to die in the course of futile aggressive treatment.

Glass v UK is a rare case in which the doctors were held to have given insufficient weight to the parents' wishes. The mother believed that the doctors were intending, through the provision of diamorphine and 'Do Not Resuscitate' Orders, to covertly 'euthanase' her son. Relations between the medical staff and the mother were extremely poor, but the hospital did not make an application to the court to resolve the question of the child's treatment. The European Court of Human Rights found that treatment in defiance of the parent's objections, without the authorization of a court, gave rise to an interference with the child's right to respect for his private and family life, and amounted to a violation of Article 8. It should however be remembered that the breach of Article 8 in the *Glass* case would have been prevented if the doctors had made a timely application to the court. And of course it is clearly possible, perhaps even probable, that the court would have granted the declaration authorizing non-treatment of this severely disabled child.

Glass v UK[131]

The first applicant was a severely mentally and physically disabled child requiring 24-hour care. The second applicant was his mother. The mother opposed the use of morphine and expected him to receive resuscitation should his heart stop. The treating doctors did not agree. The child's condition deteriorated and the doctors wanted to administer diamorphine as pain relief. The

---

[130] [2005] EWHC 693 (FAM), [2005] All ER (D) 278 (Apr).
[131] (Application No 61827/00) [2004] 1 FLR 1019 European Court of Human Rights.

mother wished to take her son home. A 'do not resuscitate' (DNR) order was put on the child's case notes without the mother's consent. The mother believed that her son was being covertly euthanased and a fight broke out between the doctors and the family. The mother successfully resuscitated her son who later improved and was discharged home. The applicants alleged, amongst other matters, that domestic law and practice failed to ensure effective respect for the first applicant's right to physical and moral integrity within the meaning of 'private life' under Article 8 of the European Convention for the Protection of Human Rights and Fundamental Freedoms 1950.

ECHR

[I]t is clear that, when confronted with the reality of the administration of diamorphine to the first applicant, the second applicant expressed her firm opposition to this form of treatment. These objections were overridden, including in the face of her continuing opposition. It considers that the decision to impose treatment on the first applicant in defiance of the second applicant's objections gave rise to an interference with the first applicant's right to respect for his private life, and in particular his right to physical integrity . . .

The court is not persuaded that an emergency High Court application could not have been made by the Trust when it became clear that the second applicant was firmly opposed to the administration of diamorphine to the first applicant. However, the doctors and officials used the limited time available to them in order to try to impose their views on the second applicant. It observes in this connection that the Trust was able to secure the presence of a police officer to oversee the negotiations with the second applicant but, surprisingly, did not give consideration to making a High Court application even though 'the best-interests procedure can be involved at short notice' . . .

The court considers that, having regard to the circumstances of the case, the decision of the authorities to override the second applicant's objection to the proposed treatment in the absence of authorisation by a court resulted in a breach of article 8 of the Convention.

(3) THE 'CONJOINED TWINS CASE' RE A

(a) Re A [132]

As we have seen, the reason why doctors who discontinue life-prolonging treatment are not routinely charged with murder is that treatment withdrawal is treated in law as an omission. When the courts were first asked to authorize the separation of conjoined twins, a new problem arose. In Re A,[133] the weaker twin (known as Mary) would die as a result of the operation to separate her from her twin sister (known as Jodie).

At first instance, Johnson J attempted to justify the operation by describing it as an omission: the operation would, he said, interrupt or withdraw the blood supply which Mary was receiving from Jodie. This explanation was rejected by the Court of Appeal who robustly admitted that invasive surgery is unquestionably an action, and that this meant the doctors carrying out the operation would be guilty of murdering Mary, unless they could avail themselves of a defence.

Each of the four judges who heard the case appeared to start from the utilitarian presumption that saving one life must be preferable to losing two lives. The problem,

---

[132] [2001] Fam 147 CA.   [133] Ibid.

of course, was that Jodie's life could only be saved by doing something that would kill Mary. So the judgments can be read as different attempts to justify a course of action which, on the face of it, is impermissible in order to achieve 'the lesser of two evils', that is the death of one child rather than two.

In Re A (Children) (Conjoined Twins: Surgical Separation)[134]

Conjoined twins, referred to as Jodie and Mary, were born in Manchester to devout Roman Catholic parents from the small Mediterranean island of Gozo. They were joined at the pelvis and each had her own brain, heart and lungs and other vital organs and her own arms and legs. The medical evidence was that Mary's heart and lungs were too deficient to pump blood through her own body, and that Jodie, the stronger twin, was sustaining Mary's life. If they were not separated Jodie's heart would fail and they would both die. However, if they were separated the doctors were convinced that Jodie would have a relatively normal life, although Mary would die within minutes. The parents refused to consent to the operation on religious grounds. The hospital applied for a declaration that it could lawfully carry out separation surgery. The judge held that, although regard had to be had to the parents' wishes, the proposed operation was not a positive act, which would be unlawful, but rather, by analogy with the situation where a court authorized the withholding of food and hydration, represented the withdrawal of Mary's blood supply, and therefore could be lawfully performed. The parents appealed to the Court of Appeal, which rejected Johnson J's reasoning, but for different reasons, declared that the separation operation should go ahead.

Ward LJ

Just as the parents hold firm views worthy of respect, so every instinct of the medical team has been to save life where it can be saved. Despite such a professional judgment it would, nevertheless, have been a perfectly acceptable response for the hospital to bow to the weight of the parental wish however fundamentally the medical team disagreed with it. Other medical teams may well have accepted the parents' decision. Had St Mary's done so, there could not have been the slightest criticism of them for letting nature take its course in accordance with the parents' wishes. Nor should there be any criticism of the hospital for not bowing to the parents' choice. The hospital have care of the children and . . . there can be no doubt whatever that the hospital are entitled . . . to seek the court's ruling . . .

Family Law

The question of Mary's best interests is one of the key and one of the difficult issues in the case and it calls for thorough exposition. That Mary's welfare is paramount is a trite observation for family lawyers. . . .

The question is whether this proposed operation is in Mary's best interests. It cannot be. It will bring her life to an end before it has run its natural span. It denies her inherent right to life. There is no countervailing advantage for her at all. It is contrary to her best interests. Looking at her position in isolation and ignoring, therefore, the benefit to Jodie, the court should not sanction the operation on her . . .

If the duty of the court is to make a decision which puts Jodie's interests paramount and that decision would be contrary to the paramount interests of Mary, then, for my part, . . . [g]iven the conflict of duty, I can see no other way of dealing with it than by choosing the lesser of the two evils and so finding the least detrimental alternative . . .

Mary may have a right to life, but she has little right to be alive. She is alive because and only because, to put it bluntly, but none the less accurately, she sucks the lifeblood of Jodie and she

134 Ibid.

sucks the lifeblood out of Jodie. She will survive only so long as Jodie survives. Jodie will not survive long because constitutionally she will not be able to cope. Mary's parasitic living will be the cause of Jodie's ceasing to live. If Jodie could speak, she would surely protest, 'Stop it, Mary, you're killing me.' Mary would have no answer to that. Into my scales of fairness and justice between the children goes the fact that nobody but the doctors can help Jodie. Mary is beyond help.

Hence I am in no doubt at all that the scales come down heavily in Jodie's favour. The best interests of the twins is to give the chance of life to the child whose actual bodily condition is capable of accepting the chance to her advantage even if that has to be at the cost of the sacrifice of the life which is so unnaturally supported. I am wholly satisfied that the least detrimental choice, balancing the interests of Mary against Jodie and Jodie against Mary, is to permit the operation to be performed.

Criminal Law

The test I have to set myself is that established by [*R v Woollin*]. I have to ask myself whether I am satisfied that the doctors recognise that death or serious harm will be virtually certain, barring some unforeseen intervention, to result from carrying out this operation. If so, the doctors intend to kill or to do that serious harm even though they may not have any desire to achieve that result. It is common ground that they appreciate that death to Mary would result from the severance of the common aorta. Unpalatable though it may be . . . to stigmatise the doctors with 'murderous intent', that is what in law they will have if they perform the operation and Mary dies as a result . . .

[The doctors] are under a duty to Mary not to operate because it will kill Mary, but they are under a duty to Jodie to operate because not to do so will kill her . . . What then is the position where there is a conflict of duty? . . . What are the doctors to do if the law imposes upon them a duty which they cannot perform without being in breach of Mary's right to life if at the same time the respecting of her right puts them in breach of the equally serious duty of respecting Jodie's right to life? A resort to a sanctity of life argument does not enable both rights to receive the equal protection the doctrine is supposed to provide each of them equally. In those circumstances it seems to me that the law must allow an escape through choosing the lesser of the two evils . . . The respect the law must have for the right to life of each must go in the scales and weigh equally but other factors have to go in the scales as well . . .

[T]he proposed operation would not in any event offend the sanctity of life principle . . . The reality here—harsh as it is to state it, and unnatural as it is that it should be happening—is that Mary is killing Jodie. . . . Mary uses Jodie's heart and lungs to receive and use Jodie's oxygenated blood. This will cause Jodie's heart to fail and cause Jodie's death as surely as a slow drip of poison. How can it be just that Jodie should be required to tolerate that state of affairs? . . . I can see no difference in essence between . . . resort to legitimate self-defence and the doctors coming to Jodie's defence and removing the threat of fatal harm to her presented by Mary's draining her lifeblood. The availability of such a plea of quasi-self-defence, modified to meet the quite exceptional circumstances nature has inflicted on the twins, makes intervention by the doctors lawful . . .

Lest it be thought that this decision could become authority for wider propositions, such as that a doctor, once he has determined that a patient cannot survive, can kill the patient, it is important to restate the unique circumstances for which this case is authority. They are that it must be impossible to preserve the life of X without bringing about the death of Y, that Y by his or her very continued existence will inevitably bring about the death of X within a short period of time, and that X is capable of living an independent life but Y is incapable under any circumstances, including all forms of medical intervention, of viable independent existence.

Brooke LJ

[T]he doctrine of double effect can have no possible application in this case, as the judge rightly observed, because by no stretch of the imagination could it be said that the surgeons would be acting in good faith in Mary's best interests when they prepared an operation which would benefit Jodie but kill Mary . . . It follows from this analysis that the proposed operation would involve the murder of Mary unless some way can be found of determining that what was being proposed would not be unlawful . . .

Mary is, sadly, self-designated for a very early death. Nobody can extend her life beyond a very short span. Because her heart, brain and lungs are for all practical purposes useless, nobody would have even tried to extend her life artificially if she had not, fortuitously, been deriving oxygenated blood from her sister's bloodstream . . .

There are sound reasons for holding that the existence of an emergency in the normal sense of the word is not an essential prerequisite for the application of the doctrine of necessity. The principle is one of necessity, not emergency . . . There are also sound reasons for holding that the threat which constitutes the harm to be avoided does not have to be equated with 'unjust aggression' . . .

According to Sir James Stephen there are three necessary requirements for the application of the doctrine of necessity: (i) the act is needed to avoid inevitable and irreparable evil; (ii) no more should be done than is reasonably necessary for the purpose to be achieved; (iii) the evil inflicted must not be disproportionate to the evil avoided. Given that the principles of modern family law point irresistibly to the conclusion that the interests of Jodie must be preferred to the conflicting interests of Mary, I consider that all three of these requirements are satisfied in this case.

Finally, the doctrine of the sanctity of life respects the integrity of the human body. The proposed operation would give these children's bodies the integrity which nature denied them.

Robert Walker LJ

In truth there is no helpful analogy or parallel to the situation which the court has to consider in this case. It is unprecedented and paradoxical in that in law each twin has the right to life, but Mary's dependence on Jodie is severely detrimental to Jodie, and is expected to lead to the death of both twins within a few months. Each twin's right to life includes the right to physical integrity, that is the right to a whole body over which the individual will, on reaching an age of understanding, have autonomy and the right to self-determination . . .

The surgery would plainly be in Jodie's best interests, and in my judgment it would be in the best interests of Mary also, since for the twins to remain alive and conjoined in the way they are would be to deprive them of the bodily integrity and human dignity which is the right of each of them . . .

In this case the purpose of the operation would be to separate the twins and so give Jodie a reasonably good prospect of a long and reasonably normal life. Mary's death would not be the purpose of the operation, although it would be its inevitable consequence. The operation would give her, even in death, bodily integrity as a human being. She would die, not because she was intentionally killed, but because her own body cannot sustain her life . . . The proposed operation would not be unlawful. It would involve the positive act of invasive surgery and Mary's death would be foreseen as an inevitable consequence of an operation which is intended, and is necessary, to save Jodie's life. But Mary's death would not be the purpose or intention of the surgery, and she would die because tragically her body, on its own, is not and never has been viable.

In deciding whether the separation operation should take place despite the parents' objections, the test the court had to apply was, of course, the welfare principle: that is, the child's best interests had to be the court's paramount consideration. Here, however, there were two children whose best interests could not be reconciled. The operation was clearly in Jodie's best interests, because it was the only way in which she could survive. But—according to Ward and Brooke LJJ—it was equally clearly *not* in Mary's best interests, because it would kill her. Robert Walker LJ tried to argue that the operation would in fact be in Mary's best interests too because it would restore her bodily integrity, and allow her to die with the dignity of a separated body.

What should the court do when faced with two children whose interests are diametrically opposed? Ward and Brooke LJJ agreed that Jodie's interests should take priority because Mary was 'destined for death'. But while they believed that the operation would be consistent with family law principles, the problem that it might nevertheless be murder remained. Ward LJ's solution was to say that Mary was effectively killing Jodie, by 'draining her lifeblood', and that the operation could be justified as quasi self-defence. Brooke LJ, on the other hand, attempted to invoke the defence of necessity: here he said the doctors were entitled to operate because it was the lesser of two evils. Robert Walker LJ appeared to justify the operation through the doctrine of double effect: Mary's death is a foreseen but unintended consequence of saving Jodie's life.

Following the Court of Appeal's judgment, an appeal to the House of Lords was anticipated, and seven Law Lords (as opposed to the normal five) were convened to hear the appeal. The parents had, however, had enough, and decided to accept the Court of Appeal's decision. The operation went ahead leading to Mary's death and Jodie's survival. Jodie—whose real name is Gracie Attard—appeared not to need any further surgery, and returned to Gozo with her parents the following year.

(b) Commentary on *Re A*

Unsurprisingly *Re A* has generated considerable academic controversy. In the next extract John Harris rejects the Court of Appeal's reasoning and instead argues that the operation could be justified because Mary was not yet, and never would be a 'person', and death would therefore not deprive her of a life which she would be capable of valuing.

John Harris[135]

[T]he alleged right or entitlement to bodily integrity . . . seems to have been plucked, literally from the air, by the Court of Appeal as a new basic right. This supposed justification for a separation which will afford bodily integrity to one individual at the cost of her life deserves short shrift. It is cited, apparently as one of a group of decisive reasons, by Brooke LJ, '. . . The proposed operation would give these children's bodies the integrity which nature denied them'. The kindest way to interpret Brooke LJ's thinking here is that he has simply confused two senses of 'integrity'. Bodily

---

[135] 'Human Beings, Persons and Conjoined Twins: An Ethical Analysis of the Judgment in *Re A*' (2001) 9 Medical Law Review 221–36, 226–7, 232–3.

integrity protects individuals . . . from violations of their person. It does not mean that the body must be 'separated from all life preserving contact with other bodies or things'—how could it? Someone on a life-support system, or on dialysis, or fitted with a pacemaker, or with prosthetic limbs, arguably lacks bodily integrity, but the sanctity of life doctrine could hardly require that she be separated from these things . . .

The idea that Mary was 'dying anyway' and could not long survive is I believe tenacious . . . Where the individual with short life expectancy has a life to lead and wants to lead it for whatever time is left, . . . it would seem inconceivable that they would be killed against their will by a decision of the courts. It is not then life expectancy *per se* that makes a difference; but perhaps the *sort of life* that is available may be relevant?

If we say that Mary is going to 'die anyway' we may not be concentrating on the *duration* of the life expectancy but on some other feature of that life expectancy. I believe that there is something about Mary's life expectancy that makes plausible the decision in *Re A* . . . It is that the life expectancy of Mary between the time when the operation would take place and her inevitable death, would not have been expectancy of what might be called 'biographical life', not the life of a person. Indeed neither Mary nor Jodie had started living biographical lives, neither were persons properly so called at the time of the operation. On this analysis, the life Mary would lose by the performance of the operation which would kill her, would not have been life from which she could benefit significantly, not life that could ethically be distinguished from her life *in utero*.

Raanan Gillon criticizes the decision from a different perspective, arguing that the parents' view that it would be wrong to kill one daughter in order to save the other's life was not 'eccentric' and should have been accorded greater respect.

Raanan Gillon[136]

This alternative way of dealing with the moral dilemma does not result from an eccentric religious position held only by a small group or sect; on the contrary it results from a standard line of moral reasoning common not only to Roman Catholicism but to many, probably most, societies, both secular and religious. In its most obviously relevant form it forbids (under English law, for example) the killing of one innocent infant, even if already dying, to save another.

Consider the following thought experiment. Two identical twins are born. One will incurably die within a few months, but has healthy lungs and a healthy heart. The other has a feeble heart and poor lungs, and will also soon die unless she is given a compatible heart lung transplant in which case she is likely to survive. Only her identical twin's heart and lungs are compatible with her own tissue type, and in any case no other transplant donor is available in the time left before she will die. Either an early heart lung transplant is carried out using her identical twin sister as 'donor' which would kill her—but she was going to die soon anyway—or both twins will die, one of whom could have been saved by killing the other. Imagine the outrage of the English Court of Appeal, if a lower court had judged that in such a case, though the best interests of the incurably dying twin precluded being killed prematurely in order to provide a life-saving heart lung transplant for her sister, none the less the best interests of the other twin were to obtain such a transplant, and since without medical intervention both children would die, whilst with intervention using the twin as donor at least one child would be saved, 'there was no other way of dealing with it than by choosing the lesser of the two evils and so finding the least detrimental alternative'. . . .

It seems to this writer morally far preferable for the court, having spelled out the moral dilemma, to have ruled that there was no legal obligation—and perhaps no legal justification—in

---

[136] 'Imposed separation of conjoined twins—moral hubris by the English courts?' (2001) 27 Journal of Medical Ethics 3–4.

this case for removing the normal responsibility and right of parents to make health care decisions for their children. The parents were neither incompetent nor negligent—the standard justifications for depriving parents of such authority—and their reasoning was not eccentric or *merely* religious, but was widely acceptable moral reasoning—as was the contrary moral reasoning justifying an operation. The court should thus have declined to deprive the parents of their normal responsibilities and rights in order to impose its own preferred resolution of the moral dilemma, and should have allowed the parents to refuse medical intervention—while still ruling as it did, that such separation would not have been unlawful had the parents consented.

Jenny McEwan suggests that despite the Court of Appeal's attempt to confine their decision in this case to its very special and perhaps unique facts, the decision might have much wider application.

Jenny McEwan[137]

[H]ard cases are known to make bad law. Here we find Family Division judges making a fundamental change to criminal law doctrine. It is not clear whether *Re A* will be regarded as an authoritative judgment for the purposes of subsequent criminal trials. If it were, the effect would be profound. Allowing necessity as a defence in murder cases would not only create enormous uncertainty; it would inevitably draw criminal courts into many cases involving difficult moral issues. The defence of necessity works in this way. If the law does not recognise the defence in a murder case (which previously it most certainly did not), the judge will not allow the jury to consider it. It is not legally available as a defence. But where it is a legal defence, the jury has to decide whether the killing was genuinely necessary. They must consider the nature of the emergency and whether means other than killing were available to deal with it. This means that a defendant could argue that the killing of a severely disabled child was necessary to put an end to her pain and suffering. How would a jury respond to a necessity plea in relation to an act of mercy? . . . The Court of Appeal has opened the door to lawful acquittal where euthanasia is the reason for a killing, and it can be only a matter of time before such cases are before the courts . . . The Court of Appeal considered that . . . the test in *Woollin*, currently the leading case on the mens rea for murder, would be satisfied. But the *Woollin* test is less than clear-cut. Evidence that a defendant foresaw death or really serious bodily harm is evidence from which a jury *may*, not *must*, infer intention . . . If Mary's surgeons were tried for murder, the jury would make a decision on the facts as to whether intent was present at the time of the operation. They would be likely to conclude that the surgeons foresaw Mary's death as being a virtually certain consequence of their actions. Whether or not their wish to save Jodie would lead the jury to conclude that they did not intend to kill Mary is a matter of guesswork.

Finally, Barbara Hewson draws attention to Ward LJ's comment that it would have been equally legitimate for the doctors to comply with the parents' wishes and let both children die. This comment may have been prompted by media interviews with paediatric surgeons from Great Ormond Street Hospital in London, who said that if the twins had been born there, the medical staff would have respected the parents' decision. Hewson argues that Ward LJ's apparent willingness to condone an entirely different course of action undermines resort to the doctrine of necessity, since logically something cannot be both necessary and optional.

---

[137] 'Murder by Design: The "Feel-Good Factor" and the Criminal Law' (2001) 9 Medical Law Review 246–58, 247–8, 257.

Barbara Hewson[138]

The most surprising aspect of [his] judgment is Ward LJ's assumption that it would have been appropriate for the hospital to do nothing. Thus the whole case turned on a contingency: the fact that the twins happened to be in Manchester, rather than London. On any view, this is arbitrary, and cannot but undermine the application of a doctrine of necessity. By definition, necessity cannot properly apply to a course of action which is entirely optional and which only comes into play if one happens to live in town A rather than in town B. Another striking aspect of Ward LJ's judgment is his use of pejorative langauge, both about Mary and her parents. Initially, he cites a consultant's evidence that 'Mary does very little and her twin does all the work'. Subliminally, this description creates an impression of unworthiness. Mary is also described as growing normally, while Jodie remained thinner. She was thought to be 'growing at Jodie's expense'. Ward LJ seizes on these medical metaphors: 'She lives on borrowed time, all of which is borrowed from Jodie. It is a debt she can never repay.' This makes Mary seem positively culpable, in terms of conventional legal morality. By the end, in a logical leap, he portrays Mary as a killer: 'she sucks the lifeblood out of Jodie'. . . . Mary emerges from this forensic denunciation as akin to Dracula: not only monstrous, but also evil. Buoyed up by his disturbing metaphors, Ward LJ readily concludes that Mary 'has little right to be alive' . . .

Anatomically, Ward LJ's description was inaccurate: Mary was not sucking anything from Jodie. Rather the reverse: Jodie's heart was responsible for circulating blood around both of them. This was not Mary's fault.

(b) ADULTS

In Chapter 4, we saw that when an adult patient is incompetent, doctors can give her treatment which is in her best interests. Usually, of course, it will obviously be in the incompetent patient's best interests to receive life-prolonging medical treatment. But our ability to sustain life artificially means that patients who are permanently unconscious or insensate may now be able to 'live' for many years. Thus medical progress has presented us with a new dilemma. Are doctors *always* under a duty to sustain life for as long as possible, or could there ever be circumstances in which prolonging life ceases to be in an incompetent patient's best interests?

(1) *AIREDALE NHS TRUST v BLAND*[139]

(a) The facts

Tony Bland, then aged 17, was very seriously injured in the disaster which occurred at the Hillsborough football ground on 15 April 1989. His lungs were crushed and punctured and the supply of oxygen to the brain was interrupted. As a result, he sustained catastrophic and irreversible damage to the higher centres of the brain, which had left him since April 1989 in a condition known as a persistent vegetative state (PVS). The medical opinion of all who had been consulted about his case was unanimous in the diagnosis, and also all were agreed that there was no hope of any improvement in his condition or recovery. At no time before the disaster had Tony Bland

---

[138] 'Killing Off Mary: Was the Court of Appeal Right?' (2001) 9 Medical Law Review 281–98, 284–5, 288, 290, 293–4.
[139] [1993] AC 789 HL.

indicated his wishes if he should find himself in such a condition, but his father was convinced that his son would not 'want to be left like that.'

With the agreement of Tony Bland's family and the support of independent physicians, the authority responsible for the hospital where he was being treated sought declarations that they might (i) lawfully discontinue all life-sustaining treatment and medical support measures designed to keep the patient alive including the termination of ventilation, nutrition and hydration by artificial means; and (ii) lawfully discontinue and thereafter withhold medical treatment except for treatment which would enable Tony Bland to die peacefully with the greatest dignity and the least pain, suffering and distress. The trial judge granted the declarations sought, and his decision was upheld by the Court of Appeal. The Official Solicitor appealed to the House of Lords.

(b) The legal and ethical questions raised by *Bland*

The *Bland* case raised a number of novel and extremely complex legal and ethical questions. First, as we saw earlier, a doctor who breaches his duty to provide life-prolonging treatment to a patient may be guilty of murder. Since the doctors were proposing to withhold artificial nutrition and hydration from Tony Bland, knowing that this would lead to his death, might they satisfy both the *actus reus* and *mens rea* for murder? Secondly, even if we allow that doctors are sometimes entitled to withdraw futile medical treatment from patients, is artificial hydration and nutrition 'medical treatment', or is it more accurately described as basic care, which—by definition—cannot be futile? Thirdly, we know that doctors must treat incompetent patients, like Tony Bland, in their best interests. Since the result of the proposed course of action would be Tony Bland's death, could this be said to be in his best interests? Can death ever be in a patient's best interests? Would withdrawing Tony Bland's feeding tube be tantamount to saying that his life has ceased to have any value, and is this incompatible with respect for the sanctity of human life?

(c) The decision

The House of Lords unanimously rejected the Official Solicitor's appeal, and confirmed that Airedale NHS Trust was entitled to the declarations sought. Although there are some important differences between the judgments (Lord Mustill for example, was especially critical of the law which he was forced to apply), the points of agreement can be summarized as follows. First, the Lords were unanimous that the principle of the sanctity of life, while important, was not absolute. Secondly, artificial nutrition and hydration was agreed to be medical treatment and not basic care. Thirdly, the Lords—with some notable reservations—accepted that withdrawing artificial nutrition and hydration was an omission rather than an action. (Recall that an omission can only constitute the *actus reus* of murder if the doctor is under a pre-existing duty to act.) Fourthly, prolonging Tony Bland's life had ceased to be in his best interests. Fifthly, since treatment was no longer in his best interests, the doctor is no longer under a duty to prolong his life, and treatment withdrawal could not therefore constitute the *actus reus* of murder. Indeed Lord Browne-Wilkinson and Lord Lowry went further and suggested that if continued treatment was not in Tony Bland's best interests, the doctor might actually be under a duty to cease treatment.

Lord Keith

In the case of a permanently insensate being, who if continuing to live would never experience the slightest actual discomfort, it is difficult, if not impossible, to make any relevant comparison between continued existence and the absence of it. It is, however, perhaps permissible to say that to an individual with no cognitive capacity whatever, and no prospect of ever recovering any such capacity in this world, it must be a matter of complete indifference whether he lives or dies . . . Given that existence in the persistent vegetative state is not a benefit to the patient, it remains to consider whether the principle of the sanctity of life, which it is the concern of the state, and the judiciary as one of the arms of the state, to maintain, requires this House to hold that the judgment of the Court of Appeal was incorrect. In my opinion it does not. The principle is not an absolute one . . . In my judgment it does no violence to the principle to hold that it is lawful to cease to give medical treatment and care to a PVS patient who has been in that state for over three years, considering that to do so involves invasive manipulation of the patient's body to which he has not consented and which confers no benefit upon him.

Lord Goff

I start with the simple fact that, in law, Anthony is still alive. It is true that his condition is such that it can be described as a living death; but he is nevertheless still alive . . .

It is on this basis that I turn to the applicable principles of law. Here, the fundamental principle is the principle of the sanctity of human life—a principle long recognised not only in our own society but also in most, if not all, civilised societies throughout the modern world . . . But this principle, fundamental though it is, is not absolute. . . .

I must however stress, at this point, that the law draws a crucial distinction between cases in which a doctor decides not to provide, or to continue to provide, for his patient treatment or care which could or might prolong his life, and those in which he decides, for example by administering a lethal drug, actively to bring his patient's life to an end. As I have already indicated, the former may be lawful . . . But it is not lawful for a doctor to administer a drug to his patient to bring about his death, even though that course is prompted by a humanitarian desire to end his suffering, however great that suffering may be . . . So to act is to cross the Rubicon which runs between on the one hand the care of the living patient and on the other hand euthanasia—actively causing his death to avoid or to end his suffering. Euthanasia is not lawful at common law. It is of course well known that there are many responsible members of our society who believe that euthanasia should be made lawful; but that result could, I believe, only be achieved by legislation which expresses the democratic will that so fundamental a change should be made in our law, and can, if enacted, ensure that such legalised killing can only be carried out subject to appropriate supervision and control. It is true that the drawing of this distinction may lead to a charge of hypocrisy; because it can be asked why, if the doctor, by discontinuing treatment, is entitled in consequence to let his patient die, it should not be lawful to put him out of his misery straight away, in a more humane manner, by a lethal injection, rather than let him linger on in pain until he dies. But the law does not feel able to authorise euthanasia, even in circumstances such as these; for once euthanasia is recognised as lawful in these circumstances, it is difficult to see any logical basis for excluding it in others . . .

I agree that the doctor's conduct in discontinuing life support can properly be categorised as an omission. It is true that it may be difficult to describe what the doctor actually does as an omission, for example where he takes some positive step to bring the life support to an end. But discontinuation of life support is, for present purposes, no different from not initiating life support in the first place. In each case, the doctor is simply allowing his patient to die in the sense that he is desisting from taking a step which might, in certain circumstances, prevent his patient from dying as a result of his pre-existing condition; and as a matter of general principle an omission such as this will not be unlawful unless it constitutes a breach of duty to the patient. I also agree that the doctor's conduct is to be differentiated from that of, for example, an interloper who maliciously switches off a life support machine because, although the interloper may perform exactly the same act as the doctor who discontinues life support, his doing so constitutes interference with the life-prolonging treatment then being administered by the doctor. Accordingly, whereas the doctor, in discontinuing life support, is simply allowing his patient to die of his pre-existing condition, the interloper is actively intervening to stop the doctor from prolonging the patient's life, and such conduct cannot possibly be categorised as an omission . . .

[F]or my part I cannot see that medical treatment is appropriate or requisite simply to prolong a patient's life, when such treatment has no therapeutic purpose of any kind, as where it is futile because the patient is unconscious and there is no prospect of any improvement in his condition. It is reasonable also that account should be taken of the invasiveness of the treatment and of the indignity to which, as the present case shows, a person has to be subjected if his life is prolonged by artificial means, which must cause considerable distress to his family—a distress which reflects not only their own feelings but their perception of the situation of their relative who is being kept alive. But in the end, in a case such as the present, it is the futility of the treatment which justifies its termination.

Lord Browne-Wilkinson

Where a case raises wholly new moral and social issues, in my judgment it is not for the judges to seek to develop new, all embracing, principles of law in a way which reflects the individual judges' moral stance when society as a whole is substantially divided on the relevant moral issues. Moreover, it is not legitimate for a judge in reaching a view as to what is for the benefit of the one individual whose life is in issue to take into account the wider practical issues as to allocation of limited financial resources or the impact on third parties of altering the time at which death occurs . . .

For these reasons, it seems to me imperative that the moral, social and legal issues raised by this case should be considered by Parliament. The judges' function in this area of the law should be to apply the principles which society, through the democratic process, adopts, not to impose their standards on society. If Parliament fails to act, then judge-made law will of necessity through a gradual and uncertain process provide a legal answer to each new question as it arises. But in my judgment that is not the best way to proceed . . .

Murder consists of causing the death of another with intent so to do. What is proposed in the present case is to adopt a course with the intention of bringing about Anthony Bland's death. As to the element of intention or mens rea, in my judgment there can be no real doubt that it is present in this case: the whole purpose of stopping artificial feeding is to bring about the death of Anthony Bland.

As to the guilty act, or actus reus, the criminal law draws a distinction between the commission of a positive act which causes death and the omission to do an act which would have prevented death. . . . Apart from the act of removing the nasogastric tube, the mere failure to continue to do what you have previously done is not, in any ordinary sense, to do anything positive: on the contrary it is by definition an omission to do what you have previously done. The positive act of removing the nasogastric tube presents more difficulty. It is undoubtedly a positive act, similar to switching off a ventilator in the case of a patient whose life is being sustained by artificial ventilation. But in my judgment in neither case should the act be classified as positive, since to do so would be to introduce intolerably fine distinctions. If, instead of removing the nasogastric tube, it was left in place but no further nutrients were provided for the tube to convey to the patient's stomach, that would not be an act of commission. Again, as has been pointed out . . . if the switching off of a ventilator were to be classified as a positive act, exactly the same result can be achieved by installing a time-clock which requires to be reset every 12 hours: the failure to reset the machine could not be classified as a positive act. In my judgment, essentially what is being done is to omit to feed or to ventilate: the removal of the nasogastric tube or the switching off of a ventilator are merely incidents of that omission . . .

In my judgment, there is a further reason why the removal of the nasogastric tube in the present case could not be regarded as a positive act causing the death. The tube itself, without the food being supplied through it, does nothing. The removal of the tube by itself does not cause the death since by itself it did not sustain life . . .

Finally, the conclusion I have reached will appear to some to be almost irrational. How can it be lawful to allow a patient to die slowly, though painlessly, over a period of weeks from lack of food but unlawful to produce his immediate death by a lethal injection, thereby saving his family from yet another ordeal to add to the tragedy that has already struck them? I find it difficult to find a moral answer to that question. But it is undoubtedly the law.

Lord Mustill

The conclusion that the declarations can be upheld depends crucially on a distinction drawn by the criminal law between acts and omissions . . . The acute unease which I feel about adopting this way through the legal and ethical maze is I believe due in an important part to the sensation that however much the terminologies may differ the ethical status of the two courses of action is for all relevant purposes indistinguishable. By dismissing this appeal I fear that your Lordships' House may only emphasise the distortions of a legal structure which is already both morally and intellectually misshapen. Still, the law is there and we must take it as it stands . . .

The whole matter cries out for exploration in depth by Parliament and then for the establishment by legislation not only of a new set of ethically and intellectually consistent rules, distinct from the general criminal law, but also of a sound procedural framework within which the rules can be applied to individual cases. The rapid advance of medical technology makes this an ever more urgent task, and I venture to hope that Parliament will soon take it in hand . . .

Unlike the conscious patient [Anthony Bland] does not know what is happening to his body, and cannot be affronted by it; he does not know of his family's continuing sorrow. By ending his life the doctors will not relieve him of a burden become intolerable, for others carry the burden and he has none. What other considerations could make it better for him to die now rather than later? None that we can measure, for of death we know nothing. The distressing truth which must not be shirked is that the proposed conduct is not in the best interests of Anthony Bland, for he has no best interests of any kind . . .

Thus, although the termination of his life is not in the best interests of Anthony Bland, his best interests in being kept alive have also disappeared, taking with them the justification for the non-consensual regime and the co-relative duty to keep it in being . . . Since there is no longer a duty to provide nourishment and hydration a failure to do so cannot be a criminal offence . . .

I must recognise at once that this chain of reasoning makes an unpromising start by transferring the morally and intellectually dubious distinction between acts and omissions into a context where the ethical foundations of the law are already open to question. The opportunity for anomaly and excessively fine distinctions, often depending more on the way in which the problem happens to be stated than on any real distinguishing features, has been exposed by many commentators . . . All this being granted we are still forced to take the law as we find it and try to make it work.

(d) Commentary on the legal and ethical issues raised in *Bland*

A Best interests

The decision to withdraw artificial nutrition and hydration from Tony Bland was based upon an assessment of his best interests. It could, however, be argued that the best interest test is not especially helpful when the patient has effectively ceased to have any interests at all. This, as we saw earlier, was Lord Mustill's view in *Bland*:

The distressing truth which must not be shirked is that the proposed conduct is not in the best interests of Anthony Bland, for he has no best interests of any kind . . . Thus, although the termination of his life is not in the best interests of Anthony Bland, his best interests in being kept alive have also disappeared.

Treatment does not benefit a permanently insensate patient like Tony Bland, but nor is it burdensome to him. If, from the patient's perspective, it is a matter of complete indifference whether treatment is continued or withdrawn, how could we base the decision to withdraw treatment upon his best interests? One possibility is to argue that such individuals do have an interest in the manner of their death, and in its impact upon their relatives. In the Court of Appeal judgment in *Bland*, for example, Hoffmann LJ was of the opinion that Tony Bland did have an interest in putting 'an end to the humiliation of his being and the distress of his family':

It is demeaning to the human spirit to say that, being unconscious, he can have no interest in his personal privacy and dignity, in how he lives or dies. Anthony Bland therefore has a recognisable interest in the manner of his life and death.[140]

But regardless of whether we think the best interests test useful or not once a patient has irrevocably lost the capacity for consciousness, a decision about whether to continue the treatment of a PVS patient who has not made his own wishes known cannot be made without imposing *our* judgment about whether a permanently insensate life is worth living. This inescapably involves making a quality of life judgment. It is, as Rebecca Dresser has observed,

conceptually impossible to keep the best interests evaluation completely focused on the individual patient. The only way to decide what is best for a patient is by reference to broader definitions of what is good and bad for human beings.[141]

Coming to different conclusions, in the next extracts Jonathan Glover and Sanford H Kadish ask whether a permanently unconscious life is 'worth living'.

Jonathan Glover[142]

I have no way of refuting someone who holds that being alive, even though unconscious, is intrinsically valuable. But it is a view that will seem unattractive to those of us who, in our own case, see a life of permanent coma as in no way preferable to death. From the subjective point of view, there is nothing to choose between the two . . . Those of us who think that the direct objections to killing have to do with death considered from the standpoint of the person killed will

---

[140] [1993] AC 789 HL, 829.

[141] Rebecca Dresser, 'Missing Persons: Legal Perceptions of Incompetent Patients' (1994) 46 Rutgers Law Review 609, 662.

[142] *Causing Death and Saving Lives* (Penguin Harmondsworth 1977) 45–6.

find it natural to regard life as being of value only as a necessary condition of consciousness. For permanently comatose existence is subjectively indistinguishable from death, and unlikely often to be thought intrinsically preferable to it by people thinking of their own future.

Sanford H Kadish[143]

A fundamental objection [to the best interests standard] arises from what is implicit in the standard . . . that in certain circumstances the quality of a person's life may be so low that it is not worth living. This stands in stark opposition to the tradition that human life is always valuable. It is one thing for courts to defer to the patient's choice to die. This has proved difficult enough for some courts . . ., but at least the decision requires no judgment by the court or some other agent that the patient's life is no longer worth living—only that this is the choice of the patient whose life it is. It is quite different when the best-interests standard is applied independently of the patient's inferred preferences, because this requires the deciding authority itself—the court or some other agent—to make the substantive judgment of whether what is left of the patient's life is worth the candle . . .

First, what makes a life not worth living anyway? Loss of the patient's cognitive powers, his ability to function independently, his ability to interact with others, his dependence on constant medical intervention? How much ability to sense and take comfort from experiences is required before we can say his life is not worth living? At bottom, the difficulty is that we have no way to make confident judgments about how far cognitive and physical deterioration must go before life ceases to be worth living . . . Second, there is the challenge of 'donning the mental mantle of the incompetent,' understanding and judging his experiences as he lives and feels them, rather than from the biased perspective of a normally healthy person with unimpaired faculties. Finally, courts are often troubled by the specter of the slippery slope—the fear that once the precedent is established that a person may be left to die because someone judges his life not satisfying enough to be worth living, there will be nothing, or at least less, to stand in the way of that judgment being made of socially, mentally, and physically handicapped people on the margins of society.

Once it has been decided that prolonging life is no longer in a patient's best interests, and that conduct which will cause her death is the preferred course of action, it is, as Lord Browne-Wilkinson pointed out in *Bland*, difficult to see why the law insists that such patients must die slowly from starvation, rather than permitting doctors to administer a single lethal injection.

B Acts and omissions

A majority of the judges in the House of Lords explicitly accepted that the doctors' intention in withdrawing artificial nutrition and hydration was to 'bring about the death of Anthony Bland'.[144] Had withdrawing the nasogastric tube been an act rather than an omission, this would have been a straightforward case of murder. Given that the doctors' intention was to cause death, it was, as JC Smith explains, vitally important that withdrawing the tube be characterized as an omission.

JC Smith[145]

It was acknowledged that, whatever the circumstances, to kill by administering a lethal injection,

---

[143] 'Letting Patients Die: Legal and Moral Reflections' (1992) 80 California Law Review 857, 881–2.

[144] *Per* Lord Browne-Wilkinson; see also Lord Lowry: 'the intention to bring about the patient's death is there'; and Lord Mustill: 'the proposed conduct has the aim . . . of terminating the life of Anthony Bland'.

[145] 'Case Comment *Airedale NHS Trust v Bland*' (1993) Crim LR, 877–80, 879–80.

or by any similar act, would be murder. So there was no possibility of justification or excuse unless the discontinuance of feeding could be categorised as an omission. This seems to be the substance of the matter though it was elaborated by all the judges—by Lord Goff as follows:

> The question is not whether the doctor should take a course which will kill his patient, or even take a course which has the effect of accelerating his death. The question is whether the doctor should or should not continue to provide his patient with medical treatment or care which, if continued will prolong his patient's life.

Lord Goff answered the second question by holding that the doctor should not (or need not) continue the treatment; but he would presumably have answered the first question in the negative. 'Not continuing' is not, apparently, 'taking a course.' Why not? Only, it seems, because it is an omission, not an act,

> it may be difficult to say that it is in [the patient's] best interests that the treatment should be ended. But, if the question is asked, as in my opinion, it should be, whether it is in his best interests that the treatment . . . should be continued, that question can sensibly be answered to the effect that it is not in his best interests to do so.

The distinction is between 'ending' and 'not continuing' which look uncommonly like the same thing—except that the former expresses the conduct as an act and the latter expresses it as an omission. Omissions may be justified or excused when acts may not. Lord Browne-Wilkinson expressed the dilemma clearly:

> How can it be lawful to allow a patient to die slowly, though painlessly, over a period of weeks from lack of food but unlawful to produce his immediate death by a lethal injection, thereby saving his family from yet another ordeal to add to the tragedy that has already struck them?

Lord Browne-Wilkinson thought, nevertheless, that this was undoubtedly the law and he was, with respect, undoubtedly right.

It was not only Lord Browne-Wilkinson who expressed dissatisfaction with the act/omissions distinction which underpinned the decision in *Bland*; Lord Mustill robustly described it as 'intellectually and morally dubious'.

C Is artificial nutrition and hydration medical treatment?

The Lords' categorization of artificial nutrition and hydration (ANH) as medical treatment, as opposed to basic care, is also controversial. JM Finnis, for example, argues that this was a thinly veiled attempt to justify deliberately ending Tony Bland's life.

JM Finnis[146]

To desist from medical treatments designed to prevent, retard or cure illness, on the ground that for invalids such as Bland these treatments will achieve a benefit too limited to warrant this resort to medical resources, need involve neither intent to terminate life nor a will to cease caring for such invalids. But to desist from providing at least food and basic hygiene to invalids whose death is not imminent, and to whom the processes involved are no significant burden, seems to be either (1) to intend and bring about their death as a means, e.g. to saving the other costs involved in their continued existence, or (2) to make a choice (however hidden by benign sentiments and palliative

---

[146] 'Bland: Crossing the Rubicon' (1993) 109 Law Quarterly Review 329–37, 335–6.

accompaniments) to cease providing care for them. And in an affluent society—unlike a society, e.g. after a nuclear attack, where attending to the needs of the able-bodied might reasonably be preferred—the latter is willy-nilly a choice to deny the personhood of these invalids by breaking off human solidarity with them at its root . . .

The fact that Bland could indeed have been subjected to indignities, e.g. by being treated as a sex object or thrown, living, into the hospital rubbish, confirms that he remained a person, with some interests, and could be harmed, or benefited. But, pace the courts' incautious rhetoric, the nurses' devoted care for him did not humiliate or demean him or treat him without respect for his value as a person. On the contrary. As Lord Mustill acknowledged, the proposed discontinuance of care was going to require them to act 'contrary to all their instincts, training and traditions'. Their relationship to Bland was one of (largely unreciprocated) human solidarity between persons; as such it benefited both them and him.

John Keown further points out that the reason for categorizing ANH as treatment was so that it could legitimately be withdrawn.

John Keown[147]

Why was tube-feeding not basic care, which the hospital and its medical and nursing staff were under a duty to provide? The Law Lords held that tube-feeding was part of a regime of 'medical treatment and care.' The insertion of a gastrostomy tube into the stomach requires a minor operation, which is clearly a medical procedure. But it is not at all clear that the insertion of a nasogastric tube is medical intervention. And, even if it were, the intervention had already been carried out in Tony Bland's case. The question in such a case is why the pouring of food down the tube constitutes medical treatment. What is it supposed to be treating? . . .

Their Lordships placed great weight on the fact that the medical profession regards tube-feeding as medical treatment. But whether an intervention is medical is not a matter to be determined by medical opinion, nor by the mere fact that it is an intervention typically performed by doctors. A doctor does many things in the course of his practice, such as reassuring patients or fitting catheters, which are not distinctively medical in nature. And, if it is opinion that is crucial, the answer one gets may well depend on whom one asks. Tube-feeding may be regarded as medical treatment by many doctors, but many nurses regard it as ordinary care. . . . Dr Keith Andrews, . . . a leading authority on pvs, recently wrote 'it is ironic that the only reason that tube feeding has been identified as "treatment" has been so that it can be withdrawn'.

(4) DEVELOPMENTS SINCE *BLAND*

A year after the *Bland* case, a slightly different question was raised in *Frenchay Healthcare NHS Trust v S*.[148] Here the tube through which S, a patient in a persistent vegetative state, was being fed had become dislodged. It was not practicable to reinsert it, rather an operation would be required. The consultant involved in S's care recommended that it was in S's best interests for no action to be taken, and that he should be allowed to die naturally. It was agreed that there was no prospect of recovery. The hospital applied to the court for a declaration authorizing the hospital not to replace the gastrostomy tube, and this was granted.

---

[147] 'Restoring Moral and Intellectual Shape to the Law after Bland' (1997) 113 Law Quarterly Review 482–503, 491–2.

[148] [1994] 1 WLR 601.

The question for the Court of Appeal was whether this expedited process had offered S adequate protection. The Court of Appeal agreed that while a full exploration of the facts would normally be desirable, in an emergency it would not necessarily be possible. Sir Thomas Bingham MR explained that:

It is however to be observed that cases must from time to time arise in which this procedure [application to the Court] simply cannot be practicable. I have in mind the acute emergency when a decision has to be taken within a matter of minutes, or at most hours, as to whether treatment should be given or not, whether one form of treatment should be given or another, or as to whether treatment should be withheld. In such situations it is of course impossible that doctors should be obliged or able to come to the court and seek a decision. I think it is therefore inevitable that there must be emergencies in which application to the court is simply not possible, even though this case is not one of them.

Here there had been an opportunity to apply to the court for a declaration, and although the hearing had been comparatively brief, the Court of Appeal held that there was no reason to question the conclusion of S's consultant that it was in his best interests for no action to be taken and for him to be allowed to die naturally.

Applying the *Bland* judgment in subsequent cases, the courts have had to confront two important questions. First, is *Bland* compatible with the Human Rights Act 1998? Could the withdrawal of artificial nutrition and hydration violate a patient's right to life (Article 2), or, because the patient will die from starvation, could it amount to inhuman and degrading treatment (prohibited by Article 3)? In one of the first cases to be brought after the Human Rights Act came into force, the court determined that withdrawing artificial nutrition and hydration from a PVS patient was compatible with Convention rights.

NHS Trust A v M, NHS Trust B v H[149]

The evidence of medical specialists showed that the patient in each case was in a permanent vegetative state within the guidelines set out by the Royal College of Physicians. It was accepted that it would not be in the best interests of either patient, who had been in such a condition for over three years and over nine months respectively, to continue artificial nutrition and hydration treatment, and that withdrawal of such treatment would not cause pain and discomfort. The applicant hospital trusts, supported by the patients' families and the hospital staff, applied for declarations that discontinuing artificial feeding would not contravene Articles 2 and 3 of Schedule 1 of the Human Rights Act 1998.

Dame Elizabeth Butler-Sloss, P

Although the intention in withdrawing artificial nutrition and hydration in PVS cases is to hasten death, in my judgment the phrase 'deprivation of life' must import a deliberate act, as opposed to an omission, by someone acting on behalf of the state, which results in death. A responsible decision by a medical team not to provide treatment at the initial stage could not amount to intentional deprivation of life by the state. Such a decision based on clinical judgment is an omission to act. The death of the patient is the result of the illness or injury from which he suffered and that cannot be described as a deprivation . . . I cannot see the difference between that situation and a decision to discontinue treatment which is no longer in the best interests of the

---

[149] [2001] Fam 348 Fam Div.

patient . . ., even though that discontinuance will have the effect of shortening the life of the patient . . .

Article 2 therefore imposes a positive obligation to give life-sustaining treatment in circumstances where, according to responsible medical opinion, such treatment is in the best interests of the patient but does not impose an absolute obligation to treat if such treatment would be futile. This approach is entirely in accord with the principles laid down in *Airedale NHS Trust v Bland* . . . In a case where a responsible clinical decision is made to withhold treatment, on the grounds that it is not in the patient's best interests, and that clinical decision is made in accordance with a respectable body of medical opinion, the state's positive obligation under article 2 is, in my view, discharged

I am, moreover, satisfied that article 3 requires the victim to be aware of the inhuman and degrading treatment which he or she is experiencing or at least to be in a state of physical or mental suffering. An insensate patient suffering from permanent vegetative state has no feelings and no comprehension of the treatment accorded to him or her. Article 3 does not in my judgment apply to these two cases

Given that the 'right to life' had been a background consideration in cases decided before the incorporation of the ECHR, Dame Elizabeth Butler-Sloss's conclusion that 'a reasonable clinical decision . . . to withhold treatment' could not violate Article 2 is not surprising. Her judgment that Article 3 can only be violated if the victim is aware of the inhuman and degrading treatment is, with respect, more controversial. Failing to provide insensate patients with basic care, such as clothes, hygiene measures, and a catheter and/or colostomy would unarguably be to treat them in an inhuman and degrading fashion. And, despite the fact that they would know nothing about it, we would not allow their bodies to be used by medical students learning how to conduct internal examinations; again, regardless of their lack of awareness, this might be described as 'inhuman or degrading' treatment.

Secondly, should *Bland* be confined to PVS cases, or might there be patients who are not in a persistent vegetative state but whose condition nevertheless justifies the withdrawal of life-prolonging treatment? Following the *Bland* case, the House of Lords' Select Committee on Medical Ethics recommended that the persistent vegetative state should be defined and a code of practice developed. A working group of the Royal College of Physicians produced a set of guidelines, *The Permanent Vegetative State*, in April 1996. These guidelines have, however, caused problems in subsequent cases. In both *Re D* and *Re H* (below) the courts authorized the withdrawal of artificial nutrition and hydration from patients whose conditions were judged to be functionally indistinguishable from the persistent vegetative state, albeit that they did not quite fit within the standard clinical definition.

Re D[150]

D had suffered serious head injuries in a road traffic accident. She recovered sufficiently to be nursed at her parents' home with the assistance of a full-time carer, but 6 years later she sustained further very serious brain damage in unexplained circumstances and her condition deteriorated. She was in a permanent vegetative state, though there was some disagreement about the depth and prognosis of her vegetative state. The hospital trust responsible for her care sought a

[150] [1998] 1 FLR 411 Fam Div.

declaration that it would be lawful to withdraw the artificial feeding and hydration which was sustaining her life.

Sir Stephen Brown P

It seems to me that, for all practical purposes . . . that this patient is in fact in what would be, in Professor Jennet's terms, a permanent vegetative state. It is merely—and it is not lightly stated by me—the fact that one of the paragraphs [in the Royal College's guidelines] . . . is not actually fulfilled. However, it must be recalled that every single witness . . . [has] made it clear that this patient has no awareness whatsoever. She is, in the words of Lord Goff in *Bland*, suffering what he described as 'a living death'. I do not, therefore, believe that, if a declaration were to be granted in this case, it would be extending the range of cases in which a declaration might properly be considered. . . . The court recognises that no declaration to permit or to sanction the taking of so extreme a step could possibly be granted where there was any real possibility of meaningful life continuing to exist.

In this case, all the evidence establishes, to my satisfaction, that there is no evidence of any meaningful life whatsoever. This sad, tragic patient is suffering what is rightly termed 'a living death'. Accordingly, I am driven to the conclusion . . . that it is not in this patient's best interests artificially to keep her body alive and that the declaration sought should be granted.

Re H (Adult: Incompetent)[151]

H was a 43 year old woman who had suffered very serious brain damage following a road traffic accident. Expert evidence by several doctors was unanimous that H had been in a permanent vegetative state for the past three years. However, she did not fit fully within the criteria for the establishment of permanent vegetative state issued by the Royal College of Physicians in 1996. On occasions, she appeared able to focus on an object, and could be aroused by noise or touch. The NHS trust, in whose care H had been, applied for the declaration that it would be in her best interests for the administration of life-sustaining treatment, including the artificial administration of nutrition and hydration, to cease.

Sir Stephen Brown P

In this instance it may be that a precise label is not of significant importance . . . There is no doubt, in the view of all the witnesses who have given evidence, that . . . the patient is wholly unaware of herself or of her environment and that there is no possibility of any change . . . I am quite satisfied . . . that this is a case of a vegetative state which, although it may not fall precisely within the Royal College guidelines, is, and can properly be described as being, permanent . . . These are very anxious cases. The sanctity of life is of vital importance. It is not, however, paramount, and, in this case, I am satisfied that it is in the best interests of this patient that the life sustaining treatment presently being artificially administered should be brought to a conclusion.

In *NHS Trust v H*,[152] Dame Elizabeth Butler-Sloss preferred the guidance produced by the *International Working Party Report* in 1996 which acknowledged that not all PVS patients present the same diagnostic indicators, and that some response to stimulation, and some visual tracking may be compatible with a diagnosis of PVS. Paraphrasing one of the expert witnesses, Dame Elizabeth Butler-Sloss suggested

that the valuable report from the Royal College of Physicians in 1996 did not make the situation entirely clear and that it may be that it is time to review in 2001 the advice that is to be given in respect of these worrying and extremely sad cases.

---

[151] [1998] 2 FLR 36 Fam Div.   [152] [2001] 2 FLR 501.

The courts have also had to consider whether a complete and permanent lack of awareness is a precondition for treatment withdrawal, or whether it might be lawful to withdraw life-prolonging treatment from patients who have some level of awareness. As we can see from *Re R*, it appears that it could be lawful to withhold life-prolonging treatment, such as cardio-pulmonary resuscitation, from patients who retain some ability to interact with their environment, although it is less clear that such patients could also lawfully be deprived of artificial nutrition and hydration. This is because there are two important differences between the decision to withdraw artificial nutrition and hydration and the decision to withhold life-prolonging treatment if the patient suffers a life-threatening event. First, Do Not Resuscitate orders will only result in the patient's death *if* she has suffered a life-threatening event, so it could more plausibly be argued that the cause of death is the respiratory or cardiac arrest, as opposed to the decision to withhold treatment. Second, because resuscitation is invasive and traumatic—broken ribs, for example, are not uncommon—it would also be more straightforward to argue that the decision to withhold treatment has been taken in the patient's best interests.

Re R (Adult: Medical Treatment)[153]

R, a 23 year old man, had a serious malformation of the brain and cerebral palsy. He had no consistent interactions with the social environment, was unable to walk or to sit upright. He was believed to be blind and deaf; was incontinent and unable to chew. He was not in a persistent vegetative state, but had minimal awareness. R's psychiatrist was concerned that another admission to hospital would not be in R's best interests, and signed a direction headed 'Do not resuscitate'. The NHS trust sought a declaration that it was lawful to withhold CPR and antibiotics in the event of R developing a potentially life-threatening condition.

Sir Stephen Brown P

The extensive medical evidence in this case is unanimous in concluding that it would not be in the best interests of R to subject him to cardio-pulmonary resuscitation in the event of his suffering a cardiac arrest . . . I agree that this declaration should be made.

The withholding in the future of the administration of antibiotics in the event of the patient developing a potentially life-threatening infection which would otherwise call for the administration of antibiotics is a decision which can only be taken at the time by the patient's responsible medical practitioners in the light of the prevailing circumstances.

The General Medical Council has issued guidance on the withholding and withdrawing of artificial nutrition and hydration (ANH):

General Medical Council[154]

81. Where death is imminent, in judging the benefits, burdens or risks, it usually would not be appropriate to start either artificial hydration or nutrition, although artificial hydration provided by the less invasive measures may be appropriate where it is considered that this would be likely to provide symptom relief.

Where death is imminent and artificial hydration and/or nutrition are already in use, it may

---

[153] [1996] 2 FLR 99 Fam Div.
[154] Withholding and Withdrawing Life-prolonging Treatments: Good Practice in Decision-making (GMC London Aug 2002).

be appropriate to withdraw them if it is considered that the burdens outweigh the possible benefits to the patient.

Where death is not imminent, it usually will be appropriate to provide artificial nutrition or hydration. However, circumstances may arise where you judge that a patient's condition is so severe, and the prognosis so poor that providing artificial nutrition or hydration may cause suffering, or be too burdensome in relation to the possible benefits. In these circumstances, as well as consulting the health care team and those close to the patient, you must seek a second or expert opinion from a senior clinician (who might be from another discipline such as nursing) who has experience of the patient's condition and who is not already directly involved in the patient's care. This will ensure that, in a decision of such sensitivity, the patient's interests have been thoroughly considered, and will provide necessary reassurance to those close to the patient and to the wider public.

83. Where you are considering withdrawing artificial nutrition and hydration from a patient in a permanent vegetative state (PVS), or condition closely resembling PVS, the courts in England, Wales and Northern Ireland currently require that you approach them for a ruling. The courts in Scotland have not specified such a requirement, but you should seek legal advice on whether a court declaration may be necessary in an individual case.

This guidance was challenged in *R (on the application of Burke) v The General Medical Council*[155] by a patient who believed that to withdraw ANH, once he became incompetent, against his express wishes would breach his rights under the Human Rights Act 1998. At first instance, Munby J held that the GMC's guidance was incompatible with the claimant's right under Article 3 not to be subjected to inhuman and degrading treatment, and his right under Article 8, not to have his physical and psychological integrity and dignity infringed. Controversially, Munby J appeared to suggest that there might be times when a patient would have the *right* to demand that his doctors gave him treatment, even when this was contrary to their clinical judgment. With respect, it is probably unsurprising that his judgment was overturned by the Court of Appeal.

R (on the application of Burke) v The General Medical Council[156]

The claimant, Mr Burke, was 45 years old and suffered from cerebellar ataxia, a degenerative brain illness. In the future, as his condition worsens, he will need to receive food and water by artificial means, known as artificial nutrition and hydration (ANH). He sought clarification of the circumstances in which ANH may lawfully be withdrawn, and contended that the General Medical Council (GMC)'s guidance on the withdrawal of treatment was incompatible with his rights under Arts 2, 3, 6, 8 and 14 of the European Convention for the Protection of Human Rights.

Lord Phillips

There are great dangers in a court grappling with issues such as those that Munby J has addressed when these are divorced from a factual context that requires their determination. The court should not be used as a general advice centre. The danger is that the court will enunciate propositions of principle without full appreciation of the implications that these will have in practice, throwing into confusion those who feel obliged to attempt to apply those principles in practice. This danger is particularly acute where the issues raised involve ethical questions that any court should be

---

[155] [2005] EWCA Civ 1003.   [156] Ibid.

reluctant to address, unless driven to do so by the need to resolve a practical problem that requires the court's intervention. . . .

We have come to the clear view that this appeal must be allowed, and the declarations made by the judge set aside. It is our view that Mr Burke's fears are addressed by the law as it currently stands and that declaratory relief, particularly in so far as it declares parts of the Guidance unlawful, is both unnecessary for Mr Burke's protection and inappropriate as far as the Guidance itself is concerned. . . .

The proposition that the patient has a paramount right to refuse treatment is amply demonstrated by the authorities cited by Munby J. The corollary does not, however, follow, at least as a general proposition. Autonomy and the right of self-determination do not entitle the patient to insist on receiving a particular medical treatment regardless of the nature of the treatment. Insofar as a doctor has a legal obligation to provide treatment this cannot be founded simply upon the fact that the patient demands it.

We have indicated that, where a competent patient indicates his or her wish to be kept alive by the provision of ANH any doctor who deliberately brings that patient's life to an end by discontinuing the supply of ANH will not merely be in breach of duty but guilty of murder. Where life depends upon the continued provision of ANH there can be no question of the supply of ANH not being clinically indicated unless a clinical decision has been taken that the life in question should come to an end. That is not a decision that can lawfully be taken in the case of a competent patient who expresses the wish to remain alive . . .

There is one situation where the provision of ANH will not be clinically indicated that is not relevant to Mr Burke's concern but which received a disproportionate amount of attention in this case. In the last stage of life the provision of ANH not only may not prolong life, but may even hasten death. As we understand Munby J's judgment, he considered that in this situation the patient's wish to receive ANH must be determinative. We do not agree. Clearly the doctor would need to have regard to any distress that might be caused as a result of overriding the expressed wish of the patient. Ultimately, however, a patient cannot demand that a doctor administer a treatment which the doctor considers is adverse to the patient's clinical needs.

The Court of Appeal was concerned that it would be inappropriate to offer an opinion on the withdrawal of ANH in the abstract, divorced from the facts which may or may not justify such a decision. They also held that the patient's concerns were adequately addressed by the GMC's guidance, and that where a competent patient expresses his wish to receive ANH, a doctor who nevertheless withheld it might be guilty of murder.

Finally, it is worth mentioning that when the Mental Capacity Act 2005 was being debated in parliament, there was considerable interest in whether it would introduce 'euthanasia by the back door' for incapacitated adults. This concern was addressed by a rather curious amendment to section 4, which specifies the matters to be taken into account by the person making the determination about whether treatment is in an incapacitated person's best interests. Section 4(5) states that:

Where the determination relates to life-sustaining treatment he must not, in considering whether the treatment is in the best interests of the person concerned, be motivated by a desire to bring about his death.

What does this mean? The use of the word 'desire' is strange, since it would be extremely difficult to conclusively determine what anyone actually 'desires'. However, the intention here is clear. Section 4(5) effectively means that although the decision to withhold or withdraw life-sustaining treatment can be in a person's best interests, ending the patient's life must not be the doctor's sole intention. Rather, the decision-maker, normally the doctor, must be motivated by the 'desire' to relieve pain or end suffering, and not by the 'desire' to bring about the patient's death. Of course, if there are circumstances in which it is in a patient's best interests to have their life brought to an end by non-treatment, the doctor may in fact have two goals in mind: ending suffering *by* ensuring that the patient dies. But the Act requires doctors to be able to separate out these two outcomes, and insists that the doctor must 'desire' only the former.

5. CONCLUSION

As we have seen in this chapter, end of life decision-making raises some extraordinarily difficult and ethically contentious questions. In relation to competent adult patients, the most important question, in my view, is whether the law should move towards allowing doctors to help their patients to die, through the explicit legalization and regulation of euthanasia and/or doctor-assisted suicide. Will this happen? It is too early to predict the impact of the House of Lords Select Committee's cautious interest in the approach adopted in Oregon, and the BMA's recent change of policy, from outright opposition to neutrality. But it is certainly true that legalization looks like a less remote possibility in 2005 than it did ten years ago.

In relation to incompetent patients, the law is, as we have seen, heavily swayed by medical opinion about when it is appropriate to discontinue the treatment of profoundly incapacitated adults and children. In general, if doctors judge treatment to be futile, there is little chance of a court demanding that such treatment should nevertheless be given.

Finally, it is, in my view, interesting to contrast concern about the possible abuse of vulnerable patients if euthanasia were to be legalized, with the relative lack of interest in the much more common and *lawful* ways in which doctors are routinely involved in ending their patients' lives.

Emily Jackson[157]

The safeguards in place to protect vulnerable patients from prematurely requesting the termination of life support are fairly minimal, and certainly much less restrictive than the strict conditions which would apply to legalised euthanasia. The doctor must simply ensure that the patient is competent, and that her decision is not the result of coercion or undue influence. . . . Once these largely procedural tests have been satisfied, the *content* of the patient's decision is not open to any scrutiny at all. An otherwise completely healthy competent adult with a long and happy life ahead of her who wants to make a wholly irrational decision to refuse a simple life-saving procedure is fully entitled to do so. . . .

In contrast, the safeguards which would exist were euthanasia to be legalised would scrutinise the patient's competence *and the reasonableness of her choice*. Unlike competent treatment refusals which are governed only by the principle of patient autonomy, in relation to legalised

---

[157] Emily Jackson, 'Whose Death is it Anyway? Euthanasia and the Medical Profession' (2004) 57 Current Legal Problems 415–42, 439–40.

euthanasia the principles of beneficence and non-maleficence would trump patient autonomy. The doctor would only be acting properly if she had considered not only the patient's wish to die, but also her own ethical responsibility for the promotion of wellbeing, and her duty to do no harm. Unless the doctor genuinely *and reasonably* believed that death would benefit the patient by relieving her unbearable distress, there could be no justification for deliberately causing her death. . . .

Insofar as the potential for abuse exists, it is surely *incompetent* rather than competent patients who are most at risk. Yet, again, comparatively few safeguards exist when doctors take decisions, such as the withdrawal of artificial ventilation, which will end the lives of their incompetent patients . . .

The lack of transparency and openness about decisions justified by the doctrine of double effect, where death is disingenuously described as an incidental *side-effect* of pain relief, when in reality death is the *means* to alleviate pain, is much more likely to threaten patient trust and confidence than the set of clear and rigorous legislative criteria which would have to be satisfied before a patient could receive a lethal injection.

In short, the lawful means that doctors may employ to shorten their patients' lives are almost certainly *more* open to abuse than legalised euthanasia . . . Not only do fewer safeguards exist for the entirely lawful life-shortening practices, but they are also far more common than legalised euthanasia would ever be. In the Netherlands, 2.6% of deaths are caused by euthanasia and assisted suicide, while 20.2% follow a decision to withdraw or withhold treatment, and 19.1% result from giving patients steadily increased doses of painkilling drugs. If we are genuinely concerned to protect patients from having their lives ended prematurely against their wishes, it is perhaps these common and comparatively unregulated practices which should be our primary focus.

6. FURTHER READING

Assisted Dying for the Terminally Ill Committee, *Assisted Dying for the Terminally Ill Bill— First Report* (2005) <http://www.publications.parliament.uk/pa/ld/ldasdy.htm>.

PABST BATTIN, MARGARET, *Ending Life: Ethics and the Way We Die* (OUP Oxford 2005).

DWORKIN, GERALD, FREY RG and BOK, SISSELA, *Euthanasia and Physician-Assisted Suicide: For and Against* (CUP Cambridge 1998).

GLOVER, JONATHAN, *Causing Death and Saving Lives* (Penguin Harmondsworth 1977).

JACKSON, EMILY, 'Whose Death is it Anyway? Euthanasia and the Medical Profession' (2004) 57 Current Legal Problems 415–42.

KEOWN, JOHN, *Euthanasia, Ethics and Public Policy: An Argument against Legalisation* (CUP Cambridge 2002).

MAGNUSSON, RS, 'Euthanasia: above ground, below ground' (2004) 30 Journal of Medical Ethics 441–6.

McCALL SMITH, ALEXANDER, 'Euthanasia: The Strengths of the Middle Ground' (1999) 7 Medical Law Review 194–207.

OTLOWSKI, MARGARET, *Voluntary Euthanasia and the Common Law* (OUP Oxford 2000).

TUR, RICHARD, 'Legislative Technique and Human Rights: The Sad Case of Assisted Suicide' (2003) Criminal Law Review 3–12.

INDEX